CW01272478

# OXFORD HANDBOOK OF
# PENSIONS AND RETIREMENT INCOME

# Oxford Handbook of
# PENSIONS AND RETIREMENT INCOME

*Edited by*

GORDON L. CLARK,
ALICIA H. MUNNELL

AND

J. MICHAEL ORSZAG
WITH THE ASSISTANCE
OF KATE WILLIAMS

OXFORD
UNIVERSITY PRESS

# OXFORD
UNIVERSITY PRESS

Great Clarendon Street, Oxford OX2 6DP

Oxford University Press is a department of the University of Oxford.
It furthers the University's objective of excellence in research, scholarship,
and education by publishing worldwide in

Oxford New York

Bogota Buenos Aires Mexico City Toronto Sao Paulo
Delhi Bombay Calcutta Madras Karachi
Bangkok Kuala Lumpur Singapore Hong Kong Taipei Tokyo
Shanghai Auckland Melbourne
Cape Town Nairobi Dar es Salaam Mumbai
Athens Florence Istanbul Madrid Paris Warsaw
and associated companies in
Berlin Ibadan

Oxford is a registered trademark of Oxford University Press in the UK and in certain
other countries. Published in the United States by Oxford University Press Inc

© Gordon L Clark, Alicia H Munnell and J. Michael Orszag 2006

All rights reserved. No part of this publication may be reproduced,
stored in a retrieval system, or transmitted, in any form or by any means,
without the prior permission in writing of Oxford University Press.
Within the UK, exceptions are allowed in respect of any fair dealing for the
purpose of research or private study, or criticism or review, as permitted
under the Copyright, Designs and Patents Act, 1988, or in the case of
reprographic reproduction in accordance with the terms of the licenses
issued by the Copyright Licensing Agency. Enquiries concerning
reproduction outside these terms and in other countries should be
sent to the Rights Department, Oxford University Press,
at the address above.

This book is sold subject to the condition that it shall not, by way
of trade or otherwise, be lent, re-sold, hired out or otherwise circulated
without the publisher's prior consent in any form of binding or cover
other than that in which it is published and without a similar condition
including this condition being imposed on the subsequent purchaser.

British Library Cataloguing in Publication Data

Data available

Library of Congress Cataloguing in Publication Data

Pensions & Retirement Income
1. Ageing—Solidarity—Globalization
2. Pensions–Social Security–Welfare
3. Finance–Governance–Investment

Typeset by SPI Publisher Services, Pondicherry, India
Printed in Great Britain
on acid-free paper by
Biddles Ltd, King's Lynn

ISBN 0-19-927246-8   978-0-19-927246-4

1 3 5 7 9 10 8 6 4 2

*For Peter and Shirley, and Henry*

# Preface

The macroeconomic burden of paying for the retirement of the baby-boom generation has focused attention on one of the most important issues facing the developed economies over the next 50 years. Already, within the budgets of many OECD countries, choices are being made between the conflicting priorities of current expenditures on the education and opportunities of younger generations on the one hand, and the health and welfare of retirees and those approaching retirement on the other. As macroeconomic costs of supporting the elderly increase proportionally with the ageing of the population, the budgets of the developed world will experience increasing strain in meeting the income expectations of their elderly populations. This tension is already introducing dissention into the relationship between younger and older populations.

At the same time, expectations about population growth in the developing world have changed dramatically. Those who might have imagined the global population growing beyond the 10 billion mark have been forced to reassess their forecasts over the last ten years. Of course, the Chinese and Indian populations will grow substantially in the next 25 years, and this growth will affect the balance of trade between developed and developing economies and environmental conditions both locally and globally. On the other hand, rapid urbanization, combined with remarkable changes in fertility, seem likely to put substantial brakes upon the rate of population increase. While other changes—in productivity, in the social and political environment, and in the underlying economic infrastructure—will play their part, looking beyond the next 25 years, population ageing will almost certainly become a crucial issue in the developing world, and the funding of retirement will loom large in domestic and international politics.

The provision of retirement income is of enormous importance for countries, whether developed, developing, or undergoing structural and economic transformation. We are concerned with technical issues regarding the design and structure of retirement income systems and with the equity and efficiency consequences of different types of retirement income systems. Most importantly, we believe that planning for future intergenerational obligations is a vital ingredient in any comprehensive commitment to social justice. To think otherwise, to imagine that these issues will be accommodated by incremental political decisions over the decades, may be simply to repeat the mistakes so obvious in the historical record of developed economies during the eighteenth and nineteenth centuries.

Remarkably, some countries have taken significant steps toward being explicit about intergenerational welfare and the balance of income and expenditure. Both the World

Bank and the OECD deserve credit for bringing these issues to the top of the domestic and international policy agendas over the last decade. These efforts were not always welcomed, especially by domestic political and economic elites and other entrenched interests. Over the past few years, however, a number of countries have grudgingly accepted the notion that we have a commitment to our children and their children and not only to current constituencies. Around the world a number of nation-states are publishing intergenerational accounts that bring to the fore issues that were otherwise submerged in annual national budgets. Most importantly, countries have recognized that welfare policy is not just an issue of income distribution but involves issues of financial stability, long-term economic growth, and development.

On the other hand, the contributions to this book as a whole indicate that there are no settled solutions, no obvious templates, and no real consensus on many issues involved in the financing of retirement income. Many systems around the world remain pay-as-you-go (PAYG), although a number of countries, particularly in Latin America and Eastern Europe, have adopted funded pension arrangements. Understanding the diversity of interests and the advantages and disadvantages of different systems is a most important goal of this particular volume. The *Handbook* attempts to provide this understanding by bridging the academic debate and the real world of working men and women, their fathers and mothers, and their children.

This volume is at once interdisciplinary and committed to a rigorous understanding of the most important issues. The editors have very different backgrounds and experience. Gordon Clark is an economic geographer most interested in comparative pension systems and especially the intersection between the institutions providing retirement income and financial markets. Alicia Munnell is an economist with extensive government experience and a significant reputation for research on US social security and the structure and performance of employer-provided pension systems. And Michael Orszag combines the skills of an economist with experience around the world on issues such as pension funding. The editors share a commitment to a broader understanding of the social, historical, and political dimensions of pensions and retirement income. At the same time, by integrating economic analysis with these broader dimensions, this volume differs from those that focus on social welfare and the politics of social insurance.

We hope that the reader will draw on the book both for a comprehensive analysis of pensions and retirement income and as a reference text on specific issues. We hope that the reader will look carefully at the contributions on the historical and social development of pension systems, and equally, at the contributions on private pension systems, their design, and allocation of risk. Many pension systems carry with them the legacy of reform in the late nineteenth century and immediately after the Second World War, and nation-states have evolved quite different solutions to the common problem of funding retirement income. Taking seriously history and geography is of course a vital ingredient in any understanding of current debate.

In sum, we hope this volume sets the stage for further debate and analysis about an issue that is here and will be with us for the next 50 years.

# Acknowledgements

Most importantly, we would like to thank our contributors for showing enthusiasm for the project and making a commitment in the first stages of its development. We were able to assemble a remarkable set of experts spanning the world, a variety of disciplines, and a vast array of topics. Without their support, and without their forbearance in each and every phase of the project, the book could not have been completed. We hope the final result comes close to their expectations and their recognition of the significance of the project.

A number of institutions and individuals sustained the book. Early on, Credit Suisse First Boston (London) showed an immediate interest in the project and provided tangible support that enabled us to bring Kate Williams into its development. Simon Ford and Giles Keating recognized the complexity of the issues embraced by the *Handbook* just as they recognized the challenge of managing such an ambitious project with contributors from around the world. Importantly, they enabled us to meet regularly together, making real what would otherwise have appeared to be a virtual community of interest in cyberspace. Furthermore, they encouraged the development of the project both as an academic manifesto and as a volume that could contribute to better understanding of the issues in the world of commerce, finance, and public policy. We are most grateful for their support.

We would also like to acknowledge the support of our home institutions. In this regard, the facilities and resources of the Oxford University Centre for the Environment was an important base from which to develop the project. Here, we would like to acknowledge the efficient and timely commitment of Mrs Jan Burke, and related staff. We also acknowledge Boston College; we were fortunate to draw upon the resources of the Center for Retirement Income in the Carroll School of Management. Not only did they provide secretarial support for the project in North America, they were also able to help sustain the links between the editors across the world. Likewise, Watson Wyatt also provided similar administrative support as well as use of offices for editorial meetings.

Of course, the whole book project has relied upon the commitment of Oxford University Press and especially the support of David Musson, the business editor of the Press. We would also like to acknowledge the help and assistance of Jenni Craig and Matthew Derbyshire who together took the initial planning of the volume and its manuscript through to completion. The Press has also been very congenial and helpful hosts as the editors have planned and executed the entire project.

Ultimately, the project would not have been possible without the assistance of our editorial manager, Kate Williams. As usual, she demonstrated the keen eye, organisational skills, and ability to reach out to each and every contributor, so vital for sustaining such large-scale projects. The book project would not have been possible without her help. Similarly, we would wish to acknowledge the critical eye and intellectual challenges posed by Steve Sass from Boston College. He is a contributor to the book, but he also made important interventions early in the planning of the volume that gave it its shape and its logic. We are pleased to say that he is a most valued colleague.

# Contents

| | |
|---|---|
| List of Figures | xvii |
| List of Tables | xx |
| Editorial Team | xxiii |
| List of Contributors | xxv |

**Introduction**     1

1. The Agenda     3
   *Gordon L. Clark, Alicia H. Munnell, and J. Michael Orszag*

2. Pension and Retirement Income in a Global Environment     10
   *Gordon L. Clark, Alicia H. Munnell, and J. Michael Orszag*

## I. RETIREMENT IN CONTEXT     29

*Creating Modern Retirement*     31

3. The History of Retirement     33
   *Pat Thane*

4. The Development of Public Pensions from 1889 to the 1990s     52
   *Camila Arza and Paul Johnson*

5. The Development of Employer Retirement Income Plans: from the Nineteenth Century to 1980     76
   *Steven Sass*

6. Changing Work Patterns and the Reorganization of
   Occupational Pensions    98
   *Ewald Engelen*

7. Gender, the Family, and Economy    121
   *Vickie L. Bajtelsmit*

8. Social Solidarity    141
   *Johan J. De Deken, Eduard Ponds, and Bart van Riel*

   *The Economic Context*    161

9. Demography and Ageing    163
   *Naohiro Ogawa and Noriyuki Takayama*

10. Life-Cycle Options and Preferences    183
    *Florence Legros*

11. Funding, Saving, and Economic Growth    201
    *E. Philip Davis and Yu-Wei Hu*

## II. PUBLIC RETIREMENT PLANS    219

   *State Old-Age Pension Programs*    221

12. Structure and Performance of Defined Benefit Schemes    223
    *Warren McGillivray*

13. The Structure and Performance of Mandated Pensions    241
    *Adam Creighton and John Piggott*

14. Actuarial-Based Public Pension Systems    268
    *Richard Disney*

   *Entitlements and Pensions*    291

15. Citizenship, Entitlement, and Mobility    293
    *Robin Ellison*

| | | |
|---|---|---|
| 16. | Early Retirement<br>*David A. Wise* | 310 |
| 17. | Meeting Health and Long-term Care Needs in Retirement<br>*Marilyn Moon* | 336 |

## III. EMPLOYER-SPONSORED RETIREMENT PLANS 355

*Structure of Employer-Sponsored Pensions* 357

| | | |
|---|---|---|
| 18. | Employer-Sponsored Plans: The Shift from Defined Benefit to Defined Contribution<br>*Alicia H. Munnell* | 359 |
| 19. | Organized Labor and Pensions<br>*Teresa Ghilarducci* | 381 |
| 20. | Corporate Finance and Capital Markets<br>*J. Michael Orszag and Neha Sand* | 399 |

*Pension Plan Investments* 415

| | | |
|---|---|---|
| 21. | Asset Liability Management<br>*Rob Bauer, Roy Hoevenaars, and Tom Steenkamp* | 417 |
| 22. | Strategic Asset Allocation for Pension Plans<br>*John Y. Campbell and Luis M. Viceira* | 441 |
| 23. | Pension Fund Management and Investment Performance<br>*Ian Tonks* | 456 |

*Pension Plan Governance* 481

| | | |
|---|---|---|
| 24. | Regulation of Pension Fund Governance<br>*Gordon L. Clark* | 483 |

25. Regulatory Principles and Institutions ... 501
   André Laboul and Juan Yermo

26. Accounting Standards for Pension Costs ... 521
   Geoffrey Whittington

## IV. INDIVIDUAL AND HOUSEHOLD RETIREMENT PROVISION ... 539

*Individual Pensions, Insurance, and Saving* ... 541

27. Occupational Pension Scheme Design ... 543
   David McCarthy

28. Annuity Markets ... 562
   James M. Poterba

29. Personal Pensions and Markets ... 584
   Tryggvi Thor Herbertsson

*Individual and Household Retirement Planning* ... 601

30. Choice, Behavior, and Retirement Saving ... 603
   Steven F. Venti

31. Housing Wealth and Retirement Savings ... 618
   William C. Apgar and Zhu Xiao Di

32. The Elderly and Ethical Financial Decision-Making ... 638
   Julian Savulescu and Tony Hope

## V. LOOKING AHEAD ... 659

*Prospective Models* ... 661

33. Structural Pension Reform—Privatization—in Latin America ... 663
   Carmelo Mesa-Lago

34. Private Pensions and Public Policy: The Public–Private
    Divide Reappraised                                                  684
    *Noel Whiteside*

35. Unending Work                                                       702
    *Annika Sundén*

    *Challenges*                                                        719

36. Productivity, Compensation, and Retirement                          721
    *David Neumark*

37. Poverty and Inequality                                              740
    *Gary Burtless*

38. The Politics of Pension Reform: Managing Interest Group Conflicts   759
    *Bernhard Ebbinghaus*

    *Emerging Economies*                                                779

39. Pensions for Development and Poverty Reduction                      781
    *Armando Barrientos*

40. Retirement Income Systems in Asia                                   799
    *Hanam S. Phang*

41. Pensions in Africa                                                  816
    *Anthony Asher*
    *Coda*                                                              837

42. Sustainable and Equitable Retirement in a Life Course Perspective   839
    *Gosta Esping-Andersen and John Myles*

*Index*                                                                 859

# List of Figures

| | | |
|---|---|---|
| 4.1 | The structure of pension schemes in selected countries | 60 |
| 4.2 | Level of public pension expenditure, 1990 | 64 |
| 4.3 | Growth of public pension expenditure, 1960–1989 | 65 |
| 4.4 | Pension structure in the United Kingdom since 1908 | 67 |
| 4.5 | Pension structure in the United States since 1935 | 69 |
| 4.6 | Pension structure in Argentina since 1904 | 70 |
| 5.1 | Private sector employer plan coverage in the United States, 1940–1974 | 84 |
| 5.2 | Capital income from employer plans and household financial assets in 'Anglo-Saxon' and 'Bismarckian' nations | 90 |
| 5.3 | Capital income from employer plans and household financial assets by income group in 'Anglo-Saxon' and 'Bismarckian' systems | 92 |
| 5.4 | The income of the elderly (age 65–74) in comparison to that of working-age adults | 93 |
| 7.1 | Ratio of women's median annual earnings to men's for full-time year-round workers, United States, 1960–2000 | 128 |
| 7.2 | Labor force participation of women, 1950–2000 | 130 |
| 9.1 | World population growth, 1950–2050 | 165 |
| 9.2 | Population growth by region, 2000–2050 | 167 |
| 9.3 | Changes in the proportion aged 60 and over in developed and developing regions, 1950–2050 | 168 |
| 9.4 | Changes in the median age in developed and developing regions, 1950–2050 | 169 |
| 9.5 | Growth of population aged 60 and over in developed and developing regions, 1950–2050 | 170 |
| 10.1 | The basic model of the Life-Cycle Hypothesis (LCH) | 185 |
| 10.2 | A more complex LCH model of an individual's wealth profile | 186 |
| 13.1 | Classification of retirement policies | 245 |
| 14.1 | Internal rates of return (IRRs) to pension contributions, by country and cohort (generation) | 274 |
| 14.2 | Effective tax components, from inter-household variations in replacement rates | 276 |

| | | |
|---|---|---|
| 16.1 | Ratio of population aged 65+ to population aged 20 to 64 | 312 |
| 16.2a | Labor force participation trends for men aged 60 to 64 | 313 |
| 16.2b | Labor force participation trends for men aged 60 to 64 | 313 |
| 16.3 | Unused productive capacity: men aged 55 to 65 | 314 |
| 16.4 | United States retirement hazard rates for men by pension plan coverage | 316 |
| 16.5 | United Kingdom percentage of men and women remaining in the labor force, by age | 317 |
| 16.6 | Germany: base versus actuarial adjustment | 318 |
| 16.7 | Germany: pathways to retirement for men, 1960–1995 | 319 |
| 16.8 | Sum of tax rates on work from early retirement age to 69 | 321 |
| 16.9 | Unused capacity versus tax force to retire | 321 |
| 16.10 | Unused capacity versus tax force to retire (logarithm) | 322 |
| 16.11 | OLF change, 25 percent age plus 4 years, base versus 3-year delay: OV-S3 | 323 |
| 16.12 | OLF change, 25 percent age plus 4 years, base versus common reform: OV-S3 | 324 |
| 16.13 | Germany: base, three-year increment, actuarial adjustment, common reform | 326 |
| 16.14 | Total fiscal effect of three-year increment, as a percentage of base cost | 327 |
| 16.15 | Total fiscal effect of actuarial reform, as a percentage of base cost | 327 |
| 16.16 | Total fiscal effect of common reform, as a percentage of base cost | 328 |
| 18.1 | Percentage of US private sector workers covered by a pension plan, 1940–2001 | 362 |
| 18.2 | Percentage of non-earned US retirement income by source, population 65 and over, 2001 | 363 |
| 18.3 | Percentage of wage and salary workers with pension coverage, by type of plan, 1981–2001 | 366 |
| 18.4 | 401(k)/IRA actual and simulated accumulations, by age group, 2001 | 369 |
| 20.1 | Relationship between funding level and volatility for the Nikkei 500 in Japan | 407 |
| 20.2 | Pension liability to market capitalization for the UK FTSE 350 | 409 |
| 20.3 | Pension deficit to market capitalization for the UK FTSE 350 | 410 |
| 21.1 | Balance sheet pension fund (liquidation basis) | 419 |
| 21.2 | Factors influencing the surplus | 420 |
| 21.3 | Probability distribution of nominal funding ratio and pension result of ALM study D | 431 |
| 21.4 | Asset-liability and asset-only risks | 432 |

| | | |
|---|---|---|
| 21.5 | Average generational accounts as percentage of nominal liabilities in 2004 for all age cohorts from 1898 to 1979 | 435 |
| 23.1 | Illustrating the problem of market timing | 471 |
| 23.2 | Evidence on performance of pension funds | 475 |
| 24.1 | Regimes of pension fund governance | 493 |
| 25.1 | Defined benefit funding ratio in 2003 | 509 |
| 25.2 | Pension fund investment in equities in 2003 | 510 |
| 29.1 | Cash flow for a unit-linked life insurance policy | 589 |
| 32.1 | The necessary criteria for the diagnosis of dementia | 642 |
| 32.2 | Four models of the adviser–client relationship | 648 |
| 32.3 | Summary of ethically relevant grounds for taking over someone's financial affairs | 652 |
| 32.4 | Some key legal principles relating to competence | 653 |
| 32.5 | Outline of the assessment of competence | 656 |
| 35.1 | Labor force participation aged 55–64 in the OECD, 2003 | 704 |
| 37.1 | Relation between pension entitlement and worker's past earnings in six industrialized countries | 745 |
| 37.2 | Expected age at death among Americans surviving to age 25, by family income | 750 |

# List of Tables

| | | |
|---|---|---|
| 4.1 | Date of first pension laws in selected countries | 54 |
| 6.1 | Male and female labor market participation rates | 107 |
| 6.2 | Share of standard and non-standard employment contracts, 2003 | 107 |
| 7.1 | Sources of income by gender and marital status for individuals aged 65 plus, 2000 | 123 |
| 7.2 | Incidence of poverty, United States, 2000 | 124 |
| 7.3 | Average pension accumulation and the gender pension gap, United States, 1998 | 125 |
| 7.4 | Gender differences in life expectancy | 126 |
| 7.5 | Gender and marital status of the elderly, 2000 | 127 |
| 8.1 | Risks facing individuals in retirement | 145 |
| 10.1 | Changes in asset allocation due to the ageing process, 2000–2050 | 189 |
| 13.1 | Decumulation phase of FDC schemes | 251 |
| 13.2 | Returns over various asset classes, Australia, 1993–2004 | 257 |
| 13.3 | Returns of various share markets, 1993–2004 | 259 |
| 13.4 | Comparative impact of asset, benefit, and contribution charges over varying periods | 260 |
| 14.1 | Cumulated pension wealth accruals for single people on average earnings | 278 |
| 18.1 | Pension assets as a percentage of GDP 2001, OECD | 361 |
| 18.2 | Estimated social security replacement rates (RR) for the average earner, 2003 and 2030 | 364 |
| 18.3 | Percentage of UK workers with second-tier pension coverage, 1978/9–2001/1 | 372 |
| 19.1 | Changes in compensation for union and non-union workers, 1988–2002 | 383 |
| 19.2 | Pension coverage rates of all workers and union workers by income, sex, and firm size | 384 |
| 20.1 | Pension liabilities and deficits of the world's 500 largest companies in 2004 | 400 |
| 21.1 | Four different pension deals | 424 |

| | | |
|---|---|---|
| 21.2 | Output of ALM studies | 425 |
| 21.3 | Output of ALM study D | 430 |
| 21.4 | Average generational account as percentage of liabilities for three age groups | 436 |
| 23.1 | Private pension funding in major developed countries, 1996 | 458 |
| 23.2 | Assets under management for eight countries, 1999 | 459 |
| 23.3 | Institutionalization of the UK equity market to 1999 | 460 |
| 23.4 | Fund management fees charged in different countries for a £100 million mandate | 461 |
| 23.5 | Distribution of managers across pension funds by category of manager | 463 |
| 23.6 | Average annual returns on median UK pension fund by asset class, 1994–2003 | 466 |
| 23.7 | Average asset allocation across UK pension funds, 1993–2003 | 466 |
| 23.8 | Average asset allocation of occupational pension funds in major markets, 2003 | 467 |
| 23.9 | Performance evaluation of UK pension funds, 1983–1997 | 474 |
| 23.10 | Performance of UK pension funds, 1980–2000 | 474 |
| 25.1 | Market structures of private pension systems in OECD countries, 2001–2002 | 518 |
| 27.1 | Factors affecting pension valuation for employers and employees | 552 |
| 28.1 | Money's worth estimates for single premium immediate annuity at age 65 | 572 |
| 28.2 | Money's worth of immediate annuities in various nations, nominal contract | 574 |
| 31.1 | Wealth holdings of older homeowners grew rapidly in the 1990s | 621 |
| 31.2 | Seniors now hold more mortgage debt | 622 |
| 32.1 | Prevalence of dementia by age | 642 |
| 33.1 | Percentage of the labor force covered by the public system before the reform and by private and public systems in 2004 | 669 |
| 33.2 | Percentage of affiliates who contributed to the private system in the last month, December 1998 to December 2004 | 671 |
| 33.3 | Size of insured market, number of administrative firms, and concentration in the largest two and three firms, December 2004 | 672 |
| 33.4 | Managerial cost of the private system: deposit, costs, total deduction, and administrative burden, December 2004 | 674 |
| 33.5 | Capital accumulation in the private system in US million dollars in December 2004, and as percentage of GDP in June 2004, and average capital return in December 2003–2004 | 676 |

| | | |
|---|---|---|
| 33.6 | Portfolio diversification: percentage distribution of total pension fund by financial instrument in December 2004 | 678 |
| 35.1 | Percentage of employees aged 55 and older working part-time in selected OECD countries, 1999 | 709 |
| 37.1 | Income inequality and reduction of inequality through government redistribution and pensions in 12 industrialized countries | 743 |
| 39.1 | Old-age poverty indicators for Latin America and Africa | 784 |
| 39.2 | The contribution of non-contributory pension income to poverty reduction | 787 |
| 39.3 | Summary information on non-contributory pension programs for selected countries | 790 |
| 42.1 | Poverty rates among the population 65+, c. 2000 | 843 |

# Editorial Team

**Gordon L. Clark** is the Halford Mackinder Professor of Geography at the University of Oxford. He is also affiliated with the Institute of Ageing and the Said Business School at Oxford. Recent publications include *Pension Fund Capitalism* (Oxford University Press, 2000), *European Pensions & Global Finance* (Oxford University Press, 2003), the co-edited *Pension Security in the 21st Century* (Oxford University Press, 2003) and 'Pension fund governance', *Journal of Pension Economics and Finance* (2004). He has been involved in many research programs on private pensions sponsored by governments and various financial service companies. Current research is on the UK pensions 'crisis' for the French government, and the governance and competence of pension fund decision-making for the National Association of Pension Funds. Address is Oxford University Centre for the Environment, Dyson Perrins Building, South Parks Road, Oxford, OX1 3QY, UK. Email: gordon.clark@ouce.ox.ac.uk

**Alicia H. Munnell** is the Peter F. Drucker Professor at the Carroll School of Management and Director of the Center for Retirement Research at Boston College. She has combined a career in government with academia, serving as Senior Vice President and Director of Research at the Federal Reserve Bank of Boston, Assistant Secretary of the US Treasury for Economic Policy, and a Member of the President's Council of Economic Advisers. Her most recent books are *Coming Up Short: The Challenge of 401(k) Plans* (Brookings Institution Press, 2004), *Death and Dollars: The Role of Gifts and Bequests in America* (Brookings Institution Press, 2003), and *Framing the Social Security Debate: Values, Politics and Economics* (Brookings Institution Press, 1998). Address is Main Campus, Boston College, 140 Commonwealth Avenue, Chestnut Hill, MA 02467, USA. Email: munnell@bc.edu

**J. Michael Orszag** is Head of Global Research Services and Chairman of the Global Research Committee of Watson Wyatt Worldwide. Mike Orszag is a founding editor of the Journal of Pension Economics and Finance (Cambridge University Press). He is also Visiting Professor at Imperial College Business School, Fellow of the Institute for the Study of Labor (IZA) in Bonn, and a member of the scientific advisory board of the Center for Pensions and Superannuation at the University of New South Wales, Sydney, Australia, the Center for Retirement Research, Boston

College, USA and the Swedish Premium Pension Fund (PPM). Address is Watson Wyatt Worldwide, Watson House, London Road, Reigate, Surrey, RH2 9PQ, UK. Email: michael.orszag@watsonwyatt.com

**Kate Williams** is a teacher, writer, and editor. She has set up a study advice center for students at Oxford Brookes University, and runs writing programs for postgraduate students at Oxford University and elsewhere on a freelance basis. Her publications include *Study Skills*, a vintage text in the field, and *Developing Writing*. She has been Managing Editor of the *Oxford Handbook of Economic Geography* and *Pension Security in the 21st Century*. Email: katemwilliams1@btopenworld.com

# LIST OF CONTRIBUTORS

**William C. Apgar** is a Lecturer in Public Policy at the Harvard's Kennedy School of Government and a Senior Scholar at the Joint Center for Housing Studies. From 1997 to 2001, Apgar took a leave of absence from Harvard and served as the Assistant Secretary of Housing at the US Department of Housing and Urban Development (HUD). His research interests are in housing, community and economic development, as well as housing finance and capital markets. He leads the Joint Center's Credit, Capital, and Communities Project, an ongoing evaluation of the impact of the changing structure of the mortgage banking industry on efforts to expand access to affordable homeownership and rental housing opportunities. Address is Kennedy School, Joint Center for Housing Studies, 79 John F. Kennedy Street, Cambridge, MA 02138, USA. Email: William_Apgar@Harvard.edu

**Camila Arza** is Marie Curie Fellow at the Robert Schuman Centre (European University Institute, Florence) and researcher at the Economics Department of the Latin American School of Social Sciences (FLACSO-Argentina). She is currently conducting a research project dealing with comparative analysis of pension reform trajectories in European countries, with a focus on the distributional outcomes of the latest reforms in Italy, Sweden, Poland, and the United Kingdom. Previous research focused on the social and distributional impacts of social policy, structural reform, and privatization both in developed and developing countries. Address is VF008, Villa La Fonte, Via delle Fontanelle, I-50016 San Domenico di Fiesole, Italy. Email: camila.arza@iue.it

**Anthony Asher** is a Senior Policy Manager with the Australian Prudential Regulation Authority, and a Visiting Fellow at Macquarie University. Recent publications include chapters on benefit design and pricing in *Understanding Actuarial Management: The Actuarial Control Cycle* (Institute of Actuaries of Australia, 2003) and on old age pensions and the financing of social security in *Social Security—a Legal Analysis* (Butterworths, 2003). He was previously Professor of Actuarial Science at the University of Witwatersrand, Johannesburg. Research interests include prudential capital and superannuation administration costs. Address is APRA, Level 26, 400 George St., Sydney NSW 2000, Australia. Email: anthony.asher@apra.gov.au

**Vickie L. Bajtelsmit** is a Professor in the Department of Finance and Real Estate at Colorado State University and First Community Bank Faculty Fellow. She holds a Ph.D. in Insurance and Risk Management from the University of Pennsylvania's Wharton School of Business (1994) and a J.D. from Rutgers University School of Law (1982). Dr Bajtelsmit has published in a variety of academic and professional journals, including the *Journal of Risk and Insurance, Journal of Pension Economics and Finance,* and *Benefits Quarterly.* She is also the author of two books, *The Busy Woman's Guide to Financial Freedom* (AMACOM, 2002) and *Personal Finance* (John Wiley & Sons, 2005). Address is Department of Finance and Real Estate, Colorado State University, Fort Collins, CO 80523, USA. Email: Vickie.Bajtelsmit @business.colostate.edu

**Armando Barrientos** is Research Fellow at the Institute of Development Studies at the University of Sussex in the UK and Senior Researcher at the Chronic Poverty Research Centre. His research interests cover the interaction of labor markets and welfare production, pensions and ageing, and social protection in developing countries. His articles have appeared in journals such as *World Development, Applied Economics,* and *Geneva Papers in Risk and Insurance,* and he is the author of *Pension Reform in Latin America* (Ashgate, 1988). He has acted as an adviser to the ILO, the World Bank, DFID, UNRISD, IADB, and the Caribbean Development Bank. Address is Institute of Development Studies, University of Sussex, Brighton, BNI 9RE, UK. Email: a.barrientos@ids.ac.uk

**Rob Bauer** is Manager of the Research Department of ABP Investments and Professor of Finance at Maastricht University in the Netherlands. His present research focus is on asset liability management, risk budgeting, stock selection models, socially responsible investments (SRI), and corporate governance. His recent work has been published in *The Journal of Banking and Finance* and *Financial Analysts Journal.* He is a member of the board of the postgraduate course on investments at the Free University of Amsterdam, and teaches on various executive courses, among others IIR, TIAS, AIF, and the Dutch Financial Analysts Association (VBA). Address is Limburg Institute of Financial Economics, University of Maastricht, PO Box 616, 6200 MD Maastricht, Netherlands. Email: rob.bauer@abpinvestments.nl

**Gary Burtless** holds the Whitehead Chair in Economic Studies at the Brookings Institution, Washington, DC. His research is on issues connected with public finance, ageing, saving, labor markets, income distribution, social insurance, and the behavioral effects of government tax and transfer policy. Burtless graduated from Yale College in 1972 and earned a Ph.D. in economics from the Massachusetts Institute of Technology in 1977. Before coming to Brookings in 1981, he served as an economist in the US Departments of Labor and of Health, Education, and Welfare. In 1993 he was Visiting Professor of Public Affairs at the University of Maryland.

Address is The Brookings Institution, 1775 Massachusetts Ave, N.W., Washington, DC 20036, USA. Email: gburtless@brookings.edu

**John Y. Campbell** is the Morton L. and Carole S. Olshan Professor of Economics at Harvard University. Campbell has published over 60 articles on various aspects of finance and macroeconomics, including fixed-income securities, equity valuation, and portfolio choice. His two books, *The Econometrics of Financial Markets* (with Andrew Lo and Craig MacKinlay, Princeton University Press, 1997) and *Strategic Asset Allocation: Portfolio Choice for Long-Term Investors* (with Luis Viceira, Oxford University Press, 2002), each won Paul Samuelson Awards for Outstanding Scholarly Writing on Lifelong Financial Security from TIAA-CREF. Campbell has co-edited the *American Economic Review* and the *Review of Economics and Statistics*, and was the 2005 President of the American Finance Association. He is a founding partner of Arrowstreet Capital, LP, a Cambridge-based quantitative asset management firm specializing in global equities. Address is Department of Economics Littauer 213, Harvard University, 1875 Cambridge Street, Cambridge, MA 02138, USA. Email: john_campbell@harvard.edu

**Adam Creighton** is a Senior Analyst at the Reserve Bank of Australia and a Research Associate of the Centre for Pensions and Superannuation. He has produced a UNSW School of Economics Discussion Paper on Australia–New Zealand currency union and co-authored a Reserve Bank of Australia Research Discussion Paper on credit rating agencies in Australia. He holds a B.Econ. (Hons.) from the University of New South Wales, a B.A. from the University of Wollongong, and a diploma in music performance from the Australian Music Examinations Board. In 2005 he was awarded a Commonwealth Scholarship to study economics at Oxford University. Address is Reserve Bank of Australia, GPO Box 3947, Sydney, Australia. Email: CreightonA@rba.gov.au

**E. Philip Davis** is Professor of Economics and Finance at Brunel University. He is also a Visiting Fellow at the National Institute for Economic and Social Research and has academic links with the Pensions Institute at Cass Business School, the Financial Markets Group at LSE, and the Royal Institute of International Affairs. Recent books include *Financial Structure* (with Joseph Byrne, Cambridge University Press, 2003), *Foundations of Pension Finance* (edited jointly with Zvi Bodie, Edward Elgar, 2000), and *Institutional Investors* (with Benn Steil, MIT Press, 2001). Davis has published widely in the fields of pensions, institutional investment, euromarkets, banking, corporate finance, financial regulation, and financial stability. Recent research linked to pension issues includes estimation of the impact of demographic change on asset prices, links of pension funds to economic growth, UK pension issues and studies of the regulation of annuity markets. Address is Economics and Finance, Brunel University, Uxbridge, Middlesex, UB8 3PH, UK. Email: e_Philip_davis@msn.com

**Johan J. De Deken** is a Lecturer in the Department of Sociology at the University of Amsterdam. Before coming to Amsterdam he taught at the Humboldt University in Berlin. Recent publications include 'Christian democracy, social democracy and the paradoxes of earnings-related social security', *International Journal of Social Welfare* (2002) and 'Pensions and non wage labour costs: modelling a decade of reforms in Germany', *Journal of European Social Policy* (2002). His main current research interests include the assessment of the costs of mandated and private social security and issues of pension fund governance. Address is Department of Sociology and Anthropology OZ Achterburgwal 185 1012 DK Amsterdam, Netherlands. Email: J.J. DeDeken@uva.nl

**Zhu Xiao Di**, a Senior Research Analyst at Harvard University's Joint Center for Housing Studies, has authored and co-authored numerous Joint Center publications, including *Housing Wealth and Household Net Wealth in the United States* (2003), *The Importance of Housing to the Accumulation of Household Net Wealth* (2003), and *Intergenerational Wealth Transfer and its Impact on Housing* (2002). He is the author of *Thirty Years in a Red House, a Memoir of Childhood and Youth in Communist China* (University of Massachusetts Press, 1998) and a contributor to the anthology, *Father: Famous Writers Celebrate the Bond between Father and Child* (Pocket Books, 2000). Address is Joint Center for Housing Studies, Harvard University, 1033 Massachusetts Avenue, Cambridge, MA 02138, USA. Email: Zhu_Xiao_Di@Harvard.edu

**Richard Disney** is Professor of Economics at the University of Nottingham, having previously been a Professor of Economics at Queen Mary College, University of London, and at the University of Kent at Canterbury. He is also a Research Fellow of the Institute for Fiscal Studies in London. He has published numerous articles on the economics of labor markets, and social security and pensions in particular. Books include *Can We Afford to Grow Older? A Perspective on the Economics of Ageing* (MIT Press, 1996) and *Pension Systems and Retirement Incomes across OECD Countries* (edited with Paul Johnson, Edward Elgar, 2001). Address is Experian Centre for Economic Modelling, School of Economics, University of Nottingham, University Park, Nottingham, NG7 2RD, UK. Email: richard.disney@nottingham.ac.uk

**Bernhard Ebbinghaus** is Professor of Macrosociology at the Faculty of Social Sciences, University of Mannheim, Germany. His research covers comparative social policy, industrial relations, and labor market developments in Europe, Japan, and the USA. Before being appointed to a Chair in Mannheim in 2004, he was Senior Researcher at the Max Planck Institute for the Study of Societies in Cologne, Kennedy Fellow at Harvard University, as well as Visiting Professor at the Universities of Wisconsin–Madison and Jena. He is the co-author (with Jelle Visser) of *Trade Unions in Western Europe since 1945* (Macmillan, 2000), co-editor (with Philip Manow) of *Comparing Welfare Capitalism* (Routledge, 2001), and author of

*Reforming Early Retirement in Europe, Japan and the USA* (Oxford University Press, forthcoming). Address is Chair in Macrosociology, University of Mannheim, D-68131, Mannheim, Germany. Email: bebbinghaus@sowi.uni-mannheim.de

**Robin Ellison** is a partner in Pinsent Masons, a UK law firm specializing in the development of pensions and related financial services products for insurers and other providers, and in European and international pensions, pensions trustee law, and pensions in matrimonial matters. He is a director of the boards of a number of companies, including as Chairman of Pendragon Professional Information, which provides technical information to pension funds and financial services advisers, Chairman of London & Colonial Insurance, and is a trustee of several pension funds, both as independent trustee and as chairman. He is the author of numerous books on pensions including a four volume loose-leaf *Pensions Law and Practice* (Sweet & Maxwell), the *Pension Trustees Handbook* (Thorogood) and *Family Breakdown and Pensions* (Butterworths, 2001, 2nd edn.) and is editor of *Pensions Benefits Law Reports*. He is also Chairman of the UK National Association of Pension Funds. Address is Pinsent Masons, Dashwood House, 69 Old Broad Street, London, EC2M 1NR, UK. Email: robin.ellison@pinsentmasons.com

**Ewald Engelen** is currently cross-posted as researcher at the Scientific Council for Policy Research in the Hague and is affiliated with the Department of Geography, Planning and International Studies of the University of Amsterdam. Trained as a political philosopher with an empirical slant he has written extensively on economic issues. His articles have appeared in journals such as the *Journal of Ethnic and Migration Studies, Economy and Society, Politics and Society,* and *Environment and Planning A*. He is currently preparing a multidisciplinary research program on the Amsterdam financial services in a global context. Address is Department of Geography, Planning and International Studies, Faculty of Human and Behavioral Sciences, University of Amsterdam, Nieuwe Prinsengracht 130, 1018 VZ Amsterdam, Netherlands. Email: e.r.engelen@uva.nl

**Gosta Esping-Andersen** is Professor of Political and Social Sciences at the Universitat Pompeu Fabra (Barcelona). His research has centered on comparative social policy, labor markets, and on social inequality. He is author and co-author of numerous books, among which the most recent include *Social Foundations of Postindustrial Economies* (Oxford University Press, 1999), *Why Deregulate Labour Markets?* (Oxford University Press, 2001) and *Why We Need a New Welfare State* (Oxford University Press, 2002). He has also worked extensively with international organizations, including the OECD, World Bank, and the UN, and governments, including the Portuguese and Belgian presidencies of the EU. Address is Department of Political and Social Science, Universitat Pompeu Fabra, Plaça de la Mercè, 10–12, E-08002 Barcelona, Spain. Email: gosta.esping@upf.edu

**Teresa Ghilarducci** is Associate Professor of Economics at the University of Notre Dame and director of the Higgins Labor Research Center at the University. Her new book *The Attack on Retirement* (Princeton University Press, forthcoming), investigates the effect of pension losses on older Americans. Her book *Labor's Capital: The Economics and Politics of Employer Pensions* (MIT Press) won an Association of American Publishers award in 1992. She co-authored *Portable Pension Plans for Casual Labor Markets* in 1995. Professor Ghilarducci testifies frequently before the US Congress, and served on the Pension Benefit Guaranty Corporation's Advisory Board from 1995–2002, and the Board of Trustees of the State of Indiana Public Employees' Retirement Fund from 1997–2002. Address is 510 Flanner Hall, Department of Economics and Policy Studies, University of Notre Dame, Indiana 46556, USA. Email: ghilharducci.1@nd.edu

**Tryggvi Thor Herbertsson** is the Director of the Institute of Economic Studies and Professor of Economics at the University of Iceland. His areas of expertise include pensions and social security, demographics, macroeconomic policy, and economic growth. Herbertsson has published extensively in academic journals and books. He has been a consultant to private companies, institutions, international organizations, as well as number of governments around the world. Professor Herbertsson is a regular commentator on economic policy in the press and is a public speaker on issues regarding pensions and social security. Address is Institute of Economic Studies, University of Iceland, Aragata 14, IS-101 Reykjavik, Iceland. Email: tthh@hi.is

**Roy Hoevenaars** is Senior Researcher ALM at the financial and risk policy department, of ABP. He joined the research department of ABP Investments in 2001 where he did equity research and he was in the strategic and tactical issues group. He is also a Ph.D. candidate at Maastricht University where he does research on asset liability management and strategic asset allocation. He graduated from Maastricht University with an M.A. in econometrics and operations research. Address is PO Box 2889, 6401 DJ Heerlen, Oude Lindestraat 70, The Netherlands. Email: roy.hoevenaars@abp.nl

**Tony Hope** is Professor of Medical Ethics at the University of Oxford, Honorary Consultant Psychiatrist, and Founder of the Ethox Centre. He has carried out research in basic neuroscience and Alzheimer's Disease. Since 1990 his work has focused on medical ethics in clinical practice. He was associate editor of the *Journal of Medical Ethics* for almost 20 years. In addition to papers in the fields of neuroscience, Alzheimer's disease and medical ethics, he has written a number of books including: the *Oxford Handbook of Clinical Medicine* (editions 1–4, with Murray Longmore and others, Oxford University Press, 1985–98); *Manage Your Mind* (with Gillian Butler, Oxford University Press, 1995); *Medical Ethics and Law: The Core Curriculum* (with Julian Savulescu and Judith Hendrick, Churchill Livingstone, 2003) and *Medical Ethics: A Very Short Introduction* (Oxford University

Press, 2004). Address is The Ethox Centre, Departments of Public Health and Primary Health Care, Old Road Campus, Oxford, OX3 7LF, UK. Email: tony.hope@ethox.ox.ac.uk

**Yu-Wei Hu** is currently studying for a Ph.D. in economics at Brunel University, UK. Prior to that, he received a master's degree in Accounting and Finance from the University of Leeds, UK. His current research deals with the extent to which pension reform, pension-fund growth, economic growth, and financial development are linked together across both OECD countries and emerging market economies. In addition, issues on pension fund investment and regulations are investigated, with a particular focus on China. Address is Economics and Finance, Brunel University, Uxbridge, Middlesex, UB8 3PH, UK. Email: Yu-Wei.Hu@brunel.ac.uk

**Paul Johnson** is Professor of Economic History and Deputy Director of the London School of Economics. He has written extensively on the history of welfare, and on the economics of ageing and pensions. His most recent publication is the co-edited *Cambridge Economic History of Modern Britain* (3 vols., Cambridge University Press, 2004). He has served as an adviser on pension reform to the World Bank and the UK government. Address is Department of Economic History, London School of Economics, Houghton Street, London, WC2A 2AE, UK. Email: p.a.johnson@lse.ac.uk

**André Laboul** is the Head of the Financial Affairs Division at the Organisation for Economic Co-operation and Development (OECD). This Division is in charge of financial markets, insurance, and private pensions and services eight OECD-related financial Committees and Groups. He is also the Secretary General of the International Organisation of Pensions Supervisors (IOPS) and the Managing Editor of the *Journal of Pension Economics and Finance* (Cambridge University Press). Before joining the OECD in 1987, he worked in Belgium at the Centre for European Policy Studies (CEPS), the Centre for Law and Economic Research (CRIDE), and the Prime Minister services for Science Policy. Address is OECD, 2, rue André Pascal, 75775 Paris Cedex 16, France. Email: Andre.LABOUL@oecd.org

**Florence Legros** is Professor of Economics at the University Dauphine in Paris. Her research is on issues connected with ageing, pensions, social policies, savings and their effects on economic growth, and financial flows. Legros has served as senior economist in Caisse des depots et consignations, a major French financial institution, has been professor in Perpignan, deputy director of CEPII (a French economic think-tank) before joining Dauphine. She also chairs the prospective council of AF2I (French association of institutional investors) and acts as consultant for various international organizations in the field of retirement, pensions, and macroeconomics. As a specialist in retirement pensions schemes, savings, and financial markets, she has written numerous publications, papers, and books dealing with these topics. Address is University Dauphine, Place du Maréchal de Lattre de Tassigny, 75009 Paris, France. Email: florence.legros@dauphine.fr

**David McCarthy** is a Lecturer of Finance at the Tanaka Business School at Imperial College London. He has researched, taught, and lectured widely on pension fund issues including annuities markets, pension scheme design, pension guarantee funds, and the role of pensions in household portfolios. Current research includes work on mandatory annuitization, the valuation of defined benefit pension promises, and optimal risk sharing in pension scheme design. Address is Tanaka Business School, Exhibition Road, South Kensington, London, SW7 2AZ, UK. Email: dg.mccarthy@imperial.ac.uk

**Warren McGillivray** is an overseas Policy Associate of the Caledon Institute, Ottawa, Canada. From 1993 to 2004 he was Chief of the Studies and Operations Branch of the International Social Security Association in Geneva. After lecturing at the Universities of Dar es Salaam and Lagos, in 1976 he joined the Social Security Department of the International Labour Office. He has undertaken social security advisory assignments in numerous countries and participated in projects involving social security policy and financing. His publications focus on financing social security, actuarial topics, and pensions reform. He is a graduate of the University of Saskatchewan and a Fellow of the Society of Actuaries. Address is 26 Belvédère du Moland, Chemin de la Planche Brûlée, FR-01210 Ferney-Voltaire, France. Email: mcgillivray@caledoninst.org

**Carmelo Mesa-Lago** is Distinguished Service Professor Emeritus of Economics and Latin American Studies at the University of Pittsburgh and has been a visiting professor/researcher in seven countries and a lecturer in 36 countries. The author of 60 books and more than 200 articles/chapters published in eight languages in 33 countries, half of them on social security, his most recent is *Las Reformas de Pensiones en América Latina y los Principios de la Seguridad Social* (Santiago: ECLAC, 2004). He has worked in all countries of Latin America as a regional adviser for ECLAC, a consultant with most international financial organizations, as well as with various UN branches and national and foreign foundations. He was President of the Latin American Studies Association, is a member of the National Academy of Social Insurance and of the Board of the International Social Security Review. He has received the Alexander von Humboldt Stiftung Senior Prize, two Senior Fulbrights, the Arthur Whitaker and Hoover Institution Prizes, and OISS and CISS Homages for his life's work on social security. Address is 1902 Beechwood Blvd., Pittsburgh, PA 15217, USA. Email: cmesa@usa.net

**Marilyn Moon** is Vice President and Director of the Health Program at the American Institutes for Research. A nationally known expert on Medicare, she has served as Senior Fellow at the Urban Institute, senior analyst at the Congressional Budget Office, and public trustee for the Social Security and Medicare trust funds. Marilyn Moon has written extensively on health policy, for both the elderly and the population in general, and on social insurance issues. From 1993 to 2000, Moon wrote a column for the *Washington Post* on health reform and coverage issues. Address is Health Program, American Institutes for Research, 10720 Columbia Pike, Suite 500, Silver Spring, MD 20901-4400, USA. Email: mmoon@air.org

**John Myles** is Canada Research Chair and Professor of Sociology at the University of Toronto and Visiting Research Scholar at Statistics Canada. He is the author of *Old Age in the Welfare State: The Political Economy of Public Pensions* and numerous papers related to the comparative politics of income security. He recently collaborated with Gosta Esping-Andersen, Duncan Gallie, and Anton Hemerijck on a report for the Belgian Presidency of the EU entitled *Why We Need a New Welfare State* (Oxford University Press, 2002). Address is Department of Sociology, 725 Spadina Ave., Room 396, Toronto, ON M5S 2J4, Canada. Email: john.myles@utoronto.ca

**David Neumark** is Professor of Economics at the University of California–Irvine, and a Senior Fellow at the Public Policy Institute of California. A labor economist, his research interests include minimum wages and living wages, affirmative action, gender differences in labor markets, the economics of ageing, the employment relationship, and school-to-work programs. He recently published *Sex Differences in Labor Markets*, and an edited volume titled *The Economics of Affirmative Action*. Prior to joining UCI, Neumark was an economist at the Federal Reserve Board, and held appointments at the University of Pennsylvania and Michigan State University. He is also a Research Associate of the National Bureau of Economic Research, and a Research Fellow at IZA. Address is Department of Economics, 3151 Social Science Plaza, UCI, Irvine, CA 92697, USA. Email: dneumark@uci.edu. Policy Institute of California, 500 Washington Street, Suite 800, San Francisco, CA 94111, USA. Email: neumark@ppic.org

**Naohiro Ogawa** is Professor of Economics and is Deputy Director of the Population Research Institute at Nihon University, Tokyo. Over the last 25 years, he has been written extensively on population and development in Japan and other Asian nations. His numerous papers have been published in international journals including *Population and Development Review, Population Studies, American Economic Review*, and *Journal of Labor Economics*. Address is Population Research Institute, Nihon University, 1-3-2 Misaki-cho, Chiyoda-ku, Tokyo 02-8360, Japan. Email: ogawa@eco.nihon-u.ac.jp

**Hanam S. Phang** is a Senior Fellow at the Korea Labor Institute. He is also an Adjunct Professor of Sociology at the Chung-Ang University in Seoul, Korea. Recent publications include 'The past and future of Korean pension system: a proposal for a coordinated development of the public-private pensions', in *Pensions in Asia* (Maruzen Co., Ltd., 2005) and 'Rapid ageing and labor force changes in

Korea' (International Seminar on Low Fertility and Rapid Ageing, Seoul, Korea). He has been responsible for conducting a long-term research project aimed at introducing a corporate pension system in Korea and has been involved in various international policy initiatives on pension reform in Asian countries. He is currently a visiting scholar at the Institute for Social Research, the University of Michigan. Address is Korea Labor Institute, Yeoido PO Box 518, Seoul, Korea. Email: phang@kli.re.kr

**John Piggott** is Professor of Economics and Director of the Centre for Pensions and Superannuation at the University of New South Wales (UNSW). At UNSW, he is also Associate Dean (Research), Faculty of Commerce and Economics, and from 1999 to 2003 was a Director of UNSW Professorial Superannuation Ltd. His publications include more than 70 journal articles and chapters in books, as well as two co-authored books on pension issues published by Cambridge University Press. Professor Piggott has served on several committees related to superannuation and pension reform in Australia. Internationally, he has consulted with the Government of Mauritius on a World Bank-sponsored pension reform project, and for the last four years has been working on ageing issues with the Cabinet Office, Government of Japan. Address is School of Economics, University of New South Wales, Sydney 2052, Australia. Email: J.Piggott@unsw.edu.au

**Eduard Ponds** is Head of Strategy in the Finance Department of ABP Pension Fund in the Netherlands. He is involved with strategic issues in pension plan design, ALM, and risksharing. Dr Eduard Ponds is also associated with Tilburg University (Netspar) and the University of Amsterdam as lecturer and researcher. His research interests are related to pension fund issues, in particular risk-sharing (*Supplementary Pensions, Intergenerational Risk-sharing and Welfare*, Tilburg University, 1995), pension plan design (*Pensions*, 2003), and generational accounting (*Journal of Pension Economics and Finance*, 2003). He is the author of many publications in Dutch related to the pension debate in the Netherlands. Email: e.ponds@abp.nl

**James M. Poterba** is the Mitsui Professor of Economics at the Massachusetts Institute of Technology. He is also the Director of the Public Economics Research Program at the National Bureau of Economic Research, a Fellow of the American Academy of Arts and Sciences, and the Econometric Society, and is one of the editors of the *Journal of Public Economics*. Dr Poterba's research focuses on the economic analysis of taxation and financial markets. His recent work has emphasized the effect of taxation on the financial behavior of households, and in particular on accumulation and spend-down behavior in tax-deferred retirement saving programs such as 401(k) plans. Address is MIT Department of Economics, E52-350, 50 Memorial Drive, Cambridge, MA 02142-1347, USA. Email: poterba@mit.edu

**Neha Sand** is an economist in the Watson Wyatt research centre in Delhi. She has an MA in economics from the Delhi School of Economics. At Watson Wyatt, she has led various projects on pension accounting and pension corporate finance. Her research interests also include pension communication and financial education. Address is Watson Wyatt Insurance Consulting Private Limited, 9th Floor, JMD Regent Square, Mehrauli Gurgaon Road, Gurgaon 122001, India. Email: neha.sand@watsonwyatt.com

**Steven Sass** is Associate Director for Research at the Center for Retirement Research at Boston College. Before coming to Boston College he was an economist at the Federal Reserve Bank of Boston. Sass is the author of *The Promise of Private Pensions* (Harvard University Press, 1997) and co-edited *Social Security Reform: Links to Saving, Investment, and Growth* (Federal Reserve Bank of Boston, 1997). He is currently working on the reform of national retirement income systems, the labor market for older workers, and housing as a retirement income asset. Address is Center for Retirement Research, Boston College, 550 Fulton Hall, Chestnut Hill, MA 02467, USA. Email: steven.sass@bc.edu

**Julian Savulescu** is the Uehiro Chair in Practical Ethics and Director of the Oxford Uehiro Centre for Practical Ethics at Oxford University. Previously, he was Director of the Ethics of Genetics Unit at the Murdoch Children's Research Institute, Royal Children's Hospital, Melbourne, Australia. Julian Savulescu is qualified in medicine, bioethics, and analytic philosophy. He has published many articles in journals such as the *British Medical Journal, Lancet, Australasian Journal of Philosophy, Bioethics*, the *Journal of Medical Ethics, American Journal of Bioethics, Medical Journal of Australia and Philosophy*, and *Psychiatry and Psychology*. Address is Oxford Uehiro Centre for Practical Ethics, Littlegate House, St Ebbes, Oxford, OX1 1PT, UK. Email: julian.savulescu@philosophy.ox.ac.uk

**Tom Steenkamp** is Head of Allocation and Research and member of the board of ABP Investments. He is also (part-time) Professor of Investments at the Vrije Universiteit Amsterdam where he is responsible for the postgraduate course in Investments and Finance. Recent publications include 'Simulation for the Long Run', in *Asset and Liability Management Tools* (ed. B. Sherer, Risk Books, 2003), *Asset Allocation and Portfolio Construction* (Riskmatrix, 2004), and 'Dynamic commodity Timing Strategies', a working paper in review. Research interests are in the field of strategic asset allocation and asset and liability management. Address is PO Box 2889, 6401 DJ Heerlen, Oude Lindestraat 70, the Netherlands. Email: t.steenkamp@abp.nl

**Annika Sundén** is a Senior Economist at the Swedish Social Insurance Agency. Previously, Dr Sundén was the Associate Director of Research at the Center for Retirement Research at Boston College. She has also worked as an Economist at the Federal Reserve Board in Washington, DC. Dr Sundén's research interests include the economics of social insurance, retirement, and household savings behavior. Recent publications include *Coming Up Short: The Challenge of 401(k) Plans*

(Brookings Institution Press, 2004 with Alicia Munnell), and 'Portfolio choice, trading and returns in a large 401(k) plan', *The American Economic Review*, 2003. Address is Swedish Social Insurance Agency, 103 51 Stockholm, Sweden. Email: annika.sunden@sofi.su.se

**Noriyuki Takayama** is Professor of Economics at Hitotsubashi University, Tokyo. He is Director General and CEO of the Project on Intergenerational Equity (PIE). He has published numerous books and articles in international publications including *Econometrica* and *American Economic Review* and he edited the book titled *Taste of Pie: Searching for Better Pension Provisions in Developed Countries* (Maruzen Co., Ltd., 2003) and *Pensions in Asia: Incentives, Compliance and Their Role in Retirement* (Maruzen Co., Ltd., 2005). He works as a key player on the pension policy of Japan. Address is Institute of Economic Research, Hitotsubashi University, 2-1, Naka, Kunitachi, Tokyo, 186-8603, Japan. Email: takayama@ier. hit-u.ac.jp

**Patricia Thane** is Leverhulme Professor of Contemporary British History and Director of the Centre for Contemporary British History at the Institute of Historical Research, University of London. Relevant publications include: *Old Age in English History: Past Experiences, Present Issues* (Oxford University Press, 2000), *Women and Ageing in British Society since 1500*, co-edited with Lynn Botelho (Longman, 2001), and *Old Age from Antiquity to Post-Modernity*, co-edited with Paul Johnson (Routledge, 1998). Address is Institute of Historical Research, University of London, London, WC1E 7HU, UK. Email: pat.thane@sas.ac.uk

**Ian Tonks** is Director of the Xfi Centre for Finance and Investment at the University of Exeter. His research focuses on pension economics, fund manager performance, market microstructure and the organization of stock exchanges, directors' trading, and the new issue market. He is a consultant to the Financial Markets Group, and the Centre for Market and Public Organisation. He has previously held positions at the University of Bristol, and the London School of Economics, and has held visiting positions at University of British Columbia, Solvay Business School, Brussels; City University Business School; Ecole Nationale Des Ponts et Chaussées, Paris; and LSE Summer Schools at Moscow and St Petersberg teaching finance courses. He has acted as a consultant to a number of commercial and regulatory organisations, and has advised the Department of Work and Pensions and the House of Commons Select Committee on issues in pensions. Address is Xfi University of Exeter, Xfi Building, Rennes Drive, Exeter, EX4 4ST, UK. Email: i.tonks@exeter.ac.uk

**Bart van Riel** is Senior Policy Officer at the Netherlands Social-Economic Council (SER). He was involved in preparing several SER-advisory reports on pensions, population ageing, and economic and social aspects of European integration. He also participates in the European Studies Programme at Leiden University and is a fellow of the Amsterdam Institute of Advanced Labour Studies. Recent publications include (together with Anton Hemerijck and Jelle Visser) 'Is there a Dutch way to pension reform?', in Gordon L. Clark and N. Whiteside (eds.), *Pension Security in the 21st Century* (Oxford University Press, 2003) and (together with Kees Goudswaard) 'Social protection in Europe: do we need more coordination?' (*Tijdschrift voor Arbeidsvraagstukken, 2004*). Address is Social and Economic Council, P.O. Box 90405, 2509 LK, The Hague, The Netherlands Email: b.van.riel@ser.nl

**Steven F. Venti** is the DeWalt H. Ankeny Professor of Economic Policy and Professor of Economics at Dartmouth College. He is also a Faculty Research Associate at the National Bureau of Economic Research. Professor Venti's research focuses on the relationship between tax policy and saving, the effectiveness of saving incentives, housing policy, and the process of wealth accumulation. Address is Department of Economics, Dartmouth College, 6106 Rockefeller Center, Hanover, NH 03755, USA. Email: steven.f.venti@dartmouth.edu

**Luis M. Viceira** is an Associate Professor at the Harvard Business School. His research focuses on the analysis of asset allocation strategies for long-term investors, both individuals and institutions, in the face of changing interest rates, risk premia, and risk. His book, co-authored with Professor John Y. Campbell, *Strategic Asset Allocation* (Oxford University Press), received the TIAA-CREF Paul Samuelson Award for 'outstanding scholarly writing on lifelong financial security'. Professor Viceira is also the author of multiple articles published in leading academic finance journals, and of Harvard Business School cases on the investment and organizational problems of large, long-term institutional investors. He is a member of the Academic Advisory Board of ABP Investments in the Netherlands, a Faculty Research Fellow of the NBER, a Research Affiliate for the Centre for Economic Policy Research, and a member of the Scientific Council of Netspar, the network for research on the economics of pensions, ageing, and retirement. Address is Graduate School of Business Administration, Harvard University, Morgan Hall 395, Boston, MA 02163, USA. Email: lviceira@hbs.edu

**Noel Whiteside** is Professor of Comparative Public Policy and Senior Fellow at the Institute of Governance and Public Management at Warwick University, UK. She works on labor markets and social security in historical and comparative perspective, including the public regulation of private systems. Recent publications include the co-edited *Pension Security in the 21st Century* (Oxford University Press, 2003) and numerous academic articles addressing income security in old age. Recent research, co-funded by government and Zurich Financial Services, has focused on European pension debates and the promotion of public value. She is currently writing a book on European welfare and the politics of capability. Address is Department of Sociology, University of Warwick, Coventry, CV4 7AL, UK. Email: N.Whiteside@warwick.ac.uk

**Geoffrey Whittington** is a member of the International Accounting Standards Board with responsibility for liaison with the UK standard-setting body (the ASB). He is also a Senior Associate of the Judge Institute of Management Studies at Cambridge. He has held chairs of accounting at the Universities of Edinburgh, Bristol, and Cambridge, and has served as a member of the UK Monopolies and Mergers Commission. Honours include the ACCA/BAA Distinguished Academic of the Year Award in 1994, an honorary doctorate from the University of Edinburgh, and a CBE. In 2003, he was awarded the Founding Societies' Centenary Award of the Institute of Chartered Accountants in England and Wales. His interest in accounting for pension costs dates from his service on the ASB at the time when FRS 17 was being developed. Address is IASB, 30 Cannon St., London, EC4M 6XH, UK. Email: gwhittington@iasb.org.uk

**David A. Wise** is the Stambaugh Professor of Political Economy at the John F. Kennedy School of Government at Harvard University. He is also the Area Director of Health and Retirement Programs, and Director of the Program on the Economics of Aging, at the National Bureau of Economic Research, and a Senior Fellow at the Hoover Institution at Stanford University. He has written extensively about the saving effect of personal retirement programs—such as Individual Retirement Accounts and 401(k) plans in the United States—and more recently has been evaluating the implications of the rapid spread of these programs, which now are the dominant form of saving for retirement in the Unites States. He has also written extensively on the retirement incentives of defined benefit pension programs in the Unites States. In addition, he has been analyzing the incentive effects and features of employer-provided health insurance programs, the financial implications of housing wealth for the elderly, social secutiry reform, and other economics of aging issues. He is currently engaged in analysis of the retirement incentives in public social security programs around the world. He can be reached at the National Bureau of Economic Research, Cambridge, MA 02138, USA. Email: dwise@nber.org

**Juan Yermo** is a Principal Administrator in charge of private pensions projects in the OECD's Financial Affairs Division. He is the secretary of the Working Party on Private Pensions, a body that brings together policy-makers and the private sector from the 30 member countries. He manages a broad research program on various issues related to the operation and regulation of privately managed retirement income systems. Previously, he was a consultant for the World Bank Group on pension reform projects in Latin America. He was educated at Cambridge and Oxford Universities. Address is OECD, 2, rue André Pascal, 75775 Paris Cedex 16, France. Email: juan.yermo@oecd.org

# INTRODUCTION

CHAPTER 1

# THE AGENDA

## GORDON L. CLARK, ALICIA H. MUNNELL, AND J. MICHAEL ORSZAG

Nation-states around the world are growing increasingly uneasy about their capacity to deliver retirement income to those approaching retirement age. In most cases, the implicit or explicit compact between generations and between different groups in societies will be rewritten to lower benefits. Sometimes quietly discussed and other times disputed in the pages of the financial press, the inability to sustain the living standards of an ageing population may prompt a long drawn-out conflict between generations. In a world of increasing economic integration and head-to-head competition for markets, few countries can afford to impose upon working people and their enterprises the taxes necessary to sustain long-term living standards for retirees. The risk is not that of poverty in the industrialized world—paying to keep the elderly out of poverty in the OECD is affordable—but that expectations about replacement rates will be difficult if not impossible to manage.

For the developed and industrialized economies these changes have been well documented. Think-tanks, governmental inquiries, lobby groups, and academics have all pointed to the ageing of the population as the most challenging issue confronting pension and retirement income institutions over the next 25 years. We know that demographic ageing is the result of lower fertility rates in younger and successively smaller age cohorts on the one hand, and increased longevity of older workers on the other. Compounding these trends, of course, have been restrictions upon migration to many European countries and the concentration of migrant streams to certain jurisdictions within those nations. It is inevitable that the baby-boom generation now approaching retirement and future generations will have to work longer than expected and retire on lower-than-expected incomes.

For the less developed world, transition economies, and the rapidly developing economies of Asia, issues of ageing and pension costs also loom large, though farther into the future so they have more time to deal with the problems. For example, what kind of pension and retirement income institutions ought to be introduced to replace state-sponsored institutions? Can systems modeled on the theories and experience of North America and Western Europe improve long-term standards of living? For that matter, in the two largest populated economies of the world—China and India—can inherited theoretical frameworks provide insights about the pension and retirement income consequences of industrialization, urbanization, and ultimately (even if delayed) demographic ageing?

Recent volatility in global financial markets has raised the spectre of wholesale changes in the structure and value of employer-provided pension plans and private insurance arrangements across the Anglo-American world. These circumstances are, in effect, accelerating long-term trends as the shift from defined benefit plans to defined contribution systems and private insurance contracts expose beneficiaries to the full force of market risks previously assumed by employers and other financial and political institutions

# 1 Goals of the *Handbook*

The *Oxford Handbook of Pensions and Retirement Income* offers a comprehensive overview of the major intellectual frameworks and principles, analytical methods and techniques, and policy-related tools regarding nation-state pension and retirement income institutions. Demographic ageing, changing financial circumstances of nation-states, and the forces of globalization compel us to reassess our inherited institutions and policies. We must rethink the accepted frameworks and principles underpinning retirement income institutions to provide the basis for academic, industry, and policy-related research to move forward in the future.

To carry out this re-evaluation, we need to identify the relevant issues in relation to the structure and performance of different types of pension systems and to assess recent research so as to cast a critical eye over contemporary issues. We also need to be conscious of what was inherited from the past and how the past casts both an institutional and intellectual shadow over what may transpire in the future. In this regard, the goals of the *Handbook* can be summarized as follows:

- to bring together in one book a comprehensive statement on the theoretical frameworks used to understand the structure and performance of pension and retirement income institutions;
- to demonstrate the significance of the historical, social, and demographic context in which these institutions have developed, and an appreciation of the economic and financial drivers of pension and retirement income benefits;
- to report the latest research on these topics in a manner that is accessible to a non-technical academic audience from social sciences, economics, and finance, thereby being *the* reference point for research and teaching at the advanced undergraduate, graduate, and professional levels;
- to reach out from the developed world, with its own theoretical frameworks and methods of analysis, to the transition economies, developing economies, and the less developed economies facing similar issues;
- to be a source of information, commentary, and expertise relevant to policy-makers, financial institutions, and the financial services industry involved in the provision of pension and retirement income.

These goals are ambitious given the variety of pension and retirement income institutions around the world. But, of course there are important commonalities, overlapping points of reference, and related programs of pension reform. One of the challenges of the book has been to relate commonalities with differences, drawing on shared intellectual frameworks and traditions. As a consequence, the book is large and full of argument and analysis provided through 42 chapters and more than 50 contributors. It will be up to our readers to judge whether we have achieved our goals.

## 2 THE THEORETICAL CHALLENGE

Hidden just below the surface of this brief commentary is a complex world of nation-state institutions, social and political expectations, and financial markets. We hope that the selection of topics, contributors, and disciplinary perspectives provides the reader with an understanding of the significance of these institutions and their intersection. Our point in making these observations is twofold: across the world, the prospects for pension and retirement income are quite uncertain, and the consequences of current and prospective economic circumstances combined with long-term demographic strains have raised profound intellectual and policy-related questions about the sustainability of our inherited institutions.

It would be misleading to suggest that academics have ignored these types of issues. Quite the contrary. Considerable research has been devoted to the introduction, evolution, and current problems facing national welfare states. See, for example, the remarkable literature prompted by Esping-Andersen (1990). At the same time, an increasing body of research has addressed the impact of changing economic, demographic, and social organizations on the value and structure of retirement incomes. See, for example, the related literature on gender and inequality (Whiteside 2003). Similarly, a rather technical literature has developed in economics on comparative pension systems, the financial aspects of private pensions, and the cost and consequences of annuities. See, for example, the volume edited by Feldstein and Siebert (2002). For those seeking detailed knowledge of national social security institutions, researchers have produced compendiums on the rules and regulations governing retirement systems. See, for example, Gillian (2000).

In the next chapter, we review the literature of the most important research themes, institutions, and academic perspectives that define the field. Since our goal is to provide the reader with broad-ranging perspectives on pension and retirement income across disciplines, we draw on literature from the humanities, social sciences, and a number of disciplines in the life sciences, rather than remaining sheltered behind the walls of any one discipline. One of the challenges in the development of the academic field of pension and retirement income is the need to sustain a broad perspective of the relevant issues as well as a deep technical understanding of the design and implementation of particular pension systems.

Furthermore, much of the literature has treated pension and retirement income questions as being entirely contained within nation-state borders. Looking forward, however, any comprehensive understanding of pension and retirement income systems must be set within the context of globalization. A global perspective recognizes the movement of people across borders, competition between corporations within industries, and the allocation of rights and entitlements by citizenship or geographical location.

And yet, for all the significance of increased globalization, our pension and retirement income systems have come out of twentieth-century nation-states. Deeply embedded in this volume, therefore, is a tension between the heritage of pension and retirement income systems set against current and prospective trends. The challenge is to simultaneously recognize our inherited institutions and practices, while looking forward to new kinds of intellectual frameworks and institutions. Only by combining these two aspects can we find inventive solutions to the challenges posed by global competition and demographic ageing. Our intention is that the structure of the book, the topics identified, and our contributors provide the groundwork necessary for this ambitious intellectual enterprise.

## 3 Structure and Organization

In designing the book with respect to both its contents and its contributors, we were mindful that understanding the challenges facing pension and retirement income institutions requires an appreciation of the past, present, and future. At the same time, this enterprise requires a detailed understanding of the structure and performance of particular kinds of pension and retirement income systems. In what follows, we sought to present these elements in ways that allow the reader to use the book as a general text as well as a reference point. As a consequence, we have recruited contributors with a variety of skills and perspectives.

To begin, we (as the editors) use the Preface and this chapter to set the book in a most general and broad-ranging context, applicable, we hope, to readers around the world. Inevitably, we begin from our own experience and knowledge of developed economies over the past 50 years or so. We can hardly do otherwise. At the same time, contributors from around the world with extensive experience in both developed and developing economies enable readers to appreciate the variety of pension and retirement income systems. Having set the agenda in this chapter, we go on to look at pension research over the past 40 or 50 years in order to provide academics and those with an interest in the development of the field with a better understanding of where we have come from and where we might be going.

Thereafter, the book is organized into five major parts, with each part being organized around a series of sections and themes. Part I provides the reader with important historical, social, and economic perspectives on the field. It is vital to understand both the history of retirement and the significance of pension and retirement income systems as social and economic institutions. The origins of these institutions are rooted in debates stretching back over at least a century. And yet, of course, one lesson of Part I is that the past is not necessarily the future. In many respects, the future of pension and retirement income systems is increasingly on a collision course with the economics of demographic ageing. These systems are increasingly in play as the objects of political argument and dispute. We return to this issue in Part V of the book.

In Parts II, III, and IV we look at the provision of retirement income through public pensions, employer, or third-party pension provision, and then individual or household saving. This structure reproduces the logic to be found in many other reports on pension and retirement income provision. These three 'pillars' hardly ever exist alone; almost all countries provide pension and retirement income through a combination of these three types of pension systems. Of course, the combination of pension institutions and their relative contributions to total retirement income vary considerably between countries in the developed world, and can be very different indeed in the underdeveloped world where family and household systems provide the bulk of old-age support.

Public retirement plans often provide more than retirement income and include bundles of benefits and obligations. Likewise, employer-sponsored retirement plans should be thought of as financial systems as well as systems of negotiation and accountability. We emphasize this kind of institution precisely because of its contemporary significance in the debate over social security reform. Another important issue is the role that housing wealth may play in the long-term welfare of middle-class retirees. Likewise, longer life and restricted nation-state budgets may imply far greater family responsibilities than commonly assumed over the past 50 years or so.

The last part of the book looks ahead. This section is by necessity speculative because whatever happens in the future will depend on the interplay between politics, economics, and social welfare forces. Looking back to the nineteenth century, we can see in debate about old-age pension provision just how fragile were coalitions of support for retirement income provision and the remarkable juxtaposition of events, personalities, and economic imperatives in reform initiatives. Surely one of the most important developments affecting the provision of pension and retirement income will be globalization, its effects on nations' revenue and expenditures, industry competition, and political conflict. Although we do not have a crystal ball, we asked our contributors to think about prospective models of pension provision and important research frontiers that a new generation of researchers might take seriously. In thinking about the future, it is also important to understand what is happening in Latin America, East Asia, and Africa. In conclusion, we have asked two contributors to look back and forward about the most problematic issue of securing retirement itself.

## 4 OUR READERS

It is anticipated that the *Handbook* will have three main groups of readers. Its primary market will be upper-level undergraduates, graduate students, and academics in economics, finance, social policy, economic geography, and politics (in that order). It will also have considerable appeal for policy-makers and pension regulators and supervisors around the world. Finally, we expect that it will have a limited, but nonetheless important, market in the global financial services industry.

The audience for the *Oxford Handbook* cuts across the social science disciplines. Readers will recognize the importance of historical, sociological, and economic issues as well as crucial theoretical concepts of system design and performance. Our readers will also include those whose interests lie less in economics and finance and more in institutional structure and performance. Finally, our readers will also include those who have an interest in research on the pension and retirement income institutions in transition economies, developing economies, and less developed economies.

The intellectual agenda on pensions and retirement income is increasingly being set by multidisciplinary research programs inside and outside of universities. The constituencies with an interest in pension and retirement income institutions include the advocates of old-age welfare, their lobby groups, governments who face an enormous burden of accumulated benefit commitments, and financial institutions near and far that see markets for retirement welfare growing at the margins of existing institutions.

All these groups and organizations seek answers or at least clarity regarding the most important questions concerning pensions and retirement income, and it is to this broad constituency of interest groups that this *Handbook* is addressed.

# REFERENCES

ESPING-ANDERSEN, G. (1990). *The Three Worlds of Welfare Capitalism.* Oxford: Polity Press.
FELDSTEIN, M., and SIEBERT, H. (eds.) (2001). *Social Security Reform in Europe.* Chicago: University of Chicago Press.
WHITESIDE, N. (2003). 'Historical perspectives and the politics of pension reform', in G. L. Clark and N. Whiteside (eds.), *Pension Security in the 21st Century.* Oxford: Oxford University Press, 21–43.

CHAPTER 2

# PENSION AND RETIREMENT INCOME IN A GLOBAL ENVIRONMENT

GORDON L. CLARK,
ALICIA H. MUNNELL,
AND J. MICHAEL ORSZAG

## 1 INTRODUCTION

With the prompting of the World Bank (1994, 2005), and the OECD (1998, 2000), policy analysts and the public at large have come to recognize that the ageing of the population raises difficult questions as to the funding of the generous pension benefits promised in the wake of the Second World War. Because of dramatic increases in longevity and declines in fertility, by 2050 the ratio of elderly to working age population will be at unprecedented levels. In many countries, this dramatic increase in the dependency ratio threatens not only the fiscal integrity of the pension system but perhaps even the solvency of the nation-state (Tanzi and Schuknecht 2000).

The ageing of the population and the pressure that it puts on the pension systems raises a host of issues spread across academic disciplines. In terms of comparative economics, countries vary significantly in their ability to fund prospective entitlements. If the past is a guide to the future, in some countries that future could impoverish both young and old. Not surprisingly, such differences between nation-states are grist for the academic mill (Boeri *et al.* 2001). Furthermore, increasing economic integration may also limit the ability of nation-states to fulfill their pension promises. In terms of philosophy, the projected shortfall in funding raises important issues of social justice and inter-generational equity. In terms of political science, large numbers of older citizens will form a formidable political bloc. Pensioner poverty and the extent to which younger generations owe their parents and grandparents a living income will be on the political agenda in ways unimagined 25 years ago.

As policy-makers and the public consider reform of their pension systems, it is important to remember what was inherited from the past, including the bargains struck between social and political interests at a time of institutional innovation. That is not to say that the past is necessarily the future, despite the veritable scholastic industry demonstrating the inexorable power of path dependence (Hall and Soskice 2001). Indeed, the experience in different parts of the world shows the ability of institutions, regulatory regimes, and customs and conventions to change even if in the face of entrenched interests committed to preserving the past. Our own research has demonstrated the responsiveness of market actors to financial imperatives, such as the unanticipated adjustments of German corporations to global financial markets (Clark and Wojcik forthcoming). Of course, a few assertions and citations hardly overturn the notion of path dependence but they do raise questions about claims of historical inevitability.

As with inheritance from the past, globalization is also a vital part of the pension story, even if public and private pension systems have been relatively insulated from the immediate effects of global competition. The intersection between demographic trends, domestic fiscal and financial systems, and global competition for the fruits of economic growth has not been adequately conceptualized. Many analysts write as if pension and retirement income systems are firmly ensconced behind the 'high walls' of national borders. This perspective is not surprising, given that much of the literature comes from sociology and political science over the formation of the welfare state. Close scrutiny of nation-state pension systems themselves began in earnest only in the last 20 years, so few researchers have placed national systems in the global environment. This is part of our research agenda.

This chapter begins with the past—with the late nineteenth-century British debate over the proper provision, nature of benefits, and funding of old-age pensions. This debate has been widely discussed elsewhere (see e.g. Thane 2000, and Chapter 3 this volume). Nevertheless, it provides two important points of reference that should inform academic research. First, the size of the elderly population has changed dramatically. In the world's wealthiest economy at the turn of the twentieth century, those aged 65 years or older were only about 5 percent of the population, compared to about 18 percent in 2000, and 37 percent forecast for 2050. Second, the British debate is the first instance where the theories and methods of social science enquiry were put to use for policy purposes. The skills and experience of leading reformers, academics, and government officials informed the discussion about old-age pension provision. The chapter then works through issues related to the evolution of pension and retirement income provision over the twentieth century. Finally, it reviews the components of the retirement income system, beginning with PAYG (pay-as-you-go) social security (Pillar I), employer-sponsored supplementary schemes (Pillar II), and, finally, individual retirement products (Pillar III).

# 2 THE GREAT PENSIONS DEBATE

London in the nineteenth century was the dominant international financial center. Then, as now, it attracted migrants from the rest of the UK, Europe, and the world. For all its imperial wealth, however, many residents were poor. According to Gareth Stedman Jones (1971), the incidence of poverty was directly related to the competitive nature of the labor market. Recurrent waves of inwards migration, highly variable rates of economic growth, and limited job tenure in the hundreds of thousands of small enterprises that dominated London all contributed to fierce competition for jobs. The scramble for a living preoccupied men, women, and children in ways consistent with the experience of residents in today's mega-cities of the developing world.

Although social reformers were acutely aware of the cruel conditions in which many people lived, much of the debate about urban poverty was about individual virtue. Commentators stressed the need to develop amongst the working classes the virtues of thrift, industriousness, and self-help. Few argued that the state had any responsibility for the welfare of those most at risk from the vicissitudes of market capitalism. The vulnerable elderly had few refuges from poverty. Most families could scarcely cope with their children's needs let alone the needs of their elderly relatives. Charities were thinly spread, and, at best, proffered only modest aid.

The nineteenth century debate in the UK over old-age poverty provides a crucial reference point for understanding the nature and scope of inherited institutions in the developed world (Sires 1954). This debate was very much informed by the methods and techniques of analysis associated with the social sciences. Indeed, recent debate about the prospects for PAYG pension and retirement income institutions over the twenty-first century has grappled with the same issues then analyzed in parliamentary hearings. The analysis presented by the Parliamentary Select Committee on Age Deserving Poor in 1899 regarding the structure and long-term cost of an old-age PAYG pension scheme offers a wonderful example.

After an introduction devoted to previous reports disputing the need for an old-age pension scheme, the Committee argued that 'cases are too often to be found in which poor and aged people, whose conduct and whose whole career has been blameless, industrious, and deserving, find themselves for no fault of their own, at the end of a long and meritorious life, with nothing but the workhouse or inadequate outdoor relief, as a refuge for their declining years'. A wide range of reformers, government officials, and experts submitted evidence on behalf of the 'deserving poor'. Experts offered empirical tests to discredit the idea that the aged were poor because of moral laxity. As well, the Committee drew upon the advice and evidence of Charles Booth and his extensive surveys of poverty in and around London. Members examined tables of data on the incidence of old-age poverty drawn from survey data to build a comprehensive picture of destitution. Finally, underpinning the whole enterprise was the advice of leading government actuaries and economists, including testimony on urban poverty by Professor Alfred Marshall from Cambridge University.

To provide a comparative reference point, and evidence that old-age pension schemes could be successfully introduced in ways consistent with British standards, the Committee reported upon evidence gleaned by a government official's visit to Denmark. (Danish pensions were viewed as more relevant than the German social insurance system because they were of similar value to those anticipated by the Committee.) The Committee evidenced considerable interest in the indexing of Danish pension benefits to price changes in different types of communities, differentiating, for example, between rural areas, small towns, and large cities (especially Copenhagen). Members also scrutinized the administrative costs of the Danish pension system, and heard evidence about the use of qualifications in the Danish system to determine eligibility for a pension, and especially three disqualifications: a prison sentence, moral turpitude, and the receipt of Poor Law relief. And, most importantly, the Committee discussed the need to maintain incentives for individuals to save for their own future rather than relying entirely upon the pension institution.

With evidence on the incidence and causes of poverty and the template for a system consistent with British interests, the Committee argued that to do nothing about old-age poverty would intensify cruelty and great suffering. The Committee recommended the establishment of a national scheme where eligibility for a pension would be based on seven conditions. These were (1) being a British subject, (2) being 65 years of age or over, (3) having not been convicted and imprisoned for an offence over the past 20 years, (4) having not received poor relief over the past 20 years except for exceptional reasons, (5) with proof of residence in a district,

(6) being not in receipt of an income from any source of more than 10 shillings a week, and (7) with proof to the effect that they had made provision for themselves and immediate dependents to the best of their ability with 'reasonable providence' and thrift. This proposal was not enacted, but was clearly important in framing the 1908 Act.

The Committee then sought to determine the likely current and future cost of its proposal to the Exchequer. To determine how many people were 65 years of age or older, they began with the Population Census of 1891 and extrapolated those figures through to 1921. This process gave due regard to the most important components of any population forecast including the birth-rate, the death-rate, emigration, and immigration (compare with Preston *et al.* 2001). It was acknowledged that unexpected variations in each component could make a big difference to long-term population projections. It was determined that in 1899 there were 31.7 million people in England and Wales of which 1.4 million—4.7 percent—were aged 65 or older. The Committee then made estimates for the number of people who met the other eligibility criteria. Determining the numbers of people who had made reasonable efforts to look after themselves was considerably more difficult. The decision was to determine eligibility on a case-by-case basis through a Pension Authority with offices in districts throughout the UK.

Here are the rudiments for a systematic approach to pension and retirement income policy-making: data on need, expert evidence on current circumstances, an assessment of reform options, a comparative perspective to learn from other countries, and the methods and models necessary to estimate the costs of a new policy. The Committee recognized the importance of demography for estimating the costs of PAYG entitlements. Despite the relatively small number of people over the age of 65, for cost reasons the 1908 Act set the pension age at 70 years, not 65 years as recommended by the 1899 Select Committee (or 60 years as in the Danish case). This simple story, told without reference to the politics of policy-making, demonstrates how reformers set aside nineteenth-century morality and gained important insights as to the industrial and urban causes of old-age poverty.

# 3 Social Solidarity in the Twentieth Century

The nineteenth-century UK debate over the development of state pensions raises three issues relevant for understanding twentieth-century social policy. Most obvious is the terms and conditions potential recipients must meet in order to qualify for benefits. By 1945, vestiges of nineteenth-century morality had been expunged from nation-state pension and welfare systems. For example, nothing in the Beveridge Report of 1944 referred to turn-of-the-century conditions such as thriftiness and moral character. Nevertheless, even with the introduction of the welfare state immediately after the Second World War, the British social security system was more concerned with basic 'need' than income replacement on the basis of work-related contributions. The reasons for this distinctive feature of UK pension policy when compared to continental Europe and other countries such as the United States have been discussed extensively (see e.g. Budd and Campbell 1998).

The second issue raised by the nineteenth-century debate was the relationship between employers and employees (in modern parlance), which had been disturbed by a combination of urban residential segregation, burgeoning labor supply, economic instability, and new forms of industry and economic organization. The nineteenth-century reformers grappling with the consequences of urban and industrial capitalism were forced to acknowledge that the paternal concern of owners for the well-being of their workers could not be relied upon as it had been for so many past centuries. Furthermore, those giving evidence to parliamentary inquiries recounted time and again the inadequacies of the existing welfare system, based, as it was, on institutions derived from the agrarian revolution rather than the industrial revolution.

Finally, the debate about pension need and entitlement was also a debate about the past, present, and future social and economic organization of welfare. The idea that the nation-state was to stand in place of paternal relationships, local systems of welfare, and charitable organizations represented a remarkable moment in the consolidation of the power of the nation-state (Bayly 2004). It also reflected a realization that the elderly *deserved* the protection of the nation-state. This is not to say that the nation-state wholly replaced past institutions and forms of pension welfare. In the Anglo-American world at least, employer-sponsored pension systems and other kinds of pension and retirement income institutions persisted alongside each new initiative.

National pensions systems introduced in the aftermath of the Second World War reflected a commitment to universality growing out of the enormous economic and political upheavals of the first four decades of the twentieth century. The mass poverty of the Great Depression in many countries of the developed world undercut vestiges of nineteenth-century liberal virtues: self-reliance and cooperative institutions could not deal with urban and rural poverty on a grand scale. At the same time, those countries that experienced hyperinflation during the 1920s and 1930s witnessed the wholesale discounting of private savings and pension benefits. By the end of the 1930s, a lethal combination of unemployment and financial instability had impoverished the European middle classes. This devastation helps explain why, in continental Europe at least, private pension and retirement income systems have had so little political support.

In the aftermath of the Great Depression and the Second World War, pension reform was an important component in the creation of welfare states across the world. The shape and structure of each welfare state owed much to national political and social coalitions. Although the UK looked to Denmark in its nineteenth-century debate over social security, nation-specific compromises determined the structure of each country's system. Indeed, more often than not, nation-state welfare institutions were designed to 'regulate' the relationships between social classes in the context of their experience of the 1930s and the postwar settlement of the mid-1940s. In many countries, the population had a sense of obligation to the elderly, who had endured the privations of the Great Depression and had survived the war. Furthermore, since official population forecasts replayed earlier assumptions that nation-state populations would be stable or even declining over the coming decades, the costing and design of nation-state welfare systems paid little heed to the emerging baby-boom generation.

It is important to emphasize that nation-state welfare systems were often comprehensive sets of overlapping entitlements conceived for social and political purposes more so than for their economic consequences. These systems accommodated unemployment and under-employment without regard to the long-term financial viability of each system of entitlement. Being pay-as-you-go and dependent upon the flow of nation-state tax revenue, the value of welfare state benefits was more a question of income distribution than it was an issue of fiscal budgeting. For much of continental Europe, on the front line of the Cold War, social and political stability in conditions of considerable economic uncertainty were arguably the most important goals of the welfare state and its pension and retirement income institutions. With each period of unemployment and job displacement, the welfare state ameliorated the burdens of adjustment.

In a number of countries, notably France, pension systems bore the burden of industrial restructuring. In the Netherlands, early retirement funded by retirement income institutions limited the number seeking employment when job creation slowed. In Italy, public sector pensions were quite generous, in part because the public sector was an important employer of last resort and in part because the public did not appreciate the long-term costs of greater longevity among the retired. In short, postwar pension and retirement income institutions, situated under the umbrella of the welfare state, played important roles in the regulation of labor supply and the distribution of income (Gruber and Wise 1999). Only in the last two decades of the twentieth century did policy-makers begin to understand the enormous fiscal burden created by these systems (compare Esping-Anderson 1999 with Tanzi and Schuknecht 2000).

The first steps taken to reform PAYG pensions systems tended to be modest. Governments have reduced benefits, in many cases, by a combination of increasing the number of years required to obtain maximum amount and by switching from wage to price indexation after retirement. Some reforms have tightened the link between contributions and benefits and capped benefits for higher income groups. Others have dampened incentives for early retirement and put in place incentives to encourage continued employment. Finally, some countries have considered some forward funding, albeit at modest levels, of long-term retirement income obligations. Even these modest reforms have been widely contested, precipitating political upheaval in the largest European economies. Major structural reform, such as that undertaken in Australia and Sweden, has been widely studied but rarely incorporated into pension reform movements (Edey and Simon 1998; Palme 2003).

It is only recently that experts have analyzed nation-state pension and retirement income institutions with the same clarity and focus as in the last decade of the nineteenth century. Idealism combined with entrenched interests at first denied the need to consider the long-term viability of many countries' PAYG pensions systems. Indeed, in a number of cases, politicians used remarkably optimistic assumptions about long-term economic growth rates to mute claims about the inability of the nation-state to fund prospective benefits. At the same time, once reform was placed on the agenda, many governments have been unable politically and socially to sustain the sacrifices needed to maintain public systems. While no doubt a laudable ideal, universality has often paralyzed political debate. In some countries, the issue of 'need' as opposed to 'entitlement' is back on the agenda. Continental European traditions may be on a collision course with Anglo-American institutions (Bonoli 2000).

# 4 Employer-Sponsored and Occupational Pensions

The intellectual history of the welfare state has been preoccupied both with its achievements and its roots in political movements during the twentieth century. The literature has stressed nation-state solutions to the provision of pension and retirement income, with a focus on the social and political coalitions underpinning national institutions. For all the advantages of this perspective, it has not always provided sufficient recognition of demographic imperatives and the fiscal limits of the nation-state. Furthermore, its emphasis on universality and income replacement has sidelined consideration of other kinds of pension institutions whether employer-based or market in origin. One potential approach to the enormous fiscal burden of public PAYG schemes may involve redrawing the boundaries between nation-state, employer, and individual contributions to total retirement income (see Clark and Whiteside 2003).

Employer-sponsored and occupational pension schemes owe their origins partly to companies' needs to manage their workforce. These institutions have existed for centuries in various forms, and have co-existed with nation-state PAYG schemes through much of the twentieth century (Clark 2003). For centuries, employers rewarded long-standing service by family retainers, servants, and tenants with gratuities and other gestures of beneficence. But these types of 'retirement benefits' were few in number and were at the discretion of the employer.

By the late eighteenth century, the British government had introduced pension schemes for Customs and Excise officers (amongst a small number of other important servants of the Crown). The efficiency of the tax collection process was very important for the emerging imperial power and could only be sustained through the competence and loyalty of tax officials. Government inquiries into the tax collection process noted that Customs and Excise officers lacking a formal system of retirement often 'sold' their jobs to others in exchange for support once they were too infirm to continue in their jobs. The pension system for these government tax officials served to manage orderly retirement. During the nineteenth century, this kind of employer-sponsored occupational scheme was extended to other British government employees and was the basis for related developments by private employers in the late nineteenth and early twentieth centuries (Hannah 1986).

Although some see this innovation as a distinctively British and American phenomenon, a number of employer-sponsored and occupational pension schemes were introduced in continental European during the late nineteenth century (see e.g. Clark 2000 and Sass 1997). These employer-sponsored schemes were especially important in the emerging German industrial conglomerates. Many of these schemes were effectively bankrupted in the inter-war years through hyperinflation and mass unemployment, but a number have survived into the twenty-first century, even if their relative contribution to total retirement income has been slight, and declining over the last 50 years. Other countries of continental Europe, such as the Netherlands, Denmark, Sweden, and Switzerland, have encouraged the provision of funded employer-sponsored and occupational pension schemes as supplements to nation-state PAYG retirement income benefits. While these countries are quite unlike Anglo-American countries in terms of their commitment to the welfare state (see Esping-Andersen 1990), their commitment to employer-sponsored and occupational schemes is quite consistent with Anglo-American experience.

Generally speaking, employer-sponsored and occupational pensions began in government, manufacturing corporations, and craft industries, before spreading somewhat unevenly elsewhere. Distilling the historical record, three forces have fostered the provision of such schemes. First, employers wanted to maintain the loyalty of valued employees with job-specific skills and expertise. In effect, employers sum up the labor productivity benefits of extended job tenure against the costs of providing retirement income (Lazear 1995). Furthermore, assuming that retirement income is a form of deferred wage, both employers and employees may have a common interest in distributing earned income over a person's expected lifetime.

Second, employer-sponsored pension plans were intimately connected with labor–management relationships. In many countries, employer-sponsored pension plans were introduced through the collective bargaining process, and labor contracts regulated the value of benefits, contribution rates, and grievance procedures over benefit eligibility (Ghilarducci 1992). For many years the extent to which employers offered such plans was a function of their industry affiliation, the density of union representation, and the spillover effects of collective bargaining within and between industries. These private arrangements, typically in the form of defined benefit plans, were formalized into legislation and regulation after the Second World War, reflecting the public interest in regulating these institutions and extending private pension coverage to other industries. In some countries, governments required employers to offer retirement benefits, effectively bypassing the need for union representation and even the collective bargaining process.

Finally, once employer-sponsored pension plans became matters of public policy, governments sought to ensure that employers' interests were regulated by broader commitments to the equitable treatment of different classes of workers. Government had a stake in these plans because it provided favorable tax benefits on employer and employee contributions. Furthermore, as supplementary pension benefits became more important in terms of their contribution to retirement income, governments sought to indemnify workers (as plan participants) against the risk that promised pension benefits would not materialize because of the financial circumstances and status of the sponsoring organization. This was important in Anglo-American countries where PAYG pension benefits have been modest (Clark 1993).

Employer-sponsored defined benefit plans were well suited to an environment in which large manufacturing firms dominated their domestic markets and were able to insulate workers and retirees from the vicissitudes of market competition by virtue of their oligopolistic status. In some cases, firms and whole industries used their defined benefit pension plans to retire employees in the face of increasing competition. These declining firms and industries ultimately faced enormous financing problems as the number of retirees rocketed and the number of workers declined sharply. The run-up in financial markets over the 1990s masked the full extent of these problems.

The changing industrial structure, costly regulation, and employers' increasing unwillingness to accept financial risk led to a dramatic change in the nature of pension coverage at the end of the twentieth century. Defined benefit plans were particularly important to older workers whose human capital was so firm-specific that there was little to be gained by switching between employers. These were replaced by defined contribution arrangements, which, with their greater flexibility, seemed more tangible to an increasingly well-educated, younger, and more mobile workforce. As with defined benefit plans with their heavy administrative costs and management regimes, the financial services industry has grown to accommodate these pension and retirement income institutions. The expansion of this industry makes Anglo-American economies very different from continental European economies (Hawley and Williams 2000). Some analysts claim that this is a vital clue to the differential performance of these economies over the latter half of the twentieth century (Clark 2003).

Over the coming decades, the future of defined benefit plans is quite uncertain. Looking forward to a world of increasingly limited labor resources, especially in the OECD economies, it is possible to imagine the hybrid defined benefit plans such as cash balance plans being an essential part of provision in the private sector. In the state sector, there has also been a move away from final salary pensions to defined contribution arrangements but this is by no means universal. For example, in the UK, the arrangements for civil servants are moving to career average plans.

Looking forward, labor shortages will be increasingly common in the wealthiest economies: lower fertility and lower rates of immigration may place a premium on the value of younger generations (Nyce and Schieber 2005). Hybrid defined benefit schemes could be important for retaining valued employees, notwithstanding the costs of such schemes (Cahill and Soto 2003). Whether new types of defined benefit institutions can be sustained given the changing fortunes of private employers in the global economy remains to be seen.

## 5 Retirement Income as a Financial Product

Many individuals are increasingly reliant upon markets rather than employers for supplementary pension and retirement income. In part, this is a defensive strategy by those seeking to insulate themselves from the risks of poor and inadequate pension income from institutions they no longer entirely trust. Investment in housing and other similarly long-lived assets, apparent among the middle classes in many developed economies, may reflect a lack of confidence in the pension promises of PAYG and employer-sponsored institutions. Similarly, in some instances those reliant upon these institutions opt out so as to reduce the risks of institutional failure. In the UK, of course, this was actively encouraged by previous governments allowing individuals to opt out of employer-sponsored supplementary pension schemes in favor of the private market for individual pensions. This strategy proved more expensive and carried higher risks than remaining with employer-sponsored pension plans.

In some countries, the retail market for investment products such as mutual funds and unit trusts has been an alternative source of savings for pension and retirement income. Granted, this is not as popular as sometimes implied by the financial press but these products continue to play a role in North America and in some countries of continental Europe such as France where employer-sponsored institutions are largely absent for many of the middle class in private employment. During the 1990s this strategy was strongly advocated in the UK by the financial industry seeking to encourage middle-class investors to bypass social security and insurance markets. Relying on private products creates some moral hazard in that, should this strategy fail, state-sponsored social security would become the backup source of pension and retirement income.

Significantly, these types of pension and retirement income strategies deny both the ethos of entitlement and the commitment to universality that underpinned the introduction of comprehensive nation-state social security systems during the twentieth century. Implied is a world in which all citizens have a claim on a minimum income but are left to fend for themselves in terms of their desired standard of living in retirement. Of course, some kinds of employer-sponsored pensions such as 401(k) plans that have developed in the United States combine a commitment to the welfare of whole classes of individuals with a recognition of individual autonomy and responsibility (Munnell and Sundén 2004). Individuals have the option to assume more or less risk, make choices amongst different types and providers of investment products, and plan their own retirement income. Of course, they also bear the risks of less-than-expected income should their plans not be realized.

The future value of market-based pension and retirement income is a function of the rate of return in global financial markets, the cost-efficiency of product providers, and the contribution rate. Moreover, the future value of retirement income is a function of the competence and expertise of individuals, who must make difficult choices in conditions of considerable risk and uncertainty. If individuals are to rely upon global financial markets, they must cope with the ups and downs of the global financial system as well as its capacity to adjust to shocks from the periphery of the global marketplace. The evidence suggests that first-world financial markets differ in their efficiency and their transparency. First-world markets and third-world markets also differ markedly in terms of their institutional integrity (Stiglitz 2002). Not surprisingly, first-world retirees have an enormous stake in the development of global financial and commodity markets (Shiller 2003).

Consider, in the first instance, the issue of the cost-efficiency of product providers in first-world financial markets. In many respects, efficiency is a function of size. Size allows for the pooling of individual accounts into much larger units of management that can take advantage of the economies of scale in processing and managing the flow of assets within and between financial intermediaries. More often than not, individuals are unable to distinguish between competing product providers on issues such as cost-efficiency. More often than not, the virtues of one firm as opposed to another are simply an issue of immediate past returns and implied future returns. Too often, fees are charged against individual accounts without regard to the most efficient systems of control and trading. Too often, individual account holders remain with firms that are not able to offer competitive economies of scale.

Individuals are rarely expert consumers of financial products. Competency in this regard requires considerable education, time, and resources. Moreover, service providers are reluctant to provide the information necessary to discriminate between competing financial institutions on the basis of the true cost of their services. Even sophisticated consumers find it difficult to uncover the full range of costs charged against their accounts, and are unable to marshall sufficient evidence or contact others similarly affected to make an impact on the practices of financial services providers. Governments have been reluctant to intervene to set standardized charges and reporting practices. Transparency is essential if individuals are to play the role of informed, critical, and evaluative consumers.

Consider the purchase of an annuity. This product, which is generally offered by a life insurance company, pays monthly amounts for as long as an individual lives in exchange for an initial upfront premium. Obviously, the best time to purchase an annuity is when bond rates are relatively high, so that the price of the annuity is relatively low. This can be quite problematic. People may not have the option to choose when to purchase an annuity. In any event, it is difficult to time the market.

The market provision of pension and retirement income depends, in part, on the rationality, knowledge, and decision-making capacities of consumers. But such an assumption is rarely justified by empirical research about actual behavior in psychology and the decision sciences (see Kahneman and Tversky 1979; Thaler 1993). There is also an assumption that people can be trained to be more rational—to operate by codes of practice leading to specific outcomes. In conditions of risk and uncertainty, however, many people use heuristics and short-cuts in their decision-making, thereby economizing on the use of time and resources rather than expending enormous effort on large and small issues (Gigerenzer and Todd 1999). Moreover, most people are not concerned with achieving optimal outcomes but are more often satisfied with approximations to the best outcome (if that can be known) (see Bröder 2003). Consequently, any appeal to 'informed' consumers of pension and retirement income products must come to terms with the fact that consumers operate in a world of systematic information and knowledge asymmetries in which the providers of financial services hold all the cards.

One of the virtues of PAYG social security has been its role in standard-setting with respect to the contributions necessary to ensure the minimum (in some countries) and the desired rate of income replacement. Similarly, one of the virtues of defined benefit pension plans has been the collective, albeit decentralized, process of setting benefit levels across different types of employees and different incomes. In many cases, social justice (Pillar I) and equitable treatment (Pillar II) have together set a rate of income replacement far higher than that available through the purchase of pension and retirement products (Pillar III). The evidence suggests that, left to themselves, individuals save less than they should for retirement either because they over-value current income or because their earnings are so low that they rightly discount the value of accumulated assets against the costs of appropriate retirement income products, or because they have no access to such saving opportunities (Munnell and Sundén 2003).

The implications of these observations are far-reaching. First, the nation-state may have to set mandatory contribution rates while providing access to retirement income products at a reasonable cost. Second, the nation-state may have to provide income-related incentives to encourage the working poor to contribute to their future income, given the prospect of increasing income inequality between social classes. Third, the financial services industry may need to be regulated with respect to both the cost-efficiency of services and access to its products at an effective price. All these may be necessary ingredients in any comprehensive policy aimed at ensuring that all people have an adequate retirement income. Otherwise, nineteenth-century idealism about the 'thriftiness' of individuals may reappear in the guise of twenty-first-century idealism regarding the competence and rationality of individuals in the market for financial services.

# 6 CONCLUSIONS

The most compelling argument in favor of state responsibility for the welfare of the elderly came from those who were able to show that many of the elderly were poor for no fault (moral or otherwise) of their own. Even if debate focused upon the costs of demography, the rules of entitlement, and learning from other jurisdictions, it was a debate that sought to reject nineteenth-century idealism in favor of dealing with the reality of pensioner poverty. It is remarkable that the debate about pension provision in OECD countries has shifted back to some measure of individual responsibility. While no doubt qualified, of course, by national sentiments and values regarding social solidarity and individual autonomy, twenty-first-century idealism lauds the competence of individuals in financial markets. Governments of all political persuasions have encouraged individuals to plan for the future, making them responsible for more-than-need pension and retirement income aspirations.

Clearly, the past is not a reliable guide to the future. The debate over the goals of pension reform in the OECD countries—particularly the Anglo-American countries—has concluded that the public provision of pension and retirement income should aim to maintain a basic standard of living consistent with need rather than income replacement. The public sector has relied on the private sector to make up the difference between basic need and individuals' income aspirations. It is not clear, however, that this approach is consistent with a reasonable standard of living for many future retirees. Equally, it is clear that in a number of countries in continental Europe, high rates of income replacement have been pruned back through successive incremental reforms to the entitlement formula underpinning nation-state pension systems. Private provision may now be the only way of making up the shortfalls in European pension aspirations.

Looking forward, the cost of pensions will also be accompanied by rapidly rising healthcare costs of an ageing population. Here, two issues affecting pension provision will challenge the fiscal capacity of nation-states: the composition of government spending, and the limits on revenue raising in the context of globalization. Many countries' budgets will reflect incremental political responses to the demands of an ageing population. Many countries, whether dominated by private or public provision of health care, will face difficult choices between further expenditure on pensions and health care on the one hand, and education, or even defence on the other. The tax revenue available to a country is a function of economic growth. In addition, any country's tax burden is regulated by global capital flows and the relative tax burden of other countries. Reconciliation of these issues with the provision of pension and retirement income will depend upon the respective responsibilities of public and private institutions for benefits and income for the elderly.

This is much the same as the issue posed in the late nineteenth-century in the British Parliament, which was at the heart of twentieth-century debate over the role of the state in capitalist and non-capitalist societies. After the Second World War, the consensus was that the government would play an important role in all areas of social life including the provision of social security. This consensus, which was driven by the experience of the Great Depression and then the Cold War, appears to be crumbling in the early twenty-first century. At the same time, it remains unclear how nation-states should provide incentives for middle and upper-class taxpayers to provide for themselves in retirement and how income should be distributed in the future between the generations and within the generations. The Great Depression and the Cold War seem too distant in time to be the litmus tests of institutional design and political coalitions.

# References

BAYLY, C. A. (2004). *The Birth of the Modern World 1780–1914*. Oxford: Blackwell.

BLACKBURN, R. (2002). *Banking on Death or Investing in Life: The History and Future of Pensions*. London: Verso Press.

BLAKE, D. (2003) *Pension Schemes and Pension Funds in the United Kingdom*, 2nd edn. Oxford: Oxford University Press.

BOERI, T., BÖRSCH-SUPAN, A., BRUGIAVINI, A., DISNEY, R., and PERACCHI, F. (eds.) (2001). *Pensions: More Information, Less Ideology*. Dordrecht: Kluwer Publishers.

BONOLI, G. (2000). *The Politics of Pension Reform: Institutions and Policy Change in Western Europe*. Cambridge: Cambridge University Press.

—— and TAYLOR-GOOBY, P. (2000). *European Welfare Futures: Towards a Theory of Retrenchment*. Oxford: Polity Press.

BRÖDER, A. (2003). 'Decision making with the "adaptive toolbox": influence of environmental structure, intelligence, and working memory load'. *Journal of Experimental Psychology: Learning, Memory, and Cognition*, 29: 611–25.

BUDD, A., and CAMPBELL, N. (1998). 'The roles of the public and private sectors in the UK pension system', in M. Feldstein (ed.), *Privatizing Social Security*. Chicago: University of Chicago Press, 99–134.

CAHILL, K. E., and SOTO, M. (2003). 'How do cash balance plans affect the pensions landscape?' Issue Brief 14. Center for Retirement Research. Chestnut Hill, Boston College.

CLARK, G. L. (1993). *Pensions and Corporate Restructuring in American Industry*. Baltimore: Johns Hopkins University Press.

—— (2000). *Pension Fund Capitalism*. Oxford: Oxford University Press.

—— (2003). *European Pensions & Global Finance*. Oxford: Oxford University Press.

—— and WHITESIDE, N. (eds.) (2003). *Pension Security in the 21st Century*. Oxford: Oxford University Press.

—— and WÓJCIK, D. (forthcoming). 'Path dependence and the alchemy of finance'. *Environment and Planning A*.

DAVIS, E. P. (1995). *Pension Funds: Retirement Income Security and Capital Markets: An International Perspective*. Oxford: Oxford University Press.

DISNEY, R. (1996). *Can We Afford to Grow Older?* Cambridge, Mass.: MIT Press.

EDEY, M., and SIMON, J. (1998). 'Australia's retirement income system', in M. Feldstein (ed.), *Privatizing Social Security*. Chicago: University of Chicago Press, 63–97.

ESPING-ANDERSEN, G. (1990). *The Three Worlds of Welfare Capitalism*. Oxford: Polity Press.

—— (1999). *Social Foundations of Postindustrial Economies*. Oxford: Oxford University Press.

GHILARDUCCI, T. (1992). *Labor's Capital: The Economics and Politics of Private Pensions*. Cambridge, Mass.: MIT Press.

GIGERENZER, G., and TODD, R. (1999). *Simple Heuristics that Make Us Smart*. Oxford: Oxford University Press.

GRUBER, J., and WISE, D. (1999). 'Introduction and summary', in J. Gruber and D. Wise (eds.), *Social Security and Retirement around the World*. Chicago: University of Chicago Press, 1–35.

GUSTMAN, A. L., and STEINMEIER, T. L. (2004). 'Older workers and the labor market/labor market policies for the older worker'. Mimeo. Hanover, NH.: Dartmouth College.

HALL, P., and SOSKICE, D. (eds.) (2001). *The Varieties of Capitalism: The Institutional Foundations of Comparative Advantage*. Oxford: Oxford University Press.

HANNAH, L. (1986). *Inventing Retirement: The Development of Occupational Pensions in Britain*. Cambridge: Cambridge University Press.

HAWLEY, J. P., and WILLIAMS, A. T. (2000). *The Rise of Fiduciary Capitalism*. Philadelphia: University of Pennsylvania Press

KAHNEMAN, D., and TVERSKY, A. (1979). 'Prospect theory: an analysis of decision under risk', *Econometrica*, 46: 171–85.

LAZEAR, E. P. (1995). *Personnel Economics*. Cambridge, Mass.: MIT Press.

MUNNELL, A., and Sundén, A. (2003). *Coming-Up Short: The Challenge of 401(k) Plans*. Washington, D. C.: Brookings Institution.

NYCE, S., and SCHIEBER, S. (2005). The Economic Implications of an Aging Population. Cambridge: Cambridge Press.

OECD (1998). *Maintaining Prosperity in an Ageing Society*. Paris: OECD.

—— (2000). *Reforms for an Ageing Society: Social Issues*. Paris: OECD.

PALME, J. (2003). 'Pension reform in Sweden and the changing boundaries between public and private', in Clark and Whiteside (2003), 144–67.

PRESTON, S. H., HEUVELINE, P. and GUILLOT, M. (2001). *Demography*. Oxford: Blackwell.

SASS, S. (1997). *The Promise of Private Pensions*. Cambridge, Mass.: Harvard University Press.

SCHLESINGER, H. (2000). 'The theory of insurance demand', in G. Dionne (ed.), *Handbook of Insurance*. London: Kluwer Academic Publishers, 131–51.

SHILLER, R. J. (2000). *Irrational Exuberance*. Princeton: Princeton University Press.

—— (2003). *The New Financial Order*. Princeton: Princeton University Press.

SHLEIFER, A. (2000). *Inefficient Markets: An Introduction to Behavioural Finance*. Oxford: Oxford University Press.

SIRES, R. (1954). 'The beginnings of British legislation for old-age pensions'. *Journal of Economic History*, 14: 229–53.

STEDMAN JONES, G. (1971). *Outcast London*. Oxford: Clarendon Press.

STIGLITZ, J. (2002). *Globalization and its Discontents*. New York: Norton.

STRANGE, S. (1997). 'The future of global capitalism; or, will divergence persist forever?', in S. Crouch and W. Streeck (eds.), *Political Economy of Modern Capitalism*. London: Sage, 182–91.

TANZI, V., and CHU, K.-Y. (eds.) (1999). *Income Distribution and High-Quality Growth*. Cambridge, Mass.: MIT Press.

—— and SCHUKNECHT, L. (2000). *Public Spending in the 20th Century*. Cambridge: Cambridge University Press.

THALER, R. H. (ed.) (1993). *Advances in Behavioural Finance*. New York: Russell Sage Foundation.

THANE, P. (2000). *Old Age in English History: Past Experiences, Present Issues.* Oxford: Oxford University Press.

WORLD BANK (1994). *Averting the Old Age Crisis: Policies to Protect the Old and Promote Growth.* Oxford: Oxford University Press.

—— (2005). *Old-Age Income Support in the 21st Century: An International Perspective on Pension Systems and Reform.* Washington, D. C.: World Bank.

# PART I
# RETIREMENT IN CONTEXT

# CREATING MODERN RETIREMENT

CHAPTER 3

# THE HISTORY OF RETIREMENT

PAT THANE

## 1 INTRODUCTION

The purpose of this chapter is to complement and offer a context for the two chapters to follow by taking a longer-run view of occupational and state pensions and retirement. All three chapters take as their starting point the belief that the complex international variations across present-day pension systems can be better understood if we analyze their origins and development.

First, the chapter takes further Sass's historical analysis of the development of employer pensions (Chapter 5, this volume), locating their origins in the growing bureaucracies of pre-industrial European states in the eighteenth century. Like Sass, I emphasize the close relationship between economic change and employer pensions. The initial spurs to the growth of modern efficient bureaucracy were the growth of commerce and the prosecution and finance of war. Only later was industrialization a major factor. From the later nineteenth century, however, industrialization drove the spread of employer pensions through big business firms and among state employees. Since that time, employer pensions have become prominent in high and medium income economies in a complex variety of relationships with state pensions. The study of this relationship is a central theme of all three chapters.

The chapter then moves on to examine the other side of the relationship: state pensions, providing a more detailed account of their early history than that of Arza and Johnson. These authors rightly argue that politics as well as economics have profoundly influenced the implementation and form of state pensions, though pensions have largely been confined to high and middle income countries and their emergence went hand in hand with economic growth in these countries from the later nineteenth century. Economic growth *per se* rather than industrialization was a trigger for the introduction of state pensions, along with the democratization of political systems, as indicated by the early introduction of pensions in the predominantly agricultural, but democratized and relatively high income countries of Denmark, Australia, and New Zealand. The form taken by pension schemes was influenced by political pressures and the existing institutional legacy, especially that of institutions of poor relief and private saving.

Finally, the chapter surveys and analyzes the relationship between state and occupational pensions, and the history of retirement up to the later twentieth century, examining its shift from being an abnormal and sometimes unwelcome phase of the life-cycle for most people to becoming a taken-for-granted fact of life for most people in high and middle income countries, occurring at steadily earlier ages.

The chapter focuses upon high and middle income countries since the level and coverage of pensions and the incidence of retirement were much lower in low income countries in the period under consideration. Every attempt has been made to draw examples from as wide a range of countries as possible but an analysis of this kind is inevitably limited by the data available. The number of countries for which there are in-depth studies of the history of pensions and retirement remains few. In consequence we should be cautious about generalizing too readily about the long-run characteristics of social security regimes in clusters of countries. Nor should we assume that our knowledge of the histories of certain pension regimes can necessarily be applied to those of other countries with different political, economic, and cultural histories. It is the very specificity of the structure of each national pension system and the particularities of the political and cultural systems within which they operate which pose problems for national governments and international institutions as they contemplate contemporary pension and retirement policies.

# 2 THE LONG VIEW

Retirement and income have always, not surprisingly, been indissolubly linked. Throughout history those with access to sufficient resources have been able to chose when to give up working for an income. The rest—the great majority in all populations in all recorded time until the very recent past—worked for as long as they were physically able, though often in increasingly irregular, low-skilled, and low-paid work as their abilities declined. If they were lucky they might have children able to support them. More probably, until into the twentieth century (well into it in all too many poorer countries), their children were dead, had migrated out of easy contact in search of work or land; or were themselves too poor to assist their parents.

Even in medieval Europe, ageing people with sufficient resources could buy rest and the care of servants in old age. Monarchs, bishops, and aristocrats provided pensions and perhaps a retirement home in a monastery for favoured retainers too old for service. The not-so-wealthy, with some land or goods to trade, made agreements, sometimes formal contracts, with younger people, who might or might not be relatives, to provide them with house-room, food, and other necessities until death in return for guaranteed inheritance of their property—an early form of equity release. Shrewdly, those who made such contracts did not normally hand over formal ownership before death: a gloomy genre of medieval folklore warned of the dismal fates of those who made this mistake (Shahar 1997). Such practices continued in rural areas of northern Europe, including Ireland (Kennedy 1991) and Scandinavia (Gaunt 1987) into the late nineteenth and twentieth centuries. With the developing cash economy, by the seventeenth century landholders seeking to retire could sell their tenure, professionals or merchants their businesses, clergymen their livings, army and naval officers and civil servants their positions, for cash annuities which allowed them independent control of where and how they lived.

# 3 The Emergence of Modern Occupational Pensions

Such transactions kept the decision as to when to retire in the hands of the retiree. With the growing scale, first of government, then, much later, of private business, as described by Sass in Chapter 5, employers sought to control when an employee should retire, generally prioritizing the needs of the organization over those of the worker. Pensions were established, initially on a discretionary basis, sometimes as an act of paternalistic generosity, sometimes as a convenient management tool for removing someone who became unfit for work, sometimes as both. At a later stage, pensions and fixed retirement ages were introduced as a technique for management to evade the invidious task of telling an employee that he (or, much more rarely, she) was past work and of overcoming the inequity between those who did and did not receive pensions (Russell 1991; Fitzgerald 1988). Such procedures were established first in the expanding state bureaucracies of Britain in the eighteenth century (Raphael 1964), then of France (Troyansky 1989) and Prussia in the early nineteenth, prioritizing key, higher level employees. The efficiency of the state machine took precedence over the needs and wants of the worker. Pensions for civil servants were established and systematized in all developed countries over the course of the nineteenth century, gradually overcoming the resistance of state employees in most countries to fixed retirement ages, normally 60 or 65.

Pensions and retirement spread to other public employees, such as schoolteachers, postal workers, and local government officials in the later nineteenth and early twentieth century as their competence also came to be perceived as vital to the functioning of an efficient modern state. In most countries, veterans' pensions were paid to ex-servicemen from an early date. In the United States, pensions for veterans of the Civil War, and increasingly for their dependents also, were paid to about one-third of all, mainly white, men aged 65 and over by 1900 (Skocpol 1992). During the First World War, similar pensions were paid in Britain and the Empire for injured veterans and for their dependents and those of servicemen killed in action, including hundreds of thousands of parents of young servicemen who were dependent upon their earnings (Thane 2000: 302–4; Thomson 1998: 172).

The scale of private sector companies grew more slowly than that of state bureaucracies and their pension arrangements are not recorded so systematically. Discretionary payments to favored retiring employees had a long history and were of more than casual importance to management, since the prospect of such a payment might improve employee loyalty and efficiency. But they were by no means the norm anywhere. Formal pension schemes with retirement ages were introduced from the later nineteenth century by the minority of firms which had grown too large to employ more informal practices effectively. Pensions were normally provided only for more senior white-collar employees and employers frequently retained an element of discretion, for example to withdraw pensions from workers who took strike action, as, at least in Europe, white-collar workers did on occasion. Pensions for blue-collar workers were more common in the United States than in Europe where they were confined to the highest skilled male workers in railways and other very large undertakings.

Sometimes pensions were introduced in order to attract high-quality labor in a competitive market. This occurred in the British banking industry, for example, in the early years of the twentieth century. The demand of both the public and the private sector for clerical labor was outstripping supply and pensions were part of the banks' strategy to attract and keep good clerks. By the 1920s the costs of these schemes were such that the banks adopted a new strategy: appointing female clerical staff for low-level routine tasks. The reservoir of educated, under-employed women was vastly greater than that of suitably qualified men and they were much cheaper to employ. Not only were they paid less but they were required to retire on marriage with a gratuity in lieu of a (more costly) pension. Men were appointed in the expectation of promotion to senior positions which were effectively closed to women, a situation which continued in British banking until at least the 1960s (Savage 1993).

In lower status, blue-collar, occupations (and in Japan at higher levels also, where this continues to be so), the common alternative to a pension was to keep the worker on in posts reserved for older workers which were less demanding and less well paid than their previous occupations but were essential for the running of the business, such as cleaning, security, carrying messages (Ransom and Sutch 1986, 1988). Similar 'retirement posts' were long established in rural employment. They survived well into the twentieth century though they declined after the Second World War when modern technology provided more efficient methods of cleaning and security than the labor of old men.

The mining industry in Britain, Prussia, and elsewhere developed from the late eighteenth century distinctive systems of workers' mutual aid funds. Funded by a combination of employer and employee contributions and managed by miners, they provided benefits in sickness, accident, and old age in one of the most hazardous occupations. They were attractive to employers partly due to the need to attract and keep workers in a hard, though relatively well-paid, occupation in often remote and inhospitable locations. Similar schemes were initiated by employers in other areas of German heavy industry as it expanded from the 1860s (Ritter 1986; Fitzgerald 1988).

## 4 SAVING AND MUTUAL AID

Other workers had to provide for themselves as best they could, hence the proliferation in the nineteenth century of non-profit, mutual savings organizations for working and lower-middle-class savers. Voluntary, collective, mutual organizations emerged in most countries undergoing industrialization during the nineteenth and early twentieth centuries. These were privately initiated and managed by groups of people who were exposed to specific risks against which they could not otherwise protect themselves, including seamen (an occupation with an exceptionally high death and accident rate) and other blue-collar workers who risked losing their livelihoods and their capacity to support their dependents due to accident, illness, old age, or unemployment. They developed mainly among better, regularly paid workers, whose incomes were too low to enable them to insure individually against risk, but who were paid sufficiently well and (equally important) regularly enough to allow them to make weekly contributions to a fund which gave payments on an agreed basis to all members when in need, though not normally to their wives or other relatives. Spreading the risk over large numbers of individuals of variable age and circumstances reduced the cost to each contributor. Examples of such institutions are the Friendly Societies which flourished in Britain, Australasia (Thomson 1998), and Canada between the late eighteenth and mid-twentieth centuries (Johnson, 1985). Similar mutual funds were common throughout Europe, though less so in the United States.

In most countries the only other sources of support available to such people or their families, and to those too poor or too irregularly employed to join such schemes, were charity or publicly funded poor relief. The former was highly variable in availability, quantity, and quality. Poor relief was normally minimal and granted on punitive terms.

The overriding assumption in all societies before the mid-twentieth century was that individuals should make all possible effort to provide for their own needs and those of their immediate families. As industry, commerce, and government grew in the nineteenth century, new institutions emerged to encourage small savers to protect themselves against the hazards of sickness and old age. One such institution was the British Post Office Savings Bank, founded in 1861 to offer secure provision for financial transactions to small savers in whom commercial banks were uninterested. These flourished also in the British colonies of white settlement. The publicly owned Post Office later extended this service to include life insurance (a means of providing for surviving spouses) and old-age annuities. However, the problem everywhere was that only the better off, regularly employed, and normally male worker, or those with independent means, could afford to insure or to save. The British Post Office schemes attracted mainly middle-class savers, including widows and unmarried women who had, often small, independent incomes (Johnson 1985). The great mass of poorer male workers and women, whether or not they were in paid employment, could not afford to save. Women were the majority in most national populations, were more likely to survive to old age than men, but were less likely to receive a pension from any source. They were likely to have lesser lifetime incomes and hence had less surplus for saving and were more prone to suffer poverty in old age.

## 5 THE EMERGENCE OF STATE PENSIONS

Against this background, in the later nineteenth century pressure grew in most developed countries for governments to make some provision for the visibly large numbers of poor aged people. There is no sign that older people were *more* likely to be impoverished in urban, industrial societies than in pre- or non-industrial ones (Haber and Gratton 1993). Indeed, there were greater opportunities to accumulate savings and children were more likely to be able to assist as the living standards and survival rates of younger people slowly rose. Even if children migrated to the other side of the world, mechanisms for transmitting cash improved and were much used, for example by migrants to New Zealand or Australia to support ageing parents back in Britain, or by migrants from Italy and many other European countries to the United States. This does not imply that living conditions were necessarily dramatically better for older people in the urban, industrialized societies of the later nineteenth century but there are no clear signs that they deteriorated.

But not everyone gained and the gap between the very poor—generally those who could not work regularly, which included many older people—and the increasing numbers of working people whose living standards were rising was large, visible, and increasingly quantified and described by social researchers, such as Charles Booth in London in the 1890s. The large numbers of poor older people in particular caused increasing disquiet in the most prosperous countries in the later nineteenth century. Also the numbers of older people were slowly rising. The proportions who were above the conventional age boundary of old age, 60, were lower than today, but not insignificant: in the United Kingdom, c.6 percent of the whole population in 1901; in France, with its exceptionally low birth-rate, 10 percent in 1860, 12 percent by around 1900 (Bourdelais 1998); in the United States 6.4 percent of the white population in 1900 (fewer African Americans lived to old age; the numbers among native Americans are unknown) (Achenbaum 1978); in Ontario, Canada 8.4 percent in 1901 (Montigny 1997); in New Zealand, 1 percent of white settlers in 1870, 4 percent by 1900 (Thomson 1998). But it should be remembered that in the harder world of the nineteenth century many people 'aged' earlier in life than do most in developed countries today. Hence they were physiologically 'old' and had the needs of old people at earlier ages than today. People who 'looked old' were more visible than the crude statistics suggest.

The campaign for state action to diminish the problem of the aged poor developed first in the richest country in the world at the time—Britain. It was initiated in the 1870s by a clergyman, Canon William Blackley, who had become concerned about the numbers of old people who were in poverty because they could no longer work for a living. He was convinced, in keeping with contemporary values, that the problem lay in the absence of appropriate savings institutions. He advocated the establishment by the state of a fund into which all young people would be obliged to make fixed payments between the ages of 18 and 21. These contributions, he believed, would mature to provide an adequate pension for the working classes (only) when they reached old age. Better-off young people would contribute but not receive a pension. The scheme was designed to encourage the virtue of philanthropy in better-off young people and the virtue of saving among the poor. He believed that young workers had, at this stage of their lives, surplus income for saving which, currently, they were wasting on idleness and drink.

This proposal was reviewed very seriously by the British government in an official enquiry lasting three years. This enquiry discovered that many young people, especially females, did not earn enough for regular saving; that very many of them paid their earnings over to their families until they married and so had no surplus for saving; and that Blackley had overestimated potential interest rates and hence the probable yield. Blackley's proposal was discredited, but it put state action on old-age poverty, and the problems of finding an effective means to reduce it, onto the British political agenda. Through the 1880s and 1890s it gave rise to further proposals to assist saving and to further government enquiries which made detailed investigations into the incomes and living conditions of the poor, into existing savings institutions, the degrading inadequacy of the publicly funded poor relief system, and the difficulty of improving it while it remained under the control of local government with its generally limited sources of revenue. They all failed to find workable proposals. They foundered over the difficulty that too many people, especially women, simply could not afford to save for old age as well as provide for the more immediate needs of life (Thane 1978, 2000).

Meanwhile in 1884, the German Chancellor, Bismarck, introduced the world's first system of compulsory national insurance against disability due to accidents at work and sickness. This covered wage-earners who earned no more than 2,000 marks (c.$500) a year. In effect it provided pensions for those permanently disabled from work. These payments were funded by contributions from employers and workers. Both contributions and pensions were related to workers' earnings and subsidized from national taxation. Most regularly employed German blue-collar workers thereafter paid weekly contributions into a national fund and received, when needed, health care and weekly benefits, though the amounts were low. In 1889 the scheme was extended to include old-age pensions, payable at age 70, financed by further contributions. Like workers' mutual schemes, the German system was open only to those in regular employment, since only they could afford the required regular contributions. Hence it excluded some of the poorest men, since they were irregularly employed or too low paid to afford contributions, and the great majority of women for similar reasons. Classical contributory social insurance—compulsory saving—fitted excellently with cultures which valued private saving, but they are not an effective means of remedying severe poverty. Alleviating poverty was not, however, Bismarck's chief concern. His explicit aim was to prevent the spread of socialism among German workers by demonstrating that their needs could be met by the liberal state. Socialism was most appealing to those male workers whose lives were not dominated by grinding poverty and these were the workers who benefited from the scheme. Bismarck's actions stood in a long-established Prussian tradition. Since the late eighteenth century, Prussia had provided certain social benefits, for example social insurance for miners, whilst vigorously suppressing labor dissidence. The German social insurance scheme was extended in 1911 to include white-collar workers. This again mainly benefited males (Ritter 1986; Hennock 1987).

Imperial Austria followed the German model, building on pre-existing schemes for state employees and for miners. It introduced compulsory sickness insurance in 1886 and compulsory pensions insurance in 1906, both on Bismarckian lines, covering mainly industrial labor—a minority of workers in the Empire. These measures applied throughout the Austrian part of the Dual Monarchy and, from 1907, were applied also in Hungary, fueled by fear of contagion from the 1905 revolution in Russia. This was the legacy inherited by the new states of Czechoslovakia and Hungary after the First World War (Lindberg 2003).

Following the German initiative, the problem of poverty amongst the aged was widely discussed in developed countries. The next national scheme to be introduced, in 1891 in Denmark (the wealthiest of the Nordic countries at this time, with a largely agricultural base), was quite different in being targeted at the poorest. It aimed to reform the poor relief system by removing old people from it, on the grounds that very many of them were not legitimate objects of the punitive provisions of poor relief because they were poor due simply to their misfortune in living long, often after exemplary records of hard work and coping with risk on low incomes. The pension was funded wholly from taxation. It was means-tested and granted to full citizens aged 60 or above who had records of socially acceptable behavior, that is, no record of crime, drunkenness, or failure to work. Denmark was predominantly rural and most workers were too poorly paid for contributory insurance to be an option, especially for those at risk of greatest need in old age. The amount of the pension was locally determined, according to local needs.

Similar, though somewhat more generous, schemes were introduced in the prosperous, largely agricultural, British colonies of New Zealand, in 1898, and the Australian states of New South Wales in 1900, Victoria in 1901, and Queensland in 1907. These were extended to the whole of Australia in 1908. Throughout Australasia the introduction of pensions was driven forward by the world's first Labor governments. Neither country had a well-established poor relief system and, as immigrant countries, the proportion of old people among their white and predominantly male, settler populations was low. Excluded from the pension in both countries were their indigenous populations; all residents who were not British subjects; and 'asiatics' (primarily Chinese) who were British by virtue of having been born within the Empire (Thomson 1998).

Similar proposals eventually emerged in the very different setting of highly urbanized, long settled, Britain. First, the social investigator, Charles Booth, following research into the incomes of a national sample of older people, concluded that unmerited poverty in old age could only be minimized by a pension that was non-contributory, tax-funded, and paid universally to everyone at a certain age. He first proposed 65 as the closest approximation to the age at which most people ceased to be able to support themselves. He later retreated and proposed 70 when faced with calculations of the cost of his initial proposal. He argued, however, that a universal pension need not be more costly than a targeted one, in view of the costs of selecting qualified applicants. Also that it was, in reality, difficult to apply equitably the tests both of income and of 'character' and hard work which were deemed essential for any targeted scheme. William Beveridge, who was already active in social policy debates at the beginning of the twentieth century, agreed and proposed that if the government found the costs of universal pensions unacceptable they might consider paying them only to women: the target population was unmistakable and the need overwhelming (Thane 2000).

This was too much for the British government to accept, though for them also the clinching argument against an insurance scheme was that the majority of the neediest old people were women and no way could be found to include the great majority of women in a social insurance system. For this reason also trade unions and friendly societies supported state non-contributory pensions for those unable to afford to join their own mutual funds, including their own wives. Very few working men could afford to contribute for their wives as well as for themselves.

Having accepted the principle that a manifestly needy and deserving section of the population should be paid a non-punitive cash benefit (itself a major shift in the accepted responsibilities of government), the concern of the British government was above all with cost, at a time when an outdated fiscal system was already straining to cope with the expanding activities of government. Hence the pensions were paid at age 70, despite overwhelming testimony that 65 was the age at which need most often became apparent. The sum paid—a maximum of 5 shillings per week—was deliberately set at below subsistence level, explicitly to provide an incentive to save and/or for children to assist. In addition, pensioners had to demonstrate that they had not been imprisoned for any offence, including drunkenness, during the ten years preceding their claim and could satisfy the authorities that they had not been guilty of 'habitual failure to work according to his ability, opportunity or need, for his own maintenance and those of his legal relatives'. Attempts were made to implement this clause, though it proved difficult. Also contentious was the restriction of benefits, as in Denmark and Australasia, to naturalized citizens (or, rather, in Britain 'subjects' of the Crown) and the wives of citizens/subjects. Initially this excluded mainly the large numbers of recent Jewish immigrants from Eastern Europe and the British wives of non-naturalized male immigrants. Protests forced modification of the scheme in 1911 to include them but not British-born wives whose husbands survived (Feldman 1994). As the twentieth century went on and flows of international migration intensified, the range of excluded groups increased (Thane 1998).

However, as with all other pension schemes of this period, contributory or non-contributory, pensioners were not required to retire from work. Work was encouraged, provided that it was miserably enough paid to keep the pensioner within the stringent limits of the means test. Strict though the conditions were, almost half a million old people qualified immediately for the British pension, two-thirds of them female. According to the census, the pension had little effect on employment rates. It may, however, have enabled some old people to give up casual work, which was often unrecorded in the census. In effect the pension served as a substitute for some of the low-paid casual work with which old people had struggled to survive, while subsidizing other 'retirement jobs'.

The government immediately realized that it had underestimated the cost even of these far from generous pensions because they had underestimated the numbers who would meet the stringent qualifications. They had estimated 572,000 claims in the first year, on the mistaken assumption 'that people will not rush for these pensions in the first year'. There were 650,000 claims within the first three months and the Treasury had to increase the allocated expenditure (Thane 2000: 226–7). Partly in consequence, when health and unemployment insurance were introduced in 1911, it was on the less costly national insurance basis, though this was designed less to reduce poverty than to maintain the efficiency of key, mainly better-paid workers.

Similar non-contributory pensions were introduced in the Netherlands and Sweden in 1913. Nowhere was it expected that such schemes would be permanent. Rather they were envisaged as short-term solutions to poverty, on the assumption that in future generations all old people would have the advantage of higher capacity for saving during their working lives.

In France non-contributory assistance for impoverished people aged 70 and above, funded locally by the départements, was introduced in 1905. In 1910 it was supplemented by compulsory sickness and old-age insurance for 8 million low-paid, mainly urban, workers, essentially, as in the British schemes of 1911, providing state subsidies for existing mutual funds. As elsewhere, this excluded the large, self-employed peasant population and most poorer and female workers (Bois 1989: 389–91). The scheme was strenuously opposed by trade unions. Eligible workers were reluctant to contribute and the scheme had very little effect before it was disrupted by the onset of war in 1914.

# 6 THE SPREAD OF RETIREMENT

The pensions that were slowly introduced in Europe and Australasia in the late nineteenth and early twentieth centuries generally provided, minimally, for some of those who had already been forced by decrepitude to 'retire' from regular paid work. Since they rarely provided sufficient income to live on, they generally did not prohibit supplementary earnings. There is a major difference between retirement enforced by physical incapacity, which was the experience of very many people who survived to old age in developed economies before the Second World War, and retirement stipulated by legislative or management regulations. Retirement before it was physically imperative was not a common or an eagerly anticipated phase of the life-cycle before the Second World War, except for the comfortably off, for white-collar workers, and a small number of senior blue-collar employees of governments or large private-sector undertakings. It is only since the Second World War that 'retirement', or its linguistic equivalents, has become a normal term of everyday discourse and a normal expectation of life for most people in medium and high income countries. Most people came to experience an abrupt shift from full-time work to full-time leisure in place of the more gradual transition that had previously been commonplace.

Census statistics are an imperfect guide to the pattern of retirement before the Second World War since they depended upon self-ascription of work status and older people were often reluctant to admit to census takers that they would never work again. However, they give an indication of trends. In the British census of 1891 about 65 percent of men were recorded as being in employment at age 65; in 1901, 61 percent; in 1911, 56 percent; by 1931, 47.5 percent. These figures are, and were at the time, sometimes interpreted as evidence of the increasing obsolescence of older workers with the advance of technology. They appear however to be, rather, evidence of the decline of agriculture, from which rates of retirement were higher than in industry throughout the more developed economies of Europe and in the United States from the 1860s. In the United States, rates of retirement of men from industry were flat from 1860–1930 (Haber and Gratton 1993: 32), as they were in Britain (Johnson 1985) and in Germany and France between the 1880s and the 1920s (Conrad 1996) and the Netherlands (Bulder 1993). In most countries the employment of older people plunged in the inter-war years due not to industrial advance but to the high unemployment of the Depression years. Older workers were not more likely than younger men in the same occupation to become unemployed, but they had greater difficulties in finding work again once they were unemployed. Also they were especially heavily concentrated in the older industries, such as textiles and mining, which were particularly hard hit by unemployment; and they were less likely than younger people to be recruited into the new expanding industries such as electricals and motor-car manufacture. In both world wars demand for the labor of older people increased, to replace younger men absent at war.

Rates of retirement among women are harder to assess since in all countries many of them were in casual or part-time work which they either preferred not to declare to the census takers or which were overlooked. Censuses up to the Second World War tended to show those women who were recorded as employed admitting to retirement at later ages than men. This probably expresses both the greater longevity and the greater poverty, and hence greater need for work, of women.

Retirement at around the state pension age increased dramatically in developed countries after the Second World War. The statistical picture in Britain is clear and similar to that of other industrialized countries. According to the censuses, 31 percent of men over 65 were in paid work in 1951; 23 percent in 1961; 19 percent in 1971; 13 percent in 1980. The percentage of women over 60 (the female pension age in Britain from 1940) recorded as being in paid employment fell from 13 to 5 percent from 1901 to 1951; by 1991 it had risen to about 7 percent, most of them employed part-time and in service occupations, an outcome of the general increase in female employment in these sectors in the postwar years. The bulk of older people in paid work after 1945 were in their first five years past the state pensionable age (Johnson and Falkingham 1992).

# 7 Averting the Old Age Crisis? 1920s–1950s

The chief reason for the spread of retirement in the second half of the twentieth century was higher retirement incomes, mainly from pensions. Postwar state and occupational pensions normally assumed, and sometimes mandated, that the pensioner must retire from work. The spread of retirement was not due to low levels of demand for labor in the 'golden age' of postwar full employment from 1945 to the early 1970s. Indeed the British government, among others, sought, unsuccessfully, to encourage workers to stay on at work past the pensionable age.

The urge to keep older people at work was reinforced by the fact that from the 1920s to the 1950s, Europe was seized by panic about the ageing of its population. Pessimistic forecasts were published of the coming increase in the proportions of older people, as birth-rates fell and life expectancy rose. In Britain it was estimated that the percentage of over 65s would rise from 7.2 in 1931 to 17.5 in the late 1970s (Thane 1990). Similar calculations caused alarm in France, where the birth-rate was even lower (Sauvy 1948; Bourdelais 1998); and led Nazi Germany and fascist Italy to introduce rewards for mothers of numerous children and tax penalties on the infertile (Quine 1996). Politicians and economists (including Keynes and Beveridge) warned of the coming burden on a shrinking younger workforce of the costs of health care and pensions. William Beveridge's Report of 1942, which provided the blueprint for British social insurance reforms after the war, recommended that, to help remedy the looming crisis, incentives should be built into the social security system to keep people at work past the minimum pension age: the rate of pension should rise with every year worked past the minimum pension age.

## 8 Retirement Becomes the Norm

The postwar Labour government in Britain was sympathetic in principle to these arguments, but in practice had been long committed to earlier retirement for working people and was under trade union pressure to honor this commitment. Also employers, in Britain and elsewhere, were unconvinced of the value of older workers. The British government urged older workers to remain in the workforce and employers to keep them on. It funded campaigns to seek to persuade employers and research into the work capacities of older people which demonstrated their continuing value, but provided no serious incentives. The new pension system introduced in 1946 gave higher payments to late retirees, but the increments were small and the earnings permitted to those receiving pensions were tiny.

Whether similar concerns about the level of retirement emerged in other countries is unclear and I am aware of no comparative research on the matter. Generally, however, improved, though low, state pensions and perhaps more help from children who were benefiting from full employment, enabled more older people to contemplate giving up work with a greater sense of security and optimism than at any previous time.

However, British research at the time revealed that not everyone was happy to give up work at a time not of their choosing and many would have preferred to have continued in part-time or lighter work, but this was becoming harder to find. Many among this first generation of working men who retired while still quite fit and active felt bewildered and depressed by the unaccustomed prospect of limitless leisure. They might have been open to more serious incentives to delay retirement. Later cohorts of retirees, with time to prepare for retirement, adjusted more easily and came to expect this period of leisure in later life (Thane 2000). Retirement became a conventional luxury of the developed world, still unavailable in the many countries with large subsistence and informal economies.

In the absence of systematic research on the topic, it seems that professional people, such as lawyers and doctors, and others with independent control of their working lives, such as politicians, sometimes (but by no means routinely) resisted earlier retirement and worked to late ages. Winston Churchill had reached the state pension age of 65 when the Second World War began in 1939 and he sustained a punishing workload as leader of a country at war for the next six years. He became Prime Minister again in 1951, aged 77, though by then he was in poor health and he retired, reluctantly, four years later. Charles de Gaulle became President of France in 1958, aged 68, and remained in office for 11 years. Dictators have been notoriously reluctant to retire for any reason but death. Stalin died in office in 1953, aged 74; Francisco Franco in 1975, aged 83.

In the 1960s even British governments stopped trying to stem the tide of retirement. Concern about old age went out of fashion in the youth decade of the 'swinging sixties', largely because the worst predictions had not been fulfilled. The 30-year panic about the ageing of populations was forgotten. Birth-rates rose after the war (though it took a while for this to register) and remained above pre-war levels, until another sustained fall began in the later 1960s. Labor needs were supplied by the increased employment of female labor and migration of young workers from poorer to richer countries: from Turkey to Germany, North Africa to France, the Caribbean and South Asia to Britain, where, initially at least, they were welcomed as relieving the labor shortage. The belief that it was no longer necessary to try to keep older people in the labor force was reinforced by the fashionable belief of the 1960s that modern technology would soon reduce the demand for labor of all ages, creating a future problem of surplus leisure rather than surplus of work (Thane 2000; Bagrit 1966).

Retirement at 65, 60, or earlier became an unquestioned, normal fact of life in developed countries and an aspiration elsewhere until in the 1980s the world again woke up to the statistics of population ageing and panicked, again, about an 'old age crisis' (World Bank 1994), forgetting that it had been there before. Yet through the 1980s and 1990s the trend continued toward even earlier retirement. By the mid 1990s almost one-third of West European workers had retired permanently by the age of 60 (Kohli et al. 1991). Some left the workforce willingly, on comfortable pensions, to enjoy relaxation, travel, consumption. As both savers and spenders they contributed to the economy of their own and other countries. Others left reluctantly, feeling forced out, when they still had much to contribute to the economy. There were occasional moves against the grain: retirement ages were abolished for the academic faculty in the United States and for public servants in New South Wales, but these were rare before 2000.

It has been argued that this process of ever earlier retirement was the unavoidable consequence of changing technology: skills and knowledge became obsolescent ever faster in a 'runaway world' and older people could not keep pace. But evidence has also accumulated at a rapid pace pointing in the opposite direction. Older workers suffered from the belief of employers and others that their capacities were limited and they were not adaptable. But, wherever it was put to the test, older people proved highly adaptable and capable of learning new skills (e.g. with IT) in their seventies and beyond. In fact, they were better adapted to the changing labor market than earlier generations because, not only were they much fitter, but the high-tech labor market of the late twentieth century required less physical power. There was strong and growing evidence that people were not only living longer but were remaining physically and mentally fit to later ages (Kirkwood 2001; Bass 1995). Older workers were rejected largely because they were more costly than younger people for firms that were downsizing. But by the end of the century it was increasingly recognized that when older people left an organization, their experience went too and also their often greater reliability compared with younger workers. Younger people were not necessarily more competent. Enterprises and governments also became concerned about the growing costs of pensions. Their first moves were to cut back their pension schemes. In the first years of the twenty-first century they were, again, increasingly looking for ways to keep workers in the labor force to later ages and the trend to earlier retirement slowed and began to reverse.

# 8 Conclusions

At their inception, both employer and state pensions were driven forward by the twin imperatives of governments and employers in democratizing, economically growing countries: governments to win the trust of key voters, and employers concerned to win the trust of workers. The responses to these imperatives varied in the differing political, economic, institutional, and cultural contexts of each country. At the same time, mass retirement, at progressively lower ages, gradually became a normal fact of later life in high and medium income countries. In all countries tensions surrounded all episodes of policy change, but in general they were resolved peaceably because this period of 150 years brought the most dramatic improvements in quality and length of life in history. But these very improvements were the seed-bed for what was seen as the 'pensions crisis' of the late twentieth century. More people were living to later ages. Lower birth-rates, and hence smaller populations of people of conventional working age, were, internationally, a feature of these modern improved life-styles. People had higher expectations of desirable living standards at all stages of their lives, including in later life. Maintaining these standards was very costly. In consequence the challenge for policy makers was no longer how to keep pensions and retirement patterns moving forward in what could be widely accepted as a progressive direction, but how to reverse what were widely seen as improvements in quality of life, in particular early retirement and pensions subsidized by the taxpayer or the employer. Such reversals are hard to implement in democratic societies except in situations of extreme crisis. It is difficult to think of successful precedents. Proposals for change were likely to provoke tension and clearly are doing so in most countries in the early twenty-first century.

Yet though much changed over time, certain things remained the same. A central problem faced by all poor relief systems historically was that a significant section of all populations have been unable, even with all due effort, to save for more than a minimal contribution to their incomes in old age. This remains a problem for modern pension systems. Even in prosperous Britain in 2004 the average income of working age adults is only £24,000 per year, which leaves little margin for saving—even for the most risk averse. In consequence, it is not impossible that the future will look like the past we thought we had left behind, with poorer older people having, involuntarily, to work to ever later ages to survive as state and employer pensions are cut back, while the better off retain, indeed enhance, their freedom of choice about retirement.

The majority of poor old people, indeed of all old people, have always been and continue to be female. Despite real improvements in women's access to employment, income, and employer pensions in the later twentieth century, gender inequality in all these respects continues to be stark in all countries. The extent to which gender inequality in earlier life continues into later life and impacts upon the costs of supporting the elderly population, as well as being undesirable in itself, requires more prominence in the discourse around pensions and retirement than it normally receives.

# REFERENCES

ACHENBAUM, A. (1978). *Old Age in the New Land: The American Experience since 1790.* Baltimore: The Johns Hopkins University Press.

BAGRIT, L. (1966). *The Age of Automation: The BBC Reith Lectures.* London: Pelican.

BASS, S. A. (ed.) (1995). *Older and Active: How Americans over 55 are Contributing to Society.* New Haven and London: Yale University Press.

BOIS, J.-P. (1989). *Les Vieux: de Montaigne aux premières retraites.* Paris: Fayard.

BOURDELAIS, P. (1998). 'The ageing of the population: relevant question or obsolete notion?', in P. Johnson and P. Thane (eds.), *Old Age from Antiquity to Post-modernity.* London: Routledge, 110–31.

BULDER, E. (1993). *The Social Economics of Old Age: Strategies to Maintain Income in Later Life in the Netherlands, 1880–1940.* Tinbergen: Tinbergen Institute Research Series No. 50.

CONRAD, C. (1996). 'Mixed incomes for the elderly poor in Germany, 1880–1930', in M. B. Katz and C. Sachsse (eds.), *The Mixed Economy of Social Welfare: Public/Private Relations in England, Germany and the United States 1970s to 1930s.* Baden-Baden: Nomos, Verlaggesellschaft, 340–68.

FELDMAN, D. (1994). *Englishmen and Jews: Social Relations and Political Culture, 1840–1914.* New Haven: Yale University Press.

FITZGERALD, R. (1988). *British Labour Management and Industrial Welfare, 1846–1939.* London: Gower.

GAUNT, D. (1987). 'Retirement in Northern and Central Europe', in R. Wall, J. Robin, and P. Laslett (eds.), *Family Forms in Historic Europe.* Cambridge: Cambridge University Press, 249–79.

HABER, C. and B. GRATTON (1993). *Old Age and the Search for Security: An American Social History.* Bloomington, Ind.: Indiana University Press.

HENNOCK, E. P. (1987). *British Social Reform and German Precedents: The Case of Social Insurance, 1880–1914.* Oxford: Oxford University Press.

JOHNSON, P. (1985). *Saving and Spending: The Working-Class Economy in Britain, 1870–1939.* Oxford: Oxford University Press.
—— and FALKINGHAM, J. (1992). *Ageing and Economic Welfare.* London: Sage.
KENNEDY, L. (1991). 'Farm succession in modern Ireland: elements of a theory of inheritance'. *Economic History Review,* 44: 477–99.
KIRKWOOD, T. (2001). *The End of Age: Why Everything about Ageing is Changing.* London: Profile Books.
KOHLI, M., GUILLEMARD, A.-M., REIN, M., and VAN GUNSTEREN, H. (1991). *Time for Retirement: Comparative Studies of Early Exit from the Labour Force.* Cambridge: Cambridge University Press.
LINDBERG, G. (2003). 'Welfare state regimes in East-Central Europe: western vanity or eastern reality? A comparative study of the Czech Republic and Hungary'. University of Sussex D.Phil. thesis, unpublished.
MONTIGNY, E.-A. (1997). *Foisted upon the Government? State Responsibilities, Family Obligations and the Care of the Dependent Aged in Late Nineteenth Century Ontario.* Montreal and Kingston: McGill–Queens University Press.
QUINE, M. S. (1996). *Population Politics in Twentieth Century Europe.* London: Routledge.
RANSOM, R. and SUTCH, R. (1986). 'The labor of older Americans: retirement of men on and off the job, 1870–1937'. *Journal of Economic History,* 46: 1–30.
—— —— (1988). 'The decline of retirement in the years before social security: United States retirement patterns, 1870–1940', in R. Campbell and E. Lazear (eds.), *Issues in Contemporary Retirement.* Stanford, Calif.: Stanford University Press, 3–37.
RAPHAEL, M. (1964). *Pensions and Public Servants: A Study of the British System.* Paris: Mouton.
RITTER, G. (1986). *Social Welfare in Germany and Britain: Origins and Development. Translation.* New York: Berg.
RUSSELL, A. (1991). *The Growth of Occupational Welfare in Britain.* Aldershot: Ashgate.
SAUVY, A. (1948). 'Social and economic consequences of ageing of Western populations'. *Population Studies,* 2/1: 115–24.
SAVAGE, M. (1993). 'Career mobility and class formation: British banking workers and the lower middle class', in A. Miles and D. Vincent, *Building European Society: Occupational and Social Mobility in Europe, 1840–1940.* Manchester: Manchester University Press.
SHAHAR, S. (1997). *Growing Old in the Middle Ages.* London: Routledge.
SKOCPOL, T. (1992). *Protecting Soldiers and Mothers: The Political Origins of Social Policy in the United States.* Cambridge, Mass.: The Bellknap Press of Harvard University Press.
THANE, PAT (1978). 'Contributory versus non-contributory old age pensions, 1878–1908', in P. Thane (ed.), *Origins of British Social Policy.* London: Croom Helm.
—— (1990). 'The debate on the declining birth-rate in Britain: the "menace" of an ageing population 1920s–1950s'. *Continuity and Change,* 5/2: 283–305.
—— (1998). 'The British Imperial State and the Construction of National Identities', in B. Melman (ed.), *Borderlines: Genders and Identities in War and Peace, 1870–1930.* London: Routledge.
—— (2000). *Old Age in English History: Past Experiences: Present Issues.* Oxford: Oxford University Press.
THOMSON, D. (1998). 'Old age in the New World: New Zealand's Colonial Welfare Experiments', in P. Johnson and P. Thane, *Old Age from Antiquity to Post-Modernity.* London: Routledge, 146–79.

TROYANSKY, D. G. (1989). *Old Age in the Old Regime: Image and Experience in Eighteenth Century France.* Ithaca, N.Y.: Cornell University Press.

WORLD BANK (1994). *Averting the Old Age Crisis: Policies to Protect the Old and Promote Growth.* Oxford: Oxford University Press.

CHAPTER 4

# THE DEVELOPMENT OF PUBLIC PENSIONS FROM 1889 TO THE 1990S

CAMILA ARZA
AND PAUL JOHNSON

## 1 INTRODUCTION

In 1889 Germany became the first country in the world to introduce a compulsory national public old-age pension scheme. Over the following 100 years, public pensions were adopted by almost every country as part of a global expansion of social security systems. The long-run development of public pensions is, therefore, intimately linked with the twentieth-century extension of state activity into social and economic affairs, and thus with the political economy of state power. Political considerations have been an important influence on the evolution of public pension systems, and they are likely to remain a central determinant of the scope for public pension reform in the twenty-first century.

This chapter begins with a brief review of the pattern of public pension development over the century from 1889, and follows this with a discussion of the reasons for expansion. The following section examines in some detail the variation between countries and over time in the structure and purpose of public pension systems, and this is followed by some national case studies which illustrate both the incremental nature of system development, and the importance of the political context in which this development has taken place. The chapter concludes with a discussion of the role of historical legacy in setting the parameters within which current discussions of public pension reform take place.

## 2 Public Pensions: Patterns of Growth

In 1889 the German Chancellor, Bismarck, introduced a contributory old-age pension system for industrial and lower-paid white-collar workers. Workers and employers paid income-related contributions (a payroll tax), the state added a small flat-rate subsidy, and earnings-related benefits were paid to contributors who reached the age of 70. The scheme was administered by local committees of employers and employees who were required to follow clear government guidelines. Pension benefits were set at a below-subsistence level, but there was no requirement that pensioners need retire in order to qualify for benefit, so the scheme can be seen as being as much a form of wage subsidy for older workers as a retirement pension. No additional benefits were paid for dependents, and no survivors', benefits were offered—this was a pension scheme focused entirely on full-time workers, and thus almost entirely on males.

Bismarck's 1889 pension scheme was not the first example of compulsory old-age insurance. In 1844 Belgium introduced a compulsory sickness, invalidity, old-age, widows' and orphans' insurance scheme for seamen; Italy introduced a similar scheme for this same group of workers in 1861. However, these sector-specific schemes operated more in the manner of friendly societies than of social insurance systems, offering low, usually lump-sum, benefits to a highly restricted membership that was exposed to unusual occupation-specific risks. The German old-age pension system, by contrast, covered a large part of the workforce (40 percent at inception, 54 percent by 1895), and represented just one part of an extensive package of social protection measures for German workers, inaugurated in 1881, which included unemployment, sickness, and invalidity insurance. Over the following three decades many other European countries followed Germany's example by introducing public pension systems as part of an evolving set of social protection measures. This social innovation was not confined to Europe. Australia and New Zealand were both early pioneers of public pension provision, as was

Argentina, which, at the beginning of the twentieth century, was one of the world's richest economies.

Table 4.1 reports the date at which a selection of countries around the world took their first legislative steps to introduce public pension schemes. There is a general, but by no means precise, relationship between the level of economic development of a country and the timing of pension legislation. Perhaps the most striking outlier here is the United States, which was a chronological follower of, among others, South Africa, Brazil, and Greece. By the 1970s some form of public pension scheme had been introduced even in the poorer nations of Africa and Asia. It should be noted, however, that the coverage of many of these schemes was very narrow. For example, among 20 sub-Saharan African countries (excluding South Africa) surveyed by the International Social Security Association in 1976, the proportion of the total population covered by old-age insurance ranged from a high of 10 percent in Gabon to a low of 0.37 percent in Upper Volta; across the 162 million people living in these 20 countries, coverage was just 2.39 percent. In these poorer economies, old-age insurance was restricted primarily to urban white-collar workers, and often further limited to white-collar workers in government employment.

Table 4.1 Date of first pension laws in selected countries

| | |
|---|---|
| **EUROPE** | |
| Germany | 1889 |
| UK | 1908 |
| France | 1910 |
| Sweden | 1913 |
| Italy | 1919 |
| Netherlands | 1919 |
| Spain | 1919 |
| Poland | 1927 |
| Greece | 1934 |
| **OCEANIA** | |
| New Zealand | 1898 |
| Australia | 1908 |
| **LATIN AMERICA** | |
| Argentina | 1904 |
| Brazil | 1923 |
| Chile | 1924 |
| Costa Rica | 1941 |
| Mexico | 1943 |
| (continued) | |

| **NORTH AMERICA** | |
| --- | --- |
| United States | 1935 |
| Canada | 1927 |
| **ASIA** | |
| Japan | 1941 |
| Turkey | 1949 |
| China | 1951 |
| India | 1952 |
| Singapore | 1953 |
| Saudi Arabia | 1962 |
| Pakistan | 1972 |
| **AFRICA** | |
| South Africa | 1928 |
| Egypt | 1955 |
| Tunisia | 1960 |
| Nigeria | 1961 |
| Ethiopia | 1963 |
| Gabon | 1963 |
| Kenya | 1965 |

*Source*: Compiled from Social Security Worldwide database, International Social Security Association.

# 3 Explanations of Public Pension Growth

The reasons for the establishment and growth of public pension systems, and the related growth of broader social welfare policies, have been much debated. At one level these developments appear to be part of a general process of economic growth and modernization, and reflect Wagner's law (1883) that the size of the public sector relative to the private sector will increase as real per capita income rises. However, in the context of public pension growth this economic 'law' says little more than that public pensions are a luxury good; it does not provide an explanation of why countries chose to introduce pension schemes at different times, why they implemented their national schemes on the basis of widely varying principles and organizational structures, and why the subsequent development paths have differed.

One factor which seems not to be of direct importance is demographic pressure. Although European societies were beginning to experience a pronounced reduction in fertility at the end of the nineteenth century, the proportion of older persons in their populations at this time was historically low—as it was also in many African and Asian countries when they introduced public pension schemes in the 1950s and 1960s. Furthermore, pension schemes have typically been introduced during periods of rising real incomes, so an increase in poverty among the older population as a whole again seems to be an unlikely motivating factor. It has been suggested that rapid industrialization and urbanization may have been a common force in both late-nineteenth-century Europe and mid- and late-twentieth-century Asia and Africa in creating a specific problem of redundancy and poverty among the older urban population—a problem to which governments responded with a set of welfare measures. While it is certainly true that industrial employment in general offers less flexibility to aged workers than does subsistence farming, or even agricultural wage labor, there is little evidence that older persons as a group were becoming significantly poorer relative to prime-age workers in early twentieth-century Europe or America. Yet old-age poverty certainly rose up the political agenda toward the end of the nineteenth century. It did so partly because the simultaneous development of social statistics began to reveal the extent and systematic nature of social problems that hitherto had been viewed as largely the result of individual weakness of character, and partly because the attenuation of family ties through large-scale domestic and international migration created a small subset of dependent elderly persons who had few social support networks upon which they could draw.

There were, however, many pressing social issues affecting European and other societies in the late nineteenth and early twentieth centuries, and few of them became the focus of large-scale and costly government intervention. Public old-age pensions were introduced because the welfare of older persons became politicized. The specific processes varied across countries. Bismarck's 1889 pension scheme was part of a set of social insurance measures deliberately designed to weaken popular support for socialist parties by ameliorating the social conditions of industrial workers, and by directly linking their welfare to the security and economic strength of the central state; it was introduced with little initial enthusiasm from organized labor. The United Kingdom's 1908 scheme for a non-contributory old-age pension, by contrast, emerged from a lengthy debate in which social commentators, labor representatives, employers, and politicians sought to find a better and more systematic way of delivering assistance to genuinely needy older people than by means of a stigmatizing Poor Law. In the United States, federal pensions for civil war veterans were being paid to almost one-third of men (mainly native-born whites) aged 65 and above by 1901, but thereafter mortality among veterans reduced coverage, and the action by a number of individual states in the 1920s to introduce voluntary non-contributory pensions achieved only limited coverage. The contributory federal old-age pension introduced in 1935 owed a good deal to the progressive sentiment of President Roosevelt's administration, though it also drew on significant support from larger manufacturing businesses, which were keen to reduce their financial commitment to occupational pension schemes.

The processes by which the pensions issue became politicized clearly varied across countries, even though there were some common elements. Historians and social theorists have made a number of attempts to identify within this complexity a determining reason for the introduction of social insurance and public pensions: the industrial and political power of organized labor and leftist political parties in newly emerging democratic polities; the need of governments to incorporate a new working-class electorate; the desire of capitalists to offload some of the costs of employment onto workers and taxpayers. Each of these explanations is plausible, none is complete, and detailed investigation of the national policy-making process reveals the significance of specific historical contingency in every case (Baldwin 1990). It is perhaps easier to identify reasons for the spread of social insurance, including public pensions, from a European core to other countries. The establishment of both the International Labour Organization in 1919 and the related International Social Security Association in 1927 created important agencies for the global dissemination of social insurance ideology and good practice. Initial membership was confined to European states, but the first ISSA members from Latin America, Asia, and Africa joined in 1938 (Peru), 1949 (Turkey), and 1957 (Egypt) respectively. Furthermore, in a number of Asian and African countries one legacy of European imperialism was a state bureaucracy that benefited from its own pension system, and which provided a model for the extension of pension benefits to other groups of workers.

Academic debate about the reasons for the establishment of public pension systems has been more extensive than consideration of the reasons for subsequent growth and development, but it is this subsequent growth that led to concern about a pensions 'crisis' by the end of the twentieth century. Almost all public pension schemes have been limited in coverage and modest in expenditure at inception. As noted above, the contributory German pension system covered less than half the workforce in 1889; 60 years later coverage had risen to two-thirds, and it did not become comprehensive until the mid-1980s. A similarly gradual process has affected public pension expenditure. In the United Kingdom, for example, public pension expenditure accounted for just 0.44 percent of GNP in 1910, and did not rise above 1 percent until the late 1920s and 2 percent until the late 1940s, following which there was fairly constant, but gradual, expenditure growth to reach almost 6 percent of GNP by the early 1980s.

Part of the explanation for the growth in expenditure lies in the general improvement in mortality rates at older ages across the twentieth century, and thus a rise in the proportion of older persons in the population: between 1901 and 1985 the population aged 65 and above increased from 4.7 percent to 15.1 percent in the United Kingdom, from 4.9 to 14.8 percent in Germany, from 4.1 to 11.9 percent in the United States. But expenditure has risen much faster, particularly since the 1960s. This is a consequence of three factors: wider coverage, higher real benefits, and system maturity. The gradual extension of coverage to previously uninsured workers inevitably raises pension expenditure in the long run, but in the short run it provides the public pension system with windfall revenues, since each new group of workers has to pay contributions for many years before qualifying for a pension. Thus extension of coverage generates revenue which, in a pay-as-you-go pension system, allows for immediate increases in the real value of benefits without any corresponding increase in per capita contributions. This creates the appearance of a 'free lunch', which has proved extremely attractive to politicians eager to provide inducements to electors for their continued support. By the 1960s almost all of the workforce was enrolled in the social insurance systems of the industrialized countries, although the entry into the labor market of large numbers of married women provided a temporary additional stream of social insurance contributions. By the 1980s, however, social insurance systems in most industrialized countries had reached maturity—the number of contributors was stable, and meanwhile the number of persons retiring with a full pension entitlement was high and rising. What had once seemed like a free lunch was now turning into a very expensive meal. Public pension systems faced the dilemma of either cutting the rations of pensioners or increasing the service charge on contributors in order to maintain financial balance; neither option looked attractive to politicians or to voters.

## 4 PROGRAM VARIATION

The worldwide development of public pension policy was not based on a single or common institutional model. As national governments set up new systems of old-age income protection, a variety of mechanisms were developed to administer pension resources, determine eligibility, and set the value and distribution of benefits. Comparative welfare research has focused on these differential institutional designs and the extent to which they could signal diverse underlying policy aims, political forces, and prospective policy outcomes (e.g. Esping-Andersen 1990; Castles 1993; Ferrara 1996). The balance, within any retirement system, between private and public administration, flat-rate and earnings-related benefits, universal, employment-based and means-tested access, could provide evidence on the principles underpinning pension policy and the different roles for the family, the state, and the market in providing for the elderly. As pension provision was reformed, additional elements were combined with the remains of original systems in a dynamic process that often resulted in new and more complex arrangements.

Figure 4.1 sets out the institutional characteristics of mandatory pension systems in a number of selected countries. Most countries have tended to organize old-age income security on the basis of publicly administered contributory earnings-related schemes. In some cases, earnings-related benefits were complemented with flat-rate contributory or means-tested non-contributory benefits. Among developed countries, Italy and France provide non-contributory means-tested benefits for poor workers ineligible for contributory pensions at roughly half the value of the minimum pension. In the Netherlands and the United Kingdom a contributory flat-rate pension is the core of the system, but while in the Netherlands eligibility is based on residence, in the United Kingdom it is based on covered employment, and since 1928 workers with insufficient contribution records have been dependent on means-tested social assistance. In contrast, Australia has always provided means-tested non-contributory benefits, which are largely complemented with occupational pensions (Knox 1998). Although private occupational pensions have been a key element in old-age protection in a number of countries (e.g. Netherlands, United States, and United Kingdom), mandatory individual saving schemes were less common. Recent reforms in East-Central and South-Eastern European countries such as Poland, Hungary, Croatia, and Bulgaria have tended to introduce funded individual accounts in previously fully pay-as-you-go systems (Muller 2003). Similarly, recent pension reforms in the United Kingdom and Sweden have given greater importance to individual savings for old-age income protection (although in the United Kingdom affiliation continues to be voluntary—see below).

Pension schemes in Latin America were largely created on the social insurance model (Mesa-Lago 1978). Given that this type of pension arrangement bases eligibility on employment and contribution records, a long-standing problem throughout the region has been that even when old-age pension schemes were in place, a large share of the population working in the informal sector continued to be ineligible for benefits (Mesa-Lago 1994). As was also the case in other developing countries where the informal economy is large, in Latin America the pure existence of pension schemes of general coverage was not necessarily a good indicator of the level of old-age income security. In some countries, existing pay-as-you-go schemes were combined or replaced in the 1980s and 1990s with mandatory private savings. Chile, the worldwide pioneer, introduced private pensions in 1980–1, while Argentina, Mexico, Bolivia, El Salvador, Peru, Colombia, and Uruguay followed in the 1990s (Barrientos 1998; Mesa-Lago 2001). At the end of the century, pension schemes in the region had become complex combinations of the existing pay-as-you-go earnings-related schemes operating in parallel (at least during the transition period), or even in conjunction, with funded and privately administered defined-contribution schemes.

Public pension development in Asia has been remarkably diverse across the region. While in many countries old-age security continues to be provided largely by the family, in others like Japan and Singapore, public pension schemes created in the 1940s and 1950s covered a significant share of the labor force. In many

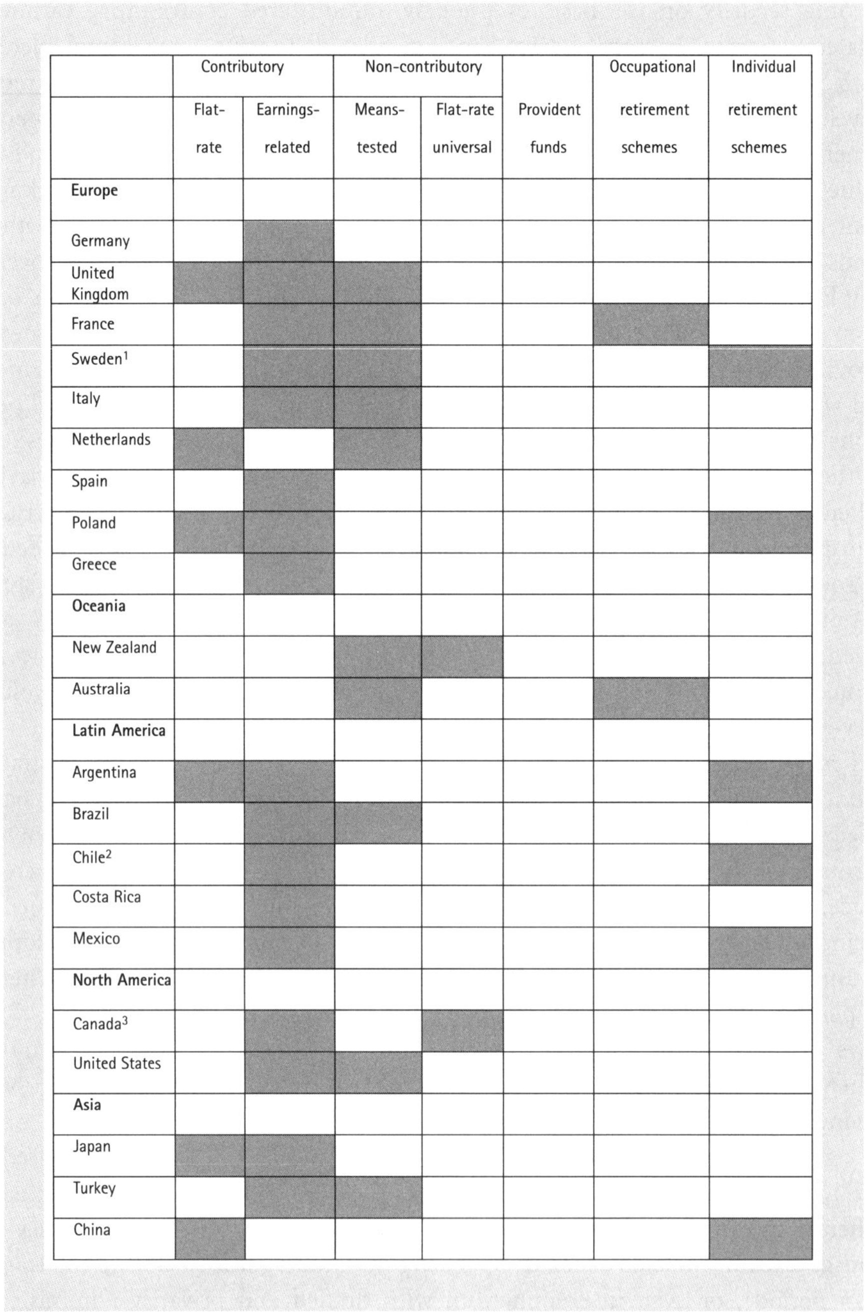

|  | Contributory | | Non-contributory | | Provident funds | Occupational retirement schemes | Individual retirement schemes |
|  | Flat-rate | Earnings-related | Means-tested | Flat-rate universal | | | |
| --- | --- | --- | --- | --- | --- | --- | --- |
| **Europe** | | | | | | | |
| Germany | | ■ | | | | | |
| United Kingdom | ■ | ■ | ■ | | | | |
| France | | ■ | | | | ■ | |
| Sweden[1] | | ■ | ■ | | | | ■ |
| Italy | | ■ | | | | | |
| Netherlands | ■ | | ■ | | | | |
| Spain | | ■ | | | | | |
| Poland | ■ | | | | | | ■ |
| Greece | | ■ | | | | | |
| **Oceania** | | | | | | | |
| New Zealand | | | | ■ | | | |
| Australia | | | ■ | | | ■ | |
| **Latin America** | | | | | | | |
| Argentina | ■ | ■ | | | | | ■ |
| Brazil | | ■ | ■ | | | | |
| Chile[2] | | ■ | | | | | ■ |
| Costa Rica | | ■ | | | | | |
| Mexico | | ■ | | | | | ■ |
| **North America** | | | | | | | |
| Canada[3] | | ■ | | ■ | | | |
| United States | | ■ | | | | | |
| **Asia** | | | | | | | |
| Japan | ■ | ■ | | | | | |
| Turkey | | ■ | ■ | | | | |
| China | ■ | | | | | | ■ |

**Fig. 4.1 The structure of pension schemes in selected countries**

*Notes*:
[1] The means-tested benefit is a guaranteed minimum pension.
[2] The earnings-related scheme is closed and being phased out.
[3] The universal pension is increased by an income test.

*Source*: Compiled from Social Security Worldwide database, years 2002–4, International Social Security Association.

|  | Contributory | | Non-contributory | | Provident funds | Occupational retirement schemes | Individual retirement schemes |
|---|---|---|---|---|---|---|---|
|  | Flat-rate | Earnings-related | Means-tested | Flat-rate universal | | | |
| India |  | ■ |  |  | ■ |  |  |
| Singapore |  |  |  |  | ■ |  |  |
| Saudi Arabia |  | ■ |  |  |  |  |  |
| Pakistan |  | ■ |  |  |  |  |  |
| Africa |  |  |  |  |  |  |  |
| South Africa |  |  | ■ |  |  |  |  |
| Egypt |  | ■ |  |  |  |  |  |
| Tunisia |  | ■ |  |  |  |  |  |
| Nigeria |  | ■ |  |  |  |  |  |
| Ethiopia |  | ■ |  |  |  |  |  |
| Kenya |  |  |  |  | ■ |  |  |

**Fig. 4.1 Continued**

countries (Singapore, Malaysia, Sri Lanka, India) pension policy was built on the legacy of the British Empire, which had set up defined-benefit pension schemes for government employees and provident funds (publicly managed defined-contribution and funded pension schemes) for industrial and urban sector workers (Linderman 2002). Singapore's provident fund was created in 1955 and by 1995 covered roughly 50 percent of the labor force (Asher 1998). Unlike the individual saving schemes which exist in some Latin American countries, the rates of return to savings in Singapore's provident fund result from governmental investment decisions and are part of an administrative process (Barrientos 2003: 700). India also set up a provident fund in the 1950s, although the high incidence of informal employment has restricted coverage to roughly 10 percent of the working population (Goswami 2002). A different type of organization is found in Japan, where a publicly administered contributory system provides basic flat-rate and earnings-related benefits which, as in the UK, can be 'opted-out' of when an occupational pension is available (Estienne and Murakami 2000). China, the most populated country in the region, set up a retirement scheme in 1951 to cover urban workers (mostly those in state-owned enterprises). In 1986 this was transformed into the current 'Basic Pension Scheme', which combines a pay-as-you-go defined-benefit system with publicly administered individual savings accounts (Zhu 2002).

Most African countries set up public social protection systems in the second half of the century. Given the large incidence of informal economic arrangements and subsistence agriculture in the region, coverage of formal retirement schemes has always been limited. In many countries, pension plans were originally oriented to certain ethnic or occupational groups only. Even where schemes of general coverage existed, they typically reached a very small proportion of the elderly (International Labor Office 2000: 300–6), leaving most of old-age income security to be provided through the traditional extended family system. In South Africa, where public non-contributory means-tested pensions were created in 1928 (State Old-Age Pension), the Indian and black population only became eligible in 1943, and their benefit entitlements were lower than those for the white population until the end of the century (Devereux 2001; van Zyl 2003). With the generalization of eligibility to the whole population, coverage expanded: the non-contributory basis of the scheme meant access to benefits did not depend on the formality of employment. Non-contributory benefits also existed in Botswana, Mauritius, and Namibia, where take-up has depended mostly on geographic factors (distances and population densities) and administrative resources. In another group of countries (Kenya, Tanzania, Zambia, and Swaziland), old-age pensions were originally organized in publicly administered mandatory saving schemes similar to the provident funds in Asian countries, with similar problems of limited coverage and low (often lump-sum) benefits (Fultz and Pieris 1999). Some of these provident funds have been, or are in the process of being, transformed into social insurance schemes, but coverage limitations remain (Dau 2003).

Program diversity across countries is not a feature peculiar to the end of the twentieth century. Indeed, the main elements of the organization of pension schemes have tended to prevail over time. The core of pension policy in Europe has been made up of schemes that were contributory, publicly administered, and pay-as-you-go since they were set up. Similarly, non-contributory pensions in Canada, Australia, New Zealand, and South Africa have prevailed since their creation in the first years of the century (even earlier in New Zealand) (see Liu 2001). Once installed, pension systems create 'policy feedbacks' that have an impact on future public action (Pierson 1993, 1994). Although radical reform is not ruled out, and has actually occurred in a number of countries, any attempt to reform existing systems has to cope with accrued entitlements and expectations that are politically difficult to reverse. New policies tend to build on existing institutional arrangements, reshaping and adapting them to changing aims and context, rather than replacing them altogether. Governments often find it easier to either apply parametric reforms which adjust the main elements of existing systems (e.g. contribution rates, age of retirement, or replacement rates), or create new entitlements (new layers of the system) without eliminating previous ones. This rebounds in often complex arrangements because of extremely long transition periods for a reform fully to take effect. Even in cases where radical reform replaced original systems, as in some Latin American and Eastern European countries, mixed or parallel systems were often adopted. When reform 'closed' the old system to new entrants, the overall social security system continued to be a mix of old and new arrangements until the end of the transition period. This helped to reduce the individual short-term costs of reform (or their visibility), and thus mitigate political opposition.

While institutional arrangements are indicators of pension policy aims and expected outcomes, the concrete effects of each model for individual pensioners depend on a number of more specific factors, such as the generosity of benefits in defined-benefit systems, and the performance of pension funds in defined-contribution systems. Outcomes also depend on the way in which formal schemes are actually implemented on the ground, and the influence the labor market and the broader socio-economic context of a country have on the operation of public pension systems. In terms of measuring the availability, distribution, and impact of old-age income protection, the actual spread of coverage and the value of benefits can be as important as the institutional design. Both coverage and benefit levels tend to determine, together with the population structure, the 'pension effort' made by each country, that is, the level of pension expenditures.

Figure 4.2 presents a comparative illustration of pension spending as a proportion of gross domestic product (GDP) in selected countries. Even though, by the end of the century, most countries around the world had developed some kind of old-age protection arrangement, major differences remained in the amount of resources allocated to pay benefits. In less developed countries in Africa and Asia the aggregate value of benefits has always been, and remains, very small. Middle income countries in Latin America allocate a somewhat higher share of GDP to pay for retirement, with the exception of Mexico where expenditure levels remain among the lowest. European countries are at the top of the distribution, with expenditures close to or over 10 percent of GDP in 1990. In the United States, Canada, and Australia, the pension budget is smaller than in European countries. Among developed countries, where full coverage usually exists, differences are mostly related to demographics, but also to the institutional structure of pension schemes, particularly the rules regulating eligibility and benefit levels. Institutional and demographic structures also affect the evolution of pension expenditures (Fig. 4.3). Countries with high expenditure growth typically face the challenge of ageing populations on generous pension systems. These are mostly European countries with earnings-related benefits and broad coverage. Countries with middle-low to low expenditure growth tend to contain expenditures via means-testing (Australia), low benefit levels (United Kingdom), or a combination of the two (Canada, United States). In contrast, most countries with low expenditure growth have young demographic structures and an effectively restricted level of pension coverage (Mexico, Kenya, Ethiopia, India).

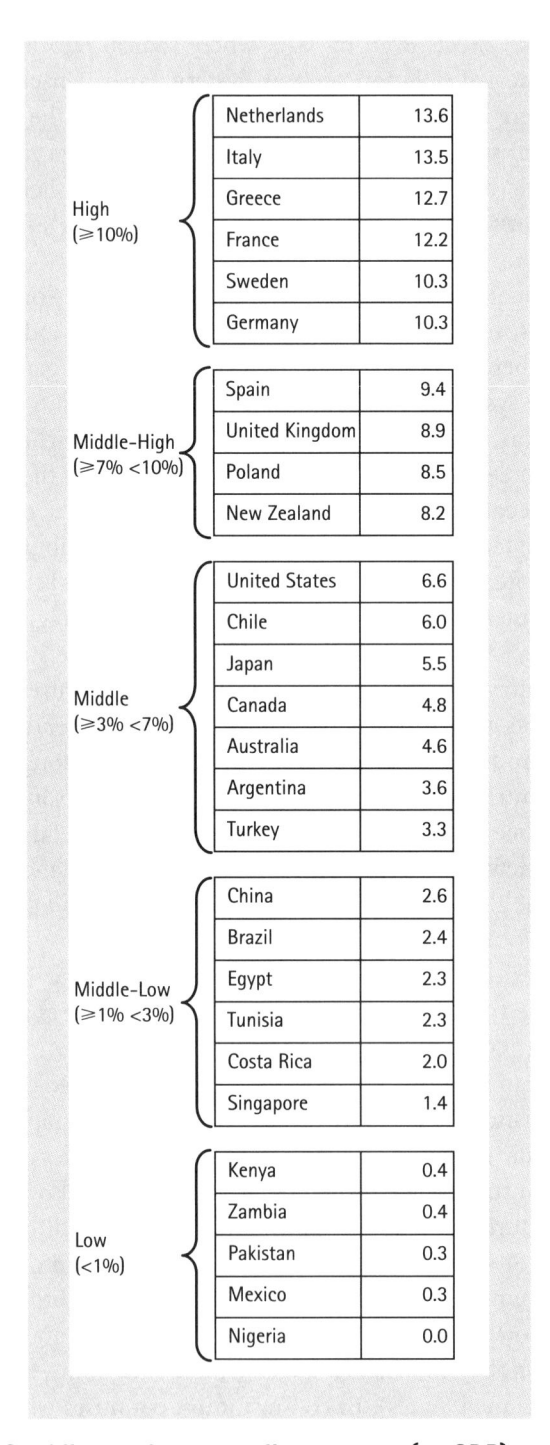

| High (≥10%) | Netherlands | 13.6 |
| | Italy | 13.5 |
| | Greece | 12.7 |
| | France | 12.2 |
| | Sweden | 10.3 |
| | Germany | 10.3 |
| Middle-High (≥7% <10%) | Spain | 9.4 |
| | United Kingdom | 8.9 |
| | Poland | 8.5 |
| | New Zealand | 8.2 |
| Middle (≥3% <7%) | United States | 6.6 |
| | Chile | 6.0 |
| | Japan | 5.5 |
| | Canada | 4.8 |
| | Australia | 4.6 |
| | Argentina | 3.6 |
| | Turkey | 3.3 |
| Middle-Low (≥1% <3%) | China | 2.6 |
| | Brazil | 2.4 |
| | Egypt | 2.3 |
| | Tunisia | 2.3 |
| | Costa Rica | 2.0 |
| | Singapore | 1.4 |
| Low (<1%) | Kenya | 0.4 |
| | Zambia | 0.4 |
| | Pakistan | 0.3 |
| | Mexico | 0.3 |
| | Nigeria | 0.0 |

**Fig. 4.2 Level of public pension expenditure, 1990 (% GDP)**

*Source*: International Labour Office, *World Labour Report: Income Security and Social Protection in a Changing World*, 2000.

| High (≥8%) | Sweden | 10.3 |
| | Italy | 8.6 |

| Middle-High (≥5% <8%) | Netherlands | 7.4 |
| | France | 7.3 |
| | Spain | 6.1 |
| | Chile[2] | 5.3 |

| Middle (≥3% <5%) | New Zealand | 4.7 |
| | Japan | 3.7 |
| | Poland | 3.6 |
| | Germany | 3.3 |

| Middle-Low (≥1% <3%) | Canada | 2.7 |
| | United States | 2.2 |
| | United Kingdom | 1.8 |
| | Costa Rica | 1.6 |

| Low (<1%) | Australia | 0.9 |
| | Mexico[1] | 0.3 |
| | Kenya[1] | 0.2 |
| | Ethiopia | 0.1 |
| | India | 0.1 |

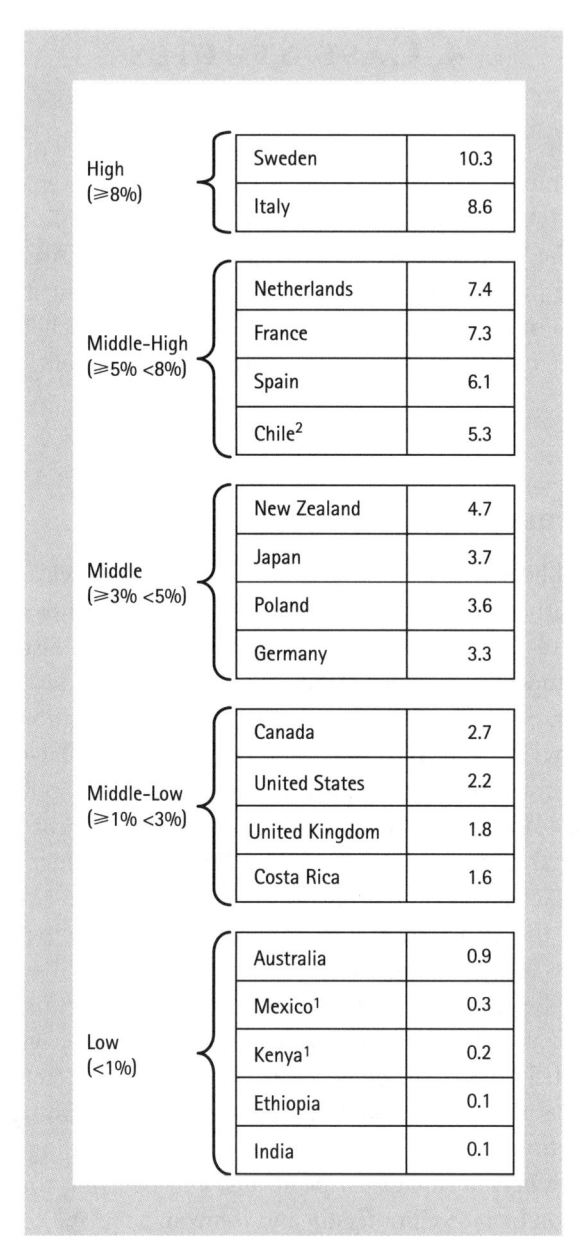

**Fig. 4.3 Growth of public pension expenditure, 1960–1989 (% GDP points)**

*Notes*: Figures exclude special social insurance schemes for public employees.
[1] 1961–89.
[2] 1963–89.

*Source*: Calculated from International Labour Office, *The cost of social security*, various years.

# 5 Case Studies

Within each country, the actual organization and performance of pension systems is often more complex and intricate than summary measures or classifications might suggest. This section studies the dynamic process of public pension policy in three countries: the United Kingdom, the United States, and Argentina. These are three cases where public pension policy developed on a contributory basis, but where the process of creation and expansion, the resulting scheme type, and the operation and outcomes of pension systems have been different.

## 5.1 United Kingdom

The history of public pensions in the United Kingdom starts with the 1908 Pension Act, which established means-tested non-contributory benefits for the elderly of 'good moral character', thus still reflecting the Poor Law distinction between 'deserving' and 'undeserving' poor (Williamson and Pampel 1993: 50). From then on, public pension policy developed incrementally, by the addition of new layers to the existing system (Fig. 4.4). In 1925, a new law established a flat-rate contributory scheme (effective from 1928) supplemented by means-tested public assistance. A significant move toward comprehensive social insurance occurred in the 1940s, after the influential impact of the Beveridge Report (Beveridge 1942). The 1946 Social Insurance Act incorporated old-age pensions into the National Insurance system, unifying the social insurance program and extending coverage to all workers, regardless of type of employment or level of earnings. Beveridge envisaged that a fund would be accumulated over a 20-year period before pensions were paid at their full rate, but political pressure forced the immediate payment of full (but still low-level and flat-rate) pensions. From its inception, therefore, the postwar national insurance pension operated, in effect, on a pay-as-you-go basis. Simultaneously, occupational schemes continued to develop, providing top-up pensions for workers in the best occupational positions, and covering roughly half of the working population by 1960 (Emmerson and Johnson 2001: 296). A divide between privileged and non-privileged workers became evident: workers included in occupational schemes obtained higher total pension benefits than those covered only by the basic state pension. This encouraged the creation of an earnings-related second tier in the public pension system. In 1959, the first earnings-related component was set up (applied in 1961). In 1975, it was replaced with the State Earnings Related Pension Scheme (SERPS), which established a fully indexed earnings-related pension equivalent to 25 percent of earnings on top of the basic state pension (with effect from 1978). In order not to 'crowd out' private pensions, a provision was

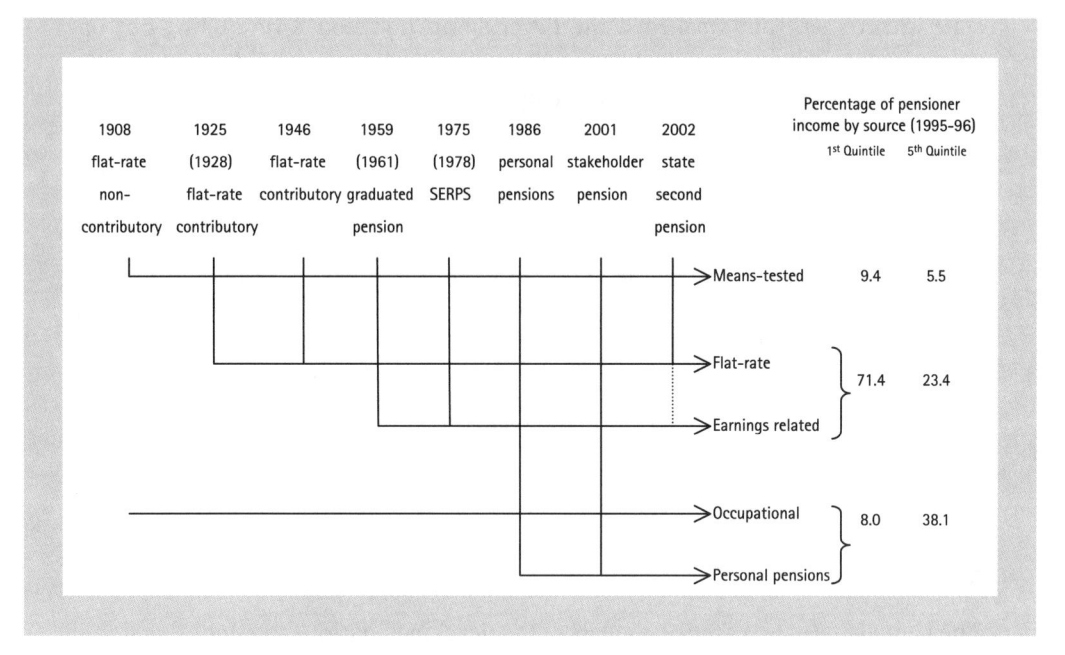

## Fig. 4.4 Pension structure in the United Kingdom since 1908

*Note*: Year of implementation in parentheses. The remaining income to add up to 100 percent originates in earnings, returns from investment or savings, and other benefits

*Source*: Authors. Percentages of pensioner income from Emmerson, and Johnson (2001), 330

made for workers with an occupational scheme to contract out of SERPS. Workers on occupational pensions would, however, continue to get the basic state pension, as well as state-provided inflation protection of a guaranteed minimum on occupational pension schemes (Williamson and Pampel 1993: 55). In 1986 workers were allowed to opt out of both the SERPS and their designated occupational pension, and join a defined-contribution personal pension plan instead, thus boosting private pension arrangements. Two pension reforms under New Labour also contributed to shifting additional pension provision to the private sector. First, SERPS was replaced with a State Second Pension which, in the long run, may become a flat-rate top-up for the basic state pension, thus reducing the role of the state in income replacement pensions. Second, a new form of private personal pension (Stakeholder Pension) was created with the aim of providing a low-cost personal pension for low income workers.

Over time, this combination of different mechanisms of old-age protection (non-contributory and contributory pensions; flat-rate and earnings-related benefits; public, occupational, and private provision) made the UK an often difficult case to classify in one or another typology. Private insurance-based schemes have always been important, and public pension expenditures have been limited as compared to other European countries. The introduction of SERPS increased state involvement but weakened the Beveridgean tradition. Contracting-out options to both occupational and personal pensions indicated a residual role for the state in pension provision for most employees. In the long run, these frequent policy changes resulted in a multilayered arrangement. Whereas the costs of reforming the whole system are large, the addition of new elements to address specific policy aims and problems is an effective short-cut. In the process, however, the pension system has become increasingly complex. In a context in which personal decisions have become more and more important, system complexity has emerged as a substantial barrier to informed individual choice. Issues of portability, financial performance, administrative costs, and so on are difficult to evaluate—risks of mis-choosing can be high and the ability of individuals to reverse negative choices can be limited (Blake 1997).

## 5.2 United States

The United States was among the last of the developed nations to establish a public pension scheme for private sector workers. Although the history of public pensions started with special schemes for military and civil servants in the late nineteenth and early twentieth century (Clark *et al.* 2003), the Old-Age Insurance system (OAI, later OASDI with the introduction of survivor and disability benefits) was not created until 1935. After the Great Depression, the risk of poverty was increasingly regarded as a result of social and economic forces that were beyond the control of the individual. As unemployment grew, poverty spread, and private saving institutions exhibited increased instability, the state took a greater role in old-age income security. Originally, OAI covered only workers in commerce and industry, but was extended to almost the whole working population in the following decades. Unlike in the United Kingdom, public social insurance in the United States has always been contributory and earnings-related: the structure of pension provision has remained largely unchanged over time. Similarly, as in the United Kingdom, private pensions have always been of major importance. Before the creation of OAI/OASDI, occupational schemes had already achieved a significant level of development. These started in railway companies, and extended to utilities, banking, and manufacturing. While early occupational pensions tended to be non-contributory and leave benefit levels to the discretion of employers, contributory arrangements started to predominate after OAI was established. When public social insurance was created, it was not designed to replace private pensions but largely to cover the rest of the labor force (Williamson 1995). However, it was not possible for workers to 'opt out' of the public system (as in the United Kingdom). Existing private pensions continued to operate and new ones were created after the Social Security Act was passed, covering roughly 45 per cent of the labor force through the

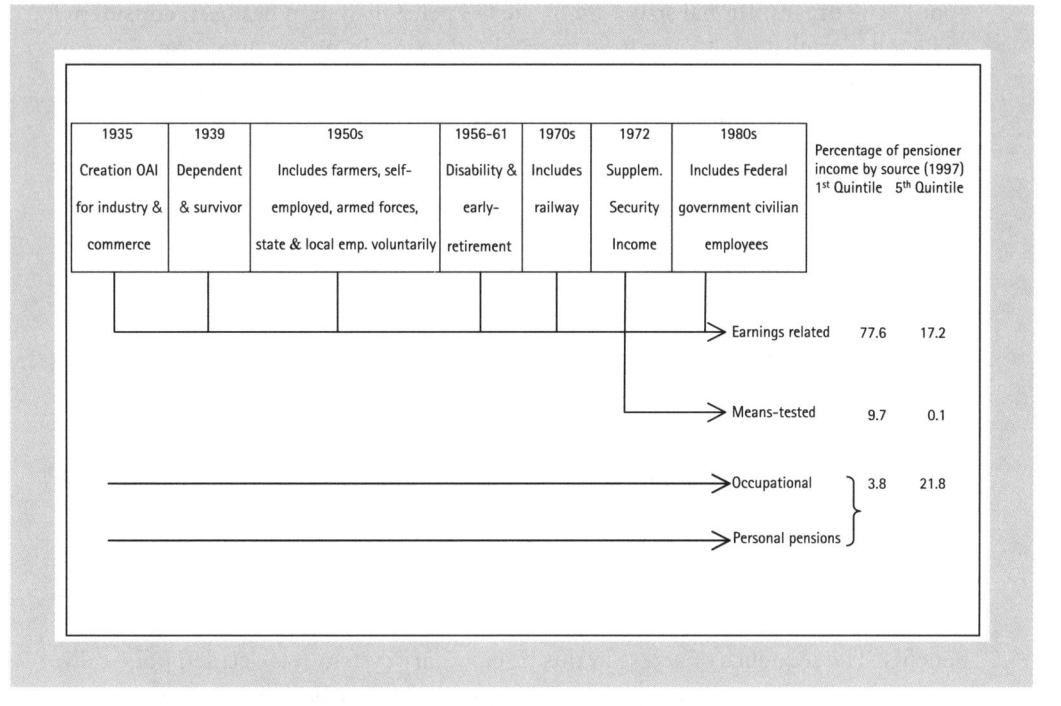

## Fig. 4.5 Pension structure in the United States since 1935

| 1935 | 1939 | 1950s | 1956-61 | 1970s | 1972 | 1980s | Percentage of pensioner income by source (1997) | |
|---|---|---|---|---|---|---|---|---|
| Creation OAI for industry & commerce | Dependent & survivor | Includes farmers, self-employed, armed forces, state & local emp. voluntarily | Disability & early-retirement | Includes railway | Supplem. Security Income | Includes Federal government civilian employees | 1st Quintile | 5th Quintile |
| | | | | | | → Earnings related | 77.6 | 17.2 |
| | | | | | | → Means-tested | 9.7 | 0.1 |
| | | | | | | → Occupational | 3.8 | 21.8 |
| | | | | | | → Personal pensions | | |

*Note*: The remaining income to add up to 100 percent originates in earnings, returns from investment or savings, and other benefits. There is no possibility of opting out OASDI to personal or occupational pensions

*Source*: Authors. Percentages of pensioner income from Jousten (2001), 359

1980s and into the 1990s (Jousten 2001). As eligibility under OASDI is based on contributory history, workers with short or discontinuous working lives can complement their pension with Supplementary Security Income, a means-tested non-contributory benefit created in 1972 and financed through general taxation. Given the strict means-testing, the incidence of these benefits in total pensioner's income is only important in the lowest income quintile.

Benefit administration under OASDI has operated on a pay-as-you-go basis, although the original intent of the 1935 Act was to establish a funded insurance scheme. However, amendments introduced in 1939 began to shift the scheme onto a pay-as-you-go basis, and the ratio of reserves to expenditure fell from 33:1 in 1940 to just 2:1 by the early 1960s (Weaver 1982: 129). Unlike many European public pensions in which benefits are closely related to individual earnings, the benefit structure of the US system is somewhere between a fully earnings-related and a flat-rate model whereby replacement rates are higher for lower income groups. Substantial reform has been absent from the US pension system. Adjustments were mainly parametric: automatic cost of living uprating in 1972, changes in the benefit structure in 1977, gradual increase in the retirement age in 1983 (applicable from

2000). The organizational structure of the US pension system has been considered to be a major obstacle to any fundamental reduction in public provision (Pierson 1994). The system works as an integrated unit, which generates unified interests and makes retrenchment more visible and more likely to produce widespread opposition. Over the last decade a growing debate has emerged around the transformation of the public pay-as-you-go pension into privately administered individual accounts, but it is unclear whether sufficient support would be achieved for a major shift of this kind.

## 5.3 Argentina

The first pension scheme in Argentina was introduced as early as 1904 for civil servants only. From then on, there was a process of phased extension to other occupational groups (Fig. 4.6). These were not occupational schemes but special public schemes segmented by sector of activity and based on a social insurance model, with contributions from workers and employers, and earnings-related benefits. The sequence of access in this fragmentary system was decided politically: powerful and influential occupational groups obtained earlier access to benefits and under better conditions (Mesa-Lago 1978). In 1968–9 all schemes were combined into a single pension system covering all employed workers. The most important

| 1904 | 1915 | 1921 | 1930 | 1939 | 1944–46 | 1955 | 1968–69 | 1993–94 |
|---|---|---|---|---|---|---|---|---|
| Civil servants scheme | Railway scheme | Utility scheme | Bank & Insurance scheme | Journalists & seamen schemes | Commerce Industry Air worker schemes | Rural, domestic, self-employed schemes | Centralised public pay-as-you-go system | Mixed state–private partly funded system |

→ Earnings related
→ Flat-rate
→ Private pensions

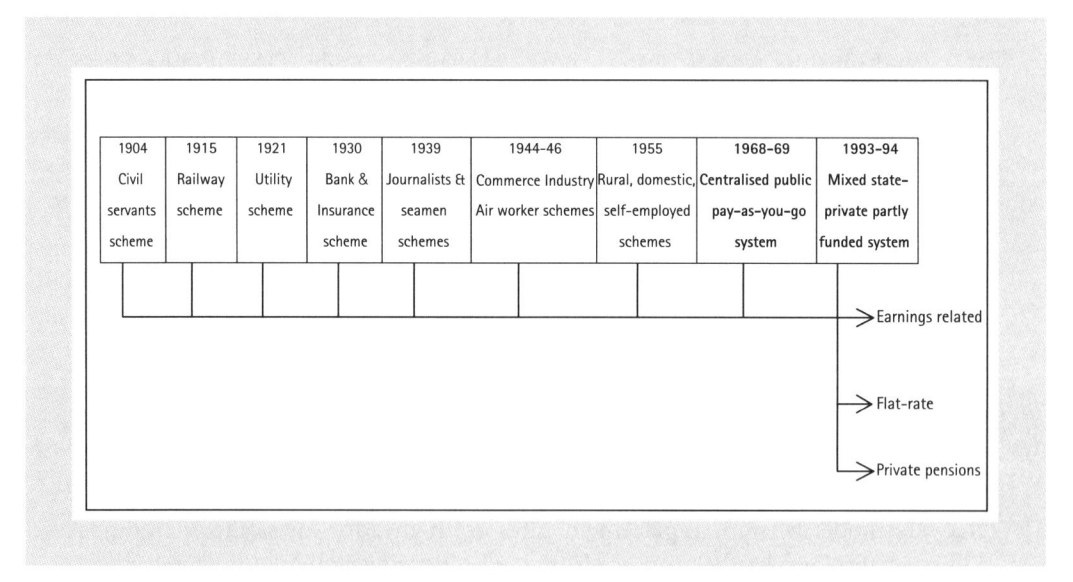

Fig. 4.6 Pension structure in Argentina since 1904

*Source*: Authors, based on relevant legislation

elements of existing schemes prevailed, including eligibility based on covered employment, contributory earnings-related benefits, and public administration. In 1993–4 a wide-ranging pension reform redefined the structural basis of the system by introducing private administration, and partially shifting from a defined-benefit to a defined-contribution model, and from pay-as-you-go to funding.

Initially, Argentine public pensions were funded, but this did not last long. Generous benefits (particularly in terms of the low number of contribution years required to gain entitlement) rapidly distributed start-up resources, and a substantial fund depreciation followed the investment of pension resources in public bonds which yielded returns below the rate of inflation. The shift to pay-as-you-go gave only temporary financial respite. Structural factors continued to affect financial equilibrium; pension schemes were often created on the basis of high benefit levels, limited contributory requirements, and inadequate actuarial valuations. Financial equilibrium was also affected by the restructuring of the labor market, where formal salaried positions tended to be replaced with informal hiring typically implying social security tax evasion. In the mid-1980s the social security crisis exploded. High pension deficits in a context of deep financial constraints forced the government to apply *de facto* cuts in benefits and increases in contributions to re-equilibrate the system. As benefits started to be paid at levels below legal entitlements, a number of pensioners initiated legal action against the state, and often received positive pronouncements.

The extent of the social security crisis was probably a key factor in making reform politically viable. In 1993, in the context of wider economic restructuring, the National Parliament approved a bill that radically changed pension provision. The existing pay-as-you-go defined-benefit scheme was replaced with a mixed pension system which included flat-rate pensions provided by the state, and supplementary pensions that could be provided either by the state (in a pay-as-you-go, earnings-related, defined-benefit model), or by private companies (on individual, funded, defined-contribution arrangements). A long process of transition followed. Entitlements derived from past contributions were maintained but, unlike in Chile, where pensioners received state bonds to compensate for past contributions, in Argentina a deferred benefit continued to be directly paid by the state upon retirement. The economic impact of transition on public finance was strong: it was estimated that the overall fiscal costs of the reform were 1.4 percent of GDP in 1995 (Bertranou *et al.* 2003: 107), mostly explained by the fall in revenues resulting from the redirection of personal contributions to individual private accounts (the so-called 'double payment' problem of shifting from pay-as-you-go to funding).

In the context of fluctuating returns to pension assets, high administrative costs, and typically discontinuous contribution histories, it is still unclear whether pension funds will generate a reasonable income for the majority of the working population. Political interference in private pensions has affected the value of individual savings: temporary reductions in personal contribution rates designed to boost domestic consumption during a long economic recession, and compulsory purchase by pension funds of government bonds on which the state later defaulted, are two examples of the 'political risks' faced by private pension schemes. Because the effect of political interference in pension systems is often only visible many years later when benefits are collected, there is a risk that politicians may remain unaccountable in the short term. Naturally, as shown by the history of financial crisis in the Argentinian system in the 1980s, publicly administered schemes also face political risks. In both cases, there tends to be an incentive to shift the costs of policies into the future and onto younger generations who are either unaware of or still uninterested in pension matters.

# 6 The Historical Legacy

After a century of almost uninterrupted growth and development, public pensions in most high income countries were seen by the 1990s to be facing multiple problems—population ageing, system maturity, and rising costs. In middle income countries with mature pension schemes, such as many Latin American countries, financial constraints have also pushed pension reform onto the political agenda. The tone of the debate was set by the title of a World Bank report published in 1994: *Averting the Old Age Crisis*. By the end of the twentieth century, old-age pensions were almost invariably the costliest element of social security. Alarming prospects of growing expenditures over the next 50 years raised concerns about the impact of ageing on public finance and economic growth. Pension reform and retrenchment started to be viewed as an essential element of a wider economic strategy, and were advocated by international agencies which focused more on the achievement of balanced budgets than on the maintenance of welfare among the older population.

National governments, however, have found it extremely difficult to reduce substantially their commitments to public pension expenditure. The incremental nature of public pension development has produced complex patterns of individual pension entitlement which vary both within and between birth cohorts, and which make it difficult to devise reform packages that are effective as well as perceived to be fair. Furthermore, the unique administrative and structural characteristics of each national public pension system, together with the local peculiarities of the political context within which every government operates, have largely negated the desire by the World Bank and others to devise and implement generic reform packages. Politicians recognize that contributions need to be raised, the retirement age increased, or benefits cut in order to maintain the financial viability of many public pension systems. But they also recognize that both delayed retirement and higher taxes and contributions are immediately unpopular with workers, and that a reduction in pension benefits breaches an implicit contract that governments have previously made with workers over several decades. Politicians are, to a significant degree, 'locked in' to national pension structures that have evolved over many decades and which, at any moment in time, mediate the pensions expectations and obligations of successive cohorts of persons born throughout the twentieth century. In order to safeguard the financial futures of workers and contributors in the later part of the twenty-first century, governments need to take action now to limit future public pension promises, but there is little electoral incentive for politicians to suffer the wrath of today's older citizens in order to benefit the as yet unborn workers (and voters) of tomorrow.

It is noteworthy that the first country to achieve radical reform and privatization of public pension commitments was Chile, where a military dictatorship could largely ignore or suppress political opposition. Argentina in the early 1990s was among the first cases where a deeply rooted pension arrangement was radically reformed in a democracy. This was carried out in the wake of the hyperinflation of the 1980s which dramatically reduced the purchasing power of public pension payments and undermined trust in government promises. Similar challenges to public trust in government following regime change throughout Eastern Europe in the late 1980s and early 1990s lay behind the partial privatization of pension systems in these countries. In politically stable, high income countries, however, radical reform of this kind was rare. Even in West European countries, where the pension budget was large and growing, reform has often been restricted to successive parametric adjustments which aimed to progressively reduce future pension expenditures. Original institutional structures influenced the reform path chosen to address the 'old age crisis'. While many countries tended to strengthen private provision, research has shown that retrenchment of public pension commitments has operated by tightening the link between contributions and benefits in countries with Bismarckian systems, and by expanding the incidence of means-testing in countries with Beveridgean systems (Myles and Quadagno 1996).

The overwhelming focus on the financial sustainability of public pension programs has led issues of poverty prevention, accessibility, and income security to take a minor place in recent discussions of pension reform, even though it is these welfare issues which had been the primary drivers of public pension development around the world in the twentieth century. However, in countries with young populations and low levels of coverage, financial issues are not as important as the consolidation of a wider and more adequate social protection net for the elderly. In some African and Asian countries, where provident funds provide only lump-sum benefits, the main problem has been to transform these schemes into annuities that can secure a stable source of income upon retirement. In developing countries at large, where informal employment, low wages, and contribution evasion are common, a primary challenge for retirement schemes based on the insurance model is how to extend the pooling of risks to uncovered populations. The variation of pension system institutions across countries, and the different socio-economic and demographic contexts into which they are inserted, establish the nature and size of the problems to be addressed and the political viability of different reform alternatives. No single model of public pension provision has suited all countries in the past, nor is it likely to in the future.

# REFERENCES

ASHER, MUKUL (1998). 'The future of retirement protection in Southeast Asia', *International Social Security Review*, 51/1: 3–30.

BALDWIN, PETER (1990). *The Politics of Social Solidarity: Class Bases in the European Welfare State 1875–1975*. Cambridge: Cambridge University Press.

BARRIENTOS, ARMANDO (1998). *Pension Reform in Latin America*. Aldershot: Ashgate.

—— (2003). 'Pensions and development in the south'. *The Geneva Papers on Risk and Insurance*, 28/4: 696–711.

BERTRANOU, FABIO, ROFMAN, RAFAEL, and GRUSHKA, CARLOS (2003). 'From reform to crisis: Argentina's pension system'. *International Social Security Review*, 56/2: 103–14.

BEVERIDGE, WILLIAM (1942). *Social Insurance and Allied Services: Report*. London: HMSO.

BLAKE, DAVID (1997). 'Pension choices and pensions policy in the United Kingdom', in Salvador Valdés-Prieto (ed.), *The Economics of Pensions: Principles, Policies, and International Experience*. Cambridge: Cambridge University Press.

CASTLES, FRANCIS (1993). *Families of Nations: Patterns of Public Policy in Western Democracies*. Brookfield, Vt.: Dartmouth.

CLARK, ROBERT, CRAIG, LEE, and WILSON, JACK (2003). *A History of Public Sector Pensions in the United States*. Philadelphia: University of Pennsylvania Press.

DAU, RAMADHANI (2003). 'Trends in social security in East Africa: Tanzania, Kenya and Uganda'. *International Social Security Review*, 56/3–4: 25–37.

DEVEREUX, STEPHEN (2001). 'Social pensions in Namibia and South Africa'. Institute of Development Studies, Sussex University, *IDS Discussion Paper*, 379.

DISNEY, RICHARD, and JOHNSON, PAUL (eds.) (2001). *Pension Systems and Retirement Incomes across OECD Countries*. Cheltenham: Edward Elgar.

EMMERSON, CARL, and JOHNSON, PAUL (2001). 'Pension provision in the United Kingdom', in Richard Disney and Paul Johnson (eds.), *Pension Systems and Retirement Incomes across OECD Countries*. Cheltenham: Edward Elgar, 296–333.

ESPING-ANDERSEN, GOSTA (1990). *The Three Worlds of Welfare Capitalism*. Cambridge: Polity.

ESTIENNE, JEAN-FRANCOIS, and MURAKAMI, KIYOSHI (2000). 'The Japanese experience of review and reform of public pension schemes', in Emmanuel Raynaud (ed.), *Social Dialogue and Pension Reform*. Geneva: International Labour Office, 49–66.

FERRARA, MAURIZIO (1996). 'The "southern model" of welfare in social Europe'. *Journal of European Social Policy*, 6/1: 17–37.

FULTZ, ELAINE, and PIERIS, BADHI (1999). 'Social security schemes in Southern Africa'. *ILO/SAMAT Discussion Paper*, 11.

GOSWAMI, RANADEV (2002). 'Old age protection in India: problems and prognosis'. *International Social Security Review*, 55/2: 95–121.

INTERNATIONAL LABOUR OFFICE (various years), *The Cost of Social Security*. Geneva: ILO.

—— (2000). *World Labour Report: Income Security and Social Protection in a Changing World*. Geneva: ILO.

INTERNATIONAL SOCIAL SECURITY ASSOCIATION, Social Security worldwide database at http://www-ssw.issa.int

JOUSTEN, ALAIN (2001). 'Pension provision in the United States', in Richard Disney and Paul Johnson (eds.), *Pension Systems and Retirement Incomes across OECD Countries*, Cheltenham: Edward Elgar, 334–62.

KNOX, DAVID (1998). 'Australia's retirement income'. Mimeo. Institute of Economic Affairs.

LINDERMAN, DAVID (2002). 'Provident funds in Asia: some lessons for pension reformers'. *International Social Security Review*, 55/4: 55–70.

LIU, LILLIAN (2001). 'Foreign social security developments prior to the Social Security Act', US Social Security Administration, *Research Notes & Special Studies by the Historian's Office*, 8.

MESA-LAGO, CARMELO (1978). *Social Security in Latin America: Pressure Groups, Stratification and Inequality*. University of Pittsburgh Press.

—— (1994). *Changing Social Security in Latin America: Toward Alleviating the Social Costs of Economic Reform*. Lynne Rienner Publisher.

—— (2001). 'Structural reform of social security pensions in Latin America: models, characteristics, results and conclusions'. *International Social Security Review*, 54/4: 67–92.

MULLER, KATARINA (2003). *Privatising Old-Age Security. Latin America and Eastern Europe Compared*. Cheltenham: Edward Elgar.

MYLES, JOHN, and QUADAGNO, JILL (1996). 'Recent trends in public pension reform: a comparative view', in Keith G. Banting and Robin Boadway (eds.), *Reform of Retirement Income Policy: International and Canadian Perspectives*. Kingston, Ontario: School of Policy Studies, Queen's University.

PIERSON, PAUL (1993). 'When effects become cause: policy feedback and political change'. *World Politics*, 45/4: 595–628.

—— (1994). *Dismantling the Welfare State? Reagan, Thatcher, and the Politics of Retrenchment*. Cambridge: Cambridge University Press.

VAN ZYL, ELIZE (2003). 'Old age pensions in South Africa'. *International Social Security Review*, 56/3–4: 101–20.

WEAVER, CAROLYN (1982). *The Crisis in Social Security*. Duke University Press.

WILLIAMSON, JOHN, and PAMPEL, FRED (1993). *Old Age Security in Comparative Perspective*. Oxford: Oxford University Press.

WILLIAMSON, SAMUEL (1995). 'The development of industrial pensions in the United States'. World Bank Policy Research Working Paper 1542.

WORLD BANK (1994). *Averting the Old Age Crisis*. Oxford: Oxford University Press.

ZHU, YUKUN (2002). 'Recent developments in China's social security reforms'. *International Social Security Review*, 55/4: 39–54.

CHAPTER 5

# THE DEVELOPMENT OF EMPLOYER RETIREMENT INCOME PLANS: FROM THE NINETEENTH CENTURY TO 1980

STEVEN SASS

## 1 INTRODUCTION

Employer pension plans are creatures of the modern industrial economy. They took shape in the nineteenth century and by the end of the 1930s were standard in large government and business organizations. Only after the Second World War, however, and only in a subset of nations, did employer plans become an important component of national retirement systems. In these nations they became major providers of old-age income, especially for middle and upper income workers.

Whether retirement plans created and maintained by employers maintain this role in the future, however, is far from certain.

In modern industrial economies, workers generally gain their livelihood by working for others, and primarily for large, rationally organized employers. In return for their labor they mainly get wage and salary earnings, which they use to purchase market-supplied goods and services. The ability to generate wage and salary income, however, grows increasingly uncertain as workers age. This was especially so from the mid-nineteenth century forward, as enterprises became larger, more capital-intensive, and more rationally managed. Such enterprises require a certain level of output merely to cover the fixed costs of plant, equipment, and supervision. To maximize profits, workers must deliver a specific contribution and maintain the organization's pace of production. Employers thus became increasingly intolerant of an ageing worker's declining capabilities. Even if most workers could meet employer expectations at age 50 or 60, they rarely could at 70 or 80. Workers over age 50 were not especially prone to lose their jobs. But if unemployed, even workers of this age encountered far more difficulty than someone younger in finding another job. In the modern economy's increasingly large and impersonal urban labor markets, age discrimination, in addition to any decline in productivity, limited re-employment opportunities. Most ageing workers in industrial economies thus eventually faced permanent unemployment and a complete loss of wages. Nor did workers in industrial economies naturally acquire assets that could provide an income when they could no longer work or find employment. They had no ownership interest in their workplace, as they had in family farms and handicraft businesses. Industrialization divorced the process of gaining a livelihood from the process of acquiring income-producing property. To build up such assets, industrial workers had to consciously set aside a portion of their current earnings and use those funds to purchase income-producing property. This saving and investing process required a good deal of foresight, discipline, and skill. If done to provide an old-age income, it also required a significant aversion to risk. As late as the first decade of the twentieth century, only one in three Americans who reached age 10, and thus had survived childhood diseases, could expect to reach age 70. Given the difficulty in acquiring income-producing assets and the low likelihood of becoming too old to work, it is not surprising that less than half of the Massachusetts elderly in 1910 had *any* income from savings to offset a decline or cessation of earnings (Sass 1997). The earliest modern response came from large employers—the central institution of modern industrial economies. For various pragmatic reasons, these organizations decided to provide their employees with old-age pensions; they would use their resources to replace the earnings their workers would lose when they could no longer keep pace. Long before Bismarck introduced the first national old-age pension program in 1889, governments (as employers), then railroads and public utilities, had set up pension plans for their workers. By the time the United States created the nation's Social Security program in 1935, employer plans had become a standard feature of corporate personnel systems, covering 15 percent of the private workforce (Chandler 1977 and 1990; Latimer 1932).

The creation of public old-age pension programs, primarily in the first half of the twentieth century, and then the general growth of government during and after the Second World War dramatically altered the landscape for employer programs. So did the macroeconomic instability of the inter-war decades and destruction wrought by the conflict. Many plans on the European continent failed to survive the war and were largely displaced by public social insurance pensions, or quasi-public arrangements negotiated at the national level by the representatives of management and labor and reinforced as a matter of law by the state. Employer plans remained important primarily, though not exclusively, in Anglo-Saxon nations such as the United States, the United Kingdom, Australia, and Canada. Postwar retirement income systems where employer plans remained important are thus commonly called 'Anglo-Saxon' as opposed to the 'Bismarckian' Continental systems. These 'Anglo-Saxon' nations were spared the hyperinflations on the Continent and worst ravages of the Second World War. Their political culture was typically far more resistant to an expansive role for the state. And they were early industrializers with a long employer plan tradition. In these nations, employer plans were not displaced but developed a symbiotic relationship with government pension programs, tax regimes, and industrial relations initiatives (Clark 2000 and 2003; Esping-Andersen 1990; Whiteside 2003).

Toward the end of the long postwar boom, from about 1965 to about 1980, the general adequacy of old-age incomes emerged as a major policy concern in Anglo-Saxon nations. Government pensions were meager and left a substantial part of the elderly population poor or near poor. By contrast, the working-age population enjoyed the rapidly rising incomes of the postwar prosperity. Workers without an employer pension, however, would also face a sharp decline in living standards when they in turn grew old. Anglo-Saxon governments responded by increasing public benefits for the elderly. They also enacted a variety of initiatives to make employer pensions a widespread, secure, and reliable source of old-age income. By the early 1980s, they largely succeeded in making employer plans a key component in an expanded national retirement income system. For the first time in the history of industrial economies, these systems, like those on the Continent, allowed the elderly to enjoy a reasonably comfortable income across an increasingly lengthy and well-defined stage of life called 'retirement'.

## 2 Employers Find an Interest in Providing Old-Age Pensions: 1800–1950

The majority of employers in industrial economies had no interest in giving their workers an old-age pension. Most remained small to mid-sized family firms whose workers rarely stayed on for more than a few years. Nor could these workers rely on the promise of such employers to pay an old-age income, decades in the future. So the standard labor contract in such firms largely remained the simple exchange of cash wages for hours of labor service.

But a handful of very large employers, with a large permanent staff and very different personnel needs, emerged in the nineteenth century and quickly came to dominate the production process in modern industrial economies. These employers, such as governments, railroads, utilities, universities, hospitals, and business corporations in industries ranging from manufacturing to finance and retailing would come to employ many if not most of an industrial nation's workforce. Such employers could make a credible promise to provide their workers with an old-age pension. They also sought to develop employment relationships with their workers that made the promise of an old-age pension a valuable instrument of personnel management.

The first such relationship involved the development of career civil servants and managers. The term 'career' assumed its modern usage in the early nineteenth century, in the notion of a 'diplomatic' (1803) or 'public' (1815) career (*Oxford English Dictionary*). As Chandler and other business historians clearly illustrate, the large organizations that came to characterize the modern industrial economy increasingly delegated authority to this special class of career employees. Governments and far-flung commercial enterprises had previously relied on personal relationships—primarily court retainers or family members—to oversee their operations. They now asked workers with whom they had no such ties to invest in organization-specific skills and relationships, to make decisions and execute responsibilities in the best interest of the organization, and to do so with limited oversight and over their entire working lives. And these organizations, both public and private, had a position in the marketplace that allowed them to assure such workers a permanent career, and an ample reward at the other end (Chandler 1977 and 1990).

The British civil service pension plan of 1859 became the model in the use of old-age pensions for developing a career managerial workforce. Governments had long granted pensions, especially to soldiers and others in the military, and the British eighteenth-century plan for customs officials is generally seen as the precursor to later civil servant plans. The 1859 plan, however, provided a template widely imitated by other large employers, both public and private. Participation in such plans was limited to white-collar workers; the plans often required employee contributions; and the pension was based on the worker's salary and years of service. Workers who remained in service to the 'normal retirement age' got an annuity for life worth far more than their accumulated contributions plus interest. The British plan paid 1.67 percent of salary for each year of service, up to two-thirds of salary for a 40-year career. Workers who left early, however, left with only their own contributions without interest. The pension thus functioned as an incentive to remain with the organization and rise in the ranks. The value of the pension, over and above the worker's accumulated cash contributions plus interest, thus reflected the value of a career to the employer. It served as compensation for the worker's contribution of this long and diligent service (Raphael 1964; Hannah 1986).

Pensions proved valuable in developing a second employment relationship, this time with blue-collar workers. In industries such as railroads, urban transit, and manufacturing, firms employed large numbers of blue-collar workers to operate their capital-intensive, high-throughput operations. In a bid to attract better workers, win their loyalty, and fend off unions, these employers already paid above-market wages. But this strategy had its limits. Beyond a certain point, these employers found they could better achieve their personnel management objectives by providing 'industrial insurance' rather than ever higher wages. This insurance protected workers and their families against the loss of earnings due to accident, death, illness, or growing too old to work. Given the new dependence on earnings in industrial economies, and the significant risk of accident, death, illness, and becoming too old to work, blue-collar workers whose basic economic needs had been satisfied placed a significant value on such protection. In exchange for the stability this insurance brought to the lives of their workers, employers expected increased loyalty and diligence. Unions and workmen's friendly societies often offered such protection, so these plans fended off competing claims to their worker's allegiance. Employers could also expect this compensation package to attract workers with a greater sense of responsibility and foresight—the type of workers they desired (Sass 1997; Hannah 1986).

Blue-collar industrial insurance programs generally required employee contributions, with higher paid workers contributing more to insure their higher wages against death, disability, accident, or age. These plans nevertheless replaced a relatively small share of earnings in the event of a loss. Pensions were often just 1 percent of earnings times years of service—barely half the amount found in most white-collar plans. They provided a floor of protection, not enough to retire in comfort. The main reason was the need to reduce 'moral hazard'—the risk that the availability of insurance will induce behavior that increases the likelihood of a claim. If benefits were too high, perfectly able workers might feign an illness or a decline in stamina to claim an old-age or disability pension (Sass 1997).

Toward the end of the nineteenth century, however, the opposite problem became the concern of many large employers. Their offices, machine shops, and locomotives were increasingly staffed by older workers whose productive abilities had clearly declined. So beginning in the 1890s in Britain, and at the turn of the century in the United States, large employers began to introduce mandatory retirement at a specified age. To remove these workers without damaging their relations with the rest of the workforce or with the public at large, they retired these workers on pension. Because employers wanted no employee interference in this mandatory retirement policy, they also paid the full cost of the 'benefit' rather than requiring employee contributions. As companies with pre-existing pension plans saw the number of older employees steadily rise, most introduced compulsory retirement, on pension, and likewise assumed the full cost of the plan (Graebner 1980; Sass 1997; Lazear 1995).

By the end of the 1930s, employer plans had become standard in governments and mature big businesses throughout the industrial world. They covered up to 15 percent of the workforce in the United Kingdom and the United States and other industrial nations. Employer plans, however, were clearly not the solution to the old-age income problem. They still covered a small percentage of the workforce. Most of those covered would leave their employer prior to retirement, voluntarily or not, and fail to qualify for an old-age pension. For this reason, and because employer plan coverage was expanding quite rapidly and older cohorts had much lower coverage rates, a much smaller percentage of the elderly were actually receiving employer pensions than the percentage of workers covered (Hannah 1986; Sass 1997; Commonwealth Treasury 2001).

# 3 THE GREAT DIVIDE: EMPLOYER PLANS IN AND OUT OF POSTWAR RETIREMENT INCOME SYSTEMS: 1945–1965

The economics of ageing changed dramatically after the Second World War. The availability of government pensions in essentially all industrial nations, typically at age 65 for men and often at an earlier age for women, provided the elderly with a basic income without the need to work. Government thus assumed much of the minimal 'industrial insurance' responsibility from employer plans. Incentives built into these public pension programs, moreover, also encouraged older workers to withdraw from the labor force. They generally had an earnings test that denied benefits to anyone who earned more than a trivial amount. This reflected both the notion that public old-age pensions were insurance against an inability to work or find employment and a Depression-era impulse to reduce the supply of labor. Public old-age pension programs, like employer plans, also encouraged retirement by not increasing benefits beyond the 'normal retirement age' (NRA). This effectively cut the compensation for remaining employed to the worker's wage less the foregone pension.[1] The combination of an assured old-age income and these incentives to retire produced a sharp drop in the percentage of the elderly who remained in the labor force. As longevity was also rising rapidly, retirement soon emerged as an expected, extended, and well-defined stage of life.

The elderly nevertheless remained a distinctly poor population. In Britain, old-age incomes in 1950 averaged only about 40 percent of the average male wage—far less than the rule-of-thumb estimate of 65 to 80 percent of pre-retirement earnings needed to maintain pre-retirement living standards. In the United States, over a third of the elderly in 1959 were actually classified as poor. The industrial world meanwhile was enjoying the long economic boom over the three decades following the Second World War. The financial standing of the elderly thus stood in increasingly sharp contrast to the rising prosperity of most working-age adults. A consensus gradually emerged that the elderly should share in this prosperity and that income should be spread more evenly across the lifespan, assuring active workers of a reasonable continuation of their living standard when they in turn grow old. The question was how.

Nations on the European continent opted for an expansion of public social insurance pensions and quasi-public arrangements negotiated by the national representatives of management and labor 'under government auspices and covered by the overarching umbrella of labor law' (Whiteside 2003). The Depression and war had destroyed much of the net worth of private employers as well as the value of assets held in employer pension funds or annuity providers, so only government pay-as-you-go transfers, or similar arrangements mandated and regulated by the government, could increase the incomes of the elderly. These Continental nations had comparatively strong traditions of publicly provided welfare and negotiated labor-market institutions, deriving variously from autocratic, Catholic social welfare, or social-democratic political traditions. Many also institutionalized national wage bargaining after the war, with the outcomes legally enforceable, and these negotiations became the platform for establishing quasi-public mandatory social insurance arrangements that would cover all workers (Esping-Andersen 1990; Whiteside 2003).

These 'Bismarckian' programs—so named because benefits were closely tied to earnings and contributions, as in Bismarck's 1889 program—were substantially expanded in the second decade following the end of the war. Pensions provided by the state and/or quasi-mandated negotiated arrangements came to replace 60 percent or more of average indexed lifetime earnings. This was generally enough to maintain pre-retirement living standards with little or no supplementation. Only those with low earnings and patchy work histories would need supplementary public support. Households who entered retirement owning their home outright or with some financial assets could actually see their living standards rise. Except for highly paid corporate and government officials, this expansion of public or publicly supervised old-age pensions effectively crowded out the need for employer plans or individual retirement savings (see Arza and Johnson in this volume).

The alternative postwar approach to the old-age income problem, adopted by Anglo-Saxon nations such as the United States, the United Kingdom, Australia, and Canada, relied on an expansion of employer plans. The conservative parties in Anglo-Saxon nations had a much more restrictive view of the proper role of the state. The United Kingdom and the United States, both early industrializers, also had long employer-plan traditions. A common Anglo-Saxon corporate-financial culture and extensive cross-border investments facilitated the spread of employer pensions to large private enterprises in Australia and Canada. The Anglo-Saxon nations were also spared the worst ravages of the Second World War. So compared to most nations on the European Continent, they entered the postwar period with far more resources in the private sector that could provide retirement incomes. Employer plans would thus remain a significant source of income in what came to be known as 'Anglo-Saxon' as opposed to 'Bismarckian' retirement income systems.

The immediate postwar years did see pitched political battles in Anglo-Saxon nations over the economic role of the state. Politicians on the left generally advocated a larger government role and increased government pensions. Politicians on the right generally advocated a restoration of private control, and often sought to replace social insurance with self-reliance, employer plans, and a means-tested safety-net. The actual postwar settlements were quite varied. Britain nationalized coal, steel, and other basic industries and created the National Health Service; the United States restored corporate management of the economy, restrained its unions, and blocked new social welfare initiatives. There was far less variance, however, in the area of old-age pensions. Anglo-Saxon nations generally continued their pre-war programs with little or no increase in benefits, but expanded coverage to include essentially all workers. In Britain, the 1946 Basic State Pension extended the 1925 plan, which paid a flat 20 percent of the average wage, to include white-collar as well as clerical and blue-collar workers. In the United States, the critical 1950 Social Security Amendments retained pre-war replacement rates—30 percent for the model average worker—while expanding coverage and easing requirements for the receipt of full benefits (Sass 1997; Ball 1947; Hannah 1986; Whiteside 2003; Commonwealth Treasury 2001).

Given the widespread acceptance of 'retirement' and the low level of government benefits, a significant expansion of employer plans was critical to the success of the Anglo-Saxon approach. Most government workers had old-age pensions even prior to the war, and government employment expanded dramatically in the postwar period. In the private sector, coverage rates shot up dramatically. At most only 15 percent of the private workforce was covered by an employer plan at the end of the 1930s. But coverage approached 40 percent of private-sector workers in the United States and Great Britain by 1960, and by the mid-1980s in Australia (Fig. 5.1). This critical increase can be traced to three factors: the expansion of large corporate employers; the growing importance of pensions as tax-advantaged compensation; and, most significantly, to the growth of collectively bargained plans. (Sass 1997; Hannah 1986; Commonwealth Treasury 2001).

The postwar decades were the heyday of corporate big business. The long postwar boom was indeed largely driven by giant mass-production mass-distribution enterprises. This included enterprises in manufacturing—in industries such as autos, steel, and consumer goods—and services—in industries such as telecommunications, banking and insurance, transportation, and public utilities. As employer plans had become an essential component of corporate personnel

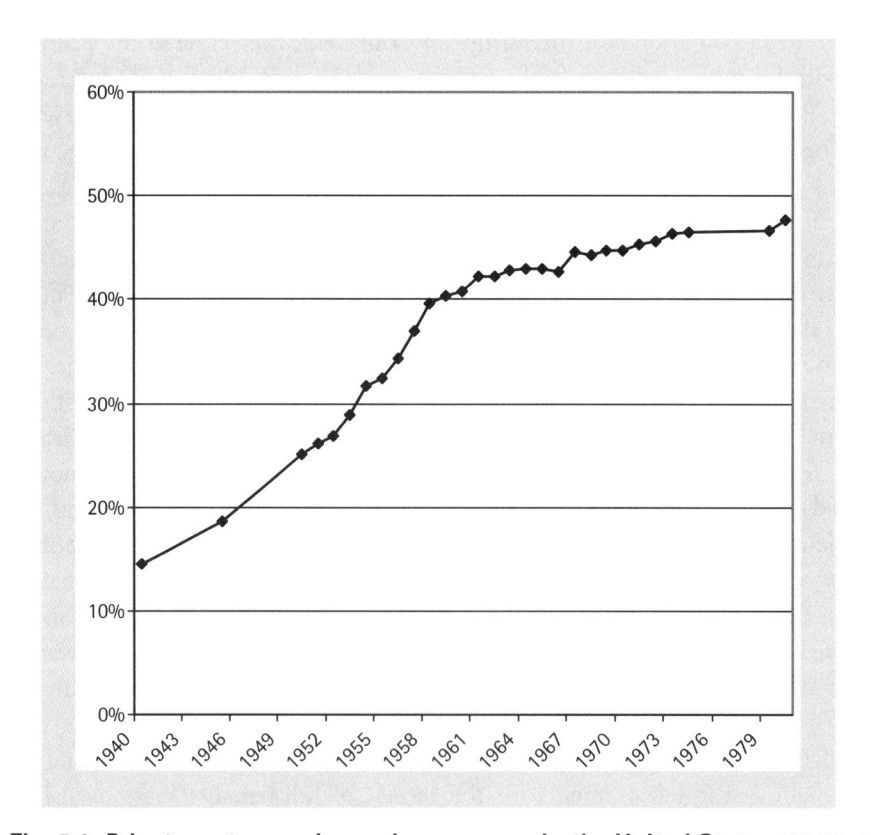

Fig. 5.1 Private sector employer plan coverage in the United States, 1940–1974

*Notes*: Pension coverage as a percentage of private wage and salary workers (excludes federal, state, and local government employees and self-employed workers).

*Source*: Author's calculations based upon Skolnik (1976) and Bureau of Labor Statistics.

systems, coverage expanded in line with the growth of big business (Chandler 1977 and 1990).

The special tax treatment of employer pensions also became significantly more attractive in the postwar era. These treatments, largely enacted in the 1920s, typically exempted employer contributions and pension fund investment income and only taxed beneficiaries on pensions paid out in retirement. In effect this was an interest-free loan of all taxes due prior to retirement, with benefits then taxed at the retiree's typically lower rate. In the United Kingdom and Australia retirees had an added tax advantage: they were allowed to take tax-free a lump sum equal to a portion of their pension benefit—25 percent in the United Kingdom and 95 percent in Australia. Before the war, however, this tax treatment had a limited effect on coverage, as less than 10 percent of the adult population typically paid tax. Only with the postwar growth of mass income taxation did these treatments have a significant effect on coverage. The government in effect became a major funder of employer plans, making them far less costly to employers and workers, and encouraging their spread.[2]

The progressive nature of income taxation made pensions an especially attractive tax shelter for high income professionals, managers, and business owners. In the United States, the 'anti-discrimination' requirements in the Revenue Act of 1942 forced business owners and employers using pensions to attract professionals and managers to distribute benefits broadly and include the lower paid. The government thus traded tax shelters for the well-to-do for expanded retirement income benefits for the rank-and-file.

The key factor in the postwar growth of employer pensions, however, was the growth of collectively bargained plans. Labor unions, worker associations, and friendly societies had long sought to provide their members with old-age pensions. But the largely voluntary nature of these organizations and their limited financial resources had restricted their ability to do so. In the United States, very few union plans survived the Depression and friendly society plans were never significant. While worker organizations in other industrial nations were often more important providers of old-age pensions, benefits were typically quite low. After the Second World War, however, unions throughout the industrial world found themselves in a much stronger position. They had gained powerful collective bargaining rights, represented a significant portion of the workforce—often a majority—and were closely affiliated with the major left-wing political parties.

Throughout the industrial world, unions used their new position to expand old-age income benefits within the larger postwar political settlement. On the Continent, they successfully pressed for expanded government pensions and mandatory employment-based plans that provided supplementary top-ups. In Anglo-Saxon nations, the unions negotiated generous employer plans, often with the help of government. These bargained plans made the employer, not the union, responsible for providing old-age pensions. They also involved an acceptance by the labor movement of limited government pensions. And by making worker old-age pensions dependent on the success of the employer, these plans helped secure union commitments to labor peace. In the United States, the big industrial unions won generous pensions in 1949 and 1950 as part of a political settlement that included long-term labor agreements, controls on labor militancy, and the passage of the 1950 Social Security Amendments. In the decade that followed, pensions became a standard component of labor agreements throughout the unionized sector. In the United Kingdom, unions in the 1950s won generous pensions in Britain's nationalized industries from a Conservative government intent on strengthening the role of employer plans and forestalling the expansion of public programs (Sass 1997; Hannah 1986; Whiteside 2003).

## 4 Employer Plans in the Expansion of Anglo-Saxon Systems: 1965–1980

The Anglo-Saxon approach to the retirement income problem had clearly taken root by the mid-1960s. But the results were clearly limited. Employer plans at best covered half the workforce. Many of these covered workers would quit or lose their jobs before gaining a pension benefit. Others would see their plans go bust and their benefits lose much or all of their value. As public pensions provided meager, even welfare-level benefits, old age remained a stage of life generally characterized by a sharp decline in living standards. Women, in particular, were poorly served. Public and employer pensions were typically based on earnings, and women earned far less than men. Employer pensions were also based on tenure, and women also had far shorter tenures. Married women were largely dependent on benefits earned by their husbands, which typically came to an end when the husbands died. Nor did public programs typically give widows adequate survivor benefits.

In response to these shortcomings, Anglo-Saxon governments launched a series of initiatives to enlarge and strengthen their retirement income programs. This expansion largely came between 1965 and 1980, at the end of the long postwar boom. It included a significant increase in public programs for the elderly. It also included a variety of new initiatives designed to make employer pensions so secure and broadly distributed that they functioned as the earnings-related second tier in the national retirement income system.

In Canada and the United States, the government sought to achieve this objective by imposing an extensive set of regulations on tax-favored employer plans.

Government officials had taken note of the large and growing size of pension 'tax expenditures'—the revenue foregone by the Treasury as a result of the special treatment afforded employer plans. The precise size of such 'expenditures' is difficult to calculate: current contributions and investment income are typically exempt while future benefit payments are not, introducing a timing problem in measuring the size of the expenditure. In addition, governments might not be able to capture the entire foregone amount as taxpayers could often employ other tax shelters. Most official enumerations of government tax expenditures nevertheless had pensions at the top of the list. Such a large apparent revenue loss could only be justified by a comparable contribution to public welfare. And this would be accomplished only if employer plans allowed a large portion of the workforce to shift income from their years of employment to their years of retirement. As these tax preferences had become a major influence on employer behavior, imposing requirements on tax-qualified plans became a major instrument of retirement income policy: in exchange for government tax benefits, the Canadian Pension Benefits Acts of 1965–7 (enacted at the national and provincial level) and the US Employee Retirement Income Security Act of 1974 (ERISA) established new vesting, funding, and fiduciary standards on employer plans.

The government vesting requirement insisted that covered workers be given a 'vested' right to a pension within a specified amount of time. The regulations allowed different vesting schedules, but the most popular was full vesting after ten years for workers aged 45 or over in Canada and after ten years in the United States. Such requirements responded to the fact that workers typically changed employers over the course of their careers. So even if continually covered by a plan, workers often failed to gain an employer pension. The vesting requirement meant that a much larger share of the workforce would get at least a small employer pension to supplement their government benefits. As expanding coverage beyond large employers and unionized workers appeared quite difficult, vesting seemed the most effective way to expand the contribution of employer plans to retirement income security for the elderly (Sass 1997; Coward 1995).[3]

The Canadian Pension Acts and ERISA also imposed a set of funding requirements on employer plans to increase benefit security. In the earliest plans, employers had merely paid benefits to retirees as an ongoing, operating expense. If the employer went bust, so would the benefits of current and future pensioners. In the 1920s and 1930s, however, sponsors came to recognize that pension benefits were properly treated as part of an active worker's current compensation—that workers had acquired a substantial financial claim by the time they retired. Employers thus recognized the accrual of pension benefits by the active workforce, not benefits paid out to retirees, as their current operating pension expense. Some employers recorded this expense in a book reserve, a bookkeeping entry that recognized the obligation and allocated a portion of the sponsor's net worth to offset the liability.

But most governments denied employers favorable tax treatment for book-reserve funding. So most employers chose to fund their plans externally. The largest employers set up separate pension funds; smaller employers generally used insurance companies, which developed a variety of deferred annuity products for employer plans (Sass 1997; Coward 1995).[4]

Insured plans were regulated and for the most part financially sound. So the funding problems were concentrated in plans controlled and managed by the sponsor. Requirements that these sponsors adequately fund their plans came slowly. As self-managed plans became increasingly popular in the postwar period, due largely to their greater flexibility in funding and benefit design, funding shortfalls became a more general concern. In the United Kingdom, funding was largely left to the discretion of the sponsor's consulting actuary, a policy that proved generally effective in assuring the solvency of employer plans. The United States first imposed a limited fund requirement in the Revenue Act of 1942. Sponsors thereafter had to fund their expense for currently accrued benefits and prevent any current shortfall—their accumulated obligation less accumulated assets—from widening. But the failure of the Studebaker pension plan, in 1963, illustrated the continuing vulnerability of plans with insufficient funding. One of the key provisions of ERISA and the Pension Benefits Acts was thus the requirement to pay down any shortfall—within 30 years in the United States and within 25 years in Canada (Sass 1997; Coward 1995).

The United States and Canada also imposed new requirements on plan governance. Trust law, which had previously governed fiduciary conduct, assumed a community of interest between the grantor (the employer) and the beneficiary (the worker) and imposed fiduciary requirements only on trustees. In pension plans, the misconduct was primarily done by the corporate and union grantors, and not the trustees. To protect the interests of workers, Canada required at least one trustee to be independent of the sponsor. ERISA defined a variety of 'prohibited transactions' and required everyone associated with a plan, from the trustees (typically officers of the sponsor) to their consultants and agents, to act solely in the interest of the beneficiaries. This effectively outlawed investments that advanced the interests of corporate and union sponsors but undermined benefit security. ERISA also made employers liable for the plan's benefit obligations up to 30 percent of their net worth and created a pension insurance fund, the Pension Benefit Guaranty Corporation. The PBGC protected up to a specified level the pensions in plans that went bust, primarily by imposing levies on continuing employer plans (Sass 1997; Coward 1995).

The United Kingdom took a different tack to strengthening employer plans. In 1961 and again in 1978 it introduced an earnings-related government pension benefit on top of the universal flat Basic State Pension enacted after the war. Unlike public pension programs in nearly all other nations, these earnings-related public programs were designed first as residual plans, for those without employer coverage, and second as incentives for employers to 'contract out'. They did that by offering employers a 'rebate' of social insurance contributions if they assumed the government's new earnings-related pension obligation, including the obligation for workers who left prior to qualifying for a vested employer benefit. To encourage the expansion of employer plans, the government set this rebate above the employer's estimated cost of providing the benefit. The Graduated Retirement Benefit program, introduced in 1961, was slight, ill-designed, and widely suspected of being a Conservative political ploy rather than a bona-fide retirement income initiative. The State Earnings Related Pension Scheme, introduced in 1978, was a far more ambitious program and a major factor in the expansion of Britain's retirement income system (Hannah 1986).[5] Japan introduced a similar scheme in 1966, offering employers with more than 500 employees a rebate of social insurance contributions if they provided pensions equal to 130 percent or more of the government's earnings-related benefit (Casey 2004).

Australia took a third approach to expanding employer plans. The Labor Party had long advocated an increase in public pensions and replacing the country's 1908 means-tested program with social insurance. But oil shocks, stagflation, and the general weakening of the Australian economy had effectively blocked these options when Labor came to power, in 1983. So labor pushed for the expansion of employer plans as a source of old-age income. Substituting pension contributions for increased cash wages also increased saving and helped the government achieve more immediate macroeconomic policy objectives: declines in consumer demand, inflation, interest rates, and the nation's widening trade deficit. Together with the unions, the government succeeded in including pension benefits in the 1986 standard labor contract negotiated at the national level by labor and management representatives (Bateman and Piggott 2001; Commonwealth Treasury 2001).

The Australian national labor bargain did not carry the same authority as similar agreements on the European Continent. Coverage nevertheless reached 72 percent of wage and salary workers by the end of the decade. Australia's national bargaining system could not impose a national defined benefit pension program, like those in Europe, that subsumed employer and union-controlled multi-employer plans. Instead the model contract included a uniform 3 percent 'award superannuation' contribution in lieu of a comparable increase in wages across all industries and firms. The plans to emerge were thus defined contribution arrangements.[6] To strengthen the new system as a broad-based source of old-age income, the government also enacted regulations that required full and immediate vesting of award superannuation contributions; equal labor–management representation on the boards overseeing the multi-employer 'industry funds'; and the 'prudent man' fiduciary standard to govern investment management[7] (Bateman and Piggott 2001; Commonwealth Treasury 2001).

# 5 The Contribution of Employer Plans at the End of the Age of Expansion

Employer plans emerged at the end of the twentieth century as the earnings-related 'second-tier' of Anglo-Saxon retirement income systems. Contributions made by or on behalf of workers during their working years would provide a critical source of income when they in turn grew old. Because employer plans were now largely funded in advance, the capital market became a major source of support for much of the elderly population in Anglo-Saxon systems. As shown in Figure 5.2, income from employer plans and household financial assets now provides 40 percent or more of the income of the elderly in the United States, United Kingdom, and

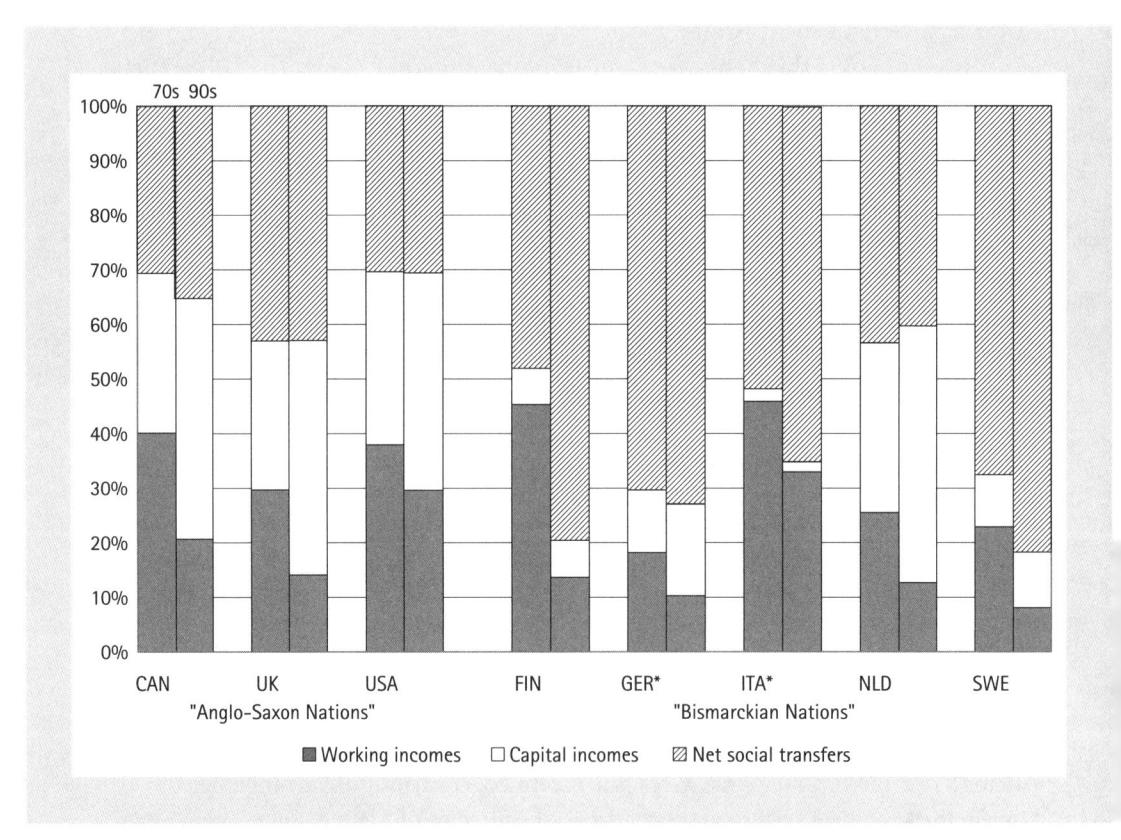

Fig. 5.2 Capital income from employer plans and household financial assets in 'Anglo-Saxon' and 'Bismarkian' nations (Disposable income by source, age 65 and over, 1970s[1] and 1990s)

Note: [1] Data for Germany and Italy are for the mid-1980s.

Source: Yamada (2002).

Canada.[8] About half of this investment income in the United States, and more than half in the United Kingdom, comes from employer plans. Other than in the Netherlands, which advance-funds its mandatory quasi-public 'second-tier' program, the income of the elderly in Bismarckian systems relies almost entirely on pay-as-you-go funding.

The recipients of employer pensions in Anglo-Saxon systems are concentrated in the middle and upper end of the income distribution. Employer plans provide earnings-related top-ups for middle income workers, with public pensions functioning as the basic source of financial security. For those in the upper income brackets, employer plans and investment income are the dominant sources of support. Only those at the bottom rely on government benefits for nearly all their old-age income. In nations with Bismarckian retirement income systems—other than the Netherlands—investment income is a minor source of support even for upper income groups (Fig. 5.3).

The expanded retirement income systems, both Anglo-Saxon and Bismarckian, have succeeded in allowing the elderly, on average, to maintain a reasonable approximation of their pre-retirement living standard. After adjusting for their lower tax burden and smaller household size, the disposable income of individuals age 65–75 in both systems is not much less than that of working-age adults (Yamada 2002; see Fig. 5.4). Even in Britain, a clear outlier, disposable incomes by this measure are reasonably close. And younger adults still have to pay working expenses, save for retirement, and make do with less leisure. Incomes in both systems tend to decline over time and older women remain a disadvantaged group. Anglo-Saxon systems also have greater disparities in the distribution of old-age income. Nevertheless, these systems now provide a far more rational distribution of income between the generations and across a worker's lifespan.

# 6 Conclusion

The expanded retirement income systems in both Bismarckian and Anglo-Saxon nations are clearly quite expensive. While costs varied from one nation to the next, Bismarckian programs toward the end of the twentieth century generally required about 20 percent of covered earnings. Costs in Anglo-Saxon systems were comparable. Contributions to government programs were typically about half the amount in Bismarckian systems; pension tax expenditures were about a fourth of contributions to public plans; and contributions to employer plans were about 7 to 8 percent of covered payroll.[9]

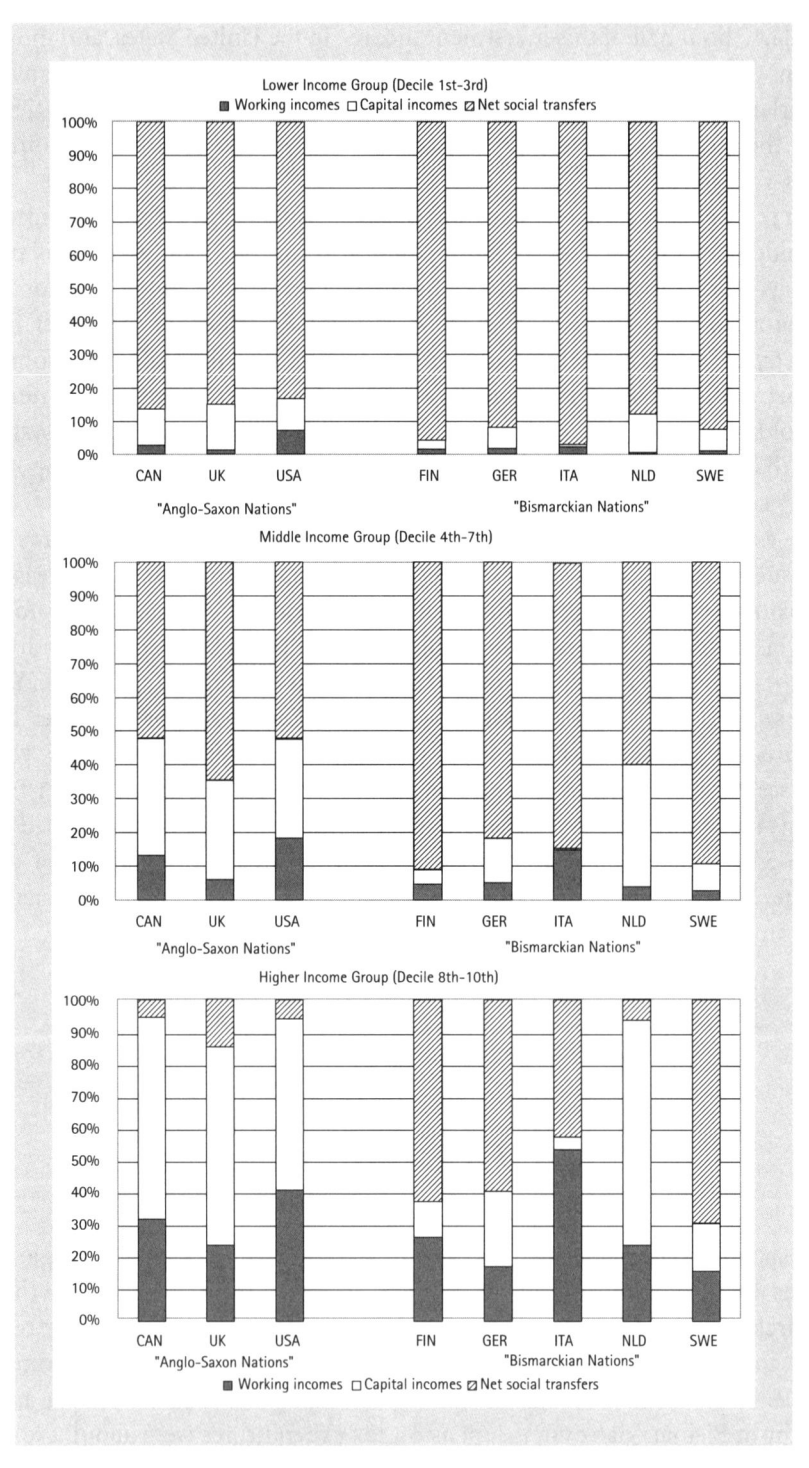

Fig. 5.3 Capital income from employer plans and household financial assets by income group in 'Anglo-Saxon' and 'Bismarkian' systems

*Source*: Yamada (2002).

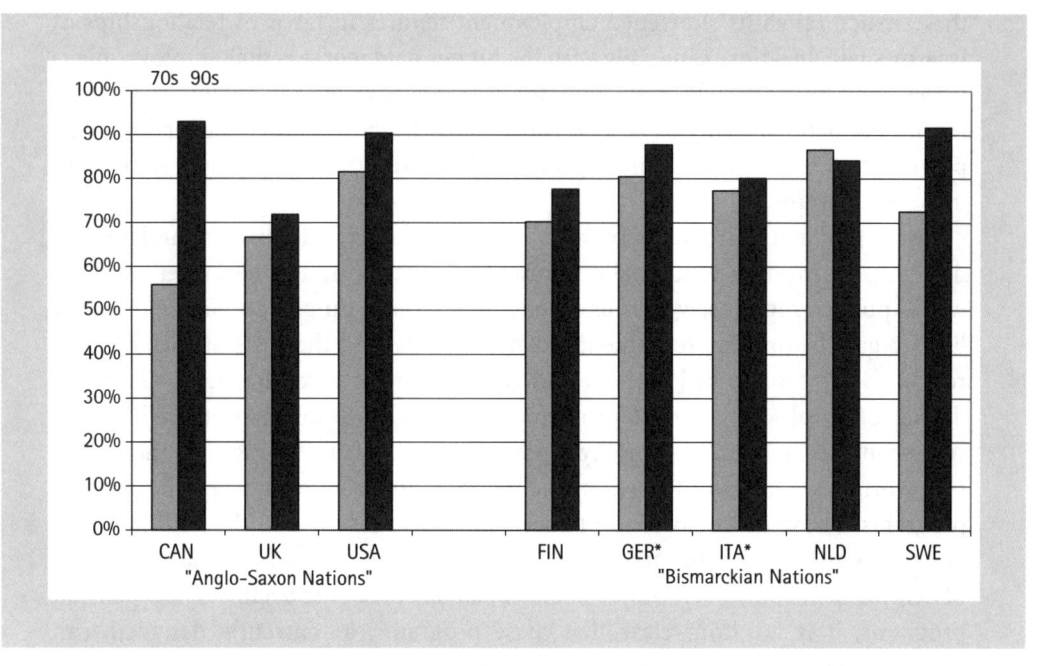

**Fig. 5.4** The income of the elderly (age 65–74) in comparison to that of working-age adults (Ratio of income adjusted for taxes and household size of people aged 65 to 74 to that of people aged 18 to 64, mid-1970s[1] and 1990s)

*Note:* [1] Data for Germany and Italy are for the mid-1980s.

*Source:* Yamada (2002).

Soon after these new systems took root, however, it became clear that the cost of pay-as-you-go government plans would dramatically rise. Rapid population ageing would place enormous pressure on public old-age pension programs in both Anglo-Saxon and Bismarckian systems. Advance-funded employer plans, as a result, appeared increasingly attractive.

But structural economic shifts seriously weakened employer plans in the years after 1980. Globalization and sharp increases in the educational attainment of the labor force, in the technical level of production, and in the employment of married women had various corrosive effects. First, globalization and the increased technical level of production undermined the market power of large corporate and union pension sponsors, which in turn undermined their ability to underwrite and manage long-term retirement income programs. Second, globalization, higher technology, and the entry of highly educated workers and married women into the paid workforce diminished the labor-market value of older less educated men. It thus became increasingly difficult for employers to keep such workers gainfully employed, at a decent wage, until the specified 'normal retirement age'. Finally, these structural shifts shortened employment tenures in favor of relationships of intermediate duration, especially with the higher paid workers that employer plans target. Employers would thus find far less justification for maintaining their traditional defined-benefit (DB) pension plans, which rewarded career long employment, or indeed for continuing any large contribution to employee retirement income programs.

Just as national retirement income systems had largely addressed a fundamental defect in the modern industrial economy, the contribution of employer plans, as well as public programs, were thus called into question. Employers had increasingly little to gain by offering retirement income benefits, and the costs of such benefits rose with the growth of longevity and government-imposed burdens. The withdrawal of employers is most problematic in 'Anglo-Saxon' nations, with their significant dependence on employer plans. Policy-makers throughout the industrial world have largely focused on the demographic challenge to public pension programs. Those in Anglo-Saxon nations must also respond to the withdrawal of employers as key contributors to the retirement income system. While the growth of defined contribution employer plans has largely offset the decline of DB pension programs, it is far from clear that these programs, as currently designed, can provide today's workers a reasonably secure and comfortable old age.

# NOTES

1. More precisely, the additional income from remaining employed was the worker's wage *plus* non-pension benefits *less* income and payroll taxes on wages, out-of-pocket working expenses, *and* the foregone pension less income taxes on the pension (which were zero on Social Security benefits). As the British economy rebounded after the Second World War and labor shortages emerged, the government did offer increased benefits to those who deferred receipt or who were denied a pension due to the earnings test (Whitehouse 1998). But this was rather unusual and had limited effect.
2. As James Wooten points out, the fact that very few rank-and-file workers paid tax in the 1920s, when these treatments took shape, argues against the notion that they were enacted as a favor or inducement to expand pension coverage. Wooten suggests that this special treatment was enacted, in part, to level the playing field between pension and wage compensation—to avoid taxing compensation taken as pensions (at the employer and pension trust level) for workers who would not be taxed on their wages (Wooten 2005).
3. In both the United States and Canada, participation requirements have since been significantly shortened. In addition to vesting, ERISA increased the number of employer plan beneficiaries, specifically to elderly widows who were poorly served by earnings-based retirement income systems, by making a joint-and-survivor annuity the default annuity form. Unless specifically waived, the surviving spouse (nearly always a widow)

would receive half the worker's pension, which would be actuarially reduced to pay for this survivor benefit.
4. Although these claims were recognized and increasingly funded by large corporate sponsors, active workers typically had a legally enforceable claim only to benefits provided by an insurance company. In uninsured plans, corporate lawyers typically defined pension benefits as a 'gratuity' that the employer was under no legal obligation to provide. Prior to 1938, pension funds in the United States could be held in a revocable trust, allowing the sponsor to reclaim the assets at will. After the Second World War, the courts and then the legislatures made pension benefits a legally enforceable claim.
5. Employers did not have to take on the entire SERPS liability as the government retained the riskier portions of the obligation, such as inflation proofing. To encourage contracting out, the government set the contribution rebate at about 0.5 percent of earnings point above the estimated private cost of providing the benefit. The estimate included administrative expenses, which increased costs above the government alternative; and assumed a significant use of equities in funding the benefit, which reduced costs far below the present value of the benefit discounted at the riskless government rate (Daykin 2001).
6. Essentially all US collectively bargained plans had a defined benefit rather than a defined contribution format. This was the case even though cost of these benefits was carefully priced at the bargaining table, and in multi-employer plans where the labor contract required employers to contribute a specific monetary amount per hour. But in these US negotiated plans, costs and benefits varied dramatically and employers bore the risk that their contributions and pension fund investment income would be insufficient to fund the benefits promised. A nationwide agreement to contribute a fixed percentage of earnings to pension plans that covered a wide variety of employer or industry groups, even in the United States, would all but inevitably result in plans with a defined contribution format (Sass 1997).
7. The prudent man standard is common in Anglo-Saxon trust law. In the formulation specified in ERISA, 'a fiduciary shall discharge his duties with respect to a plan solely in the interest of the participants and beneficiaries and ... with the care, skill, prudence, and diligence under the circumstances then prevailing that a prudent man acting in a like capacity and familiar with such matters would use in the conduct of an enterprise of like character and with like aims ...'.

In one area, the government cut back its support of employer plans. The expansion resulting from the award superannuation agreement resulted in a sharp decline in tax revenues. In response, the government rescinded the enormously generous tax treatment afforded employer plans—a treatment that allowed recipients to receive their entire pension as a lump sum and pay tax on only 5 percent of the value—a tax at most equal to 3 percent of the total amount. The new treatment imposed a tax, which was generally low compared to that imposed on other types of income, on contributions, investment income, and lump-sum distributions, as well as on pension payouts.
8. The data on Japan reported by Yamada do not properly illustrate the contribution of employer plans in the nation's retirement income system. In other 'Anglo-Saxon' nations, the elderly primarily get their benefits in the form of an annuity, and the entire annuity payment is recorded as income. Japanese employer plans distribute benefits primarily in the form of lump-sum payments before the age of 65. Only the investment income generated from such distributions, not the consumption of the underlying asset nor the imputed income from such assets, such as imputed rent from purchased

housing, is classified as income from capital. Thus only a small amount of old-age income appears to derive from employer plans or other forms of saving.

9. In the United States, the contribution for Social Security old-age and survivors', pensions is currently 10.6 percent of covered earnings, split evenly between employers and employees, realizing $450 billion in 2003; the pension tax expenditure for 2003, as reported by the Office of Management and Budget (for employer plans, Keogh plans for small businesses, and Individual Retirement Accounts, which are primarily roll-overs from employer plans) was $125 billion, nearly a third of the amount contributed to Social Security. This tax expenditure figure, however, is generally seen as too high an estimate of the actual revenue loss.

## REFERENCES

BALL, R. M. (1947). 'Social insurance and the right to assistance'. *The Social Service Review*, 21/3 (Sept.).

BATEMAN, H., and PIGGOTT, J. (2001). 'The Australian approach to retirement income provision'. Prepared for the International Seminar on Social Security Pensions, Tokyo, (5–7 Mar.).

CASEY, B. (2004). 'Reforming the Japanese retirement income system: a special case?' Boston: Center for Retirement Research at Boston College.

CHANDLER, A. D. (1977). *The Visible Hand: The Managerial Revolution in American Business*. Cambridge, Mass.: Harvard University Press.

—— (1990). *Scale and Scope: The Dynamics of Industrial Capitalism*. Cambridge, Mass.: Harvard University Press.

COMMONWEALTH TREASURY OF AUSTRALIA (2001). 'Towards higher retirement incomes for Australians: a history of the Australian retirement income system since federation'. *Economic Roundup Centenary Edition 2001*.

COWARD, L. (1995). *Private Pensions in OECD Countries: Canada*. Paris: OECD.

CLARK, G. L. (2000). *Pension Fund Capitalism*. Oxford: Oxford University Press.

—— (2003). *European Pensions & Global Finance*. Oxford: Oxford University Press.

DAYKIN, C. (2001) 'Contracting out: a partnership between public and private pensions'. *Pensions Management Institute News* (July).

ESPING-ANDERSEN, G. (1990). *The Three Worlds of Welfare Capitalism*. Oxford: Polity Press.

GRAEBNER, W. (1980). *A History of Retirement*. New Haven: Yale University Press.

HANNAH, L. (1986). *Inventing Retirement: The Development of Occupational Pensions in Britain*. Cambridge: Cambridge University Press.

LATIMER, M. (1932). *Industrial Pension Systems in the United States and Canada*, 2 vols. New York: Industrial Relations Counselors.

LAZEAR, E. P. (1995). *Personnel Economics*. Cambridge, Mass.: MIT Press.

RAPHAEL, M. (1964). *Pensions and Public Servants: A Study of the Origins of the British System*. Paris: Mouton.

SASS, S. (1997). *The Promise of Private Pensions*. Cambridge, Mass.: Harvard University Press.

SKOLNIK, A. (1976). 'Private pension plans, 1950–1974'. *Social Security Bulletin*, 39/6 (June): 3–17.

WHITEHOUSE, E. (1998). 'Pension reform in Britain'. Discussion Paper No. 9810. Washington, D. C.: The World Bank.

WHITESIDE, N. (2003). 'Historical perspectives and the politics of pension reform', in G. L. Clark and N. Whiteside (eds.), *Pension Security in the 21st Century*. Oxford: Oxford University Press.

WOOTEN, J. (2005). *The Employee Retirement Income Security Act of 1974: A Political History*. Berkeley: University of California Press.

YAMADA, A. (2002). *The Evolving Retirement Income Package: Trends in Adequacy and Equality*. Paris: OECD.

CHAPTER 6

# CHANGING WORK PATTERNS AND THE REORGANIZATION OF OCCUPATIONAL PENSIONS

EWALD ENGELEN

## 1 INTRODUCTION

Despite huge institutional differences, most developed economies have evolved a three-tiered model of pension provision to prevent the scourge of old-age poverty (see Davis 1995; Clark 2003a for general overviews). Throughout the 'three worlds of welfare capitalism' (Esping-Andersen 1990, 1999), the state provides some form of basic retirement payment. These may be in the form of tax rebates, direct payments or public services; they can be financed by either social levies or general taxation, and can be either universal or contribution-based. Moreover, there are huge differences between countries concerning their generosity and their accessibility. Some offer flat-rate benefits, others provide high levels of income replacement; some require residency, while others demand fully fledged citizenship. Despite this variety, each and every national pension system is built on the bedrock of a state-managed or state-initiated pillar.

The second pillar consists of occupational pensions. These too have many different organizational and institutional shapes: they may be either funded or unfunded, may be private, public, or semi-public, and may be corporate-based or industry wide. Occupational pensions can be found in almost every developed economy. Historically, they have been used to 'buy' the loyalty of the workforce in order to stem job mobility and reap the returns on investments in human capital. The third pillar, finally, concerns individual pension savings. Here too a wide variety of institutional shapes can be observed, ranging from different modes of participation (mandatory or voluntary), legal statuses (private or public), goals (commercial or non-profit), and different modi operandi (funded or unfunded). The share of private savings for the level of overall pensions differs widely between countries, depending on the coverage and the generosity of the first two pillars. However, as I will argue in this chapter, there are good reasons to expect that third pillar pensions will become more conspicuous in the overall mix of pension arrangements in the coming decades. The main argument is that the insurance schemes that embody notions of social or industrial citizenship (Marshall 1964), which include most first and second pillar pensions, are premised on a well-defined and stable population of contributors and beneficiaries, implying fairly high access and exit thresholds. The rationale is that the insurance mechanisms are redistributive, presupposing strong ties of solidarity, based on shared risks or clearly perceived interdependencies (Beckert et al. 2004). What is at stake here are the 'boundaries' of the insured aggregates.

Public pension systems are usually distinguished according to whether they are universal or contribution-based. In the first instance access is determined by residency or nationality, implying that the subjects of insurance are either all legal residents or all citizens. In the second instance employment status is the determinant, implying that only workers have full access. The former are truly 'citizens' pensions', while the latter are strictly speaking 'occupational pensions'. Occupational pensions, in turn, encompass either all employees, irrespective of their contract, or only workers with full tenure. The final relevant dimension concerns the mode of financing. In the case of a pay-as-you-go system, full responsibility for the economic sustainability of the plan falls on the sponsoring firm or the state. In the case of pre-funded systems, however, there are two options for the distribution of risks and responsibilities. Still dominant are plans that allocate the risks of insufficient returns to the fund itself, its sponsor(s), and/or the state. However, increasingly these 'defined-benefit' plans (DB plans) are being replaced by so-called 'defined-contribution' plans (DC plans) that place the burden of risks entirely on the shoulders of the beneficiary. In the case of third pillar schemes, insurance schemes are no longer vertically redistributive (between classes) but only horizontally (over the life-cycle). Hence, no predetermined population of insurable subjects can be identified. In principle, everyone can participate, although in practice only those who are willing (i.e. possessing a sufficient degree of risk-aversion) and able (having a sufficient level of income to save) will do so. Evidently, there is some conceptual overlap between individual saving plans and occupational DC plans, the only difference being the voluntary nature of 'pure' third pillar schemes and the binding nature of 'pure' occupational ones.

It is widely observed that first and second pillar pensions have increasingly come under pressure because of a number of macro social changes that appear to have 'denaturalized' the boundaries of the risk categories they cover, a development that is especially conspicuous in Continental Europe (Clark 2003a, 2003b). Due to migration, 'citizens' pensions' face a series of difficult and pressing moral and prudential questions (Whiteford 1996; Engelen 2003). Given the need for increasing migration, either to facilitate economic growth or to counter the socio-economic effects of demographic change, how is the turbulence of migration flows to be absorbed? How to deal with non-contributing residents who lack adequate citizenship rights? How to deal with contributors residing elsewhere? Is continuing exclusion a viable option or should states strive for inclusion? In which case, how? Which types of thresholds are morally acceptable and prudentially wise?

In the case of occupational pensions, the question is how to absorb the effects of changing job structures, increasing job mobility, the growing incidence of non-linear career patterns, and the growth of non-standard employment contracts. Since too much mobility is irreconcilable with vertically redistributive insurance schemes, job mobility is either dampened by the current design of occupational pensions or increased labor market flexibility has resulted in a growing segregation between primary and secondary labor market segments, implying growing inequalities in terms of social rights and hence the increasing exclusion of outsiders. Pre-funded private pensions in general and third pillar arrangements in particular have increasingly been presented as a solution to these sorts of problems (World Bank 1994; Sass 1997).

Here I focus on the changes in the sectoral composition of economies, firm strategies, and labor markets respectively to argue that occupational pensions will gradually be transformed into individual saving accounts. The challenges facing public retirement plans are the topic of Part II of this volume. I conclude with a brief discussion of the policy challenges and open research questions involved.

## 2 CHANGING POLITICAL ECONOMIES

During the twentieth century the advanced political economies of the West have undergone two 'great transformations'. Despite the Polanyian overtones of this phrase, the developments I have in mind are somewhat different from

Polanyi's own (Polanyi 1944). While Polanyi's *first* transformation referred to the transformation of the feudal 'moral economy' into an 'amoral' capitalist one and the *second* to the totalitarian backlashes against free market liberalism in the 1920s and 1930s, the two transformations I have in mind concern shifts in the sectoral composition of advanced political economies. In the course of little more than two decades (1945–70), predominantly agrarian economies were transformed into overwhelmingly industrial ones. During this period agricultural employment diminished by more than 3 million jobs in Germany, 4 million jobs in France, nearly 350,000 jobs in Sweden, and more than 4 million jobs in the United States. Despite the magnitude of the transformation, most economies were able to absorb the workers that were being displaced relatively easily in the expanding manufacturing sector. Over the same period the increase in industrial jobs amounted to more than 4 million in Germany, 300,000 in Sweden, and a stunning 8 million in the United States, suggesting substantial surpluses in overall employment in some economies (United States) and small deficits in others (Sweden).[1] Only France and Italy were troubled by more sizeable deficits in this regard, initiating a difficult and politically highly charged trajectory of economic transformation in which the state was heavily involved.

Most advanced economies reached the zenith of industrialization in the mid-1960s. At that time, employment in agriculture had dropped to levels below 10 percent of overall employment. While the share of industrial employment had reached 40–42 percent in Germany, the United Kingdom, and Scandinavia, due to a less decommodified labor market and a lower level of public services, it reached only 34 percent in the United States (Esping-Andersen 1999: 27). It is hard to overestimate the societal effects of these changes. Not only did industrialization imply a substantial rise in the overall standard of living, it was also accompanied by a rapid process of urbanization—changing landscapes, cities, and traditional ways of life—and a notable standardization of working practices, consumption habits, and family life. In almost every advanced political economy, the nuclear family, headed by a full-time, fully tenured male breadwinner, became the model of social and economic reproduction.

It was under these socio-economic conditions that the welfare state took shape. Most of the arrangements that were introduced in the 1950s and 1960s served to guarantee minimum income levels for dependents in case the breadwinner failed. First pillar arrangements clearly fall in this category. Another important piece of legislation in this period concerned the nationwide codification of industry or firm-based insurances against work-related risks, such as disability, sickness, unemployment, and old age. Here lie the roots of state-initiated or facilitated occupational pensions. These insurances were based on the assumption of exogenous risks, assumed a high level of similarity among the insured, stable employment relations, and low job mobility (Rosanvallon 2000; Baldwin 1990). Or as Crouch concludes after elaborate statistical testing: 'Industrialization is associated with a rise in the proportion of the working population, and in particular the male population, engaged in full time employee status' (1999: 60). As such, the mid-century 'social compromise', as it is referred to by Crouch, presupposes a gendered division of labor, a well-guarded border between social and economic reproduction, a stable economic structure, fully tenured employment contracts, a low level of job mobility, and, last but not least, a growing economy. These designate the outlines of the Fordist settlement between state, capital, and labor that has been adulated by some as the 'Golden Age of Capitalism' (Marglin and Schor 1990).

From the mid-1960s onward, however, economic development changed direction once more. A number of authors at that time noted the growing economic importance of services (Bell 1973; Kumar 1978; Gershuny 1978; Rose 1991). As a result of technological change, changing life-styles, rising living standards, and increased competition, the overall share of manufacturing—in terms of value-added as well as employment—was seen to decline relative to that of services. Individuals, households, and organizations were perceived to spend growing amounts of their budgets on non-material goods such as education, financial advice, culture, social services, tourism, and other types of personal and producers' services. Moreover, to differentiate their products from those of their competitors, manufacturers were constantly upgrading their products by advertising, branding, and after-sales services. Next, due to market-driven concentration and growing complexity as a result of more sophisticated consumer demands, management became a more difficult task, resulting in its professionalization, a relative growth of managerial jobs, and an increasing service intensity of the manufacturing sector as such. Finally, as a consequence of automation, the job content of the average industrial worker became more similar to that of his service sector counterpart (Offe 1985).

All advanced political economies have since witnessed a decline of jobs in the manufacturing sector, while service sector employment has steadily increased. From 1973 to 1990 the number of industrial jobs fell by more than 1 million in Germany, while the service sector grew by a little less than 4 million jobs. In France the shift was even more pronounced. Between 1973 and 1993 the number of manufacturing jobs declined by 1.7 million, while employment in the service industries grew by 4.3 million. Greatest of all was the transformation of the American economy. Over the same period employment in industry shrunk by 1.4 million jobs, while service employment increased with a stunning 32 million jobs (Esping-Andersen 1999: 26).

Figure 6.A1 (see Appendix) gives a graphical overview of the rise of the service economy in six advanced political economies. A number of observations can be made from this. First, in all economies where the total number of jobs has grown, that growth was primarily owed to the expansion of the service sector. This is especially true for the Netherlands and the United States. Second, the share of the service sector in total employment differs widely between political economies. In the United States and the Netherlands service employment accounts for over 70 percent of total employment, while in Germany it only just exceeds the 50 percent mark. Sweden and Denmark fall in between these extremes. Third, the label of 'deindustrialization' properly speaking is applicable only to some political economies. The most clear-cut case is the United Kingdom, where the share of industrial employment fell from 40 percent in the late 1960s to a mere 20 percent in 2003. Least pronounced is Germany, where industrial jobs still account for approximately 35 percent of total employment. In the cases of the Netherlands and the United States it is doubtful whether 'deindustrialization' is the proper label at all. In both countries, the number of industrial jobs has always been rather limited and has remained stable over time. Only in relative terms is there such a thing as a decline, suggesting that what has actually occurred in both countries is not so much 'deindustrialization' as a further intensification, sophistication, and specialization of a number of already well-developed service sectors such as personal services and especially financial services. However, despite different manifestations, a gradual reorientation of national political economies away from manufacturing toward services is observable across the board. In all six economies, the largest number of people is currently employed in services. And that represents a transformation that is just as radical as the industrial revolutions of the eighteenth and nineteenth centuries.

## 3 Changing Company Strategies

Another way of looking at these developments is to focus on the shifts in strategies that firms have pursued in response to them. The dominant model of work organization until the mid-1970s was the Taylorist firm. According to this model, the organization of work followed three principles. First, every task was to be subdivided and reduced to its constituent parts. Second, every execution task had to be stripped of its planning dimensions. Third, planning and execution tasks were to be delegated to different categories of workers who specialized in as few tasks as possible. The fine-grained intra-organizational division of labor and the large-scale firm in which Taylor's principles of 'scientific management' resulted, fitted perfectly with the Fordist compromise between state, capital, and labor described above. It made ever more standardized consumer goods available to growing numbers of workers, who in turn, because of the efficiency gains of Taylorism, saw their living standards rapidly rise, and the routinization and standardization of jobs on which it was premised allowed for easy quantification of productivity gains, wages, and social rights. The wage administrations of large firms became private extensions, so to speak, of the fiscal apparatus of the welfare state.

In due course, the principles of 'scientific management' were not only transferred from large-scale industry to large-scale services, but also started to cross the ocean, especially after the Second World War had proven the economic superiority of the American way (Berghahn 1986; Djelic 1998; Zeitlin and Herrigel 2000). However, in Europe the spread of Taylorist principles did not pass uncontested. In the late 1960s a wave of labor conflicts highlighted the increasing dissatisfaction of European workers with the loss of job autonomy as a result of the Taylorization of work practices (Crouch and Pizzorni 1978). Moreover, around the same period, ICT and market deregulations started to confront large firms with a degree of variability and complexity that forced them to adapt or perish.

With hindsight it is easy to see that the postwar successes of Taylorism were premised on three background conditions which gradually evaporated from the mid-1970s onward (Grint 1994). First, it presupposed homogeneous consumer and producer markets. Only when consumers prefer quantity and low price over quality and uniqueness will firms be able to recoup the huge investments in specialized machinery that are the hallmark of Taylorism. As soon as effective demand starts to splinter into many small market niches, firms become unable to reap the required economies of scale. Because of a confluence of social developments—overproduction in a number of crucial consumer markets (automobiles, radios, televisions, and kitchen appliances), rising living standards, rising expectations, individualization, and new technologies—economies of scale became increasingly hard to achieve (Sabel 1982).

Second, Taylorism presupposed high and stable economic growth. The pernicious effects of Taylorism for workers were largely offset by the promise (and reality) of increasing consumer rights. This in turn fed into economic growth and an increased fiscal intake. As a result capital and labor had a shared interest in policies of counter-cyclical demand management in order to ensure rising incomes, growing demand, and a constantly growing economy. Because of rising energy prices and market saturation, profits started to decrease, investments to decline, and inflation to rise in the late 1970s. In the early 1980s, governments worldwide started to pursue 'sound monetary policies', and raised interest rates to double-digit levels (Marglin and Schor 1990; Kitschelt *et al.* 1999). Compounded by a fierce international monetary conflict over the postwar distribution of global demand (Brenner 2002), the mid-century compromise started to unravel, resulting in much lower economic growth and rising unemployment figures.

Third, Taylorism presupposed at least marginal benefits of the ongoing division of intra-organizational labor. In order to offset financially the adverse effects of routinization, the Taylorist firm had to book constant efficiency gains. In the beginning that was easy. Over time, however, Taylorist firms increasingly became immune to improvement and even started to encounter constraints of scale and specialization, in the form of rising organization, information, and control costs. As a result, many firms lacked the ability to respond to new competitors, in particular from the Japanese, who used new organizational models that allowed them to accelerate product cycles and increase the number of product varieties.

Since the early 1980s, firms across the globe have frantically experimented with new organizational models, spawning a vibrant cottage industry of management and organization studies. Some firms have tried to increase product diversity, speed up delivery times and production processes by dividing up large corporations into smaller business units, devolving decision-making to the factory floor, organizing workers into work teams, and enhancing job quality. Others have pursued strategies that aim primarily at a reduction of labor costs by introducing variable working times, hiring non-standard workers, and offering different types of performance payments. The distinguishing characteristic of these two strategy types is whether or not they break with the divisional logic of Taylorism, suggesting the analytical distinction between 'post-Taylorist' and 'neo-Taylorist' strategies.

Currently, we observe different varieties of these strategies being pursued in different parts of the global economy. Under the rubric of post-Taylorism fall strategies like 'flexible specialization' (Piore and Sabel 1984) and 'diversified quality production' (Streeck 1992) that aim for 'functional flexibilization' by lengthening the production tract, recombining conceptual and execution tasks, reducing the number of managerial layers, and cutting back on inventorial redundancies. 'Lean production', on the other hand, is a strategy that clearly falls into the category of neo-Taylorism. Its overarching aim is to achieve flexibility by speeding up production processes by aiming for simple tasks and simple organizations, and, especially, by reducing standstills and redundancies (Womack et al. 1990). The same is true for outsourcing. Here, the firm tries to keep its Taylorist work organization largely intact by focusing on core competencies and externalizing the risks of market fluctuation on suppliers and subsidiaries. Another version is the strategy of numerical flexibilization, the defining characteristic of which lies in the externalization of market risks on a secondary ring of precarious workers (Lane 1989).

The choice of strategy is constrained by the institutional context, forcing German firms, for example, to pursue quality strategies instead of price strategies while the United States is instead seen to favour the latter (Whitley 1999; Hall and Soskice 2001). In almost all advanced political economies, however—Germany as well as the United States, Sweden as well as the Netherlands—there is a tendency toward a bifurcated or polarized economic structure, consisting of innovative, quality-oriented firms that offer stable employment and excellent working conditions for highly educated workers on the one hand, and on the other, a growing number of firms that pursue predominantly cost-cutting strategies and hire low-skilled workers on a temporary or part-time basis. The institutional effect is manifest only in the size of the precarious segment; large in 'Liberal Market Economies' like the

United States, the United Kingdom, Ireland, Australia, and Canada; much smaller (albeit growing) in 'Coordinated Market Economies' such as Germany, the Nordic Countries, France, and Belgium.[2] As such, neo-Taylorist and post-Taylorist firms appear to be able to coexist within the space of one national political economy.

## 4 Changing Labor Markets

Labor market changes have been both an effect and a driver of the service revolution and the spread of neo-Taylorist working patterns described above. Since the mid-century 'social compromise' came unstuck, capital has been pressing governments worldwide to pursue a supply-side strategy that is based on a cost-cutting conception of global competition. Insofar as this lobby has been successful, states have sought to enhance overall labor participation by deregulating labor markets. As a result, some of the decommodifying arrangements that were set up during the 'Trente Glorieuse' were scaled back. As such, changes in the institutions surrounding the labor market encouraged firms to pursue neo-Taylorist strategies and hence have indirectly caused the labor market changes that are the topic of this section.

Two things stand out if one looks at changes over time in the employment structure of advanced political economies. First, there has been a marked decrease in male employment. The share of male workers in total employment of the non-dependent population has declined almost everywhere. Except for Sweden, where the decrease in male employment has partly to do with increased gender equality, the overall losses in male employment have been caused by high levels of male unemployment since the early 1980s. The small decline in the United States, in turn, is attributable to high overall employment levels. And second, there has been a marked increase in female labor participation. Although there are still substantial differences between political economies regarding the level of female labor participation, it is striking that it has increased everywhere (Table 6.1).

If the 'demasculinization' and 'feminization' of working life is one development distinguishing current labor markets from those of the mid-twentieth century, another is the rise of atypical employment patterns (Table 6.2). Although much has been made of the increasing precariousness of employment contracts as a result of labor market deregulation, full tenure nevertheless remains the dominant type of employment contract. Moreover, there are no indications of a rise over time. In the second half of the 1990s—arguably the deregulatory high tide in Europe—the share of temporary workers in the total workforce rose from 6 percent in 1995 to 6.9

Table 6.1 Male and female labor market participation rates

|  | Male | | Female | |
| --- | --- | --- | --- | --- |
|  | 1960 | 1995 | 1960 | 1995 |
| Denmark | 95 | 81 | 39 | 61 |
| Germany | 89 | 71 | 43 | 48 |
| Netherlands | 87 | 74 | 24 | 50 |
| Sweden | 85 | 67 | 35 | 63 |
| United Kingdom | 87 | 69 | 38 | 53 |
| United States | 83 | 80 | 37 | 64 |

Source: Crouch (1999: 428).

percent in 2001 (EC 2004: 161). However, temporary employment is not the only form of precarious labor. In many political economies, part-time work too gives access to marginal social security rights only. So, if we add part-time workers to workers with a temporary contract, the picture changes. According to the latest EU employment monitor, the percentage of workers with a non-standard employment contract[3] in the EU 15 amounted to 22.5 in 2001 (EC 2004). In other words, the employment careers of a substantial number of workers, many of whom are employed in the service industries and many of whom are female,[4] do not conform to the mid-century model of full-time, full tenured contracts and hence do not give access to the social security rights that could protect them from the risks of sickness, disability, unemployment, and old age.

Table 6.2 Share of standard and non-standard employment contracts, 2003

|  | Full tenure | Fixed term | Total non-standard employment contracts[1] |
| --- | --- | --- | --- |
| Denmark | 62 | 5.4 | 30.6 |
| Germany | 45 | 8 | 34.6 |
| Netherlands | 56 | 6.7 | 59.6 |
| United Kingdom | 58 | 3 | 31.3 |

Note: [1] Figures do not add up since the category of 'full tenure' refers to all employment contracts of unlimited duration, many of which are part-time.
Source: EC (2004: 161, 237).

A third feature of contemporary labor markets is their increased dynamism. Compared to the stable one-firm-career path of the male breadwinner of the 1950s and 1960s,[5] post-industrial career patterns are much more diverse and unstable (Esping-Andersen *et al.* 2002). Although reliable data are hard to come by, there is some evidence of a decline in job tenure and a concomitant rise in job mobility, especially since the mid-1990s. According to the 1994 OECD *Employment Outlook*, average job tenure in 1991 was 10.48 years in Germany, 7 years in the Netherlands, 7.9 years in the United Kingdom, and 6.7 years in the United States, while the share of jobs with a tenure of less than one year amounted to 12.8 percent in Germany, 24 percent in the Netherlands, 18.6 percent in the United Kingdom, and 28.8 percent in the United States (OECD 1994: 23). Since then an upward trend in terms of mobility rates has been observable. In Denmark mobility increased from 14.6 percent in 1997 to 17.8 percent a year later.[6] For the Netherlands, the figures are 8.8 percent versus 14.3 percent, while in Sweden mobility increased from 10.3 percent to 11.8 percent (Stimpson 2000: 8). Since the share of temporary contracts increased during the 1990s, it is obvious that overall mobility too must have increased. According to figures from 2000, 57.6 percent of all temporary workers employed in the OECD have job tenure of below 1 year, while only 11.6 percent have tenure of more than 5 years. For workers with permanent employment contracts the comparable figures are 13.2 and 59.8 percent respectively (OECD 2002: 154).

Developments in the labor market thus seem to strengthen the conclusion drawn earlier, that advanced political economies are undergoing a bifurcation of their economic structure. In the arena of the labor market, the division is between, on the one hand, low-skilled, predominantly young, female and immigrant workers, working in the personal services sector, where they overwhelmingly occupy temporary and/or part-time jobs and hence build up only precarious social security rights. On the other are highly skilled, male workers with full-time labor contracts of unlimited duration, working in business services and manufacturing, where they have access to the full panoply of social security rights (see also Leisering and Leibfried 1998).

# 5 Redesigning Occupational Pension Rights

All institutional arrangements reflect the socio-economic wisdoms of their time. During the 'golden age of capitalism' stability was all. As historical reconstructions have shown, the rationale behind occupational pensions was to buy the loyalty of the worker in order to reap the returns on investment in schooling and training (Jackson 2003). Further considerations had to do with cost and solidarity. The costs of setting up and applying actuarially sound funding principles were too high to allow for quick job changes, while vertical redistribution implied pre-funded pension plans which required a level of solidarity that could only be expected from workers with a sense of shared socio-economic risks, however minimal. This is reflected in the vesting requirements of occupational pension plans. In Denmark, workers have to be older than 30 and to be employed for 5 years or more before their savings are vested. In Ireland, the vesting period is 5 years too, whereas in the United Kingdom vesting follows after only 2 years of employment. In the Netherlands, vesting requirements are relatively liberal: 1 year of employment suffices. Obviously, workers with temporary contracts are excluded from participating, while part-time workers build up only part-time pension rights (Andrietti 2001: 74).

The stability bias built into occupational pensions hinders job mobility and as such stands in the way of an efficient allocation of labor, which is increasingly seen as a prerequisite for economic growth.[7] In fact, portability issues rank high on the EU policy agenda, especially since the mobility of workers within the EU has been enshrined in the Treaty of Rome. Although the level of mobility in the EU is still relatively low, intra-national studies show that this effect can be considerable. Andrietti has demonstrated that job mobility is considerably higher among workers without occupational pension plans than among workers with such a plan. This was confirmed for the Netherlands, the United Kingdom, Spain, Ireland, and Denmark (Andrietti 2001).

However, as a result of a confluence of causes—increasing beneficiaries and decreasing contributors; new accountancy rules; lower returns on investment—a growing number of pension funds are at present transforming their defined-benefit plans into defined-contribution plans. In the United States, arguably the most mobile and flexible labor market worldwide, this has turned into a veritable trend. While DB plans were roughly twice as large in terms of participants as DC plans in the late 1970s, by the late 1990s the number of participants in DCs had clearly overshadowed those of DBs (Clark 2003*b*: 1345; see also Chapter 18 in this volume). In the UK, which has the oldest occupational pension system in the world, more than three-quarters of British DB plans have been closed to new members (Langley 2005). Instead, workers are offered so-called 'money purchase accounts', which are broadly similar to US 401(k) plans (see Munnell in Chapter 18 of this volume).

In the Netherlands—an advanced political economy which combines corporatist labor market institutions with a largely pre-funded pension system and as such can be seen as a test case for future developments in other Continental European economies—a similar development seems to be taking place, albeit not on the same scale as in the United States and the United Kingdom. While the number of DC participants was still a mere 28,000 in 1998, in 2004 their number had risen to 190,000 (www.statistics.dnb.nl).[8] Moreover, since contributions are subject to adaptations, Dutch DB plans actually share some similarities with DC plans (see Chapter 18 of this volume). Finally, the pre-funded plans that are currently being introduced in France, Germany, and Italy to relieve the demographic pressures on existing pay-as-you-go plans, are usually of a DC nature, as are the individual accounts introduced in public pay-as-you-go systems like the Swedish (Sundén in Chapter 35 of this volume). Hence, it seems as if third pillar solutions to old-age poverty are triumphing, both in Europe and in the United States, for being more in line with the preferences and needs of post-industrial firms and post-modern workers (see Chapters 18 and 35).

A second potential effect of the stability bias of DB plans is that it increases precariousness among categories of workers—female, young, and immigrant workers—that already occupy the most vulnerable socio-economic positions in our societies (Whiteford 1996). Since their work careers do not give access to the full set of social security rights, and the remuneration they receive for their efforts is generally insufficient for substantial private savings, the divide that is already visible within the labor market will over time also become visible in the distribution of pension rights and hence in old-age poverty. In other words, defenders of DB plans pursue the interest of well-vested 'insiders' only at the cost of those of marginal 'outsiders', even though they can amount to over one-third of the total workforce (see Chapter 7 in this volume).

However, despite the greater functionality of DC plans under current economic conditions, we should not be blind to their downsides. As has been argued for the United States, DC plans bring more not less old-age insecurity for the masses. The main advantage of DC plans is that they allocate the risk of insufficient returns on investment squarely on the shoulders of the participant instead of the employer. Whereas DB plans entail costly promises on the part of the employer to pay a fixed amount at a pre-arranged date, disregarding the actual amount contributed, DC plans offer no such thing. Instead they are built around the principle that what you pay is what you get. As a result of the increasing popularity of DC plans in the United States, workers have become much more exposed to the risks of the financial market. So despite rising coverage, labor market participation of older Americans has increased in the last 15 years to offset the pension 'gap' that the shift from DB to DC plans helped to create. According to Ghilarducci, there is a correlation between the increasing incidence of DC plans and the historical reversal of the growth of leisure of older males at the end of the millennium (Ghilarducci 2004; see also Chapter 35 of this volume).

Another downside of DC coverage is the high transaction cost of managing individual accounts. Since DB plans are of a collective nature and use already existing administrative infrastructures, costs can be kept at a minimum while investment costs, with a more equal balance of power between funds and investment banks, can also be kept in check. No such advantages are available to customized pensions. As Blackburn has estimated, administrative costs can amount to

20 percent of total savings, while penalties for switching amount to a stunning 40 to 50 percent. As a result, total savings have to be much higher to provide old-age income security than they would need to have been if costs were lower. In the UK, every annuity of £100,000 generates a mere £8–9,000 interest annually. In the United States it is estimated that couples would need a pot of US$1 million to be able to continue a middle-class life-style during old age, while another million is required to ensure private health coverage. The fact that the average holding in the 401(k) category—one of the most popular US saving instruments—amounts to a mere US$20,000 while many do not even reach the US$10,000 threshold, gives some indication of the pension gaps caused by the staggering charges imposed by the financial industry (Blackburn 2004: 21–2; see also Chapter 1 by Clark et al. in this volume).

# 6 RESEARCH AGENDA

Although much in this story is well known, there are a number of issues that are still in uncharted territory. I will conclude this chapter with a list of things to do. First, as I noted above, we lack robust data on job mobility over time. We know that labor market dynamics must have increased substantially since the 1950s and 1960s and expect job mobility to increase even further in the next decades. However, in the absence of standardized data we can only know this intuitively. Here, a concerted effort within the context of the OECD to set up comparable surveys would be most helpful. Currently, we only possess data on job in- and outflows for Denmark, the United States, and the Netherlands from 1999 onward.

Second, we lack information on the effects of the current design of occupational pensions on cross-border job movements, both within and outside the EU. It would be very interesting to study the effects of EU directives in this area on cross-border job mobility compared to job mobility outside the EU. Closely related is the issue of institutional and organizational impediments to cross-border job mobility. We lack an overview of the number and nature of these barriers. Nor do we possess good insights into current attempts by states and private agents to circumvent them.

Third, we lack systematic data on the life chances of precariously employed workers. Even though more than one-third of all workers are precariously employed (i.e. has either a part-time and/or fixed-term contract), there appear to be huge national differences with regard to the accrual of social rights by precarious workers. More research is needed to be able to link precarious employment contracts to socio-economic outcomes over the life-cycle and to distinguish better labor market institutions in this regard from worse ones.

Fourth, we lack data on developments within the field of pensions itself. Is there indeed robust information on the replacement of DB with DC plans? Because of institutional variety there is no generally accepted definition of pension pillars. As a result, we are unable to make international comparisons. Moreover, in many countries the privatization of pension provision is still in its infancy, implying the absence of time series. Hence, we are very much in the dark about what is going on here. The same is true for the cost profiles of individual and collective savings. There is near unanimity that the latter are cheaper than the former, but we do not know exactly by how much nor whether these price differentials are universal. Our ignorance in this field is caused by accountability gaps. However, as a result of the increasing professionalization of financial oversight there is reason to hope that in the near future some of these gaps will be filled.

What these lacunae demonstrate are the limitations of current methods of data collection in a globalizing world. Since the construction of statistics has been driven by the state's interest in the monopolization of violence and taxation (Porter 1986; Alonso and Starr 1987), many of its categories reflect the state's interests as it perceived them during the epoch of 'high modernity'. Hence, the same stability bias that features in first and second pillar pensions is to be found in the statistical apparatus of contemporary states. In a period of increasing international movements—of goods, services, capital, and people—this is increasingly turning into a liability, not only for scholars but also for the states themselves. The challenge is to find new methods of data construction that do not fall victim to the fallacy of 'methodological nationalism'. In some fields, notably finance, this task has been taken up by supranational organizations, such as the Bank of International Settlements (BIS). In other fields, no such initiatives are appearing. Of course, this is a problem of collective action, having to do with diverging interests and high costs. Alas, no easy solutions are at hand.

Finally, there are some serious moral issues at stake here. How to combine flexibility and security or openness and protection? In a world in which labor is increasingly becoming mobile, workers can no longer rely to the same extent on the social security arrangements that states set up during the 'golden age of capitalism'. Since the security of yesteryear was based on the immobility of yesteryear, defensive strategies merely appear to set in motion a pernicious cycle of worsening exclusion. The security of some will come at the cost of the insecurity of many. Shifting risks and responsibilities to the shoulders of the worker, as seems to be happening, goes some way toward a more equal distribution of both security and uncertainty. However, the individualization of pension savings to accommodate and even facilitate labor mobility is not a gift from heaven. How to find a mix between individualism and collectivism in the organization of pension provision is set to become the institutional design challenge of the twenty-first century.[9]

## Notes

1. In the United States the shortage of low-skilled industrial workers in the early twentieth century was solved by mass migration from Eastern and Southern Europe, while in Sweden the state dealt with the lack of jobs for displaced farmers by initiating a trajectory of active labor market policies and an expansion of public services and hence public employment.
2. The dichotomy 'Liberal Market Economies' versus 'Coordinated Market Economies' is Hall and Soskice's (2001).
3. That is: either a part-time or a fixed-term contract.
4. Nearly 70 percent of all temporary jobs within the OECD area are to be found in the service industries (OECD 2002: 139), while the incidence of part-time employment in the service sector as a ratio of average incidence in all sectors is 1.68 for personal services and 1.10 for social services (OECD 2001: 118). Women's share in part-time employment in 2002 was 66.2 percent in Denmark, 83.7 percent in Germany, 70.4 percent in the Netherlands, 71.8 percent in Sweden, 78.8 percent in the United Kingdom, and 68.2 percent in the United States (OECD 2003: 321), while their share in total temporary employment in 2000 was 55.5 percent in Denmark, 46.2 percent in Germany, 53.4 percent in the Netherlands, 58.5 percent in Sweden, 53.8 percent in the United Kingdom, and 49.9 percent in the United States (OECD 2002: 139).
5. And—one should add—'one wife' marriage careers. See Esping Andersen et al. (2002) for an analysis of the socio-economic effects of the increasing incidence of divorce for women and children.
6. Mobility rates refer to the share of workers changing jobs in relation to the total number of workers in any year.
7. Of course, portability problems do not occur in political economies where the state provides most of the pension income, while portability problems are partly solved by industry-wide pension plans. Nevertheless, even in well-organized, highly institutionalized occupational pension systems like the Dutch, portability losses cannot be prevented, since there are substantial transaction costs involved in the construction and maintenance of the five clearing houses, or 'transfer circuits' as they are called, that were set up in the mid-1990s to solve portability problems. Portability across borders only compounds these problems, as Andrietti (2001) shows.
8. The preferred strategy of Dutch pension funds to face up to their post-2001 funding problems appears to have been a more sober benefit benchmark. Recently a large number of end-of-career plans have been transformed to mid-career plans in an attempt to alleviate their burdens. A further explanation for the less pronounced shift to DC plans is the later introduction of the new IASC accountancy rules that will oblige firms to consolidate the market values of their pension liabilities.
9. Some of these issues will be taken up in the concluding chapter of Esping-Andersen and Myles in this volume. The sectoral employment figures provided by the ILO LABORSTA database are based on the industrial categories of the International Standard Classification of all Economic Activities (ISIC 2). I have added Divisions 2–5 to calculate total industrial employment and Divisions 6–9 to calculate total service employment. Except for US data, ISIC 2 was replaced by ISIC 3 in the mid-1990s. Since the nine classifications of ISIC 2 were substituted by 23 classifications in ISIC 3 there are some discontinuities. In

the case of ISIC 3 data, I have calculated total agricultural employment by adding A and B, to calculate total industrial employment C–F, and to calculate total service employment G–Q. For information on the empirical referents of the two classificatory systems see laborsta.ilo.org/applv8/data/isic2e.html and laborsta.ilo.org/applv8/data/isic3e.html respectively.

# References

ALONSO, W., and P. STARR (eds.) (1987). *The Politics of Numbers*. New York: Russell Sage Foundation.

ANDRIETTI, V. (2001). 'Portability of supplementary pension rights in the European Union'. *International Social Security Review*, 54/1: 59–83.

BALDWIN, P. (1990). *The Politics of Social Solidarity: Class Bases of the European Welfare State 1875–1975*. Cambridge: Cambridge University Press.

BECKERT, J., ECKERT, J., KOHLI, M. and STREECK W. (eds.) (2004). *Transnationale Solidarität*. Frankfurt am Main: Campus Verlag.

BELL, D. (1973). *The Coming of Post-Industrial Society: A Venture in Social Forecasting*. New York: Basic Books.

BERGHAHN, V. R. (1986). *The Americanisation of West German Industry 1945–1973*. Cambridge: Cambridge University Press.

BLACKBURN, R. (2004). 'The global pension crisis: from grey capitalism to responsible accumulation'. Paper presented at the Sixth Real Utopias-Conference, University of Wisconsin–Madison, 25–7 June.

BRENNER, R. (2002). *The Boom and the Bubble: The US in the World Economy*. London: Verso.

CLARK, G. L. (2003a). *European Pensions and Global Finance*. Oxford: Oxford University Press.

—— (2003b). 'Pension security in the global economy: markets and national institutions in the 21st century'. *Environment & Planning A*, 35/8: 1339–56.

CROUCH, C. (1999). *Social Change in Western Europe*. Oxford: Oxford University Press.

—— and PIZZORNI, A. (eds.) (1978). *The Resurgence of Class Conflict in Western Europe since 1968*. London: Holmes & Meier.

DAVIS, E. P. (1995). *Pension Funds: Retirement Income, Security and Capital Markets: An International Perspective*. Oxford: Oxford University Press.

DJELIC, M.-L. (1998). *Exporting the American Model: The Post-War Transformation of European Business*. Oxford: Oxford University Press.

EC (2004). *Employment in Europe 2004: Recent Trends and Prospects*. Luxembourg: Office for Official Publications of the European Communities.

ENGELEN, E. (2003). 'How to combine openness and protection? Citizenship, migration and welfare regimes'. *Politics & Society*, 31/4: 503–36.

ESPING-ANDERSEN, G. (1990). *Three Worlds of Welfare Capitalism*. Oxford: Polity Press.

—— (1999). *Social Foundations of Postindustrial Democracies*. Oxford: Oxford University Press.

—— (with D. Gallie, A. Hemerijck, and J. Myles). (2002). *Why We Need a New Welfare State*. Oxford: Oxford University Press.

GERSHUNY, J. (1978). *After Industrial Society: The Emerging Self-Servicing Economy*. London: Macmillan.

GHILARDUCCI, T. (2004). 'The political economy of 'pro-work' retirement policies and responsible accumulation'. Paper presented at the Sixth Real Utopias-Conference, University of Wisconsin–Madison, 25–7 June.

GRINT, K. (1994). *The Sociology of Work*. Oxford: Polity Press.

HALL, P., and D. SOSKICE. (2001). *Varieties of Capitalism: The Institutional Foundations of Comparative Advantage*. Oxford: Oxford University Press.

JACKSON, G. (2003). 'Corporate governance in Germany and Japan: liberalization pressures and responses during the 1990s', in K. Yamamura and W. Streeck (eds.), *The End of Diversity? Prospects for German and Japanese Capitalism*. Ithaca, N.Y.: Cornell University Press, 261–305.

KITSCHELT, H., LANGE, P., MARKS, G. and STEPHENS, J. (eds.) (1999). *Continuity and Change in Contemporary Capitalism*. Cambridge: Cambridge University Press.

KUMAR, K. (1978). *Prophecy and Progress: The Sociology of Industrial and Post-Industrial Society*. London: Allen Lane.

LANE, CHRISTEL. (1989). 'Industrial change in Europe: the pursuit of flexible specialization in Britain and West Germany'. *Work, Employment & Society*, 2/2: 141–68.

LANGLEY, P. (2005). 'In the eye of the "perfect storm": the final salary pensions crisis and financialisation of Anglo-American capitalism'. *New Political Economy*, 9/4: 539–58.

LEISERING, L., and LEIBFRIED, S. (1998). *Time, Life and Poverty: Social Assistance Dynamics in the German Welfare State*. Cambridge: Cambridge University Press.

MARGLIN, S., and SCHOR, J. (eds.) (1990). *The Golden Age of Capitalism: Reinterpreting the Post-War Experience*. Oxford: Oxford University Press.

MARSHALL, T. H. (1964). *Class, Citizenship, and Social Development*. London: Heinemann.

OECD (1994). *Employment Outlook*. Paris: OECD.

—— (2001). *Employment Outlook*. Paris: OECD.

—— (2002). *Employment Outlook*. Paris: OECD.

—— (2003). *Employment Outlook*. Paris: OECD.

OFFE, C. (1985). *Disorganized Capitalism: Contemporary Transformations of Works and Politics*. Oxford: Polity Press.

PIORE, M., and SABEL, C. (1984). *The Second Industrial Divide: Possibilities for Prosperity*. New York: Basic Books.

POLANYI, K. (1944). *The Great Transformation*. Boston: Beacon Press.

PORTER, T. M. (1986). *The Rise of Statistical Thinking 1820–1900*. Princeton: Princeton University Press.

ROSANVALLON, P. (2000). *The New Social Question: Rethinking the Welfare State*. Princeton: Princeton University Press.

ROSE, M. (1991). *The Post-modern & the Post-industrial: A Critical Analysis*. Cambridge: Cambridge University Press.

SABEL, C. (1982). *Work and Politics: The Division of Labor in Industry*. Cambridge: Cambridge University Press.

SASS, S. (1997). *The Promise of Private Pensions*. Cambridge, Mass.: Harvard University Press.

STIMPSON, A. (2000). 'Preliminary results from the HRST mobility analysis'. 15. Paris.

STREECK, W. (1992). *Social Institutions and Economic Performance*. London: Sage.

WHITEFORD, E. A. (1996). *Adapting to Change: Occupational Schemes, Women and Migrant Workers*. The Hague: Kluwer Law International.

WHITLEY, R. (1999). *Divergent Capitalism: The Social Structuring and Change of Business Systems*. Oxford: Oxford University Press.

WOMACK, J. P., JONES, D. T., and ROOS, D. (1990). *The Machine that Changed the World*. Oxford: Maxwell Macmillan International.

WORLD BANK (1994). *Averting the Old Age Crisis: Policies to Protect the Old and Promote Growth*. New York: Oxford University Press.

ZEITLIN, J., and HERRIGEL, G. (ed.) (2000). *Americanization and its Limits: Reworking US Technology and Management in Post-War Europe and Japan*. Oxford: Oxford University Press.

# APPENDIX

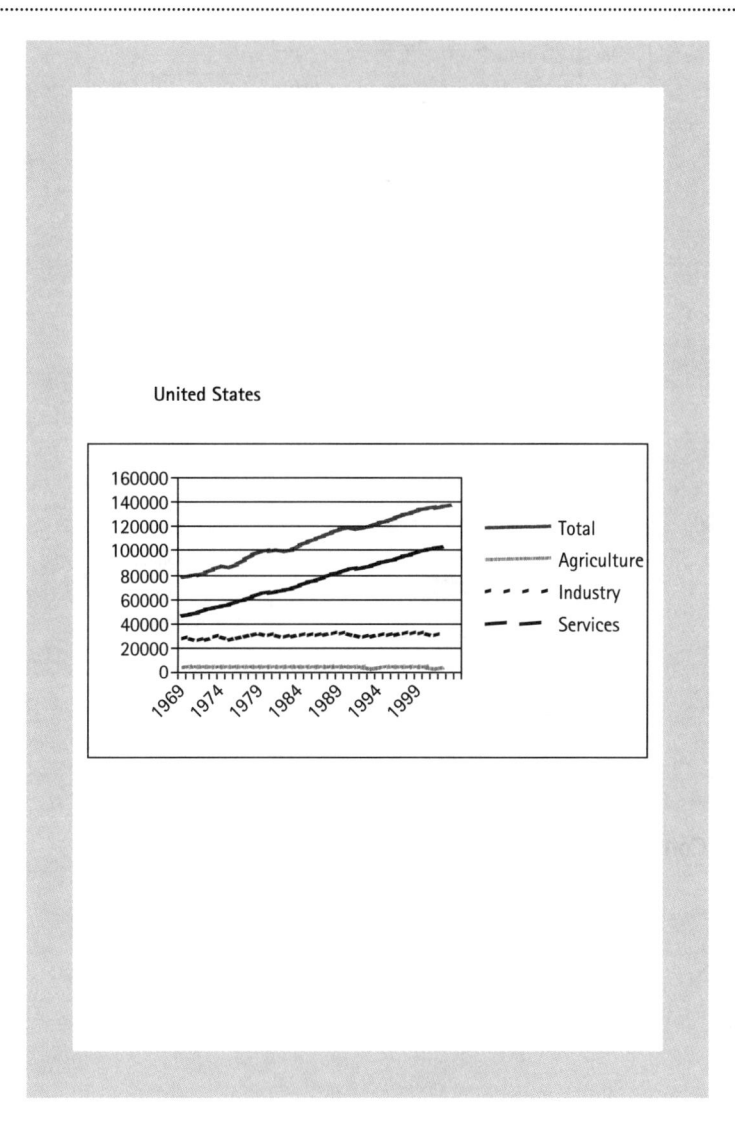

**Fig. 6.A1 Sectoral Change over time**

*Source*: ILO Geneva, Labour Statistics Database, 1998–2005.

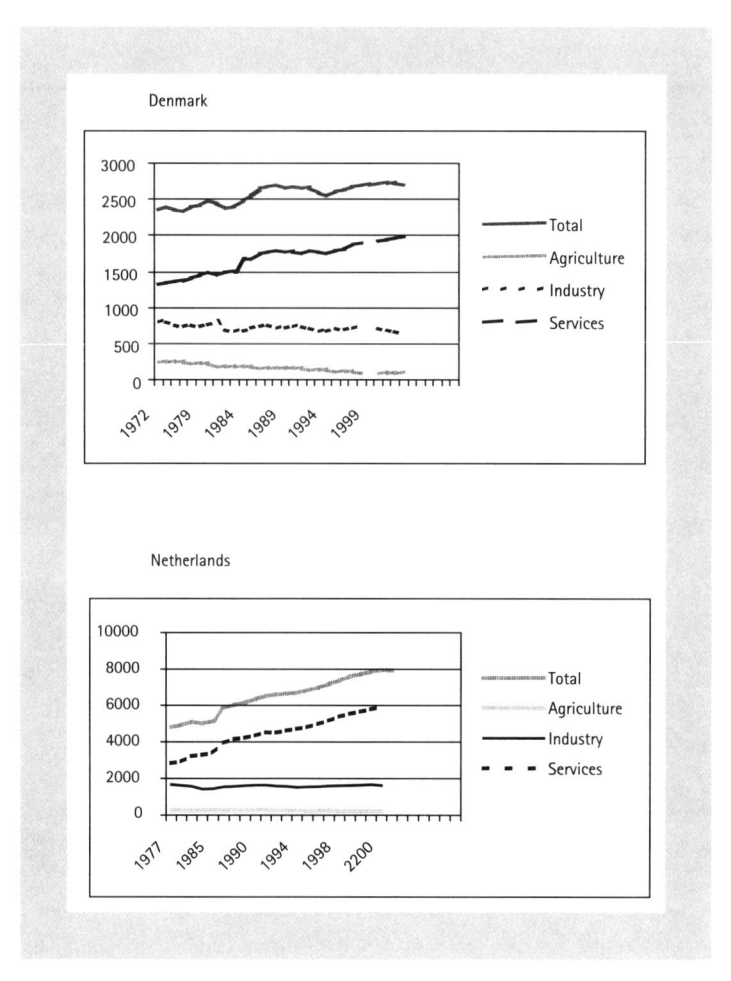

Fig. 6.A1 Continued

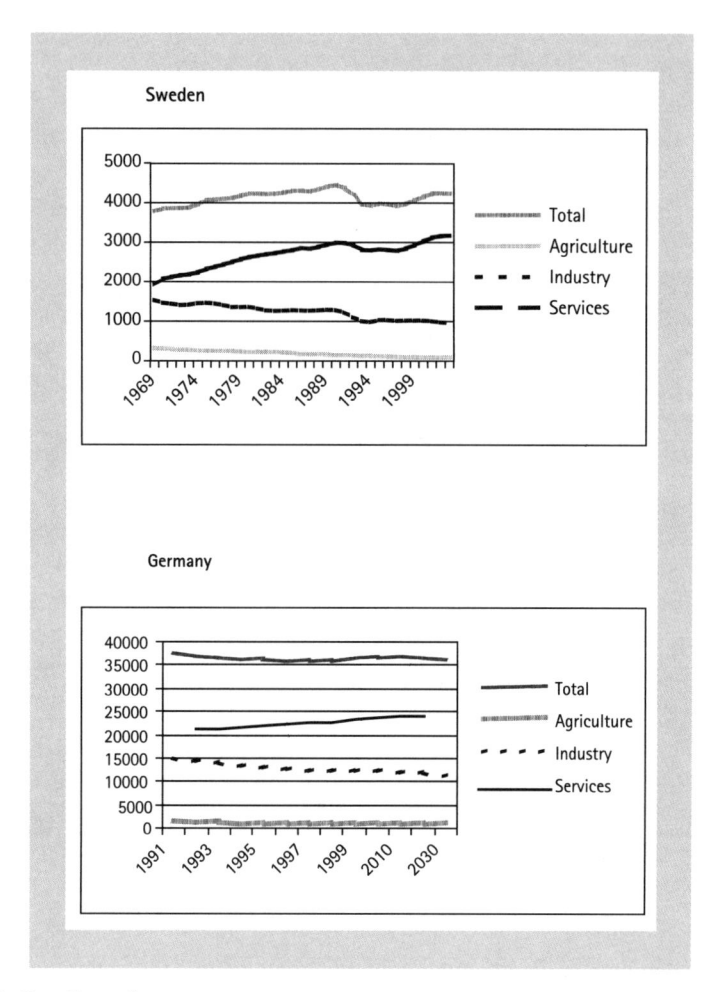

**Fig. 6.A1 Continued**

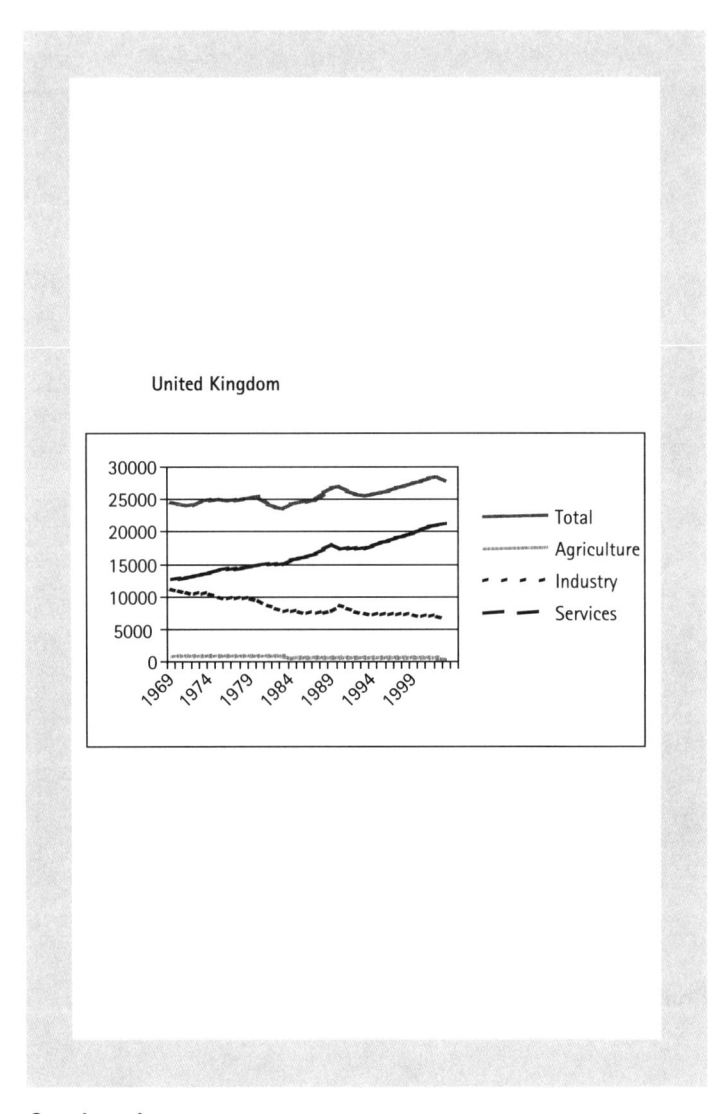

**Fig. 6.A1** Continued

CHAPTER 7

# GENDER, THE FAMILY, AND ECONOMY

VICKIE L. BAJTELSMIT

## 1 INTRODUCTION

It is impossible to discuss pension and retirement issues without consideration of gender and family. Despite improvements in recent decades, there are still persistent differences in the retirement experience of women, as compared with men, in the United States and elsewhere. Women are more likely to have inadequate retirement income and wealth as a result of differences in labor market experience, access to employment-based retirement plans, and their role in the family.

Research by numerous individuals from a diverse set of disciplines, including economics, sociology, psychology, education, and finance, have focused recent attention on the continued need for retirement policy initiatives aimed at improving the prospects for women's retirement in the coming decades. The purpose of this chapter is to summarize this wide-ranging body of literature in an effort to draw together our current state of knowledge regarding the impact of gender and family on retirement outcomes. The following section provides the motivation for the remainder of the chapter by quantifying the very significant differences in retirement outcomes for men and women. Section 3 then outlines the demographic, sociological, and regulatory factors that may be responsible for these observed differences. In addition to the obvious factors such as life expectancy and marital status, it is important to emphasize that labor market experience is a fundamental determinant of retirement outcomes. If women continue to earn less than men, have shorter working lives, and subpar benefits packages, there is little doubt that these factors will have a negative impact on their retirement.

The final section offers some suggestions for future policy direction related to gender, family, and retirement. Although much has been accomplished in retirement policy over the last few decades, the point of this chapter is that there is still much that needs to be done. If the policy goal is to enable individuals to prepare adequately for retirement, the methods by which we attempt to accomplish that goal should be motivated by an understanding of how the current system is failing to meet the needs of women.

# 2 GENDER DIFFERENCES IN RETIREMENT OUTCOMES

There is little dispute that women fare substantially worse in retirement than men. This section provides a summary of gender differences in retirement income, reliance on social security, and incidence of poverty among current retirees, as well as the differences in retirement preparation by younger workers.

## 2.1 Income Adequacy of the Elderly

Several recent studies have examined the retirement income of the elderly and near-elderly (e.g. Levine *et al.* 1999; McDonnell 2001). Although average real income for the elderly has increased over time in the United States, continued reliance on social security benefits by a significant proportion of the population is cause for concern, particularly in light of the long-term actuarial imbalance of that program, which is discussed elsewhere in this volume. In other developed countries, as in the United States, extensions in coverage of social security schemes and increased relative generosity of benefits since the 1940s have resulted in improved standards of living for the elderly (Gillion *et al.* 2000). For less developed countries, old age is still highly correlated with poverty.

The distribution of income and wealth among the US elderly, as shown in Table 7.1, shows marked differences between men and women. US women aged 65 and over have substantially lower retirement income than men in the same age group

Table 7.1 Sources of income by gender and marital status for individuals aged 65 plus, 2000

| Sources of income | Men Income ($) | % | Women Income ($) | % | Married couples % | Singles % |
|---|---|---|---|---|---|---|
| Social security | 10,004 | 35.0 | 7,571 | 49.8 | 37.7 | 47.0 |
| Pensions and annuities | 6,043 | 21.1 | 2,426 | 16.0 | 19.8 | 17.9 |
| Income from assets | 4,473 | 15.6 | 3,150 | 20.7 | 17.3 | 18.7 |
| Earnings | 7,389 | 25.8 | 1,831 | 12.0 | 23.5 | 13.9 |
| Other | 688 | 2.4 | 219 | 1.4 | 1.7 | 2.5 |
| **Total Income** | **$28,597** | **100.0** | **15,197** | **100.0** | **100.0** | **100.0** |

Source: McDonnell (2001, table 2 and chart 3), based on tabulations of the March 2001 Current Population Survey.

($15,197 as compared with $28,597). They also rely much more heavily on social security, which provides nearly half of average income for older women, but only 35 percent of average income for older men. As compared to men, women have much lower income from pensions and earnings on assets as well.

Such low average income levels imply that a large proportion of the retired population are poor. Poverty rates for the elderly continue to exceed those for the general population, despite noted improvement since the advent of social security programs around the world. Although this is a concern for both men and women, older women are more likely to be poor or near-poor than older men, and the incidence of female poverty increases with age. As quantified in Table 7.2, fully one-third of US women over age 75 qualify as near-poor, with income less than 150 percent of the poverty level, as compared with 20 percent of men over age 75. The probability of poverty is much higher for divorced older women (Butrica and Iams 2000).

Williamson and Sneeding (2004) examine elderly poverty (defined as 50 percent of median disposable income) in five developed countries and find the incidence of poverty for both men and women to be higher in the United States than in Canada, Sweden, Australia, or the United Kingdom. The gender difference is greater in the United States than in any of the other countries. In the United States, United Kingdom, and Australia, female poverty increases for the oldest old, whereas poverty rates are relatively flat with age in Canada and Sweden, where social program benefits are more generous. In all five countries, social retirement benefits represent at least 60–70 percent of disposable income for those over age 65.

**Table 7.2** Incidence of poverty, United States, 2000

|  | Percent of population with Retirement income < 150% poverty level | |
| --- | --- | --- |
| Age | Men | Women |
| 60–64 | 16 | 20 |
| 65–74 | 17 | 24 |
| 75+ | 20 | 33 |

*Source*: Current Population Survey, March 2001.

## 2.2 Retirement Wealth of Future Retirees

The evidence of retirement income inadequacy for those who are already in retirement leads to the obvious questions of whether younger households are preparing adequately for the future and, more specifically, whether there are gender differences in retirement preparation. Recent studies on this topic have reached different conclusions depending on the data used for the analyses and the assumptions used in the forecasts. Although most studies conclude that current workers are saving too little, there is disagreement on the degree to which they are undersaving. Bernheim and Scholz (1993), for example, estimate that the savings rates are far too low, whereas Uccello (2001) finds that the current savings rate is adequate.

A recent simulation study (VanDerhei and Copeland 2003), using the EBRI-ERF Retirement Security Projection Model, suggests that American retirees will be short by at least $400 billion of the funds necessary to cover their basic living and healthcare costs during the decade beginning in 2020, assuming current patterns of tax-preferred saving and current social security rules. Although younger middle- and upper-income individuals could remedy the problem by saving more, the study concludes that single women are most at risk of income shortfall since they would have to save an improbable amount, exceeding 25 percent of their annual pay, in addition to current savings, in order to afford basic expenses in retirement.

Levine *et al.* (1999) use the first wave of the Health and Retirement Study, which surveyed households with at least one person aged 51 to 61 in 1992, to project annual retirement income for a sample of older households. They estimate mean projected total annual retirement income (including social security, pension income, and earnings on assets) for single female households to be 63 percent of that for single men and 34 percent of married couples' mean household income. Black and Hispanic women are projected to have even less retirement income. Although women have lower income from all three sources, differences in retirement plan savings are clearly an important component of the differential. By comparing male and female accumulations in retirement accounts for different age cohorts in the

**Table 7.3** Average pension accumulation and the gender pension gap, United States, 1998

| Age Cohort | Average accumulated DC balance | | Gender pension gap | Average accumulated IRA balance | | Gender pension gap |
| --- | --- | --- | --- | --- | --- | --- |
| | Men | Women | (Women/men) | Men | Women | (Women/men) |
| All | 57,239 | 25,020 | 44% | 56,429 | 26,307 | 47% |
| 18–26 | 4,532 | 2,794 | 62% | 8,009 | 17,415 | 217% |
| 27–35 | 28,152 | 11,875 | 42% | 22,956 | 10,260 | 45% |
| 36–44 | 50,761 | 23,074 | 45% | 33,614 | 20,874 | 62% |
| 45–53 | 72,621 | 45,412 | 63% | 64,826 | 33,816 | 52% |
| 54–62 | 123,625 | 25,557 | 21% | 105,482 | 38,579 | 37% |

*Source*: Bajtelsmit and Jianakoplos (2000, table 2) (tabulations of the 1998 Survey of Consumer Finances with sample weighting).

1998 Survey of Consumer Finances, Bajtelsmit and Jianakoplos (2000) concluded that women in all age groups have significantly less savings in employer-sponsored retirement plans and individual retirement accounts than men in the same age groups. The ratio of female to male retirement accumulations, or the gender-pension gap, is detailed in Table 7.3. Notably, the defined contribution wealth of working women aged 27–35 and aged 36–44 was only 42 percent and 45 percent respectively of men in their same age group. The existence of a significant gender-pension gap for these younger age groups is important, since it belies the common wisdom that gender differences apply only to older generations of women. This is clearly a cross-generational problem.

# 3 Factors Affecting the Retirement Income Adequacy of Women

The previous section paints a dire picture of women's current and future retirement income security. Public policy aimed at rectifying this problem must necessarily address the underlying factors that make it more difficult for women to prepare adequately for retirement. The gender literature suggests that differences in life expectancy, marital status in retirement, labor market experience, household responsibilities, family make-up, and financial decision-making are all potential explanations for observed differences in retirement outcomes. Better understanding of the challenges faced by women in these areas is necessary to develop policy initiatives that can improve future outcomes. This section identifies and explains these gender differences.

## 3.1 Differences in Life Expectancy

Well-known demographic trends are creating pressures on public and private retirement systems around the world and particularly in developed nations. Life expectancies are on the increase, and women tend to live longer than men in most countries. The extent of this difference differs by country and region, as shown in Table 7.4, with OECD countries having the greatest longevity and the largest gender difference.

Whereas the average life expectancy of a child born in the United States in 1929 was only 59.2 (57.5 for men and 60.9 for women), the average life expectancy of a child born in 2001 is now 77.2 years (74.4 for men and 79.8 for women). This represents a gain of 16.9 years for men and 18.9 years for women and is primarily attributable to the availability of antibiotics and vaccines for many previously fatal illnesses and infections. Even compared to the baby-boom generation, today's children are likely to live at least six years longer on average. More importantly, however, individuals who live to the age of retirement today can expect to live much beyond the average life expectancy, well into their eighties or even nineties.

Table 7.4 Gender differences in life expectancy

| Country or region | Age 60 | | Age 65 | | Age 70 | |
|---|---|---|---|---|---|---|
| | Male | Female | Male | Female | Male | Female |
| Africa (5) | 16.2 | 18.1 | 13.1 | 14.6 | 10.3 | 11.4 |
| Arab states (3) | 21.1 | 19.4 | 17.7 | 15.5 | 14.4 | 11.4 |
| Asia and Pacific (9) | 16.7 | 18.8 | 13.6 | 14.9 | 10.6 | 11.6 |
| Eastern Europe and Central Asia (23) | 15.4 | 19.6 | 12.5 | 15.8 | 10.0 | 12.4 |
| Latin and Central America (19) | 17.9 | 20.6 | 14.5 | 16.8 | 11.5 | 13.4 |
| OECD countries (23) | 18.6 | 23.0 | 15.0 | 18.8 | 11.7 | 14.9 |

Source: Gillion et al. (2000, table A-2). Simple average of countries sampled from United Nations, *Demographic Yearbook*, various issues. Note that average does not include all countries in a particular region.

The importance of increasing life expectancy to retirement policy is obvious. As people live longer and potentially healthier lives, the strains on retirement savings, pension, and social security systems will increase. Women are particularly vulnerable in this respect, since they will, on average, need to support a longer retirement period than men. Unfortunately, evidence suggests that financial planning and retirement income payout decisions are often based on average life expectancy, increasing the risk of undersaving or overspending.

## 3.2 Differences in Marital Status

The institution of marriage has been linked to better health, longer life (at least, for men), and higher lifetime household income. However, there is some disagreement as to whether these factors are the *benefits* of marriage (e.g. through specialization of labor and economies of scale) or simply the result of a selection bias in the marriage markets that makes it more likely for individuals with positive traits to marry (Waite 1995).

Marital status also plays an important role in retirement income adequacy of women. Not only is it generally easier to live on two incomes than one, but the pension coverage rate for two-person households is greater than that for singles of either sex (Even and Turner 1999). Table 7.5 shows the distribution of the elderly in the United States by gender and marital status. Women are more likely to be single in retirement, most often as a result of divorce or widowhood. Although nearly 80 percent of men aged 65 to 74, and 69 percent of those over 75, are married, elderly women are less likely to be married. Nearly two-thirds of women over 75 in the United States are divorced or widowed. Divorce and widowhood both result in

**Table 7.5** Gender and marital status of the elderly, 2000

|  | Age 65–74 | | Age 75+ | |
| --- | --- | --- | --- | --- |
|  | Male | Female | Male | Female |
| Number | 8,051,000 | 9,748,000 | 5,838,000 | 8,989,000 |
| Divorced | 7.76% | 9.29% | 3.85% | 4.87% |
| Widowed | 8.28% | 31.34% | 22.73% | 60.46% |
| Married | 79.63% | 55.64% | 69.27% | 31.14% |
| Single | 4.32% | 3.72% | 4.15% | 3.53% |

*Source*: Table 51, Statistical Abstract of the United States, 2001, US Census Bureau.

significant declines in standard of living and have been statistically linked to income differentials in retirement (Butricia and Iams 2000). Smeeding and Sandstrom (2005) use the Luxembourg Income Study to examine poverty among the elderly in seven developed countries and find poverty rates for women over 65 living alone to be nearly double the overall poverty rate (defined as 50 percent of the national median disposable income level). Single women aged 75 and over had an even higher incidence of poverty.

## 3.3 Differences in Labor Market Experience

It is also well-established that differences in labor market experience between demographic groups influence retirement income security. Individuals with greater lifetime income are more able to save and invest to accumulate wealth to support their retirement. The annuities provided by social security pensions and employer-sponsored defined-benefit pensions are dependent on average lifetime earnings as well, so lower earners and those with a more sporadic work history will qualify for lower annuities on their own earnings. Lastly, many workers do not have access to employer-sponsored retirement plans and pensions.

There is substantial evidence that women earn less than men, both in the United States and elsewhere. Robinson (2001) examines pay differentials in specific occupations for a diverse set of countries and finds that, while there are inter-country differences, the tendency is for women to be paid less than men in all countries, regardless of the occupation being considered. In the United States, the ratio of women's average wages to men's has been increasing, but there is still a significant wage gap. Figure 7.1 shows continued persistence of this gender wage gap, despite

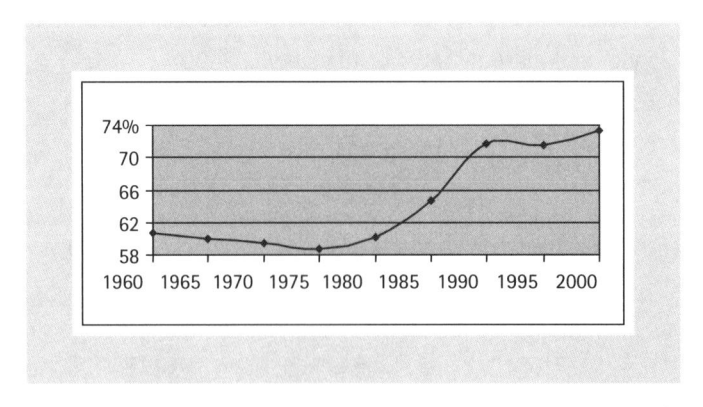

**Fig. 7.1** Ratio of women's median annual earnings to men's for full-time year-round workers, United States, 1960–2000

*Source*: US Department of Commerce, Census Bureau, *Historical Income Tables.*

improvements since 1960. The most recent US Census statistics indicate that, in 2000, women in full-time employment on average earned 73.3 percent of what men earned. The differential is actually much larger when all working women are compared to all working men (Bajtelsmit and Jianakoplos, 2000), since a larger percentage of women are part-time workers.

Despite its persistence over time, there is considerable disagreement regarding the causes for the gender-earnings gap. Differences in the average pay of women and men in the same occupation may be the result of discrimination, but may also be related to lower labor force participation by women. Women tend to work fewer hours than men and they are less likely to participate in shift work and overtime, both of which tend to improve average hourly earnings. Although overt discrimination in hiring, promotion, and pay raises is relatively less likely in today's US work environment, there is some evidence that men are paid higher salaries than women in similar positions and that upper management positions are disproportionately held by men. The compensation literature suggests that a large part of the wage differential is due to differences in starting salaries and that these differences may be attributable to women's failure to negotiate effectively (Kaman and Hartel 1994).

Recent studies suggest that occupational and industrial segregation and individual choice are also important factors in gender-related pay differentials (Macpherson and Hirsch 1995; Levine *et al.* 1999). A higher percentage of women than men tend to work in traditionally female-dominated occupations and industries which pay lower wages and salaries (Anker 1998). At least in the United States, these female-dominated occupations also tend to have lower pension coverage rates. In 2000, 70 percent of all working women in the United States were concentrated in only two industries: services (49.0 percent) and wholesale/retail trade (20.9 percent). The retirement plan sponsorship rates for these two industries are 52.8 and 43.9 percent respectively, significantly lower than the overall plan sponsorship rate.

Another possible explanation for the wage gap is individual choice. If women choose to have shorter working lives and work fewer hours, on average, they will never reach the same pay levels based on job tenure as their male counterparts. While it is true that women's labor force participation still lags behind that of men, the difference in the United States is much smaller than it was in past generations. As illustrated in Figure 7.2, more than 60 percent of all women today are in the workforce, compared with only 34 percent in 1950. At the same time, the proportion of men in the labor force has declined from nearly 87 percent in 1950 to about 75 percent today. While women's job tenure levels are still lower than men's, with women aged 55–64 having a median job tenure of only 9.9 years in 2000, this is double the 4.5 years that women in that age group had in 1951 (EBRI 2001).

Lifetime earnings are also affected by individual choice related to fulfillment of gender-based role expectations and these differences appear to be more pronounced in certain countries where gender roles are more rigidly defined. Studies

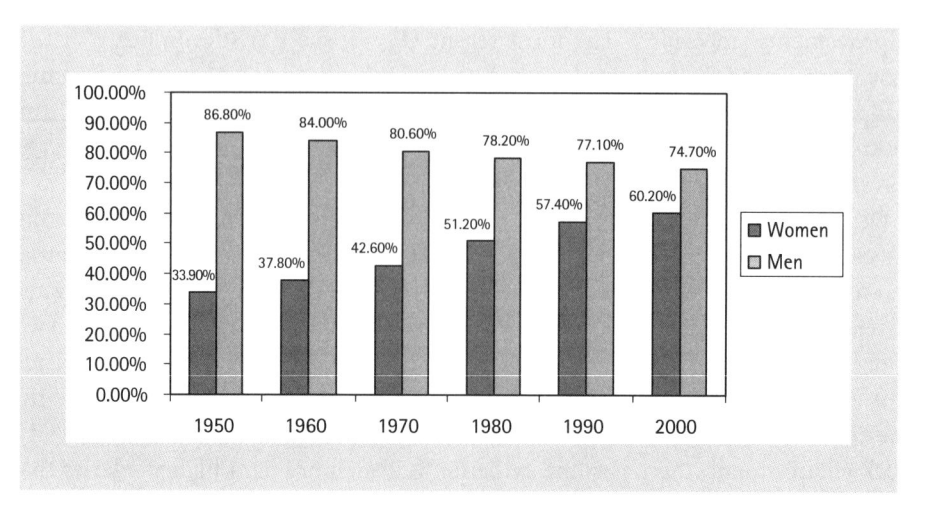

**Fig. 7.2** Labor force participation of women 1950–2000

*Source*: US Department of Labor, Bureau of Labor Statistics.

of the division of household labor show that, as women's labor force participation in developed countries has increased, men's share of family and household responsibilities has not increased proportionately (Blau 1998). Women are more likely to engage in unpaid labor, both at home and as volunteers (McGarry 1998), and to have breaks in their employment due to child and elder-care responsibilities (Beneria 2001). Seaward (1999) reports that 72 percent of the 22.4 million family caregivers in the United States are women. A recent study concludes that 81 percent of the retirement income gap between men and women is attributable to differences in lifetime labor market earnings, years worked, and occupational segregation (Levine *et al.* 1999). Job switching and breaks in employment adversely impact annuities payable from public and private defined-benefit plans and limit women's ability to continuously contribute to retirement savings programs.

Regardless of the cause of the gender-earnings gap, the impact on lifetime savings is obvious. Lower lifetime earnings can be expected to result in reduced retirement wealth and lower public and private pension annuities. It is interesting to note that some countries allow women to receive pension benefits at an earlier age than men, in theory compensating for women's role in unpaid caregiving. In Algeria and Tunisia, for example, child-rearing responsibilities are considered in setting the minimum retirement age for women. Until 1997 Belgium applied more favorable accrual rates for women than for men (1/40th per year as compared with 1/45th per year) (Gillion *et al.* 2000). However, the equality movement in the United States, the European Union, and elsewhere is gradually causing countries to equalize pension ages and accrual rates. In some cases, even more detrimental to women's retirement income, sex-based actuarial tables are being used to calculate benefits (Luckhaus 2000).

## 3.4 Differences in Employer Plan Sponsorship and Participation

In the United States, regulatory change has made it easier for employers to sponsor employment-based retirement plans and pensions. The non-discrimination rules under the Employee Retirement Income Security Act of 1974 (ERISA), which limit tax preferences to employers sponsoring plans in which all workers, including the lower paid, are eligible to participate, appear to have been somewhat successful in reducing the correlation of wage rates and pension coverage. While US regulatory change has resulted in an increase in pension coverage across the board, low-wage, part-time, and small-firm workers still tend to have lower rates of coverage. Since women represent a large share of those groups, it should come as no surprise that a significant percentage of women are not covered by employer retirement plans and many of those who are will find the retirement income generated by their plans insufficient to meet their needs. In their tabulations of the Survey of Consumer Finances, Kennickell and Sundén (1997) find that pension coverage increases with both education and income.

In other developed countries, the picture is much the same. In their five-country comparison, Williamson and Smeeding (2004) find that only 30 to 50 percent have an occupational pension and these pensions provide about 30 percent of disposable income for retirees.

US gender differences in sponsorship are declining with the increasing labor force participation of women. Younger men and women are generally equally likely to work for an employer that sponsors a plan, but older women have lower sponsorship rates. Of more concern, though, is finding that, among employees who work for an employer who sponsors a plan, women of all ages are less likely than men to participate in their employers' plans. Based on analysis of the 1993 Survey of Income and Program Participation, Shaw and Hill (2001) find that the most common reasons for lower participation rates among women are short job tenure and part-time employment (which may not be sufficient to qualify them for participation in the plan). Married women may have spousal coverage through their husband's plans, which implies that single women are the most at risk of retiring without an employment-based plan.

## 3.5 Differences in Employer Plan Types and Features

An important structural change, discussed elsewhere in this text (Chapter 18), is the shift from employer-sponsored defined-benefit (DB) plans, which promise a lifetime retirement income, to defined-contribution (DC) retirement plans, which make no such promise. As described in more detail in that chapter, approximately

60 percent of Americans with employer retirement plans were covered exclusively by a DB plan in 1981, but by 2001, that number had dropped to less than 15 percent, and more than 60 percent were by that time exclusively covered by a DC plan. Even though workers have generally favored this shift, presumably because it provides easier portability and the perception of greater control, it has serious implications for both men and women. Traditional defined-benefit pension plans provide protection against outliving one's assets, an element of insurance that has even greater value to women, whereas defined-contribution plans place the investment risk on the workers who are generally less able to bear that risk. The trend toward self-directed investment of plan assets is also detrimental to retirement income security, given that many participants do not have the financial skills necessary to make wise long-term investment decisions.

In addition to gender differences in plan participation discussed above, women's use of certain plan features may interfere with their ability to prepare adequately for retirement. As compared with men, female participants tend to have lower amounts accumulated in their DC plans and, upon separation from an employer, they are less likely to roll over lump-sum distributions into another tax-qualified savings vehicle, instead using it to meet other household needs. When their plan offers a loan option, the average amount borrowed is slightly lower for women, but it is much larger as a percentage of the average account balance (Copeland 2002). These are all behaviors that make it less likely that women will accumulate sufficient savings over their lifetime.

Compounding the risks associated with shifts in plan type, many employers have also reduced or eliminated previously promised retiree health benefits. As healthcare expenditures become a larger percentage of the household budget, the ability of retirees to maintain their standard of living in retirement will depend on the availability of both employer pension income and health insurance. Rather than looking to a paternalistic government or employer to provide an adequate retirement income, the workers of the future will be expected to take personal responsibility for these household expenditures.

## 3.6 Differences in Social Security Programs

The US Social Security Administration estimates that, not counting continued employment in retirement, 25 percent of aggregate retirement income comes from earnings on assets, 22 percent from government and private retirement plans and pensions, and 53 percent from social security. For two-thirds of current retirees, social security represents at least half of their retirement income and 31 percent rely on it to provide 90 percent of their retirement income. Whereas social security was originally designed to be a only a 'safety net,' supplementing income from private savings and employer pension plans, for many Americans, it has taken on a role of much greater importance. This is consistent with patterns found in other developed countries which have provided relatively generous social program benefits.

Social security programs around the world which have been designed to provide certain protections for women have been credited with the large reduction in female elderly poverty rates over the last 50 years. Demographic shifts and social change (increasing divorce rates and labor force participation of women) are providing the impetus for revision of social insurance programs in many countries, but the distributional effects of these changes are not always easy to predict.

To understand fully the potential impact of future programmatic changes in the United States, it is important to understand the existing rules and to observe the outcomes in countries which have already implemented similar changes. Consistent with the time period in which social security programs originated in many countries, the governments imagined a household in which the male head-of-household was fully employed throughout his working life and was married to a woman who stayed home to raise the children and manage the household, entering the workforce at an older age, if at all. Since women in that era were likely to have lower earnings as well as a shorter earnings history than their husbands, many programs were designed to allow women to qualify for social security retirement benefits based on her husband's participation. In the US system, a woman can be eligible to receive a benefit either on her own earnings history or calculated as 50 percent of her husband's benefit amount, whichever is greater. Thus, the minimum couple's benefit is 150 percent of the greater of the two individual benefits.

Under the current US social security system, there are also protections for divorcees. A divorced woman who is married for at least ten years can still qualify for a spousal benefit based on 50 percent of her ex-husband's benefit provided she does not remarry. A widow qualifies for 100 percent of her husband's benefit, which implies that the death of a spouse results in at least a 33 percent benefit decline in household income (from 150 percent of the spousal benefit to 100 percent), generally more than the usual estimated reduction in expenses experienced by a widow upon the death of her spouse. Many countries, in the interest of equality, have instituted widower benefits as well. Some countries require that a divorced woman be receiving income maintenance from her ex-husband at the time of retirement as a condition of receiving benefits based on his income.

Although current US Social Security benefit calculations provide income protection for women with certain characteristics, they also result in some inequities across different household types with equivalent total income. For example, a retired single-earner couple will generally qualify for a larger joint monthly benefit than a retired dual-earner couple which had the same total household average earnings. Similarly, widows and divorcees will qualify for a higher spousal benefit if they were previously in a single-earner household. This is an artifact of a view of the family that is no longer the norm and inherently penalizes working women.

A widely discussed option for reform of public pensions, and one that has been implemented in several countries, is to shift from a pay-as-you-go DB system to a partially or fully funded DC system in which workers accumulate funds in individual accounts. While it is possible to divert some level of payroll taxes to provide a retirement income floor as well as survivor and disability insurance in such a system, these types of features significantly reduce the 'return' on invested payroll taxes. The greater these often poorly understood insurance components, the more difficult it is for participants to build sufficient wealth to fund their retirement. Thus, it is highly likely that non-working spouses and widows will have less protection in an individual account system. For example, many countries' public retirement plans provide only a limited death benefit instead of a lifetime income upon the death of a spouse. In both public and private DC retirement plans, the spend-down of household assets to support the final illness of the first-to-die makes it more likely that a widow will end her years with insufficient wealth and income.

James *et al.* (2003) examine the impact of public pension reforms in Chile, Argentina, and Mexico, all of which involve a shift to private investment accounts and away from a traditional DB model. Using household-level survey data to simulate the retirement income under the old and new rules, they find that women accumulate private annuities that are only 30–40 percent of their male counterparts. However, in all three countries, continued redistributive elements of the programs and mandatory joint annuity payouts for married couples make up the difference for low-earning women. It should be noted, however, that these types of comparisons are not entirely fair in that the old systems have generally been insolvent at the time of change, so the previously promised benefits were unlikely to have been paid at the original level.

## 3.7 Differences in Financial Decision-Making

With the shift to defined contribution pensions, individuals are increasingly being called upon to make savings and investment decisions designed to support their own future retirement income needs. This implies that gender differences in risk aversion, financial literacy, and financial decision-making can have important implications for investment outcomes.

In the last ten years, several studies have explored differences in risk aversion and investment choices by gender, controlling for other factors such as income, wealth, age, and education. (See e.g. Jianakoplos and Bernasek 1998; Hinz *et al.* 1997; Sundén and Surette 1998.) This body of research generally is consistent with the conclusions that women are more risk averse than men and that women are less likely to invest in risky assets than men. However, there is evidence that this gender difference is lessening over time. Bajtelsmit and Jianakoplos (2000) compared 1989 and 1998 stock investment allocations in DC pension plans by men and women and found that, although women were still less inclined to invest in stock than men in 1998, the gap had narrowed over the decade. As might be expected, gender differences were most pronounced for older age groups and increased with age. Gerrans and Clark-Murphy (2004) find similar evidence of gender differences in retirement saving decisions of Australian participants in the country's superannuation program.

Differences in financial literacy are more difficult to measure. Several studies, summarized in Alcon (1999), document women's self-professed lack of confidence in their financial abilities and avoidance of financial planning tasks. The results of the Retirement Confidence Survey, sponsored by the Employee Benefit Research Institute, the American Savings Education Council, and Mathew Greenwald & Associates, show that women are less confident than men in their overall retirement income prospects. In the 2001 survey, for example, 59 percent of women said they were very confident or somewhat confident in having enough money to live comfortably throughout retirement compared with 69 percent of men (EBRI 2001). In that same survey 64 percent of women compared with 54 percent of men said they were behind schedule when it comes to planning and saving for retirement.

Despite the growing literature on gender and risk-taking, less is known about how financial decisions are made within households. Most studies of household finances are based on large surveys that are conducted at the household level (such as the Survey of Consumer Finances and the Health and Retirement Study). Although some information in these surveys is individual specific, as in the case of retirement account balances, most household assets are assumed to be owned jointly. For this reason, risk aversion studies have commonly compared single women to single men and married couples. Since household decisions may be made jointly and individual decisions may be influenced by others, it may be the case that these studies have actually underestimated gender differences in risk aversion.

Neoclassical economics considers the household decision-making problem in the context of a household utility maximization where each person in the household specializes according to their comparative advantage (Becker 1981). In previous generations, for example, we might hypothesize a 'typical' husband who provided and managed household income and his 'typical' wife who took care of the house and children. Today's households cover a much wider spectrum and modern economic and sociological models of household decision-making envision a bargaining process based on non-cooperative game theory. In these models, relative access to income, education, and paid work outside the home are hypothesized to increase the likelihood of involvement in household financial decisions. Women who provide a larger share of total household income and wealth are therefore expected to have more influence on household financial decisions. Recent empirical studies have found that women have decreasing involvement in financial decisions as household wealth increases (Dobbelsteen and Kooreman 1997) and increasing involvement in financial decisions as their share of household income increases (Bernasek and Bajtelsmit 2002).

Although it is clear that we still do not have a full understanding of the household financial decision-making process, evidence seems to contradict the Becker model of the family. Whether this implies a joint decision-making process or some other, these results should be taken into consideration in future household finance research and in applying research results to achieve change. For example, if the unit of decision-making is the individual rather than the household, it will be necessary to revise the way in which we collect large national data sets for analysis. It is also apparent that surveys should specifically identify the household decision-maker rather than assume that it is the male head-of-household, a common default. As women become more involved in household financial decisions over time, it will be interesting to see how this increased involvement affects decisions related to saving and investment.

## 3.8 Differences Due to Marital Sorting

The proportions of both dual-earner and dual-pension households have been increasing. For example, the proportion of dual-earner households among married couples with at least one worker aged 21 to 55 increased from 52.8 to 65.5 percent from 1979 to 1993, while the proportion of dual-pension households increased from 16.7 to 21.7 percent over the same period (Even and Macpherson 1994).

The increase in women's labor force participation and, hence, the greater likelihood of two-earner households, have prompted researchers to consider the impact of the second earner on the distributions of household earnings and pension wealth to see if the tendency of men and women to marry those with certain characteristics, also called 'assortative mating', magnifies inter-household inequality. Although there are numerous reasons to expect the distributions of income and wealth to be unequal, the degree of inequality can have important implications for the economic well-being of households. The empirical results have been mixed, with Cancian and Reed (1999), for example, finding that wives' earnings lead to greater equality of household income and Burtless (1999) concluding that the growing correlation of husband and wives' earnings contributes to greater income inequality. Hyslop (2001) estimates that 25 percent of the increase in earnings inequality between 1979 and 1985 was the result of assortative mating.

If individuals with employer-sponsored retirement plans are more likely to be married to individuals who also have such plans, it could be hypothesized that the existence of this type of sorting behavior could affect the distribution of total wealth, and ultimately the distribution of earnings in retirement. Given the assortative mating literature which finds that those with higher levels of education and earnings are more likely to marry each other, it would make sense to assume that the greater incidence of dual pensions among this group would widen the distribution of retirement wealth and income. On the contrary, Jianakoplos and Bajtelsmit (2002) find that, although there is evidence of assortative pensions, public and private pensions actually act as equalizers. Since middle-class households are more likely to have dual pensions and greater total pension wealth than other income groups and social security provides greater replacement rates to the lowest wealth households, the differential impact of private and public pensions tends to equalize the wealth distribution.

# 4 Public Policy

This chapter identifies an important problem for pension and retirement policy: women are more likely than men to have inadequate retirement income and wealth. This is not surprising, given their lower labor force participation, lower lifetime income, lower rates of pension sponsorship and participation, lower retirement savings, and more conservative investment behavior. Continued improvement in the labor market experience of women, their pay scales, education, and skill development are obviously part of the solution. With greater workforce participation, more women will have access to employment-based retirement plans and will qualify for public retirement benefits based on their own earnings.

It would be a mistake, however, to conclude that time will heal the entire problem. Retirement policy needs to recognize the continued differences in social roles and family-motivated decisions that make retirement saving more difficult for women. Working women continue to shoulder a greater proportion of family responsibilities than men and therefore can be expected to work fewer hours and move up the career ladder more slowly. In addition, as women continue to outlive their husbands, they are more likely to be left impoverished in old age after spending down family resources during their husband's final illness. For these reasons, women's future retirement prospects depend on the continuance of an adequate safety net. Increased maximums on tax-deferred contributions to retirement plans do little to benefit women who are not currently participating in plans or who are not contributing to the current maximum. Transitioning public retirement programs from traditional pay-as-you-go to individual account systems is also likely to have a negative effect on women's retirement. Given current trends, women will be likely to contribute for fewer years, make more conservative investment decisions, and spread the payout over a greater number of years. Some of these negative outcomes can be minimized by maintaining an adequate level of guaranteed benefits, by providing credits for child-rearing years, and by retaining protections for widows and divorcees.

Future public policy directions should be guided by informed research and cogent argument. The body of research in this area is still relatively sparse and there is room for new approaches and better analysis of existing data. Some of the questions that remain to be answered include the following. Why do women continue to earn less than men? And what can be done to change this? Is there a viable way to incorporate household labor in pension benefit calculations? Is it feasible to maintain a retirement safety net for widows and divorcees? What impact would an individual account approach to social security have on retirement outcomes for women? Why do women invest more conservatively than men? How are household financial decisions made and what impact does that have on retirement income and wealth? Research addressing these issues will contribute to our knowledge in this important area of pensions and retirement and will improve retirement prospects for future generations of women.

# REFERENCES

ALCON, ARNAA (1999) 'Financial planning and the mature woman'. *Journal of Financial Planning*, 12/2: 82–8.

ANKER, RICHARD (1998). *Gender and Jobs: Sex Segregation of Occupations in the World.* Geneva: International Labour Office.

BAJTELSMIT, VICKIE L., and JIANAKOPLOS, NANCY A. (2000). 'Women and pensions: a decade of progress?' *EBRI Issue Brief*, No. 227 (Nov.). Washington, D.C.: Employee Benefit Research Institute.

BAXTER, MARIANNE (2002). 'Social security as a financial asset: gender-specific risks and returns'. *Journal of Pension Economics and Finance*, 1/1: 35–52.

BECKER, GARY (1981). *A Treatise on the Family.* Cambridge, Mass.: Harvard University Press.

BENERIA, LOURDES (2001). 'The enduring debate over unpaid labour', in Martha Fetherolf Loutfi (ed.), *Women, Gender, and Work.* Geneva: International Labour Office.

BERNASEK, ALEXANDRA, and BAJTELSMIT, VICKIE (2002). 'Predictors of women's involvement in household financial decision-making'. *Financial Counseling and Planning*, 1–9.

BERNHEIM, B. DOUGLAS, and SCHOLZ, JOHN KARL (1993). 'Private saving and public policy'. *Tax Policy and the Economy*, 7: 73–110.

BLAU, FRANCINE D. (1998). 'Trends in the well-being of American women, 1970–1995'. *Journal of Economic Literature*, 36/1: 112–65.

BURTLESS, GARY (1999). 'Effects of growing wage disparities and changing family composition on the US income distribution'. *European Economic Review*, 43 (4–6 Apr.): 853–65.

BUTRICA, BARBARA A., and IAMS, HOWARD M. (2000). 'Divorced women at retirement: projections of economic well-being in the near future'. *Social Security Bulletin*, 63/3.

CANCIAN, MARIA, and REED, DEBORAH (1999). 'The impact of wives' earnings on income inequality: issues and estimates'. *Demography*, 36 (2 May): 173–84.

COPELAND, CRAIG (2002). 'Retirement plan participation and features, and the standard of living of Americans 55 or Older', *EBRI Issue Brief*, No. 248 (Aug.). Washington, D.C.: Employee Benefit Research Institute.

DOBBELSTEEN, S., and KOOREMAN, P. (1997). 'Financial management, bargaining, and efficiency with the household: an empirical analysis'. *De Economist*, 145/3: 345–66.

EBRI (2001). 'Women in retirement'. *Facts from EBRI*. Washington, D.C.: Employee Benefit Research Institute.

EVEN, WILLIAM E., and McPHERSON, DAVID (1994). 'Gender differences in pensions'. *The Journal of Human Resources*, 29/2: 555–87.

—— and TURNER, JOHN A. (1999). 'Has the pension coverage of women improved?' *Benefits Quarterly*, 15/2: 37–40.

FOX, LOUISE, and CASTEL, PAULETTE (2001). 'Gender dimensions of pension reform in the former Soviet Union'. Working Paper No. 2546. World Bank.

GERRANS, PAUL, and CLARK-MURPHY, MARILYN (2004). 'Gender differences in retirement savings decisions'. *Journal of Pension Economics and Finance*, 3/1: 145–64.

GILLION, COLIN, TURNER, JOHN, BAILEY, CLIVE, and LATUPILLE, DENIS (eds.) (2000). *Social Security Pensions: Development and Reform*. Geneva: International Labour Office.

HINZ, RICHARD P., McCARTHY, DAVID D., and TURNER, JOHN A. (1997). 'Are women conservative investors? Gender differences in participant-directed pension investments', in *Positioning Pensions for the Twenty-First Century*. Philadelphia: Pension Research Council and University of Pennsylvania Press.

HYSLOP, DEAN R. (2001). 'Rising U.S. earnings inequality and family labor supply: the covariance structure of intrafamily earnings'. *American Economic Review*, 91/4: 755–77.

JAMES, ESTELLE, EDWARDS, ALEJANDRA COX, and WONG, REBECA (2003). 'The gender impact of pension reform'. *Journal of Pension Economics and Finance*, 2/2: 181–219.

JIANAKOPLOS, NANCY, and BAJTELSMIT, VICKIE L. (2002). 'Dual-pension households and the distribution of wealth in the United States'. *Journal of Pension Economics and Finance*, 1/2: 131–55.

—— and BERNASEK, ALEXANDRA (1998). 'Are women more risk averse?' *Economic Inquiry*, 36/3: 620–30.

KAMAN, VICKI S., and HARTEL, CHARMINE E.J. (1994). 'Gender differences in anticipated pay negotiation strategies and outcomes'. *Journal of Business and Psychology*, 9/2: 183–97.

KENNICKELL, ARTHUR B., and SUNDÉN, ANNIKA E. (1997). 'Pensions, social security, and the distribution of wealth'. Federal Reserve Working Paper.

LEVINE, PHILIP, MITCHELL, OLIVIA and PHILLIPS, JOHN (1999). 'The impact of pay inequality, occupational segregation and lifetime work experience on the retirement income of women and minorities'. Report No. 9910. Washington, D.C.: AARP.

LUCKHAUS, LINDA (2000). 'Equal treatment, social protection, and income security for women'. *International Labour Review*, 139/2.

McDONNELL, KEN (2001). 'Income of the elderly population'. *EBRI Notes* (Nov.): 5–9.

McGARRY, KATHLEEN (1998). 'Caring for the elderly: the role of adult children', in David A. Wise (ed.), *Inquiries in the Economics of Aging*. Chicago: University of Chicago Press.

MACPHERSON, DAVID, and HIRSCH, BARRY (1995). 'Wages and gender composition: why do women's jobs pay less?' *Journal of Labor Economics* (July): 426–71.

PRESSMAN, STEPHEN (2000). 'Explaining the gender poverty gap in developed and transitional economies'. Luxembourg Income Study Working Paper No. 243.

ROBINSON, DEREK (2001). 'Differences in occupational earnings by sex', in Martha Fetherolf Loutfi (ed.), *Women, Gender and Work*. Geneva: International Labour Office.

SEAWARD, MARY R. (1999). 'The sandwich generation copes with eldercare'. *Benefits Quarterly*, 15/2: 41–8.

SHAW, LOIS, and HILL, CATHERINE (2001). 'The gender gap in pension coverage: what does the future hold?' Institute for Women's Policy Research Publication No. E507.

SNEEDING, TIMOTHY, and SANDSTROM, SUSANNA (2005). 'Poverty and income maintenance in old age: a cross-national view of low income older women'. Luxembourg Income Study Working Paper.

SUNDÉN, ANNIKA, and SURETTE, B. J. (1998). 'Gender differences in the allocation of assets in retirement savings plans'. *American Economic Review*, 88/2: 207–11.

UCCELLO, CORI E. (2001). 'Are Americans saving enough for retirement?' Issue Brief, Center for Retirement Research at Boston College, No. 7 (July).

VANDERHEI, JACK, and COPELAND, CRAIG (2003). 'Can America afford tomorrow's retirees: results from the EBRI-ERF Retirement Security Projection Model'. *EBRI Issue Brief*, No. 263 (Nov.). Washington, D.C.: Employee Benefit Research Institute.

WAITE, LINDA J. (1995). 'Does marriage matter?' *Demography*, 32/4: 483–507.

WILLIAMSON, JAMES, and SNEEDING, TIMOTHY, M. (2004). 'Sliding into poverty? Cross-national patterns of income source change and income decay in old age'. Center for Retirement Research at Boston College, Working Paper 2004–25.

# CHAPTER 8

# SOCIAL SOLIDARITY

## JOHAN J. DE DEKEN, EDUARD PONDS, AND BART VAN RIEL

## 1 INTRODUCTION

In all industrialized countries the bulk of old age income provision results from collective arrangements. Such arrangements can either be run on a pay-as-you-go (PAYG) scheme or on a funded basis. They can be run as public schemes or the state can mandate private agencies to administer occupational and firm-based schemes. All these collective forms of pension provision have in common that they may be seen as the institutional expression of some form of solidarity as they all have distributional implications that go beyond a mere actuarial redistribution of good and bad risks. In Europe in particular, social solidarity is an important concept in the debate over pensions.

In this chapter we discuss why and under what conditions people are willing to share risks collectively and accept the resulting distributional implications. We explore whether these conditions will change because of individualization, ageing, and globalization. Will these trends erode social solidarity and therefore also the institutional basis for sustaining pensions income?

As a first step toward understanding solidarity as the social basis for collective pension provision, the chapter starts with a definition of solidarity in general (Section 2), exploring how this principle has found its institutional expression in different types of pension regimes. The chapter develops a broad analytical framework for understanding the different dimensions of social solidarity and in which way these different dimensions are linked to collective pension provision (Section 3).

In the course of history, solidarity has acquired a variety of meanings. For some social solidarity has to do primarily with risk-sharing, for others social solidarity equals redistribution. This distinction is intimately intertwined with accounts that seek to explain the development different kinds of pension schemes (Section 4). The theoretical building blocks of Sections 3 and 4 will also be helpful for thinking about future changes in social solidarity (Section 5), and directions for future research (Section 6).

## 2 Defining Social Solidarity

Solidarity refers to networks of social relationships that involve mutual dependencies, responsibilities, and entitlements within a defined group of people or a community. It is a structure through which fortunes and misfortunes are reapportioned. In pre-modern societies, these networks were embedded in extended families, in religiously integrated communities, in guilds, and in corporations. Facing an erosion of these traditional institutions, governments have sought to redefine the networks of mutual support, and respecify the group in which fortunes and misfortunes are redistributed.

It is difficult to define the concept of solidarity simply and unambiguously. Like so many central concepts in sociology, the term has acquired a variety of meanings (see Stjernø (2005) for an overview). On the one hand, this means that the concept has become 'essentially contested': the meaning attributed depends upon one's political or philosophical orientation. On the other hand, it has been argued that it is precisely this multitude of meanings that has allowed the concept to survive throughout history (Hayward 1959).

It is possible to distinguish two main interpretations of the concept: an individual and a collective interpretation (Spicker 1991). In both interpretations, solidarity essentially comes down to an acceptance of responsibility for others. In the individual interpretation, this acceptance is rooted in mechanisms that depend upon mutual self-interest, whereas the acceptance in the collective interpretation is seen as embedded in the social cohesion of the collectivity.

The individual interpretation approximates the pooling of risks as being modeled by the risk redistribution paradigm, so there are some affinities with the notion of solidarity as advocated by rational choice theory. This perspective assumes that people are only prepared to go beyond the one-sidedness of charity and altruism if they have a vested interest in structuring a social solidarity that is mutually advantageous, and where solidarity is considered to be 'the child of interdependence' (Baldwin 1990).

Philosophically, this form of solidarity has its roots in the liberal tradition and was first manifested in self-help initiatives, or 'mutualism' as Spicker describes it. However, the introduction of compulsory social insurance meant a clear break with this liberal heritage as the state assumed an active role in fostering the recognition of mutual interdependence. Social insurance pensions came to be distinguished from private arrangements (i.e. those offered by commercial insurance companies or by mutual benefit societies), in that they became politically generated. The state used its legislating power to impose statutory arrangements that applied to certain categories of the population of a country or sometimes even to the entire nation. In practical terms this meant that insurance became compulsory (initially only for certain segments of the working class, later for all wage earners, and ultimately for most people in gainful employment), and that it placed the costs not simply in terms of the insurance of the risks covered, but to some extent in accordance with the ability to bear them. The social element in social insurance thus in part depends upon the extent to which the orthodoxy of actuarial logic is transcended. But even under compulsory social insurance, people only support others who support them. Those who are unable to contribute to the pooling of resources (e.g. a typical workers, migrants, long-term unemployed, housewives, people with disabilities, etc.), are either excluded altogether, or at best, they are included on inferior terms.

The mutualistic pattern of solidarity produces a horizontal redistribution within a group of people who are subject to the same types of risk. Such horizontal redistribution implies, for example, that groups are diversified according to occupation and income differentials. The higher contributions of higher income groups are used only to grant higher benefits for those groups. The lower contributions of low income groups severely limits the level of their benefits, and those lower strata therefore often end up with an inadequate coverage of the risks to which they are exposed. A mutualist system of solidarity thus generally leads to fragmented and stratified social welfare programs.

The collective interpretation of social solidarity, on the other hand, has affinities with Emile Durkheim's conception of solidarity and can be adequately captured by the metaphor of 'fraternity'. Under this form of solidarity, people are expected to support one another because they are equal members in the same community. With the development of nation-states, this membership came to be defined in terms of citizenship. Thus in the modern age fraternal solidarity came to manifest itself in the form of a social security system based on citizenship entitlements. Under such a system all citizens are covered on the same terms by a comprehensive national benefit system. Solidarity as fraternity leads to a vertical redistribution that goes from the rich to the poor, and from high risk groups to low risk groups.

If such a system is based on contributions, then the higher contributions are used to increase the level of the benefits for high-risk and/or low income groups.

Solidarity as fraternity should be clearly distinguished from altruism. Both imply a generosity toward the unfortunate that, in contrast to mutualist solidarity, does not rely on the expectation of reciprocal kindness. Both are motivated by empathy toward persons who belong to a disadvantaged group. But whereas in the case of altruism, the personal characteristics of the targeted individuals are the central driving force behind this empathy, for fraternal solidarity they are not an issue (Arnsperger and Varoufakis 2003).

As Glazer (2000, p. ix) notes, only the first two principles of the French revolution—freedom and equality—have received the wholehearted support of Americans. Fraternity and solidarity are not familiar terms in American political rethoric. As a possible explanation for this, he points to the presence of a large racial minority that was kept in slavery and kept down by prejudice and discrimination. One can also point to the fact that the US population never experienced the kind of devastation of savings and property brought about by two world wars in Europe, which created a solid foundation for solidaristic arrangements. This does not necessarily imply that there are no solidaristic elements in the American pension system, though it should be noted that collective pension provision plays a smaller role in old-age income provision in the United States as compared to Europe.

# 3 Solidarity and Pensions

Social solidarity can be defined as the willingness to share risks collectively and accept the resulting distributional implications. In this section we look first at the risks being shared in old-age income provision and the reason why this might be done collectively. Subsequently, we examine the factors determining the distributional consequences of collective risk-sharing.[1]

## 3.1 Solidarity and Risk-Sharing

Individuals who seek to provide for themselves in retirement are faced with two types of risks: income and longevity. Both risks are manifested at the micro and macro levels. At the micro level, the income risks are to some extent endogenous in that they depend upon decisions the individual makes throughout his or her life course (Shiller 1998). Longevity risks involve uncertainties both regarding each individual lifespan, as well as regarding future trends in average mortality. But at the micro level, this risk is far more exogenous than the income risk. The macro risks are by definition of an exogenous nature. Table 8.1 identifies a number of these risks.

To some extent, individual lifespan risks can be insured in the private market. But without government regulation imposing fair annuities and mandatory participation, the resulting form of solidarity will at best resemble a highly fragmented form of mutualist solidarity and will be limited to that section of the population with a minimum level of income. Moreover, this subset of the population will be segmented into a multitude of narrowly delimited risks categories to which vastly different premiums are charged. The contribution rates of life annuities are typically based on the remaining lifespan of an age cohort to which the individual belongs. As men and women, for example, differ in life expectancy, insurance companies end up differentiating between, in this case, low-risk men and high-risk women when setting contribution rates.[2] Adverse selection problems may further prevent the development and sustainability of voluntary mutualist schemes, as individuals will be better informed about their life expectancies than insurance companies and insurance companies will be confronted with the fact that their customers live longer than the reference population as a whole.

The main economic risks in pension finance, whether the micro risk of wage path or the macro risks of the real rate of return and stability of purchasing power, cannot be insured via the market (Ponds 2003).[3] Some have argued that intergenerational risk-sharing overcomes private market failures (Merton 1983).[4]

Table 8.1 Risks facing individuals in retirement

|       | Income | Longevity |
|-------|--------|-----------|
| Micro | *individual wage path* the risk of having a non-standard employment career with resulting fluctuations in earnings | *individual lifespan*: the risk of living longer than average |
| Macro | *investment returns and economic growth*: uncertainty about the resources that will be available to finance pension claims *purchasing power*: uncertainties about the development of wage levels and prices once a cohort enters retirement | *average mortality and fertility*: uncertainty regarding the future old-age dependency ratio: how many pensioners will there be in relation to the working population? The development of the old-age dependency ratio is determined by average mortality and fertility |

Intergenerational risk-sharing usually is analyzed in the face of uncertainty with respect to factor rewards: wages and rental income (Gordon and Varian 1988). Long-term wage risk and rental-income risk are not diversifiable within an age-cohort because these risks affect individuals of the same age simultaneously. But as in the long run wage income and rental income are negatively correlated, it would be possible to accomplish welfare improvement by sharing both risks between generations. Intergenerational solidarity thus would make it possible to exchange the human capital of young workers in the form of wages, and the financial capital of pensioners in the form of savings. Solidarity would thus take the form of an income redistribution from high rental income to low wage income, and vice versa.

## 3.2 The Distributional Consequences

What determines the distributional consequences of collective risk sharing? In this context three factors[5] can be identified:

- the risks covered;
- the way benefits are determined;
- the constituency within which the solidaristic logic of risk redistribution operates.

### 3.2.1 *The Risks Covered*

The extent to which micro and macro risks are covered respectively has intra- and intergenerational distributional consequences. The vertical redistribution of income within pension schemes that redistributes the micro income risks at the heart of fraternal solidarity, tends to be confined to public and mandated pension schemes. Such schemes are often characterized by a number of deviations from actuarial orthodoxy. These include provisions such as additional allowances for dependents, and various floors or ceilings on benefits and contributions (Disney 2004).[6] Such deviations give rise to a vertical redistribution from high income to low income. In contrast, the coverage of the individual longevity risk may result in a vertical redistribution from low income to high income. In general, upper income groups enter the labor force later in life and live longer after retirement, so that, compared to low income groups, over a lifetime they contribute less and receive more in schemes in which benefits are independent of life expectancy (World Bank 1994). The overall intra-generational distributional consequences of the coverage of microeconomic risk may therefore well be limited. The coverage of macro risks, however, has by definition intergenerational consequences. The reapportionment of macro risks depends on the way in which benefits are determined.

## 3.2.2 Determining Benefits

A typology developed by Musgrave to characterize various PAYG systems (Musgrave 1981) can be expanded to describe the way benefits are determined. The distinction between PAYG and funding, though, is only of secondary importance. What matters more is (1) the contrast between defined contribution (DC) and defined benefit (DB), and (2) the way in which the benefits are being defined. Of course, the decision to opt for orthodox funding precludes a DB formula, just as PAYG cannot be reconciled with a true DC formula—in the end even a so-called notional defined contribution PAYG plan remains a kind of DB scheme that at best emulates some of the distributional principles of a funded DC scheme. It is, however, possible to distinguish four approaches toward setting benefits, which all have their distinct way of reapportioning macro risks:

1. Funded Defined Contribution (FDC): in the case of an orthodox funded defined contribution scheme, there is hardly any sharing of macro risks involved, as retirees individually have to bear the risks. Their individual contributions determine their individual benefits, and the costs of both demographic changes and of economic fluctuations fall on the retirees.
2. DB with Fixed Contribution Rate (FCR): the working population is required to contribute a fixed fraction of its income to support retirees. Taxes drive benefits and benefits are the dependent variable. The costs of demographic changes fall on retirees. A typical example of such an arrangement is the notional defined-contribution system of the reformed Swedish scheme.
3. DB with Fixed Replacement Rates (FRR): retirees are entitled to a given fraction of their earnings plus an adjustment factor reflecting inflation, productivity gains (wage indexation), and/or inflation (price indexation) in the subsequent generation. Under such a system, benefits drive taxes and the tax rate is the dependent variable. All costs (or nowadays less likely benefits) of demographic changes and economic developments fall on the contributing generation. A typical example of such a scheme was the German statutory pensions up to 1992 and the defined-benefit schemes that can be found in the sector-wide pension funds of the second pillar in the Netherlands. As pensions are related to wages, the welfare of retirees is linked to productivity gains achieved by the working population. In the case of price indexation, pensioners will benefit less from productivity increases but will be shielded from possible economic decline.[7]
4. Fixed Relative Position (FRP): contributions and benefits are set to hold constant the ratio of per capita earnings of those in the working population (net of contributions) to the per capita benefits (net of taxes) of retirees. The tax/contribution rate is adjusted periodically to reflect population and productivity changes. As the population ages, tax rates rise, but benefits also fall, so that both parties end up footing the bill of ageing at the same rate. This

type of arrangement has come to be known as the Musgrave condition. It seems to serve as a guiding principle of recent cost-containing reforms in the German statutory scheme.

### 3.2.3 *The Basic Universe of Solidarity*

The third factor which determines the distributional consequences of collective risk-sharing concerns the unit within which the fortunes and misfortunes of life are being redistributed. The risks can be reapportioned across several generations of the population of an entire country (as is the case in general schemes such as the basic pension in Denmark); it can be limited to the entire class of wage earners (as is the case in wage-earner schemes such the Belgian statutory pension insurance); or it can be further limited to specific sectors of the economy (as is the case with sector-wide pension funds in the Netherlands), or to specific occupational categories (as was the case in the original myriad of schemes in the corporatist Italian pension regime prior to the reform started in 2002). This 'basic universe of solidarity' is the group or the community which forms the constituency within which the solidaristic logic of risk redistribution operates (Esping-Andersen 1987). The members of the groups in question recognize their obligation in this respect: each member can invoke the group's solidarity as a matter of principle.

### 3.2.4 *The Governance of Solidarity*

Funded DB schemes have in common with PAYG arrangements that, in contrast to orthodox funded DC schemes, it is not the individual participant who has to bear the macroeconomic and demographic risks, but the stakeholders of the basic universe of solidarity. The crucial question here is which stakeholder is responsible for closing the balance of the fund. In most corporate pension plans it is ultimately the shareholders and employees of the sponsoring company who have this responsibility, as back-servicing can lower future profits, dividends, or wages and even lead to job losses. In most public sector pension funds and industry-wide pension funds, these risks are formally borne jointly by all the stakeholders: that is, the shareholders and active participants of all the affiliated firms, and by the retirees. Such differences are also reflected in the governance of solidarity. Most Anglo-American corporate plans are run as a trust that is legally required to act in the financial interest of the current and future pensioners. Trustees are nominated by management as representatives of the shareholders. Employees and retirees have no influence on the governance of their pension fund. In some industry-wide funds, such as the ones found in the Netherlands and Denmark, employees formally do have a say in the decision-and rule-making.

# 4 Explaining Solidarity

Explanations of social solidarity in pension schemes can be sought at two levels. On the one hand, one can look at the level of individual motives, where one can try to understand the conditions under which people are willing to accept the redistributive consequences of the reapportionment of risk. On the other, one can address the issue at the level of institutions, where one can seek to specify how these individual motives are being translated into a collective voice, and under what conditions this collective voice in turn leads to formal institutions.

## 4.1 Individual Motives

To some extent, solidaristic redistribution is the result of the demands for different risk categories in societies confronted with various types of market failures, including asymmetric information and interdependent risks, which may prevent them from obtaining insurance through commercial channels. However, this cannot explain majority support or the legitimacy of pension regimes in which solidarity goes beyond a mere mutualist self-interest in redistribution. As Øverbye has pointed out, given the positively skewed distribution of risks, the median risk in a population is lower than the average risk (Øverbye 1998). But in a solidaristic pension system it is the latter that forms the basis for determining contribution rates. Persons with a medium risk may end up contributing far more than they would do if they chose to take out an individual contract in the insurance market. A number of complementary explanations have been advanced to explain this paradox.

A first set of explanations focuses on uncertainty, risk aversion, and myopia. Both providers and potential buyers of insurance may be unable to assess the risk they are facing. This is more likely to be the case if a society is subjected to random shocks, such as wars or severe economic depressions, or in times of rapid social changes, as such events increase the interdependence of risks, modify the risk structure, and make it hard to foresee one's future station in life. More generally, common vulnerability and the uncertainty each individual faces about the likelihood of ending up amongst the disadvantaged leads to a willingness to support pension schemes that go beyond merely correcting market failures. Because of what Rawls has referred to as the 'veil of ignorance', rational actors with little knowledge about their station in life and impelled by a fear of misfortune are said to be willing to conclude a 'social contract' that institutionalizes aid for the neediest (Rawls 1971). This 'veil of ignorance' makes it possible to develop empathy for the condition of others and thus forms the basis for a more fraternal form of solidarity (Schokkaert and Van Parijs 2003).

Individual myopia can lead young people to give inadequate consideration to their consumption needs in retirement and save too little. Decisions about making adequate provisions for retirement differ from other inadequate economic judgments because they are being made at such an early stage in life. By the time people discover their mistake they are no longer in a position to escape the consequences and have a vested interest in continuing existing arrangements (World Bank 1994). Such myopia can be offset by compulsory inclusion in a solidaristic scheme, which has the added advantage of functioning as a safeguard to protect prudent members of a society against those who are imprudent and are tempted to bank on a means-tested social minimum (Thompson 1998). Countries that seek to encourage more mutualist forms of solidarity by means of excessive means-testing, thus often face the problem of people close to retirement deliberately impoverishing themselves by spending most of their savings prior to retirement or donating their savings to their children in order not to miss out on the means-tested benefits (Binstock and George 1996). On the other hand, it can be argued that most people tend to overestimate their lifespan risks: in contrast to other social risks such as illness or unemployment most people prefer to see themselves as belonging to a high-risk category that lives longer than average. Finally, fraternal solidaristic pensions can also be seen as a form of risk-sharing not only against one's own longevity risk, but as much against the risks of having parents who live longer than average and who need to be supported by their children through an extended old age (Myles 2003).

A second set of explanations starts out from the idea that solidaristic redistribution is embedded in notions of equity and justice (Baldwin 1990). Underlying these notions are the social preferences of individuals: caring not only for the resources allocated for oneself but also for the resources allocated to other relevant reference agents. Until recently, these preferences were all gathered under the rather imprecise term of 'altruism'. Recent progress in experimental economics and evolutionary biology has established the importance of these preferences and contributed to understanding their nature, forms, and evolution (Bowles 2003). Two types of social preferences seem to be specially relevant for understanding social solidarity: reciprocal fairness and inequity aversion. It is important to note that not everybody exhibits social preferences and it is likely that people in general care more about others with whom they can in one way or another identify through a shared religion, nationality, occupation, ethnicity, race, and so on (Lindert 2004). Differences in the size of government redistribution in the United States as compared to European countries have been linked to the degree of racial heterogeneity and racial prejudice as these factors tend to increase the distance between the poor and the rest of society (Alesina and Glaeser 2004). Thus, whereas Americans are said to believe that the poor are lazy, Europeans believe they are unfortunate.

## 4.2 Institutions, Collective Actors, and Path Dependency

Institutional explanations seek to understand how individual motives are being translated into a collective voice, and under what conditions such a voice leads to formal arrangements. Such questions become particularly puzzling whenever the preferences that underpin those motives are heterogeneous, and it becomes difficult to explain solidarity in terms of a clear-cut bilaterally advantageous reciprocity. Majority support for extending solidaristic redistribution beyond mutual self-interest has been explained in terms of the weight of elderly voters in the population (Pampel and Williamson 1985). However, even though the relative weight of the elderly population in the electorate does say something about the salience of the pension issue, it cannot explain the extent of fraternal redistribution between pensioners. Others have pointed to the extension of political suffrage and a 'logic of democracy' that has allowed the class struggle to move from the industrial context into the political arena (Hewitt 1977; Lindert 2004). This argument has been further developed by the so-called 'power resources model' that sees solidaristic redistribution as the product of the struggle of a social-democratic labor movement (Shalev 1983). In some countries, political movements of the center (such as Christian Democratic parties) have shared the fraternal redistributive inclinations of social democracy, endorsing a mutualist interpretation of solidarity. Added to this are the effects of World War II and the ensuing Cold War, which created a level of national solidarity and catapulted the labor movement into the center of political decision-making. More generally, it has been argued that social security systems have been established or extended whenever an economy has had to experience the effects of an adverse event such as war or a depression, or when the economy has experienced a high level of growth or anticipates future growth (Blinder 1988).

Another set of explanations builds upon the idea of path dependency. Many public pension plans originated in the 1930s and the first decade after World War II. They reflected the economic, social, and political conditions of that period, and were financed on a PAYG basis. The adoption of this method of financing created a cohort of retirees that received benefits without having contributed to an earlier generation of pensioners. This generosity led to inter-cohort transfers and has created a 'legacy debt' (Diamond 2004). At the time, it was assumed that, given a steady population growth, the PAYG model would make everybody better off (Samuelson 1958). However due to the fall in fertility and mortality rates, the rate of return in the PAYG model has fallen below the capital market rate of return. Several authors have shown that, even in the case of an unbalanced population growth, a move from a PAYG system to a funded system cannot, in terms of income, be a Pareto gain (Breyer 1989; Barr 2001; Sinn 2000). When a PAYG system is introduced, the income gain of the privileged generations is exactly equal to the capital value of the income losses to all subsequent generations. This result holds regardless of the size of the difference between the rate of return in the PAYG model and the capital market.

# 5 Prospects for Pensions Solidarity

Pessimism about the future for social solidarity is widespread: its basis is perceived to be undermined by societal fragmentation, itself the consequence of increasing individualization and heterogeneity resulting from immigration. In addition, it is often argued that the twin pressures of an ageing population and globalization will make social solidarity too costly to sustain. In this section we give a critical review of the impact of these 'mega-trends' on social solidarity.

## 5.1 Individualization, Fragmentation, and Heterogeneity

In the socio-political debate on welfare solidarity, individualization and solidarity are often seen as mutually exclusive and contradictory phenomena. The basis for this view, which goes back to de Tocqueville, is that individualism ultimately leads to egoism. However, a contrasted view would argue that the increase in the options for individual choice strengthens responsibility and thus may well contribute to solidarity (Arts and Verburg 2001). Classical sociology sees individualization not so much as a process of dismantling solidarity, but rather as one that gives rise to other types of solidarity (Van Oorschot and Komter 1998). Close and often personal ties are gradually replaced by more abstract notions based on interdependence, reciprocity, and equality. Given its secular character, the question is what is new in the process of individualization.

A relatively new trend is the decline in household size, in particular the growing number of people living alone, often seen as made possible by the welfare state. It has been argued that the breakdown of family bonds has undermined feelings of reciprocity and solidarity. Even if we accept this, it might be argued that, because of the growth of single-person household units, people find themselves more dependent on collective arrangements (Pierson 2001), which could strengthen the 'selfish' motives for supporting solidaristic arrangements. This also holds true of another aspect of individualization, namely the increasing demands for flexibility in the labor market and the erosion of the standard working career. Where people are less able to count on a standard employment career, the building up of pension rights in second-tier occupational pensions becomes precarious and makes certain segments of the labor market more dependent upon a first-tier pension with a strong element of horizontal solidarity.

Thus, the arguments for believing that individualization will inevitably lead to a decline of solidarity are not well founded theoretically. There is also little empirical evidence that support for solidaristic arrangements is on the wane. For example, a survey among people in France, Germany, Italy, and Spain found that a majority of Continental Europeans supported existing collective arrangements, and were strongly averse to the neoliberal social model (Boeri *et al.* 2001). Immigration has become an issue in relation to support for solidaristic arrangements in most European countries. The discussion, however, seems to concentrate on restricting access to welfare to new immigrants; there are no signs that increased heterogeneity in European countries is eroding support for collective pension provisions.

## 5.2 Ageing

By shifting the balance between younger and older generations, ageing has made solidarity between the younger and older generations more costly. This applies to PAYG and, more indirectly, to funded systems as well (Barr 2001). However, there is no compelling reasons why this should lead to a break-up of solidarity. A logical response would be to reapportion the demographic risk in such a way that the burden for the youngest generations is reduced, while their relative position remains the same. One obvious instrument for this is a gradual rise in the retirement age (Myles 2003).

Early retirement schemes, in particular, tend to be actuarially highly unfair and are based on redistribution from young to old, without the young being aware of this. In the past such arrangements might have been legitimate, as younger generations might also have benefited from the labor market opportunities that resulted from the reduction in the labor supply. However, it is likely that in the future demographic changes may well lead to a shortage of labor, and the argument of making room for the young may no longer be convincing. More generally, given the demographically induced increases in the cost of solidarity, a critical review of all kinds of 'hidden' forms of redistribution in pension schemes is required (e.g. from those with short-term or intermittent careers to those with long-term careers in final salary schemes). In addition, an appeal could be made to intra-generational solidarity among elderly persons by taxing affluent pensioners more heavily and reconsidering the general character of tax breaks given to the elderly (Bovenberg 2002).

Partly in response to their ageing populations, countries have reformed their public pensions schemes. The question remains, however, whether these reforms will spread demographic costs fairly. Most countries have reacted by shifting from wage indexation to price indexation. As a result, the average net replacement rate in the EU will fall from its present level of 74 percent down to 58 percent in 2050 (see Van Riel *et al.* 2003). The move in some countries from a classical PAYG pension scheme to a notional defined-contribution scheme will lead to a fall in replacement rates as the costs of demographic changes fall entirely on retirees (Oksanen 2004). Moreover, these schemes are largely devoid of horizontal solidarity. They are less likely to assure adequate pension benefits for women, low-wage workers, and other workers with irregular employment histories (Williamson 2004). It should be noted that the consequences of these reforms are rarely spelt out by governments; it is doubtful whether these consequences will fit in with existing notions of fairness and be politically feasible given the increased proportion of elderly voters (Galasso and Profeta 2004).

## 5.3 Globalization

The idea that increased economic integration will lead to a decline of the welfare state rests on the assumption that social spending increases wage costs and will pose a threat to the competitiveness of a national economy. This view has been refuted in a number of studies (e.g. Castles 2004). One explanation is that social expenditure premiums mainly affect the composition of wage costs, and their level is affected to a much lesser extent. From this perspective, there is no compelling reason to expect that social solidarity, insofar as it is expressed in levels of welfare state spending, will become too costly, nor that globalization will have an eroding impact on first pillar pensions. Still, one could argue that changes in the composition of the social wage, such as the abandoning of parity financing in an attempt to lower non-wage labor costs, can indeed reduce the solidaristic nature of the first pillar. This seems to be especially the case if unions lack the capacity to press for higher wages across the board, and individual households are differently burdened with footing the bill depending upon their income and occupational status.

The integration and re-regulation of global financial markets might, however, have an impact on supplementary pension funds. In company-based pension plans, the sponsoring firm is usually held responsible for the funding position. The funding risks are borne by the shareholders and the active employees of the firm. With the advent of new global accounting rules, the former are no longer willing to bear those risks, and the reported financial position of companies is likely to become very unstable due to the volatility of pension funds' assets and liabilities. The new accounting rules will require pension liabilities to be booked using the so-called 'fair value basis'. Corporations will therefore seek to limit the impact of pension fund risks on their performance and financial position. One route is to minimize mismatch risk by holding an appropriate mix of nominal bonds and index-linked bonds (Exley *et al.* 1997). Another route is to switch from defined-benefit to defined-contribution schemes. Such a transition implies a switch from collective risk-sharing to individual risk-taking. This may well lead to an end to solidarity in funded occupational pensions, at least when it comes to sharing macro-level risks. This trend will be reinforced by closing down defined-benefit funds in the United States, a process which has been going on for some time (Clark 2003). Shareholders might increasingly demand that European firms emulate the new American standards of minimizing pension risk to safeguard the financial position of the companies they have invested in. The change in occupational pensions will set limits to the attempts in countries like the United Kingdom to shift old-age income provision from public pensions to occupational pensions by gradually discounting public pensions (Pensions Commission 2004).

# 6 Conclusions

Solidarity in old-age income provision is rooted in a combination of market failures, social norms, risk aversion, myopia, and path dependency. We therefore expect social solidarity never to disappear altogether. However, because of the 'mega-trends' discussed in Section 5, it is likely to be redefined, as has already happened several times in the past. Such changes occur mainly as a reaction to the erosion of existing institutions. The framework we presented in Section 3 might be helpful in analyzing and predicting the directions of these changes: the risks that are covered; the way benefits are determined; and the constituency within which the logic of solidarity operates. We conclude that the integration and regulation of global financial markets will, in combination with an ageing population, make it harder to cover macroeconomic risks via occupational pension plans. Will solidarity in this respect therefore be more limited to the first pillar? The way benefits are determined will change primarily as a result of population ageing. Here a new balance of burden sharing will have to be found between the young and older generations. Given social norms of fairness and the increased proportion of elderly voters, we remain skeptical about the ability of government to gradually lower net replacement rates as a way of limiting the budgetary costs of ageing.

Future research may lead to a better understanding of why people show solidarity, how solidarity might change, and what the effect of this will be on old-age income provision. The relationship between the insurance and distributional motives needs further exploration: do people accept distributional consequences as a side product of the advantages of social insurance; or are distributional motives important in their own right, because they are rooted in notions of fairness? For a better understanding of the forces driving changes in solidarity, more should be known about differences over time and between countries with respect to the risk covered in old age, the rules for determining benefits, and the constituency within which the logic of solidarity operates.

Cross-national differences in old-age poverty rates; and the extent to which such differences are related to the type of solidarity that is embedded in a country's pension system are issues that will inform future policy development. Related to this, more research would be welcome on the micro-empirical consequences of various pension designs on the re-apportionment of macroeconomic income risks and of macro-longevity risks, that is, to identify the categories of persons that effectively shoulder the burdens of macroeconomic fluctuations and of an ageing population. The re-apportionment of the risks related to pension income will remain a hotly debated issue in the years to come. A better understanding of social solidarity will be essential for the quality of this debate.

# NOTES

1. For some authors social solidarity has to do primarily with risk-sharing and therefore equals social insurance (e.g. Disney and Wakefield 2004 for the British context), while for others social solidarity equals redistribution and is conceptually different from social insurance (e.g. Rosanvallon 2000). In accordance with the double dimension of solidarity discussed in Section 2, we think that social solidarity is about both collective insurance and redistribution. Moreover, these cannot be seen as independent from each other because an important motive for collective insurance might be to avoid the distributional consequences of insurance through the market; social insurance has distributional consequences. Finally, if one adopts a Rawlsian perspective, vertical redistribution can be seen as a form of lifetime income insurance.
2. Some countries prescribe unisex mortality tables. Thus the low-risk male population is forced to cross-subsidize the high-risk female population. However, this may be seen as being a consequence of a larger social contract: women generally bear the costs of men's inferior physical endowment in the form of additional care provision as their husbands grow older (Myles 2003).
3. The private market fails to provide insurance products based on intergenerational risk-sharing. The reason for this is straightforward: current and future generations are not both alive prior to the outcome of the income risks. The current young generation is not able to pre-commit the future young generation, although from an *ex ante* perspective both generations may benefit. Whenever the current young generation of workers wants to commit itself to an insurance contract, the other party to the hedge is not born. By the time the next young generation is able to commit to the contract, the *ex post* outcome of the contract will be known. The support of the future young generation will be

contingent on the *ex post* outcome of the contract. They may not accept voluntarily a contract that will lead to a loss of welfare for them.

4. Merton (1983) points to the role of a public scheme in improving diversification of lifetime income resources. Because human capital is non-tradable, individuals are forced to hold too much of their wealth in human capital in relation to financial capital, that is, retirement wealth, while on retirement all capital is only available as financial capital. Merton shows that a public pension scheme in which retirees are entitled to a share of current-wage income, and the young are taxed accordingly, provides diversification of income risk across wages and profits and increases welfare by improving the efficiency of risk-bearing in the economy.

5. It should be noted though that pension schemes often contain redistributive elements which are hidden for participants (such as redistribution from dual wage-earner families to single wage-earner families, or from young workers to older workers to early retirement schemes) and which might on closer scrutiny be considered 'unfair' by most participants (World Bank 1994).

6. The degree of vertical redistribution of social security programs is usually measured in terms of the extent to which differences in replacement rates correlate with income and work histories. The underlying assumption is that in an orthodox actuarial scheme, contributions are proportional to past earnings and employment tenure. In countries where replacement rates decline as the earnings and tenure enjoyed in the past rises, pension schemes come closer to representing the fraternal ideal of solidarity. In contrast, countries with a public scheme in which benefits are more linked to past income and employment tenure, vertical redistribution is less and the model of solidarity comes closer to the mutualist pattern. Whereas the first group of countries (e.g. Denmark, the Netherlands, New Zealand, and the United Kingdom) is often called Beveridigean, the second group (e.g. Germany, Italy, and France) is associated with Bismarck, but this nomenclature seems to have lost much of its classifying power as:

- most countries with a flat-rate public scheme developed earnings-related occupational pensions etc. private or state mandated supplementary arrangements; those arrangements can either be voluntarist or state mandated, but are almost always encouraged by tax benefits and have for most wage-earners resulted in an income package that is similar in its equivalence to the packages typical of Bismarckian schemes (e.g. the Netherlands);
- many countries with a public scheme that might have been Bismarckian in origin, over time implemented a number of floors and ceilings, on either the benefit or contribution side, that have dramatically blurred the equivalence of the scheme and have resulted in a decline of the replacement rate with income that is similar to the one found in Beveridgean-type schemes (e.g. Belgium); and
- even in countries in which the public pension scheme exhibits a high degree of equivalence (i.e. replacement rates scarcely change with income), the leveling effect may be accomplished through other branches of the transfer system—most notably the social assistance scheme for which eligibility conditions have been liberalized for the elderly (e.g. Germany).

7. Once established, a wage-indexed PAYG scheme provides insurance against the risks inherent in the factor rewards that are related to fluctuations in the rate of population growth. This type of risk can result in the bad luck of being born into an unusually large cohort or of being retired when the younger cohorts are unusually small, because these large cohorts are confronted with relatively low wages as well as a relatively low rate of return on their savings. A social insurance contract between the retirees and the workers with fixed benefits will be beneficial from an *ex ante* point of view. A fixed benefit system has the effect of creating net transfers in lifetime income from lucky (small) to unlucky (large) generations (Smith 1982).

# References

Alesina, A., and Glaeser, E. (2004). *Fighting Poverty in the US and Europe: A World of Difference*. Oxford: Oxford University Press.

Arnsperger, C., and Varoufakis, Y. (2003). 'Toward a theory of solidarity'. *Erkenntnis*, 59/2: 155–87.

Arts, W., and Verburg, R. (2001). 'Modernisation, solidarity and care in Europe: The Sociologist's Tale', in R. ter Meulen, W. Arts, and R. Muffels (eds.), *Solidarity in Health and Social Care in Europe*. Deventer: Kluwer Academic Publishers, 15–39.

Baldwin, P. (1990). *The Politics of Social Solidarity: Class Bases of the European Welfare State 1875–1975*. Cambridge: Cambridge University Press.

Barr, N. (2001). *The Welfare State as a Piggy Bank*. Oxford: Oxford University Press.

Binstock, R. H., and George, L. K. (eds.) (1996). *Handbook of Aging and the Social Sciences*, London: Academic Press.

Blinder, A. S. (1988). 'Why is the government in the pension business?', in S. M. Wachter (ed.), *Social Security and Private Pensions*. Lexington, Mass. and Toronto: D. C. Heath.

Boeri, T., Börsch-Supan, A., and Tabellini, G. (2001). 'Would you like to shrink the welfare state: a Survey of European citizens'. *Economic Policy*, 32: 9–50.

Bovenberg. L. (2002). 'Pension systems in ageing societies', in H. Siebert (ed.), *Economic Policy for Ageing Societies*. Berlin: Springer Verlag, 183–206.

Bowles, S. (2003). *Microeconomics: Behavior, Institutions and Evolution*. New York: Russell Sage Foundation.

Breyer, F. (1989). 'On the intergenerational Pareto efficiency of pay-as-you-go financed pension systems'. *Journal of Institutional and Theoretical Economics*, 145: 643–58.

Castles, F. G. (2004). *The Future of the Welfare State: Crisis Myths and Crisis Realities*. Oxford: Oxford University Press.

Clark, G. L. (2003). 'Twenty-first-century pension (in)security', in G. L. Clark and N. Whiteside (eds.), *Pension Security in the 21st Century*. Oxford: Oxford University Press, 225–51.

Diamond, P. (2004). 'Social Security'. *American Economic Review*, 94/1: 1–24.

Disney, R. (2004). 'Are Contributions to Public Pensions Programmes a Tax on Employment?' *Economic Policy*, 39: 267–311.

—— and Wakefield, M. (2004). 'Solidarity and the free market in UK pension provision: how much risk-sharing in a multi-pillar programme'. Paper presented at the conference, Second-Pillar Pension Schemes, Between Market and Solidarity, Amsterdam, Nov.

Esping-Andersen, G. (1987). 'The comparison of policy regimes: an introduction', in M. Rein, Rainwater, and G. Esping-Andersew (eds.), *Stagnation and Renewal in Social Policy: The Rise and Fall of Policy Regimes*. Armonk, N.Y.: M. E. Sharpe, 3–12.

—— (1990). *The Three Worlds of Welfare Capitalism*. Cambridge: Polity Press.

Exley, J., Mehta, S. J. B., and Smith, A. D. (1997). 'The financial theory of defined benefit schemes'. *British Actuarial Journal*, 3/4: 835–966.

Galasso, V., and Profeta, P. (2004). 'Lessons for an ageing society: the political sustainability of social security systems'. *Economic Policy*, 39: 63–115.

Glazer, N. (2000). Foreword to P. Rosanvallon, *The New Social Question*. Princeton: Princeton University Press.

Gordon, R. H., and Varian, H. R. (1988). 'Intergenerational risk sharing'. *Journal of Public Economics*, 37/4: 605–63.

Hayward, J. E. S. (1959). 'Solidarity: the social history of an idea in nineteenth century France'. *International Review of Social History*, 4: 261–84.

Hewitt, C. (1977). 'The effect of political democracy and social democracy on equality in industrial societies: a cross-national comparison'. *American Sociological Review*, 42/3: 450–64.

Lindert, P. H. (2004). *Growing Public: Social Spending and Economic Growth since the Eighteenth Century*. Cambridge: Cambridge University Press.

Merton, R. C. (1983). 'On the role of social security as a mean for efficient risk sharing in an economy where human capital is not tradable', in Z. Bodie and J. Shoven (eds.), *Financial Aspects of the US Pension System*. Chicago: Chicago University Press.

Musgrave, R. (1981). 'A reappraisal of social security financing', in F. Skidmore (ed.), *Social Security Financing*. Cambridge, Mass.: MIT Press, 89–127.

Myles, J. (2003). 'What justice requires: pension reform in ageing societies'. *Journal of European Social Policy*, 13/3: 264–9.

Oksanen, H. (2004). 'Pension reform: an illustrated basic example'. *European Economy, Economic Papers*, no. 201.

Øverbye, E. (1998). *Risk and Welfare: Examining Stability and Change in 'Welfare' Policies*. Oslo: NOVA.

Pampel, F. C., and Williamson, J. B (1985). 'Age structure, politics, and cross-national patterns of public pension expenditures'. *American Sociological Review*, 50: 782–99.

Pensions Commission (2004). *Pensions: Challenges and Choices: The First Report of the Pensions Commission*, Norwich: TSO.

Pierson, P. (2001). 'Post-industrial pressures on mature welfare states', in P. Pierson (ed.), *The New Politics of the Welfare State*. Oxford: Oxford University Press, 80–104.

Ponds, E. H. M. (2003). 'Pension funds and value-based generational accounting'. *Journal of Pension Economics and Finance*, 2/3: 295–325.

Rawls, J. (1971). *A Theory of Justice*. Oxford: Oxford University Press.

Rosanvallon, P. (2000). *The New Social Question: Rethinking the Welfare State*. Princeton: Princeton University Press.

Samuelson, P. A. (1958). 'An exact consumption-loan model of interest with or without the social contrivance of money'. *The Journal of Political Economy*, 64/6: 467–82.

Schokkaert, E., and Van Parijs, P. (2003). 'Social justice and the reform of Europe's pension systems'. *Journal of European Social Policy*, 13/3: 245–63.

Shalev, M. (1983). 'The social democratic model and beyond: two generations of comparative research on the welfare state'. *Comparative Social Research*, 6: 315–51.

SHILLER, R. (1998). *Social Security and Institutions for Intergenerational, Intragenerational and International Risk Sharing.* NBER Working Paper W6641.

SINN, H. W. (2000). *Why a Funded Pension System is Useful and Why it is Not Useful.* Washington, D.C.: NBER Working Paper 7592.

SMITH A. (1982). 'Intergenerational transfers as social insurance'. *Journal of Public Economics*, 19: 97–106.

SPICKER, P. (1991). 'Solidarity', Graham Room (ed.), *Towards a European Welfare State.* Bristol: SAUS Publications, 17–37.

Stjernø, S. (2005). *Solidarity in Europe: The history of an idea.* Cambridge: Cambridge University Press.

THOMPSON, L. (1998). *Older and Wiser: The Economics of Public Pensions.* Washington, D.C.: The Urban Institute Press.

VAN OORSCHOT, W., and KOMTER, A. (1998). 'What it is that ties...? Theoretical perspectives on social bond'. *Sociale Wetenschappen*, 41: 5–24.

VAN RIEL, B., HEMERIJCK, A., and VISSER, J. (2003). 'Is there a Dutch way to pension reform?', in G. L. Clark and N. Whiteside (eds.), *Pension Security in the 21st Century.* Oxford: Oxford University Press, 64–92.

WILLIAMSON, J. B. (2004). 'Assessing the pension reform potential of a notional defined contribution pillar'. *International Social Security Review*, 57/1: 47–63.

WORLD BANK (1994). *Averting the Old Age Crisis: Policies to Protect the Old and Promote Growth.* Oxford: Oxford University Press.

# THE ECONOMIC CONTEXT

CHAPTER 9

# DEMOGRAPHY AND AGEING

NAOHIRO OGAWA AND
NORIYUKI TAKAYAMA

## 1 INTRODUCTION

Longer life expectancy has been a long-cherished dream throughout history, and today we can expect to live longer than ever, with many of us remaining healthy well beyond the age of 80. It is a great achievement to be celebrated. However, longer life expectancy also increases the proportion of the elderly in the total population, a trend known as population ageing. Besides increased life expectancy, declining fertility plays an important role in determining the level and speed of population ageing. Developed regions of the world have been experiencing population ageing for more than 40 years, and this trend is expected to continue for several decades. Furthermore, a growing number of developing countries will experience population ageing in the first half of the twenty-first century.

Population ageing represents a major challenge that is unprecedented in human history: a shrinking working population is forced to support a growing number of economically inactive persons. This phenomenon gives rise to a multitude of pressing issues. How long will declining fertility persist in years to come? How rapidly will the number of older people grow? How high will the proportion of the elderly be in, say, 2050? What socio-economic impacts can be expected as a result of population ageing? Will economic growth slow down in an ageing world? What policies should be pursued to maintain economic growth to allow all segments of society to benefit? Can younger people no longer achieve a higher standard of living than their parents? Will a vast majority of older persons have to live on an inadequate income? How great are the increased costs required to support an increasing number of retirees? Who shares them and when? How are they shared? Can the cost-sharing be equitable between different generations? Will the existing social security system for pensions be financially sustainable in the long run? Is it possible for us to avoid adverse economic effects by reforming social security pensions? Do we indulge the present at the expense of children living and unborn? What will be a time-consistent policy for social security pensions, given the significant uncertainties about the likely shape of the world decades into the future? Are we wise enough to find solutions to the difficulties arising from longer life expectancy?

This chapter addresses these problems, identifying what is known and what is not known. The chapter particularly addresses two questions: first, how significant is demographic ageing; and second, whether there are any effective solutions. Section 2 deals with demographic trends and future prospects from global and regional perspectives. Section 3 examines the economic implications of population ageing. Section 4 discusses pension funding issues, and Section 5 presents concluding remarks.

# 2 Demographic Trends and Prospects

## 2.1 Global and Regional Demographic Perspectives

In 2004, the total world population reached 6.4 billion persons. Its current annual growth rate is estimated at 1.3 percent, considerably lower than its peak value of 2.1 percent during 1965–70. This slowing of global population growth has been primarily due to the almost universal reduction of fertility in recent decades. The number of countries with fertility levels above five children per woman dropped from 55 in the early 1990s to 34 ten years later. In contrast, the number of countries with below replacement levels of fertility increased from 51 to 62 over the same time period. It is also important to note that although most of these low-fertility countries are in the developed regions, the number of countries in the developing regions with below-replacement fertility doubled to 20.

Because of such reduced population growth rates for the world as a whole in the late twentieth century, the outlook today is substantially different from the one that demographers had a few decades ago. The twentieth century was a century of explosive population growth, consequently causing unprecedented impacts on various socio-economic aspects. In contrast, the twenty-first century is likely to see the end of world population growth and become the century of population ageing (Lutz *et al.* 2004).

Despite the lower fertility projected for the majority of populations and the increased mortality risks for some, the population of the world is projected to increase from 6.1 billion in 2000 to 8.9 billion by 2050, as shown in Figure 9.1. This is an expected net increase of 2.8 billion persons during the first half of the twenty-first century.

These projected net additions suggest that the potential still exists for significant population growth in the next few decades. It should also be stressed that population dynamics among the regions of the world will be increasingly diversified. At present, the population of the more developed regions is growing at an annual rate of 0.25 percent, approximately one-sixth of the 1.46 percent annual rate for the less developed regions, and almost one-tenth of the 2.4 percent for the 49 least developed countries. It is important to note, as can be seen in Figure 9.1, that the population of the more developed regions is projected to decline after 2030, amounting to 1.22 billion persons in 2050, which is only marginally larger than 1.19 billion persons in 2000. This implies that most of the net additions to the world

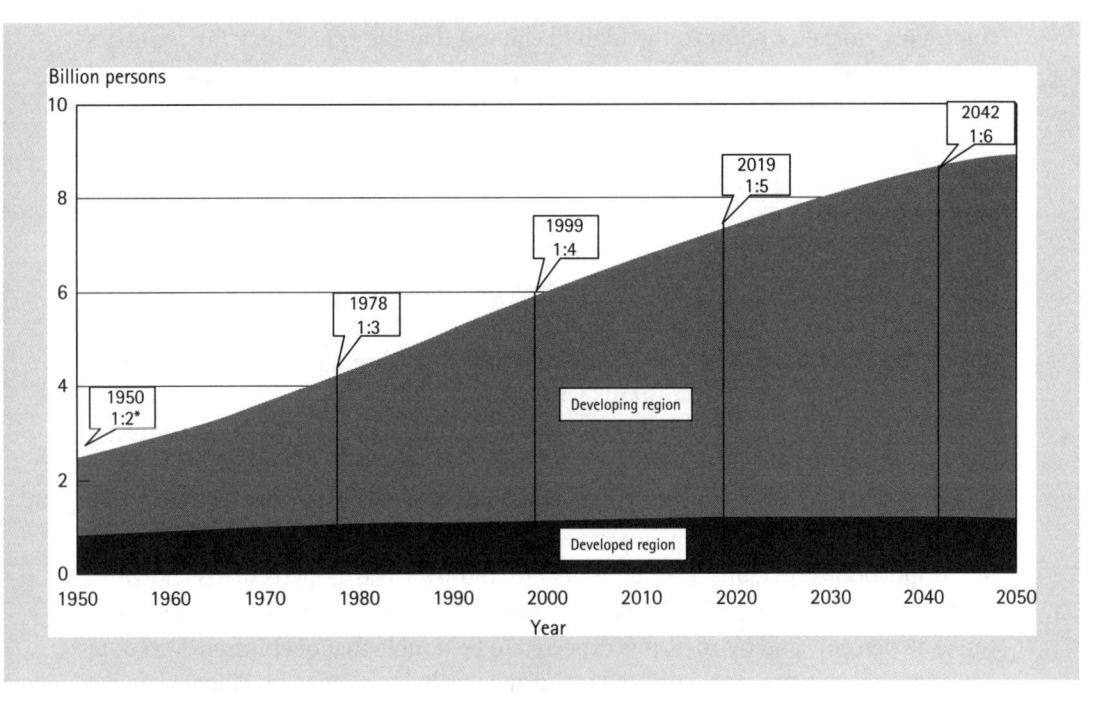

**Fig. 9.1 World population growth, 1950–2050**

*Note:* *Indicates ratio of population size in the developed region to population size in the developing region.

*Source:* United Nations (2003).

population will be in the less developed regions, with their proportion of the world population increasing from 80 percent in 2000 to 86 percent in 2050. Among the more developed regions, the population share of Europe will fall from 12 percent in 2000 to 7.1 percent in 2050, as depicted in Figure 9.2, while that of North America will change little, remaining at approximately 4 percent for the next 50 years.

The total fertility rate for the developed regions is expected to decline slightly from 1.58 children per woman in 1995–2000 to 1.56 in 2005–10. It is anticipated, however, that it will recover gradually to 1.85 by 2050. In contrast, in the less developed regions as a whole, fertility stood at 3.11 in 1995–2000 and is projected to decline to 2.22 in 2030–5, further declining to reach 2.04 by 2050. It is also interesting to note that approximately three-fifths of both developed and developing countries are currently concerned about their level of fertility for totally opposite reasons. According to United Nations projections, 28 out of 48 developed countries are concerned about the persistence of below-replacement fertility, while 84 out of 146 developing countries report that their fertility is too high (United Nations 2004).

Life expectancy at birth was 75 years in the more developed regions in 1995–2000, whereas it was 63 years in the less developed regions. The gap between the two groups of countries is expected to narrow over the next 50 years, reaching 82 years for the former and 73 for the latter. It should be noted, however, that a few recent studies on mortality point to the high likelihood that life expectancy for countries in the developed regions will improve at a considerably faster rate than anticipated (e.g. Keilman 1997).

The United Nations report *World Population Policies 2003* finds that high mortality is the most significant population concern for developing countries; more than 80 percent of developing countries list infant and child mortality, maternal mortality, and HIV/AIDS as the most imminent population and development concerns. These mortality risks will be directly influenced by the degree to which modern medical care services and public health measures become available to the poverty-stricken segment of the population in the developing countries, making it difficult to predict future conditions with any certainty.

This report also finds that the most significant demographic concern of developed countries relates to low fertility and its consequences, including population ageing and a decrease in the working-age population. The population in the more developed regions has been ageing at a rapid rate over the past few decades. In 1950, the proportion of persons aged 60 years old and over was 12 percent, as shown in Figure 9.3. By 2000, it had overtaken that of children aged 0–14 years (19 percent versus 18 percent) and by 2050, it is expected to be double that of children aged 0–14 years (32 percent versus 16 percent). Consequently, as shown in Figure 9.4, the median age in the more developed regions rose from 28.6 years in 1950 to 37.3 in 2000 and is expected to reach 45.2 years in 2050.

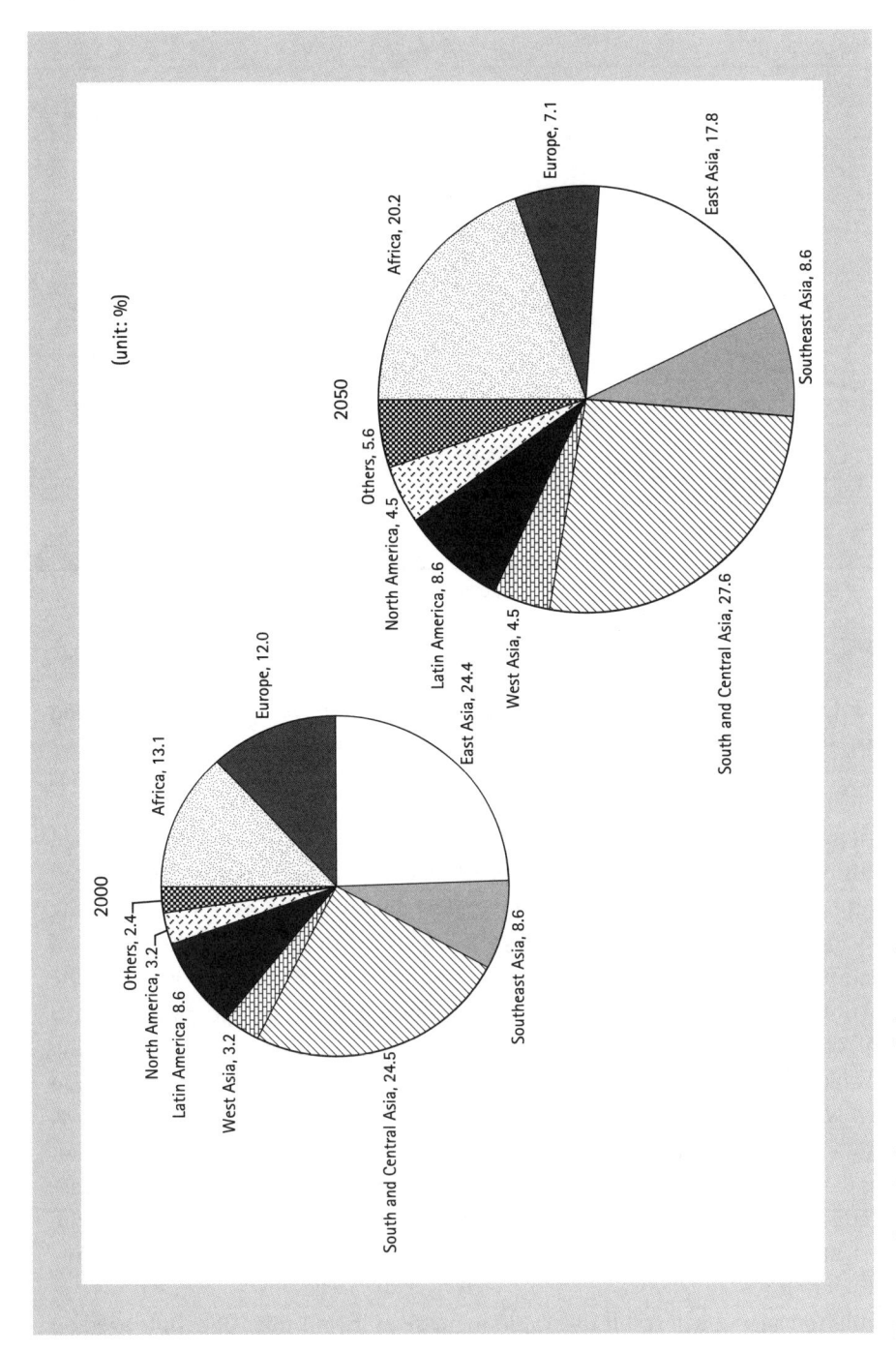

**Fig. 9.2 Population growth by region, 2000–2050**

*Source*: United Nations (2003).

2000 (unit: %)
- South and Central Asia, 24.5
- East Asia, 24.4
- Southeast Asia, 8.6
- West Asia, 3.2
- Latin America, 3.2
- North America, 8.6
- Others, 2.4
- Africa, 13.1
- Europe, 12.0

2050
- South and Central Asia, 27.6
- East Asia, 17.8
- Southeast Asia, 8.6
- West Asia, 4.5
- Latin America, 8.6
- North America, 4.5
- Others, 5.6
- Africa, 20.2
- Europe, 7.1

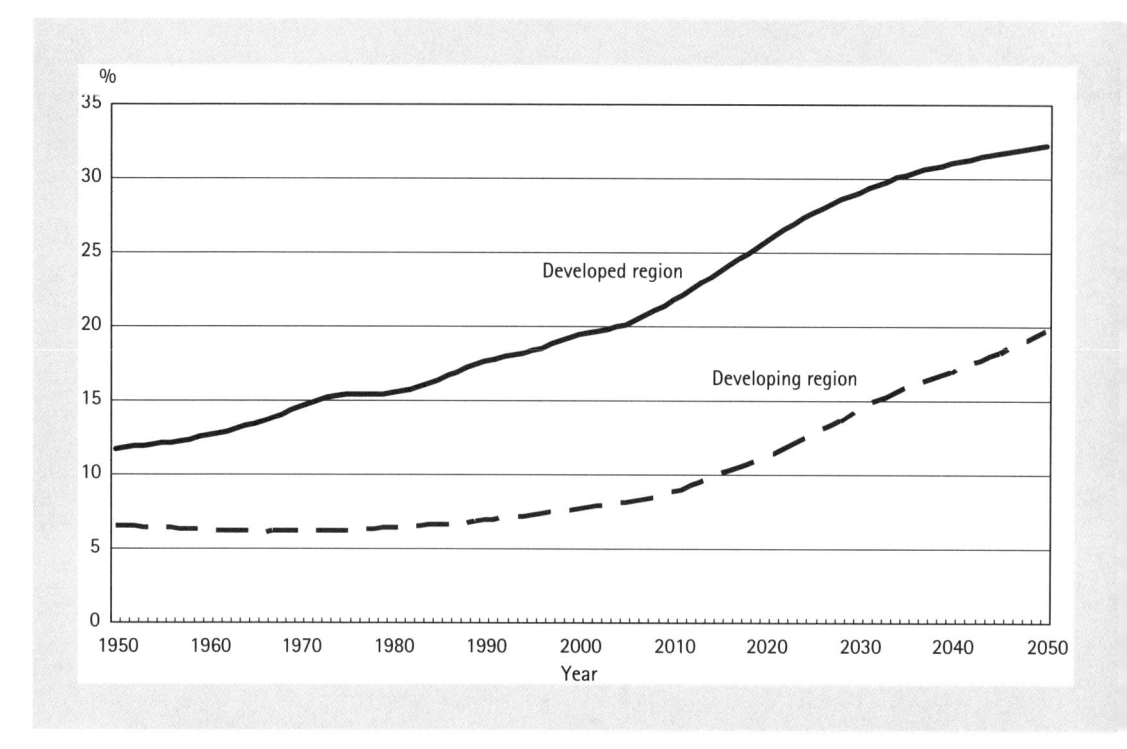

Fig. 9.3 Changes in the proportion aged 60 and over in developed and developing regions, 1950–2050

*Source*: United Nations (2003).

Until recently, many of the governments of developing countries perceived population ageing as an issue only for developed countries. However, as depicted in Figure 9.3, the proportion of older persons aged 60 and over in developing regions increased from 6 percent in 1950 to 8 percent in 2000, and the tempo of population ageing is anticipated to accelerate in the years to come. By 2050, the proportion of older persons is expected to rise to 19 percent, highly comparable to that of contemporary developed regions. The median age in these developing regions had changed only marginally from 21.4 years in 1950 to 24.3 years in 2000 (United Nations 2002), but it is expected to increase by almost 11 years to reach 35 by 2050, as shown in Figure 9.4. Subsequent to the United Nations' designation of 1999 as 'The Year of Older Persons', many developing countries have been increasingly concerned about various population ageing problems that require more focused attention in the process of formulating long-term development plans (Ogawa 2003).

Population ageing will result in a rapid increase in the number of people aged 60 and over. At the global level, the number will rise from 606 million in 2000 to 1.9 billion in 2050, as presented in Figure 9.5. Because of their sheer population size,

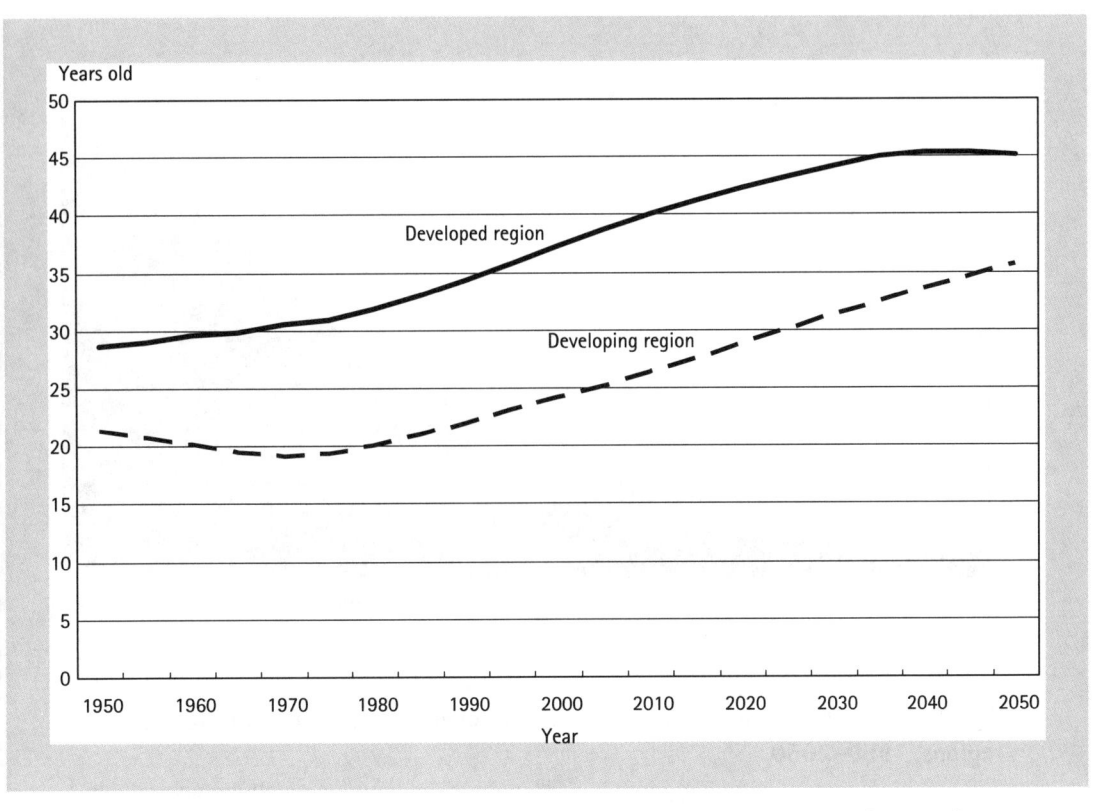

**Fig. 9.4** Changes in the median age in developed and developing regions, 1950–2050

*Source*: United Nations (2003).

the developing regions are expected to undergo a substantially larger increase in the number of older persons than the developed countries. The older population in developing countries is projected to increase more than four times from 375 million in 2000 to 1.5 billion by 2050.

Population ageing has been most marked in Europe. By 2050, those aged 60 and over will account for more than one-third of its population. At present, by country, the population of Japan is the oldest in the entire world, with a median age of 41.3 years. Japan's population is expected to remain the oldest in the world over the next half century, with a median age reaching 53.2 years in 2050.

A number of East and Southeast Asian countries, including Japan, the Republic of Korea, China, and Singapore, will face very rapid population ageing in the next 50 years. The driving force behind such rapid ageing is an unprecedentedly fast decrease in fertility. These four countries have all experienced a similar decline in fertility, although the time period for each differs considerably. In the case of Japan, the total fertility rate declined by 50 percent, from 4.5 children in 1947 to 2.0 children in 1957. Comparable reductions in fertility were recorded in Singapore

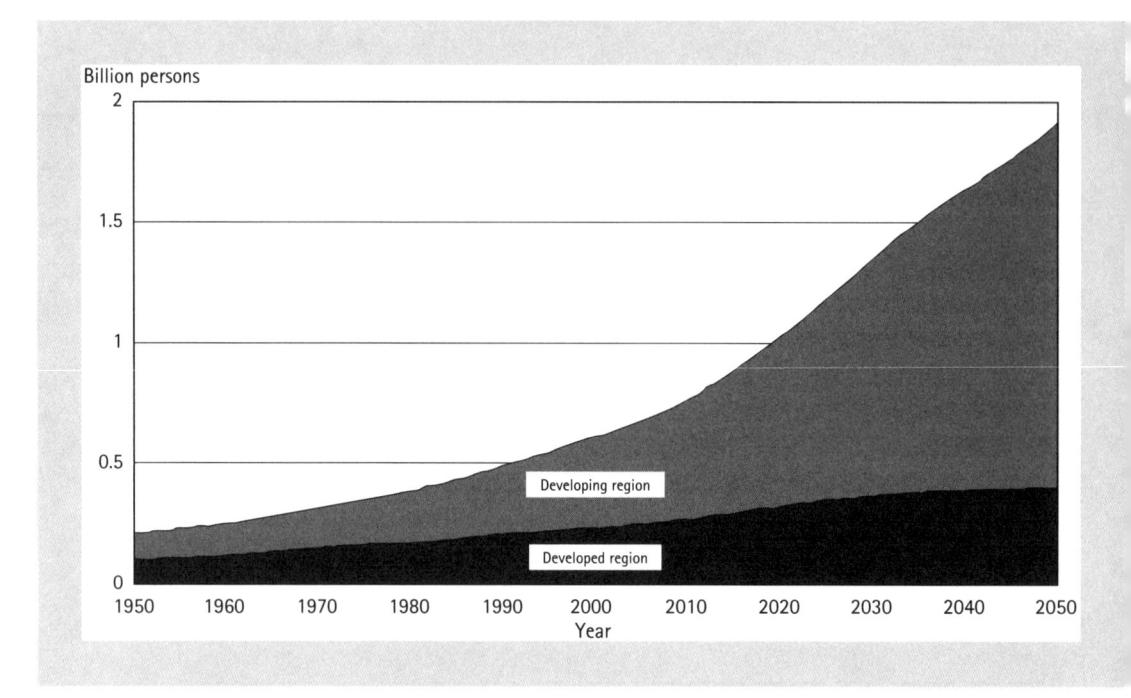

**Fig. 9.5** Growth of population aged 60 and over in developed and developing regions, 1950–2050

*Source*: United Nations (2003).

from 1966 to 1976, the Republic of Korea from 1971 to 1981, and China from 1973 to 1983. This decline in fertility is a serious cause of concern to policy-makers. In 2003, the total fertility rate was well below replacement level in all these countries: 1.19 children for the Republic of Korea, 1.25 for Singapore, and 1.29 children for Japan. The corresponding figure for China in 2004 is estimated to be 1.69 children. Furthermore, there is no definite indication of a recovery in fertility rates in the foreseeable future.

As a consequence of their rapid reduction in fertility, these Asian countries enjoyed or are still enjoying the so-called 'demographic bonus', the mechanism of which works as follows. In the process of slowing population growth, the labor force continues to grow some years after fertility has started to decline, thus increasing the percentage of the population engaged in productive activities. Moreover, as a result of reduced fertility, more economic resources can be allocated to those in the labor force in order to equip them with better physical capital. In addition, increased economic resources facilitate improvements not only in the coverage of the education program but also in its quality (Mason 2001).

It is important to bear in mind that the patterns of population ageing are broadly similar in most countries, but the timing differs substantially. For example, among the more developed regions, Japan, Germany, and Italy are forerunners, having the highest old-age dependency ratios at the present moment, followed by other EU countries. The population of the United States, by comparison, is relatively young among developed countries. These differences in the stages of population ageing among various countries will be sure to stimulate international movements of capital, goods, and labor, moderating any possible adverse economic effects arising from population ageing within each country.

The number of international migrants increased worldwide by 21 million persons between 1990 and 2000, the majority of whom moved from developing to developed nations (United Nations 2004). On the one hand, a sizeable proportion of these international migrants are making substantial contributions to their host nations. On the other, it is often the case that international migration entails the loss of qualified human resources for many developing countries and may become a source of political instability and socio-economic tensions in a number of developed countries of destination.

## 2.2 Alternative Population Projections

The medium variant of the United Nations population projection provides a useful base for gaining a rough perspective on population change at global, regional, and national levels. It is often the case, however, that national population projections prepared by each country produce more reliable and realistic estimates than those prepared by the United Nations, as the former are based on relatively rich data compiled from population censuses and numerous sample surveys.

In their population projections, the United Nations applies the same set of assumptions on future longevity and fertility to countries at comparable development stages. For example, in the case of the medium variant of the most recent population projection prepared by the United Nations, the total fertility rate is assumed to become 1.85 in 2045–50 for all developed countries. However, in their national projection, the government of Japan assumed a fertility rate of 1.39 in 2050. As a result, Japan's own estimates of its future demographic trajectory is considerably more problematic than the United Nations' projection.

## 2.3 Remaining Issues

There still remains a reliability issue with demographic projections. Short-run demographic projections are likely to be more accurate in comparison to economic projections, but longer-run projections are far from satisfactory. One of the primary reasons for this is a lack of reliable statistical data, especially in the less developed regions where long time-series data on mortality, fertility, and migration are least likely to be available.

In order to enhance the reliability of projected results, there is a long list of research studies that need to be conducted. For example, it is not entirely clear why some countries have a lower fertility rate than other countries, and why some regions within each country have lower fertility than others. Still controversial are the links between the social security system and fertility, and the link between female labor force participation and fertility. Least known are the quantitative effects of global ageing on migration. Another area for investigation is whether any family-friendly policies will induce a steady increase in fertility.

# 3 Economic Implications of Population Ageing

This section considers how population aging is likely to affect the economic well-being of each country; if patterns of likely losers and winners can be discerned, and how policies adopted can influence economic outcomes.

## 3.1 A Closed Economy

Economists usually discuss the effects of ageing in two ways: adopting either a macroeconomic approach, or an individualistic one. The macroeconomic approach often implies a pessimistic view on population ageing, while the individualistic approach is more likely to induce an optimistic scenario.

The macroeconomic approach assumes the following production function ($F$):

$$Y = A \cdot F(L,K)$$

where $Y$ is national output (or gross domestic product, GDP) of a country, $L$ the labor force, and $K$ the capital stock. As the population ages, the relative size of the labor force over the total population will be reduced. In some countries, the labor force will even decrease in absolute size. Unless this is compensated by an increase in total factor productivity ($A$) and/or an increase in the capital stock, the national output will decline. The economic presence of these countries in the world will then shrink. This line of thinking implies a pessimistic view.

Smaller countries are not necessarily poorer ones, however. An individualistic approach considers not the *absolute* size of national output, but the *per capita* output ($Y/N$), where $N$ is the total population:

$$Y/N = A \cdot f(L/N, K/L)$$

Per capita output can even increase in spite of a shrinking population with a falling national output, if labor force participation ($L/N$) or the capital-labor ratio ($K/L$) increases. People can be wealthier even when the population is ageing or declining. This can be a cause for optimism, and thus the absolute size of the population does not always matter in an individualistic context. What really matters is labor force participation, capital intensity, and the speed of increases in factor productivity. Economic implications will vary depending on different speeds of changes in these factors. Astute policies can bring about preferable results by affecting these factors.

The first important factor is labor force participation. Labor force participation rates vary among different age and gender groups. The dominant factors are labor market entry and exit ages along with child-raising circumstances. Participation rates can be increased by earlier labor market entry ages through structural education reform and later labor market exit ages through pension reform. Pensions often have the incentive effect of inducing early retirement (see Chapters 10 and 16 of this volume). Pension reform to encourage later retirement is crucial for an ageing society, to minimize the economic damage resulting from population ageing. Female labor force participation can rise, if child-raising does not deter women from engaging in paid employment. The established gender roles between men and women in employment and work within the home need to be reconsidered, and difficulties in reconciling paid employment with child-care responsibilities can be mitigated through more family-friendly policies.

The second important factor is capital intensity. Population ageing will have a negative effect on increases in the labor force, directly leading to a higher capital-labor ratio. If population ageing induces a lower saving rate, then it will usually reduce the capital-labor ratio through decreased investment. The overall change in capital intensity is then determined by these two opposing factors. Empirical studies verify their net effect, which differs country to country.

A simple life-cycle model implies that population ageing will lead to a decrease in national saving rates (Modigliani and Brumberg 1954). Still controversial is its empirical evidence, however, since in some developed countries no reduction in savings has been observed (Börsch-Supan 2003). National savings depend not only on a retirement motive (individuals saving for their own retirement), but also on other saving motives, including precaution, bequest, education, and housing. National savings depend on the public–private mix of pension schemes. More pre-funding for retirement through increased private initiatives might induce more savings. It should be remembered, however, that a higher saving rate means sacrificing consumption to some extent, possibly leading to lower utility or well-being. The maximum per capita consumption is attained when the economy is on the Golden Rule (Phelps 1966). A higher saving rate will be necessary if the existing capital-labor ratio is below the optimal level on the Golden Rule. If not, people will opt for a lower rate of savings (Auerbach and Kotlikoff 1983).

The third important factor is productivity. Productivity growth can bring higher economic well-being even with an ageing population. There is no reliable data currently available, however, on age-specific labor productivity. Higher productivity may be possible through human capital investment (a higher quality of education) and market-oriented job training with fuller labor mobility. Needless to say, technological innovation is also significant in this area. An ageing economy needs stronger incentives for building a higher innovative capacity. More research is urgently needed to enable us to understand whether ageing societies are likely to suffer from a productivity decline.

## 3.2 An Open Economy

People in a country with an ageing population can enjoy capital income from foreign direct investment. GNP (gross national product) is larger than GDP if foreign direct investment creates large returns. GNP might be the more relevant indicator of when the country enjoys a substantial income from foreign direct investment. Capital usually moves with much less friction than labor across countries. With a deregulation policy on foreign direct investment, a country with an older population can benefit from greater returns from direct investment than countries whose population is just beginning to age, or is still relatively young. Moreover, the international nature of the flow of capital may lessen the possible melt-down of the asset market when the baby boomers decumulate their assets after retirement.

Thus, the degree of capital mobility is quite crucial. Obviously, there is home bias in international portfolio choice, due to capital market frictions including tax provisions, different levels of information on country risks, and instabilities in global financial markets. An open economy also facilitates the international flow of goods and services, through which domestic consumers usually benefit. This too could mitigate the economic difficulties induced by population ageing in any country. Migration is the other positive source of well-being for people in an ageing country. Our understanding is still quite primitive, however, as to how much global ageing will affect migration.

In summary, smoother international movements of capital, goods and services, and labor can moderate any adverse economic effects of population ageing (Börsch-Supan 2004). Deregulations for stimulating these international movements will be required, together with reforms of existing socio-economic systems which were established when the country had younger populations. Overall, we understand the basic channels through which population ageing will exert economic effects, but lack intensive empirical research studies that would generate more specific quantitative data for individual countries with ageing populations.

# 4 Ageing and Pensions Funding

As ageing becomes a global phenomenon, the big challenge for the twenty-first century will be to provide an adequate income for older persons in ageing societies. In a few decades' time, the overwhelming majority of the world's older populations will live in developing countries, which at present have no or only limited social protection in old age. Establishing and extending appropriate social security programs will be an absolute priority in the national agenda of these countries.

The situation is quite different in developed countries. Most of them set up social security programs when their populations were young enough, thereby providing an adequate retirement income to the majority of retirees. The coverage of social security is a comparatively minor issue in these countries at present, although a growing number of atypical employment patterns and migrant workers are inducing serious drop-out, thus threatening the base of participation in some countries. Instead, they will face the prospect of unsustainable pension obligations as their population ages. Some economists warn that, if governments continue on the course they have currently set, people in most developed countries will see skyrocketing rates of social security contributions, drastically reduced retirement benefits, high inflation, and a ruined domestic currency (Kotlikoff and Burns 2004). These difficulties form the so-called 'demographic time-bomb'.

Can pension reforms ensure that the old-age security systems of developed countries will be financially sustainable in the long run? To achieve this, developed countries need to contain the increasing costs of social security pensions, while maintaining the adequacy of pension benefits. This section addresses these problems, highlighting gaps and disputed issues in our current knowledge.

## 4.1 Growing Anxieties

Most developed countries have a pay-as-you-go defined benefit system for social security pensions. This system was a success story when the economy enjoyed a relatively high speed of growth with a relatively young population. It has been effective in reducing poverty among the elderly and also in providing people with a stable standard of living after retirement. Since 1980 or a little earlier, however, the pay-as-you-go defined benefit plans for pensions have been facing serious and growing criticisms in these countries. Among other issues, the financial burden is becoming very severe with the declining rate of economic growth associated with population ageing. The system is losing popularity with younger people.

It is becoming difficult and undesirable for these countries to increase the contribution rate for social security pensions. Contributions to social security pensions operate as 'penalties on employment'. Further hikes in the contribution rate run the risk of damaging domestic companies that are facing mega-competition on a global scale, with adverse effects on the economy, including a higher unemployment rate, lower economic growth, lower saving rates, and so on. Hikes in the contribution rate will also induce an incentive compatibility problem. For younger cohorts, the internal rate of return in the social security pension system is likely to be relatively low or even negative, leading contributors to find that their participation in the system does not pay. The Japanese case is a typical example (Takayama 2003).

Another criticism leveled at the current pay-as-you-go defined-benefit plan is that it exerts a perverse redistribution effect. Through a massive transfer of income by social security pensions, the rich elderly are becoming richer, while other elderly people are still suffering from low incomes. Political resistance to cutting the benefits level or to further increasing the normal pensionable age has been very strong. Many people feel that the government is breaking its promise to them, leading to a loss of credibility, as people increasingly mistrust the commitment of their governments to providing them with an adequate retirement income.

## 4.2 Pension Debate

The publication of the World Bank's *Averting the Old Age Crisis* in 1994 prompted a heated debate on pensions worldwide. It identified three functions of old-age security programs: redistribution, saving, and insurance, claiming that each function should be separated. It proposed a recipe involving three pillars: a publicly managed mandatory first pillar to combat poverty, a privately managed mandatory savings second pillar, and a third voluntary saving pillar.

The 1994 World Bank approach faced immediate counter-criticisms by social security experts who contended that the recipe would require individuals to bear significant risks (Beattie and McGillivray 1995). A rejoinder followed (James 1996) and a vast literature has been built up dealing with all aspects of retirement income provisions (Arnold *et al.* 1998; Diamond 1996; Feldstein 1998; Fultz 2002; Gill *et al.*

2004; Gruber and Wise 1999; ILO 2001; OECD 1998, among others). The debate centered on the design of the second pension pillar. The World Bank held a conference on new ideas about old-age security five years later, in order to re-examine both the evidence and the thinking on pensions and retirement security (Holzmann and Stiglitz 2001).

There are several points of agreement which seem to have been reached through the pension debates of the past ten years. First, the pay-as-you-go defined-benefit system has been working not as a pure insurance system but rather as a tax-and-transfer system involving huge amounts of income transfers between generations. To some extent it is a problem between managers and trade unions, but mainly it is a problem *between generations*. This produces a political difficulty: older people are committed voters while younger people and future generations currently have decidedly weak or no political powers. The interests of future generations are likely to be neglected in the political arena.

Second, the nature of the intergenerational contract is difficult for many people to understand. Maintaining a fixed rate of replacement in gross income terms is by no means 'a contract'. It is actually quite risky, pushing its costs entirely onto actively working generations or future generations. The benefits and contributions in pay-as-you-go defined-benefit plans need some flexibility to respond to changing circumstances. The replacement rate embedded in the law is less a 'promise' in a strict sense, but the starting point of an ongoing process of adaptation to a changing and unpredictable world. Constant adjustments will be required to keep the system viable, and these will be viewed as 'political risks' (Diamond 1996).

Considerable efforts have already been made in some developed countries including Sweden, Germany, and Japan to prevent political risks in the future. An automatic balance mechanism or a sustainability factor has been introduced to adjust pension benefits to respond flexibly to never-ending changes in demographic and economic conditions (Heller 2003; Settergren 2001; Takayama 2005). Financial sustainability is often accomplished at the price of income adequacy after retirement. For instance, the United Kingdom succeeded in reducing social security benefits by 1996 to make the system financially sustainable. The system may face another problem of political sustainability in the future, however, since its benefit level will not be sufficient for many people to maintain a decent life after retirement.

Third, social security pensions are consumption allocation mechanisms, transferring resources from workers to pensioners when pensions are paid. Under the pay-as-you-go system, the transfer is direct through contributions or taxes paid by workers. Under the funded scheme, pensioners liquidate their accumulated assets by selling to workers. In both cases, the disposable income of workers is reduced by the amount of resources transferred to retirees.

Supporting an increasing number of retired persons is possible if output grows. Economic output depends crucially on the supply of workers, and thus increasing the labor force participation of elderly persons, women, and young adults will be required to maintain this supply (see Chapter 12 of this volume). In the light of this, we need to approach the question of funding from the perspective of circumventing constraints on economic growth. We must ask which revenue sources will slow down growth the least. Is the answer a wage (or payroll) tax or not? It should be remembered that the tax on consumption does not function as a direct levy on the saving and investment that powers the economy. It will make sense in some countries to fund part of the increased costs of a greying society by raising the rate of consumption-based tax.

Fourth, people in the more developed countries are increasingly concerned with the 'taste of pie' rather than the 'size of the pie' or the 'distribution of the pie' (Takayama 2003). When it comes to social security pensions, the most important question is whether or not they are worth buying. It has become of secondary concern how big or how fair they are. The basic design of the pension program should be incentive-compatible. Contributions should be much more directly linked with old-age pension benefits, while an element of social adequacy should be incorporated in a separate tier of pension benefits financed by other sources.

The incentive-compatibility problem can be avoided with the notional defined contribution (NDC) plan, which has already been introduced in Sweden, Italy, Poland, and Latvia. It will demonstrate to the public that everybody will get a pension equivalent to his/her own contribution payments. 'Every penny counts' was the selling phrase in Sweden when the NDC plan was advocated in early 1990s. Unfunded DC schemes can make transparent the relationship between contributions and benefits, thereby deterring evasion and other distorting behavior, and can also eliminate undesirable redistribution within the same cohort of individuals (Holzmann and Palmer 2006).

On the other hand, the NDC plan does have some disadvantages. Risks will be entirely on the shoulders of pensioners as there is no risk-sharing between old parents and their children. Nor will it be easy for NDC plans to provide social security in the event of the invalidity or death of the breadwinner. Furthermore, the *notional* rate of return is usually set to equal wage increases, long-term averages of which are likely to be lower than long-term interest rates. If this is to be the case in the future, NDC benefit levels will be potentially lower than those under real DC plans.

## 4.3 Strengthening Private Initiatives

The majority of people in almost all developed countries are reluctant to accept further increases in taxes and/or social security contributions. Under these circumstances, people must be encouraged to become self-reliant after retirement.

With stronger tax incentives, private initiatives will grow in due course. If this occurs, the future picture of distribution of income after retirement may be quite different.

Obviously the funded defined-contribution scheme has some advantages such as understandability (or transparency) and offers a flexible response to increasing diversity of life-style (increasing heterogeneity, increasing freedom to choose the place of work, working hours, and working periods, widening choices of no-kids, divorce, and remarriage, and so on). It also encourages people to be responsible and self-reliant, penalizing irresponsible behavior that imposes cost on others, especially on future generations who have no political influence today.

Funded defined-contribution plans will face several difficulties, however. First, the market rate of return is quite volatile in the short term, producing large differentials. The rate of return from the financial market may decline with ongoing population ageing, and with an ample supply of funded money. It is not inflation-proof. Consequently insured people will face an investment risk (Campbell and Feldstein 2001). The income disparity after retirement will widen, and an increasing proportion of the elderly will suffer from low income. Some of the current retirees, namely asset-holders, will also suffer loss from a possible decline in the market rate of return on their assets.

Second, we must have appropriate regulations for funded schemes. We can learn from the experiences of the Anglo-Saxon countries, but so far our knowledge about them remains insufficient. A particular gap in understanding concerns institutions against investment risks (see Chapter 25 of this volume). Third, the problem of administrative costs (Shoven 2000) will particularly affect low income earners who will be forced to accept a relatively low rate of return.

Voluntary pre-funding seems inevitable. Better instruments to minimize risks involved in the funded system are needed, as well as better understanding of individual behaviors induced by different provisions, the macroeconomic impacts, and the distributional outcomes from increased pre-funding.

## 4.4 No Single Solution

Each country faces the dilemma that policy-makers seek to make pensions the vehicle for too many policy objectives. Japan, Singapore, and China are typical examples (Takayama 2005; Asher 2005; Chen 2005). This runs counter to the standard theory of policy assignment, which suggests that each policy objective can be best attained only if it is matched with a different policy instrument.

Different objectives are often competing. Promoting later retirement may induce higher unemployment for younger people. Encouraging occupational and individual pensions can lead to early retirement. Tax smoothing or advance increases in the contribution rate for sound financing in the long term will cause higher unemployment in the short term. Financial sustainability often comes at the price of income adequacy in retirement. Solutions will be different depending on which objective is more important.

For an ageing society, increased costs are inevitable to secure a stable income for people after retirement, and to prevent poverty. We have no painless solutions for the future; no reforms without tears. The type of pain that we will have to bear will be different from country to country. It depends on a whole host of variables: the potential for economic growth; the balance between solidarity and self-reliance; perceptions about income disparity after retirement; understanding of intergenerational equity; the credibility of the government commitment; regulatory competence against investment risks, the development of the capital market, and so on.

# 5 Conclusion

Ageing is taking place on a global scale in the twenty-first century. The economic implications of ageing can be seen in both a pessimistic and an optimistic light, depending on different analytical frameworks, each country's specific conditions, and policies to be adopted. Increasing and smoother international movements of capital, goods and services, and labor can moderate any adverse economic effects of population ageing. Overall, higher economic growth can mitigate the difficulties in ageing societies, and employment with increasing labor force participation of elderly persons, women, and young adults carries the crucial key to financing adequate retirement income in the future.

Providing adequate income to senior citizens is a big challenge for the world with its ageing populations. Enormous efforts will be necessary for developing countries to extend the coverage of social protection in old age in order to prevent insufficient retirement income for the vast majority of older people. Developed countries have been struggling to contain social security pension costs with the focus on increasing the normal pensionable age and introducing an automatic balance mechanism, together with giving a minimum income guarantee to older persons. Scenarios of bankrupt schemes for social security pensions will turn out to be overly simplistic and groundless. There are no magic bullets, however. No painless solutions for the future. No single policy will be sufficient on its own in addressing the long-term challenges.

No one can claim to see clearly all the changes that lie in the decades ahead, but the challenge is hard to ignore. Missing from the picture is a more explicit consideration of economic consequences arising from population ageing. Missing, as well, is a far greater commitment to research on the magnitude of the principal long-term risks in an ageing society, their sensitivity to key assumptions, and their implications.

In the end, life is still risky. We have to realize that we cannot completely eliminate all the risks associated with living longer. What we can do is to make greater efforts to control these risks at a minimum level.

# References

ASHER, M. G. (2005). 'Retirement financing in Singapore', in N. Takayama (ed.), *Pensions in Asia*. Tokyo: Maruzen Co., Ltd.

ARNOLD, R. D., GRAETZ, M. J., and MUNNELL, A. H. (eds.) (1998). *Framing the Social Security Debate: Values, Politics and Economics*, Washington, D.C.: Brookings Institution.

AUERBACH, A. J., and KOTLIKOFF, L. J. (1983). 'National savings, economic welfare and the structure of taxation', in M. S. Feldstein (ed.), *Behavioral Simulation Methods of Tax Policy Analysis*, Chicago: University of Chicago Press.

BEATTIE, R., and MCGILLIVRAY, W. (1995). 'A risky strategy: reflections on the World Bank Report *Averting the Old Age Crisis*'. *International Social Security Review*, 48/3–4: 5–22.

BÖRSCH-SUPAN, A. (ed.) (2003). *Life Cycle Savings and Public Policy*. New York: Academic Press.

—— (2004). 'Global aging: issues, answers, more questions'. DP-55-04, Mannheim Research Institute for the Economics of Aging.

CAMPBELL, J. Y., and FELDSTEIN, M. (eds.) (2001). *Risk Aspects of Investment-Based Social Security Reform*. Chicago: University of Chicago Press.

CHEN, V. Y. (2005). 'A macro analysis of China pension pooling system', in N. Takayama (ed.), *Pensions in Asia*. Tokyo: Maruzen co., Ltd.

DIAMOND, P. (1996). 'Proposals to restructure social security'. *Journal of Economic Perspectives*, 10/3: 67–88.

FELDSTEIN, M. S. (ed.) (1998). *Privatizing Social Security*. Chicago: University of Chicago Press.

FULTZ, E. (2002). *Pension Reform in Central and Eastern Europe*, 2 vols. Budapest: International Labour Organization.

GILL, I. S., PACKARD, T., and YERMO, J. (2004). *Keeping the Promise of Social Security in Latin America*. Washington, D.C.: World Bank.

GRUBER, J., and WISE, D. (1999). *Social Security and Retirement around the World*. Chicago: University of Chicago Press.

HELLER, P. S. (2003). *Who Will Pay?* Washington, D.C.: International Monetary Fund.

HOLZMANN, R., and PALMER, E. (eds.) (2006). *Non-financial Defined Contribution (NDC) Pension Schemes: Concept, Issues, Implementation, Prospects*. Washington, D.C.: World Bank.

—— and STIGLITZ, J. E. (eds.) (2001). *New Ideas about Old-Age Security*. Washington, D.C.: World Bank.

INTERNATIONAL LABOUR OFFICE (2001). *Social Security: A New Consensus*. Geneva: ILO.

JAMES, E. (1996). 'Providing better protection and promoting growth: a defense of *Averting the Old Age Crisis*'. *International Social Security Review*, 49/3: 3–17.

KEILMAN, N. (1997). 'Ex-post errors in official population forecasts in industrialized countries'. *Journal of Official Statistics*, 13: 793–810.

KOTLIKOFF, L. J., and BURNS, S. (2004). *The Coming Generational Storm: What You Need to Know about America's Economic Future*. Cambridge, Mass.: The MIT Press.

LUTZ, W., SANDERSON, W. and SCHERBOV, S. (2004). *The End of World Population Growth in the 21st Century: New Challenges for Human Capital Formation and Sustainable Development*. London and Sterling, Va.: Earthscan.

MASON, A. (2001). *Population Change and Economic Development in East Asia: Challenges Met, and Opportunities Seized*. Stanford, Calif.: Stanford University Press.

MODIGLIANI, F., and BRUMBERG, R. (1954). 'Utility analysis and the consumption function: an interpretation of cross-section data' in K. K. Kurihara (ed.), *Post-Keynesian Economics*, New Brunswick, N.J.: Rutgers University Press, 388–436.

OGAWA, N. (2003). 'Ageing trends and policy responses in the ESCAP region'. *Population and Development: Selected Issues*. Asian Population Studies Series, No. 161: 89–127. New York: United Nations.

ORGANIZATION FOR ECONOMIC COOPERATION AND DEVELOPMENT (1998). *Maintaining Prosperity in an Aging Society*. Paris: OECD.

PHELPS, E. S. (1966). *Golden Rules of Economic Growth*. New York: Norton.

SETTERGREN, O. (2001). 'The automatic balance mechanism of the Swedish pension system'. *Wirtschaftspolitische Blätter*, No. 4, available at www.rfv.se

SHOVEN, J. (ed.) (2000). *Administrative Aspects of Investment-Based Social Security Reform*. Chicago: University of Chicago Press.

TAKAYAMA, N. (ed.) (2003). *Taste of Pie: Searching for Better Pension Provisions in Developed Countries*. Tokyo: Maruzen Co., Ltd.

—— (ed.) (2005). *Pensions in Asia: Incentives, Compliance and their Role in Retirement*. Tokyo: Maruzen Co., Ltd.

UNITED NATIONS (2002). *World Population Ageing 1950–2050*. New York: United Nations.

—— (2003). *World Population Prospects: The 2002 Revision*. New York: United Nations.

—— (2004). *World Population Policies 2003*. New York: United Nations.

UNITED NATIONS POPULATION FUND (2004). *State of World Population Report 2004*. New York: United Nations Population Fund.

WORLD BANK (1994). *Averting the Old Age Crisis: Policies to Protect the Old and Promote Growth*. New York: Oxford University Press.

HELP SPMAP  Thursday September 4 17:20:04 2014   Page 14

```
100 . do "C:\Users\cenv0386\AppData\Local\Temp\STD06000000.tmp"

101 . mlogit calling_behaviour gender year_dob balance_cat salary_cat av_years_fund fundid web_user sta¹
>  )

Iteration 0:   log pseudolikelihood = -329249.1
Iteration 1:   log pseudolikelihood = -305928.29
Iteration 2:   log pseudolikelihood = -299787.06
Iteration 3:   log pseudolikelihood =   -299582
Iteration 4:   log pseudolikelihood = -299580.89
Iteration 5:   log pseudolikelihood = -299580.89

Multinomial logistic regression                   Number of obs   =     286663
                                                  Wald chi2(24)   =   40915.24
                                                  Prob > chi2     =     0.0000
Log pseudolikelihood = -299580.89                 Pseudo R2       =     0.0901
```

| calling_beh~r | Coef. | Robust Std. Err. | z | P>\|z\| | [95% Conf. Interval] |
|---|---|---|---|---|---|
| **0** | | | | | |
| gender        | .1540302  | .0106717 | 14.43  | 0.000 | .133114   .1749464 |
| year_dob      | .0079656  | .0005265 | 15.13  | 0.000 | .0069338  .0089975 |
| balance_cat   | -.0577833 | .0031902 | -18.11 | 0.000 | -.0640361 -.0515306 |
| salary_cat    | -.0361588 | .0014716 | -24.57 | 0.000 | -.0390432 -.0332744 |
| av_years_fund | -.1069958 | .0020413 | -52.42 | 0.000 | -.1109966 -.102995 |
| fundid        | -.0000628 | .0000137 | -4.59  | 0.000 | -.0000896 -.000036 |
| web_user      | -.2130796 | .0118845 | -17.93 | 0.000 | -.2363728 -.1897864 |
| state         | .0003469  | .002131  | 0.16   | 0.871 | -.0038297 .0045235 |
| _cons         | -13.8582  | 1.040867 | -13.31 | 0.000 | -15.89826 -11.81814 |
| **1**         | (base outcome) | | | | |
| **2**         | | | | | |
| gender        | -.0186759 | .0121445 | -1.54  | 0.124 | -.0424788 .0051269 |
| year_dob      | -.0170614 | .0005873 | -29.05 | 0.000 | -.0182125 -.0159102 |
| balance_cat   | .0678693  | .0027691 | 24.51  | 0.000 | .062442   .0732966 |
| salary_cat    | .0168607  | .001503  | 11.21  | 0.000 | .0139149  .0198065 |
| av_years_fund | .0438822  | .0019957 | 21.99  | 0.000 | .0399706  .0477937 |
| fundid        | -.0000422 | .0000154 | -2.75  | 0.006 | -.0000723 -.0000121 |
| web_user      | .3516858  | .0140135 | 25.10  | 0.000 | .3242197  .3791518 |
| state         | -.0050404 | .0024002 | -2.10  | 0.036 | -.0097447 -.0003361 |
| _cons         | 33.16023  | 1.159841 | 28.59  | 0.000 | 30.88698  35.43347 |
| **3**         | | | | | |
| gender        | -.0587579 | .0232238 | -2.53  | 0.011 | -.1042758 -.01324 |
| year_dob      | -.0709855 | .0011183 | -63.48 | 0.000 | -.0731772 -.0687937 |
| balance_cat   | .1147053  | .0035919 | 31.93  | 0.000 | .1076653  .1217452 |
| salary_cat    | .0326283  | .002508  | 13.01  | 0.000 | .0277127  .0375438 |
| av_years_fund | .0944788  | .0032495 | 29.08  | 0.000 | .08811    .1008477 |
| fundid        | .0001115  | .0000272 | 4.10   | 0.000 | .0000581  .0001648 |
| web_user      | 1.208367  | .0324334 | 37.26  | 0.000 | 1.144799  1.271936 |
| state         | -.0248252 | .0043556 | -5.70  | 0.000 | -.0333621 -.0162884 |
| _cons         | 135.9424  | 2.194281 | 61.95  | 0.000 | 131.6417  140.2431 |

```
102 . end of do-file

103 . do "C:\Users\cenv0386\AppData\Local\Temp\STD06000000.tmp"
```

CHAPTER 10

# LIFE-CYCLE OPTIONS AND PREFERENCES

FLORENCE LEGROS

## 1 INTRODUCTION

Until the 1980s, economic literature provided only limited explanations about the allocation of households' financial portfolios. For decades, economists had been considering savings as a homogeneous aggregate and concentrated their studies on its volume and not on its components. Most of the theories were dedicated to the study of household consumption, which explains why savings were considered as a 'residual'. The Life-Cycle Hypothesis theory (LCH), developed by Modigliani and Brumberg in 1954, marked a departure from this perspective and considered saving as a voluntary and rational behavior. Since the end of the 1970s, LCH has been considered as a useful tool in explaining the patterns of behavior in saving.

The increasing diversification of households' portfolios led economists to another question: how do households allocate their financial wealth? With LCH, households became forward looking; their behavior as asset managers raised the question of their attitude toward risk. The problem became one of their preferences and differing attitudes toward risk and the future.

One can understand that—faced with an ageing population—the issues of both savings determinants and portfolio allocation became central. In the near future, a serious decline in the generosity of public pensions is expected to raise the problem of the revenues of retirees. Are they saving enough? How do they and should they save? Because LCH explicitly takes into account the changes in revenues throughout the life-cycle, it is the favorite tool for answering these kinds of questions. According to LCH, people should try to smooth their intertemporal consumption—in other words, to save in order to consume as much as they want even after the drop in their revenue when they retire. That means that, still according to LCH, a huge increase in saving rates must be expected. Equally, the nature of the ageing process is very important. The key factor at present is the increase in life expectancy. Intuitively, it seems that this should lead to higher ownership of equities or risky assets, whose risk decreases with the duration of ownership.

The main purpose of this chapter is to show that these conclusions are not well supported by empirical studies, which leads the observer to approach these theories with caution. The chapter proposes some alternative explanations for households' behaviors. The first section deals with the basic LCH model; the second discusses households' intrinsic attitude toward risk; and the chapter concludes with a consideration of the difficulties in distinguishing these attitudes from the specific environment in which they are embedded. The last section examines the effect of so-called 'background risks'.

## 2 THE LIFE-CYCLE HYPOTHESIS AND WEALTH COMPOSITION

The basic LCH model, as Modigliani and Brumberg show in their seminal paper, is usefully enriched by additional assumptions or variables, such as uncertainty, or the existence of bequests, that do not change—according to the authors—the general principle of wealth accumulation. LCH, however, remains of very little use in explaining portfolio composition; as noted by Modigliani and Brumberg 'This composition will also be affected by the current and prospective total resources, by the nature of the available alternatives, and, last but not least, by "social" pressures' (1954: 119–20). While they suggest some link between composition of assets and risk aversion, they implicitly propose a study of individuals' preferences, one of the extensions central to this chapter.

## 2.1 Life-Cycle Hypothesis

At its simplest, the life-cycle hypothesis (LCH) makes very simple behavioral assumptions. The accumulation strategy adopted by a consumer during his or her active life is to smooth the consumption profile: individuals accumulate wealth during their working lives which will guarantee them a stable standard of living throughout life—during both active and retirement periods.

Two variables will determine the agent's saving behavior: age and permanent income. This income is determined by the sum of an individual's discounted anticipated income including retirement pensions. In the basic model, people know their exact date of death, do not care about other generations, have time-invariant preferences, and deal with non-risky financial markets. Basic behaviors with no real link with reality result from this model. In order to introduce phenomena like voluntary or non-voluntary bequests, economists introduced uncertainty over life expectancy and altruism; they also introduced liquidity constraints and various imperfections in the financial markets, such as labor market, supply, and rational behaviors (Arrondel 1993).

Various kinds of consumers/savers can be represented diagramatically. Figure 10.1 shows the basic model when the date of death is known with certainty, the individual is left with and leaves no inheritance, begins his active life in $t_0$, retires in $t_1$ and dies in $t_2$. Income is $w$ (as 'wage') during his active life and $p$ (as 'pension') in retirement. Figure 10.1 shows the wealth profile, $W$, which smoothes life-cycle consumption, $c$. The wealth profile is the well-known reversed V curve, maximum wealth being reached when the individual retires, at point $t_1$, and begins to consume his wealth, which decreases until it is nil, in $t_2$.

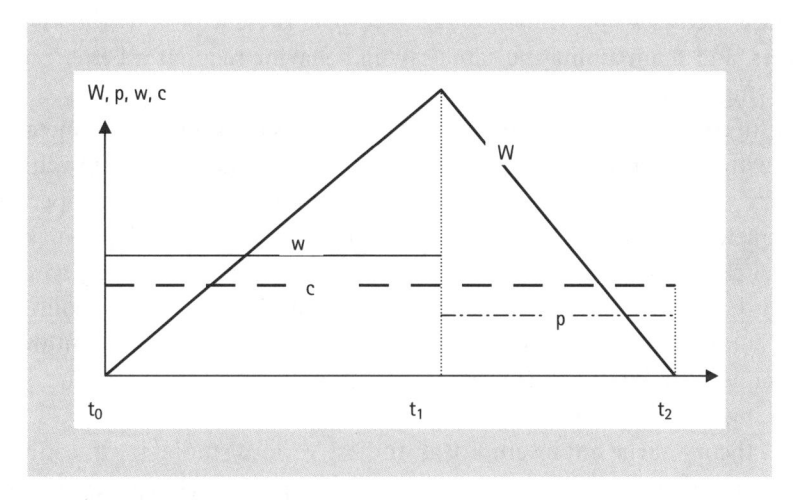

**Fig. 10.1** The basic model of the Life-Cycle Hypothesis (LCH)

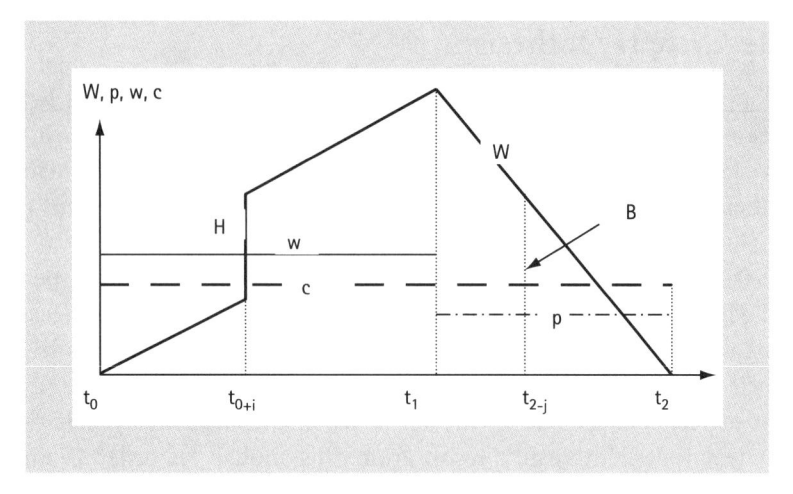

**Fig. 10.2 A more complex LCH model of an individual's wealth profile**

Figure 10.2 shows an individual's wealth profile when this individual gets an inheritance, $H$, in $t_{o+i}$ and overestimates his life expectancy (targeting his wealth profile in order to smooth consumption until $t_2$ but he will die in $t_{2-j}$); the result is that this individual will leave an involuntary bequest, $B$.

One problem that arises is the variation in individuals' expectations of the future. The usual illustration of the impact of time preference comes from Robinson Crusoe. At a given moment, Crusoe decides to consume only part of his harvest and to seed the remaining part of the wheat: in economic terms, he saves and invests. That means that he takes into account his future and gives a value to it: his time preference favors future consumption. An intuitive first result is the relationship between time preference, savings, and interest rate: when the time preference increases (when individuals favor the present period) the saving rate decreases, and maintaining the same saving behavior requires a better return for these savings, that is, a higher interest rate.

A useful concept is the discount rate; it transforms the value of $X$ monetary units earned within $T$ periods at the present value. For example, the present value of 100 monetary units within one year if the discount rate is 10 percent per year is 90.9 monetary units ($100/[1 + 0.10]$). A crucial point is that people make intertemporal choices according to how they value the future; if they have to trade off between the present and the future for the allocation of financial resources, they have to compare the interest rate (the value of their resources in the future if they are remunerated by the financial sector) and their preferences (the price of renouncing immediate consumption).

Is this theory borne out by empirical studies? Various studies try to compare the age-wealth profile with the life-cycle hypothesis perspective. They generally conclude that the theory—*per se*—is unable to explain individuals' saving behavior. In the

United States, Bernheim *et al.* (1997) point to marked discontinuities in consumption at retirement, but these discontinuities do not correlate with income profiles (including retirement pensions), an independence that leads the authors to conclude that households do not use savings in order to smooth their life-cycle consumption. In France, the reversed V curve is truncated for the oldest age group, the wealth profile being flat after the age of 69. In addition, if we divide the components of households' wealth between risk-free assets and risky assets, the reversed V shaped profile can be seen to be caused by financial assets (non-liquid ones). As an aside, the share of risky assets in portfolios shows a constant increase over ten years.

An international comparison highlights very different behaviors in different countries, confirming the idea of an institutional component and/or cultural differences. Arrondel and Masson (2003) show that inequalities in wealth levels depend on the countries under consideration: France is comparable to Canada and Germany, is more equal than the United Kingdom or United States, but with wealth levels less concentrated than in Northern European countries. They add that the differences in wealth levels are actually quite independent of age and income: for France, variables such as income, age, and the existence of a bequest explain less than 50 percent of inequalities in wealth levels. In Japan, Kitamura *et al.* (2001) confirm that the differences in saving behaviors across income classes are much wider than across age groups; they also find a huge heterogeneity of saving behaviors among elderly households.

To sum up, there is no real agreement among the empirical studies. Despite the fact that they all indicate that there is a wealth effect, cultural differences remain, leaving a serious need for further work about individuals' preferences. Nevertheless, at the end of the 1970s, LCH was considered to be powerful theory in explaining the saving rate. This theory is still very useful, as indicated by the huge theoretical and empirical literature about expected changes in the savings rate as the population ages or when the generosity of public retirement pensions decreases.

Studies of interactions between savings and pensions have been the source of abundant economic literature and debates among policy-makers since Feldstein's article, published in 1974, established a negative link between the existence of a public pension scheme and household savings. Subsequently, numerous economists have tried to test Feldstein's findings empirically but the results do not provide any clear conclusion.

Feldstein maintains that the creation of the OASDI (Old Age, Survivors and Disabled Institution) in 1937 in the United States prompted a huge decrease in Americans' saving rate (minus 50 percent). The argument is as follows: given the assumption that a pay-as-you-go public pension scheme provides the same yield as a fully funded scheme (a pension scheme that functions on a capitalization basis), the social security subsidies of the pay-as-you-go public scheme are a perfect substitute for the saving products. That means that each time the government increases social security pensions, the saving rate decreases. Feldstein adds that if social security contributions are so high as to cause people to work less, people will save more in order to finance a longer inactive period. However, according to his empirical results, the substitution effect dominates the income effect. These developments prompted a long economic debate (see Caussat 1992, or Jafari-Samimi 1984), notably between Feldstein and Barro. According to Barro (in Barro and Feldstein 1978), these social security transfers are neutral. The argument is the same as for public debt and holds for all negative transfers toward future generations: if public debt increases (through a public deficit that is caused by increased social transfers, for example), or if pension subsidies are generous, the current generation is aware that subsequent generations will have to pay for it, whether by taxes, or by contributions. The current generation will not consume the transfers and will have a higher saving rate in order to bequeath more to their children, a behavior called 'altruism', or 'Ricardian neutrality', which implies voluntary bequests. Altruism then increases the saving rate thoughout the life-cycle including retirement. This is one explanation for the particularly high saving rate of elderly people in Japan.

If there is a difference in the returns between fully funded and pay-as-you-go schemes (for example, the interest rate is higher than the rate of economic growth because there is a lack of capital due to a low saving rate), it is clear that the effect described by Feldstein is strengthened: an increase in the contribution rate impoverishes contributors and increases the deficit in both savings and productive capital.

The LCH theory is elegant but is clearly not powerful enough to explain the saving behaviors of households. A simple comparison between countries requires a lot of characteristics to be integrated. First, cultural differences are often neglected. A comparison between time preference in the French and American studies (Blanchet and Mahieu 2001) shows a much higher psychological discount rate for Americans than for the French population and a higher risk aversion in the French case. These two characteristics can explain the differences between saving rates. Second, altruism questions the link between age, savings, and intergenerational transfers; for example, it has often been suggested that the high saving rate among Japanese people over 75 is due to a high public deficit. Third, some authors have found that the recent increase in the ownership of risky assets can be attributed to the higher financial literacy of younger generations, highlighting the role of information.

## 2.2 Some Preliminary Views about Asset Allocation and Age

The first questions financial advisers ask clients often deal with the client's investment horizon: while equities are more risky in the short run, they are less risky in the long run and could be considered—at first glance—as the first-choice savings vehicle for retirement.

This is reflected in the forecasts made by financial experts when they write about the ageing process and its consequences. Because the number of retirees will increase relative to the number of contributors, the share of equities in institutional investors' portfolios will decrease while the share of bonds increases—a phenomenon that will be detrimental to equities prices. Table 10.1, drawn from Mantel (2000) for Merril Lynch, illustrates this kind of study.

At a more microeconomic level, financial advisers generally consider that older people should invest less in stocks than younger people (Mankiel 1996); a typical rule of thumb is that the equity share should be equal to 100 minus one's age. The three basic arguments that underpin this advice have been criticized by Jagannathan and Kocherlakota (1996). First, the fact that the risk of common stock declines with long-term ownership does not compensate for the fact that people are generally concerned by the huge loss that they can face with stock ownership.

Second, the argument which says that people have to draw on their wealth in order to fulfill their mid-life obligations such as children's education would lead people to save to meet these obligations and to switch from stocks to bonds when they age. However, families react differently when faced with these commitments. The only valid argument is the third one: while young people can diversify risk with their wages, or with the incomes that they will earn over a long period of activity, this is not possible for older people. They note that this is true only if the risks associated with their stock portfolio and their human capital are not correlated.

The debate is important, and draws on different arguments: financial advice relies on the statistical behavior of financial series while the criticisms levelled by Jagannathan and Kocherlakota are based on economic and psychological issues linked to risk aversion, personal life, social constraints, and position in the labor market. The main difficulty is to identify the different influences in order to extract from the debate the issues relevant to a discussion of what stems from individuals' preferences.

Table 10.1 Changes in asset allocation due to the ageing process, 2000–2050

|  | UK | | USA | | Netherlands | | Japan | |
| --- | --- | --- | --- | --- | --- | --- | --- | --- |
|  | 2000 | 2050 | 2000 | 2050 | 2000 | 2050 | 2000 | 2050 |
| Equities | 72% | 60% | 62% | 54% | 45% | 30% | 40% | 28% |
| Non-equities | 28% | 40% | 38% | 46% | 55% | 70% | 60% | 72% |

Source: Mantel (2000) for Merril Lynch.

# 3 Individual Preferences and Age

The diversification of households' wealth and portfolio according to age and life expectancy has become a huge topic in economic studies; first, it is of increasing importance for economists and policy-makers, and second, financial institutions have every incentive to understand this phenomenon, and its relationship to an ageing population. Despite their interest in maintaining demand for stocks, financial analysts advise people to reduce the share of stocks in their portfolios as they age. Do people follow this advice? While empirical analysis suggests that the answer is negative, theoretical analysis provides some interesting studies about age, risk perception, and portfolio selection.

While the LCH model has played a major part in explaining wealth accumulation with respect to age, the ideal model would link these life-cycle decisions to a portfolio selection model (see Markovitz 1959). This synthesis was done at the end of the 1960s by the lifetime portfolio selection theory after the seminal paper by Samuelson (1969). In his model, Merton (1969) studies the wealth accumulation and asset allocation of an individual who wants to maximize his expected utility according to his risk aversion. Merton's model is probably most relevant to professional portfolio managers but it still provides a good reference point for the key issues in this discussion.

## 3.1 The Influence of Age on the Composition of Portfolios: Empirical Studies

Most studies are based on panel studies but two types of analyses can be distinguished. First, virtual experiments (laboratory experiments where the situations are simulated) measure consumers' risk aversion or tolerance and link these indicators with the decisions individuals take in order to allocate their portfolios. A second type of analysis is based on surveys that provide effective portfolio allocation linked with other variables such as age, profession, and education. Within the first family of analyses, Barsky *et al.* (1997) and Guiso and Paiella (2001) draw two important conclusions:

- first, the agent's preferences cannot be represented with certainty by a simple function; and
- second, even after controlling for a number of variables, behavioral heterogeneity cannot be explained.

The results of studies of the relationships between age, preferences, and the holding of risky assets are more divergent. In a sample of 3,458 individuals, Guiso and Paiella find that absolute risk aversion is a decreasing function of consumers' resources—the richer individuals are, the less risk averse they are. They also find that risk tolerance is an increasing and concave function of wealth, which means that rich people take more risks than poor people but the increase in risk-taking is not proportional to the increase in wealth. This leads them to reject both isoelastic utility functions (characterized by constant relative risk aversion) and constant absolute risk aversion functions, the two types of functions that are supposed, in economic theory, to represent the consumer/saver's behavior. The implication is that the age risky portfolio should be upwardly sloping. The results are consistent with this: the share of risky assets increases with age, with portfolio share increasing by two points every ten years of age increase.

In a sample of 11,707 persons, Barsky *et al.* (1997) show a clear correlation between the risk tolerance index and stock holding while risk-free assets are characteristic of risk averse people. The relationship between risk tolerance and age is less clear since they show a slight U shape; but their sample is restricted to people over 50. They also try—but fail—to solve the 'equity premium puzzle' and suggest that many more variables than simply risk aversion characteristics need to be introduced in order to reproduce the saver's behavior. Effectively, according to theory, the aggregate risk aversion must be very high in order to explain the six points excess return of equities above the Treasury bills rate of return during the last century. This is obviously not the case in their measures of risk aversion.

Of course, this kind of 'virtual' study has to be treated with caution. A second group of studies aims to correlate observed behaviors with other variables. For France, and using data from the 'wealth survey' of 1998, El Mekkaoui-de Freitas *et al.* (2001) show that age has a clear influence on the ownership of risky assets—the probability of owning a diversified financial portfolio increases with age. Equally, individuals aged between 26 and 35 are less likely to own an entirely risk-free portfolio than those aged between 35 and 39, which shows the effect of linking the age and generation effects.

Ameriks and Zeldes (2002) separate these generation and age effects. Their data are based on five surveys of consumer finances to which they add the TIAA-CREF (the largest American private pension fund) data. They confirm the heterogeneity across individuals in portfolio allocations and the low activity of transfers for individuals. When looking at the whole sample, the authors observe a mild hump shape in the age pattern in equity shares in more recent years, and a strictly downward sloping age profile, and find that the proportion of stocks is constant with age. This shows, at least, a sensitivity to the period of estimation. The authors follow each cohort through time and find that equity allocation increases with age, while the time effect shows that most of the stock held has been 'pushed' by the recent high yields.

These studies, however, are of little help in explaining savers' preferences. At most, it appears that older people seem to be more risk tolerant than younger people, and people do not follow the advice they are given by their financial advisers. This clearly indicates that individuals make their own choices, according to their preferences. The pattern of these preferences now has to be clarified.

## 3.2 Individual Horizon and Financial Decision: The Theory

Merton's model is an extension of the portfolio choice theory to the continuous time case. As noted by Arrondel and Masson (1989), this rather technical formulation provides some advantages: on the one hand, it offers the possibility of reallocating the portfolio when necessary, and not at predetermined periods as in the discrete time model; on the otherhand, it can apply without restrictive assumptions such as normally distributed yields or quadratic preferences. This flexibility in the choice of the utility function is a very valuable card.

Merton made a number of assumptions: that information about assets and their yields, and the capital market is perfect; that there are no transaction costs, and human capital incomes are certain. This set of assumptions implies that the only source of uncertainty is asset prices and yields. These prices are generated by a stochastic process, which means that they are time independent and not self-correlated.

Merton first confirms Samuelson's separation theorem: for isoelastic marginal utility, consumption behavior is independent of past asset prices and consumption path. Finally, the asset allocation decision and the consumption decision are independent. The intuition of this result is that with an additive utility function, preferences will be time independent (with no age effect), which is why these portfolio choices are generally described as static. The isoelasticity of the preference function (the Constant Relative Risk Aversion or CRRA) entails an attitude toward financial risk that is independent of an individual's level of wealth. In addition, for the same CRRA utility function, Merton finds the same portfolio as Markovitz: the asset demand only depends upon the mean and variance of their yields.

Finally, in this model, the optimal portfolio selection rule is constant and depends only upon the degree of risk aversion: when relative risk aversion increases, the share of the portfolio which is invested in risky assets decreases, and is independent of the individual's age and accumulated wealth. That would mean that, in order to prepare for their retirement, all individuals own the same amount of risky assets and differ only in the amount of their savings. This seems at odds with the empirical evidence of diversity in households' portfolios and prompts calls for a better model. It also points to the important variables: individuals' preferences and the way they vary through the life-cycle, and individuals' environment, the so-called 'background risks'.

Ameriks and Zeldes (2002) take a simple example from Jagannathan and Kocherlakota (1996) in order to show how different preferences can generate an investment horizon or age effect. They imagine an individual whose utility function (representing his preferences) is such that his/her satisfaction depends on a target represented by a minimum level of wealth (fixed *ab initio*) that has to be reached at a given horizon. If the effective wealth is below this target, the individual's satisfaction drops to an infinitely negative level; if the effective wealth is over this target, satisfaction will grow proportionally to the difference between the effective level of wealth and the target. The result of the individual's choice is quite simple to understand: in order to avoid any possibility of ending up with less than the target, at each period the individual will place in the risk-free asset the discounted value of the target, taking as discount rate the risk-free return. If the risky asset return is greater than the risk-free return, total wealth will tend to grow, and the wealth invested in the risky asset will tend to grow as the horizon approaches. If the total wealth is constant, however, the wealth invested in the risky asset will shrink as the horizon approaches; the preferences and horizon effects depend upon the size of wealth. This purely mechanical approach lacks rationality; if wealth is really constrained so as not to increase, there are no incentives for having any risky assets even if their expected returns are very high.

Another example is given in a paper by Bommier and Rochet (2004) exploring the reasons why older people hold more risky assets than theory would indicate. They take a simple non-additive model where consumers' preferences depend on past preferences. In this case, a clear relationship between horizon length and risk aversion appears. The intuition can be found in a parallel with addictions in consumption; when past consumption of a good raises the marginal utility of present consumption, obviously the length of addiction influences present consumption (Becker and Murphy 1988).

Finally, Merton's CRRA utility function appears to be a very specific representation of preferences (Hanoch 1977) and the only function that provides two results: first, wealth has no impact on optimal portfolio; second, there is a separation between decisions about portfolio allocations and decisions about consumption and saving. The difficulty of representing the consumer/saver's psychology is compounded by the difficulty of taking into account his/her environment, the 'background risks'.

The trade-off between preferences and background risks faced by agents is perfectly represented by the 'Duration Enhances Risk' clause (Gollier and Zeckhauser 1997). The decisions of both young and older savers (or wealth owners) to invest in more or less risky assets will come from two factors acting in opposite ways. On the one hand, a longer horizon is synonymous with more flexibility, which means that young people will invest in more risky assets because they expect to live long enough to be able to reallocate their portfolio. On the otherhand, these young persons will face 'background risks' because they are still involved in the labor market: they risk unemployment, a decrease in the work for which they are paid, and so on. Portfolio composition is based on a consideration of these various phenomena. Gollier and Zeckhauser showed that the 'Duration Enhances Risk' (DER) clause is valid when the first factor (flexibility) dominates the second (labor market risks). This is the case when the risk tolerance is convex and a decreasing function of consumers' resources, when the young are less risk adverse than the old.

These results are interesting if compared to the empirical findings of Guiso and Paiella (2001): they find that the young are more risk averse than older consumers. This leads to a conclusion about the role of preferences: absolute risk aversion is a decreasing function of a consumer's resources, and risk tolerance, which is the opposite, is concave and increasing. Relative risk aversion appears to be an increasing function of wealth, allowing the wealth effect to moderate the decrease in absolute risk aversion. Of course, this shows that neither the CARA (Constant Absolute Risk Aversion) function nor the CRRA (Constant Relative Risk Aversion) function accurately represents household preferences, a finding consistent with the fact that young households face more background risks than the more mature.

Finally, two conclusions can be drawn. First, it appears to be impossible to set a simple and representative preference function (the so-called 'utility function') which explains an individual's savings and portfolio choices at any age; second, it is clear that these choices are the result of interactions between unconstrained preferences and background risks.

## 4 Individuals and 'Background Risks'

The study of background risks leads to a consideration of the risk that affects the consumer's resources and not only the variance of these resources. For example, a pension fund manager generally has a higher but more risky wage than a civil servant. Should we conclude that the civil servant should have a more risky financial portfolio? Or that the decisions are linked and that the civil servant is a civil servant precisely because he or she is risk averse and consequently holds a large share of risk-free assets. This is one of the conclusions by Barsky *et al.* (1997). They find that the degree of risk aversion depends on a range of factors including religion and ethnic origin, and this in turn influences behaviors: a smoker is more risk tolerant than a non-smoker, males are more risk tolerant than females, and risk tolerant individuals would accept a more risky situation in the labor market and a more risky financial portfolio.

## 4.1 Background Risks: What are They?

For Merton (1969), portfolio choices are independent of age. That means that age has no direct or indirect influence on portfolio choices. An indirect influence would be, for example, the influence of anxiety over job insecurity, especially if this increases with age. In Merton's model such influences do not exist for four reasons:

H1. the CRRA utility function implies an independence between wealth and portfolio choices (via an independence between wealth and preferences);

H2. the list of assets is reduced to financial assets (no human capital, i.e. no wages and no uncertainty over these wages);

H3. the yields of these assets are independently distributed over time; and

H4. the financial market is perfect.

We have already discussed the form of the utility function, and shown that the CRRA preferences are questionable. A consideration of background risks shows that some variables related to wealth may have an influence on portfolio choices. People have a life aside from their financial behavior and may experience uncertain income. Thus, the individual's total wealth, $W$, is seen as the sum of financial wealth ($W_{FI}$) and human wealth ($W_{HU}$). Human capital includes wages and other forms of income (e.g. self-employed persons' incomes, pensions, and retirement incomes). Human capital is deeply correlated with age since at the beginning of one's lifespan human capital is at its maximum and decreases with age. With a CRRA preference function, the total share of risk-free assets will be constant over the life-cycle, keeping constant the total share of risk-free assets (human and financial) with a declining amount of (risk-free) human capital, which implies an increase in the share of risk-free assets in the portfolio. In fact, both may have uncertain yields: financial returns, of course, and human capital incomes like wages, pensions, and various social subsidies because social policies can change. A household's human capital can also be affected by exogenous events such as divorce or health problems. The portfolio pattern will then depend on the correlation between the assets' yields. If financial yields are perfectly correlated with human wealth yields then—in order to keep constant the share of risky assets—the share of risky financial assets will increase with age (again because human wealth, which is now risky, decreases with age). If financial yields are not correlated with human capital yields, in order to keep constant the risky asset share, individuals will increase the share of risky financial assets while (risky) human capital stock decreases. These considerations show that even with a structure of preference that would imply independence between portfolio choices and age, the introduction of background risks provides age effects.

Another type of risk concerns future incomes of children and grandchildren. If the altruism assumption holds—if individuals care about the welfare of future generations—they will organize their wealth accumulation and allocation in order to bequeath. This radically changes the time horizon of their portfolio and will radically change their asset allocation. When the altruism hypothesis holds, an individual takes care of his/her children and future descendents, and includes their welfare in his/her utility function arguments. The implication of this is that these people will act as if their lives were infinite. In these circumstances, reference to age has no meaning unless there are breaks in the time horizon, like succession taxes, differences in preferences between parents and children. This could explain, for example, a preference for bequeathing equities to real estate.

Do background risks matter? Empirical studies do not succeed in showing an adequacy between data and theory. For France, El Mekkaoui-de Freitas *et al.* (2001) look at various variables including professional status. Theoretical considerations would suggest that the self-employed have a smaller share of risky assets than civil servants. In fact, they have a larger share of risky assets, providing confirmation that they are less risk averse than civil servants. Again, the theory is not confirmed if we look at household composition: single people and couples with no children are more likely to own risky assets than households with children; the risks of unemployment and disease appear not to influence the holding of risky assets. The only significant variable is home ownership, which increases the probability and the share of risky assets. A possible explanation is that home ownership can be perceived as a cover against background risks. For Italy, Guiso and Paiella (2001) reach similar conclusions—these variables explain little. Finally, these studies seem to confirm that households are not really active in their allocation of assets but passive, one of the main findings of Ameriks and Zeldes (2002).

The share of risky assets is smaller for individuals with a low degree of education. Here again it is quite difficult to capture the true mechanism: is it a consequence of low human capital or because managing a financial portfolio requires financial literacy? This meets the 'experienced saver argument': stock markets have high entry costs which tend to ensure that only experienced savers get in. These arguments are mainly based on the idea of a degree of imperfection in the financial markets.

## 4.2 The Effects of Market Imperfections and Institutional Framework

This leads us to the last assumption made by Merton (1969) about perfection of the markets. In reality, markets are far from perfect so that the composition of wealth can be far from the theoretical optimum. Adjustment costs on assets markets, transaction costs, liquidity constraints, information costs, and institutional environment are some of the factors that ensure that actual portfolio choices differ from those that would result from the application of economic theory. Many countries, for example, organize their fiscal policy in order to produce a particular saving behavior: incentives for pension funds, life insurance, savings for housing like the German *Bausparkassen* or French *Epargne logement*.

The weight of information costs and the need for a degree of financial literacy if one wants to hedge on the financial markets have been evaluated by Clark and d'Ambrosio (2002). They found a positive and significant relationship between financial literacy, on the one hand, and saving behavior and asset allocation, on the other. According to them, informed individuals adopt saving behavior which is more consistent with population ageing and the anticipated financial imbalances in public pension schemes, and adopt an asset allocation which is closer to their real needs. A financial culture, linked with a lower risk aversion, is often given as a reason for the higher ownership of risky assets by American or British savers compared to households in Continental Europe. According to some authors, these information costs are the source of the so-called 'stock holding puzzle'. This 'puzzle' is rooted in the idea that everyone should hold some equities in their financial portfolio, which is not the case. This 'experienced saver argument' was used by King and Leape (1987) to explain why older people hold more risky assets than younger ones.

# 5 Conclusions

Does the theory work? Modigliani's life-cycle theory is a very powerful framework to explain how agents should save rationally, and provides some explanation for observed changes in saving rates, with the addition of certain assumptions and external factors such as expectations and cultural characteristics.

Portfolio selection raises some other problems. At first glance, it appears impossible to represent households' preferences in terms of the usual utility function. On closer inspection, it seems that these behaviors are based on a whole range of factors, the implications of which are hard to distinguish. These factors can be placed in three groups:

1. The preferences themselves. Despite a review of the literature in this chapter, it is still not clear if individuals are more or less risk adverse as they age. In addition, if they care about their children and grandchildren they can be considered as immortal as economic players, throwing into doubt the whole age/risk relationship.
2. Even if we assume that individuals' relative risk aversion is constant over age, the population and its habits change. Let's imagine a demographic change that produces a higher proportion of males in the population. As males are

less risk averse than females, macroeconomic studies would show increasing risk tolerance, but would not learn anything about individuals' preferences.
3. Even microeconomic studies dealing with individuals and controlling for the above problems have difficulty in capturing the rationality of behaviors because of 'background risks' and the variability of the effects of these risks upon individuals.

In the end, the mix of characteristics and preferences makes the perfect model difficult to build and the agent's preferences difficult to summarize, a conclusion borne out by the enormous heterogeneity of behaviors in portfolio choices. And what about institutional characteristics such as changes in legislation, macroeconomics, differences in financial engineering? Artus (2005) noticed that portfolio allocations are deeply influenced by macroeconomics and by regulations; in Europe and the United States, the share of bonds and real estate within institutional investors' portfolios has increased since 2000. He links this to increasing public deficits and the new accounting principles (IFRS), which are detrimental to equity ownership by households who direct their savings toward institutional investors. Another explanation is that institutional investors follow their own advice; in this case, the structure of portfolio changes comes from the increased share of intermediated savings in household portfolios. But this change remains unexplained.

Two issues emerge as important territory for future research. The first is the altruism hypothesis. This has been widely used to explain why the saving rates of older people are often higher than LCH theory would admit. However, as far as we know, it is used to a lesser extent when trying to solve the 'portfolio allocation puzzle': if people care about future generations, they will leave them some wealth to meet any increase in taxes. But what about portfolio composition? If people really care about their children, why should they bequeath them a financial portfolio that may be inappropriate because it is illiquid or constraining?

The importance of the second issue is reflected in the large number of papers devoted to 'behavioral finance' following Kahneman and Tversky's publication in 1979. Since then this line of inquiry into modern finance has tried to capture the psychological factors which result in actual financial portfolios being very far removed from the teachings of economic theory. Undoubtedly, there are some interesting inquiries to be made in this promising line of research.

# References

AMERIKS, J., and ZELDES, S. P. (2002). 'How do household portfolio shares vary with age?' *TIAA-CREF Institute Working Paper*, No. 6-120101.

ARRONDEL, L. (1993). *Cycle de vie et composition du patrimoine: un regard théorique.* Paris: Economica.

—— and MASSON, A. (1989). 'Déterminants individuels de la composition du patrimoine: France 1980'. *Revue économique*, 40/3: 441–502.

—— —— (2003). 'Le patrimoine et ses logiques d'accumulation'. Delta-CNRS Working paper, No. 2003-26.

ARTUS, P. (2005). 'Les effets théoriques du vieillissement s'observent-ils dans la realité?' Flash IXIS, No. 2005-19.

BARRO, R., and FELDSTEIN, M. S. (1978). *The Impact of Social Security on Private Saving: Evidence from the U.S. Time Series*. Washington, D.C.: American Enterprise Institute.

BARSKY, R. B., JUSTER, F. T., KIMBALL, M. S., and SHAPIRO, M. D. (1997). 'Preference parameters and behavioral heterogeneity: an experimental approach in health and retirement study'. *The Quarterly Journal of Economics*, 112/2: 537–79.

BECKER, G. S., and MURPHY, K. M. (1988). 'A theory of rational addiction'. *Journal of Political Economy*, 96/4: 675–700.

BERNHEIM, B. D., SKINNER, J., and WEINBERG, S. (1997). 'What accounts for the variation in retirement wealth among U.S. households?' Stanford University Working Paper, No. 97–035.

BLANCHET, D., and MAHIEU, R. (2001). 'Une analyse microéconometrique des comportements de retraits d'activité'. *Revue d'économie politique*, special issue, *Epargne et retraite*, 9–30.

BOMMIER, A., and ROCHET, J.-C. (2004). 'Risk aversion and planning horizon'. Paper presented at the RTN project workshop on 'Financing retirement in Europe', 13–15, May Louvain-la-Neuve.

CAUSSAT, L. (1992), 'Retraite et épargne dans la littérature américaine'. *Revue d'économie financière*, No. 23: 159–72.

CLARK, R. and L., d'AMBROSIO, M. (2002). 'Saving for retirement: the role of financial education'. TIAA-CREF Institute Working Paper No. 4-070102-A.

EL MEKKAOUI-DE FREITAS, N., LAVIGNE, A., and MAHIEU, R. (2001). 'La détention d'actifs risques selon l'age: une étude économetrique'. *Revue d'économie politique*, special issue, *Epargne et retraite*, 59–78.

FELDSTEIN, M. (1974). 'Social security, induced retirement and aggregate capital accumulation'. *Journal of Political Economy*, 82: 905–26.

GOLLIER, C., and ZECKHAUSER, R. (1997). 'Horizon length and portfolio risk'. NBER Working Paper, No. 216 (Oct.).

GUISO, L., and PAIELLA, M. (2001). 'Risk aversion, wealth and background risk'. CEPR Discussion Paper, No. 2728.

HANOCH, G. (1977). 'Risk aversion and consumer preferences'. *Econometrica*, 45/2 (Mar.): 413–26.

JAFARI-SAMIMI, A. (1984). 'Social security and private savings: empirical analysis'. *Public Finance*, No. 2: 226–45.

JAGANNATHAN, R., and KOCHERLAKOTA, N. R. (1996). 'Why should older people invest less in stocks than younger people?' *Federal Reserve Bank of Minneapolis Quaterly Review*, 20/3 (summer): 11–23.

KAHNEMAN, D., and TVERSKY, A. (1979). 'Prospect theory: an analysis of decision under risk'. *Econometrica*, 47/2: 263–91.

KING, M. A., and LEAPE, J. I. (1987). 'Asset accumulation, information and the life cycle'. *NBER Working paper*, No. 2392.

KITAMURA, Y., TAKAYAMA, N., and ARITA, F. (2001). 'Household savings and wealth distribution in Japan'. Institute of Economic Research, Hitotsubashi University. Project on Intergenerational Equity, Discussion Paper, No. 2001–38.

MANKIEL, B. (1996). *A Random Walk down Wall Street Including a Life Cycle Guide to Personal Investing*, 6th edn. New York: Norton.

MANTEL J. (2000). 'Demographics and the funded pension system, ageing populations, mature pension funds and negative cash flow'. Merril Lynch, 30 Oct.

MARKOVITZ, H. (1959). *Portfolio Selection*. New York: Wiley.

MERTON, R. C. (1969). 'Life time portfolio selection under uncertainty: the continuous time case'. *Review of Economics and Statistics*, 51/3: 247–57.

MODIGLIANI, F., and BRUMBERG, R. (1954). 'Utility analysis and the consumption function: an interpretation of the cross-section data', in K. K. Kurihara (ed.), *Post-Keynesian Economics*. New Brunswick, N. J.: Rutgers University Press, 388–436.

SAMUELSON, P. A. (1969). 'Lifetime portfolio selection by dynamic stochastic programming'. *Review of Economics and Statistics*, 51/3: 239–46.

CHAPTER 11

# FUNDING, SAVING, AND ECONOMIC GROWTH

E. PHILIP DAVIS AND YU-WEI HU

## 1 INTRODUCTION

It is anticipated that by 2050, one in four people worldwide will be aged above 65 (United Nations 2002). Rising longevity, declining fertility rates, and the unfunded nature of pay-as-you-go (PAYG) systems are posing financial difficulties for governments in both OECD countries and emerging market economies (EMEs), leading many countries to rethink their pension systems. Typically, they switch partially or wholly from unfunded pay-as-you-go (PAYG) systems to funded systems, such as the three-pillar World Bank model (1994), or from defined-benefit (DB) systems to defined-contribution (DC) systems.

A key issue in pension reform is whether such a shift from PAYG to funding is largely a matter of reallocation of the financial burden of ageing (with the risk of a generation paying twice), or whether funding improves economic performance sufficiently to generate some or all of the resources required to meet the needs of an ageing population. The underlying issue is that with characteristics such as greater actuarial fairness, transparency, and flows of funds to securities markets, a funded system may prompt greater economic efficiency than

PAYG, which is of wider benefit to the economy. There are several aspects to this question. One is whether funding leads to an increase in saving, which permits higher capital formation. A second is whether, independently of the impact on saving, there are effects of funding which lead to higher economic growth, for example via positive externalities generating more efficient capital and labor markets. A third is whether a direct impact of funding on growth can be discerned. We investigate the literature on these issues and seek to draw conclusions.

# 2 Saving and Funding

In this section, we analyze theory and empirical work on pension funding and saving, looking successively at personal saving and national saving. It should be noted at the outset that population ageing will of itself generate changes in saving which may have a major macroeconomic impact. See for example Disney (1996), who noted that, consistent with the life-cycle, savings rates tend to decline in countries where there are a larger number of retired people. These changes in savings rates will undoubtedly be channeled via pension funds, but pension funds may not be the causal factor in such shifts.

## 2.1 Personal Saving

On a superficial view, it seems unlikely that funding has a significant effect on savings. Empirically, the countries where pension funds are most important—the United States and the United Kingdom—are also known for low personal saving. Indeed, in the United Kingdom there is thought to be a major 'savings gap', reflecting underestimation of saving needs for retirement (Davis 2004). There are also theoretical objections. The basic argument against funding having any effect on saving is that individuals choose a lifetime savings pattern separately from its distribution, so a rise in one component of wealth (such as pension funds) should be fully offset by falls elsewhere, either by reducing forms of discretionary saving or by borrowing. This offset will be particularly likely to occur when pension wealth and discretionary savings are close substitutes. Nevertheless, in principle, funding could generate increased saving via the following channels (for an overview, see Kohl and O'Brien 1998):

- Illiquidity of pension assets may mean that other household wealth may not be reduced one-to-one when pension assets increase, because households do not see such claims as a perfect substitute for liquid saving such as deposits. This argument is supported by the fact that many pension laws prohibit pensioners from mortgaging their future pension benefits.
- There may be liquidity constraints, whereby some households are not free to borrow. These may imply that any forced saving (such as pension contributions) cannot be offset either by borrowing or by reducing discretionary saving.
- The interaction between the need for retirement income and retirement behavior may increase saving in a growing economy, as workers increase their saving to provide for an earlier planned retirement.
- As unfunded social security is typically seen to reduce saving because it implies an accumulation of implicit claims on future income, a switch toward funding of pensions should increase it.
- There might be a 'recognition effect' as people who witness the transition via pension reform from PAYG to funded systems realize the importance of saving for retirement regardless of whether they are directly affected.
- Tax incentives that raise the rate of return on saving via life insurance or pension funds may encourage higher aggregate saving (McCarthy and Neuberger 2004). This tax deferral arrangement is designed to encourage pension saving.

Empirical research suggests that growth in funded pension schemes does appear to boost personal saving, but not one-to-one, as it is offset by a decline in discretionary saving. Much of the literature is focused on the impact on household saving of the growth of US defined-benefit funds, and on balance it suggests an increase in personal saving of around 0.35–0.5 percent results from every unit increase in pension fund assets (Pesando 1992), though the cost to the public sector of the tax incentives to pension funds reduces the overall benefit to national savings to around 0.2 percent.

Effects are less marked for defined-contribution funds, in which the worker is more likely to be able to borrow against pension wealth and participation is generally optional. On the other hand, Poterba *et al.* (1996) suggest that 401(k)[1] accounts in the United States have added to aggregate saving. Tax incentives are one important factor in encouraging net saving by this route, but employer matching of contributions, payroll deduction schemes, and information seminars may also be relevant. For example, for families accumulating both IRAs and 401(k) between 1987 and 1991, mean total financial assets increased from $37,882 to $44,432 while there was no decline in non-pension financial assets.

Whereas funding has a positive effect on personal saving, evidence also suggests that unfunded systems have a damaging effect on savings. Edwards (1995) finds that unfunded social security appears to lower private saving in developing countries. In addition, Feldstein (1995) suggests that personal saving rises 0.5 percent for every unit decrease in US social security wealth (and vice versa).[2] Rossi and Visco (1995) find a comparable figure of 0.66 percent for Italy.

Kohl and O'Brien (1998) argue that the displacement of private saving by pay-as-you-go is more likely, the more imperfect capital markets are. For example, Reisen and Bailliu (1997) used data from 11 countries, including both OECD and non-OECD nations, and found that the impact of reform on saving is eight times larger for non-OECD countries, which have more imperfect capital markets, than in OECD countries. On the other hand, even in a liberalized financial system, credit constraints will affect lower income individuals particularly severely, as they have no assets to pledge and less secure employment. Therefore, forced institutional saving will tend to boost their overall saving particularly markedly (for evidence, see Bernheim and Scholz 1992). This point is of particular relevance in countries with compulsory private pensions, such as Australia, which could thus anticipate a rise in personal saving (Edey and Simon 1996) and also in poorer countries such as Chile.

## 2.2 National Saving

James (1996), the principal author of *Averting the Old Age Crisis* (World Bank 1994), argues that one main advantage of the World Bank multi-pillar model is that national saving as well as personal saving could be boosted. But the effect of pension fund growth on personal saving could be offset at the level of national saving by the impact on public finances of the costs involved in the transition to a privately funded system, as well as the costs of tax subsidies to personal saving.

A key aspect of this issue is how pension-reforming governments finance existing social security obligations. If the government tries to finance the implicit pension debts by public debts, then public savings would decrease, so the overall national saving rate might be unchanged or even fall. For example, a simulation study by Hviding and Merette (1998) shows that debt-financed transitions may not have material effects on national saving and output; all that may happen is that the government has altered the form of the debt. If such transition burdens are partly financed by tax, they are more likely to increase national saving, as public saving would not decline significantly, other things being equal. But even tax-financed transitions may, according to some authors, have at most a small positive effect on national saving in the long term (Cifuentes and Valdes Prieto 1997). Of course, a further key issue is the *size* of the transition burden, which depends on the generosity of the system and the benefits accrued, linked in turn to the scope of ageing.

Samwick (1999), working with a panel of countries, found that no countries except Chile experienced an increase in gross national saving rates after pension reform moved towards non-PAYG systems. He included control variables such as the log of per capita income, per capita income growth, the private credit to income ratio, demographic indicators, and the urbanization rate to avoid omitted variables bias. On the other hand, cross-section evidence, based on data of 1990 and averages of 1991–4, suggested that countries with PAYG systems had lower saving rates than other countries. This finding is consistent with Orszag and Stiglitz's claim (2001) that it is entirely possible that the introduction of a PAYG scheme reduces national saving, but a shift to an individual account system does not necessarily increase national saving.

# 3 Wider Impacts on Financial Markets

## 3.1 Pension Funds and Financial Development

Pension reform can also be viewed more broadly as aiding financial development, which may also in turn stimulate growth.[3] A quantitative impact of development of pension funds on capital markets must arise mainly from differences in behavior from the personal sector. Pension funds in most cases hold a greater proportion of equities and bonds than households.[4] These differences can be explained partly by time horizons, which for households are relatively short, whereas given the long-term nature of liabilities, pension fund portfolios may concentrate on long-term assets yielding the highest returns. But given their size, pension funds also have a comparative advantage in compensating for risk by pooling and diversifying across assets whose returns are imperfectly correlated, an advantage linked also to lower transactions costs for large deals and the ability to invest in large indivisible assets such as property. Unlike banks, pension funds tend to rely on public rather than private information in investment and hence seek relatively liquid assets.

The implication is that, even if there were no increase in saving and wealth, a switch to funding could increase the supply of long-term funds to capital markets. There might be increases in the supply of equities, long-term corporate bonds, and securitized debt instruments, and a reduction in bank deposits, so long as individuals do not adjust the liquidity of their portfolios to fully offset the effects of growth of pension funds—and so long as the macroeconomic environment favors long-term financing. Full offsetting is unlikely, especially if pension assets are defined benefit or substitute for highly illiquid implicit social security wealth. Empirical work by King and Dicks-Mireaux (1988) found no such offset by households for Canada, while Davis (1988) obtained similar results for the G-5.

Catalan *et al.* (2000) sought to identify whether there is a Granger-causality relation between capital markets and contractual savings. They use two capital market indicators, stock market capitalization and stock market value traded across 26 countries, among which six are developing countries. They give evidence that contractual saving institutions, for example pension funds, Granger-cause capital market development. The potential benefits of developing contractual saving sectors are, unsurprisingly, stronger for developing countries than for developed countries.

Such overall shifts to long-term assets tend to reduce the cost and increase the availability of equity and long-term debt financing to companies, and hence may raise productive[5] capital formation. Particularly for existing firms with small equity bases, there may be important competitive advantages to be reaped from equity issuance from growth potential as well as reducing the risks of financial distress in case of economic downturn; Furthermore, long-term debt finance correlates with higher growth for manufacturing firms (Caprio and Demirgüç-Kunt 1998). Economically, efficient capital formation could in turn raise output and growth itself, independently of a change in saving (Holzmann 1997). Higher growth will feed back on saving. 'Endogenous growth' effects of an increase in capital investment on labor productivity may be particularly powerful in developing countries if a switch from pay-as-you-go to funding induces a shift from the labor-intensive and low productivity 'informal' sector to the capital-intensive and high productivity 'formal' sector (Corsetti and Schmidt-Hebbel 1997).[6]

In this context, a panel study focused on 33 EMEs by Walker and Lefort (2002) finds that pension fund growth accompanies a decreased dividend yield and increased price-to-book ratio, implying a drop in the cost of capital. This result is robust when pension funds are proxied by four sets of variables, that is (a) a dummy variable, (b) the share of stock in pension portfolios, (c) the ratio of pension investment in stocks and private bonds to total market capitalization, (d) the ratio of pension fund assets to GDP. Other explanatory variables are inflation, per capita income, bank assets/GDP, and a dummy variable for the region.

In terms of bond markets, in recent years governments have tried to attract foreign pension funds by modernizing the infrastructure of their public bond markets as well as facilitating private bond issuance. In a cross-country study, Impavido *et al.* (2003) find a positive relationship between contractual saving assets and bond market capitalization/GDP, whereby a 1 percent increase in the former leads to a 0.4 percent rise in the latter. On the other hand, they use the value of aggregate outstanding public and private bond issuance to proxy bond market development, when the former is driven by government needs. Hu (2004) shows that in a panel error correction model, growth of pension funds also stimulates *private* bond finance, notably in developing countries, both in the short and long run.

Besides inducing shifts to longer-term assets, funding also increases international portfolio investment if permitted. On the one hand, international investment may be seen as a loss of potential to develop domestic capital markets. On the other, by generating inflows of profits, interest, and dividends, holdings of assets offshore can actually help to contribute to greater stability of national income (Fontaine 1997). This may in turn benefit growth, since fixed investment responds negatively to uncertainty.

Besides the quantitative effects noted above, the development of pension funds is also likely to trigger qualitative developments in financial markets which may benefit growth via better resource allocation. These developments are in general subject to positive externalities, as, once instituted, other investors may also benefit from them. One qualitative improvement is financial innovation, which early on in financial development may include equities, junior markets, corporate bonds, securitization, Certificates of Deposit (CDs), derivative markets, and indexed instruments. In OECD countries, pension funds' need for hedging against shortfalls of assets against liabilities has led to the development of a number of recent financial innovations such as zero coupon bonds and index futures (Bodie 1990). Similarly, immunization strategies and the development of indexation strategies by and for pension funds has increased demand for futures and options.

Modernization of the infrastructure of securities markets, as required by pension funds, should entail improved clearing and settlement on the one hand, and provide more sensitive price information on the other, thus improving resource allocation. As a consequence, it may help to reduce the cost or increase the availability of capital market funds, and aid industrial development and growth as well as facilitating privatizations. In developing countries, pension funds' influence may be seen in terms of the development of the overall market infrastructure (such as trading and settlement systems) and enhancement of liquidity. In OECD countries, given their focus on liquidity[7] and lesser emphasis on investor protection, pension funds offer benefits to wholesale equity markets, as opposed to heavily regulated retail markets. They are footloose in their trading, and thus make the business of trading 'contestable' rather than monopolistic, and facilitate its concentration. Increased pension-funding would raise the proportion of 'wholesale' trading activity which would be willing to shift between markets. It would also put pressure on cartels in bond issuance and price-fixing in equity trading.

There may be important indirect benefits in this context, as pension funds press for improvements in the 'architecture of allocative mechanisms' (Greenwald and Stiglitz 1990), including better accounting, auditing, brokerage, and information disclosure. The development of modern banking and insurance supervision, new securities and corporate laws, junior equity markets, and credit rating agencies are also stimulated. Such improvements are crucial for financial development and growth more generally.

Development of equity markets and their dominance by pension funds would have implications not just for companies' balance sheet structure—with potentially lower debt–equity ratios—but also for corporate governance, implying a greater degree of control by capital markets and pension funds. In this context, the 'corporate governance movement' in OECD countries reflects dissatisfaction among pension funds with the costs of the takeover mechanism, and preference for direct influence as equity holders on management (Davis 1995, 2002). It also links to indexation by large funds which seek to improve the performance of firms they have to hold, as well as more generally where pension funds are very large and cannot readily sell their participations without significant market movements against them. In practice, however, the scope of 'direct influence' is limited in most EMEs; Brazil and South Africa are two exceptions.

There is a growing literature on the impact of corporate governance initiatives on performance, albeit mainly focusing on the effects on share prices *per se*. Positive results may be favorable to economic growth via efficiency gains. For example, on the positive side, Wahal (1996), in a sample of 43 cases in the United States, found that efforts by institutional investors to promote organizational change via negotiation with management (as opposed to proxy proposals) are associated with gains in share prices. On the negative side, Del Guercio and Hawkins (1999) found no evidence that activism had a significant effect on stock returns over the three years following the proposals. Evidence from outside the United States on the effectiveness of corporate governance initiatives is sparse, but Faccio and Lasfer (2000) show that the monitoring role of UK pension funds is concentrated among mature and low-performing firms. Furthermore, in the long run, the firms in which pension funds have large stakes markedly improve their stock returns.

These studies are based on micro evidence and hence only indirectly bear on the issue of whether pension funding affects growth. Davis (2002, 2003) undertook macro work based on the share of equities held by pension funds and life insurers. The results are complementary to micro work if the view is taken that the effects of takeovers, institutional activism, and so on are not just apparent in the performance of targeted firms but also in the wider economy. This may plausibly be the case if managers of 'unaffected' firms nonetheless change their behavior in response to the threat of such action. Davis found results consistent with a disciplining role of institutions, particularly life insurers and pension funds, in the Anglo-Saxon countries. They exert restraint of investment, and lead to a boost to dividends and to total factor productivity, while they are favourable to R & D (research and development). The trend for corporate use of equity to rise, for equity shares of institutions to increase, and for traditional corporate governance structures to break down in Continental Europe and Japan suggests these results could hold there in the future as well as in EMEs.

## 3.2 Developments in Chile

A number of the phenomena highlighted in the section above are illustrated by the experience of Chile. It provides a test-bed for the effects of pension reform on a relatively simple financial system. Holzmann (1997) points to the fact that Chilean pension funds grew from zero in 1980 to 39 percent of GDP in 1995, rising to over 60 percent in 2002. As of 2000, 65 percent of government debts, 12 percent of time deposits and bank bonds, 56 percent of mortgage bonds, 40 percent of corporate bonds, and 7 percent of equity were held by pension funds (Walker and Lefort 2002). Pension funds may have played a major role in stimulating the rise in private saving observed over this period (Morandé 1998). This accompanied an expansion of overall financial assets from 28 percent of GDP in 1980 to 68 percent in 1993 (Fontaine 1997), with pension assets accounting for a third of this total. Initially, funds were invested mainly in debt securities, owing to regulatory prohibition of equity investment, but not solely those of the government—also bank certificates of deposit (CDs) and mortgage bonds. Debt maturities increased as a consequence of the development of pension funds to 12 to 20 years by 1990. Equity investment was permitted in 1985 and holdings have grown to over 30 percent of assets. This accompanied and encouraged a marked expansion of equity market capitalization from 32 percent of GDP in 1988 to 90 percent in 1993. In the early 1990s, closed companies were encouraged by high price/earnings (P/E) ratios to go public and accept standard record-keeping and auditing practices, thanks to better access to pension fund financing. In 1991 the pension funds held one-third of public bonds, two-thirds of private bonds, and 10 percent of equities.

Fontaine (1997) also notes that pension fund development facilitated internal resource transfers. It enabled the Chilean government to service its international debts without extreme fiscal adjustment, which was elsewhere damaging to the real economy, by providing a domestic source of borrowing without requiring excessively high interest rates (in fact the debt was generally CPI-indexed). Correspondingly, public sector debt rose from 5 percent of GDP in 1980 to 28 percent in 1990. Later, the demand of pension funds enabled debt conversion—by both private and public institutions—to occur smoothly. In addition, the fact that pension funds were not permitted to invest internationally till 1989, and then only in a limited way, explains why the capital markets in Chile grew in size and depth so rapidly. Again, given the existence of domestic long-term institutions and the high domestic saving that pension reform helped to stimulate, Chile is probably better insulated from the shifting behavior of international investors; it had a lower correction after the 1994 Mexican crisis than other Latin American markets. Hansell (1992) suggests development of pension funds has been a major factor behind Chile's bonds being rated investment-grade, the first Latin American country to be so rated since the debt crisis.

Schmidt-Hebbel (1999) estimated that pension reform in Chile raised the saving rate. Given the difficulty of pinning down how the pension reform was financed in

Chile, he considered three cases, that is, fiscal contraction financing of pension reform at the levels of 100, 75, and 50 percent. On balance, he suggests that between 10 and 45 percent of the rise in national saving could be explained by pension reform, with the remainder being explained by structural reform, such as tax reform and so on.

## 3.3 Potential Costs of Pension Fund Growth for Financial Markets

An aspect that could weaken the growth benefits of funding is pension funds' direct effect on liquidity and price volatility. In normal times, pension funds, being willing to trade, having good information, and low transactions costs, should speed the adjustment of prices to fundamentals. It need hardly be added that such market sensitivity generates an efficient allocation of funds, and acts as a useful discipline on lax macroeconomic policies. Again, the liquidity that institutional activity generates may dampen volatility, as is suggested by lower average share price volatility in countries with large institutional sectors.[8] And evidence on average day-to-day asset price fluctuations shows no tendency for such volatility to increase (Davis and Steil 2001).

It has been shown that the growth of pension funds reduces security price volatility for 33 EMEs (Walker and Lefort 2002). This negative link between pension funds and market volatility might be justified by the large investors' ability to access more information, thus restraining prices from deviating too far away from fundamentals. In contrast, Davis (2003), using a data set covering both pension and life insurance assets across G-7 countries, found a positive link between equity price volatility and the share of equity held by pension funds and life insurance across both Anglo-Saxon countries and Continental European countries and Japan (CEJ). He notes, however, that such a link might reflect a shift in sectoral holdings of equities rather than institutional holdings *per se*.

Besides these average patterns, periodically some unfamiliar systemic risks may arise in institutionalized and securitized financial systems, about which regulators need to learn, and which will not be captured by econometric assessments depicting long-term average behavior (Davis and Steil 2001). One is extreme price volatility after a shift in expectations and asset allocations (such as the 1987 crash and the 1992 European Monetary System crisis). Another is a protracted collapse of market liquidity and issuance after similar portfolio shifts (as for Russia/Long-Term Capital Management in 1998). Such periodic market-crisis events were characterized by heavy involvement of pension funds in both buying and selling waves; international investment, and signs of overreaction to the fundamentals, and excessive optimism prior to the crisis. Underlying factors appear to be influences on fund managers that induce herding behavior. In countries such as Chile, 'herding' may also be stimulated by regulations which require pension funds to obtain similar returns.

The growth of pension funds is likely to entail increased competition for the banking sector. Such competition may lead to heightened efficiency of banks, thus aiding economic development. Disintermediation, however, may also help to generate banking problems; the lessons of history from OECD countries suggest a need for vigilance, particularly if disintermediation coincides with deregulation and hence heightened competition within the banking sector.

Evidence that pension funds are reticent in investing equity in small firms is also a cause for concern, despite the fact that small firms' potential for innovation, growth, and job creation is widely seen as crucial for economic growth.[9] For example, Sias (1996) shows that institutional holding of the largest US firms is over 47 percent on average over the period 1977–91, and for the smallest, only 8 percent. The consequence of neglect of small firms by pension funds (assuming individual investors do not fill the gap) may be biases in the economy toward sectors with larger firms (for even if small firms can obtain bank loan finance, growth potential via debt is likely to be more restricted than with equity in addition). This may be contrary to the comparative advantage of the economy as a whole. It suggests a need for venture capital funds, junior equity markets, and appropriate pension fund regulation, as well as an ongoing role for banks.

Regular performance evaluation of pension fund managers by trustees is said to underpin the short-termist hypothesis, entailing undervaluation of firms with good earnings prospects and a willingness of funds to sell shares in takeover battles. This in turn is held to discourage long-term investment or R & D as opposed to distribution of dividends, which would imply a suboptimal transfer and allocation of resources. Some recent empirical research seems to confirm the existence of short-termist effects in the UK, with overvaluation of profits in the short term (Miles 1993).

## 4 PENSION FUNDING AND LABOR MARKETS

During 1950–70, there was a very sharp fall in participation rate for those men over state pension age (65+) in EU countries. Early retirement has also become endemic—for men aged 55–64, there was a sharp fall in labor market participation during 1970–90, although this trend was less clear for women aged 55–64. One contributing factor is the disincentives to labor supply embedded in public pension systems (Blondal and Scarpetta 1998). In view of such problems, James (1998) notes 'the close linkage between benefits and contributions, in a defined-contribution plan is designed to reduce labor market distortions'. It also motivates the defined-contribution PAYG schemes recently introduced in some European countries such as Sweden and Italy.

Early retirement is also prevalent in the UK, although PAYG is not generous and defined-benefit occupational schemes were historically dominant. Davis (2004) suggests that early retirement there to some extent reflects social preferences to retire early by those with occupational pension funds and the relative generosity of the public scheme of disability benefits. But it also reflects long-term restructuring of manufacturing, where closure of firms has left many older workers with inappropriate skills, lack of demand in the local labor market, and/or unwillingness to accept lower pay than younger workers, even if they are less productive. These aspects interact with early retirement provisions of defined benefit occupational pension schemes. In some cases, firms were seeking to avoid the large accrual of benefits in defined-benefit funds close to retirement—but most commonly early retirement is used simply to deal with redundancy via voluntary severance, often on actuarially generous terms. From this it would seem that it is the type of pension (defined benefit or defined contribution) and not the funding *per se* that has an impact on labour supply. Meanwhile, UK pension reform in the 1980s and 1990s was closely and positively linked to job mobility, as people who opted out of occupational pension schemes (largely defined-benefit plans) and switched to personal pensions appear to be more mobile than those who did not (Disney 2004).

Disney (2004) argues that public pension contributions can affect not only labor supply but also the demand for labor. If employers view PAYG contributions as one form of payroll tax, they tend to replace labor recruitment with capital investment, therefore reducing labor demand. In an imperfectly competitive product market, the employee can pass on the burden of their pension contributions to consumers, for example via product prices, thus reducing the demand for labor at a given wage. If the labor market is not fully competitive and unions play an important role in setting wages this may affect employment. This effect will be most marked in advanced countries with generous PAYG systems. It is likely to be less important when tax rates are not high, when the population is young for example, and only a relatively small proportion of the population are elderly dependents.

## 5 Funding and Growth

Empirical work that focuses directly on the relationship of funding to growth (i.e. not indirectly via saving, financial development, or labor market performance) is relatively sparse. Barr (2000) argues that there are three steps whereby funding could induce economic growth; first, pension reform may lead to a higher saving rate. Second, the higher saving needs to be translated into more productive investment (which requires allocative efficiency, notably via financial development). Third, investment results in an increase in output. He argues that all of these three links do not necessarily hold. On the other hand, we have argued that funding can also induce growth via improved market efficiency and incentives operating outside the saving–investment nexus.

A tentative empirical study by Holzmann (1997) indicates a positive relationship between pension reform and economic growth in Chile. With the simple Solow residual specification of total factor productivity (TFP), it is found that improving financial market conditions following pension funds reform have a significantly positive effect on TFP. Meanwhile, Schmidt-Hebbel (1999) reached the conclusion that pension reform in Chile boosted private investment, the average productivity of capital, and TFP, even after allowing for the rise of each variable attributed to structural reform (e.g. tax reform).

A transnational study by Davis (2002) found an insignificant direct effect of institutional assets—including pension funds, life insurance, and mutual funds—on economic growth for 16 OECD countries, although the size of the banking industry was found to be positively linked to economic growth. The equation Davis employed is the standard five-year average economic growth model, where explanatory variables included bank lending/GDP, stock market turnover, institutional assets/GDP, equity market capitalization/GDP, and as a variant the share of institutions in total financial assets.

Hu (2004) empirically analyzed two relationships, first that between pension reform in the direction of the World Bank model and economic growth, and second that between pension fund assets and economic growth. The logic of separating reform and asset growth is that reform may have a signaling effect on expectations before assets are built up and that some reforms do not generate assets (e.g. defined-contribution PAYG). Data from 59 countries showed pension reform is negatively linked to such growth indicators as TFP and investment (as well as saving) in the short run, and positively in the long run. This non-linearity might reflect the fact that people need time to get used to dramatic changes in the public pension systems, and that such reforms may initially engender uncertainty. Where reform is voluntary, it may for example take a few years for people to switch to private systems, when they are confident about the new system.

A clear link between pension fund assets and economic growth indicators can be made: a contemporaneous estimation (for five-year averages 1981–2000) covering 35 countries suggests a strong positive link between pension assets and TFP. More directly (in addition to the effect via financial development), there seems to be a reduction in labor distortions following pension reform, and pension funds' increasing participation in corporate governance, thus improving corporate performance at the firm level and economic productivity on the macro level.

A further regression for growth over 1996–2002 based on initial pension fund assets in 1996 is successful in terms of all three indicators.

Davis and Hu (2004) used a data set covering 38 countries to investigate the direct link between pension assets and GDP growth, using the framework of a modified Cobb-Douglas production function with the inclusion of pension assets/GDP as a shift factor. A cointegrating relationship was found between pension assets, the capital stock, and output, where pension funds and output are positively related. In addition, impulse response tests in the related Vector-Error-Correction-Mechanism show that a rise in pension assets boosts output per worker initially, followed by a gradual decline, but during the whole specified period, the effect remains positive. The positive effect on output per worker of a shock to pension assets is larger in EMEs and also remains significant for longer. Furthermore, a positive average long-run relationship between pension assets and output across four countries is suggested by dynamic heterogeneous models and dynamic ordinary least squares models estimated with the same data set.

# 6 Conclusions

This chapter has focused on the issue of whether a shift from PAYG to funding is largely an accounting matter concerning the allocation of the burden of ageing, or whether funding improves economic performance. We have addressed several aspects to this question. One is whether funding leads to an increase in saving which permits higher capital formation. As regards personal saving, both theory and empirical evidence indicate that pension reform has a positive effect on saving, although such an effect is not one-to-one and appears to be less in more advanced countries. In addition, there is evidence that unfunded social security leads to lower private saving, which further justifies a shift to funding. In relation to national saving, empirical results are mixed, and the ultimate impact depends on whether tax or debt finance is chosen to deal with the transition burden. The transition itself is of course costlier, and the more generous the system, the higher the accrued benefit obligation.

A second issue is whether, independently of the impact on saving, there are effects of funding which lead to higher economic growth, for example via more efficient capital and labor markets. Our literature survey has indicated that pension reform has strong impacts on capital markets in both quantitative and qualitative matters, again notably in EMEs. Quantitatively, funding has led, for example, to higher stock market capitalization in reforming countries such as Chile. The benefits of funding on the qualitative side, among others, include financial innovation, and improvements in the 'architecture of allocative mechanisms' (Greenwald and Stiglitz 1990). There may also be costs, in terms of new types of financial instability but this is not considered a major drawback. In addition, the move in pension reform toward funding leads to lesser labor market distortions, to an extent that depends notably on the degree of actuarial fairness between pension contribution and retirement benefits.

A third aspect is whether a direct impact of funding on growth can be discerned. Research on this issue is sparse. One exception is Davis and Hu (2004), who found that across 38 countries, covering both advanced OECD countries and EMEs, there exists a positive and direct linkage between pension assets and growth, suggesting positive effects from funding. A single country study of Chile by Schmidt-Hebbel (1999) found an impact of reform on growth indicators even allowing for the effect of the tax reform that accompanied the pension reform. On balance, a direct link between funding and growth has been justified theoretically and validated empirically, across both advanced OECD countries and EMEs, albeit more strongly in the latter. The implication for policy-makers is that early pension reform toward more funded systems is warranted in many countries to minimize costs of transition and allow the benefits of transition, such as higher economic growth, to be realized as soon as possible.

The impact of funding on the wider economy is under-researched and warrants more attention generally, especially as experience of pension reform in a range of countries develops. There are also a number of specific areas which warrant further research. These include further work on the general issue of funding and growth, which must partly underlie the benefits of a reform strategy, the appropriate design of funded schemes (in terms of structure and regulation) to maximize the benefits to the wider economy, and the best transition strategy for countries dependent on PAYG in order to maximize gains to economic efficiency.

# NOTES

1. 401(k)s are a form of personal pension provided by US employers, who make contributions in addition to those of their employees.
2. Lower figures than Feldstein's are found by other studies of the United States, such as Gale (1997), who found an elasticity of social security wealth to saving of $-0.11$, and Hubbard (1986), who found $-0.33$.
3. As background we may cite extensive work that suggests financial development aids growth, and in particular that equity market development is a positive factor for growth (such as Levine and Zervos 1998).

4. Differences in portfolios link to a variety of factors, notably regulation and historical developments. See Byrne and Davis (2003).
5. This also requires allocation of funds to their most profitable uses and adequate shareholder-monitoring of the investment projects, which, as detailed below, should also tend to occur in capital markets dominated by pension funds.
6. One note of caution is that if governments force pension funds to absorb the significant issues of bonds that may be needed in a debt-financed transition strategy, or if government issuance crowds out corporate issues, many of the benefits outlined will not be realized. An extreme example was in the Argentina financial crisis when the government forced pension funds to buy government bonds, which rapidly devalued.
7. Liquidity may be less important where pension funds focus on buy-and-hold strategies, as in Chile.
8. This is not to deny that markets may be subject to forms of excess volatility relative to fundamentals, but that the scope of average volatility does not seem to be linked to institutionalization.
9. This tendency may link to illiquidity or lack of marketability of shares, levels of risk which may be difficult to diversify away, difficulty and costs of researching firms without track records, and limits on the proportion of a firm's equity that may be held. The development and improvement of stock markets for small company shares is one initiative that may make such holdings more attractive to pension funds.

# References

Barr, N. (2000). 'Reforming pensions: myths, truths, and policy choices'. Working Paper WP/00/130. International Monetary Fund.

Bernheim, B. D., and Scholz, J. K. (1992). 'Private saving and public policy'. National Bureau of Economic Research Working Paper No. 4213.

Blondal, S., and Scarpetta, S. (1998). 'The retirement decision in OECD countries'. Economics Department Working Papers No. 202. Paris: OECD.

Bodie, Z. (1990). 'Pension funds and financial innovation'. *Financial Management*, autumn: 11–21.

Byrne, J. P., and Davis, E. P. (2003). *Financial structure*. Cambridge: Cambridge University Press

Caprio, G., and Demirguc-Kunt, A. (1998). 'The role of long term finance: theory and evidence'. *World Bank Research Observer*, 13: 171–89.

Catalan, M., Impavido, G., and Musalem, A. R. (2000). 'Contractual savings or stock market development: which leads?' Social Protection Discussion Paper Series No. 0020. The World Bank.

Cifuentes, R., and Valdes Prieto, S. (1997). 'Pension reforms in the presence of credit constraints', in S. Valdes-Prieto (ed.), *The Economics of Pensions*. Cambridge: Cambridge University Press.

Corsetti, G., and Schmidt-Hebbel, K. (1997). 'Pension reform and growth', in S. Valdes-Prieto (ed.), *The Economics of Pensions*. Cambridge: Cambridge University Press.

Davis, E. P. (1988). 'Financial market activity of life insurance companies and pension funds'. Economic Paper No. 21. Bank for International Settlements.

—— (1995). *Pension Funds, Retirement-Income Security and Capital Markets: an International Perspective.* Oxford: Oxford University Press.

—— (2002). 'Institutional investors, corporate governance, and the performance of the corporate sector'. *Economic Systems,* 26: 203–29.

—— (2003). 'Financial development, institutional investors and economic performance', in C. A. E. Goodhart (ed.), *Financial Development and Economic Growth.* Basingstoke: Palgrave.

—— (2004). 'Is there a pensions crisis in the UK?' *Geneva Papers on Risk and Insurance,* 29: 343–70.

—— and Hu, Y. (2004). 'Is there any link between pension fund assets and economic growth?—A cross-country study'. Economics and Finance Working Paper 04-23, Brunel University.

—— and Steil, B. (2001). *Institutional Investors.* Cambridge, Mass.: MIT Press.

Del Guercio, D., and Hawkins, J. (1999). 'The motivation and impact of pension fund activism'. *Journal of Financial Economics,* 52: 293–340.

Disney, Richard (1996). *Can We Afford to Grow Older?* Cambridge, Mass.: MIT Press.

—— (2004). 'Are public pension contributions a tax on employment?' *Economic Policy,* 19: 267–311.

Edey, M., and Simon, J. (1996). 'Australia's retirement income system: implications for saving and capital markets'. Working Paper No. 5799. National Bureau of Economic Research.

Edwards, S. (1995). 'Why are saving rates so different across countries?' NBER Working Paper No. 5097.

Faccio, M., and Lasfer, M. A. (2000). 'Do occupational pension funds monitor companies in which they hold large stakes?' *Journal of Corporate Finance,* 6: 71–85.

Feldstein, M. (1995). 'Social security and saving, new time series evidence'. NBER Working Paper No. 5054.

Fontaine, J. A. (1997). 'Are there good macroeconomic reasons for limiting external investments by pension funds? The Chilean experience', in S. Valdes-Prieto (ed.), *The Economics of Pensions.* Cambridge: Cambridge University Press.

Gale, W. (1997). 'The effect of pension wealth: a re-evaluation of theory and evidence'. Washington, D.C.: Brookings Institution.

Greenwald, B. C., and Stiglitz, J. E. (1990). 'Information, finance and markets, the architecture of allocative mechanisms'. NBER Working Paper No. 3652.

Hansell, S. (1992). 'The new wave in old age pensions'. *Institutional Investor,* Nov. 57–64.

Holzmann, R. (1997). *Pension Reform, Financial Market and Economic Growth: Preliminary Evidence from Chile.* International Monetary Fund Staff Papers (June). Washington, D.C.: International Monetary Fund.

Hu, Y. (2004). 'Pension reform, economic growth and financial development—an empirical study'. Mimeo. Brunel University.

Hubbard, R. G. (1986). 'Pension wealth and individual saving, some new evidence'. *Journal of Money, Credit and Banking,* 18: 167–78.

Hviding, K., and Merette, M. (1998). 'Macroeconomic effect of pension reforms in the context of ageing: OLG simulations for seven OECD countries'. OECD Working Paper No. 201.

Impavido, G., Musalem, A. R., and Tressel, T. (2003). 'The impact of contractual savings institutions on securities markets'. World Bank Policy Research Working Paper 2948 (Jan.). The World Bank.

JAMES, E. (1996). 'Providing better protection and promoting growth: a defence of averting the old age crisis'. *International Social Security Review*, 49/3.

—— (1998). 'Pension reform: an efficiency-equity tradeoff?', in Nancy Birdsall, Carol Graham, and Richard Sabot (eds.), *Beyond Tradeoff*. Washington, D.C.: Brookings Institution Press. Cited by Orszag and Stiglitz (1999).

KING, M. A., and DICKS-MIREAUX, L. (1988). 'Portfolio composition and pension wealth: an econometric study', in Z. Bodie, J. B. Shoven, and D. A. Wise (eds.), *Pensions in the US Economy*. Chicago: University of Chicago Press.

KOHL, M., and O'BRIEN, P. (1998). 'The macroeconomics of ageing, pensions and savings: a survey'. Economic Department Working Paper No. 200. Paris: OECD.

LEVINE, R., and ZERVOS, S. (1998). 'Stock markets, growth and economic development'. *American Economic Review*, 88: 537–58.

MCCARTHY, D., and NEUBERGER, A. (2004). 'Pensions policy: evidence on aspects of savings behaviour and capital markets'. London: Centre for Economic Policy Research.

MILES, D. K. (1993). 'Testing for short termism in the UK stock market'. Bank of England Working Paper No. 4.

MORANDÉ, F. G. (1998). 'Savings in Chile; what went right?' *Journal of Development Economics*, 57: 201–28.

PESANDO, J. E. (1992). 'The economic effects of private pensions', in *Private Pensions and Public Policy*. Paris: OECD.

POTERBA, J., VENTI, S., and WISE, D. (1996). 'How retirement savings programs increase savings'. *Journal of Economic Perspectives*, 10: 91–112.

REISEN, H., and BAILLIU, J. (1997). 'Do funded pensions contribute to higher aggregate savings: a cross-country analysis'. OECD Development Centre Technical Papers No. 130. Paris: OECD.

ROSSI, N., and VISCO, I. (1995). 'National savings and social security in Italy'. *Temi di Discussione del Servizio Studi*. Rome: Banca d'Italia.

SAMWICK, A. A. (1999). 'Is pension reform conducive to higher saving?' (Nov.) The World Bank.

SCHMIDT-HEBBEL, K. (1999). 'Does pension reform really spur productivity, saving and growth'. The World Bank.

SIAS, R. W. (1996). 'Volatility and the institutional investor'. *Financial Analysts Journal*, Mar.–Apr.: 13–20.

UNITED NATIONS (2002). *World Population Prospects: The 2002 Revision and World Urbanization Prospects*. Population Division of the Department of Economic and Social Affairs of the United Nations Secretariat.

WAHAL, S. (1996). 'Public pension fund activism and firm performance. *Journal of Financial and Quantitative Analysis*, 31: 1–23.

WALKER, E., and LEFORT, F. (2002). 'Pension reform and capital markets: are there any (hard) links?' Social Protection Discussion Paper No. 0201 (Jan.). The World Bank.

WORLD BANK (1994). Averting the Old Age Crisis: Policies to Protect the Old and Promote Growth. New York: Oxford University Press.

# PART II

# PUBLIC RETIREMENT PLANS

# STATE OLD-AGE PENSION PROGRAMS

CHAPTER 12

# STRUCTURE AND PERFORMANCE OF DEFINED BENEFIT SCHEMES

## WARREN MCGILLIVRAY

After Germany introduced a scheme towards the end of the nineteenth century, contributory defined benefit (DB) public pension schemes gradually became the foundation of social protection for retired wage earners and their dependents in industrialized countries and most developing countries.[1] As these public pensions have matured, they have helped retired persons to enjoy a financially independent retirement, and they have largely relieved their children from the need to provide direct financial support to them. Everywhere since they were introduced, DB schemes have undergone continuous modifications in order to take into account emerging national social and economic realities. In recent years, population ageing has brought into question the future sustainability of public DB schemes, and sometimes this has led to precipitate reforms which dismantled the DB schemes.

This chapter first describes the nature of these public DB pension schemes and how they operate. The second section focuses on the financing of these plans, which generally operate on a pay-as-you-go basis. The third section uses Germany and France as examples to explain how today's public pension schemes emerged in their current form. Section 4 explores the demographic, economic, and political risks faced by DB schemes. Section 5 discusses the fundamental ways that governments can respond to the challenges of financing DB pensions. The conclusion is that the options are limited and difficult.

# 1 Description, Design, Operation

Defined benefit pension schemes provide a periodic pension at pensionable age as a flat rate benefit or as a function of an individual's employment and earnings history. In its simplest form, a flat rate benefit is a universal benefit based on residence or citizenship, and consists of a fixed amount payable to a pensioner, usually with supplements for dependents.[2] Generally, public DB schemes are contributory, and the pension is related to a participant's attachment to the labor force and earnings. Most plans impose a ceiling on earnings which are taken into account for contributions and calculation of benefits. A typical benefit formula consists of two components. The first is a basic benefit calculated as a percentage (generally 20 to 30 percent) of final average earnings for a specified period of service. The second component is an additional percentage (usually 1 or 2 percent) of final average earnings for each additional year of service up to a maximum.

There is much variation around this general structure. Sometimes there is no basic benefit. In Germany and in the mandatory complementary schemes in France, participants' annual contributions are applied to purchase points that are converted into a pension at retirement.[3] Another variation of the DB approach is the notional defined contribution system.[4] Compared to (funded) defined contribution (DC) schemes, traditional DB schemes have the advantage of offering predictable pensions, even though the schemes are subject to modifications on the basis of a political consensus.

Pension benefit formulas are subject to manipulation. Final average earnings can be artificially increased, and participants can contrive to contribute for the least years so as to receive the basic benefit based on their highest final earnings. Most DB schemes provide for a minimum pension, and some participants try to make only enough contributions to qualify for this benefit. Manipulation has become less of a problem in recent years as modern information technology systems enable reliable records to be maintained over long working careers. This technology makes it possible to replace final average earnings by career average earnings adjusted for wage increases. This approach links benefits more closely to contributions.

What should be the target replacement rate (annual pension/annual earnings at retirement)? In countries with strong occupational pension systems to supplement the public scheme, the replacement rate from the public schemes is in the order of 40 to 45 percent of the average wage (e.g. Canada, the United States). A long-standing guideline was set by the International Labour Organization Social Security (Minimum Standards) Convention in 1952, which advocated a replacement rate of 40 percent for a man with a wife of pensionable age and 30 years of contributions to a scheme. Many countries in Western Europe, the former Soviet Union and its satellites, and in the developing world adopted benefit formulas which can yield substantially higher replacement rates of 70 percent or more of average earnings (thereby 'crowding out' supplementary schemes).[5] Many of these schemes have become financially unsustainable due their ageing populations, and require difficult reforms.

DB pension formulas can be redistributive within a generation, by applying higher replacement rates to low-income earners than to high-income earners (e.g. Philippines, the United States). In some countries, contributions are attributed for periods when none are made (e.g. during military service or parental leave). After retirement, DB scheme pensions are normally adjusted annually to take into account increases in the cost of living, or if pensioners are to benefit from workers' productivity gains, to increases in wages, or to a combination of both.

DB schemes normally provide survivors and invalidity benefits, and the benefit formulas are related to the old-age pension benefit formula. Invalidity pensions can be abused at the upper ages if they are substituted for early retirement pensions (when the latter are lower than invalidity pensions), or if invalidity pensions are substituted for unemployment benefits which are payable for limited periods.

The key to the cost of any pension scheme is the pensionable age, the age from which pensions are paid. Pensionable ages set decades ago remain in effect despite significant increases in life expectancy at older ages. Sometimes pensions are payable after a specified number of years of participation in the scheme. Whereas in the 1950s in the industrialized countries a male worker might expect his retirement years to be about one-quarter of his working years, now in many countries the proportion is 40 percent or more.[6] Despite their longer expectation of life at higher ages, pensionable ages for females are often up to five years lower than for males. Raising retirement ages has proved to be difficult. In 1983 the United States raised its retirement age to 67, but the full impact of this change will not take effect until 2027.[7] Changes in pensionable age must be implemented gradually so as not to disrupt the plans of persons nearing retirement.

In fact, the real retirement age is lower than the pensionable age since substantial numbers of participants in DB schemes opt for early retirement.[8] If early retirement pensions are actuarially reduced, they do not increase the cost to the scheme. It was expected that applying actuarial reductions would discourage early retirement, and actuarial increases in pensions for deferring retirement to after pensionable age would encourage continued attachment to the labor force. In practice neither of these incentives has proved to be particularly effective. Raising the earliest retirement age and the pensionable age may be the only ways of extending persons' working careers (assuming, of course, that they can find employment).

Public DB schemes are generally contributory with workers and employers contributing equally, or with employers contributing a greater share of the total contribution. Self-employed persons are sometimes assessed a contribution less than the total worker and employer contribution. In some schemes the state is obliged to make a specific contribution (other than as an employer when civil servants are covered by the public DB scheme). A state contribution from general revenues is defensible when the public DB scheme covers most of the labor force. Evasion of contribution obligations occurs in all public pension schemes. Principal reasons for evasion are employers' desire to reduce their labor costs and workers' myopia and current consumption needs. Evasion threatens the adequacy of pensions, the financing of a DB scheme, and the state, which may be importuned to supplement the resulting inadequate pensions (McGillivray 2001).

The state provides an implicit (and sometimes explicit) guarantee of the benefits promised under a public DB scheme which it has enacted. The perpetuity of the scheme is founded on the scheme's statutory authority to collect contributions and the state's capacity to level taxes. The strength of this foundation is brought into question—often in a dramatic and sometimes deceptive manner—by pessimistic analyses of the consequences of population ageing on DB schemes, thereby undermining the confidence of the public in their DB schemes. Critics sometimes characterize revisions to public DB schemes to take into account emerging national social and economic realities as defaults of pension promises by the state, forgetting that in democratic states decisions are taken following public consultations.

## 2 Financing of Defined Benefit Public Pension Schemes

The financial organization of a social security scheme refers to how the scheme receives and manages income and then allocates its income to meet benefit and administration expenditures. In a pension scheme, the financial system which is applied can range from full funding to pay-as-you-go (PAYG)—sometimes called 'assessment'—which implies no advance funding. The financial system does not affect the amount or timing of benefit payments; rather it establishes the basis for determining whether the scheme is in 'financial equilibrium' in the short and long terms (i.e. whether it is solvent).

## 2.1 Financial Systems

For social security benefits, which are payable in respect of short-term risks (e.g. sickness and maternity cash benefits, work injury benefits other than invalidity and survivors' pensions), the annual frequency of occurrence and severity (average duration of benefit payment period) of the risks are relatively constant from year to year. Hence, the annual ratios of benefits and administration expenses to earnings subject to contributions will be relatively constant, and a PAYG system of finance is appropriate for these benefits. Under the PAYG system of finance, current benefits are paid out of current contributions (where the ratio establishes the contribution rate). Aside from a contingency reserve, which might be set up to smooth cash flows and excess benefit payments resulting from catastrophic events, no funds need be set aside in advance to pay benefits.

If, in year $t$, $p$ is the number of beneficiaries and $n$ the number of contributors, $TB_t$ is the total amount of benefits (including administration expenses) and $TE_t$ is the total earnings on which contributions are paid, then $AB_t$ and $AE_t$ are the average amounts of benefits and contributory earnings, and the PAYG contribution rate, $C_t$, in year $t$ is:

$$C_t = \frac{TB_t}{TE_t} = \frac{p^*}{n} \frac{AB_t}{AE_t}.$$

Pensions, in contrast to benefits for illness or other short-term contingencies, are long-term obligations characterized by increasing annual expenditures. Each year new persons qualify for pensions, and new pensions are greater than those in payment due to higher earnings on which the pensions are based, and in immature schemes due to longer periods of service. In addition, existing pensions are increased to take into account inflation. Added to this automatic escalation is the effect of increasing life expectancy at older ages. Consequently, using a PAYG financial system to finance pensions results in steadily increasing annual expenditures relative to earnings subject to contributions, and thus for many years annual increases in the contribution rate.

Since contribution rates in the early years of a DB scheme are low, PAYG financing of public DB schemes can lead myopic or opportunistic governments to implement generous schemes. Applying the PAYG financial system to public DB pensions means that the cost of pensions for the current generation is transferred to subsequent generations. Hence, in the future the pension system dependency ratio ($p/n$) must not rise above the capacity of the economy to provide the goods and services to meet the consumption needs of both pensioners and the working population (contributors) and their dependents. Eventually PAYG financing can require increases in contribution rates that are unacceptable to worker and employer contributors.

In theory, after two or three generations public pension schemes will mature and eventually reach a 'relatively stationary state' when the financial ratio, $AB_t/AE_t$, and the system dependency ratio, $p/n$, are relatively stable resulting in a contribution rate, $C_t$, which varies little thereafter. In practice, this state is seldom reached due to changes in demographic factors (birth rates, expectation of life), coverage of the scheme, employment patterns and benefit provisions.

At the other extreme, a fully funded financial system could be applied to a public DB pension scheme.[9] Under the open fund 'general average premium' system, at any time the scheme would hold reserves equal to the present value of all future expenditures in respect of current and future pensioners minus the present value of all future income in respect of current and future contributors. Applying this system would result in a high initial contribution rate, which would theoretically remain constant, and enormous reserves would be accumulated in the early years of the scheme and for many years thereafter.[10]

While neither PAYG nor full funding of public DB schemes is entirely appropriate, it is widely assumed that public DB pension schemes are financed on the PAYG system.[11] Indeed, this is generally true of countries in Western Europe. Elsewhere, in Canada, Cyprus, Japan, and the United States, and in most developing countries with public DB schemes, systems of partial funding which fall between the extremes of PAYG and full funding are applied.

A multitude of systems of partial funding of public DB schemes can be designed. The simplest is the requirement that reserves be maintained over a number of years at a specified multiple (funding ratio) of the current annual expenditure of the scheme. If the funding ratio is zero, the system is PAYG in that the money coming in equals the money going out each year. For the Canada Pension Plan, in 1998 the desired funding ratio was raised from two to approximately five over a 75-year period.

A more sophisticated system of partial funding, the 'scaled premium' system, was advocated by the International Labour Office when it assisted developing countries to set up their schemes. Under the scaled premium system, over a predetermined period of time (10 to 20 years) the contribution rate was set so that the reserves would not decrease. That is, contributions plus investment income would be sufficient to pay pensions every year throughout the period of equilibrium (Thullen 1964; Iyer 1999). At the conclusion of a period of equilibrium, the contribution rate would be increased for a subsequent period of equilibrium. This system allows contribution rates and/or periods of equilibrium to be set taking into account the capacities of scheme participants to contribute and the reserves to be invested domestically.

Adopting a system of partial funding implies acceptance that in the future the contribution rate must be increased. In reality, in different economic circumstances from when the schemes were set up, implementing increases in contribution rates has proved to be difficult. Even though increases in the contribution rates to partially funded schemes were originally foreseen, they are resisted, thereby putting the sustainability of the schemes in jeopardy. Nevertheless, Canada gradually raised the contribution rate to the Canada Pension Plan/Québec Pension Plan from 5.85 to 9.9 percent of contributory earnings over six years from 1998. In Japan, the contribution rate to Employees' Pension Insurance is being raised gradually from the 13.58 percent of covered wages in 2004 to 18.3 percent in 2017.

Other factors affect the financing of a DB scheme. Virtually all DB schemes are founded on the principle of intergenerational solidarity whereby resources are transferred from the current generation's contributors to preceding generations' pensioners. At the same time, the principle of equity among generations requires that each generation's contributors pay roughly the same share of their disposable incomes for pensions and enjoy replacement rates equivalent to those of preceding generations. Intergenerational equity is a contentious issue. For example, to what extent should pensioners share in the increase in living standards, which may be attributed to investment of reserves arising from their contributions? When a scheme is set up, contributors in the early years normally receive pensions under favorable conditions so that the scheme can become fully operational in a few years rather than after one or two generations. Consequently, early entrants to the scheme receive pensions which violate the equity principle.

## 2.2 Investment of Reserves

Generally, public DB pension schemes that adopt systems of partial funding rapidly accumulate substantial reserves. In developing countries, these schemes often have reserves equal to a significant proportion of the national GDP. The social security scheme thus becomes the most important financial institution in the country. Unless the reserves can be properly invested—taking properly into account security and rate of return—the rationale for accumulating substantial reserves is questionable. The social and economic utility of investments can be an additional subsidiary investment objective for most social security schemes. Clearly, national infrastructure investments in education, health care, transportation, communications, and so on can spur economic growth, which will enable the schemes to meet their future obligations (see ISSA 2004, Guideline 14).

Public pension schemes in developing countries often accumulate reserves that their national economies cannot absorb productively. Unlike industrialized countries, for developing countries with limited appropriate domestic investment options, placing substantial investments abroad is not viable since foreign investments will not enhance national economic growth and they are unlikely to be offset by inward direct investments. Moreover, chronic trade deficits mean that foreign investments can affect the national currency exchange rate.

This situation has led some governments to plunder the reserves of social security schemes by treating them as substitutes for taxation to meet recurrent expenditures. Social security schemes have often been obliged to accept government securities at lower-than-market interest rates. And they have faced even less satisfactory terms at the time the securities are refinanced or if the government effectively defaults on the debt. Some contend that public pension schemes that invest in government securities are in effect PAYG financed. This need not always be the case. Sometimes the buildup in the pension plan actually does lead to increased national saving. But often when pension scheme reserves are invested in public securities, tax rates can be kept low since government expenditure can be financed by excess social security contributions. Eventually, responsible governments must redeem their debt from current revenues, and at that time taxes must be increased or government expenditures curtailed. The apparent financial rectitude of high levels of funding can thus create a parlous situation for both social security schemes and governments.

## 2.3 Adjustment of Pensions in Payment

Pensions must be adjusted to take into account changes in the cost of living or wages, or a combination of both, if they are to maintain the purchasing power of pensioners. If pensions are adjusted to reflect changes in the average wage level of contributors, in a PAYG system changes in the average wage level will automatically cause a scheme's income to rise or fall by an amount sufficient to adjust pensions in payment by the same rate (provided any ceiling on contributory earnings is also adjusted). Similarly, PAYG schemes can normally adjust pensions for changes in the cost of living since over time wages tend to rise faster than prices. If wages do not keep pace with inflation, in order to maintain the cost of living adjustment to pensions, additional funds are required if pensioners are to be protected against a fall in their living standards resulting from the decline in real wages.

While adjustment of pensions is relatively straightforward in PAYG schemes, it is more difficult in funded schemes. The challenge is to maintain the same funding ratio when pensions in payment are increased, and the higher the level of funding, the more difficult this becomes. For funded schemes, assumptions of future pension increases can be made in the actuarial projections used to calculate the contribution rate. Alternatively, excess investment income over that assumed in the calculations can be applied to fund expected future increases. But, since inflation is neither regular nor predictable, these means of financing increases in pensions and reserves are undependable. Investing in inflation-indexed bonds where the principal and interest are indexed to the cost of living allows adjustments to pensions in payment and to the level of the reserves to be made. These bonds are issued almost exclusively by governments. They introduce a PAYG financing element to funded schemes since the commitment to meet the indexed bond interest is met by future taxpayers (Thompson 1998: 159).

## 2.4 Economic Effects of PAYG Financing

Saving and the resulting investments, provided they are productive, are prerequisites for economic growth, which is necessary for public pension schemes to be sustainable. The effect of PAYG and funding financial systems on saving has been much studied. The results are conflicting and inconclusive; the most that can be stated is that a PAYG scheme probably does not reduce savings, but a funded scheme might increase them. (For further discussion of this issue see Chapter 11.)

Public pension schemes are sometimes regarded as means of developing domestic capital markets. Clearly, this is a desirable result of the investment of social security funds, but equally clearly, it is not a priority objective of a public pension scheme. Countries have other means of developing capital markets (e.g. tax policy). The schemes distort national capital markets when their principal borrower, the government, abuses them by requiring that they purchase government securities at below-market rates of interest. Similarly, when participants exploit deficiencies in DB benefit formulas and contribution arrangements they can create distortions in labor markets.

Pension plans are consumption smoothing mechanisms, and according to the 'life-cycle' theory, individuals save during their working years so that they will have resources available for consumption during retirement. In a public DB scheme, when the contributions of early entrants (who join under favorable transitional conditions) are related to their pensions, it is inevitable that the rate of return on their contributions is much higher than it is for later entrants who contribute to the scheme throughout full working careers. If the support which early entrants had provided to their elders who were not covered by the scheme is ignored, this 'windfall profit' is criticized. From a rate of return viewpoint, the criticism is valid, but it ignores the social dimension of public DB pension schemes. While alternative investments of later entrants' contributions might produce greater rates of return, this would not apply to all of them, and supporters of public DB schemes cite the dependability and predictability of pensions as justifications for DB schemes.

# 3 Evolution of the Financing of Public Pension Schemes

In the context of the debate on the appropriate method of financing and organizing the provision of public pensions, the examples of Germany and France are instructive. Both countries set up schemes with the intention of having high levels of funding. Germany, following 1888 legislation establishing a DB public pension scheme, adopted a financial system that set contributions for a specific period at a level that would fully fund (capitalize) all future payments arising from pensions becoming payable in the period and cover other expenditure. The first period was 10 years, and thereafter 15-year periods were to be used. This system of 'average premiums for a fixed period' was chosen since applying the general average premium system over an indefinite period was considered likely to create excessive reserves. By 1913 the reserves were nearly nine times annual expenditures. As a result of the First World War and depreciation of the currency, the reserve funds almost entirely disappeared, and following the period of postwar inflation, in 1924 the financial system which provided for building up reserves was abandoned.

In France, 1910 legislation established a contributory pension scheme for industrial and agricultural workers based on a financial system of capitalization in individual accounts supplemented by state subsidies.[12] For various reasons, including the erosion of pensions by inflation, the 1910 legislation was only partially applied. In 1930, France introduced a scheme with a minimum pension guarantee after 30 years of contributions of 40 percent of the average basic wage on which contributions were paid. A financial system of capitalization in individual accounts was applied, whereby deferred annuities were purchased annually with each individual's contributions. Participants were free to choose from among approved institutions to manage their accounts. The State provided a subsidy and set the maximum interest rate for calculating annuities and the maximum level of administration expenses. The system of funding was jeopardized in 1934, however, when the State diverted social security funds to public works projects to relieve unemployment. This, and the inflation of the late 1930s, led the Vichy government to abandon the system in 1941 and effectively confiscate the reserves. Subsequently, DB public pensions in France have been financed on the PAYG system (répartition).

Elsewhere in Western Europe, public schemes are generally DB with PAYG financing, often with state subsidies. In the Soviet Union, DB pensions were paid from the State budget, and similar systems were applied in its satellite countries. During the 1990s in these countries, the Russian Federation, and the former Soviet Union, the schemes were replaced, often with a combination DB and DC scheme.

In South America, public DB schemes were set up in many countries early in the twentieth century (among the earliest, in Argentina (1904), Brazil (1923), and Chile

(1924)). These schemes were generally financed on a partial funding basis. By the 1980s, in a number of South and Central American countries, the DB schemes were failing to deliver the promised benefits. In some countries, the reserves of schemes were victims of currency devaluations and inflation, often the result of macroeconomic mismanagement of national economies. Sometimes, political interference and mismanagement of the schemes contributed to the depletion of schemes' reserves and loss of confidence in the schemes. This led to the replacement of the failed DB schemes by privately managed individual account DC schemes in a number of countries in the region.

In many developing countries of Africa, Asia, and the Caribbean, public retirement benefit schemes were set up around the time the countries became independent. In former British possessions, provident funds (mandatory state-managed individual account DC schemes) were established. Since the provident funds were fully funded, contribution rates had to be sufficiently high to produce worthwhile lump sums at retirement, thereby creating substantial reserves. Often the reserves could not be invested productively, leading to low or negative real rates of return and sometimes their misappropriation. Beginning in the 1970s, nearly all provident funds have been converted into partially funded DB schemes or to DB schemes with a DC component.[13] In many francophone countries in Africa, partially funded DB schemes were set up with provision for periodic actuarial reviews and increases in contribution rates. Some governments have subsequently been either reluctant or unable to apply the financial system, with the result that their schemes have effectively reverted to PAYG financing, sometimes, where possible, with support from general government revenues.

# 4 Risks of Defined Benefit Schemes

While DB schemes are relatively insensitive to changes in rates of growth in average earnings or in investment returns, they are sensitive to changes in birth rates and life expectancy. Making necessary adjustments to take into account demographic and other changes, which usually involve increasing the contribution rate or reducing pensions, or more likely, a combination of both measures, requires political intervention. While this can result in a collective response, thereby reducing individual risk, the lack of political will and the inability to reach a consensus can result in a 'reform deadlock' and, hence, financial disequilibrium in the DB scheme.

## 4.1 Demographic Risks

The simultaneous falls in the birth rate and increases in the expectation of life can have a dramatic effect on the number of contributors available to support each pensioner ($n/p$) in a PAYG or partially funded DB scheme. But neither of these demographic changes occurs suddenly. They develop over long periods, and the necessary actuarial and other studies can identify emerging trends and provide the basis for remedial measures to maintain the financial integrity of the scheme.

Lower birth rates begin to affect the relative size of the labor force after 15 or 20 years. Thereafter, the support ratio will gradually decrease. Declines in birth rates affect PAYG financed and partially funded DB schemes, but have no direct impact on DC schemes.[14] In contrast, increases in the expectation of life at the upper ages, which also decrease the support ratio, affect both DB and DC schemes, but in different ways. In any scheme, an increase in the average period during which pensions are payable raises the cost of providing the pensions. In order to control the cost increase contributions must be increased and/or pensions must be reduced. To the extent increases in life expectancy are related to rapid economic development, the cost increases may be more affordable. DC schemes are not immune to demographic changes which affect the relative number of persons wishing to buy or sell financial assets to fund or pay their pensions.

Consequently, the problem of an increasing demographic burden is not solved by replacing a PAYG scheme by a funded scheme. In both cases uncertainty remains. The uncertainty faced by participants in PAYG DB schemes is whether declining relative proportions of active workers will have the capacity to pay the pensions of increasing numbers of pensioners. In funded schemes the uncertainty is whether there will be inflation in asset values followed by a systemic decline when pensioners sell their assets to finance their retirement consumption to a relatively smaller active population. Rates of return could also decline. The fallacy of composition is cited to explain why in a microeconomic sense individuals can save for their own retirement, but in aggregate, societies—the collectivity of individuals—cannot (Brown 1997: 4).

## 4.2 Economic Risks

Changes in the structure of the labor market (e.g. level of employment, voluntary intermittent employment, informal employment) affect the coverage of pension schemes. In DB schemes, one issue is whether the benefit formula properly accounts for gaps in participation in the scheme during which no contributions were made. As discussed earlier, the opportunities for abuse of final earnings benefit formulas and possible destabilization of PAYG schemes has led to the introduction of formulas based on career average earnings adjusted for wage inflation. Possible variations in the number of workers who will be contributing to the scheme ('annual density of contributions') are taken into account in setting contribution rates to PAYG and partially funded DB schemes.

Unlike DC schemes, in DB schemes individuals do not bear risks such as rates and timing of wage growth and investment returns, asset values, and inflation. In all public pension schemes, the fundamental issue is not the financial system used to determine how output is divided between workers and pensioners, but whether economic growth is sufficiently robust to generate the resources to be transferred to pensioners without unduly depriving active workers.

## 4.3 Political and Institutional Risks

Public DB schemes are created by governments and managed by a government department or a statutory body over which the government has oversight. Faulty or opportunistic policies or good policies poorly implemented jeopardize the promised pensions. Myopic politicians can ignore the fiscal implications of pension promises which they make to curry favor, especially when schemes are first established. When the time comes for adjustments to the scheme to have to be made, the political system may be unable to organize a consensus, thereby leaving the scheme in financial disequilibrium and undermining confidence in it. The reserves of partially funded DB schemes may be exploited for political ends.

Institutions administering public pension schemes must operate with rectitude and set up efficient and effective administrative arrangements. A serious problem for many schemes is enforcing the contribution collection conditions of the scheme. Contribution evasion creates the risk that persons who evade their contribution obligations will have inadequate pensions and that the state will be called upon to remedy the shortfall. Clearly, social security schemes must be administered by institutions capable of reliably maintaining individual records over long periods. Unfortunately this has not always been the case.

Political interference and mismanagement of public pension schemes have led to increasing attention to the governance of the schemes. In a public pension scheme the stakeholders include the state, the management institution, the contributors (workers and employers), and pensioners. While boards of directors of the schemes have included these stakeholders in the past, it is necessary to expand the capacity of board members and the scope of their oversight. Given its national social and financial importance, no social security scheme can operate entirely independent of the government. The government's legitimate interest must be balanced with sufficient autonomy for the scheme and independence of its board so that the board can properly exercise its fiduciary responsibility and protect the interest of members of the scheme.

## 4.4 Individual Risks

Individuals face the impact of demographic, economic, political, and institutional risks to the scheme and personal risks such as unemployment, illness, and retrenchment to lower paying work, all of which can affect their pensions. DB pension schemes can provide some protection against personal risks by allowing non-contributory ('drop-out') periods, and by providing minimum pensions (financed by the scheme, not from general government revenues). DB schemes generally provide predictable pensions. They are sensitive to demographic changes, but can spread the effect of such changes throughout the working and retired population covered by the scheme. In a DC scheme, on the other hand, all risks are borne by individual participants (unless the scheme provides minimum pensions). But DB schemes also involve political risk. Changes to a DB scheme require informed political leadership. DB scheme participants bear the risk that the polity is unable to reach a consensus on amendments to the scheme.

# 5 Challenges for Defined Benefit Schemes

Ultimately, no matter how they are financed, pensions are transfers of resources from active workers to inactive pensioners at the time the pensions are paid. Amounts paid in pensions, which pensioners then convert into goods and services that they consume, are equal to consumption (and investment) that workers forego. The goods and services that workers and pensioners share must almost all be produced by workers at the time pensions are paid. In DB schemes, under the PAYG system the transfer is direct through contributions. Under a funded DC system, pensioners liquidate assets which they have accumulated by selling their assets to workers. In both cases workers' disposable income is reduced by the amount of resources transferred to retired persons. The economic cost of pensions is thus independent of the system applied to finance them.

In order to finance a given pension, Samuelson (1958) and Aaron (1966) show that the internal rate of return on contributions to a PAYG scheme is equal to the rate of growth of the labor force plus the rate of growth of wages. If population growth rates decline and the implicit return on contributions to a PAYG scheme falls below the market rate of return, it is inferred that pensions could be financed better by funding through the capital market. The question is then whether meeting the cost of public pensions should be based on labor markets and PAYG financed, or whether the individual risk which can occur in a funded scheme can be ignored and the cost of pensions met (wholly or in part) through funding in the capital market. In practice, while many DB schemes are partially funded, the change from PAYG financing to full funding is extremely difficult. Such a change means that the generation involved would have to fund its own pensions and pay those under the (former) PAYG system, unless the government takes on the enormous fiscal charges for many years to pay the PAYG financed pensions.

Rather than a structural change from a PAYG DB public pension scheme, most countries have sought to make parametric changes to their DB schemes to ensure their sustainability, sometimes with the addition of a funded DC component. The alternatives for modifications to DB schemes are limited. Thompson (1998: 49) provides a disaggregation of the retirement burden which identifies where changes can be made to public pension schemes to reduce the burden of retirement pensions. If $Y =$ total income, $C =$ aggregate consumption, $C_p =$ aggregate consumption of retired persons, $n =$ total population, and $p =$ number of retired persons (pensioners), then:

Number of retirement pensioners/Total population $= p/n$;
Average consumption of retired persons $= C_p/p$;
Average consumption of total population $= C/n$;
Retired persons living standards ratio $=$
 Average retiree consumption/Average total consumption $= (C_p/p)/(C/n)$;
hence the Retirement Burden $= C_p/Y = C/Y * p/n * [(C_p/p)/(C/n)]$.

Clearly, one can seek to increase output, $Y$, or to decrease overall consumption, $C$. In theory, this goal could be accomplished in a number of ways. The population, $n$, can be increased by higher birth rates and immigration. Heretofore, governments' efforts to increase birth rates have been largely unsuccessful. Immigration at the levels which would be required to sustain economic growth is apt to be socially and politically unacceptable. Alternatively, the number of pensioners, $p$, can be reduced by curtailing retirements before pensionable age (unless early retirement pensions are actuarially equivalent to pensions at pensionable age, in which case this is irrelevant). Most important, the number of pensioners can be reduced by raising pensionable age. The average living standards of retired persons relative to the total population, $(C_p/p)/(C/n)$, can be reduced by measures such as lowering replacement rates and deferring or omitting inflation adjustments to pensions.

# 6 CONCLUSION

Thus, the alternatives are limited and difficult.[15] Modifications to public DB schemes are contentious, and it is difficult to reach a consensus on acceptable changes. Increasingly, however, it is recognized that from an economic point of view all public pension schemes are PAYG transfers. Taking into account the risks and uncertainty of the allegedly superior funded DC schemes, the advantages of DB schemes lead those responsible to eschew radical structural reforms and to make modifications to their public PAYG or partially funded DB schemes in order to ensure their sustainability.

# NOTES

1. The coverage of contributory schemes in developing countries is very limited since most workers are not wage earners. In these countries, low coverage is a problem for all systems of social protection based on contributions.
2. For example, in Canada, Denmark, Mauritius, and New Zealand.
3. In the complementary DB schemes in France (AGIRC and ARRCO), contributions are applied annually to purchase points at the cost of a point for the year. At retirement, the number of points credited to an individual is converted into a pension based on the value of a point at that time. Thus, the pension at retirement is not known in advance as it depends on the amount of contributions collected each year. The PAYG financial equilibrium of the scheme is maintained by annually adjusting the value of a point. (See Gillion et al. 2000: 52–3.)
4. In a notional defined contribution system, contributions are accumulated in individual accounts just as in a funded DC scheme, but the contributions are used to pay pensions on a PAYG basis. The accounts are revalued annually, not with interest, but according to a factor such as the rate of real wage growth or the rate of GDP growth. At retirement, the balance in an individual's notional account is converted into a pension, taking into account the life expectancy of the cohort retiring at that time.
5. In practice, actual replacement rates are lower due to earnings ceilings which are taken into account in the calculation of pensions and failure to complete long contribution periods to qualify for full pensions.
6. The broader question of maintaining or increasing output with relatively smaller labor forces as a result of population ageing is beyond the scope of this chapter.
7. In the former Soviet Union and its satellites, where the male retirement age was typically 60 (females 55), many countries have recently moved towards a pensionable age of 65.
8. This is less of a problem in DC schemes where persons' decisions to retire depend on the amount of pension their balances in the schemes can provide. An inadequate pension is a powerful incentive to continue working.
9. The Kuwait public scheme is an example.
10. If $V_t$ is the reserve at the beginning of year $t$, $v = 1/(1+i)$ where $i$ is a constant rate of interest, and the summation runs from $t=0$ to $t=\infty$, then at time $t=0$, a simplified equation for $C$, the theoretical indefinite level contribution rate is:

$$C = \left[\sum TB_t * v^t - V_0\right] / \sum TE_t * v^t.$$

11. Occupational or private schemes apply systems of funding since the scheme sponsors do not have the same perennity as a public scheme.
12. Since 1912 public pensions in France have had a normal retirement age of 60.
13. Notable exceptions are the provident funds in Malaysia and Singapore.
14. In notional defined contribution schemes, the effect depends on the basis for the annual revaluation of the individual accounts.
15. See chapter 1 of the Pensions Commission (2004).

# References

AARON, H. (1966). 'The social insurance paradox'. *Canadian Journal of Economics and Political Science*, 32: 371–7.
BARR, N. (1998). *The Economics of the Welfare State*, 3rd edn. Oxford: Oxford University Press.
—— (2000). 'Reforming pensions: myths, truths and policy choices'. *International Social Security Review*, 55/2: 3–36.
BEATTIE, R., and MCGILLIVRAY, W. (1995). 'A risky strategy: reflections on the World Bank Report: *Averting the Old Age Crisis*'. *International Social Security Review*, 48/3–4: 5–22.
BROWN, R. L. (1997). 'In defense of pay-as-you-go (PAYG) financing of social security'. *North American Actuarial Journal*, 1/4: 1–20.
CHARLTON, R., and MCKINNON, R. (2001). *Pensions in Development*. Aldershot: Ashgate.
FÉRAUD, L. (1940). *Actuarial Technique and Financial Organisation of Social Insurance*. Geneva: ILO.
GILLION, C., TURNER, J., BAILEY, C., and LATULIPPE, D. (eds.) (2000). *Social Security Pensions: Development and Reform*. Geneva: ILO.
HOLZMANN, R. (1997). *On the Economic Benefits and Fiscal Requirements of Moving from Unfunded to Funded Pensions*. Washington, D.C.: American Institute for Contemporary German Studies.
—— PALACIOS, R., and ZVINIENE, A. (2000). 'On the economics and scope of implicit pension debt: an international perspective'. Presented at IAES Session on 'Public Sector Debt: International Experiences', ASSA Meetings, Jan. New Orleans.
INTERNATIONAL LABOUR OFFICE (ILO) (1952). Social Security (Minimum Standards) Convention, 1952 (No. 102). Geneva: ILO.
—— (2000). *World Labour Report: Income Security and Social Protection in a Changing World*. Geneva: ILO.
INTERNATIONAL SOCIAL SECURITY ASSOCIATION (ISSA) (2004). *Guidelines for the Investment of Social Security Funds*. Geneva: ISSA. www.issa.int/pdf/GA2004/2guidelines.pdf
IYER, S. (1999). *Actuarial Mathematics of Social Security Pensions*. Geneva: ILO.
LA LETTRE DE L'OBSERVATOIRE DES RETRAITES (2001). 'Reserves and pay as you go', No. 12 (Nov.). Paris. www.observatoire-retraites.org/versionanglaise/letters/lor12.pdf
MCGILLIVRAY, W. (2001). 'Contribution evasion: implications for social security pension schemes'. *International Social Security Review*, 54/4: 3–22.
—— (2003). 'Ten years of public pensions reform', in N. Takayama (ed.), *Taste of Pie: Searching for Better Pension Provisions in Developed Countries*. Tokyo: Maruzen Co., 401–17.

PENSIONS COMMISSION (2004). *Pensions Challenges and Choices: The First Report of the Pensions Commission.* London: The Stationery Office. www.pensionscommission.org.uk/publications/2004/annrep/index.asp

SALY, P. (1999). Chapter 7 in M. Laroque (ed.), *Contribution à l'histoire financière de la Sécurité sociale.* Paris: La Documentation Française.

SAMUELSON, P. (1958). 'An exact consumption loan model of interest with or without the social contrivance of money'. *Journal of Political Economy,* 66: 467–82.

THOMPSON, L. (1998). *Older and Wiser: The Economics of Public Pensions.* Washington, D.C.: Urban Institute Press.

THULLEN, P. (1964). 'The scaled premium system for the financing of social insurance pension schemes'. *International Review on Actuarial and Statistical Problems of Social Security,* 10. Geneva: ISSA.

WORLD BANK (1994). *Averting the Old Age Crisis: Policies to Protect the Old and Promote Growth.* Oxford: Oxford University Press.

ZÖLLNER, D. (1982). 'Germany', in P. Köhler and H. Zacher (eds.), *The Evolution of Social Insurance 1881–1981.* London: Frances Pinter, 1–92.

CHAPTER 13

# THE STRUCTURE AND PERFORMANCE OF MANDATED PENSIONS

## ADAM CREIGHTON
## AND JOHN PIGGOTT

> The only purpose for which power can rightly be exercised over any other member of a civilized community, against his will, is to prevent harm to others. His own good, either physical or moral, is not sufficient warrant.
>
> (J. S. Mill, 'On Liberty', 1859)

## 1 INTRODUCTION

Government-mandated pensions have become increasingly popular since the early 1980s. The idea of mandating individual pensions arose largely as a response to problems that afflict traditional PAYG schemes, demographic change, and from governments' desire to maintain a role in their citizens' retirement arrangements. Mandated pension schemes exhibit significant differences, yet all follow the same general framework: workers have *individual* pension *accounts* to which they or their employers or both make *compulsory* and *periodic defined* contributions from their *employment* income. These amounts accrue until retirement, and then become available for consumption. This chapter deals with the context and impetus for mandated pensions, using existing national programs for illustration where possible, and addresses three questions. What structures have mandated pensions taken internationally? What factors affect the performance of mandated pensions? What are some potential design pitfalls?

The argument is that the demographic transition has primarily been responsible for the development of mandated pension schemes, and that three core types have emerged as a response: funded defined contribution plans—with and without private sector involvement—and the government-managed, but unfunded, variety. Most of the following discussion revolves around the first arrangement (the most common and promising), and offers a comprehensive catalog of issues (relating to both structure and performance) that need to be *directly* considered when designing mandated pensions. As the discussion implies, no existing mandated system has adequately addressed all these issues. Indeed, the final suggestions for future research include issues that have not been addressed at all by public policy, yet they will become increasingly important as mandated pensions become more common and demographic change progresses.

## 2 Context

In the field of social security, governments have been flouting Mill since Germany introduced a state-administered retirement scheme for private sector employees in the late nineteenth century. By the mid-twentieth century, economic growth and increased life expectancy had facilitated the introduction of old-age pension schemes in most developed countries. Many of these schemes were expanded after the Second World War to include a generous earnings-related pay-as-you go (PAYG) component. This development resulted in large increases in government spending as a proportion of national output. Around 70 percent of the increase in OECD governments' spending between 1953 and 1975 was due to greater social security expenditures, of which public retirement schemes were the major component (Feldstein and Liebman 2001).

While these developments were acceptable in times of robust postwar economic growth and growing working populations, demographic and behavioral developments later put pension reform on the agenda. Life expectancy is now almost 80 years in many OECD countries. Those who retire at 65 can expect to live even longer—especially women. Moreover, the working age population is shrinking. Fertility has fallen since the 1970s, and is now 20 percent below that required to maintain a constant population. And workers are retiring earlier. Participation rates for males aged 60–64 have fallen from between 70 and 90 percent in the 1970s to between 20 and 50 per cent today.[1] OECD workers can now reasonably expect to spend 30 or more years in retirement.

These developments will see dependency ratios in Western countries increase dramatically over the next 30 years.[2] The OECD average dependency ratio in 2000 was 21 percent, and this is set to increase to 37 percent by 2030. Some countries will fare worse—Italy, France, Germany, and Japan's ratios are set to exceed 45 percent. In this context, PAYG schemes become untenable—unless society is willing to endure a significant increase in taxation or reduce retirement benefit levels substantially. Mandated pensions, on the other hand, force people to save for their own retirement, and therefore break the transfer between those who work and those who are retired.

Although the primary impetus is demographic, other arguments can be made for a shift to mandated pensions. For instance, mandated pensions can offer potentially higher rates of return if appropriately invested, improve labor market productivity, insulate retirement benefits from government interference, and provide individuals with a greater range of investment options. Moreover, funded schemes can improve national saving and investment, and can have a salutary effect on financial-system development. Individual retirement accounts can also offer greater portability in increasingly mobile workforces.

Of course, governments could abrogate their involvement in retirement provision. As Mill suggests, there are philosophical reasons for doing so. Yet both PAYG and mandated pension systems either implicitly or explicitly compel individuals to provide for their retirement. There are three primary reasons why. First, these schemes exist to mitigate the empirically documented tendency to undersave. Second, private financial markets might not otherwise provide the types of financial products required for retirement. Third, compulsory retirement systems provide a mechanism for redistribution. Further, to prevent segments of society from taking advantage of basic means-tested pensions, government can force all income groups to save. Although a few commentators lament governments' willingness to get involved and downplay the importance of the above reasons (Agulnik 2000), some form of government involvement will likely continue.

At least 15 countries now operate some type of mandated pension scheme, with over 100 million potential contributors, up from around 10 million in the early 1990s. Prominent adherents include Australia, Chile, and Switzerland, while at least another 12 Latin American and Central European countries have also mandated private pensions. The World Bank has been a strong advocate of the mandated pension model since 1994, and encourages many developing and transition countries to take this approach. Additionally, the United Kingdom has moved toward a mandated pension structure; and the United States, China, and India are all considering the benefits of instituting mandated pensions.

# 3 Structure

Retirement schemes are frequently discussed in terms of different 'pillars' (Fig. 13.1).[3] The first pillar generally involves minimum 'safety-net' retirement benefits funded out of general government revenue which are paid to retirees whose income is below some threshold. These benefits are generally not linked to participation in the formal economy, and can either be means-tested as in the United Kingdom, or universal as in New Zealand. The second pillar can be thought of as compulsory labor income replacement: mandated pensions and PAYG schemes. These compulsory schemes are funded from forced saving or specific taxes, and retirement benefits are linked—either directly through a formula or indirectly through a contribution rate—to lifetime labor income. The third pillar encompasses individual, discretionary saving for retirement, sometimes comprising supplementary, voluntary contributions to a second-pillar account, or to a separate vehicle supported by tax incentives. Countries need not have a policy for each pillar. The following section addresses the structure of mandated pensions in terms of the accumulation and decumulation phases of the life-cycle.

## 3.1 Accumulation Phase

Pensions are 'mandated' during the working, or accumulation, phase of the life-cycle in the sense that workers *must* provide for their *own* retirement pensions. The chronological structure of mandated pensions is essentially this:

- individual accounts are established for employees upon entering the workforce;
- compulsory contributions are put in these accounts, by employees or employers or both;
- the accumulated funds are invested, and the returns credited to the respective accounts;
- individuals receive periodic updates on the size and performance of their accumulated assets;
- the preserved assets become available at retirement.

## First Pillar:
- Safety Net
  - Universal
  - Means-tested

## Second Pillar: Compulsory Employment Related
- Publicly Mandated Individual Accounts *(Discussed in Chapter 13)*
  - Funded Defined Contribution (privately managed)
  - Funded Defined Contribution (publicly managed)
  - Notional Defined Contribution* (publicly managed)
- Publicly Provided (no individual accounts)
  - PAYG (unfunded)
  - Funded

*NDC Schemes also contain elements of public provision; they are difficult to classify neatly.

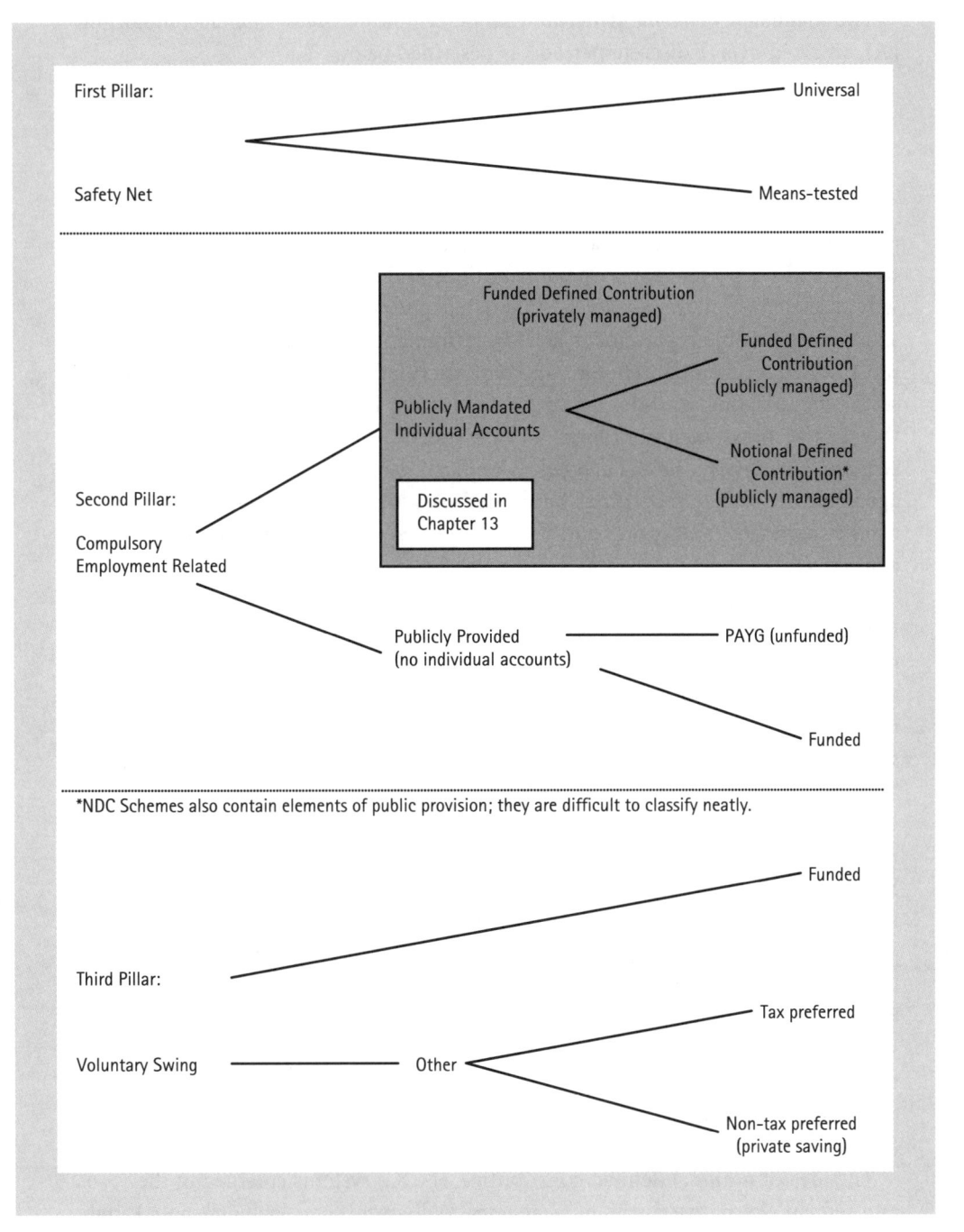

## Third Pillar: Voluntary Swing
- Funded
- Other
  - Tax preferred
  - Non-tax preferred (private saving)

**Fig. 13.1 Classification of retirement policies**

*Note*: Discussed in Chapter 13.
*NDC schemes also contain elements of public provision; they are difficult to classify neatly.

The mandated pensions structure that determines retirees' final accumulations (A), amassed over T discrete periods, is described below:

$$A \sum_{i=1}^{T} \left\{ C \cdot W \cdot (1+w)^{i-\pm 1} \cdot (1 - \beta_c - \tau_c) \cdot [1 + (\mu - \beta_A) \cdot (1 - \tau_A)] \right\}^{T-i} \quad (1)$$

$C$ is the contribution rate, $W$ the wage, and $w$ the wage growth rate; $\beta$ represents the contribution and asset management fees, $\mu$ is the investment return, and $\tau$ represent taxes on contributions and earnings. Each of these factors will crucially affect the ability of mandated pension schemes to provide for a satisfactory income replacement level in retirement. This algebraic description is most suited to funded defined contribution (FDC) schemes where the private sector has a significant role: the form encouraged by the World Bank. Although this is the most common form of mandated pension structure, two major structural variations have emerged. Mandated pensions may be publicly managed; and if so, they may either be funded or simply notional defined contributions (unfunded). Singapore[4] and Italy[5] are representative of these two structures, respectively.

Singapore has the world's oldest national, publicly managed defined contribution scheme, established in 1955. Almost all employed Singaporean permanent residents are required to contribute to the Central Provident Fund (CPF), a statutory body whose board is appointed by the Ministry of Labor.[6] Like the national provident funds of other Asian countries, the CPF has wider goals than simply providing retirement income. Contributors can access the fund to purchase 'socially desirable' goods, whose range has progressively increased since 1968 to include housing, insurance, and tertiary education. Such broad goals have resulted in very high contribution rates, which peaked at 50 percent of income in 1984, but have since fallen to below 40 percent to accommodate economic downturns. Legislation provides that assets of the CPF be invested in special, non-tradable government securities whose interest rates are determined by a weighted average of local, short-term, commercial deposit rates; interest is directly credited to members' accounts, subject to a 2.5 percent per annum minimum return. After considering inflation, returns on members' balances are often negative, and averaged zero percent per annum in the ten years to 1997. Poor returns have also been symptomatic of other national provident funds, for similar reasons (Asher 1999).

The idea of notional defined contribution (NDC) systems emerged in the 1990s as a reform alternative to the FDC system (Williamson and Williams 2003). Italy became the first country (1995) to introduce this system. Italian employees' payroll tax contributions[7] are used to finance the retirement benefits of current retirees, but unlike PAYG schemes each employee is given an account that records the amount of individual payroll tax paid. Regular 'interest' adjustments are made to account balances during the accumulation phase using GDP growth rates. Upon retirement, the notional amount in the account, together with life expectancy, is used to determine the size of retirement benefits. Although NDC schemes have not reached maturity—and still operate in complicated tandem with obsolescent PAYG systems—they better accommodate demographic transitions and discourage early retirement, since unlike PAYG schemes, they provide a direct link between individual contributions and eventual benefits.

The most common form remains the FDC system, where the private sector takes a significant administrative and prudential role.[8] Chile (1981) and Australia (1992) were relatively early to establish FDC systems. In general, workers' individual accounts are credited with compulsory contributions equal to around 10 percent of their income, and these contributions are managed by private pension funds, which have fiduciary responsibilities to their members. Workers may have the right to choose their fund, or at least have some choice in relation to their investment choice within funds. That investment choices are left up to individuals and pension funds is a crucial distinction between FDC systems and publicly managed or NDC systems. Two broad structural considerations need to be addressed in FDC systems: contribution issues and governance.

The issue of contributions refers not only to the level, but also to coverage, legal responsibility for contributions, and collection arrangements. Contribution rates can range from 5 percent of labor income in Denmark to 18 percent in Switzerland. There can be a range within schemes: in Switzerland workers near retirement pay 18 percent, while young workers pay 7 percent. Most FDC countries enforce a contribution rate of around 10 percent, although contribution limitations can apply. In Chile contributions are required after one hour's paid work per week, in Australia contributions are limited to those aged 18–70 who earn more than A$450 per month (or about 11 percent of average earnings), and except for Hong Kong, the self-employed have not been required to contribute. Although contribution levels are determined with reference to employee labor income, in practice employers make the actual contributions to funds on behalf of their employees, and so employees' periodic labor income is received 'net' of contributions. In Australia, the 9 percent contribution is gross of taxes and administration charges (which can defray actual contributions significantly). Latin American FDC plans generally specify a rate *net* of such charges. Collection arrangements can be centralized, as in Argentina where the authorities are responsible for allocating funds to asset managers, or decentralized, as in Australia where government has no such custodial role.

Given private sector involvement in FDC schemes, governance—the structure of the pension funds and the regulations surrounding their decisions—is crucial. Pension funds are created to administer accounts, manage retirement assets, and select support services, yet governance arrangements differ considerably across schemes. Chile is indicative of the more tightly regulated Latin American FDC schemes. There, pension fund administrators, or AFPs, are profit-making entities managed by boards of directors that have responsibilities to both shareholders and fund members. Each AFP needs to be approved by the government (which limits numbers to around ten) and can only manage one pension fund. There is little outsourcing of support functions. The arrangements are more varied in OECD FDC systems. Pension funds are often established as trusts, whose trustees have legally binding fiduciary responsibilities to fund members. In Australia, these trusts can be not-for-profit 'industry' funds, where both employees and employers are represented on the fund's board. These funds compete with for-profit trusts, often established by major financial institutions. It is necessary to specify the composition and responsibilities of pension boards, be they trusts or limited liability companies. Indeed, research shows that these stipulations matter for fund performance. For example, it appears that transparency of investment decisions and the professionalism of pension fund boards can have significant effects on returns (Yang and Mitchell forthcoming).

The most significant regulatory constraints on pension funds' decisions relate to asset allocations and performance. Again, there are significant differences across FDC regimes. Most countries enforce specific limits for particular asset classes. In Argentina only 10 percent of assets may be foreign but up to 65 percent of assets may be held in Argentine government securities. The Netherlands, the United Kingdom, and Australia—countries with well-developed fiduciary or 'prudent-man' legal frameworks—have no asset limits, and do not specify performance guarantees. In Chile no fund is allowed to return below 50 percent of the average real return of all AFPs; Switzerland imposes a 4 percent nominal return floor. Asset and performance regulations have encouraged manager herding, and have produced poorer returns than in freer jurisdictions.

## 3.2 Decumulation Phase

Upon reaching some stipulated 'preservation' age, which has varied from 55 in Australia (but 60 for those born in 1964 or later) to 65 in most other FDC countries, workers may have access to their accumulated assets to provide for their retirement:

- These assets may either be partly or fully converted to an annuity.
- Assets that are not converted to an annuity may be re-invested or drawn down, at discretion or subject to limits.
- Workers with insufficient accumulations may be eligible for further (first-pillar) government assistance.
- Residual assets at death can form part of a bequest, or can revert to the deceased party's spouse.

There is little regulation surrounding choices in decumulation. Pensions are only 'mandated' to the extent that workers' accumulated assets *must* be used to partly or fully fund their retirement.

Retirees are subject to three main risks *during* their retirement: inflation, longevity, and investment risk. Contributions and investment performance in the accumulation phase will have already determined the initial replacement rate. Ideally, individuals would mitigate the three risks by purchasing a particular annuity, calculated in the following manner:

$$y = \frac{f \cdot A}{\sum_{t=1}^{X} tp_x \left[ \frac{(1+\pi)^{(t-1)}}{(1+R)^t} \right]} \quad (2)$$

$A$ is the accumulation, and $y$ is the yearly income that can be thus derived, assuming a positive annual adjustment factor $\pi$. $R$ is the risk-free rate, $\chi$ is the maximum possible life expectancy, and $_tp_x$ is the probability that a particular retiree will live until that maximum. Each individual would only annuitize some fraction, $f$, of his accumulated balance, given a desire for liquidity or a bequest. Such an arrangement would guarantee both a regular, inflation-adjusted income until death, and accessible precautionary savings. Indeed, retirees may wish to accept some investment risk over the course of their annuity in return for potentially greater income. Economists have demonstrated that these types of arrangements provide the optimal structure for individuals' decumulation phase, where financial markets accommodate individual preferences for optimum retirement income streams.

These arrangements, however, do not arise in practice; the policy environment surrounding the decumulation phase in all FDC countries is quite undeveloped (Table 13.1). Most Latin American FDC countries have a choice between a *phased withdrawal* of retirement benefits—subject to predetermined limits based on life expectancy—and the purchase of a nominal life annuity. Phased withdrawals offer some exposure to market returns but little longevity insurance. Broadly similar arrangements exist in Singapore, the United Kingdom, and elsewhere. Additionally, almost all FDC countries maintain a means-tested safety net pension, so that retirees whose income genuinely falls below a certain threshold can maintain an acceptable standard of living. Indeed, in Australia, especially until the superannuation system matures, many workers will need to rely on funding from the first-pillar age pension to supplement their retirement income from the second-pillar superannuation scheme.

A key structural issue for FDC schemes is their interaction with the unfunded first pillar. In particular, governments would like to prevent the first pillar from being abused by retirees whose accumulations fall close to the income or assets threshold at which they become eligible for the minimum pension. For these retirees, an additional dollar of saving is subject to very high marginal tax rates, owing to the consequent reduction in pension payments that would ensue. Australia offers an unusual case in that it imposes no compulsion whatsoever upon reaching retirement, and around 75 percent of the value of retirees' accumulations is taken as a lump sum (for large accumulations there are tax incentives to purchase an annuity). In practice, many of these lump sums are reinvested in phased withdrawal programs, but nevertheless without compulsion it is easier for retirees to engineer their financial affairs so as to become eligible for first-pillar support. From this angle alone, some constraint on spending of accumulated assets appears sensible.

Going forward, *the* key structural consideration for policy-makers is how to facilitate an effective market for annuities. Given the desirability of inflation-indexed, permanent income streams, a well-functioning annuities market is important for FDC schemes. Yet few people purchase annuities. Retirees may not annuitize their accumulation in order to leave a bequest or maintain precautionary balances, or because they already possess implicit annuity income. The bequest motive has been downplayed in recent research, as many people without children or with significant housing assets still do not annuitize their financial assets. The desire for precautionary balances, on the other hand, is seen as more feasible, particularly as unexpected health costs can be large in old age. Over-annuitization refers to the availability of a first-pillar minimum pension. The evidence from Australia and the United States suggests that minimum social security benefits reduce the demand for annuities (Doyle *et al.* 2001). Conversely, insurance companies are reluctant to supply annuities given uncertainty about future payouts. For example, significant medical advances could render life insurance companies insolvent.

Nevertheless, most research has examined the annuity market itself—specifically, the existence of adverse selection. Adverse selection refers to the 'bad' set of risks that present themselves to life insurance companies when annuity purchase is voluntary—a process that progressively increases prices until few find purchase worthwhile. Even in developed financial systems like Australia, the United Kingdom, and the United States, annuities can be up to 11 percent more expensive than actuarial fair value would imply (Finkelstein and Poterba 1999).

So how can policy-makers best structure the decumulation phase to attenuate adverse selection? Mandatory annuitization can reduce annuity prices by mitigating the preponderance of 'bad' risks. Indeed, evidence suggests that annuities in the United Kingdom (where annuity purchase is compulsory at age 75) are better value than equivalent voluntary annuities in the United States (McCarthy and Neuberger 2003). But important structural issues arise. Which types of annuities are acceptable, and how much should be annuitized? At what age should people annuitize, and to what extent could annuity issuers price-discriminate using buyers' health records and sex, and the current economic climate? Few governments offer inflation-

Table 13.1 Decumulation phase of FDC schemes

| Country | Preservation Age (Longevity)[1] | Benefit Type | Replacement Rate (RR) | Taxation |
|---|---|---|---|---|
| Australia | Male (FM): 55 years. To be increased to 55 years by 2025.<br><br>Life exp: M(FM): 25.4 (29.4) yrs.<br><br>Pre-retirement withdrawals are restricted. | Choice of a lump sum or an income stream. Lump sums are popular (73%). | Annual retirement income of about A$ 19,800[2].<br><br>Poor integration. Retirement age is not co-ordinate with public pension eligibility age. | 15% tax on lump sums above an indexed threshold. |
| Poland | Male (FM): 65 (60) years.<br><br>Pre-retirement withdrawals are restricted.<br><br>Life exp: M (FM): 14 (26.3) yrs. | Annuity only. | Around 59.9 in 2000.<br><br>Fully indexed to inflation and partially to wage.<br><br>Well integrated with universal basic pension.<br><br>Minimum pension is guaranteed. | Benefits are taxable. |
| Switzerland | Male (FM): 65 (62) years.<br><br>Pre-retirement withdrawals: permitted for home buyers.<br><br>Life exp at age 65: M (FM): 16.3 (20.3) yrs. | Annuity or Lump sum.<br><br>Pre-retirement withdrawals are restricted. | Pension should be higher than the guaranteed minimum pension.<br><br>Well integrated with public pension. | Benefits are fully taxed. |

(Continued)

Table 13.1 (Continued)

| Country | Preservation Age (Longevity)[1] | Benefit Type | Replacement Rate (RR) | Taxation |
|---|---|---|---|---|
| UK | Male (FM): 65 (60) years. Pre-retirement withdrawals: permitted. Life exp: M (FM): 14 (26.3) yrs. | Minimum mandatory annuitization. Accepted amount of lump sum. | RR above 60%, if contribute 10% of salary for 40 years. Well integrated with public pension. | Annuity payments are taxed. Lump sums are tax free. |
| Argentina | Male (FM): 65 (60) years. Pre-retirement withdrawals: for high accumulators. Life exp: M (FM): 13.3 (20.4) yrs. | Choice of programmed withdrawal, life annuity, or a combination. Lump-sum withdrawals: for high accumulators. | Total RR of around 63% (35% from DC scheme). Well integrated with universal basic pension. Minimum pension is guaranteed. | Benefits subject to income tax. |
| Bolivia | Male (FM): 65 years. Pre-retirement withdrawals: for high accumulators. Life exp: M (FM): 12.7 (14.0) yrs. | Annuity only. | Minimum pension is guaranteed. | No taxation on benefits (or contributions). |
| Chile | Male (FM): 65 (60) years. Pre-retirement withdrawals: for high accumulators. Life exp: M (FM): 15 (22) yrs. | Choice of programmed withdrawal, life annuity or a combination. Lump-sum withdrawals: for high accumulators. | Average RR of around 78% (82% for early retirees). Benefits are indexed to inflation. Well integrated with universal basic pension. Minimum pension is guaranteed. | Benefits subject to income tax. But the tax-free threshold is high. |

| | | | |
|---|---|---|---|
| El Salvador | Male (FM): 60 (55) years. | Choice of programmed withdrawal, life annuity. | Benefits are tax free. |
| | Pre-retirement withdrawals: for high accumulators. | Lump-sum withdrawals are permitted. | Minimum pension is guaranteed. |
| Mexico | Male (FM): 65 (60) years. | | Benefits above the threshold are taxed. |
| | Pre-retirement withdrawals: for high accumulators. | Choice of programmed withdrawal, life annuity, or a combination. | Annuity should be higher than the minimum salary. |
| Peru | Male (FM): 65 years. | | Minimum pension is guaranteed. |
| | Pre-retirement withdrawals: for high accumulators. | Choice of programmed withdrawal, life annuity, or a combination. | Pension benefits are taxed. |
| | Life exp: M (FM): 14.7 (16.5) yrs. | | No public pillar or minimum pension guarantee. |
| Uruguay | Male (FM): 60 years. | Annuity only. | |
| | Pre-retirement withdrawals: not permitted. | | No public pillar or minimum pension guarantee. |
| | Avg life exp at age 60: 19.8 yrs. | | |
| India | Male (FM): 60 years. | Lump sum only. | Member balances are insufficient. Benefits are tax free. |
| | Life exp: M (FM): 14.9 (16.2) yrs. | Highly vulnerable for inflation and longevity risks. | No indexation. |
| | | | No integration with public safety nets. |

*(Continued)*

Table 13.1 (Continued)

| Country | Preservation Age (Longevity)[1] | Benefit Type | Replacement Rate (RR) | Taxation |
|---|---|---|---|---|
| Malaysia | Male (FM): 55 years. Pre-retirement withdrawals: permitted. Life exp: M (FM): 19.9 (22.6) yrs. | Lump sum only. Benefits can be withdrawn in two stages at age 50 and 55. | Do not provide sufficient balances. Vulnerable to inflation and longevity risks. No integration with public safety nets. | Benefits are tax free. |
| Singapore | Male (FM): 60 years. Pre-retirement withdrawals: permitted. Life exp: M (FM): 18.8 (21.7) yrs. | Minimum mandatory annuatization. Rest as a lump sum. | Member balances are insufficient. Avg RR of about 26%. No integration. Means-tested safety nets are limited. | Benefits are tax free. |
| Sri Lanka | Male (FM): 55 years. Pre-retirement withdrawals: permitted for housing. Life exp: M (FM): 21.4 (23.7) yrs. | Lump sum only. Highly vulnerable for inflation and longevity risks. | Member balances are insufficient. Avg CAR[3] of about 4.52. No integration with public safety nets. | Benefits are tax free. |

Notes:
[1] Longevity (years): measured as life expectancy at retirement.
[2] For average income earner with 9% contributions for 30 years. ASFA, 2004.
[3] CAR: Capital Accumulation Ratio (accumulated balance at retirement/final annual wage) for an average income earner.

Sources: Various; contact authors for details.
ASFA (2004); Natali (2004); Cannon and Tonks (2003); Karunarathne and Goswami (2002); Rofman (2002); Kay and Kritzer (2001); UN (2001); McCarthy et al. (2000).

linked bonds, yet such products might be necessary to pique insurance firms' interest in such products.

Finally, policy-makers need to consider other sources of retirement income which might complement annuity income from mandated accumulations and supplement reliance on the first pillar. Reverse mortgages, for example, can allow retirees to remain in their home, and to receive payments indefinitely until death. These could be particularly useful in countries with significant housing wealth. Additionally, the benefits of group self-annuitization, in which employment or other groups of people can self-annuitize without recourse to a third party, are yet to be tested in practice.

One paradox of FDC schemes is the important role of government regulations. Although not publicly managed, the prudential framework, governance structure, and constraints on workers' and retirees' choices require far more consideration than in a centrally administered PAYG system. Moreover, given that workers are forced to save, governments might be partly obliged to guarantee retirement savings. The extent of this support could introduce moral hazard and distort investors' choices.

## 4 Performance

The ultimate aim of second-pillar pension schemes is to replace labor income during retirement. There is no consensus on the most appropriate replacement rate, yet many commentators would agree with the US Department of Labor that between 60 and 80 percent of gross pre-retirement income needs to be replaced to maintain a familiar standard of living. Replacement rates can be set precisely in PAYG systems, since final pensions are determined with reference to labor income. In FDC schemes (and to a much lesser extent NDC schemes), however, initial contribution rates will not correlate perfectly with final replacement rates because asset markets and efficiency levels will affect final accumulations. This uncertainty might explain the lack of official target replacement rates in FDC systems—although the World Bank (2004) believes between 50 and 60 percent is appropriate for developing countries, and a 60 percent target has been officially suggested in Australia.

Nevertheless, the relationship between contribution rates and replacement rates is simple: other things equal, the greater the initial contribution rate the greater the eventual replacement rate. Policy-makers can easily alter the former, which will be justified by normative considerations about what is the 'best' replacement rate. Therefore, simply comparing replacement rates across FDC schemes is not always useful. It ignores the performance of a given system; the best-performing FDC scheme produces the highest replacement rate for a *given* level of contributions. Indeed, it is clear from equation (1) that the three main factors that affect *performance* of FDC schemes are investment returns ($\mu$), administration fees and changes ($\beta$), and taxation ($\tau$).

## 4.1 Investment Returns

Investment returns are an important factor in privately managed FDC schemes. In public schemes, such as those exemplified by Southeast Asian provident funds, assets are invested mostly in government debt securities, the returns of which are relatively low and certain. By contrast, in private FDC schemes, individuals and pension funds have some choice over their investments. Investment returns in these FDC schemes will be directly determined by two factors: the performance of the underlying assets, and the allocation of assets across different classes. These issues apply equally to investments in the decumulation phase, to the extent that retirees maintain some exposure to investment markets.

A voluminous literature has captured the risk-return trade-off between asset classes. Equities are considered the most risky but can offer the high upside potential (Table 13.2). In Australia, international equities have returned around − 8 percent per annum on average in the four years to end 2003 compared to 20 percent to end 1999, although currency movements can undermine foreign investments and funds need to determine to what extent they will hedge. Nevertheless, over different time periods relative returns can vary significantly: in the three years to June 2004 property and bonds returned far more than any other asset class, and with lower volatility. More recently, hedge funds, which are leveraged entities that seek arbitrage opportunities and speculate on price changes in financial markets, have become popular with pension funds. In the first six months of 2004 US pension funds invested almost $90 billion in hedge funds. Hedge funds have exhibited comparatively high returns over the past ten years, and may become a 'fifth' major asset class, positioned at the high end of the risk-return spectrum. Generally, any diversified pension fund with access to these asset types could have performed well over a 20-year period.

Nevertheless, returns over a 40 to 50 year period, the approximate working life of members, are more relevant for pension funds, and so assumptions about long-term asset returns are crucial. For instance, the expectation that equities will generate superior returns over the long term will have a very significant impact on the performance of FDC schemes. Yet there is uncertainty about this assumption's validity. The demographic transition may reduce equity returns, as retirees sell their accumulated assets during retirement. History shows that equity markets had performed relatively poorly for decades before the 1980s. And the constant evolution and expansion of financial markets, to which the growth of pension funds will themselves contribute, make it difficult to extrapolate asset returns into the future (Davis 2004).

The second factor that will affect fund investment returns is the allocation of assets across investment classes. Pension funds traditionally invest in all major asset classes but the weightings will be critical, as the above discussion demon-

Table 13.2 Returns over various asset classes, Australia, 1993–2004

| Period | Returns (percent) | | | | |
| --- | --- | --- | --- | --- | --- |
| | Australian equities[1] | International equities[2] | Aust. listed property securities[3] | Australian fixed interest[4] | Cash[5] |
| 1993 | 45 | 19 | 30 | 16 | 5 |
| 1994 | −9 | −2 | −6 | −5 | 5 |
| 1995 | 20 | 18 | 13 | 19 | 8 |
| 1996 | 15 | 15 | 14 | 12 | 8 |
| 1997 | 12 | 21 | 20 | 12 | 6 |
| 1998 | 12 | 19 | 18 | 10 | 5 |
| 1999 | 16 | 27 | −5 | −1 | 5 |
| 2000 | 5 | −11 | 18 | 12 | 6 |
| 2001 | 10 | −16 | 15 | 5 | 5 |
| 2002 | −9 | −25 | 12 | 9 | 5 |
| 2003 | 15 | 23 | 8 | 6 | 5 |
| Average | 12.1 | 7.9 | 12.5 | 8.6 | 5.8 |
| Standard deviation | 14.55 | 18.04 | 10.48 | 7.00 | 1.06 |

Notes:
[1] Australian Equities: S&P/ASX 200 Accumulation Index.
[2] International Equities: MSCI World (ex Australia) Index.
[3] Australian Listed Property Securities: S&P/ASX 300 Listed Property Trust Accumulation Index.
[4] Australian Fixed Interest: UBS Warburg Composite All Maturities Index.
[5] Cash: UBS Warburg Bank Bill Index.
Sources: Various.

strates. Three stylized facts are observed in relation to asset allocation. First, FDC pension funds exhibit a strong home bias in their investments, even without government stipulations. In Australia, around 50 percent of all assets are held in domestic equities, despite the Australian market's much smaller global weighting. Second, there is no consensus on what is the best portfolio to hold. And third, the trend is for funds to be managed passively rather than actively.

Home bias here refers to the preponderance of domestic financial assets in the portfolios of pension funds, where it is seemingly desirable (and possible) to invest overseas and obtain the same expected return with a lower expected volatility. As much as 90 percent of US financial assets are held domestically, even though it comprises less than 50 percent of the world's capitalization, and similar ratios can be given for other countries. To some extent these 'biases' might be explained by the additional or uncertain transaction costs that investing overseas entails, or the information disadvantage that outside investors might have, but it is difficult to believe that large biases can be explained by these phenomena alone. Home bias clearly can have a large impact on the performance of FDC schemes: Table 13.3 shows the returns of five national equity markets over different periods of time. Relatively more exposure to international equity markets may enhance the expected risk-adjusted returns of pension funds, although the need for pension funds to reduce the exposure to equities of fund members nearing retirement has wide acceptance.

Finally, given some prescribed investment allocation across classes, there is considerable debate about whether pension funds should be 'actively' managed at all. In the United States, the evidence clearly shows that index funds outperform actively managed mutual funds over the long term (Shah and Fernandes 2001). Certainly, index funds have grown significantly over the past 20 years—now around a quarter of the assets of UK and US pension funds are attached to index managers. This growth augurs well for FDC systems, since index funds can lower aggregate long-term transaction costs yet maintain the same exposures to equities.

## 4.2 Fees and Costs

Fees and underlying costs are crucially important when discussing the efficacy of FDC schemes, yet they have received very little attention in the literature.[9] Fees arise from the three core functions of pension funds—collecting contributions, investing and managing assets, and paying benefits to retirees—and sometimes

Table 13.3 Returns of various share markets, 1993–2004

| Period | Returns (percent) | | | | |
|---|---|---|---|---|---|
| | United States S&P 500 | Japan Nikkei | United Kingdom FTSE 100 | Hong Kong Hang Seng | Singapore Straits Times |
| 1993 | 7 | 15 | −1 | 116 | 63 |
| 1994 | −2 | 27 | 8 | −31 | 2 |
| 1995 | 34 | −2 | 10 | 23 | 5 |
| 1996 | 20 | 1 | 13 | 34 | −1 |
| 1997 | 31 | −23 | 29 | −20 | −42 |
| 1998 | 27 | −21 | 21 | −6 | −8 |
| 1999 | 20 | 55 | 9 | 69 | 78 |
| 2000 | −10 | −35 | −5 | −11 | −25 |
| 2001 | −13 | −33 | −17 | −25 | −21 |
| 2002 | −23 | −11 | −14 | −18 | −12 |
| 2003 | 26 | 39 | −3 | 36 | 34 |
| 2004 | 9 | 8 | 8 | 11.8[1] | 14.9[1] |
| Average | 11 | 2 | 5 | 15 | 6 |
| standard deviation | 19 | 28 | 13 | 46 | 37 |

Notes:
[1] At the end of November 2004.
Source: EIU Country Data.

from the profit motive. Fees are normally charged as some percentage of contributions, benefits, assets under management, or as annual fixed amounts. It is possible to convert all these different types of charges into a single percentage fee. Such standardization can allow comparison across funds, and highlights the relative impacts of different charges. Table 13.4 shows the relationship for different charges, rates of return ($\mu$), and different periods of accumulation. A 1 percent asset charge over 35 years is equivalent to an ongoing contributions charge of around 22 percent. The potency of asset charges derives from their ever-increasing relationship with contributions, investment returns, and length of contribution period. Even small differences in asset charges can have large impacts over time. These relationships imply a strong case for ensuring members understand the impact of different charges.

Table 13.4 Comparative impact of asset, benefit, and contribution charges over varying periods

|  | Charges as proportion of assets under management | Equivalent contribution or benefit charge (%) | Equivalent contribution or benefit charge (%) |
|---|---|---|---|
|  |  | $r = 5\%$ | $r = 10\%$ |
| 15 years of contributions | 0.5 | 4.2 | 4.7 |
|  | 1.0 | 8.3 | 9.1 |
|  | 2.0 | 15.8 | 17.3 |
|  | 3.0 | 22.7 | 24.6 |
| 25 years of contributions | 0.5 | 7.2 | 8.2 |
|  | 1.0 | 13.8 | 15.6 |
|  | 2.0 | 25.4 | 28.6 |
|  | 3.0 | 35.1 | 39.4 |
| 35 years of contributions | 0.5 | 10.3 | 20.0 |
|  | 1.0 | 19.3 | 22.4 |
|  | 2.0 | 34.4 | 39.6 |
|  | 3.0 | 46.2 | 52.6 |

Source: Adapted from Bateman et al. (2001).

In practice, overall charge ratios vary dramatically across FDC regimes and also within jurisdictions. For example, given some simplifying assumptions about asset returns and contributions, the Australian Master Trust member's final accumulation will be almost 30 percent lower than his Bolivian contemporary's. Fees and costs are the main disadvantage of privately managed FDC schemes.

Almost all FDC jurisdictions have placed regulations on the types of charges allowed. Typically, asset management charges are banned (as in Chile and Colombia) or capped (Poland and Hungary). Other restrictions include limits on contribution charges, and competitive bidding for asset management whereby the government chooses the ultimate manager(s) (Sweden and Bolivia). Australian and some United Kingdom pension funds are subject to little fee regulation (apart from standard disclosure requirements), perhaps owing to the inertia of having a long-standing (pre-mandatory) funded pension industry. Perhaps surprisingly, though, Whitehouse's (2000) investigations show that the existence of regulation neither standardizes nor necessarily reduces overall fees and charges. Indeed, Australian 'industry' funds have some of the lowest overall fees of any FDC scheme, while Argentinian FDC pensions, having limits on charge types, are comparatively expensive. Evidence suggests the existence of regulation is not sufficient or even necessary to ensure efficient FDC schemes.

Governance has an impact on fees. Australia's 'industry' funds, originally set up by trade unions for the exclusive use of members in a particular industry and governed by a mixture of employer and employee representatives, are both not-for-profit and historically closed to new members. These traits have ensured low marketing costs and charges. By contrast, the profit motives and marketing costs of Master Trusts and AFPs have facilitated a cost disadvantage. Although these funds are quick to point out that they offer higher levels of service, there is little evidence of consistently superior investment returns. The ability of industry funds to prosper has been predicated on their having a captive 'market' based on workers' occupations. Forthcoming free 'choice of fund' rules in Australia may render the advantages of industry funds obsolete, because these funds will have to compete with for-profit retail funds. More broadly, the extent of member choice of fund will be a crucial determinant of marketing costs in any given FDC system. On the other hand, simply having a regime where employers choose funds introduces agency issues, since employers have no incentive to choose the right fund for their employees. The Australian industry funds offer the best of both worlds, yet would be difficult to replicate given their unique historical evolution (Bateman *et al.* 2001).[10]

Given the trend toward individual choice of fund, some options can reduce overall fees. First, transparency may be the best strategy to encourage competition and efficiency. Unlike Australian and UK arrangements, Latin American schemes generally specify that contributions be paid net of fees, thus drawing members' attention to additional payments. Moreover, charges should be consolidated into a single measure so consumers can make better-informed choices. In Australia, the confusion over fund charges has led the government to force funds to compute a 'single fee' so that consumers can readily compare funds. Second, the government can become involved in the provision of custodial, collection, and bookkeeping service—where clear and intuitive economies of scale emerge. Bolivia and Sweden have pursued this latter strategy, where members still have ultimate choice of fund.

## 4.3 Taxation

The compulsory nature of FDC schemes offers much scope for governments to extract revenue. Although almost all FDC schemes are taxed, differences in form can have significant equity and efficiency effects. Two key issues arise in relation to pension taxation, and only the first engenders any *theoretical* agreement. First, governments need to decide at which point retirement flows are to be taxed—when contributions are made, when benefits are paid, or while the assets are earning income during accumulation. Second, to what extent should pension taxation be concessional—and more broadly, should participants be able to make additional contributions at concessional tax rates?

The debate about pension taxation falls within the broader discussion of income versus consumption taxation. Although income tax is a firmly entrenched pillar of government revenue, it facilitates the 'double taxation' of saving and can thus discourage saving for retirement: income is taxed, and the income generated from whatever is saved is taxed again. Therefore, taxation of pension fund earnings is considered a relatively egregious policy, particularly given the evidence of significant undersaving and declines in consumption upon retirement. In particular, the volatility of investment markets renders the compounding effect of earnings taxation unpredictable, and would significantly undermine the incentive to join a fund that exhibits good returns. Moreover, in order to put pension saving on an equal footing with owner-occupier housing—from which income and capital gains are not taxed—it might be sensible to exempt pension earnings from taxation.

The taxation of investment earnings can also distort first-best asset allocations within funds, since assets that pay income in different forms may be subject to idiosyncratic tax credits and thus cause funds to favor particular assets. In Australia, for example, domestic equity investments often lead to a tax 'imputation' credit that makes these a relatively attractive investment: almost 50 percent of Australian funds invest in domestic equities. Finally, investment earnings taxes can encourage an early retirement, since larger pension accumulations will produce greater investment earnings. Moreover, investment earnings taxes penalize workers whose careers are marked by part-time employment later in life (mainly women), who consequently depend more on investment earnings to augment their savings.

Given the problems with earnings taxation, most FDC policy frameworks tend to exempt fund investment earnings from taxation and to tax either contributions or benefits or both. Although the two are equal in present value terms, benefits taxation might be preferred for three reasons. First, it entails more investment risk-sharing by the government. Second, if private sector investments have a higher marginal benefit than public investments, then benefits taxes allow money to be invested privately for longer. And third, progressive income tax structures during retirement will take account of variability in investment performance. On the other hand, contribution taxes are likely to produce more revenue, as they are made when workers are generally within higher marginal tax brackets. The World Bank supports either (Holzmann and Hinz 2005). Australia is one of the very few countries to tax all three flows, while Singapore stands out for taxing none. Whichever method is chosen, it is important for policy changes to be consistent, as uncertainty about rules will stifle confidence in the system, potentially reducing additional contributions in favor of other assets. Substantive changes in taxation policy can entail significant transfers across generations and within cohorts.

Concessional pension fund taxation itself is based on the premise that tax exemptions will reduce future first-pillar payouts, and simultaneously encourage (and signal to) workers to save more. Thus, these concessions for FDC schemes are normally extended to voluntary saving within FDC schemes—in Australia such contributions comprise over 20 percent of total contributions. Economists, however, do not agree whether concessional voluntary taxation really increases saving, or merely displaces it from elsewhere. Indeed, the *Journal of Economic Perspectives*, 10/4 devoted a volume to the arguments for and against. Determining the answer empirically is very difficult, owing to lack of data and the standard inability to conduct counterfactual scenarios. Nevertheless, even if voluntary saving diverts 'saving' from elsewhere, the very diversion will highlight to myopic workers the importance of retirement saving, and indeed the propensity to consume out of these voluntary contributions is likely to be lower.

## 5 Pitfalls and Research Suggestions

The efficacy of mandated pension schemes relies on their ability to force people to save, which in turn requires that workers will not adjust their saving behavior to accommodate mandatory saving rules. After all, workers could conceivably offset any forced saving by increased borrowing, and thus ensure that their chosen consumption paths remain unchanged. Recent thinking from the behavioral finance literature suggests deeper reasons why mandatory saving rules will not be flouted. It is likely that people do not know their optimal consumption path. This path is inherently difficult to know, as the interplay of taxation, income, saving, and investment returns must all be estimated, together with the probabilities of different events occurring. Second, saving for retirement offers neither opportunities for learning through repetition nor rules of thumb. Moreover, people might be reluctant to think about retirement planning for ingrained psychological reasons: the distasteful self-images such a topic evokes. In fact, the evidence is that these plans have increased household saving in Australia and the United Kingdom (Connolly and Kohler 2004; Attanasio and Rohwedder 2001). Nevertheless, in view of increasing financial sophistication, it will be necessary to monitor the extent to which the mandated pension system interacts with private discretionary saving.

Behavioral finance also sheds light on potential pitfalls in FDC design. Two developments can be seen as potential problems: choice of fund and saving rates, and asset allocation. Now-famous evidence suggests that individuals can be subject to too much choice (Seth-Iyengar 2003)—in the face of an abundant choice of jams, consumers show little interest in making purchases, in contrast to the scenario with only a few jams. Notwithstanding the need for funds to present financial performance and fees in clear and comparable terms, in a fully privatized FDC scheme the existence of thousands of pension funds may not be optimal. The problem is exacerbated when it is not just firms or governments having to choose funds, but all workers, each of whom must potentially sift through hundreds of pages of documents in order to find the 'best' fund. Indeed, the evidence is that people's saving decisions are heavily influenced by the default setting of their saving plan, even when they have the option of easily increasing their saving rate (Madrian and Shea 2001). The corollary of this is that contributors will trust policy-makers (and employers) to choose the most appropriate saving rate.

Moreover, in a fully privatized FDC scheme, workers will have some say over the asset allocation of their retirement saving. This is a very important decision that will dramatically affect their retirement, yet it requires some fairly sophisticated knowledge about asset returns and projections. Again, individuals are heavily influenced by default allocations (Bernatzi and Thaler 2001). For instance, contributors tend to choose an investment allocation based on the range of funds on offer as opposed to the assets in which particular funds choose to invest: a set of offered funds that was in general riskier would result in participants having a higher exposure to equities than a group of funds which was on average invested mainly in bonds. Moreover, Mitchell and Utkus (2003) have noted a propensity for a large minority of US pension funds investors to place a significant proportion of their pension assets in the stock of their employer. Given their existing exposure to their employer, this would be counter-intuitive in relation to modern asset allocation theory.

Therefore, FDC schemes need to at least acknowledge the problems that free consumer choice can have for completely free-market implementation. In relation to choice of fund, investment allocation, and savings rate, it is incumbent on employers but ultimately policy-makers to ensure that people's default decisions are roughly appropriate. Perhaps the most important complement for FDC schemes is compulsory financial education, potentially during secondary school. There is some evidence that this can be effective (Bernheim *et al.* 1997). If governments mandate saving and give consumers choice, then it is also necessary to equip them with the basic financial skills required to make informed decisions about a subject that will have a significant impact on their lives. It is unlikely the market alone will provide this information in an unbiased manner, and the 1980s United Kingdom pension mis-selling crisis is ample testament to that.

Insights from behavioral finance for pension design have now been well addressed, yet other crucial areas should also be part of the research agenda. First, the appropriate retirement income needed by retirees needs to be further analyzed. The ubiquitous 60 percent replacement rate may well overstate the real requirement—particularly when significant tax and transport concessions may need to be taken into account. On the other hand, retirees' health costs may rise significantly in retirement, particularly in the later stages. Second, the types of financial instruments available in even the most advanced markets are not ideal for facilitating good retirement outcomes. Governments need to facilitate the development of new financial products that are geared ultimately to supporting retirees. Inflation-indexed bonds are obvious contenders, but there are others. For example, might life insurance policies, or health insurance policies, be able to be securitized? Both developments would serve to spread risk more evenly, and attenuate the reluctance insurance companies might feel to write such long-term business. Finally, the macroeconomic consequences of FDC systems have only been tentatively addressed. Pension fund dynamics may have a significant impact on financial stability, monetary policy, exchange rate dynamics, and asset prices.

# 6 Conclusion

FDC schemes offer a timely and practicable alternative to traditional PAYG retirement schemes, regardless of their particular features. Both the accumulation and decumulation phases will be affected by investment performance, the types of fees and charges levied, and the taxation regime. The crucial point here is that small annual differences can compound to make a large difference to the final accumulation. Going forward, investment returns will prove to be a crucial determinant of the success and spread of FDC schemes. Successful implementation also requires a pragmatic recognition of the average worker's likely behavior and response to FDC schemes. In particular, policy-makers should acknowledge the likelihood of significant inertia in fund and investment choice on the part of workers. Many political and vested interests are at stake in changing to a new regime, even if all the objective evidence points to the benefits. Indeed, when put to referendums, such policies are likely to receive a resounding 'no' as they did in the case of New Zealand in 1997—and so arguments need to be put strongly but tactfully. Nevertheless, FDC schemes are well within the bounds of sensible libertarian government policy. Far from simply looking out for workers' 'own good', Mill would have approved of such policy that reduces the ability of individuals to 'harm' their future selves and government finances at large.

# Notes

The views expressed in this chapter are those of the authors and do not necessarily reflect the views of the Reserve Bank of Australia or the University of New South Wales. We would like to acknowledge the helpful research assistance provided by Wasana Karunarathne.

1. Japan is a notable exception; here participation rates remain around 80 percent.
2. The *dependency ratio* is the ratio of retirees and children to those of working age.
3. More recently, the World Bank has started classifying policy into *five* pillars, although the framework remains essentially the same (see Holzmann and Hinz 2005). The potential for PAYG and mandated pensions to operate in parallel resulted in their becoming the 'first' and 'second' pillars, respectively. This rendered the flat-rate pension the 'zero' pillar, and the somewhat neglected need for the elderly to have access to health care and housing has become the 'fifth' pillar.
4. Indonesia, Malaysia, Philippines, and Thailand also embody similar retirement structures.
5. Sweden, Poland, Latvia, Mongolia, and the Kyrgyz Republic also operate NDC schemes.
6. Certain classes of civil servants and politicians are instead provided for in retirement by a generous unfunded PAYG system. The assets of the CPF amount to around 55 percent of Singapore GDP, or over S$80 billion.
7. Thirty-three percent, and capped at 2.5 times average salary (other countries use wage growth).
8. Countries are not limited to operating one second-pillar scheme. For instance, Poland and Sweden operate NDC and FDC schemes concurrently. In both cases, however, the FDC scheme is secondary.
9. Whitehouse (2000) makes a useful distinction between fees and costs.
10. Nevertheless, the UK's new 'stakeholder pensions' aim to increase the role of employers in fund choice in order to mitigate marketing costs.

# References

AGULNIK, P. (2000). 'Maintaining incomes after work: do compulsory earnings-related pensions make sense?' *Oxford Review of Economic Policy*, 16: 45–56.

ASHER, M. (1999). 'South East Asian provident and pension funds: investment policies and performance'. Working Paper. National University of Singapore. Nov.

ATTANASIO, O., and ROHWEDDER, S. (2001). 'Pension wealth and household saving: evidence from pension reforms in the UK'. IFS Working Paper w01/21. Institute for Fiscal Studies.

BATEMAN, H., KINGSTON, G., and PIGGOTT, J. (2001). *Forced Saving: Mandating Private Retirement Income*. Cambridge: Cambridge University Press.

BERNATZI, S., and THALER, R. (2001). 'Naïve diversificaiton strategies in defined contribution saving plans'. *American Economic Review*, 91/1: 79–98.

BERNHEIM, D., GARRETT, D., and MAKI, D. (1997). 'Education and saving: the long-term effects of high school financial curriculum mandates'. NBER Working Paper 6085.

CHOI, J., LAIBSON, D., MADRIAN, B., and METRICK, A. (2005). 'Optimal defaults and active decisions'. NBER Working Paper 11074.

CONNOLLY, E., and KOHLER, M. (2004). 'The Impact of superannuation on household saving'. Reserve Bank of Australia Research Discussion Paper 2004/01.

DAVIS, E. P. (2004). 'Demographic and pension-system challenges to financial and monetary stability'. Paper presented at the Austrian Central Bank Conference, Vienna, 27–2 May.

DOYLE, S., MITCHELL, O., and PIGGOTT, J. (2001). 'Annuity values in defined contribution retirement systems: the case of Australia and Singapore'. NBER Working Paper 8091.

FELDSTEIN, M., and LIEBMAN, J. (2001). 'Social security'. NBER Working Paper 8451.

FINKELSTEIN, A., and POTERBA, J. (1999). 'Selection effects in the market for individual annuities: new evidence from the United Kingdom'. NBER Working Paper 7168.

HOLZMANN, R., and HINZ, R. (2005). *Old Age Income Support in the 21st Century: An International Perspective on Pension Systems and Reform*. Washington, D.C.: World Bank Publications. Available online at http://www1.worldbank.org/sp/incomesupportfiles/oldAgeSupportPrelimWeb.pdf

MCCARTHY, D., and NEUBERGER, A. (2003). *Pensions Policy: Evidence on Aspects of Savings Behaviour and Capital Markets*. London: Centre for Economic Policy Research.

MADRIAN, B., and SHEA, D. (2001). 'The power of suggestions: inertia in 401(k) participation and savings behavior'. NBER Working Paper 7682.

MITCHELL, O., and UTKUS, S. (2003). 'Lessons from behavioural finance for retirement plan design'. Pension Research Council Working Paper. The Wharton School.

SETHI-IYENGAR, S. (2003). 'How much choice is too much?'. Paper presented at Developments in Decision-Making under Uncertainty: Implications for Pensions, Wharton Impact Conference. Pension Research Council, 28–9 Apr.

SHAH, A., and FERNANDES, S. (2001). 'The relevance of index funds for pension investment in equities', in R. Holzmann and J. Stiglitz (eds.), *New Ideas about Old Age Security: Toward Sustainable Pension Systems in the 21st Century*. Washington, D.C.: World Bank Publications.

WHITEHOUSE, E. (2000). 'Paying for pensions: an international comparison of administrative charges in funded retirement-income systems'. Financial Services Authority Occasional Paper 13. Nov.

WILLIAMSON, J., and WILLIAMS, M. (2003). 'The notional defined contribution model: an assessment of the strengths and limitations of a new approach to the provision of old age security'. Working Paper. 2003–18. Center for Retirement Research at Boston College.

YANG, S. T., and MITCHELL, O. S. (forthcoming). 'Public pension governance, funding and performance: a longitudinal appraisal', in J. Evans and J. Piggott (eds.), *Shortchanged: Pension Fund Governance and Retirement Provision*. Cheltenham: Edward Elgar.

# CHAPTER 14

# ACTUARIAL-BASED PUBLIC PENSION SYSTEMS

## RICHARD DISNEY

## 1 INTRODUCTION

In employer-provided pension plans and individual retirement saving accounts, contributions over the working lifetime are used to purchase assets that are drawn down after retirement. In contrast, public pension systems typically use pay-as-you-go (PAYG) finance. With PAYG finance, current revenue to the program, which may be derived from a tax on payroll or from general taxation, is used to finance current pension expenditure. Such a pension program is therefore a form of tax-and-transfer system, akin to other elements of the public welfare program.

With certain exceptions such as Australia, public PAYG pension systems differ from public welfare programmes that compensate those with inadequate private resources. Analogous to private pension plans, public program entitlements are contribution-based. Participants through their contributions accrue implicit 'rights' to a specific benefit upon retirement that will be paid by later taxpayers.

In the United Kingdom, for example, the National Insurance system, initiated in 1911 and extended universally in 1946, is a 'social insurance' program that differs from a private program insofar as it pools risks (of differential longevity) across contributors. Contributions levied on payroll are notionally allocated to a 'National Insurance Fund' (which in fact only contains a few months of reserves).

The value of the participant's contributions determines his or her benefits on retirement based on an explicit formula related to annual earnings levels, years of contributions, and indexation factors.

In France (since 1945) and Germany (in more recent times), this link between contributions and pensions has been even more explicit through a points-based system. Each year's individual contributions accumulate 'points' which, on an individual's retirement, are converted into a pension by an explicit formula. By making explicit the link between generations, European pension systems reflect intergenerational 'solidarity', whether funded or tax-financed.

It could be argued that portraying public pension systems as 'social insurance' or 'solidaristic' vehicles is merely a revenue-raising device. Governments can arbitrarily change the value of 'accumulated' contributions, as the Conservative administrations did in the UK during the 1980s and early 1990s and as the French government did when it arbitrarily revalued individual accumulated 'points'. Nevertheless, the analogy between public and private contribution-based systems raises interesting questions for public pension policy that are the focus of this chapter. Does it matter whether tax-financed public pension systems look more like private insurance-based programs or operate as tax-and-transfer programs? The distinction might matter if public pension programs that mimic private insurance-based programs had favorable incentive effects on participant's behavior. Let us designate those systems with a closer link between an individual's contributions and benefits as *actuarial-based* systems. Since individuals do not normally perceive contributions to a retirement saving program in the same way as they perceive taxes, the stronger the 'actuarial basis' of the system, the greater the potential for positive incentive effects on, for example, labor supply. This point is formally illustrated in the next section, although its practical significance is an empirical matter.

Second, tax-financed actuarial-based public pension systems might have features that enable them better to absorb macroeconomic 'shocks', such as demographic ageing. The well-known 'Aaron–Samuelson' condition (Aaron 1966; Samuelson 1958) states that, in the long run, a country can afford a public pension system that, on average, pays contributors a 'return' equal to the growth of the labor force (in real efficiency units). The question is whether a formula can be found, and implemented automatically, that ensures that this condition is met. Intuitively, it would seem that it is easier to do this in an actuarial-based system than in a tax-and-transfer system. Actuarial-based systems may therefore be more sustainable in the long run.

These points are not simply of abstract interest. Several countries have in recent years attempted to move their public pension systems closer toward actuarial-based systems in many dimensions whilst maintaining PAYG finance rather than funded provisions. This trend is most explicit in those countries, including

Sweden, Italy, Poland, and Latvia, that in the mid to late 1990s introduced what are sometimes termed 'notional accounts'.

Given these general issues, the plan of this chapter is as follows. Section 2 describes an actuarial-based system and contrasts it with an explicitly redistributive program. It then delineates four dimensions in which public pension systems diverge from this actuarial benchmark, providing actual illustrations for OECD countries. Section 3 considers the limited empirical evidence on whether, in practice, deviations from an actuarial basis to the public pension system actually affect household behavior. Section 4 briefly describes some actual reforms in the mid-1990s designed explicitly to move public pension systems toward an actuarial basis. It is too early to use these reforms as 'quasi-experiments' in order to examine household responses to actuarial-based reforms, but it is possible to consider the issue of macroeconomic sustainability in this context. Finally, Section 5 provides a brief conclusion.

# 2 ACTUARIAL-BASED SYSTEMS: PRINCIPLES AND DEFINITIONS

## 2.1 Actuarial versus Tax-Based Public Pension Systems: An Illustration

Lindbeck and Persson (2003) provide a useful notation to examine the distinction between actuarial and non-actuarial-based public pension systems. Assume that a household lives for two periods with employment income $y$ in the first period, on which the government levies a proportional contribution to a pension program, denoted by $\tau$. Households can consume or save post-tax income. In the second period, the household does not work and consumes its saved resources from the first period and a benefit from the pension program, $b$. Define the market rate of interest as $r$ and consumption as $c$. The subscript denotes the time period. The consumption possibilities in the two periods can be written as:

$$c_{t+1}^2 = [y_t(1-\tau) - c_t^1](1+r) + b_{t+1}$$
$$c_t^1 \leq y_t(1-\tau) \tag{1}$$

The first equation, which simply derives from the lifetime budget constraint with no bequests, states that second period consumption comprises accumulated saving from the first period (plus interest earned at the market rate) and the pension benefit. The second equation states that individuals cannot borrow against their future pensions. If the latter constraint exists, some individuals may be *liquidity constrained* in the sense that their contributions to the pension program exceed the amount that they would have saved and may alter the timing of the labor supply and/or consumption. This constraint may bind whether the program is public or private, and funded or unfunded.

Now assume that the pension program is 'actuarial-based' in the following senses: (i) an individual's contributions are exactly matched by the program to his or her individual pension benefits and (ii) contributions 'earn' the market rate of interest $r$. The pension benefit is then:

$$b_{t+1} = (1+r)\tau y_t \qquad (2)$$

Substitution of (3) into (1) yields the revised budget constraint:

$$c^2_{t+1} = (y_t - c^1_t)(1+r) \qquad (3)$$

We can see that (3) does not include the tax rate $\tau$. Because benefits exactly correspond to contributions plus market returns, the marginal effective tax from the pension contribution is zero. As the lifetime budget constraint is not affected by this actuarial-based pension system, the individual's savings and labor supply choices are independent of the level of the pension contribution as long as liquidity constraints are not binding.

Now consider a very different scenario. Assume that the public pension system, as before, levies a contribution rate proportional to earnings, $\tau$, but then pays everyone the same benefit, $\bar{b}$ in the second period. Then second period consumption in (1) can be written as:

$$c^2_{t+1} = [y_t(1-\tau) - c^1_t](1+r) + \bar{b} \qquad (4)$$

Here each individual receives a benefit totally unrelated to contributions. In this 'non-actuarial' program, the effective marginal tax on the individual's work effort is $\tau$. The smaller rewards to work can affect both labor supply and saving—the former because the positive tax rate will induce the household to alter its labor supply so that the marginal disutility of work equals the net-of-tax wage rate (as in Sheshinski 1978), the latter because the substitutability of pension benefits for other retirement saving depends on the extent to which the pension program is actuarial-based.

Of course, every public pension system exhibits deviations from an actuarial system, such as floors and ceilings to benefits and contributions, additional allowances for dependents, and so on. In general, it can be said that each program contains an *effective tax component*, which lies between 0 and $\bar{\tau}$, the average payroll contribution.

## 2.2 Is an Actuarial-Based System Possible with Pay-As-You-Go Finance?

Can a PAYG-financed public pension system *ever* be actuarial-based in the sense defined here? In a fully funded pension system, the present value of net wealth invested in the pension plan discounted at the market rate of interest, $r$, equals the present value of liabilities. This constitutes an 'actuarial' program in the sense described in equations (1) to (3). In a PAYG program, in contrast, the only requirement for balance is that *current* receipts equal current outgoings—that is:

$$n_{t-1}\hat{b}_t = \hat{\tau} n_t \hat{y}_t \tag{5}$$

where $n$ denotes the number of contributors, with those working at $t-1$ now retired and receiving pension benefits, so that $n_t/n_{t-1}$ is the ratio of workers to pensioners. As before, $b$ is the pension benefit, $y$ earned income, and $\tau$ the contribution rate, with hats denoting averages. Thus $\hat{b}/\hat{y}$ is the average replacement rate, and the equilibrium contribution rate is the average replacement rate divided by the support ratio.

A 'generational' imbalance arises if contribution rates are forecast to rise over time in order to satisfy PAYG equilibrium in future years and for future generations. The only *sustainable* long-run 'return' on contributions is where projected $\hat{\tau}$ is constant for given $\hat{b}$ in (5) above. As suggested previously, this sustainable return is approximately equal to the sum of the rate of growth of the labor force, $n$, and the rate of growth of real income (productivity), $y$. Call this combined growth rate $g$.

When this growth rate falls short of the rate of return on private investment (i.e. when $r > g$, which is the condition when an economy is dynamically efficient), a PAYG system cannot be wholly actuarial-based. Again following the notation of Lindbeck and Persson (2003), assume that contributions earn the sustainable 'return' $g$: that is:

$$b_{t+1} = (1+g)\tau y_t \tag{6}$$

Then substituting into (1), as before, a PAYG system in long-run equilibrium gives second period consumption of:

$$c_t^2 = y_t[(1-\tau)\frac{r-g}{1+r} - c_t^1](1+r) \tag{7}$$

In a dynamically efficient economy, the average effective tax rate on each successive generation is $\tau(r-g)/(1+r)$ even if the program has no 'generational imbalance' and even if it is sustainable in the long run. Fenge and Werding (2003) call this difference in pension benefits between a sustainable PAYG system earning $g$ and a funded program earning $r$ the 'implicit tax' arising from PAYG financing (although, as shown in (4), this need not be the only tax arising from program design).

## 2.3 Intergenerational Equity

Although the only sustainable return on contributions to a public tax-financed pension system in the long run is $g$, actual returns to any generation of retirees can differ from $g$. The first generation in the program will earn an effective return greater than $g$ simply because they typically receive benefits on retirement without a lifetime of contributions into the system. But program generosity can also vary over time due to the introduction of new benefits, differential indexation procedures, changes in the real value of ceilings and floors, and so on. These departures from generational equity can be measured as divergences from an intergenerational benchmark of an actuarial-based system.

How large are such departures from generational equity in practice? We can examine this by calculating average internal rates of return (IRRs) to contributions for successive generations in OECD countries for a number of retiring generations and see how the returns differ across countries and over time. As a general benchmark, $g$, the sustainable rate of return, is likely to lie in the range of 1 percent to 3 percent. This seems a sensible benchmark if the productivity growth averages around 1.5 to 2 percent per annum in the long run and the labor force growth depends on both demographic change and changes in economic activity rates (and may therefore be positive or negative).

Disney (2004) calculates average IRRs to public pension contributions for 22 OECD countries for three cohorts—that is, for generations retiring in the late 1970s and early 1980s and born in 1920 ('Cohort 1920'), the late 1980s and early 1990s ('Cohort 1930'), and the late 1990s on ('Cohort 1940'). It is assumed that the first cohort (born 1920) retires with an incomplete earnings record but receives full benefits, and that contribution rates adjust over time to ensure PAYG balance. As a result, higher IRRs derive not from greater generosity of replacement rates (since taxes adjust to finance such benefits on a PAYG basis) but from differences across countries and over time in the average expected length of retirement and from differences in the generosity of post-retirement indexation of benefits.

Figure 14.1 reproduces the results of this exercise. Some countries, such as Australia, Canada, and New Zealand, have IRRs between 1 to 4 percent, declining slightly with later cohorts, reflecting both the generosity of treatment of earlier retiring cohorts and declining labor force growth (i.e. declining $g$). Given likely measurement error, such countries are probably close to intergenerational equity, which is our intergenerational benchmark of an actuarial-based system. A few countries, such as Ireland, the United Kingdom, and the United States, actually

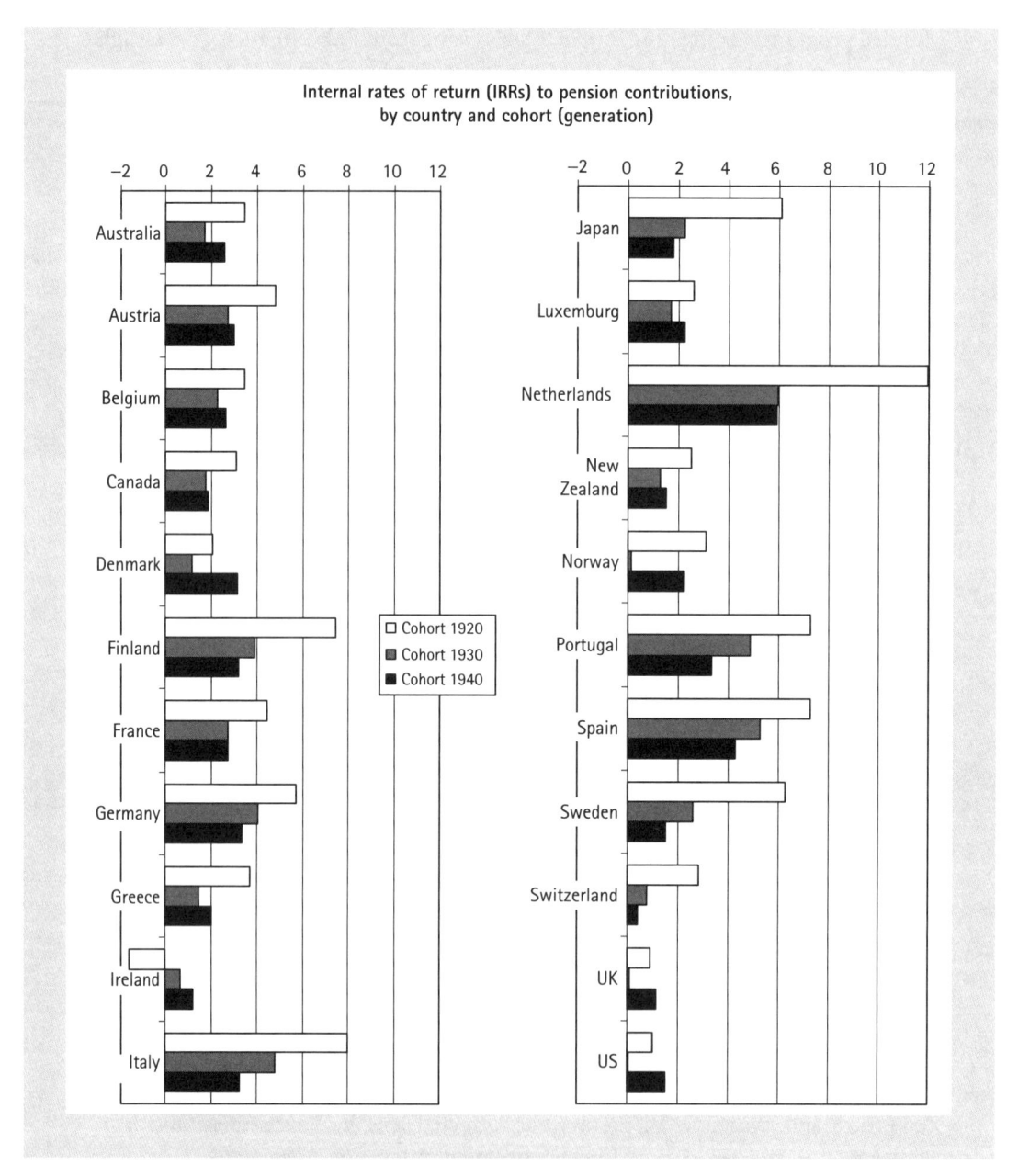

**Fig. 14.1 Internal rates of return (IRRs) to pension contributions, by country and cohort (generation)**

*Source*: Disney (2004, fig. 1).

exhibit IRRs that are probably *below* a likely value of *g*. It is of interest to note that both these groups of countries are generally associated with an Anglo-Saxon (sometimes termed 'Beveridge') form of social security program in which benefits are generally not related to contributions and are floor-based, and in which substantial benefits are provided through employer-based pensions.

Now consider many of the other countries in Figure 14.1, notably those from Continental Europe that operate a 'Bismarck' form of social security. In many of these, IRRs are much higher but show a distinct pattern of decline for later cohorts. These are mostly countries that are not actuarial-based (in an intergenerational sense) and where the requirements of PAYG equilibrium from equation (5) above have required rising contribution rates over time.[1] It is no coincidence that many of these countries are facing strong pressure to introduce a stronger actuarial basis to the public pension system.

## 2.4 Actuarial Fairness

Implicit in the earlier discussion of an actuarial-based system was another dimension of system design. This concerns differences in benefits relative to contributions *within* generations, that is, the *intra*generational features of a public pension system. Compare an *actuarially fair* program that pays benefits to all proportional to contributions (as in equations (2) and (3) above) with a program that departs from actuarial fairness and pays a fixed pension benefit to all, as in equation (4). The latter exhibits strong within-generation redistribution, not just by risk-pooling across different classes of longevity risk (which is intrinsic to social insurance programs) but also because the benefit formula gives greater replacement rates to households with lower lifetime income.[2] ('Equity' and 'fairness' here should not be treated as constituting any social welfare judgments but merely as providing benchmarks against which to judge an actuarial-based program.)

How large are these departures from 'actuarial fairness'? As stated in Section 1, every program in practice contains some departures from actuarial fairness. Blöndal and Scarpetta (1998) report expected pension replacement rates for four categories of 55-year-old contributors: single people and couples, on average earnings and at 66 percent of average earnings. In 1995 the replacement rate in Belgium for singles both at average earnings and 66 percent of average earnings was 60 percent: for couples both at average earnings and 66 percent of average earnings it was 75 percent. The Belgium system thus was actuarially fair with regard to earnings level but not with regard to family composition (singles versus couples). Compare this with Australia where the system departs in both dimensions.

A useful quantitative indicator of the relevant differences can be computed as follows (Disney 2004). If the four Blöndal and Scarpetta expected replacement rates are identical for each country-time observation, the program is approximately actuarially fair (in this dimension). If the rates vary, then the coefficient of variation of the replacement rates gives an approximate measure of the departure from actuarial fairness in each country and time period. Figure 14.2 illustrates these calculated 'tax components' for each country and each year.

Again, what is striking is the difference between 'Beveridge' and 'Bismarck' regimes: the former tends (by design) to exhibit significant departures from 'actuarial fairness', the latter is much closer to this benchmark. By the criterion discussed in Section 1, therefore, 'Beveridge' or Anglo-Saxon-type programs

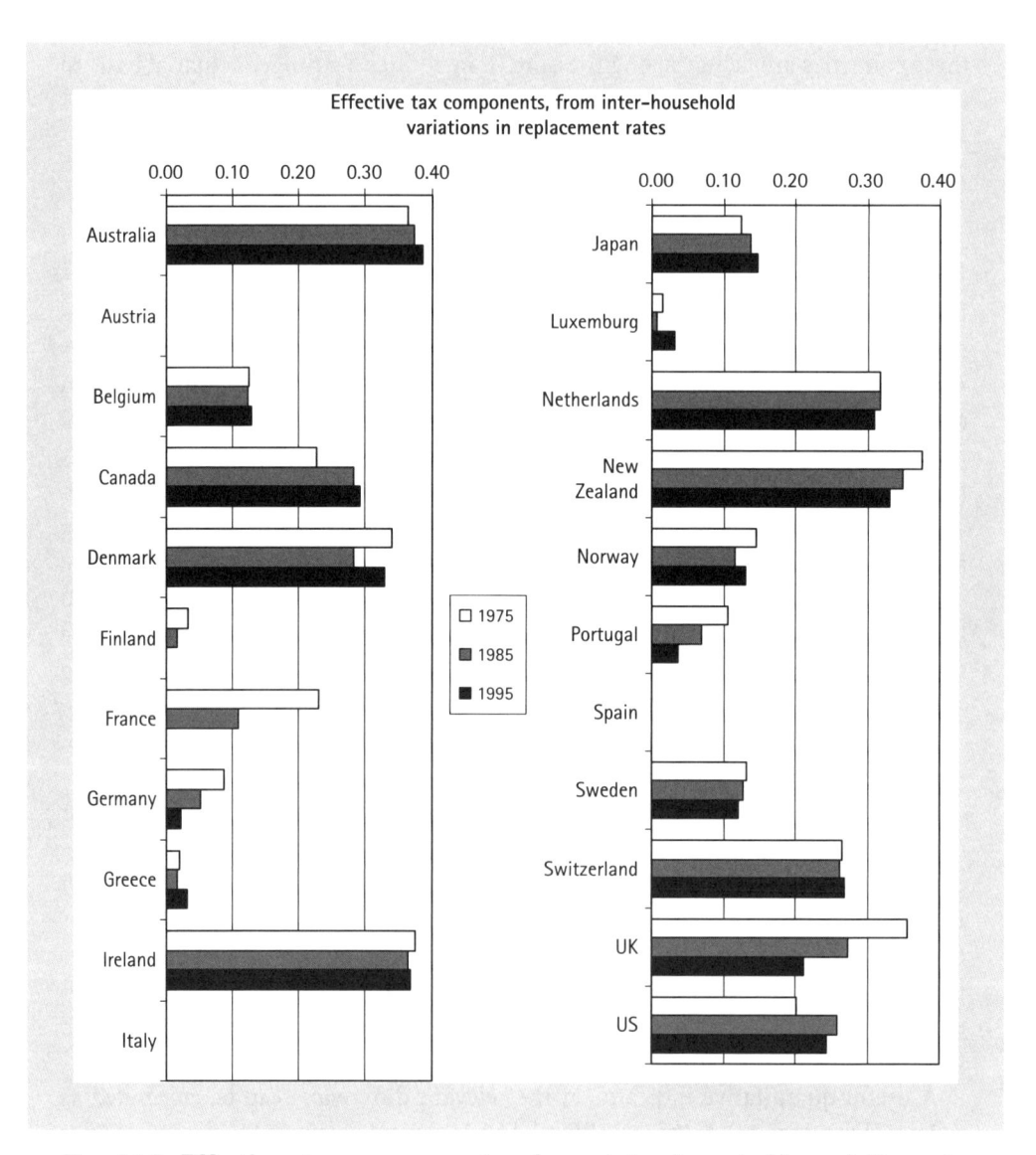

**Fig. 14.2 Effective tax components, from inter-household variations in replacement rates**

Source: Disney (2004, fig. 4). The dates refer to the date at which the generation member reaches age 55.

exhibit a high tax component, although generally not suffering the ever-rising contribution rates exhibited by 'Bismarck' programs which, with the notable addition of the Netherlands, depart from 'intergenerational equity'.

## 2.5 Actuarial Neutrality

A final criterion for judging the actuarial basis of a public pension system is the incentive to retire. Intrinsically, the retirement decision should be forward-looking—examining the opportunity cost of continuing to work relative to current and expected benefits (which may themselves be affected by postponing the retirement decision) after the age at which the individual is first entitled to a public pension. In OECD terminology this is commonly described as the (marginal) implicit tax rate on (continued) employment. *Actuarial neutrality* occurs when this implicit tax rate is zero and the individual's budget constraint gives an equal value to continuing to work and retiring now (in which case the retirement decision will wholly be determined by preferences and expected individual mortality risk).

To illustrate this, define the expected effective tax rate, $m$, from one more year's work at age $a$ at some time $t$ as the *marginal implicit tax rate* $= m(t,a) = -\Delta p(t,a)/w(1-x_w)(t,a)$ where the change in pension wealth at age $a$ is $\Delta p$, the wage is $w$, and both are defined net of other personal taxes, $x$. Clearly the sign of $m$ depends on the sign of $\Delta p$. If $s_i$ is the individual probability of surviving from one period to the next, then:

$$\Delta p = \sum_{i=a+1}^{\infty} s_i [p_{a+i} - p_a](1-x_p)(1-\delta)^{-(i-a)} - [c_a + p_a(1-x_p)]$$

where $c$ is the contribution rate and $\delta_i$ is the individual's discount rate. The first term represents the increased prospective pension benefit stream times the probability of surviving from $a$ to $a+1$ (parameter $s$), and the second term is the cost of continuing to work, which consists of the contribution plus foregone pension at that age. When these two terms are equal, $\Delta p$ is zero and so is $m$.

Note that the marginal implicit tax rate does not directly determine the retirement decision. It defines the budget constraint for every future date at which the individual faces a choice between work and retirement ($p_a$ gives the 'wealth effect', as a current annuity value). Within the window during which the retirement date can be chosen, the pension accrual $\Delta p$ will depend on the benefit formula (e.g. whether an extra year of contributions 'count' toward benefits) as well as the possibility of deferring benefits, and at what rate. And the individual's decision as to when to retire will depend on the distributions of $s$ and $\delta$ across individuals as well as accumulated wealth.

What do these marginal implicit tax rates on continued work look like in practice? Table 14.1 uses data from Blöndal and Scarpetta (1998) to examine whether postponing retirement increases prospective public pension wealth. A positive sign indicates a positive incentive to continue working, zero indicates 'actuarial neutrality' (at the assumed discount rate of 3 percent) and a negative sign indicates a disincentive to continue in work. In almost all cases, the sign is negative and has risen between 1967 and 1995 despite some efforts to reform public pension systems to encourage people to retire later. Note that these calculations ignore other early retirement 'routes' in the public pension welfare program such as disability pensions. When these, too, are taken into account, the disincentives to postpone retirement increase correspondingly (Gruber and Wise 1999).

Table 14.1 Cumulated pension wealth accruals for single people on average earnings

|  | Postponing retirement 55 to 64 | | Postponing retirement 55 to 69 | |
| --- | --- | --- | --- | --- |
|  | 1967 | 1995 | 1967 | 1995 |
| United States | −0.8 | −1.2 | −1.9 | −2.5 |
| Japan | −1.0 | −2.8 | −2.1 | −3.9 |
| Germany | −0.4 | −1.4 | −2.9 | −3.4 |
| France | −0.2 | −1.4 | −1.2 | −3.7 |
| Italy | −3.0 | −7.9 | −4.5 | −11.8 |
| United Kingdom | −0.6 | −0.5 | −1.4 | −1.5 |
| Canada | 1.5 | −0.6 | −0.1 | −1.6 |
| Australia | 0 | 0 | −0.8 | −0.9 |
| Austria | −3.1 | −3.4 | −6.5 | −7.0 |
| Belgium | 0.2 | −2.3 | −2.3 | −5.0 |
| Denmark | 0 | 0 | −0.6 | −0.8 |
| Finland | 0 | −2.2 | −1.3 | −4.9 |
| Ireland | −0.5 | −1.4 | −0.6 | −2.6 |
| Netherlands | −0.9 | −1.3 | −2.3 | −2.9 |
| New Zealand | 0 | −0.9 | −0.5 | −2.3 |
| Norway | −0.3 | −1.5 | −0.3 | −3.3 |
| Portugal | −0.5 | −0.4 | −3.8 | −3.7 |
| Spain | – | −1.4 | – | −5.9 |
| Sweden | 0.9 | −1.8 | 0 | −3.3 |
| Switzerland | 0.2 | 0 | −0.7 | −1.5 |

Source: Blöndal and Scarpetta (1998, table III.6).

# 3 The Effects of Deviations from Actuarial-Based Public Pensions

Public pension systems depart from actuarial-based systems in a number of respects—the 'implicit tax' arising from PAYG funding and departures from intergenerational neutrality, actuarial fairness, and actuarial neutrality. In principle, all these deviations affect household labor supply and incentives to save. But how important are these effects in practice and do they suggest that moving programs closer to an actuarial basis will generate significant efficiency gains? And if so, what are the most relevant margins?

Economists have extensively discussed the first issue—the implicit tax implied by PAYG financing where $r > g$. Feldstein (1996) is the seminal account of the welfare losses arising from PAYG financing rather than full funding of pension programmes. The subsequent literature tends to focus on two issues: how large is the disparity between $r$ (the 'return' on contributions to a funded programs) and $g$ (the 'return' on contributions to a tax-financed program), and what is the magnitude of the transition cost in moving from PAYG financing to full funding? These issues are discussed elsewhere in this volume.

Departures from 'intergenerational equity' and 'actuarial fairness' have received somewhat less attention. Nevertheless these might be significant to the extent that public pension systems are perceived as having a substantial 'tax component' (and look less like mandatory retirement saving programs), thereby affecting both labor supply and saving behavior.

In testing this general hypothesis, one possibility is to ask people about what type of pension programme would encourage them to save more (as in Boeri *et al.* 2001) but such studies cover only a limited number of countries and the interpretation of responses is not always straightforward. An alternative is to construct some form of econometric test, in which an economic variable such as the economic activity rate or the saving rate is linked to cross-country or temporal differences in the design of the public pension system.

Disney (2004) undertakes a panel analysis of economic activity rates of different sex and age groups across OECD countries, in which these activity rates are linked to macroeconomic variables and institutional indicators, including the extent to which public pension systems are actuarial-based. He shows that the labor force activity rates of women of different ages are typically higher (other things being equal) where the program has a lower intragenerational tax component, the internal rate of return to pension contributions is higher, and the expected pension replacement rate is lower. However, these indicators of pension system design had no significant impact on the labor force activity of men.

Does this imply that countries should move closer to an actuarial-based program if they want to achieve higher employment growth? For 'Beveridge'-type programmes, these results give conflicting signals. On the one hand, such programs deviate substantially from 'actuarial fairness' (Figure 14.2). On the other hand, 'floor-based' programs of this type typically have a low absolute tax burden. These effects may offset one another. Conversely, 'Bismarck'-type programs typically depart from intergenerational equity, from actuarial neutrality (in terms of retirement incentives) and also have a higher tax cost given high replacement rates. These factors may slow down employment growth in such countries and give rise to pressure for an even closer link between contributions and entitlements.

The link between type of public pension system and savings rates has not, to my knowledge, been analyzed. The seminal work of Feldstein (1974) on the impact of public pension wealth on household saving has been followed up on a cross-country basis by a number of studies (summarized in Disney 2000a). These suggest that more generous public pension systems tend to crowd out private retirement saving both at a macro level (i.e. cross-country) and across households, the latter exploiting differential changes in pension wealth across households arising from pension reforms (Attanasio and Brugiavini 2003; Attanasio and Rohwedder 2003). However, no paper has as yet linked these offset effects to the differential design of pension programs across countries or over time periods. Programs which depart significantly from actuarial fairness, and in particular where pension entitlements are income or asset-tested, might be expected to have a significant impact on retirement saving (Disney and Emmerson 2004).

Finally, the evidence strongly suggests that departures from actuarial neutrality in terms of retirement incentives may have adverse effects on activity rates of older people. Blöndal and Scarpetta (1997, 1998), using a cross-country fixed effect model, conclude that 'a 10 percentage points reduction in the implicit tax on continued work from 55 to 65 years of age would lead to an increase in participation rates among older males of about 1.8 percentage points'. They contend that the fall between 1967 and 1995 (see Table 14.1) of pension wealth accruals from deferred retirement accounts for substantial drops in labor force participation in Finland, Italy, the Netherlands, and Portugal (1998).

In similar vein, the country studies in Gruber and Wise (1999) calculate implicit tax rates on marginal earnings at the first date at which retirement is possible and find a strong negative relationship across countries in the mid-1990s between these implicit tax rates and the economic inactivity rates in the age range 55 to 65. In later microeconometric analyses (Gruber and Wise 2004), the authors confirm that these incentive effects have a major explanatory role in models of retirement based on household data.

# 4 ACTUARIAL-BASED REFORMS OF PUBLIC PENSION SYSTEMS

Although the literature does not give a clear-cut answer as to whether actuarial-based programs are welfare-improving, in the late 1990s several countries—most notably Sweden and Italy, introduced 'notional accounts' as part of a comprehensive pension reform. These reforms were primarily designed to introduce greater intergenerational equity, actuarial fairness, and actuarial neutrality into the public pension program and therefore form a sort of natural experiment. The Swedish reform proposal also precipitated two 'test-bed' reforms in Latvia and Poland—the former almost explicitly a trial run for the Swedish reform, the latter containing a number of additional features. Since the reforms largely eschew greater funding (although small funded components form a part, or an ideal future part, of each reform), they do not handle the 'implicit tax' issue arising from PAYG finance.

Of course, movement toward an actuarial-based system need not involve the whole notional account apparatus. For example, many countries in the late 1990s reduced the marginal implicit tax on postponing retirement. More strikingly, the 2004 public pension reform in Germany indexes benefits to earnings growth ($g$) and a 'sustainability formula' ($n$) without introducing individual accounts (Börsch-Supan and Wilkie 2003). Moreover, despite their 'defined contribution' name, notional accounts are primarily reformed defined benefit systems where pension accruals and indexation procedures are formula-based. Nevertheless, the 'individualization' of the pension account is presumably designed to promote different incentives, perhaps reflecting the behavioral economics notion that saving and consumption decisions are partly influenced by the form in which saving opportunities are presented. The following discussion briefly describes the introduction of notional accounts in Italy, Sweden, Latvia, and Poland.

## 4.1 Italy

The Italian reform of 1995 (implemented in January 1996) introduced a new public pension system that directly related pension entitlements to accumulated payments, rather than to age or years of service (for descriptions, see Fornero and Castellino 2001; Brugiavini and Fornero 2001; Gronchi and Nisticò 2003). Contributions are notionally accumulated in individual accounts that are revalued in line with a moving average of GDP growth. Since contributions are approximately proportional to earnings, this feature moves the system closer to 'actuarial fairness' (although in practice the system includes a benefit floor and other milder non-linearities). Additional revaluations linked to the PAYG feasible long-run rate of return also move the system toward 'intergenerational equity'.

The annuity value of the contribution balance at retirement is then calculated as a product of these revaluations and a 'transformation coefficient' conditional on the age of retirement. These 'transformation coefficients' are the products of what would normally be called annuity factors—the rate of pension conditional on life expectancy at each age of retirement within a cohort—and are therefore designed to move the program closer to 'actuarial neutrality'. Once in payment, pensions will be indexed to prices.

The Italian reform therefore has two key features. First, it is formula-driven and the formula and its values are public knowledge, whether or not fully understood by the public. Second, individual benefits are driven by accumulated notional pension wealth although still tax-financed on a PAYG basis.

Several features of the Italian reform, however, enhance the scope for discretionary changes and political manipulation. First, the program still has a window of retirement ages (currently 57 to 65), which is to be reconsidered at regular intervals. Of course, with increasing longevity, the age of first retirement has to be raised regularly on the basis of actuarial projections of longevity of future generations. This retirement age is potentially (and has proved in practice to be) a source of continued political negotiation.

Second, the transition period to the new program is extremely long. New labor market entrants from 1996 onward belonged wholly to the new system, those with between 1 and 18 years of contributions in 1996 will retire with a mixture of benefits from the new and the old systems, and those with 18 years or more contributions will retire under the rules of the 'old' system. This means that the system will not be in 'steady state' until well into the 2040s, which gives plenty of scope for subsequent political manipulation. Indeed, in the transition, the program remains out of fiscal balance since non-contributory tax revenues are used to augment contributions in order to finance some of the existing ongoing liabilities.

Finally, the program still contains features, such as a minimum pension, that provide a departure from an actuarial basis within generations. Inevitably, given an existing institutional setting, it is difficult to introduce a 'pure' actuarial-based program, even allowing for continued tax-based finance. Current (2004) measures to eradicate some of these features, notably to raise the retirement age, seem likely to be implemented only with concessions that might erode some other actuarial-based features of the post-1995 program. The major defense of the Italian reform was that it moved Italy away from a trend toward a deficit-financed unsustainable public program that had only been halted by the ad hoc and therefore potentially reversible 1992 reforms.

## 4.2 Sweden

The Swedish pension reform was initiated in 1994, but the majority of the required legislation was not passed until 1998 (Palmer 2000). As in Italy, the new program establishes a set of individual accounts, one novelty being that a small proportion of the contribution (2 percent of 18.5 percent) will be invested in a funded component, the rest being put into the PAYG program. The accounts are indexed to earnings growth but make no allowance for changes in the labor force growth rate—which may be positive or negative. The growth rate of the labor force does enter into the *post-* retirement calculation for indexing benefits, which takes account of any deviation of real wage growth from a growth 'norm' (set at 1.6 percent per annum).[3] As with Italy, a formula links annuity factors at retirement to published life expectancy tables.

Also as in the case of Italy, the Swedish system is introduced gradually, so that individuals born between 1938 and 1953 (i.e. aged 45 to 60 in 1998) accrue rights under a mixture of the old and new rules. For those aged 45 and below, all rights are accrued under the new system. So the transition to the 'steady state' is much faster than in Italy. A major departure from 'actuarial fairness', to be expected in the social welfare environment of Scandinavia, is that individuals can accumulate notional contributions to the new plan from periods of economic inactivity: for women bringing up young children, spells of unemployment, sickness and disability, periods of military conscription, and post-school education.

## 4.3 Latvia and Poland

Although the reforms in these countries are also of interest, they can be summarized briefly given that many of their features have already been discussed. The Latvian reform was introduced in 1995–6 and bears all the hallmarks of a 'test-bed' for the Swedish reform (see Fox and Palmer 1999) bar two important features. First, the accounts are revalued in line with, not the growth of earnings or GDP, but the growth of the contribution base. Whilst this is technically a 'better' measure of the underlying PAYG 'feasible' rate of $g$, the contribution base is highly volatile in a transition economy such as Latvia (Disney 1999). Consequently, the value of notional accounts in Latvia in the period after 1995 fluctuated 15 to 20 percent from one year to another, on a par with fluctuations in the values of funded accounts. If one rationale for *not* funding pensions is the lower volatility of accumulated funds, indexation procedures of this type are not helpful. Second, and also inevitable in a transition economy, the minimum pension remains very important and its value will probably determine pension values for a long time to come.[4]

The Polish reform, introduced in 1999, has several features similar to the Latvian system, but it also has a very interesting funded component (for details, see Chlon et al. 1999). Again, the idea is that in the long run, the PAYG 'pillar' will be comprised of individual accounts, indexed to the growth of the real wage bill but with a significant and relatively generous minimum pension. Again, the system contains 'carrots and sticks' designed to persuade people to defer taking their pension. These provisions include a significant rise in the minimum pension age and deferral rates that broadly reflect differences in life expectancies at different retirement ages. Pensions in payment will be indexed to price inflation, unless real wages are falling in which case they will be indexed to nominal wage growth.

The Polish system also includes a second pillar of individual funded accounts that involves a much greater share of the total contribution than in Sweden. One's intuition is that, in the long run, the notional account component of the Polish program may turn out to be less important than in the other countries, depending on what happens to (i) the value of the minimum PAYG pension, (ii) the retirement age, and (iii) the value of individual funded accounts. In this sense the program is not as 'full blooded' a shift to a tax-financed actuarial-based program as in the other countries described here.

## 5 Do Actuarial-Based Program Guarantee Sustainability?

One of the claims most often advanced for a shift to an actuarial-based program is that it introduces automatic macroeconomic stability. One of the major problems of existing defined benefit public programs is that, as populations age, and without the types of adjustment mechanisms described here, pension costs inevitably rise as a share of GDP over time (Disney 2000b).

In the long run, linking the 'return' on contributions in a public program to $g$, whether done through a macroeconomic formula as in Germany or by individual accounts, should arrest this tendency to rising costs. Although in some cases, such as Italy, this stability might require a retrenchment in pension costs and not just a cap on their growth. However, advocates of actuarial-based programs sometimes go beyond this general statement to assert that implementation of these regimes removes the need for even short-term discretionary stabilization of the program. Is this correct?

The essential problem can be simply stated. Linking benefit entitlements to *g* is treating the program, by analogy, as if it were a funded program, albeit earning a lower return. But the analogy, while attractive, is misleading. PAYG finance is not like funding, and the equilibrium requirement is that current pension expenditure equals current tax receipts. In a static environment, or where all variables perpetually grow at their steady state values, a rule can be implemented that eliminates the need for discretionary actions to restore fiscal balance. Many 'proofs' of propositions concerning actuarial-based systems use models (e.g. propositions from comparative statics) of this type. The picture is quite different where pension programs face macroeconomic and demographic 'shocks'.

Faced with shocks, what formula, if any, could guarantee short-run stability? Valdés-Prieto (2000) considers the issue formally and comprehensively, but the results are fairly intuitive. The issue partly depends on the timing of new information, and on whether the shocks are primarily macroeconomic (i.e. arising from earnings, productivity, or labor force growth, or from inflation) or demographic (arising from changes in longevity, assuming that the impact of fertility rate changes can be predicted and that changes in net migration are too small to 'matter').

If the shocks only come from the macroeconomic side, the first possibility is to index claims on the system to aggregate contribution revenues. This would 'work' insofar as it is the dynamic analogy to PAYG equilibrium. Since total accumulated contributions and the number of pensioners are both known from the size of the past workforces, a formula that automatically indexed interest on accumulated contributions and pension benefits to changes in contribution revenue would indeed automatically stabilize the program. It is like first differencing the formula and netting out a constant tax rate. Unfortunately, changes in contribution revenue are generally an outcome variable that cannot be observed in time to alter announced interest rates on accumulated contributions and to index pension benefits. If lagged contribution revenues are used, then *ex post* adjustments of interest on accumulated contributions will never guarantee actuarial balance. However, so long as any discrepancies between changes in contribution revenues are serially uncorrelated and relatively small, and the PAYG program retains a small reserve fund, such fluctuations can be absorbed. In fact, this is how PAYG programs operate in practice, subject to the major constraint that they are pre-committed to a certain level of benefits.

Valdés-Prieto shows that other indexation formulae do not have this property. Intuitively, indexing benefits to the growth of covered wages, as in Sweden, will not suffice (although Sweden then has a balancing formula in determining the post-retirement indexation of benefits). Indexing contributions and the pension benefit to the growth of the wage *bill*, as in most of the other countries that have introduced notional account-type programs, will be more effective. However, in the Valdés-Prieto set-up of the problem, the relationship between the growth of the wage bill and the indexation of pension rights would be proportional but not unitary since the outcome also depends on the contribution rate. In steady state growth (constant contribution rate), indexing to the covered wage bill does ensure macroeconomic stability, but not if the contribution rate varies over time.

These stabilization measures may or may not 'work' in the face of macroeconomic shocks. But if the system faces demographic shocks, a second instrument is needed which adjusts the annuity rates at retirement to changes in expected longevity. The concern here is not the difficulties in doing this (private annuity markets are supposed to handle exactly this sort of problem) but that government actuaries seem to have rather a poor record in forecasting aggregate longevity changes (Disney 2000*b*).

Looking at individual countries that have moved toward actuarial-based programs, these problems of automatic stabilization have not been completely solved, although it is at least arguable that the presence of some stabilizers are better than none. Sweden and Germany have attempted, or are attempting, to introduce demographic adjustments to either benefits or retirement ages that handle demographic shocks. It is not clear that this has been done in Italy, other than in a somewhat ad hoc way by raising retirement ages. On the other hand, indexing pension claims to GDP growth or the growth of the wage bill, which has taken place in all notional account-type countries except Sweden, is probably closer to what is required for macroeconomic stabilization. Sweden indexes to covered earnings and therefore is still required to make periodic discretionary adjustments to program finances in order to maintain PAYG equilibrium.

# 6 Conclusion

This chapter has considered actuarial-based public pension systems—that is, tax-financed public programs that, in one way or another, impose contributory requirements or other design mechanisms that imitate, however imperfectly, a funded retirement saving program. It considered some rationalizations for such procedures—primarily enhanced revenue-raising capacity, elimination of perceived tax distortions to labor supply and saving, and built-in macroeconomic stabilization, especially in the face of financing problems created by adverse demographic shocks.

The chapter then explored the dimensions in which PAYG programs depart from this actuarial basis (Section 2). The fundamental point is that a PAYG program can never 'earn' the same return on contributions to the program as a funded system when an economy is dynamically efficient. But public plans also deviate from actuarial-based programs in other dimensions, including intergenerational equity, actuarial fairness, and actuarial neutrality. These deviations have been discussed at great length at a theoretical level, but it is interesting to note that very few empirical studies have attempted to address this practical issue. However, such studies as exist were discussed in Section 3.

Section 4 then considered 'Notional Account' or 'Notional Defined Contribution' (NDC) reforms in practice in a number of other countries—how they worked and the extent to which they had successfully handled the intrinsic components of actuarial-based programs described in Section 2.

The last section considered the important issue of whether switching to actuarial-based pension regimes allows countries to absorb both long-run changes and short-run 'shocks' to macroeconomic and demographic variables.

As with other generic reform packages, notional account-type reforms are not a 'magic wand' to solve the problems of financing pensions. They provide some transparency, a degree of stability, and avoid some of the issues involved in moving toward greater pre-funding. More generally, shifts to actuarial-based programs can improve incentives. However such programs inherently reduce the redistributive capacity of social welfare policy, which may or may not be an objective of government. And they may have the harmful effect of persuading contributors that, somehow, their pension 'rights' are no longer dependent on the willingness to pay of future taxpayers. Actuarial-based programs are, ultimately, tax-and-transfer programs and dependent on the intergenerational solidarity of taxpayers. Coping with ageing populations remains a challenge to many countries whatever the pension program that is chosen.

# Notes

My grateful thanks to Elsa Fornero and Alicia Munnell for helpful suggestions.

1. In fact a number of these countries, such as Greece and Italy, have consistently run deficits on their public pension system, financed out of general revenue. Since the incidence of general taxation may differ from a fully financed contribution-based system, this calculation may slightly understate IRRs in those countries.
2. Since mortality is generally negatively related to lifetime wealth, these two facets of the program may offset one another.
3. This example is from Sundén (1998). Suppose inflation is 2 percent p.a. and actual real wage growth is 0.5 percent p.a. Then actual indexation is $(2-(1.6-0.5)) = 0.9$ percent p.a.

Thus, slower real wage growth than average GDP growth is reflected in a fall in the real value of the pension. This is an alternative to the indexation of the account to real GDP growth (Italy) or real earnings growth plus a 'sustainability formula', as in the 2004 German reform.

4. A personal view is that it is undesirable to use transition economies as 'test-beds' for 'extreme' reforms—whether shifts to fully actuarial-based programs, or indeed fully privatized programs. In this sense, the 'multi-pillar' strategy seems a better option.

# REFERENCES

AARON, H. (1966). 'The social insurance paradox'. *Canadian Journal of Economics*, 32 (Aug.): 371–4.

ATTANASIO, O., and BRUGIAVINI A. (2003). 'Social security and households' saving'. *Quarterly Journal of Economics*, 118: 1075–119.

—— and ROHWEDDER, S. (2003). 'Pension wealth and household saving: evidence from pension reforms in the U.K.' *American Economic Review*, 93/5: 1499–521.

BLÖNDAL, S., and SCARPETTA, S. (1997). 'Early retirement in OECD countries: the role of social security systems'. *OECD Economic Studies*, No. 29, Paris.

—— —— (1998). 'The retirement decisions in OECD countries'. OECD Economics Department, Working Paper 202, Paris.

BOERI, T., BÖRSCH-SUPAN, A., and TABELLINI, G. (2001). 'Would you like to shrink the welfare state? The opinions of European citizens'. *Economic Policy*, 16 (Apr.): 7–50.

BÖRSCH-SUPAN, A., and WILKIE, C. (2003). 'The German public pension system: how it was, how it will be'. Mimeo. Mannheim Research Institute for the Economics of Ageing, Mannheim, Germany.

BRUGIAVINI, A., and FORNERO, E. (2001). 'Pension provision in Italy', in R. Disney and P. Johnson (eds.), *Pension Systems and Retirement Incomes in OECD Countries*. Cheltenham: Edward Elgar.

CHLON, A., GÓRA, M., and RUTKOWSKI, M. (1999). 'Shaping pension reform in Poland: security through diversity'. World Bank, SP Discussion Paper 9923, Washington, D.C.

DISNEY, R. (1999). 'Notional accounts as a pension reform strategy: an evaluation'. World Bank SP Discussion Paper 9928, Washington, D.C.

—— (2000*a*). 'Declining public pensions in an era of demographic ageing: will private provision fill the gap?' *European Economic Review*, 44/4–6: 957–973.

—— (2000*b*). 'Crises in OECD public pension programmes: what are the reform options?' *Economic Journal Features*, 110 (Feb.): F1–F23.

—— (2004). 'Are contributions to public pension programmes a tax on employment?' *Economic Policy*, 39 (July): 267–311.

—— and EMMERSON, C. (2004). 'Public pension reform in the United Kingdom: what effect on the financial well being of current and future pensioners?' Mimeo. London: Institute for Fiscal Studies.

FELDSTEIN, M. (1974). 'Social security, induced retirement and aggregate capital accumulation'. *Journal of Political Economy*, 82/5: 75–95.

—— (1996). 'The missing piece in policy analysis: social security reform'. *American Economic Review Papers and Proceedings*, 86 (May): 1–14.

FENGE, R., and WERDING, M. (2003). 'Ageing and fiscal imbalances across generations: concepts of measurement'. CESifo Working Paper 842, Jan.

FORNERO, E., and CASTELLINO, O. (2001). *La Riforma del Sistema Previdenziale Italiano.* Bologna: I Mulino Studi e Richerche.

FOX, L., and PALMER, E. (1999). 'Latvian pension reform'. World Bank SP Discussion Paper 9922, Washington, D.C.

GRONCHI, E., and NISTICÒ, C. (2003). *Fair and Sustainable Pay-As-You-Go Pension Systems: Theoretical Models and Practical Realizations.* Rome: Consiglio Nazionale dell'Economia e del Lavoro.

GRUBER, J., and WISE, D. (eds.) (1999). *Social Security and Retirement around the World.* Chicago: Chicago University Press for National Bureau of Economic Research.

—— —— (eds.) (2004). *Social Security and Retirement around the World: Micro-estimation.* Chicago: Chicago University Press for National Bureau of Economic Research.

LINDBECK, A., and PERSSON, T. (2003). 'The gains from pension reform'. *Journal of Economic Literature,* 41 (Mar.): 74–112.

PALMER, E. (2000). 'The Swedish pension reform—framework and issues'. World Bank SP Discussion Paper 0012, Washington.

SAMUELSON, P. (1958). 'An exact consumption-loan model of interest with or without the social contrivance of money'. *Journal of Political Economy,* 66 (Dec.): 467–82.

SHESHINSKI, E. (1978). 'A model of social security and retirement decisions'. *Journal of Public Economics,* 10: 337–60.

SUNDÉN, A. (1998). 'The Swedish pension reform'. Mimeo. Federal Reserve Board, Apr.

VALDÉS-PRIETO, A. (2000). 'The financial stability of notional account pensions'. *Scandinavian Journal of Economics,* 102/3: 395–417.

# ENTITLEMENTS AND PENSIONS

CHAPTER 15

# CITIZENSHIP, ENTITLEMENT, AND MOBILITY

ROBIN ELLISON

One of the major issues for social security, as migration becomes more widespread, is the question of whether protection follows the individual. This issue has a long history. As far back as the Poor Laws in the UK—at the time of Shakespeare and Queen Elizabeth I—local parishes sought relief from beggars traveling into their area in some form of ancient social security arbitrage (Poor Law Board 1853). More recently, newspapers in the UK have objected to the movement of economic migrants traveling allegedly not so much because of the fear of persecution as the enjoyment of social security benefits (Walters 2001).

In order to control costs, most social security systems set down criteria in relation to the entitlement to benefits that involve some form of proof of contribution record, or citizenship, or residence. But as much of the case law of jurisdictions—especially in certain groupings such as the European Union—demonstrates, minor disputes about the entitlement to benefits have been incessant.

This chapter explores some of the issues that have emerged in both public and private social security arising as a consequence of attempts to arrange cover despite lack of residence or nationality. The chapter is in three sections, dealing separately with:

- the questions of residence and nationality;
- the question of mobility and transfer of rights; and
- the more recent influence of human rights case law on rights and expectations.

The chapter attempts to develop some coherent political and legal framework, but in reality few of the rules in many countries reflect a rigorous policy structure, based on any serious logical principles. The one acknowledged framework, that of the European Union, is however considered at some length.

# 1 Residence and Nationality

The old UK poor law of the seventeenth century was firmly based on residence. Beneficiaries had to reside in the parish to have a chance of the workhouse. It was not until the beginning of the twentieth century that the UK devised a national social security and pensions system that avoided domestic geographical issues—although it still required UK residence. These requirements (and those of other jurisdictions), however, have in recent times failed to meet the contemporary needs of multinationals and migrant workers. As a result, some approximate solutions have been attempted using reciprocal agreements and, within the EU, for example, coordinating regulations.

Modern social security involves not only benefits, of course, but also contributions. Residence has a part to play in the collection of contributions where the scheme is a contributory one; without presence it is difficult to enforce contributions. But benefits generally require no positive requirement as to residence. All that is usually needed is participation in the scheme for a specified number of years. While many jurisdictions seem to disqualify absent individuals, even where they have paid contributions, pensions is a special area where particular rules apply (see below). Sometimes schemes relax restrictions for those forms of benefits like pensions where the entitlement bears no relationship to the ability to work. For example, sometimes benefits are payable (e.g. UK bereavement benefits) even though the beneficiary is not resident—but any enhancements or increases to the benefits since the absence began will not be applied. And it is not always easy in practice to determine for the payment of benefits whether an individual is 'resident' for benefit purposes or not. The definition of residence differs in each jurisdiction and even within jurisdictions for different purposes. In the UK, for example, there is 'resident', 'ordinarily resident', 'habitually resident', 'normally resident', 'present', and 'domiciled', each of which carries a slightly different nuance—and to which different rules may (or may not) apply.

Emigrés have faced particular problems, especially in times of inflation. It has been common, for example, for UK pensioners or New York pensioners to retire to more restful climes, either for health or family reasons. Like many jurisdictions, the

UK continues to pay state old-age pensions to those entitled to it, even if their residence is moved abroad, but has conventionally frozen the pension at levels payable at the time of leaving. The justification for this is never very clear. It could be argued that the benefit is a social security benefit, and since social security (e.g. unemployment benefit or child support) is only payable to residents it should cease to be payable once residence ceases. On the other hand, if it is treated as a right acquired as an asset by virtue of long-term contributions, then presumably it should be paid at the same rate as residents regardless of residence. In many cases, social security conventions require the payment of domestic pensions to subjects of contracted states. But in the absence of such arrangements, the UK, for example, adopts some particularly schizoid logic.

For example, in *Carson v Secretary of State for Work and Pensions (CA)*,[1] Mrs Carson was a British pensioner entitled to a UK state pension who emigrated on retirement to live in South Africa. Once she became no longer resident in the UK, her social security pension was frozen at the rate it was paid at the time of emigration. Pensioners who remained resident in the UK or in the EU and other countries with reciprocal recognition agreements did not have their pension frozen, but periodically uprated, largely in line with UK inflation.

For many years, no legislation or principle of law seemed to provide a base upon which to base a case for uprating overseas. However, following the introduction of human rights law into UK legislation, Mrs Carson claimed that this amounted to discrimination contrary to the provisions of the UK Human Rights Act 1988. The High Court held that the perception that a pension is the fruit of the pensioner's contributions was incorrect. If it were, a claimant would have a right protected by Article 1 of the First Protocol of the European Convention. The application by Mrs Carson was denied, and she appealed to the UK Court of Appeal.

The Court of Appeal held that in many countries specific restrictions exist on the payment of social security benefits to foreign countries, and they do not amount to a deprivation of possessions infringing Article 1 of the Protocol to the European Convention on Human Rights. The Court of Appeal concluded that the UK pension provisions were geared to the impact on the pension of price inflation in the UK. Price inflation, said the court, in other countries where expatriate UK pensioners might have made their home was unlikely to have a comparable effect on the value of the pension. Such pensioners might do better or worse, particularly in the face of variable exchange rates. An award across the board to all such pensioners would have random effects. A refusal by government to introduce such a measure does not need justification by reason of comparing it with the clear and certain effects of the uprate for UK-resident pensioners. In the event, the appeal was dismissed.

On the other hand, the UK does provide uprated pensions for those in the European Economic Area and in States with which the UK has entered into bilateral agreements requiring such payments. Between 1948 and 1992, the UK entered into bilateral agreements, or reciprocal social security agreements, with a number of foreign States. With one minor exception, the agreements entered into after 1979 fulfilled earlier commitments given by the UK government. Agreements with Australia, New Zealand, and Canada came into force in 1953, 1956, and 1959 respectively; but even they did not require payment of uprated pensions. The agreement with Australia was terminated effective March 2001, because of the refusal of the UK government to pay uprated pensions to its pensioners living in Australia. Uprating never applied to those living in South Africa, Australia, Canada, and New Zealand. The EC Regulations on Social Security for Migrant Workers require uprating of benefits throughout the European Union. In practice, the entry of the UK into the EC had little effect on the provision for uprating pensions in the Member States, because the UK had pre-existing reciprocal agreements with all of them except Denmark providing for payment of uprate.

The Court of Appeal concluded that the overall position was a haphazard consequence of events, including not least the conclusion of the various bilateral agreements, happening over time, but that did not give grounds for a claim. The government was slightly shamefaced, but unrepentant. On 13 November 2000, the Minister of State said in the House of Commons:

I have already said I am not prepared to defend the logic of the present situation. It is illogical. There is no consistent pattern. It does not matter whether it is in the Commonwealth or outside it. We have arrangements with some Commonwealth countries and not with others. Indeed, there are differences among Caribbean countries. This is an historical issue and the situation has existed for years. It would cost some £300 million to change the policy for all concerned...

The Court had taken notice of what was said in a House of Commons inquiry: (House of Commons Social Security Committee 1997): 'It is impossible to discern any pattern behind the selection of countries with whom bilateral agreements have been made providing for uprating'. Some explanation of these bilateral agreements was given in a Department of Social Security Memorandum:

17 The main purpose of reciprocal agreements so far has been to provide a measure of social protection for workers, and the immediate members of their families, when moving from one country to the other during their working lives. In effect, they generally prevent such workers from having to contribute to both countries' Social Security schemes at the same time while ensuring that they retain benefit cover from either one country or the other. On reaching pensionable age, such workers who have been insured in two or more countries' schemes can receive a pension from each which reflects the amount of their insurance in each.

18 Whether a reciprocal Social Security agreement with another country is entered into depends on various factors, among them the numbers of people moving from one to the other, the benefits available under the other country's scheme, how far reciprocity is possible and the extent to which the advantages to be gained by an agreement outweigh

the additional expenditure likely to be incurred by the UK in negotiating and implementing it. Where an agreement is in place, the flow of funds may differ depending on the level of each country's benefits and the number of people going in each direction.

19 Since June 1996, the Government's policy has been that future reciprocal agreements should normally be limited to resolving questions of liability for social security contributions...

At paragraph 38 of the same document, observations were made which foreshadowed the UK Minister of State's words on 13 November 2000:

Surely no one would have deliberately designed a policy of paying pensions to people living abroad intending to end up in the position we are at today... It is impossible to discern any pattern behind the selection of countries with whom bilateral agreements have been made providing for uprating.

## 2 MOBILITY AND TRANSFER

In Europe, attempts to ensure continuity of coverage for individuals moving between states developed early in the twentieth century both because social security arrangements themselves began then to emerge—and because transport and events, such as major conflicts, allowed and encouraged significant movements of labor across Europe. In practice, the early developments involved bilateral and sometimes multilateral agreements (the first one being a Franco-Italian agreement in 1904). But it was not really until 1971 and the introduction of the EU Regulation 1408 that modern sophisticated arrangements emerged—almost at the very time that major inter-EU migration fell significantly.

The then Article 42 of the Treaty of Rome, which was part of the Treaty that dealt with the free movement of workers, required the European Council of Ministers to ensure there was a system of aggregation of social security benefits derived from service in individual member states—and then pay benefits to persons resident in the territories of those states. Residence was even then the key, and later coverage was extended to refugees and stateless persons who were not citizens—provided they were resident.

Critical to the effective implementation of the Regulation was the system of coordination of the schemes—and the payment of benefits. The EU system employs four techniques: (1) the prohibition of discrimination on the grounds of nationality; (2) the aggregation and apportionment of benefit rights; (3) the removal of territorial restrictions on continued access to benefit; and finally (4) the application of a single legal system to the benefit entitlement. Although the legislation, Regulation 1408/71, has been subject to a battery of case law and interminable bureaucratic difficulties in implementation by some Member States, it has been remarkably successful—witness the fact that it stands still as the core legislation after around 35 years.[2]

## 2.1 Pensions and Taxes

Pensions in particular offer slightly more complicated issues—largely because they are often regarded less as social security than as a form of deferred income that has been paid for by labor or contributions or both. Over the last few years, the provision of pensions has become an important economic and political issue in most of the industrialized economies. In practice, coping with international mobility in pensions poses special problems because unlike much social security, it has more of an 'asset' feel to it than a 'support' feel.

Tax has been a major issue in private pension arrangements. The problem of 'fiscal coherence' has fascinated and obsessed national tax authorities ever since the first of a series of cases[3] in the European Court of Justice discussed whether cross-border tax relief on contributions meant loss of income to national treasuries. In practice, many employers, particularly those with only a small number of multinational employees, attempt to use their existing retirement benefit arrangements as far as possible.

The tax treatment of private pension provision and the obligation to pay social security contributions vary significantly from jurisdiction to jurisdiction. Issues amongst others that are likely to affect the employer's approach to providing an occupational pension arrangement include tax and social security.

In practice, several issues concern both employers and employees in relation to tax:

- whether the employer receives a tax deduction for its contributions to the plan;
- whether the employee is subject to income tax on the employer's contributions;
- whether the employee receives a tax deduction for contributions to the plan;
- whether the investment return of the plan's assets (income and capital gains) are taxable; and
- whether the emerging benefits are taxable.

Modern European Court of Justice case law now makes it clear that, generally, national treasuries should not impede such cross-border relief (see below).

## 2.2 European Union Arrangements

A core principle of the Treaty of Rome was (is) the removal of obstacles to freedom of movement between Member States (Articles 42 and 308 (51 and 235) EC). In pursuit of this aim, social security rules had to be developed that prevented people who work and reside in a Member State other than their own from losing some or all of their social security rights when they exercise that freedom of movement.

In 1958, the Council issued two regulations on social security of migrant workers, later replaced by Regulation 1408/71, and even later by Regulation 574/72. Nationals from Iceland, Liechtenstein, and Norway are also covered via the European Economic Area (EEA) Agreement. The idea was to coordinate the Member States' social security legislation, rather than harmonize their social security schemes. In practice Member States' very different social security schemes offer a wide variety of rights and levels of benefit to employees and the self-employed.

The rules now determine which country's legislation applies in the event of a conflict between the laws of two or more Member States; the principle is that a person is subject to only one country's legislation, which, as a rule, is that of the Member State in which he or she is employed or self-employed. The State of employment is thus the 'competent State' and the rights of the worker/self-employed person to social security benefits are decided by that State. Different rights apply to exporting cash benefits (e.g. sickness benefit or pensions) and benefits in kind (e.g. medical assistance). As a rule, benefits in kind are governed by the rules of the country in which the person entitled to them resides or stays. If the 'competent State' is not the State of residence, the 'competent State' must reimburse the institution in the State of residence or stay its expenditure on benefits in kind.

Originally, Regulation 1408/71 only covered employees but from 1982 it also covered the self-employed (Regulation 1390/81). The Regulation also covers members of workers' and self-employed persons' families and their dependents, as well as stateless persons and refugees, and nowadays civil servants, students, and others not in gainful employment. Generally, the benefits of the Regulation are not available to nationals of third countries working in the Union, although occasionally suggestions are made that they should. Benefits largely covered include:

- sickness and maternity benefits;
- invalidity benefits, including those intended for the maintenance or improvement of earning capacity;
- old-age benefits;
- survivors' benefits;
- benefits in respect of accidents at work and occupational diseases;
- unemployment benefits; and
- family benefits.

Pension arrangements have their own painfully complex rules. If an employed or self-employed person has been subject to the legislation of two or more Member States, the regulation's special rules apply for the calculation of the pension. Such a person receives a proportional pension from each of the States in which he was insured for at least one year, for example, from States A and B. That is, the national rules of State A apply to the payment of that part of the pension and in the country in question. Likewise with the payment of pension by State B. Retirement age does not therefore need to be the same in both countries. If the retirement age in State A is 67 and in State B 60, the person must wait until he has reached the age of 67 before receiving his pension from State A. If the period of insurance completed in State B is not of sufficient duration to give entitlement to a pension in that country, the regulation provides that periods of insurance completed in other countries, in this case in State A, should be taken into account (the aggregation principle). The rules in the regulation for calculating the amount of pension to be paid by each of the States in which the person concerned was insured are extremely technical. Generally, however, they are based on a principle that each of the countries pays a proportional pension benefit. On 29 June 1998, the Council adopted Directive 98/49/EC on safeguarding the supplementary pension rights of employed and self-employed persons moving within the European Community. The aim of this Directive is to protect the rights of members of supplementary pension schemes who move from one Member State to another, thereby contributing to the removal of obstacles to the free movement of employed and self-employed workers within the Community.

In the meantime a stream of other provisions (including the Migrant Workers Directives and the European Pensions Directive) uses the issue of residence as a criterion. The European Pensions Directive in particular attempts to remove (at least in the case of workplace pension systems) issues of citizenship and residence following a series of cases in the European Court of Justice, which insisted that Member States grant cross-border tax relief on contributions by employers and employeres (and individuals) to pension systems in other Member States.[4]

# 3 Human Rights and International Law

Some commentators have made reference to the European Court of Human Rights in relation to pensions claims, and occasional references in the European Court of Justice (the EU court) to human rights law in pensions matters (particularly equal treatment issues), though less so in relation to issues of citizenship and residency. In the UK, the Human Rights Act 1998 created directly enforceable rights against public bodies (and quasi-public bodies which have some public functions) by introducing a ground of illegality into proceedings brought by way of judicial review. Individuals have a cause of action against public bodies that fail to act compatibly with the Convention, and Convention rights are available as a ground of defense in cases brought by public bodies against private bodies (in both criminal and civil cases).

## 3.1 International Treaties

While the European Convention on Human Rights has been a significant source of international influence on UK domestic pensions policy, other international influences include the International Labour Organization (ILO 1962, 1967, 1977; Zelenka 1974) and the Council of Europe (Council of Europe 1965), predominantly of course in relation to social security pensions rather than private pensions. For example, the ILO's Social Security (Minimum Standards) Convention does not apply directly to private schemes, but has been held to have been influential (Jenks 1960): '[there] has been misapprehension in some quarters concerning the relationship between the Convention and voluntary private insurance. The Convention is not material to, and does not interfere with, voluntary private insurance in any way'. Nonetheless, this does not mean that it is without influence on the private sector (Jenks 1960): 'It provides for a basic code of protection on which voluntary private insurance can and should build'. Similarly the European Code of Social Security provides (Council of Europe 1969):

Article 25: Each contracting party for which this part of the Code is in force shall secure to the persons protected the provision of old-age benefit in accordance with the following articles of this part.

Article 26: The prescribed ages shall be not more than 65 years of age or than [sic] such higher age that the number of residents having attained that age is not less than 10 per cent of the number of residents under that age but over 15 years of age.

Other studies have been carried out by the Organization for Economic Cooperation and Development (OECD 1977) and the International Social Security Association (ISSA 1973, 1977; Masini 1974) and even the Universal Declaration of Human Rights has something to say about pensions (Council of Europe 1965; Taubenfeld and Taubenfeld 1978).

## 3.2 Grounds for the Application of Human Rights Principles

Whether pension rights and benefits are eligible to be protected under human rights legislation has been considered in a number of cases. While the European Convention on Human Rights has many articles and protocols that set out a series of rights (e.g. prohibition of torture, freedom of thought, and so on) four provisions have been considered as directly applicable to the protection of pension rights and indirectly examine the issues of residence and citizenship in relation to pension claims, namely (Council of Europe 1998):

(a) Article 6 (whether a pension is a 'civil right' such that in the determination of his civil rights an individual is entitled to a fair and public hearing);
(b) Article 10, which requires freedom of expression (whether the government must disclose information which might lead to a pension being granted);
(c) Article 14, which prohibits discrimination (whether a pension right is a right protected under the Convention);[5] and
(d) Article 1 of the First Protocol (whether a pension is a possession which everyone is entitled to peaceful possession of).

In a dispute concerning a widow's pension arising out of her husband's death following an industrial injury it was held that the classification of pension rights as public law rights in German law was not conclusive for the purposes of art 6(1) of the European Convention on Human Rights. No common European standard existed on the classification of such rights. The dispute, the court held, had the features of a public law character: the character of the legislation, the compulsory nature of the insurance, the assumption by the state of responsibility for social protection. These features were, however, outweighed by features of a private law nature: the personal and economic nature of the right, the close connection with the contract of employment, and the affinity with insurance under ordinary law. The right asserted by the applicant was therefore a civil right within the meaning of art 6(1).[6]

## 3.3 State Pensions

No right to receive a pension under the national insurance scheme of a country is included as such amongst the rights and freedoms guaranteed by the European Convention on Human Rights. In *X v The Netherlands*[7] members of the Women's Action Committee for Advanced Old Age Pensions, created in May 1962 in order to obtain advanced old-age pension rights for unmarried and divorced women, laid a complaint against the Dutch government. The grounds were that the Dutch scheme appeared to discriminate against women, since widows of men who died after the age of 65, and who themselves were under the age of 65, could draw on the old-age pension. Their unmarried and divorced women colleagues, however, could not draw a pension until age 65. Since the contributions paid by all three types of women, namely married, unmarried, and divorced, were the same, it was argued that the benefits paid under the pension scheme discriminated against certain women.

A second argument, based on allegations of discrimination, was also declined by the Commission. It found that the difference in the treatment of men and women in the pensions sphere:

Insofar as it can be said to amount to an inequality, inequality of treatment between married and unmarried and divorced women is justified as being based on the legislators' appreciation of the general family pattern while making allowances for the generally different situation of a married couple in comparison with that of a single person.[8]

Discrimination is explored in the texts mostly in relation to sex and race discrimination, at great length (Ellison 1978). Article 14 of the Convention provides:

The enjoyment of the rights and freedoms set forth in this Convention shall be secured without discrimination on any ground such as sex, race, colour, language, religion, political or other opinion, national or social origin, association with a national minority, property, birth or other status.

Some of these issues have been explored in other jurisdictions. Studies of the Canadian experience (Smolkin 1999; McAauley 2000; Bermuda 1999; Kohn 1999) and the New Zealand position (where the New Zealand Human Rights Commission has issued Superannuation Guidelines, intended to provide guidance on the Commission's views on the provisions of the New Zealand Human Rights Act 1993 on pensions (Cochrane 1999) ) can be instructive. In *Coburn*,[9] the trustees of the New Zealand pension scheme sought a declaratory judgment on a range of issues put to the court after widespread industry consultation. Obviously, the terms of the New Zealand and the UK legislation differ, but not that much. That litigation explored whether to:

- remove marital and family status discrimination by equalizing benefits (notably death benefits) for those with and without spouses, children, or other dependents;
- remove discrimination between legal and *de facto* spouses;
- provide for contributions and benefit accruals to continue to at least age 65;
- ensure that early retirement benefit reduction factors could be justified on actuarial or statistical grounds;

and a series of other questions. Amongst other decisions of the court, one of the most interesting from the UK's point of view was that which held that providing secondary pensions exclusively for spouses was unlawful discrimination. Similar developments are taking place in Canada.[10]

## 3.4 Pensions as Property

Several cases in the European Court have explored the issue of whether a pension rights is property subject to the protection of the First Protocol. This Protocol provides:

Every legal or natural person is entitled to the peaceful enjoyment of his possessions. No one shall be deprived of his possessions except in the public interest and subject to the condition provided for by law and by the general principles of international law.

The preceding provisions shall not, however, in any way impair the right of a State to enforce such laws as it deems necessary to control the use of property in accordance with the general interests or to secure the payment of taxes or other contributions or penalties.

In most cases, the Court and Commission have taken a relaxed view, being reluctant to intervene in pensions matters. Even where the contributions to a state pension scheme bear a relationship to proprietary rights, if for example they are voluntary, the Commission has refused to intervene.

Residence and citizenship have however remained at the heart of the issues raised. In *Muller (Christian) v Austria*[11] the applicant had been employed in Austria by a number of employers and had been a member of the Austrian workers' old-age insurance scheme. He was born in 1905 and for 32 years until 1963 he worked in Austria. The period was not sufficient to ensure a full pension, and in 1963 he started working as a locksmith in Liechtenstein while continuing to live in Austria. During this time, he continued to make voluntary payments to the Austrian scheme, in order to ensure that he would receive a full pension when he retired in 1970. In 1969, however, the Austrian and Liechtenstein governments signed a social security convention that prohibited anyone compulsorily insured in Liechtenstein to pay voluntary contributions to the Austrian scheme.

In its decision, the Commission again refused to accept jurisdiction. However, it distinguished between public and private pension arrangements, and excluded state arrangements from its competence, since the social security system must take account of political considerations, in particular those of financial policy. It was conceivable, for instance, that a deflationary trend could oblige a state to reduce the nominal amount of pensions, and fluctuations of this kind have nothing to do with the guarantee of ownership as a human right. Finally, a worker could be, and indeed had to be, a member of the scheme of the country in which he worked, so that he was not deprived of the right to a pension, even though the amount of the pension would be affected.

### 3.4.1 *Reduction of State Pensions*

The reduction of a state pension, not uncommon where individuals have built rights in various different states, and fail to aggregate rights, is probably not a ground for complaint under the European Human Rights Convention. In *X v Sweden*[12] the applicant was a retired employee of the Swedish Railways who during his period of employment had subscribed to a pension scheme. As a result when he took early retirement he was granted a state pension in advance, as well as an old age pension, the latter under the social insurance system. As from March 1982, however, when the applicant attained the normal retirement age of 65, his state pension rights were 'coordinated' with the social insurance benefits. This meant that his state pension was reduced. His request to the government for 'non-coordination' was rejected with the explanation that without such a 'coordination' the cumulative benefits would exceed what the pensioner had received when he was working. The applicant alleged a violation of Protocol No 1, art 1 of the European Convention.

The Commission held:

> The applicant has complained that he does not receive full pension in accordance with the agreement he had with his employer, the Swedish Railways. He alleges a breach of Protocol No 1, article 1. A question may be raised whether the applicant has exhausted domestic remedies in respect of his complaint as required by article 26 of the Convention. However, the Commission does not find it necessary to analyse this question in greater depth since the application is in any case inadmissible for the following reasons. The Commission recalls its consistent case law, according to which the right to a pension is not as such guaranteed by the Convention. At the same time the Commission has frequently held that the payment of contributions to a pension fund may in certain circumstances create a property right in a portion of such fund and of the pension rights under such a system and could therefore in principle raise an issue under Protocol No 1, article 1. The Commission has added, however, that 'even if it is assumed that Protocol No 1, article 1 guarantees persons who have paid contributions to a special insurance system the right to derive a benefit from the system it cannot be interpreted as entitling that person to a pension of a particular amount'.[13] The Commission also considers that the right to a pension which is based on employment can in certain circumstances be assimilated to a property right, and this can be the case, whether special contributions have been paid or the employer has given a more general undertaking to pay a pension on conditions which can be considered part of the employment contract.

### 3.4.2 *The Juridical Nature of State Pensions*

In October 1997 the European Court looked at *Szrabjer and Clarke v UK*[14] where two pensioners stopped receiving their pension under the UK State Earnings

Related Pension Scheme whilst in jail. The curious feature of this scheme is that it can be provided either by the State (if full social security contributions are paid to the State) or by a private pension scheme. They complained to the European Commission of Human Rights, since they had no remedy in the UK, and suggested that the failure to pay by the government was a breach of Article 1 of Protocol 1 of the European Convention. This article provides that everyone is entitled to 'peaceful enjoyment of his possessions'. Normally a person can only be deprived of his possessions where the deprivation is in the public interest or for taxation and related purposes.

By way of contrast, in *Gaygasuz v Austria*[15] an advance on a pension was held to constitute a property right; the pension was linked to the payment of contributions.

Other questions are bound to emerge in due course; one will no doubt be whether a forfeiture clause breaches the property rights upheld by the Convention, and such clauses, especially in public sector schemes, are commonly inserted to protect the public (rather than as in private schemes to protect the pensioner), or whether the non-availability of widow's benefits to men is a breach.[16]

### 3.4.3 Tax and Discrimination

Discrimination can apply not only to gender and racial discrimination but also to sectors of the community. One case on alleged discrimination against the self-employed has already been mentioned (*Iceland*). More recently, in *R v Commissioners of Inland Revenue ex p Professional Contractors' Group* (UK High Court, Queen's Bench Division, Administrative Court, 10 October 2000), Gibbs J gave permission for judicial review of changes made by the Welfare Reform and Pensions Act 1999 ss 75 and 76 requiring special tax treatment of one-man companies on the grounds that this was discrimination against such companies in favor of larger ones, and hence amongst other things a breach of the Protocol. And discrimination against individuals seeking tax relief on contributions to pension systems outside the domestic jurisdiction has already been explored above. Member States of the EU nonetheless continue to attempt to discriminate (witness for example the UK Finance Act 2004 Schedules 33 and 34) but over time such discrimination is expected to be outlawed by the European Court and the European Commission.

The provisions relating to human rights under the European Convention may not necessarily apply to anti-discrimination provisions under EC law (Ellison 1995). This is not the place for an analysis of EU jurisprudence, but to date it has affected pension issues largely in the areas of equal treatment, particularly gender discrimination, and issues of residence and citizenship. At the Nice summit in December 2000, the European Union adopted the Charter of Fundamental Rights, which is largely regarded as declaratory rather than a basis for an extended EU social policy agenda.

## 4 CONCLUSIONS

It may well be that the requirement of citizenship as a prerequisite to entitlement to income protection by the state in old age is becoming as arcane and obsolete as the former English poor law requirements on residence. With increases in migration, with the development of larger and more liberal free-trade areas, and with decline in the cost of record-keeping, citizenship at least looks to be becoming a non-factor in benefit entitlement. Curiously, as part of the drive to reduce administrative costs and encourage simplification, the UK is exploring replacement of the contribution requirements with a simple residence and age test, disregarding contribution records and citizenship requirements completely. It is too early to determine whether this trend will emerge elsewhere in the world, but it seems likely. Both the states and the individuals have an economic interest in making presence alone the basis for entitlement to protection in old age.

## NOTES

1. *Carson v Secretary of State for Work and Pensions (CA)* ([2003] 45 PBLR [2003] EWCA Civ 797) (United Kingdom: England and Wales: Court of Appeal: Civil Division 2003 June 17 (Human rights—Discrimination—Persons living abroad—Whether breach of European Convention on Human Rights to pay uprating to state pensioners resident in the UK and not to pensioners not resident in the UK)).
2. European Union 1971 Regulation 1408 EEC on the application of social security schemes on employed persons to self-employed persons and to members of their families moving within the Community OJ L28 30.01.1997, 1–229.
3. See e.g. *Wielockx v Inspecteur Der Directe Belastingen* (ECJ Case C-80/94); [1995] 16 PBLR (006); [1996] 1 WLR 84; [1995] All ER (EC) 769; [1995] STC 876; [1995] ECR I-2493; [1995] 3 CMLR 85.
4. *Safir v Skattemyndigheten I Dalarnas Län* (ECJ Case 118/96); [1998] 11 PBLR (09); [1999] QB 451; [1999] 2 WLR 66; [1998] STC 1043; [1998] ECR I-1897; [1998] 3 CMLR 739; [1998] BTC 8028; *Danner* [2002] 53 PBLR (017); (ECJ Case C-136/00) [2002] ECR I-8147.
5. There has been a pensions case (which failed) under the International Convention; see e.g. *Kaaber v Iceland* [1999] 20 PBLR (07) (International Commission on Human Rights Industry-wide schemes—Self-employed—Compulsory contributions) where a Reykjavik lawyer complained that the tax reliefs on pension contributions for the self-employed were discriminatory when compared with employed lawyers.
6. In the UK see Human Rights Act 1998; see frequent press articles in the UK in March 1999 and discussions in Parliament during the passage of the Financial Services and Markets Act 2000, which also raise the issues of human rights in regulatory procedures.
7. *X v Netherlands*, Application No 4130/69 (1971) 14 *Yearbook of European Convention* 224.

8. Cf. definition of discrimination under EC law. Note also that the circumstances of another case might justify a finding that the making of compulsory contributions to a pension fund may create rights amounting to possessions within the meaning of article 1 of Protocol 1, ibid.
9. *Coburn v Human Rights Commission* [1994] 3 NZLR 323.
10. *Dwyer v Metropolitan Toronto (Municipality)* [1996] 27 CHRR D/108; *Laesoe v Air Canada* [1996] 27 CHRR D/1; *Leshner v Ontario (No 2)* [1992] CHRR D/184; *Rosenberg v Canada (Attorney General)* [1998] OR (3rd) 577 (Ont CA). For an exploration of whether there is a breach in the UK of the Convention in the non-availability of a state survivors' pension to men as to women see *Willis v UK* (1999) 4 EHRLR.
11. *Muller (Christian) v Austria* (1976) 19 Yearbook of European Convention 994.
12. *X v Sweden* Application No 10671/83, 8 EHRR 269.
13. See *Muller v Austria* Application No 5849/72, 3 D&R 25. The only exception seems to be *Schuler-Zgraggen v Switzerland* (1993) *The Times*, 21 Oct. European Court of Human Rights [1995] 12 PBLR.
14. *Szrabjer & Clarke v UK* [1998] 18 PBLR (10) (1997 10 23) European Commission of Human Rights: United Kingdom: First Chamber (Definition of a pension—Rights of prisoners to property—Pension—Whether a pension is 'property' European Convention on Human Rights, Article 14 and Protocol No 1 Article 1—Nature of state pension—Nature of state earnings related pension—Nature of contracted-out state earnings-related pension—Equal treatment—Discrimination—Whether non-payment of pension while in prison is breach of Convention).
15. *Gaygasuz v Austria* (1996) 23 EHRR 364. A Turkish national who had worked and paid contributions in Austria was refused an advance on his retirement pension because he was not an Austrian national. It was held that there had been a breach of the First Protocol article 1, in a decision that indicated that provision applied only to insurance-based benefits (as opposed to safety-net benefits).
16. Explored in *Willis v UK* (1999) 5 EHRLR. There is also discussion of whether discrimination in the provision of benefits to same-sex couples may be a breach of Article 8 which provides for the respect for private and family life which has been held to include not only marriage-based relationships, cf. *Botta v Italy* (1999) 2 CLR 61.

# References

Bermuda (1999). Bermudan National Pension Scheme (Occupational Pensions) Act 1999. (Removed the spouse, however defined, as a compulsory beneficiary of a deceased participant's pension.)

Cochrane, David (1999). *Human Rights in the Workplace: A New Zealand Perspective.* IPEBLA Conference, 24–8 May 1999. Wellington: Chapman Tripp.

Council of Europe (1961). European Social Charter, Council of Europe (1961) Treaty Series, no 38.

—— (1965). Cmnd 2643.

—— (1969). Treaty Series, no 10; (1969) Cmnd 3871; European Treaty Series no 48; *European Yearbook*, XII: 397.

—— (1998). *Convention for the Protection of Human Rights and Fundamental Freedoms as amended by Protocol No 11* (date of entry into force 1 Nov. 1998).

ELLISON, ROBIN (1978). *Pensions Law and Practice.* London: Longmans, chapter 22.

—— (1995). *Pensions: Europe and Equality*, 2nd edn. London: Sweet & Maxwell.

FERAUD, L. (1975). *Les Pensions Complémentaires* Geneva: ISSA.

FRANCE FRENCH CODE CIVILE, Book One, Title XII. (Establishing the 'pacte civil de solidarité' and 'concubinage'.)

HOUSE OF COMMONS SOCIAL SECURITY COMMITTEE (1997). *Third Report* (Jan.). London: HMSO.

ILO (1962). Convention Concerning Equality of Treatment of Nationals and Non-Nationals in Social Security, ILO Convention No 118 (1962) ILO Official Bulletin, XLV.

—— (1967). Invalidity Old-Age and Benefits Convention, ILO Convention No. 128 (1967), ILO Official Bulletin, L, Supp 1, no. 3: 4.

—— (1977). *Pensions and Inflation* Geneva: ILO.

—— (1979). Minimum Standards on Social Security, ILO Convention No. 102 (1979), ILO Official Bulletin, XXXIV: 45.

ISSA (1973). Complementary Pension Institutes, Geneva.

—— (1977). *Implications for Social Security of Research on Ageing and Retirement.* Geneva: ISSA.

JENKS, WILFRED C. (1960). *Human Rights and International Labour Standards.* London: Stevens, 108.

KOHN, SALLY (1999). *The Domestic Partnership Organising Manual for Employee Benefits.* Washington: National Gay and Lesbian Task Force, June.

MCAULEY, MICHAEL (2000). 'The unconsciousness of the law: sexuality and the regulation of close personal relationships'. Paper to the International Bar Association, 2000 Conference, Amsterdam, 17–22 Sep.

MASINI, CARLO ALBERTO (1974). *General Compulsory Old Age Insurance Schemes for Employees in the Member States in the EEC* Geneva: ISSA.

OECD (1977). *Old Age Pension Schemes.* Paris: OECD.

POOR LAW BOARD (1853). 1853 Poor Law Return, House of Commons, 11 Feb. 1853.

SMOLKIN, SHERYL (1999). *Human Rights in the Workplace: A Canadian Perspective.* IPEBLA Conference, 24–8 May. Toronto: Watson Wyatt Worldwide.

TAUBENFELD, R., and TAUBENFELD, S. (1978). *Sex-Based Discrimination: International Law and Organisation*, vol. I. Dobbs Ferry, N.Y.: Oceana Publications.

WALTERS, SIMON (2001). 'Britain's immigration service "close to collapse"'. *Mail on Sunday* 2 Sept. and seriatim.

ZELENKA, A. (1974). *Les Systèmes des Pensions dans les Pays Industrialisés.* Geneva: ILO.

CHAPTER 16

# EARLY RETIREMENT

DAVID A. WISE

In the United States, the labor force participation rate of men over 60 fell continuously from about 65 percent in 1940 to about 30 percent by 1980. The reduction in the labor force participation was made possible by social security benefits and by firm pension plans. Social security was introduced under the Social Security Act of 1935. Company pensions were spurred by the Revenue Act of 1942 that granted tax incentives to firms to establish pension plans. The percentage of persons 65 and over receiving social security benefits increased from about 20 percent in 1940 to 85 percent in 1960; now about 95 percent receive social security benefits. The proportion of the workforce covered by an employer-provided (or a federal or state or local government) pension plan increased from 23.8 to 48.6 percent between 1950 and 1979, and remains at that level today. The public and private pension plans did just what they were intended to do. They allowed workers to retire with a secure source of income thereafter. The major reason for retirement programs is to do just this. Thus, it should be expected, and welcomed, that increased pension coverage allows workers to retire earlier.

But in addition to allowing workers to retire, public and private pension plans often penalize work. This is the issue addressed in this chapter. It considers not the accumulation of pension benefits that allows retirement, but rather the pattern of benefit accumulation that often penalizes continued labor force participation of older workers. Pension plans often impose a very substantial 'implicit tax' on work. This chapter draws heavily on illustrations and results generated though an international social security project that I organized with Jonathan Gruber. Indeed much of the discussion is a summary of the results for that project. Research groups from 12 countries participate in the ongoing project. Thus, the results discussed in this chapter should be credited not only to my co-organizer but to participants in each of the countries as well.

The country authors are listed below. Most have participated in all phases of the project.

| | |
|---|---|
| Belgium | Arnaud Dellis, Raphaël Desmet, Alain Jousten, Sergio Perelman, Pierre Pestieau, Jean-Philippe Stijns |
| Canada | Michael Baker, Jonathan Gruber, and Kevin Milligan |
| Denmark | Paul Bingley, Nabanita Datta Gupta, and Peder J. Pedersen |
| France | Dider Blanchet, Ronan Mahieu, Louis-Paul Pelé, and Emmanuelle Walraet |
| Germany | Axel Börsch-Supan, Simone Kohnz, Giovanni Mastro buoni, and Reinhold Schnabel |
| Italy | Agar Brugiavini and Franco Peracchi |
| Japan | Takashi Oshio, Akiko Sato Oishi, and Naohiro Yashiro |
| Netherlands | Arie Kapteyn and Klaas de Vos |
| Spain | Michele Boldrin, Sergi Jiménez-Martín, and Franco Peracchi |
| Sweden | Mårten Palme and Ingemar Svensson |
| United Kingdom | Richard Blundell, Carl Emmerson, Paul Johnson, Costas Meghir, and Sarah Smith |
| United States | Courtney Coile, Peter Diamond, and Jonathan Gruber |

# 1 Social Security and Work: What's the Problem?

Under pay-as-you-go (PAYG) social security systems governments around the world have made promises they can't keep. The systems were not sustainable. Social reform discussions are ongoing in almost all developed countries. Some proposals call for fundamental reform, often funding through personal social security accounts. Other proposals call for 'incremental' reform, suggesting increases in retirement ages and other changes without changing the basic pay-as-you-go structure of the systems.

What caused the problem? It has been commonly assumed that the problem was caused by population ageing. The number of retirees is now increasing very rapidly relative to the number of younger persons in the workforce. In addition, persons are living longer, so that persons who reach retirement age will be receiving benefits longer than they used to. The ratio of the number of persons aged 65 and over to the number aged 20 to 64—based on data for a number of countries that provide the backbone of the discussion below—is shown in Figure 16.1, now and in future years. The increase is striking in almost every country. In Japan, with the most rapid population ageing, the ratio will more than double by 2020 and will almost triple by 2050. These demographic trends have placed enormous pressure on the financial viability of the social security systems in these countries, increasing the number of retirees relative to the number of employees who must pay for the benefits for retirees.

The financial pressure caused by demographic trends was compounded by another trend. In virtually every country employees were leaving the labor force at younger and younger ages, further increasing the ratio of retirees to labor force participants who must pay for the benefits. The labor force participation (LFP) rates of men aged 60 to 64 for the years 1960 to 2003 are shown for each of the 12 countries in Figures 16.2a and 16.2b. A vertical line divides the data before 1996 from the data for 1996 and later years because the discussion below suggests an apparent change in trend in many of the countries at about this time. Through 1995, the decline was substantial in each of the countries, but was much greater in some countries than in others. In the early 1960s, the participation rates were above 70 percent in all but one of the countries and above 80 percent in several countries.

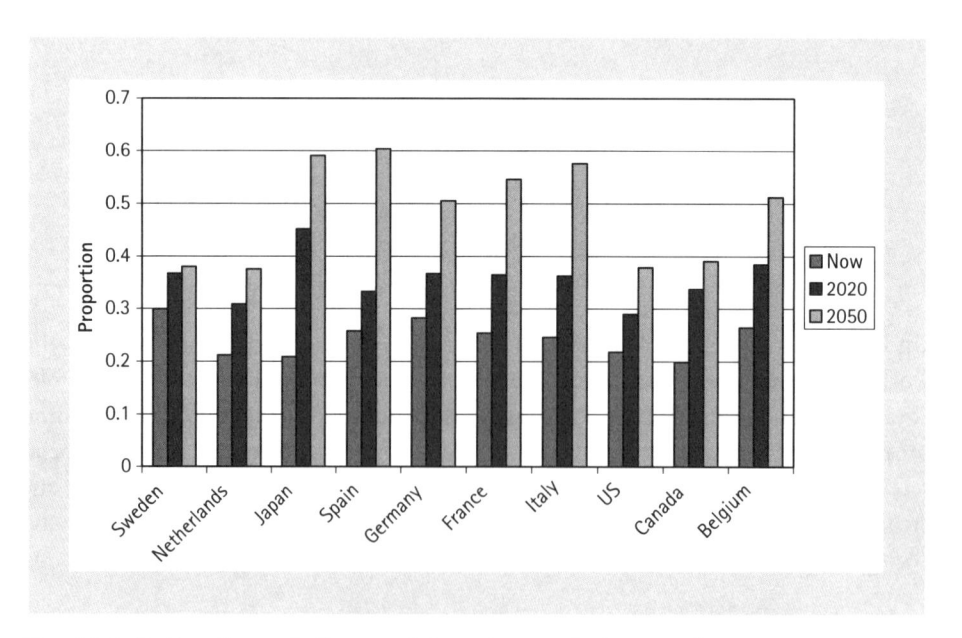

**Fig. 16.1** Ratio of population aged 65+ to population aged 20 to 64

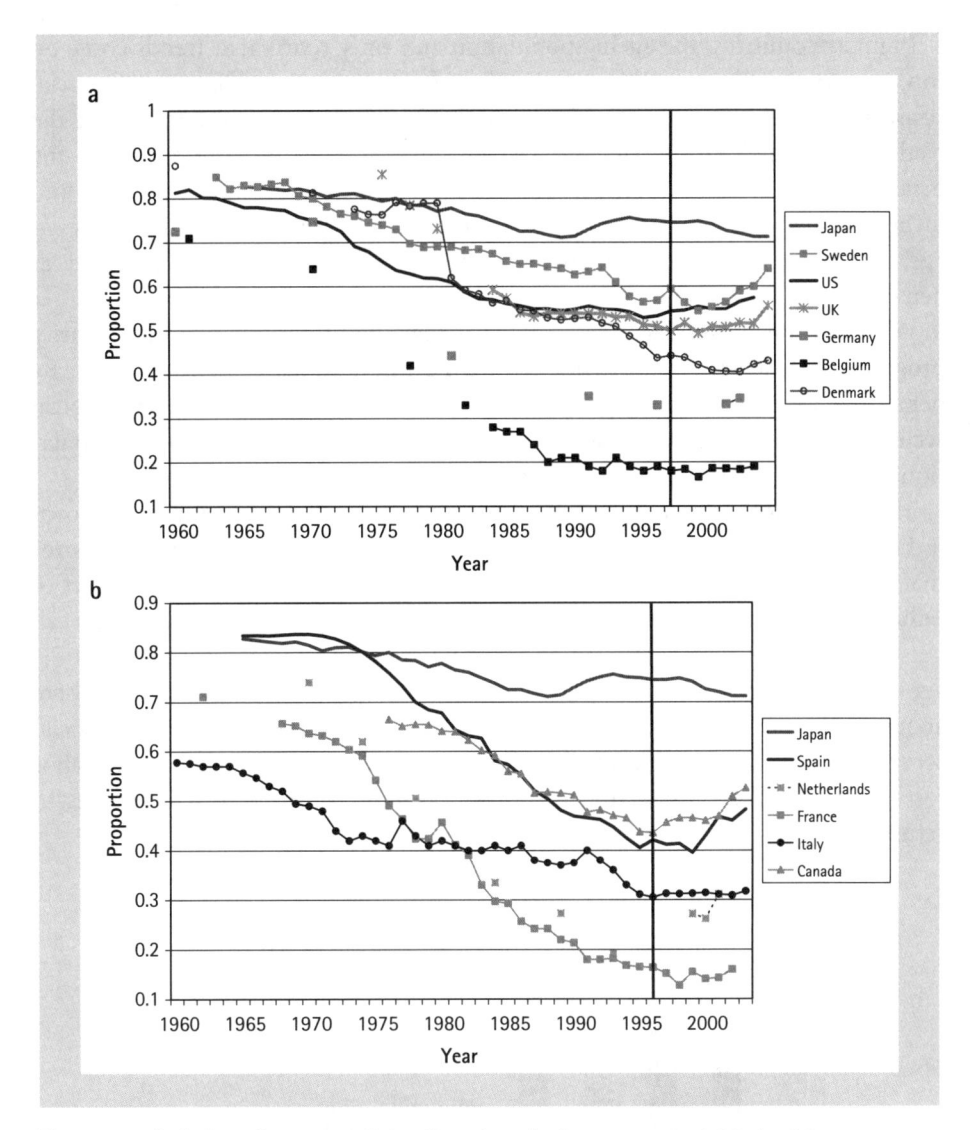

Fig. 16.2a,b Labor force participation trends for men aged 60 to 64

By the mid-1990s, the rate had fallen to below 20 percent in Belgium, Italy, France, and the Netherlands. It had fallen to about 35 percent in Germany and 40 percent in Spain. Although US analysts have often emphasized the 'dramatic' fall in that country, the US decline from 82 percent to 53 percent was modest in comparison to the much more precipitous declines in these European countries. The decline to 57 percent in Sweden was also large, but modest when compared to the fall in other countries. Japan stands out with the smallest decline of all the countries, from about 83 percent to 75 percent. Labor force participation rates of 45- to 59-year-old men, as well as those aged 60 and older, have also declined substantially.

In many countries, the ageing population and early retirement trends come on top of very generous retirement benefits, further compounding the financial consequences of these trends. For example, in Belgium, France, Italy, and the Netherlands the social security replacement rates at the early retirement age—the benefit relative to final earnings—average 77 percent, 91 percent, 75 percent, and 91 percent respectively. In contrast the replacement rate at the early retirement age in Canada is only about 20 percent; in the United States it is about 41 percent.

What has not been widely appreciated is that the provisions of social security programs themselves often provide strong incentives to leave the labor force. By penalizing work, and creating a reserve of 'unused labor force capacity', social security systems magnify the increased financial burden caused by ageing populations and thus contribute to their own insolvency.

The proportion of men out of the labor force between ages 55 and 65 is shown in Figure 16.3 for 11 countries. The term 'unused labor force capacity' emphasizes that incentives to induce older persons to leave the labor force have the effect of reducing national economic production, recognizing of course that not all persons in these age ranges want to work or are able to work. For the 55 to 65 age group the proportion ranges from close to 0.7 in Belgium to somewhere about 0.2 in Japan. Subsequent results will show the relationship between social security plan provisions to leave the labor force and this measure of unused labor force capacity. The next section describes the social security plan incentives to retire.

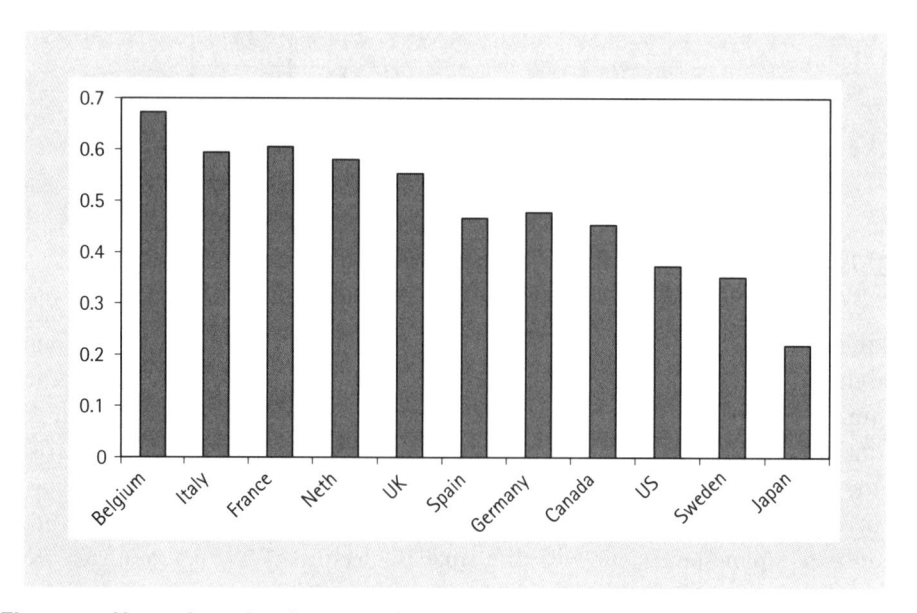

Fig. 16.3 Unused productive capacity: men aged 55 to 65

## 2 Incentive Effects of Plan Provisions

Three key features of social security systems have an important effect on the labor force participation of older persons.

### 2.1 Eligibility Age

The first is the age at which benefits are first available. This is called the early retirement age, or the age of first eligibility. Across the countries noted in Figures 16.2a and 16.2b, the first eligibility age ranges from about 53 for some employee groups in Italy to 62 in the United States. The 'normal' retirement age—for example, 65 in the United States—is also important, but typically much less important than the early retirement age. Now in most countries, few people work until the 'normal' retirement age.[1]

In each country retirement rates are strongly related to specific eligibility ages prescribed in country-specific plan provisions. Perhaps most important is that retirement rates increase sharply at ages of first eligibility for benefits. The age of first eligibility may differ from person to person and varies by program (social security, disability, unemployment, for example) in many countries. In the absence of eligibility for benefits retirement is rare in each of the countries. One way to see this relationship is to consider retirement hazard rates. The hazard rate shows the proportion of persons employed at a given age who retire over the subsequent year. The empirical regularity between hazard rates and eligibility ages across countries is shown in some detail in Gruber and Wise (1999b).

The importance of eligibility can be seen clearly in Figure 16.4. This figure shows hazard rates for the United States by pension plan coverage. The hazard rates for men who have no private pension coverage, and are covered only by the social security program are indicated by the line with round markers. The hazard rates for these persons are very close to zero until the social security early retirement age, when they are first eligible for retirement benefits. At that age, the departure rate increases sharply. The important feature of the pattern is that there is essentially no retirement before that age.[2]

The other line in the figure shows the hazard rates for men who are covered by an employer-provided defined benefit pension plan. The early retirement age under these plans is often age 55 and is rarely over age 60. The hazard rates are very low before age 55. But for these employees, the hazard rate jumps sharply at age 55, when many in this group are first eligible for benefits, and then jumps again at 62, when social security benefits are first available.[3]

The second example is for the United Kingdom, where the social security program has different provisions for men and women. Men can begin to receive

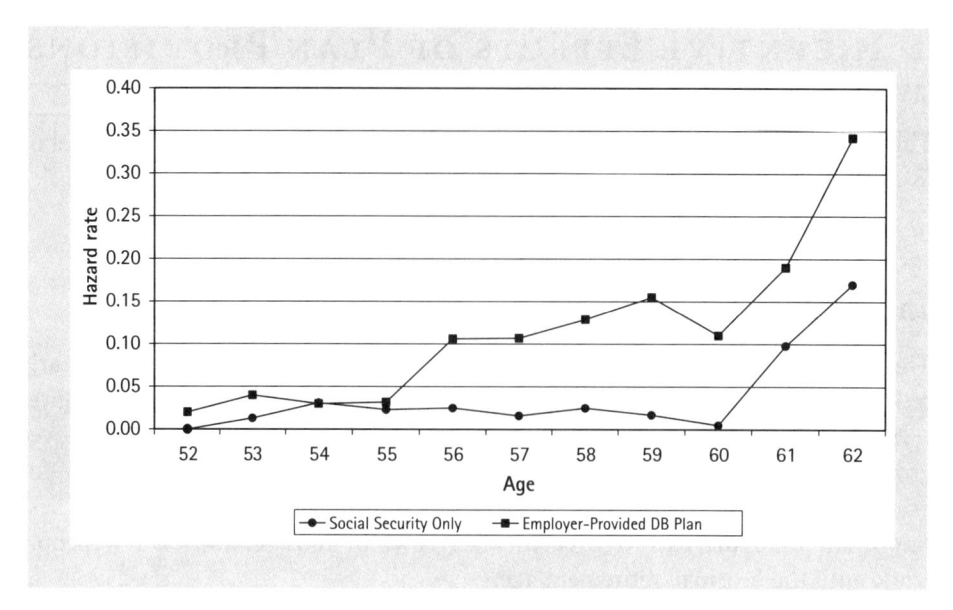

**Fig. 16.4 United States retirement hazard rates for men by pension plan coverage**

benefits under the public social security program at age 65. Women can begin to receive benefits at age 60. These differences are clearly reflected in the retirement patterns of men and women, as shown in Figure 16.5. The proportion of women employees still in the labor force drops by about 20 percentage points (from 60 to 40 percent) at the age of 60. But there is essentially no decline for men at this age. On the other hand, labor force participation drops by 20 percentage points (from about 40 to about 20 percent) for men at age 65, when they can receive benefits.

Thus, within-country differences in labor force departure rates by gender and by pension plan coverage show clearly that retirement is strongly influenced by eligibility ages. It seems clear that differences in labor force departure rates among countries are also strongly influenced by differences in eligibility ages.

## 2.2 Benefit Accrual after Eligibility

The second important feature of plan provisions, which is strongly related to work after the early retirement age—and which is discussed below—is the pattern of benefit accrual after the age of first eligibility. The idea can be explained this way: consider two components of total compensation for working an additional year. One component is current wage earnings. The other component is the 'increase' in future promised social security benefits. Consider a person who has attained the social security early retirement age (when benefits are first available) and suppose

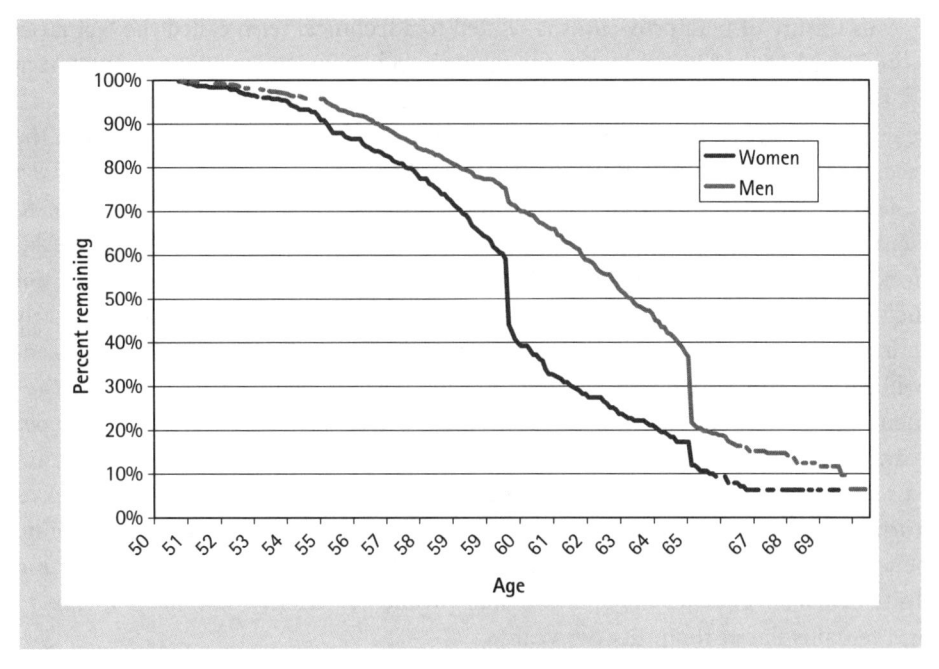

Fig. 16.5 United Kingdom percentage of men and women remaining in the labor force, by age

that a person is considering whether to work for an additional year. It is natural to suppose that if benefit receipt is delayed by a year, benefits when they are received might be increased, to offset the receipt of benefits for one less year. But in most countries this is not the case. Once benefits are available, a person who continues to work for an additional year will receive less in social security benefits over his lifetime than if he quit work and started to receive benefits at the first opportunity. That is, the present value of expected social security benefits declines. In many countries, this loss of social security benefits can offset a large fraction of the wage earnings a person would receive from continued work. Thus, the system imposes an implicit tax on work, and total compensation can be much less than net wage earnings.

A bit more formally, consider the difference between the expected discounted value of social security benefits (social security wealth) if retirement is at age $a+1$ and the present value if retirement is at age $a - SSW(a+1) - SSW(a)$. This difference is called the accrual of benefits between age $a$ and age $a+1$. If the accrual is positive it adds to total compensation from working the additional year; if the accrual is negative, it reduces total compensation. The ratio of the accrual to net wage earnings is an implicit tax on earnings if the accrual is negative and an implicit subsidy to earnings if the accrual is positive. As it turns out, the pension accrual is typically negative at older ages and in many countries exceeds 80 percent the first year after benefit eligibility.

This feature of plan provisions is related to a technical term called the 'actuarial adjustment'. In the United States, for example, if benefits are taken at 64 instead of 65, they are reduced just enough to offset the receipt of benefits for one additional year. If they are taken at 63 instead of 65 they are reduced just enough to offset the receipt of benefits of two additional years, and so forth.[4]

The importance of actuarial adjustment can be illustrated with reference to Germany. Germany made no actuarial adjustment before the 1992 reform legislation, and until recently most employees still retired under provisions that did not include actuarial adjustment. The magnitude of the combined effect of early retirement under the disability program in Germany and no actuarial adjustment is illustrated conceptually in Figure 16.6. The official social security normal retirement age in Germany is 65. Suppose that at that age, benefits were 100 units per year. Many employees can receive benefits at age 57 through the disability program (discussed below). The disability benefits at age 57 are essentially the same as normal retirement benefits at age 65. That is, a person 'eligible' for disability benefits at age 57 who did not take the benefits at that age would forego 100 units per year. This results in a baseline profile of benefits that starts at age 57 and remains flat at 100 units per year.

On the other hand, suppose benefits were reduced actuarially if taken before age 65 and increased actuarially if taken after age 65. Then benefits taken at 57 would be about 60 instead of 100. Benefits if taken at 70 would be about 140 instead of 100. Under this system, there would be no incentive to take benefits early. Indeed there would be no social security incentive to take benefits at any specific age, once benefits were available.

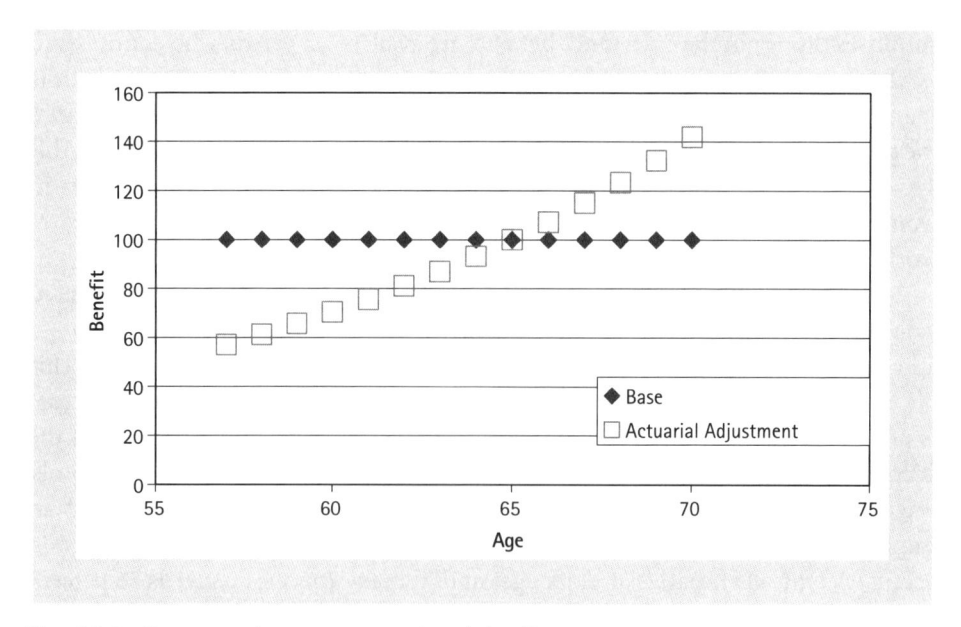

Fig. 16.6 Germany: base versus actuarial adjustment

## 2.3 Disability Insurance, Unemployment Programs, and Early Retirement

A third important feature of social security systems is that in many European countries disability insurance and special unemployment programs essentially provide early retirement benefits before the official social security early retirement age. Germany provides a good example. The pathways to retirement in Germany are shown in Figure 16.7. In 1995 about 65 percent of men entered retirement by way of a disability program or a special unemployment program. As explained above, these programs are closely tied to the explicit social security program. For example, benefits taken at 57 through the disability program are the same as benefits taken at age 65, the 'normal' social security retirement age. To understand the incentive effects of the inclusive social security program, these programs must be treated as part of the social security system. (They are included in the social security incentive calculations discussed below.)

# 3 RETIREMENT INCENTIVES AND LABOR FORCE PARTICIPATION

The Gruber–Wise project used a simple measure to summarize the social security incentive to retire. At each age, beginning with the early retirement age, the implicit

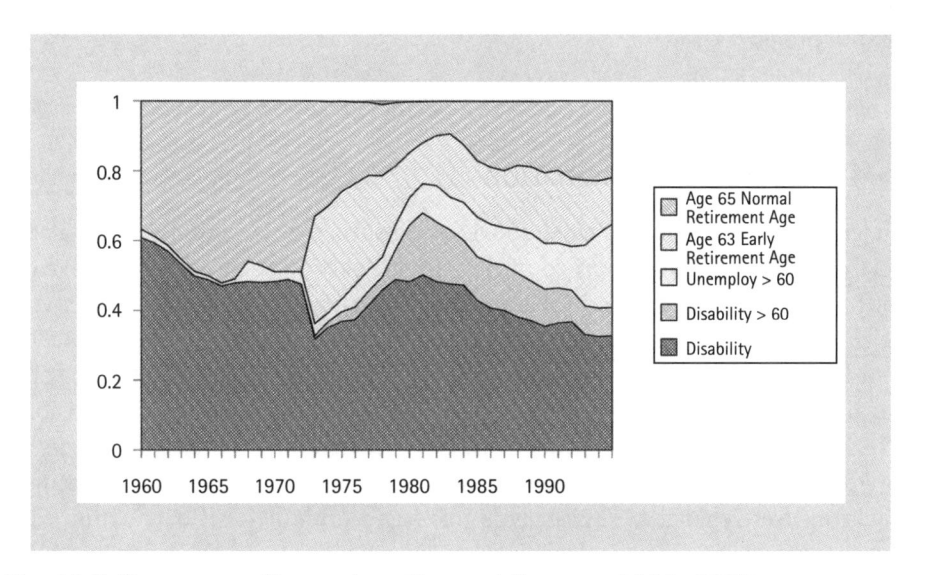

Fig. 16.7 Germany: pathways to retirement for men, 1960–1995

tax on work was calculated in each country. These implicit tax rates on work were then summed beginning with the early retirement age and running through to age 69. This measure was called the 'tax force' to retire. The sum is shown for each of the countries in Figure 16.8. This tax force to retire ranges from over 9 in Italy to about 1.5 in the United States.

The tax force to retire is strongly related to the proportion of older persons in the labor force. This is the key finding from the first phase of the Gruber–Wise project. The relationship is shown in Figures 16.9 and 16.10. Figure 16.9 shows the relationship between the tax force to retire and unused labor force capacity—the proportion of men between ages 55 and 65 that is out of the labor force. It is clear that the two correspond very closely. Figure 16.10 shows the same data for all of the countries except Japan, and rescales the tax force measure to achieve a linear relationship between the tax force to retire and unused labor force capacity. The relationship between the two is perhaps even more evident. The proportion of variation in unused labor force capacity that is explained by the tax force to retire is 86 percent (as indicated by the R-squared value).

# 4 Fiscal Implications of Labor Force Participation

Changes in program provisions can have very important implications for the labor force participation of older workers and thus for the financial position of social security programs.

## 4.1 Labor Force Participation

The empirical findings discussed above established two key results: (1) that the social security systems in many countries provide enormous incentives to leave the labor force at older ages; and (2) that there is a strong correspondence between social security incentives to retire and the withdrawal of older workers from the labor force. These relationships, however, do not provide a means of estimating the magnitude of the effect on labor force participation of changes in plan provisions.

In the second phase of the Gruber and Wise project, the country participants set out to estimate how much the retirement age would change if social security provisions were changed. This analysis was based on individual data within each country, considering the relationship between retirement and the incentives faced

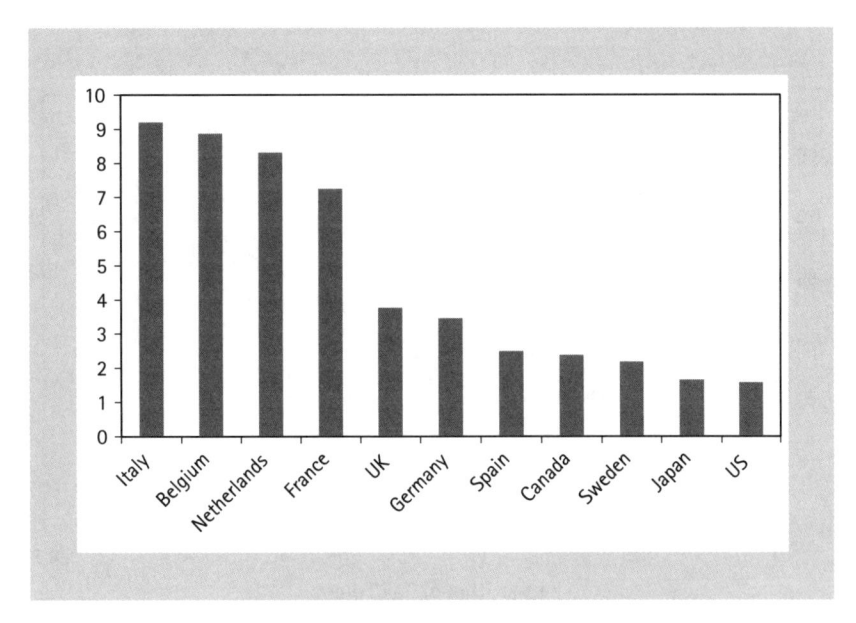

**Fig. 16.8 Sum of tax rates on work from early retirement age to 69**

by individual employees. That is, rather than considering system-wide incentives for representative persons (such as those with median earning histories), and comparing these incentives with aggregate labor force participation across

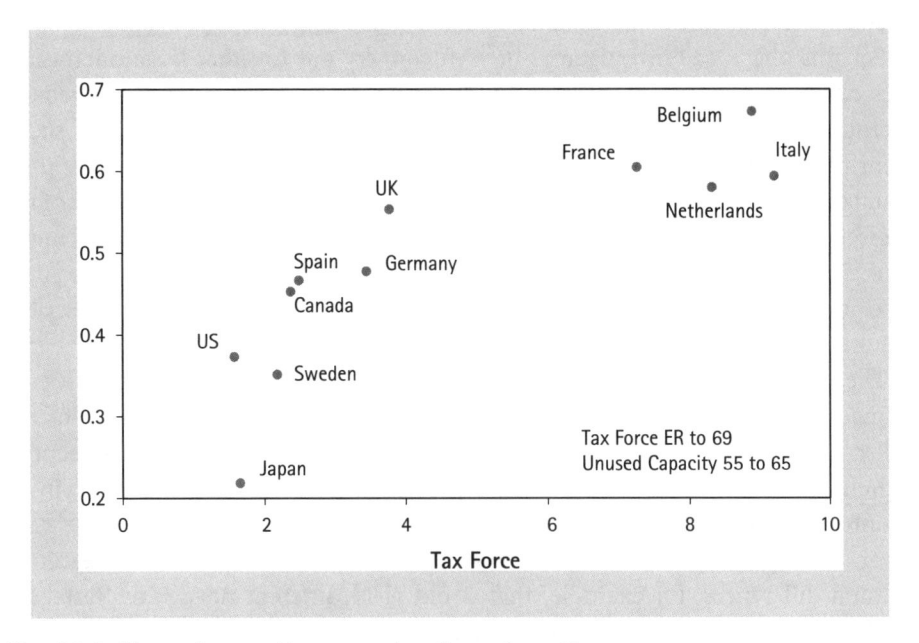

**Fig. 16.9 Unused capacity versus tax force to retire**
*Note*: Tax force ER to 69; unused capacity 55 to 65.

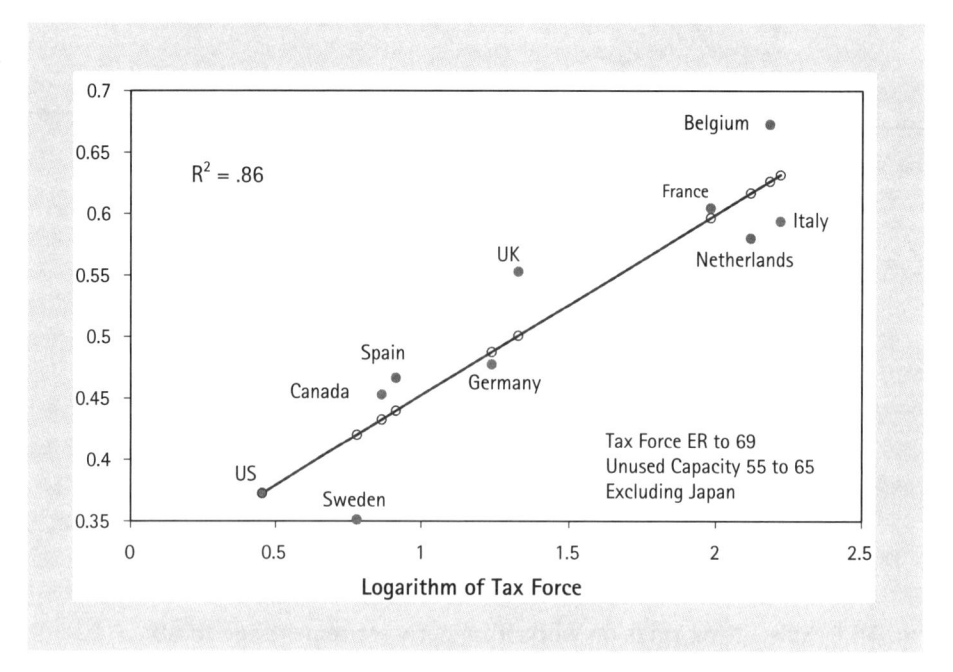

**Fig. 16.10 Unused capacity versus tax force to retire (logarithm)**
Note: $R^2 = 0.86$ Tax force ER to 69; unused capacity 55 to 65 excluding Japan.

countries, the results of these analyses are based on differences in individual circumstances within a given country.

For this phase, the investigators in each country put together large micro data files combining information on individual retirement decisions with retirement incentives (together with other individual data). Individual measures of social security retirement incentives—which vary substantially across persons within a country—were calculated based on the methods developed for the first phase of the project. The key incentive measure was the 'option value' of delayed retirement. This measure is based on the potential gain (or loss) in social security wealth if receipt of benefits is delayed. That is, this constructed economic variable describes the financial gain or loss from continuing to work.[5]

The key advantage of the micro estimation is that in each country the effects of changes in plan provisions could be predicted. The first striking feature of the collective analyses based on within-country micro data is that social security retirement incentives have very similar effects on labor force participation in all countries. In particular, the results strongly confirm that the relationship between labor force participation and retirement across countries is not the result of cultural differences, for example, that could yield different norms, or 'taste' for work, at older ages across countries. The within-country analyses show similar responses to retirement incentive effects, even though the countries differ with respect to cultural histories and institutions.

To demonstrate the effect of plan provisions on retirement, the country authors used the estimates for each country to simulate the effect of three illustrative changes in plan provisions: (1) The three-year increment in eligibility ages increases all eligibility ages by three years, including the early retirement age, the normal retirement age, and the ages of receipt of disability benefits—in countries in which disability, unemployment, or other retirement pathways are important, the eligibility age for *each* of the programs is delayed by three years. (2) The common reform is intended to predict the effect of the same reform in each country. Under the common reform, the early retirement age is set at age 60 and the normal retirement age at 65. Benefits taken before age 65 are reduced 'actuarially', by 6 percent for each year before age 65. Benefits taken after age 65 are increased by 6 percent for each year the receipt of benefits is delayed. In addition, the replacement rate at age 65 is set at 60 percent of (projected) age 60 earnings. (3) The actuarially fair reform reduces benefits actuarially if taken before the normal retirement age and increases benefits actuarially if taken after the normal retirement age. Actually, only the first two reforms were simulated at this stage of the analysis; the third is discussed below.

The findings can be illustrated in two figures. Figure 16.11 shows the effect of the three-year increment in eligibility ages.[6] To help to standardize for the wide variation across countries in the age at which retirement begins, each bar shows the reduction in the fraction of the population out of the labor force four years after the age at which a quarter of the population has retired (which is an 'effective retirement age'). This figure has two notable features. The first is that the average

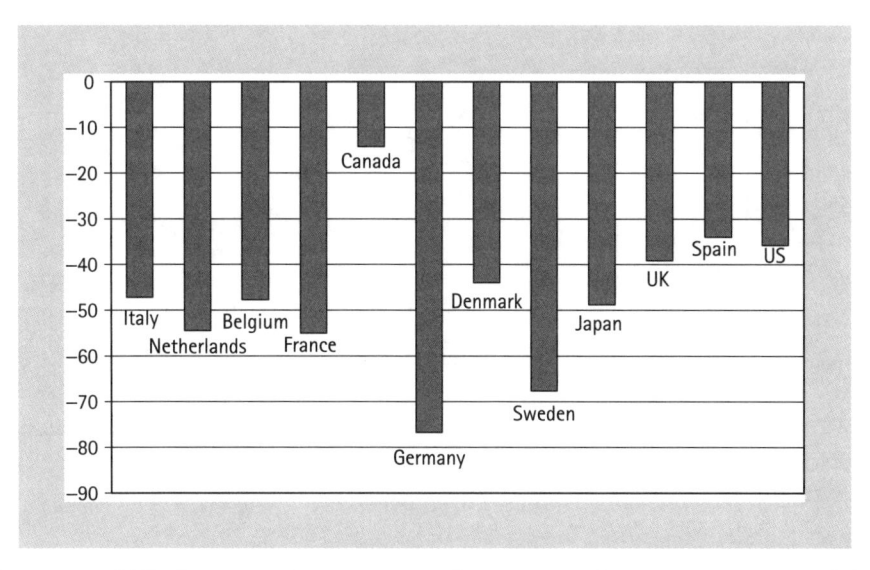

Fig. 16.11 OLF change, 25 percentage plus 4 years, base versus 3-year delay: OV-S3 (OV option value: S3 Simulation method 3)

reduction in the proportion of the population out of the labor force is very large—47 percent. The second notable feature of the figure is the similarity across countries. The reduction is between 34 and 55 percent in nine of the 12 countries. In Germany and Sweden, the reductions are 77 and 68 percent respectively.[7]

Figure 16.12 shows the effect on the out-of-the-labor force proportion of the common reform. In this figure, it is clear that the greatest reductions in the out-of-the-labor force proportion under the common reform are realized in the countries with the youngest effective retirement ages. For the six countries with substantial retirement before age 60, the average *reduction* in the out-of-the-labor force proportion is 44 percent. For the six countries in which most retirement is after age 60, the *increase* in the out-of-the-labor force proportion averages 4 percent.

The systematic pattern of these results shows a strong correspondence with intuition. For the six countries with the youngest effective retirement ages, the common reform represents a substantial *increase* in the youngest eligibility age, and the actuarial reduction means that benefits at this age are much lower than under the base country plans. Thus, for these countries, the OLF proportion should decline under the reform, and that is the case for every country but Canada. But for the six countries with older retirement ages, the common reform may reduce the earliest eligibility age—as in the United States—and may provide a greater incentive to leave the labor force. In addition, the 60 percent replacement rate at the normal retirement age represents an increase for some countries, like the United States, and a reduction in the replacement rate for other countries. Consequently, in three of these six countries, the proportion out of the labor force increases under the common reform simulation, and on average the out-of-the-labor-force proportion increases.

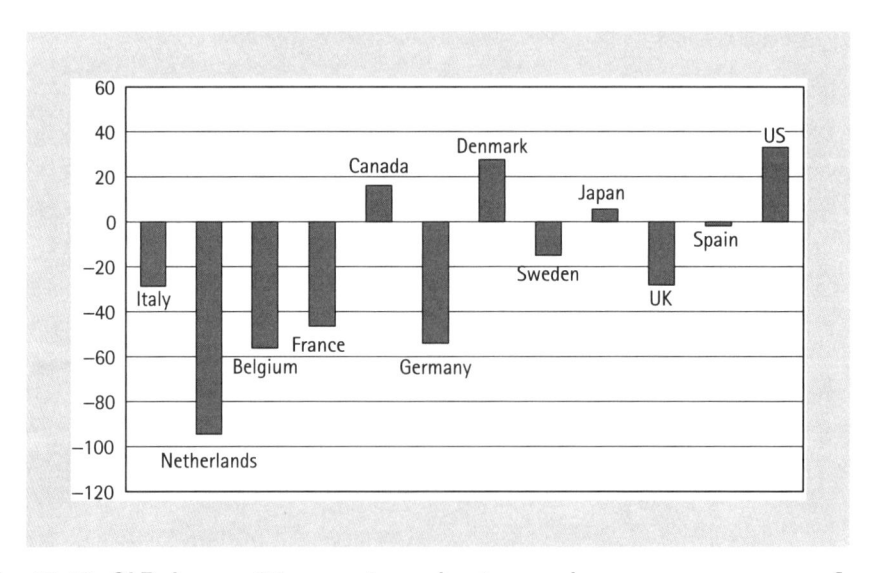

Fig. 16.12 OLF change, 25 percentage plus 4 years, base versus common reform: OV-S3

## 4.2 Fiscal Implications

Increasing the labor force participation rates of older workers can have very substantial implications for the financial footing of social security systems. In the third phase of the Gruber and Wise project, the country participants estimated the fiscal effects of changes in plan provisions. The results relied on the retirement model estimates obtained in the second phase and discussed above. Again, the results are demonstrated by simulating the fiscal effects of illustrative reforms.

The goal of these analyses is to illustrate the fiscal implications of reform for a specific cohort or for a group of cohorts. For example, in the United States, the calculations show what the fiscal implications would have been had the social security provisions been changed for the cohort born between 1931 and 1941 (reaching age 65 between 1996 and 2006). The fiscal implications are measured in terms of the government budget and include the change in social security benefits and the change in tax revenues from prolonged (or decreased) labor force participation. The fiscal implication is defined as the change in benefits minus the change in taxes. This change is stated as a percentage of the base cost of the social security program.

The country participants simulated the effects of each of the three illustrative reforms. The effect of the reforms of course depends on the current system in each country. An increase in eligibility ages will reduce expenditures and increase tax revenues in all countries (with a couple of aberrant exceptions). The actuarial reform, which has large effects in Germany, should have little effect in countries like the United States and Canada where the system is already actuarially fair.

The results are illustrated in three figures. Like the results reported above, these results are also taken from the individual country papers. The papers with these results have not yet been published, however, so these results are taken from the country working papers.

To understand the potential implications of the reforms, the following discussion focuses on the effect of the common reform in Germany. Figure 16.13 illustrates conceptually the effect of each of the components of the common reform. Since the common reform in Germany would increase the age of first eligibility by three years, the common reform incorporates the three-year increment in eligibility. In addition, the common reform incorporates actuarial reduction in benefits before and actuarial increase in benefits after the normal retirement age. Finally, the common reform in Germany implies a substantial reduction in benefits at the age 65 normal retirement age. As the diagram suggests, the combined effect of these changes can be large in Germany. Benefits before age 60 are no longer available. When they are available at 60, the system provides no financial incentive to take benefits then as opposed to at some later age. And, when the normal retirement age is reached, again the system provides no financial incentive to take benefits at that age as opposed to at some later age. As seen in Figure 16.12, the common reform reduces very substantially the proportion of older persons that is out of the labor

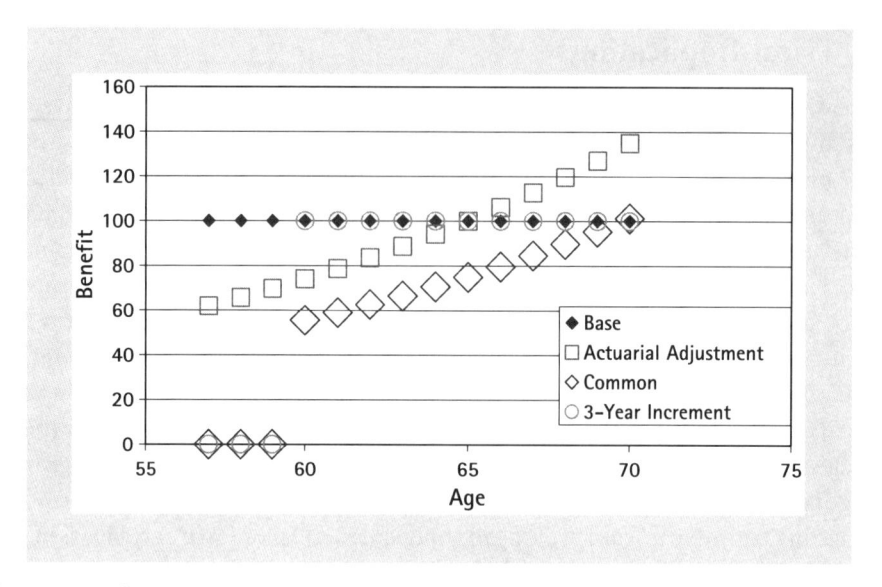

Fig. 16.13 Germany: base, 3-year increment, actuarial adujstment, common reform

force. The fiscal implication of the increase in the labor force participation that is predicted from the common reform is also very substantial.

Figure 16.13 also highlights once again that the effect of illustrative reforms will depend on the current plan provision in a country. For example, the actuarial adjustment will have no effect if the current system is already actuarially fair. First eligibility at age 60 will be an increase in the eligibility age in some countries and a reduction in others. A replacement rate of 60 percent is lower than the current replacement rate in some countries and greater than the current rate in other countries.

Figure 16.14 shows the total fiscal effect of the three-year increment in eligibility ages. For example, in Germany, the decrease in social security benefits minus the increase in government tax revenue resulting from a three-year increment in all eligibility ages would be equivalent to about 36 percent of the current cost of the program. Across all countries, the average increase in revenue is equivalent to 27 percent of current program cost—reported as a reduction in government expenditures minus revenues. The average increase in revenue over all countries is equivalent to 0.72 percent of GDP—again reported as a reduction in government expenditures for benefits minus the increase in tax revenues.

Figure 16.15 shows the fiscal effect of actuarial adjustment, as a percentage of base cost. As expected, the variations are large across countries. In the United States and Canada, for example, where adjustment is close to actuarial already, the effect is small. In Germany, which until recently had no actuarial adjustment, the effect is very large, as explained in detail above. In France, actuarial increase in benefits after

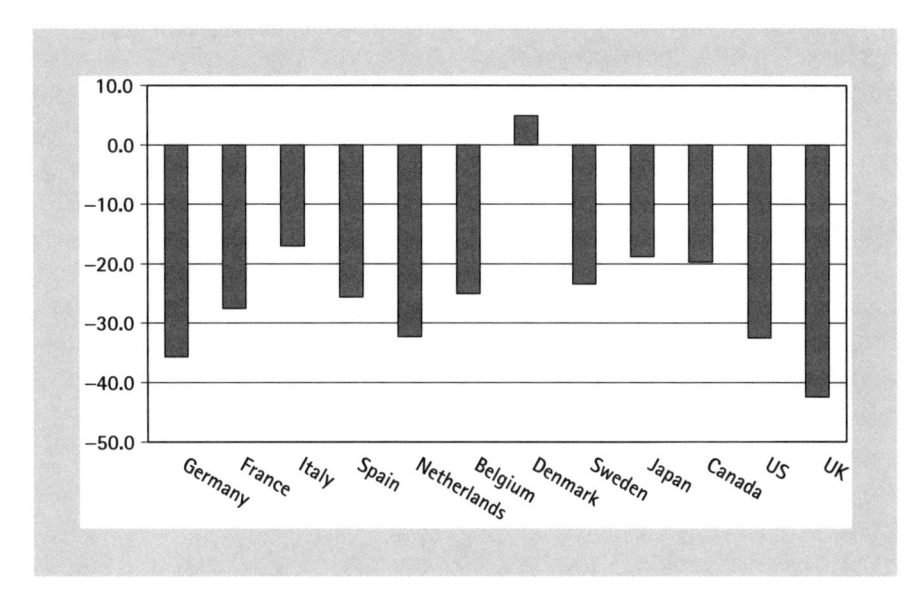

**Fig. 16.14 Total fiscal effect of three-year increment, as a percentage of base cost**

the age 60 normal retirement age would increase cost.[8] On average the decrease in government expenditure minus revenue is about 26 percent.

Figure 16.16 shows the fiscal effect of the common reform, as a percentage of base cost. In accord with intuition, the total net government revenue as a percentage of program base cost varies greatly. In the United States and Canada, for example,

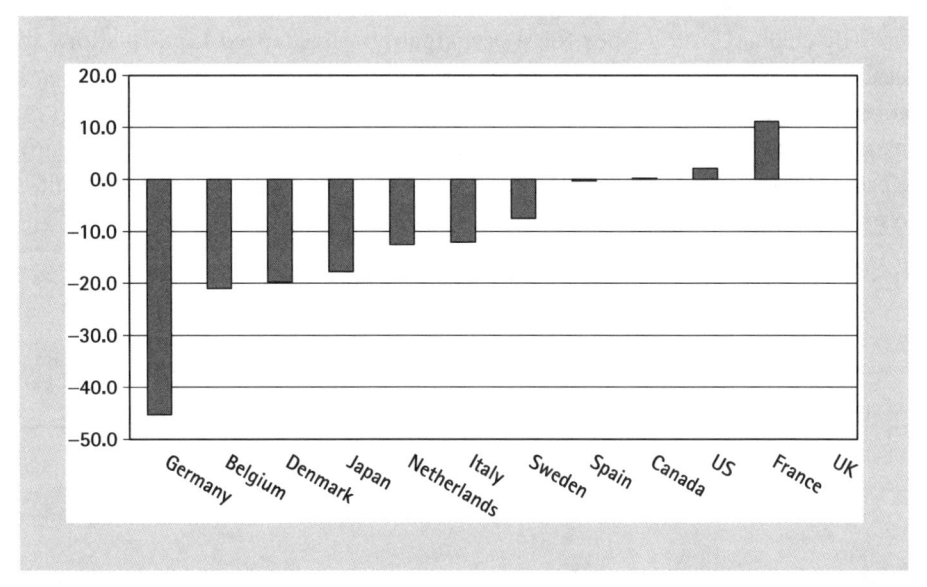

**Fig. 16.15 Total fiscal effect of actuarial reform, as a percentage of base cost**

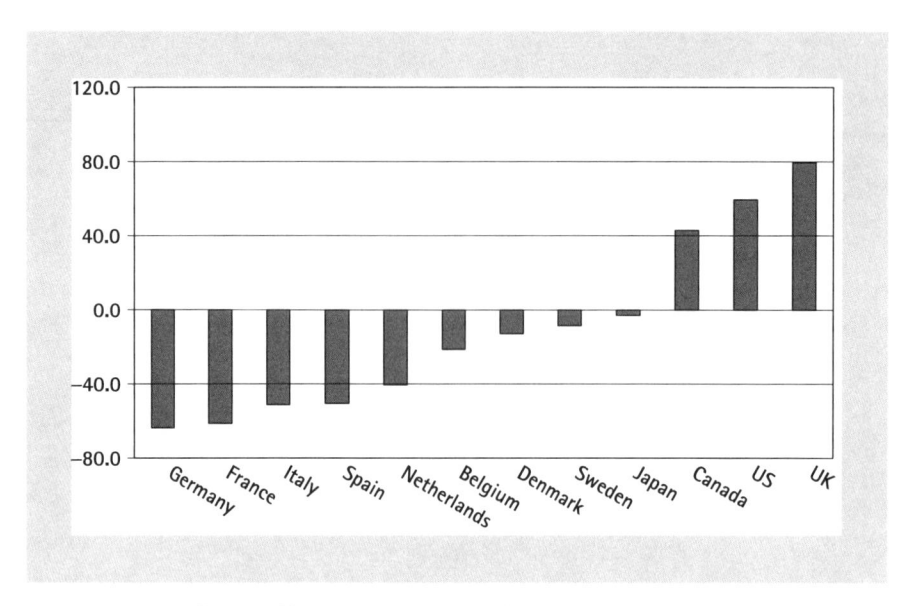

Fig. 16.16 Total fiscal effect of common reform, as a percentage of base cost

benefits under the common reform are more generous than current benefits, and they are available at age 60 instead of the current age 62 early retirement age. Also in the United Kingdom, the common reform benefits are much more generous than current benefits and the age 60 early retirement age is younger than the current early retirement age for some participants.

Thus, reforms like those considered here can have very large fiscal implications for the cost of social security benefits as well as for government revenues engendered by changes in the labor force participation of older workers. In short, the fiscal effects of reform can be very large. Some combination of increases in the early retirement age, actuarial adjustment of benefits, and change in the benefit level can change net government revenue substantially. In many countries, the *illustrative* reforms yield increases in government revenue minus expenditures equivalent to 20 to 50 percent of current program cost.

# 5 Are Social Security Work Penalties Being Reduced?

Having emphasized the potential for changes in plan provisions to increase the labor force participation of older workers and to relieve the financial pressure on social security systems, this section considers, provisionally, whether social security systems may already be moving to reduce work penalties. As discussed earlier, Figures 16.2a and 16.2b were marked to distinguish years before and after 1996. In many of the countries the decline in labor force participation seems to reverse around that time. In some countries the reversal can be traced to changes in social security provisions, while in others it seems to be associated with economy-wide trends in labor market conditions.

Consider Denmark first. Except for updating the series, the only other change is the addition of data for Denmark, which was added to the project after the first phase. In 1999, the Post Employment Wage (PEW) program was changed to provide incentives to stay in the labor force until 62. (When the PEW program was introduced in 1979 it induced an almost immediate drop of 17 percentage points in the labor force participation rate of men aged 60 to 64.)

In Sweden, the explanation for the increase in the labor force participation of men aged 60 to 64 lies primarily in changes in the eligibility requirement for the disability program. The provision that unemployed workers older than age 60 were eligible for a disability pension was abolished in 1991, and the provision that these unemployed workers were eligible because of a combination of medical and labor market reasons was abolished in 1997. The most important change was likely the 1995 provision that enabled the social security administration to reconsider the right to a disability pension. Consistent with these changes, from 1993 to 2002 the percentage of men aged 60 to 64 with a disability pension was reduced from 30 to 23 percent. In addition, the Swedish economy has recovered from the 1990s recession that limited labor force demand.

In Germany, the reversal of the downward trend in the labor force participation of men aged 60 to 64 that began in 1997 coincides with the introduction of partial actuarial reduction in benefits taken before the early retirement age. In the United States the downward trend was reversed about 1995. While the reason for the reversal is unclear, it seems likely that the decline in employer-provided defined benefit pension plans—with strong incentives to retire early—and the rapid spread of personal retirement plans—with no retirement incentive effects—have been part of the explanation.

In the United Kingdom, labor force participation rates have increased at all ages, but there was no apparent change in social security plan provisions that might have led to an increase for men aged 60 to 64. In Canada, there were no changes in social security provisions that could account for the increase in the labor force participation of men aged 60 to 64. There was, however, a general improvement in labor market conditions after the mid-1990s, with a fall in the overall unemployment rate from 10.4 percent in 1995 to 7.6 percent in 2003. In Spain, the reforms during the 1997 to 2002 period did not change substantially the retirement incentives faced by older workers. However, the labor force increased substantially—from about 12.5 million in 1995 to over 17 million in 2004—apparently due to an increase in the demand for labor. And during this period, labor force participation increased from 50.8 to 55.7 percent.

The increase in the labor force participation in the Netherlands is also difficult to explain. Early retirement provisions in the Netherlands are the result of collective bargaining by sector, or even by firm, and hence it is hard to easily identify and summarize changes in plan provisions.

# 6 A More Comprehensive Understanding of Reform

Social security is the largest social insurance program in most developed countries. The vast differences in social security program provisions across countries have provided a natural laboratory to study the influence of program provisions on individual behavior. The finding that social security provisions penalize work, and thus distort retirement decisions, is a critical foundation for understanding the effects of social security provisions and in particular the implications of system reform. But a comprehensive assessment of the implications of reform also requires an understanding of the relationship between social security provisions and the well-being of the elderly, and the young. If reforms that remove work penalties also reduce income, this trade-off must be considered in evaluation of the reform. If, on the other hand, a decline in social security benefits is completely offset by other forms of support such as labor income or greater personal saving, reform may have little effect on the well-being of the elderly.

A comprehensive assessment of reform also requires evaluation of the implications of reform for the employment of the young. Indeed, a common explanation of provisions that induce the elderly to retire, and a common argument in opposition to reform, is that the departure of older persons from the labor force will improve the employment prospects of younger workers. To what extent do labor markets operate in this 'boxed' fashion?

In addition, to understand the implications of reforming disability insurance programs, it is necessary to understand how the truly disabled would be affected by such changes. In particular, how do program provisions affect the relationship between health status and employment? As the international project goes forward, the goal is to expand understanding of these issues and thus to provide further understanding of the implications of social security reform.

# 7 Employer-Provided Pension Plans and Incentives to Retire

The social security retirement incentives described above result from the way in which the social security defined benefit is determined in each country. Employer-provided defined benefit pension plans typically have similar retirement incentives. Defined benefit pension plans are still common in the United States, although the proportion of employees covered by personal retirement plans such as 401(k) plans is rising rapidly. Defined benefit plans are also common in Canada and in the United Kingdom. Such plans are also the basis of the employer-based system in the Netherlands. Thus, in some countries the incentive effects inherent in these plans can also have a large effect on labor force participation.

Just like social security incentives, the key issue is this: if the receipt of benefits is delayed for a year, are benefits increased enough to offset their receipt for one less year? Is the benefit formula actuarially fair? Under the typical employer-provided defined benefit plan in the United States, the answer is no. Benefits are not increased enough to offset their receipt for one less year. Thus, the plans impose no implicit tax on work, just like the implicit tax described above for social security defined benefits. Indeed, the analysis of the retirement incentives inherent in employer-provided defined benefit plans led to the international comparison project that produced the results discussed above. The following discussion provides some information on the incentive effects of employer-provided plans. It does not attempt to cover the large number of studies that address this issue, but only describes the work that more narrowly prompted the comparative analysis of the retirement incentives inherent in social security plan provisions.

One of the most striking economic trends in the United States over the past several decades has been the withdrawal of older persons from the labor force. As noted at the outset of this chapter, this trend was surely made possible by the advent of the social security program and by the concurrent spread of employer-provided pension plans. Most of the pension plans were defined benefit plans, in which the employee pension benefit at retirement depended on years of service with the employer and earnings, typically earnings in the last years of employment. In the early 1980s, the retirement incentive effects of these plans began to be understood. The first description (of which I am aware) of the incentives inherent in the plan provisions was by Jeremy Bulow (1981). Edward Lazear (1983) then wrote an influential paper proposing that the incentives were intended to induce older workers to leave the labor force, based on the proposition that, when old, they were paid more than their marginal product.

In a series of papers Kotlikoff and Wise (1985, 1987, 1988, 1989a) used data from the Bureau of Labor Statistics—which provided information on the precise provisions of a large sample of employer-provided plans—to describe the incentive effects over a broad range of pension plans in the United States and we emphasized the enormous variation across plans. These data, however, contained no information on the retirement decisions of individuals covered by the plans. To obtain plan provisions together with data on individual retirement choices, we turned our attention to firm personnel records. These data included information on individual retirement decisions as well as information on their earnings histories, in addition to a precise description of their firm pension plan provisions. Again with Larry Kotlikoff (Kotlikoff and Wise 1989b) we used such data to describe the striking relationship between pension plan provisions in a firm and retirement from that firm.

Then Stock and Wise (1990a, 1990b) used firm data to develop and estimate an option value retirement model. The central feature of this model is recognition of the important effect on retirement of the future accrual pattern of pension benefits. That is, retirement benefits could be much larger, or much smaller, if retirement is delayed and thus the 'option value' of delaying retirement can have an important effect on individual retirement decisions. A series of subsequent papers found very similar behavioral responses to pension plan incentives by men and women and by different types of employees.[9]

Considering social security systems in different countries was analogous to considering the effects of different employer-provided pension plans—with varying provisions—in the United States. Indeed, the retirement responses to social security plan incentives to retire correspond very closely to the incentive inherent in the employer-provided defined benefit plans.

# 8 Conclusion

The social security programs in many countries induce older employees to leave the labor force. By penalizing work, these social security systems magnify the increasing financial burden caused by ageing populations and thus contribute to their own insolvency. Removing the incentives to retire early can increase substantially the labor force participation of older workers. In turn, the increase in labor force participation of older persons can relieve the financial pressure faced by social security systems. The gain from leveling this playing field is not to make people work longer but rather to remove the penalty for working. Employees can then make retirement decisions based on individual circumstances and preferences.

## Notes

1. The normal retirement age in the United States is scheduled to increase to 67 by 2002.
2. These rates are based on labor force participation rates of Health and Retirement Study respondents. The precise age of departure from the labor force is obscured by the two-year interval between survey waves, and thus the jump in the hazard rate does not match the age 62 early retirement age exactly.
3. The data for the figure come from the Health and Retirement Study and the two-year survey interval means that the jumps in the hazard rates may not correspond exactly to ages 55 and 62.
4. Now, benefits in the United States are actuarial between 62 and 65, but are increased less than actuarially if the receipt of benefits is delayed beyond age 65, thus providing an incentive to leave the labor force at 65. Under current law, benefits will eventually slowly become actuarial by 2009.
5. Estimation using this measure goes back to the Stock and Wise (1999a, 1999b) procedure we used to analyze the effect on retirement of employer-provided defined benefit pension plans in the United States, as discussed below. Estimates were also obtained based on the peak value measure proposed by Coile and Gruber (2000).
6. These estimates are based on the method that is most likely to reflect the long-run effect of such a reform.
7. The average reduction is 28 percent using the simulation method, which is likely on average to substantially underestimate the response to the three-year increment.
8. Because of particular features of the current system in the United Kingdom, the actuarial reform has not been simulated for that country.
9. Analyses by Lumsdaine *et al.* (1992) of the option value model in comparison with a stochastic dynamic programming specification were also based on firm data. The conclusion of this paper was that the option value model seemed to capture the retirement decisions of employees just as well or perhaps better than the closely related, but more complex, dynamic programming model. This result was confirmed by Ausink and Wise (1996). Several additional papers by Lumsdaine, Stock, and Wise (1990, 1991, 1994, 1996, 1997) compared results from several different firms, for men and women, and for different types of employees.

## References

AUSINK, JOHN, and WISE, DAVID A. (1996). 'The military pension, compensation, and retirement of U.S. Air Force pilots', in David A. Wise (ed.), *Advances in the Economics of Aging*. Chicago: University of Chicago Press.

BULOW, J. (1981). 'Early retirement pension benefits'. NBE Research Working Paper 654.

COILE, COURTNEY, and GRUBER, JONATHAN (2000). 'Social security incentives for retirement', in David Wise (ed.), *Themes in the Economics of Aging*. Chicago: University of Chicago Press, 311–41.

GRUBER, JONATHAN, and WISE, DAVID A. (eds.) (1999a). *Social Security and Retirement around the World*. Chicago: University of Chicago Press.

—— —— (1999b). 'Social Security and Retirement around the World: introduction and summary', in Jonathan Gruber and David A. Wise (eds.), *Social Security and Retirement around the World*. Chicago: University of Chicago Press. Also published in *Research in Labor Economics*, 18. JAI Press Inc, 1999.

—— —— (eds.) (2004a). *Social Security and Retirement around the World: Micro-Estimation*. Chicago: University of Chicago Press.

—— —— (2004b). 'Social Security and Retirement around the World: Micro-Estimation: introduction and summary', in Jonathan Gruber and David A. Wise (eds.), *Social Security and Retirement around the World: Micro-Estimation*. Chicago: University of Chicago Press.

—— —— (eds.) (forthcoming a). *Social Security and Retirement around the World: Fiscal Implications*. Chicago: University of Chicago Press.

—— —— (forthcoming b). 'Social Security and Retirement Around the World: Fiscal Implications: introduction and summary', in Jonathan Gruber and David A. Wise (eds.), *Social Security and Retirement Around the World: Fiscal Implications*. Chicago: University of Chicago Press.

KOTLIKOFF, LAURENCE, SMETTERS, KENT, and WALLISER, JAN (1999). 'Privatizing social security in the United States—comparing the options'. *Review of Economic Dynamics*, 2: 532–74.

—— and WISE, DAVID A. (1985). 'Labor compensation and the structure of private pension plans: evidence for contractual versus spot labor markets', in D. A. Wise (ed.), *Pensions, Labor and Individual Choice*. Chicago: University of Chicago Press.

—— —— (1987). 'The incentive effects of private pension plans', in Z. Bodie, J. B. Shoven, and D. A. Wise (eds.), *Issues in Pension Economics*. Chicago: University of Chicago Press.

—— —— (1988). 'Pension backloading, wage taxes, and work disincentives', in L. Summers (ed.), *Tax Policy and the Economy*, vol. 2. Cambridge, Mass.: MIT Press.

—— —— (1989a). *The Wage Carrot and the Pension Stick*. Kalamazoo, MI: W. E. Upjohn Institute.

—— —— (1989b). 'Employee retirement and a firm's pension plan', in David A. Wise (ed.), *The Economics of Aging*. Chicago: University of Chicago Press.

LAZEAR, E. (1983). 'Pensions as severance pay', in Z. Bodie and J. Shoven (eds.), *Financial Aspects of the United States Pension System*. Chicago: University of Chicago Press.

LUMSDAINE, ROBIN, STOCK, JAMES H., and WISE, DAVID A. (1990). 'Efficient windows and labor force reduction'. *Journal of Public Economics*, 43/2: 131–59.

—— —— —— (1991). 'Fenêtres et retraites (Windows and retirement)'. *Annales d'Économie et de Statistique*, 0/20–1: 219–42.

—— —— —— (1992). 'Three models of retirement: computational complexity versus predictive validity', in D. A. Wise (ed.), *Topics in the Economics of Aging*. Chicago: University of Chicago Press.

—— —— —— (1994). 'Pension plan provisions and retirement: men and women, Medicare, and models', in D. A. Wise (ed.), *Studies in the Economics of Aging*. Chicago: University of Chicago Press.

—— —— —— (1996). 'Why are retirement rates so high at age 65?', in D. A. Wise (ed.), *Advances in the Economics of Aging*. Chicago: University of Chicago Press.

—— —— —— (1997). 'Retirement incentives: the interaction between employer-provided pension plans, social security, and retiree health benefits', in M. D. Hurd and N. Yashiro (eds.), *The Economic Effects of Aging in the United States and Japan*. Chicago: University of Chicago Press.

SAMWICK, A. (1998). 'New evidence on pensions, social security, and the timing of retirement'. *Journal of Public Economics*, 70: 207–36.

STOCK, JAMES H., and WISE, DAVID A. (1990a). 'The pension inducement to retire: an option value analysis', in David A. Wise (ed.), *Issues in the Economics of Aging*. Chicago: University of Chicago Press.

—— —— (1990b). 'Pensions, the option value of work, and retirement'. *Econometrica*, 58/5: 1151–80.

## PHASE III WORKING PAPERS

BAKER, M., GRUBER, J., and MILLIGAN, K. (2003). 'Simulating the response to reform of Canada's income security programs'. NBER Working Paper 9455 (Jan.).

BINGLEY, P., GUPTA, N. D., and PEDERSEN, P. J. (2003). 'Fiscal implications of reforms in retirement systems in Denmark'. Jan.

BLUNDELL, R., and EMMERSON, C. (2003). 'Fiscal effects of reforming the UK state pension system'. July.

BÖRSCH-SUPAN, A., KOHNZ, S., and SCHNABEL, R. (2003). 'The budget impact of reduced early retirement incentives on the German public pension system'. Jan.

BOLDRIN, M., and JIMÉNEZ-MARTIN, S. (2003). 'Evaluating Spanish pension expenditure under alternative reform scenarios'. Sept.

BRUGIAVINI, A., and PERACCHI, F. (2003). 'Fiscal implications of pension reforms in Italy'. Jan.

COILE, C., and GRUBER, J. (2003). 'Fiscal effects of social security reform in the United States'. Mar.

DESMET, R., JOUSTEN, A., PERELMAN, S., and PESTIEAU, P. (2003). 'Micro-simulation of social security reforms in Belgium'. NBER Working Paper 9494 (Feb.).

KAPTEYN, A., and DE VOS, KLAAS (2003). 'Simulation of pension reforms in the Netherlands'. Feb.

OISHI, A. S., and OSHIO, T. (2002). 'Financial implications of social security reforms in Japan'. Nov.

PALME, M., and SVENSSON, I. (2003). 'Financial implication of income security reforms in Sweden'. Dec.

WALRAET, E., and MAHIEU, R. (2002). 'Simulating retirement behavior: the case of France'. Nov.

CHAPTER 17

# MEETING HEALTH AND LONG-TERM CARE NEEDS IN RETIREMENT

## MARILYN MOON

Although it is common to focus more on income support issues for persons in retirement, access to good health care coverage is also essential. It is likely to be a less debated issue outside of the United States since all OECD countries provide for the health care needs of their elderly as part of their comprehensive national health care systems. But the United States has taken a much different direction. While largely depending on employers to provide for the needs of workers and their families, once people reach the age of 65, they shift to a public program for basic coverage. This basic program, Medicare, offers a minimal benefit package; as a result, a mixed public/private system has evolved to meet the acute care needs of the elderly in the United States. Thus, individuals considering retirement need to focus on how well their acute health care needs will be met; the answer will vary substantially depending upon people's work histories, level of income, and, to some extent, health status. This system creates complexity and inefficiency that certainly does not make Medicare a model for others to follow.

Further, access to long-term care services is more severely means tested in the United States than in many European countries, again creating a number of problems. The joint federal/state Medicaid program is based on a welfare model with strict income limits that vary across the United States. Yet, even with these inadequacies for both acute and long-term care, the United States is considering cutting back on its public health care insurance promise to older Americans in order to address the projected higher costs of Medicare and Medicaid over time.

This chapter explores how the United States meets the health care needs of older Americans, highlighting the extent to which the US model differs from that of other countries. It also examines whether greater reliance on the private sector and eventually shifting from a defined benefit to a defined contribution approach will be effective in holding down the costs of health care over time while still meeting the needs of older Americans. As other countries may also consider adding market incentives to their systems, the US experience can highlight problems that may arise from such changes. Further, the financing challenges in the United States pose an additional element of uncertainty that can be instructive to other countries if attitudes toward the public sector erode over time.

# 1 US Health Care System for the Elderly

Although the United States does not provide public health insurance for the general population, it has two programs that provide health insurance for older Americans. The publicly supported Medicare and Medicaid programs ease the burdens on individuals financing health care independently and on employers offering retiree health plans. As such, Medicare and Medicaid are a critical part of the retirement system in the United States. Like Social Security, many observers are concerned about the future of these publicly supported health programs and society's willingness to fund them. In fact, solving the financial problems of Social Security likely will prove substantially easier than the problems facing Medicare and Medicaid. In addition to the demands that changing demographics create, Medicare and Medicaid costs tend to rise faster than incomes or per capita GDP.

The Medicare program serves persons aged 65 and over eligible for any form of Social Security benefit and persons with disabilities who have been on Social Security for two years. Medicare does not provide fully comprehensive coverage and is usually supplemented by private sources. Many employers, reluctant to take on the full risks of health insurance for their retirees, nonetheless chose to supplement these benefits after Medicare's passage in 1965. For about a third of all Medicare beneficiaries, the combination of Medicare and retiree benefits generates good acute health care coverage. A smaller proportion—about 17 percent—of Medicare beneficiaries receives Medicaid, a joint federal/state program that serves low-income seniors. This group accounts for a substantial share of Medicare's expenditures since its members tend to be sicker (MedPAC 2002). And although not intended originally to provide long-term care (particularly institutional) coverage, Medicaid has become the major source of such protection for those with low incomes and some persons with modest incomes who have exhausted their resources.

Although the Medicare program is extremely popular, its future is nonetheless unclear. The pressures of financing over the last 25 years have resulted in many cutbacks to the program. In part because past changes have already pared back payment levels to providers of services and limited the comprehensiveness of coverage, many policy-makers are now looking for more dramatic ways to change the program to hold down its long-term costs as the baby-boom generation approaches eligibility age. The Medicaid program is even more stringent in its payments to providers of care, often resulting in limited access by patients who would otherwise be eligible. Concurrently, the distrust of government and reluctance of politicians to consider expanding financing for the program have contributed to a sense of the need for change. And since these programs, particularly Medicare, do not provide universal coverage, critics often argue that 'too much' is spent on the elderly. Interestingly, the ratio of spending on health care for the elderly versus the young is not higher in the United States as compared to other industrialized countries where everyone is in the same system.

The current 'magic bullets' for reducing costs that have captured the imagination of many policy-makers are reliance on private insurance to help curb spending costs and shifting Medicare's commitment from a defined benefit to a defined contribution. The first is more immediately on the horizon, while the second is often viewed as a logical next step. Other options—such as a higher eligibility age, income-tested premiums, direct reforms to fee-for-service, or increased financial support—are less often mentioned, in part because they highlight that painful choices will be required. Most of this chapter explores the future of Medicare and whether the strategy of giving individuals a limited stipend with which to purchase insurance in the private market is likely to be a viable option. Anticipating what will happen to Medicaid is even more difficult. This program involves two levels of government and recipients whose incomes are generally well below the poverty line, which makes it difficult to shift a large share of program costs to Medicaid beneficiaries.

## 2 Origins of Medicare and Medicaid

When Medicare was established in 1965, many supporters believed that covering persons aged 65 and over was a precursor to a national system of health insurance. But a national health insurance system never materialized. Instead, Medicare has become the largest single public program of health insurance. Medicaid, which was also passed in 1965, now has combined spending about equivalent to that of

Medicare. However, the program varies by state and covers more than just the elderly population (Moon 1996).

Initially, everyone over the age of 65 was eligible to participate in Medicare when it began in July of 1966. After 1968, eligibility was limited to persons over the age of 65 who qualified for some type of Social Security benefit, usually as a worker or dependent. Even with this limitation, Medicare covers about 97 percent of all persons aged 65 and older. In 1972, the program's scope was expanded to include persons who receive Social Security Disability Insurance after a two-year waiting period. In 2003, 41 million people, nearly one in every eight Americans, were enrolled in Medicare (Boards of Trustees 2004).

The benefits covered by Medicare have changed little since 1965, but changes in the delivery of care in the United States have affected the size of the various components of the benefit package. Part A of Medicare, also called Hospital Insurance, covers inpatient hospital services, up to 100 days of care in a skilled nursing facility following a hospital stay, and hospice care. Part B of Medicare, Supplementary Medical Insurance, covers physician services, outpatient hospital care, laboratory, testing, and other ambulatory services. Home health care services—skilled care such as rehabilitation services provided to persons who are homebound—have been subject to a number of changes in recent years; presently most of these services are now under Part B. In 2006, a new Part D of Medicare will offer a prescription drug benefit. It, like Part B, will be voluntary; for those who enroll, a little less than half of drug costs will be covered.

Part A of Medicare is financed by a payroll tax of 1.45 percent of all wages assessed on both employers and employees. When the program began, that tax rate was 0.35 percent, and gradually increased over time. The rate of the tax has not changed since 1986, however, although the amount subject to tax has risen over time. In 1993, the upper limit on the tax was eliminated so that all wages are subject to the Medicare payroll tax. Part B is voluntary and financed by premiums on beneficiaries and by general revenues sufficient to make up the level of spending required. That premium initially paid 50 percent of the costs of Part B, but legislation reduced that share beginning in 1972 because Medicare's costs were growing substantially faster than incomes of beneficiaries. It was set at 25 percent of the costs of an aged beneficiary's benefits on a temporary basis starting in 1982, and became a permanent requirement in 1997. Part D will use the same funding structure as Part B (Boards of Trustees 2004).

## 2.1 Benefits and Payments in the Fee-for-Service Portion of Medicare

When Medicare began, inpatient hospital care accounted for about two-thirds of all spending. Indeed, most of the focus of debate before Medicare's passage was on Part A of the program. Today, care in hospital outpatient departments and in physicians' offices has replaced many surgeries and treatments formerly done only in inpatient settings. As care has moved out of the inpatient setting, Part B has become a much larger share of the program. In addition, skilled nursing facility care and home health—referred to as post-acute care—have also increased in importance over time. When individuals leave a hospital after only a few days, post-acute care is often needed as a transition. The increased reliance on care outside of the hospital has changed the composition of Medicare spending and financing, with a larger share coming from general revenues over time.

The nature of how Medicare treats providers has also changed. Originally, the goal was to avoid interfering with the practice of medicine, so payments were designed to be as much like standard insurance policies then in place as possible. But costs for the program rose rapidly almost from the beginning, and in the mid-1970s it became clear that the government needed to slow spending growth. To accomplish this goal, the government adopted new payment policies, which affected both how much would be paid and the item to be priced. Beginning in the mid-1980s, the hospital payment—the biggest component of Medicare—was restructured to be based on the diagnosis, regardless of length of stay in a hospital or the actual costs of a particular case. This new system encouraged hospitals to be more efficient, and to move away from long inpatient stays and deliver more care outside of hospitals. Although it also resulted in some premature discharges, this payment system has been judged to be relatively successful (MedPAC 2000).

Physician reform came later and established payments on the basis of a set of relative values, limiting payments to specialists and increasing them for primary care physicians (PPRC 1987). Many other health care insurers now use Medicare's physician 'relative value' payment system. Both hospital and physician payments require periodic updating, and Medicare is sometimes criticized for falling behind. But Medicare has been a major player affecting the delivery of care, and has fundamentally changed the way that hospitals and doctors are paid in the United States—and in some cases in other countries as well.

The 1997 Balanced Budget Act (BBA) contained a number of additional changes, significantly slowing the growth in Medicare spending. Nearly all areas of the program were affected, with a particular emphasis placed on post-acute care (i.e., skilled nursing facility and home health benefits). The basis for payments for post-acute care services was changed from per visit or day to per episode of care. Further, some post-acute care was being used to help support long-term care needs, so Congress placed limits on use over time. After these changes, spending on home health benefits actually fell in nominal dollars. These reforms on the fee-for-service side of the program have helped to slow per capita Medicare costs relative to the private sector, particularly during the 1980s when private employers were paying little attention to health care costs (Boccuti and Moon 2003).

## 2.2 Private Plan Options

Beneficiaries under the Medicare program can choose to enroll in a participating private plan if they agree to get all of their Medicare-covered services from that plan. A private plan—so far, usually a health maintenance organization (HMO)—agrees to provide care to Medicare beneficiaries in a given area for a fixed monthly payment. That is, while other countries have sometimes used global budgets for hospitals or various parts of the system, the US version of this is to set a budget for an individual consumer. When HMOs began to take on the risk of serving Medicare beneficiaries in 1985, the goal was to save money for Medicare by paying HMOs 95 percent of the costs of average enrollees.

When the HMO option began, private plans attracted only a small share of Medicare beneficiaries because HMOs require beneficiaries to use only plan-approved doctors and hospitals. Medicare lagged behind the rest of the health care system in adopting managed care, in part because beneficiaries could choose to remain in fee-for-service with no penalties attached. To be more competitive with fee-for-service, many HMOs offered beneficiaries services in addition to those covered by Medicare such as prescription drugs. Plans have been able to offer more benefits in part because of the restricted network of doctors, hospitals, and other health care providers. And HMOs also did well under the Medicare payment system since they attracted healthier than average enrollees but were paid as if they were serving the average population. Many studies have concluded that the reduction in costs was substantially larger than the 5 percent 'discount' in payments, resulting in overpayments to private plans (GAO 2000).

In 1997, Congress introduced a new Part C of Medicare called Medicare+Choice to replace the managed care option. The intent was to move Medicare further away from its traditional role as insurer and expand its role as a purchaser of private insurance. But this legislation also slowed the growth in payments to plans in response to evidence that Medicare was overpaying private plans (MedPAC 2000). This payment slowdown overshadowed all other legislative changes and led to an exodus of plans from the Medicare program. Some of the 1997 changes were modified in 1999, but HMOs remained critical of the severity of the cutbacks.

In 2003, about 4.7 million beneficiaries participated in Medicare+Choice plans—down from a peak of 6.2 million in 2000 (Boards of Trustees 2004). In response to the declining role of private plans, the 2003 Medicare Prescription Drug, Improvement and Modernization Act (MMA) substantially increased payments—again assuring payment levels greater than would be necessary under the traditional fee-for-service option. In addition, the legislation also once again changed the name of the private plan option—to Medicare Advantage. Plans seem to be slowly returning, but so far they are mostly plans with a history of participating in Medicare.

## 2.3 Medicare Cost Sharing and Supplemental Insurance

Coverage under Part B of Medicare is voluntary; participants who sign up have to pay a premium that equals 25 percent of the costs. Most who are eligible choose to enroll. In addition to the Part B premium, Medicare beneficiaries are required to pay an array of cost-sharing charges. Both parts A and B have a deductible, and most of the services are subject to some type of coinsurance. The Part A deductible—$916 in 2005—is particularly high. The required cost sharing and the exclusion of some benefits from coverage have resulted in a less comprehensive benefit package than what many younger families receive through their employer-sponsored health insurance. For example, in 2002, estimates indicated that in addition to $260 billion of Medicare expenditures, payments by beneficiaries or supplemental insurance to fill in the gaps totaled another $180 billion (MedPAC 2002). Thus, it is not surprising that a market for supplemental insurance arose shortly after Medicare's passage, paid for either by employers as part of a retirement package or by individual beneficiaries (and referred to as Medigap). Even the addition of a limited drug benefit package in 2006 is unlikely to eliminate the desire to purchase supplemental coverage to achieve more comprehensive insurance. Consequently, acute care services for the elderly and disabled will remain a fragmented and complicated system.

Again, the US system differs from other countries. For those services covered by Medicare, access is good and few people go outside the system for those services (as compared to countries in which supplemental insurance is used to reduce waiting times for care). Rather, they seek supplemental coverage to pay for Medicare's required cost sharing and for services not covered by Medicare.

Persons covered by employer-subsidized retiree benefits have the best coverage. The extra coverage is usually quite comprehensive, and the employer generally subsidizes any premiums that retirees must pay. This coverage fills in most of Medicare's required cost sharing and benefits, such as prescription drugs. Although these plans are quite generous for those who have them, fewer and fewer retirees are covered by these employer-sponsored retiree health plans (Kaiser and HRET 2004). A major policy question is whether the 2003 prescription drug legislation will accelerate this trend.

In contrast, Medigap plans, which are generally purchased by individuals, protect against unusually high medical expenses, but tend to be very expensive. Regulations on the Medigap market established controls on what could be offered but not on the costs of plans. These costs tend to be very high for the oldest beneficiaries, and the plans are often not available to beneficiaries under age 65.

As noted above, beneficiaries also can obtain additional benefits to supplement Medicare's basic package by enrolling in Medicare Advantage. Cost sharing is lower and some additional benefits are usually offered for less than the price of a Medigap plan. But these plans also are becoming more expensive and less comprehensive over time.

Gaps in coverage for some low-income beneficiaries are made up through Medicaid, the joint federal/state program available to Medicare beneficiaries with limited financial resources. Run by the states, Medicaid coverage and benefits vary substantially across the United States. For those who qualify, Medicaid does a good job of serving their needs. But many critics contend that Medicaid does a poor job of assuring access to those with the lowest incomes. Further, since it is the only program that offers substantial amounts of long-term care coverage, these costs create a major issue for the states. Long-term care coverage usually extends higher up the income scale than the rest of the program, but again varies by state and excludes most seniors until they impoverish themselves in order to qualify. Variation in enforcement of rules requiring individuals to spend their assets on care rather than giving them to relatives have also resulted in inequities in eligibility across states. While Medicaid has received less attention than the Medicare program, its ability to keep up with an ageing population is even more uncertain. Its crisis will come in another 20 to 25 years.

Legislation in 1988 established a Qualified Medicare Beneficiary Program, which helps fill in Medicare's cost sharing or premium requirements for persons with low income who do not qualify for full Medicaid benefits. Since then, several other pieces of coverage have been added so that some protection extends above the formal poverty level. However, participation remains a problem. The elderly are much more willing to participate in a universal program (Medicare) than in a welfare-based program. As a result, coverage for older Americans and eligible disabled persons varies considerably in this complicated environment of patchwork supplemental benefits.

The lack of a comprehensive Medicare benefit also creates a substantial financial burden for beneficiaries who end up paying for their own care. On average, older Americans devote over 22 percent of their incomes to acute health care, including Part B premiums, payments for supplemental insurance, and direct expenses for care not covered by any insurance (Maxwell *et al.* 2001). Participants in the Medicare Advantage program face smaller but not insignificant burdens.

In 1965, when Medicare was instituted, individuals paid about 19 percent of their income for acute health care. Medicare reduced that share, but it has gradually risen over time as the costs of health care have gone up faster than the incomes of older Americans. Even without further requirements on beneficiaries to pay more for their care, that share will likely continue to rise over time as health costs continue to outpace retirement incomes. The new prescription drug benefit will help, but only modestly, in reducing these burdens. Further, these estimates exclude costs of institutional care for the disabled; for if the costs of institutional care were included, they would absorb nearly all of an average person's income.

# 3 Challenges for the Future of Medicare

No one doubts that the Medicare program must change. Projections of greater numbers of beneficiaries and higher per capita spending ensure that either financing sources must be expanded or benefits reduced. But policy-makers have engaged in very little serious discussion on these issues. Instead, the debate has focused on how to restructure the program. This restructuring would rely upon contracting with private insurance plans that would compete for enrollees. Another approach—although distinctly less comprehensive—would focus on continuing to improve both private plan options and fee-for-service Medicare.

## 3.1 Private Plans and Competition

Those who support shifting Medicare more to a system of private insurance contend that such a restructuring will save money for two reasons. First, proponents claim that the private sector is more efficient than Medicare. Second, they contend that competition among plans will generate more price sensitivity on the part of beneficiaries and plans alike, also resulting in savings. The way the restructuring would work is that the federal government would subsidize a share of the costs of an average plan, and beneficiaries would pay the remainder. If participants wanted more expensive plans—with more comprehensive coverage and more choice—they would have to pay higher premiums. The goal of such an approach is to make both plans and beneficiaries sensitive to the costs of care, leading to greater efficiency.

A particularly crucial issue regarding such restructuring is the treatment of the traditional Medicare program. Under the current Medicare Advantage arrangement, beneficiaries are automatically enrolled in traditional Medicare unless they choose to go into a private plan. Alternatively, traditional Medicare could become just one of many plans that beneficiaries choose—likely paying a substantially higher premium if they choose to do so. The 2003 prescription drug legislation included the funding for a large demonstration of such an approach beginning in 2011 (Boards of Trustees 2004).

Restructuring could profoundly affect Medicare's future and the well-being of future beneficiaries. In particular, the traditional Medicare program could be priced beyond the means of most beneficiaries, leaving only private plan options from which to choose. Further, if plans begin to sort into groups of higher cost and lower cost plans, beneficiaries are likely to choose plans on the basis of their ability to afford care. This would be quite different than today where at least the basic program treats all beneficiaries alike. As compared to other countries, Medicare would become even less of a universal public program.

## 3.2 Inherent Advantages of Private Plans

Some supporters of a private approach assume that private plans inherently offer advantages that traditional Medicare cannot achieve. But there is no magic bullet to holding the line on the growth in health care spending. Per capita spending rises because of increased use of services, higher prices, or a combination of the two. Medicare has already demonstrated that it can hold down payments to doctors and hospitals, so the debate centers on its relative ability to control the use of services.

What evidence do studies of managed care provide about the ability of the private sector to control the use of services? Most studies have concluded that managed care plans generally have saved money by obtaining price discounts for services and not by changing the practice of health care (Strunk *et al.* 2002). Reining in the use of services represents a major challenge for private insurance as well as Medicare in the future, and it is not clear whether the public or private sector is better equipped to do this. Proponents for the private sector claim that such an approach will avoid the government's 'micromanaging' of health care. That is, the government will no longer set prices and will allow private plans to adopt innovations and make changes in coverage of benefits without as much oversight. Proponents add that private plans have the ability to be flexible and even arbitrary in making decisions. This allows private insurers to respond more quickly than a large government program to adopt innovations and to intervene where insurers believe too much care is being delivered. But critics of that approach argue that what looks like cost-effective activities from an insurer's perspective may be seen by a beneficiary as the loss of essential care. Further, to date, private plan competition has produced few examples of truly innovative techniques or organizational strategies. Some managed care plans, for example, rely solely on price discounts and do not develop the data or administrative mechanisms to attempt any care coordination.

The newest plans suggested as an improvement for Medicare beneficiaries are preferred provider organizations (PPOs). These plans, in addition to obtaining discounts, get their savings by paying very little for patients who go outside the network for care. Thus, their strategy is often one of cost shifting onto beneficiaries. This may hold down PPO premiums, but from society's standpoint, does little to help reduce health care costs (GAO 2004).

Private plans are also not in a position to achieve larger social goals, such as making sure that the sickest beneficiaries get high quality care if they cannot afford it. Under the traditional Medicare program, beneficiaries do not need to fear loss of coverage when they develop health problems. In contrast, private insurers are interested in satisfying their own customers and generating profits for stockholders. If they receive a flat amount for each participant, any profit-making entity has a strong incentive to weed out the sick. Once avoiding the sick and seeking out the healthy becomes the dominant approach, even insurers who would like to treat sicker patients are penalized by the market if they do so. Segregating beneficiaries does not limit overall costs to either the federal government or to society as a whole; it simply puts some participants at great risk. Thus, it is important to understand the impact of competition on health care delivery.

Finally, private insurers will almost surely have higher administrative costs than does Medicare. Insurers need to advertise and promote their plans. They also face a smaller risk pool that may require them to make more conservative decisions regarding reserves and other protections against losses over time. These plans expect to return a profit to shareholders. All of these factors cumulate and work against private companies performing better than Medicare.

## 3.3 Competition among Plans

Reform options, such as paying beneficiaries a flat amount, seek savings not only by relying on private plans but also on competition among those plans. The theory is that since beneficiaries have to augment the government payment to get a more generous plan, they will become more price conscious and choose lower cost plans. The increased demand for lower-priced products, in turn, will reward those private insurers able to hold down costs. And some evidence from the federal employees' system and the CalPERS system in California suggests that this approach has disciplined the insurance market to some degree in the 1990s.

On the other hand, evidence from the Medicare experience suggests that the approach may be much less successful with the retiree population (GAO 2000). Studies that have focused on retirees show much less sensitivity to price differences among older Americans. Older persons may be less willing to change doctors and learn new insurance rules in order to save a few dollars each month. Thus, what is not known is how well this will work for Medicare beneficiaries.

For example, for a competitive private plan model to work, at least some beneficiaries must be willing to change providers and learn new rules in order to reward the more efficient plans. Without that shifting, savings will not occur. A further question is how private insurers will respond. Will they seek to improve service or instead focus on marketing and other techniques to attract a desirable, healthy patient base? It simply is not known if competition will really do what it is supposed to do. In fact, undesirable outcomes may be as common as desirable ones.

One example is the repercussions from beneficiaries shifting between plans. Shifting across plans is not necessarily good for patients; it is not only disruptive, it can raise costs of care. Studies have shown that having one physician over a long period of time reduces costs of care. And if only the healthier beneficiaries switch plans, the sickest and most vulnerable beneficiaries may end up being concentrated in plans that become increasingly expensive over time. Studies of retirees left in the federal employees' high-option Blue Cross plan and of retirees in California suggest that even when plans become very expensive, beneficiaries may be fearful of switching and end up substantially disadvantaged when premiums rise to a very high level (Buchmueller 2001).

Another potential problem is equal access to care and plans. For example, if private plans sort out into higher cost and lower cost options, not all beneficiaries will be assured access to high quality care and responsive providers. People with lower incomes or greater health problems will be at a disadvantage in such a system. Moving away from a 'one-size-fits-all' approach is a prescription for risk selection problems. About one in every three Medicare beneficiaries has severe mental or physical health problems. In contrast, the healthy and relatively well-off (with incomes over $35,000 per year for singles and $47,000 per year for couples) make up less than 10 percent of the Medicare population. Moving to a market approach is likely to put the sickest at greater risk relative to the healthy.

If the advantages of one large risk pool (such as the traditional Medicare program) are eliminated, other means will have to be found to make sure that insurers cannot find ways to serve only the healthy population. Although this very difficult challenge has been studied extensively, as yet researchers have not developed a satisfactory measure of a beneficiary's potential health risk (Newhouse *et al.* 1999). On the other hand, insurers have developed to a fine degree marketing tools and mechanisms to select risks. High-quality plans that attract people with extensive health care needs are likely to be more expensive than plans that focus on serving the relatively healthy. If risk adjustors are not powerful enough to provide sufficient government subsidies for those with a greater likelihood of high medical expenditures, then those with health problems, who also disproportionately have lower incomes, would have to pay the highest prices under many reform schemes.

The emphasis on private plans, competition, and choice tends to ignore the need for standardization. The difficulty is that without standardization of the most important benefits, such choice will lead to risk selection. Young healthy 65 year olds will pass on home health coverage, for example, in exchange for other benefits or a lower premium. But until risk adjusters get much better (if ever), standardization is important. Moreover, to get plans to compete on price, consumers must be able to compare plans—another strong argument for standardization. It is not possible to realistically expect both variation in options and health competition.

In short, increasing reliance on private plans to serve Medicare beneficiaries is likely to produce modestly lower costs as a result of some increased competition, but also to lead to some loss of protection. Creating in a private plan environment all the protections now available in the traditional Medicare will be very challenging and cannot promise success. For example, in 2003, after six years, many of the provisions in the 1997 legislation that would be essential in any further moves to private insurance—generating new ways of paying private plans, improving risk adjustment, and developing information for beneficiaries, for example—still had not been successfully implemented. None the less, major additional changes to emphasize private plans were included in the drug legislation in 2003.

In addition, it is not clear that policy-makers or the public at large understand all the consequences of a competitive market. Choice among competing plans and the discipline that such competition can bring to prices and innovation are often stressed as potential advantages of relying on private plans for serving the Medicare population. But choice and competition also mean that some plans will not do well in a particular market, and as a result they will leave. In fact, if no plans ever left, that would likely be a sign that competition was not working well. But plan withdrawals will result in disruptions and complaints by beneficiaries—much like those that have occurred with the withdrawals from Medicare+Choice. Beneficiaries must then find another private plan or return to traditional Medicare. They may have to choose new doctors and learn new rules. Not only will beneficiaries be unhappy, but political pressures may emerge to keep federal payments higher than a well-functioning market would require. A more realistic approach would be to emphasize improvements in *both* the private plan options and the traditional Medicare program, basically retaining the current structure in which traditional Medicare is the primary option.

# 4 A LESS COMPREHENSIVE APPROACH TO IMPROVING MEDICARE

Rather than using private insurance to make needed changes in Medicare, the emphasis could be placed on innovations necessary for improvements in health care delivery regardless of setting. At present a number of areas in Medicare need attention.

## 4.1 Possible Reforms to the Provision of Benefits

### 4.1.1 *Improving the Benefit Package*

Critics of Medicare rightly point out the inadequacy of its benefit package. This inadequacy has led to supplemental insurance arrangements so that most beneficiaries rely on two sources of insurance to meet their needs. Some argue that improvements in coverage can only occur in combination with structural reform. And some advocates of a private approach to insurance go further, suggesting that the structural reform itself will naturally produce such benefit improvements. This debate implicitly holds the debate on improved benefits hostage to accepting other unrelated changes.

The logic should run in the other direction. It is not reasonable to expect any number of other changes to work without first offering a more comprehensive benefit package for Medicare. In that way, payments made to private plans can improve, allowing them to better coordinate care. And the fee-for-service system will also be able to change in ways that might encourage better care delivery. For example, it is not reasonable to ask patients to participate in a program to reduce hypertension (which can save costs over the long run) without covering the prescription drugs that are likely to be an essential part of that effort. In addition, a better benefit package will also allow at least some beneficiaries to forego the purchase of inefficient private supplemental insurance. That itself should be a goal of reform. The addition of a prescription drug benefit in 2006 will help, but not fully address the issues arising from an inadequate benefit package in Medicare.

### 4.1.2 *Improving Norms and Standards*

In addition, better norms and standards of care are needed to ensure quality of care protections to all Americans. Investment in outcomes research, disease management, and other techniques that could lead to improvements in treatment of patients will require a substantial public commitment. This investment is much better done by the government than by proprietary for-profit entities, which are unlikely to share any new findings on better ways to coordinate care.

Private plans can play an important role and may develop some innovations on their own, but in much the same way that we view basic research on medicine as requiring a public component, innovations in health delivery also need such support. Further, innovations in treatment and coordination of care should focus on those with substantial health problems—exactly the population that many private plans seek to avoid. Some private plans might be willing to specialize in individuals with specific needs, but they are not likely to do so in the face of aggressive price competition and barely adequate risk adjustors. Innovative plans would likely suffer in that environment.

A good area to begin improvements in knowledge about the effectiveness of medical care would be with prescription drugs. Realistically, the new prescription drug benefit will require major efforts to hold down costs over time. Part of that effort needs to be based on evidence of the comparative effectiveness of various drugs. Establishing rules for coverage of drugs should reflect good medical evidence rather than manufacturers' discounts. Undertaking such studies and evaluations represents a public good and needs to be funded on that basis, but the 2003 prescription drug legislation provided no resources.

### 4.1.3 *Engaging Patients in their Own Care*

Within the fee-for-service environment, it would be helpful to energize both patients and physicians in helping to coordinate care. Patients need information and support as well as incentives to become involved. Many caring physicians, who have often resented the low pay in fee-for-service and the lack of control in managed care, would likely welcome the ability to spend more time with their patients. One simple way to do this would be to give beneficiaries a certificate that spells out the care consultation benefits to which they are entitled and allow them to designate a physician who will provide those services. In that way, both the patient and the physician (who would get an additional payment for the annual or biannual services) would know what they are expected to provide and could likely reduce confusion and unnecessary duplication of services that go on in a fee-for-service environment. This change should be just one of many in seeking to improve care coordination.

Additional flexibility to manage and develop payment initiatives aimed at using competition where appropriate also could result in long-term cost savings and serve patients well. In the areas of durable medical equipment and perhaps even some testing and laboratory services, contracting could be used to obtain favorable prices.

## 4.2 Possible Improvements on the Financing Side and the Issue of Long-Term Care

More resources will be needed to finance Medicare and Medicaid over time (Gluck and Moon 2000). For Medicare, the resources can come from asking either beneficiaries to pay more or taxpayers to increase their contributions. It is simply not feasible to absorb a doubling of the population over the next 30 years without dealing with the financing issue. In fact, avoiding discussions of higher taxpayer revenues has already led to cost shifting onto beneficiaries—which represents an implicit financing decision.

A wide range of mechanisms can be used to explicitly or implicitly require beneficiaries to contribute more to the costs of their care. For example, increased premiums or cost-sharing requirements can be and have been applied over time to shift costs onto those who use the program. The 2003 legislation includes not only an increased across the board Part B deductible in 2005, but also will begin phasing in a higher premium for persons with annual incomes above $80,000 beginning in 2007 (Boards of Trustees 2004). As described above, a voucher approach through private plan payments would also essentially result in cost shifting onto beneficiaries by asking them to bear a greater share of both the costs and risks of higher prices for insurance over time.

Efforts to raise the age of eligibility for the program also implicitly shift costs to beneficiaries. Because of problems in the private insurance market, those ineligible for Medicare who would have to buy private plans could quickly find that coverage very expensive or even unaffordable (Pollitz et al. 2001). And since raising the age of eligibility to, say, 67 excludes Medicare's least expensive patients on average, the 5 percent reduction in beneficiaries would cut Medicare costs by only about 2 percent (Waidmann 1998).

In terms of Medicaid, it is not feasible to ask beneficiaries—who have by definition lower incomes—to bear a greater share of the costs of their care. Indeed, the way that Medicaid works for long-term care services is to require that individuals devote most of their incomes to the costs of institutionalization, with the government then only filling in the gaps. This program will be increasingly important to retirees who need long-term care in the future, and is likely to face a real crisis as members of the baby-boom generation approach their eighties and nineties. As a combined state and federal program, politicians are likely to jockey over which level of government will bear this responsibility.

To what extent is it realistic to raise additional Medicare money from taxpayers? This will be difficult to do in the current environment in Washington, especially since Medicare can cover its obligations for a number of years. Moreover, since Medicare is a program restricted to seniors and some persons with disabilities, the question of generational equity inevitably arises. In countries with a system covering persons of all ages, the equity issues can be dealt with directly. In the case of the public programs on health care in the United States that so strongly affect persons aged 65 and over while others get care in a variety of ways, it is difficult to know whether greater spending on Medicare, as some have claimed, will truly reduce access to health care for others.

The advantage of raising taxes sooner rather than later is that baby-boomers who will be drawing heavily on Medicare in the future would make a major contribution. In addition to the timing element, the nature of the tax is also important. For example, payroll taxes remain relatively popular with the general public, probably because they serve as dedicated revenues for particular programs. But critics claim the payroll tax is not particularly progressive, and, by raising the costs of workers to employers, discourages employment. General revenues, the other major source of income for Medicare, are more progressively distributed and require that older persons as well as the young contribute. Medicaid relies on general revenue contributions from both the federal and state governments. Other taxes—such as those on alcohol and tobacco—often do not bring in enough revenue to resolve the financing issues. Whatever choices are made, this is likely to be a last resort approach given the political costs often associated with raising taxes.

But it is also the case that someone will need to pay more to provide care for an ageing population. Issues of fairness raise important considerations about how much beneficiaries can be asked to pay and how much should be required from others. The key question facing the financing of the US health care system will be how to share that burden, not whether it will increase over time, as it surely will. Other countries are likely to find it more feasible to address these issues directly and thereby avoid some of the search for cost savings that will occupy the debate in the United States for some time to come, but that are likely to prove unrealistic.

## 5 Conclusion

An examination of the public programs serving America's elderly population is likely to be more of a case study in what to avoid rather than a role model for other countries. Experience with a mixed public/private approach in health care has generated substantial complexity and inequities in access to care for seniors. Reluctance to improve the benefit package is understandable given the high and rising costs of care, but has led to a system of gap filling that is often inadequate. Moreover, providing health insurance is more complicated than providing pensions. Two or more pensions can often simply be added together; the existence of multiple insurance plans increases inequities and administrative costs.

Despite enthusiasm for greater reliance on private market forces for holding down costs in Medicare, the evidence points in the opposite direction. Private plans have not done a better job of controlling costs or of creating innovative new strategies. In part this is because the practical application of managed care falls far short of the promise that coordinated care holds if done well. Ultimately, reliance on the private sector may simply reflect a desire to pass costs off onto beneficiaries by putting them at risk in a defined contribution approach while holding the line on tax increases. In this way, policy-makers may be able to avoid having the honest discussion of who should pay that needs to go on in an ageing society.

## References

BOARDS OF TRUSTEES (2004). *2004 Annual Report of the Boards of Trustees of the Federal Hospital Insurance and Federal Supplementary Medical Insurance Trust Funds*. Washington, D.C.: US Government Printing Office.

BOCCUTI, C., and MOON, M. (2003). 'Comparing Medicare and private insurance: growth rates in spending over three decades'. *Health Affairs*, 22: 230–7.

BUCHMUELLER, T. (2000). 'The health plan choices of retirees under managed competition'. *Health Affairs*, 35: 949–76.

GENERAL ACCOUNTING OFFICE (2000). *Medicare+Choice: Payments Exceed Cost of Fee-For-Service Benefits: Adding Billions to Spending*. Washington, D.C.: GAO.

GLUCK, M., and MOON, M. (2000). *Financing Medicare's Future: Final Report of the Study Panel on Medicare's Long Term Care Financing*. Washington, D.C.: National Academy of Social Insurance.

GOVERNMENT ACCOUNTABILITY OFFICE (2004). *Medicare Demonstration PPOs: Financial and Other Advantages for Plans, Few Advantages for Beneficiaries*. Washington, D.C.: GAO.

KAISER FAMILY FOUNDATION AND HEALTH RESEARCH AND EDUCATIONAL TRUST (2004). *Employer Health Benefits 2004 Annual Survey*. Menlo Park, Calif.: Kaiser Family Foundation.

MAXWELL, S., MOON, M., and SEGAL, M. (2001). *Growth in Medicare and Out-of-Pocket Spending: Impact on Vulnerable Beneficiaries*. New York: The Commonwealth Fund.

MEDICARE PAYMENT ADVISORY COMMISSION (MedPAC) (2000). *Report to Congress: Medicare Payment Policy*. Washington, D.C.: USGPO.

—— (2002). *Report to Congress: Assessing Medicare Benefits*. Washington, D.C.: USGPO.

MOON, M. (1996). *Medicare Now and in the Future*, 2nd edn. Washington, D.C.: Urban Institute Press.

NEWHOUSE, J., BUNTIN, M. B., and CHAPMAN, J. (1999). *Risk Adjustment and Medicare* New York: The Commonwealth Fund.

PHYSICIAN PAYMENT REVIEW COMMISSION (PPRC) (1987). *Medicare Physician Payment: An Agenda for Reform. Annual Report to Congress*. Washington, D.C.: US Government Printing Office.

POLLITZ, K., SORIAN, R., and THOMAS, K. (2001). *How Accessible is Individual Health Insurance for Consumers in Less-Than-Perfect Health?* Washington, D.C.: The Henry J. Kaiser Family Foundation.

STRUNK, B. C., GINSBURG, P. B., and GABEL, J. R. (2001). 'Tracking Health Care Costs'. *Health Affairs*, Web Exclusive, W39–W50.

—— —— —— (2002). 'Tracking Health Care Costs: Growth Accelerates Again in 2001'. *Health Affairs Web Exclusive*, W299–W310.

WAIDMANN, T. (1998). 'Potential Effects of Raising Medicare's Eligibility Age'. *Health Affairs*, 17 (Mar.–Apr.): 156–64.

# PART III

# EMPLOYER-SPONSORED RETIREMENT PLANS

# STRUCTURE OF EMPLOYER-SPONSORED PENSIONS

CHAPTER 18

# EMPLOYER-SPONSORED PLANS: THE SHIFT FROM DEFINED BENEFIT TO DEFINED CONTRIBUTION

ALICIA H. MUNNELL

In a number of countries—particularly the United States and the United Kingdom—*voluntary* employer-sponsored pensions play a major role in supplementing relatively modest pay-as-you-go public pensions. And in both of these countries the nature of these supplementary plans has changed dramatically, as coverage has shifted from defined benefit to defined contribution arrangements. Understanding the strengths and weaknesses of alternative employer-sponsored pension schemes is useful for two reasons. First, in both the United States and the United Kingdom the shift to defined contribution plans has occurred against a backdrop of retrenchment of the relatively modest pay-as-you-go public social insurance programs, so it is important to determine the extent to which future retirees may be at risk. Second, many Continental European countries with generous pay-as-you-go public schemes have signaled an interest in moving some responsibility for retirement income to funded private plans, primarily using a defined contribution format, so it is helpful to learn what works and what does not.

# 1 NARROWING THE DISCUSSION

Table 18.1, which shows employer-provided pension assets as a percentage of GDP, helps to narrow the discussion of this chapter in three ways. First, the focus here is on *voluntary* supplementary systems. Mandatory systems, such as that currently used in Australia, are really an alternative—rather than a supplement—to government pay-as-you-go programs.[1] These programs are discussed in Chapter 14 of this *Handbook* under 'Public Retirement Programs'. Second, the voluntary program must be significant. Voluntary employer-sponsored systems with assets equal to roughly 50 percent or more of GDP reduces the sample to four countries—the Netherlands, United Kingdom, United States, and Canada.

Finally, the discussion centers on those countries experiencing major change from the 1980 situation described in Chapter 4. Neither Canada nor the Netherlands falls into this group. The movement from employer-sponsored defined benefit to defined contribution plans in Canada has been minimal; in 2000 less than 15 percent of members of Registered Retirement Plans were covered by a defined contribution arrangement. And the number of contributors to individual retirement savings accounts (Registered Retirement Savings Plans) has remained roughly constant since the mid-1990s (Statistics Canada 2003). Moreover, the earnings-related public pension system underwent reform in 1997, and the replacement rate for the typical worker has stabilized at about 25 percent of pre-retirement earnings (Statistics Canada 2003). Thus, all seems relatively calm in Canada.

Similarly, the Netherlands has not seen any dramatic reform in its pension system (De Gier 2003). The occupational pensions in the Netherlands, while technically defined benefit, often look more like a defined contribution plan to the employer (Yermo 2003). In most cases, the extent of benefit indexation is determined by the pension fund's board on the basis of the fund's solvency rather than established in the plan documents. Further, in some plans, such as the APB that covers government and educational workers, the state's responsibility is defined in terms of contributions rather than benefits. If solvency deteriorates, plan members can be called upon to increase their contributions. The ability to redefine employers' obligations and increase employee contributions in periods of financial stress

Table 18.1 Pension assets as a percentage of GDP 2001, OECD

| Country | Assets as a percentage of GDP | |
| --- | --- | --- |
| | Voluntary | Mandatory |
| Switzerland | | 113.5 |
| Netherlands | 105.1 | |
| Iceland | | 87.3 |
| Australia | | 67.5 |
| United Kingdom | 66.4 | |
| United States | 63.0 | |
| Canada | 48.3 | |
| Denmark | 23.8 | |
| Japan | 18.5 | |
| Portugal | 11.4 | |
| Spain | 8.2 | |
| Belgium | 5.6 | |
| Norway | 5.6 | |
| Italy | 4.4 | |
| Mexico | | 4.3 |
| Hungary | | 3.9 |
| Austria | 3.8 | |
| Sweden | 3.7 | |
| Finland | | 3.4 |
| Germany | 3.3 | |
| Korea | 3.2 | |
| Poland | 2.6 | |
| Czech Republic | 2.5 | |

*Source*: ISSA and INPRS (2003).

means that employers enjoy many of the advantages of a defined contribution plan and have not had the incentive to shift the nature of pension coverage.

Thus, the focus of this chapter is the United States and the United Kingdom, where supplementary employer pensions play a major role in the retirement income system, and where the nature of those pensions has changed dramatically. The evidence suggests that the shift from defined benefit to defined contribution plans in these countries has put the future retirement security of many at risk.

## 2 THE EMERGENCE OF 401(K) PLANS IN THE UNITED STATES

As discussed in Chapter 4, employer-sponsored pension plans in the United States date from the last quarter of the nineteenth century when the large prosperous and increasingly regulated transportation industry pioneered the development of these plans. During this time, trade unions also established benefit arrangements for their workers, and by 1928 about 40 percent of union members had some form of old age and disability benefits. But the Great Depression devastated union plans and saw the enactment of the Social Security program. So after the Second World War business and labor had to re-create a large portion of the pension system.

The re-creation of the employer-sponsored pension system occurred within a favorable tax environment. The approach of federal pension policy as far back as the 1940s has been to provide tax incentives that will encourage highly paid employees to support the establishment of employer-sponsored pension plans that provide retirement benefits to the rank and file. The tax incentives arise because employer contributions to an employee's pension plan are deductible as a business expense when made, and the employee is not taxed until receipt of pension benefits. In addition, the pension fund is not taxed on its earnings. These provisions, which permit tax deferral on both employer contributions and the earnings

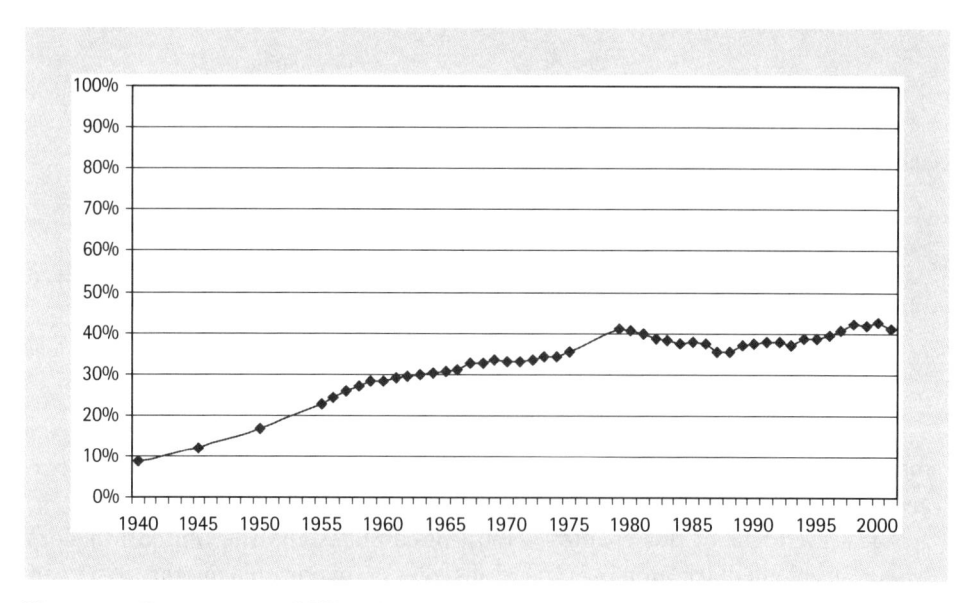

**Fig. 18.1 Percentage of US private sector workers covered by a pension plan, 1940–2001**

*Source*: Author's calculations from the March Current Population Survey (1979–2002); Author's calculations from Skolnik (1976): 4 (1940, 1945, 1950–74); Author's calculations from Yohalem (1977): 27 (1975).

on those contributions, are equivalent to exempting from taxation the earnings on the money that would have been invested after tax, assuming the employee remains in the same tax bracket.

Although in the immediate postwar period employees focused on cash wages to cover ground lost during the wartime period of wage stabilization, in 1949 pensions became a major issue in labor negotiations. Pension coverage expanded dramatically during the 1950s primarily through the establishment of new plans, and grew in the 1960s and 1970s primarily due to expansion of employment in firms that already had pension coverage. Since the late 1970s, coverage has been virtually stagnant (Fig. 18.1). Currently less than half of the private sector workforce in the United States participates in a pension plan; coverage rates are higher for government workers. In 2001, supplementary pension benefits accounted for about one-quarter of non-earned income of those 65 and over (Fig. 18.2). Supplementary pensions are much more important for higher paid workers; those in the lowest quintile of the income distribution receive almost no pension benefits. Before exploring recent developments in the second tier of employer-sponsored pensions, it is useful to consider the outlook for the first tier of support—namely, the Social Security program.

## 2.1 The Outlook for the US Social Security System

The US Social Security program covers virtually all workers and provides benefits based on lifetime earnings at the Normal Retirement Age and reduced benefits at 62. The program is financed on a pay-as-you-go basis by a payroll tax levied on

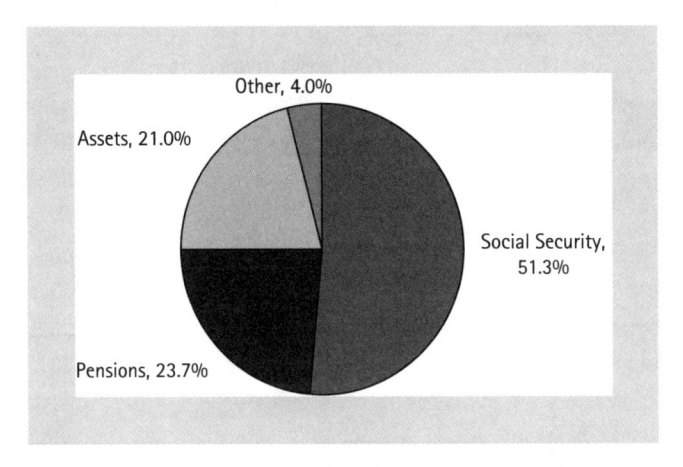

**Fig. 18.2** Percentage of non-earned US retirement income by source, population 65 and over, 2001

*Source*: US Social Security Administration (2003).

wages up to a taxable maximum. Social Security benefits are kept up to date with wages before retirement, which stabilizes the ratio of benefits to earnings over time. After retirement, benefits are indexed to prices in order to maintain their purchasing power. In addition, Social Security provides a non-working spouse with an amount equal to half of the worker's benefit. For the average earner, retiring at age 62—the typical retirement age—Social Security today replaces 33 percent of pre-retirement earnings, or 30 percent after deduction of Medicare Part B premiums, which go to cover doctor's visits, and which are automatically deducted from Social Security benefits.

Going forward, Social Security's relatively modest benefits will decline relative to earnings for four reasons. First, the Normal Retirement Age is in the process of increasing from 65 to 67. This increase is equivalent to an across-the-board benefit cut. For those who continue to retire at age 62, this cut takes the form of lower monthly benefits; for those who continue to work to the normal retirement age, it takes the form of fewer years of benefits. Second, Medicare premiums are scheduled to increase. Third, benefits will be subject to increased taxation under the personal income tax, because the thresholds determining taxation are not indexed for inflation—much less wage growth.[2] Finally, the Social Security system faces a long-term financing gap, and some benefit cuts will inevitably be part of any package to restore long-term balance. Taken together, these developments are likely

Table 18.2 Estimated US Social Security replacement rates (RR) for the average earner, 2003 and 2030 (percent)

| Development | Percentage of Pre-Retirement Earnings | |
| --- | --- | --- |
| | Age 62 | Age 65 |
| *2003* | | |
| Reported replacement rate (RR) | 33.0 | 41.3 |
| After Medicare Part B deduction | 30.2[1] | 38.5 |
| Net replacement rate | 30.2 | 38.5 |
| *2030* | | |
| RR after extension of Normal Retirement Age | 28.7 | 36.3 |
| After deduction for Medicare Part B | 25.0[1] | 32.6 |
| After personal income taxation | 22.8 | 29.9 |
| After hypothetical 10% benefit cut | 19.9 | 26.3 |
| Net replacement rate | 19.9 | 26.3 |

Note: [1] For the individual retiring at age 62, the Medicare Part B premium will not begin until age 65.
Source: Author's calculations.

to reduce the net replacement rate for the average earner who retires at age 62 from 30 percent to 20 percent (Table 18.2). This is the background against which to assess the changing nature of employer pensions.

## 2.2 The Changing Nature of Employer Pension Coverage

Until recently, most people with a pension were covered by a traditional defined benefit plan that paid benefits in the form of an annuity. Pay-related plans, which are generally used for salaried employees, state the benefit as a percentage of the employee's pay over the entire career or over the period just prior to retirement. For example, a plan might provide 1.5 percent of final three-year average pay for each year of employment, so that an employee with 20 years of service would receive a benefit equal to 30 percent (20 years at 1.5 percent) of final salary for as long as he lives. The other type of defined benefit plan, which is common in collectively bargained plans for hourly paid employees, states benefits in terms of flat dollar amounts per year of service. For example, the plan might provide $50 per month for each year of service, so that an employee with 20 years would receive a lifetime pension of $1,000 per month. The employer finances these benefits by making pre-tax contributions into a pension fund; employees typically do not contribute. The employer holds the assets in trust and directs the investment. For employees who remain with one firm throughout their working lives, defined benefit plans can offer a predictable and substantial stream of monthly benefits. Mobile employees, however, often forfeit a significant amount of future pension income when they change employers, because their pension credits apply to earnings at termination rather than retirement.

From the employer's perspective, defined benefit plans help manage the workforce by encouraging longer tenure and efficient retirement (Lazear 1985). Since pension benefits based on final earnings increase rapidly as job tenures lengthen, these plans motivate workers to remain with the firm. Defined benefit plans also encourage workers to retire when their productivity begins to decline. But for employers, these plans also have two disadvantages: exposure to financial market risk, including both investment risk during the accumulation phase and interest rate risk when purchasing annuities, and sometimes a less than desired rate of employee turnover.

Today the world of pensions in the United States looks very different. Most people with pensions have a defined contribution plan, most often a 401(k). This shift is evident in Figure 18.3. In 1981, roughly 60 percent of those with pensions relied exclusively on a defined benefit plan; in 2001, the percentages had reversed and nearly 60 percent relied solely on a 401(k) or similar defined contribution plan.

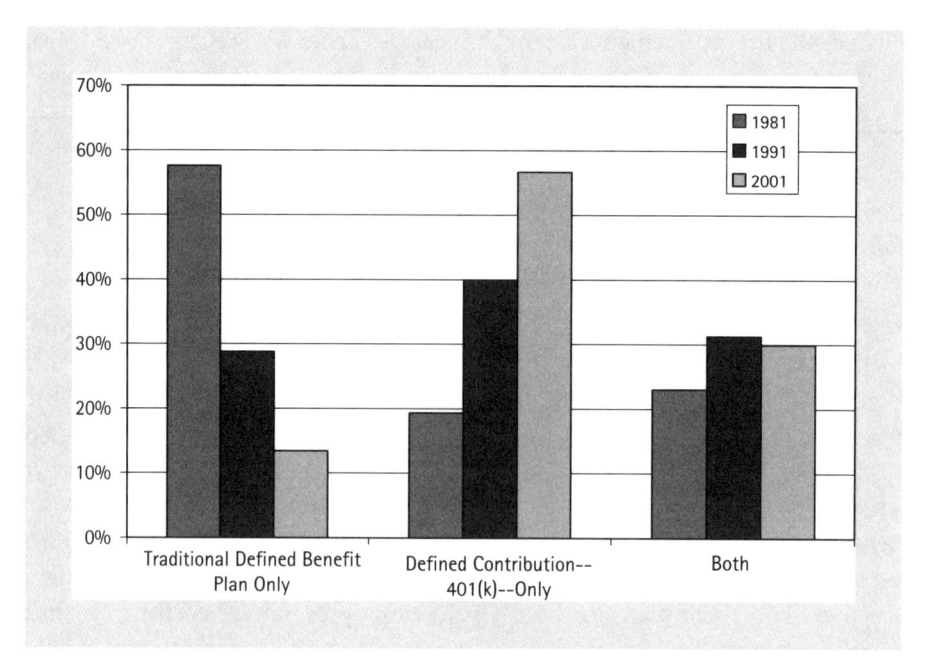

**Fig. 18.3** Percentage of wage and salary workers with pension coverage, by type of plan, 1981–2001

*Source*: US Department of Labor (2002). Percentages for 2001 are based on authors' calculations from Survey of Consumer Finances (2003) data.

The defining characteristics of a 401(k) plan are that participation in the plan is voluntary and that the employee as well as the employer can make pre-tax contributions to the plan. These contributions are invested, usually at the direction of the employee, mostly in mutual funds consisting of stocks and bonds. Upon retirement, the worker generally receives the balance in the account as a lump sum. These characteristics shift virtually all the burden for providing for retirement to the employee; the employee decides whether or not to participate in the plan, how much to contribute, how to invest the assets, how to adjust those investments over time, and how to use the assets at retirement. In addition, workers have some access to 401(k) plan funds before retirement, adding another element of individual responsibility.

## 2.3 Reasons for the Shift from Defined Benefit to 401(k) Plans

It is easy to understand the popularity of 401(k) plans. They are portable, which means that mobile workers can take their balances with them. Employees get statements several times a year, and many have daily access to pension benefit data through the World Wide Web, which makes their benefits seem more tangible. As the plans allow employees to choose investments that match their tolerance for risk, it also gives them a sense of control over their retirement funds. Finally, 401(k) plans emerged on the scene in 1981, the year before the beginning of an extended stock market boom.[3] As stock values soared, rapidly rising account balances greatly enhanced the popularity of these plans.

Employers also like 401(k)s. These plans are a tangible benefit that employees appreciate. Employers can use 401(k) plans to attract workers who value saving and who, some economists argue, are presumably more conscientious and productive than non-savers (Ippolito 1997). And employers' contributions are controllable and do not hinge on stock market and interest rate swings. This means that when the stock market plummets, the employee, not the employer, loses money. And when interest rates fall, the employee realizes a lower retirement income, rather than the employer paying more for an annuity. And the cost of a 401(k) plan is highly predictable, which became increasingly important after 1980 as the economic environment became more competitive.

At the same time that 401(k) plans emerged, employment was shifting to sectors of the labor market in which defined benefit plans were less attractive. Employment was declining in large hierarchic firms and unionized industries, which typically offered defined benefit plans, and was growing in high-tech firms and small, non-unionized companies, which typically did not. Defined benefit plans are a sensible arrangement for large, well-established firms and unionized industries with lots of long-service workers. They are ill suited to industries where companies come and go and the workforce is mobile. Several studies find that changes in industry composition, unionization, and firm size account for about half the decline in defined benefit coverage.[4]

The regulatory environment also caused many companies to opt for a 401(k). In 1974, in response to abuses in defined benefit plans that deprived participants of benefits, Congress passed a major pension reform—the Employee Retirement Income Security Act (ERISA). ERISA imposed minimum standards that were particularly stiff for defined benefit plans. ERISA also established the Pension Benefit Guaranty Corporation (PBGC), a mandatory insurance program that imposes premiums on defined benefit plans to insure workers against the loss of basic retirement benefits. In addition to ERISA, during the 1980s Congress passed significant legislation affecting defined benefit plans every few years. The increased regulation was aimed at making pensions, which are supported by federal income tax preferences, fairer. But it also made the pension system more complex and more costly to administer.

Finally, developments beginning in 2000 suggest that the decline in coverage under traditional defined benefit plans is likely to continue. These plans have been hit by the perfect storm of stagnant equity markets and falling interest rates. Defined benefit plans were ill prepared for such an onslaught because the government had enacted funding limitations in the 1980s to preserve government tax revenues in an era of huge budget deficits.[5] Many plan sponsors were forced to take a 'funding holiday' in the 1980s and 1990s rather than building up surpluses in good times to serve as a buffer in periods of economic stress. As a result, the recent drop in bond yields, which raised the present value of liabilities, and the fall in equity prices, which lowered the value of assets, pushed many corporate plans from overfunded to underfunded status.

In addition, regulators have refocused on the accounting and funding rules for these plans. A number of reform proposals are currently under discussion. These include: (1) changing the discount rate for funding purposes; (2) improving disclosure rules; (3) imposing mark-to-market for pension fund assets and liabilities; and (4) imposing risk-adjusted PBGC premiums based on the amount of equity holdings. If these changes were enacted, the inherent volatility of equity investments would become more evident, as has been the case in the United Kingdom. In all likelihood, defined benefit plans would reduce their holdings of equities and increase their holdings of fixed income securities. Since fixed income securities have a lower expected yield than equities, this portfolio shift would increase funding costs and exacerbate the decline in defined benefit plans. Thus, going forward an even larger proportion of the working population will rely on defined contribution plans for their supplementary retirement income.[6]

## 2.4 Implications of the Shift to 401(k) Plans for Retirement Income Security

In theory, workers could do equally well under either a defined benefit or a 401(k) plan. Simple simulations suggest that a worker with a history of average earnings could accumulate roughly $300,000 by age 62 either through continuous employment under a typical defined benefit plan or from steady contributions by the employee (6 percent of earnings) and the employer (3 percent of earnings) in a 401(k) plan. In fact, balances in 401(k) plans are coming up short (Munnell and Sundén 2004). As shown in Figure 18.4, 401(k) participants are approaching retirement with only a fraction of the simulated accumulations. The typical older worker covered by a 401(k) has less than $50,000 instead of the $300,000 suggested by the simulations.

The reason for these low balances is that the shift in coverage to 401(k) plans has transferred all the responsibility for retirement income from the employer to the employee and that at every step along the way a significant fraction of participants make serious mistakes. A quarter of those eligible to participate in a plan choose not to do so. Less than 10 percent of those who do participate contribute the maximum. Over half fail to diversify their investments, many over-invest in company stock, and almost none re-balance their portfolios in response to age or

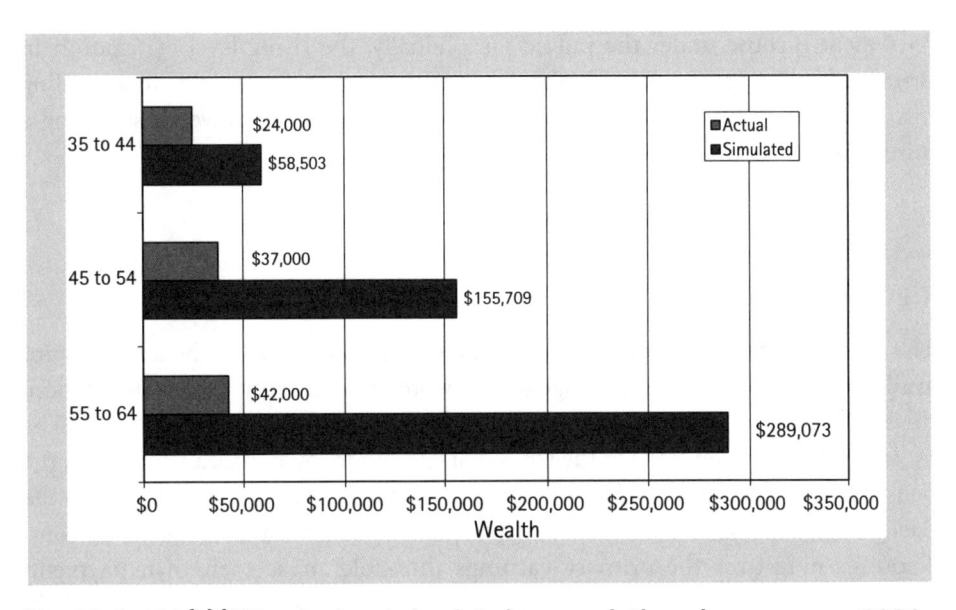

**Fig. 18.4** 401(k)/IRA actual and simulated accumulations, by age group, 2001

*Note*: IRAs (Individual Retirement Accounts) are tax-favored vehicles introduced in 1974 that allow individuals with incomes below $160,000 (for joint filers) and $110,000 (for singles) in 2005 to make annual contributions of up to $4,000 per person.

*Source*: Munnell and Sundén (2004).

market returns. Most importantly, many cash out when they change jobs. And very few annuitize at retirement. In short, the lesson from 401(k) plans is that leaving individuals to save on their own does not produce very satisfactory outcomes.

# 3 THE SHIFT TO MONEY PURCHASE PLANS IN THE UNITED KINGDOM

The United Kingdom has the oldest employer-sponsored pension system in the world. Defined benefit pensions developed throughout the nineteenth century in large firms mostly to retain experienced white-collar workers. Employer plans covered 5 percent of British employees by 1900, 13 percent by the 1930s, and 33 percent by 1956, roughly comparable to growth in the United States (Sass 2004).[7] As in the United States, this expansion can be attributed to several factors. First, increasing numbers of large employers found pensions a valuable instrument for managing their workforce. Second, powerful trade unions successfully bargained with employers to establish plans for employees who would not receive adequate retirement income under the public plan. Finally, the rising level of taxation in Britain after the Second World War made tax-advantaged pensions an appealing form of compensation.[8] Before discussing the second tier, it is worth spending a minute on the first tier.

## 3.1 The Basic State Pension

The Basic State Pension, which was enacted in 1946, is a flat benefit amount available at age 65 for men and age 60 for women. As a result of 1995 legislation, the age for women will gradually rise beginning in 2010 so that by 2020 it too will be 65. In contrast to provisions in the United States and many European countries, the pension is payable whether the individual has actually retired or not. Rights to the Basic State Pension are established through National Insurance Contributions. Those earning over the primary earnings threshold make their own payment; some people with low or no earnings have contributions made on their behalf. The Basic State Pension is financed on a pay-as-you-go basis.

Between 1948 and 1975, the Basic State Pension was increased periodically and actually grew relative to average earnings. The Social Security Act of 1975 formally linked increases in the Basic State Pension to the growth in prices or average earnings, whichever is larger. This arrangement lasted only until 1980, however, when the indexing was changed to prices alone. Price indexing means that the Basic State Pension will replace a declining share of pre-retirement earnings over time, since wages grow faster than prices. By the end of the 1990s, the replacement rate had declined from 25 percent to 16 percent of average earnings and was projected to decline below 10 percent by 2030 (Whitehouse 1998). However, under the current government, the rate of increase of the Basic State Pension has exceeded the consumer price index because the benefit is indexed to the Retail Price Index, which includes rapidly rising housing costs. The government has also introduced a generous Minimum Income Guarantee scheme.

## 3.2 The Introduction of Money Purchase Accounts

Employer defined benefit plans supplemented the Basic State Pension. In 1970, these plans covered half the workforce and two-thirds of male workers. But their limitations were becoming apparent. They functioned best for workers in long-term employment relationships. But mobile employees, the self-employed, those employed in small firms, and part-time and low-wage workers got few benefits and had inadequate old-age incomes. The government responded in 1975 by enacting the State Earnings Related Pension Scheme (SERPS), essentially a residual scheme for workers outside the mainstream.[9] Employers who already had a suitably generous plan were allowed, indeed encouraged, to 'contract out' and get a rebate on part of their national insurance contribution.

The expansion of social insurance was short lived. In 1979, only a year after SERPS went into effect, the Conservatives returned to power, promising to privatize the economy and reduce the national tax burden. The national insurance contribution was a major component of taxation, especially for middle-income workers. In 1986 the government sharply cut SERPS benefits and returned more of the responsibility for providing retirement income to employer plans that contracted out. Employers had to vest benefits after two years of service, and also became partially responsible for indexing the benefits of 'leavers' and retirees to inflation. The privatization campaign was stymied, however, by the decline in employer-plan coverage, which had peaked at 53 percent of the workforce in 1967 (Davis 1997).

As an answer to the coverage problem, the 1986 legislation that diminished SERPS allowed firms and workers to contract out using defined contribution as well as defined benefit plans. These defined contribution plans could be either individual 'personal pensions' offered by insurance companies or self-administered employer schemes. To encourage the adoption of personal accounts, the government offered an additional 2 percent over the normal rebate amount for contracting out. In addition to their rebate, workers could transfer their accumulated rights from their defined benefit plan to a personal pension. The privatization effort appears to have increased somewhat the share of private sector workers who contracted out (see Table 18.3).

## 3.3 Scandal and Reform of Money Purchase Accounts

The government's aggressive promotion of private pensions sparked financial service firms to sign up individuals. Insurance agents, driven by the prospect of large commissions, convinced millions of Britons to take out private pensions. They also convinced 500,000 to switch from an employer defined benefit plan, and many of these workers were misadvised (Blake 2000).

Workers who opted out of an employer plan lost the employer's contribution, the plan's risk pooling and administrative economies, as well as ancillary disability and life insurance benefits. Moreover, most of the purchased personal pensions had very low cash values in the early years since the bulk of the initial contributions went to pay commissions and set-up fees.

The complaints of former defined benefit participants sparked the 'mis-selling' scandal in 1993. In response, the government took steps to ensure compensation for individuals who were ill-advised. These compensation claims cost the insurance industry over £11 billion (Davis 2000). The scandal also led to much tougher controls on the selling of financial products. For example, to transfer accruals from an employer defined benefit plan to a private pension, a worker needed a written explanation,

Table 18.3 Percentage of UK workers with second-tier pension coverage, 1978/9–2000/1

| Type of Coverage | 1978–9 | 1987–8 | 1994–5 | 2000–1 |
|---|---|---|---|---|
| Total with second-tier coverage | 69.3 | 70.3 | 74.2 | 83.2 |
| Public Sector: employer-sponsored DB plan | 14.1 | 15.0 | 14.6 | 16.5 |
| Private Sector[1] | 55.2 | 55.3 | 59.6 | 66.7 |
| SERPS | 34.3 | 27.7 | 26.6 | 32.0 |
| Contracted out | 22.6 | 29.8 | 36.4 | 35.3 |
| Distribution of the private-sector, contracted-out pension schemes[2] | | | | |
| Employer-sponsored DB plan | 100.0 | 58.9 | 38.4 | 34.0 |
| Appropriate personal pension | – | 41.1 | 58.4 | 58.6 |
| Money purchase plan | – | – | 2.9 | 3.2 |
| Mixed benefit | – | – | – | 4.2 |
| Addendum: | | | | |
| Total workers (millions) | 24.6 | 25.8 | 25.8 | 27.7 |

Notes: [1] The percentage of the workforce covered by SERPS and 'Contracted out' exceeds the percentage of the private sector workforce with second-tier coverage because some people participate in both arrangements if they have more than one job.
[2] The distribution of private sector workers is based on 'membership' rather than number of workers because workers can participate in a number of arrangements if they have more than one job.
Source: United Kingdom Department for Work and Pensions (2003). Employment data come from the United Kingdom Office for National Statistics (2004).

prepared by a trained expert and checked by the insurer, demonstrating the gain. In addition, private pension providers had to disclose commissions and surrender values over the first five years of the contract (Davis 2000 and Blake 2000, 2002).

Most of the workers who opted for personal pensions switched not from defined benefit plans but from SERPS. And most of these workers were under age 45 because of the way the government rebate was structured (Disney and Whitehouse 1997). Prior to 1997, the government provided essentially the same national insurance rebate for all workers regardless of age, so young workers with many years to retirement had the chance for substantial investment earnings. Over the first ten years of the program, the government lost about £6 billion on personal pension rebates as young workers snapped up the offer (Davis 1997); employer plans also lost as younger employees opted out and took their mis-priced rebates with them. The government did not introduce fully age-adjusted rebates until 1997.

Despite the scandals and difficulties with the private system, the Conservatives continued to pursue their goals of privatization. In 1995, they cut the value of

SERPS benefits significantly by gradually raising the retirement age for women from 60 to 65, narrowing covered earnings, and other steps. Raising the retirement age also reduced the cost of the Basic State Pension.

## 3.4 Labour's Reaffirmation of Private Plans

In 1997, the Conservative government proposed the elimination of both the Basic State Pension and SERPS in favor of mandatory participation in a private plan. The drastic privatization proposals were never enacted because the Labour Party returned to power in 1997. Labour, however, reaffirmed the nation's commitment to private employment-based pensions, declaring that private plans should provide 60 percent of old-age income by the middle of the twenty-first century (Sass 2004).

To make personal pensions more attractive, the Labour government in 2001 introduced the 'stakeholder pension' that addressed shortcomings that surfaced in the mis-selling scandal. By sanctioning the design and by requiring employers without their own plan to offer workers a stakeholder option, the government hoped to dramatically increase personal pension coverage (UKDWP 1998, 2000). The take-up of stakeholder pensions, however, has been low. Some explanations include: the 1 percent cap on fees made them unprofitable for many companies; several target groups already had personal pensions; and small firms were not required to participate.

As insurance, in the face of diminished public programs and the limited reach of private plans, the Labour government also reformed the nation's means-tested program for the elderly. In 2003, it introduced the 'Pension Credit', which reduced the implicit tax from 100 percent to 40 percent on earnings and savings above the guaranteed level. This reform improved incentives for work and saving among low-income workers, but also will draw more people into the welfare net and the program's benefit withdrawal rate. By mid-century, when the Basic State Pension is projected to fall below 10 percent of average earnings, 65 to 80 percent of retirees will qualify for means-tested payments and be subject to disincentives (the implicit 40 percent tax) on work and saving (PPI 2003).

Labour also replaced SERPS with the 'State Second Pension', which increased benefits for low-wage workers without private pension coverage. The benefit for all workers with lifetime earnings below 45 percent of the average wage was set at a flat amount—equal to twice the SERPS benefit for the 45 percent earner. Benefits for higher earners are somewhat greater, gradually returning to the SERPS accrual rate at the level where most workers contract out. Thus, while low earners gained some protection, most middle and upper earners will be left with a dwindling Basic State Pension, incentives to contract out of the State Second Pension, and declining employer defined benefit coverage.

## 3.5 The Decline in UK Defined Benefit Plans

As in the United States, the growth of personal pensions in the United Kingdom has been accompanied by a sharp decline in traditional defined benefit plans. This decline reflects the popularity of money purchase plans as well as reforms to the employer plan institution and external economic shifts that have reduced the size and strength of defined benefit pensions.

Like the US situation, funding limitations to preserve tax revenue contributed to the precariousness of private plans. The Finance Act of 1986, enacted at a time of serious budget pressures, limited overfunding of defined benefit plans to at most 5 percent. As a result, sponsors of defined benefit plans took 'funding holidays' instead of building up surpluses during the boom years of the 1980s and 1990s.

Various reforms then shifted more of the risk associated with the provision of retirement income to these plans. In the early 1990s, it was revealed that Robert Maxwell, who controlled a large publishing empire, had used assets in company defined benefit plans to prop up shares in some of his other businesses. In response, the 1995 Pension Act imposed stricter rules on fiduciary conduct of defined benefit plans, created new enforcement mechanisms, and set up an insurance fund to protect participants against fraud. Importantly, the legislation also required plans that contract out to index pension payments and leavers' accruals up to 5 percent inflation (formerly 3 percent).

The 1995 legislation also established minimum funding requirements, albeit relatively weak ones. Former rules only required an actuarial certificate that the plan could pay the Guaranteed Minimum Pension required to contract out of SERPS. The new law required assets sufficient to meet the entire obligation should the plan terminate. However, problems with the legislation meant that in most cases assets were significantly below termination liability.

And the status of defined benefit plans was of increasing interest to the investor community. In response, the accounting profession issued Financial Reporting Standard 17 in 2000, requiring sponsors to report the current market value of assets and liabilities in their financial statements.[10] While a move from equity to bonds would have avoided sharp surplus/deficit swings associated with 'mark to market' accounting. Such movement was relatively limited. At the end of 2003, of the Financial Times Stock Exchange (FTSE) 100 companies equities averaged 62 percent of total pension assets. Only one company in the FTSE 100 had less than 30 percent of its assets in equity (see Chapter 20).

Changes in the labor market also reduced the appeal of defined benefit plans. Defined benefit plans were ill-suited to firms adopting more fluid, American-style employment relationships that did not involve lifetime career attachments. In addition, pension legislation had diminished the value of pensions in personnel management, since employers had to give leavers increasingly generous benefits as a condition of contracting out, in effect reducing the pension they paid only to those remaining with the firm.

The pressures on defined benefit plans came to a head, as in the United States, in the financial storm that began in 2000. Funding levels fell sharply as asset values declined (plans were still heavily invested in equities) and as liabilities ballooned with the fall in interest rates. By year-end 2002, funding levels at Britain's top 100 firms averaged about 80 percent of plan liabilities. At the time, only seven FTSE 100 companies had fully implemented Financial Reporting Standard 17 but they were nevertheless required to make footnote disclosure of their liabilities. Government funding rules also required sharply increased contributions—at a time when the operating business was struggling (Davis 2003).

The response has been a significant move away from defined benefit pension plans. As early as the mid-1990s, 80 percent of new employer plans have been money purchase, and employers covering over half of all private-sector defined benefit participants have recently closed their plans to new entrants. Workers in government agencies and enterprises have retained their defined benefit plans. But in the private sector, retirement plans will increasingly be organized around individual money purchase accounts, either as personal or stakeholder pensions or in an employer-sponsored plan.

## 3.6 The Current State of the UK Retirement Income System

The British system has four components, two private and two public: (1) employer defined benefit pensions; (2) money purchase accounts; (3) the Basic State Pension and the State Second Pension; and (4) a means-tested welfare program. The system is both complex and unstable—a problematic arrangement for workers who have to make plans years in advance of retirement.

The Basic State Pension benefit is projected to decline below 10 percent of the average wage by 2030. With the introduction of the State Second Pension in 2002, the government essentially transformed its second tier pension into a flat benefit program for lower wage workers that will cushion the erosion of Basic State Pension benefits. But more than half of private sector workers 'contract out' of the second tier pension, and today two out of three (67 percent) are covered by a money purchase plan provided either through their employer or an insurance company.

Money purchase plans raise many of the issues involved in 401(k) plans. The most obvious is financial risk. As in US 401(k) plans, where much of the investment is undertaken through diversified mutual funds, risk in the accumulation phase in the United Kingdom is reduced by the widespread use of pooled investment funds. Diversification, however, cannot avoid the possibility that returns will be low or even negative during the crucial ten or so years prior to retirement.

The other type of financial risk is low interest rates at the time of retirement, which either reduce the stream of income or raise the price of an annuity. As a response, the British government allowed individuals to postpone until age 75 the mandatory annuitization of assets attributable to contracting out. Extending the period for annuitization enabled individuals to avoid annuitizing when interest rates were particularly low. On the other hand, allowing individuals to wait to age 75 also introduces adverse selection—the likelihood that unhealthy individuals will postpone so that their heirs can inherit their account balances should they die before age 75—and this reduces the income that a given account balance could purchase at age 65. Under new tax rules to be implemented in 2006, mandatory annuitization will cease to exist. Pensioners will still have to take some action to secure a stream of income by age 75, but they will have a broader array of options, such as the 'Alternative Secured Pension'. Under this plan, the retirees can keep their assets but can withdraw only an amount equal to 70 percent of that provided by the flat-rate single-life annuity at age 75.

The UK system requires workers to make a series of complex decisions. As in the United States, those who opt for a money purchase plan have to decide how much to contribute, and contribution levels to money purchase plans appear low—roughly half of that going into defined benefit plans. Participants also have to make a host of complicated investment decisions, including the challenge of reallocating their investments over time. In addition, low and middle earners have to decide whether to stay in the government earnings-related program and how to optimize access to means-tested benefits.

In short, personal pensions now account for two-thirds of the arrangements for those who opt out, and the growth of money purchase plans has shifted the responsibility for the provision of retirement income from the employer to the employee. The low level of contributions and risks associated with these plans raise serious questions about their ability to maintain living standards in retirement.

# 4 CONCLUSION

This chapter has examined the shift from defined benefit to defined contribution plans in the second tier of the US and UK pension systems. Income provided through the second tier will be crucial in allowing individuals to maintain their pre-retirement standard of living given the scheduled decline in both the US and UK public first tier pension programs. Yet, neither the US nor UK system appears to be functioning very effectively.

As structured, both the US and UK defined contribution accounts place virtually all the risk and responsibility for retirement income on the worker. In the United States, participation is totally voluntary, and one-quarter of those eligible to participate in a plan choose not to do so. These individuals have nothing else other than Social Security. In the United Kingdom, the public earnings-related tier provides some additional protection for everyone. But those who opt out face the same tough investment decisions as 401(k) participants—how much to contribute, how to allocate contributions among stocks, bonds, and fixed income securities, and how to change those allocations over time. The evidence suggests that most people do not make good investment decisions.

At retirement, individual accounts raise other issues. In the absence of annuitization, workers risk either outliving their resources or living excessively frugally. The United Kingdom has responded initially by mandating annuitization and later by limiting the annual withdrawal beginning at age 75. The United States has relied on individual initiatives, and current patterns suggest that few will annuitize. In both cases, retirees will bear the risk that inflation will dramatically erode their purchasing power. This risk is a step backward for UK workers who previously enjoyed inflation-indexed benefits under their publicly provided or contracted-out SERPS benefits. While they can still select inflation-adjusted payments when they annuitize their money purchase accumulations, few do. Defined benefit plans in the United States generally did not provide any inflation adjustment.

The fundamental problem with individual accounts is that most individuals lack the experience or training to make wise saving, investment, and withdrawal decisions. For the vast majority of the population, their retirement saving is the only area where financial issues arise. They find the array of choices overwhelming and to many the costs of understanding the options appear greater than the benefits. Education might help some, but research suggests the gains are modest.

An approach with a potentially bigger payoff, at least in the United States, is to make the process simpler for the employee by building on the inertia so evident in human behavior. Public policy could leverage this inertia by setting the defaults in 401(k) plans to the desirable outcome. Under such an approach, all eligible participants would be automatically enrolled; their contributions set to maximize the employer match; the portfolios diversified and automatically re-balanced as they age; lump-sum distributions automatically rolled over; and retirement benefits paid in the form of a joint-and-survivor inflation-indexed annuity. Setting these defaults would eliminate the cost for participants of trying to figure out what to do, and it would help workers avoid mistakes by pointing them in the right direction. Of course, individuals could opt out at any stage, allowing them the flexibility to make different decisions if their circumstances warrant it.

But even if both the United States and the United Kingdom got their second tier pensions to work better, future retirees in both countries are likely to have inadequate retirement income. Some of the shortfall could be addressed by keeping workers in the labor force longer. Retiring later allows people to accumulate more assets and face a shorter period over which they have to support themselves. Extended worklives may become an increasingly realistic option as labor force growth slows reflecting the marked decline in fertility rates. But more will probably be needed. Both countries will have to consider either enhancing existing layers of protection or adding new ones.

The important lesson for countries thinking of transferring some of the responsibility for retirement from generous pay-as-you-go public to funded private plans is that the design of those plans matters a lot. The more that can be made automatic, the more effective will be the arrangement.

# Notes

The author would like to thank Greg Wiles for superb research assistance and Richard Disney for valuable comments. My colleague Steve Sass should have been a co-author but declined.

1. The classification of employer-sponsored pensions as mandatory or voluntary is based on that presented in ISSA and INPRS (2003).
2. Individuals with less than $25,000 and married couples with less than $32,000 of 'combined income' do not have to pay taxes on their Social Security benefits. (Combined income is adjusted gross income as reported on tax forms plus non-taxable interest income plus one half of Social Security benefits.) Above those thresholds, recipients must pay taxes on either 50 or 85 percent of their benefits.
3. Commentators often refer only to the bull market of the 1990s, but stocks posted strong gains for a much longer period. Between 1982 and 2000, stock prices rose at an annual nominal rate of 16.9 percent compared to 7.6 percent between 1963 and 1981, the previous 18-year period.
4. See, for example, Andrews (1985); Gustman and Steinmeier (1992); Ippolito (1995).
5. The full funding limitation generally makes it impossible for firms to make any contributions to overfunded plans. Beginning in 1987, if employers make tax-deductible contributions in excess of the permissible limits, they are subject to a 10 percent penalty tax.
6. In addition to the shift in pension coverage from defined benefit to defined contribution plans, some employers have converted their pensions to so-called cash balance plans. Legally, cash balance arrangements are defined benefit plans where employers make the contributions, own the assets, select the investments, and bear the risk. To the employee, however, cash balance plans look very much like a defined contribution plan. Contributions made for the employees are recorded in separate 'notional' accounts for each worker. As of 1999, government data report about 1,300 cash balance plans, which accounted for 15 percent of all defined benefit plan participants and 20 percent of all defined benefit assets.
7. The following discussion is based almost entirely on the overview of the UK retirement income system presented in Sass (2004).

8. The benefits of pension plans became so attractive that workers began to take advantage of the tax laws in order to receive tax-free compensation. In 1947 the government had to impose limits on pension amounts and accrual rates to stem this trend (Hannah 1986).
9. The SERPS was targeted primarily at women and others with intermittent work histories. As such it required only 20 years of service to qualify and based benefits on earnings in the highest 20 years. SERPS replaced 25 percent of indexed covered earnings—earnings between a 'lower' and 'upper' amount. Thus, the average earner with 20 years of service would get a benefit replacing somewhat more than 40 percent the average wage at retirement—roughly half from the Basic State Pension and half from the SERPS.
10. Although FRS 17 only became mandatory in 2005, most employers voluntarily adopted the provisions soon after the standard was issued.

# REFERENCES

ANDREWS, EMILY S. (1985). *Changing Profile of Pensions in America*. Washington, D.C.: Employee Benefit Research Institute.

BLAKE, DAVID (2000). 'Two decades of pension reform in the UK: what are the implications for occupational pension schemes?' Discussion Paper PI-0004. London: Pensions Institute, Birkbeck College, University of London.

—— (2002). 'The United Kingdom pension system: key issues'. Discussion Paper PI-0107. Pensions Institute, Birkbeck College, University of London.

BOARD OF GOVERNORS OF THE FEDERAL RESERVE SYSTEM (2003). *2001 Survey of Consumer Finances*. Washington, D.C.

BUREAU OF LABOUR STATISTICS (1979–2002). *Current Population Survey*.

DAVIS, E. PHILLIP (1997). 'Private pensions in OECD countries—the United Kingdom'. OECD. Labour Market and Social Policy Occasional Papers No. 21. Paris: Organisation of Economic Co-operation and Development.

—— (2000). 'Regulation of private pensions—a case study of the UK'. Discussion Paper PI-0009. Pensions Institute, Birkbeck College, University of London.

—— (2003). 'Is there a pension crisis in the UK?' Draft keynote address for the Japan Pension Research Council meeting, Tokyo, 18–19 Sept.

DE GIER, ERIK (2003). 'The future of the Dutch pension system'. Presented at the Fourth International Research Conference on Social Security. Antwerp, Belgium (May).

DISNEY, RICHARD, and WHITEHOUSE, EDWARD (1997). 'Personal pensions and the review of the contracting-out terms'. *Fiscal Studies*, 13 (Feb.): 35–53.

GUSTMAN, ALAN, and STEINMEIER, THOMAS (1992). 'The stampede toward defined contribution pension plans: fact or fiction?' *Industrial Relations*, 31/2: 361–9.

HANNAH, LESLIE (1986). *Inventing Retirement: The Development of Occupational Pensions in Britain*. Cambridge: Cambridge University Press.

HM REVENUE AND CUSTOMS (2005). 'Pensions Tax Simplification'. Available at: http://www.hmrc.gov.uk/pensionschemes/pts.htm

INTERNATIONAL SOCIAL SECURITY ASSOCIATION (ISSA) and International Network of Pension Regulators and Supervisors (INPRS) (2003). *Complementary and Private Pensions Throughout the World 2003*. Geneva: ISSA/INPRS.

IPPOLITO, RICHARD A. (1995). 'Toward explaining the growth of defined contribution plans'. *Industrial Relations*, 34/1: 1–19.

—— (1997). *Pension Plans and Employee Performance*. Chicago: University of Chicago Press.

LAZEAR, EDWARD (1985). 'Incentive effects of pensions'. David A. Wise (ed.), in *Pensions, Labor, and Individual Choice*. Chicago: University of Chicago Press, 253–82.

MADRIAN, BRIGITTE C., and SHEA, DENNIS F. (2002). 'The power of suggestion: inertia in 401(k) participation and savings behavior'. *Quarterly Journal of Economics*, 116/4: 1149–87.

MUNNELL, ALICIA H. (1982). *The Economics of Private Pensions*. Washington, D.C.: The Brookings Institution.

—— and SUNDÉN, ANNIKA (2004). *Coming Up Short: The Challenge of 401(k) Plans*. Washington, D.C.: Brookings Institution Press.

PENSIONS POLICY INSTITUTE (2003). 'The Pensions Landscape'. London: Pensions Policy Institute.

SASS, STEVEN A. (2004). 'Reforming the UK retirement system: privatization plus a safety net'. *Global Issue Brief*, 3. Center for Retirement Research at Boston College (June).

SKOLNIK, ALFRED M. (1976). 'Private Pension Plans'. *Social Security Bulletin*, 39/6: 3–17.

STATISTICS CANADA (2003). *Canada's Retirement Income Programs: A Statistical Overview (1990–2000)*. Income Statistics Division, Pensions and Wealth Program. Ottawa, Ont.: Statistics Canada.

UNITED KINGDOM DEPARTMENT FOR WORK AND PENSIONS (UKDWP) (1998). *A New Contract for Welfare: Partnership in Pensions*. London: The Stationery Office Ltd.

—— (2000). *The Changing Welfare State—Pensioner Incomes*. London: Department of Social Security.

—— (2003). *Second Tier Pension Provision*. Available at: http://www.dwp.gov.uk/asd/asd1/dsu/second_tier/second_tier.asp

UNITED KINGDOM OFFICE FOR NATIONAL STATISTICS (2004). *Labour Force Survey*. Available at: http://www.statistics.gov.uk/

US DEPARTMENT OF LABOR (2002). *Private Pension Plan Bulletin: Abstract of 1998 Form 5500 Annual Reports*. Employee Benefits Security Administration.

—— (2004). *Private Pension Plan Bulletin 12: Abstract of 1999 Form 5500 Annual Reports*. Pension and Welfare Benefits Administration, Office of Policy and Research. Available at: http://www.dol.gov/ebsa/PDF/1999pensionplanbulletin.pdf

US SOCIAL SECURITY ADMINISTRATION (2003). *Income of the Aged Chartbook, 2001*. Available at: http://www.ssa.gov/policy/docs/chartbooks/income_aged/2001

WHITEHOUSE, EDWARD (1998). 'Pension reform in Britain'. World Bank Discussion Paper No. 9810, June.

WHITESIDE, NOEL (2002). 'Constructing the public-private divide: historical perspectives and the politics of pension reform'. Working Paper WP102. Oxford Institute of Ageing.

YERMO, JUAN (2003). 'Recent developments in occupational pension plan accounting'. *OECD National Accounts and Economic Statistics*.

YOHALEM, MARTHA R. (1977). 'Employee Benefit Plans, 1975'. *Social Security Bulletin*, 40.

CHAPTER 19

# ORGANIZED LABOR AND PENSIONS

TERESA GHILARDUCCI

## 1 INTRODUCTION

This chapter addresses the role of organized labor in shaping pension design and retirement policy. Several distinctive aspects of American organized labor's experience with pensions—heavy reliance on an employer-based pension system,[1] limited union bargaining power, shifts in pension design towards individual-based accounts, union association with 'legacy costs', and investment activism by labor unions—serve as models for many international pension reform ideas. Moreover, since international pension reform generally aims to reduce government pension benefits, proposals often involve diminishing state obligations by expanding employer-based pensions. In this regard, the American unions support the defined benefit design (Solomon 2003),[2] and international unions have very similar principles for pension design. Thus, although this chapter focuses on the United States, much of US experience is relevant to labor's advocacy for pensions in Europe and Latin America.

All union movements reject privatizing government pensions and developing pension systems that rely on voluntary individual accounts. This shift has generally not occurred in Europe (except for the United Kingdom and Sweden), and American trade unions are among those leading the opposition to individualizing pension accounts in the United States. Where individual accounts have been implemented—Chile, Argentina, El Salvador, Mexico—the unions support reforms so that workers can collectivize the decisions about investments and bargain with managers to lower fees and improve services. As a result, this chapter explores the role of unions in establishing, maintaining, and controlling defined benefit pension plans.

The first section describes how US trade unions dramatically changed the composition of compensation between cash wages and pensions, and how the decline in union membership can be linked to the decline in the defined benefit plans and the rise of defined contribution plans. The second section explores how the US labor movement adapted to employers using pensions as one tool to generate higher productivity and demanded that pension plans similar to those already provided for management be extended to their members. The third section addresses the source of 'legacy costs' and trade union concerns for the financial future of secure pensions. The fourth section presents the US labor movement's argument that workers' pension funds should be invested to meet workers' needs since a full 50 percent of the $6 trillion in pension assets is derived from collective bargaining.[3] But ownership is not control, and unions have developed strategies to cope with that disconnect.

The conclusion brings together these threads and argues that organized labor will continue to swap cash for income security, to advocate for more employer-based pensions if they have defined benefit features, and to inculcate a role for organized labor as a legitimate pension investor.

## 2 UNIONS AND THE COMPOSITION OF PAY

The United States relies much more heavily than other countries on employers for pensions and health insurance. Many decades before other trade unions, American unions supported a complementary employer-based layer of pension provision (Klein 2003). The goal is twofold: government pensions provide basic income in a mandatory universal system and occupational pensions ensure a secure retirement.

Fewer than half of American workers were covered by employer pension plans in 2003 (Congressional Research Service 2004). However, union members are twice as likely as non-union workers to be covered. Not only are union pension costs a higher proportion of total pay; union workers receive higher levels of pension coverage for workers across a range of earnings. Unionization boosts pension coverage by approximately 20 percent for workers earning below the average wage and by 11 percent for workers earning above average annual earnings.[4]

In addition to receiving a greater portion of their compensation in pensions, union workers also enjoy a higher level of total compensation than their non-union counterparts. Union members earned, in 2002, over $30 per hour in total compensation, of which 65.5 percent constituted cash wages. Average non-union workers earned much less, $21.03, of which 73.9 percent was in cash wages (Employment Cost Index 2002). This differential is called the union premium (Mishel et al. 2000).

In addition, the rate of increase in employer spending reveals significant differences by union status. Between 1988 and 2002, the rate of growth for pension spending was 42 percent for non-union workers compared to 95 percent for union workers (see Table 19.1).

## 2.1 Unions and Low Pension Coverage in Small Firms

A worker's chances of being covered by a pension if working for a small firm (fewer than 100 employees) is 33 percent (for the lowest earners) and 27 percent (for the highest earners), which is half the coverage rate in larger firms (Ghilarducci and Lee 2005). But even in small firms, unions significantly increase the rates of pension coverage. Unions are especially effective in obtaining pensions for lower middle-class workers (earning $15,000 to $35,000 per year) in small firms. Being in the

Table 19.1 Changes in compensation for union and non-union workers, 1988–2002

| Component of compensation | Union workers | | | Non-union workers | | |
|---|---|---|---|---|---|---|
| | Dollar amounts | | Percentage change | Dollar amounts | | Percentage change |
| | 1988 | 2002 | | 1988 | 2002 | |
| Total compensation | 18.16 | 30.06 | 65.5 | 12.9 | 21.03 | 63.0 |
| Wages | 12.04 | 19.69 | 63.5 | 9.61 | 15.55 | 61.8 |
| Total benefits | 6.12 | 10.37 | 69.4 | 3.29 | 5.48 | 66.6 |
| Paid leave | 1.35 | 2.13 | 57.8 | 0.89 | 1.37 | 53.9 |
| Supplemental pay | 0.64 | 1.05 | 64.1 | 0.26 | 0.55 | 111.5 |
| Health, life, and disability insurance | 1.45 | 2.9 | 100.0 | 0.64 | 1.27 | 98.4 |
| Pensions | 0.86 | 1.68 | 95.4 | 0.36 | 0.51 | 41.7 |
| Other | 0.06 | 0.08 | 33.3 | 0.005 | 0.02 | 300.0 |

Source: Employment Cost Index (various years).

union significantly raises the likelihood of pension coverage. About 54 percent of middle-class men and 58 percent of middle-class women working in small firms are offered a pension. If the firm is unionized, however, pension coverage rates rise to 72 percent and 70 percent respectively (see Table 19.2). The unions' effect is strongest for workers in the lower-middle end of the distribution and for workers in small firms.

The strong relationship between unionization and pension coverage has meant that the decline in unions has produced a decline in pension coverage—the portion of the labor force represented by unions fell from 35 percent to 9 percent from 1953 to 2003 (Lichtenstein 2000). Although workers in medium and large firms have higher rates of pension coverage than those in small firms, their coverage has declined in recent years—down from 91 percent in 1985 to 70 percent in 2000 (Bureau of Labor Statistics 2004). And, since the 1980s, many firms which have had traditional defined benefits plans are making defined contribution pension plans the primary pension plan.[5] The percentage of employees participating in defined benefit plans declined from 80 percent in 1985 to 39 percent in 2002. Meanwhile, during the same period, the percentage of employees in defined contribution plans changed more modestly, increasing from 41 percent to 50 percent. Also, new firms are unlikely to sponsor a traditional defined benefit plan and are unlikely to be unionized.

Table 19.2 Pension coverage rates of all workers and union workers by income,* sex, and firm size

| Income Group[1] | Percentage of workers with pension coverage | | | | | | | |
| --- | --- | --- | --- | --- | --- | --- | --- | --- |
| | All firms | | | | Small firms (under 100 employees) | | | |
| | All workers | | Union workers | | All workers | | Union workers | |
| | Men | Women | Men | Women | Men | Women | Men | Women |
| Low | 33.8 | 39 | 70.7 | 69.8 | 17.0 | 21.0 | 42.1 | 37.5 |
| Low-middle | 55.2 | 64.2 | 74.0 | 80.0 | 35.1 | 43.2 | 53.6 | 62.6 |
| High-middle | 75.1 | 78.7 | 86.9 | 89.8 | 54.0 | 58.3 | 72.4 | 70.6 |
| High | 80.4 | 82.2 | 88.3 | 86.7 | 62.3 | 62.1 | 78.1 | 58.3 |

Notes: [1] Income Levels Definitions: low is under $15,000 per year, which is 45 percent of the Social Security Average Wage (SSWA); low-middle is between $15,000 and 35,000, which is between 45 percent of the SSWA; high-middle is $35,000 and $54,700, which is between the SSA wage and 160 percent of the SSWA; high is over over $54,700 annually or 160 percent of the SSWA.

Source: Author's calculations from the 2003 Current Population Survey (CPS) and discussed in Ghilarducci and Lee (2005).

## 2.2 Explaining the Union Pension Premium

Economists attribute the existence of the union pension premium to at least six factors: the voice effect, unions' effect on individuals' preferences for saving, the impact of solidarity, efficiency wage theory, gift exchange, and power effects. Economists' explanation of how unions and defined benefit pensions affect productivity are complementary; both increase a worker's likelihood of staying longer with a particular employer. The complementarity can partially explain why unions create an environment for defined benefit pensions and defined benefit pension plans create an environment for unions. When one is diminished, the other is similarly affected. (See Chapter 36 in the *Handbook* for the effect of pensions on productivity.)

Freeman (1981) argues that unions provide an example of the superiority of 'voice' over 'exit' as devices in market transactions. Unionized workers who want workplace improvements have 'voice' because of collective bargaining. Without the ability to complain and bargain for workplace improvements periodically, workers would exit (resign) to find a better job. Through the mechanism of 'voice', unions reduce turnover. This reduction in turnover increases productivity by creating long-term workplace relationships between workers and their employers and among workers themselves. Long-term workplace relationships boost productivity by improving employers' chances of reaping the rewards of expensive training, because the trained worker will likely not leave the firm. Similarly, workers may accept lower pay at times, such as during their training, knowing that seniority will yield a pension. In sum, the voice effect predicts that unionized workplaces will have benefits, like pensions, that encourage tenure and relatively lower turnover, which encourages employer training (Ghilarducci and Reich 2001; Miller and Mulvey 1992; Freeman 1981).[6]

Another method whereby unions affect employee benefits is by creating group processes that enable workers to overcome short-sightedness and psychological denial of unpleasant realities. Many people significantly discount the future and downplay the real risks of poor health, disability, and living in old age without enough income. The process of collective bargaining brings workers together every few years to determine their salient demands for pay, hours, and working conditions. These deliberative group processes create analytical rather than emotional decisions, which shifts preferences toward different forms of compensation. In other words, unions create 'educable' moments about the importance of savings and insurance that help to expand time horizons, which results in union members placing relatively more value on future consumption (Ghilarducci *et al.* 1995).

In addition, unions operate on the principles of solidarity—a context of shared interests, responsibilities, and fellowship. This context can explain why unions prefer defined benefit plans to individualistic defined contribution plans. Shiller (2000) argues that without solidarity, which includes a desire to share risks, demands for some form of defined benefit pensions are replaced by demands for cash or individual accounts. Thus, he contends, individualized pensions—primarily 401(k) plans—have replaced defined benefit plans because unions have lost influence in setting pay and benefits. In his words, 'a key factor appears to be an erosion of solidarity and loyalty among workers and an attitude that has come to be replaced by an individual business ethic' (23).

Economists have also introduced the concept of 'efficiency wage' to explain why employers provide pensions. In this framework, pensions that encourage tenure are 'discipline devices'. Defined benefit pensions raise the cost of workers losing their jobs. Middle-aged valuable employees, who are covered by pensions, the theory holds, work hard and shirk less because they fear losing their rapidly accumulating pensions (Lazear 2000).

The notion of 'gift exchange' to explain pension coverage is slightly different. This notion refers to valuable transfers of some type of pay that does not require a response—that is, 'gifts'. Pensions, in these models, reflect the loyalty that employers feel toward their older workers, and the gift exchange stabilizes relations and improves the workplace (Akerlof 1982). As the profitability of long-term contracts fades, employers adopt defined contribution plans but for reasons different than those embodied in the 'voice' or 'solidarity' explanations.

Finally, economists have explored the implications of power in explaining pension coverage. A justification for government encouraging unions and collective bargaining is that the process 'levels the playing field' by balancing the power between workers and employers, which, the thinking goes, generates more efficient markets. The idea is that unions countervail the inherently stronger position of capital in setting wages, hours, and other conditions of employment (Kaufman 1989). Under this view unions are able to extract pensions from employers through bargaining power.

In sum, unions and unionized employers provide different 'compositions of compensation'. Pensions meet employees' needs as well as help employers solve labor problems. How unions and employers established pension agreements is discussed below.

# 3 Unions Fight for Retirement Benefits

The historical debate within the labor movement over the nature of pensions affected how unions argued for pensions and how they identified who should pay for those pensions. The competing metaphors were whether pensions represent 'deferred wages' or whether they represent an employer's payment for the 'depreciation' of workers' bodies and minds after long periods of work. Harbrecht

(1959) described the differences in the pension approaches of the progressive industrial workers, CIO, and the more established craft unions in the AFL. The CIO tended to describe pensions as a 'payment for depreciation', whereas the AFL viewed pensions as 'deferred wages'. The payment for depreciation model infers that the employer owes a payment to workers. The idea underlying the deferred wage metaphor is that employers are rather neutral, and employer pensions merely help workers save for the future. Pensions help facilitate an intertemporal transfer of consumption. The deferred wage metaphor implies that workers pay for pensions by accepting a reduced wage.

If pensions are deferred wages, then joint control of the pension fund makes sense. Workers should have a say in how 'their money is invested', but they are not entitled to a defined benefit promise. In other words, one is entitled to control one's savings account, but not to a guaranteed return or outcome. On the other hand, if pensions represent payments for depreciation, then consumers and employers owe replenishment, owe secure income and retirement. In that way, the unfunded past liabilities, the so-called 'legacy costs' have a flip side. The legacy costs are accompanied by the legacy benefits of the value of the work that employers and consumers enjoyed, which took a toll on human beings.

In the three decades after the Second World War, the US employer-based benefit system grew to cover two-thirds of the working population for health insurance, and one-half of the working population for pensions. Non-union companies frequently matched the unionized firms' benefit offerings in order to thwart unionization efforts. While employers may have agreed to provide employee benefits and accede to union demands for business reasons, they also profoundly changed social expectations and beliefs about what good employers do. Namely, good employers provide pensions and health insurance.

At the same time, being able to garner social approval for retiring without being disabled and/or superannuated—that is, discharged or disqualified on account of old age—constituted a sea change in society's vision of retirement. Retirement became viewed as an entitlement to healthy leisure at the end of a working life— leisure enjoyed while one could still work. This view swept all developing wealthy nations with labor movements.

Notably, organized labor's demands for pensions were accompanied by a new entitlement claim. Organized labor demanded that old but healthy workers should be able to retire just as the wealthy are able. Unions demanded retirement as a state that was worthwhile for its own sake, not because old workers would happen to be more at risk of infirmity or superannuation. In other words, the claim that workers were entitled to leisure in old age because they were 'too old to work and too young to die'[7] evolved into a claim for socially legitimate retirement. The US labor movement's evolution, from self-help efforts to advocacy for retirement and a government pension system, is similar to the history of organized labor's retirement income agenda internationally. The major exception is the American labor movement's substantial attention to expanding employer-based benefits. This is because 'welfare capitalism' expressed itself more fully in the United States than anywhere else (Jacoby 1997).

A reprise of the history of the American labor movement's pension agenda emphasizes that labor unions were not a powerful force in creating the American welfare state. Labor did not become a sophisticated political organization until well after the New Deal social programs in the 1930s were formed and businesses formulated employee benefits. So, despite the crucial role in expanding pension rights to workers, organized labor in the United States did not initially have a major role in constructing US Social Security. However, in 2005, the American labor movement is a major part of a coalition opposing partial privatization efforts by President Bush. In the 1880s, labor unions began as 'mutual aid' societies, with their major function the collection of funds from members to provide self-help aid, such as funeral benefits. The concept of linking 'trust funds' contributions directly to payroll was an extension of this concept of self-help. (The Brotherhood of Electrical Workers and Electrical Contractors (Local 3) of New York was probably the first union to establish a multi-employer pension plan in 1929 (EBRI 1997).)

From the 1900s to the 1920s, the very largest American corporations introduced a number of programs, including pensions, that improved the welfare of their workers. These benefits were linked to wide-ranging efforts to rationalize work and involved newly created personnel management departments. Their aim was to both induce loyalty among certain workers and to ease out older managerial employees. Sass (1997) found that over 300 plans, covering 15 percent of the workforce, had been established by 1919, and by 1924 just four firms—two railroads, AT&T, and US Steel—covered one-third of all pension plan participants. Of course, most workers would die or leave the firms before the age of compulsory retirement (age 60 at many firms) and ordinary workers were less likely to ever receive a benefit than were management employees. Company plans in the 1920s became more mature—and thus more expensive—and collapsed in the Great Depression.

Early disappointment in the security of employer-based systems led to a growing push for a government retirement income security program similar to social security programs found in Europe by the 1920s. In the United States, organized labor did not initiate, but joined with other groups, to advocate a universal, mandatory government program, which became Social Security in 1935. One of the reasons that organized labor was not a key player in Social Security's passage is that labor unions were engaged in forming their own versions of social insurance. At first organized labor's pension efforts (in the United States and elsewhere) were aimed at alleviating poverty among superannuated workers. Union efforts were devoted to creating self-help programs that evolved into scattered successes at persuading employers to extend managerial employer-based pensions to the rank and file. The US labor movement linked demands for employer-based pension systems to its demand for an entire system of social insurance, such as unemployment and disability insurance.

Also, many unions looked to the pensions provided to workers of local state and federal governments as a model. Pensions offered to New York City and Massachusetts State workers, Civil War veterans and dependents, to teachers' pensions in some states set the standard for private sector workers wanting a pension that was not vulnerable to firm failures and volatile employment relationships.

In fact, many union and employer pension plans disappeared during the 1930s Depression. Thirteen international union pension funds also collapsed; only four survived after the Second World War. The survivors consisted of multi-employer plans for craft workers—electricians, carpenters, typographers, typesetters, and printers. As industrial workers organized new firms in the postwar period, unions in collective bargaining negotiations demanded to get the same type of plans provided to management.

Industrial unions worked to make pension bargaining legitimate and advanced 'depreciation' as the rationale for pensions. Although the United Mineworkers of America (UMWA) was not the first union to negotiate pensions, it significantly helped define the union role in establishing workplace pensions after the Great Depression.[8] The UMWA story highlights the special ways unions strive to obtain job security from the collective bargaining process and not just higher wages and more consumption. Declining coal demand and automation of dangerous coal mining jobs caused substantial miner displacement after the Second World War. In 1945, the UMWA demanded a fully employer-paid $100 per month pension for old and retiring miners. The union characterized its demand as 'payment for past service'. Instead of arguing that pensions were deferred wages (payment for services rendered) that had to be accumulated before being paid out, the UMWA (and many other industrial (CIO) unions afterward) argued that pensions were depreciation payments owed to labor and thus were analogous to employer expenses for 'wear and tear' (depreciation) on capital. That is, pensions represented 'legacy benefits'. Pensions then are complements to, rather than substitutes for, higher wages,[9] and something employers, customers, or citizens are obligated to pay.

During the Second World War, the government introduced wage and price control policies to raise money and curb inflation. Defense-related firms, desperate for workers, were making enormous and socially unsavory profits out of the war and were bidding up wages and putting pressure on prices. The government put a tax on 'excess' profits but deemed that profits spent on employee benefits, such as pensions, heath insurance, vacations, that did not cause labor costs to rise immediately and consumer demand to spike would be exempt from the large profit tax. This exclusion encouraged firms to make increasing payments to workers in the form of non-cash wages. The government further encouraged the growth of pensions when in the late 1940s and 1950s, the Supreme Court agreed with unions—because employers resisted negotiating over them—that pensions were mandatory subjects of bargaining (Stevens 1986: 17–19).

Organized labor in the United States linked collective bargaining demands to the changes in the new Social Security program. That is, pensions were viewed as supplements to the Social Security program. Because the early negotiated pension plans allowed the employee to reach a target benefit including Social Security, these integrated plans allowed employers to pay virtually nothing for lower paid employees because the Social Security benefit exceeded the employer promise. The United Autoworkers (UAW) purposefully negotiated the pension in this way so that workers and firms would lobby for a higher Social Security system. When Congress increased benefits in the 1950s some workers' pensions benefits were diminished. They revolted against their fast-learning union leaders. Integrated plans in collectively bargained pensions began to disappear as union leaders responded.

In summary, in the three decades after the Second World War, the US employer-based benefit system grew to cover two-thirds of the working population for health insurance, and one-half of the working population for pensions. Non-union companies frequently matched the unionized firms' benefit offerings in order to thwart unionization efforts. While employers might have agreed to provide employee benefits and accede to union demands merely to attract and retain scarce workers, these developments profoundly changed social expectations and beliefs that good employers provide pensions and health insurance.

## 4 Unions and Legacy Costs

In 2002, a beleaguered analyst at Morgan Stanley set off a customer relations disaster when he wrote that collective bargaining causes large pension liabilities and lowers profits (Morgan Stanley 2002). The bank's chief US strategist warned that a tough economic environment is likely to penalize businesses with high fixed costs, pension-funding issues, and rising healthcare obligations, which are associated with unionized companies. Union clients fire-stormed the company and threatened to terminate millions of dollars of business because of the report. In a sense, however, the analyst was right. The average ratio of assets to liabilities is smaller in defined benefit plans in unionized companies than in non-union companies.

The most recent poster child for expensive union legacy costs is the airline industry. Older airlines—mostly all unionized—have 10 percent of the DB system's total unfunded pension liabilities. But the connection between unions and legacy costs is not always complete. Unionized Southwest Airlines is one of the financially healthy airlines, bringing down airline fares and threatening airlines with large legacy costs. Although Southwest is a unionized carrier, it provides only a DC plan. Southwest is one example that supports the view that it is the combination of unions and DB plans and not unionization *per se* that is associated with unwieldy expenses. The relevant characteristic of financially troubled airlines is that they are older than the financially secure airlines, which are mainly point-to-point carriers that cherry pick the most profitable routes.

In some cases, union workers have demanded full funding. For example, the Railroad Retirement fund, established in the 1930s, grew out of workers' demands for their mature defined benefit pensions be fully funded (Sass 1997). At the turn of the last century, the pensions at the legacy railroads were amassing huge unfunded liabilities because the workforces were ageing and the recession had severely reduced demand for their services. Moreover, young lower-cost carriers were pushing down prices. The railroad retirees and unions sought a federal solution that became an industry tax on both the legacy railroads and the young non-union railroads. The solution was the Railroad Retirement system. The underlying argument was that the young railroads had the advantage of what the legacy railroads had produced and should fairly share the costs of those benefits.

In a similar move 70 years later, the UAW were active in designing the defined benefit pension insurance agency—the Pension Benefit Guaranty Corporation (PBGC). The PBGC was included in the comprehensive legislation regulating most aspects of defined benefit pension plans: the Employee Retirement Income Security Act (ERISA) (Wooten 2001). The labor movement is at the time of writing developing a defense of the PBGC and a rationale for the PBGC to be reinsured. Reinsurance is common in other insurance systems. Insurers buy insurance for themselves (Lloyd's of London is a well-known example of a reinsurer) to cover catastrophic events for which the normal insurance company is not prepared. For example, house insurers can cover one house burning down, but not a whole city. In the case of a metropolitan area, the government steps in effectively reinsuring the home insurance company. The PBGC is designed as insurance in case of the collapse of a company, not if an entire set of defined benefits companies collapse at the same time in the same industry.

The point of these two examples is that unions understand the security they gain when defined benefit plans are fully funded or at least insured in a secure fashion.

# 5 Labor's Capital

The US labor movement stands out from other national union movements in having an extensive history of being sophisticated pension fund managers and of being prominent pension investment and shareholder activists. Ironically, the US trade unions' strong presence as pension activists stems from their unusual weakness. The US labor movement's economic and political strength has always been among the weakest in the developed world. And, in the last 20 years, it has diminished the fastest (Lichtenstein 2000). The combination of large and growing pensions and wizened and diminishing unions is like the fate of the Cheshire cat: all that is left of the disappearing body of the US labor movement is the gleaming smile of the pension funds. European national unions are strong in terms of bargaining and political power, yet many are just beginning to exert significant influence over their pension funds' investment practices.

In the last 30 years, the sheer size of pension assets, accompanied by the weakness of traditional union tactics and developments in finance regarding shareholder rights, has given American unions an opportunity to challenge corporate behavior in new ways. Labor partially owns (under both the 'deferred compensation' and 'depreciation payment' rationales) pension assets. But ownership does not necessarily confer control (Blackburn 2002). American unions, and increasingly international unions, want control of workers' pension funds. Note that in the single employer world, American labor unions bargained successfully for defined benefit pension promises but lost their demands for control of investments. In multi-employer plans, unions and management are legally viewed as joint owners and share control (Ghilarducci *et al.* 1995). A well-known (and misunderstood) case of unions and management jointly managing pension funds is the Teamsters. Some history of this union's engagement in pensions helps illustrate how aiming both to secure pensions and to manage the funds has always been part of organized labor's pension agenda.

In the 1940s, the International Brotherhood of Teamsters (IBT) was one of the leading union innovators to use pension funds strategically to strengthen their members' bargaining position. The sophisticated and robust pension systems the IBT crafted were remarkable given that at the time trucking companies and warehouses were small, fledging, and undercapitalized and their workers were among the most underprivileged in society. Often President James Riddle Hoffa and trustees awarded the business of administering the growing IBT pension funds to banks in the community. These activities did not involve any shady investments. Rather, the goal was to divide the interests and loyalties of local businesses and thus blunt community resistance to the unions' organizing efforts (James and James 1965; Sloane 1991).

On the other side of the equation, many employers did not initially fight unions controlling pension investments in multi-employer plans. A partial reason for the acquiescence is that the early plans operated on a pay-as-you go basis—that is, contributions collected were immediately paid out and the money did not accumulate in a trust fund. As discussed above, the UMWA President, John L. Lewis, argued that since employers garnered the benefits and workers paid the costs of automation, workers should be compensated with pension contributions based on tonnage mined per hour rather than work hours. This caused contributions to explode, swelling the pension fund. Since the union already dominated the UMWA pension fund administration (though the fund had equal numbers of employer and union trustees) the union ended up dominating pension investment policies.

The unions in the large rubber, steel, and auto industries were aware of the importance of having a say in pension funding and investment decisions of single employer plans. Lane Kirkland, former president of the AFL-CIO, as a young researcher in the newly formed AFL-CIO in 1955 issued a ten-point pension bargaining agenda for unions. The tenth point was to bargain for joint control of investments. Although the unions wanted joint control of investments, they did not have the bargaining strength to achieve this goal. Instead, they focused on something that turned out to be more valuable—'past-service' credits—credits for pension based on service before the pension plan was implemented.

Since the 1970s, the labor movement's pension tactics have grown in many directions as organized labor lost traditional sources of power. For example, unions are prominent members of the Council of Institutional Investors, which was formed in the late 1970s by state pension funds. California took the lead in setting up this organization because its pension funds were so large. These large funds had become too big to 'exit' a stock. If they sold a stock to protest about a firm's management—the old-fashioned way to complain—the stock price would fall precipitously. Corporate engagement was the solution for pension funds that wanted a 'voice' in how corporations are managed (Hebb and Clark 2003). Unions wanting a voice work through the Council of Institutional Investors.

Unions also use an updated version of the 'Hoffa tactic' to influence the behavior of companies. Pension funds are important clients of banks and money managers and unions leverage these financial institutions to pressure their corporate clients to make certain pro-worker decisions. Launching shareholder resolutions against a company often initiates discussion with worker and other activist organizations. Union pension funds also invest in construction projects and own buildings to ensure the construction and the building management work is unionized or union neutral.

In 1995 this type of union activity was institutionalized with the formation of the AFL-CIO's Department of Corporate Affairs when John Sweeney became president in a rare contested AFL-CIO presidential election. The Department aims to make the AFL-CIO a sophisticated analyst of corporate behavior.[10] AFL-CIO General Counsel Damon Silvers et al. (2001) argue that legal, prudent investment conforms more closely to a worker's view of investing than 'Wall Street's conventional wisdom'. The conventional principles of efficient market theory reward short-term-oriented behavior with exaggerated managerial compensation. Silvers et al. argue that long-term growth and productivity are not pursued under the current system, and thus union engagement in corporate decisions helps all investors.

Unions submitted 28 percent of all shareholder resolutions in the 2000 proxy season and 18 percent in 2003—far more than any other institutional investor (Hebb 2001). Unions submitted resolutions on auditor independence at 33 companies. Union shareholder activists were among the first to challenge Stanley Works—through the press and the bully pulpit—for its attempt to avoid taxes by moving to Bermuda (*Business Week* 2002).

How does the AFL-CIO resolve its paradoxical roles? On the one hand, it is redistributing profits from owners to workers. On the other, as a shareholder, its goal is to maximize profits for owners. The paradox is more easily reconciled than it would first appear. The AFL-CIO Proxy Guidelines clearly state that the trustee 'must not subordinate the interests of the pension participant to any other interest' (p. 2)—such as to a striking union.[11] Union trustees may vote proxies to serve the interests of trustees if their actions concern a decision that affects the long-term value of the company. Such decisions include corporate policies that affect (1) employment security and wage levels of plan participants; (2) local economic development and stability; (3) growth and stability of the overall economy; (4) corporate responsibility to employees and local communities; and lastly, (5) safety and health considerations at the workplace. Since proxies must be couched in terms that serve the interests of shareholders, labor's demands are couched in terms of goals to maximize shareholder value, but the route to do this is assumed to be through prudent long-term decision-making (Hawley *et al.* 1997).

# 6 CONCLUSION

Another logical consequence of organized labor's decline is the shift from the traditional form of primary pensions—employer and government-guaranteed defined benefit plans to the more individualistic defined contribution plans.

In the early part of the twenty-first century, America's labor movement is actively engaged in both public and private pension issues. President Bush's most prominent second term domestic policy goal is to reduce the role of Social Security by allowing younger workers to divert part of their Social Security payroll taxes into individual accounts. Tax hikes have been ruled out as an option to pay for the transition costs. Bush's plan diminishes Social Security benefits. As expected, the American labor movement is coupling its support of defined benefit pensions with support for Social Security.

The US labor movement has an important role in bringing retirement to the working classes because it has linked bargaining for employer-provided pensions to legislative goals for establishing and improving the Social Security system. The peculiar stinginess of public social insurance programs in the United States made employers an important source of retirement income (and health insurance) and a focus for union efforts and bargaining power. The dependence on protections at the workplace also led to legacy costs. One aspect of organized labor's role in the development of the US pension system is unexpected. By changing the composition of compensation, the US labor movement promotes savings and because of its role as saver and investor, unions have become one of the most ardent representatives of capital owners in the United States.

# Notes

1. The private sector's prominent role in providing pensions in the United States stands apart from most nations (with some exceptions in Anglo nations). The replacement rate, the ratio of retirement benefits to pre-retirement earnings, for an average worker after 35–44 years of work ranges in Europe's six largest nations from a low 38 percent in the United Kingdom to a typical 70 percent (Peagle 2004: 14). The average US replacement rate is 43 percent and falling (Munnell 2003).
2. The key distinction between defined benefit (DB) (either traditional or cash balance) and defined contribution (DC) plans is who bears the risk regarding the availability of funds when retirement occurs. Prior to the 1980s, most employer-sponsored pension plans were traditional defined benefit plans. A firm guarantees a monthly or lump-sum payment to workers after retirement in DB plans. The company bears the risk of making pension payments. A cash balance plan is technically still a defined benefit plan because the employer completely funds the payments. However, the dollar value of the account is derived from contributions made by the employer (usually a fixed percentage of one's salary) and a guaranteed rate of return on those contributions (either a fixed interest rate or one tied to a given index rate). One benefit of a cash balance plan to an increasingly mobile workforce is that workers can take a lump-sum distribution if they leave the firm prior to retiring (Brown et al. 2000). The most common form of DC plan are 401(k) plans. Employees make pre-tax contributions to DCs and employers are not required to contribute.
3. Fifty percent of these workers are in plans that are under a union contract or influence. Excluding the monies in individual retirement accounts, like 401(k)s, there is $1.8 trillion in corporate accounts and over $2 trillion in state and local pension funds. $300 billion are in accounts managed jointly by union and management representatives (Ghilarducci 2001: 166).
4. Another way to see unionization's effect on pension coverage is to compare differences in averages by group: only 33.8 percent of low income men are offered a pension at work but of the small percentage of low income men who are unionized, 6.71 percent, a full 70.67 percent have pensions. For all men and women, regardless of income, the union effect is of the same large magnitude. For example, of the high-middle income workers (earning between the average wage and 160 percent of the average wage), 75 percent of middle-class men, and 78.7 percent of middle-class women, are offered a pension at work. If they are unionized, the pension coverage rates rise to 86.9 percent and 89.8 percent respectively (Ghilarducci and Lee 2005).

5. Some employers are finding a middle ground and offering a version of a defined benefit plan, called a cash balance plan, where an employer guarantees a defined rate of interest on a defined periodic contribution to an individual account. The employees do not direct the investments nor can they access the cash balance account as they can with a DC account, and the account balance is guaranteed by the government agency insuring DB plans, the Pension Benefit Guaranty Corporation (PBGC). Cash balance plans provide attractive features of both DB and DC plans (Brown *et al.* 2000).
6. An employee benefit that increases in value with increases in a worker's service with a firm is called 'tenure-weighted' and includes defined benefit pensions and vacation periods that increase with seniority.
7. A well-known songwriter dealing with subjects regarding the labor movement, Joe Glazer, sometimes referred to as 'Labor's bard', recorded a song in 1959 supporting the Chrysler workers' demands that a pension system similar to one offered to management employees be extended to line workers.
8. In the 1930s and 1940s the UMWA covered a majority (80 percent) of mineworkers. The union was so wealthy that it helped organize emerging unions in the Congress of Industrial Organization (CIO), which covered workers in the rubber, steel, and auto industries. In the mid-1940s, the UMWA directed its bargaining power toward pensions.
9. President Truman delegated his Secretary of Interior to mediate the negotiations in the coal industry, and thus the US government encouraged the relatively weak employers in this vital industry to settle with the powerful union. The result was a multi-employer pension and a powerful trend and 'expectation' setter that unions negotiate pensions (Ghilarducci 1992).
10. One of the chief features of the AFL-CIO's website is the executive pay watch link (http://www.aflcio.org/paywatch/ceou.htm). A worker in a number of large companies can enter their salary at the website and their hourly wage is compared to the bosses'. I selected Abbott Laboratories at random and entered $40,000 as my salary. I got this message back: 'You would have to work 8 years to equal Peter Caswell's 2001 compensation. *"You'd better get working, because you can't take a vacation until 2010 A.D."*'.
11. The AFL-CIO's Proxy Voting Guidelines further justify the labor movement's involvement with proxy voters because pension law requires that pension fiduciaries consider proxy votes as trust assets. The AFL-CIO gently warns union trustees if their pension fund does not have guidelines and the trustees do not hold managers accountable for voting according to guidelines they eventually might develop, since then the trustees could be violating federal pension regulations.

# References

Akerlof, George A. (1982). 'Labor contracts as partial gift exchange'. *Quarterly Journal of Economics*, 97/4 (Nov.): 543–6.

Blackburn, Robin (2002). *Banking on Death or Investing in Life: The History and Future of Pension Funds*. London: Verso.

Brown, Kyle N., Goodfellow, Gordon P., Hill, Tomeka, Joss, Richard R., Luss, Richard, Miller, Lex, and Schieber, Sylvester J. (2000). 'The unfolding of a predictable surprise: a comprehensive analysis of the shift from traditional pensions to hybrid plans'. Watson Wyatt Worldwide Research Report. Bethesda, Md.: Watson Wyatt Worldwide.

BUREAU OF LABOR STATISTICS (BLS) (2004). 'Employee participation in defined benefit and defined contribution plans, 1985–2000', 16. June http://www.bls.gov/opub/cwc/cm20030325tb01.htm

—— (Various years). Employment Cost Index. Washington, D.C.: United States Department of Labor.

BUSINESS WEEK (2002). 'Getting the boss to behave, big labor has led the charge for corporate-governance reform'. *Business Week*, 15 July.

CONGRESSIONAL RESEARCH SERVICE (2004). 'Pension sponsorship and participation: summary of recent trends'. Order Code RL30122, Sept. Written by Patrick Purcell.

EMPLOYEE BENEFITS RESEARCH INSTITUTE (EBRI) (1997). *Fundamentals of Employee Benefit Programs*, 5th edition. Washington, D.C.: Employee Benefit Research Institute, 149–62.

EMPLOYMENT COST INDEX (2002). 'Employer costs for employee compensation 1986–2002'. Bureau of Labor Statistics, US Department of Labor BLS Statistics. http://www.bls.gov/ncs/eci/home.htm

FREEMAN, RICHARD, B. (1981). 'The effect of unionism on fringe benefits'. *Industrial and Labor Relations Review*, 34/4 (July): 489–509.

GHILARDUCCI, TERESA (1992). *Labor's Capital: The Economics and Politics of Private Pensions*. Cambridge, Mass.: MIT Press.

—— MANGUM, GARTH, PETERSEN, JEFFREY S., and PHILIPS, PETER (1995). *Portable Pension Plans for Casual Labor Markets: Lessons from the Operating Engineers Central Pension Fund* Greenwich, Conn.: Quorum Books, Greenwood Publishing Group, Inc.

—— (2001). 'Small benefits, big pension funds, and how corporate governance reforms can close the gap', in Archon Fung, Tessa Heb, and Joel Rogers (eds.), *Working Capital: The Power of Labor's Pensions*. Ithaca, N.Y.: Cornell University Press, 158–80.

—— and LEE, MARY (with Lance Wescher). (2005). 'Small firm pension coverage, multi-employer plans, and middle class workers'. University of Notre Dame, presented at the Industrial Relations Research Association at the Allied Social Sciences Association Annual National Meeting, Philadelphia.

—— and REICH, MICHAEL (2001). 'Complementarity of pensions and training under multiemployer plans'. *Journal of Labor Research*, 22/3 (summer): 615–34.

HARBRECHT, PAUL P. (1959). *Pension Funds and Economic Power*. New York: Twentieth Century Fund.

HAWLEY, JAMES, WILLIAMS, ANDREW, and GHILARDUCCI, TERESA (1997). 'Labor's paradoxical interests and the evolution of corporate governance'. *Journal of Law and Society*, 24/1 (Mar.): 26–43.

HEBB, TESSA (2001). 'Introduction: the challenge of labor's capital strategy', in Archon Fung, Tessa Hebb, Joel Rogers, (eds.), *Working Capital: The Power of Labor's Pensions*. Ithaca, NY: Cornell University Press, 1–13.

—— and CLARK, GORDON L. (2003). 'Understanding pension fund corporate engagement in a global arena'. Working Paper, School of Geography and the Environment, University of Oxford.

JACOBY, SANFORD (1997). *Modern Manors*. Princeton: Princeton University Press.

JAMES, ESTELLE, and JAMES R. (1965). *Hoffa and the Teamsters: A Study of Union Power*. Princeton: D. Van Nostrand.

KAUFMAN, BRUCE. E. (1989). 'Labor's inequality of bargaining power: changes over time and implications for public policy'. *Journal of Labor Research*, 10/3. (summer): 285–99.

KLEIN, JENNIFER (2003). *For All these Rights: Business, Labor, and the Shaping of the American Public-Private Welfare State*. Princeton: Princeton University Press.

LAZEAR, EDWARD T. (2000). 'The future of personnel economics'. *Economic Journal*, 110: F611–39.

LICHTENSTEIN, NELSON (2000). *The State of the Unions*. Princeton: Princeton University Press.

MILLER, PAUL, and MULVEY, CHARLES (1992). 'Trade unions, collective voice and fringe benefits'. *Economic Record*, 68/201 (June): 125–41.

MISHEL, LAWRENCE, BERNSTEIN, JARED, SCHMITT, and JON (2000). *The State of Working America*. Ithaca, N.Y.: Cornell University Press.

MORGAN STANLEY (2002). 'Look for the union label... and run the other way'. *Investment Perspectives*, 14 Nov. Written by analyst Steve Galbraith.

MUNNELL, ALICIA (2003). 'The declining role of social security'. An Issue in Brief for Retirement Research at Boston College, N. 6 (Feb.).

OSTERMAN, PAUL (1999). *Securing Prosperity*. Princeton: Princeton University Press.

PEAGLE, NIGEL (2004). 'European pension reform and private pensions: an analysis of the EU's six largest countries'. Association of British Insurers, May. Tables 4 and 6.

SASS, STEVEN (1997). *The Promise of Private Pensions*. Cambridge, Mass.: Harvard University Press.

SHILLER, ROBERT J. (2000). *Irrational Exuberance*. Princeton: Princeton University Press.

SILVERS, DAMON, PATTERSON, WILLIAM, and MASON, J. W. (2001). 'Challenging Wall Street's conventional wisdom: defining a worker-owner view of value?', in Archon Fung, Tessa Hebb, and Joel Rogers (eds.), *Working Capital: The Power of Labor's Pensions*. Ithaca, N.Y.: Cornell University Press, 203–23.

SLOANE, ARTHUR (1991). *Hoffa*. Cambridge, Mass.: MIT Press

SOLOMON, JOEL (2003). *Retirement in the Balance: The Crucial Role of Defined Benefit Pension Plans in Achieving Retirement Security in the United States*. Washington, D.C.: Center for Working Capital, AFL-CIO, May.

STEVENS, BETH (1986). *Complementing the Welfare State: The Development of Private Pensions, Health Insurance and Other Employee Benefits in the United States*. Geneva: International Labour Office.

WOOTEN, JAMES A. (2001). 'The most glorious story of failure in the business: the Studebaker-Packard Corporation and the origins of ERISA'. *Buffalo Law Review State University of New York—Law School*, 49: 683.

CHAPTER 20

# CORPORATE FINANCE AND CAPITAL MARKETS

## J. MICHAEL ORSZAG AND NEHA SAND

Pension fund assets in the OECD in 2001 represented roughly 9 trillion euros and on average about 25 percent of GDP and about 33 percent of market capitalization (Salou 2004, 2005).[1] Outside the OECD, private pension assets tend to be relatively small.[2] Inside the OECD, the countries with the largest pension assets are also those with strong occupational pensions: the United States, Japan, the Netherlands, Switzerland, Canada, Denmark, and Portugal.

Regardless of whether pensions are defined benefit or defined contribution, pension assets are an important segment of financial markets. But the implications for corporate finance are dramatically different if the pension benefit structure is defined benefit or defined contribution. If pensions are defined contribution, the employer provides no explicit or implicit guarantee and therefore its pension arrangements do not contribute to its debt. Even in systems with insured defined contribution arrangements such as are predominant in Denmark, the direct guarantee obligation lies with insurance companies and not with employers. Low levels of funding, however, may require increased employer contributions, thereby creating, to an extent, an implicit liability. Where pensions are defined benefit, the pension liability is a direct part of the capital structure of the sponsoring employer.

This chapter provides a broad overview of the corporate finance of pensions, starting with the theoretical contributions of Sharpe (1976) and others. After reviewing the theory, the chapter summarizes the empirical evidence, and then discusses unresolved issues in the literature.

# 1 AN OVERVIEW OF FUNDING

Among the top 500 OECD companies by market capitalization,[3] 371 reported defined benefit liabilities on their 2003–4 accounts.[4] In aggregate, these liabilities amounted to 1.8 trillion euros, with aggregate underfunding at 392 billion euros.[5] Table 20.1 reports summary liabilities and deficits by country for the data set.[6]

According to Table 20.1, pension liabilities amount to roughly 21 percent of market capitalization on average for US firms, 29 percent for Japanese firms, and 35 percent for the firms in the UK. But a few companies report pension liabilities significantly more than market capitalization. Also, as companies with high levels of

Table 20.1 Pension liabilities and deficits of the world's 500 largest companies in 2004

| Country | Number of companies | Pension liabilities (billion euros) | Pension deficit (billion euros) | Pension liabilities to market capitalization (average) (%) | Pension deficits to (total debt + pension deficits) (%) |
|---|---|---|---|---|---|
| USA | 167 | 727 | 72 | 20.5 | 7.5 |
| Japan | 58 | 294 | 126 | 29.0 | 26.7 |
| United Kingdom | 42 | 360 | 59 | 35.2 | 15.5 |
| Germany | 18 | 166 | 79 | 40.5 | 21.7 |
| Canada | 17 | 44 | 4 | 18.3 | 6.6 |
| France | 17 | 52 | 19 | 15.0 | 15.8 |
| Switzerland | 11 | 65 | 8 | 13.9 | 9.3 |
| Hong Kong | 3 | 1.7 | 0.2 | 3.4 | 0.0 |
| Other | 38 | 117 | 24 | | |

Note: Statistics cover only firms with positive pension liabilities reported on their balance sheets.

pension liabilities may have a lower market capitalization, it is not surprising to have found ratios of pension liability of over 10 in some cases.

As pension deficits can be viewed as debt to the employer, the far right column in Table 20.1 captures the average ratio of pension deficits to total pension and non-pension debt. This ratio averages 7 percent in the United States, 16 percent in the UK and 27 percent in Japan, but this masks considerable variation across companies. Five of the 42 UK companies have over a third of their financing effectively from pension debt. And in Japan, 12 of the 58 companies in the sample achieve over half their financing from pension debt. If indeed pension deficits are viewed as corporate debt, the impact on leverage seems to be greatest for Japan (roughly 27 percent) as compared to the UK and the United States.

The figures in Table 20.1 are of course not without caveats. They depend on accounting standards which differed by country at the time of analysis, though as noted in Chapter 26 (Whittington), accounting standards are indeed coming together. Even the most rigorous accounting standards probably still understate to a degree the true termination liability to employers in most geographies. And the imperfect nature of the accounting standards means that even within a given country, cross-company comparisons need to be examined carefully.

Despite these caveats, it is clear that pensions are an important part of corporate finance. But despite the importance of pensions for corporate finance, the economics and finance literature in the area is both dated and largely based on US evidence. This is a shame because corporate pensions raise important corporate finance and empirical issues, and improved accounting and financial data are available to shed light on these questions.

# 2 Theories of Corporate Finance and Pensions

William Sharpe's (1976) is one of the first attempts in the literature to shed light on the corporate finance of pension provision. Using the basic principles and assumptions of the Modigliani–Miller (1958) theorem, Sharpe considers a model in which firms can invest their autonomous pension fund in either bonds or equity. The firm is operating in a US institutional framework in which the Pension Benefit Guaranty Corporation (PBGC) guarantees a large fraction of pensions in the case of bankruptcy. The PBGC guarantee means pension liabilities resemble a put option. If firms invest more in equity, the value of their pension liabilities decreases (because the embedded volatility in the option has increased and the option value increases as volatility rises). However, because workers realize this, they bid up their wages to compensate for the decline in the value of their pension-related compensation, and the value of the firm remains unchanged, which is the Modigliani–Miller proposition.

Exley *et al.* (1997) apply many of Sharpe's ideas to an actuarial context, particularly in the UK. At the time of the study, the UK had no equivalent to the PBGC and application of Modigliani–Miller principles hence led to the broad conclusion that the value of the firm was invariant to the asset allocation of the pension fund.

Some aspects of the application of the Modigliani–Miller theorem to pensions can be challenged on a number of grounds. First, Sharpe (1976) assumes all members of a pension scheme can bargain over their wages, whereas in practice, deferred members and pensioners, who are not earning wages, do not have bargaining power. This argument seems more significant in light of the fact that in the UK, for instance, about two-thirds of all liabilities relate to deferred members and pensioners. Where options are embedded and members lack bargaining power, more risky investment does reduce the level of liabilities and increase the value of the firm, because wage rates will not rise to compensate for the reduction in liabilities. Second, the structure of pension benefits often embeds very complex option structures which are not easily matched by bond investments. In particular, money put into pension funds is often difficult to take out in the case of surpluses, because of either reversion taxes or legal ambiguities.

In addition, pension funds operate in a relatively long-term setting in which hedging is difficult if not impossible. Mortality risk is a common feature faced by many pension funds, particularly in environments such as the UK and the Netherlands, where benefits are indexed to keep pace with prices or wages. Some mortality risk can be hedged through reinsurance contracts and a limited quantity of mortality-backed securities, but the ability to hedge mortality-based liabilities remains limited.

Another important point raised in Exley *et al.* (1997) is the appropriate way in which to discount corporate pension liabilities. A good summary of the literature appears in Sutcliffe (2005). The economic cost of pension liabilities is the buy-out cost of pension liabilities on the market. Unfortunately, the market for pension liabilities suffers from lack of capacity because of risks involved and also from lack of transparency about the underlying pension liabilities because it is often unclear who will be paid first in the event of bankruptcy or who gains from emergent surpluses. As a result, bond interest rates are treated as a reasonable proxy. This issue is often confused with the process of calculation of 'actuarial valuations' in which the actuary seeks to compute the contribution rate necessary on average to fund the pension plan. These actuarial valuations are essentially a funding exercise. As such, they can be done in two equivalent ways. The first is by computing liabilities on a bond basis and adjusting contribution rates downwards, based on risk taken in investment strategy. The second is by computing liabilities based on discount rates tied to actual investment strategy and analyzing how much risk may be involved in future funding positions and contribution rates. The second is viewed by most actuaries as easier to communicate.

Whichever approach is appropriate, basic financial economics says little about how to fund a pension plan—in a Modigliani–Miller world the level of funding is just as irrelevant to the value of the firm as the asset allocation of the pension plan. One market imperfection that leads to more definitive conclusions is the introduction of tax effects. Black (1980) shows that if pension savings are tax-advantaged, tax arbitrage is possible if one borrows on the market at a bond rate and invests in corresponding bonds in the pension plan on a tax-free basis. The differential taxation of bonds and equity is an important consideration (Tepper 1981; Tepper and Affleck 1974); if equity is taxed less than bonds, pensions serve as more of a tax shield and therefore bond investment adds value.

Harrison and Sharpe (1983) develop a theoretical analysis that says the optimal asset allocation is either entirely in bonds (because of tax effects) or entirely in equity (because of the effects of guarantee funds such as the PBGC). But the predictions of this analysis are somewhat unsatisfactory because in practice corporate pension funds rarely invest in such extreme portfolios. Part of the reason that corporate pension plans invest in less safe instruments such as equity may have to do with the risk-return trade-off that individuals face. Pension funds are in a sense delegated decision-makers for individuals, and individuals may prefer higher expected returns to more secure pensions. Individuals may also undervalue pensions as part of their compensation package, and this may explain why individuals may prefer more cash (and lower contributions on average) to more secure pension arrangements (and higher average costs). Bicksler and Chen (1985) explore limitations on the marginal value of the tax shield at different levels of funding. At high levels of funding, the tax shield may be mitigated because of limits on tax relief on funding pensions or because of the progressive nature of the tax system. At low levels of funding, government intervention and pressure from labor and financial markets may lower the overall marginal benefits of reducing funding further. These imperfections mean that the optimal funding strategy is not the corner solution of Harrison and Sharpe (1983) but a mixed equity-bond portfolio.

Sundaresan and Zapatero (1997) look at optimal asset allocation of pension plans in the context of issues such as early retirement. Using a model which integrates retirement decisions with asset allocation, they find that pension funds should invest in a mixed portfolio. With their choice of utility functions, mandatory retirement makes the asset allocation riskier, perhaps because workers need to be induced to retire when economic conditions are bad. Black (1989) discusses bond-based asset allocations for a floor of accumulated obligations and more flexibility above that level.

Cooper and Ross (2002) look at optimal funding when pensions serve as collateral to back the promise made by firms. They find that with perfect capital markets, firms should fully fund pensions. In their analysis, funding is related to whether an employer has sufficient access to capital markets to finance investments and also to what return can be earned on pension investments. When pensions are underfunded, they predict upward-sloping wage profiles. Upward-sloping wage curves have a number of implications, including the potential for forced early retirements as workers become too expensive at older ages. A similar model in Cooper and Ross (2003: 281) is used to show that guarantee funds, which are presumably in place to protect workers, may not enhance welfare because they induce more risk-taking and less funding of pensions.

Ippolito (1985a, 1985b) argues that pensions are underfunded to moderate wage demands, particularly from unions. Through underfunding, workers essentially own some of the debt of the firm and share part of the risk of the firm performing poorly. A risk-sharing argument for underfunding is also made in Arnott and Gersovitz (1980).

McMillan (1986) assesses how the level of funding affects market risk premia in an environment where pension risks cannot be hedged. An increase in benefits increases the risk of the firm, whereas an increase in funding decreases it. A fully funded increase in benefits has no effect on the risk premium. The analysis however makes some key assumptions such as investment of pension portfolios in risk-free securities.

Though quite a bit has been written on the theoretical aspects of pension financing, much more needs to be done. In particular, a theory of funding of public pensions developed by D'Arcy *et al.* (1999) and Merton (1983), which examines trade-offs between growth rates and financial market returns, may well be applicable to corporate pensions. That is, in more mature industries with lower growth, pensions may need to be closer to fully funded.

# 3 EMPIRICAL EVIDENCE

Much of the empirical evidence on pension corporate finance relies on accounting data. While these data are improving dramatically, they still remain flawed by incomplete disclosure of assumptions such as mortality, potential biases in assumptions, and lack of disclosure of liabilities by subclasses of members or by national jurisdiction. Until recently, equity allocation of pension funds was not included in the United States FAS accounting disclosures, though it has been part of FRS17 in the UK for accounting years after June 2001. Other key sources for research data besides accounting disclosures have been US Form 5500 disclosures and US Pension Benefit Guaranty Corporation records. Both have been made available only with significant time lags and are complex data sets for researchers to work with.

## 3.1 Assumptions and Accounting

Calculations of pension liabilities are notoriously sensitive to assumptions because pensions are long-dated instruments. Hence, analysis of the assumptions used in financial reports is important for understanding the nature of companies' pension exposure. Thies and Sturrock (1988) examine the assumptions used by a sample of defined benefit sponsors in 1980–3 and find that those with weak financial circumstances choose assumptions which place too low a value on their pension liabilities. This assumption bias is also found in Feldstein and Morck (1983) and Bodie (1985). If assumptions used to calculate liabilities depend on the financial status of the company, then the data really need to be corrected before analysis of corporate finance issues to avoid bias.

These early studies predate the enactment of FAS87 in the United States, which standardized assumptions, and subsequent assumptions seem much less related to the financial circumstances of companies. This is similar to the UK, where very little relationship has been found between the market circumstances of companies and the assumptions used or their changes over time. Chen and D'Arcy (1986) look at the response of the market in the United States in 1980 on mandating the disclosure of interest rate assumptions. The paper finds that low interest-rate assumption firms did outperform, suggesting that the new information available to the market was taken into account by investors and that the additional disclosure added value.

In the United States, plan sponsors are permitted to smooth liabilities and to discount at rates higher than bond yields. It has been argued that the market does not see through this accounting veil. Coronado and Sharpe (2003) look empirically at the effect of accounting on stock market valuations using data from the late 1990s. Their model separates out core earnings from pension earnings and includes a transparent non-smoothed net asset value. They find that the market weights accounting pension earnings even more than core earnings and does not seem to pay sufficient attention to the higher quality non-smoothed information available in footnote disclosures. The results hence suggest that investors do not see through accounting veils.

The specific details used in the above study are tricky to replicate for the UK, yet anecdotal evidence suggests that the UK market seems to be acting somewhat differently than the US. The UK in 2001 introduced footnote disclosure for pension liabilities on a particularly transparent basis, yet until 2004 most companies continued to report on the legacy SSAP 24 basis. Press and analyst attention in the UK focused exclusively on the transparent FRS 17 numbers, whereas the traditional SSAP 24 numbers were virtually ignored, even though these numbers are used to calculate earnings.

## 3.2 Effect of Pension Liabilities and Pension Risk on Enterprise Value

Quite a bit of evidence suggests that pension liabilities and deficits do affect the way markets value companies. Feldstein and Mørck (1983) estimate a regression in which the ratio of value of the firm to the equity value of its physical assets is related to the earnings–asset ratio, growth, R & D expenditure relative to assets, beta, the debt-asset ratio and unfunded pensions relative to assets. They work with data from a cross-section of 132 manufacturing firms in 1979 and conclude that the market treats pension deficits as debt, even though the debt coefficients do not seem to work very well. Similar conclusions that the market takes into account unfunded pension liabilities were also obtained in Feldstein and Seligman (1981), Bodie and Papke (1992), and Bulow et al. (1987). This last study used data from several cross-sections and illustrates that the effects are not due to biases from interest rate assumptions. Carroll and Neihaus (1998) find that debt ratings are significantly affected by unfunded pension liabilities.

Li et al. (2005) use the Form 5500 tax filings of US pension funds from 1993 to 1998 and look in a panel regression at how a firm's betas (which measure the sensitivity of a particular security in relation to the market index's return) are affected by pension variables. They find that the betas of the firm respond at least as strongly to pension risk as suggested by financial theory.

One of the issues, however, is that while markets empirically seem to respond significantly to pension deficits, the addition of a pension liability variable to regressions makes debt effects insignificant in some cases. More generally, it is the case that pension liability to market capitalization matters in regression results whereas the simple corporate finance theory suggests it should not matter.

These results may be due to the fact that pension liabilities do have a real effect, because it is difficult for the pension funds to hedge large liabilities, even if they are well funded. However, it may also be due to analysts and institutional investors paying attention to headline figures such as ratios of pension liabilities to market capitalization rather than regarding pensions purely as a debt of the employer. In a panel setting, the market capitalization effect does not appear as strong but the deficit effect is also not so strong. Such an outcome suggests that firm-specific effects could be behind many of the observed cross-sectional results. Hence, these studies do not provide conclusive evidence for corporate finance theories.

Another potential analytical approach is the use of volatility measures (either implied or historical) to capture the effect of pensions on market value as high volatility implies a high premium set by the market. Implied volatility figures provide a clear indication of how risky the company is perceived to be on a prospective basis.

Figure 20.1, for instance, displays data for the Nikkei 500 on pension funding versus historical volatility of returns.[7] The evidence does not indicate that underfunded pension plans are associated with more volatile returns. Because volatile returns are connected with a market premium, the market does not appear to penalize underfunded pension plans. Indeed, in Japan the funding level for AA or above rated companies was slightly lower than BBB rated companies.

The impact of regulatory change on the value of firms who are more exposed differentially to pensions is also an interesting area for explanation. Munnell and Soto (2004) find that over the 20-year period 1982–2001, changes in the stock

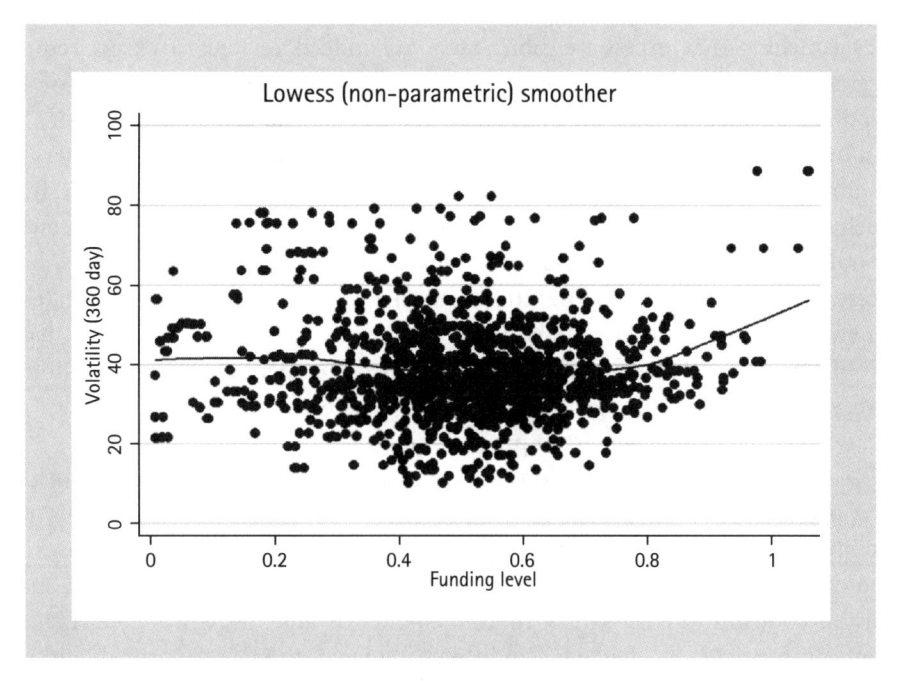

**Fig. 20.1** Relationship between funding level and volatility for the Nikkei 500 in Japan (accounting years June 2002–June 2003)

*Note*: Bandwidth = 0.8.

market and legislative changes reduced contributions, which would have been 50 percent more in the absence of these changes boosting corporate profits by 5 percent.

## 3.3 Asset Reversions

If assets and liabilities of pension funds are regarded as part of the corporate balance sheet, then asset reversions of pension money back to the firm should not affect shareholder value. Alderson and Chen (1986) look at excess returns prior to reversions and afterwards for 58 US firms for 1980–4. They find significant effects of asset reversions, suggesting that markets consider pension funds to be somewhat separate from companies rather than an integral part of their corporate finance.

Mittelstaedt and Regier (1990) take issue with these results, attributing them to reversion dates being imprecise, or specific confounding circumstances such as mergers or acquisitions, and reversions associated with policy changes. They find little impact on excess returns, though some of this may be due to the use of later data after the clarification of some legal issues.

Bowers and Moore (1995) focus exclusively on acquisitions from 1979–88 and examine the extent to which firms with overfunded pensions earn excess returns. They conclude that excess pension assets are indeed related to excess returns, suggesting that markets may value pension assets as an integral part of the corporate balance sheet. However, this may not be the case. For example, the firm might violate an implicit labor contract and hence create shareholder wealth. Assuming there are excess shareholder returns—and the evidence is far from conclusive—this would mean that the market views the pension fund as somewhat separate from the corporation as otherwise a full takeover would not have been necessary to release value. The literature on reversions in the United States is somewhat inconclusive but the issue of whether the pension fund is an integral part of corporate finance remains a critical one. The evidence from other countries is very limited, even though in some cases such as in the UK, companies did occasionally recover money from pension funds.

Because the analysis of reversions has produced inconclusive results, it is helpful to consider other approaches to assessing how integrated pension assets and liabilities really are on the corporate balance sheet. Rauh (forthcoming) uses US 5500 data to examine what happens to investment with firms who need to make pension contributions to satisfy funding standards and finds that investment is significantly negatively affected. This interesting separate evidence provides limited support for the idea that pensions are an important part of a company's balance sheet. Analysis of contribution holidays and the effects on corporate finance (e.g. investment) may also help shed further light on this question.

## 3.4 Equity Allocation of the Pension Fund

As noted in Section 2, the theoretical basis for equity allocation of pension funds has proven illusive. Still it remains surprising that the pension funds, which are large relative to their market capitalization or who have large deficits relative to their market capitalization, do not tend to be less invested in equity than other funds. For example, in accounting years between June 2002 and June 2003 in the UK, five of the FTSE 100 had ratios of pension liabilities to market capitalization of over two and their average portfolio share in equity was over 50 percent. Where pension liabilities or deficits are large relative to market capitalization and the pension fund is invested largely in risky securities, a good portion of the total risk of the company may come from its pension fund, something outside the core business of most firms and often not fully integrated into risk management systems.

To illustrate these points, Figure 20.2 displays the equity allocation of pension funds in the FTSE 350 in UK for accounting years June 2003–June 2004 against the ratio of pension liabilities to market capitalization. Figure 20.3 shows the relationship over the same time period for pension deficits to market capitalization. Contrary to what one may expect given the scale of risks involved, both the figures

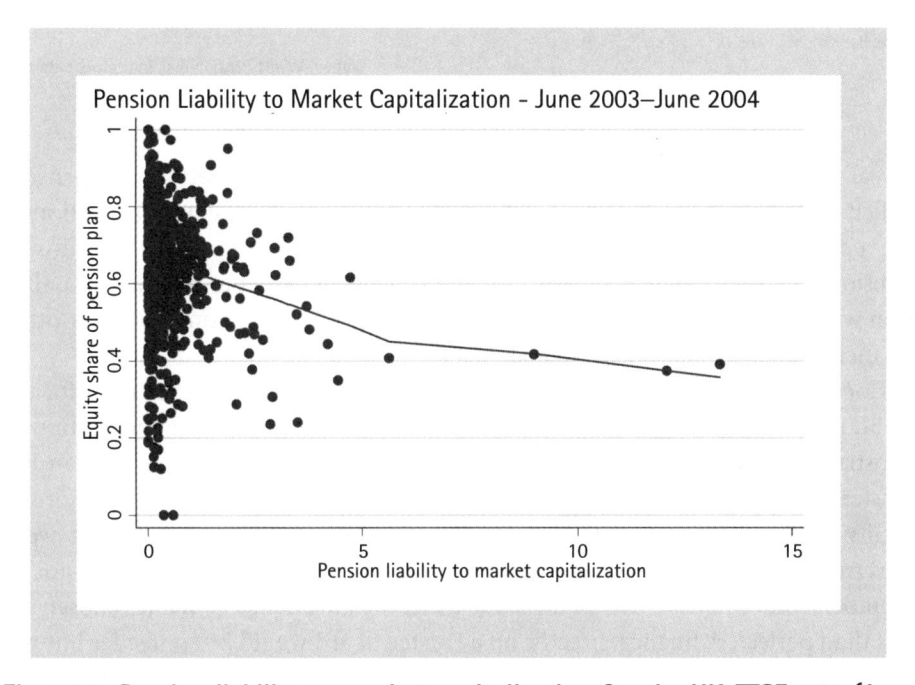

**Fig. 20.2** Pension liability to market capitalization for the UK FTSE 350 (June 2003–June 2004)

*Note*: Bandwidth = 0.8.

*Source*: Watson Wyatt Pension Risk Indicators database.

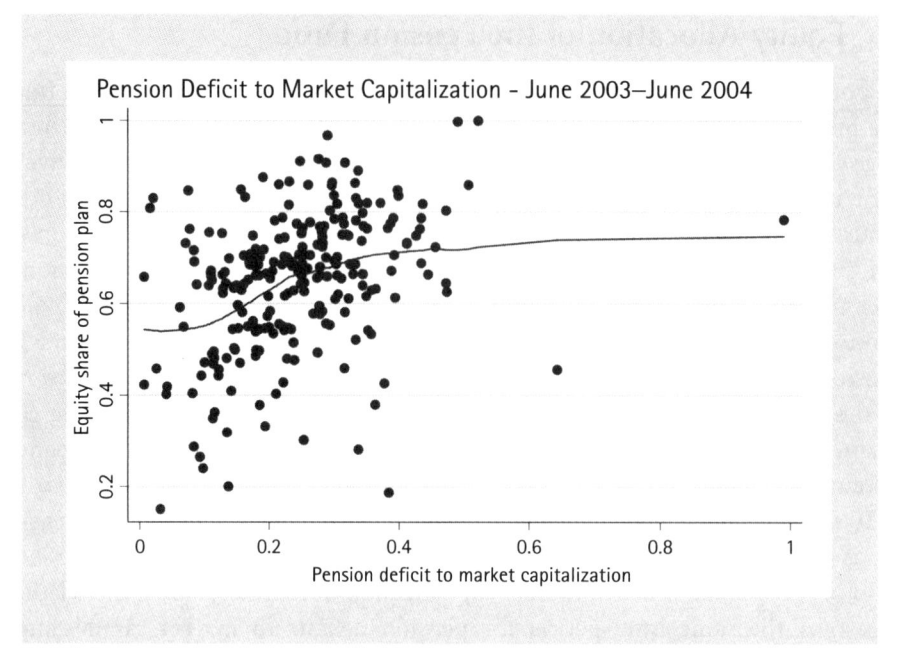

**Fig. 20.3 Pension deficit to market capitalization for the UK FTSE 350 (June 2003–June 2004)**
*Note:* Bandwidth = 0.8.
*Source:* Watson Wyatt Pension Risk Indicators database.

reveal that high ratios of pension liability to market capitalization and pension deficit to market capitalization can be associated with a high equity allocation in the pension funds. The economic relationship between the financial ratios of pension liability to market capitalization and pension deficit to market capitalization with equity allocation of pension funds is weak and the same holds for other financial variables and for panel analysis.

Cocco and Volpin (2005) find similar results using UK pension accounts for the FTSE 100 in calendar year 2003. However, they also use an industry publication to construct governance variables based on the degree of insider involvement on UK trustee boards. They find that firms with insider trustees tend to invest more in equity and contribute less to the pension plan. This result suggests that weak governance leads to risk-taking by occupational pension plans which is not in members' best interests. Yet, at the same time, the governance variables chosen are less than perfect. A finance director on a trustee board would be an insider but not someone who works in the finance department and reports to the finance director. And because the data are only from a cross-section, it is difficult to infer causality. A low level of funding and large deficits may induce attention and concerns from insiders rather than vice versa.

## 4 CONCLUSION

Because a significant portion of corporate financing is implicitly handled through pension vehicles, pensions are quite an important part of corporate finance and corporate financial policy. Yet many aspects of the interaction between pensions and corporate finance are imperfectly understood at both the theoretical and empirical levels.

An early literature did develop many of the foundations of a theory of corporate finance for pensions built on the ideas of Modigliani–Miller. However, particularly in countries such as the United Kingdom and the Netherlands, where there is clearest legal separation between the plan sponsor and the management of the plan, the application of the basic corporate finance theory which abstracts away these governance and agency issues is quite problematic. If the plan sponsor does not have absolute control over the governance of the plan, the plan's independence may create problems for the sponsor in implementing an optimal financial strategy. For example, consider a financial institution whose pension trust arrangements give only limited say to the bank in investment matters and the pension fund invests largely in equity. The financial institution may either be limited in the scope of other risks it can reasonably take or be faced with the situation in which it wishes to reverse or offset the risks taken in the pension plan but is unable to do so.

The most fundamental questions in pension finance are how much to fund pensions and how to invest. As yet, modern finance theory does not provide an answer to these questions. One branch of the literature ties funding to labor market considerations and financial market imperfections but this needs to incorporate more fully the structure of pension benefits and designs. Another branch suggests why pension assets should be invested in equities or bonds but this literature does not provide sufficient analysis of the optimal asset allocation in the case where access to long-term bonds or other risk reduction instruments is limited. Researchers also need to address more fully the background risk from sources such as mortality which pension funds are not able to hedge.

The introduction of new accounting standards such as IAS 19 and FRS 17 is at the same time an important opportunity for empirical researchers both to extend and confirm earlier results from the US literature. It also offers the opportunity to look in detail at how corporate finance factors operate in different market structures such as Japan and Germany.

Results in the literature indicate that markets take into account pension deficits in valuing companies. Pensions do matter quite a bit, and this is not surprising given their importance. However, some evidence suggests that these markets operate imperfectly. Asset allocation may be dependent on governance, and investors may look at pension factors other than purely the scale of pension debt. While not surprising to practitioners and experts in the area, it remains to be seen whether pensions are simply no different from any other form of corporate finance or whether pension liabilities and pension governance have some unique characteristics. Both theory and empirical research have exciting challenges ahead in this area.

# NOTES

1. These estimates exclude Japan whose institutionally invested private pension assets at the end of 2004 were US$3.1 billion.
2. Although the coverage of non-OECD countries in Salou (2005: 191–4) is limited, the pension assets in those countries covered in aggregate amount to only about 10 percent of those of the OECD.
3. Using the FT Global 500 as of 25 March 2004.
4. Pension disclosures for reporting year ends from 30 June 2003 to 30 June 2004. Most reporting dates in the sample are 31 December 2004. Data was hand-collected and checked by Watson Wyatt research.
5. Pension liability figures exclude post-retirement and medical obligations.
6. Because the table reports those liabilities only for the top 500 companies in the world, these figures will clearly differ from aggregate pension liabilities in the countries listed.
7. Bloomberg data.

# REFERENCES

ALDERSON, M., and CHEN, K. C. (1986). 'Excess asset reversions and shareholder wealth'. *The Journal of Finance*, 41/1: 225–41.

ARNOTT, R., and GERSOVITZ, M. (1980). 'Corporate financial structure and the funding of private pension plans'. *Journal of Public Economics*, 13: 231–47.

BICKSLER, J., and CHEN, A. (1985). 'The integration of insurance and taxes in corporate pension strategy'. *Journal of Finance*, 40/3: 943–55.

BLACK, F. (1980). 'The tax consequences of long run pension policy'. *Financial Analysts Journal*, 36/1: 3–10.

—— (1989). 'Should you use stocks to hedge your pension liability?' *Financial Analysts Journal*, 45/1: 10–12.

BODIE, Z. (1985). 'Corporate pension policy: an empirical investigation'. *Financial Analysts Journal*, 41/5: 10–16.

—— and PAPKE, L. E. (1992). 'Pension fund finance', in Z. Bodie and A. Munnell, *Pensions and the Economy*. Philadelphia: University of Pennsylvania Press.

BOWERS, H., and MOORE, N. (1995). 'Market valuation of excess pension assets: evidence from the market for corproate control'. *Journal of Risk and Insurance*, 62/2: 214–29.

BULOW, J., MØRCK, R., and SUMMERS, L. (1987). 'How does the market value unfunded pension liabilities?', in Z. Bodie, J. Shoven and D. Wise, *Issues in Pension Economics*. Chicago: University of Chicago Press, 81–103.

CARROLL, T., and NEIHAUS, G. (1998). 'Pension plan funding and corporate debt ratings'. *Journal of Risk and Insurance*, 65/3: 427–43.

CHEN, K. C., and D'ARCY, S. P. (1986). 'Market sensitivity to interest rate assumptions in corporate pension plans'. *Journal of Risk and Insurance*, 53/2: 209–25.

COCCO, J., and VOLPIN, P. (2005). 'Corporate governance of defined benefit pension plans in the United Kingdom'. London Business School.

COOPER, R. W., and ROSS, T. (2002). 'Pensions: theories of underfunding'. *Labour Economics*, 8: 667–89.

—— —— (2003). 'Protecting underfunded pensions: the role of guarantee funds'. *Journal of Pension Economics and Finance*, 2: 247–72.

CORONADO, J. L., and SHARPE, S. (2003). 'Did pension plan accounting contribute to a stock market bubble?' *Brookings Papers on Economic Activity*, 1.

D'ARCY, S. P., JAMES, D., and OH, P. (1999). 'Optimal funding of state employee pension systems'. *Journal of Risk and Insurance*, 66/3: 345–80.

EXLEY, J., MEHTA, S., and SMITH, A. (1997). 'The financial theory of defined benefit pension schemes'. *British Actuarial Journal*, 3/4: 835–966.

FELDSTEIN, M., and MØRCK, R. (1983). 'Pension funding decisions, interest rate assumptions and share prices,' in Z. Bodie and J. Shoven, *Financial Aspects of the United States Pension System*. Chicago: University of Chicago Press.

—— and SELIGMAN, S. (1981). 'Pension funding, share prices and national saving'. *Journal of Finance*, 36: 801–24.

HARRISON, J. M., and SHARPE, W. (1983). 'Optimal funding and asset allocation rules for defined benefit pension plans,' in Z. Bodie and J. Shoven, *Financial Aspects of the United States Pension System*. Chicago: University of Chicago Press.

IPPOLITO, RICHARD (1985a). 'Economic function of underfunded pension plans'. *Journal of Law and Economics*, 28: 611–51.

—— (1985b). 'Labour contract and true economic pension liabilities'. *American Economic Review*, 75: 1031–43.

LI, J., MERTON, R., and BODIE, Z. (2005). 'Do a firm's equity returns reflect the risk of its pension plan?' Harvard Business School.

MCMILLAN, H. (1986). 'Nonassignable pensions and the price of risk'. *Journal of Money, Credit and Banking*, 18/1: 60–75.

MERTON, R. (1983). 'On the role of social security as a means for efficient risk sharing in an economy where human capital is not tradeable', in Z. Bodie and J. Shoven, *Financial Aspects of the United States Pension System*. University of Chicago Press.

MITTELSTAEDT, F., and REGIER, P. (1990). 'Further evidence on excess asset reversions and shareholder wealth'. *Journal of Risk and Insurance*, 57/3: 471–86.

MODIGLIANI, FRANCO, and MILLER, MERTON H. (1958). 'The cost of capital, corporation finance and the theory of investment'. *American Economic Review*, 48: 261–97.

MUNNELL, A., and SOTO, M. (2004). 'The outlook for pension contributions and profits in the United States'. *Journal of Pension Economics and Finance*, 3/1: 77–97.

RAUH, J. (Forthcoming). 'Investment and financing constraints: evidence from the funding of corporate pension plans'. *Journal of Finance*.

SALOU, JEAN-MARC. (2004). 'Global pension statistics project: measuring the size of private pensions with an international perspective'. *OECD Financial Market Trends*, 87: 229–39.

—— (2005). 'Global pension statistics project: data update'. *OECD Financial Market Trends*, 88: 191–4.

SHARPE, W. (1976). 'Corporate pension funding policy'. *Journal of Financial Economics*, 3/2: 183–93.

SUNDARESAN, S., and ZAPATERO, F. (1997). 'Valuation, optimal asset allocation and retirement incentives of pension plans'. *Review of Financial Studies*, 10/3: 631–60.

SUTCLIFFE, C. (2005). 'The cult of the equity for pension funds: should it get the boot?' *Journal of Pension Economics and Finance*, 4/1.

TEPPER, I. (1981). 'Taxation and corporate pension policy'. *Journal of Finance*, 36/1: 1–14.

—— and AFFLECT, A. (1974). 'Pension plan liabilities and corporate financial strategies'. *Journal of Finance*, 29/5: 1549–64.

THIES, C. F., and STURROCK, T. (1988). 'The pension-augmented balance sheet'. *Journal of Risk and Insurance*, 55/3: 467–80.

# PENSION PLAN INVESTMENTS

# CHAPTER 21

# ASSET LIABILITY MANAGEMENT

## ROB BAUER, ROY HOEVENAARS, AND TOM STEENKAMP

## 1 INTRODUCTION

In the past few years, falling stock returns and low interest rates resulted in a deterioration of the financial position of many pension funds. Regulatory bodies across the world responded by evaluating and adapting the existing monitoring frameworks. This resulted in new and updated regulations in a large number of countries. A well-known example is the recent shift toward fair valuation of both assets and liabilities. Market valuation of assets is a topic that has been discussed for quite some time now, but the valuation of pension contracts including all embedded options is a major challenge for pension fund policy-makers. On top of that, pension fund beneficiaries are increasingly demanding more transparency with regard to the exact nature of their pension arrangement, or their *pension deal*.

This chapter will shed some light on the management of the current and future financial health of a defined benefit public pension fund.[1] Most funds conduct a so-called Asset Liability Management (ALM) study which investigates the impact of decisions with regard to investment, contribution, and indexation policy on the various stakeholders of the fund (employees, employers, retired and future generations). Prominent examples of research on asset liability management for pension funds are Boender (1995), Boender *et al.* (1998), Dert (1995, 1998), Mulvey (1994, 1996), Mulvey *et al.* (2000), Ziemba and Mulvey (1998), and Ziemba (2003).

Although this chapter will focus on ALM for pension funds, it should be noted that ALM can be equally important to other organizations and institutional investors. For instance, university endowments have to consider their long-run financial goals when managing their assets. ALM is also a challenging task for the banking and insurance industries, which have to deal with complex embedded options in their liability structure. Well-known examples of ALM studies in an insurance context are Carino *et al.* (1994), Carino and Ziemba (1998) and Consiglio *et al.* (2000). Furthermore, individuals are more involved in financial planning to evaluate their long-term financial asset position, financial goals, and liabilities as retirement, mortgages, and education.

Throughout this chapter we will show that pension fund board members, representing the stakeholders of the fund, face several dilemmas when deciding on investment, contribution, and indexation policy. In particular, we will focus on the appropriate discount rate for the fair valuation of pension liabilities and the choice of the investment horizon. Samuelson (1969) and Merton (1969, 1971) showed that optimal portfolio decisions are horizon dependent under time-varying investment opportunities. As a consequence, the optimal portfolio choice of long-term investors would differ from that of short-term investors. Campbell and Viceira (2005) describe how changes in investment opportunities can alter the risk-return trade-off of bonds, stocks, and cash. Recently, Hoevenaars *et al.* (2005) have explicitly shown that horizon effects in volatilities and correlations are also relevant for asset liability investors. Furthermore, their findings suggest that there are horizon effects in inflation and real interest rate hedge properties as well. Many other studies explore the implications of the changing investment opportunity set for long-term investors. We refer to Brennan *et al.* (1997), Barberis (2000), Campbell *et al.* (2003), Wachter (2002), Brandt and Santa-Clara (2004), Brennan and Xia (2004), and especially Campbell and Viceira (2002).

Recently, several papers have proposed generational accounting to make an ALM study even more transparent, as it verifies whether all generations are treated fairly in a particular pension deal or in the case of an intermediate policy change. Good examples of this strand of the literature are Ponds (2003), Teulings and De Vries (2004), and Cui *et al.* (2004). In the empirical section we will show how certain policy decisions of the board might influence the accounts of several generations.

The remainder of this chapter is structured as follows. Section 2 describes the basic elements of an ALM process and provides a brief literature overview on the various components of an ALM study. In Section 3, we will present a stylized example in which we evaluate four alternative pension deals. The output presented will be discussed from the perspective of various stakeholders of the fund. Subsequently, Section 4 will address the dilemmas pension board members face in evaluating alternative pension deals. In Section 5, we focus on a particular pension deal and introduce the concept of generational accounting. Finally, Section 6 concludes.

## 2 MANAGING THE FUTURE BALANCE SHEET

By conducting an ALM study, policy-makers manage and model the future financial position of the pension fund. Generally, the current balance sheet is the starting point of the analysis. Figure 21.1 displays a balance sheet in its most basic form. Assets (A) on the left-hand side refer to the investment portfolio, Surplus (S) on the right-hand side to pension (and possibly other) obligations, and Liabilities (L) indicates the financial health of a fund. Note that the funding (or coverage) ratio of a pension fund is equal to $1 + (S/L)$. Usually, this balance sheet is analyzed on a so-called liquidation basis, which implies that only current liabilities and assets are taken into account.[2] With the current balance sheet as a reference point, an ALM study gives insight into the future development of assets, pension liabilities, and—as a result—the surplus and the funding ratio (see also Leibowitz et al. (1994), who approach asset liability management from a funding ratio return perspective). Future values of the surplus are influenced by a great number of exogenous variables and policy decisions.

Figure 21.2 indicates that the future financial position is dependent on certain key (exogenous) economic variables like interest rates and inflation, and the content of three (endogenous) policy decisions: contribution, indexation, and

| BALANCE SHEET | |
|---|---|
| Assets (A) | Liabilities (L) |
| | Surplus (S) |

Fig. 21.1 Balance sheet pension fund (liquidation basis)

investment policy. We will first focus on the valuation of liabilities and subsequently discuss the asset side of the balance sheet.

The value of pension liabilities on the balance sheet is calculated as the current (discounted) value of earned pension rights. Changes in this value can therefore be due to three factors: actuarial, (nominal or real) interest rates, and inflation. Actuarial factors are somewhat of a misnomer for those factors influencing the level and length

| | | | |
|---|---|---|---|
| Δ(Surplus) = | Δ(Assets) | −/− | Δ(Liabilities) |

| | | |
|---|---|---|
| Contribution policy | Contributions (+) | |
| Indexation policy | Pension payments (−) | |
| Investment policy | Gross investment return (+ or −) | |
| | Costs (−) | |
| Exogenous actuarial and economic factors | | Actuarial factors (+ or −) |
| | | Interest rate (+ or −) |
| | | Inflation (+) |

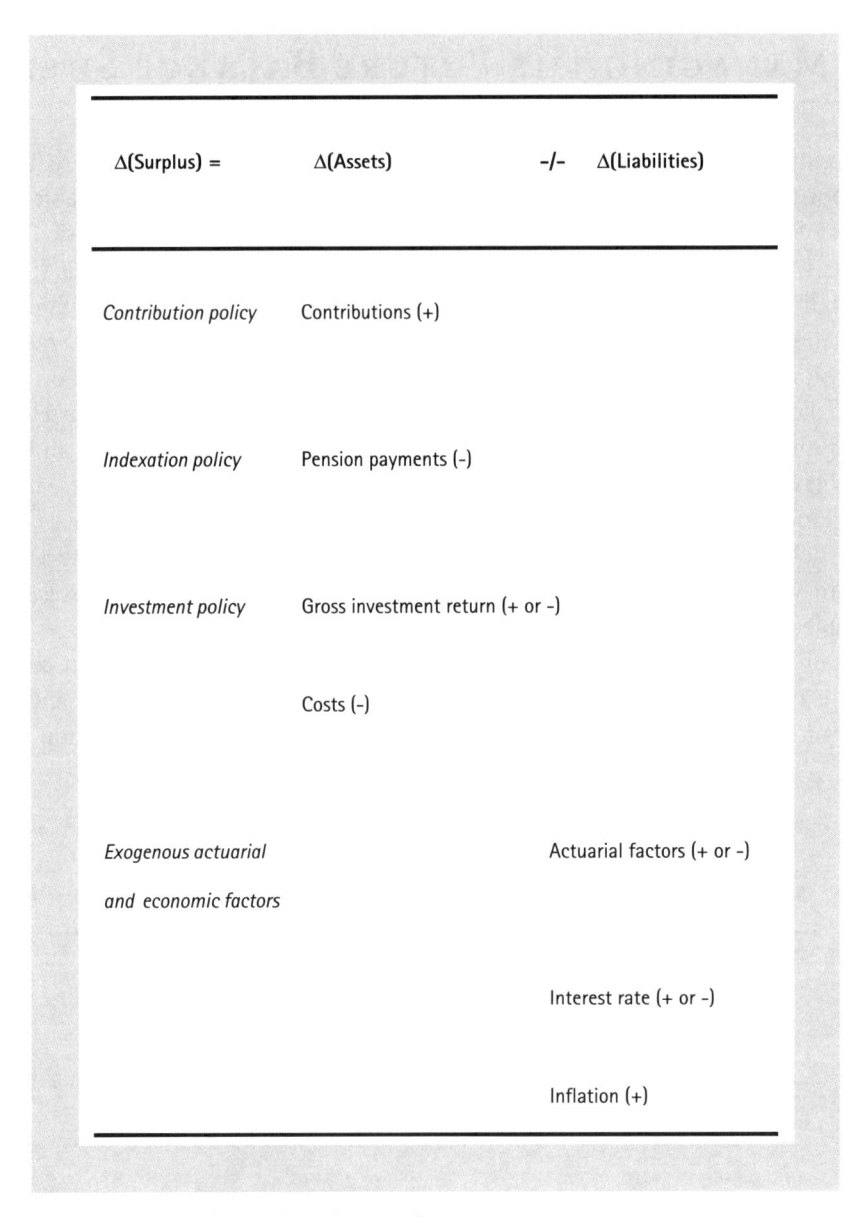

Fig. 21.2 Factors influencing the surplus

of nominal cash flows of earned pension rights. Usually, factors of this sort represent demographic trends. Some factors, like for instance retirement age, job promotion, and discharge, are indirectly influenced by economic forces. Actuarial factors are generally modeled as Markov processes where transition probabilities indicate the likelihood that someone, for example, dies next year. The ageing of the population is taken into account and current active, retired, and sleeping participants are integrated as well. The underlying transition probabilities (e.g. mortality rates) therefore determine the length of the cash flow series. For example, people could start working and accruing pension rights from 20 years onwards, and they could die around the age of 100. In this case the cash flow would be 80 years.

Changes in real or nominal interest rates have a direct impact on the valuation of pension liabilities as those variables are used as discount rates for future cash flows of nominal earned pension rights. Choosing the appropriate discount rate is a delicate and somewhat arbitrary issue. Historically, a lot of countries (e.g. the Netherlands) have used a fixed discount rate for all liabilities at all future horizons. Most new regulatory frameworks require fair market valuation of liabilities. This can be interpreted as the value against which liabilities could be sold to a third party. Under the assumption that liabilities are only guaranteed in nominal terms, the appropriate discount rate is a term structure of nominal yields. These nominal yields could be government bond yields or swap rates and an additional risk premium reflecting the default probability of the pension fund. Similarly, when liabilities are guaranteed in real terms, hence there is full (wage or price) inflation compensation, a real term structure of interest rates is required.

The third variable influencing the value of liabilities is inflation. Pension funds can aim to index pension payments fully, either by wage or by price inflation. This would ensure that retirement income rises with economic welfare. Some pension funds however only guarantee nominal pensions. Additionally, liabilities could be inflation-indexed conditional on the financial position of the fund. The health of the fund is then measured for instance by the funding ratio, or fully determined by the discretion of the Board.

The value of the left-hand side of the fund is influenced by pension payments (cash outflow), contributions (cash inflow), and investment returns (on average cash inflow). Pension payments are considered to be reasonably predictable and determined by the same actuarial factors as mentioned above. Contribution levels are set in the contribution policy of the fund. The contribution level is usually dependent on the current and future financial health of the pension fund. In some countries contribution levels have to comply with certain rules set by the regulator. Investment returns clearly depend on the chosen investment policy, which usually selects the strategic asset mix and defines the expected returns on the assets in the investment portfolio. Additionally, it contains decisions made by the board on the currency hedging policy and the rebalancing strategy of the strategic mix, for example, buy and hold versus dynamic rebalancing (see Perold and Sharpe (1988) for a discussion of dynamic rebalancing strategies). Furthermore, the management of downside risks is reviewed here as well. For example, equity risks can be dealt with using equity derivatives, while interest rate risks can be managed by interest rate swaps. The board should also decide on the duration of the assets in order to match the duration of the nominal or real liabilities, as interest rate changes could affect both the investment portfolio and liabilities through the discount rate.

Managing the future balance sheet of a pension fund is a difficult task. As the future is inherently uncertain, we need different future scenarios for the key economic variables in the ALM study. There are many ways to generate economic scenarios. A traditional method is to generate one central future scenario and some limited stress scenarios, most often based on both qualitative and quantitative input. In most ALM studies, a very large number of scenarios are generated with the help of a stochastic model. These stochastic models can be of a widely varying nature. For instance, an unconditional correlation matrix can be used to impose relationships on return drawings from a multivariate standard normal distribution. Furthermore, Wilkie (1987, 1995) suggests the cascade approach, whereas Mulvey (1994; Mulvey et al. 2000) proposes a stochastic differential equation approach for generating these scenarios. Recently, vector autoregressive (VAR) models are used more frequently in this context. A good example, among others, is the recent work of Campbell and Viceira (2002, 2005).[3] All approaches have their merits and pitfalls, but it is beyond the scope of this chapter to discuss these methods in too much detail. In the stylized example in Section 3, we will use the VAR technique to simulate scenarios for bonds and stocks in the long term. We refer to Ziemba and Mulvey (1998) for an extensive survey of ALM in general. For readers particularly interested in scenario generation techniques, we refer to Hoevenaars et al. (2003) for an overview and the impact of different VAR methods on an ALM study. Furthermore, we describe a basic VAR in the Appendix.

The outcome of an ALM modelling process is a set of probability distributions of the main decision variables for the board. Asset returns and the asset mix policy are used to determine the returns on the asset mix. Nominal interest rates are used to compute the present value of nominal liabilities and a similar procedure is applied for the valuation of liabilities in real terms. Furthermore, the inflation scenarios are used to index the liabilities, and the indexation and contribution policy in each simulation is derived. Subsequently, the ratio between assets and liabilities (funding ratio), the ratio of cumulated actual indexation and cumulated wage inflation (pension result), and the contribution rate can be determined in each simulation. The use of a large number of scenarios (in our example 5,000) enables us to derive a probability distribution of all relevant ALM output variables at each future year. In this way we assess the probability that the funding ratio or pension result will exceed a certain threshold value in, for instance, five years from now.

In order to analyze the relevant ALM output variables, the preferences of the various stakeholders and a probability distribution of the relevant decision variables are required. Determining the preferences of the beneficiaries of a pension fund is an extremely debatable issue as there are stakeholders with different interests. Exley *et al.* (1997) extensively describe the agency costs that exist between the different stakeholders. The employer and the current employees benefit from low contribution rates, while the retired prefer a high degree of inflation indexation of their pension liabilities to guarantee their welfare. Besides, regulators require that several solvency restrictions have to be met to maintain the financial health of the pension fund. As it is tentative to assign different weights to the diverse objectives of the stakeholders, we evaluate the output of the ALM study for each of these stakeholders. Therefore we consider the contribution rate, the degree of indexation, and the ratio of assets divided by liabilities (funding ratio). Obviously, a further decomposition of the stakeholders could give even more interesting insights into the effects of the main policy decisions of a pension fund. As such, we will elaborate on these implications for different generations in Section 5.

In the stylized example we perform the ALM study using a simulation approach. The benefit is that a simulation study can easily deal with highly non-linear and company-specific decision rules in the investment, contribution, indexation, and pension policy. We do not explicitly optimize a utility function, but instead we show the simulation output of the variables of interest to the stakeholders. Board members can evaluate this output in light of their own perspective and preferences. Consequently, it is not subject to a pre-specified utility function, as is the case in for example mean variance analysis (see Markowitz 1952), power utility, HARA utility or Epstein-Zin (see Campbell and Viceira 2002) or stochastic programming models (see Carino *et al.* 1994; Dert 1995, 1998; Kouwenberg 2001; and Ziemba 2003). In stochastic programming the optimal decision for investment, indexation, and contribution policies is derived for each node in the scenario structure, given the information available up to that point in time.

To summarize, an ALM model uses stochastic scenarios to construct probability distributions of the key decision variables for the board of a pension fund for each future year. We will evaluate this output in terms of expectations, downside risks, and upward potential. This enables us to study the impact of a particular strategic asset mix, indexation and contribution policy, on the interests of the main stakeholders of a pension fund.

# 3 A Stylized Example

In the previous section, we described the ALM process for a defined benefit pension fund. In this section we apply this procedure by presenting a stylized example. We will discuss the output of an ALM study in terms of the preferences of the various stakeholders. In particular, we consider a mature defined benefit, final wage (70 percent) pension plan with four alternative 'pension deals'. In these deals, we will vary the amount of equities in the asset mix and we will investigate the impact of making both the contribution policy and the indexation policy conditional on the financial position of the fund. Furthermore, the pension fund rebalances its asset mix to a constant mix each year. For reasons of simplicity and space we additionally assume that the investment universe consists of two asset classes: equities and government bonds. Scenarios are generated using the VAR methodology assuming that equities and bonds on average have a long-term return of 7.25 and 4.25 percent respectively. In line with the current funding situation of most pension funds, we assume that this particular pension fund is underfunded in real terms (85 percent) and overfunded in nominal (125 percent) and fixed 4 percent (110 percent) terms. Table 21.1 briefly summarizes the four alternative pension deals (A–D).

In Table 21.2 we evaluate the ALM output of each pension deal in terms of the relevant variables of interest for the different stakeholders. In particular, we show the effect on the funding ratio (F), the contribution rate (CR), and the pension result (PR). Here we define the funding ratio as the ratio between the market value of assets and the present value of the liabilities. We distinguish between a fixed (F 4 percent), a nominal (F nom.), and a real funding ratio (F real). These ratios differ depending on which discount rate is used to calculate the present value of the liabilities. The pension result is computed as the ratio of actual indexation received and full (or 100 percent) indexation. This implies that the pension result is always between 0 and 100 percent and that a PR of 90 percent means that the participant receives 90 percent of the 70 percent final wage promise as a pension payment (therefore 63 percent of the final wage). We provide both the median outcomes of the probability distribution of all ratios and downside risks and upward potential, thus the probability of low funding (F < 100 percent) or very high funding ratios

Table 21.1 Four different pension deals

| Pension deal | Asset mix | Contribution policy | Indexation policy |
|---|---|---|---|
| A | 0% Equities<br>100% Bonds | Fixed: 21% | Full indexation |
| B | 60% Equities<br>40% Bonds | Fixed: 21% | Full indexation |
| C | 60% Equities<br>40% Bonds | Fixed: 21% | No indexation |
| D | 60% Equities<br>40% Bonds | Conditional on<br>financial position | Conditional on<br>financial position |

### Table 21.2 Output of ALM studies

ALM output variables in year 2018 for four different pension policies

| | | median | < 85% | < 100% | < 105% | < 125% | < 150% |
|---|---|---|---|---|---|---|---|
| F nom. | A | 1.00 | 11.52% | 49.40% | 64.24% | 95.86% | 99.98% |
| | B | 1.36 | 7.16% | 16.40% | 20.06% | 38.98% | 62.18% |
| | C | 2.18 | 0.06% | 0.26% | 0.50% | 2.66% | 10.32% |
| | D | 1.43 | 0.34% | 2.72% | 4.96% | 25.90% | 58.38% |
| F real | A | 0.77 | 70.86% | 94.36% | 97.06% | 99.92% | 100.00% |
| | B | 1.05 | 26.88% | 44.66% | 49.64% | 69.32% | 84.94% |
| | C | 1.68 | 1.04% | 4.10% | 5.98% | 17.36% | 36.20% |
| | D | 1.09 | 11.18% | 36.08% | 44.22% | 69.20% | 86.14% |
| F 4% | A | 0.89 | 38.98% | 78.72% | 87.34% | 99.32% | 100.00% |
| | B | 1.21 | 13.94% | 28.08% | 34.00% | 54.32% | 75.52% |
| | C | 1.93 | 0.14% | 0.90% | 1.60% | 5.96% | 19.32% |
| | D | 1.26 | 1.52% | 11.28% | 17.02% | 48.68% | 75.84% |
| | | | < 85% | < 100% | < 105% | < 125% | < 150% |
| F nom. within | A | | 17.32% | 71.56% | 86.28% | 99.98% | 100.00% |
| | B | | 20.68% | 51.06% | 62.38% | 93.16% | 99.78% |
| | C | | 1.76% | 16.44% | 26.48% | 76.20% | 98.52% |
| | D | | 3.72% | 30.36% | 46.52% | 93.04% | 99.82% |
| | | median | < 70% | < 80% | < 90% | < 99% | < 100% |
| PR | A | 1.00 | 0.00% | 0.00% | 0.00% | 0.00% | 0.00% |
| | B | 1.00 | 0.00% | 0.00% | 0.00% | 0.00% | 0.00% |
| | C | 0.69 | 56.22% | 91.18% | 99.68% | 100.00% | 100.00% |
| | D | 1.00 | 0.96% | 7.82% | 22.78% | 47.40% | 51.88% |
| | | median | < 18% | < 20% | < 22% | < 24% | < 28% |
| CR | A | 0.21 | 0.00% | 0.00% | 100.00% | 100.00% | 100.00% |
| | B | 0.21 | 0.00% | 0.00% | 100.00% | 100.00% | 100.00% |
| | C | 0.21 | 0.00% | 0.00% | 100.00% | 100.00% | 100.00% |
| | D | 0.18 | 63.36% | 75.30% | 85.90% | 93.52% | 100.00% |

(F > 100 percent). Moreover, we consider the within probability (F nom. within), as suggested by Kritzman and Rich (2002), for the nominal funding ratio. This measure provides the probability that the funding ratio is below a certain value across a period of years at least once, instead of in a particular year only. Note that the ALM study can be used to analyze the balance sheet for several years into the future. In this example, however, we present output for the future year 2018.

The first pension policy setting A assumes that the pension fund's asset mix contains 0 percent equities and 100 percent government bonds. Deal A furthermore has fixed contribution rates (i.e. 21 percent) and it guarantees full indexation with wage inflation. In this deal both employees and employers in the plan benefit from a fixed contribution rate, and the retired benefit from full indexation. This ensures a stable standard of living for all participants. In addition, the asset mix with 100 percent bonds can be regarded as a low risk mix. However, all these benefits come at the cost of the financial position of the pension fund, which deteriorates substantially. All median funding ratios in Table 21.2 decrease relative to the starting position: 100 percent for the nominal case, 77 and 89 percent for the real and the 4 percent case, respectively. This implies that the pension fund would barely have enough assets to pay out all future nominal pension rights, but that there is no money left for any indexation. However, in a fixed 4 percent regime the pension fund would be in serious trouble because it is not solvent enough from this perspective. Additionally, downside risks are high. The probability that the nominal funding ratio is below 100 percent is almost 50 percent. This number is significantly higher for the real and 4 percent case: 94.36 and 78.72 percent respectively. There is also hardly any upward potential in terms of the probability that the funding ratio exceeds 125 percent. An even worse picture is given by the within probability (F nom. within) of Kritzman and Rich (2002): the probability that the nominal funding is below 100 percent in at least one of the next 15 years is 71.56 percent. This is actually considerably higher than the 49.40 percent probability of underfunding in the year 2018.

The second pension deal B has the same indexation and contribution policy as A. Deal B shows the impact of a more risky asset mix: 60 percent in equities and 40 percent in government bonds. Just as in deal A, the participants benefit from full indexation and a stable contribution rate. The higher expected return of equities and diversification between equities and bonds results in a substantial improvement of the funding ratios. Although downside risks remain considerable and the financial position of the fund deteriorates, the probability of underfunding in real funding ratio terms decreases from 94.36 to 44.66 percent. Consistently, the probability that the nominal funding ratio is below 100 percent in one of the next 15 years reduces from 71.56 to 51.06 percent. The financial position in terms of funding ratios and downside risks has improved relative to pension deal A, but it remains poor and a regulator will most probably not allow such a situation to continue. This suggests that for this pension fund, with this particular starting position, changing the investment policy is not a sufficient measure to achieve a healthy financial situation. In the following two examples we additionally adapt the indexation and contribution policies.

The third pension deal C differs from B with respect to the indexation policy. The pension fund decides not to index the pension payments, the contribution rate on the other hand remains fixed at 21 percent, and the asset mix does not change. This implies that the pension result will be considerably below 100 percent. In this case the median pension result is 69 percent, which means that participants will on average receive 69 percent of 70 percent of their final wage (i.e. $<$ 50 percent). Obviously, this difference can be explained by the inflation gap. The flipside of this is that the fund is in a healthy position in terms of both median funding ratios and downside risks. There is even upward potential. Whereas the median real funding ratio is at 105 percent under policy B, it is at 168 percent under pension policy C. In addition, in nominal terms, there is hardly a probability of underfunding. It reduces from 16.4 percent under B to 0.3 percent under C. Also the probability of underfunding within the next 15 years reduces to 16.4 percent. Note, however, that in this pension deal the financial position of the fund is kept healthy at the cost of retired participants, who will receive no indexation at all, whereas employers and employees still pay a stable contribution rate at the same level as in B. Deal C will therefore never survive a well-represented boardroom.

In the fourth pension, policy D employers, employees, and retired participants all contribute to a balance sheet which satisfies the solvency restrictions of the regulator. In this system the contribution and indexation policy is directly related to the financial position of the fund in terms of nominal and real funding ratios. Whenever the nominal funding ratio reaches a threshold value of less than 100 percent, the contribution rate will be set at its *ex ante* defined maximum of 25 percent and pension payments are no longer indexed by wage inflation. If the nominal funding ratio is above 100 percent and the real funding ratio is below 100 percent, the contribution rate declines linearly from 25 percent towards 18 percent and the degree of indexation increases from 0 to 100 percent of wage inflation. Whenever the real funding ratio exceeds 100 percent, contribution rates decline further and pension payments are fully indexed. Additionally, any foregone indexation of past pension payments—the nominal funding ratio was less than 100 percent—will be made up. The investment policy does not change.

Clearly, system D is the fairest system of the four deals considered. The median contribution rate paid by employers and employees is even lower than the fixed 21 percent in the other three deals. The probability that the contribution rate is below 18 percent is 63.36 percent. The retired still have a median pension result of 100 percent, which means that most pensions will be fully indexed by wage inflation. However, as the degree of indexation depends on the financial position, there are some downside risks. The probability that the pension result is below 90 percent is still 22.78 percent. At the same time, the financial position of the pension fund seems pretty healthy. The nominal, real, and 4 percent funding ratios have medians of 1.43, 1.09, and 1.26 respectively. Downside risks have reduced compared to B, and there is still space for upward potential. Nevertheless, the probability of underfunding within the next 15 years is 30.36 percent. The output of this fourth pension deal suggests that such a risky asset mix provides a fairer trade-off between the interests of the different stakeholders in terms of the financial health of the fund, the degree of indexation, and contribution rates. Moreover, it is more transparent who pays when for the pension risks. The expectations in terms of medians as well as the downside risks and upward potentials seem at acceptable levels.

# 4 Board Dilemmas

In evaluating an ALM study and making decisions on investment, contribution, and indexation policy the board of trustees of a pension fund faces a lot of difficult questions. This section addresses some of these dilemmas. We will then discuss horizon effects in the investment policy and life-cycle investing. Finally, we will elaborate on the fair valuation of liabilities by comparing funding ratios based respectively on fixed 4 percent, nominal, and real discount rates. All questions in this section will be based on pension deal D.

## 4.1 Increasing Contributions or Reducing Indexation?

The indexation and contribution policy can be used to recover from financially stressful periods and to extricate from deficits. However, the impact of an indexation reduction or an increase in contribution levels depends on the liability structure. Contributions are paid as a percentage of the salary sum of all working participants in the fund. Evidently, raising contribution levels creates more inflow into the fund when the gross salary sum is high. In general, the gross salary sum is higher for younger pension funds, which have more working participants than mature pension funds. The ratio of the total asset value and the gross salary sum is illustrative in this context. For the mature pension fund in example D, we assume that this ratio is 10, which indicates that a 10 percent increase in the contribution rate is required in order to compensate for a 1 percent reduction of the return on the asset mix. The multiplier is lower for younger funds because their gross salary sum is relatively higher and consequently the inflow from contributions is much more powerful. The opposite line of reasoning applies to the indexation policy, which is more effective for mature funds, simply because they have more pension payments than younger funds. Consequently, the indexation policy is much more powerful than the contribution policy in deal D.

From a social perspective the board has to decide *who* pays *when* for the pension fund risks of financial distress: employers and employees in terms of contributions, or the retired in terms of indexation. If the pension fund is in a sound financial position with a high funding ratio, the board could even decide to index the liabilities fully and to allow the contribution rate to be (near) zero.

## 4.2 Which Investment Horizon should be Considered?

Horizon effects in risk properties as volatilities of and correlations between asset classes imply that an asset mix could potentially be attractive in the long term, but not necessarily in the short term (see e.g. Barberis 2000; Campbell *et al.* 2003; Campbell and Viceira 2002). Time diversification in equity returns, for example, makes this asset class less risky in the long run. Furthermore, the correlation between equities and bonds changes substantially across investment horizons. This makes it possible to benefit not only from risk diversification between asset classes, but also from time diversification within an asset class.

Campbell and Viceira (2005) recently showed that there is a term structure of the risk-return trade-off for bonds, stocks, and cash. Hoevenaars *et al.* (2005) extend their asset-space with credits, hedge funds, commodities, and real estate and find that there are not only horizon effects in volatilities and correlations, but also in inflation and real interest rate hedge properties. In particular, they show that these findings are relevant for asset liability investors and that the costs of ignoring the liabilities in the strategic asset allocation decision are substantial.

At this point it is important to mention that collective defined benefit pension funds in practice do not have one fixed investment horizon. Liabilities are paid at all horizons. Nonetheless, they typically invest in just one asset mix motivated by the average age of the fund. Teulings and De Vries (2004) show that one asset mix could be too restrictive and they suggest that younger generations should have a higher equity exposure. The investment policy should therefore be appropriate and acceptable in risk terms at all horizons. As a consequence this is an important aspect in evaluating the ALM study.

Table 21.3 shows the ALM output for pension deal D at a short (1 year), medium (7 years), and long (15 years) horizon. Additionally, Figure 21.3 demonstrates the probability distribution of the nominal funding ratio and the pension result at all horizons up to 15 years. This illustrates how horizon effects in the asset categories, for example mean reversion in stocks, work out in an ALM context and whether a pension policy is acceptable for the stakeholders at all horizons.

### Table 21.3 Output of ALM study D

ALM output variables in short, medium and long term for pension policy D

|   |   | median | < 85% | < 100% | < 105% | < 125% | < 150% |
|---|---|---|---|---|---|---|---|
| F nom. | 2004 | 1.23 | 0.04% | 3.46% | 8.00% | 55.40% | 94.98% |
|  | 2010 | 1.33 | 0.24% | 3.80% | 7.14% | 35.78% | 73.82% |
|  | 2018 | 1.43 | 0.34% | 2.72% | 4.96% | 25.90% | 58.38% |
| F real | 2004 | 0.85 | 48.84% | 92.00% | 96.08% | 99.88% | 100.00% |
|  | 2010 | 0.99 | 18.40% | 52.44% | 61.90% | 85.12% | 96.36% |
|  | 2018 | 1.09 | 11.18% | 36.08% | 44.22% | 69.20% | 86.14% |
| F 4% | 2004 | 1.09 | 0.26% | 17.26% | 33.38% | 90.96% | 99.92% |
|  | 2010 | 1.16 | 1.84% | 16.38% | 25.32% | 67.02% | 90.66% |
|  | 2018 | 1.26 | 1.52% | 11.28% | 17.02% | 48.68% | 75.84% |
|   |   |   | <85% | < 100% | < 105% | < 125% | <150% |
| F nom. within | 2004 |   | 0.04% | 3.46% | 8.00% | 55.40% | 94.98% |
|  | 2010 |   | 1.80% | 20.80% | 34.20% | 87.46% | 99.52% |
|  | 2018 |   | 3.72% | 30.36% | 46.52% | 93.04% | 99.82% |
|   |   | median | <70% | <80% | <90% | <99% | <100% |
| PR | 2004 | 0.99 | 0.00% | 0.00% | 0.00% | 55.30% | 90.74% |
|  | 2010 | 0.98 | 0.00% | 1.48% | 19.02% | 54.42% | 61.46% |
|  | 2018 | 1.00 | 0.96% | 7.82% | 22.78% | 47.40% | 51.88% |
|   |   | median | < 18% | < 20% | <22% | < 24% | < 28% |
| CR | 2004 | 0.21 | 0.00% | 0.00% | 100.00% | 100.00% | 100.00% |
|  | 2010 | 0.18 | 46.60% | 61.80% | 78.30% | 90.40% | 100.00% |
|  | 2018 | 0.18 | 63.36% | 75.30% | 85.90% | 93.52% | 100.00% |

Although the pension liabilities are expected to be fully indexed in 2018, the median pension result is 98 percent in 2010. Moreover, Figure 21.3 shows that the median pension result has a convex shape, which reaches 100 percent after 15 years, but partial indexation is expected at intermediate horizons. It should also be noted that the contribution rate in 2004 is set at 21 percent, whereas the probability on lower contribution rates rises for a longer horizon. It can also be observed that the median nominal funding ratio rises steadily over time, because the expected return on the asset mix is above the growth of the liabilities. However, the table also indicates that the downside risks are higher in the short term than in the long term. Typically, the probabilities of underfunding have to be acceptable for the board—and regulator—at all horizons.

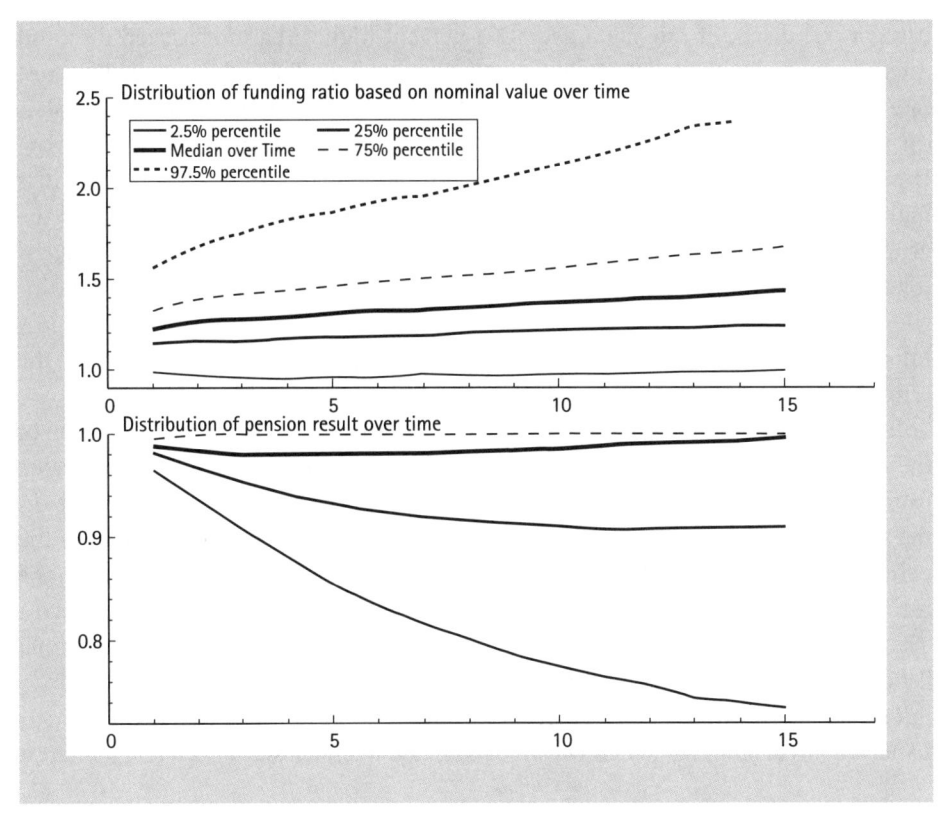

Fig. 21.3 Probability distribution of nominal funding ratio and pension result of ALM study D

## 4.3 Nominal, Real or Fixed Discount Rates?

We have already discussed the valuation of liabilities against nominal, real, and fixed discount rates in Section 2. Figure 21.4 shows the accompanying asset-liability risks and the asset-only risk for 15 years into the future. The latter is computed as the standard deviation of the return on the asset mix. The asset-liability risks are provided for the 4 percent, nominal, and real discount rates, computed as the standard deviation of the difference in the growth of assets and liabilities. The asset-liability risks are commonly known as mismatch or surplus risks.

The growth of the assets does not only depend on the return on the asset mix, but also on the inflow from contributions and the outflow from pension payments. The growth of the liabilities is based on changes in the discount rate, inflation, and the degree of indexation, and the liability growth as a result of demographical aspects like, for instance, participants entering or leaving. In the case of a fixed discount factor, the discount rate does not introduce volatility and consequently there are only two risk factors left in the growth of the liabilities. For this reason, the mismatch risk is lowest in the case of a fixed discount rate. The mismatch risk using a real discount rate is on average 1 percent higher than for a fixed discount rate. This is due to the volatility of the real discount rate. Since the nominal interest rate is much more volatile than the real interest rate, the nominal mismatch risk is on average 2 percent higher: approximately 14 percent for a 20-year horizon. Despite the fact that there is no liability component in the asset-only risk, it is higher than the mismatch risk using a fixed rate. Clearly, extremes are less and the growth of assets is in line with the growth of liabilities. This could be explained as follows. In high inflation scenarios, asset returns are high as well, funding ratios rise, and the liabilities are fully indexed by inflation. The opposite occurs in low inflation scenarios. As a consequence, assets and liabilities partially move in the same direction in the extremes, which reduces the (mismatch) risk.

In general, mismatch risk can be reduced substantially by matching the duration of the assets to that of the (nominal or real) liabilities. In this way, a rise in asset value from a fall in interest rates is cancelled, in terms of funding ratio, by an identical rise in the value of the liabilities. A next step would be to match the cash flow pattern of the pension payments. As the depth in the real bond market is not sufficient to match the real liabilities of most pension funds, the real liabilities cannot be matched perfectly. The nominal bond market is much more developed and consequently nominal liabilities could be perfectly matched. However, this introduces another type of risk: inflation risk. Although the pension fund is matched in nominal terms, the participants are worse off in real terms because a decrease in asset value (from rising interest

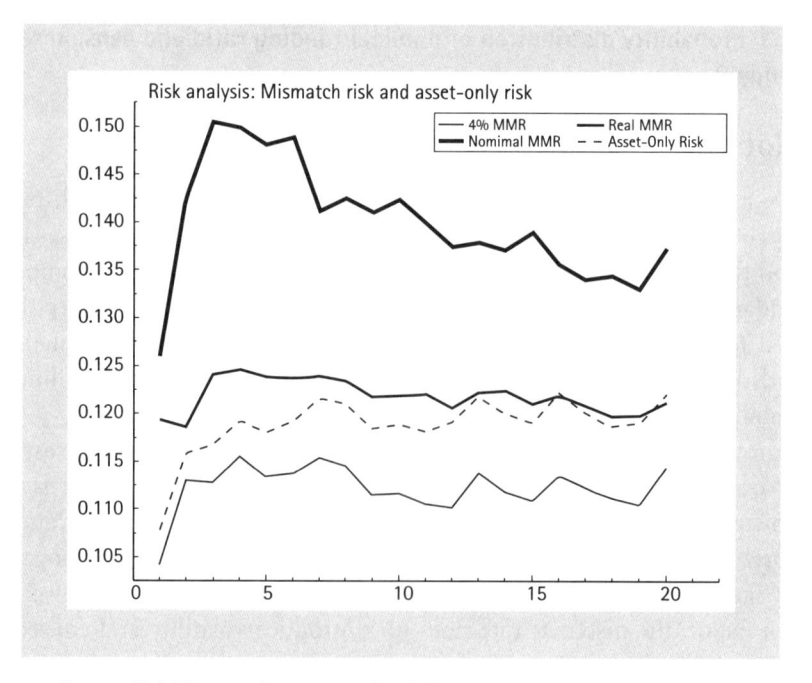

Fig. 21.4 Asset-liability and asset-only risks

rates) is not sufficient to index the liabilities. This introduction of real risks has to be taken into account in matching the nominal liabilities.

We have seen that the risks vary substantially between 10.5 and 15.0 percent. Furthermore, the effect of policy changes could work out positive in nominal terms, but negative in real terms. So, which of these risks and funding ratios should the pension board look at? In a pension fund context the appropriate risk measure of course depends on the regulatory framework and the ambition of the pension plan, but it should reflect the mismatch between assets and liabilities. An asset-only risk measure does not take into account the right-hand side of the balance sheet (see Fig. 21.1).

# 5 GENERATIONAL ACCOUNTING

In the contribution and indexation policy in example D, it is clear when the retired pay in terms of indexation and when employers and employees pay in terms of contributions in case of a substantial pension deficit. However, as the ALM study above is conducted on an aggregate level, it is not really transparent whether particular generations (or cohorts) are worse off than others. In order to analyze possible wealth transfers between stakeholders in the pension fund more extensively, the concept of generational accounting can be applied. Generational accounting makes the consequences of policy changes on the various stakeholders more transparent, which enables the board of trustees to create a more sustainable, transparent, and fair pension deal.

Generational accounting was developed originally in the area of public finance by Auerbach and Kotlikoff (1987) and Auerbach, *et al.* (1994) as a method of long-term fiscal analysis. Ponds (2003) applies the concept of generational accounting in a pension fund context. He analyzes the transfers of economic value (not wealth) between generations, specifically investigating which age cohorts lose and which gain from alternative funding and indexation policies. Cui *et al.* (2004) formally model these transfers and the corresponding distribution of value across generations. They calculate the pension deal from the point of view of each cohort. Teulings and De Vries (2004) suggest that political tensions between generations can best be solved by the introduction of so-called generational accounts.

Generational accounting analyzes the impact of different policies on the well-being of different generations. Moreover, it verifies whether each generation receives the indexed pension payments for which it has paid in terms of contributions. A generational account is defined as the difference between the present value of future pension payments plus possible current pension payments minus the present value of contributions. This should be (near) zero in a fair pension system, or else some generations pay for others. If it turns out, for example, that younger generations pay for the older generations, younger generations will probably not join the pension system voluntarily. We provide the intuition of generational accounting by showing how pension deal D transfers wealth between generations. This makes the pension deal even more transparent and shows whether, and if so which, generations pay for other generations. We assume that a generation is based on age cohorts. People belong to the same generation if they have the same birth year. We consider 151 cohorts ranging from 2044 to 1894, which implies that cohorts from 2005 onwards are generations that are not born yet, but will enter the fund in the future.

Several facts appear in the cash flow structure of the generations. Retirement income is only received by people older than 65. However, all people can receive a relative or family member pension payment before they reach the age of 65. This explains the jump in pension payments for people older than 65 and why cohorts younger than 65 receive positive pension payments even if they have not retired yet. Since people who are younger than 65 are still working, the growth of their liabilities is positive. On the other hand, people aged 65 and older receive pension payments and consequently their future liabilities are reduced. Such a pattern is also observed in contributions. Only the working population pays contributions. Note that the individuals within a cohort could still have different pension claims. This could happen, for example, when someone has worked abroad for some time and starts working at a later age than someone else in the same cohort. Such differences are not represented in the cohort data that we use. However, we do not expect this to change our general conclusions. Note also that more detailed data would in the end result in *individual* accounting instead of *generational* accounting.

The average generational account, $\overline{GA\%}_t^c$, over all scenarios S is calculated for each cohort $c$ at time $t$ as in equation 1.

$$\overline{GA\%}_t^c = \frac{1}{S} \sum_{s \in S} [L_{s,t}^c - L_{s,t-1}^c - C_{s,t}^c + U_{s,t}^c]/L_{s,t-1}^c \qquad (1)$$

It is the average difference between benefits and costs, for example the increase in nominal liabilities, $L_{s,t}^c - L_{s,t-1}^c$, during the year minus contributions paid, $C_{s,t}^c$, plus pension payments, $U_{s,t}^c$, in the particular year. Subsequently, the generational account is expressed as a percentage of the nominal value of the liabilities (VOR) at the beginning of the year of the particular cohort. The mean generational account as a percentage of the liabilities makes them more comparable. Figure 21.5 shows the average generational accounts in 2004 for all age cohorts from 1898 to 1979. The figure shows that all participants who are born before 1967 benefit from the pension policy D in 2004: the increase of their liabilities and possible pension payments is

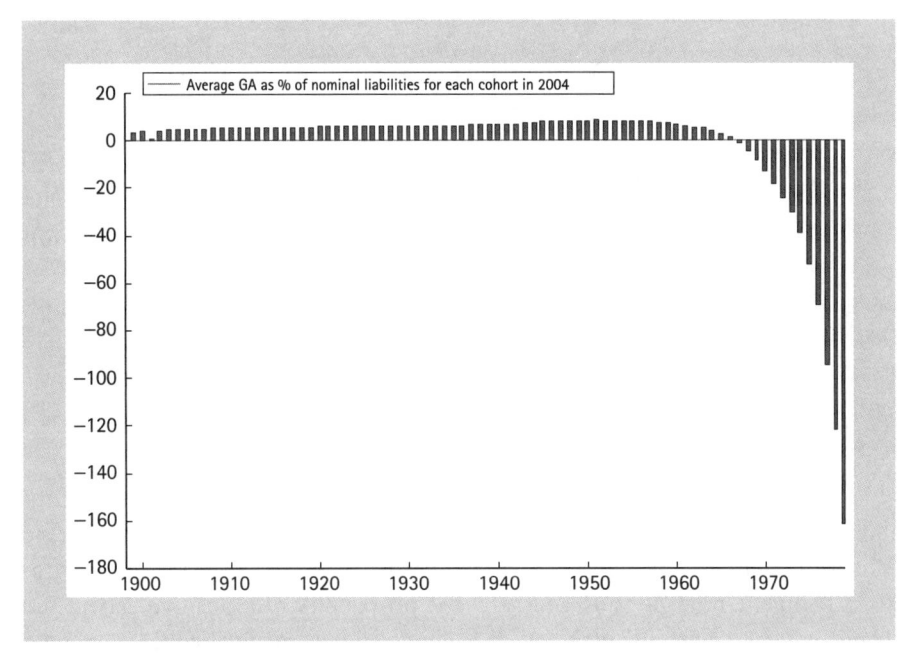

**Fig. 21.5** Average generational accounts as percentage of nominal liabilities in 2004 for all age cohorts from 1898 to 1979

higher than the contributions that they pay in 2004. It can be seen that the younger cohorts are much worse off. They seem to pay in 2004 for the benefits of the older cohorts, because the rise of the present value of their liabilities is less than the contributions they pay in 2004.

Table 21.4 shows the average generational accounts as a percentage of their liabilities for three age groups: Young, Workers and Retired. We have aggregated the cohorts with birth year 1970 to 1975 to create the Young group, people born in 1955 to 1960 form the Workers, and the Retired group consists of people born in 1930 to 1935. The results can be interpreted as follows. The values in the table represent the benefit (positive) or loss (negative) for a certain age group as a percentage of its liabilities due to the pension policy in that particular year in the column heading. A positive value indicates that the liability payments and growth of liabilities through indexation compensation is greater in money terms than the contributions that they pay in that year. In 2004, for example, the younger cohorts born between 1970 and 1975 seem to pay more in terms of contributions than they earn in future pension rights.

Based on the pension policy decisions regarding indexation and contribution rates in 2004, the young age group receives 201 million euros less than the 2004 contributions, which is 25.08 percent of the present value of its accrued pension rights. More specifically, this generational account can be decomposed in to three terms. In 2004 the cohort pays 487 million euros in contributions, it receives 1.1

**Table 21.4** Average generational account as percentage of liabilities for three age groups

Average generational account (%) for three age groups

|  | Year 2004 | Year 2007 | Year 2010 | Year 2014 | Year 2018 |
| --- | --- | --- | --- | --- | --- |
| Young 1970–75 | −25.08 | −17.51 | −8.30 | −0.83 | 3.12 |
| Workers 1955–60 | 7.82 | 4.99 | 6.09 | 7.22 | 7.78 |
| Retired 1930–5 | 6.34 | 6.59 | 6.86 | 7.00 | 7.00 |

million in pension payments (in this case relative pension payments), and its future liabilities increase by 284 million euros. This is the 2004 present value of the increase of future liabilities. The opposite pattern seems to be the case for working and retired people. Under pension policy D the probability of a positive generational account increases with people's age. It is above 50 percent for people born before 1966. The generational account of the young age group changes from −25.08 percent in 2004 to +3.12 percent in 2018. The fact that the young group of today (2004) will be the working group in 15 years from now explains this finding. So, under the same pension policy the current young cohort benefits from the system whereas the new young cohort with birth years between 1984 and 1989 will pay for them.

Although Table 21.4 and Figure 21.5 give some interesting insights we need to compute the present value of all future generational accounts whenever we want to evaluate and compare the effects of different investment, contribution, and indexation policies on the generations. Ponds (2003) suggests the use of stochastic discount factors (deflators) for the present value calculation. Deflators make it possible to value the generational accounts against fair market value through explicitly taking into account the risk of cash flows underlying the generational accounts. For a further elaboration on stochastic discount factors we refer to Cochrane (2005).

# 6 Concluding Comments

By explicitly considering the interests of the different stakeholders, an ALM study can be used as a steering device to compose a fair, transparent, and sustainable pension deal acceptable for all major stakeholders of the fund. We have shown that an ALM study can particularly be applied to get insights into the dilemmas and trade-offs a pension board faces in deciding on appropriate investment, contribution, and indexation policies. Using ALM tools we can obtain a 'term structure' of the financial position of the fund as the deal should be acceptable for stakeholders and regulators in both the short run and the long run. An ALM exercise can also clarify the magnitude of downside risks at all relevant investment horizons and the choice of the appropriate asset mix.

The analysis on generational accounting showed that key policy decisions made by the board of trustees eventually lead to value transfers between generational cohorts. A defined benefit pension scheme can only be sustainable in the long run when all generations feel comfortable with these transfers. In our view, future research on ALM should therefore further investigate issues related to generational accounting. One particularly interesting area is how to discount future value transfers in order to obtain present values. Another is that differences in present value do not necessarily imply equal differences in the utility of beneficiaries. Moreover, the valuation of embedded options in pension deals will be a major challenge for both practitioners and academic researchers. Finally, in the ultimate pension deal it should be clear *ex ante* how value imbalances between generations will be treated. All these efforts most likely will contribute to fairer and more transparent pension deals.

# Notes

1. Although most of our analysis also holds for corporate DB plans, the existence of, for instance, agency relations between beneficiaries and shareholders of the company can influence some of our general conclusions. See Exley (2004) for more details.
2. An alternative would be to use the going concern basis in which the current value of future contributions (on the left-hand side) and future pension liabilities (on the right-hand side) are additional items on the balance sheet.
3. See previous chapter.

# References

AUERBACH, A. J., GOKHALE, J., and KOTLIKOFF, L. J. (1994). 'Generational accounting: a meaningful way to evaluate fiscal policy'. *Journal of Economic Perspectives*, 8: 73–94.
—— and KOTLIKOFF, L. J. (1987). *Dynamic Fiscal Policy*, Cambridge: Cambridge University Press.
BARBERIS, N. (2000). 'Investing for the long run when returns are predictable'. *Journal of Finance*, 55: 225–64.

BOENDER, C. G. J. (1995). 'Hybrid simulation/optimisation scenario model for asset/liability management'. *European Journal of Operational Research*, 99: 126–35.

—— VAN AALST, P. C., and HEEMSKERK, F. (1998). 'Modelling and managment of assets and liabilities of pension plans in the Netherlands', in W. T. Ziemba and J. M. Mulvey (eds.), *Worldwide Asset Liability Modeling*. Cambridge: Cambridge University Press.

BRANDT, M. W., and SANTA-CLARA, P. (2004). 'Dynamic portfolio selection by augmenting the asset space'. NBER Working Paper No. 10372.

BRENNAN, M. J., SCHWARTZ, E. S., and LAGNADO, R. (1997). 'Strategic asset allocation'. *Journal of Economic Dynamics and Control*, 21: 1377–403.

—— and XIA, Y. (2004). 'Persistence, predictability, and portfolio planning'. Working Paper. Wharton School of University of Pennsylvania.

CAMPBELL, J. Y., CHAN, Y. L., and L. M. VICEIRA, (2003). 'A multivariate model for strategic asset allocation'. *Journal of Financial Economics*, 67: 41–80.

—— and VICEIRA, L. M. (2002). *Strategic Asset Allocation: Portfolio Choice for Long-Term Investors*. Clarendon Lectures in Economics. Oxford: Oxford University Press.

—— —— (2005). 'The term structure of the risk-return tradeoff'. *Financial Analyst Journal*, 61: 34–44.

CARINO, D. R., KENT, T., MYERS, D. H., STACY, C., SYLVANUS, M., TURNER, A. L., WATANABE, K., and ZIEMBA, W. T. (1994). 'The Russel-Yasuda Kasai model: an asset liability model for a Japanese insurance company using multistage stochastic programming'. *Interfaces*, 24/1: 29–49.

—— and ZIEMBA, W. T. (1998). 'Formulation of the Russel-Yasuda Kasai financial planning model'. *Operations Research*, 46: 443–9.

COCHRANE, J. H. (2005). *Asset Pricing*. Princeton: Princeton University Press.

CONSIGLIO, A., COCCO, F., and ZENIOS, S. A. (2000). 'Scenario optimization asset and liability modelling for endowments with quarantees'. Working Paper. HERMES European Center of Excellence on Computational Finance and Economics.

CUI, J., JONG DE, F., and PONDS, E. H. M. (2004). 'Intergenerational transfer within funded pension schemes', in *Proceedings of International AFIR Colloquium 2004*, Boston, 8–10 Nov.

DERT, C. L. (1995). 'Asset liability management for pension funds: a multistage chance constrained programming approach'. Ph.D. thesis. Erasmus University, Rotterdam.

—— (1998). 'A dynamic model for asset liability management for defined benefit pension funds', in W. T. Ziemba and J. M. Mulvey, (eds.), *Worldwide Asset Liability Modeling*. Cambridge: Cambridge University Press.

EXLEY, J. (2004). 'Stakeholder alignment and agency issues in pensions management'. Presentation to the Centre for Pension Management Colloquium, 5–6 Oct.

—— MEHTA, S. J. B., and SMITH, A. D. (1997). 'The financial theory of defined benefit schemes'. *British Actuarial Journal*, 3/4.

HOEVENAARS, R. P. M. M., MOLENAAR, R. D. J., SCHOTMAN, P. C. and STEENKAMP, T. B. M. (2005). 'Strategic asset allocation with liabilities: beyond stocks and bonds'. Working Paper. Maastricht University.

—— —— and STEENKAMP, T. B. M. (2003). 'Simulation for the long run', in B. Scherer (ed.), *Asset and Liability Management Tools*. London: Risk Books.

KOUWENBERG, R. R. P. (2001). 'Scenario generation and stochastic programming models for asset liability management'. *European Journal of Operational Research*, 134: 51–64.

Kritzman, M., and Rich, D. (2002). 'The mismeasurement of risk'. *Financial Analyst Journal*, May–June: 91–9.

Leibowitz, M. L., Kogelman, S., and Bader, L. N. (1994). 'Funding ratio return'. *Journal of Portfolio Management*, Fall: 39–47.

Markowitz, H. (1952). 'Portfolio selection'. *Journal of Finance*, 7: 77–91.

Merton, R. C. (1969). 'Lifetime portfolio selection under uncertainty: the continuous time case'. *Review of Economics and Statistics*, 51: 247–57.

—— (1971). 'Optimum consumption and portfolio rules in a continuous-time model', *Journal of Economic Theory*, 3: 373–413.

Mulvey, J. M. (1994). 'An asset-liability investment system'. *Interfaces*, 24:22–33.

—— (1996). 'Generating scenarios for the Towers Perrin investment system'. *Interfaces*, 26: 1–15.

—— Gould, G., and Morgan, C. (2000). 'An asset and liability management system for Towers Perrin-Tillinghast'. *Interfaces*, 30: 96–114.

Perold, A. F., and Sharpe, W. F. (1988). 'Dynamic strategies for asset allocation'. *Financial Analysts Journal*, Jan.–Feb.: 16–27.

Ponds, E. (2003). 'Pension funds and value-based intergenerational accounting'. *Journal of Pension Economics and Finance*, 2/3: 295–325.

Samuelson, P. (1969). 'Lifetime portfolio selection by dynamic stochastic programming'. *Review of Economics and Statistics*, 51: 239–46.

Teulings, C. N., and De Vries, C. G. (2004). 'Generational accounting, solidarity and pension losses'. CEPR Discussion Paper 4209.

Wachter, J. (2002). 'Optimal consumption and portfolio allocation under mean-reverting returns: an exact solution for complete markets'. *Journal of Financial and Quantitative Analysis*, 37: 63–91.

Wilkie, A. D. (1987). 'A stochastic investment model for actuarial use'. *Transactions of Actuaries*, 39: 391–403.

—— (1995). 'More on a stochastic asset model for actuarial use'. Presented to the Institute of Actuaries and Faculty of Actuaries, London.

Ziemba, T. Z. (2003). 'The stochastic programming approach to asset, liability, and wealth management'. The Research Foundation of the Association for Investment Management and Research.

—— and Mulvey, J. M. (1998). *Worldwide Asset and Liability Modelling*. Cambridge: Cambridge University Press.

# APPENDIX: SCENARIO GENERATION

The scenario generation technique used in the stylized example is based on a vector autoregressive (VAR) model and is given in (A1):

$$y_{t+1} = c + By_t + e_{t+1} \tag{A1}$$

A VAR model describes next period returns and yields, represented by $y_{t+1}$, out of a linear combination of their current values, represented by $y_t$. $c$ is a constant term in the linear combination and $e_{t+1}$ is the unexplained random error term, which is stochastic and normally distributed with zero mean and covariance matrix $\Sigma$. The coefficients $c$, $B$, and $\Sigma$ are estimated from the available historical data using econometric techniques. The merits of a VAR for long-run simulation are various. It is an intuitive linear model that describes stochastic time series, but more importantly it captures the long-term dynamics out of the data. The estimated coefficients reflect variances, cross-correlations between asset classes, autocorrelation within a return series, and cross-correlations between shocks in the residuals of different asset classes. Moreover, these are conditional effects, which means that the relationship between two variables simultaneously also accounts for the presence and influence of the other variables in the VAR system. Another attractive property of this time-series approach is that it enables us to distinguish short-run risk characteristics of asset classes from long-run risk characteristics as shown by Campbell and Viceira (2005).

$$y_{t+t^*} = \sum_{i=0}^{t^*-1} B^i c + B^{t^*} y_t + \sum_{i=0}^{t^*-1} B^i e_{t+t-i} \tag{A2}$$

5,000 scenarios are created by a VAR for 20 years in the future by forward iterating equation (A1). Future asset returns and interest rates $t^*$ periods from now are created as in equation (A2). We refer to Hoevenaars *et al.* (2003) for a further elaboration on scenario generation for ALM.

CHAPTER 22

# STRATEGIC ASSET ALLOCATION FOR PENSION PLANS

JOHN Y. CAMPBELL AND
LUIS M. VICEIRA

## 1 INTRODUCTION

Academic research on asset allocation has had a strong influence on the investment policies of large institutional investors, particularly endowments and pension funds. This chapter summarizes recent research on asset allocation, and discusses its implications for the management of pension plans.

The first part of this chapter asks a basic question about pension investing: who controls the asset allocation decision? One view is that the asset allocation decision for a pension fund is made by those responsible for funding the plan liabilities ('plan sponsors'), or agents acting on their behalf. An alternative view is that the decision is made by the beneficiaries of the plan, or fiduciaries acting on their behalf. In defined contribution (DC) pension plans, there is no conflict between these two views because the same individuals are plan sponsors and beneficiaries. In defined benefit (DB) pension plans, however, plan sponsors are the shareholders of corporations (in corporate plans) and taxpayers (in public plans), while the beneficiaries of the plan are employees. The fiduciaries who manage the fund have a legal obligation to respect the interests of the employees, even though they report to and are paid by the plan sponsors.

We begin by considering the corporate DB asset allocation problem from the plan sponsor's perspective, assuming that the plan sponsor must fully cover the promised benefits to employees. We then introduce the possibility that the corporate plan sponsor may default on some portion of those benefits, and consider the problem from the point of view both of the plan sponsor and of a fiduciary acting in the interests of employees. Finally, we consider public DB plans, and DC plans where there are no fixed benefits at all.

It is important to ask why pension fund investment decisions have relevance for plan sponsors. Pension fund investing is irrelevant in a hypothetical world with no taxes or transaction costs and where all investors have perfect information, identical investment expertise and opportunities, and unlimited liability. In such a world, those responsible for funding the plan—shareholders and taxpayers in the case of DB plans, and individuals saving for retirement in the case of DC plans—can use their own portfolios to undo whatever asset allocation the pension plan decides upon, to obtain the exposure to risk and return they deem optimal, given their resources and risk preferences. This is the well-known Miller–Modigliani capital structure irrelevance theorem, applied to pension fund investing. Of course, taxes, transaction costs, and differences in information and expertise are facts of life, and not all investors have the same access to all asset classes. These imperfections have the potential to justify the existence of pension funds, and make pension fund investment policies relevant for pension fund sponsors.

Section 3 of this chapter discusses alternative approaches to computing optimal investment policies for pension plans, taking into account that these plans have liabilities and long investment horizons. We start with mean-variance analysis, which is the most popular model in the practice of asset management. One standard implementation of mean-variance analysis ignores changes in expected returns and risk over time, so it rules out any response to changing market conditions. An alternative implementation, 'tactical asset allocation', recognizes that market conditions change, and calculates the optimal response using current estimates of short-term expected returns and risks. A more sophisticated approach to asset allocation is available for long-horizon investors. 'Strategic asset allocation' builds on the idea that long-term investors should choose their portfolios taking into account both short-term risk and long-term risk. It tilts portfolios toward those assets that can help investors meet their liabilities when investment opportunities deteriorate.

# 2 Imperfections and the Pension Investment Problem

## 2.1 Taxation

In most countries, asset return taxation differs across assets: typically the tax burden on assets whose return comes mostly in the form of income, such as fixed-income securities, is higher than the tax burden on assets whose return comes mostly from capital gains, such as equities. Additionally, contributions and returns in retirement accounts of DC plans and in corporate DB plans are often tax-exempt. Investors can minimize their tax burden by locating their most heavily taxed assets in their tax-exempt accounts and their lightly taxed assets in their taxable accounts.

Black (1980) and Tepper (1981) were among the first to make this point in the context of optimal asset allocation for corporate pension plans. They note that a pension fund is economically an integral part of the balance sheet of a corporation, since the corporation is responsible for funding the plan on behalf of the shareholders. Within the corporation, the pension fund works effectively as a tax-exempt investment account. Tax optimization makes it optimal for corporations to contribute as much to the plan as regulations allow, to place fixed-income assets in the pension fund, and to hold equities in the taxable part of the balance sheet. This can be achieved by investing pension assets in bonds, and simultaneously implementing a share buy-back program. This location of assets creates shareholder value in the form of interest tax shields. It also makes future contributions to the plan less volatile; in fact, if there is no uncertainty about the average longevity of the group of pension beneficiaries, and if no new benefits accrue, this policy requires no additional contributions after the initial funding of the plan.[1] Viceira and Mitsui (2003) studies the implementation of a Black–Tepper investment strategy by the British retailer Boots PLC.

## 2.2 Transactions Costs and Portfolio Constraints

From a shareholder risk perspective, a shift into bonds in the pension fund combined with a share repurchase program is not necessarily equivalent to a simple swap or change of location of assets in the balance sheet. This is particularly true in the realistic case where risky assets in the pension plan are held in the form of a well-diversified portfolio of equities. By moving those assets into bonds, the corporation effectively delevers the balance sheet and consequently reduces systematic equity risk. By repurchasing shares, the corporation relevers the balance sheet and increases equity risk. But this increase affects total equity risk, both idiosyncratic and market risk, because the corporation buys back its own shares instead of a portfolio of well-diversified equities. An increase in idiosyncratic risk is inconsequential for shareholders who can offset it by trading in their own portfolios, but can be material for shareholders who face binding short-sales constraints or employees who contractually must hold a large fraction of their wealth in company stock.

More generally, there are many reasons why individual investors may have a limited ability to optimally diversify their portfolios on their own. These reasons, which may be described as 'transactions costs', include investors' limited information or financial expertise, lack of self-discipline, limited access to certain asset classes, transaction fees, and short-sales and borrowing constraints. DB pension funds can be cost-efficient vehicles for corporate shareholders, particularly those of modest net worth, to implement their optimal asset allocation.

DB plans tend to be large relative to almost any individual investors. They also have predictable inflows and outflows. These attributes make them well suited to hold asset classes where large investments are required and where liquidity is limited, such as private equity and alternative investments. These asset classes are not generally available to individuals, unless they have high net worth. DB pension plans can take short positions and use leverage at a fraction of the cost a small investor would have to pay, if he could do it at all. They can hire investment professionals whose information and expertise is not available to most individual investors. These professionals can also provide investors with disciplined investing, which may be important in light of the empirical evidence that individuals tend to sell equities to institutions when expected stock returns are highest, and conversely buy stocks when their expected return is lowest (Cohen 2003).

There are two objections to the idea that corporate DB plans should provide investment services to shareholders. First, alternative institutions could provide such services on a stand-alone basis without any connection to a non-financial corporation. Second, corporate pension plans lack transparency; pension accounting rules are complex and do not make it easy for shareholders to understand the impact of pension plan investments on the financial health of the parent corporation.[2] As we discuss below, the case that pension plans should provide general investment services may be stronger for public DB and DC plans than for corporate DB plans.

## 2.3 Limited Liability: Shareholder Perspective

So far we have assumed that shareholders have an absolute obligation to pay the benefits promised by a corporate DB pension plan. In fact, however, shareholders have limited liability and this can have an important effect on the optimal pension plan investment strategy.

Building on the work of Merton (1974, 1977) on the structure and valuation of corporate liabilities, Sharpe (1976) and Treynor (1977) note that the pension liabilities in a corporate DB plan are not intrinsically different from the rest of the liabilities in the corporate balance sheet: shareholders are responsible for funding them only to the extent that there are assets in the corporation. Limited liability makes it optimal for shareholders to hold risky assets in a pension fund, because they may lower future contributions to the plan if realized returns are positive. Equally, shareholders are not liable beyond the assets of the firm if those returns are negative and as a result firm assets are not enough to fund the plan liabilities. In short, limited liability gives shareholders an option to default on the payment of pension fund benefits, which of course is valuable to them.

Functionally, the shareholder position with respect to the pension plan is akin to holding simultaneously a put option on the assets of the plan, with strike price equal to the value of the plan liabilities, and a short position in default-free bonds with value equal to the plan liabilities. Of course, this option is most valuable to shareholders when the plan assets are most volatile, and also when the option is most in the money, that is, when the plan is severely underfunded. Investing in risky assets increases the volatility of the plan assets and the value of the put option to shareholders.[3] Taxes on the one hand, and limited liability on the other hand, create an asset allocation trade-off for corporate DB plans which must be evaluated in each particular case.

The incentive to invest pension plan assets in risky assets is exacerbated in countries whose governments insure failed pension plans. In the United States the Pension Benefit Guaranty Corporation (PBGC), a government-sponsored agency, collects insurance premia from pension plans in exchange for taking over the assets and liabilities of those that fail. The United Kingdom is creating a Pension Protective Fund (PPF), a pension agency similar to the PBGC. Even in countries without formal pension-protection agencies, there may be implicit government guarantees if governments tend to take over failed plans.

A pension insurance program gives a corporation an option to sell its pension assets to the pension agency at a price equal to its pension liabilities. This put option becomes more valuable as pension plan assets become riskier. If the agency collects a pension insurance premium based on a fair valuation of the put option, the incentive to hold risky assets in the pension plan is offset. However, in practice pension insurance premia are similar for all corporations, regardless of their credit risk, and are relatively low. Thus underfunded pension plans, which are most likely to fail, have a strong incentive to undertake risky investments.

An additional effect of limited liability is that the tax minimization strategy for a corporate pension plan makes existing bondholder claims riskier. This is so because pension claims typically have much lower priority than senior debt on assets outside the pension plan. By funding the pension plan and investing the pension plan assets in bonds, the corporation is effectively making pension liabilities senior to on-balance sheet debt, thus shifting risk from pension beneficiaries to bondholders.

## 2.4 Limited Liability: Fiduciary Perspective

In the presence of limited liability, pension beneficiaries share in the downside risk of the pension fund investment results. Fiduciaries acting on their behalf should limit this risk. In addition, fiduciaries should consider the effect of pension fund asset allocation on the behavior of the plan sponsor. For example, a Black–Tepper investment policy of placing bonds in the pension fund is risk-free if no further contributions are required from the sponsor, but not if the pension plan is underfunded. In this case there is even a possibility that the reduction of risk in the pension plan assets actually increases the risk to plan beneficiaries, if the plan sponsor responds with a share buyback plan that greatly increases idiosyncratic risk and thus increases the probability of corporate bankruptcy (Oberhofer 2003).

We have assumed so far that pension beneficiaries hold a fixed claim against the sponsor, and that sponsors have the right to appropriate fund surpluses, for example through 'contribution holidays'. In practice, however, many DB plans involve some flexibility to adjust benefits over time. Workers are in effect offered a combination of a fixed benefit and a benefit that is linked to the overall performance of the fund. In this context, beneficiaries may share to some extent in the upside as well as the downside results of the fund investment decisions. Thus pension beneficiaries will be as interested as plan sponsors in using the pension fund as an efficient vehicle to optimally diversify their portfolios, and pension fund investment in risky assets makes some sense for them too.

## 2.5 Asset Allocation for Public DB Pension Plans

Many of the considerations that are relevant for corporate pension plans do not apply to publicly sponsored DB plans. These are tax-exempt institutions whose ability to default on their pension obligations is probably very limited—though they may have the power to reduce pension benefits through legislation.

Asset allocation for public DB plans is relevant largely because they may be able to invest on behalf of taxpayers in illiquid asset classes, and to provide investment expertise at low cost. This role may be more important for public DB plans than for corporate DB plans. The ultimate sponsors of corporate DB plans are corporate shareholders, who by definition are participants in equity markets; they are likely to have at least some financial expertise and access to alternative investment vehicles. The ultimate sponsors of public DB plans are taxpayers, some of whom may have no other exposure to the diversified investment opportunities available in financial markets.

## 2.6 Asset Allocation for DC Pension Plans

Some of the same considerations that we have discussed for DB plans also apply to DC plans. First, the returns on DC pension plans are untaxed until the assets are withdrawn from the plan. Dammon *et al.* (2004) have argued that this should lead individuals with DC pension plans to hold bonds in their retirement accounts, and equities in their taxable accounts, following a strategy that is analogous to the Black–Tepper strategy for DB plans.[4] Second, DC plans can in principle offer individual investors access to otherwise unavailable asset classes. In current practice, however, DC plans have built-in liquidity requirements which make them unsuitable for investments requiring lockup periods. They tend to be offered as simple tax-exempt vehicles for mutual fund or company stock investing.

# 3 Asset Allocation for Long-Term Investors

The arguments we have laid out so far imply that pension fund investment decisions are relevant to sponsors and beneficiaries alike. We now assume that the pension fund investment problem can be written as an optimization problem of maximizing expected utility subject to constraints. The utility function captures the notion that there is diminishing marginal benefit of a pension surplus and increasing marginal cost of a pension shortfall. The constraints of the problem reflect the influences of investment returns, pension contributions, and pension benefits on the value of the pension fund.

The academic model which has been most influential in the practice of asset management is Markowitz's (1952) mean-variance analysis. The success of the mean-variance model derives from its simplicity, with a clear and intuitive connection between inputs—investors' expectations of future returns, volatilities, and correlations—and the output—a recommended portfolio, and its useful emphasis on portfolio diversification to control risk. This has made the model the basic paradigm in asset allocation, upon which academics and practitioners alike have built numerous refinements and extensions.[5]

The model suffers, however, from two important limitations in its practical application to pension fund investing. First, it focuses only on the financial assets in a portfolio, abstracting both from liabilities and from non-financial income. Second, it assumes that all investors have a short-term investment horizon. For a given set of expectations of future returns and their variances and correlations, the model recommends the same portfolio of risky assets for all investors.

## 3.1 Pension Fund Liabilities

By their very nature, pension funds have important liabilities. A DB pension plan, for example, must finance a promised stream of benefits. One way to handle this, while preserving the simplicity of the mean-variance approach, is to specify the objective function in terms of the pension plan surplus, the value of assets less the value of liabilities, at some future date. One can write $S_T = A_T - L_T$, where $A_T$ is the value of assets at future date $T$ and $L_T$ is the value of liabilities at date $T$, and define a utility function over $S_T$ to capture the idea that the marginal benefit of a surplus is diminishing in the level of the surplus. Mean-variance analysis then seeks to maximize a linear function of the mean and variance of $S_T$.[6]

This approach implies that the risk of any individual investment with return $R_{iT}$ to horizon $T$ should be measured by its covariance with the surplus:

$$\text{Cov}(R_{iT}, S_T) = \text{Cov}(R_{iT}, A_T) - \text{Cov}(R_{iT}, L_T).$$

In standard mean-variance analysis, an asset's risk is measured by its covariance with the value of the total portfolio of assets, but here one must also take account of covariance with the value of liabilities. An asset that covaries positively with the value of liabilities hedges those liabilities and should be given credit for this. For example, if liabilities take the form of long streams of fixed nominal payments to retirees, then they increase in value when nominal interest rates decline. Long-term nominal bonds also move inversely with nominal interest rates, so they hedge long-term nominal liabilities. Similarly, inflation-indexed bonds hedge liabilities that require long streams of real (inflation-adjusted) payments.

A variant of this approach assumes that there is an infinite utility cost to a pension shortfall, that is, a negative value of $S_T$. In this case it is optimal first to find a portfolio of assets that perfectly hedges liabilities, and then to invest the remainder of the portfolio, trading off risk and return in the usual manner. This approach requires that liabilities be perfectly hedgeable, and at a cost less than the value of the total portfolio. That is, the pension plan must be overfunded.[7]

In practice, many pension plans are underfunded and have some ability to reduce benefits in bad states of the world (perhaps by threatening bankruptcy). This suggests that one should allow for the possibility of a pension shortfall, and should invest with due regard to the cost of a shortfall, but without assuming that the cost is infinite. One popular approach is to impose a constraint that there is only a small probability (often chosen to be 5 percent) that a shortfall exceeds some given amount (the 'value at risk'). The weakness of this approach is that it treats all shortfalls greater than the value at risk as equivalent, whereas it seems likely that the cost of a shortfall is increasing in the size of the shortfall. This makes it preferable to specify a utility function that penalizes large shortfalls more than smaller ones.

An even more sophisticated approach recognizes that surpluses may be more welcome, and shortfalls may be more painful, in some states of the world than in others. For example, the marginal cost of a shortfall in a corporate DB plan may be greater when the corporate sponsor is currently unprofitable, because then the sponsor must rely on costly external finance to fund the plan; the marginal cost of a shortfall in a public DB plan may be greater when the local economy is weak, because then the local government sponsor of the plan has a reduced tax base. Effects of this sort can be modeled using state-dependent utility, or by treating the condition of the sponsor as an implicit asset of the pension plan whose risks can be hedged by the financial assets of the plan. In either case the lesson is that the financial portfolio should be used to hedge these additional risks. For example, public DB plans should avoid holding local stocks whose value will be correlated with the local tax base.[8]

## 3.2 Long-Term Investment Horizon

Pension funds are distinctive not only because they have liabilities, but because they must invest over a long period of time. The investment horizon $T$ discussed above is likely to be more than one year from the present; indeed, the fund may need to consider multiple horizons rather than just a single horizon. Financial economists have understood at least since the work of Samuelson (1969) and Merton (1969, 1971, 1973) that long-term investing may differ from short-term investing when investment opportunities vary over time. In this situation long-term investors will care about shocks to investment opportunities—the productivity of wealth—as well as shocks to wealth itself. As Merton emphasized, long-term investors may wish to hedge their exposures to wealth productivity shocks, giving rise to intertemporal hedging demands for financial assets. Brennan et al.

(1997) have coined the phrase 'strategic asset allocation' to describe this far-sighted response to time-varying investment opportunities.

Unfortunately, in contrast to the appealing simplicity of mean-variance analysis, strategic asset allocation models can be difficult to solve in practice: investors' risk preferences, spending needs, and investment horizons interact in complex ways with investment opportunities and risk. For many years, practically usable solutions to strategic asset allocation models were unavailable. As a result, the Merton model did not become a usable empirical paradigm, and did not displace the Markowitz model as the leading model in the practice of asset management. A contributing factor to this situation may have been the view that prevailed in academic literature and applied finance until the late 1980s that investment opportunities were approximately constant. Under this view, one might see Merton's model as an important conceptual advance, but much less important in practice.

Since the 1980s this situation has changed as a result of several related developments. First, a large body of research in empirical finance has established not only that investment opportunities change over time, but also that changes in expected returns on bonds and equities and in real interest rates are highly persistent (e.g. Campbell and Shiller 1988; Fama and French 1988; Hodrick 1992; Campbell et al. 1997). Second, this shift in perception has motivated new research into long-term investing, and financial theorists have discovered some new closed-form solutions to the Merton model. These solutions, while still based on stylized models, offer important analytical insights into the importance for long-term asset allocation of long-term risk (e.g. Kim and Omberg 1996; Campbell and Viceira 1999, 2001; Schroder and Skiadas 1999; Wachter 2002). Third, computing power and numerical methods have advanced to the point at which realistic multi-period portfolio choice problems can be solved numerically. One particularly appealing approach is to combine approximate analytical solution methods with numerical methods; this greatly increases the realism of the investment problems that can be solved numerically, while also making the solutions easier to interpret. Campbell and Viceira (2002) provide a book-length survey and integration of this literature, and Campbell et al. (2003) is an extensive empirical application to the problem of optimal asset allocation across US stocks, bonds, and Treasury bills.

One particularly simple approach to long-term investing modifies the mean-variance analysis only by replacing short-term means and covariances with long-term means and covariances. This approach, which is discussed by Barberis (2000) and Campbell and Viceira (2005), is appropriate for a long-term 'buy-and-hold' investor who must make a single portfolio decision today and then must hold the portfolio without further rebalancing. Assets that offer temporarily high returns are less attractive to such an investor than assets that are expected to deliver high returns over the long term. Assets with mean-reverting returns are relatively more attractive to such an investor. For these assets, short-term risks will tend to cancel out over the longer term as unusually high initial returns are offset by lower average subsequent returns. Empirically, stock returns appear to be mean-reverting, as are inflation-indexed bond returns and nominal bond returns in periods of relatively stable inflation. Bill returns, on the other hand, exhibit persistent fluctuations so bills are riskier in the long term than the short term. Campbell and Viceira (2005) show how these effects lead a buy-and-hold investor to hold more bonds and stocks than an equally risk-averse short-term investor.

Of course, even investors with a long horizon have frequent opportunities to rebalance their portfolios. An asset with a temporarily high expected return is attractive to an investor who can exploit the short-term opportunity and then rebalance when normal conditions resume. 'Tactical asset allocation' strategies use mean-variance analysis with time-varying expected returns derived from some return forecasting model, and short-term risk estimates. But these strategies ignore the difference between short-term and long-term risks. The correct investment approach for a long-term investor who can rebalance frequently is to respond to short-term expected returns, while measuring the risk of each asset using not only its covariance with the total portfolio return, but also its covariance with changes in investment opportunities. A conservative long-term investor should favor assets that do well when investment opportunities deteriorate—that is, when expected returns decline—for such assets protect the portfolio against the effects of prolonged periods of poor returns. This 'strategic asset allocation' strategy leads conservative long-term investors to increase their average allocations to mean-reverting assets. A mean-reverting asset is one whose expected return tends to decline when its price increases; thus it hedges the variations in its own expected return. Equities, inflation-indexed bonds, and nominal bonds in periods of stable inflation all appear to be mean-reverting, and so they play a major role in strategic asset allocation just as they do in long-term mean-variance portfolios.

Strategic asset allocation investors should value assets not only for hedging their own expected returns, but also for hedging the variations in the expected returns of other attractive assets. Growth stocks, for example, appear to be good hedges against low returns on the aggregate stock market, and may be attractive to strategic asset allocation investors despite their low average returns (Campbell and Vuolteenaho 2004).

# 4 Conclusion

Much work remains to be done to make strategic asset allocation usable for pension funds and other long-term institutional investors. The goal is to build practical tools to derive optimal strategic portfolio weights given an investor's beliefs about investment opportunities. The challenge is that strategic asset allocation requires an investor to specify beliefs not only about investment opportunities today, but also about how those opportunities may evolve in the future. The reward is that, given such beliefs, a strategic asset allocation portfolio can have much better long-run properties than a mean-variance portfolio (Campbell and Viceira 1999, 2002).

One promising approach is the use of Bayesian methods to model investors' uncertainty about the process governing investment opportunities. Uncertainty about the mean return on a risky asset increases its long-term risk relative to its short-term risk and reduces the portfolio allocation of a conservative long-term investor (Brennan 1998). Bayesian methods can also be used to impose prior beliefs about the validity of asset pricing models (Pastor and Stambaugh 2000) or about the predictability of stock returns (Xia 2001).

Another important task is to integrate the analysis of liabilities with the analysis of time-varying investment opportunities. If interest rates are constant, fixed nominal liabilities can be hedged using either short-term bills or long-term nominal bonds. If interest rates are arbitrarily time-varying, fixed nominal liabilities at a given future date can only be hedged by nominal bonds that mature at the same date. If interest rates are time-varying in a manner that can be captured by a parsimonious term structure model, then such liabilities can be hedged using a small number of short-term and long-term bonds. Indexation of benefits to wages or prices and uncertain lifetimes of pension beneficiaries further complicate the management of liabilities. The integration of liability management with strategic asset allocation is a leading investment challenge for pension plans.

## Notes

1. In practice, longevity risk is a significant issue (Blake and Burrows 2001; King 2004). A recent financial innovation that will help pension plans to manage this risk is the creation of 'longevity bonds', whose payoffs depend on the longevity of a large demographic group. The European Investment Bank and BNP Paribas, for example, have announced a 25-year issue linked to the longevity of senior citizens in England and Wales.
2. Jin et al. (2004), however, present evidence that corporate stock prices do reflect information about the investment risks of corporate pension plans.
3. Equivalently, we can interpret the plan beneficiary position as equivalent to holding the assets of the plan while giving shareholders the option to buy them at a strike price equal to the value of the plan liabilities. Increasing the volatility of the plan assets makes this option more valuable to shareholders.
4. This view has been challenged by Poterba et al. (2004) for the case of high-income taxable investors who save in actively managed equity funds. They argue that it might be optimal for those investors to hold these funds in their retirement (non-taxable)

account, because they tend to impose substantial tax burdens on their investors, while at the same time it is possible to hold forms of fixed-income investments with low tax burdens such as municipal bonds in the United States.

5. Much work by practitioners has sought to address the problem that arises when a mean-variance optimization falsely identifies some combination of risky assets as almost riskless, based on the historical pattern of returns. In this circumstance the optimization will often place excessive weight on what it perceives to be a near arbitrage opportunity. One approach is to constrain portfolio weights (e.g. Frost and Savarino 1988; Jagannathan and Ma 2002); another is to use prior information to influence the mean-variance estimates (e.g. Treynor and Black 1973; Black and Litterman 1992; Pastor and Stambaugh 2000). Brandt (forthcoming) surveys this literature.

6. In implementing this approach, an important question is whether to measure only those pension liabilities that have been incurred to date (accumulated benefit obligation, or ABO, in US terminology), or whether to include also liabilities that will be incurred by the ongoing operations of the plan sponsor in the future (projected benefit obligation, or PBO). One view is that future ongoing liabilities will be covered by future contributions from the plan sponsor, in which case plan assets need only be matched to ABO in calculating the plan surplus. An alternative view is that plan assets must cover both past and future accumulated benefits, in which case the PBO may become relevant. Viceira and Tung (2005) discusses these issues and the related US accounting rules in the context of the General Motors pension plan.

7. See Rubinstein (1976a, 1976b) for the theory of optimal investment with fixed liabilities and an infinite shortfall cost. Dybvig (1999) considers the case of an endowment that can increase discretionary spending but never reduce it; such an endowment has variable, endogenous liabilities but again an infinite shortfall cost.

8. These points are related to the large literature on optimal investment in the presence of non-financial income, for example, labor income for individuals or donations for universities. See, for example, Bodie *et al.* (1992), Merton (1983, 1993), and Campbell and Viceira (2002, ch. 6).

# REFERENCES

BARBERIS, NICHOLAS (2000). 'Investing for the long run when returns are predictable'. *Journal of Finance*, 55: 225–64.

BLACK, FISCHER (1980). 'The tax consequences of long-run pension policy'. *Financial Analysts Journal* (July–Aug.).

—— and LITTERMAN, ROBERT (1992). 'Global portfolio optimization'. *Financial Analysts Journal*, 48: 28–43.

BLAKE, DAVID, and BURROWS, WILLIAM (2001). 'Survivor bonds: helping to hedge mortality risk'. *Journal of Risk and Insurance*, 68: 339–48.

BODIE, ZVI, MERTON, ROBERT C., and SAMUELSON, WILLIAM (1992). 'Labor supply flexibility and portfolio choice in a life cycle model'. *Journal of Economic Dynamics and Control*, 16: 427–49.

Brandt, Michael (forthcoming). 'Portfolio choice problems', in Yacine Ait-Sahalia and Lars Hansen (eds.), *Handbook of Financial Econometrics*. Amsterdam: Elsevier Science.

Brennan, Michael J. (1998). 'The role of learning in dynamic portfolio decisions'. *European Finance Review*, 1: 295–306.

—— Schwartz, Eduardo S., and Lagnado, Ronald (1997). 'Strategic asset allocation'. *Journal of Economic Dynamics and Control*, 21: 1377–403.

Campbell, John Y., Chan, Yeung Lewis, and Viceira, Luis M. (2003). 'A multivariate model of strategic asset allocation'. *Journal of Financial Economics*, 67: 41–80.

—— Lo, Andrew W., and MacKinlay, A. Craig (1997). *The Econometrics of Financial Markets*. Princeton: Princeton University Press.

—— and Shiller, Robert J. (1988). 'The dividend-price ratio and expectations of future dividends and discount factors'. *Review of Financial Studies*, 1: 195–228.

—— and Viceira, Luis M. (1999). 'Consumption and portfolio decisions when expected returns are time varying'. *Quarterly Journal of Economics*, 114: 433–95.

—— —— (2001). 'Who should buy long-term bonds?' *American Economic Review*, 91: 99–127.

—— —— (2002). *Strategic Asset Allocation: Portfolio Choice for Long-Term Investors*. New York: Oxford University Press.

—— —— (2005). 'The term structure of the risk-return tradeoff'. *Financial Analysts Journal*, 61: 34–44.

—— and Vuolteenaho, Tuomo O. (2004). 'Bad beta, good beta'. *American Economic Review*, 94 (Dec.): 1249–75.

Cohen, Randolph (2003). 'Asset allocation decisions of individuals and institutions'. Working Paper 03–112. Harvard Business School.

Dammon, Robert M., Spatt, Chester H., and Zhang, Harold H. (2004). 'Optimal asset location and allocation with taxable and tax-deferred investing', *Journal of Finance*, 59: 999–1037.

Dybvig, Philip H. (1999). 'Using asset allocation to protect spending'. *Financial Analysts Journal* (Jan.–Feb.): 49–62.

Fama, Eugene F., and French, Kenneth (1988). 'Dividend yields and expected stock returns'. *Journal of Financial Economics*, 22: 3–27.

Frost, Peter A., and Savarino, James E. (1988). 'For better performance: constrain portfolio weights'. *Journal of Portfolio Management*, 15: 29–34.

Hodrick, Robert J. (1992). 'Dividend yields and expected stock returns: alternative procedures for inference and measurement'. *Review of Financial Studies*, 5: 357–86.

Jagannathan, Ravi, and Ma, Tongshu (2002). 'Risk reduction in large portfolios: why imposing the wrong constraints helps'. *Journal of Finance*, 58: 1651–84.

Jin, Li, Merton, Robert C., and Bodie, Zvi (2004). 'Do a firm's equity returns reflect the risk of its pension plan?' NBER Working Paper No. 10650.

Kim, Tong Suk, and Omberg, Edward (1996). 'Dynamic nonmyopic portfolio behavior'. *Review of Financial Studies*, 9: 141–61.

King, Mervyn A. (2004). 'What fates impose: living up to uncertainty'. Annual Lecture, British Academy.

Markowitz, Harry (1952). 'Portfolio selection'. *Journal of Finance*, 7: 77–91.

Merton, Robert C. (1969). 'Lifetime portfolio selection under uncertainty: the continuous-time case'. *Review of Economics and Statistics*, 51: 247–57.

—— (1971). 'Optimum consumption and portfolio rules in a continuous-time model'. *Journal of Economic Theory*, 3: 373–413.

—— (1973). 'An intertemporal capital asset pricing model'. *Econometrica*, 41: 867–87.

—— (1974). 'On the pricing of corporate debt: the risk structure of interest rates'. *Journal of Finance*, 29: 449–70.

—— (1977). 'On the pricing of contingent claims and the Modigliani–Miller theorem'. *Journal of Financial Economics*, 5: 241–9.

—— (1983). 'On consumption-indexed public pension plans', in Z. Bodie and J. Shoven (eds.), *Financial Aspects of the US Pension System*. Chicago: University of Chicago Press, 259–76.

—— (1993). 'Optimal investment strategies for university endowment funds', in C. Clotfelter and M. Rothschild (eds.), *Studies of Supply and Demand in Higher Education*. Chicago: University of Chicago Press.

OBERHOFER, GEORGE (2003). 'Boots PLC's all-bond pension portfolio: will the world follow?' *Frank Russell Company Viewpoint*, Mar.

PASTOR, LUBOS, and STAMBAUGH, ROBERT F. (2000). 'Comparing asset pricing models: an investment perspective'. *Journal of Financial Economics*, 56: 335–81.

POTERBA, JAMES, SHOVEN, JOHN, and SIALM, CLEMENS (2004). 'Asset location for retirement savers', in William G. Gale, J. Shoven, and M. Warshawsky (eds.), *Private Pensions and Public Policies*. Washington, D. C.: The Brookings Institution, 290–331.

RUBINSTEIN, MARK (1976a). 'The strong case for the generalized logarithmic utility model as the premier model of financial markets'. *Journal of Finance*, 31: 551–71.

—— (1976b). 'The valuation of uncertain income streams and the pricing of options'. *Bell Journal of Economics*, 7: 407–25.

SAMUELSON, PAUL A. (1969). 'Lifetime portfolio selection by dynamic stochastic programming'. *Review of Economics and Statistics*, 51: 239–46.

SCHRODER, MARK, and SKIADAS, COSTIS (1999). 'Optimal consumption and portfolio selection with stochastic differential utility'. *Journal of Economic Theory*, 89: 68–126.

SHARPE, WILLIAM F. (1976). 'Corporate pension funding policy'. *Journal of Financial Economics*, 3: 183–93.

TEPPER, IRWIN (1981). 'Taxation and corporate pension policy'. *Journal of Finance*, 36: 1–13.

TREYNOR, JACK L. (1977). 'The principles of corporate pension finance'. *Journal of Finance*, 32: 627–38.

—— and BLACK, FISCHER (1973). 'How to use security analysis to improve portfolio selection'. *Journal of Business*, 46: 66–86.

VICEIRA, LUIS M. and MITSUI, AKIKO (2003). 'Pension policy at The Boots Company PLC'. Case 203–105, Harvard Business School.

—— and TUNG, HELEN H. (2005). 'General Motors US Pension Funds'. Case 9-206-001, Harvard Business School.

WACHTER, JESSICA (2002). 'Portfolio and consumption decisions under mean-reverting returns: an exact solution for complete markets'. *Journal of Financial and Quantitative Analysis*, 37: 63–91.

XIA, YIHONG (2001). 'Learning about predictability: the effects of parameter uncertainty on dynamic asset allocation'. *Journal of Finance*, 56: 205–46.

# CHAPTER 23

# PENSION FUND MANAGEMENT AND INVESTMENT PERFORMANCE

## IAN TONKS

## 1 INTRODUCTION

Pension schemes may be unfunded or funded, and the detailed working of these is discussed elsewhere in this *Handbook*. In an unfunded pay-as-you-go scheme, the pension represents a transfer made between the current working population and the current retired population. In a funded scheme the working population makes contributions into a pension fund which, during the accumulation phase, grows in value up to retirement. After retirement, the fund enters the decumulation phase and pays out a pension to the retired pensioners for the remainder of their lives. The management of investment funds in these pension schemes is the topic of this chapter.

During the accumulation phase, the pension fund will tend to increase in value because of additional contributions made into the fund, and also due to the investment returns generated by the assets in the fund. For example, in a pension scheme that requires annual contributions of $1,000 over 40 years, the fund's assets would build up to $120,800 in value at retirement if the return on cumulated funds was 5 percent per year; but the same contributions over the same period if the rate of return was 6 percent would grow to $154,800. This simple numerical example illustrates that small changes in the return on assets can have a dramatic impact on the size of the pension fund at retirement, and hence on the pension that can be paid from this accumulated fund. In practice the returns on pension fund investments will vary every period, hence introducing some risk into the size of the pension fund at retirement, and types of pension schemes differ according to who bears this investment risk.

Private pension schemes can be classified by type in two dimensions: whether the pension is paid on a defined contribution or a defined benefit basis, and whether the pension scheme is constituted on an individual or a group basis. Individual pension schemes are always *funded* and pay a pension at retirement on a *defined contribution* basis. This means that the individual receives a pension which depends on the accumulated assets in the fund. Personal pensions in the UK and 401(k) pension plans or individual retirement accounts in the United States are examples of such schemes, and individuals may have some choice over the type of investments in the fund. Under any defined contribution scheme, the pensioner bears the risk of fund underperformance. Group pension schemes are arranged for more than one individual, and there may be some sharing across generations of the accumulated assets in the pension fund. In most countries, occupational schemes provided by an employer are examples of group pension schemes, and may pay on a defined benefit or a defined contribution basis. Papke *et al.* (1996) note the shift in the United States from defined benefit to defined contribution pension schemes and particularly 401(k) plans. Similarly, in the UK there has been a substantial growth in UK individual defined contribution schemes over the last 20 years. According to the Sandler Report (2002) between 1988 and 1995 the share of total pensions assets represented by personal pensions increased from 12 to over 20 percent.

The return earned by assets in the pension fund depends upon the investment strategy and asset allocation decisions of the pension fund. These investment decisions can be made by individual pension contributors, or delegated to professional fund managers. The purpose of this chapter is to analyze the investment management process of funds invested in pension schemes.[1] The chapter focuses particularly on measuring the performance of investment returns earned by pension funds. Although investment performance is considered within a global context, in fact only a small number of countries have sizeable funded pension schemes. Table 23.1 shows the stock of pension assets for major developed countries in 1996. The United States, UK, and the Netherlands have large amounts of pension fund assets relative to GDP in their economies, reflecting the importance of funded schemes in these countries.[2] In contrast major economies such as Japan, France, and Germany have a relatively small percentage of pension fund assets, reflecting the fact that these economies' pension schemes are predominantly unfunded pay-as-you-go systems.

Table 23.1 Private pension funding in major developed countries, 1996

| | US $bn | % of GDP |
|---|---|---|
| Belgium | 11 | 4 |
| Canada | 213 | 45 |
| Denmark | 38 | 22 |
| Finland | 18 | 14 |
| France | 69 | 5 |
| Germany | 137 | 6 |
| Ireland | 32 | 43 |
| Italy | 32 | 3 |
| Japan | 943 | 22 |
| Netherlands | 349 | 89 |
| Spain | 22 | 4 |
| Sweden | 38 | 33 |
| UK | 966 | 76 |
| USA | 4,763 | 62 |
| EU total | 1,730 | 21 |

Source: Davis (1998).

The next section discusses the investment management industry in general, and explains how it relates to the pensions management industry. Section 3 explains the measurement of investment returns; Section 4 introduces a number of risk-adjusted performance measures, and Section 5 discusses some problems with these measures. Sections 6 and 7 report the results of empirical evidence of pension fund investment performance. Section 8 concludes.

## 2 THE PENSIONS MANAGEMENT INDUSTRY

Pension fund management is only one part of the very large global investment management industry, which represents the management of investment portfolios by professional fund managers.[3] Such delegated portfolio management also includes unit trusts (mutual funds), investment trusts (closed-end funds), investment policies (life assurance, endowment policies). Franks *et al.* (2003) report that it is estimated that the extent of global assets under external management during 1999 was of the order of €33 trillion. Table 23.2 shows the assets under management in seven European countries and the United States. Franks *et al.* report that in all of these countries the amount of assets managed has increased substantially throughout the 1990s. In the UK, United States, France, Germany, the Netherlands over the period 1994–9 the amount of assets managed more than doubled; net assets of Spanish institutional investors trebled over the same period; and assets under management in Italy in 1999 were six times greater than in 1994. Davis and Steil (2001) produce similar estimates, and suggest that the recent increase is part of a longer trend of institutionalization of the savings markets around the world. In 1970 the total financial claims of the financial sector were 4 percent of GDP for the G-7 countries. By 1998 this figure had almost doubled to 7.91 percent.

Pension assets are a significant part of the global investment management industry: pension funds, mutual funds, and insurance funds account for roughly equal shares of total assets, though both mutual funds and insurance funds will include some pension savings. Pension funds are relatively important in the UK and the United States, and we can see from Table 23.2 that in the United States mutual funds are also important institutional investors, which is not the case for the UK. Table 23.3 shows the percentage of UK corporate equity owned by institutional investors, and shows that pension funds are major investors in the

Table 23.2 Assets under management for eight countries, 1999 (billion euro)

| Country | Pension funds | Insurance companies | Mutual funds |
| --- | --- | --- | --- |
| France | 66 | 830 | 705 |
| Germany | 129 | 673 | 515 |
| Ireland | 47 | 32 | 150 |
| Italy | 65 | 169 | 412 |
| Netherlands | 397 | 220 | 83 |
| Spain | 32 | 62 | 219 |
| UK | 1,270 | 1,266 | 345 |
| Total Euro-7 | 2,006 | 3,252 | 2,429 |
| USA | 7,225 | 2,403 | 6,388 |

*Source*: Franks *et al.* (2003).

## Table 23.3 Institutionalization of the UK equity market to 1999

| | End year (%) | | | | | |
| --- | --- | --- | --- | --- | --- | --- |
| | 1963 | 1975 | 1981 | 1989 | 1994 | 1999 |
| Pension funds | 6.4 | 16.8 | 26.7 | 30.6 | 27.8 | 19.6 |
| Insurance companies | 10.0 | 15.9 | 20.5 | 18.6 | 21.9 | 21.6 |
| Unit and investment trusts and other | 12.6 | 14.6 | 10.4 | 8.6 | 10.1 | 9.7 |
| Banks | 1.3 | 0.7 | 0.3 | 0.7 | 0.4 | 1.0 |
| Total UK institutions | 30.3 | 48.0 | 57.9 | 58.5 | 60.2 | 51.9 |
| Individuals | 54.0 | 37.5 | 28.2 | 20.6 | 20.3 | 15.3 |
| Other personal sector | 2.1 | 2.3 | 2.2 | 2.3 | 1.3 | 1.3 |
| Public sector | 1.5 | 3.6 | 3.0 | 2.0 | 0.8 | 0.1 |
| Industrial and commercial companies | 5.1 | 3.0 | 5.1 | 3.8 | 1.1 | 2.2 |
| Overseas | 7.0 | 5.6 | 3.6 | 12.8 | 16.3 | 29.3 |
| Total | 100 | 100 | 100 | 100 | 100 | 100 |

*Source*: Myners (2001), based on ONS 'Share Ownership: A Report on the Ownership of Shares at 31/12/99', 8.

equity markets, owning about 40 percent of the UK's equity sector. Table 23.2 also shows that although France and Germany do not have large funded pension schemes, they have relatively large insurance and mutual fund sectors. It is important to recognize that individuals in different countries may be making provisions for their retirement through other savings vehicles. UCITS (Undertaking for Collective Investment in Transferable Securities) are important savings vehicles in France and Germany (Franks *et al.* 2003).

The difference between pension schemes and other saving vehicles is the long-term nature of a pension scheme under which the savings cannot be accessed until retirement. Del Guercio and Tkac (2002) find that the flow of funds into pension funds is less sensitive to past performance than for mutual funds and suggest that this is because of the long-term nature of pension schemes.

A fund manager is an individual (or company) that performs a range of activities centered around a core service of investing clients' assets, in particular managing an investment portfolio. The client–manager relationship is an example of the principal–agent framework where the client employs a fund manager to invest the client's assets in order to maximize returns for a given level of risk or obtain the lowest level of risk to achieve a targeted return. In terms of mean-variance analysis, the objective of the fund manger is to locate the client's portfolio on the efficiency frontier or in the case of active fund management to generate abnormal returns above some benchmark, that is, to do better than the efficiency frontier. With respect to occupational pension funds, Lakonishok *et al.* (1992) refer to a 'double agency' problem, since the employee, who will eventually become the recipient of the pension, is also principal, and delegates pension fund decisions to the company, which in turn delegates the investment allocation decisions to a fund manager.

Why does the client delegate investment management to the fund manager? There are two reasons: first the fund manager may have superior investment skills, through information-processing abilities. The second reason is due to economies of scale in the fund management process: buying and selling securities may be expensive for a small fund, and pooling these funds under the jurisdiction of a single fund manager may be efficient. Of course the disadvantage of delegated portfolio management is that the client needs to monitor the fund manager. Bhattacharya and Pfleiderer (1985) and Stoughton (1993) discuss the structure of fund manager contracts within the context of delegated portfolio management.

There are two basic types of delegated investment management: bespoke and pooled fund management. In a bespoke vehicle the client hires a fund manager to make the investment decisions on its behalf according to some specified mandate and specific return expectation. The fund manager acts as the custodian of the investor's capital, and will typically report back to the client in a personal capacity on a regular basis on the performance of the fund. In a pooled vehicle, the client simply purchases units of a diversified investment from a financial institution, such as an insurance company or a unit trust, and this approach involves the commingling of investment capital from many clients. The fund manager will again report back to the client, but in a less personal manner. Not surprisingly, the costs of

Table 23.4 Fund management fees charged in different countries for a £100 million mandate

|  | Basis points per annum | | | | | | | |
|---|---|---|---|---|---|---|---|---|
|  | Canada | | UK | | Australia | | USA | |
|  | Equities | Fixed interest | Equities | Fixed interest | Equities | Fixed interest | Equities | Fixed interest |
| Upper quartile fee | 28 | 22 | 48 | 23 | 47 | 22 | 50 | 30 |
| Median fee | 24 | 18 | 40 | 18 | 44 | 19 | 42 | 26 |
| Lower quartile fee | 21 | 16 | 30 | 17 | 40 | 18 | 33 | 23 |

*Source*: Frank Russell quoted in Myners (2001).

running a bespoke service will be more than the pooled vehicle, and for that reason the bespoke vehicle is only likely to be used by clients with large amounts of funds to be managed. Typical fees charged by fund managers for managing a segregated fund across a number of countries are given in Table 23.4. The median fee for managing an equity portfolio is about 50 basis points or 0.5 percent per year of the funds under management.

The fund manager manages the client's investment portfolio, with an appropriate mix of asset classes, and selects securities, with the typical objective of maximizing returns subject to a specified level of risk, and will adjust the portfolio through time, as expectations of returns change. Under pooled fund management, the fund manager sets the long-term policy of the fund, and then investors such as pension funds can choose to purchase shares in this investment vehicle. Under bespoke asset management, the fund manager will agree a long-term policy or strategy with the pension fund, and this will involve specifying a relevant benchmark against which the portfolio performance will be judged. Traditionally, fund managers were assessed in relation to a peer-group benchmark such as outperforming the median performance of similar funds. However, Myners (2001) reports a long-run trend away from peer-group benchmark to customized benchmarks. This trend reflects trustees increasingly taking asset-allocation decisions on the basis of advice from consultants, and then allocating management of a class of assets to a specific fund manager. The customized benchmark for that manager might then be the relevant index for that asset class. The bespoke investment management process is seen as dynamic, with the mandate evolving over time as the performance of the fund or asset class varies, and expectations of future returns change.

Individual pension schemes that have delegated investment management will typically be constituted on a pooled basis, unless the individual is particularly wealthy. The type of fund management chosen for occupational pension schemes will depend in part on the advice given by consultant actuaries who assess the financial viability of the occupational pension scheme. Under an insured scheme, contributions are made into a pooled vehicle which guarantees to pay a pre-defined benefit at a pre-defined time. The risk of a funding shortfall (ignoring default risk) is borne by the fund manager (typically an insurance company), and not the individual or the corporation.

Most small schemes will be run as insured fund management. Under a self-administered scheme, where the pension fund sponsors have some control over the investment management, fund management may be outsourced to one or more external managers, or managed in-house. If the performance objectives are met, the pension scheme should meet all actuarially defined future liabilities. The risks of a contribution shortfall are thus borne by both the sponsoring company and by the external fund manager (to the extent that a failure to meet the benchmark will result in a loss of assets under management). A self-administered scheme may either opt to join a pooled investment fund, which typically offers a lower fee structure though no mandate flexibility. Alternatively, the fund may be managed on a segregated basis, offering greater mandate flexibility but at a higher price. If the scheme is managed on a segregated basis, the pension fund employs one or more fund managers, who are given a mandate to manage assets against a predetermined benchmark. This method may be discretionary, whereby the asset composition is left up to the fund manager, or non-discretionary, whereby the trustees decide upon the asset allocation. In the non-discretionary case the pension fund sponsors would typically rely on the advice of consultants (actuaries) on the appropriate asset allocation, and then employ specialist fund managers in different sectors.

Very large pension schemes are typically managed by a team of in-house professionals. This allows the fund complete flexibility in terms of asset/liability matching. However, the risk of a contribution shortfall lies solely with the scheme sponsor. Tonks (2005) reports on the distribution of fund managers (external and internal) across 2,175 UK occupational pension funds from 1984–97 (see Table 23.5), and provides evidence on the concentration of pension fund management.

The top-ranked fund manager (1RMan) manages 10.8 percent of observations in the sample, the second-ranked manages 5.6 percent and the third manages 4.8

### Table 23.5 Distribution of managers across pension funds by category of manager

| FMan category | Overall | | Between Funds | | Within Funds |
|---|---|---|---|---|---|
| | Freq. | % | Freq. | % | % |
| Multi-manager | 17,299 | 29.07 | 659 | 30.3 | 78.10 |
| 1RMan | 6,410 | 10.77 | 244 | 11.22 | 81.04 |
| 2RMan | 3,318 | 5.58 | 184 | 8.46 | 59.55 |
| 3RMan | 2,881 | 4.84 | 116 | 5.33 | 73.40 |
| 4RMan–17RMan[#] | 13,758 | 23.14 | 681 | 31.31 | 68.16 |
| 18RMan–188RMan | 15,595 | 26.22 | 965 | 44.65 | 58.84 |
| ΔMan | 248 | 0.42 | 225 | 10.34 | 2.64 |
| Total | 59,509 | 100.0 | 3,074 (n = 2,175) | 141.33 | 63.43 |

*Notes*: Sample consists of 2,175 pension funds 1984–97 with 59,509 quarterly observations, with 190 categories of fund manager. Total within = (659 * 78.1 + 244 * 81.04 +...) /3,074; Multi-manager denotes a multiple manager mandate for the pension fund, where more than one manager is employed by the pension fund; n RMan denotes nth Ranked Manager by frequency of observations. For example, 1RMan denotes the first-ranked fund manager, and 188RMan is the 188th-ranked fund manager. ΔMan denotes a change of fund category, when the identity of the fund manager for that quarter is unclear, because the pension fund is changing fund managers during the quarter.[#] denotes that each of these fund managers had greater than 1% of the overall frequency.
*Source*: Tonks (2005).

percent, and another 14 fund managers (4RMan–18RMan) manage a total of 23.14 percent of observations. 1RMan manages across 244 funds, and 81.04 percent of these funds' observations are using 1RMan. There is also a multi-manager category and a change of manager category ($\Delta$Man). Most funds use a single fund manager in any quarter, but 659 funds have multiple fund managers at some time, and 29.07 percent of all observations have multiple fund managers. Only 85 funds use the same fund manager over the fund's life.

There are a number of different fund management styles. The traditional mandate given to a fund manager is a balanced mandate under which the fund manager manages across all asset classes, and then selects securities within each asset class. The asset allocation decision has a strategic component, in which the global mix of asset classes are based on long-term expectations of expected returns and global macroeconomic factors. In the short term, fund managers may make tactical asset allocation decisions, moving away from the strategic asset allocation decision, to take advantage of short-term fluctuations in asset returns.

Within each asset class a fund manager will make security selection decisions. This may involve active fund management, based on better information or the better investment skills of the fund manager, in order to earn a return above the efficiency frontier. As distinct from balanced fund management, the pension fund may employ specialist managers or apply specialist mandates to specific sectors, having made the asset allocation decision separately. An alternative to active management is passive fund management, whereby the fund manager adopts a stock selection strategy that tracks the market portfolio, proxied by an appropriate index. Pension funds may also employ specialist fund managers who apply quantitative investment management techniques, such as programme trading, or using hedge funds.

# 3 Return Calculations Methods and Benchmarks

Investors such as pension funds who have delegated their portfolio to a portfolio manager will want to assess the portfolio's performance in terms of its realized risk and returns characteristics. The return to a pension fund's investments over a period $(t, t+1)$, provided there are no net cash inflows into the pension fund during the period is defined as

$$r_i = \frac{mv_{i,t+1} + divs_{i,t} - mv_{i,t}}{mv_{i,t}}$$

where $r_i$ is the return on the pension fund over the period, $divs_{i,t}$ are the dividends received by the pension fund from its investments at the end of the period, $mv_{i,t}$ is the market value of the fund at time $t$. However, suppose that there are net inflows $NI_{i,t}$ representing cash coming into the fund through contributions, and cash going out in the form of pensions. A mature pension fund, with a high percentage of pensioners to active members, is likely to have negative net inflows. We need to allow for these cash flows in the return calculation, since they do not reflect the investment performance of the fund manager.

$$r_i = \frac{mv_{i,t+1} + divs_{i,t} - NI_{i,t} - mv_{i,t}}{mv_{i,t}}$$

There are two methods for allowing for within-period cash flows: time-weighted return (TWR), and money-weighted return (MWR). TWR calculates the return achieved from a time point immediately after each cash flow until the next cash flow and compounds the returns to get the total return. MWR treats the investment as a project with positive and negative cash flows, and calculates the internal rate of return (IRR) of these cash flows. The IRR is called the MWR when applied in this manner. In general TWR and MWR differ because TWR is a pure percentage return, taking no account of the size of the actual cash value on which the percentage is based.

The Chartered Financial Analysts (CFA) Institute (formerly the Association of Investment Management Research (AIMR)) has developed a comprehensive set of Global Investment Performance Standards (GIPS) in order to promote a common set of guidelines for portfolio performance measurement: these standards recommend the use of TWR in performance calculations. There may, however, be times when the portfolio assessment would like to take account of the amount of funds under management, in which case the MWR would be more appropriate. So the moral is that in calculating returns ensure that cash inflows and outflows are appropriately allowed for, and then use either TWR or MWR consistently to compute returns.

Table 23.6 reports the average return on the median UK pension fund over the period 1994–2003 as 6.1 percent per annum. Part of the investment return will be due to movements on the stock market as a whole. In order to isolate the performance of the fund manager, the performance of the investment portfolio may be separated from the return on an appropriate benchmark portfolio. One candidate benchmark is a stock market index such as the S&P 500, or the FTSE 100. However, this may be a poor proxy for the asset allocation of the whole pension fund, if the fund is invested in a variety of asset classes. Tables 23.7 and 23.8 illustrate the asset allocation of UK pension funds from 1993–2003, and of the pension funds

Table 23.6 Average annual returns on median UK pension fund by asset class, 1994–2003

|  | Median pension fund return (%) 1994–2003 | Index return (%) 1994–2003 | Index definition |
|---|---|---|---|
| UK equities | 6.3 | 6.1 | FTSE All-Share |
| Overseas equities | 3.4 | 5.3 | FTSE All-World Ex-UK |
| UK gilts | 7.1 | 7 | FTSE A All Stocks Gilts |
| Overseas bonds | 4.9 | 4.7 | JP Morgan (Global Ex-UK) Traded |
| UK index-linked | 6.5 | 6.5 | FTSE A ILG |
| property | 11.2 | 9.8 | CAPS Property |
| Total fund | 6.1 | | |

Source: RussellMellonCAPS Fund Returns (2004).

of a number of major economies in 2003. Table 23.8 suggests that the asset allocation of pension funds is similar across countries: approximately 50 percent in equities, 25 percent in bonds, and the remainder in cash, property, and other assets. There are some differences in the split between foreign and domestic equities and bonds, but Table 23.7 shows how the median UK pension

Table 23.7 Average asset allocation across UK pension funds, 1993–2003

| As at 31 December (%) | 1993 | 1994 | 1995 | 1996 | 1997 | 1998 | 1999 | 2000 | 2001 | 2002 | 2003 |
|---|---|---|---|---|---|---|---|---|---|---|---|
| UK equities | 57.3 | 56.0 | 54.9 | 54.7 | 54.3 | 52.0 | 53.6 | 51.0 | 47.4 | 43.4 | 41.5 |
| Overseas equities | 24.4 | 23.0 | 22.0 | 21.0 | 18.6 | 18.9 | 22.8 | 22.5 | 25.0 | 25.1 | 26.7 |
| UK bonds | 4.8 | 6.1 | 7.4 | 7.9 | 9.4 | 11.3 | 10.3 | 12.8 | 14.8 | 18.2 | 19.4 |
| Overseas bonds | 4.7 | 4.6 | 4.9 | 3.7 | 4.0 | 4.6 | 3.9 | 3.7 | 2.9 | 2.1 | 1.1 |
| Index-linked bonds | 3.0 | 3.8 | 3.8 | 3.9 | 4.1 | 4.0 | 4.0 | 5.0 | 5.7 | 7.1 | 7.5 |
| Cash | 3.5 | 3.7 | 4.6 | 6.6 | 7.5 | 7.2 | 3.5 | 3.2 | 2.3 | 2.0 | 1.6 |
| Property | 1.9 | 2.5 | 2.1 | 2.0 | 1.9 | 1.9 | 1.7 | 1.7 | 1.8 | 2.0 | 2.0 |
| Other | 0.4 | 0.3 | 0.3 | 0.2 | 0.2 | 0.1 | 0.2 | 0.1 | 0.1 | 0.1 | 0.2 |
| Total fund | 100.0 | 100.0 | 100.0 | 100.0 | 100.0 | 100.0 | 100.0 | 100.0 | 100.0 | 100.0 | 100.0 |

Source: RussellMellonCAPS (2004).

Table 23.8 Average asset allocation of occupational pension funds in major markets, 2003

| (%) | Australia | Japan | Netherlands | Sweden | Switzerland | UK | USA | Average |
| --- | --- | --- | --- | --- | --- | --- | --- | --- |
| Domestic equities | 31 | 27 | 7 | 21 | 12 | 39 | 48 | 26 |
| Overseas equities | 22 | 17 | 36 | 16 | 13 | 28 | 14 | 21 |
| Domestic bonds | 17 | 32 | 8 | 29 | 30 | 12 | 33 | 23 |
| Overseas bonds | 5 | 13 | 32 | 26 | 16 | 3 | 1 | 14 |
| Cash | 6 | 5 | 4 | 2 | 10 | 3 | 1 | 4 |
| Property | 12 | 1 | 5 | 6 | 15 | 6 | 2 | 7 |
| Other | 7 | 5 | 8 | 0 | 4 | 9 | 1 | 5 |
| **Total fund** | 100 | 100 | 100 | 100 | 100 | 100 | 100 | 100 |

Source: UBS Pension Fund Indicators (2004).

fund has moved toward its recent asset allocation: a substantial reduction in UK equities, partially offset by an increase in overseas equities, and a substantial increase in bonds.

In order to assess performance of the portfolio, we could use a market index appropriate to the particular asset class, such as in the second column of Table 23.6. However market indices still suffer from a number of problems. The sector market index may exhibit survivorship bias from assets that have been removed due to poor performance, so that returns on the index will be upward biased. It would not be possible to generate the returns on an index by continuously replicating the exact asset composition of the index without incurring substantial trading costs. Bailey et al. (1990) point out that pension funds may hire fund managers with specific investment mandates which are related to the liabilities of the pension fund. The market index may not reflect the divergent style of the managers. Other alternative benchmarks are the median return of a sample of fund managers in a similar asset class, or a normal portfolio. Bailey (1992) makes a number of criticisms of median managers including: the subjective selection of the sample; the different risks and styles between managers; the lack of transparency in such a benchmark; and the difficulty in replicating the same investment strategy. Normal portfolios are customized benchmarks designed to reflect the style of an individual manager, but these may be difficult to implement, and are subject to manipulation from an underperforming fund manager. Blake (1998) and Blake and Timmermann (2002) suggest the use of liability-driven benchmarks. However, this raises the issue of the valuation of pension liabilities, and it is often unclear how to obtain the appropriate discount rate for valuing pension liabilities.[4]

# 4 Risk-Adjusted Portfolio Performance Measurment Measures

In making a comparison in terms of realized returns it is important to make an adjustment for the risk of the portfolio. What is the appropriate measure of risk? If the portfolio is the only portfolio held by the pension fund then the total risk of the portfolio would be the measure of risk. If the portfolio is held along with a number of other portfolios, then the non-diversifiable risk of the portfolio will be the appropriate measure.

## 4.1 Sharpe Measure: Excess Return to Variability

To assess the portfolio returns, Sharpe (1966, 1994) proposed computing $S$ for the portfolio under consideration and also for the benchmark portfolio

$$S = (r_p - r_f)/\sigma_p$$

where $r_p$ is the return on the portfolio, $r_f$ is the risk-free rate, and $\sigma_p$ is the standard deviation of the returns on the portfolio. The Sharpe measure uses the Capital Market Line as a benchmark and is appropriate for a pension fund that has invested its wealth in the one portfolio under consideration. Lo (2002) has examined the properties of the Sharpe ratio taking account of estimation risk.

## 4.2 Excess Return to Beta: Treynor Measure

Treynor (1965) proposed using the Security Market Line as a benchmark and $T$ is appropriate for funds that have invested their wealth in a number of portfolios

$$T = (r_p - r_f)/\beta_p$$

where $\beta_p$ is the beta of the portfolio. Again to assess the performance of a portfolio, $T$ is computed for both the portfolio and a benchmark.

## 4.3 Jensen Differential Performance Index

Jensen (1968) proposed measuring the performance of a portfolio by its abnormal return above the Security Market Line

$$\alpha_p = \{r_p - \{r_f + \beta_p(Er_m - r_f)\}\}$$

where $Er_m$ is the expected return (sample average) on the market portfolio, and $\alpha_p$ is the Jensen-alpha measure of outperformance. Alternatively, we may regress the excess return $(r_p - r_f)$ of a portfolio against the excess return on the market and interpret the intercept as the Jensen measure. The Jensen-alpha specifically evaluates the active fund management by the portfolio manager, as opposed to the passive fund management of investing in the risk-free asset and the market portfolio.

Although both the Treynor and Jensen measures are based on the Security Market Line, when comparing two portfolios, they can give conflicting assessments of performance. This is because the Treynor measure evaluates a portfolio based on the excess return per unit of risk, measured by the portfolio beta. In contrast, the Jensen-alpha measures the absolute excess return for the level of risk adopted by the portfolio. These three measures of portfolio performance can be interpreted as investment returns, in the following way. The Sharpe measure $S$ shows the return per unit of volatility to the zero investment portfolio formed by borrowing $1 and investing it in the portfolio. The Treynor measure $T$ shows the return per unit of beta-risk to the zero investment portfolio formed by borrowing $1 and investing it in the portfolio. The Jensen-alpha shows the return earned by the zero investment portfolio formed by selling short $\beta_P$ dollars in the market portfolio and $(1 - \beta_P)$ dollars in the risk-free asset and investing $1 in the portfolio.

The Jensen-alpha measure has the advantage that it can easily be extended to alternative asset-pricing models, such as the Arbitrage Pricing Theory. The multi-factor Jensen-alpha with $n$ factors can be written as:

$$\alpha_p = r_p - r_f - b_{p1}F_1 - b_{p2}F_2 - \ldots - b_{pn}F_n$$

where $F_k$ is the risk premium on the kth factor.

## 4.4 Information Ratio

The information ratio is similar to the Sharpe ratio but compares the performance of a portfolio to its benchmark:

$$I = (r_p - r_b)/\sigma_{ER}$$

where $r_p$ is the average return for portfolio $p$ over some period, $r_b$ is the average return on a benchmark portfolio over the same period, so that $(r_p - r_b)$ is the excess return on the portfolio over the benchmark; $\sigma_{ER}$ is called the tracking error, and is the standard deviation of the excess returns during the period. The information ratio compares the return over the benchmark with the 'risk' taken—where risk is the tracking error, defined as the deviation from the benchmark.

# 5 Problems with Performance Measurement

## 5.1 The Market Index

A potential problem with the risk-adjusted performance measures outlined above is that the benchmark used for comparison may be inappropriate. For example, it is an unresolved question whether the CAPM is the correct asset pricing model that can explain the cross-sectional distribution of asset prices in an economy (Fama and French 1996). Even if the correct asset pricing model is specified, Roll (1978) points out that the chosen index may not represent the entire universe of securities: in fact it is likely that equity indices such as the S&P 500 will have a large capitalization bias. In this case the performance measure may be comparing the performance of the fund with a benchmark that itself is inefficient. Grinblatt and Titman (1993) suggest a method of assessing portfolio performance without requiring a benchmark. This involves comparing the performance of the selected assets in the portfolio with a reference period when these same assets were not in the portfolio.

## 5.2 Market Timing

The original Jensen technique made no allowance for the market-timing abilities of fund managers when fund managers change the composition of their portfolio on the basis of expected market movements. When portfolio managers expect the market portfolio to rise in value, they may switch from bonds into equities and/or they may invest in more high beta stocks. When they expect the market to fall, they will undertake the reverse strategy: sell high beta stocks and move into 'defensive' stocks. If managers successfully engage in market timing, then returns to the fund will be high when the market is high, and also relatively high when the market is low.

If there were no market timing, then a regression of $R_p - r_f$ against $R_m - r_f$ would produce points scattered around the solid line in Figure 23.1. If there is market timing, then the correct model specification will be a different dotted line in the good and bad market conditions. A simple Jensen-alpha intercept will conclude that there is negative performance. If managers successfully market time, then a quadratic plot would prove a better fit (Treynor and Mazuy 1966). A test of market timing is a significant value of $\gamma_p$ in the following regression, for the single factor model:

$$R_{pt} - r_f = \alpha_p + \beta_p(R_{mt} - r_f) + \gamma_p (R_{mt} - r_f)^2 + \varepsilon_{pt}.$$

An alternative test of market timing for the single factor model suggested by Henriksson and Merton (1981) is:

$$R_{pt} - r_f = \alpha_p + \beta_p(R_{mt} - r_f) + \delta_p(R_{mt} - r_f)^+ + \eta^{pt}$$

where $(R_{mt} - r_f)^+ = Max(0, R^{mt} - r_f)$. The market timing test is easily extended to a multi-factor framework, assessing the timing on each of the style components.

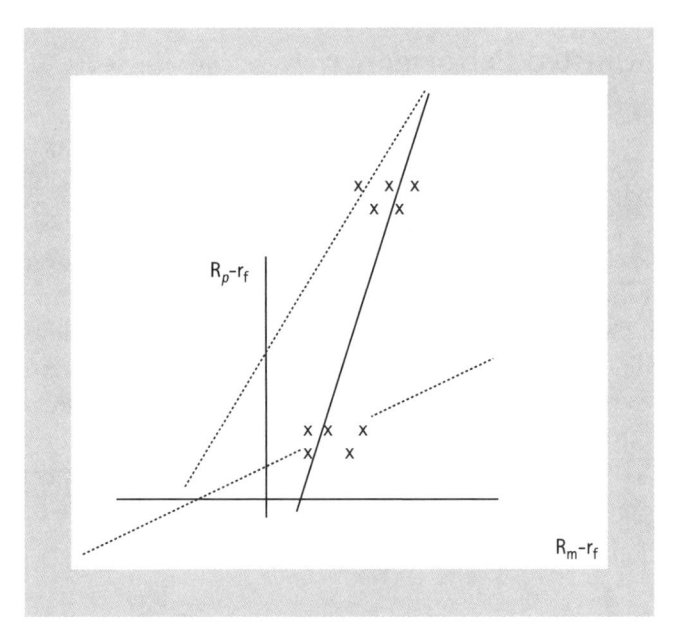

**Fig. 23.1** Illustrating the problem of market timing

## 5.3 Conditional Performance Evaluation

In order to distinguish fund managers' skills from simply taking advantage of predictable market or factor movements, Ferson and Schadt (1996) advocate allowing for the benchmark parameters to be conditioned on economic conditions. Allowing the market parameters to be time-varying, the Jensen regression becomes:

$$R_{it} - r_{ft} = \alpha_i + \beta_i(Z_{t-1})(R_{mt} - r_{ft}) + \gamma_i F_t + \varepsilon_{it}$$

where $Z_{t-1}$ is a vector of instruments for the information available at time $t$ (and is therefore specified as $t-1$) and $\beta_{i*}(Z_t)$ are time-conditional betas, and their functional form is specified as linear:

$$\beta_i(Z_t) = b_o + B'z_{t-1}$$

where $z_{t-1} = Z_{t-1} - E(Z)$ is a vector of deviations of the Zs from their unconditional means. Implementing this approach involves creating interaction terms between the market returns and the instruments. Typical instruments used are: lagged Treasury bill rate, dividend yield, default premium (difference between low and high quality corporate bonds), slope of the term structure (difference between long- and short-run government bond yields).

## 5.4 Style-Adjusted Performance

The benchmark portfolio can be a single index or because investment style is important, a 'customized' benchmark can be developed specifically for the portfolio in question (Daniel et al. 1997). For example, if the portfolio holds on average 20 percent US government bonds and 80 percent US equities, we may form a customized benchmark as 0.8 × S&P 500 + 0.2 × Merrill Lynch Government Bond Index. Usually the customized benchmark is based on an effective mix style analysis (Sharpe 1992). This is achieved by performing an 'effective mix' style analysis on the fund and finding the style exposures. For example, suppose a regression is run on the portfolio returns against various factors, and suppose the following factor-loadings are estimated: 0.4 for large value stock portfolio; 0.2 for growth stock portfolio; 0.3 for small capitalization portfolio; and 0.1 for government bond. Then we can form a customized benchmark for the fund as 0.4 * Large + 0.2 * growth + 0.3 * Small cap + 0.1 * Bonds.

# 6 Evidence on Investment Performance

The early evidence on the performance of mutual funds in the United States found that simple tests of abnormal performance did not yield significant returns. Jensen (1968) examined the performance of 115 mutual funds over the period 1955–64, using the Security Market Line as the basis for comparison. Jensen's technique is to regress the excess returns on the individual fund (above the risk-free rate) against the excess return on the market ($R_{mt} - r_{ft}$):

$$R_{it} - r_{ft} = \alpha_i + \beta_i(R_{mt} - r_{ft}) + \varepsilon_{it}$$

for each fund $i$ over the $t$ data periods, and save the coefficients $\alpha_i$ and $\beta_i$. Under the null hypothesis of no-abnormal performance the $\alpha$ coefficient should be equal to zero. For each fund we may test the significance of $\alpha$ as a measure of that fund's abnormal performance. In addition, we may test for overall fund performance by testing the significance of the mean $\alpha$:

$$\bar{\alpha} = \frac{1}{N} \sum_{i=1}^{N} \alpha_i.$$

The appropriate $t$-statistic is

$$t = \frac{1}{\sqrt{N}} \sum_{i=1}^{N} \frac{\alpha_i}{SE(\alpha_i)}.$$

Jensen examined the abnormal return for each fund net of expenses, and found that the average abnormal return was approximately 1 percent per annum: if expenses were added back into the gross return, average abnormal return was approximately zero. Hence Jensen's conclusions were that market professionals do not appear to be able to beat the market.

Applying this same methodology to the average performance of pension funds, Ippolito and Turner (1987) examined returns on 1,526 US pension funds and find underperformance relative to the S&P 500 Index. Lakonishok et al. (1992) provide evidence on the structure and performance of the money management industry in the United States in general, but focus on the role of pension funds, examining 769 pension funds, with total assets of $129 billion at the end of 1989. They find the equity performance of funds underperformed the S&P 500 by 1.3 percent per year throughout the 1980s. They emphasize that although there is a long literature on the underperformance of mutual funds, pension funds also underperform relative to mutual funds on average. Coggin et al. (1993) investigate the investment performance of a random sample of 71 US equity pension fund managers for the

### Table 23.9 Performance evaluation of UK pension funds, 1983–1997

|  | No. funds | α | α t-stat. | δ (Market timing) | δ t-stat. |
|---|---|---|---|---|---|
| **Panel A: CAPM benchmark** | | | | | |
| Average values | 1,714 | 0.00017 | 0.966 | | |
| No. coeffs > 0 |  | 898 | | | |
| No. of signif. coeffs. |  |  | 165 | | |
| Treynor–Mazuy | | | | | |
| Average values | 1,714 | 0.0008 | 11.055 | −0.0013 | −21.152 |
| Merton–Henriksson | | | | | |
| Average values | 1,714 | 0.0018 | 19.412 | −0.0493 | −27.14 |
| **Panel B: three-factor benchmark** | | | | | |
| Average values | 1,714 | 0.0001 | 4.526 | | |
| No. coeffs > 0 |  | 940 | | | |
| No. of signif. coeffs. |  |  | 142 | | |

*Source*: Thomas and Tonks (2001) and Tonks (2002).

period January 1983 through December 1990, and find that the average selectivity measure is positive and average timing ability is negative, though both selectivity and timing are sensitive to the choice of benchmark when management style is taken into consideration. For example, they find that funds that target value strategies yielded outperformance of 2.1 percent per annum, but funds that adopted growth strategies underperformed by −0.96 percent.

### Table 23.10 Performance of UK personal pensions 1980–2000

|  | No. funds | α | α t-stat. | δ (Market timing) | δ t-stat. |
|---|---|---|---|---|---|
| **Panel A: CAPM benchmark** | | | | | |
| Average values | 399 | −0.00013 | −6.43 | | |
| Average values | 399 | 0.00033 | −1.07 | −0.1538 | −14.12 |
| **Panel B: three-factor benchmark** | | | | | |
| Average values | 399 | 0.00029 | −1.68 | | |
| Average values | 399 | 0.00030 | 0.68 | 0.1081 | −7.75 |

*Source*: Gregory and Tonks (2004).

In the UK, Blake *et al.* (1999) examine the asset allocations of a sample of 364 UK pension funds that retained the same fund manager over the period 1986–94. Following the methods suggested by Brinson *et al.* (1986), they find that the total return is dominated by asset allocation. Average return from stock selection is negative, and average return to market timing very negative. In one asset class, UK equity managers are comparatively good at selecting equities, but only 16 percent of the sample beat the peer group average. Thomas and Tonks (2001) investigate the performance of the UK equity portfolios of 2,175 segregated UK pension funds over the period 1984–97, and the results are presented in Table 23.9. They find that over the whole period and across all funds average outperformance was not very different from zero, and there were negative returns to market timing, though the significance of selectivity increased with the addition of the market timing variable. The distribution of the Jensen-alphas across funds is given in Figure 23.2. Gregory and Tonks (2004) examine the performance of individual personal pensions (exempt unit trusts) in the UK from 1980–2000. They examine those personal pension schemes that invest predominantly in UK equities, and in Table 23.10 report that average performance is not significantly different from zero.

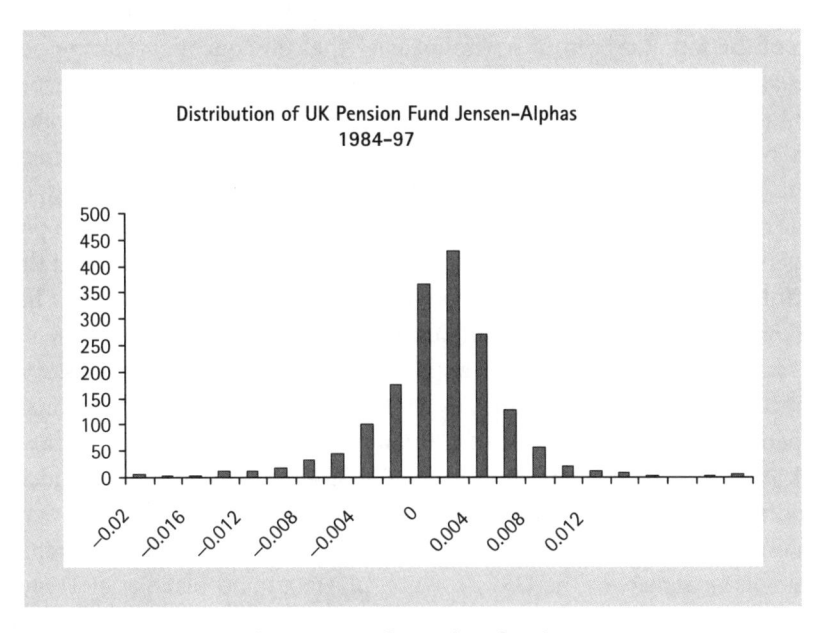

**Fig. 23.2 Evidence on performance of pension funds**

*Source*: Thomas and Tonks (2001).

# 7 PERSISTENCE IN INVESTMENT PERFORMANCE

Although on average fund managers do not outperform, in any sample there is a distribution to the performance as shown in Figure 23.2, and more recently research on performance measurement has investigated whether the outperformers in the sample continue to outperform in the future. Grinblatt and Titman (1992) find that differences in mutual fund performance between funds persist over five-year time horizons and this persistence is consistent with the ability of fund managers to earn abnormal returns. Carhart (1997) demonstrates that common factors in stock returns (including a momentum factor) and investment expenses explain persistence in equity mutual funds' mean and risk-adjusted returns. The only significant persistence not explained is concentrated in strong underperformance by the worst return mutual funds. His results do not support the existence of skilled or informed mutual fund portfolio managers. There are a number of tests for persistence, and Carpenter and Lynch (1999) have assessed the power of these difference tests particularly in the presence of different types of survivorship bias. Carpenter and Lynch classify persistence tests into two types: performance-ranked portfolio strategies, and contingency tables.

Performance-ranked portfolio tests sort fund managers each year into portfolios based on past performance, and then form portfolios of the top and bottom managers (by decile or quintile). The equally weighted average portfolio abnormal return of the top and bottom portfolios over the subsequent evaluation period is then evaluated. These procedures are followed for overlapping periods throughout the full period of the data set, and the difference between the average abnormal return on the series of top and bottom portfolios is computed. From their simulations, Carpenter and Lynch find that the persistence test based on a *t*-statistic of the difference between the performance of the top and bottom portfolio managers is the best specified under the hypothesis of no persistence, and the most powerful against the alternatives considered. These persistence tests can be computed on the basis of alternative ranking and evaluation time periods, since it may be the case that persistency is only apparent at particular time intervals.

Contingency tables classify funds as winners or losers in each of two consecutive time periods, and examine the distribution of winner–loser combinations. Lakonishok *et al.* (1992), in their study of 769 all equity pension funds, undertake a contingency analysis with funds divided into quartiles, and conclude that evidence of persistence is weak since there is only a 26 percent probability of repeat top quartile performance. In the UK, Brown *et al.* (1997) and Blake *et al.* (1999) have examined consistency in UK occupational pension fund performance. Both studies find only weak evidence of persistence in performance. In constructing their data samples, both the Brown *et al.* (1997) and Blake *et al.* (1999) studies of UK pension funds specify that the pension fund have the same single fund manager over the length of their respective samples. Tonks (2005) argues that this specification of the data set may have induced survivorship bias in these data samples, since Grinblatt and Titman (1992) and Hendricks *et al.* (1993) have argued that if fund survival depends on average performance over several periods, then survivorship induces spurious reversals: first-period losers must subsequently win in order to survive, and this biases persistence downwards. Tonks (2005) examines persistence in pension fund manager performance using data on UK occupational pension funds irrespective of whether they change manager. He finds strong evidence of persistence in abnormal returns generated by fund managers over one-year time horizons. He found that the returns on a zero investment portfolio of a long position in a portfolio of fund managers that performed well over the previous 12 months and a short position in a portfolio of fund managers that performed poorly, would have yielded an annualized abnormal return of 1.56 percent. He then compares his sample with a restricted sample that imposes the Brown *et al.* (1997), and Blake *et al.* (1999) criteria that specify that the pension fund has the same fund manager over the length of their respective samples. With the restricted sample, he finds that the evidence on persistence is weaker. Gregory and Tonks (2004) in their study of personal pension funds also examine persistence in performance of these pension schemes and identify negative persistence at short horizons, but at time intervals of six months to one year they find significant positive persistence, though this positive persistence weakens at longer time intervals.

# 8 Conclusions

This chapter has provided a survey of pension fund management industry and how it relates and interacts with individual and occupational private pension funds. We have focused on the performance of pension funds whose assets are managed by fund managers. In a funded scheme the pension paid to a retired person will depend on the accumulated value of the assets in the pension fund at retirement. This is clearly the case for a defined contribution scheme where the relationship between the value of the fund and the pension is explicit. But this same annuitization is implicit in a defined benefit scheme, since although there may be some risk-sharing across generations, ultimately the defined benefit scheme is only able to pay out a pension that is a proportion of the value of the assets in the scheme.

The value of the pension fund will increase over time due to contributions and the investment returns on the fund. These investment returns depend on the asset allocation and portfolio decisions of fund managers. Small changes in the investment returns compound up to large changes in the value of the pension fund at retirement. The evidence on fund manager performance is that on average they do not add very much value over and above a passive strategy of investing in the market index. However, this average disguises the fact that some fund managers perform well, and others perform poorly. Identifying and understanding the persistence of the poor performance of some fund managers is an important issue in the pensions area, and one in which further research would be worthwhile.

## Notes

1. Blake (2003) provides a detailed description of the development of funded pensions in the UK, and a discussion of recent policy initiatives.
2. Palacios and Pallares-Miralles (2000) identify these three countries plus Australia, South Africa, Switzerland, and Iceland as being the only countries in the world with private pension fund assets greater than 50 percent of GDP. A combination of generous tax allowances on pension contributions (Dilnot and Johnson 1993) and a liberal regulatory regime for pension investments (Davis 1995) probably explains the dominance of funded pensions in these countries.
3. Investment management is also referred to as fund management, asset management, portfolio management, and money management.
4. Speed *et al.* (2003) and Hill (2003) discuss the use of liability-based benchmarks in the context of pension fund returns.

## References

Bailey, J. V. (1992). 'Are manager universes acceptable performance benchmarks'. *Journal of Portfolio Management*, 18/3: 9–13.

—— , Richards, T. M. and Tierney, D. E. (1990). 'Benchmark portfolios and the manager/plan sponsor relationship', in Frank Fabozzi and T. Dessa Fabozzi (eds.), *Current Topics in Investment Management*. New York: Harper & Row.

Bhattacharya, S., and Pfleiderer, P. (1985). 'Delegated portfolio management'. *Journal of Economic Theory*, 36 (June): 1–25.

Blake, D. (1998), 'Measuring the performance of pension funds using liability-driven performance attribution'. *Journal of Pensions Management*, 3: 105–9.

—— (2003). *Pension Schemes and Pension Funds in the UK*, 2nd edn. Oxford: Oxford University Press.

—— LEHMANN, B., and TIMMERMANN, A. (1999). 'Asset allocation dynamics and pension fund performance'. *Journal of Business*, 72: 429–61.

—— and TIMMERMAN, A. (2002). 'Performance benchmarks for institutional investors', in J. Knight and S. Satchell (eds.), *Performance Measurement in Finance*. Oxford: Butterworth-Heinemann, 342–64.

BRINSON, G. P., HOOD, L. R., and BEEBOWER, G. L. (1986). 'Determinants of portfolio performance'. *Financial Analysts Journal* (July/Aug.): 39–48.

BROWN, G., DRAPER, P., and MCKENZIE, E. (1997). 'Consistency of UK pension fund performance'. *Journal of Business Finance and Accounting*, 24 (Mar.): 155–78.

CARHART, M. (1997). 'On persistence in mutual fund performance'. *Journal of Finance*, 52: 57–82.

CARPENTER, J. N., and LYNCH, A. W. (1999). 'Survivorship bias and attrition effects in measures of performance persistence'. *Journal of Financial Economics*, 54: 337–74.

COGGIN, T. D., FABOZZI, F. J., and RAHMAN, S. (1993). 'The investment performance of US equity pension fund managers: an empirical investigation'. *Journal of Finance*, 48: 1039–55.

DANIEL, K., GRINBLATT, M., TITMAN, S., and WERMERS, R. (1997). 'Measuring mutual fund performance with characteristic based benchmarks'. *Journal of Finance* (July).

DAVIS, E. P. (1995). *Pension Funds: Retirement-Income Security, and Capital Markets: An International Perspective* Oxford: Clarendon Press.

—— (1998). 'Pension fund reform and European financial markets'. LSE Financial Markets Group Special Paper No. 107.

—— and STEIL, B. (2001). *Institutional Investors*. Cambridge, Mass.: MIT Press.

DEL GUERCIO, D., and TKAC, P. A. (2002). 'The determinants of the flow of funds of managed portfolios: mutual funds vs pension funds'. *Journal of Financial and Quantitative Analysis*, 37/4: 523–57.

DILNOT, A., and JOHNSON, P. (1993). *The Taxation of Private Pensions*. London: Institute for Fiscal Studies.

FAMA, E., and FRENCH, K. (1996). 'The CAPM is wanted, dead or alive'. *Journal of Finance*, 51: 1947–58.

FERSON, W., and SCHADT, R. W. (1996). 'Measuring fund strategy and performance in changing economic conditions'. *Journal of Finance*, 51: 425–62.

FRANKS, J., MAYER, C., and DA SILVA, L. C. (2003). *Asset Management and Investor Protection: An International Analysis*. Oxford: Oxford University Press.

GREGORY, A., and TONKS, I. (2004). 'Performance of personal pension schemes in the UK'. *UBS/FMG Discussion Paper*, No. 486 (Mar.).

GRINBLATT, M., and TITMAN, S. (1992). 'Persistence in mutual fund performance'. *Journal of Finance*, 47: 1977–84.

—— —— (1993). 'Performance measurement without benchmarks: an examination of mutual fund returns'. *Journal of Business*, 66/1: 47–68.

HENDRICKS, D., PATEL, J., and ZECKHAUSER, R. (1993). 'Hot hands in mutual funds: short run persistence of relative performance, 1974–1988'. *Journal of Finance*, 48: 93–130.

HENRIKSSON, R., and MERTON, R. (1981). 'On market timing and investment performance. II. Statistical procedures for evaluating forecasting skills'. *Journal of Business*, 54/4: 513–33.

HILL, J. (2003). *Submission on the Relationship between Pension Assets and Liabilities*. London: Staple Inn Actuarial Society.

IPPOLITO, R. A., and TURNER, J. A. (1987). 'Turnover, fees and pension plan performance'. *Financial Analysts Journal*, 43: 16–26.

JENSEN, M. C. (1968). 'The performance of mutual funds in the period 1945–1964'. *Journal of Finance*, 23/2: 389–416.

LAKONISHOK, J. A., SHLEIFER, A., and VISHNY, R. W. (1992). 'The structure and performance of the money management industry'. *Brookings Papers on Economic Activity*, 339–91.

LO, A. W. (2002). 'The statistics of Sharpe ratios'. *Financial Analysts Journal*, 58/4 (July–Aug.): 36–52.

MALKIEL, B. G. (1995). 'Returns from investing in equity mutual funds 1971 to 1991'. *Journal of Finance*, 50: 549–72.

MYNERS, P. (2001). *Report on Institutional Investment*. HM Treasury. London: The stationery office.

OCCUPATIONAL PENSIONS REGULATORY AUTHORITY (2001). *Annual Report 2000/2001*. Brighton: OPRA.

PALACIOS, R., and PALLARES-MIRALLES, M. (2000). 'International Patterns of Pension Provision'. Social Protection Discussion Paper No. 0009. Washington, D. C.: World Bank.

PAPKE, LESLIE E., PETERSEN, MITCHELL, and POTERBA, JAMES M. (1996). 'Did 401(k) plans replace other employer-provided pensions?', in David Wise (ed.), *Advances of the Economics of Aging*. Chicago: University of Chicago Press.

ROLL, R. (1978). 'Ambiguity when performance is measured by the securities market line'. *Journal of Finance*, 33: 1051–69.

RUSSELL/MELLON (2004). *CAPS Fund Returns 2004*.

SANDLER, R. (2002). *Medium and Long-Term Retail Savings in the UK: A Review* HM Treasury. London: The Stationery office.

SHARPE, W. F. (1966). 'Mutual fund performance'. *Journal of Business*, 39/1 (part 2): 119–38.

—— (1992). 'Asset allocation, management style and performance measurement'. *Journal of Portfolio Management* (winter): 7–19.

—— (1994). 'The Sharpe ratio'. *Journal of Portfolio Management*, 21/1: 49–59.

SPEED, C., BOWIE, D., EXLEY, J., JONES, M., MOUNCE, R., RALSTON, N., SPIERS, T., and WILLIAMS, H. (2003). *Note on the Relationship between Pension Assets and Liabilities*. London: Staple Inn Actuarial Society.

STOUGHTON, N. M. (1993). 'Moral hazard and the portfolio management problem'. *Journal of Finance*, 47: 2009–28.

THOMAS, A., and TONKS, I. (2001). 'Equity performance of segregated pension funds in the UK'. *Journal of Asset Management*, 1/4: 321–43.

TONKS, I. (2002). 'Measuring pension fund performance in the UK', in J. Knight and S. Satchell (eds.), *Performance Measurement in Finance*. Oxford: Butterworth-Heinemann, 342–64.

—— (2005). 'Performance persistence of pension fund managers'. *Journal of Business*, 78/5 (Nov.): 1917–42.

TREYNOR, J. L. (1965). 'How to rate management of investment funds'. *Harvard Business Review*, 43 (Jan.–Feb.): 63–75.

—— and MAZUY, F. (1966). 'Can mutual funds outguess the market?' *Harvard Business Review*, 44: 131–6.

UBS (2005). *UBS Pension Fund Indicators 2005*. UBS Global Asset Management.

# PENSION PLAN GOVERNANCE

CHAPTER 24

# REGULATION OF PENSION FUND GOVERNANCE

GORDON L. CLARK

## 1 Introduction

Pension funds collect contributions, invest accumulated assets, and distribute income to beneficiaries through their retirement. These are simple functions, easily mapped (Clark 2000). As such, it is arguable that pension funds are like other economic organizations in that they have goals and objectives as well as procedures by which those goals and objectives are realized. There is an enormous literature on the economic form and structure of organizations making it hard to summarize that literature in any meaningful way. Even so, it can be observed that some theorists believe that the most efficient organizations are those with the simplest well-defined objective functions (Jensen 2000). By contrast, other theorists suggest that whatever the principles that legitimize an organization, they cannot be reduced to the rational input-output machines of neoclassical theory (March 1994). Governance matters.[1] Pension funds, like the administrative organizations of social security systems, are hardly ever unitary profit-maximizing entities. More likely, they are beneficial organizations combining various administrative and organizational tasks with a vaguely defined but widely accepted mandate—that they act on behalf of beneficiaries' best interests (the so-called 'exclusive benefit' rule). This can be a most problematic combination. For some critics, moral commitment may be just a convenient cover for favoritism and sweetheart deals that benefit all but the intended beneficiaries (Romano 1993). On the other hand, market idealism may be unjustified in the face of speculative behavior; witness the comments of Allen *et al.* (2003), Clark *et al.* (2004), and Shiller (2002) on the scope and nature of the peer-related benchmarks used to assess investment performance and their contribution to the dot.com bubble. Understanding the nature of pension fund regulation in the ground between morals and the market is a vital task in any comprehensive framework for the provision of pension and retirement income.

Few plan participants are in the position to disagree with or dispute the actions and intentions of trustees. Exit, voice, and loyalty are more abstract than real, given the unequal distribution of information between plan trustees, their agents, and beneficiaries as well as profound differences between them in terms of financial expertise. One way forward may be the formation of larger pension institutions more focused upon transparency and more capable of overseeing the performance of their service providers (Clark 2004). Another way forward is through public regulation (the topic of this chapter). Clearly, we are dealing with two sides of the same problem but from different perspectives—one the internal organization of funds and the other being about the accountability of funds to their public and private mandates. In this chapter, I survey the relevant literature and provide a theoretical perspective on the relationship between the various models of public regulation in Western economies. Anglo-American regulatory regimes are guided by a basic principle: inherited from trust law, fiduciary duty is the golden rule (model 1) even if its elaboration typically runs to many thousands of pages in statute. Pension fund trustees have significant discretion in choosing the means by which they set about enhancing and protecting the welfare of others. In many respects, regulatory frameworks (model 2) that cover private pension funds provide a mandate and a set of constraints; such regulatory regimes are often silent on the issue of how best to fulfill the mandate. I argue that both models of regulation are insufficient—the market (model 3) has a vital role to play in 'regulating' pension funds. Various regimes of regulation exist, combining in different ways the three models noted above. In the penultimate section of the chapter, the implications of these different regimes are considered with reference to the need to balance the interests of plan participants (beneficiaries and retirees) with current employees and plan sponsors. Finally, implications are drawn for the design of regulatory regimes.

## 2 THE GOLDEN RULE AS REGULATION

The origins of fiduciary duty are to be found in the English common law of trusts. There have been innumerable histories of trust law and its subsequent application to Anglo-American pension and investment management. See, for instance, the related essay by Langbein (1997) on the significance of the trust institution for modern capitalism. Basically, trust law established a set of principles that define the responsibilities of third parties who undertake to protect the welfare of those reliant upon their judgment and expertise. Often cited in this regard is the opinion of the Massachusetts Supreme Judicial Court in *Harvard College v Amory* 26 Mass 446 (1830). There it was held that trustees should act on behalf of the beneficiaries of the trust institution, eschewing their own interests in favor of the interests of those for whose welfare they are responsible.[2]

With the passage of the Employment Retirement Income Security Act (ERISA) in 1974, the principles of trust law were deliberately and explicitly established as the *first-order* rules by which fiduciaries are to discharge their duties. As noted by the US Supreme Court in *Pegram v Herdrich* 530 US 211 (2000), pension plan fiduciaries are required to act 'solely in the interest of the participants and beneficiaries' and 'for the exclusive purpose of (i) providing benefits to participants and their beneficiaries; and (ii) defraying reasonable expenses of administering the plan'.[3] Underpinning the principle of fiduciary duty is a set of moral standards of behavior including duties of care, loyalty, and fidelity (in contrast with the opportunism and selfishness often thought to characterize individual interests). Thus, trustees are properly 'held to something stricter than the morals of the market place' as indicated by the US Supreme Court in *Herdrich* citing Justice Cardozo's opinion in *Meinhard v Salmon* 249 NY 458, 464 (1928).

Notice that the trust model of fiduciary duty does not capture the full scope of who is accountable to the golden rule. ERISA not only covers pension plan trustees but all those who exercise 'discretionary control or authority over the plan's management, administration, or assets' *Mertens v Hewitt Associates* 508 US 248 (1993). All kinds of agents who act on behalf of pension fund trustees are accountable to the golden rule including the financial services industry (Black 1992). At the same time, it should be observed that the historical sense of the trust relationship was one of paternalism—in the *Harvard* case, as in much of trust law, relatives knowledgeable about investment and real estate undertook to care for a designated beneficiary unable to care for herself. This ethic or moral obligation is closely related to the 'prudent man' rule and is sometimes assumed to be an entirely Anglo-American ideal. But it can also be found in Continental European legal traditions that emphasize fathers' family responsibilities (Brydon 2000).

Modern treatments of fiduciary duty rarely if ever refer to paternalism (Hawley and Williams 1999). Liberal democracies care more for individual autonomy and responsibility than traditional views about family hierarchy and the internal distribution of authority; the presumption in law favors the former rather than the latter.[4] Modern interpretations of fiduciary duty refer to widely held social expectations regarding proper behavior. To care for the welfare of others, to remain loyal to freely undertaken obligations and responsibilities whatever the intervening opportunities, and to act according to common standards of decency is to act with respect to normative ideals that transcend everyday life. Assuming that standards of behavior are socially constructed and are systematically communicated to each new generation, moral imperatives have two related institutional forms: being a normative framework setting the terms and conditions for social relationships, and being a mechanism for penalizing those who stray from expected behavior. Neither is ironclad and inviolate. Both may be disputed, circumvented, and even subverted at will. So why take them seriously?

For Rescher (1987: 3) 'ideals are important both because of their critical guiding role at the level of personal decision making and because of their utility in rendering the behavior of rational agents amenable to explanatory understanding'. This does not mean, as Rescher points out, that the moral imperative of how people 'ought' to behave always determines how people actually behave. Whatever people's best intentions, the real world is complicated and quite diverse morally speaking (Bader and Engelen 2003). The real world is also difficult to control, especially if we rely upon other agents not so concerned for the welfare of others and not so respectful of community standards. Its very complexity may encourage the proliferation of rules thereby undercutting the coherence of rule-based regulation. The consequences of augmentation may be to weaken the virtues of moral imperatives and introduce the need for other models of regulation. There are limits to the power of golden rules.

## 3 Virtues and Vices of Golden Rules

One important virtue of a golden rule is its so-called formal status (Kennedy 1976: 1687–8). This refers to the quality of a rule that enables one to apply that rule directly to a situation without recourse to another set of rules or standards. So, for example, the exclusive benefit rule has the virtue of formality because it is presumed to be sufficient in its own right as guidance for all relevant situations. This virtue or quality guards against opportunism on a case-by-case basis while promising certainty from situation to situation. This quality also guards against the introduction of other criteria by which to make decisions, whether these be about pension eligibility, or the investment of pension plan assets. It promises consistency whatever the circumstances and whatever the immediate interests of those involved.

Related to this virtue is the virtue of generality (Kennedy 1976: 1689–70) or universality (following Kant). This refers to a quality of rules that enables one to apply a rule to a class of related issues or situations and is apparent in both narrowly defined rules and in broadly defined rules. The scope of a rule is one issue. Its generality, however, is the quality of rules whatever their scope. Of course, there may be virtues in a rule that has broad scope as well as generality. In theory, this would minimize administrative procedures, eschewing the detail of specific cases in favor of the application of the rule across cases. At the same time, generality may sustain the underlying principle in the face of counter-claims regarding the relevance of particular circumstances. Furthermore, generality may enable decision-makers to resolve jurisdictional questions regarding the applicability of competing or overlapping rules by reference to one rule rather than many rules. There is little doubt that the exclusive benefit rule has this virtue.

A third virtue of rule-based decision-making is that it enables decision-makers to remain independent of the competing interests implied by a choice between alternative courses of action. Instead of accounting on a case-by-case basis for the consequences of those actions, the existence of a rule should resolve a priori any debate about the particular decision taken. Over the long term, decisions should be simplified because those involved in sequential decision-making would learn to exclude consideration of the alternatives in the face of the compelling claim of rule-based principle. This may be most important where those involved in pension fund decision-making are nominally representative of various stakeholders brought together in a plan. The appeal to a rule is an appeal to independence justified by its formality, generality, and non-partisan qualities.

There is no use in having rules unless there are penalties or sanctions when decision-makers break those rules. Assuming rules are clear and unambiguous, and that the sanctions for breaking rules are known to those concerned, then the application of a rule to a situation may carry the force of its virtues as well as the prospect of penalty if not observed. There may be a broad range of penalties. For example, to break a rule may incur the approbation of the community, acknowledging the moral imperatives noted above that underpin expected standards of behavior. To break a rule may prompt review of the appointment process and the fitness to serve of those responsible for decision-making. And to break a rule may prompt legal prosecution and the prospect of civil or even criminal penalties. By this account, the virtues of a rule are necessarily protected by the costs of non-compliance. This is consistent with Rescher's (1987) argument that the power of an ideal is to be found in the public accountability of those responsible.

For every virtue, there is a vice. For example just as formal 'realizability' has the virtue of certainty from situation to situation, it also carries the possibility of arbitrariness. By treating all situations the same whatever their distinctive circumstances, there is a risk that the application of a rule will be deemed arbitrary and indeed damaging to the long-term interests of those involved. Furthermore, the generality of a rule of broad scope carries with it the danger of including rather different situations that deserve closer scrutiny on their own terms. Indeed, while independence of the competing interests involved in alternative courses of action is a virtue, independence may translate into isolation from the circumstances in which people find themselves. And finally, the existence of a regime of sanctions is premised upon the need for rules that are clear and unambiguous. But this may not be the case. In fact, for rule-makers the existence of a sanctions policy may represent such a threat to their well-being that their decision-making becomes timid and isolated from the 'hard' problems posed by the boundaries of rules. To follow a rule slavishly may be to impose injustice on those affected in the name of virtue.

# 4 Rules, Regulation, and the Public Interest

At one level, statutory rules and regulations are a recent phenomenon. Passage of the US ERISA (1974) and the UK Pension Reform Act (PRA) (1995) were prompted and sustained through the legislative processes by the high-profile failure of company pension schemes—respectively, the bankruptcy of the Studebaker auto company and the subsequent loss of employees' retirement benefits, and Robert Maxwell's diversion of the Mirror Group's pension plan assets into various corporate financial arrangements designed to sustain his empire rather than the retirement incomes of his employees. Both legislative initiatives sought to separate the financial commitments inherent in pension plans from the corporate competitive and financial strategies of plan sponsors. And both sought to define explicitly the fiduciary responsibilities of pension fund trustees, referring to the principles of trust law while establishing civil and criminal penalties for wrongdoing. In this sense, the regulation of pension funds became a formal topic of statute going beyond inherited case law custom and practice.[5]

One response to the vices associated with model 1 (above) has been to introduce a set of constraints or legislative requirements relating to public standards of justice. So, for example, embedded in ERISA are public standards of equitable treatment including clauses drawn from civil rights legislation outlawing discrimination on the basis of age, gender, and race (Clark 1993). Furthermore, regulations have been introduced so as to ensure that the different types of workers of a plan sponsor are treated equitably as regards their eligibility for certain types of pension benefits. These kinds of regulations have effectively reduced the scope of rule-based decision-making substituting the public interest in protecting the welfare of those considered at risk if private interests were to dominate the decision making process.

There is no doubt that these regulations have vastly complicated the application of the golden rule. And it can be argued that these types of regulations have slowly but profoundly altered the balance between private and public interests in the provision of pension and retirement benefits across the Anglo-American world.[6]

At the same time, legislative frameworks have sought to protect the accumulated retirement assets of plan participants from those that would exploit their privileged positions as guardians of beneficiaries' interests. One approach has been to seek ways of distinguishing between the interests of plan sponsors and plan trustees in the hope of driving a wedge between corporate finance and the control and management of plan assets and liabilities. Another approach has been to broaden the applicability of the golden rule, including financial service providers as fiduciaries, thereby adding accountability and compliance to the functions of private agents responsible for the flow of assets between tasks. Yet another approach has been to develop governmental institutions that would guarantee or in some way insure the benefits or even the assets of plan beneficiaries. In recent years, of course, these institutions have been exposed to the vicissitudes of finance capitalism—such guarantees are very problematic if risk is systematic (industry or economy wide) instead of idiosyncratic (company specific) (Clark 1993).

These types of second-order rules have become very complex, covering more and more aspects of what might be thought historically to be the domain of private interests. Indeed, it could be argued that the public interest in private pension systems has effectively neutered the historical connection between employer-offered pension benefits and employee compensation. In doing so, fiduciaries' discretion has been progressively narrowed and more explicitly demarcated—trustee decision-making is increasingly dominated by formal procedures set out in peer-reviewed manuals and handbooks designed according to expert advisers' interpretations of statute and case law.

This approach to pension fund regulation ignores the fact that pension benefits need not be offered to employees in the same manner as before, nor need they even be offered at all. The benefits and costs of model 2 are asymmetrically distributed in time: the benefits in terms of beneficiary protection are short term whereas the social costs of such protection in terms of static coverage rates and greater uncertainty over the value of private pension benefits are long term.

## 5 MARKETS, INFORMATION, AND ACCOUNTABILITY

As we have seen, both model 1 (the golden rule) and model 2 (statutory frameworks) of pension fund regulation have virtues and vices. One obvious limitation of the golden rule is that it may be difficult to rely upon one rule without amending and adding rules to increasingly complex and different circumstances. Another problem may be the fragility of moral imperatives, especially in circumstances where social conflict and dispute over core moral commitments spill over into the regulation of private institutions. This model of pension fund regulation has slowly replaced the employment relationship with the rights of citizenship. Legislative frameworks tend to be static rather than dynamic, comprehensive and highly prescriptive in form, and subject to judicial oversight. In effect, statute tends to replicate history and react against it rather than look forward to new forms of compensation, and new types of relationships between plan sponsors and their beneficiaries.

By this logic, a third model of pension fund regulation is required, one that relies upon contractual negotiation between the parties immediately affected rather than moral imperatives or the state-based protection of rights (Besley and Prat 2003). The market model of pension provision co-exists in many countries with conventional models of pension fund regulation. In this model, pension funds 'govern' service providers by performance standards such as cost-efficiency, the rate of return, and client-responsiveness. This requires consistent and timely reporting of performance as well as mechanisms that can identify and distinguish between aberrant and systematic failures in performance. Indeed, much of the financial services industry is 'regulated' by measures of relative performance as opposed to absolute performance. For some critics such as Allen et al. (2003), however, relative measures of performance tend to encourage herd behavior and tend to reward mediocrity rather than exceptional performance. External consultants may also play a vital role in maintaining the integrity of the evaluation and regulation process (Clark 2004).

There are dangers in such close relationships with market actors. The apparent gap in compensation paid to pension fund employees as opposed to the employees of financial service providers for similar functions is one source of tension. Whatever the moral virtues of representing the welfare of others, a twofold or threefold difference in compensation may be reason enough to seek sweetheart deals that benefit both sides of the transaction without benefiting beneficiaries. On the other side of the equation, the apparent cost-efficiency of the market may not be recognized by pension fund officers more concerned with their own interests in controlling the flow of assets than the interests of beneficiaries. Consequently, regulators may introduce the market as a regulation mechanism, requiring the publication of comparable performance data amongst pension funds and between funds and market providers. If beneficiaries are offered the option to switch between internal and external service providers and even switch out of funds to market providers, it is arguable that the discipline imposed on both sides of the market may enhance standards of pension fund regulation.

For consumers of pension and retirement income products, a similar logic may apply.[7] With sufficient information, with the option to switch between service providers, and with an abiding interest in their own welfare, it is possible that the virtues of the institutional market for financial services could be replicated in the retail market. To make the market work on behalf of individual consumers, the integrity of market transaction and contract are essential ingredients in any regulatory regime. So, for example, individuals should be well informed about current and future prospects with the option to renegotiate should unexpected circumstances change the calculus of consent. Coercion would violate both the legal institution of contract and would invoke otherwise suppressed moral standards of behavior.[8] In effect, another guiding principle has crept into the judicial interpretation of contract: it should contribute to social welfare (Posner 1986). Inevitably, contract must be more flexible and subject to renegotiation than moral theorists would accept.

Historically, at least, *caveat emptor* has also been an important principle for individual consumers of financial products. Assuming individuals are rational decision-makers, they are also responsible for the results (good and bad) of their actions.[9] But as is well appreciated, the market for financial services is far from perfect. Not only are many financial products opaque in structure, operation, and cost, the comparability of such products is often obscured by product providers. Information asymmetries are characteristic of model 3 whether institutional or retail based. Even in situations where there is adequate information about literally thousands of products, consumers use short cuts to make decisions rather than make the sophisticated comparisons that academics believe and regulators hope they might employ.

All this has been recognized by regulators. In the UK, the Financial Services Authority has sought to improve consumer decision-making focusing on education, idealized decision trees, and improved market information. In the United States, the Securities Exchange Commission (SEC) has long sought to protect individual consumers in financial markets, being most concerned with the consequences of consumer distrust for market liquidity and performance. So, for example, Section 10(b) of the US Securities Exchange Act of 1934 'makes it "unlawful for any person ... [t]o use or employ, in connection with the purchase or sale of any security... any manipulative or deceptive device or contrivance"' as recently cited in *SEC v Zandford* 536 US 862, 867 (2002). The recent history of the tech-bubble is surely evidence of the continuing significance of this provision.

## 6 REGIMES OF PENSION FUND REGULATION

Up to this point, each model of pension fund regulation has been treated as distinct and separate; each model could be *the* model of pension fund regulation. In fact, it is arguable that there are distinctive regimes of regulation, combining the three models in different ways for different reasons. Regimes of regulation may not be chosen at a particular point in time so much as accreted through compromise amongst economic, political, and social elites (as suggested by Roe 1994 for corporate governance). This is a well-worn analytical logic, articulated in a variety of settings including studies of national welfare regimes (notably Esping-Andersen 1990 and Goodin *et al.* 1999). Here, I present three regimes of pension fund regulation assuming they have evolved rather than been designed and implemented at a particular point in time and space. A 'reform' may be structural in the sense that new regimes are often designed and implemented against history and geography.

Figure 24.1 is organized in the following fashion. At each corner of the triangle is one of the three models of pension fund regulation identified above. There may be countries whose regime of pension fund regulation is just one model rather than a combination of models. This seems unlikely, at least with respect to current circumstances. For instance, notwithstanding the historical significance of the golden rule of fiduciary duty for Anglo-American economies, this rule never stands by itself. Likewise, the market is not used as the exclusive mechanism of pension fund regulation even if recent reforms in Central and Eastern Europe have used it to introduce defined contribution (DC) and related schemes. In some circumstances, notably those countries that depend entirely on social security for citizens' retirement incomes, it is arguable that statute is an exclusive model of regulation. Yet even in these circumstances, trustees may be guided by a moral framework of obligations and responsibilities that go beyond their powers as enumerated in statute. At the centre of the triangle is a point of reference allowing us to distinguish between each of the three regimes. In what follows, I look at each of the regimes of pension fund regulation explaining their core characteristics in theory and in practice.

*Regime 1: Moral commitment with back-up* This regime of pension fund regulation is the dominant regime in Anglo-American economies. It is termed 'moral commitment with back-up' recognizing the historical significance of the left-hand corner of the triangle in relation to the development of legislative frameworks designed to solve problems and deal with issues not easily accommodated within the inherited common law framework. As noted above, legislative initiatives gained prominence during the second half of the twentieth century and now incorporate many aspects of common law as statutory requirements. This regime of pension

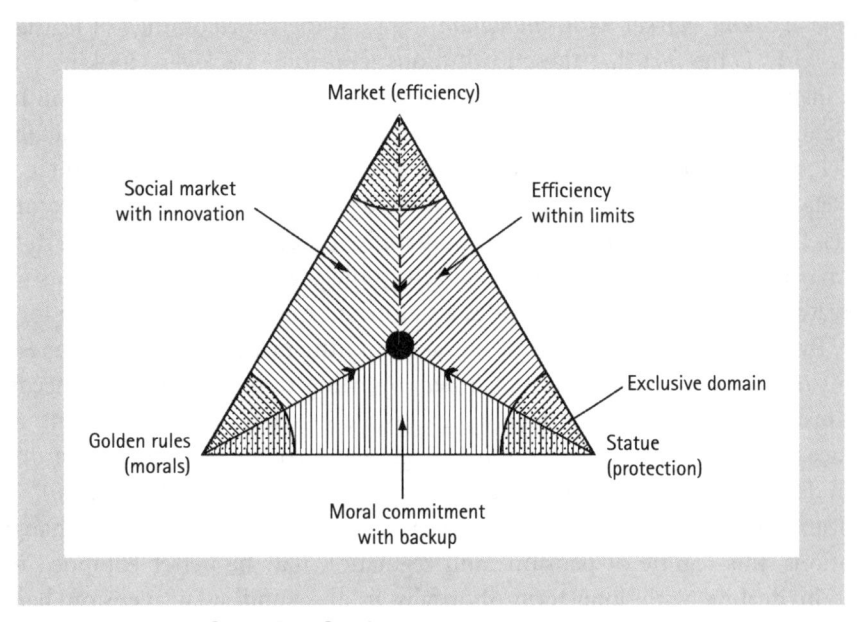

**Fig. 24.1** Regimes of pension fund governance

fund regulation can also be characterized as a regime designed to enhance the public good: the market has a minor role in this regime although it is not entirely absent from the framework (especially in relation to DC schemes). Most importantly, it combines two sources of the public interest, one in background moral commitments and the other in the public purpose embedded in legislation. Whatever role the market plays thereafter, it should not be as the servant of the public good.

That being the case, it is quite possible that the public good would be served by balancing the interests between current younger workers, older workers, and retired pension plan beneficiaries. If we assume that a long-term shortfall in the funding of current defined benefit (DB) pension benefits can be met either by introducing and even increasing contributions by younger workers and/or decreasing the level of current paid pension benefits, the public good may be served by introducing a measure of sacrifice by one, or two, or all three generations of plan participants. Notice that 'balance' is hardly a moral value equal in strength or historical significance to duty and obligation. Even so, it is hard to believe that duty and obligation should be allowed to bankrupt the whole institution. In this respect, the legislative side of the equation is a means of legitimately deliberating over the distribution of costs and benefits in such institutions. The introduction of cash-balance pension schemes may be a recipe for 'balance' notwithstanding its age-related discriminatory tendencies.[10]

*Regime 2: Social market with innovation* One of the shortcomings of legislative frameworks is the fact that these institutions tend to be backward looking rather than instruments for innovation at the local level. In this regime of pension fund regulation, the virtues of model 1 are combined with model 3, with a modicum of model 2 in that discretion remains at the local level drawing upon the advantages of markets while being regulated by widely held and deep-seated moral commitments. Duty and obligation imply accountability (Dietze 1985). Most importantly, this may mean that plan participants use the judiciary to enforce their rights to be so treated. This kind of logic provides a significant but circumscribed role for the state. By contrast, assuming robust moral commitments, the market becomes the means of enhancing the welfare of others by being responsive to their needs as circumstances change. If this seems implausible in relation to the current significance of legislative frameworks, it is an argument that has preoccupied European social democratic governments over the past decade or so (see Clark 2003*b*).

Clearly, in circumstances where innovation is needed to respond to changing situations, this regime of pension fund regulation may be better equipped than most in dealing with long-term shortfalls in the funding of pension benefit obligations. Furthermore, it locates decisions about balancing the interests between different generations of plan participants fairly and squarely with those most affected. At the same time, it places a heavy burden upon social solidarity and the robustness of local institutions in the extent to which they are able to make independent but responsible decisions. This regime of pension fund regulation is very sensitive to the constitution of boards of trustees, their expertise, the protocols and customs underpinning collective decision-making, and the degree to which decisions can be justified by reference to community principles.

*Regime 3: Efficiency within the limits* This regime of pension fund regulation relies upon a legislative framework to sustain market solutions to pension and retirement income issues. In this regime, the virtues of the market for innovation and individual welfare are paramount; moral imperatives are at best background issues and more likely deliberately discounted in favor of bilateral contractual relationships. In this kind of regime, there is a significant premium attached to sustaining market efficiency: legislative frameworks are more likely to be mechanisms for enhancing market efficiency rather than embodying moral expectations about the public good. Most importantly, the integrity and performance of contract would be a crucial element in any public policy framework. If the public good is relevant at all, it is simply the sum of individual transactions. In this regime, pensions and retirement income have no greater status than the status accorded to any other contractual savings institutions. Pension fund regulation may be no more than the regulation of market contracts (Besley and Prat 2003).

How would this regime of pension fund regulation deal with a long-term shortfall in funding and the relationship between younger and older workers and current retirees? Lacking widely shared and deeply held moral commitments to the welfare of others, it is doubtful that this regime would take seriously the issue of distributing equitably the costs and benefits of a pension fund system amongst different categories of current and potential beneficiaries. Indeed the 'best' solution may be to divide and separate their interests, introducing DC and other hybrid options that locate risk with the individual. If so, we may be in a world so aptly described by Posner (2003); a world in which the ruling ethos is simply and only individual interest. This may be entirely consistent with those who stand to benefit the most from such an arrangement, including market agents that provide DC services. But it is a regime of pension fund regulation that stands against the collective interest in the welfare of others.

# 7 CONCLUSIONS

In this chapter, I assessed the virtues and vices of three current models of pension fund regulation. The historical significance of these models can be clearly seen from recent experience in the Anglo-American world. These models do not stand entirely alone—they have complementary relationships with one another in part because statute and market models of regulation are often seen to be solutions to the apparent problems of the golden rule model. Indeed, it is hard to identify any regime of pension fund regulation that is just one model; the three regimes of pension fund regulation noted in Figure 24.1 are combinations of the three models recognizing their distinctive qualities and characteristics.

If the history of Anglo-American pension fund regulation can be written as common law heritage amended by statute and market interests, over the last couple of decades deliberate attempts have been made to design efficient and equitable regimes of regulation. As part of the process of rethinking the national provision of pension and retirement incomes in the context of globalization and the emerging hegemony of neoliberal capitalism, the introduction of private pension systems around the world has been accompanied by debate about what would be the best regime of regulation rather than that which was inherited. In this respect, the history of policy response is hardly the best indicator of which regime to adopt. What lessons can be drawn from this analysis for structural reform and institutional innovation?

One lesson is surely that no one model of pension fund regulation is sufficient in its own right. To rely upon one model would be to give undue weight to an idealized notion of the power of any one approach: the proper role of moral imperatives in society; the public interest embedded in national legislation; or the functions and efficiency of markets. It is tempting, of course, to idealize while denigrating the power and prospects of alternatives. For many years the efficient market hypothesis was effectively used to discount the role for governments in regulating financial markets. Likewise, it is easy enough to denigrate moral imperatives, believing that individual psychology is at best selfish and avaricious in nature and at worst destructive of any sense of collective identity and commitment. To do so, whatever the evidence drawn from surveys of individual preferences, would miss the disciplining effects of duty, obligation, and responsibility. These ideals matter, particularly if we recognize the cost-effectiveness of social discipline.

A second lesson is that regimes of regulation must allow for local discretion. One of the problems of legislative models of pension fund regulation is that they tend to respond to past problems while reducing the scope for local innovation. Their virtue is, of course, the common framework and expectations imposed upon private agents. But one lesson to be drawn from static coverage rates and the systematic shift away from defined benefit to defined contribution plans is that the burdens imposed by a standard framework are such that private agents have sought alternatives. Just as defined contribution plans are subject to the burdens of increasing regulation, so private agents have sought other options. We may be dismayed about this type of behavior. And it is more than possible that those who seek alternatives outside existing legislative frameworks do so for reasons unrelated to the best interests of plan beneficiaries. Yet all kinds of private agents have an interest in private pension plans that can adapt to their own circumstances rather than those that impose a straitjacket upon the responsiveness of plan administrators to their interests and ambitions.

A third lesson is that, whatever the regime of pension fund regulation, information problems loom large. Indeed, it could be argued that the public good regime is a response to the inability of plan participants to observe the intentions of pension plan officers and trustees *and* a reflection of their distrust of market options. In this respect, plan participants require an enormous amount of information if they are to understand and act in their best interests. In one corner of the regulation regime is a premium on trust; the expectation that all things being equal, those responsible for plan beneficiaries' welfare act in accordance with their duties and obligations. In the other corner of the regulation regime is recognition that trust is fragile, and intervening opportunities unobserved by plan beneficiaries may subvert duty and obligation. In this regime of regulation the costs of market information for individuals are assumed to be higher than the costs of checking on the behavior by those responsible for the welfare plan of participants.

Not so clear, however, are the underlying assumptions or principles that should guide the design process. Here, I suggest two basic principles. In the first instance, moral duties and obligations remain an important foundation for any regulation regime. Making the connection to widely held and deeply felt moral expectations is an essential element in any regulation regime that has as its core responsibility for the welfare of others. In this respect, there is little reason to agree with Posner (2003), who suggests that Western societies are so divided that widely shared moral commitments cannot function as a means of discipline on behavior. Second, the commitment to the welfare of others, especially to those who are aged and infirm, is a moral imperative that transcends income, race, and gender etc. To think otherwise, to imagine that individual interests could drive such a wedge between people in their concern for others will take us back to the dark days of the nineteenth century and the poverty prompted by the failure of voluntary retirement schemes (see Chapters 2 and 3 in this volume).

The design of any regime of pension fund regulation must take these lessons seriously. At the same time, care must be used so that the checks and balances needed to maintain discipline, responsiveness, and oversight do not in combination become so unwieldy as to cut against efficiency and equity. In some respects, each of the three regimes of pension fund regulation identified in Figure 24.1 holds one model at bay (being of less significance) while relying upon the combination of the two other models to drive the regulation process. When the three models of pension fund regulation are combined in a regulatory regime, the design process must be clear about the balance between each model and what each model seeks to achieve within the overarching regime. There is a real danger that the inclusion of elements of several models within a regime may put in play competing and antagonistic goals in the decision-making process and effectively paralyze decision-making.

# Notes

This chapter was prepared as a background paper for a project with John Marshall and Emiko Wakasugi on pension fund trustee decision-making sponsored by the UK National Association of Pension Funds. A version was first presented to the World Bank's conference on 'Contractual savings: supervisory and regulatory issues in life insurance and private pensions', Washington, D. C., November 2003. Thanks are also due to the insights and knowledge of my colleagues near and far including Ewald Engelen, Tessa Hebb, Alicia Munnell, and Noel Whiteside. None of the above should be held responsible for any errors or omissions.

1. The term 'governance' is used to refer to the formal mechanisms by which an institution makes decisions, is held accountable to its stakeholders and beneficiaries, and acts in accordance with public and private standards (Clark 2004). There are other related definitions, including one from the OECD that refers to 'a robust, process-oriented decision-making framework' including administrative and oversight functions as well due regard to the investment of pension fund assets (Galer 2002: 62).

2. The suit was brought by Harvard College and Massachusetts General Hospital, beneficiaries of the trust upon the death of the surviving spouse. These parties argued that the trustees had failed in their fiduciary duty in that the value of the trust had declined precipitously as a result of poor investment returns. The Court held that as the trustees had 'acted... according to their best skill and discretion' there was no basis for recovering the value of the trust from the trustees. Fiduciary duty does not guarantee the value of assets; it is a behavioral imperative rather than a certain outcome. This decision has had long-lasting consequences for the investment strategies of trustees.
3. In the Restatement of Trusts sponsored by the American Law Institute (1992), the related prudent man rule was augmented by a set of conditions. The Restatement (Ch 7, Section 227, p. 8) sought to recover trustees' discretion in investment noting the necessity (a) for a portfolio investment strategy with an appropriate risk and return profile, and (b) the diversification of investments. Thereafter, (c) the General Standard affirmed that 'trustees must' (1) respect 'loyalty' and 'impartiality', (2) 'act with prudence' in the delegation of authority and 'selection and supervision of agents', and (3) only incur 'reasonable' costs when undertaking their investment duties.
4. This is, of course, a sweeping statement perhaps more consistent with current expectations in social science and law than it is necessarily consistent with the history of liberal democracy (as exemplified by J. S. Mill). This is hardly the occasion to review and assess the evidence for and against this proposition.
5. Whereas moral imperatives underpin the golden rules of common law, they are less significant for statutory frameworks derived from the legislative process. Here, the legitimizing force of democratic representation and accountability provides the basis for second-order rules and regulations. In fact, statutory frameworks may deliberately eschew moral imperatives favoring 'neutral' rather than normative standards of behavior in societies that may not be able to achieve consensus on anything other than procedural democracy. See Ely (1980).
6. See, for example, Ellison's (2000, ch. 14) elaboration of UK pension fund trustee responsibilities referencing the historical origins of those responsibilities in trust law and more recent developments found in statute and the introduction of the Financial Services Authority.
7. In the UK, for example, employees have the right to opt out of company-provided pension schemes, relying upon markets for retirement income products without the governance institutions that are typical of defined benefit and defined contribution schemes. At the same time, as pension funds have increasingly relied on market agents for advanced administrative and financial services, pension funds have added to their governance tasks new functions such as the monitoring and scrutiny of agents' behavior (Clark 2004).
8. It is arguable, of course, that contract is a moral institution based upon the commitment implied by the act of promise. This would mean that there is, in fact, an intimate relationship between the moral foundations of rules (model 1) and market-related contracts (model 3). This issue was widely debated some years ago; see especially Atiyah (1981) and Fried (1981). More recently, Migotti (2003) has revisited the issue distinguishing between the types of commitment implied by the act of promise.
9. The implications of such a principle are (ideally) twofold: (1) individuals will seek out and obtain the information necessary to make 'good' decisions, and (2) individuals will be cautious in making decisions, recognizing the costs as well as the possible benefits of

one choice as opposed to others. In this manner, the market should be close to self-regulating.

10. In *Cooper et al. v The IBM Personal Pension Plan* (2003) WL 21767853 (S.D.I11), a US federal district court ruled that a company's cash balance and pension equity formula violated ERISA's Section 204(b)(1)(G) age discrimination provisions. Using hypothetical examples, the court showed that the age of an employee would have a significant impact upon his or her benefits accrued through a cash balance scheme. Older workers would be less well-off than younger workers. In doing so, the court held that cash balance schemes are similar in effect to defined benefit schemes notwithstanding the fact that their introduction over the past ten years has been driven, in part, by companies seeking to avoid the oversight and administrative procedures associated with defined benefit plans and the interests of younger workers in an accumulation fund linked to equities.

# References

ALLEN, F., MORRIS, S., SHIN, H. S. (2003). 'Beauty contests, bubbles and iterated expectations in asset markets'. Discussion Paper 1406. New Haven: Cowles Foundation, Yale University.

AMERICAN LAW INSTITUTE (1992). *Restatement of the Law. Trusts: Prudent Investor Rule*. St Paul, Minn.: American Law Institute Publishers.

ATIYAH, P. (1981). 'Review of *Contract as Promise*'. *Harvard Law Review*, 95: 509–28.

BADER, V., and ENGELEN, E. (2003). 'Taking pluralism seriously: arguing for an institutional turn in political philosophy'. *Philosophy and Social Criticism*, 29: 375–406.

BESLEY, T., and PRAT, A. (2003). 'Pension fund governance and the choice between defined benefit and defined contribution plans'. Discussion Paper 3955. London: Centre for Economic Policy Research.

BLACK, B. (1992). 'Agents watching agents: the promise of institutional voice'. *UCLA Law Review*, 39: 811–93.

BRYDON, D. (ed.) (2000). *'Prudent Man' and European Pensions*. London: European Asset Management Association.

CLARK, G. L. (1993). *Pensions and Corporate Restructuring in American Industry: A Crisis of Regulation*. Baltimore: Johns Hopkins University Press.

—— (2000). *Pension Fund Capitalism*. Oxford: Oxford University Press.

—— (2003a). 'Twenty-first century pension (in)security', G. L. Clark and N. Whiteside (eds.), in *Pension Security in the 21st Century*. Oxford: Oxford University Press, 225–53.

—— (2003b). *European Pensions & Global Finance*. Oxford: Oxford University Press.

—— (2004). 'Pension fund governance: expertise and organizational form'. *Journal of Pension Economics and Finance*, 3: 233–53.

—— THRIFT, N. and TICKELL, A. (2004). 'Global finance: the industry, the media and its image'. *Review of International Political Economy*, 11: 289–310.

DIETZE, G. (1985). *Liberalism Proper and Proper Liberalism*. Baltimore: Johns Hopkins University Press.

EISENBERG, M. A. (1988). *The Nature of the Common Law*. Cambridge, Mass.: Harvard University Press.

ELLISON, R. (ed.) (2000). *Pensions Law and Practice with Precedents*. London: Sweet and Maxwell.

ELY, J. H. (1980). *Democracy and Distrust*. Cambridge, Mass.: Harvard University Press.

ESPING-ANDERSEN, G. (1990). *The Three Worlds of Welfare Capitalism*. Oxford: Polity Press.

FRIED, C. (1981). *Contract as Promise*. Cambridge, Mass.: Harvard University Press.

GALER, R. (2002). '"Prudent person rule" standard for the investment of pension fund assets'. *Financial Market Trends*, 83: 43–78. Paris: OECD.

GOODIN, R., HEADEY, B., MUFFELS, R., and DIRVEN, H.-J. (1999). *Real Worlds of Welfare Capitalism*. Cambridge: Cambridge University Press.

HAWLEY, J., and WILLIAMS, A. (1999). *The Rise of Fiduciary Capitalism*. Philadelphia: University of Pennsylvania Press.

JENSEN, M. (2000). *A Theory of the Firm*. Cambridge, Mass.: Harvard University Press.

KENNEDY, D. (1976). 'From and substance in private law adjudication'. *Harvard Law Review*, 89: 1685–778.

LANGBEIN, J. H. (1995). 'The contractarian basis of the law of trusts'. *Yale Law Journal*, 105: 625–75.

—— (1997). 'The secret life of the trust: the trust as an instrument of commerce'. *Yale Law Journal*, 107: 160–89.

MARCH, J. (1994). *A Primer on Decision Making*. New York: Free Press.

MIGOTTI, M. (2003). 'All kinds of promises'. *Ethics*, 114: 60–87.

MUNNELL, A., and SUNDÉN, A. (2003). *Coming Up Short: The Challenge of 401(k) Plans*. Washington, D. C.: Brookings Institution.

POSNER, R. (1986). *Economic Analysis of Law*. Boston: Little Brown.

—— (2003). *Law, Pragmatism and Democracy*. Cambridge, Mass.: Harvard University Press.

RESCHER, N. (1987). *Ethical Idealism*. Berkeley: University of California Press.

ROE, M. (1994). *Strong Managers, Weak Owners*. Princeton: Princeton University Press.

ROMANO, R. (1993). 'Public pension fund activism in corporate governance reconsidered'. *Columbia Law Review*, 93: 795–853.

SCANLON, T. M. (1998). *What We Owe Each Other*. Cambridge, Mass.: Harvard University Press.

SHILLER, R. J. (2002). 'Bubbles, human judgement, and expert opinion'. *Financial Analysts' Journal*, 58/3: 18–26.

SMILEY, M. (1992). *Moral Responsibility and the Boundaries of Community*. Chicago: University of Chicago Press.

CHAPTER 25

# REGULATORY PRINCIPLES AND INSTITUTIONS

ANDRÉ LABOUL AND
JUAN YERMO

## 1 INTRODUCTION

The debate over appropriate policy responses to population ageing has intensified in recent years. The prime concern is the expected increase in the elderly dependency ratio (the ratio of workers over 65 to those between 15 and 64) over the coming decades to levels as high as 40 to 50 percent in most OECD countries and in some large developing countries such as China. Among other international organizations, the OECD has been heavily involved in the lively discussions that have taken place. The 1998 meeting of OECD Ministers, for example, called for urgent, comprehensive reform across different sectors—financial, economic, social, and fiscal—and reached the obvious conclusion that the solutions would be much more difficult and painful if needed reforms were postponed. All agreed that the responses to the pension challenges required prompt action on many fronts (OECD 1998).

Action on the ageing agenda has been forthcoming. Governments around the world are reforming public pension systems by adjusting their parameters[1] and promoting policies which are expected to help make ageing populations sustainable and improve the long-term actuarial balance of social security systems. Policy reforms are required to achieve several objectives including the promotion of faster technological progress, encouraging fertility, increasing labor force participation rates among women and the elderly, speeding the entry of young people into the labor market, and reducing disability and sickness rates. Many countries are also considering the role of immigration.

Another important axis for policy reform is related to private pensions. The OECD recommends that retirement income should be provided by a mix of tax-and-transfer systems, funded systems, private savings and earnings. The objective is risk diversification, a better balance of burden-sharing between generations, and more flexibility for individuals over their retirement decision. This implies increasing the size of advanced-funded systems in member countries and especially in those where pay-as-you-go (PAYG) systems are still dominant. Allowing people to adjust through private pension saving also requires reforms to ensure that the operation of the financial sector inspires confidence in the safety and soundness of such saving.

The development of private pensions is promoted as a complement to, and not as a substitute for, public schemes. Furthermore, whatever form they take, private schemes must be well regulated and underpinned by efficient financial markets. Regulations, which are indispensable for sustaining the confidence of beneficiaries, primarily help safeguard the rights of members and the financial security of plans. They are especially necessary because retirement systems affect people's lives. The important social role of the pension sector—which is shared with that of health care—requires governments to pay special attention to it and ensures that private firms—to which certain duties can be said to have been delegated—are properly fulfilling their obligations. The granting of fiscal advantages is also an incentive to governments to check their use.

In the academic literature, informational failures also typically call for state intervention. Employer-sponsored or occupational pension plans[2] are subject to the standard informational problems stemming from a principal–agent relationship. Employees may not understand the issues involved in pension plan design and administration. In turn, employers themselves do not always have the skills needed to administer a pension plan and, in particular, to invest the pension plan's assets. The need to delegate in turn raises the spectre of opportunistic behavior, of an agent following his or her self-interest, as opposed to that of the principal. Equally worrying, there is little guarantee even if the agent is better qualified to make decisions than the principal, that he or she has all the information needed to make appropriate decisions. In general, it could first be argued that such situations call for institutions that can enforce certain codes of behavior. An example of such codes in occupational pension plans are collective bargaining agreements involving mutual supervision by employer and employee representatives as exist in some Scandinavian countries, Sweden being the prime example.

In nearly all OECD countries, however, the trend has been toward encoding rules in pensions law and pension regulation. The development of occupational pension regulation has hardly been a well-synchronized or uniform development across countries. Nor has it always been a one-shot exercise. As argued by Gordon Clark in this volume, regulatory initiatives have sometimes been a response to major frauds or other scandals. Such events can influence policy-making and bias decision-making toward conservative outcomes.

While policy action is generally required, the temptation to overregulate must be avoided. This is especially important as private pensions systems are generally voluntary. Against this background, pension rules should provide an adequate regulatory framework for these systems to function efficiently, but they should avoid creating disincentives to employer participation and the development of private pensions in general. On the contrary, incentives for competitive pension markets, where financial institutions can operate freely, are important, as is the need to adjust to the anticipated globalization of pension markets.

Given the different social and economic roles of occupational plans in OECD countries, one may also question how much countries can learn from each other, or indeed whether one can set out basic standards at the international level that can guide countries that are in the process of establishing occupational plans. Our view, shared by the members of the OECD Working Party on Private Pensions, is that there is much to be gained from international cooperation in the field of private pensions. This group has led the development of international standards for occupational pension regulation since 1998 and also helped establish the International Organization of Pension Supervisors (IOPS) in July 2004.

In the next section, we provide some background on the development of pension regulation in OECD countries and make some passing references to non-OECD countries. Then we evaluate the role of regulation and assess the delicate question of the level of regulation needed to ensure an efficient functioning of the system. We then describe the process and thinking that led to the development of international standards for occupational pension systems. Next, we assess the related question of supervision and evaluate the emerging models of supervisory structures and methods. Finally, we take a look into what the future might hold for occupational pensions and their regulatory and supervisory frameworks.

# 2 The Development of Occupational Pension Systems

Occupational pension systems predate social security arrangements.[3] Occupational pensions originally appeared in the civil service of countries such as Germany and the United Kingdom and were adopted by the manufacturing industries starting in the mid-nineteenth century. The appearance of social security systems in the late nineteenth century might have been expected to replace these schemes. Instead, the opposite happened, and employers became even more interested in providing supplementary benefits to their employees. After the Second World War, occupational pension plans grew rapidly in Germany, Japan, the Netherlands, Switzerland, the United Kingdom and the United States among other OECD countries. In the United Kingdom, they covered only 5 percent of the workforce in the first decade of the twentieth century, but nearly half of the workforce by the 1960s. A similar trend was observed in the Netherlands, Switzerland, and the United States.

Economic theory has attempted to rationalize the growing popularity of occupational pension schemes among employers for their value in promoting long-term contracts, reducing turnover costs, and encouraging high productivity (Becker 1975; Shapiro and Stiglitz 1984). Occupational pensions have hence been interpreted as deferred wages. Workers accept lower wages during their active careers in exchange for a salary-based pension after they leave the firm.

The attraction of pension arrangements for employers in countries such as Germany or the United States was compounded by the possibility of using these deferred salaries as sources of internal finance. The state at times even encouraged such arrangements. In postwar Germany, the high financial requirements of reconstruction favored these so-called book reserve systems and to this day they have remained the preferred financing vehicle for occupational pension plans. Book reserve financing was also the standard financing method for occupational plans developed in other European countries such as Austria, Spain, and Sweden. As book reserve systems fall out of favor in practically all OECD countries,[4] occupational pension plans still play an important role in company financing through their investment in private sector securities. Sometimes, as in the United States, corporations have promoted investment of pension plans assets in their shares, allowing access to cheap capital but also important risk transfers.

Economic rationality, however, should not obscure the fact that occupational pensions were not simply a form of deferred wages or internal financing. They provided an important benefit to workers in the form of work-based retirement and disability insurance which supplemented the social security system. Given the absence of developed deferred annuities markets in most countries, occupational pension systems performed an important insurance function, and one which at times was more reliable than social security benefits.

Since 1965 in Japan and since 1978 in the United Kingdom, occupational pensions have even become an alternative to social security arrangements. The contracting-out system works in a similar way in both countries and allows employers to replace the earnings-related part of social security benefits through their own benefits in exchange for lower social security contributions. In other countries, such as Denmark, Iceland, and Sweden, occupational pension plans became in effect mandatory for both employers and employees through national collective bargaining agreements or by law. In Switzerland and Finland, while retaining their private sector status, occupational pension plans were brought under social security legislation. In the Netherlands, a combination of industry-based collective bargaining and state compulsion also led to a rapid extension of occupational plans. In all these countries occupational pension plans cover practically the whole of the labor force.

# 3 The Belated and Uneven Appearance of Pension Regulations

Despite the rapid development of occupational pensions since the Second World War, the involvement of the state was minimal until the last decades of the twentieth century. Wide-ranging pension regulation was only introduced in 1974 in Germany (Occupational Old Age Protection Act) and the United States (Employment Retirement Income Security Act, ERISA), in 1987 in Spain (Law on Pension Plans and Pension Funds), 1990 in Ireland (Pensions Act) and Austria (Company Pensions Act and Pension Fund Act), and only in 1995 in the United Kingdom (Pensions Act). With the latest legislative initiatives in Greece, Korea, and Turkey, all OECD countries now have a specific private pensions law that recognizes occupational pension arrangements.[5]

Pension legislation has been primarily driven by two objectives: protecting the rights of members and other beneficiaries and promoting the financial security of the plans (Laboul 1998). Some examples of member rights include representation in the governance of pension funds, protection of vested benefits, and disclosure of plan information. A related objective in some countries has been the promotion of an equitable distribution of benefits. For example, in the United States tax regulations play a central role in avoiding discrimination in contributions or benefits.

The second key objective of pension regulation is promoting the financial security of pension arrangements. One of the key requirements in the pensions law of most OECD countries has been the segregation of assets of the pension plan from those of the plan sponsor. In countries that have retained book reserves, pension promises are protected through external insolvency guarantee arrangements, and in some instances, through priority creditor rights.

Even within those countries that required segregation of assets, the approach to prudential regulation of pension funds differs markedly. Anglo-Saxon countries have generally allowed a much greater degree of involvement of employers in the administration of pension funds than have Continental European countries. Funding rules, which set minimum ratios of pension assets to liabilities, have also been generally laxer in the former countries while investment regulations have largely relied on the 'prudent person' standard.

The difference in regulatory approach is due to a large extent to differences in the conceptualizations of the pension fund, the division of responsibilities, and the extent of risk-sharing between employers and employees. Pension funds in countries such as Denmark, Finland, Iceland, Germany, the Netherlands, and Switzerland are independent financial institutions with their own governance and administrative structure separate from that of employers. The foundation or association, a common legal status for pension funds in these countries, gives it a significant degree of operational autonomy that is not always present in the Anglo-Saxon trust model.

At the same time, employers in these European countries have often limited responsibility in the event of underfunding of the pension plan. Indeed, in countries like Denmark or Iceland, the employer's responsibility is limited to making current contributions. From the plan sponsor's perspective, these are defined contribution systems, even though the plans aim to provide a certain replacement rate. This institutional set-up also led to a regulatory approach that is closer to that of life insurance companies than Anglo-Saxon pension funds. Pension funds in Denmark and Iceland are in fact covered by life insurance regulations and, among other things, must have a solvency margin like that of life insurance companies. Such an approach is consistent with the fact that the pension funds themselves, rather than the sponsoring employers, bear the plan's risks.

The situation in Anglo-Saxon countries in the past was usually one where employers were fully responsible for correcting situations of underfunding. In accounting parlance, these countries had defined benefit plans. Partly for that reason, policy-makers have traditionally taken a relatively permissive attitude to funding levels. Amortization periods for unfunded liabilities are long and plan actuaries are left much leeway in determining assumptions. The long-term expectation has always been that employers would eventually come round to meeting their benefit promises through additional contributions to the plan.

Yet, a series of policy decisions, as well as adverse economic developments, made these expectations increasingly less realistic. First, tax regulations set limits on overfunding that obliged companies to take contribution holidays despite the uncertainty surrounding the valuation of funding ratios. Second, countries such as Canada, the United Kingdom, and the United States introduced legislation over the ownership of any funding excess (or reversion to the sponsoring employer) that reduced the attractiveness of prudent levels of funding above the minimum required by the legislation. Corporations in several mature sectors were also affected by technological and economical progress, which brought their own viability into question, and hence the solvency of their pension funds. Company bankruptcies have exposed the frailty of these promises, as occupational plans were often severely underfunded when companies went under and there was little if any protection of plan members' claims relative to those of other creditors.

The situation in Anglo-Saxon countries, where sponsors of defined benefit plans are responsible for underfunding but must return overfunding to plan members, or reduce contributions, has been an important factor in determining the reduction of funding levels. Unless plan sponsors can be convinced of their right to the upside gains as part of their responsibility for accepting the downside risks, solid 'voluntary' funding of pension obligations is unlikely to take place.

The bursting of the stock market bubble in 2000 has had a further dampening effect on funding rules. In the United States, the upper side of the interest rate corridor for valuing assets was increased from 105 percent to 120 percent effective for 2002 and 2003, which lowered funding requirements somewhat. In Ireland, the Pensions Board has implemented a new policy that extends the three and a half year period for correcting a shortfall to as much as ten years if certain conditions hold. In Canada, the Federal Government is also considering increasing the degree of funding flexibility by permitting longer correction periods. In the United Kingdom, the government intends to replace the Minimum Funding Requirement by scheme-specific funding arrangements.

Another policy reaction to the funding problem implemented in the United Kingdom in April 2005 is the introduction of a pension guarantee agency based on the US model, the Pension Benefit Guaranty Corporation (PBGC). While it is expected that the UK guarantee fund (the Pension Protection Fund) will charge a variable risk-based premium, there are concerns over the solvency of such an arrangement. If the PBGC experience is anything to go by, there is a great risk that unless premiums are fully commensurate with the risks borne, weak companies will try to offload their underfunded plans onto the guarantee fund. Moreover, such a fund may increase the expectations that the state will bail out workers of failed sponsoring companies. The potential moral hazard of such arrangements and the consequent undesirable subsidies and inefficient allocation of capital should therefore be carefully considered. By encouraging appropriate funding rules and asset liability management, regulators can limit the likelihood of calls on the guarantee fund to exceptional circumstances. Whether appropriate funding is promoted through funding rules or risk-based premiums to a guarantee fund, it is, however, important to consider the transition costs for companies. A rapid transition may be onerous for employers, especially smaller ones.

While Anglo-Saxon countries have in general given employers greater flexibility to correct underfunding, some Continental European countries such as Austria, Denmark, the Netherlands, and Norway have taken a harder line and brought about regulatory changes with the intention of achieving a speedy recovery in funding levels. In the Netherlands, new rules to be introduced in January 2007 require schemes to have a funding ratio of at least 105 percent at any time.

A tightening of solvency rules was also observed in Denmark. The recent financial downturn and the consequent funding gaps also clearly showed that the problems came from both the asset and liabilities angles, including underestimation of the liabilities and overestimation of expected returns from investment. In this respect, it was recognized that new investment policies should include a sound risk management process that measures and seeks to appropriately control portfolio risk and the matching between assets and liabilities. The use of asset-liability management (ALM) and risk management practices and techniques need to be promoted.

Most countries have generally moved in the direction of greater consistency between the calculation of assets and liabilities. Most of these countries still use fixed discount rates but these have been adjusted downwards, in line with the decline of bond yields. In the Netherlands, the government has also proposed a market value approach to measuring liabilities, using market interest rates to calculate the present value of future benefits, rather than a fixed rate of 4 percent as has been historically the case. At the end of 2002, the Danish Financial Supervisory Authority also introduced a standardized stress test in order to test the resilience of company pension funds based on market values of assets and liabilities.

In the United States, the Administration has also supported measures that should result in more accurate valuation of pension liabilities. These measures replace the current 30-year Treasury bond interest rate that is used by employers as a benchmark to determine plan funding with a blend of corporate bond index rates for two years through 2005. A proposal has also been tabled to shift to a corporate bond yield curve to measure liabilities, where the timing of future benefit payments would determine the yield to be used.

The convergence toward market valuation of pension liabilities is not without controversy (Yermo 2005). Yet, given the risk of plan closures, it is to be expected that policy-makers are concerned with the termination value of plan liabilities using market discount rates. Similarly, regulators may wish to promote faster amortization of plan amendments and actuarial gains and losses than in the past, as a plan funded on an ongoing basis may reveal a significant degree of underfunding when it terminates.

There is also increasing convergence toward some form of the 'prudent person' rule in investment regulations and away from quantitative restrictions. Some limitations on portfolio allocation, however, may be needed. Obvious candidates are limits to self-investment by asset managers and ceilings on the portion of pension fund assets that can be invested in securities issued by the sponsoring company. Such limits exist in all OECD countries for defined benefit plans. They are also widespread for defined contribution plans, the main exception being 401(k) plans in the United States. The extent of exposure to employer stock in 401(k) plans would not be possible in the occupational pension plans of other OECD countries.

## 4 Retrenchment and Transformation of Occupational Pensions

The funding crisis faced by defined benefit occupational pension plans is at the forefront of the policy agenda of many OECD countries. Average funding levels were as low as 40 percent in Japan and less than 80 percent in the United Kingdom and the United States at the end of 2003 (see Fig. 25.1). On the other hand, funding ratios only dipped slightly below 100 percent in countries such as the Netherlands and Switzerland, in part thanks to the larger buffers built in earlier years.[6] Some pension funds, however, suffered significant investment losses and large funding gaps as a result of their exposure to equities. Indeed, the allocation to equities in these countries is not so different to that of the United Kingdom and the United States (see Fig. 25.2).

Ironically, while the funding concerns of defined benefit plans are in the vanguard of the policy debate in Anglo-Saxon countries, their constituency is slowly (or rapidly in some cases) shrinking. Currently, over three-quarters of UK occupational defined benefit plans are closed to new entrants. In the United States, employers have responded in a variety of ways. In a recent survey of 500 defined

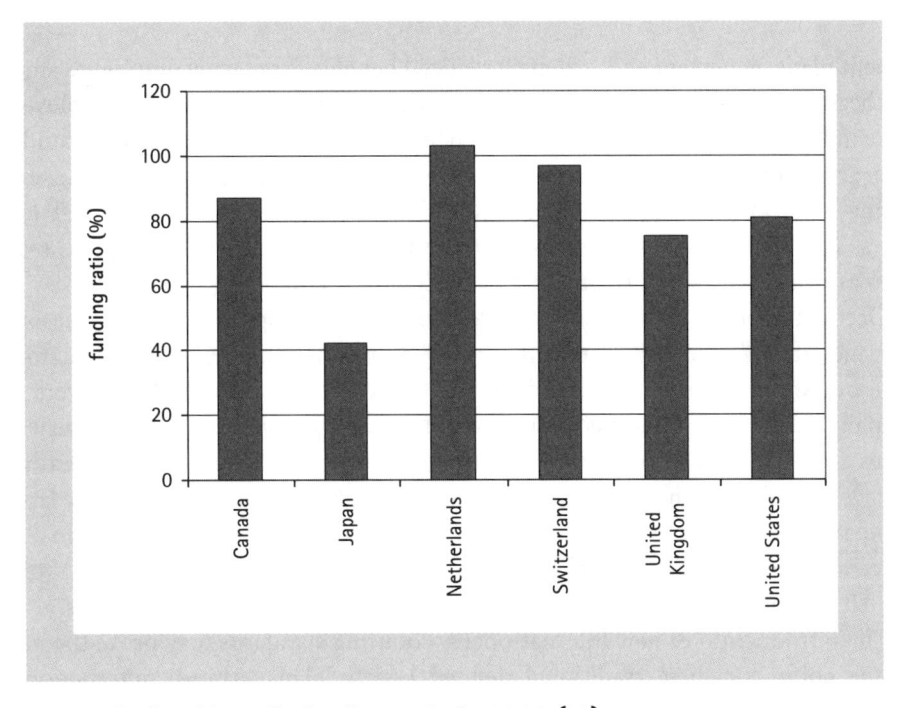

**Fig. 25.1 Defined benefit funding ratio in 2003 (%)**

*Source*: OECD Global Pension Statistics.

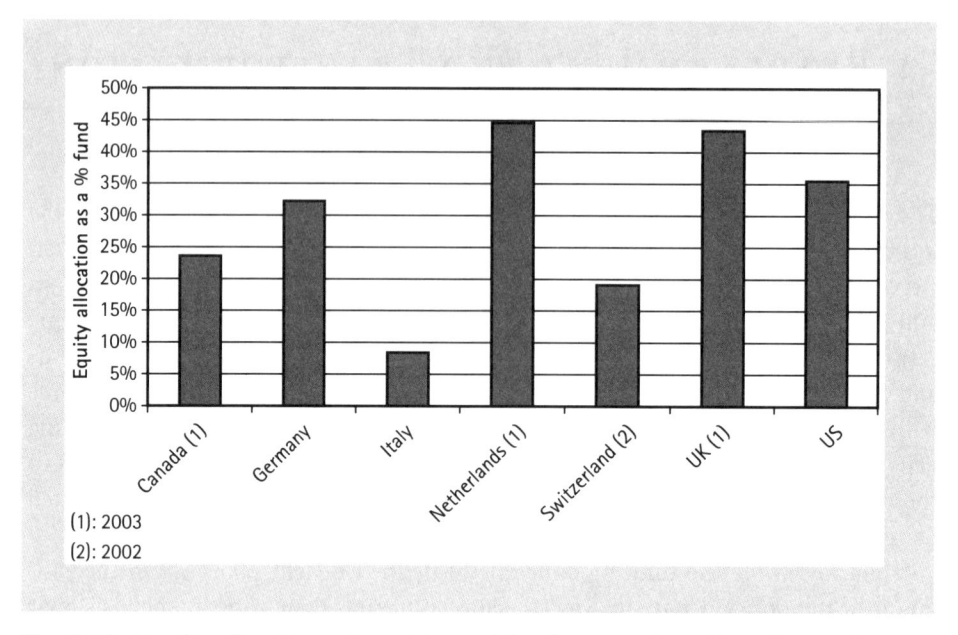

Fig. 25.2 Pension fund investment in equities in 2003 (% of total assets)

*Source*: OECD Global Pension Statistics.

benefit plans, 15 percent had frozen or reduced benefits for current employees since the beginning of 2000 and 19 percent had done so for new hires. Smaller employers were more likely to have implemented benefit freezes, which cut costs more rapidly than gradually reducing the accrual of future benefits (Shieber 2003). The demise of defined benefit plans in the United States has also accelerated over the last few years. The PBGC reports a decrease of more than 7,500 defined benefit plans over the past three years—approximately 20 percent of the total.

Occupational defined benefit arrangements have lost appeal for many reasons that include the need for greater mobility of labor, sometimes excessive regulatory zeal, but also a more general trend toward the transfer of risk from employers to employees. In Anglo-Saxon countries, the declining popularity of defined benefit plans seems to be part of a long-term trend resulting from underlying structural changes in their economies. Defined benefit plans were most popular in large companies in the manufacturing sector, which accounts for an increasingly smaller percentage of output and workforce. Compliance costs may have also played a role, as well as the policy decision to assign the pension surplus to plan members.

The introduction of new international accounting standards may prove the nail in the coffin for these traditional defined benefit plans. Already international accounting standards (IAS 19), implemented in the EU in 2005, require liabilities to be valued using a market discount rate and assets on fair values. Amortization periods for actuarial gains and losses and benefit adjustments may be no longer than the estimated remaining career service of plan members. A reform in IAS 19 in December 2004 also permits immediate recognition of gains and losses through a special income statement, as has been done in the United Kingdom since 2002 as a result of the application of FRS 17. Immediate recognition may gradually establish itself as the norm for defined benefit plans. As shareholders realize the risks that they are exposed to through corporate contributions to defined benefit plans, they are starting to push for closer matching of assets and liabilities and for a sharing of investment and longevity risks with employees.

Indeed, increases in life expectancy may yet deal a greater if a more gradual blow to these plans than the stock market crash. Life tables have historically underestimated the decline in mortality in the general population. Given that occupational plans often cover the wealthier, longer-lived workforce, there is a greater likelihood of mistakes. As pressure builds for immediate recognition of gains and losses, these plans will be forced to show in their balance sheets the extent of the increase in costs as a result of longer-lived beneficiaries.

Given these circumstances, it is therefore unlikely that traditional defined benefit plans will remain unchanged. Even in OECD countries such as Germany, Japan, and the Netherlands, with a strong defined benefit tradition and much resistance to abandoning these plans, some important steps have been taken. In the Netherlands, for example, most of the larger plans have replaced the final salary formulas in defined benefit plans by career-average formulas. It has also been made more explicit that indexation to inflation is a promise conditional on the performance of the pension fund, and therefore not a defined benefit promise. The question is whether these reforms will be enough and if not, what type of pension design will emerge to make defined benefits sustainable, if at all possible. In this respect, hybrid plans (such as cash balance plans) may prove an attractive proposition.

A career average defined benefit (DB) plan still provides full insurance against longevity risk from the moment the benefits are vested. Yet, it is difficult to rationalize the plan sponsor's role as the underwriter of longevity risk, especially over such long periods. Employers have no specific expertise as part of their daily business operations in managing biometric risks. Moreover, assuming there are well-functioning annuities markets, they may not get significant additional benefits in terms of increased worker loyalty and productivity by providing pension benefits in the form of annuities (which provide longevity protection) instead of lump sums (which do not have such protection). In some countries such as Belgium employers have accepted their role as guarantors of investment risk, but at retirement, the fund accumulated in a member's individual account is paid out as a lump sum. These defined benefit plans resemble the so-called cash balance plans in the United States. Employers in the United Kingdom and other countries are exploring similar arrangements to replace their traditional DB arrangements. While such plans may be convenient for employers and employees alike, tax and regulatory policies should encourage the conversion of these lump sums into income streams.

Another solution that may be followed in Continental Europe is the collective defined contribution model in Denmark and Iceland, where pension funds operate like mutual insurance institutions, liberating plan sponsors from their responsibility in the event of underfunding. These pension funds provide intergenerational risk-sharing, targeting a replacement rate, but adjusting benefits throughout the membership when the fund's buffer becomes too low.

Yet, the most important trend that has been observed in OECD countries is toward occupational plans that offer no investment or longevity protection for members, at least during the accumulation phase. Defined contribution plans without risk-sharing or return smoothing arrangements are now the fastest growing segment in the market in all OECD countries. Some countries, such as Hungary, Italy, or Poland, actually require all new occupational pension plans to follow this design. In this form, it is difficult to distinguish occupational pension plans from personal pension arrangements. Indeed, in Hungary, the regulations covering both types of arrangements are the same. Similar regulations apply also to occupational and personal pension plans in Spain, a country that also has predominantly defined contribution arrangements.

An important advantage of occupational arrangements for such defined contribution plans is the possible role of the employer in simplifying choice for plan members, keeping administration costs low (through economies of scale and by negotiating lower fees with pension providers), and obtaining effective professional advice and financial education for plan members and beneficiaries.

# 5 Regulatory Challenges of Defined Contribution Arrangements

The shift to 'pure' defined contribution arrangements (those without risk-sharing or return smoothing mechanisms) raises major policy concerns and regulatory challenges. First, in countries that have had a marked shift from defined benefit to defined contribution plans, employer contributions to the latter tend to be much lower. This has been widely reported in the United Kingdom, a country where private pension plans are expected to account for a large portion of retirement income. In the United States, defined benefit plans tend to be offered as part of the employment contract and have automatic enrollment, while employees must specifically request membership of defined contribution plans, such as 401(k)s. The experience of these countries points to an emerging 'retirement savings deficit', as the replacement rates achieved by workers with defined contribution plans may be much lower than those for workers covered by defined benefit plans.

Second, the absence of risk-sharing in the accumulation stage raises the question of how to invest and who should make the investment decisions. As each plan member singly bears investment risk, it may be deemed appropriate that they should make investment decisions. Yet, in many European countries such as Hungary, Italy, Poland, Portugal, or Spain, workers are affiliated to a single pension fund with a single investment portfolio. Such a structure may be inefficient as it exposes workers of different ages and preferences to the same level of risk in their retirement income.

Shifting portfolio decisions to workers, however, presumes a high degree of financial literacy and informational transparency that is rarely present in even the more financially developed countries. In addition to difficult risk-return analysis, plan members must be able to compare different fee structures. Financial education is clearly necessary to overcome some of these deficiencies. Policymakers also need to play a role in ensuring that the latest academic wisdom on retirement saving quickly filters through to the financial industry. Employers, too, could be required to play a role in educating their employees and in providing them with low cost access to annuities and to financial products that carry benefit or return guarantees.

Policy proposals that are being considered in the United States include automatic enrollments to 401(k) plans and the development of default portfolios. Such default portfolios could be designed as guaranteed investment contracts (providing a fixed or minimum investment return over a certain period) or life-cycle fund management solutions where the investment allocation is automatically shifted from riskier to more conservative asset allocations as the worker approaches retirement. Sponsoring employers could play a central role in designating one or more independent professional investment managers that offer such products.

Policy initiatives are also critical to ensure a high degree of transparency in fees between different providers. One obvious way to ensure a minimum level of comparability is to regulate fee structures, permitting only one type of fee (e.g. a fee on accumulated assets or a fee on contributions). Some countries such as Ireland, Poland, Sweden, and the United Kingdom have gone further and set limits on the fee level. Under the UK stakeholder system, for example, fees cannot be greater than 1 percent of assets under management.

Finally, further consideration should be given to the role of annuities in retirement portfolios. While social security systems and bequest motives may limit the attractiveness of such products, there is also evidence from countries such as Australia, Belgium, and the United States that adverse tax treatment of annuities has steered retirees towards lump-sum payments when deciding how to draw their retirement benefits. Such a policy is clearly inconsistent with the goal of promoting retirement income adequacy and drives an inexplicable wedge between the liquidity of tax-advantaged savings in the accumulation and the retirement phase.

Subject to appropriate tax treatment and regulation, annuities may actually become popular in the accumulation stage as well. Workers may take the decision earlier in their lives to protect themselves against the risk of longevity. Deferred annuities also reduce the risk of adverse selection, as individuals are less likely to have private information about their life expectancy earlier in their lives. The irony of the shift toward defined contribution plans is that, ultimately, workers may end up investing largely in products that provide benefit guarantees similar to those that existed under defined benefit plans. Such a development would conclude a cycle of transfers of retirement income risk from sponsoring employers to workers and then from workers to financial institutions.

# 6 Risk Management and the Need for New Financial Instruments

Further policy focus is also needed in the area of asset-liability management and public debt management. Occupational pension funds are increasingly considering the market value of their liabilities when setting out their investment strategies. A better match between assets and liabilities in defined benefit plans will require financial instruments that are currently in short supply or do not even exist. Similarly, the role of pension funds and financial institutions as providers of long-term guarantees and annuities in defined contribution plans will be determined by their ability to hedge the inherent risks adequately.

While the duration of most defined benefit plans is declining as a result of plan closures, many funds will still be paying out benefits in 50 years or even more. A liquid market of long-dated government bonds offering indexation to macroeconomic variables such as inflation and wage growth would facilitate the risk management tasks of pension funds. Life insurance companies would also benefit from such a development even if the duration of their liabilities tends to be much lower than that of defined benefit pension funds.

Another area where further policy effort is needed is in the appropriate management of longevity risk. Given the uncertainty surrounding mortality projections, it will become increasingly costly for defined benefit plans and insurance companies alike to offer guarantees that protect workers against outliving their income. Mortality bonds, which pay coupons linked to the mortality experience of a particular cohort, would ease the hedging risk for employers and pension providers.

Some observers have questioned whether there will be a sufficient supply of indexed bonds to ensure a good matching of pension plan liabilities. If a strong demand for these securities arises, however, it is likely that a rapid restructuring of government debt issues will take place. Ultimately, governments seek the lowest cost alternative for their issues. In turn, the costs are determined by the excess demand for different securities and risk management aspects of the government's long-term budget. Indexed securities can improve budgetary management as coupon payments will be more closely related to tax revenues.

Securities offering protection against macroeconomic and biometric risks seem to be most efficiently handled through the intergenerational risk-sharing mechanisms of fiscal policy. Indeed, the market for inflation-indexed bonds is dominated by sovereign issues. On the other hand, the first issues of mortality bonds have been underwritten by reinsurers. It may be just a matter of time before governments also become central to this market, at least as a catalyst in the initial stages. They have a clear risk management advantage over financial institutions as they can spread the cost of unexpected increases in life expectancy across many generations.

# 7 WHY ARE INTERNATIONAL REGULATORY STANDARDS NEEDED?

Policy consensus is hard to come by as far as occupational pensions are concerned. Countries differ in the role they assign to occupational pensions in retirement income. Governments also provide different incentives to promote such arrangements, from mandates to tax incentives. Even two countries in relative geographical and cultural proximity, such as Australia and New Zealand, have a completely different view of how much private pensions should be promoted. In Australia private pensions (which for many workers consist primarily of occupational arrangements) are mandated and subject to an advantageous tax treatment. In New Zealand, on the other hand, occupational pension plans are voluntary and do not receive any tax benefits.

Occupational pension systems themselves differ in the roles assigned to the different actors (employers, pension funds, other pension providers, and consulting firms) and the way plan risks are distributed and managed. Pension regulatory frameworks must clearly take into account the specificities and complexities of different arrangements. Indeed, in some cases, the preferred method for oversight may rely not on explicit legislation but on self-regulation in the form of codes of conduct or collective bargaining agreements. While a variety of solutions exists to ensure a smooth functioning of a private pension system, it is possible to identify a basic set of objectives that any oversight framework should aim at. Through the OECD Working Party on Private Pensions, policy-makers reached a consensus over a set of common regulatory principles and guidelines. While these standards were originally developed with a view to assisting countries at an early stage of development of their private pension systems, they have become a useful tool for regulators and supervisors when assessing the adequacy of their regulatory proposals. International standards provide an independent benchmark against which to gauge the appropriateness of different policy proposals, alongside any local cost-benefit analysis.

The 'OECD Recommendation on the Regulation of Occupational Pensions'[7] provides a comprehensive set of principles addressing areas such as the establishment of pension plans and funds, the funding of pension liabilities, the regulation of pension fund investment, the supervision of pension funds. It also addresses the rights of beneficiaries and the governance of pension funds in specific guidelines.

Amongst other things, the core principles recommend that:

- companies should create separate legal entities for their pension funds or at least that such separation is irrevocably guaranteed through appropriate mechanisms;
- the investment of a company pension fund's portfolio in securities issued by that company (or its group) should be prohibited or strictly limited;
- non-discriminatory access should be granted to private pensions schemes;
- employees should be protected from retroactive reduction of the value of accrued benefits;
- employees moving from one company to another should be able to transfer to their new employers' pension fund the pensions contributions made by themselves or their previous employer on their behalf; and
- employees should be given sufficient investment choice over their own investments.

The recommendation promotes the disclosure and availability of a large range of information, a prudent approach to investment, proper liabilities calculation, and actual powers for the supervisor, including fit and proper tests.

Other guidelines, the 'Pension Fund Governance Guidelines', draw inspiration from the OECD Principles of Corporate Governance but take into consideration the particularities of pension funds. They establish basic norms for the governance structure of pension funds, such as the identification of the governing body and its responsibilities, and stress the role of auditors, actuaries, and custodians in monitoring fund activities. The OECD is currently working on new guidelines related to investment and funding and further work is expected on risk management issues.

International standards clearly have a central role in the provision of cross-border pension services. It is much easier for policy-makers to agree to cross-border provision if it can be confirmed that the other countries involved comply with internally agreed standards. Initiatives at the international level can therefore promote better diversification and more efficient management of occupational pension plans.

# 8 THE SEARCH FOR NEW ROLE MODELS OF PENSION SUPERVISORY STRUCTURES AND METHODS

By far the greatest difficulty in supervising occupational pension systems is the large number of pension plans and funds that exist (see Table 25.1). This is especially the case in Anglo-Saxon countries, where single employer plans are the norm. In Continental European countries, the prevalence of industry-wide schemes facilitates more regular supervision and, specifically, proactive supervision.

Governments in some countries, such as Belgium and Germany, are encouraging the consolidation of the occupational pension system through industry-wide arrangements. Employers are also reviewing such options in the United Kingdom. Imposing an industry-wide arrangement can be costly, however, when the necessary bargaining agreements are not in place. A more appropriate solution in countries such as the United Kingdom where most bargaining takes place at the company level would be to rely on external pension providers to carry out the administrative operation of the pension plan. Such providers could offer their services to different pension funds, hence bringing about a consolidation in the occupational pension system.

An increased consolidation of the industry coupled with greater professionalization in the governing bodies of occupational pension plans would go a long way toward ensuring the long-term success of occupational pension systems. Supervisors could then play an increasingly central role in pension market surveillance and in the assessment of compliance with regulatory standards. Effective supervision of pension funds and plans is essential to the proper development of an

Table 25.1 Market structure of private pension systems in selected OECD countries, 2004

| Country | No. of funds | No of participants (million) | Assets (billion US$) |
|---|---|---|---|
| Australia | Over 300, 000 | 26.5 | 465 |
| Canada (1) | 3,045 | 0.7 | 446 |
| Czech Republic | 11 | 3.0 | 4 |
| Denmark | 112 | 4.4 | 73 |
| Germany | 182 | 4.1 | 104 |
| Hungary | 93 | 3.7 | 7 |
| Iceland | 48 | 0.3 | 14 |
| Ireland | 100,000 approx. | 0.6 | 77 |
| Italy | 458 | 2.2 | 44 |
| Japan | 2,017 (2) | 19.1 (1) | 661 |
| New-Zealand | 543 (2) | 0.6 | 11 |
| Portugal | 194 | 0.4 | 19 |
| Spain | 1,163 | 8.5 | 94 |
| United Kingdom | 105,000 approx. | 40 | 1,175 (1) |
| United States | 700,000 approx. | 144 | 11,090 |

Source: OECD.
(1): 2003
(2): 2002

appropriate pension framework. This requires adequate supervisory techniques, structures and methods. One of the objectives of the recently established IOPS (International Organization of Pension Supervisors) is precisely to set up high quality standards for such supervision, which will complement the OECD regulatory principles.

## 9 CONCLUSIONS

Retirement income systems were well served by occupational pension plans throughout the second half of the twentieth century. In recent years, however, the market downturn has revealed inherent imbalances in traditional defined benefit plans. Two major weaknesses are lack of consideration of plan pension liabilities and insufficient professionalism of pension plan fiduciaries in some countries.

Greater accounting and regulatory surveillance are expected to improve the institutional integrity of these plans, but they could also further undermine employers' support for defined benefit arrangements. Instead, employers are being drawn toward hybrid pension arrangement (such as the cash balance plans in the United States) and defined contribution plans. In many countries, concerns over workers' ability to make investment decisions may lead to calls for plans that ensure a high degree of protection against investment risk. Annuities markets are also likely to develop rapidly, especially if appropriate tax incentives are provided.

The development of private pension markets will also require greater international cooperation to ensure that basic benchmarks are met and that the cross-border provision of pension plans is promoted. Occupational pension plans can still make significant efficiency gains through international consolidation, an option that is currently only being opened to members of the European Union. Cooperation on private pension regulatory and supervisory standards through the OECD Working Party on Private Pensions and the IOPS could help achieve this goal in addition to serving as a basic developmental tool for countries starting their own private pension system.

# NOTES

This chapter reflects the personal view of the authors. We would like to thank Gordon Clark, Alicia Munnell, and Michael Orszag for insights and comments.

1. Parametric reforms include increasing retirement ages, linking benefits to life expectancy, providing appropriate actuarial adjustments to benefits for early/late retirement, and raising contribution rates.
2. The terms employer-sponsored and occupational pension plan are used interchangeably in this article.
3. The earliest private sector occupational pension plan in Germany (*Gutehoffnungshütte*) dates from 1832, more than 50 years before the enactment of social security legislation under Chancellor Otto von Bismarck.
4. The United Kingdom was one of the first countries to fund its occupational plans. The roots of the UK experience in the immediate postwar period can be found in various initiatives during the inter-war period which introduced tax relief on contributions to pension schemes established as trusts.
5. Not all types of occupational pension arrangements are regulated, however. For example, the friendly societies in Sweden are not subject to specific pension regulation.
6. Comparisons in funding levels remain problematic as measurement methods differ significantly between countries. See Yermo (2005) for a discussion of valuation methods.
7. The OECD recommendation and guidelines can be obtained from the website (www.oecd.org/daf/pensions). Hard copies are available from the authors upon request.

# References

Becker, G. (1975). *Human Capital.* New York: Columbia University Press.

Carvalho-Pinheiro, V. (2004). 'Supervision of pension funds: theory and practice', in *Supervising Private Pensions: Institutions and Methods.* Private Pension Series No. 6. Paris: OECD.

Laboul, A. (1998). 'Private pension systems: regulatory policies'. Financial Market Trends No. 71. Paris: OECD.

OECD (1998). *Maintaining Prosperity in an Ageing Society.* Paris: OECD.

Shapiro, C., and Stiglitz, J. (1984). 'Equilibrium unemployment as a worker discipline device'. *American Economic Review,* 74: 433–44.

Schieber, S. (2003). 'Pensions in crisis'. *Watson Wyatt Insider,* 13/9 (Sept.).

Yermo, J. (2006). 'Funding rules and accounting standards: are occupational pension plans safer?' In *Benefit Security in Occupational Pension Systems.* Private Pension Series No. 8. Paris: OECD.

CHAPTER 26

# ACCOUNTING STANDARDS FOR PENSION COSTS

GEOFFREY WHITTINGTON

## 1 Introduction

This chapter deals primarily with the problem of accounting for the cost of defined benefit pension schemes in the accounts of the sponsoring company (the employer). This is one of the most controversial issues currently being debated by accounting standard-setters, following the introduction of an innovative standard on the subject, FRS 17 (ASB 2000) by the UK Accounting Standards Board (ASB). This standard measured the pension fund deficit or surplus as the difference between the current values of the pension fund assets and liabilities, and the effects of changes in valuations were to be reported immediately in the Statement of Recognized Gains and Losses (STRGL). The introduction of FRS 17 coincided with a sharp decline in stock market prices, which reduced the value of pension fund investments, and a revision of actuarial tables to reflect the increased expectation of life, which increased pension fund liabilities. The so-called 'balance sheet approach' of FRS 17 exposed these effects very clearly, and advocates of FRS 17 believed that this transparency conveyed an important message. Opponents of FRS 17, on the other hand, argued that, by reporting short-term fluctuations in the estimate of a long-term liability, it was introducing spurious fluctuations into the accounting reports which might give a misleading picture of a company's performance and financial state. Whatever the relative merits of these views, FRS 17 certainly revealed some significant, even dramatic, pension fund deficits in the accounts of UK companies.[1]

Before exploring these matters further, it is important to explain three issues that will not be discussed in the chapter. First, accounting for defined contribution schemes will not be discussed, because a pure defined contribution scheme is a 'pay-as-you-go' scheme, in which the employer discharges all obligations through periodic contributions to the scheme: the employee bears the subsequent risks arising from the uncertainty of investment returns from the fund. Of course, there are hybrid schemes that have features of both defined benefit and defined contribution (e.g. the employer may guarantee a minimum investment return) and in such cases the accountant has either to make a judgment as to the classification of the whole scheme, or to separate out the two components (defined benefit or defined contribution),[2] but for current purposes we shall concentrate on the pure defined benefit case.

Second, accounting by pension funds, when these are entities are separate from the employer, will not be discussed. Such accounts are addressed by the trustees of the fund to the beneficiaries and to regulators and therefore adopt a different perspective to that of the accounts of the employer which will be addressed primarily to shareholders and other investors.

Third, post-retirement benefits other than pensions will not be discussed, although they raise many of the same problems as defined contribution pension plans. An example of such benefits is a post-retirement healthcare scheme. In fact, such schemes are typically regarded by accounting standard-setters as requiring similar treatment to that prescribed for defined benefit pension schemes,[3] but they also entail specific application problems which will not be addressed here.

The subsequent discussion is arranged as follows. First, the three basic alternative models of accounting for deferred benefit pension costs are considered, 'flow through', the actuarial approach, and the balance sheet approach. The balance sheet approach, which is the newest, most controversial, and currently favoured by accounting standard-setters, is then examined in greater detail from a conceptual standpoint. The practical application of the balance sheet method in the current accounting standards of the US, UK, and international accounting standard-setters is then considered. Finally, the chapter concludes with a consideration of the aspects of these standards that will require improvement in the future.

# 2 Basic Models of Pension Cost Accounting

There are three basic models of accounting for defined benefit pension costs. These are to treat the actual contribution arising in the period as the cost of the period; to base the cost on a smoothed estimate of the future payments necessary to meet the previous obligation; and, finally, to measure the assets and liabilities currently in the scheme, reporting all of the net changes in the obligations of the scheme in the employer's performance statement, but distinguishing between different elements of such changes.

The first of these models, treating the actual contribution to the pension scheme arising in a period as the cost of the period, is the simplest and the oldest. It could be characterized as a 'flow through' model. It was common practice in the UK before SSAP 24 (ASC 1988; see Wilson et al. 2001: 515). It has the advantage of objectivity, and its impact on the accounts is very simple: a single charge to the profit and loss account and no asset or liability in the balance sheet (other than any contributions owing or pre-paid). It is an appropriate method of accounting for a defined contribution scheme, in which the contribution arising in the period is the employer's only obligation. In the case of a defined benefit scheme, it will give rise to an appropriate expense charge only if the annual contribution is an accurate reflection of the increase in the burden of the defined benefit promise during the period. An obvious example of when this does not occur is the 'pension holiday', which occurs when a pension scheme becomes overfunded, enabling the employer to make no contributions for one or more periods, despite employing people and thus increasing its pension promise during those periods. This was once regarded as a form of 'creative accounting' (Griffiths 1986) that facilitated earnings manipulation.

The second model, which smoothes the periodic charge using long-run estimates of the pension payments and the contributions necessary to fund them, can be described as an 'actuarial' model, because it relies on the funding plans drawn up by actuaries. It can be regarded as an attempt to deal with the limitations of the 'flow through' approach described above, and it was the basis of the accounting standard SSAP 24 in the UK. This approach involved estimating the funding requirements to meet the defined benefit promise and expressing them as a proportion of expected salary payments. The pension cost for the current year would then be calculated as the relevant proportion of salary payments made during the year. When the actuarial funding plan was revised to incorporate changes in circumstances and expectations the resulting change in estimated costs would typically[4] be spread over the remaining working lives of current employees, by changing the proportion of salary payments used to calculate pension costs. This approach clearly avoids the main problem arising from using actual contributions as the basis of pension costs insofar as it assesses the long-term funding requirements of the pension promise made during the period, rather than the short-term funding needs arising in a particular period, as reflected in the contributions. It is therefore a method which can accommodate an unfunded defined benefit scheme, which is quite common in some Continental European countries. For such a scheme, a contributions basis would not show a charge until the pension was paid, whereas the actuarial approach would show a charge as soon as the defined benefit obligation was incurred, which seems a more appropriate treatment within the framework of accrual (as opposed to cash flow) accounting.

However, the actuarial approach can be regarded as an incomplete method because, by spreading gains and losses forward, it does not recognize the current best estimate of the deficit or surplus on the pension fund. This problem is dealt with by the 'balance sheet' approach adopted in several recent accounting standards, notably the UK's FRS 17. This method estimates the current values of the assets and liabilities in the pension scheme reporting the net deficit (and sometimes the surplus) in the employer's balance sheet, with the components of changes in that amount being immediately reported in the profit and loss account or a statement of recognized gains and losses. Critics of the balance sheet approach argue that pension obligations are a long-term commitment and that estimates of its measurement fluctuate over time and are unreliable, so that the forward spreading of the actuarial approach gives a more stable and more reliable representation of costs. Advocates of the balance sheet approach, on the other hand, accept that it may show greater volatility but argue that this is a true representation of reality: the market price of investments and the current value of the pension promise do fluctuate as current conditions change. With regard to reliability, advocates of the balance sheet approach would argue that this is no less reliable than the actuarial approach: both methods rely heavily on estimates of future cash flows.

## 3 Reporting for Pension Costs Under the Balance Sheet Method

The balance sheet approach entails measuring the surplus or deficit in a defined benefit scheme at both the beginning and the end of a period. The gain or loss in the fund is measured as the difference between these two figures, and the total amount recognized as a cost in the performance statements (the profit and loss Account (P and L), the statement of recognized gains and losses (STRGL) or a similar statement) comprises the contributions arising in the period, plus the loss or minus the gain for the period. The balance sheet records the surplus or deficit at balance sheet date subject to possible restrictions on the employer's access to the surplus.

Thus, the balance sheet approach, as its name suggests, is firmly rooted in the concept of measuring the deficit or surplus in a pension scheme at a point of time, the balance sheet date. However, in order to do that it is necessary to measure the plan assets and the plan liabilities, to assess the surplus or deficit to be recognized in the balance sheet, and to measure the components of the change in the deficit (or surplus) for the performance statements. Each of these steps is outlined in turn.

## 3.1 Measuring the Plan Assets

The logic of the balance sheet approach, that the surplus or deficit in the pension scheme should be measured at balance sheet date, suggests that the appropriate measurement of the assets in the scheme should be current value as of balance sheet date. This should ensure both consistency and relevance in the measurement process. There are practical problems to be addressed. For example, in the case of securities listed in markets, do we adopt bid, offer, or mid-market prices, and do we make adjustments to quoted prices when large blocks of the same security are held? In the case of unlisted securities and property, it is necessary to establish the relative merits of using observed market transaction data (which may be out of date) or model-based measures (using up-to-date market measures of the determinants of market value such as discount rates). However, the central objective is clear: to obtain a measure of the current (at balance sheet date) value of the assets in the marketplace. Lest this seem to be a rather obvious objective to adopt, it should be noted that some actuarial methods of assessing fund surpluses or deficits attribute to assets an amount different from their market value (see Exley et al. 1997: 850–6).

The assets in the scheme will be those assets (typically bonds, shares, or property) specifically allocated to meet the pension obligation by means of allocation to a separate fund, so that the employer cannot use them for other purposes. Another type of asset, from the perspective of the employer, is the right to claim higher future contributions for members of the scheme in order to compensate for deficits arising for past service and the right to pay lower benefits if a deficit arises. Both of these rights are usually treated as part of the measurement of the pension liability rather than as assets of the scheme. Either classification will lead to an appropriate measurement of the net surplus or deficit in the scheme, and adjustment of the pension liability enables an appropriate comparison between unfunded schemes (which are a direct obligation of the sponsoring employer and do not have separate investment assets assigned to them) and funded schemes.

## 3.2 Measuring the Plan Liabilities

The balance sheet approach requires a current valuation of the pension fund liabilities suitable for offsetting against the current value of the assets in order to establish the net current surplus or deficit of the scheme. Ideally, there would be a ready market in which pension fund liabilities could be laid off to third parties, such as reinsurers. In this case, it would be possible to establish what accounting standard-setters often call a 'fair value': the price at which the obligation would exchange in the marketplace between a willing buyer and a willing seller. Unfortunately, such markets for pension obligations do not exist[5] and it is therefore usual to estimate a current value by estimating the expected future cash flows and discounting them at an appropriate rate. If an appropriate discount rate can be established which reflects current market conditions, it can be argued that the resulting present value is a model-based estimate of what fair value would be if there were a market. There are two obvious difficulties in this approach: first, we have to identify and measure the relevant cash flows, and second, we must define and measure the appropriate discount rate.

The cash outflows of a pension scheme are, of course, characterized by uncertainty. This will be discussed in the context of the discount rate. There are also definitional problems. The most important and controversial of these is the treatment of future salary increases in final salary schemes. The current accounting standards in the UK, FRS 17, the United States, SFAS 87 (FASB 1985), and the international standard IAS 19 (IASC 1993) all use the projected unit credit method. When the pension is based on final salary, this method bases the cash flows used in measuring the pension liability on the estimated future final salary. It therefore anticipates the effect of future salary increases to which the employer is not yet committed. However, the employer is committed to increasing pension payments if salary increases are given, so that the promise of a final salary-based pension must be worth more than one based on current salary. The alternative approach, of estimating future pension payments on the basis of current salaries, accords better with the definitions of liabilities used by accounting standard-setters. These are framed in terms of present, rather than future, commitments. A question that remains to be resolved is whether the promise of an additional pension based on final salary is a commitment that justifies recognition as a liability and, if so, how it should be measured.

Another issue in defining the cash flows that has already been referred to is the treatment of the employer's options to vary the benefits to or contributions from employees. Clearly, these will affect future cash flows, but (like the final salary promise) they contain an element of optionality which may mean that they are not appropriately measured by the traditional method of taking an expected value of the cash flows and then applying a risk-adjusted discount rate.

Apart from these particular problems arising when there is a degree of optionality in the cash flows, the definition and measurement of the discount rate present difficulties even in the more straightforward case of discounting the expected pension payments arising from present commitments.

The pure time value of money, measured by the risk-free discount rate, is easily observable from markets in which government bonds are traded. These markets now include index-linked bonds, so that the real risk-free rate (which excludes compensation for anticipated inflation) is observable in addition to that nominal rate (which includes compensation for anticipated inflation). The real rate should be chosen if the cash flows being discounted are real cash flows (expressed in terms of present price levels rather than expected future price levels) and the nominal rate should be used when the cash flows are nominal (including anticipated future inflation of price levels). The rate chosen should also be appropriate to the period elapsing before the cash flow occurs. The term structure of interest rates is rarely flat (i.e. the annual rate of interest will usually vary with length of the period) and, in the case of cash flows that occur over many periods such as pension payments, there is a danger that using a single interest rate based on average maturity will lead to material measurement errors.

The main difficulty in establishing an appropriate discount rate for pension obligations is in adjusting for risk. This poses problems of both definition and measurement. The definitional problem is to decide what risks should be reflected in the discount rate. The measurement problem is to quantify those risks and is made particularly difficult by the long-run nature of pension obligations. Before entering into a discussion of risk adjustment, it is important to emphasize that this is strictly a separate issue from that of the discount rate. In principle it is possible to adjust the expected cash flows to what economists call a certainty equivalent, that is, the certain cash flow which is of equal value to the uncertain cash flow. The certainty equivalent cash flows can then be discounted at the risk-free discount rate in order to obtain a present value, so that the need to adjust the discount rate for risk is avoided. Of course, done properly, these two procedures (discount risky cash flows by a risk-adjusted discount rate, or discount risk-adjusted cash flows by a risk-free discount rate) are equivalent.[6] Adjusting the interest rate for risk may appear to be simple and have intuitive appeal, but, because the methods are equivalent, they include the same underlying complexities.

The certainty-equivalent approach makes these complexities clearer in at least two respects. First, it shows us clearly that risk adjustment has to be applied individually to the separate cash flows of each period, so that it may not be appropriate to apply the same risk adjustment to all periods. The interest rate adjustment will achieve this properly only if a different risk adjustment is applied to the discount rate for each period: otherwise, using a common risk-adjusted discount rate will produce an exponential pattern of risk adjustment through time (as a result of the compounding effect of discounting) which is arbitrary and has no particular empirical or theoretical justification. Second, the certainty-equivalent approach suggests that, if risk aversion is present, the certainty equivalent of a risky cash inflow should be lower than the amount of the expected inflow, but the certainty equivalent of a risky cash outflow should be higher than the amount of the expected outflow, that is, a risk-averse economic agent would accept a smaller asset or a larger liability than their risky equivalents, in order to be relieved of the risk. If the risk adjustment is made to the discount rate rather than the cash flows, this means that the discount rate applied in measuring assets should have a positive sign (risk-adjusted rate greater than risk-free rate, so that risk adjustment lowers present value). The discount rate applied in measuring liabilities should, however, have a negative sign (risk-adjusted rate less than risk-free rate, so that risk adjustment raises the present value) to reflect risk aversion.

Of course, risk is not always an undesirable property of a particular asset or liability even when there is general risk aversion. In the context of a portfolio, the risks of one asset or liability can offset those of another to reduce overall risk, and the Capital Asset Pricing Model (CAPM) provides a framework within which this hedging property can be evaluated. The debate on pension fund finance and accounting has been strongly influenced by one idea which is loosely based on these concepts: the belief that equities provide a hedge on pension fund liabilities. There are quite plausible reasons to believe this: pension fund liabilities are driven, at least in part and depending on the specific terms of the scheme, by inflation and the growth of salaries (although there are other important factors such as the longevity of scheme members). Equities are believed to rise in value to match inflation (in the past, they have been referred to as a hedge against inflation) and they also respond positively to economic growth, which also drives salary increases. Thus, there is a plausible prima-facie case for believing that equity returns correlate well with pension fund liabilities. This belief was used as an argument in favour of using the rate of return on equity investment as the discount rate to be applied to pension fund liabilities: the risks of the two were similar (but in opposite directions, so that the returns offset), so the risk adjustment to the discount rate should be similar (and should have the same sign because, unusually, in the case of a defined benefit pension liability the risk is benign, making the liability more valuable because it hedges an equity investment). Unfortunately, this hypothesis is not supported by empirical evidence. Extensive investigations by actuaries and economists have failed to discover the hoped-for close positive correlation between changes in pension liabilities and the return on equity investment.[7]

In addition to the risk in the pension obligation itself, arising from variations in the benefits payable, is the credit risk of the sponsoring employer. Clearly, from the point of view of the pensioner, the risk that the employer will not make up any deficiency in the scheme reduces the value of the pension promise. From the point of view of the employer, whose accounts we are considering here, the issue is less clear cut. Some argue that accounts are statements of stewardship and should not reduce the value of liabilities to allow for the fact that it might be possible to avoid payment of those liabilities by reneging on the obligation. This might be possible if the employing entity were insolvent and therefore demonstrably unable to pay its debts, but accounts are usually prepared on a going-concern assumption, which assumes that all debts will eventually be paid. On the other hand, business entities do recognize their credit risk when they initially recognize debt instruments: the market price at which they are issued reflects the risk. Furthermore, they are subsequently able to repurchase their debt in the market at prices that reflect the market's current assessment of credit risk. These considerations have led to a tentative introduction into accounting standards of the idea of reporting liabilities at current market prices which reflect credit risk, but the matter is still controversial.[8] Moreover, pension liabilities, unlike bonds, are not traded on markets, so that the arguments for allowing for credit risk in valuing liabilities that are traded have less practical appeal when applied to pension liabilities.

In summary, the valuation of defined benefit pension obligations is a complex matter and there are many unresolved issues. Whatever decisions are made about what cash flows to include and how to incorporate risk, the practical matter of measurement will involve a significant amount of estimation and uncertainty. Hence, adopting the balance sheet approach does not provide a panacea for curing all of the uncertainties of the actuarial approach, although it should provide a better discipline and a more transparent framework.

## 3.3 Assessing the Net Surplus or Deficit

The net surplus or deficit is usually calculated by deducting the liabilities of the scheme from the investments in the scheme. However, it may be the case that a surplus that arises should not be recognized fully in the accounts of the sponsoring employer when the surplus is so large that the employer has no prospect of benefiting from it through future reduction in contributions or (where the scheme permits) refunds. In such a case, the pension fund asset appearing in the employer's accounts should be limited to the extent to which the employer can benefit: otherwise it would not meet the definition of an asset from the employer's perspective. This gives rise to what, in the current international accounting standard (IAS 19), is described as an asset ceiling.

An alternative method of assessing the net surplus or deficit in the scheme would be to measure directly the employer's interest (in a net surplus) or obligation to the scheme. This could be done only if there were a market in such interests and obligations, and this is not usually the case. Moreover, if there were such a market, participants in it would be likely to need more detailed assessments of assets and liabilities in order to inform their decisions.

At the other extreme, it is possible to argue that, under some institutional arrangements for pension funds, the assets and liabilities of the fund should not be netted off against each other but should be consolidated in the employer's financial statements on an item-by-item basis, like the assets and liabilities of subsidiary companies. At present, accounting standards typically exempt pension funds from consolidation requirements, because the fiduciary duties of pension fund trustees are presumed to require them to act independently in the interests of the pensioners and not under the control of the employing entity.

## 3.4 Recognizing Changes in Pension Obligations in the Performance Statements

The change over a period in the net pension obligation (or surplus) recorded in the balance sheet consists of four distinct elements: the cost of additional pension rights granted, the return on investments, the interest cost of the pension liability, and the actuarial gain or loss arising from changed circumstances, such as a change in the expectation of life of the pensioners.

The cost of additional pension rights granted has three components. First, there is the current service cost arising from additional pension rights granted to employees for services rendered during the period. This is a cost of employment during the period and should therefore be charged as an expense in the profit and loss account. Second, there is the cost of additional pension rights granted during the period for past service. This is clearly a consequence of a decision made in the period and can therefore be regarded as an expense of the period, although some would argue that to the extent that it benefits past employees rather than current employees, it might be regarded as an adjustment to the costs of earlier periods. Third, there is the cost, or in many cases the benefit, of settlements and curtailments: reductions in pension liabilities due to employees leaving the scheme either in exchange for benefits or because they cease to qualify (e.g. by terminating the relevant employment). These also arise from events of the period and thus qualify for immediate recognition as a component of the pension cost in the profit and loss account.

The return on the pension fund investments and the interest cost represent the income and financing costs of the pension fund and are therefore appropriately recognized in the profit and loss account of the period.

The return on investments might seem to be a straightforward matter, but there are problems of definition. The return should be the total return, including capital appreciation in addition to receipts such as dividends, interest, and rents. If capital appreciation were excluded, this would lead to serious understatement of the returns on such items as equity shares and investment property, which are often held with long-term capital appreciation as a primary objective. Under some current accounting standards, the investment return recorded in the profit and loss account is an *expected* return, reflecting long-run expectations (including capital appreciation). The difference between the expected return and the actual return in the period is then reported as part of the actuarial gain or loss, which will typically not appear in the profit and loss account. This splitting of the actuarial return into an expected return and an actuarial adjustment has dubious theoretical justification, because accounting is usually based on actual rather than hypothetical events. Moreover, it has allowed scope for abuse, particularly during the recent stock market recession, when generous positive returns on investment could appear in the profit and loss account, to be offset by an actuarial adjustment in a less prominent statement.

The interest cost is the unwinding of the discount rate used in measuring the liability. As the liability comes closer in time, the effect of discounting is reduced and the value of the liability increases. This is because the pension liability is a form of borrowing, analogous to a zero-coupon bond. The initial burden of the pension promise is lower because payment is deferred, but as the payment period expires, the value of the liability increases up to the settlement value at the date of settlement. The relevant interest rate is, of course, the discount rate used in calculating the liability. We have already seen that the measurement of this discount rate raises both theoretical and practical problems but, once it is measured, it meets the needs of both the balance sheet and the profit and loss account.

The actuarial gain or loss measures the effect of changes in the assumptions that were used in measuring the net pension obligation in the opening balance sheet. They are of two types: events that have occurred during the year that were not anticipated correctly (sometimes called experience gains and losses) such as the number of members leaving the scheme, and changes of actuarial assumptions relating to the future such as the level of the appropriate discount rate.

Actuarial gains and losses will typically arise from changes in the estimated pension liability, but they can arise from other sources. As we have already seen, if an expected, rather than an actual, return on investment is reported in the profit and loss account, the difference between the actual and the estimated return, and the effect of any change in the future estimated return, may be included in the actuarial gain or loss. When a fund is in surplus and the amount of the surplus that can be recognized in the balance sheet is affected by an asset ceiling, the changes in the recognized surplus resulting from the operation of the asset ceiling will not be included in the actuarial gain or loss, but will be reported immediately in the profit and loss account.

The presentation of the actuarial gain or loss in the financial statements is possibly the most contentious issue in accounting for pension costs. The current standards of the FASB, SFAS 87 (1985), and the IASB, IAS 19 (1993), allow entities to smooth the impact on the profit and loss account by spreading gains or losses over a number of periods. The only standard to require full immediate recognition of actuarial gains or losses in the financial statements is the UK's FRS 17, but this avoids the impact on the profit and loss account by requiring actuarial gains and losses to be reported in a supplementary statement, the Statement of Recognized Gains and Losses (STRGL). Nevertheless, FRS 17 has been very controversial, because it does expose the full impact very clearly and immediately.

# 4 Current Accounting Standards

It will be apparent from the above discussion that, although the balance sheet approach has gained credibility with accounting standard-setters in recent years, it has not yet been fully implemented in its pure form. The modifications that have been made have been designed to placate those critics who wish to smooth out the volatility in the profit and loss account that would result from the immediate reporting there of actuarial gains and losses.

In historical terms, the first accounting standard to use the balance sheet approach was the US standard SFAS 87 (FASB 1985). Not surprisingly, this standard modified the impact of the balance sheet approach by offering a number of options that smoothed out the resulting fluctuations in the reported surplus or deficit. The international standard, IAS 19 (IASC 1993), which followed, adopted a similar approach to SFAS 87, although it eliminated one of the smoothing options (that related to asset values). A similar standard was adopted subsequently in Japan. The UK's FRS 17 was issued in 2000, although full implementation in the accounts (as opposed to disclosure in notes), whilst encouraged immediately, was not required until 2005. FRS 17 is the most radical of the three balance sheet approach standards discussed here, because it does not allow smoothing of the actuarial gain or loss, although it does, as indicated earlier, require that this item be reported separately in the STRGL. It should be noted that the recent Australian standard, AASB 119 (AASB 2004), originally proposed to implement the provisions of IAS 19 without the deferral options, so that actuarial gains and losses would have been reported immediately in the profit and loss account; a more radical treatment than in FRS 17. This proposal was subsequently modified to allow the other options that are available under IAS 19. The IASB has recently completed a short-term project to revise IAS 19, resulting in an amendment which allows companies to report on a basis similar to FRS 17 if they so choose (IASB 2004). A longer-term project, which is still in the planning stage, is expected to address some of the fundamental issues discussed earlier, such as the measurement of pension liabilities. The standard that emerges from this process is likely to determine practice in the European Union (which has adopted international standards for these companies from 2005) and in the United States and Japan, both of which have programs to converge their standards with those of the IASB. The question of long-term improvements will be discussed later, after examining the main features of the three 'balance sheet approach' standards.

## 4.1 The Measurement of Plan Assets

SFAS 87, the earliest of the three standards, allows the market value of assets to be averaged over a period up to the last five years. This smooths out the fluctuations of market prices to some extent, and was an obvious concession to those who objected to the volatility introduced into accounting by using current market prices. On the other hand, current market prices can be regarded as representing the economic situation at balance sheet date more faithfully and are therefore as more consistent with the objectives of financial reporting, as stated in the conceptual frameworks of the standard-setters. For this reason, the later standards, IAS 19 and FRS 17, have not allowed the arranging of asset values over past periods and have required the use of market values as at balance sheet date.

## 4.2 The Measurement of Plan Liabilities

All of the three current standards use the projected unit credit method for projecting future cash flows. As indicated earlier, this recognizes the effects of estimated future salary increases to which the employer is not yet committed, and it is not clear that such expectations meet the definition of a liability. Thus, although the three standard-setters are currently agreed on a common solution, it may be necessary to consider whether that solution can be improved.

With regard to the choice of discount rate, all three standards again choose the same solution, that a high quality corporate bond rate is the appropriate discount rate. This rate embodies a small positive risk premium and this might be regarded as a practical compromise between the wide variety of alternatives that have been proposed, ranging from a high positive premium (as in the equity return) to a high negative one (as in the case of strong risk aversion without any hedging characteristics in the risk). However, the debate between these alternatives has not been resolved, so the discount rate may be another area in which, although the three standard-setters are currently agreed on a common solution, future changes may be expected.

## 4.3 The Measurement of the Net Surplus or Deficit

All three of the current standards, SFAS 87, IAS 19, and FRS 17, calculate the net surplus or deficit as the difference between the current value of the investments in the scheme and the liabilities. In the case of the two later standards, IAS 19 and FRS 17, the amount of the surplus is restricted by the application of an asset ceiling, based on the amount that the sponsoring company could recover from the scheme. SFAS 87 does not include such a restriction; pension scheme arrangements in the United States usually give the sponsoring company access to any surpluses, so that the asset ceiling is not relevant.

## 4.4 The Recognition of Actuarial Gains and Losses

This is an area in which there is an obvious difference of approach between the earlier standards, SFAS 87 and IAS 19, on the one hand and FRS 17 on the other. All of these standards require disclosure, by way of note, of full details of the change in actuarial gains and losses, but for the purpose of recognition in the main statements (as opposed to the notes), SFAS 87 and IAS 19 both contain two options which allow the impact of the changes to be smoothed or even ignored. FRS 17 does not allow these options.

The two options are, first, the corridor, and second, forward spreading. The corridor is an option which allows actuarial gains or losses to be ignored in the financial statements if, in the relevant period, they amount to less than 10 percent of the greater of the present value of the pension liability or the current value of the assets in the scheme. The forward-spreading option allows any actuarial gain or loss that is recognized to be spread forward over a period no longer than the service lives of current employees. These two options together mean that substantial actuarial gains or losses may never be recognized and those that are recognized may not appear in the accounts until long after they occurred.

Neither of these options conforms to the conceptual frameworks of the standard-setters, and FRS 17 poses an immediate challenge to IAS 19 because UK-listed companies are being required to change from UK standards (FRS 17) to international standards (IAS 19) in 2005. Thus, the IASB has not only introduced a short-term option to allow an FRS 17 approach within IAS 19[9] but in the longer-term project, the whole question of whether smoothing should be allowed will need to be reconsidered.

## 4.5 Recognition in the Balance Sheet

This is affected by the treatment of actuarial gains and losses. Where either or both of the two smoothing options is used, both SFAS 87 and IAS 19 will show an arbitrary amount in the balance sheet, to represent the pension fund deficit or surplus. The arbitrariness will reflect the extent to which the 10 percent corridor has been applied and the period over which forward spreading has been utilized.

SFAS 87 contains an additional element of arbitrariness, arising from the option to use average prices, rather than current prices, to value fund assets. This option can be used to average over any period up to five years.

FRS 17, on the other hand, contains no averaging, forward-spreading, or corridor options. Thus, the amount appearing in an FRS 17 balance sheet is the full current amount of the deficit or surplus in the fund, calculated in accordance with the balance sheet approach. This leads to greater comparability and relevance than the other approaches, which provides a strong argument for reconsidering the justification for preserving the deferral options in SFAS 87 and IAS 19.

## 4.6 Recognition in the Performance Statements

The deferral options in SFAS 87 and IAS 19 also create a difference between these standards and FRS 17 with respect to the performance statements. The former two standards exclude deferred actuarial gains and losses, whereas FRS 17 does not allow such deferrals. On the other hand, FRS 17 recognizes the actuarial gains and losses separately in the STRGL, whereas SFAS 87 and IAS 19 recognize them, to the extent that they are recognized at all, in the main body of the profit and loss account.

Thus, the performance reporting question in relation to pension obligations is one of presentation as well as of recognition. The objections to immediate recognition that led to the deferral options in SFAS 87 and IAS 19 were based on the long-run nature of pension obligations, the difficulties of measuring such obligations, and the short-term volatility that such measurements were likely to reflect. These properties suggest that their distinctive nature justifies the separate reporting of actuarial gains and losses, so that they are not confused, for example, with the current trading activities of the business. This presentation issue raises the whole problem of the structure of the profit and loss account; for example, whether it should be a statement of comprehensive income (i.e. incorporating items that the ASB reports in the STRGL). This is currently being addressed by the IASB (in collaboration with the ASB, the ASBJ, and the FASB) in a separate project which is proving to be as controversial as the project on accounting for pension costs.

## 5 Future Directions

Accounting for pension costs is a subject in which there are a number of important unresolved issues on the theoretical level. On the practical level, existing accounting standards have inconsistencies and deficiencies that will be addressed in the near future.

The most obvious problem of current standards is the recognition of actuarial gains and losses, which can be deferred in SFAS 87 and IAS 19. The alternative FRS 17 approach, of recognizing these items immediately, gives a more comparable and representationally faithful picture of the current financial position, but it raises the presentational issue as to how and where these gains and losses should appear in the accounts. International harmonization of standards on something resembling the FRS 17 approach seems to be a desirable direction for future improvement and is now allowed as an option in the recent amendment to IAS 19 (IASB, 2004b).

The other major area that needs to be reconsidered is the measurement of the pension liability. With regard to the cash flows, the merits of the projected unit credit method need careful scrutiny: should the full effect of possible future salary increases be recognized before there is a commitment to such increases? The effect of options to vary benefits and contributions to the scheme also needs to be considered. With regard to the discount rate, the present international consensus on using a high-quality corporate bond rate will need a clearer theoretical underpinning if it is not to be changed. Alternative compromises, such as the risk-free interest rate, may have some appeal, but what is really needed is to decide precisely what risks should be allowed for: for example, should the credit risk of the employer be included? The answers to such questions may well be informed by developments in other accounting standards, such as those on financial instruments (which determine the accounting treatment of another group of risky liabilities).

Apart from these major issues, there are many others that may be less important but still require attention. These include the precise definition of a defined benefit plan, the possible consolidation of defined benefit plans, the operation of the asset ceiling (e.g. should it allow for indirect benefits, such as the ability to pay lower future contributions?), and the return on assets (expected or actual?). It is likely that all of these issues will be addressed in the context of the balance sheet approach, which is more consistent with the objectives of financial reporting than the more traditional flow through or actuarial approaches.

The fundamental objective of these changes must be to provide as realistic a picture as possible of the current pension cost and pension obligation. The balance sheet approach has been criticized because it may report volatile results. However, volatility is a feature of markets and if this is the price of realistic reporting, it is a price worth paying. It is in the interests of pensioners as well as employers that the true current cost and surplus or deficit of the pension scheme should be reported. Otherwise, employers may be unaware of the true cost of their commitments. This may damage both their shareholders, through unexpected costs, and their pensioners, through inability to meet their full obligations.

Thus, the balance sheet approach, despite its relative novelty and the opposition that it has attracted, seems likely to be the prevalent model in the future. Standard-setters should concentrate on improving the application of this approach, particularly with respect to how its results are presented in the financial statements and how the defined benefit liability is measured.

# Notes

1. Evidence will be found in the study by Harris *et al.* (2003). They estimate that at 31 December 2002, ten of the FTSE 100 companies had pension fund deficits exceeding 40 percent of their market capitalization.
2. Guidance on this subject appears in IFRIC Interpretation D9 (IFRIC 2004).
3. In the accounting standards of all three of the standard-setters compared in this chapter (the ASB, the IASB, and FASB), other retirement benefits are treated for accounting purposes in a similar manner to defined benefit schemes.
4. Exceptions explained in paragraphs 81 to 83 of SSAP 24 were cases in which the number of employees covered by the scheme was significantly reduced, circumstances in which prudence required that the consequences of major events be recognized quickly, and situations in which a refund was tax-deductible.
5. Laying off a variable defined benefit obligation to a third party would raise a moral hazard problem where the party laying off the obligation (such as an employer) had control over variations in its amount (e.g. final salaries).
6. There is an exact analogy with inflation adjustment, where the equivalent alternatives are discounting nominal cash flows by a nominal interest rate or discounting real cash flows by a real interest rate.
7. The evidence is discussed, from an actuarial perspective, in the influential paper by Exley *et al.* (1997), particularly sect. 7.2. A financial economist's perspective is given by Bodie (1991).

8. The International Accounting Standards Board's 'fair value option' in its revised standard on financial instruments, IAS 39 (IASB 2004a) is currently the subject of fierce debate. Banking regulators, in particular, are opposed to reporting apparent gains on liabilities when an entity's credit rating declines.
9. Full immediate recognition of actuarial gains and losses is already allowed by IAS 19, but the recognition has to be in the profit and loss account. FRS 17 requires recognition separately in the STRGL, the international equivalent of which would be used in the amendment to IAS 19. The amendment to IAS 19 (IASB 2004b) allows the recognition of actuarial gains and losses in full for the period in which they occur, outside the profit and loss account, in a Statement of Reorganized Income and Expense (SORIE).

# References

AASB (2004). *AASB 119, Employee Benefits*. Melbourne: Australian Accounting Standards Board.
ASB (2000). *FRS 17, Retirement Benefits*. London: The Accounting Standards Board.
ASC (1988). *SSAP 24, Accounting for Pension Costs*. London: Accounting Standards Committee.
Bodie, Z. (1991). 'Shortfall risk and pension asset allocation'. *Financial Analysts Journal*, 47/3: 57–61.
Exley, C. J., Mehta, S. J. B., and Smith, A. D. (1997). 'The financial theory of defined benefit pension schemes'. *British Actuarial Journal*, 3(iv): 835–938.
FASB (1985). *SFAS 87, Employers' Accounting for Pensions*, Stamford, Conn.: Financial Accounting Standards Board.
Griffiths, I. (1986). *Creative Accounting, or How to Make your Profits What you Want Them to Be*. London: Sidgwick and Jackson.
Harris, T., Michaelides, L., and Weyns, G. (2003). *UK Pensions: Is it just a Storm in a Teacup?* London: Morgan Stanley.
IASB (2004a). *IAS 39, Financial Instruments: Recognition and Measurement* (rev., Mar.). London: International Accounting Standards Board.
—— (2004b). *Amendment to IAS 19, Employee Benefits—Actuarial Gains and Losses, Group Plans and Disclosures* (Dec.). London: International Accounting Standards Board.
IASC (1993). *IAS 19, Retirement Benefits*. London: International Accounting Standards Committee.
IFRIC (2004). *Interpretation D 9: Employee Benefit Plans with a Promised Return on Contributions or National Contributions*. London: International Accounting Standards Board.
Wilson, A., Davies, M., Curtis, M. and Wilkinson-Riddle, G. (2001). *UK & International GAAP*. London: Butterworth-Tolley.

# PART IV

# INDIVIDUAL AND HOUSEHOLD RETIREMENT PROVISION

# INDIVIDUAL PENSIONS, INSURANCE, AND SAVING

CHAPTER 27

# OCCUPATIONAL PENSION SCHEME DESIGN

DAVID MCCARTHY

## 1 INTRODUCTION

Occupational pension schemes are pension arrangements which form part of the employment contract between employers and employees. Traditionally, there have been two main types of these arrangements: defined benefit (DB) pensions, where the benefits are set by formula rather than by reference to the actual contributions workers and employers have made to the scheme, and defined contribution (DC) schemes, where the contributions are set by formula and the benefits depend on these contributions and the investment returns they have earned in the period before retirement. Until the mid-1980s, it was common for workers in the United States and the United Kingdom who had occupational pensions to be members of defined benefit schemes. Beginning at that time in the United States, there was a large shift from these to defined contribution-type pensions, such as 401(k) plans. Today in the United States, defined benefit pensions are still prevalent at large companies and in the public sector, but most private sector workers who have pensions have DC-type pensions. Recent figures from the US Department of Labor show that in 1996–8, 32 percent of full-time private sector workers were covered by DB plans, whereas 90 percent of full-time public sector workers were (US Department of Labor 2001). In the United Kingdom, the shift to defined contribution started later than in the United States, and has been slightly more muted. The Employer Pension Provision Survey of the Department of Work and Pensions (2003) shows that 39 percent of private-sector employees were members of open salary-related schemes in 2002, while a further 9 percent were members of closed schemes, probably mainly of the DB type. However, occupational pensions coverage has been falling in the United Kingdom since the 1970s, and occupational pensions has become an area of pressing public policy concern there.

Despite these shifts in favored pension designs, relatively little academic work has evaluated different occupational scheme designs from an economic standpoint, in marked contrast to the intense academic debate on state pension design. This omission is all the more surprising given that in the United Kingdom, but also in the United States, occupational pension scheme entitlements represent a significant fraction of the portfolios of most households, in many cases greater than the value of state benefits. For instance, in the United States, Mitchell and Moore (2000) estimate that occupational pensions make up a greater fraction of personal wealth than social security for approximately 30 percent of US retirement-age households. Although household-level wealth data is lacking in the United Kingdom, given the somewhat less generous state pension, and the prevalence of contracting out of the earnings-related Second State Pension, the relative importance of occupational pensions in the United Kingdom is likely to be higher than in the United States.

Part of the explanation for this omission lies in the fact that there was no computable theory which modeled how firms and workers actually valued their pensions: realistic pension contracts were too complex for traditional theoretical economic models. The massive reduction in the cost of computing power has changed this. It is now possible to use numerical analysis to assess different pension plan designs using a coherent economic framework which is realistic enough to assist researchers and practitioners who study and design pension plans.

This chapter summarizes current economic analyses of occupational pension scheme design. The first section discusses the case of complete markets,[1] and 'spot' labor markets, in which both employees and employers are indifferent between different occupational pension scheme designs. The implication of this result is that if any optimal scheme design exists then it must be the result of market incompleteness. The second section discusses the ways in which different types of market incompleteness faced by employees affect their relative preferences for pensions and cash wages. These include uninsurable risks, such as wage risk and annuity price risk, portfolio restrictions, and the inability to borrow significantly against future income to support current consumption. In addition, workers receive significant tax benefits in the US and the UK if they take part of their compensation in pensions. This section assumes that individuals have preferences that are well described by standard discounted utility models and is theoretical in nature. A third section discusses the empirical economic evidence about the role of pensions in labor markets that deviate from 'spot' labor markets. These include the transactions costs of high job turnover, asymmetric information in the labor market between job seekers and employers, moral hazard of employees, and some effects of internal labor markets in firms on the compensation of older employees. We then discuss how a life-cycle model of employee preferences calibrated to the United Kingdom might be used to estimate the size of pensions-related labor market effects required to make different types of pension schemes efficient ways of paying employees. Readers interested in this chapter should also consult Neumark (Chapter 36, this volume), who discusses the interplay between productivty, compensation, retirement, and pensions, and Ghilarducci (Chapter 19, this volume), who discusses the role that organized labor has played in pensions in the United States.

## 2 COMPLETE MARKETS FRAMEWORK

In a seminal paper on occupational pensions, Blinder (1983) found that with no uncertainty, no taxes, and perfect capital markets, pensions are perfect substitutes for cash wages. McCarthy (2005) generalizes this result and shows that in complete capital markets (which have uncertainty), the same result obtains.

In complete markets, workers can take their pension—regardless of what type it is—and sell it to other capital market participants in exchange for cash. They are also free to purchase more of the pension if they wish, or to sell more of the pension than they have. If we assume that employees are price-takers in markets, then, at the margin, employees value their pensions at precisely the market price, or else they would adjust the quantity they hold to ensure that this is the case. Exactly the same result applies to employers if we assume 'spot' labor markets,[2] and if we assume that employers and employees trade in the same capital markets, then they will value pensions at exactly the same price. Even if pensions cannot be traded, if employees and employers can perfectly replicate pension payments by trading in capital markets, the same result applies. This is because employees and employers can hedge themselves against any pension risk on their wealth by trading in the private portfolios, and employers can do the same.

This implies that employees and employers care only about the total market value of the compensation contract they agree on, not about its constituent pieces: employers cannot create value for employees by changing how they compensate them. Hence, pensions and cash compensation are perfect substitutes. This result applies regardless of whether the pension is funded or unfunded, or invested in bonds, equities, or cash, or linked to wages or not.

If markets are incomplete, as arguably all markets are, then this result no longer obtains. If pensions are not traded, we cannot observe their market price, and must resort to preference-based models in order to determine their value in cash terms. If employers and workers have different preferences, as is very likely, then this opens up the possibility of occupational pensions creating or destroying value for employees and employers. The next section discusses different types of market incompleteness which affect how employees value pensions, and the following section discusses the case of the employer.

# 3 Incomplete Markets: Employees

The previous section showed why, in complete markets, the pension compensation decision (how much to pay workers in pensions and how much in cash), and in what form to pay pensions (equities, bonds, defined benefit pensions), is irrelevant. However, it is well known that markets are not complete: employers and employees face different tax arrangements for cash and pension compensation, and moral hazard, asymmetric information, and transactions costs prevent some risks from being traded.

This section will examine the implications of some of these market incompleteness problems from the point of view of employees. In incomplete markets, employment contracts can no longer be perfectly replicated by holding portfolios of traded securities and hence we require models of preferences rather than merely observing market prices in order to assess how market participants might value these contracts. The section relies on standard discounted utility models of employee preferences, and so is theoretical in nature. These models only provide theoretical guidance about the direction of different effects. Empirical research would be required to assess the magnitude of these effects.

## 3.1 Taxation

The first issue is taxation. In the United States, pension payments are not taxed as income in the hands of employees, and employers and employees are not required to pay FICA taxes (taxes to pay for Social Security and Medicare, named for the Federal Insurance Contributions Act) on pension compensation. In the United Kingdom, employees do not pay income tax or National Insurance (NI) contributions on pension payments, and employers do not pay NI contributions on pension compensation. In both the United States and the UK, pensions taxes can be written off against income for the purposes of corporation tax. Employees in the United States and UK pay taxes only when the pension is actually paid out at their marginal rates at that time. In addition, if it is taxed at all, investment income earned inside pensions is taxed at a lower rate than income earned outside pension accounts.

If we assume that the presence of taxation differentials does not alter the ability of employees to hedge payoffs held inside tax-preferred accounts by trading securities held outside them, then the tax preferences given to pensions make employees prefer to be compensated inside their pension accounts than outside them. If tax privileges are not rationed, employers will find it cheaper to pay workers only in the form of pensions, and workers will borrow against these pensions to finance consumption. Workers will still be indifferent to the risk characteristics of these pensions—whether they are paid in bonds, equities, or final salary form, and whether they are default-free or not. If tax privileges are rationed, as they are in the United Kingdom, then employers will minimize their wage bill by paying the maximum compensation they can in the form of pensions, and the rest as cash or in other forms. Poterba (2004) has examined the value of assets in tax-deferred accounts in the United States.

## 3.2 Basis Risk

A second source of market incompleteness relevant to pensions is basis risk: some risks—such as wage risk—cannot be traded on financial markets. This means that if workers are exposed to this risk in their pensions, they cannot hedge themselves against it by trading securities in financial markets, and hence place a value on the pension which depends on the characteristics of the untraded risk they are exposed to in their pension.

McCarthy (2005) shows that if a risk is untraded on financial markets, then differing attitudes to risk between employers and employees might cause there to be an optimal sharing of the risk between the two parties. If employers are risk neutral and employees highly risk averse, then the optimum allocation will have the employer bearing most of the risk. In this situation, the employer effectively sells insurance to employees as part of the employment contract. The risk aversion of employees allows employers to charge a high insurance premium for this insurance, implicitly by reducing employee wages by more than the expected cost of the risk, thus reducing their wage costs. Further, McCarthy (2005) shows that the presence of an untraded risk does not affect the valuation by employees and employers of traded risks: the rest of the employment contract is still valued by employers and employees at observed market prices.

It is important to discuss why employers are the optimal provider of insurance against the risk that employees face. In the absence of asymmetric information and moral hazard, if an employer is willing to take on a risk on behalf of its employees in exchange for paying them lower wages, a third company should also be willing to take on the risk at the same price. Employees would then collect a full cash salary from their employers and pay insurance premiums to the third company. In some ways, this is a better arrangement for both parties: employees would not need to renegotiate their employment contracts every time their demand for insurance changed, and employers could focus limited management expertise on core business risks.

However, there may be some circumstances in which employers are the logical place for employees to seek insurance. For instance, if there are significant asymmetric information problems which the employer is able to mitigate because it has information about its employees that a third insurance company could not have access to, if the employer could save transactions costs by dealing with employees as a group, if the employer benefits from externalities associated with having its employees covered by insurance, or if the insurance itself may expose the third party to greater moral hazard problems than the employer, then the employer may be the optimal place for the insurance. A common example is medical insurance, which is often provided by employers, presumably because individual employees who wish to buy medical insurance must pay large premiums for moral hazard reasons. Further, many firms which are large enough to benefit from diversification choose to insure themselves against small independent risks such as theft and vehicle damage. This is to save transactions costs, cut down on moral hazard by employees, and, if the firm's existing capital is large enough to bear the risks, to prevent the firm from losing the profits that insurance companies would earn on the business.

If employees cannot buy protection against a risk in the open market because employee demand for protection is very small at the price markets would charge for bearing the risk, even taking into account any informational advantage the employer has over rivals, then it makes little sense for the employer to take on this risk. If employers have no information about employees which allows them to reduce asymmetric information problems, or do not save significant transactions costs, then it also makes little sense for employers to take on risks at prices which third-party shareholders will not accept.

## 3.3 Employer Default Risk

An important source of market incompleteness to employees is the virtual absence of long-term credit insurance to protect workers against the bankruptcy of their employers. This is important given the widespread practice in the United States and the United Kingdom of paying employees with partly unfunded pension promises. If these pensions are to be paid, they require the ongoing support of the employer, which will not be forthcoming if the employer defaults. In the United States, this risk is mitigated by the presence of the PBGC, although the PBGC does not cover 100 percent of accrued benefits and imposes a cap on the level of pension benefits it will cover. In the United Kingdom, a Pension Protection Fund has been recently created which performs the same function, with similar limitations on coverage.

Uninsurable pension default risk is very similar to other forms of basis risk: differences in risk aversion between employers and employees make it possible that an optimal division of the risk between the two parties could exist. Employees are likely to be very averse to employer credit risk—as one would expect given that losing work imposes large fixed costs on employees. Employers, on the other hand, are likely to be close to risk neutral about the extra pension payments they would make if they stay in business long enough to make them: these payments are perfectly hedged by firm income. This means that the optimal risk allocation is that the employer bears all of the default risk. The only way in which the employer can credibly do this if third-party insurance markets are not available is to fully fund their pension plans. McCarthy (2005) shows that paying employees underfunded pensions is expensive for companies because they have to pay employees extra cash wages—more than the expected cost of the default—to compensate them for the risk they are exposed to.

Our conclusion differs radically from that of Sharpe (1976), who found that employees are indifferent to the funding status of their pension plan, because unlike Sharpe, we assumed that employees are unable to insure themselves against firm default. If there is pension insurance for DB pension plans such as the PBGC, there will be no wage premium for underfunding pensions and the optimal compensation strategy depends on the size of pension insurance premia for underfunded pension schemes relative to the cost of fully funding pensions. This situation has been examined by Sharpe (1976) and others.

## 3.4 Portfolio Restrictions and Liquidity Constraints

An important source of market incompleteness in financial markets is portfolio restrictions which affect the ability of employees to trade sufficient securities to reach their optimal portfolio holdings. For example, individuals are usually unable to take large short positions in most assets (a mortgage against a house is a significant exception to this). They are also unable to sell their rights to their pensions.

Assume that markets are complete except for the fact that employees cannot sell their pensions. Assume that there are no portfolio restrictions on the assets which employees hold outside their pension plans, and that employees can borrow against their pensions to finance consumption, or that the amount saved in the pension is lower than the optimal amount of savings the employees would choose if there were no pension. Then employees will be totally indifferent to the mandatory asset mix inside their pension plans: they can trade assets outside their pensions so that, overall, their optimal asset allocation is attained. Therefore, the complete markets result derived above still applies: a pension which cannot be sold does not change the value that the employee derives from the compensation.

An application of this result might be to offer employees investment choice in their DC pension plans. This could, in some circumstances, add little value to the compensation contract, if individuals are able to alter their portfolios outside their pension plans to take into account the mandatory investment mix in their pensions.

If employees cannot reach their optimum overall asset mix by changing the asset mix of their private portfolios then the complete markets result no longer applies. This may be because their private portfolios are too small relative to their pensions, or because the asset mix in the pension is too far from their optimal overall asset mix to make adjustment possible if there are restrictions on the employee's private portfolio, or because employees cannot replicate the pension payout by trading securities outside the pension plan. In these cases, employees will no longer be indifferent between two different securities of equal market value in their pension plans. We then require a model of employee preferences for the different securities in order to determine how employees value different types of pensions and hence to determine how they should be paid.

The same is true if liquidity constraints bind: the employee will no longer be indifferent between pension compensation which cannot be sold to finance consumption, and cash compensation which can be consumed, or which can be set aside as precautionary savings. Liquidity constraints arise when employees are unable to borrow against future income or pensions in order to finance current consumption.

Blinder (1983) emphasizes that pension contracts are voluntary arrangements between employers and employees. Hence, if employees are free to choose jobs, then pensions cannot result in forced savings or undesirable asset allocations: workers will optimally choose that job which offers them the optimal cash–pension trade-off and whose asset allocation perfectly matches their desired allocation. He notes that in the presence of heterogeneity among different jobs and transactions costs of finding employment, this result no longer holds.

## 3.5 Transactions Costs

An important source of market incompleteness is transactions costs. In this model, relevant transactions costs might be the cost of determining the employment contract, the cost of choosing investment policy (in other words, collecting information about the different assets which are available, their expected returns and likely risk) and the cost of changing investment policy (in other words, the cost of buying and selling different kinds of assets).

To understand the effect of transactions costs, it is useful to add a fixed transaction cost to the complete markets case. Imagine that if employers pay employees any pension at all, then employees must incur a fixed cost of investigating their options. If employees are paid purely in cash, then assume that they do not need to incur this cost. In this case, employers can minimize their employment costs by paying no pension: the transactions costs of paying a pension have caused there to be a preference for cash compensation over pension compensation, even though markets are complete. Although it is difficult to state results more generally, it is likely that differential transactions costs of different pensions arrangements would destroy the complete markets indifference result derived earlier.

In this section we have examined how the different types of market incompleteness that employees face affect the complete markets result we presented, and induce a preference in employees for pensions or cash compensation. In the first column of Table 27.1, we summarize reasons why employees might value pensions compensation and cash compensation differently. The importance of these factors varies with scheme design, and hence these factors induce a preference among employees for some scheme designs over others. In order to quantify what this preference might be, we need to specify a model of employee preferences and the types of market incompleteness that employees are exposed to. McCarthy (2005 and 2003) examines preferences for different scheme designs assuming some of the types of market incompleteness discussed here.

# 4 Incomplete Markets: Employers

We now turn to the role that pensions play in labor markets, viewed from the point of view of employers. If there were a 'spot' labor market, there would be no long-term employment contracts and perfectly rational employees would sell their labor to firms each period on an open market. Wages would always adjust to ensure that there would be no involuntary unemployment and no internal labor markets in firms—such as regular pay scales, promotion, or retirement. If this model of the labor market were correct, firms would only offer pensions as part of employment contracts because of employees' preferences. Factors discussed in the previous section, such as taxation, which make providing for retirement cheaper inside

### Table 27.1 Factors affecting pension valuation for employers and employees

In complete markets, employers and employees are indifferent to the mix of pension compensation and cash compensation in employment contracts. In incomplete markets, the following factors change this result and cause employers and employees to have preferences for different types of pension scheme and for different mixes of cash compensation and pension compensation.

| Employee | Employer |
| --- | --- |
| *Taxation* Pensions receive favorable tax treatment: in the US and the UK, they are not taxed as income in the hands of employees until the benefit is collected—when marginal tax rates are lower. Income earned on investments in pension accounts also attracts a lower rate of tax than income outside pension accounts. | *Taxation* Employers may not have to pay some forms of taxation on their employees' pension income. Examples are FICA taxes in the US and NI contributions in the UK. |
| *Basis risk* Defined benefit pensions such as final salary pensions and career average pensions cannot be replicated by trading in markets. This is because there are no markets in which the wage link of these pensions can be hedged. | *Retention benefits* Pensions may help bond workers and firms, reducing training and recruitment costs. |
| *Annuity market access* Defined benefit and defined contribution pensions may give employees cheaper access to annuity markets when they retire. | *Sorting effects* Pensions may help firms attract workers with desirable characteristics to jobs. |
| *Liquidity constraints* There are constraints on accessing pensions compensation before retirement. Therefore pensions savings cannot be used as precautionary savings. | *Productivity effects* Pensions may align the incentives of workers and firms, resulting in higher worker productivity. |
| *Portfolio restrictions* Individuals face portfolio restrictions on private assets and on pension assets. These affect their ability to reach their optimum asset allocation (and risk allocation). | *Retirement behavior* Pensions may be used to offer workers at certain ages strong incentives to retire, possibly mitigating one disadvantage of internal labor markets in firms. |
| *Default risk* Underfunded defined benefit pension plans require the ongoing support of the company in order to meet their obligations. Workers may reduce the value they place on pensions if this support is uncertain. The presence of pension guarantee insurance reduces this effect. | |

pensions than outside them, and the different types of market incompleteness, would affect how employees value pensions relative to cash, and the cost-minimizing employer would respond to these preferences and pay employees in their preferred way. However, there are considerations other than the cost of the pension benefit which affect how employers assess the total cost of paying a pension. For instance, labor market transactions costs, skills specificity, on-the-job training, customs, indenture premia, asymmetric information in the labor market and incentives, all affect the value that employers might derive from different pensions—and hence the total cost of paying different types of pensions.

These imperfections in the labor market mean that pensions may have benefits and costs for employers in addition to the cash wages they substitute for and the cost of the pension itself. Employers may not be able to hedge these additional costs and benefits away on capital markets, even if they can hedge the cost of the pension. For instance, pensions may cause employees to remain longer at the firm than they otherwise would, saving employers the costs of finding and training new staff. They may give workers an incentive to work harder by providing larger pensions to workers who do well at the firm. Underfunded pensions may change the incentives of unions in labor negotiations. Pensions may also help employers to attract staff with desirable characteristics, by attracting staff who value pensions compensation more. Pensions may also influence employees' retirement decisions, very useful if internal labor markets in the firm pay older employees more than their marginal product of labor. More detailed treatments of the role that pensions play in labor markets can be found in Gustman et al. (1994), McCarthy and Neuberger (2003), and Neumark (Chapter 36, this volume).

## 4.1 Job Turnover

Many studies have examined the connection between pensions and job turnover. Some have investigated the relationship between pension coverage on a particular job and the length of service in that job or the probability of leaving that job. These have usually found a significant negative association between pension coverage and job turnover: workers with pensions stay longer in jobs. A detailed survey is given in Allen et al. (1993).

Much econometric work has focused on trying to identify the relationship between pensions and job mobility more precisely. Some researchers have argued that the pension capital loss (PCL) associated with receiving a deferred pension, which is based on the level of wages when the worker leaves the job, rather than a pension based on the final wages the worker receives, deters workers from leaving. For instance, Allen et al. (1993) found that the PCL explained approximately 40 percent of the lower turnover of workers in jobs with DB pensions. Other researchers contend that the lower job mobility is caused by workers self-selecting into jobs with compensation arrangements which suit their own expectations about their future. Firms are probably more concerned about the effects of pensions on job turnover than about the source of the effect, although job sorting may be a separate rationale for offering pensions. Allen *et al.* (1993) also found evidence for sorting effects in pensions.

A newer study, by Gustman and Steinmeier (1995), found evidence that it was not PCLs associated with pensions that were driving lower job turnover, but rather the higher wages of workers in jobs with pensions. Higher wages are associated with lower job turnover because the higher a worker's wages, the less likely they are to find a job which pays better. Supporting their results, Gustman and Steinmeier (1995) found that DC plans are as likely to impede worker mobility as DB plans, casting some doubt over the hypothesis that PCLs are causing the decline in mobility because DC plans typically impose no PCL on departing workers. They also estimated that the PCL was likely to be no more than a small percentage of the remaining lifetime wages of the worker who was moving, meaning that a small percentage increase in wages was more than sufficient to compensate the worker for the loss. This suggests that the PCL should not be a significant deterrent to mobility.

UK evidence on the effect of pensions on job mobility is sparse. This may be the result of compulsory preservation laws in the UK—deferred pensions must be indexed to the lower of the retail price index and 5 percent in the UK—which lowers the PCL workers who change jobs are exposed to in the UK. Mealli and Pudney (1996) test the impact of pension coverage on job tenure in the UK and find that, as in the US, DB pension-covered jobs are associated with longer job tenure. Their econometric technique allows them to conclude that this is not exclusively the result of sorting effects. Similarly, Henley *et al.* (1994) find that membership of an occupational pension scheme significantly reduces hazard rates of leaving a job, but that transferability of pensions rights increases it. However, this study ignores selection into jobs with different pension schemes. Disney *et al.* (2003) present some evidence which suggests that individuals in the UK who opt out of occupational pension schemes and purchase personal pensions may be more mobile than individuals who do not opt out of their occupational schemes.

The results of Gustman and Steinmeier (1995) are important for employers because they suggest that employers could reduce job turnover simply by paying their employees more, rather than by giving employees a pension. Further, if DB and DC pensions have equivalent effects in reducing turnover, then employers should be indifferent between the two scheme designs if lowering the costs of job turnover is their objective in providing a pension. On the other hand, if Allen *et al.* (1993) are correct, then this has important implications for scheme design for employers who wish to lower job turnover.

### 4.1.1 *Pensions and Productivity*

Another reason firms might choose to offer workers pensions is because pensions might make workers more productive at their jobs by offering them an incentive to work harder. One way to test this theory is to observe the productivity of workers with pensions, and compare this to the productivity of workers without.

Unfortunately, as a practical matter, it is very difficult to observe directly how productive a particular worker is in a particular job. Consequently, there is little econometric evidence that workers with pensions are any more productive than workers without pensions, and in fact relatively little evidence on the effect of compensation policies in general on productivity. For instance, in common with other aggregate studies, Allen and Clarke (1987) were unable to reject the hypothesis that there is no relationship between pension coverage and productivity at an aggregate industry level, and no studies have examined the incentive effects of deferred compensation policies at the individual level (Dorsey et al. 1998).

However, the problem can also be approached indirectly: if workers value their compensation contracts rationally, and workers are as productive in jobs with pensions as in jobs without, it stands to reason that there should be a pension–wage trade-off: after controlling for job type, a job which offers a pension should pay a lower cash wage than a job which does not. Most studies that have compared wages in jobs with pensions and similar jobs without pensions have, surprisingly, observed a wage premium associated with pension coverage of up to 29 percent, summarized in Dorsey et al. (1998). These findings show that workers covered by pensions earn more than workers not covered by pensions, after controlling for other factors. This may imply that workers who have pensions are more productive than workers who do not.

Evidence in favor of this hypothesis is provided by Dorsey et al. (1998), who find a strong relationship between pension status and receiving on-the-job training. They also compare the productivity of labor in manufacturing firms which offer DB pensions to that of manufacturing firms who offer DC pensions or no pensions using Compustat and PBGC data. They find that while there was a significant productivity differential in 1981 (around 15 percent), by 1992 this differential had fallen to zero. However, their analysis is unable to reject the hypothesis that this differential is the result of a package of human-resource policies that are signaled by the presence of a DB pension, or that the differential is the result of efficient job matches caused by sorting effects, or the result of lower job turnover.

## 4.2 Underfunded Pensions

Several studies have examined the effect of underfunded pensions on employee–employer relationships. Underfunded pensions make employees unsecured bondholders in the firm, because any pension underfunding is effectively a loan from employees to the employer. If the employer declares bankruptcy, employees lose the loan. This may create an incentive for employees to work harder than they otherwise would to prevent bankruptcy. However, most voluntary incentive schemes tend to make employees equity holders in the firm, rather than debt holders, because the value of equity is more sensitive to the value of the firm than the value of debt unless the firm is in severe trouble. Further, pension wind-up rules, which determine the allocation of pension assets between different classes of workers if the firm winds up the pension plan, would tend to reduce any incentive effect faced by workers. This is because workers would not know in advance which class they will fall into if the firm defaults, and hence the correlation of the pension payout and firm success is lower than other possible forms of incentive compensation, probably lowering its effectiveness.

Another explanation of underfunded pension plans uses the underfunded pension plan as a technique by management to align the incentives of unionized employees and the firm. By underfunding pension plans, employers may prevent unions from holding up profitable projects and extracting rents from owners, or discourage unionization (see White 1993). Ippolito (1985) reports that union plans were more likely to be DB plans than non-union plans in the United States, and that these plans were much more likely to be underfunded than non-union plans. Bodie (1987) finds that flat-rate plans (which are commonly associated with unions in the United States) were much more likely to be underfunded than other types of plans at that time in the United States. There does not appear to be much evidence for this in the United Kingdom.

## 4.3 Pensions and Sorting

As discussed in the section on job mobility, pensions may also be used by employers as a tool to select desirable workers from the pool of job applicants. Pensions may be useful because they provide a mechanism by which employers can make a given compensation package more attractive to workers who have characteristics that the employer finds desirable. Workers who value pensions compensation will be more likely to accept a job that offers a pension than other types of workers. If workers who value pensions are also likely to have other desirable characteristics from the point of view of the firm, then offering a pension may cause these workers to self-select into jobs with pensions. For instance, DB pensions may make a job more attractive to individuals who believe that they are likely to stay at a given job for a long time than to individuals who are intending to move jobs quickly. Ippolito (1997) has expanded this theory to DC plan design, too. He divides workers into 'low' and 'high' discounters. 'High' discounters place low weight on the future, and, according to the theory, make worse employees than 'low' discounters because of the lower value they place on deferred gratification. He shows that workers who earn more are likely to take less sick leave, less likely to smoke at age 50, and are more likely to have a longer planning horizon than other workers. He finds that these same characteristics seem to be associated with higher pensions savings, even after controlling for wage differences. He supposes that the matching contribution in many US DC pension plans serves to make the employment contract more attractive to workers who save more, and hence selects 'low' discounters from the pool of available workers. If firms use pensions to attract better workers, then they will be more productive than other firms, and hence will be able to pay their workers more.

## 4.4 Pensions and Retirement

There is a substantial literature on the incentive effects of DB plans on retirement and individual responses to them. This literature is summarized in Kotlikoff and Wise (1987), Gustman and Steinmeier (1995), Quinn et al. (1990), and in Ippolito (1997). Work has examined the incentive effects provided by both the US Social Security System and those given by occupational DB plans in the United States. The almost universal conclusion of these studies is that individuals tend to respond to these incentives in planning their retirements. The evidence tends to be US-based, although there is some evidence that workers in the United Kingdom respond strongly to the retirement incentives provided by their pension plans, as presented in Blundell and Johnson (1997). Ippolito (1997) concludes his discussion of DB pension plans and retirement by saying:

Workers covered by defined benefit plans face nearly universal penalties for leaving the firm too early or too late... Firms act as though particular tenure and age distributions are important to firm productivity and they seemingly use the flexibility inherent in defined benefit pension plans to help them attain some of their desired labour force characteristics.

One reason for this may be the presence of internal labor markets in firms. Bewley (1999) presents convincing evidence that firms operate internal labor markets—pay scales, seniority pay, and lay-offs rather than pay reductions—as a response to employee concerns about fairness and to align the incentives of workers with those of their employer. However, one possibly undesirable result of internal labor markets is that workers who are near retirement or very senior may not wish to retire because they earn more than their marginal product. Therefore, firms may actually save money by offering workers strong incentives to retire at certain ages. Pensions, and DB pensions in particular, are one way of doing this. Along with preferential taxation of pensions, Blinder (1983) presents this as one of the primary motivations for occupational pensions in general.

The second column of Table 27.1 summarizes the factors which may cause employers to value pensions compensation at more or less than the cost of providing it. As discussed in the text, the importance of these factors varies from scheme design to scheme design. This may cause employers to have a preference for one scheme design over another.

## 5 Conclusion

The first section of this chapter presented a result which showed that in complete markets, the pension compensation decision is irrelevant. One section examined different types of capital market incompleteness which might affect how employees value pensions compensation relative to cash compensation, and a third section examined how different features of real-world labor markets such as asymmetric information, transactions costs, and internal labor markets might cause employers to derive value from paying pensions rather than cash to their employees.

The fact that these deviations from the perfect markets case exist creates opportunities for firms to create value by paying employees pensions rather than cash. Since different pension scheme designs impose different costs and benefits on employers, and are valued differently by employees, this implies that there may be an optimal efficient pension scheme design. This design may be different for employees and employers with different characteristics. For instance, by specifying models of employee preferences, McCarthy (2005)[3] uses the above framework to estimate how large the benefits of paying pensions rather than cash need to be in order to mitigate some of the undesirable aspects of pensions from the point of view of employees, such as illiquidity, mandatory asset mixes, and exposure to undiversifiable wage risks. He finds that for older workers and workers with less variable wage income, the labor market benefits of DB plans need to be smaller than for younger workers or workers with highly variable wage income. He also finds that career average defined benefit plans seem to require lower labor market benefits than final salary DB plans for most types of workers, and that cash balance plans and defined contribution plans require yet lower labor market effects.

It would be fair to say that the existing work on occupational pension scheme design has just scratched the surface. Arguably, until we clearly understand the rationales for providing occupational pensions in the first place—work that needs to go beyond tax considerations and embrace both the theory and empirical aspects of imperfect capital and labor markets—it will be impossible for us to understand the determinants of occupational pension scheme designs. In order to do this, we need a better understanding of employee savings behavior and employee behavior in other areas. The role of labor markets is important too: the dynamics of internal labor markets inside firms, and the implications these have for the labor market as a whole, are crucial in assessing the need for employers to provide pensions. Finally, transactions costs and asymmetric information affect how capital markets and insurance markets function. This is important because these affect whether employees can participate in these markets more efficiently through their employers or on their own. Those who study occupational pension scheme design will be able to utilize the work of the large and ongoing research programs in each of these areas. Furthermore, new techniques in the theory of financial markets, and the highly promising field of behavioral economics, may result in new and unexpected insights in the field of occupational pension scheme design.

# Notes

This chapter relies on theoretical results and numerical models originally developed as part of a research project for the Department for Work and Pensions, published in McCarthy (2005).

1. Complete markets are markets in which participants can hedge themselves against every possible event occurring by costlessly buying and selling traded securities. See, for example, Černy (2003) for details.
2. 'Spot' labor markets are labor markets which clear every period. Wages in these markets adjust each period to ensure that there is no involuntary unemployment. Hence, there can be no internal labor markets in firms—in other words, no regular pay scales, promotion, or mandatory retirement.
3. That work assumes that employees are rational, with time-separable, constant relative risk-aversion preferences, and estimates the consequences of different pensions arrangements for employee lifetime utility in the context of various forms of incomplete markets and taxation.

# References

Allen, Steven G., and Clark, Robert L. (1987). 'Pensions and firm performance', in Morris M. Kleiner (ed.), *Human Resources and the Performance of the Firm*. Industrial Relations Research Association series. Madison: Industrial Relations Research Association.
—— —— and McDermed, Ann A. (1993). 'Pensions, bonding, and lifetime jobs'. *Journal of Human Resources*, 28: 463–81.
Bewley, Truman F. (1999). *Why Wages Don't Fall During a Recession*. Cambridge, Mass.: Harvard University Press.
Blinder, Alan S. (1983). *Private Pensions and Public Pensions: Theory and Fact*. Ann Arbor: University of Michigan Press.

BLUNDELL, RICHARD, and JOHNSON, PAUL (1997). 'Pension and retirement in the UK'. *National Bureau of Economic Research Working Paper* 6154 (Septr.). http://www.nber.org/papers/w6154

BODIE, ZVI (1987). 'Funding and asset allocation in corporate pension plans: an empirical investigation', in *Issues in Pension Economics*. Zvi Bodie, John B., Shoven, and David A., Wise (eds.), National Bureau of Economic Research Project Report series. Chicago and London: University of Chicago Press.

CERNY, ALEŠ (2003). *Mathematical Techniques in Finance: Tools for Incomplete Markets*. Princeton: Princeton University Press.

DEPARTMENT FOR WORK AND PENSIONS (2003). *Employer Pension Provision Survey 2003*. Research Report 207 (Mar.). London: Department for Work and Pensions.

DISNEY, RICHARD, EMMERSON, CARL, and SMITH, SARAH (2003). 'Pension reform and economic performance in Britain in the 1980s and 1990s'. National Bureau of Economic Research Working Paper 9556 (Mar.). http://www.nber.org/papers/w9556

DORSEY, STUART, CORNWELL, CHRISTOPHER, and MACPHERSON, DAVID, (1998). *Pensions and Productivity*. Kalamazoo, Mich.: W. E. Upjohn Institute for Employment Research.

GUSTMAN, ALAN L., MITCHELL, OLIVIA S., and STEINMEIER, THOMAS L. (1994). 'The role of pensions in the labor market: a survey of the literature'. *Industrial & Labor Relations Review*, 47: 417–38.

—— and STEINMEIER, THOMAS L. (1995). *Pension Incentives and Job Mobility*. Kalamazoo, Mich.: W. E. Upjohn Institute for Employment Research.

HENLEY, A., DISNEY, R., and CARRUTH, A. (1994). 'Job tenure and asset holdings'. *Economic Journal*, 104 (Mar.): 338–349.

IPPOLITO, RICHARD A. (1985). 'The economic function of underfunded pension plans'. *Journal of Law & Economics*, 28: 611–51.

—— (1997). *Pension Plans and Employee Performance: Evidence, Analysis, and Policy*. Chicago and London: University of Chicago Press.

KOTLIKOFF, LAURENCE J., and WISE, DAVID A. (1987). 'The incentive effects of private pension plans', in Zvi Bodie, John B., Shoven, and David A. Wise (eds.), *Issues in Pension Economics*. National Bureau of Economic Research Project Report series. Chicago and London: University of Chicago Press.

MCCARTHY, DAVID G. (2003). 'A life-cycle analysis of defined benefit pension plans'. *Journal of Pension Economics and Finance*, 2/2: (July) 99–126.

—— (2005). *The Optimal Allocation of Pension Risks in Employment Contracts*, Department for Work and Pensions, *forthcoming*.

—— and NEUBERGER, ANTHONY (2003). *Pensions Policy: Evidence on Aspects of Savings Behaviour and Capital Markets*. London: Centre for Economic Policy Research.

MEALLI, F., and PUDNEY, S. (1996). 'Occupational pensions and job mobility in Britain: estimation of a random-effects competing risks model'. *Journal of Applied Econometrics*, 11: 293–320.

MITCHELL, OLIVIA S., and MOORE, JAMES F. (2000). 'Projected retirement wealth and savings adequacy in the health and retirement study', in O. S. Mitchell, B. Hammond, and A. Rappaport (eds.), *Forecasting Retirement Needs and Retirement Wealth*. Pension Research Council. Philadelphia: University of Pennsylvania Press, 68–94.

POTERBA, JAMES M. (2004). 'Valuing assets in retirement savings accounts', Boston College Working Paper 2004-11, www.bc.edu/centers/crr/wp_2004-11.shtml

QUINN, JOSEPH F., BURKHAUSER, RICHARD V., and MYERS, DANIEL A. (1990). *Passing the Torch: The Influence of Economic Incentives on Work and Retirement.* Kalamazoo, Mich.: W. E. Upjohn Institute.

SHARPE, W. F. (1976). 'Corporate pension funding policy'. *Journal of Financial Economics* (June): 183–93.

WHITE, MICHAEL D. (1993). 'Delayed payment contracts as a means of discouraging unionisation'. *Journal of Labor Research*, 14/4 (Fall): 423–38.

US DEPARTMENT OF LABOR (2001). *Report on the American Workforce, 2001*, Washington, D.C.: Department of Labor.

# CHAPTER 28

# ANNUITY MARKETS

## JAMES M. POTERBA

The prospect of reaching extreme old age with very limited resources is one of the most important risks facing the elderly, particularly those without substantial income from social security or a defined benefit pension. Annuities, which are sometimes labeled 'reverse life insurance', offer individuals insurance against the risk of outliving their resources. Annuity buyers make a large initial payment to an insurance company, and in return they receive a stream of smaller payouts for as long as they live. This chapter summarizes the current operation of annuity markets and the potential role of these markets in providing retirement security. It is divided into six sections. The first describes the basic structure of annuity products, with particular reference to those that are currently available in the United States and the United Kingdom. The second section explains the standard analysis of why annuities are attractive to individuals who face uncertainty about length of life, and describes several hypotheses that have been advanced to explain the limited size of private annuity markets. Section 3 describes the standard methodology for comparing the expected present value of annuity payouts with their cost. Section 4 examines several aspects of individual demand for annuity products. The fifth section briefly discusses the role of regulation in annuity markets. Finally, the brief conclusion considers a number of emerging issues that bear on the role of private annuity markets in providing retirement income security.

# 1 Categorization of Annuity Products

The simplest annuity is a contract under which an annuitant makes a single initial payment to an insurance company, in return for which the company promises a stream of payouts that are contingent upon the beneficiary's survival. When the payouts are fixed in nominal terms for as long as the buyer remains alive, the product is labeled a *single premium immediate life annuity*. Insurance companies sell a wide range of annuity products, with many different options for paying premiums and for receiving payouts. Annuities can vary with respect to the number and timing of premiums, the number of covered lives, the nature of the payouts, and the date at which benefits begin. The initial premium can be paid in a single lump sum, as a fixed annual premium for several years, or as a flexible payment that varies from one year to the next. The payouts can be fixed in nominal terms for the duration of the annuity, or they may increase over time according to a pre-specified schedule or to preserve the real purchasing power of the annuity payouts. Payouts can also be conditional on the survival of a single individual, or on either of two individuals, as in a joint life annuity purchased by a married couple. Brown *et al.* (2001) and Poterba (2005) explain that, historically, it was also possible to purchase annuities on the life of a nominee, an individual who was not the beneficiary of the payout stream.

Payouts from an annuity can begin immediately after the premium is paid, or with a *deferred annuity*, they can begin after some waiting period. When the premium payment occurs before payouts begin, there is an *accumulation phase* during which the value of assets held in the annuity increases. In most countries, the investment return during the accumulation phase is not taxed until the annuity enters the payout phase. The opportunity for tax-free accumulation in annuity products has stimulated the development of many annuity products that are designed at least in part to reduce the tax liability of their buyers, while also potentially providing some longevity insurance. Some annuities provide for a guaranteed payout period, usually five or ten years, so that even if the annuitant dies, his or her estate will continue to receive payments for a minimum specified period.

Immediate annuities are the annuity products that bear most directly on issues of retirement income security. Deferred annuities, which are often labeled *variable annuities* in the United States, are, in contrast, wealth accumulation vehicles that also offer some promise for providing income in old age. A range of accumulation products provides annuity buyers with many different investment options during the accumulation phase. In many cases there is no requirement that payouts from these products take the form of life-contingent annuity payouts.

The range of annuities in the marketplace enables individuals to select products that are particularly well suited to their insurance needs. For example, the choice between a single life annuity and a joint life product may depend on the other sources of retirement income support available to an individual and his spouse. The variation in annuity products also permits individuals to exploit information they have about their mortality prospects to select products that will be particularly valuable to them. An individual who is in poor health would be unlikely to purchase an annuity unless required to do so. If she was required to purchase an annuity, she might try to find a product that provided a long span of guaranteed payouts. A healthy individual, by comparison, might be willing to forego the guarantee period in return for somewhat higher annual payouts.

# 2 Annuities and Life-Cycle Consumption Planning

## 2.1 Demand for Annuities

Yaari (1965) demonstrated the value of annuities in life-cycle consumption planning. In an economy populated by single-person households with no publicly provided social security but with actuarially fair annuity markets, where individuals have no bequest motives and do not face any random shocks to their late-life consumption needs, annuitization dominates other strategies for drawing down wealth. If individuals know their date of retirement and know that they will not die until they are retired, and if they face uncertain mortality prospects beginning when they retire, then they should use their saving at each age to purchase a deferred annuity that will begin paying benefits when they reach retirement.

Each individual gains in an actuarially fair annuity market by pooling mortality risk with other individuals. Purchasing annuities offers a higher rate of return than holding bonds or other financial assets, because the insurance company selling annuities can pay a mortality premium to annuitants. A simple illustration explains this central point. If the annual rate of return on bonds is $i$, and if all individuals face the same, age-invariant, annual probability $p$ of death, then the actuarially fair annual payout on an annuity is $(i + p)$ times the annuity premium. This payout exceeds the interest payments that the annuitant could earn by holding a bond, which would be $i$ times the value of the bond principal. Because the insurance company selling annuities retains the principal of the annuitants who die within the year, it can afford to offer payouts higher than those that a stand-alone investor could earn on a bond.

For individuals like those modeled by Yaari (1965), planning a lifetime consumption trajectory *without* access to an annuity market is difficult. A full solution requires solving a stochastic dynamic programming problem. Simple heuristic rules for planning consumption can be designed in such a setting, but they all entail a trade-off between the risk of reaching extreme old age with very limited resources, and the risk of leaving a large bequest which, absent bequest motives, indicates the failure to use resources that could have been used to support lifetime consumption. If the individual consumes only interest income generated by her portfolio each year, then she preserves her principal and can consume the same amount each year regardless of how long she lives. She will never exhaust her resources but she will also leave all her principal behind when she dies; this is inefficient *ex post*. Alternative consumption profiles that involve greater consumption in the early years of retirement, along with declining principal and some risk of low consumption at extreme old age, may offer higher expected lifetime utility than the strategy of never consuming principal. The solution to the optimal consumption problem will generally involve a consumption stream that varies over time, with the specific time profile dependent on the individual's discount rate, the rate of return available in financial markets, and the age-specific pattern of mortality risk.

Yaari (1965) examined the demand for annuities in a setting with *ex ante* identical individuals and perfect markets, which rules out the potential for adverse selection in the annuity market. In the presence of individual heterogeneity and asymmetric information between annuitants and insurance companies, however, the annuity market may no longer provide actuarially fair annuities to all individuals. Imperfect competition between insurers could lead to the same outcome. Some prospective annuitants may choose not to purchase an annuity because the effective price is too high. Davidoff *et al.* (2005) analyze the demand for annuities when annuity markets are imperfect, and show that under much weaker conditions than those considered by Yaari (1965), there is still a positive demand for annuitization.

When annuity markets are imperfect, government intervention may be able to improve welfare by regulating insurance companies or by providing annuities that are actuarially fair given the population mortality rates. Diamond (1977) argues that the limited private market for inflation-indexed annuities is an important justification for the public provision of annuities in the form of social security. A number of other studies, including Abel (1986), Eckstein *et al.* (1985), Townley and Broadway (1988), and Townley (1990), also consider the potential welfare effects of government intervention in the annuity market, or the impact of government social security programs on the operation of the private annuity market. While inflation-indexed annuities are now available in some nations, in most cases, as Brown *et al.* (2002) report, the markets for these annuities are small.

## 2.2 Why Are Voluntary Annuity Markets Small?

Theoretical research suggests that annuities should feature prominently in the portfolios of retired households, yet relatively few households in the United States and most other developed nations purchase annuity contracts except when they are legally required to do so. Many research studies have tried to reconcile the limited size of the voluntary annuity market with the theoretical prediction that annuities should represent an important component of retirees' portfolios. While there is no single explanation for the limited size of annuity markets that commands universal acclaim, several potential explanations have been offered.

First, some suggest that annuities are expensive from the standpoint of most buyers, either because of profit margins in the insurance industry or because of adverse selection. If the mortality rates for annuity buyers are substantially lower than those for the rest of the population, then annuities would be unattractive to randomly chosen individuals who expect to face the population mortality curve. If individuals act on the basis of private information about their mortality prospects in deciding whether or not to purchase annuities, the pool of annuitants could face lower mortality risk than the population. The same empirical pattern could emerge if the likelihood of purchasing an annuity is positively correlated with socio-economic status, which in turn is negatively correlated with mortality risk.

A second explanation for the limited size of annuity markets is that many households already have a substantial stream of annuitized income, which limits their demand for incremental annuitization. This argument is developed by Auerbach *et al.* (2001), who point out that because Medicare is an annuitized benefit stream, promising a stream of real medical insurance for life, and because social security is an annuitized income flow, annuities already represent a substantial share of wealth for many low- and modest-income households in the United States. Bernheim (1991) presents empirical evidence suggesting that households with a higher fraction of pre-existing annuitized wealth are less likely to purchase additional annuities, and more likely to purchase life insurance. Mitchell *et al.* (1999) show that the expected utility gain from using non-annuitized wealth to purchase an actuarially fair annuity is a declining function of an individual's level of annuity income. Thus the presence of substantial public annuities may explain the limited demand for private annuities.

A related argument for limited annuity demand emphasizes the availability of non-market sources of annuity-like retirement income protection. Kotlikoff and Spivak (1981) and Brown and Poterba (2001) show that the value of an annuity to a single individual is substantially greater than the corresponding value to a married individual, under the assumption that the members of the couple face identical mortality prospects and that the second-to-die inherits the financial assets accumulated by the couple. Family ties, along with government programs, may provide many of the benefits that might be available from the insurance market.

A third explanation for small annuity markets is that households have bequest motives that make them reluctant to annuitize their wealth. A voluminous literature has developed empirical tests of competing models of bequest behavior, but there is still no research consensus on the relative importance of altruistic intergenerational linkages and other factors. The presence of bequests does not indicate that households are altruistically linked to their heirs, or that such links are the reason for limited annuitization. In the absence of annuity markets, individuals who do not know their length of life and are risk averse will never allow their stock of wealth to reach zero, so they will leave bequests even if they have no altruistic intentions.

A fourth factor that may contribute to limited annuitization is the risk of substantial medical or other late-life outlays that can only be met if the household has a substantial holding of non-annuitized wealth. In the United States, Medicare, the publicly provided retiree health insurance program, covers hospitalization and doctor visits, but it does not insure the cost of long-term stays in nursing homes. Such stays are particularly likely to develop in connection with long-term mental degeneration such as that associated with Alzheimer's disease. Purchasing an annuity may deprive the buyer of the flexibility in the timing of asset decumulation that may be needed to pay for a short stay in a high-cost medical facility.

It is difficult to judge the importance of the four alternative explanations for a limited annuity market. They are not mutually exclusive, and each may contribute to some extent. The explanation that has received the most empirical attention, particularly in recent years, is the presence of adverse selection. The next section explains the computation of the expected present value of annuity payouts, and the use of this summary statistic to evaluate the role of adverse selection.

## 3 Analyzing Annuity Prices

The pricing of annuity contracts is of substantial interest for at least two reasons. First, the price when viewed from the perspective of a random person in the population may be an important determinant of the number of annuity buyers. Pricing may therefore offer a partial explanation for the size of the annuity market. Second, when annuity markets are considered in connection with the expansion of public and private defined contribution pension programs, a key question is how close these markets come to delivering actuarially fair annuity products. Government social security programs offer annuities to the general public at close to actuarially fair rates, so this is a natural benchmark against which to compare the private market. This section describes two approaches to computing the effective price of annuities, along with empirical evidence on annuity prices.

## 3.1 The 'Money's Worth' Calculation

The economically relevant price of transforming a current stock of wealth into a future stream of annuity payments is not the premium for the annuity product, but rather the fraction of the initial wealth that must be foregone, in expected present value terms, to obtain the annuitized stream. Computing this price requires calculating the expected present discounted value (EPDV) of the annuity's payouts, and comparing this magnitude with the annuity's premium. The ratio of these two quantities is often labeled the 'money's worth' of the annuity.

The EPDV is a function of the *amount* of the annuity payout, the *discount rate* that is used to discount future payouts, and the *mortality rates* and corresponding survival probabilities facing the annuity purchaser. To formalize the calculation, let $P_{j,\alpha}$ denote the probability that someone who is $\alpha$ years old at the time when he purchases an annuity survives for at least $j$ years. The amount of the nominal annual annuity payout is $A$, and the nominal one-period discount rate that applies $k$ years into the future is $i_k$. The EPDV for an individual of age $\alpha$, purchasing an annuity that promises a nominal payout stream $A$, is then

$$EPDV_\alpha(A) = \sum_{j=1,\ T} \{A^* P_{j,\alpha} / \prod_{k=1, j-1} (1 + i_k)\}. \tag{1}$$

This calculation imposes an arbitrary upper age limit, $T$, on the horizon over which annuity payments can be received. In practice, EPDV calculations are relatively insensitive to assumptions about this upper age, which can be set at 110 or higher. While the formula in (1) applies to an annuity with a nominal payout stream, similar expressions can be used to value annuities with rising nominal payouts or with inflation-indexed payouts.

The *discount rate* that applies to future cash flows is subject to some debate. The operative choice is between riskless discount rates, typically drawn from the market for long-term government bonds, and discount rates that are derived from the prices of long-term bonds issued by corporations or other riskier borrowers. If annuities are effectively riskless from the standpoint of a buyer, either because the insurance companies selling these products are financially strong or because government regulation and risk pools provide an effective guarantee of payout, then the riskless discount rate should be used to compute the EPDV. If, however, the future payout stream is risky, it may be appropriate to choose a higher discount rate corresponding for example to the yield on corporate bonds. Many studies of annuity prices have reported EPDV calculations using both risky and riskless discount rates.

Actuarial projections of the *mortality rates* for current cohorts are used to forecast the survival probabilities for current annuity buyers. Such projections require an assumption about the rate at which age-specific mortality rates will decline in the future. In most cases these projections simply extrapolate past experience through the next few decades. Actuaries and demographers report four different types of mortality tables. Mortality tables can describe the experience of the *population* at a given point in time, or they can describe the experience of a *cohort* with a given birth date. They can also correspond to the mortality experience of the *general population*, or to the experience of a subset of the population, such as *annuitants*. Cohort and population mortality tables differ because of mortality improvement over time. They only coincide for a single mortality rate, that corresponding to the population table entry for the current age of the cohort group. For the cohort aged 65 in 2005, for example, the mortality rates in the cohort table for ages above 65 will be lower than the mortality rates in a 2005 population mortality table. Cohort mortality tables are appropriate for analyzing annuity payouts since they provide mortality rates at future ages for current annuity buyers.

The difference between the mortality rates for the general population and for the annuitant population affects annuity valuation. Both the general population and the annuitant mortality tables can lead to interesting EPDV calculations. The calculation using the general population survival rates provides insight into the price of an annuity for a randomly chosen individual in the population. The calculation using the annuitant mortality table describes the price for a typical annuitant, and it also provides evidence on the potential profit margin for insurers who sell annuities. Because the survival rates for annuitants tend to be higher than those for the general population, it is possible for existing annuity products to be actuarially fair for the individuals who purchase them, and for insurers to earn a profit on these contracts, even though a randomly chosen individual in the population would conclude that the EPDV was below the annuity premium.

The mortality probabilities for both men and women in the general population at every age are higher than the mortality probabilities for annuity purchasers. For men at age 65 in 2005 in the United States, for example, the mortality rate in the general population is slightly less than 2 percent (196 out of 10,000), while that for annuitants is just over 1 percent (105 in 10,000). For women, the proportional differences in the relative mortality rates are comparable, 0.0128 for the general population and 0.0068 for the annuitant population. The proportional differences are even larger in the data from the United Kingdom, where the annuitant mortality rates are less than half, and for women close to one-third, of the mortality rates for the general population.

Regardless of whether the difference between the mortality rates for annuitants and for the general population is the result of *active selection*, rational purchase decisions based on private information, or whether it is the result of *passive selection,* a correlation between attributes of annuity buyers and the determinants of mortality that is not mediated through selective purchasing, the differential is important for computing annuity EPDVs. Since survival rates are higher for annuitants, the EPDV is higher when it is computed using annuitant mortality rates than when it is computed using general population mortality rates.

The calculation described in equation (1) does not consider the tax burden on annuity payouts, even though many nations tax at least part of this payout. The pre-tax calculation, which is used in virtually all empirical studies of annuity valuation, is appropriate when annuitants are purchasing annuities in tax-deferred accounts. All payouts from such accounts are fully taxed, and they would be regardless of whether the account balance was used to purchase an annuity or to make periodic lump-sum distributions. For individuals considering the purchase of annuities in taxable environments, the relative tax treatment of annuities and other financial products can be a critical determinant of optimal portfolio allocation.

## 3.2 The Internal Rate of Return

Computing the EPDV of annuity payouts is the most common approach to analyzing annuities; it is not the only approach. The leading alternative is the computation of the internal rate of return (IRR) on the annuity contract. This approach is discussed in Broverman (1986) and it is used by Murthi *et al.* (2000) in their analysis of the annuity market in the United Kingdom. Computing the IRR involves solving the following equation for $\rho$:

$$\text{Premium}_\alpha(A) = \sum_{j=1,\ T} A^* P^*_{j,\alpha} (1+\rho)^{-(j-1)}. \tag{2}$$

This expression uses a single discount rate, $\rho$, to discount all future payouts from the annuity. It finds the value of this discount rate that will equate the EPDV of future payouts to the current premium cost of the policy. This rate of return can then be compared with the return on other investments to evaluate the attractiveness of the annuity. The IRR algorithm is straightforward to apply to immediate annuities that require one payment and that deliver a stream of benefits in all future years, but it may break down when applied to more complicated deferred annuity products that involve future premiums as well as payouts.

Milevsky (2005) describes a summary statistic related to the IRR, the *implied longevity yield.* This yield is defined as the internal rate of return that an annuity buyer would have to earn, over a pre-specified period, to self-annuitize using the principal that could otherwise be used to purchase an annuity. For large values of $T$ in equation (2), this approach combines a small risk of outliving one's resources with an easy-to-interpret measure of annuity returns.

One attraction of the IRR approach is that consumers are accustomed to evaluating financial products by considering rates of return. It could therefore provide a basis for making publicly useful comparisons of different annuity products. One disadvantage is that it does not provide a direct measure of the share of the annuity premium that the buyer gives up at the time of purchase. Small differences in rates of return between different products can translate into substantial differences between the EPDV of the corresponding annuity streams.

## 3.3 Empirical Evidence on Annuity Pricing: The United States

Friedman and Warshawsky (1988, 1990) were among the first to present EPDV calculations that were based on equation (1). Since their analysis, this approach has been used to compute the money's worth of annuities in a number of different countries. Table 28.1 illustrates the money's worth approach. It reports an updated version of the calculations in Mitchell *et al.* (1999). The table evaluates individual annuity products that were available in the voluntary, taxable, US annuity market in early 2005. Annuity prices and payouts are computed as the average for 14 firms reporting data on the *Annuity Shopper* database for January 2005. General population mortality rates for annuity buyers at age 55, 65, and 75 are drawn from the US Social Security Administration cohort mortality tables for the 1950, 1940, and 1930 birth cohorts, respectively. The annuitant mortality rates that are used to generate the survival probabilities for annuitants are estimated by updating the Annuity 2000 mortality table that underlies calculations in Mitchell *et al.* (1999). The discount rates for the calculation are drawn from the yield curve for 'stripped' Treasury bonds. The longest maturity currently available is 30 years, so the per-period discount rates for all cash flows more than 30 years into the future were assumed to be the same as those on 30-year bonds. The Treasury yield curve provides riskless discount rates. Risky discount rates corresponding to BAA-rated corporate bonds are computed by adding 179 basis points to the riskless discount rates. This differential corresponds to the difference between the yield on long-term Treasury bonds and long-term BAA corporate bonds in November 2004 when the price data were collected.

Table 28.1 presents four sets of estimates of the money's worth ratio for single premium immediate annuities for men and for women at various ages. The annuity prices correspond to annuities in the voluntary US annuity market, so men and women face different prices. The first two columns report estimates using the general population mortality table, while the last two columns use the annuitant mortality table. In each case the table shows a money's worth calculation using the riskless Treasury bond discount rates as well as the risky BAA bond-equivalent discount rates. In part because nominal long-term interest rates were near historic lows in the closing months of 2004, the difference between the riskless and the risk-adjusted interest rate has an important effect on the estimated money's worth of annuity products. The upper panel in Table 28.1 presents before-tax money's worth calculations, which correspond to the ratio of EPDV from equation (1) to the annuity premium. The lower panel presents after-tax money's worth values, computed using the algorithm described in Mitchell et al. (1999) and

Table 28.1 Money's worth estimates for single premium immediate annuity at age 65

| Gender and age of annuity buyer | Valuation using population mortality table | | Valuation using annuitant mortality table | |
|---|---|---|---|---|
| | Treasury yields as discount factors | BAA corporate bond yield as discount factors | Treasury yields as discount factors | BAA corporate bond yields as discount factors |
| | Before-tax calculation | | | |
| Men | | | | |
| Age 55 | 0.908 | 0.767 | 0.993 | 0.824 |
| Age 65 | 0.864 | 0.756 | 0.986 | 0.848 |
| Age 75 | 0.814 | 0.740 | 0.969 | 0.866 |
| Women | | | | |
| Age 55 | 0.919 | 0.766 | 0.985 | 0.811 |
| Age 65 | 0.879 | 0.760 | 0.972 | 0.829 |
| Age 75 | 0.840 | 0.755 | 0.951 | 0.844 |
| | After-tax calculation, Marginal tax rate = 0.28 | | | |
| Men | | | | |
| Age 55 | 0.903 | 0.789 | 0.998 | 0.861 |
| Age 65 | 0.850 | 0.767 | 0.976 | 0.870 |
| Age 75 | 0.793 | 0.739 | 0.943 | 0.869 |
| Women | | | | |
| Age 55 | 0.930 | 0.805 | 1.005 | 0.861 |
| Age 65 | 0.883 | 0.790 | 0.981 | 0.869 |
| Age 75 | 0.838 | 0.775 | 0.947 | 0.868 |

*Source*: Author's calculations based on data from *Annuity Shopper*, January 2005, corresponding to annuity prices recorded on 26 November 2004. Interest rates are those that apply for November 2004.

assuming a marginal tax rate of 28 percent. They are similar to the before-tax values in every case.

The entries in Table 28.1 illustrate the important differences between annuity valuation using general population and annuitant mortality tables. For a 65-year-old man, for example, the money's worth value using the population mortality table and the BAA discount rate is 0.756, compared with 0.864 using the annuitant mortality table. None of the estimates using the BAA discount rates and the annuitant mortality table rises above 0.870, and at age 75 the estimates for both men and women are below 0.850. When the Treasury bond yield curve is used to construct discount rates, the money's worth values rise substantially. For a 65-year-old man, the money's worth value using the general population mortality table rises from 0.767 to 0.850. For a 65-year-old woman the value rises from 0.790 to 0.883. When the annuitant mortality table is combined with riskless discount rates, the money's worth values reach their highest level.

## 3.4 Empirical Evidence on Annuity Pricing: The United Kingdom and Other Nations

The annuity market in the United Kingdom is larger than the annuity market in the United States. There is also more variation in the set of annuity policies available to potential annuitants, and in the institutional structure surrounding the annuity market. Finkelstein and Poterba (2004) explain that while the voluntary annuity market is small, like that in the United States, there is a substantial *compulsory* market because individuals who have accumulated balances in private defined contribution retirement plans must annuitize part of their account balance at retirement. They also note that inflation-indexed annuities are widely available, in contrast to the US market, in which virtually all annuities promise fixed nominal payouts.

The UK annuity market has been analyzed in several studies that have used money's worth or IRR approaches to evaluate current products. Murthi *et al.* (2000) use the IRR method to compute the difference in returns available in the annuity market and in other investment vehicles. They conclude that the IRR on compulsory annuities in the late 1990s was roughly 100 basis points lower than the return on comparably risky fixed income investments. Cannon and Tonks (2004a, 2004b) provide a time series perspective on annuity valuation in the UK market. They compute money's worth values for the period between 1957 and 2002, and find that on average money's worth values are slightly less than unity. Their analysis focuses on the voluntary annuity market, and on nominal level-payout products within this market.

While the United States and the United Kingdom are the two nations with the most-studied annuity markets, money's worth calculations have been implemented for many other nations. It is sometimes difficult, however, to obtain comprehensive data on the available set of annuities, on the mortality rates that correspond to the annuitant population, and on the discount rate that potential annuitants might use in valuing future payment streams. The most comprehensive international comparisons of money's worth values for annuity products are James and Song (2001) and James and Vittas (2001). These studies present the available information on annuity prices and money's worth calculations for a range of countries including Canada, Australia, Switzerland, Singapore, Chile, and Israel, as well as the United States and the United Kingdom. McCarthy and Mitchell (2004) also present interesting international comparisons, and provide information on both life insurance markets and annuity markets. Cardinale et al. (2002) describe the institutional structure of annuity markets in various nations. Most of the existing research on annuity markets, with rare exceptions, focuses on markets in developed nations.

Table 28.2 reports summary money's worth measures for several nations as reported by James and Song (2001). A wealth of further information on annuity markets in the various nations can be found in that study. The results are reason-

Table 28.2 Money's worth of immediate annuities in various nations, nominal contract

| Country | Male | | Female | |
| --- | --- | --- | --- | --- |
| | Population mortality | Annuitant mortality | Population mortality | Annuitant mortality |
| Discount rate = riskless rate | | | | |
| Canada | 0.914 | 0.981 | 0.950 | 0.976 |
| United States | 0.858 | 0.974 | 0.871 | 0.954 |
| Australia | 0.911 | 1.010 | 0.915 | 0.984 |
| United Kingdom | 0.912 | 0.983 | 0.926 | 0.974 |
| Switzerland | 0.916 | 1.082 | 0.969 | 1.057 |
| Discount rate = risky rate (= riskless rate + 1.4%) | | | | |
| Canada | 0.824 | 0.879 | 0.840 | 0.864 |
| United States | 0.777 | 0.873 | 0.781 | 0.847 |
| Australia | 0.819 | 0.896 | 0.813 | 0.865 |
| United Kingdom | 0.821 | 0.879 | 0.823 | 0.860 |
| Switzerland | 0.814 | 0.944 | 0.845 | 0.916 |

Source: James and Song (2001, tables 6 and 9).

ably consistent across countries, with money's worth values of between 90 and 100 cents on the dollar in virtually every country. In some nations the money's worth ratio rises above unity when annuitant mortality tables are used to estimate survival curves. This may indicate that some insurance companies are using higher mortality rates than those embodied in the annuitant mortality tables to price their policies, or it may suggest differences in the discount rates used by insurance companies and those used in the country-specific studies of annuity markets.

The diversity of annuity markets across nations provides valuable opportunities to study how external factors influence the operation of these markets. For example, Fong (2002) presents data on the money's worth of individual annuities in Singapore, and Doyle et al. (2004) present a detailed comparison of the annuity markets in Singapore and Australia. They contrast Singapore, with a limited social security program, with Australia, where there is a generous public program and consequently very limited activity in the private annuity market. They find a much greater degree of adverse selection in the Australian market.

## 3.5 Expected Utility of Annuity Purchases

Money's worth and IRR calculations do not consider the utility value associated with longevity insurance. Because insurance is valuable to risk-averse agents, even if an annuity's payouts are less in expected value than its cost, the annuity buyer may be better off with than without the policy. A number of theoretical and simulation studies have explored the value of annuitization from the standpoint of risk-averse individuals and families. Mitchell et al. (1999) compute the expected lifetime utility associated with various strategies for drawing down assets with and without access to annuity markets. They assume that individuals seek to maximize the expected present discounted value of a time-separable constant relative risk aversion utility function. They demonstrate that even when annuities are actuarially unfair, rational individuals may choose to purchase them.

Ameriks et al. (2001) and Dus et al. (2005) carry out related exercises that do not explicitly involve utility functions. They evaluate shortfall risk and study how annuitization reduces the probability of reaching various advanced ages with resource levels that fall low enough to place constraints on consumption.

The utility gain from annuitization is very sensitive to the economic environment that prospective annuitants are assumed to face, in particular to the presence or absence of other annuities. When prospective annuitants have access to defined benefit pensions provided by the government or by the private sector, or to social insurance programs that guarantee them a minimal consumption floor even if they outlive their resources, then the incremental value of annuitizing assets is much smaller than when there is no consumption floor.

# 4 Household Choice in Annuity Markets

Most of the empirical research on annuity markets has focused on the aggregate size of these markets and on the prices for annuity products. A more limited literature has explored the behavior of individuals and households who make decisions about whether to annuitize, when to annuitize conditional on annuitizing, and which annuity products to select. Research on these issues may provide important insights, however, about the potential behavior of future annuitants as defined contribution retirement plans become more ubiquitous.

## 4.1 Who Annuitizes?

Bernheim (1991), Brown (2001), Sinha (1986), and others have used stochastic life-cycle models to explore the comparative statics of annuity demand. In spite of the small number of annuity owners, several studies have found ways to study annuity demand using household-level data. One particularly contentious issue with regard to annuity demand concerns the role of bequest motives in reducing desired annuity holdings. Bernheim's (1991) analysis of data from the Retirement History Survey, and Laitner and Juster's (1996) analysis of annuitization behavior by TIAA-CREF participants, suggest that the desire to leave a bequest does attenuate the demand for annuities. In contrast, Brown's (2001) analysis of annuitization plans of survey respondents in the Health and Retirement Survey does not support an important role for bequest motives. Studies in other nations, such as the analysis of UK annuity demand by Banks and Emmerson (1999), have largely explored the degree to which the comparative static predictions of the standard stochastic life-cycle model are consistent with the observed patterns of annuitization.

## 4.2 Age of Annuitization

The timing of annuity purchase is another element of annuity demand that has attracted research attention, although there are no definitive recommendations with regard to optimal behavior. Brugiavini (1993), Dushi and Webb (2004), Milevsky (1998), and Palmon and Spivak (2002) explore this question. The first study focuses on the set of annuitants who purchase policies at different ages, and suggests that adverse selection may increase as the annuitant pool ages. In this setting, annuitizing earlier in life allows the annuity buyer to avoid a higher adverse selection premium at a later date. Palmon and Spivak (2002) investigate the welfare properties of equilibria in which individuals make voluntary annuity purchases at different ages. They find that equilibria in which deferred annuities are purchased at younger ages dominate those with immediate annuity purchase at older ages, because there is less adverse selection when buyers must wait for a substantial period before collecting payouts. Milevsky (1998) finds that deferring annuitization is likely to increase expected utility during retirement. The paper takes the age-specific pattern of annuity prices and payouts as given, and asks whether an individual would be better off purchasing an annuity today, or deferring annuitization for a number of years, investing in financial markets during that time period, and annuitizing at a later date. Given the age-specific structure of annuity prices in Canada during the 1990s, simulation results recognizing the uncertainty of financial market returns suggest that 65-year-old prospective annuitants would have had at least an 85 percent chance of having more resources for retirement if they did not annuitize at age 65, but invested and consumed the stream of income that they could have had with an annuity until they reached age 80, at which time they annuitized their remaining wealth. Dushi and Webb (2004) find something similar for the United States; they conclude that deferring annuitization is an appropriate strategy for most young retirees. These studies generally draw attention to the role of age-related variation in the money's worth of annuity products, as well as the absolute level of the money's worth, in affecting the optimal age of annuitization.

## 4.3 Which Annuity Product?

The menu of annuity products available to potential annuitants has become richer in the last two decades. In addition to level-payout nominal annuities, insurers now offer inflation-indexed annuities, graduated payout annuities with payout streams that rise over the payout period, and annuity products with various guarantee features. When households are heterogeneous, they may differ in which annuity policy offers the highest expected utility.

Yagi and Nishigaki (1993) show that when individual discount rates differ from the real rate of return available in the market, consumers will prefer time-varying consumption profiles to profiles that offer a constant level of real expenditure. The particular profile that will be most attractive will depend on the individual's discount rate. If the rate of return exceeds the time preference rate, then annuities with increasing real payouts, such as those that offer a fixed rate of nominal payout growth that exceeds the expected rate of inflation, will be preferred to level-payout policies. When the discount rate exceeds the rate of return, declining real payout streams such as those associated with products that offer a nominal payout stream that declines in real value will be preferred to a fixed real payout annuity.

Differences in subjective mortality rates may also affect annuity choices. Longer-lived individuals should find back-loaded annuities, such as those with payout streams that increase in real terms as they age, relatively more attractive than policies with fixed nominal payouts and declining real payout streams. Similarly, individuals who are in poor health should value policies with guaranteed payouts for a fixed number of years more than policies without the guarantee feature. Finkelstein and Poterba (2004) analyze data from a large insurance company in the United Kingdom and find that annuity choices are broadly consistent with these predictions. These results support the potential importance of private information about mortality prospects in affecting individual annuity purchases, and they suggest that further work along related lines may provide additional insight into the determinants of annuity choices.

# 5 REGULATION OF ANNUITY MARKETS

Annuity markets are regulated. Some regulations apply to the insurance companies that sell annuities, while others apply to the policies that insurers may offer. Regulatory rules are likely to affect the nature of annuity market equilibrium, as well as the welfare of individuals who participate in the annuity market. One of the important trends in annuity markets in the last two decades has been the rise of specialized annuity products that are available to individuals with higher than average mortality risk. This development is most evident in the United Kingdom compulsory annuity market. In the mid-1990s, UK insurers began to introduce annuities with above-normal payouts to individuals who could be certified as cigarette smokers. While smokers were the first group targeted for such *impaired life* annuities, other products have focused on coal miners and individuals who have retired from other high-mortality industries.

A central issue for annuity market equilibrium concerns the impact of growing numbers of specialized products on the annuities available to individuals who do not fall in high-mortality groups. A small but emerging literature recognizes the importance of government regulations and other policies on the equilibrium in the private annuity market. A key insight is that the extent to which different risk types are segmented in the annuity market may depend on subtle features of the contracting environment. Brunner and Pech (2005), for example, explore how changing the time path of payouts in annuity contracts may alter the feasibility of separating rather than pooling equilibrium.

While insurance companies have been introducing new products that target subsets of the potential annuitant population, one strand of regulatory policy has been reducing the extent to which insurers can use information on policy-holders to segment their pricing structure. One of the most visible such distinctions arises with respect to the use of gender in setting annuity prices. In the United States, employers cannot set different payout rules for defined benefit pensions paid to men and women in the same retirement plan. Whether gender neutrality should be required in pension payouts was an active topic of litigation during the 1970s and early 1980s, and the courts eventually ruled in favor of plaintiffs who argued for equal treatment of men and women. Since men have shorter life expectancies at all ages than women, regulations that require equal per-period payouts to men and women imply that the expected present value of the pension annuity received by a woman is greater than that of the pension annuity paid to a man. In the United States, annuities purchased by individuals may offer different gender-specific payouts, while those provided by employers to their workers must be the same for men and women. The European Union is currently considering a gender-blind regulation for financial services that would have the effect of precluding the use of gender in pricing annuities as well as other insurance products.

Crocker and Snow (1986) and Rea (1987), among others, explore the efficiency effects of restricting the use of observable characteristics, such as gender, to price policies. Finkelstein *et al.* (2005) estimate the redistribution that occurs under the naïve assumption that men and women spend the same amount on annuities that they would spend if prices were gender-specific. They also explore how the nature of equilibrium in the annuity market, including the set of policies offered and the amount that men and women spend on annuities, might adjust if gender-specific pricing was available.

# 6 CONCLUSION

Annuity markets have long attracted interest among economic researchers, in part because simple economic models of optimal life-cycle behavior suggest that annuities should play a central role in end-of-life consumption planning. In practice, however, most nations have relatively small annuity markets. Recent shifts in the structure of retirement income provision have drawn increased attention to the operation of annuity markets. The structure of employer-provided pensions in the United States and some other nations has shifted toward a defined contribution model, in which workers need to make decisions about how to draw down their assets during retirement, and some proposals for reform of public sector pensions and social security have suggested the use of individual accounts that would raise similar issues of asset draw-down. Private annuity markets offer one means of accomplishing the goal of systematic asset reduction with limited risk of poverty at extreme old ages, Blake (1999), Mackenzie and Schrager (2004), Poterba and Warshawsky (2000), Wadsworth *et al.* (2001), and others have examined the extent to which existing markets can perform this task.

This chapter has summarized the current operation of annuity markets, the theoretical analysis of annuities and their role in life-cycle wealth accumulation, and the empirical evidence on the pricing of annuity products. There are a number of important issues that have been omitted from this chapter but that warrant mention. One is the potential development of insurance products that combines annuity protection with other elements of insurance protection, such as long-term care insurance that defrays the cost of a nursing home stay. Murtaugh *et al.* (2001) explore the potential benefits of an insurance policy that combined both long-term care coverage and retirement income support.

A second important avenue for research concerns the economy-wide consequences of changes in the structure of annuity markets and the access to these products. Kotlikoff *et al.* (1986) show, for example, that both the aggregate private saving rate and the degree of consumption inequality decline when individuals have access to a well-functioning annuity market. While private saving behavior is likely to be affected by developments in the annuity market, other aspects of household decision-making may also be influenced by these markets. Philipson and Becker (1998) suggest that when the share of resources held in annuitized form increases, either through annuity purchases in the private market or through government provision, individuals have a heightened incentive to take precautions against death and to make life-extending investments. Whether such effects are empirically significant remains an open question.

A final issue concerns the allocation of the risk associated with annuity contracts. One of the key risks that an insurance company faces when it writes an annuity is the prospect that a future decline in mortality rates may increase the expected duration of the payout stream and therefore the cost of servicing the policy. The concern that the cost of bearing this risk is leading insurers to reduce the money's worth of annuity products has led to calls for the design of derivative securities that enable insurers to trade the risk associated with annuity contracts. Blake and Burrows (2001) and Lin and Cox (2005) discuss *survivor bonds* and related approaches to creating tradable claims on the risks associated with annuities. The development of such markets could have important implications not just for annuity pricing but for the pricing of other life-contingent claims more generally.

## Notes

This chapter draws heavily on insights and findings in joint research with Jeffrey Brown, Amy Finkelstein, Olivia Mitchell, and Mark Warshawsky. I am grateful to Hui Shan for outstanding research assistance, and to the National Institute of Aging and the National Science Foundation for research support.

## References

ABEL, ANDREW B. (1986). 'Capital accumulation and uncertain lifetimes with adverse selection'. *Econometrica*, 54: 1079–97.

AMERIKS, JOHN, VERES, ROBERT, and WARSHAWSKY, MARK (2001). 'Making retirement income last a lifetime'. *Journal of Financial Planning* (Dec.): 60–76.

AUERBACH, ALAN, GOKHALE, JEGADEESH, KOTLIKOFF, LAURENCE, SABELHAUS, JOHN, and WEIL, DAVID (2001). 'The annuitization of Americans' resources: a cohort analysis.' in L. Kotlikoff, *Essays on Saving, Bequests, Altruism, and Life Cycle Planning*. Cambridge Mass.: MIT Press.

BANKS, JAMES, and EMMERSON, CARL (1999). *UK Annuitants*. London: Institute for Fiscal Studies.

BERNHEIM, B. DOUGLAS (1991). 'How strong are bequest motives? Evidence based on the demand for life insurance and annuities'. *Journal of Political Economy*, 99: 899–927.

BLAKE, DAVID (1999). 'Annuity markets: problems and solutions'. *Geneva Papers on Risk and Insurance*, 24: 358–75.

—— and BURROWS, WILLIAM (2001). 'Survivor bonds: helping to hedge mortality risk'. *Journal of Risk and Insurance*, 68: 339–48.

BROVERMAN, SAMUEL (1986). 'The rate of return on life insurance and annuities'. *Journal of Risk and Insurance*, 53: 419–34.

BROWN, JEFFREY (2001). 'Private pensions, mortality risk, and the decision to annuitize'. *Journal of Public Economics*, 82: 29–62.

—— MITCHELL, OLIVIA, and POTERBA, JAMES (2002). 'Mortality risk, inflation risk, and annuity products'. in Z. Bodie, B. Hammond, and O. Mitchell (eds.), *Innovations for Financing Retirement*. Philadelphia: University of Pennsylvania Press, 175–97.

—— —— —— and WARSHAWSKY, MARK (2001). *The Role of Annuity Markets in Financing Retirement*. Cambridge, Mass.: MIT Press.

—— and POTERBA, JAMES M. (2000). 'Joint life annuities and annuity demand by married couples'. *Journal of Risk and Insurance*, 67: 527–53.

BRUGIAVINI, AGAR (1993). 'Uncertainty resolution and the timing of annuity purchases'. *Journal of Public Economics*, 50: 31–62.

BRUNNER, JOHANN, and PECH, SUSANNE (2005). 'Adverse selection in the annuity market when payoffs vary over the time of retirement'. *Journal of Institutional and Theoretical Economics*, 161: 155–83.

CANNON, EDMUND, and TONKS, IAN (2004a). 'U.K. annuity rates, money's worth, and pension replacement ratios, 1957–2002'. *Geneva Papers on Risk and Insurance: Issues and Practice*, 29: 371–93.

CANNON, EDMUND, and TONKS, IAN (2004b). 'U.K. annuity price series, 1957–2002'. *Financial History Review*, 11: 165–96.

CARDINALE, MIRKO, FINDLATER, ALEC, and ORSZAG, MIKE (2002). *Paying Out Pensions: A Review of International Annuities Markets*. London: Watson Wyatt Worldwide Research Report 2002-RU07.

CROCKER, KEITH J., and SNOW, ARTHUR (1986). 'The efficiency effects of categorical discrimination in the insurance industry'. *Journal of Political Economy*, 94: 321–44.

DAVIDOFF, THOMAS, BROWN, JEFFREY, and DIAMOND, PETER (2005). 'Annuities and individual welfare'. *American Economic Review*, 95: 1575–90.

DIAMOND, PETER (1977). 'A framework for social security analysis'. *Journal of Public Economics*, 8: 275–98.

DOYLE, SUZANNE, MITCHELL, OLIVIA, and PIGGOTT, JOHN (2004). 'Annuity values in defined contribution retirement systems: Australia and Singapore compared'. *Australian Economic Review*, 37: 402–16.

DUS, IVICA, MAURER, RAIMOND, and MITCHELL, OLIVIA (2005). 'Betting on death and capital markets in retirement: a shortfall risk analysis of life annuities versus phased withdrawal plans'. NBER Working Paper 11271, Cambridge, Mass.

DUSHI, IRENA, and WEBB, ANTHONY (2004). 'Household annuitization decisions: simulations and empirical analysis'. *Journal of Pension Economics and Finance*, 3: 109–44.

ECKSTEIN, ZVI, EICHENBAUM, MARTIN, and PELED, D. (1985). 'Uncertain lifetimes and the welfare enhancing properties of annuity markets and social security'. *Journal of Public Economics*, 26: 303–26.

FINKELSTEIN, AMY, and POTERBA, JAMES (2004). 'Adverse selection in insurance markets: policyholder evidence from the U.K. annuity market'. *Journal of Political Economy*, 112: 183–208.

—— —— and ROTHSCHILD, CASEY (2005). 'Redistribution by insurance market regulation: the effect of banning gender-based retirement annuities'. Mimeo, MIT Department of Economics.

FONG, WAI MUN (2002). 'On the cost of adverse selection in individual annuity markets: evidence from Singapore'. *Journal of Risk and Insurance*, 69: 193–207.

FRIEDMAN, BENJAMIN, and WARSHAWSKY, MARK (1988). 'Annuity prices and savings behavior in the United States', in Zvi Bodie, John Shoven, and David A. Wise (eds.), *Pensions in the U.S. Economy*. Chicago: University of Chicago Press.

—— —— (1990). 'The cost of annuities: implications for saving behavior and bequests'. *Quarterly Journal of Economics*, 105: 135–54.

JAMES, ESTELLE, and SONG, XUE (2001). 'Annuities markets around the world: money's worth and risk intermediation'. World Bank Working Paper.

—— and VITTAS, DIMITRI (2001). 'Annuities markets in comparative perspective: do consumers get their money's worth?', in *Private Pensions Systems: Administrative Costs and Reforms*. Paris: OECD.

KOTLIKOFF, LAURENCE J., SHOVEN, JOHN, and SPIVAK, AVIA (1986). 'The effect of annuity insurance on savings and inequality'. *Journal of Labor Economics*, 4: S183–207.

—— and SPIVAK, AVIA (1981). 'The family as an incomplete annuities market'. *Journal of Political Economy*, 89: 372–91.

LAITNER, JOHN, and JUSTER, F. THOMAS (1996). 'New evidence on altruism: a study of TIAA-CREF retirees'. *American Economic Review*, 86: 893–908.

LIN, JIJIA, and COX, SAMUEL H. (2005). 'Securitization of mortality risks in life annuities'. *Journal of Risk and Insurance*, 72: 227–52.

MCCARTHY, DAVID, and MITCHELL, OLIVIA (2004). 'Annuities for an ageing world', in E. Fornero and E. Luciano (eds.), *Developing an Annuities Market in Europe*. Cheltenham: Edward Elgar, 13–48.

MACKENZIE, GEORGE, and SCHRAGER, ALLISON (2004). *Can the Private Annuity Market Provide Secure Retirement Income?* International Monetary Fund Working Paper WP/04/230.

MILEVSKY, MOSHE (1998). 'Asset allocation towards the end of the lifecycle, to annuitize or not to annuitize?' *Journal of Risk and Insurance*, 65: 401–26.

—— (2005). 'The implied longevity yield: a note on developing an index for life annuities'. *Journal of Risk and Insurance*, 72: 301–20.

MITCHELL, OLIVIA S., POTERBA, JAMES M., WARSHAWSKY, MARK, and BROWN, JEFFREY R. (1999). 'New evidence on the money's worth of individual annuities'. *American Economic Review*, 89: 1299–318.

MURTAUGH, CHRISTOPHER, SPILLMAN, BRENDA, and WARSHAWSKY, MARK (2001). 'In sickness and in health: an annuity approach to financing long-term care and retirement income'. *Journal of Risk and Insurance*, 68: 225–53.

MURTHI, MAMTA, ORSZAG, J. MICHAEL, and ORSZAG, PETER R. (2000). 'Annuity margins in the U.K.' Mimeo, Pensions Institute, Birkbeck College, London.

PALMON, ODED, and SPIVAK, AVIA (2002). 'Adverse selection and the market for annuities'. Working Paper, Bank of Israel.

PHILIPSON, TOMAS, and BECKER, GARY (1998). 'Old-age longevity and mortality-contingent claims'. *Journal of Political Economy*, 106: 551–73.

POTERBA, JAMES (2005). 'Annuities in Early Modern Europe', in W. Goetzmann and G. Rouwenhorst (eds.), *Origins of Value*. New York: Oxford University Press, 207–24.

—— and WARSHAWSKY, MARK (2000). 'The costs of annuitizing retirement payouts from individual accounts', in J. Shoven (ed.), *Administrative Costs and Social Security Privatization*. Chicago: University of Chicago Press, 173–200.

REA, SAMUEL A., Jr. (1987). 'The market response to the elimination of sex-based annuities'. *Southern Economic Journal*, 54: 55–63.

SINHA, TAPEN (1986). 'The effects of survival probabilities, transactions cost, and the attitude toward risk on the demand for annuities'. *Journal of Risk and Insurance*, 53: 301–7.

TOWNLEY, PETER (1990). 'Life insured annuities: market failure and policy dilemma'. *Canadian Journal of Economics*, 23: 546–62.

—— and BROADWAY, ROBIN (1988). 'Social security and the failure of annuity markets'. *Journal of Public Economics*, 35: 75–96.

WADSWORTH, MIKE, FINDLATER, ALEC, and BOARDMAN, TOM (2001). *Reinventing Annuities*. London: The Staple Inn Actuarial Society.

YAARI, MENAHEM (1965). 'Uncertain lifetimes, life insurance, and the theory of the consumer'. *Review of Economic Studies*, 32: 137–50.

YAGI, T., and NISHIGAKI, Y. (1993). 'The inefficiency of private constant annuities'. *Journal of Risk and Insurance*, 60: 385–412.

CHAPTER 29

# PERSONAL PENSIONS AND MARKETS

## TRYGGVI THOR HERBERTSSON

### 1 INTRODUCTION

Many countries have reformed their pension systems, or are on their way to doing so, to be better prepared financially to meet upcoming demographic challenges. During these reforms many countries have moved further toward systems based on funding and private arrangements, such as individual retirement accounts, both mandatory and voluntary. It is a well-known fact that people are retiring earlier than before, even before they are entitled to public pensions. This withdrawal of workers from the workforce at a younger age suggests that retirement income is gradually increasing, or that people are being forced out of the labor market. Moreover, life expectancy is constantly increasing. This combination of earlier retirement and longer life expectancy results in a much longer span of inactivity than before, which has to be financed. This has prompted people to make private pensions arrangements.

The inability of social security to provide enough retirement income for all, especially for people high in the income distribution, has contributed to an observed increase in personal pension schemes. As pointed out by Munnell (1982), potential expansion of social security to meet the needs of all raises the philosophical issue of the government's right to infringe on individual freedom beyond assuring a basic retirement benefit. The plethora of pension system goals led the World Bank (1994) to advocate a three-tier pension model in which public pensions would focus on a minimal poverty reduction, the second tier on a fully funded, mandatory defined-contribution pension system, and a third tier on voluntary savings. This chapter is primarily concerned with the last pillar—personal pension arrangements—but also addresses parts of the second pillar where pension policies are administered by insurance companies or other financial institutions. The main focus is on problems associated with the marketing and distribution of private pension products, namely high costs and regulation.

The complexity of pension systems and the consequent high acquisition costs for consumers can lead to considerable expense. In the UK, the historical level of costs (including annuitization) for a typical personal pension account holder is assessed at over 40 percent by Murthi et al. (2001). Economies of scale are considered by James et al. (2001) to be of crucial importance. Mitchell (1999) finds costs low in Mexico where economies of scale are enforced. On the other hand, an extreme example of a lack of economy of scale is in Iceland, with its population of a little less than 300,000, where Benediktsson et al. (2001) find that charges of between 2.5 and 12 percent (depending on the provider) are considerably lower than in the UK. The Icelandic system is simple and decentralized, and the sales process is unregulated. The results, however, may also be explained by an immature market in Iceland. The bidding contest in Bolivia has led to the lowest commissions in Latin America. Finally, Dobronogov and Muthi (2005) calculate costs of individual accounts in transition economies, drawing on examples from Croatia, Hungary, Kazakhstan, and Poland. The study finds that charges are likely to reduce returns on individual account balances by around 1 percent on average.

The remainder of the chapter is organized as follows: Section 2 reviews personal pension products, especially insurance products, and their technical characteristics. Section 3 is concerned with marketing and distribution of pension products, Section 4 with regulatory issues, while Section 5 concludes the chapter.

# 2 PERSONAL PENSION PRODUCTS

The main function of personal pensions is to smooth consumption over the life-cycle. Personal pensions can take on a variety of legal structures. They can be provided by an insurance company, designed either to deliver a stream of benefits at retirement or a lump sum that can be used to purchase an annuity. They might be offered through a mutual entity or through various forms of collective investments, such as unit trusts, investment trusts, open-ended investment companies, or by other financial institutions (cf. Daykin 2002). The government's main function in personal pension arrangements is to identify incentives and promote pensions savings, often by tax-preferred instruments. This overview focuses primarily on with-profit policies offered by the insurance industry and other financial institutions. However, it begins with a brief discussion of individual retirement accounts to set the stage for Sections 3 and 4.

## 2.1 Individual Retirement Accounts

A naive perspective on pensions is the view that they are simply one form of savings. In the absence of tax advantages, the illiquidity of accumulated pension assets before retirement and the inflexibility of payments during retirement would make such pension investments unattractive relative to other savings mechanisms. In this view of the world, tax advantages or compulsory contributions are essential for the growth of pensions. This perspective naturally lends itself to pension systems that mimic other savings instruments—ultimate benefits depend primarily or perhaps even exclusively, on contributions and financial performance. Individual retirement accounts are often used in countries that have opted for pension systems of this type (cf. Herbertsson et al. 2000).

During the last 25 years, individual retirement accounts have grown in importance as a retirement saving vehicle across the world. This form of pension known as IRAs or 401(k)s in the United States, APFs in Chile, RSAs in Australia, became widespread in the pension reforms in Latin America in the 1980s and the 1990s, in the 1990s in Northern Europe, and in the late 1990s in Eastern Europe. The first comprehensive individual retirement account system was introduced in Chile in 1981—the *Administradores de Fondos de Pensiones* (AFPs)—to manage and administer workers' retirement, survivors', and disability benefits. Chile had the oldest social insurance program in the Americas, and the system was running deficits amounting to 25 percent of Chile's GDP, although 93 percent of retired people received only minimum benefits. The country therefore urgently needed to reform its retirement system.

The accounts are administered by insurance companies, and in the 1990s it became apparent that administration and acquisition costs were very high and portability losses huge. Gill et al. (2004) point out that management fees have remained stubbornly high in almost all the Latin American countries, even when administrative costs have fallen. This raises questions about the ability of governments to effectively regulate providers of pension products, an issue addressed in Section 4. It is also important to consider intergenerational fairness when discussing costs related to individual accounts. There is some evidence that the high costs observed in the past simply reflected the costs of starting up a new industry.

Initial pension scheme members paid a larger share of their contributions in costs than current contributors, indicating that the old members were subsidizing newer ones.

As with any system based on defined-contribution (DC) principles, there are both financial and policy risks associated with individual accounts. The financial risk is due to the fact that the value of assets in the accounts is often highly volatile, and consequently the benefits depend very much on the exit date from work to retirement. For example, a person who retired in, say, 2000 would have received a quite different pension to a person who retired in 2001 after the fall of stock markets. In any funded system there is also the danger that a dictatorial government or a government facing a serious crisis can abuse the schemes. In Tanzania, pension funds were used to build a new palace for the president; in Argentina the government instructed pension funds to invest in increasingly risky government bonds during the 2001 crisis; and in Bolivia funds were forced to swap dollar-dominated assets to less attractive assets in the local currency (see Gill *et al.* 2004). Consequently, it is important to allow pension fund administrators to invest funds abroad (investment regulation is discussed in Section 4.3).

## 2.2 Life Insurance

Life insurance is one of the oldest forms of insurance and comes in a variety of forms. In its simplest form it is a contract between an insurance company and an individual, where, in return for premiums paid, the insurer pays out if the policy-holder dies before the end of the contract. In general, relevant life insurance savings products are: *with-profits policies*, which allow policy-holders to participate in the profits of the life fund of which their premiums form a part and, *unit-linked policies*, which are linked to the investment funds of the life insurance company.

### 2.2.1 With-profits Policies

With-profit policies, also known as participating policies in some countries, allow policy-holders to share in the profits of the life insurance company. Usually this is achieved through the distribution of annual bonuses that are accumulated in the policy-holders' funds. Annual bonuses are calculated by the insurance company based on its own profit experience in that year. Policy-holders may also receive an additional bonus which is payable on the termination of the policy, often called a 'terminal bonus'.

With-profits products have certain features, which usually include (see FSA 2001):

- the use of premiums to invest in a pooled fund made up of a range of assets, a significant proportion of which are likely to be in the form of equities and property;
- the *smoothing* of the amount of claim payments to cushion the policy-holder from the extremes of fluctuations in the property and equity markets;
- a share in certain of the profits or losses of the insurer, often including those arising from mortality risks and expense risks, and any distributions from the inherited estate; and
- certain guarantees, which tend to increase over the lifetime of the policy; for example the payment of a guaranteed amount at maturity or retirement, or on death.

Payment of premiums is generally made in one of three ways: as a *single premium*, which is simply a lump-sum payment, as recurrent single premiums, where the policy-holder can pay a non-contractual series of lump sums, and as regular premiums where the policy-holder pays a premium regularly according to a contract. The benefits are either paid out as a lump sum at the end of contract or converted into annuities. Since the majority of new with-profits policies are now unitized, more space will be devoted here to unit-linked policies.

### 2.2.2 Unit-Linked Policies

The appeal of this type of insurance (also known as universal life insurance) is that the individual can benefit in a transparent way from asset markets while at the same time, retaining the advantages of life insurance products, such as death benefits and tax advantages. Unit-linked life insurance policies have been growing in importance as a retirement savings vehicle. Between 1997 and 2001, the share of unit-linked business as a proportion of life insurers' total business in Western Europe rose from 21 to 36 percent. At the end of 2001, investments in unit-linked policies amounted to 1,020 billion euros, equivalent to about 20 percent of the assets under management of European life insurers. This corresponded to about 11 percent of Europe's GDP (see Swiss Reinsurance Company 2003).

Unit-linked products can be divided into three categories according to the underlying investment: unit-linked (underlying investment is then equities, bonds, real estate, and money market), index-linked (investment is equities, bonds, and money market), and equity-linked (investment is only equities). Unlike guaranteed return policies, unit-linked policies leave most of the investment risk with the policy-holder. As life premiums are used to purchase units in funds, and the value of each unit depends on the underlying value of the fund, units can increase as well as decrease in value, all according to the state of the relevant asset markets.

Usually, acquisition commissions on this kind of policies are front-loaded, and the premiums are paid over the course of the following years. Administrative costs and mortality risk premiums are either—depending on the country— deducted from the premiums or paid for by selling fund units. Figure 29.1 illustrates the working of a unit-linked policy, a simple policy with annual premiums and death benefits.[1]

The policy-holder pays a premium which is split into two components, one to buy units and the other is paid into the non-unit fund to the insurer. The mortality risk premium is financed by selling units from the unit fund. At the end of each period a return is paid on the units, and a management fee is charged on the unit fund before being passed onto the insurance company to cover expenses. Interest is credited to the non-linked fund from which administration costs are paid. In the event of death or withdrawal, units are released from the unit fund and used to pay death claims and surrender benefits. Otherwise, the beneficiary will receive the maturity value of the units and can use it in his or her retirement. It is likely that pension system reforms will further drive growth of unit-linked products in the future.

### 2.2.3 Endowments

Endowments are savings products that include life insurance. They are often taken out to run alongside a mortgage as a long-term investment. At the end of the contract, accumulated returns are paid out to the policy-holder and can be used for pensions. If the insured person dies before the end of the term, the sum assured and, depending on the type of policy, any accumulated returns, are paid out to individuals.

A low-cost endowment is a combination of a decreasing term policy and an endowment. The minimum sum assured continually decreases throughout the

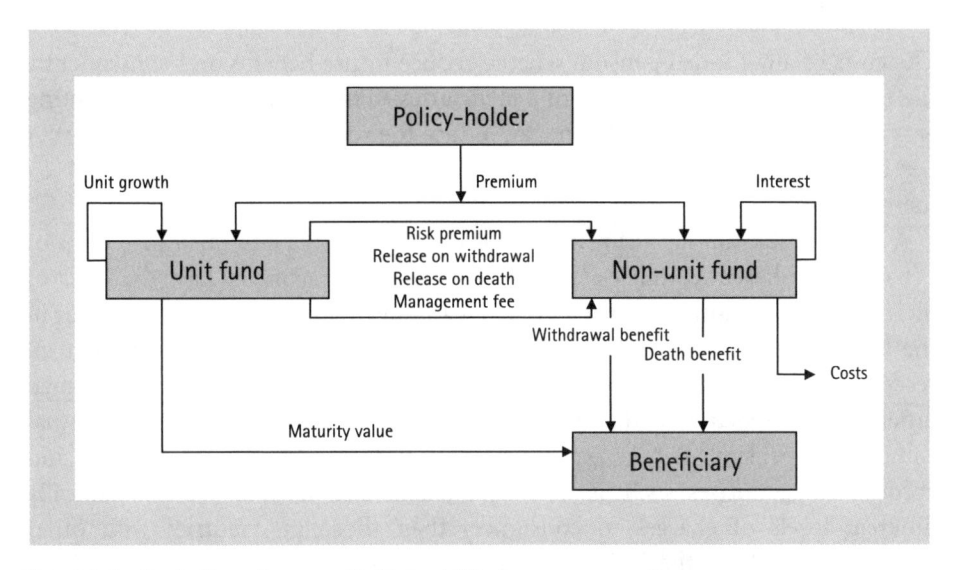

**Fig. 29.1 Cash flow for a unit-linked life insurance policy**

*Source*: Swiss Reinsurance Company.

term to cover the outstanding mortgage debt. The growth in the endowment is expected to make up the difference. The overall intention is to add bonuses to the sum assured so that it grows to match the actual mortgage. Low-start endowments offer the option to pay lower premiums at the start of a policy, which might be attractive to young, low-income workers who may be able to afford a higher premium in a few years' time.

# 3 Marketing and Distribution

Consumers in investment product markets are at a particular disadvantage: pension products are often a complex financial phenomenon, and most people do not have a good financial education. This has resulted in mis-selling where unscrupulous salesmen, often on front-loaded commissions, have advised and sold wrong pensions products to people. This mismatch has led to calls for increased regulation to protect the consumer, which in turn makes distribution complex and further drives up acquisition costs for providers.

## 3.1 Transaction Costs

The costs of any funded pension scheme reduce future benefits and consequently the future consumption options of beneficiaries.[2] For example, a cost amounting to, say, 100 basis points per annum can reduce the value of a pension by almost 21 percent, assuming 40 years of contributions.[3] Clearly it is very important to keep these costs down.

A considerable amount of research has emerged on the administrative costs of pensions in different countries.[4] Private insurance arrangements have the effect of increasing transaction costs (such as search and negotiation costs), which is not in the best interests of the individual consumer. In general, the conclusions from recent experience with supplementary pension accounts are that institutional differences in regulation and market structure have a major impact on the eventual value of the pension. Recent experiences with individual supplementary pension accounts in countries such as Bolivia, Sweden, and Iceland indicate radically different levels of charges to consumers than those in countries with other approaches, such as the UK, Argentina, Chile, and in some of the transition economies (cf. James *et al.* 2001; Dobronogov and Murthi 2005). Group or employer arrangements for supplementary pension arrangements also avoid many transaction costs and hence have considerably lower administrative costs than individual accounts.

### 3.1.1 Administrative Costs

In order to understand supplementary pension costs, Murthi et al. (1999) identified three different sources of administrative costs for individuals:

- *accumulation costs*, which capture fund management and administrative costs for a worker contributing funds to a single financial provider or pension plan throughout her career;
- *alteration costs*, which measure the additional costs of failing to contribute consistently to a single financial provider or pension plan over an entire career. This includes any costs from switching from one financial provider, or pension plan, to another or from stopping contributions altogether; and
- *annuitization costs*, which reflect the costs of converting an account to a lifetime annuity upon retirement (if required).

Murthi et al. (1999) analyze the total costs for an individual over a lifetime under the headings above. The *alteration costs* are particularly significant where there are significant up-front costs which providers recover partially or wholly by *front-loading* charges. These up-front costs are common where either complex advice is required or there are inefficient or costly sales forces. High front-loading of costs coupled with high lapse rates can lead to considerable loss for consumers. Front-loaded charges are particularly worrisome for lower-income consumers who tend to have higher lapse rates. In many countries, supplementary pensions will not have front-loaded charges because of their simple structure or because they are sold directly or in a particularly simple manner. However, in other countries there is a high degree of front-loading, which leads to high deadweight loss from consumer turnover. The issue of front-loading is also closely related to that of *portability* of benefits.

### 3.1.2 Provider Costs

Murthi et al. (1999) suggest three types of provider costs:

- *acquisition costs* include the costs of new business, which include commissions to advisers, compensation to sales forces, and any advertising costs;
- *administration costs* involve administering ongoing business, including IT infrastructure and back and front office management; and
- *asset management costs*.

Of these, asset management costs are the smallest component. In a recent study Fletcher and Orszag (2002) report that acquisition costs run at about 50 percent of total costs for providers in the UK, while administration costs amount to a little over 35 percent, and asset management costs are under 15 percent of the total cost.

### 3.1.3 Clearing-House

In order to deal with the high costs often associated with financial institutions administrating individual accounts, the Premium Pension Authority (PPM) in Sweden introduced the concept of a clearing agency for the funded part of the new public pensions system. It is modeled on a unit-linked insurance company. It acts as a clearing-house for the system as a whole, with individual members choosing up to five different private funds in which to invest. The PPM will collect funds and transfer them to the relevant private fund managers. A key design feature of the PPM is that the fund managers administering investments will not know the identity of the investors.

Marketing and acquisition costs have traditionally been a high component of private pension costs and regulatory problems; the PPM's anonymity rules are an attempt to lower costs to consumers. At the same time, the PPM anonymity rules probably lower entry costs to the Swedish market because entrants need only provide investment management services and need not spend as much effort on buying up distribution channels. Indeed, at the outset in the spring of 2000, the PPM offered a choice of 453 different funds provided by 67 different fund managers, most of them based outside Sweden. In addition, for those not choosing funds to invest in, a special low-risk government fund called the Premium Savings Fund (Premieparfonden) competes with the private sector. The organization along unit-linked lines also makes private pension provision accessible to both fund managers and life insurance companies. The PPM charges individuals 30 basis points for its management services.

## 3.2 Transparency and Disclosure

In the pensions and insurance markets information is asymmetric: consumers who generally lack the knowledge to understand the products are at a disadvantage in relation to the companies selling the product. This raises costs and creates problems of mismatch. One way to address the problem is to regulate; another is to increase consumer knowledge through transparency and advice.

Fee-based advice is one solution to the problem of asymmetric information, but in general, individuals in Europe have not been willing to pay directly for financial advice, whereas fee-based advice is common in the United States. One of the issues may be that where commission payments are not subject to value-added tax, remuneration for advice is at a substantial tax disadvantage. Another issue is that it is difficult to determine the proper market price for information goods such as financial advice, because if individuals knew how to calculate the value of the advice, they would probably not need it.

In many countries product disclosure is often the most detailed regulatory measure as it represents the final opportunity in the sales process to help the consumer to make informed decisions. It is clearly in consumers' interests that sellers of financial products give full, clear, fair information and are not misleading in any way. It is also important to allow consumers to make informed decisions about the products they are buying and to make it easier for them to understand the consequences of their purchase.

However, given that individuals do not know the value of advice in imperfect markets, it is an open economic question whether transparency and disclosure of charges would improve consumer welfare. On the one hand, consumers may not buy what is good for them if they know the high commission income that they are providing to a salesperson or an independent adviser. On the other hand, disclosure allows consumers to buy the lowest-cost products and compare financial service products on the basis of cost. The United Kingdom originally regulated the sales process for direct sales forces so that voluntary disclosure was limited,[5] but in 1995 a new regime of mandatory disclosure was introduced. In general, disclosure has had the effect of reducing the dispersion of costs rather than reducing costs overall.

However, without disclosure requirements firms would provide products of less value and also offer less information about them. It is also important to remember that some of the positive effects of transparency do not depend only on consumers' use of the information. Research carried out by the Financial Supervisory Authority (2003) in the United Kingdom has shown that in practice, written information rarely forms part of the process of shopping around. The most important point is that consumers' attention should be drawn immediately to the most significant costs and risks, and that they can also find their way to all information about the potential downsides of a product. Consumers are often either unwilling to read the material (largely because they prefer to rely on what they are told by advisers), or they have difficulty understanding and using it. The provider may ultimately choose where and how to explain the downsides.

# 4 REGULATION

While informing consumers is important in regulating the sales process, there are other ways to protect them. Regulation is also important[6] in protecting accumulated contributions and reducing the risks associated with investment decisions of pension funds and insurers.

## 4.1 Consumer Protection

In competitive markets with perfect information, economic theory suggests that there is no need for regulation of the sales process. However, as discussed above, where there is imperfect information or information is costly for individuals to obtain, there may be welfare gains from either regulation of the disclosure of information to particular consumers, or direct regulation of the sales process itself.

A commonly cited example of the need for regulation of the sales process is the UK experience with *mis-selling* personal pensions. The UK introduced Personal Pensions in 1988, and high-pressure sales tactics were subsequently used to persuade members of good occupational pension schemes (especially older, long-serving members) to switch into unsuitable personal pension schemes. Sales agents had often sought too little information from potential clients to provide proper advice, and their firms did not keep adequate records to defend themselves against subsequent claims of mis-selling. The total amount of investor compensation resulting from the mis-selling scandal is estimated to be about £15 billion. There is at present no single system of sales authorization or regulation in Europe although for life insurance there is a single market in which EU companies authorized to provide life insurance products in one country can do so in another under the same solvency regulations.

The UK sales process itself is, and has been, heavily regulated relative to most other European countries. The Financial Services Act of 1986 introduced strict regulation of the sales process, including a principle of *polarization*, so that independent advisers and salespeople must either sell the product of one company or sell products of all providers.[7] In general, supplementary pension provision in most European countries involves heterogeneous marketing channels: independent advisers, direct sales forces, bank assurers, appointed representatives, and, increasingly, direct sales by telephone and e-commerce. In such an environment, multiple ties between salespeople and advisers and companies can increase consumer information costs about whether an adviser is independent or not.[8] Therefore, polarization can increase consumer welfare. On the other hand, polarization may restrict competition and raise costs for new entrants because they need to either pay high commissions to independent advisers or build an independent sales network from scratch.

Polarization in the UK has not been so successful at lowering consumer costs—there is some evidence that sales-weighted average commissions are higher than unweighted average commissions, indicating that independent advisers tend to suggest high commission plans. In addition, the regulatory regime has independent costs, which raise the un-weighted industry costs. Another problem is that, because of the front-loading of commissions, salespeople and advisers have less of an incentive to make sure individuals hold a policy for a long period of time. Commissions spread over longer periods of time and salary-based remuneration are becoming more common and will help relieve these problems. These solutions are, however, often not advantageous to sales forces and advisers (especially in the short run) and are difficult to implement in practice without explicit or implicit regulatory pressure.

Another way of reducing the costs of information to consumers in the sales process is to regulate product design. The UK's new Stakeholder Pensions have a mandatory maximum 1 percent annual charge, and no other charges can be imposed. Such simple, commoditized products lead providers to compete on price rather than product characteristics. Single-premium retirement annuities are another example of simple commoditized products. The economic issue with such commoditized products is that while margins can be driven down, consumers can also be worse off with product regulation if they gain from the product diversity.

Companies are also very sophisticated at marketing to the most profitable consumers and cost or product regulation very often hurts the least profitable consumers who are also the least well off (see Marsh 1988). Finally, it is important not to overregulate for the sake of consumer protection. That will make distribution complex and can drive up acquisition costs.

## 4.2 Solvency Regulation

An important issue for supplementary provision is protection of accumulated contributions held by pension funds or insurers. The Maxwell scandal of the early 1990s in Britain, the Studebaker Company scandal in the US in 1964, and recently the Enron scandal are just the most prominent of a number of high profile examples where individual pension rights were compromised by corporate performance and reliance on pension funds as a source of capital.

A number of different approaches are used to ensure the solvency of accumulated pension funds. For funds held with life insurers in Europe, the EU-wide solvency regulations and reserving requirements apply. These regulations provide security of capital for individual investors and insured corporate pensions. These solvency guarantees are particularly important for book reserve pensions.

Solvency regulations for pension funds can be quite different to life insurance solvency regulations and differ considerably across countries. In 1997 the Minimum Funding Requirement (MFR) rule, which requires pension funds to be at least at the level of funding on a discontinuance basis, was introduced in the UK. It uses a prescribed method of calculation, so that if funding is below 90 percent of the discontinuance basis, a more rapid schedule of contributions is required. A Pension Compensation Fund is available to make up shortfalls and criminal penalties for employers failing to make contributions to a scheme on time.

In other countries, pension funds are insured or guaranteed centrally. Smalhout (1996) reviews the economics of pension guarantees and examples throughout the world. The German Pensions-Sicherungs-Verein (PSVaG) insures book reserve pensions on an essentially pay-as-you-go basis. Other countries with insurance arrangements for pension fund insolvency include Finland, the Netherlands, Sweden, and Switzerland. General lessons about guarantee programs seem to be:

- These arrangements come under pressure primarily when there are large aggregate shocks, which create large numbers of employer insolvencies. In Finland claims against the insurance fund rose by a factor of 40 between 1988 and 1992 (see Smalhout 1996). If the guarantee system is privatized, some sort of central government guarantee or external reinsurance program is important to insure against aggregate risks.
- Risk-related insurance premiums are important in reducing disincentive effects to employers to underfund. Without risk-related premiums, underfunded schemes (bad risks) have to be subsidized, and problems may be exacerbated by wind-ups of solvent schemes.
- Solvency regulation and intervention/supervisory powers are also very important.
- Public disclosure of funding status can also be useful. The Netherlands are illustrative in this respect.

Providing guarantees for pension benefits is a complex economic area, not only because any form of insurance introduces incentive problems, but because the risks are not only aggregate but also long term in nature. Private solutions for guarantees have been tried in many countries but are most successful if backed up by additional regulation and government guarantees.

## 4.3 Investment Regulation

Various restrictions exist on portfolios of pension funds across the world. While these might appear at first glance to be regulatory constraints which unambiguously lower consumer welfare, the issues of investment freedom and solvency regulation for pension funds can be quite intertwined. For instance, if pension liabilities are in one currency, there may be some justification for mandating these liabilities to be appropriately matched with assets of an appropriate risk class in the same currency. This particularly applies if there are government guarantees whether implicit or explicit.

At the same time, international investment of pension funds conveys many important benefits including potentially higher returns and better risk reduction. A greater variety of investment opportunities increases the scope for high asset returns and by moving investment funds abroad, pension funds can effectively insure against adverse country-specific shocks.

Restrictions that prevent pension funds of employers from investing excessively in the sponsoring employers' business form another example of where investment freedom regulation is closely intertwined with solvency regulation. The Maxwell scandal points to the importance of careful regulation of the custody of pension fund assets, designed to ensure that no more than a small percentage of assets can be held with the employer.

Such asset restrictions are good for solvency but can be a problem for small and medium-sized enterprises, which may find pensions a good source of capital for business expansion. The UK has lighter employer investment regulation for very small pension funds, called SSASs, which are self-administered schemes for groups of 12 or fewer individuals. There are similar provisions in other countries for small and medium-sized enterprises to help provide them with low-cost access to capital, with the extreme example being the book reserve systems of many countries. The trade-off between the costs and the security of capital is hence an important one to consider in the design of supplementary pensions. The capital needs of small businesses, particularly in underdeveloped financial markets, are important to consider in such design. Whether pension funds of employees are the appropriate vehicle to solve problems of capital market imperfections, or whether other forms of explicit or implicit subsidy might be better, remains an issue. Easy access to capital may deter competitiveness and slow down development of capital markets. It has been claimed, for example, that the book reserve system in Germany is partly responsible for the lack of development of German equity capital markets (cf. Taverne 1995).

# 5 CONCLUSIONS

The main message of this chapter is that costs associated with personal pensions have to be understood clearly in order to guarantee future retirement benefits. A cost that lowers net returns by only a small fraction can substantially reduce an individual's pension wealth in the long run. Consequently, it is very important to keep these costs down. Mis-selling is another problem. Consumer education is one way of addressing this difficulty, but regulation of sales tactics and consumer protection is probably a more efficient solution. However, overregulation will make distribution complex and can drive up acquisition costs. Finally, efficient investment and solvency regulation are important in order to minimize the risk inherently associated with the volatile financial assets of pension funds.

Future research on personal pension arrangements will have to focus on these issues. The connection between the regulatory framework and costs associated with retirement products is less than well understood. It is, for example, not obvious why costs in the UK, Chile, and the Balkan countries are so high in comparison with costs observed in Bolivia, Iceland, and Sweden. Research on consumer behavior in financial retail markets is also needed as is research on risk associated with private pension products. By better understanding these issues policy-makers will be better equipped to promote policies and regulation that will safeguard retirement benefits in the future.

# Notes

This chapter was written during my stay at the Center for Research on Pensions and Welfare Policies, University of Turin in September and October 2004. I would like to thank the center's director Elsa Fornero and the staff for their hospitality during my stay. I would also like to thank Carolina Fugazza, Gylfi Zoega, and the editors for useful comments.

1. This example is taken from the Swiss Reinsurance Company. The cash-flow structure can vary from the one illustrated here, depending on the charging structure, design of funds, etc.
2. This section and the next are based on Herbertsson and Orszag (2001).
3. Additional assumptions in the calculations are a 2 percent annual wage increase and a 5 percent rate of return.
4. Relevant comparative work includes Mitchell *et al.* (1994), Valdes (1994), and Mitchell and Sundén (1994).
5. Securities and Investments Board (1986) is a publication reviewing the initial considerations on disclosure.
6. This section is based on Herbertsson and Orszag (2001).
7. An excellent review of the regulatory issues behind the UK Financial Services Act 1986 is Abrams *et al.* (1989).
8. A related issue emphasized by the Forum of European Securities Commissions (FESCO) is making sure that 'ownership' of the provider is transparent (http://www.fsa.gov.uk/pdf/fesco.pdf).

# References

Abrams, Charles, Michael Ashe, and Barry Rider (1989). *Guide to Financial Services Regulation*. London: CCH.

Benediktsson, Haukur C., Herbertsson, Tryggvi Thor and Orszag, J. Michael (2001). 'Cost on individual retirement accounts and savings plans in Iceland'. *Journal of Applied Economics*, 33/8 (June): 979–87.

DAYKIN, CHRIS (2002). 'Trends and challenges in pension provision and regulation', in *Regulating Private Pensions Schemes: Trends and Challenges*. OECD Private Pensions Series, No. 4.

DOBRONOGOV, ANTON, and MUTHI, MAMTA (2005). 'Administrative fees and costs of mandatory private pensions in transition economies'. *Journal of Pension Economics and Finance*.

FLETCHER, FRANK, and ORSZAG, J. MICHAEL (2002). 'Distribution and private pensions: lesson from the United Kingdom experience', in *Regulating Private Pensions Schemes: Trends and Challenges*. OECD Private Pensions Series, No. 4.

FSA (2001). 'A description and classification of with-profits policies'. FSA (Oct.).

—— (2003). 'Informing consumers: product disclosure at the point of sale'. FSA Consultation Paper No. 170 (Feb.).

GILL, INDERMIT S., PACKARD, TRUMAN G., and YERMO, JUAN (2004). *Keeping the Promise of Social Security in Latin America*. World Bank.

HERBERTSSON, TRYGGVI THOR, and ORSZAG, J. MICHAEL (2001). 'Policy options and issues in reforming European supplementary pension systems'. *Journal of Pensions Management*, 7/2.

—— —— and ORSZAG, PETER (2000). *Retirement in the Nordic Countries: Prospects and Proposals for Reform*. A report to the Nordic Council of Ministers (ECOFIN), TemaNord No. 2000:548, Nordic Council of Ministers, Copenhagen.

JAMES, ESTELLE, SMALHOUT, JAMES, and VITTAS, DMITRI (2001). 'Administrative costs and the organization of individual account systems: a comparative perspective', in Robert Holzmann and Joseph Stiglitz (eds.), *New Ideas about Old Age Security*. Washington, D.C.: The World Bank.

MARSH, JOHN (1988). *Managing Financial Services Marketing*. London: Pitman.

MITCHELL, OLIVIA (1999). 'Evaluating administrative costs in Mexico's AFORES system'. Pensions Research Council (Jan.).

—— and SUNDÉN, ANNIKA (1994). 'An examination of social security administrative costs in the United States'. Pensions Research Council, Wharton School.

—— —— and HSIN, PING-LUNG (1994). 'An international comparison of social security administrative costs'. *International Compensation and Benefits*.

MUNNELL, ALICIA H. (1982). *The Economics of Private Pensions*. Brooking Studies in Social Economics. Washington, D.C.: Brookings Institution.

MURTHI, MAMTA, ORSZAG, J. MICHAEL, and ORSZAG, PETER (2001). 'Administrative costs under a decentralized approach to individual accounts: lessons from the United Kingdom', in Robert Holzmann and Joseph Stiglitz (eds.), *New Ideas about Old Age Security*. Washington: The World Bank.

SECURITIES AND INVESTMENTS BOARD (1986). *Life Assurance Companies Disclosure of Expenses and Charges* (Dec.). London: Securities and Investment Board.

SMALHOUT, JAMES (1996). *The Uncertain Retirement*. London: Irwin.

SWISS REINSURANCE COMPANY (2003). 'Unit-linked live insurance in Western Europe: regaining momentum?' *Sigma*, No. 33.

TAVERNE, DICK (1995). *The Pension Time Bomb in Europe*. A Federal Trust Report. London: Federal Trust.

VALDES, SALVADOR (1994). 'Administrative charges in pensions in Chile, Malaysia, Zambia, and the United States'. World Bank Policy Research Working Paper No. 1372 (Oct.).

WORLD BANK (1994). *Averting the Old Age Crisis: Policies to Protect the Old and Promote Growth*. A World Bank Policy Research Report. Washington, D.C.: World Bank.

# INDIVIDUAL AND HOUSEHOLD RETIREMENT PLANNING

CHAPTER 30

# CHOICE, BEHAVIOR, AND RETIREMENT SAVING

## STEVEN F. VENTI

## 1 INTRODUCTION

How much to save for retirement is one of the most difficult decisions a household faces. The outcome is so important that all countries assist people in the provision of retirement security through mandated public sector pension plans, and many countries also provide generous tax advantages to private sector saving. Despite these efforts, there is evidence that some households—even those with substantial financial resources—fail to save 'enough' for retirement. Concern about levels of household saving for retirement is likely to grow in the future as benefits from unsustainable public sector pensions are trimmed in many countries. The decline of traditional employer-based defined benefit (DB) pensions and rise of defined contribution (DC) and other personal account plans has given added importance to how households make retirement saving decisions.

Conventional economic theory predicts that consumers should be forward-looking and smooth consumption (or more technically, the marginal utility of consumption) over their lifetimes. In this framework, saving is a purely a function of the economic and financial fundamentals of the planning problem. The theory is silent about the difficulties agents may face planning for the future or carrying out their saving plan.

A growing research literature suggests that actual retirement savings decisions are complicated by behavioral and psychological factors that may interfere with the ability of persons to make and execute plans in accord with the conventional theory. Persons may not be well-informed agents able to correctly process information and make choices based solely on financial considerations. Given the complexity of the saving decision, it is questionable whether most people can solve the saving problem in the manner prescribed by conventional models. Instead they may decide how much to save in a variety of other ways that are susceptible to behavioral factors. Other people may simply become paralyzed by the complexity of the problem and not save at all. Still other people may be able to solve the standard model and formulate a saving plan, but for a variety of non-economic reasons they cannot follow through to achieve their saving goals.

One consequence of the intrusion of psychological and behavioral factors into the saving decision is that households may fail to save adequately for their retirement. Another consequence is that seemingly inconsequential features of the consumer's decision environment—defaults, deadlines, or cues, for example—often have substantial effects on actual savings behavior. In the context of the conventional theory, these 'behavioral' effects are puzzling. These features have no effect on the financial fundamentals of the saving problem and should thus be irrelevant. However, their importance in actual saving decisions suggests that policies designed with psychological and behavioral factors in mind may help individuals who find it difficult to save.

This chapter focuses the effect of behavioral and psychological factors on two stages of the saving decision: planning and execution. At each stage I will try to identify and provide evidence of the effects of behavioral and psychological factors on saving decisions. The aim is not to evaluate the relative importance of conventional and alternative models of retirement saving. It is acknowledged that conventional models may be very good descriptions of how consumers intend to save and for some persons may describe observed behavior. However, the conventional models are only part of the story. Our discussion focuses on the other part: why some people fail to behave according to conventional models and what kinds of policies employers, governments, and savers themselves can adopt to encourage better saving decisions.

## 2 Planning to Save

If some households save too little, it may be because they are unable to decide how much to save. A properly executed saving strategy first requires a plan. Conventional economic models assume households formulate saving plans based on expectations of future income, consumption, and mortality. Survey evidence shows that, on average, households may hold reasonable expectations for each of these components (see e.g. Hurd and McGarry 1995). However, the stochastic nature of each makes planning a difficult cognitive task—perhaps too complicated for most households to grasp. Indeed, survey evidence suggests that many households are unable to take even the first step toward calculating a saving plan. The most recent (2004) EBRI Retirement Confidence Survey finds that only about 40 percent of all workers in the United States have actually calculated how much money they will need to save by the time they retire. About one-third of the younger workers and about half of the older workers nearing retirement say they have planned. Similar results are reported in previous years. Lusardi (1999a) finds that among workers within five to ten years of retirement in 1992, about one-third had thought about retirement 'hardly at all' and less than one-third thought about it 'a lot'. For this same cohort, only 25 percent had ever attended any meetings on retirement or retirement planning. Ameriks et al. (2003) find that even in a sample of highly educated (predominately university employees) and wealthy individuals (2.5–3 times wealthier than the general population), about 27 percent had 'not formulated a specific financial plan for your household's long-term future' and over 30 percent had not 'spent a great deal of time developing a financial plan'.

The failure to formulate a plan may be the consequence of a number of factors. First, the information required to formulate a plan is often elusive. Uncertainty itself may be the most daunting obstacle to planning. Households may have only the foggiest notion of what earnings, their health, rates of return, house price appreciation, and other key planning inputs will be in the future. Second, planning is itself a difficult task. Even the simplest calculations require rudimentary familiarity with discounting, compounding, and other fundamental building blocks of intertemporal planning as well as awareness of the properties of different investments. Bernheim (1995, 1998) was among the first to document that many households display little financial literacy and do not possess the information or skills necessary to make saving decisions. In a recent survey (John Hancock 2002) three out of four respondents could not correctly identify the relationship between long-run interest rates and bond prices. Nearly two-thirds of the respondents were unaware that money market funds do not include stocks. Lusardi (1999b, 2004) and Ameriks et al. (2003, 2004) show that the set of skills and aptitudes required to plan varies considerably in the population.

Finally, much of the information needed to formulate a life-cycle saving plan may not be readily available to most households. Key inputs into any savings plan are future benefits provided by non-discretionary saving sources such as defined benefit pensions and Social Security. Yet many, if not most, workers have at best a fuzzy notion of how much to expect from these sources and when they will begin to draw on them. For example, EBRI (2004) reports that only 19 percent of all workers are able to give the correct age at which they are eligible for full Social

Security retirement benefits. This unawareness may reflect a misunderstanding of the phased increase in the age required to receive full benefits. However, 21 percent of the respondents believed they would be eligible for full benefits before the current age of 65 and 21 percent said they simply didn't know when they would become eligible. Gustman and Steinmeier (2004) compare what respondents know about their employer-provided pension plans to administrative records. In their sample of workers within ten years of retirement only half of all workers could identify plan type (defined contribution or defined benefit), and fewer than half could correctly identify, within one year, the dates of eligibility for receipt of early and normal benefits.

How might consumers overwhelmed by the planning process behave? One option is to simply not plan. For some households, particularly those at the bottom end of the income distribution, public benefits may crowd out private saving, making the need to plan debatable. There are other reasons why lack of planning may be a rational decision given certain preferences and economic circumstances. However, there seems to be some agreement that there is a 'saving problem' for some households (see the next section) so the failure to plan by some non-saver households may indicate these households are making the easiest decision rather than the best decision. Moreover, lack of planning has consequences for saving; those who do not plan have lower wealth holdings and are less likely to report that they experience a satisfying retirement (Lusardi 1999a; Ameriks et al. 2003).

Other households overwhelmed by the planning process may adopt simple rules-of-thumb in lieu of a carefully thought-out plan. If these heuristics approximate the saving path that would result from careful planning, then the failure to plan may not prevent households from achieving retirement saving goals. Thus, following a simple rule—for example, save 10 percent of income—may work for some households. However, it appears that other households save in a formulistic way that does not approximate the appropriate level of saving (Bernheim 1995). For example, an unusually large proportion of participants in 401(k) plans in the United States choose contribution rates that are even multiples of five despite any apparent rationale for this choice. Participants also display a tendency to split their contributions evenly among investment options irrespective of the number and type of options offered, a rule-of-thumb that is inconsistent with even the most primitive financial advice (Benartzi and Thaler 2001).

Still others overwhelmed by the planning process turn to financial advisers, peers, the government, or their employers for planning advice and information. Numerous recent studies show that providing people with more information may make the planning problem less complex and get at least some consumers out of the starting blocks. Bernheim and Garrett (2003), Ameriks, Caplin and Leahy (2003), Clark and d'Ambrosio (2003), Lusardi (2003, 2004), and Scott and Stein (2004) show that exposure to financial seminars and other forms of investment education can change retirement saving goals and subsequent saving behavior.

Lusardi, for example, finds that households with low levels of education save little and hold very simple portfolios containing few high return assets. Exposure to financial seminars was associated with a 20 percent increase in household net worth over all households, and sharper increases for households with low levels of education. Indeed, the promise that investor education may facilitate planning and stimulate saving prompted the US Congress to adopt several measures encouraging employers to become more involved in the saving decisions of their employees. Restrictions were loosened on the types of financial advice employers can provide and companies were granted some protections from liabilities arising from bad choices made by their employees. In sharp contrast to 20 years ago, most large employers now provide direct financial planning assistance to employees and the financial institutions administering employer-sponsored plans compete vigorously to make sophisticated planning aids accessible to mainstream investors.

There are other means of moving non-planners off the status quo when it is in their longer-term interest to do so. Behavioral economics suggests that imposing deadlines may be useful to prompt action as may rules that force employees to make 'active decisions' concerning participation in employer-provided savings plans (Choi et al. 2002). Both mechanisms may get people to act when they otherwise would not do so. More generally, consumers unable to plan on their own may look to others to provide 'cues' to appropriate saving behavior (see Bernheim and Rangel 2003). For example, governments may encourage citizens to plan by providing statements of projected benefits from public pensions. Employers may help by setting defaults, providing financial seminars, or by pressuring employees to participate in or even mandating participation in contributory saving plans.

Peers may affect a person's propensity to plan by offering advice or by providing an example of a prudent saving strategy (if everybody else is doing it, perhaps I should too). For example, Duflo and Saez (2003) compare retirement savings plan participation rates of persons working in different departments at a large research university. Some employees in randomly selected departments were offered a cash incentive to attend a benefits information fair. As expected, those who attended the fair were significantly more likely to enroll in the saving program. However, they also found that the saving choices of persons not attending the fair mirror the savings choices of peers in their department. A person not offered an incentive to attend the fair, but in a department containing members offered the incentive, was more likely to enroll than a person not offered an incentive in a department containing no members offered an incentive. Duflo and Saez offer several interpretations for this result, including peer effects at the department level and the effect of the incentive payment on the perceived value of attending the fair. However, regardless of the interpretation, the experiment suggests that relatively minor factors (small cash incentives, peer effects) that do not directly affect the financial attractiveness of saving can have a significant impact on the formulation of saving plans.

The Duflo and Saez experiment suggests that the observed choices of peers may motivate some non-planners to take action. However, it should be clear that the information in peer choices should be interpreted with caution. Persons easily influenced by peers may not necessarily be following the advice of the most financially savvy group of investors. While people can learn from colleagues, family and friends, and other peers, they can also copy their mistakes.

Finally, there is growing evidence that the complex design of many saving programs may itself hinder planning. Persons facing complex decisions may be unable to make a choice. Indeed, too much choice may just make the problem harder to solve, causing consumers to back away from a difficult problem. A recent study of over 800,000 employees found that participation is higher in 401(k) plans offering a small number of investment options, compared to plans offering ten or more options (Iyengar *et al.* 2004). Other studies (Benartzi and Thaler 2001, and Huberman and Jiang 2004) have noted that savings plan participants are unable to make financially appropriate investment choices when confronted with many investment options—they adopt the so-called '1/n strategy' whereby investors allocate equal proportions of their savings portfolio to each investment option offered. In a more direct test of 'information overload', Agnew and Szykman (2004) show that persons with low financial sophistication are more likely to choose defaults (rather than making active decisions) and are more likely to report that they are overwhelmed by the investment decision in general.

## 3 Executing a Savings Plan

With the retirement of the baby-boomers and the precarious financial state of public pension funds, the adequacy of saving has become a central policy issue and the object of a great deal of recent research. The Congressional Budget Office (2003) surveys a large numbers of studies on the adequacy of saving in the United States. These studies use a wide range of standards to assess adequacy. Several studies have documented an unanticipated drop in consumption at retirement. Other studies compare realized saving at retirement to levels predicted by life-cycle models. Still other studies evaluate adequacy by calculating replacement income in retirement. Perhaps because of the different conventions employed, these studies have produced conflicting results. However, as a whole, the research indicates that a substantial proportion, and perhaps most, households in the United States fail to save 'enough' for retirement. The European experience, at least for current retirees, shows a higher level of overall financial preparation for retirement, due primarily to the large compulsory public pension systems in most countries. Nonetheless, there are substantial differences in saving adequacy among EU countries as measured by replacement rates (see Boersch-Supan 2003).

Direct survey evidence presents a similar picture. In 2004, 68 percent of US workers say they or their spouse have saved for retirement (EBRI 2004). Of those who save, 72 percent say they can afford to save $20 more per week for retirement. Of the 32 percent of workers not saving for retirement, 54 percent say they can afford to save $20 per week for retirement. These data suggest that many, if not most, workers are comfortable with their current level of saving. Yet when asked if they are 'doing a good job preparing financially for retirement', only 26 percent of all workers agree, and only 24 percent of workers over age 55 agree. Hurd and Zissimopoulos (2000) examine subjective information about past saving behavior. When asked to evaluate their saving, a stunningly high proportion of respondents (73 percent) in their sample report having saved too little over the past 20 and 30 years. Another survey (cited by Laibson *et al.* 1998) finds that 76 percent of respondents believe they should be saving more for their retirement. Still another study (Choi *et al.* 2002) finds that 68 percent of workers say their saving rate is too low. Of these low savers, 35 percent plan to increase their saving in the short run, but only about 4 percent actually do so.

Survey evidence for Europe shows a markedly higher level of overall financial preparedness for retirement. A 2001 Eurobarometer survey asked retirees if they should have made additional contributions to pension schemes or if they otherwise should have saved more for their retirement. The proportion of the population 'undersaving' by this measure ranged from just under 10 percent in Portugal and Spain to nearly 30 percent in Sweden, France, and Ireland. The same survey also asked retirees to compare their current financial situation to that prior to retirement. In all countries a large fraction of respondents indicated that they were 'a bit worse' or 'much worse' off in their current situation, with country-level responses ranging from 30 percent in Luxembourg to 57 percent in France and Ireland.

In the United States and Europe, most analytical research and survey evidence on saving adequacy pertains to persons either just before or just after retirement. In part this is due to the difficulty of judging adequacy for younger cohorts when future public sector benefits cannot be projected with much certainty. If cuts in future benefits are substantial, the saving problem may be more severe for persons currently far from retirement.

Why is saving so low for some households, particularly in light of intentions to save more? One explanation that has long been advanced by psychologists is that many people lack the discipline, will-power, or self-control required to implement a saving plan. People want to save for the future, but they lack the capacity to carry out their intentions. Schelling (1978) noted long ago that the problem is not unlike that faced by people unable to follow through on plans to diet, exercise, or quit smoking.

The psychological and behavioral basis for self-control problems has long occupied the research agenda of psychologists (see references in Laibson 1998 and Ameriks *et al.* 2004). Experimental evidence has shown that for some people near-term discount rates are much higher then longer-term discount rates, that is, people do not discount exponentially (see the references in Frederick *et al.* 2002). Attempts to incorporate this behavior into economic models have been more recent. Strotz (1956) was the first to recognize that many predictions of the standard life-cycle model fail to hold when the discount rate is not constant over time. He showed that if discounting is not exponential, then consumers will exhibit time-inconsistent preferences. Typically, time inconsistency is observed as a declining discount factor as the time horizon increases. People may prefer $10 today to $12 tomorrow, but at the same time prefer $12 in 101 days to $10 in 100 days. One mathematical function that fits this temporal pattern of discounting is the hyperbolic functional form (Ainslie 1992; Laibson 1997; Laibson *et al.* 1998). It should be noted that hyperbolic discounting is simply a convenient analytical function that fits observed outcomes arguably better than exponential discounting. It is not a model of the deeper psychological decision-making process that underlies self-control or will-power deficiencies. Nonetheless, it has proven to be a useful means of incorporating some behavioral factors into utility maximization models.

Laibson and his co-authors have explored some of the features of saving in this class of models. Chief among these is the divergence between plans and actions. Time-inconsistent consumers may formulate the same future saving plan as a conventional life-cycle planner, but engage in short-term behavior that violates the plan. This is the so-called 'self-control' problem. Sophisticated consumers— those aware that they have self-control problems—can overcome this problem by engaging in commitment mechanisms that restrict future actions. In principle, employers, governments, or financial institutions can also improve welfare by providing similar self-control safeguards. One example is the penalty applied to pre-retirement withdrawals in most retirement saving plans. This feature allows individuals who are aware of their limited self-control to commit themselves to saving by placing funds 'off limits'. Another example is the automatic payroll deduction feature of most employer-based plans. This feature helps individuals by removing saving from the day-to-day decision-making. In the United States, automatic payroll deduction is often cited as one of the reasons for the high participation rate in 401(k) saving programs. The IRA program widely available in the United States in the mid-1980s had tax advantages similar to the 401(k), but was not employer based and thus lacked the automatic payroll deduction feature. Instead the IRA required an active decision to save each year. Despite the similar financial advantages offered by the two programs, participation rates in IRAs were only about one-quarter of those in 401(k)s. Other examples of commitment devices include advice from financial planners to cut up your credit cards, and 'forced' saving by having excess income tax withheld from pay, and so-called 'Christmas club' accounts. Each of these mechanisms in some way restricts short-term spending. In light of self-control issues faced by households, it is thus not surprising that programs that make saving non-discretionary—compulsory employer pensions, mortgage payment plans, and public pensions—are perhaps the most effective saving devices. Empirical evidence has shown that households heavily engaged in these activities are the least likely to be financially unprepared for retirement.

Another behavioral impediment, also an implication of time-inconsistent preferences, is the impact of procrastination or inertia on saving choices. Again, psychologists have extensively studied the tendency of persons to defer action if there are immediate costs even if the long-term gains are substantial. As mentioned before, agents can face substantial planning or informational costs in making saving decisions. Only recently has this behavior made its way into economic models of decision-making (O'Donoghue and Rabin 1999*a*, 1999*b*). The key insight is that persons will not always make decisions that are in their best long-term interest when short-run costs are involved. This problem had become more relevant as the pension structure shifts from the types of pensions where employers make all of the decisions to newer 'self-directed' pensions that require employees to make choices. For example, new employees may have to take action to enroll in their employer-sponsored plan, to choose a contribution rate, or to choose from among the many investment options in their DC or 401(k) pension plans. These choices involve immediate time costs as well as mental anguish for some persons. In far too many cases procrastination appears to take over.

One way to increase saving in these circumstances is to redesign plans to automatically enroll employees as in so-called 'autopilot' 401(k) plans. Madrian and Shea (2001) show that automatic enrollment in the employer's plan can have large effects on saving. In their study the employer had a plan that originally required employees to make an affirmative decision to enroll in the 401(k) plan. The plan was then redesigned to automatically enroll new employees, although they were permitted to affirmatively 'opt out'. The results are striking. Automatic enrollment raised the participation rate of new employees from 37 percent to 86 percent. Moreover, much of the gap persisted over time. Although employees hired under the original plan increased their participation over time, the enrollment rates of even the most senior employees under the old regime continued to be below the enrollment rates of new hires under automatic enrollment. Choi *et al.* (2004) extend the analysis to a longer time horizon and find that the enrollment gap is still substantial after four years. They also note that automatic enrollment is particularly successful in raising the participation rate of lower-paid employees. Indeed, the company used in their studies adopted automatic enrollment to satisfy IRS non-discrimination rules.

Automatic enrollment is a form of 'default' choice and the tendency of employees to stick with company defaults extends to decisions involving the amount contributed and how these funds are invested. The default may be particularly powerful because it involves no immediate costs associated with decision-making and because employees may view default parameters as suggestions from the employer. In the Madrian and Shea study (2001), the pension redesign that implemented automatic enrollment also established a default contribution rate of 3 percent of compensation and a default investment allocation of 100 percent of contributions to a money market fund. Defaults for these choices did not exist in the original plan. About two-thirds of the new employees adopted these defaults despite the fact that they were probably too conservative to generate adequate retirement saving. In particular, the 3 percent contribution default led to a dramatic shift away from higher rates chosen by participants enrolled under the original plan. As is the case with enrollment, once the initial choice is made, subsequent changes are infrequent. In terms of wealth accumulation, the beneficial effects of automatic enrollment were roughly offset by harmful effects of defaults on contribution rates and investment allocations. Similar results from a broader array of firms and for longer time horizons are reported in Choi et al. (2002 and 2004).

Another study (Choi et al. 2003) compared participation in a plan that changed from a default choice not to participate to a new enrollment procedure that required employees to check one box or another, to participate or not. This redesign of the pension plan—requiring an 'active decision'—led to participation rates as much as 25 percent higher than the standard default of non-enrollment.

These and other findings from 401(k) plan design in the United States suggest that employers can make procrastination or inertia work in the employee's favor by setting more desirable defaults (the paternalistic approach) or, to a lesser extent, by requiring employees to make 'active choices'. The studies also show that how the enrollment decision is framed has not only a large effect on initial participation, but that this effect persists because once having enrolled in a plan and having selected an asset allocation (or having an asset allocation chosen for them), most employees are unlikely to make changes in the future. Again, these simple design features adopted by the firm do not affect the financial attractiveness of the plan, yet may have large effects on saving behavior.

Of course, the difficulty with defaults is that employers cannot frame each feature of a retirement saving plan to meet the needs of individual employees. Employers must choose not only whether to implement automatic enrollment, but also must set defaults for other features of a saving plan, including the contribution level, the composition of the investment portfolio, rules on investment in company stock, and whether portfolios are automatically rebalanced as participants age. One thing we've learned from the many studies on saving is that saving behavior is very heterogeneous and a 'one-size-fits-all' approach may be overly simplistic. Thus, defaults set to encourage the saving of some employees may hinder the saving of others. Similarly, forcing employees—through an 'active decision' rule—to choose when they are inexperienced or uninformed may also lead to poor saving decisions. Nevertheless, the large effects of defaults and active decision rules on saving behavior are now well documented and the current challenge is how best to use them to help people save.

Two other recent 'experiments' provide further evidence that saving products designed to address behavioral factors can have large effects on the ability of people to reach their saving goals. First, Ashraf et al. (2004) have designed a saving commitment product and tested its use in the Philippines. In cooperation with a Philippine bank they began by administering a survey to identify subjects with time-inconsistent preferences (long-term discount rates exceed short-term discount rates). Subjects were then randomly assigned to three groups—a control group, a group that was counseled on the use of existing saving products, and a treatment group that was offered a new commitment saving product that restricted access to funds, but in other respects was similar to existing products. Two findings are of particular interest. First, the survey determination of time-inconsistent preferences was highly predictive of enrollment in saving commitment plans. The only other significant predictors of take-up were education (positive effect) and income. Middle income households were more likely to enroll in commitment saving plans than either low or high income households. Twenty-five percent of households offered the product opened an account, a result that may be interpreted as a lower bound on the percentage of the population with time-inconsistent preferences under the plausible assumption that the new product would only be preferred by persons with time-inconsistent preferences. Second, the saving effects were substantial in percentage terms, although modest in nominal amounts. After six months, subjects in the treatment group increased saving by more than 20 percent relative to the control group. Among those that opened an account, saving increased by a startling 85 percent.

A second, and particularly intriguing, proposal that also addresses many of the behavioral obstacles to saving is the 'Save More Tomorrow' plan that has already been adopted by several employer-sponsored 401(k) plans (Thaler and Benartzi 2004). The plan allows employees to commit themselves today to increasing their savings rate at some later date. Enrollees pre-commit to saving a larger percentage of their salary each time they receive an increase in pay. This plan essentially makes inertia work in favor of employee saving by establishing a higher saving rate as the default each salary cycle. Workers can commit today at no near-term cost, but saving will increase if they fail to act in the future. Early implementation of the plan required each worker to meet with a financial consultant to determine the worker's saving needs. Most workers were found to be undersaving and the consultant recommended that these workers immediately increase contributions to the saving plan. Most workers rejected this advice. However, over 80 percent of the 'undersavers' were willing to accept a proposal to increase their contribution rate by 3 percent each time they received an increase in pay. The results were dramatic. After two years the savings rates of participants—erstwhile reluctant savers—nearly quadrupled.

# 4 Conclusions

The trend to defined contribution plans in many nations has placed increased emphasis on the capacity of households to make decisions about saving for retirement. Recent research documenting unanticipated drops in consumption at retirement, as well as less than ideal replacement rates after retirement, suggests that households may not be making the best saving decisions for their future. Many households fail to plan for their retirement or fail to carry out a saving plan. This chapter identifies and provides evidence on a host of psychological and behavioral factors that may impede either planning or saving itself. Many of these are shown to have large effects on saving outcomes, a puzzling result from the perspective of conventional economic models that treat these factors as inconsequential because they affect neither the financial constraints households face nor the financial reward to saving.

The challenge facing governments and employers is how to exploit the lessons of behavioral research to design saving plans to encourage individuals to make decisions that are in their own long-term best self-interest. One approach is to restrict choice. Most of the 30 public sector defined contribution plans introduced in the last two decades mandate contributions. This takes most of the problems associated with planning, self-control, procrastination, and ill-informed investment choices off the table. Some of these plans also take asset allocation decisions completely out of the hands of participants (e.g. Australia) while others (e.g. Sweden and Chile) permit a great deal of individual choice. In the latter case, behavioral research, as well as experience with these plans, shows that the menu of investment options offered and how they are presented can have substantial effects on actual saving decisions.

The lessons of behavioral research for plan design are perhaps most relevant for voluntary employer-based pension arrangements and personal saving decisions. Here the research suggests that certain key features of plan design can have significant effects on saving by addressing self-control problems, the tendency to procrastinate, and the cognitive difficulties associated with planning. In the United States, employers and other private sector plan providers have, in recent years, greatly increased the information and planning aids available to participants. Whereas in the past most 401(k)-type plans were 'take-it-or leave-it' offers to employees, most firms now recognize that leaving the retirement saving decision completely in the hands of the employee has resulted in poor financial choices by some employees, most notably low participation by low-income and less educated employees. Firms have begun to promote their saving plans among employees, and many firms now also use default options for participation, contribution levels, asset allocation, and cashing out to help their employees make prudent choices.

More generally, research on behavioral decision-making helps us understand how plan features that were considered second-order in the past—such as automatic enrollment, payroll deduction, the menu of investment options (including employer stock), deadlines, defaults, early withdrawal penalties, and mechanisms allowing participants to pre-commit—can be exploited to promote retirement saving. Researchers have only recently begun to understand how self-control, procrastination, cognitive limitations, and other behavioral traits affect economic choices. The challenge ahead is to better integrate the psychology of human behavior into conventional economic models of saving decisions.

# NOTE

The author thanks Gordon Clark, Anna Lusardi, and David Wise for valuable comments.

# REFERENCES

AGNEW, JULIE, and SZYKMAN, LISA. 2004. 'Asset allocation and information overload: the influence of information display, asset choice, and investor experience'. Center for Retirement Research, Boston College (May).

AINSLIE, GEORGE (1992). *Picoeconomics*. Cambridge: Cambridge University Press.

AMERIKS, JOHN, CAPLIN, ANDREW, and LEAHY, JOHN. (2003). 'Wealth accumulation and the propensity to plan'. *Quarterly Journal of Economics*, 1007–47.

—— —— —— and TYLER, TOM (2004). 'Measuring self-control'. NBER Working Paper 10514 (May).

ASHRAF, NAVA, KARLAN, DEAN, and YIN, WESLEY. (2004). 'Getting Odysseus to save: evidence from a commitment saving product in the Philippines'. Unpublished.

BENARTZI, SHLOMO, and THALER, RICHARD (2001). 'Naive diversification strategies in defined contribution savings plans'. *American Economic Review*, 91: 79–98.

BERNHEIM, DOUGLAS (1995). 'Do households appreciate their financial vulnerabilities? An analysis of actions, perceptions, and public policy'. *Tax Policy and Economic Growth*. Washington, D.C.: American Council for Capital Formation, 1–30.

BERNHEIM, (1998). 'Financial Illiteracy, Education and Retirement Saving', in Olivia Mitchell and Sylvester Schieber (eds.), *Living with Defined Contribution Pensions*. Philadelphia: Pension Research Council, 38–68.

—— and GARRETT, DANIEL (2003). 'The effects of financial education in the workplace: evidence from a survey of households'. *Journal of Public Economics*, 87: 487–519.

—— and RANGEL, ANTONIO (2003). 'Emotions, cognition, and savings: theory and policy'. Stanford University.

BOERSCH-SUPAN, AXEL (ed.). (2003). *Life-Cycle Savings and Public Policy*. London: Academic Press.

CHOI, JAMES, MARDRIAN, BRIGITTE, METRICK, ANDREW, and LAIBSON, DAVID (2002). 'Defined contribution pensions: plan rules, participant decisions, and the path of least resistance'. *Tax Policy and the Economy*, 16: 67–114.

—— —— —— —— (2003). 'Active decisions: a natural experiment in savings'. Unpublished (Dec.).

—— —— —— —— (2004). 'For better or for worse: default effects and 401(k) savings behavior', in David A. Wise (ed.), *Perspectives in the Economics of Aging*. Chicago: University of Chicago Press.

CLARK, ROBERT, and D'AMBROSIO, MADELINE (2003). 'Ignorance is not bliss: the importance of financial education'. *Research Dialogue*, No. 78. New York: TIAA-CREF Institute.

Congressional Budget Office (2003). *Baby Boomers' Retirement Prospects: An Overview*. Washington, D.C.: US GPO.

DUFLO, ESTER, and SAEZ, EMMANUEL (2003). 'The role of information and social interactions in retirement plan decisions: evidence from a randomized experiment'. *Quarterly Journal of Economics* 68: 815–42.

Employee Benefit Research Institute (2004). *The 2004 Retirement Confidence Survey Summary of Findings*. Washington, D.C.: EBRI.

FREDERICK, SHANE, LOEWENSTEIN, GEORGE, and O'DONOGHUE, TED (2002). 'Time discounting and time preference: a critical review'. *Journal of Economic Literature*, 40: 351–401.

GUSTMAN, ALAN, and STEINMEIER, THOMAS (2004). 'What people don't know about their pensions and social Security', in W. Gale and J. Shoven (eds.), *Public Policies and Private Pensions*. Washington, D.C.: Brookings Institution, 57–119.

HUBERMAN, GUR, and JIANG, WEI (2004). 'The 1/N Hueristic in 401(k) Plans'. Columbia Business School. Unpublished.

HURD, MICHAEL and MCGARRY, KATHLEEN (1995). 'Evaluation of the subjective probabilities of survival in the health and retirement study'. *Journal of Human Resources*, 30: S268–S292.

—— and ZISSIMOPOULOS, JULIE (2000). 'Inadequate retirement savings: an experimental approach to understanding saving behavior'. Mimeo. Rand.

IYENGAR, SHEENA, JIANG, WEI, and HUBERMAN, GUR (2004). 'How much choice is too much?', in O. Mitchell and S. Utkus (eds.), *Pension Design and Structure: New Lessons from Behavioral Finance*. Philadelphia: Pension Research Council.

John Hancock Financial Services (2002). *Eighth Annual Defined Contribution Survey*. Boston.

LAIBSON, DAVID (1997). 'Golden eggs and hyperbolic discounting'. *Quarterly Journal of Economics*, 62: 443–77.

—— (1998). 'Comment: personal retirement saving programs and asset accumulation', in D. A. Wise (ed.), *Frontiers in the Economics of Aging*. Chicago: University of Chicago Press, 106–20.

—— Repetto, Andrea, and Tobacman, Jeremy (1998). 'Self-control and saving for retirement'. *Brookings Papers on Economic Activity*, 91–196.

Lusardi, Annamaria (1999a). 'Information, expectations, and savings for retirement', in Henry Aaron (ed.), *Behavioral Dimensions of Retirement Economics*. Washington, D.C.: Brookings Institution and Russel Sage Foundation, 81–115.

—— (1999b). 'Saving for retirement: the importance of planning'. *Research Dialogue*, No. 66. New York: TIAA-CREF Institute.

—— (2003). 'Planning and the effectiveness of retirement seminars'. Unpublished. Dartmouth College.

—— (2004). 'Financial education and saving', in O. Mitchell and S. Utkus (eds.), *Pension Design and Structure: New Lessons From Behavioral Finance*. Philadelphia: Pension Research Council.

Madrian, Brigitte, and Shea, Dennis (2001). 'The power of suggestion: inertia in 401(k) saving participation and saving behavior'. *Quarterly Journal of Economics*, 116/4: 1149–87.

O'Donoghue, Ted, and Rabin, Matthew (1999a). 'Doing it now or later'. *American Economic Review*, 89/1: 103–24.

—— —— (1999b). 'Procrastination in preparing for retirement', in Henry Aaron (ed.), *Behavioral Dimensions of Retirement Economics*, Washington, D.C.: Brookings Institution and Russell Sage Foundation, 125–56.

Schelling, Thomas (1978). 'Egonomics, or the art of self-management'. *American Economic Review*, 68/2: 290–4.

Scott, Jason, and Stein, Gregory (2004). 'Retirement security in a DC world: using behavioral finance to bridge the expertise gap', in O. Mitchell and S. Utkus (eds.), *Pension Design and Structure: New Lessons from Behavioral Finance*. Philadelphia: Pension Research Council.

Strotz, Robert (1956). 'Myopia and inconsistency in dynamic utility maximization'. *Review of Economic Studies*, 23/3: 165–80.

Thaler, Richard, and Benartzi, Shlomo (2004). 'Save more tomorrow'. *Journal of Political Economy*, 112/1 (part 1): s164-s187.

# CHAPTER 31

# HOUSING WEALTH AND RETIREMENT SAVINGS

## WILLIAM C. APGAR AND ZHU XIAO DI

## 1 INTRODUCTION

The rapid rise in home prices in countries around the world has focused new attention on the role that housing and housing wealth play in enhancing the financial security for families and individuals as they move into their retirement years. This is especially true in the United States where after a decade of steady increases in home values, residential real estate has grown to become the largest single asset class held by households with heads aged 65 or older. With so much wealth tied up in owner-occupied housing, little wonder that the popular press in the United States provides extensive coverage of the 'housing bubble' and what will happen should that bubble suddenly burst.

Given the importance of housing wealth as an overall component of the wealth holdings of older homeowners, until recently, surprisingly little was known about how housing wealth influences the consumption and investment decisions of households, especially as they relate to retirees. This chapter summarizes available literature on these topics and assesses the pluses and minuses of having housing wealth play such an important role in providing for the income security of older homeowners.

There are many reasons to be concerned about the reliance on housing wealth as a source of retirement savings. Even as homeownership rates continue to rise, millions still rent. Moreover, there can be little doubt that renters in general, and low-income renters in particular, face a bleak retirement future given the relatively limited reach of current social security and other income support systems now in place. But rather than condemn renters to a life of limited wealth accumulation, it is important to create new investment vehicles that will support savings and investment by renters. Just as the current housing finance and tax system makes it relatively easy to invest in real estate, a balanced national housing and income support system should provide expanded opportunities for renters to accumulate wealth by investing in other financial assets.

While the situation facing lower-income renters merits special attention, millions of homeowning retired people also face serious challenges. Here it is important to recognize that readily available national data on wealth trends mask significant regional variation. Housing markets are distinctly local in nature. Even as home prices move up sharply in one region, they may lag behind elsewhere. As a result, there is a certain lottery-like element to the role that home equity buildup plays as a source of retirement savings, with the winners generally being those lucky enough to live in areas where home prices have appreciated most rapidly just as they prepare to move into their retirement years.

While acquiring a home can boost wealth accumulation, many retired people face unmanageable housing-payment burdens. Many own their home 'free and clear', but a growing number are burdened by the increasing amount of debt they carry into later life. Moreover, despite these affordability pressures, many elderly people are unwilling or unable to downsize their consumption of housing. What is needed is the creation of new financial instruments designed to meet the particular problems faced by 'house rich, cash poor' retirees, as well as expanded efforts to create new affordable housing options that best meet the needs of older people.

These observations are a reminder that housing wealth accumulation is no substitute for a comprehensive set of housing and income support policies designed to help households prepare for retirement. Rather than simply provide income support payments to retirees, the best retirement support policy will undoubtedly involve a mix of income transfer programs and housing assistance efforts that enable retired people to sell their homes and tap into accumulated home equity. Failure to think creatively about how best to coordinate income assistance and housing assistance efforts will most certainly result in having pension and income support systems continue to struggle to meet the retirement needs of current and future generations of retired persons, while at the same time leaving hundreds of billions of dollars of home equity to sit idly on the sidelines.

This chapter is divided into three main sections and a conclusion. The first section discusses recent trends in wealth accumulation with a particular focus on the accumulation of housing wealth by older households. The next section examines the impact of housing wealth on consumption and investment activities, and demonstrates that for most households, homeownership opens up new pathways for additional wealth accumulation. Given the fact that housing wealth is the largest component of wealth for most households, the chapter then turns to a discussion of the several significant risks that threaten to undermine the benefit that older Americans derive from accumulated housing wealth. The concluding section offers some brief observations on policy approaches designed to enhance the ability of housing wealth to add to the financial security of older people.

## 2 Residential Real Estate and the Wealth of Seniors

### 2.1 Housing Equity Key to Growing Wealth for Many Older Homeowners

Over the decade of the 1990s, much of the increase in aggregate wealth holdings was linked to the growth of wealth among homeowning households (see Table 31.1).[1] Median net wealth holdings for homeowners with heads aged 65 to 74 increased over the 1992 to 2001 period by close to $100,000 to just under $250,000. Households with heads aged 75 or older posted similar gains, while homeowning households with heads aged less than 65 added just $42,000 in median wealth over the period. In contrast, the wealth of renting households of all ages lagged far behind owners over the period.

After a decade of steady increase in home values, now residential real estate represents the largest single asset class owned by seniors.[2] According to the 2001 Survey of Consumer Finances, over 80 percent of all seniors owned a home, and these homes were valued at nearly $3.168 trillion. Including the $781 billion of other residential real estate owned by seniors (largely second homes), the total value of residential real estate owned by seniors increases to $3.95 trillion. As a result in 2001, residential real estate accounted for some 30 percent of the nearly $13.2 trillion in aggregate asset holding of seniors.

In contrast, only 21.1 percent of all households with heads aged 65 and older owned publicly traded stocks. Even expanding the concept of stock ownership to combine the direct ownership of publicly traded stocks plus stocks owned indirectly through mutual funds, retirement accounts, and other managed assets, the share of seniors owning stocks only increases to 36.8 percent. Under this expanded definition, seniors own—either directly or indirectly—nearly $3.4 trillion in stocks,

Table 31.1 Wealth holdings of older homeowners grew rapidly in the 1990s (Median net wealth in 2001 dollars)

|  | 1992 | | | 2001 | | |
| --- | --- | --- | --- | --- | --- | --- |
| Age of Head | Owners | Renters | All Households | Owners | Renters | All Households |
| Less that 65 | 112,300 | 4,400 | 48,500 | 154,100 | 4,500 | 67,900 |
| 65 to 74 | 151,800 | 4,400 | 122,200 | 249,700 | 6,000 | 176,700 |
| 74 or older | 140,400 | 7,600 | 107,500 | 243,000 | 7,000 | 151,400 |
| All ages | 123,600 | 4,600 | 62,100 | 171,800 | 4,800 | 86,100 |

*Source*: Joint Center for Housing Studies tabulations of Survey of Consumer Finances. See also discussion of these figures in Di (2003).

an amount that represents just 25.8 percent of their aggregate asset holdings.[3] Moreover, since the 2001 Survey of Consumer Finances was taken before the full brunt of the stock market crash was evident, the 25.8 percent share undoubtedly overstates the relative importance of stocks as a share of wealth holdings of older households.

## 2.2 Mortgage Debt Also Grew for Older Homeowners

Building on strong homeownership gains and house price appreciation, the aggregate value of the nation's owner-occupied housing inventory increased an inflation-adjusted 50 percent to $13.1 trillion from 1989 to 2001. Over this same period there was a corresponding 89 percent increase in mortgage debt to $4.4 trillion. By 2001, mortgage debt accounted for 33.6 percent of residential value, up from 26.4 percent in 1989. In part, this increase in mortgage debt reflects the fact that the tax reform of 1986 eliminated the deductibility of many other forms of interest, encouraging homeowners to substitute mortgage debt for unsecured consumer loans. More recently, favorable interest rates not only encouraged households to take on more debt to buy bigger and better homes, these low rates also prompted a wave of cash out refinancing that enabled homeowners to pay off higher priced credit card and other unsecured forms of debt.

Borrowers of all ages are carrying more mortgage debt, yet the increase among older households has been striking. While it appears from the cross-sectional data in Table 31.2 that mortgage debt declines at age 35–44, tracking specific age cohorts over time reveals that each succeeding generation is carrying more mortgage debt into their older years (Masnick *et al.* 2005). For example, only 41 percent of owner

Table 31.2 Seniors now hold more mortgage debt

| Age of head | Share with outstanding mortgages (Percent) | | Median outstanding balance of those with mortgages (2001 dollars) | |
| --- | --- | --- | --- | --- |
| | 1989 | 2001 | 1989 | 2001 |
| Less than 35 | 88.5 | 89.6 | 61,000 | 77,000 |
| 35 to 44 | 87.7 | 87.8 | 55,400 | 80,000 |
| 45 to 54 | 76.2 | 78.4 | 36,000 | 75,000 |
| 55 to 64 | 46.2 | 58.9 | 27,700 | 55,000 |
| 65 or older | 20.7 | 26.4 | 12,500 | 44,000 |
| ALL | 63.9 | 67.7 | 48,500 | 75,000 |

*Source*: Joint Center for Housing Studies tabulations of Survey of Consumer Finances. See also discussion of these figures in Di (2003).

households with head aged 55 to 64 in 2001 had paid off their mortgages, compared with 54 percent of their same-age counterparts in 1989. Moreover, one in four (or some 26 percent) of owner households with heads aged 65 or older had not yet retired their mortgage—nearly six percentage points higher than the 1989 figure.

Even more remarkable is the level of debt these older homeowners carry into their retirement years. After adjusting for inflation, the median mortgage debt of those older homeowners more than tripled to $44,000 in 2001, while the mortgage debt of slightly younger mortgage borrowers (aged 55 to 64) nearly doubled. Consistent with the general trend to substitute mortgage debt for non-mortgage debt, in 2001 home mortgage debt accounted for 70 percent of the total debt of owners aged 65 and older—up nearly 20 percentage points since 1989.

## 2.3 Housing Wealth is Widely Distributed

Adding to the importance of housing as a storehouse of wealth is the fact that housing wealth is more widely distributed with respect to income than is true for stock market holdings. Stock market wealth is especially concentrated in the hands of the highest income households, while home equity is an especially important source of wealth holding for those in the bottom fifth of the income distribution. While the top 1 percent of stock holders own 33.5 percent of total stock wealth, the top 1 percent of owners of residential real estate own just 13 percent of the total. In contrast, only 12.4 percent of households of all ages falling into the bottom 20 percent of the income distribution own stocks and control just 2 percent of aggregate stock wealth, while 50 percent of these lowest-income households own a home and hold 15 percent of aggregate home equity.

Many retired people fall squarely into the group of 'cash poor, house rich' households. For example, households with head aged 65 or older account for some 8.4 million of the nearly 20 million households falling in the lowest quintile of the income distribution. Of these lowest-income seniors, 5.8 million (or 70 percent) are homeowners, but only 6 percent own stocks, including stock owned indirectly through retirement accounts and mutual funds.

Of course these aggregate national statistics mask significant regional variation in the importance of housing as a storehouse of wealth. Though returns to investments in stock are more or less constant across regions, housing returns can and do vary significantly from one region to the next. While higher house prices may bring with them higher property taxes and insurance costs, they also provide greater potential for home equity buildup—an additional source of wealth accumulation that is not available to households living in regions with more limited home price appreciation.

## 2.4 Cross-National Comparisons

The importance of housing as a storehouse of wealth is hardly unique to the United States. In 2001, the aggregate value of residential real estate owned by households in the United States accounted for 32 percent of gross household asset holdings. For Canada, the comparable figure for housing as a share of gross asset holdings stood at 46 percent in 1999 (Statistics Canada 2001). Though the information is not strictly comparable, the Reserve Bank of Australia (2000) estimated in 1999 that for the United Kingdom, 'dwellings' accounted for 38 percent of total wealth, while for Australia this ratio was as high as 57 percent. Finally, data on the composition of wealth holdings in selected OECD countries for 1998 suggest that housing is also an important component of aggregate wealth holdings in six of the G-7 nations (Canada, France, Germany, Italy, the United Kingdom, and the United States). Among the G-7 (OECD 2000), the exception appears to be Japan, where housing assets apparently comprise only 19 percent of tangible assets and only 10 percent of total assets.[4]

Of course each of these estimates depends on recent trends in housing markets, stock markets, and other asset markets. Particularly problematic is assessing whether the recent runup of home prices in a diverse set of nations will persist, or will home prices move back down to levels more in keeping with longer-term trends. In its most recent report on global house price indicators for 2005, *The Economist* noted that while home prices in the United States appreciated fully 65 percent over the 1997 to 2004 period, house price appreciation over this period was even stronger in Australia, Britain, France, Ireland, the Netherlands, South Africa, Spain, and Sweden, though the same study also noted that there were some signs of softening (if not outright declines) in home prices in Australia, Britain, and New Zealand.[5]

As an element of wealth building, home price appreciation is decidedly a double-edged sword. Home price increases generally boost homeowners' equity and thus add to household wealth accumulation. At the same time, home price appreciation can also reduce housing affordability and limit the number of potential first-time homebuyers able to make the transition to homeownership. Somewhat remarkably, despite reduction in overall affordability of homebuying, the number of homeowners in the United States—and especially young homebuyers—has continued to move up more or less steadily since 1993. As a result, though the wealth holdings of older Americans moved up sharply over this period, younger generations also experienced an increase in their wealth holdings (Joint Center for Housing Studies 2005).

Elsewhere, it appears that affordability problems are having a more serious impact on the overall growth in homeownership. In Australia, for example, the share of households owning their own homes moved steadily upward from around 50 percent in the 1950s to more than 70 percent by the early 1990s. Since then, there are clear signs that the upward movement of homeownership is 'unraveling', as younger Australians struggle to purchase a home of their own.[6]

Decline in the homeownership rate among younger Australians could have implications not just for how Australians are housed today, but could also adversely impact the financial security of younger generations as they reach their retirement years. Though estimates of trends in wealth holdings by age differ, they agree that wealth accumulation among households aged 45 or less has virtually come to a halt in Australia over the past decade.[7] A future rebound of home buying by younger Australians could slow or reverse the emergence of what appears to be a growing generational gap in wealth holdings. Yet for now, the current trend has sparked a vigorous debate as to whether the social safety net will have to adjust, and particularly the role that housing policy must play to help provide for the long-term financial security of the currently less wealthy generation of young Australians.[8]

# 3 THE IMPACT OF HOMEOWNERSHIP ON CONSUMER SPENDING AND INVESTMENT

## 3.1 Using Housing Wealth to Create New Wealth

For many, purchasing a home is the first step on a pathway to wealth accumulation. Work by Di *et al.* (2003) suggests that even controlling for factors likely to account for household differences in permanent income and the marginal propensity to save and to invest, homeowners build wealth more quickly than otherwise comparable renter households.

Of course, the investment motive is just one of many reasons why people purchase a home. Families and individuals in the United States and many other Western European countries view homeowning as superior to renting for a variety of social and psychological reasons (Apgar 2004). What is important here is that once they choose to purchase a home, even if the motive hinges on reasons only marginally linked to investment and wealth accumulation, homeowners can borrow against home equity to 'cultivate' new ways to build wealth.[9]

By tapping home equity to start a business, invest in stocks, or spend their money on education, homeowners have the potential to increase income growth and provide for their financial security in their older years. In effect, home equity becomes the central focus of a household portfolio management operation, in which homeowners periodically adjust their assets and debts.[10] Of course, while it is also possible for investors to borrow against their equity in stocks, bonds, or other financial or non-financial assets, the ability of average homeowners to tap home equity to fund acquisition of other wealth-generating assets is unique. Indeed, growth of new forms of home equity loans and lines of credit liens has made borrowing against home equity a very simple, fast, and reasonably inexpensive activity (Canner *et al.* 1998).

Despite these benefits of homeownership, the observation that homeowners accumulate more wealth over time than renters is not equivalent to saying the financial returns to homeownership exceed those of other types of investment. Indeed, many argue that buying stock would be a superior investment. Depending on the time period analyzed, return on investment in a home has been shown to lead or lag behind common stocks, though returns on investment in homes generally exceed those of generally safer corporate bonds and US government securities.

In the absence of certain knowledge about future trends in the housing market and the general economy, it seems a futile exercise to even attempt to answer the question 'is home ownership or the stock market the better investment?' Instead, the better question is whether purchasing a home—along with its potential for financial leverage—is a good early step to make on the pathway to long-term wealth accumulation. Here the answer appears to be an unambiguous yes.

Even so, homeownership does not necessarily help to build wealth in all instances. Purchasing a unit with mortgage financing further magnifies the risks and rewards of investing in a durable capital asset.[11] The leverage associated with a debt-financed acquisition implies that any given percentage increase in property values will generate an even larger percentage increase in the owner's equity in the property. Yet higher leverage also means that even a relatively small decline in housing prices can leave a homeowner with a mortgage that exceeds the value of their home. For credit-impaired borrowers, higher leverage also will substantially increase mortgage interest payments. If a borrower is unable to repay outstanding mortgage obligations, or the home they purchased actually declines in value, rather than being a pathway to increased wealth accumulation, homeownership can also be the pathway to default, foreclosure, and financial ruin.

## 3.2 Housing Wealth's Contribution to Household Consumption

Much of the current empirical work on wealth and consumption still builds on the Life-Cycle Hypothesis (LCH) developed in the 1950s and 1960s.[12] The LCH predicts that in the face of variations in income over the life course, consumers will either borrow against future earnings, or spend out of accumulated wealth to smooth out consumption levels. For example, LCH implies that younger individuals will tend to borrow against expected rising future incomes. As incomes rise during mid-life, individuals will become net savers and accumulate wealth that will enable them to maintain spending in later life. Of course, the pace of drawing down assets in later life will depend on the life expectancy, whether or not they would like to make a bequest upon death, as well as how rapidly current income is projected to decline with retirement. As a result, LCH implies that consumption spending will vary not only according to changes in individual and family wealth levels, but also depending on the age of the household, desired level of bequests, projected earnings, and life expectancy.

Despite being fundamentally a theory about microeconomic behavior, early empirical tests of LCH were based on highly aggregated data. Moreover, even though particular households may have differing views about likely volatility in the future value of various assets, as well as differing views about their willingness to divest any particular asset to fund current consumption, early empirical estimates assumed that the impact on consumption did not vary by type of wealth. For example, in their path-breaking paper, Ando and Modigliani (1963) estimate that the current consumption for the United States increases by $60 for every $1,000 increase in total household wealth, regardless of the composition of that wealth.

With improvement in both available data and econometric modeling techniques, over time greater attention has been paid to disaggregating wealth into various components. Estimating differing marginal propensities to consume over varying wealth categories is no easy feat, especially in light of the fact that changes in housing wealth and stock market wealth tend to be highly collinear when measured at the national level. In an effort to overcome this collinearity issue, Case *et al.* (2001) used state level data to identify the independent effects of housing and stock market wealth, and hence were able to take advantage of the significant variation in housing price appreciation that occurs across spatially segmented markets. Using these state-level data, Case and colleagues estimated that the marginal propensity to consume out of financial wealth is 2 percent, while the marginal propensity to consume out of housing wealth is in the range of 5–9 percent.

At first blush, these results may seem counter-intuitive. Housing wealth is relatively illiquid, and the transactions costs of selling a home tend to be high, at least when compared with the cost of selling stocks or bonds. Apparently, the recent rise of a wide range of home equity loans and lines of credit has substantially increased the ability of households to translate housing wealth into cash. As a result of these financial innovations, the Joint Center for Housing Studies and Macroeconomic Advisors suggest that households spend on average 5.5 cents a year out of every dollar increase in house value. Moreover, this additional spending hits its long-term average within a year of when the increase in house value occurs—much more quickly than households spend gains in stock wealth, which they may view as less secure (Belsky and Prakken 2004).

## 3.3 Cross-National Comparisons of Housing Wealth Effects

With house prices on the rise in countries around the world, there are a growing number of cross-national studies on the impact of housing wealth on consumption, including several studies that provide separate estimates of the marginal propensity to consume housing wealth and financial wealth. For example, work completed by OECD researchers (Catte *et al.* 2004) suggests that just as in the United States, changes in housing wealth in the Australia, Canada, the Netherlands, and the United Kingdom also appear to have a significant effect on consumption with the marginal propensity to consume housing wealth ranging from 5 to 8 percent. Moreover, Catte *et al.* (2004) estimated that Australia, Canada, the Netherlands, and the United Kingdom also mirror the United States in that marginal propensity to consume housing wealth appears to be greater than the propensity to consume financial wealth.[13]

In contrast, Catte *et al.* (2004) find that the marginal propensity to consume housing wealth in France, Germany, Italy, Japan, and Spain is either small (less than 2 percent) or statistically insignificant. In addition, in these countries, the impact of housing wealth on consumption was generally smaller than that of financial wealth.[14]

Hong Kong, China presents yet another pattern (Cutler 2004). There the marginal propensity to consume housing wealth of 3 percent is more or less in the middle of the range of estimates for the countries examined by the OECD research, and statistically identical to the estimate obtained for the marginal propensity to consume financial wealth.

Though specific empirical results for individual countries undoubtedly reflect a number of factors peculiar to each country, several structural factors stand out. First, the impact of wealth on consumption seems to vary systematically with respect to the distribution of wealth holdings by people of differing income. For example, Case et al. (2001) argue that the relatively high marginal propensity to consume housing wealth in the United States reflects in part the fact that housing wealth tends to be held by households in all income segments, while stock wealth tends to be more concentrated.

Similarly, in explaining why the marginal propensity to consume housing wealth tends to be lower in Hong Kong than elsewhere, Cutler notes that this is consistent with the fact that in Hong Kong housing wealth is more skewed toward the rich. Finally Dvornak and Kohler (2003) argue that the reason that the impact of stock market wealth on consumption is generally smaller in European Countries than in the United States reflects the fact that stock ownership in the United States is more widely distributed than in Europe.[15]

Theory also suggests that the impact of housing wealth on consumption will be greater in countries with financially more sophisticated mortgage and financial markets that enable consumers to borrow against or otherwise transform illiquid housing wealth into cash. For example, unlike the United States, 'equity extraction' is relatively rare in Japan, a feature which helps explain why Japan appears to have the greatest gap between the marginal propensity to consume housing wealth and the marginal propensity to consume financial wealth of all the major industrial counties studied to date.

## 3.4 The Changing Impact of Housing Wealth Over the Life Course

The pace of wealth accumulation, and hence the 'wealth effect' is likely to vary over the life course. Families and individuals can begin acquiring assets at any age, but most households typically begin by accumulating financial assets. Starting the wealth building cycle with financial assets makes sense since mutual funds and certificates of deposit are available in small denominations. In contrast, housing is a lumpy investment. While in principle families could purchase a partial ownership share in a home (as in time share vacation homes), more typically young families draw down on any accumulated financial assets and take on substantial mortgage debt to acquire their first home. As a result, the typical first-time buyer has put most or all of its 'eggs' in one asset basket (Tracy et al. 1999).

Having made the transition from renting to owning, households are now to free reduce the share of total assets held in residential real estate. In particular as families and individuals age and begin to save for retirement, stocks, bonds, savings, and other financial assets grow as a share of total asset holdings. Moreover, as noted earlier, if the value of their home appreciates, they have the option of refinancing their home to take out cash to acquire additional financial assets and/or invest in business, education, or other income-producing assets.

Of course the extent to which the residential real estate as a share of total assets declines depends in part on housing mobility. As long as families continue to trade up to bigger and better homes, housing as a share of total assets will remain high. Once a household begins to settle into a more 'permanent' home, however, the possibility for asset diversification increases and the ratio of the value of owner-occupied housing to total assets declines. This is also true as 'empty nesters' downsize their spacious housing, though often this downsizing in space involves an increase in housing quality and hence produces little or no reduction in the aggregate value of residential real estate holdings.

Finally, with retirement, households will begin to draw down assets to offset loss of income, and their portfolio will tend to tilt back in favor of placing more weight on housing. In previous decades, this process might be halted as older owners sold their homes and either purchased a more modest house or returned to renting. While this is undoubtedly happening, many seniors are choosing instead to remain in their homes. For example, a recent study by Stephen Venti and David Wise (2000), using data from the Survey of Income and Program Participation and the Survey of Asset and Health Dynamics of the Oldest Old, finds that barring changes in household composition, households with a head over 70 typically do not use home equity to support general non-housing consumption. This behavior is consistent with an AARP survey that found that 95 percent of persons aged 75 or older agreed with the statement 'What I would really like to do is stay in my current residence as long as possible'.

# 4 Future Risks

## 4.1 Will the Housing Bubble Burst?

In light of the importance of home equity as a source of financial security for older homeowners, little wonder that policy analysts and commentators worry about the consequences of a sudden and widespread decline in home prices. In part, the recent increase in home prices simply reflects higher housing quality standards and the larger size of newly constructed homes. Even so, it has been the rapid run-up of land prices—supported in large measure by restrictive zoning and land use practices—that have pushed overall housing prices to new record highs in metropolitan areas across the country. Nationwide, the Joint Center for Housing Studies estimated that land price inflation accounted for over 75 percent of the total inflation-adjusted price increase for homes of this type over the decade 1990–2000 (Joint Center for Housing Studies 2002). Of course in areas where zoning and land use restrictions are most stringent, land and housing prices have moved up even faster over the past decade.

Given that higher home prices are rooted primarily in rising land costs, the question remains as to whether continued price pressure will stifle housing demand and precipitate a steep drop-off in housing market activity. Just as a high price-earnings ratio often signal a strong downside correction in the stock market, some pessimists argue that with median home prices rising faster than median household income, it is only a matter of time before housing demand also experiences a sharp downside correction. Once they start to fall, declining house prices could in turn undermine consumer confidence, erode home equity, and send the housing market into a tailspin.[16]

Yet the comparison between the stock market and the housing market is misleading at best. Because people live in, as well as invest in, their homes, most owners choose to stay put when prices first show signs of softening. This reduces the number of homes on the market and helps bring supply and demand back into balance, thereby forestalling faster and sharper declines. In addition, as incomes at the high end of the distribution continue to pull away from those in the middle, shifts in median income are increasingly a poor proxy for the relative purchasing power of potential home buyers. Indeed, Joint Center for Housing Studies data suggest that, despite rapid home price appreciation, various measures of housing cost burdens for higher-income home-buyer households—the group that actually constitutes the biggest share of all homebuyers—were little changed over the decade (Joint Center for Housing Studies 2005).

## 4.2 Growing Inequality in Access to Homeownership

While it seems unlikely that home prices will fall precipitously in the future, it still is true that persistent homeownership affordability problems will continue to limit the ability of low- and moderate-income families to realize the wealth building potential of homeownership. In particular, for many, down-payment remains a barrier to home ownership. Lower down-payment requirements help families get around this barrier, but only by having buyers pay higher interest rates and bear the risks associated with owning a highly leveraged asset.

While shared appreciation mortgages have existed for some time, this form of lending needs to be perfected. For example Caplin *et al.* (1997) propose the formation of 'housing partnerships', a financing arrangement where a homebuyer shares ownership with an outside investor. In effect, rather than take on a debt partner through a mortgage, the homeowner would take on an equity partner to help remove the downpayment constraint. Such partnerships would significantly reduce the up-front costs and monthly carrying costs of owning a home, and enable families to devote more income to other forms of investments to help them diversify their portfolio.

Even under the best of circumstances, however, it is unlikely that homeownership is a universally obtainable goal. Whether because of lifestyle choices, affordability constraints, or other factors, some households will always remain renters. Yet rather than condemn these remaining renters to a life of limited wealth accumulation, it is important to create new financial instruments that will support savings and investment. For example, it would be possible to create a class of reasonably secure corporate equities that could be purchased on margin and that would provide a non-housing alternative to the currently available highly leveraged opportunity to purchase a first home. With proper insurance to reduce whatever risk exists in these investments, along with subsidies that reward thrift, it would be possible to help renters accumulate financial assets just as the current housing finance system makes it relatively easy to invest in real estate.

## 4.3 The Growing Housing Cost Burden of Older Homeowners

Overall, 5.1 million lowest-income seniors—defined here as households with head aged 65 or older and an income that falls in the lowest 20 percent of the income distribution—own a home free and clear of any mortgage debt. Even so, given their limited incomes and the high cost of property taxes, utilities, and other home operating costs, one in four of these debt-free lowest-income owners pay more than 50 percent of their incomes for housing.

Having to pay down mortgage debt only further increases the housing cost burden of lowest-income older homeowners. For this group, the share paying more than 50 percent of income for housing rises to nearly 75 percent. In the past, the early age at which households became debt free served as a cushion to absorb the consequences of falling income in later life. Though improving health and life expectancy has led many to decide to remain in the labor force longer, the added pressure of having to meet mortgage payment obligations should reinforce this upward trend in elderly labor force participation.

Should an older homeowner be unable or unwilling to meet their mortgage obligations, they can always sell their home, retire their outstanding debt, and move to a smaller home or become a renter. Unfortunately, limited growth in housing subsidies, along with limited production of housing suitable for older families and individuals, especially the frail elderly, means that downsizing may not be possible in many situations. In situations where neither continued employment nor downsizing is practical, the housing-cost burdens of older homeowners could rise, squeezing out other consumption activity including increasingly important healthcare expenditures.

## 4.4 Equity Stripping and Mortgage Abuse

The growing availability of home equity loans and lines of credit presents both new opportunities and new risks to equity rich and cash poor older homeowners. In most instances, the new mortgage delivery system has expanded access to prime mortgages on favorable terms. As noted earlier, growth of new mortgage products has enabled many older homeowners to maintain relatively high level of consumption, without having to sell their home to do so.

Unfortunately, all too often the way these new mortgage products are delivered puts many lowest-income older homeowners at risk. In particular, over the past decade, the home equity lending market has been increasingly served by non-prime lenders driven by brokers, who aggressively 'push-market' loans to high risk families and individuals. Given that older homeowners often have significant equity, even owners with limited ability to repay a mortgage can still get loans, since the loan is backed by relatively high levels of collateral (Joint Center for Housing Studies 2004).

Of course, in a market where people can comparison shop, a broker may lose business if costs are too high. Unfortunately, many older homeowners apparently do not seek out loans, but rather are sold on the idea of borrowing additional amounts of money after extensive outreach or marketing by brokers. Available survey data (Kim-Sung and Hermanson 2003) suggest that these 'push-marketing' techniques often leave older borrowers with mortgage loans that are overpriced and/or contain abusive features. In the extreme case 'push-marketing' can saddle borrowers with debt that they are unable to repay; a situation that can lead to foreclosure and/or a loss of whatever remaining equity the borrower had in the home.

## 4.5 The Growing Number of 'House Rich, Income Poor' Households

Next, it is important to encourage older homeowners to make better use of their home equity. Clearly, many households are reluctant to sell their home and move as a way to tap home equity. Home equity loans can help older owners convert equity to much-needed cash, but often leave families unable to meet their mortgage payment obligations. Reverse mortgages can also help older families convert home equity to cash, but with households living longer, the risk associated with many home equity products is that the homeowner will outlive the annuity and be forced to move at an advanced age. Absent a guarantee that a senior will receive the annuity payment until they choose to move or die—as is the case with the Home Equity Conversion Mortgage (HECM) product offered by the FHA—the market for conventional reverse mortgage products has been limited indeed.

What is needed are new financial instruments designed to meet the particular problems faced by 'house rich, cash poor' households. For example, taking on an equity partner as described above is one way to reduce the payment burden associated with home equity loans. Instead of requiring a monthly payment, an investor partner would purchase a share of the future interest in the home. Not only would such a product provide much-needed resources to an equity rich and cash poor older homeowner, it would not burden the owner with greater mortgage payment burdens, nor require them to move after some specified period of time.

# 5 CONCLUSION

Housing wealth is likely to continue as the cornerstone of wealth holdings for retired people around the world for some time to come. As the baby-boomers age into their retirement years, the homeownership rate of households with heads aged 65 or higher is likely to rise, as will their housing wealth. At the same time, it is important to recognize that a growing homeownership rate is no substitute for a comprehensive set of housing and income support policies designed to enable all households—rich and poor alike—to accumulate income-producing assets that they can carry into their retirement years.

First and foremost, it is important to recognize the plight of the lowest-income elderly renters with both limited incomes and wealth holdings. Buying a home is not a wise decision for everyone. But rather than condemn renters to a life of limited wealth accumulations, it is important to create new investment vehicles that will support savings and investment by lower-income renters. At the same time, it is also important to create new methods to overcome affordability constraints to homeownership. Here it is important to create homebuying options that not only are affordable in the short run, but buffer these new buyers from the significant downside risks associated with owning a highly leveraged asset.

Next, it is important to encourage older homeowners to make better use of their home equity. Clearly many households are reluctant to sell their home and move as a way to tap home equity. Once again what is needed is creation of new financial instruments designed to meet the particular problems faced by 'house rich, cash poor' households. In addition, to help older homeowners convert their home equity to much-needed assistance, it is important that policy-makers focus on expanding the supply of affordable rental housing. Having focused so much attention on promoting homeownership, the irony is that when owners seek to cash in on their retirement nest egg, there is a severe shortage of affordable housing to accommodate the move.

And finally, even while working to improve the ability of families to accumulate housing wealth, it is important to recognize the downside of the current heavy reliance on housing wealth as a source of retirement savings. Accumulation of housing wealth undoubtedly enhances the well-being of many. At the same time, the inability of all households to realize the benefits of homeownership leaves behind gaping holes in the retirement security safety net. Enhanced coordination of income assistance and housing assistance efforts is essential if governments are to meet successfully the challenge of enabling all current and future generations to live out their retirement years with dignity.

# NOTES

1. Gross household wealth here is defined as the aggregate market value of financial and non-financial assets, and net wealth is defined as gross wealth less offsetting debt. Financial assets include retirement accounts, stocks, bonds, savings and money market accounts, and other financial assets, while non-financial includes value of real estate owned, as well as value of business, vehicles, and other real property. Offsetting debts include mortgages on residential real estate, as well as credit card and other forms of unsecured debt.
2. Throughout this chapter, seniors are defined as households with head aged 65 or older. Most seniors are retired (or at least have cut back on their participation in the labor market) but some still work. Even so, the data analysis presented in this chapter refers to seniors as a group, and does not discuss differing wealth and consumption patterns of working and non-working seniors.
3. Joint Center tabulations of 2001 Survey of Consumer Finances. See Aizcorbe et al. (2003) for more complete discussion of terms 'direct' and 'indirect' stock ownership.
4. For further discussion of these data see Doling et al. (2004). See also Claus and Scobie (2001).
5. *The Economist* (2005) reported for the five-year period 1997–2004 that home prices appreciated in Australia (113 percent), Britain (147 percent), France (90 percent), Ireland (179 percent), the Netherlands (75 percent), South Africa (195 percent), Spain (131 percent), Sweden (76 percent).

6. Berry (1999). See also Berry (2005).
7. Data presented in Apelt *et al.* (2003) suggest that from 1993 to 2002, average household wealth in Australia increased from $199,000 to $280,000, with particularly strong increases recorded for households aged 45 or older. At the same time, the wealth of households with heads aged 25 to 34 fell by $71,000 to $121,000, while for households with head aged 35 to 44 total wealth fell by $29,000 to $253,000.
8. For a discussion of the link between home equity accumulation and retirement security see Dolan *et al.* (2005). See also Apelt *et al.* (2003).
9. For further discussion of the concept of housing wealth as a 'cultivator' of new wealth see Di (2001).
10. For example, a survey of borrowers who took out cash when they refinanced in 2001–3 (Canner *et al.* 2002) found that the majority of funds were used to acquire additional assets, including investments made on home improvements (35 percent) and to purchase a business or other real estate (11 percent), or make other financial investments such as stocks and bonds (10 percent), while the rest was largely spent on repayment of other debts (26 percent) or new consumer expenditures (16 percent).
11. According to the Federal Housing Finance Board as reported in Belsky and Prakken (2004), approximately one in ten of all home mortgages made in 2002 had loan-to-value (LTV) ratios of more than 90 percent, while slightly more than one in 20 exceeded 95 percent LTV.
12. For an excellent summary of the wealth effects literature see Belsky and Prakken (2004).
13. Note that Dvornak and Kohler (2003) using a different data and estimating technique than OECD report just the opposite pattern—namely that in Australia the marginal propensity to consume out of stock wealth (0.09) is greater than out of housing wealth (0.03).
14. Similar results for France, Germany, Japan, the United States, and the United Kingdom are reported in Barrell and Davis (2004).
15. See also International Monetary Fund (2000).
16. For a general summary of 'the bubble' debate see McCarthy and Peach (2004).

## References

Aizcorbe, Ana M., Kennickell, Arthur B., and Moore, Kevin B. (2003). 'Recent changes in U.S. family finances: evidence from the 1998 and 2001 Survey of Consumer Finances'. *Federal Reserve Bulletin*, 89/1 (Jan.): 1–29.

Ando, Albert, and Modigliani, Franco (1963). 'The life-cycle hypothesis of saving: aggregate implications and tests'. *American Economic Review*, 53: 55–84.

Apelt, Linda, Hall, Greg, and Young, Peter (2003). 'Housing at the cross-roads: the case for an integrated national housing policy for Australia'. Paper Presented to 'Cities and Markets' Forty-Seventh IFHP World Congress, Vienna, Austria (Oct.).

Apgar, William C. (2004). 'Rethinking rental housing: expanding the ability of rental housing to serve as a pathway to economic and social opportunity'. Joint Center for Housing Studies at Harvard University, Working Paper W04-11.

BARREL, RAY, and DAVIS, E. PHILIP (2004). 'Consumption, financial and real wealth in the G-5'. National Institute of Economic and Social Research Discussion Paper No. 232.

BELSKY, ERIC, and PRAKKEN, JOEL (2004). 'Housing wealth effects: housing's impact on wealth accumulation, wealth distribution, and consumer spending'. Paper prepared for the National Association of Realtors National Center for Real Estate Research.

BERRY, MIKE (1999). 'Unravelling the "Australian Housing Solution": the post war years'. *Housing, Theory and Science*, 16/3 (Oct.): 106–23.

—— (2005). 'Show me the money: financing more affordable housing'. RMIT-AHUR/NATSEM Research Centre, Melbourne, Working Paper No. 5.

CANNER, GLENN B., DURKIN, THOMAS A., and LUCKETT, CHARLES A. (1998). 'Recent developments in home equity lending'. *Federal Reserve Bulletin*, 84/4 (Apr.): 241–51.

—— DYNAN, KAREN, and PASSMORE, WAYNE (2002). 'Mortgage refinance in 2001 and 2002'. *Federal Reserve Bulletin*, 88/12 (Dec.): 469–81.

CAPLIN, ANDREW, CHAN, SEWIN, FREEMAN, CHARLES, and TRACY, JOSEPH (1997). *Housing Partnership*. Cambridge, Mass.: MIT Press.

CASE, KARL E., QUIGLEY, JOHN M., and SHILLER, ROBERT J. (2001). 'Comparing wealth effects: the stock market versus the housing market'. Working Paper 8606, National Bureau of Economic Research.

CATTE, PIETRO, GIROUARD, NATHALIE, PRICE, ROBERT, and ANDRÉ, CHRISTOPHE (2004). 'Housing markets, wealth and the business cycle'. OECD, Economics Department Working Paper, No. 394 (Dec.).

CLAUS, IRIS, and SCOBIE, GRANT (2001). 'Household net wealth: an international comparision'. The Treasury of New Zealand, Wellington, New Zealand, Working Paper 2001/19.

CUTLER, JOANNE (2004). 'The relationship between consumption, income and wealth in Hong Kong'. Hong Kong Institute for Monetary Research Working Paper No. 1.

DI, ZHU XIAO (2001). 'The role of housing as a component of household wealth'. Joint Center for Housing Studies at Harvard University at Harvard University, Working Paper W01–6.

—— (2003). 'Housing wealth and household net wealth in the United States: a new profile based on the recently released 2001 SCF data'. Joint Center for Housing Studies at Harvard University, Working Paper W03–8.

—— YANG, YI, and LIU, XIAODONG (2003). 'The importance of housing to the accumulation of household net wealth'. Joint Center for Housing Studies at Harvard University, Working Paper W03–5.

DOLAN, ALEX, MCLEAN, PETER, and ROLAND, DAVID (2005). 'Home equity, retirement incomes and family relationships'. Paper prepared for the Ninth Australian Institute of Family Studies Conference, Families Matter, Melbourne (9–11 Feb.).

DOLING, JOHN, ELSINGA, MARJA, BOELHOUWER, PETER, and FORD, JANET (2004). 'Playing snakes and ladders: the gains and losses for homeowners'. A paper presented at the ENHR Conference (2–6 July). Cambridge, England.

DVORNAK, NIKOLA, and KOHLER, MARION (2003). 'Housing wealth, stock market wealth and consumption: a panel analysis for Australia'. Economic Research Department, Reserve Bank of Australia, Discussion Paper 2003–07.

INTERNATIONAL MONETARY FUND (2000). 'Asset prices and the business cycle'. *World Economic Outlook*, 77–112.

JOINT CENTER FOR HOUSING STUDIES, Harvard University in Collaboration with the Neighborhood Reinvestment Corporation (2002). *Manufactured Housing as a Community Building Strategy.*
—— (2003). *The State of the Nation's Housing.*
—— (2004). 'Credit, capital and communities'. A report prepared for the Ford Foundation (Mar.).
—— (2005). *Improving America's Housing 2005: The Changing Structure of the Home Remodeling Industry.* Cambridge, Mass.: Harvard University.
KIM-SUNG, KELLIE, K., and HERMANSON, SHARON (2003). 'Experience of older refinance mortgage loan borrowers: broker- and lender-originated loans'. *AARP Public Policy Institute, Data Digest* (Jan.).
MCCARTHY, JONATHAN, and PEACH, RICHARD W. (2004). 'Are home prices the next bubble?' *Federal Reserve Bank of New York Economic Policy Review,* 10/3 (Dec.): 1–17.
MASNICK, GEORGE S., DI, ZHU XIAO, and BELSKY, ERIC S. (2005). 'Emerging cohort trends in housing debt and home equity'. Joint Center for Housing Studies at Harvard University, Working Paper W03–5.
OECD (2000). 'House prices and economic activity'. *OECD Economic Outlook,* 68 (Dec.): 169–84.
RESERVE BANK OF AUSTRALIA (2000). *Bulletin* (May).
STATISTICS CANADA (2001). *The Assets and Debts of Canadians: An Overview of the Results of the Survey of Financial Security.* Catalogue No. 13-595-XIE.
THE ECONOMIST (2005). 'Global House Prices: Still Want to Buy?' *The Economist* (3 May).
VENTI, STEVEN F., and WISE, DAVID A. (2000). 'Aging and home equity'. National Bureau of Economic Research Working Paper No. W7882.

CHAPTER 32

# THE ELDERLY AND ETHICAL FINANCIAL DECISION-MAKING

JULIAN SAVULESCU AND
TONY HOPE

## 1 INTRODUCTION

A tension between allowing people the freedom to make their own decisions, and protecting them from harm—including harm that may result from the exercise of that very freedom—runs through many aspects of society. In different countries and in different cultures, this tension is resolved in different ways, and the relative power given to individuals, their families, and the state varies according to the prevailing political and social values. Our financial decisions have considerable potential to cause us benefit or harm. In societies that leave many personal decisions to the individual, such as those of North America, Australasia, and much of Europe, the question of when the state should intervene in a person's financial affairs in the interests of the person herself is an acute one.

The legal powers for state interference in a person's financial decision-making in England (and many other 'Western' countries) crucially involve doctors. This is because those powers can, in general, only be invoked if the person is suffering from a mental disorder, or lacks competence, and the assessment of these two related conditions is seen to lie within the realm of medical expertise. A doctor's training, however, focuses on diagnosis and management of disease. Remarkably little attention is paid, in either undergraduate or postgraduate training, to the question of how to assess a person's decision-making capacity, or to the ethical issues involved in overriding a person's own decisions in their own interests. Indeed, it is only in the last decade that ethics and law have been included in the curriculum for medical students in most British medical schools.

The question of the ethics and the practicalities of when it is right to override a person's decision in her own interests has, however, received considerable attention in recent years within the fields of medical ethics and law. In this chapter, we consider what lessons can be learnt from those fields for how we can promote better financial decision-making in the elderly.

The main focus of recent medical debates has been around the question of when it is right to override patients' treatment decisions, and in particular refusal of beneficial treatment. In English law, and in many other English language jurisdictions, there are essentially two ways of tackling the question of when doctors should override patients' refusals of beneficial treatment. The first is through common law. In both England, and the United States, an adult patient who is deemed to 'have capacity' (or to 'be competent') to refuse treatment has the right to do so even if such refusal results in a death that could have been avoided. Thus in common law the key concept is of 'capacity' or 'competence' to make the decision. The second is through mental health legislation which allows for enforced treatment of patients who are suffering from a mental disorder and for whom treatment 'is appropriate'.

The legal frameworks are blunt instruments and are aimed mainly at the 'bottom line' issue of whether or not the doctor should override refusal of treatment. They tell us little about how forceful a doctor should be when she thinks that a patient is making the wrong decision, or how much information should be provided, or to what extent the doctor should enter into discussion with the patient. These are the kinds of questions, however, that have been debated in recent years amongst those interested in medical ethics—doctors, philosophers, lawyers amongst others. Such debate takes us into questions of what is meant by a person's best interests, as well as what are the grounds for giving weight to a person's own views in complex decision-making, or, more abstractly, what it means to respect a person's autonomy. The debate has also been framed in medical ethics in terms of what is the appropriate kind of relationship between a doctor and his patients, including with regard to making decisions.

Our argument in this chapter is that the question of ethical financial decision-making is, at root, a very similar question to that of ethical medical decision-making. We have explored ethical medical decision-making elsewhere (Hope *et al.* 2003). Both financial and medical decisions are centrally involved with issues of balancing welfare, or best interests, of people with the need to respect people's own decisions; both can involve quite difficult decisions based on complex information; and both will often involve an expert professional in helping the person to come to a decision. In both situations, furthermore, there is potential for serious harm to the individual if a particular decision is made. Because of these similarities we believe that it is fruitful to draw on recent work in the ethics and practicalities of treatment decisions and of the physician–patient relationship when thinking about financial decision-making in the elderly. In the main part of this chapter this is what we will do. We will examine different conceptions of 'well-being' and of autonomy. We will also suggest that a classification of models of the physician–patient relationship into four different types sheds light on the ethical aspects of the client–financial adviser relationship and shows how different ideas about respecting autonomy have practical implications. We will go on to look at the ethical justifications for taking over a person's financial affairs before outlining the current legal approach to this in England and Wales.

None of all this is specific to the elderly, or to retirement. We will begin, however, with a brief account of how ageing, and the disorders associated with ageing, may have an effect on people's ability to manage their financial affairs. It is the impact of illness on mental rather than physical health that is of most relevance to our subsequent discussion of the ethical issues. Physical illness or disability may interfere with, for example, the collection of a pension or welfare benefit from the relevant office and may require special arrangements to be made. But it is interference with the mental abilities that are needed in order to manage one's financial affairs that raise the most difficult problems from both an ethical and a practical point of view.

## 2 THE EFFECTS OF NORMAL AGEING ON COGNITIVE FUNCTION

The first question is whether normal ageing itself, in the absence of mental disorder, can cause sufficient cognitive impairment for someone, who was previously competent, to lack the ability to manage his financial affairs.

The answer is that, although there is some deterioration in cognitive functioning with age, it is rarely of a nature, or extent, that is likely to have any relevant effect on the ability to manage financial affairs (Milwain and Iversen 2002). The elderly are less flexible in their thought processes than the young and are poorer at solving novel problems. Problem-solving skills relating to well practiced activities, however, are well maintained. An elderly, but healthy, person who has to take on the management of financial affairs for the first time (e.g. because of the death of a partner) may be less competent than she might have been had she taken on these tasks at a younger age. It will very rarely be the case, however, that age is of crucial relevance. With normal ageing, the retrieval of memories also deteriorates but again this is most unlikely to interfere with competence to manage financial affairs. Such competence does not depend on the retrieval of specific facts as these can be recorded on paper, and in any case, given adequate time to complete the task, the performance of the elderly is not markedly impaired.

# 3 Mental Disorder in the Elderly

## 3.1 Dementia

By far the most important mental disorder that interferes with the capacity to manage financial affairs in the elderly is dementia. Dementia is a syndrome (that is a collection of symptoms) and not a single disease. Just as a headache is a symptom that can have many different causes, so dementia is a collection of symptoms that can have many causes. Dementia is defined by five features all of which are necessary for the diagnosis to be made (see Fig. 32.1).

The most common cause of the dementia syndrome, accounting for 50–70 percent of cases, is Alzheimer's disease. This is a disease of the brain cells themselves. It is defined by specific pathological changes in the brain and can only be diagnosed with certainty by microscopic examination of the brain after death. Many factors appear to contribute to Alzheimer's disease but there is currently no comprehensive theory as to its cause; and also no cure.

The second most common cause (20–30 percent of cases) is thought to be vascular disease: that is, not a disease primarily of the brain substance itself but one due to problems in the blood vessels. This results in impaired blood supply to parts of the brain with resulting brain damage. Over the last few decades a large number of rarer conditions causing dementia have been recognized.

The proportion of people in the population with dementia (i.e. the *prevalence* of dementia) increases rapidly, indeed almost exponentially, with age. This is illustrated in Table 32.1. In broad terms the prevalence of dementia doubles with every five years between the ages of 60 and 90 years.

## 3.2 Other Mental Disorders in the Elderly

A stroke leaves some people with long-term cognitive problems of sufficient magnitude to interfere with competence to manage financial affairs.

> (i) Multiple cognitive deficits (i.e. deficits in intellectual abilities such as reasoning and memory). These deficits must include some memory impairment.
> (ii) Impairment in the functioning of day-to-day living. This could, for example, be impairment in the ability to organize shopping.
> (iii) A change from the previous level of cognitive ability and daily functioning. This criterion is important to distinguish dementia from learning disability.
> (iv) Duration of the above symptoms of more than six months. This criterion is to exclude those cases in which a person fully recovers from some temporary cognitive impairment—such as might occur following a stroke or from a severe illness (such as pneumonia).
> (v) The person's level of consciousness is not impaired. This is to distinguish dementia from delirium: the acute confusional state that can result from almost any acute illness in which a person's conscious level is impaired (and in extreme cases the person becomes unconscious). Such delirium will usually resolve as the acute illness resolves.

**Fig. 32.1 The necessary criteria for the diagnosis of dementia**

Acute illness (such as infection, or following an operation) is often accompanied by a period of confusion, particularly in the elderly. This may require others, temporarily, to take over the management of financial affairs. Such confusion will normally resolve following recovery from the acute illness.

Depression is common. A European survey showed a prevalence in the elderly of 14 percent for women and 9 percent for men. Only about one in eight of these people will remain depressed and the impact of depression on long-term problems with financial affairs is small. Short-term problems such as failure to pay bills because of lack of interest and energy are much more common.

**Table 32.1 Prevalence of dementia by age**

| Age (years) | Prevalence (%) |
|---|---|
| 60–4 | 1.0 |
| 65–9 | 1.5 |
| 70–4 | 3.0 |
| 75–9 | 6.0 |
| 80–4 | 12 |
| 85–9 | 20–25 |
| 90–9 | 30–40 |

*Source*: Based on Hofer *et al.* (2002).

Manic illness, which is usually associated with depressed periods as well, can be particularly problematic because during the manic phase people may spend large amounts of money and incur substantial debts. Urgent treatment, usually requiring admission to hospital, is necessary.

Other delusional and paranoid illnesses in old age are rare. They are not major causes of problems with financial management.

# 4 Ethical Financial Decision-Making

The goal of financial decision-making in the elderly is to make a good financial decision. We should set up institutions and arrangements so that the elderly are more likely to make a good financial decision and, in cases in which the elderly person lacks the ability to make a good financial decision, make that decision ethically on the person's behalf.

It might seem obvious what a good financial decision is. One might think that it is the decision which maximizes the expected return from one's investment. Or the one which a financial expert would endorse as best. A parallel in health care would be that a good medical decision is one which maximizes the chances of good health. Or the one which expert doctors would endorse as best.

This model of making a good decision in health care has been abandoned for two reasons. First, while the goal of medicine may be good health, the goal of patients receiving medical care is to promote their overall well-being. As far as the individual is concerned, the goal of medical or financial decision-making is not merely health or financial gain, but well-being.

Second, it has come to be recognized that to respect patients as persons, one must respect their right to make their own decisions, for whatever reasons. The traditional model of decision-making which focused narrowly on health and was based on the expertise of the doctor failed to respect the autonomy of the patient. In financial decisions, it is equally important to respect the autonomy of the older person.

There are thus two goals of *ethical decision-making*: promotion of the patient's well-being (or best interests) and respect for their autonomy. Ethical financial decision-making should aim at promotion of the person's best interests and respect for their autonomy. We will now explore what these concepts are and their relevance for financial decision-making.

## 4.1 Well-Being

Most of us would like our financial decisions to make our lives go well, but what do we mean by this? Three main theories can be distinguished (Parfit 1984; Griffin 1986).

### 4.1.1 Mental State Theories

Hedonism is the simplest of the mental state theories of well-being. The central aspect of hedonistic theories is that well-being is defined in terms of mental states. At its simplest this is the view that happiness, or pleasure, is the only intrinsic good and unhappiness or pain the only intrinsic bad. All other goods are to be understood as instrumental—that is that they are good (or bad) to the extent that they bring about happiness or unhappiness.

On this account of well-being, a good financial decision is one which brings a person the most pleasure over time. This of course requires an understanding of what makes the person happy (which requires knowledge of human psychology (Argyle 1987)), which will differ from person to person and from time to time.

### 4.1.2 Desire Fulfillment Theories

According to desire-fulfillment theories, well-being consists in having one's desires fulfilled. Most of us believe that we would benefit if a genie appeared from one of our old lamps and granted us three wishes. It is plausible that to maximize a person's well-being we ought to give him what he wants.

Desire-fulfillment theories are attractive because they tailor well-being to each individual's own desires. They therefore give weight to individual values and they account well for the plurality of values individuals have. Economic theory commonly employs a related notion of value, and such accounts are widespread in philosophy and the social sciences.

If desire-fulfillment theories are to provide a plausible account of well-being, it is necessary to restrict the relevant set of desires: '... [W]hen the gods wish to punish us they answer our prayers' (Oscar Wilde 1895). What we desire and what contributes to our well-being may be two separate things. Which desires should be fulfilled for a plausible theory of well-being? There are many answers. One plausible answer is those desires which are based on relevant available information and which relate to a person's stable and settled values. This approach requires providing relevant information to people and eliciting their values and derivative desires.

### 4.1.3 Objective List Theories

According to objective list theories of well-being certain things can be good or bad for a person and can contribute to her well-being, whether or not they are desired.

Examples of the kinds of things that have been given as intrinsically good in this way are pleasure, the development of one's abilities, gaining knowledge, caring for one's family, having and raising children, and so on. Good financial decision-making, on this view, requires consideration of what is good for a person, regardless of how much that person desires it or whether it would give the person pleasure.

*An example* Consider an example in which these three accounts may yield different results. Joan is considering selling her house to enter a retirement village. She prefers to keep the family home even though her husband has died and her children have moved away. She is isolated and requires her family to visit and support her. The family home provides a sound financial investment and she hopes to leave a considerable inheritance to her children. She would be happier and receive more social support in a retirement village, though this would reduce her capital worth. Her children are all sufficiently well off that they do not need her inheritance to have a good life, and supporting her is a burden at times. In this case, she will be happiest if she sells her house to move into a retirement village and this may be best objectively for her (as her children's welfare is already secured) even though she most desires to retain the home. On the mental state and objective list accounts, she may be better off selling, though on the desire fulfillment account, she may be better off remaining where she is.

What is best for a person depends on which account of well-being is adopted. What is best for a person is to be gaining pleasure from objectively worthwhile activities, and strongly wanting to be engaged in them. The very best thing would be to persuade Joan to change what she most wants so that she comes to desire to sell the family home and want to move into a retirement village. Shaping a person's desires according to hedonistic and objective list accounts of well-being is an important part of promoting a person's well-being.

## 4.2 Autonomy

Autonomy comes from the Greek *autos nomos* meaning self-rule or self-determination. It is the concept that as persons unique amongst all animals, we have the power to make normative or value judgments about how our lives should go. The German philosopher Immanuel Kant famously related autonomy to rationality. We are fully autonomous when we make stable, considered, informed, consistent judgments about how our lives should go. Autonomy is not merely making a decision—it is making a rational decision (Savulescu 1994).

The two goals of ethical decision-making can pull in different directions: sometimes people autonomously desire what is not in their best interests, even when best interests is conceived very broadly as their overall well-being.

*A case example* Mr Smith is quite poor and needs to invest his savings wisely to ensure his well-being in his last years. He has £50,000. If he invests it in plan A, he has a 50 percent chance it will rise to £100,000 over five years and a 50 percent chance it will remain static. The expected return of plan A is thus £75,000. If he invests in plan B it is certain that the return will be £60,000. Let us assume that his well-being will be tightly correlated with his assets. It is in his interests to invest in plan A. Yet Mr Smith is highly risk averse and, knowing the facts, wishes to invest in plan B. Respecting his autonomy requires investing in plan B.

Respect for autonomy and promotion of well-being can be brought together when we assist, through rational persuasion or exciting the imagination, a person to autonomously desire what is good for them. The supreme goal of ethical decision-making should be to identify, on the basis of the person's own life and values, what is best for that person and to enable a person to autonomously desire what is best for them.

## 4.3 Complexity of Financial Decision-Making and the Need for an Independent Adviser

Making investment decisions today is highly complex for several reasons. First, the decisions themselves involve complex probabilistic information with numerous alternatives and consequences. Some elderly people have the financial experience to make these decisions themselves. Yet many will not. They require the support of an adviser. This person may be a professional or expert or it may be a family member or friend or other person with appropriate experience in financial decision-making. The difference between financial decision-making and medical or legal decision-making is that there is a less well-developed structure of independent decisional support in finance which serves the best interests of the client. As individuals are forced to take greater personal control of their own financial security, one of the great challenges of the twenty-first century is to develop a better system of professional support for financial decision-making in general.

Second, as we have argued, ethical decision-making should aim to promote the client's well-being. This requires a complex evaluation of what is best overall for this individual in these circumstances at this particular time. It requires the input of both the client and the financial adviser.

Third, ethical decision-making enables the client to come to autonomously choose the decision which is expected to best promote their well-being. This requires significant interpersonal skills and development of a trusting and supportive relationship with the client.

How should financial advisers or professionals substantively support individual decision-making? Emanuel and Emanuel (1992) proposed four models of the doctor–patient relationship based on different conceptions and weighting of beneficence (promoting well-being) and respect for autonomy. These can be adapted to apply to the financial adviser (be it professional, expert, family, friend or other) and the 'client' (in this case, the elderly person). These can be represented as four points on a spectrum, and are summarized in Figure 32.2. Each model is based on particular views of the consultation, the values of well-being and autonomy, and the nature of ethical dialogue.

## 4.4 Four Models of the Financial Adviser–Client Relationship

### 4.4.1 *The Paternalistic Model (also known as the traditional model or the priestly model)*

The paternalistic model is the 'traditional' kind of professional relationship. A paternalistic relationship derives from the idea of the relationship between a father and his child. The idea is that a father tries to do what is best for his child principally as he, the father, sees it. A child, on this model, will not be sufficiently mature to be able to adequately decide what is best for herself. A good father will override the child's own wishes or choices for the child's own good.

The paternalistic model of professional relationship sees the professional, in this case the financial expert, as making the main decisions about the person's finance. In making the decisions the professional has only the best interests of the client at heart. There is no question, in the paternalistic model, of the professional making decisions for his own sake. But the client is seen as being in an analogous position to a child. The professional or expert, on this model, is seen as being in a better position than the elderly person is, to decide what is in the person's best interests.

In an extreme form of the paternalistic model, the financial expert can decide what is best for the client from knowledge of the financial facts alone. The expert's role, in the consultation, is to come to a decision about what will maximize financial return. There is little or no discussion of what the client's views and values are.

### 4.4.2 *The Informative Model (also known as the consumer model or the engineering model)*

This model is at the opposite end of the spectrum from the paternalistic model. It is based on the analogy between the elderly person and a consumer. At its most extreme, 'rampant consumerism', the adviser's role is to provide the patient with all

| | Informative | Interpretive | Deliberative | Paternalistic |
|---|---|---|---|---|
| *Client values* | Defined, fixed, and known to the client | Inchoate and conflicting, requiring elucidation | Open to development and revision through normative discussion | Objective and shared by the adviser and client |
| *Adviser's obligation* | Providing relevant factual information and implementing client's selected financial strategy | Elucidating and interpreting relevant client values as well as informing the client and implementing the client's selected strategy | Articulating and persuading the client of the most admirable values as well as informing the client and implementing the client's selected strategy | Promoting the client's well-being independent of the client's current preferences |
| *Conception of client's autonomy* | Choice of, and control over, financial management | Self-understanding relevant to financial decision | Self-development relevant to financial management | Assenting to objective values |
| *Conception of adviser's role* | Competent technical expert | Counselor or adviser | Friend or teacher | Guardian |

**Fig. 32.2 Four models of the adviser–client relationship**

*Source*: Adapted from Emanuel and Emanuel (1992).

the financial facts relevant to making the decision. The elderly person decides what she wants. The adviser implements this decision with her technical expertise.

What this model has in common with the paternalistic model is that there is little discussion between adviser and client over what is the best decision, and little if any overt acknowledgement of the client's (or the adviser's) values. In the case of the paternalistic model this is because the professional can decide the best strategy without knowledge of the patient's own values; in the case of the informative model this is because all the client requires of the adviser are the financial facts. The patient then decides the financial strategy on the basis of her own values—but she does not need to discuss these with the adviser.

The informative model derives from one view of the principle of respecting patient autonomy, whereas the paternalistic model emphasizes the principle of beneficence.

### 4.4.3 The Interpretive Model

According to the interpretive model it is often helpful for the adviser to discuss financial decisions with the client. The adviser may enable the client to clarify her values and help her make the decision that is most in keeping with those values. Furthermore, the facts that the client may need to know cannot necessarily be determined unless the adviser knows something about the patient's values. The adviser may also play a useful role in helping the client to understand the implications of the different possible decisions.

In the example above, if the adviser believed that Mr Smith was making the wrong decision, it would be appropriate, on the interpretative model, for him to discuss this further. Such further discussion would be aimed at ensuring that Mr Smith had thought clearly about the implications of choosing Option B—in particular the implications of lower expected return and the nature of the probabilities concerned. The adviser might also, on this model, challenge Mr Smith's negative view of uncertain investments, or at least he would help him think through the implications of having £50,000 rather than £60,000. It might be appropriate, too, for the adviser to tell Mr Smith which option he would advise, as long as he gave the reasons for such advice. It is important on the interpretative and deliberative models that advisers understand the psychology of choice, and the effects of, for example, different ways of presenting the same information on the choices made (known as the framing effect (Tversky and Kahneman 1981)).

### 4.4.4 The Deliberative Model

The deliberative model shares many of the properties of the interpretive model but differs in one important respect. In the deliberative model the adviser not only helps the client to clarify her values but may also discuss, and challenge, these values. According to the deliberative model the adviser should be prepared to try to persuade the patient to alter her values if the adviser thinks that these are not right, just as a teacher or friend might discuss values. This model can be derived from a concept of respect for autonomy that sees an element of moral and personal development as part of promoting autonomy. According to the deliberative model, it might be right for the adviser in the above example of Joan to challenge Joan's values relating to retaining the family home.

Thus, the deliberative model goes further than the interpretative model. On the deliberative model, even if a person understands the facts, and chooses a course of action, the adviser might challenge Mr Smith's value that security is more important than return in the example. The adviser may believe that Mr Smith is too risk averse or that Joan is attaching too much significance to the family home at the cost of her own and her family's well-being. At least in the case of Joan, he may believe that Joan would be likely to change her values were she to sell the family home and move to a retirement village.

Consider another example. Mr J has Alzheimer's disease. His wife is finding it very difficult to look after him at home, and it would be possible to find a good nursing home that would take him. His wife, however, is very reluctant for Mr J to go to the nursing home because of the costs. According to the deliberative model it might be appropriate for the adviser to assess her overall financial status and whether she can afford it, and challenge the strength of her concern for saving. According to the interpretative model, however, it would be appropriate only to help Mrs J to understand the facts and clarify what her values are.

In neither the deliberative nor the interpretative models is it envisaged that the adviser is overbearing in challenging a person's decisions or values. In the end, it is for the person to decide. The main point at issue between the models is whether an adviser should stick to helping a person to understand and think through the issues, trying to persuade only when the person appears to be making the wrong decision given the patient's own values (the interpretative model); or whether it is appropriate in some circumstances to try and persuade the person to change her own values (the deliberative model).

These models are aspirational. And different models may be preferable in different professions. For example, the deliberative model has received considerable recent support in health care. But in financial management, when the adviser's fee is tied to the choice of certain options, there may be less professional independence and it may be less appropriate to challenge the client's underlying values. The interpretative model may be more appropriate for this reason within the current system of financial decisional support. The interpretative or paternalistic models may be more appropriate where a person has some impairment of capacity for complex decision-making, and the informative least appropriate in that circumstance.

# 5 THE JUSTIFICATIONS FOR TAKING OVER A PERSON'S FINANCIAL AFFAIRS

So far, we have considered financial decision-making in the competent elderly person. At the heart of the liberal view is the principle of respect for individual autonomy: the right of individuals to control their own lives free from outside interference. While we argued in the early part of this chapter that most elderly people will have the full capacity to make their own financial decisions, we have raised at the end of the last section the possibility of impaired capacity for decision-making, which will inevitably be present in some elderly people.

The British philosopher John Stuart Mill famously wrote (1998): '...the only purpose for which power can be rightfully exercised over any member of a civilized community, against his will, is to prevent harm to others. His own good, either physical or moral, is not a sufficient warrant. He cannot rightfully be compelled to do or forbear...because in the opinion of others, to do so would not be wise, or even right.' But Mill went on to write: 'It is perhaps hardly necessary to say that this doctrine is meant to apply only to human beings in the maturity of their faculties.'

Mill's caveat raises two questions: first, what is it about those who are not 'in the maturity of their faculties' that potentially justifies compelling them to do something against their will (for their own good); and second, what is meant by not being in the maturity of one's faculty? A modern answer to this second question is that the person is not competent (or lacks capacity) to decide for himself. The equivalent answer to the first question is to say that because of the lack of competence the person's decision is not his genuine autonomous decision. Thus in compelling him against his will (but for his own good), we are not overriding his autonomous decision because his decision is not autonomous (due to his lack of competence). However, lack of competence alone is not sufficient to justify taking over someone's financial affairs.

Figure 32.3 summarizes the conditions that, we suggest, are needed in order to take over someone's financial affairs.

## 5.1 Competence

At the heart of the issue of deciding whether someone should intervene and take over a person's financial affairs is the question of competence. This is because in general adults should be able to make their own decisions about the management of their affairs. The main justification for interfering with a person's decisions is that the person lacks the competence to make those decisions. The question of

> 1. The person decides that he wants someone else to take over his financial affairs and is competent to do so.
> 2. (a) The person lacks competence to make decisions concerning the management of his financial affairs,
>
>    and is either:
>
>    (b) coming to, or is likely to come to, significant harm as a result of this;
>
>    or
>
>    (c) the consequences of the lack of ability to manage the financial affairs are likely to be significantly different from what the person would have wanted when competent. For example, the mismanagement of affairs is resulting in significantly reduced inheritance for the person's children.
> 3. If the person, when competent, nominated another person to take over his affairs in the event of his becoming incompetent, then this wish should normally be respected.

**Fig. 32.3 Summary of ethically relevant grounds for taking over someone's financial affairs**

competence can arise in a number of different situations: competence to consent to, or refuse medical treatment; competence to consent to hospitalization or to living in a nursing home; competence to complete a will; competence to manage other aspects of one's financial affairs.

Both the terms 'competence' and 'capacity' are used in this context. We will use the term competence in this chapter. This is the term that is generally used by clinicians and is in common currency. English law uses the term 'capacity' (e.g. capacity to consent to medical treatment). In the United States, the terms are used the other way round with competence being the legal term and capacity being generally favored by clinicians.

There are three approaches to determining competence: an outcome approach, a status approach, and a functional approach. Most modern jurisdictions, and most philosophers, favor a functional approach.

According to the outcome approach a person's competence is assessed in terms of the outcome of the decision that is made. The fact that a decision is a bad decision, on this view, provides sufficient grounds for concluding that the person lacks competence. This approach is generally rejected in liberal societies as overly paternalistic, and open to abuse.

According to the status approach a person is to be judged as competent or not as a result of his status. For example, a child might be regarded as lacking competence (e.g. to consent to or refuse treatment) simply on grounds of his age. An application of a status approach would be to regard anyone with dementia as *ipso facto* incompetent to make decisions regarding, for example, medical care or the management of financial affairs. The two problems with this approach are that it regards all people within the relevant category as similar with regard to decision-making ability; and regards the status as affecting competence across a wide range of decisions.

The functional approach focuses on the way in which the decision is taken, not on the outcome of that decision nor on the status of the person taking it. According to this approach the kind of issues that are important in deciding whether a person is competent to take a particular decision are whether the person is able to understand the information relevant to the decision; able to think about that information and manipulate it in a rational manner; and able to weigh up the different likely consequences of different decisions, compare them, and come to a decision. On this view, some people with dementia will be able to make decisions about their financial affairs whereas others will not; and the same person may be competent to make some decisions but not others. Figure 32.4 summarizes some of the key legal principles relating to competence (see also Fig. 32.5).

## 5.2 Enhancing Capacity

A person's competence to make a decision not only depends on the person but also on the environment. The assessment of competence must not be treated like a school exam. If patient autonomy is to be properly respected doctors should try and enable patients to have the competence to make decisions or carry out normal tasks. This might be done in several ways:

---

An imprudent decision is not, by itself, sufficient grounds for incompetence.
A person should not be regarded as lacking competence merely because she is making a decision that is unwise or against her best interests. An unwise decision might alert a doctor to the need for assessment of competence; but that assessment must be made by analyzing the way the decision is made, not from the decision itself.

Capacity is 'function specific'
A person is not 'globally' competent or incompetent. One can only talk of competence to do a particular thing. Thus a patient may be competent to make a will, but incompetent to consent, or refuse consent, to a particular operation (or vice versa).

*The presumption of capacity*
An adult is presumed competent until the contrary is proved by acceptable evidence.

*The presumption of continuance*
Once incompetence has been established, it is presumed to continue until the contrary is proved by acceptable evidence.

---

**Fig. 32.4 Some key legal principles relating to competence**

(i) by treating any mental disorder which affects capacity;
  (ii) if capacity is likely to improve—to wait, if possible, until it does improve to allow the patient to be properly involved in decisions;
 (iii) to be aware of the possibility that medication may adversely affect capacity;
 (iv) if capacity fluctuates (e.g. it depends on the time of day), to assess capacity when the patient is at her best;
  (v) if there is a need to assess capacity for different tasks or decisions, to assess these separately;
 (vi) to choose the environment which maximizes the patient's capacity—including minimizing distractions—such as excessive noise;
(vii) to consider whether the person might be helped if a relative or friend is with her;
(viii) by allowing the person time to take in and process information; and
 (ix) by making explanations simple and using aide-mémoires, written information and diagrams, where these are likely to be helpful.

## 5.3 Legal Mechanisms for Taking Over a Person's Financial Affairs

When a person becomes incompetent, there are two principal ways in English law of taking over the management of a person's financial affairs, and this is broadly similar in the laws of many other countries. The first is through the Court of Protection; the second is by means of an enduring Power of Attorney.

### 5.3.1 *The Court of Protection*

The Court of Protection is designed to protect people from significant financial harm as a result of their no longer being capable of looking after their financial affairs. The Court has the power to take over those affairs and make arrangements to deal with them even against the person's wishes. In England these powers are closely associated with the Mental Health Act and a result of this is that the powers can only be taken if the person suffers a mental disorder, and a registered medical practitioner must complete the form.

In addition to suffering a mental disorder, the person needs to 'be incapable of managing and administering his of her property or affairs'. In our view this, rather than mental disorder, is the key issue, in keeping with a focus on competence:

Silberfeld and colleagues suggest that with regard to competence to manage financial affairs it is useful to break this into four specific components:

1. knowledge of income;
2. knowledge of expenses;
3. an ability to handle everyday financial transactions;
4. the ability to delegate financial wishes (Silberfield *et al.* 1995).

This last ability has been further analyzed as raising three issues:

- Does the person have the insight and understanding that she has a problem for which she needs advice?
- Is she capable of seeking an appropriate adviser and instructing him accordingly?
- Does she have the competence to make decisions as needed?

### 5.3.2 *Enduring Power of Attorney (EPA)*

The Court of Protection can take over a person's affairs whether or not they had made prior arrangements. A Power of Attorney is a document completed by one person that appoints another person to look after his financial affairs. An enduring power remains in force even after the first person has lost the competence to look after his affairs. An enduring power can be set up by a person before they lose competence to manage their affairs to come into force in the event that they subsequently lose capacity—at which time the person appointed (e.g. the son or daughter of the person) takes over management.

Unfortunately, relatively few people use the provisions of the enduring power of attorney to ensure that their financial affairs are in safe hands were they to become incompetent themselves. It may not be until close family become aware of problems, because of early dementia, for example, that anyone thinks about creating an enduring power of attorney. This then raises the question of whether, at a point when the person is no longer able to manage their affairs reliably, they might be able to create an enduring power of attorney. This point has been tested in English law. In Lord Hoffman's judgment: The validity of the act to create an enduring power of attorney depends on whether the person understands its nature and effect and not on whether she is able to perform all the acts that it authorizes. Thus it may be possible for a person to create an EPA at a point (e.g. at the beginning of a dementing illness) when they are not able to look after their financial affairs. If, however, by the time family have been alerted to the problems, the person no longer has the capacity to complete an EPA then the only recourse in law for taking over the financial affairs is through the Court of Protection.

The advantages of EPAs are that they allow the person to make their own decision about the future management of their affairs and can ensure that there is continuity of agency. They are also cheaper than the Court of Protection. They are, however, easier to abuse because they do not have the mechanisms of protection that are included in the Court of Protection. Lush estimates that financial abuse (including both fraud and mismanagement) occurs in about 10–15 percent of cases of EPA (Lush 2002).

---

**Step 1:** *Identify the information relevant to the decision, e.g.*
That a decision needs to be made.
The nature of the various reasonable decisions.
The pros and cons of each reasonable decision.

**Step 2:** *Assess cognitive ability*
With regard to the information identified in Step 1, assess whether the person has the cognitive ability to carry out all three elements of the decision-making process:
Understanding the information relevant to the decision. This involves understanding in broad terms the nature and purpose of the information.
Ability to believe the information. A person with a delusional disorder, for example, may be able to understand the information but is not able to believe it because of a paranoid delusion that everyone is trying to deceive him.
Weighing up the information and coming to a decision. Some authorities break this criterion into two components. The first is the ability to compare risks and benefits of the various options and to come to a decision based on such comparison. The second is to appreciate how the decisions will affect the person and his family and to therefore be able to assign values to each benefit and risk.
The ability to communicate, and maintain, choices.

**Step 3:** *Assess other factors which may interfere with decision-making*
This involves ensuring that even when cognitive ability appears to be intact there is not mental disorder that has an important impact on functions outlined in Step 2. Some relevant symptoms of mental illness are delusions, hallucinations, and affective disorder (i.e. depression or manic illness).

---

**Fig. 32.5 Outline of the assessment of competence**

# 6 CONCLUSION

In this chapter, we have examined the lessons from the ethics of medical decision-making to inform the ethics of financial decision-making in the elderly. We argued that most elderly people retain the capacity to make their own financial decisions. The goal of financial decision-making is to make an ethical financial decision. An ethical financial decision is not merely one which maximizes expected financial return or one which a financial expert recommends. It is a decision which promotes the individual's global well-being and respects that individual's autonomy. Financial decision-making is becoming increasingly complex. It involves complex probabilistic information. Many elderly people, as many younger people, require support in making these complex decisions. Fully ethical decision-making requires experts not just to provide information and ensure that their clients understand this, but also to understand the person's values and circumstances, and in some cases challenge these values, to assist the person to autonomously decide on a course of action which is best for him or herself. We outlined four possible models for professional support of financial decision-making based on different understandings and weightings of beneficence and respect for autonomy: the paternalistic, the informative, the interpretative, and the deliberative.

While most elderly people retain the capacity to make their own financial decisions, illness or age may render some incompetent to manage their own affairs. We have outlined steps to enhance competence and detect incompetence. We also outlined legal mechanisms to control an incompetent person's affairs.

The problems which the elderly face in making decisions about their finances are in many ways the same as the problems which all of us now face. The opportunities for autonomy and a better life have never been greater. Yet achieving these goals has never been more complex and there is an ever increasing requirement for independent, ethically informed professional support of these decisions.

Much research is required to promote more ethical decision-making. Strategies to help the elderly deal with complex probabilistic information need to be identified. Research needs to examine the extent to which professionals evaluate competence, provide relevant information in an intelligible way, elicit client values and recommend courses of action which are in the elderly person's best interest. The extent of financial abuse needs to be documented. In short, we urgently require evaluation of the extent to which financial decision-making is ethical and how it can be improved. There is a strong moral imperative to enable the elderly to make better financial decisions.

# References

Argyle, M. (1987). *The Psychology of Happiness*. London: Methuen.
Emanuel, E. J. and Emanuel, L. L. (1992). 'Four models of the physician-patient relationship'. *Journal of the American Medical Association*, 267: 2221–6.
Griffin, J. (1986). *Well-Being*. Oxford: Clarendon Press.
Hofer, S. M., Christensen, H. Mackinnon, A. J., Korten, A. E., Jorm, A. F., Henderson, A. S., and Easteal, S. (2002). 'Change in cognitive functioning associated with apoE genotype in a community sample of older adults'. *Psychology and Aging*, 17/2: 194–208.
Hope, T. Savulescu, J., and Hendrick, J. (2003). *Medical Ethics and Law: The Core Curriculum*. London: Churchill Livingstone.

Lush, D. (2002). 'Managing the financial affairs of mentally incapacitated persons in the United Kingdom and Ireland', in R. Jacoby and C. Oppenheimer (eds.), *Psychiatry in the Elderly*, 3rd edn. Oxford: Oxford University Press, 951–65.

Mill, J. S. (1998). *On Liberty and other Essays*, ed. John Gray. Oxford World's Classics. Oxford: Oxford University Press.

Milwain, E., and Iversen, S. (2002). 'Cognitive change in old age', in R. Jacoby and C. Oppenheimer (eds.), *Psychiatry in the Elderly*, 3rd edn. Oxford: Oxford University Press, 43–79.

Parfit, D. (1984). *Reasons and Persons*. Oxford: Oxford University Press.

Savulescu, J. (1994) 'Rational desires and the limitation of life-sustaining treatment'. *Bioethics*, 8: 191–222.

Silberfield, M., Corber, W., Madigan, K. V., and Checkland, D. (1995). 'Capacity assessments for requests to restore legal competence'. *International Journal of Geriatric Psychiatry*, 10: 191–7.

Tversky, A., and Kahneman, D. (1981). 'The framing of decisions and the psychology of choice'. *Science*, 211 (30 Jan.): 453–8.

Wilde, O. (1895). *An Ideal Husband*, Act 2.

# PART V
# LOOKING AHEAD

# PROSPECTIVE MODELS

CHAPTER 33

# STRUCTURAL PENSION REFORM— PRIVATIZATION—IN LATIN AMERICA[1]

## CARMELO MESA-LAGO

In the last two decades, the most important social transformation that has occurred in Latin America is the privatization of public pension systems. By mid-2005, half of the countries in the region had implemented or approved structural pension reforms which totally or partially established private systems embracing 63 million workers. The pioneer reform began in Chile in 1981, followed a decade later by nine other countries: Peru (1993), Argentina and Colombia (1994), Uruguay (1996), Bolivia and Mexico (1997), El Salvador (1998), Costa Rica (2001), and Dominican Republic (2003–6).[1] Two other countries passed reform laws but they had not been implemented by April 2005: Ecuador, where the law (2001) has been contested at the constitutional court, and Nicaragua (2000), where implementation has been postponed indefinitely because of unsustainable transitional fiscal costs. There is no other region in the world that has undergone reforms of such scope and depth. They have influenced similar processes in many other countries and the agendas of international and regional financial organizations, as well as challenging international and regional social security agencies.

This chapter analyzes structural pension reforms in the 12 Latin American countries. Section 1 offers a brief description of the three different models of reforms applied in the region, as well as outlining the range of features of the specific reforms in each of the 12 countries. Section 2 provides a summary of the beneficial impact of such reforms. Section 3 discusses the diverse levels of pension privatization in ten countries and the reasons for this divergence. Section 4 evaluates eight assumptions about the effects of structural reforms based on statistics available for ten countries, and Section 5 concludes with a review of outstanding issues and indications of further research needed.

The essential argument of this chapter is that, contrary to the generally accepted views on the effects of structural pension reform on the social, administrative, and financial aspects of the countries concerned, data from ten Latin American countries where reform has been implemented demonstrate that eight of these effects either have not materialized or cannot be validated by empirical evidence, and have therefore become significant challenges for the reforms.

# 1 Structural Reforms and Their Differences

Public pension systems are characterized by defined benefit, pay-as-you-go financing, and are publicly managed programs, while private systems are characterized by defined contribution, fully funded financing and privately managed programs. Structural reforms completely transform the public system, replacing it wholly or partially with a private one. Non-structural or parametric reforms strengthen the public system financially in the long term by raising the age of retirement or the level of contributions or similar measures. The 12 structural reforms in Latin America have followed three different models: substitutive, parallel, or mixed.

The substitutive model has been implemented or approved in six countries: Chile, Bolivia, Mexico, El Salvador, the Dominican Republic, and Nicaragua (not in force in April 2005; SIP 2005). In this model, the public system is closed (no new members are allowed) and replaced by a private system with its three basic characteristics. Mexico is the exception: its management is multiple, a mix of private, public, and mixed institutions, and the benefits may be defined or undefined.

The parallel model has been applied in only two countries: Peru and Colombia. In this model the public system is not closed but reformed, a new private system is established, and the two compete with each other. The public system has its three typical characteristics, except that in Colombia the financing system is partial collective capitalization instead of pay-as-you-go. The private system also has its three typical characteristics, except that in Colombia the management is multiple.

The mixed system has been implemented or approved in four countries: Argentina, Uruguay, Costa Rica, and Ecuador (not yet in force). This model combines a public system which is not closed and provides a basic pension, with a private system which offers a supplementary pension. The public pillar has its three typical characteristics, as does the private pillar, except that the management of the latter is of a multiple nature in all four countries.

The other eight Latin American countries have kept their public systems. Brazil introduced parametric reforms for its private sector employees in the late 1990s, and more recently for its public employees. Venezuela passed a substitutive structural reform, but it was abolished by the current government, which instead approved parametric reforms in 2002. In Panama the government was about to pass a parametric reform in the spring of 2005. Cuba has been considering a parametric reform since 1995 but it had not yet been approved as of April 2005. Structural or parametric reforms have been considered in Guatemala, Honduras, and Paraguay.

## 2 The Beneficial Effects of Structural Reform

Among the beneficial effects of structural reforms are the following:

(a) unification of different programs in six countries (Bolivia, Chile, Costa Rica, Dominican Republic, El Salvador, and Peru), thus strengthening unity and making portability possible, although segmentation persists in the remaining four countries;

(b) equalization of conditions of access and rules for the calculation of pensions in most of the systems except for the armed forces in all countries (excluding Costa Rica) and for civil servants in various countries;

(c) increase of retirement ages in a majority of countries, more in keeping with life expectancy at retirement, thus strengthening long-term financial sustainability;

(d) establishment of a much closer relationship between contributions and the amount of the pension, and opening up the option to save additional sums that could enable middle- and high-income groups to earn higher pensions;

(e) granting of state guarantees to pay ongoing pensions in all countries, as well as recognition of the contributions made under the public system and a minimum pension in the private system in most of the countries;

(f) elimination of the public system's monopoly and introduction of competition (albeit not functioning properly in most countries);
(g) substantial accumulation of capital in the pension funds (although this must be balanced by the fiscal cost during the transition);
(h) improved efficiency in registration, individual accounts, provision of periodic information to the insured, and rapid processing of pensions;
(i) providing an option for insured persons to select an investment fund of their choice from among various alternatives (Chile); and
(j) regulation and supervision of the pension system by technical bodies endowed with relative independence ('superintendencies' or supervisory bodies).

# 3 THE IMPORTANCE OF THE PRIVATE SYSTEM

At the end of 2004, out of 63 million members of pensions schemes in the countries with structural pension reforms, an average of 86 percent were in the private system or the private component of a mixed system, and the remaining 14 percent in the public system. When disaggregating those averages, the proportion of members in the private system varied from 50 to 100 percent across the ten countries, due to the different models adopted and for other reasons explained later. One hundred percent of insured persons were in the private system in Bolivia, Mexico, and Costa Rica; 98 percent in Chile, 96 percent in Peru, 92 percent in El Salvador, 90 percent in Argentina, and 87 percent in the Dominican Republic, but 54 percent in Uruguay and only 50 percent in Colombia.[2]

Changing from the public to the private system depends not only on the virtues of the latter but also on other variables: the insured person's freedom to choose whether to stay in the public system or move to a private or mixed system, as well as (in some countries) that person's age and income; state provision of benefits and incentives to join the private system; tightening of the rules of the public system to encourage change; publicity to promote such change; the rate of return of the public system as compared with the rate of capital return in the private system, and the length of time the reform has been in effect.

In Bolivia, Costa Rica, and Mexico the law obliged all insured persons to move to the private or mixed system. In the six countries which applied the substitutive model, as well as in Costa Rica which has adopted the mixed system, new insured persons entering the labor force are obliged to enroll in the private or mixed system. Where the reform has been in operation for a long time (24 years in

Chile), this obligation to enroll, together with the gradual retirement of those who stayed in the public system, has significantly increased the number of affiliates in the private system. In El Salvador and the Dominican Republic, the younger affiliates of the public system, who were a majority, were obliged to move to the private system. In Chile and Peru, contributions in the private system were lower than in the public system; furthermore, insured persons who moved to the private system in Peru were banned from returning to the public one. In Argentina, those entering the labor market are free to choose between the public and mixed systems, but workers who do not take a decision are automatically assigned to the mixed system and those who move from the public to the mixed system cannot return to the former. Publicity has also been a crucial factor in the change, since the private system has promised higher pensions, lower management costs, and protection against government interference. Colombia still has half of the total insured population in the public system, because insured persons were initially allowed to change systems every three years and the average public pension was higher than the average private pension. To correct this situation a law was introduced in 2002 to increase the period of change to five years, and to prevent affiliates in the public system from changing in the ten years before retirement, as well as tightening the rules of retirement and reducing the pension in the public system.

# 4 AN EVALUATION OF EIGHT ASSUMED BENEFITS OF STRUCTURAL PENSION REFORM

The debate in the last five years has focused on whether the assumed effects of structural pension reforms have materialized in practice. These assumptions were initially set out by the World Bank (1994) and later ratified and expanded by scholars and experts who advocate such reforms. Orszag and Stiglitz (2001) refuted in a theoretical manner the 'myths' of the basic reform model sponsored by the World Bank; Barr (2002) expanded that analysis. The author of this chapter tested the 12 'myths' identified by Orszag and Stiglitz based on scattered data (1998–2000) from eight Latin American countries with reforms in place, albeit most of them for a relatively short time (Mesa-Lago 2002). Three experts from the World Bank have evaluated the effects of the Latin American reforms in the last decade, changing some initial views of the Bank but still supporting the fundamental principles and alleged effects of the structural reforms (Gill et al. 2005).

The reforms have now been operating in half of Latin America: for 24 years in Chile, between seven and 12 years in seven other countries, and two to four years in the remaining two countries. Abundant comparative statistics are now available to enable a thorough evaluation of the effects of these reforms. In assessing whether eight of the assumed effects of structural pension reforms have indeed materialized in the ten Latin American countries this section reaches a largely negative conclusion. The failure of these supposed effects to materialize has significantly challenged reforms in the region, as discussed in this section.

## 4.1 Declining Coverage of the Labor Force

Structural pension reforms were expected to extend labor force coverage by increasing incentives for affiliation: establishing a tight relationship between contribution and the pension level (the principle of equivalence), particularly among informal workers. Gill *et al.* (2005) affirm that, despite improvements in such incentives, coverage ratios in most countries—after rising modestly due to the reforms—stalled, with levels of about half of the labor force in the two countries with highest coverage (Chile and Mexico), but much lower coverage in the rest. They add that stagnant coverage is indicative of skepticism about the private system and even rejection by many workers.

Table 33.1 compares coverage of the labor force combining active contributors in both private and public systems in the year before the reform (or the year of the reform) and in 2004. Rather than stagnating, coverage decreased in all countries, and the weighted average coverage fell from 38 to 26 percent;[3] in Argentina and Peru coverage decreased to about one-half. This comparison confronts some methodological problems (see Mesa-Lago 2004a), but two standardized series for Chile confirm the declining trend. The first shows a maximum of 79 percent in 1973, a decrease to 64 percent in 1980 (prior to the reform) and 29 percent in 1982, a gradual increase to 58 percent in 1997, and stagnation thereafter (SAFP 2002). The second series shows a decline from 62 percent in 1975 to 48 percent in 1980, an increase to 62 percent in 1997, and a fall to 58 percent in 2000 (Arenas de Mesa and Hernández 2001). A similar comparison for Argentina shows a decline from 35 percent in 1994 to 26 percent in 2002 (Hujo 2004).

Contrary to what was expected from the reforms, its alleged incentives to join these schemes have neither stopped the flight to the informal sector nor increased the coverage, as the data in the period 1990–2002 show: seven out of ten new jobs created were in the informal sector, and only four out of those ten new jobs had social security protection. Only two out of ten workers in the informal sector had such protection (ILO 2003). Twenty-four years after the reform in Chile, coverage of self-employed workers—the most important group in the informal sector—was

Table 33.1 Percentage of the labor force covered by the public system before the reform and by private and public systems in 2004 (based on contributors)[1]

| Country | Coverage (%) before the reform (year) | Coverage (%) 2004 |
| --- | --- | --- |
| Argentina | 50 (1994) | 27 |
| Bolivia | 12 (1996) | 11 |
| Chile | 64 (1980) | 57 |
| Colombia | 32 (1993) | 22 |
| Costa Rica | 53 (2000) | 47 |
| Dominican Republic | 30 (2000) | 15 |
| El Salvador | 26 (1996) | 20 |
| Mexico | 37 (1997) | 28 |
| Peru | 31 (1993) | 12 |
| Uruguay | 73 (1997) | 59 |
| Average[2] | 38 | 26 |

*Notes:* [1] Excludes some groups of insured with separate programmes: the armed forces in all countries except Costa Rica, public employees in some countries and other small groups. If these groups were included, the percentage of the labor force covered would increase.
[2] Based on total contributors and total labor force in the ten countries.

*Sources:* Coverage before the reform from Mesa-Lago (2004b, 2005); coverage in 2004 are author's estimates based on BCU (2005); CONSAR (2005); SAFJP (2005); SAFP (2005); SBC (2005); SBS (2005); SIPEN (2005); SP (2005); SPVS (2005); SUPEN (2005), and labor force from CEPAL (2004).

5 percent; it was less than 10 percent in Colombia and less than 1 percent in Mexico. Only 4 percent of the total insured were self-employed in Bolivia in 2004 and 8 percent in El Salvador. Private and public pension systems in the region face a double challenge: to halt the fall in coverage of the formal sector and to include the expanding informal sector.

Last but not least, the minority of countries with relatively high levels of pension coverage also have the lowest levels of poverty as well as social assistance pension schemes to protect the poor (Argentina, Chile, Costa Rica, and Uruguay). The majority of countries with low levels of coverage, on the other hand, are characterized by high levels of poverty and lack of social assistance pension schemes. The reform laws approved in Costa Rica and Colombia provide for social assistance pensions, but as of April 2005 they had not yet been implemented. In the Dominican Republic, the law mandated a social assistance ('subsidized') pension for low income and other vulnerable groups to be implemented in 2004 but this has been postponed to 2006 (SIPEN 2005).

Gill *et al.* (2005) warn that the current low coverage could lead in the future to a high proportion of old people without protection despite the fact that the majority of countries have the fiscal and administrative ability to fulfill that function. Household surveys taken in 1997–2002 show that in only three countries were between 33 and 66 percent of the elderly population protected (Argentina, Chile, and Costa Rica), while in a further six countries protection was only 9–20 percent. Furthermore, in several Latin American countries the share of the elderly receiving pension benefits is actually falling. In view of these problems, the World Bank recommends giving priority to the poverty prevention pillar rather than to the mandatory saving pillar.

## 4.2 Increasing Non-compliance in the Payment of Contributions

Another assumption about the benefits of structural reform is that the ownership of individual accounts and the principle of equivalence would encourage prompt payment of contributions. The higher the amount of contributions, and the higher the return on individual accounts, the greater would be the accumulated fund and hence the higher the pension. On the other hand, increasing the worker's contribution (as has happened in seven out of the 12 countries with reforms) could lead to disincentives for affiliation and compliance. Based on surveys taken in Santiago de Chile and Lima (not at the national level), Gill *et al.* (2005) infer that there is a higher contribution density after the reforms. However, Chilean affiliates who complete the required contributions to obtain the minimum pension, usually stop contributing to the private system and give priority to less risky and costly alternatives, while in Peru the greater a member's accumulated contributions, the less likely they are to continue to contribute.

In contrast to the assumption that reform would bring about better compliance, Table 33.2 shows that the percentage of affiliates who were active contributors steadily decreased in all countries in 1998–2004 with few exceptions. The rate of compliance in 2004 ranged from 35 percent in Argentina to 66.8 percent in Costa Rica, and the weighted average of the ten countries fell from 57.9 percent in 1998 to 40.8 percent in 2004. The standardization of the last month of contribution (rather than one contribution in the last six or 12 months) led to a significant decrease in the rate of compliance: in Colombia it dropped almost ten percentage points in 2004; in Bolivia almost eight points in 2003, and in Mexico 13 points in 2001. The level of compliance decreased steadily from 76 percent in 1983 to 51 percent in 2004 in Chile, and from 73 percent in 1994 to 35 percent in 2003 in Argentina (SAFP 2005; Hujo 2004).

Table 33.2 Percentage of affiliates who contributed to the private system in the last month, December 1998 to December 2004

| Country | 1998 | 1999 | 2000 | 2001 | 2002 | 2003 | 2004[1] |
|---|---|---|---|---|---|---|---|
| Argentina | 48.9 | 44.3 | 39.1 | 29.0 | 33.2 | 35.2 | 35.4 |
| Bolivia | n.a.[3] | n.a.[3] | n.a.[3] | 47.0 | 46.9 | 39.0 | 42.7 |
| Chile | 52.8 | 53.4 | 50.9 | 53.7 | 51.0 | 51.9 | 51.0 |
| Colombia | n.a. | 51.6[4] | 48.5[4] | 48.7[4] | 47.6[4] | 48.7[4] | 39.0[4] |
| Costa Rica | | | | n.a.[5] | n.a.[5] | 73.1 | 66.8 |
| Dom. Rep. | | | | | | 65.5 | 53.5 |
| El Salvador | 67.2 | 63.7 | 55.2 | 53.2 | 47.6 | 46.3 | 42.2 |
| Mexico | 63.4[6] | 60.2[6] | 57.9[6] | 44.7 | 41.7 | 39.3 | 40.0 |
| Peru | 45.6 | 45.7 | 41.7 | 41.2 | 39.4 | 41.9 | 40.3 |
| Uruguay | 67.4 | 58.7 | 53.9 | 53.2 | 45.1 | 52.7 | 52.5 |
| Total[2] | 57.9 | 55.5 | 51.0 | 43.5 | 42.1 | 42.0 | 40.8 |

*Notes*: n.a. = not available.
[1] Figures for Bolivia, Costa Rica, and Mexico are for June.
[2] Estimate based on total affiliates and total contributors in all countries with available data.
[3] Until 2001, contributor was an affiliate who had at least one contribution since the inception of the system.
[4] In 1999–2003, contributor was an affiliate who had at least one contribution in the last six months; in 2004 in the last month.
[5] The system began in 2001, in 2001–2 contributor was an affiliate who had at least one contribution in the last year.
[6] In 1998–2000 contributor was an affiliate who had a contribution in the last two months.

*Sources*: 1998–2003 from Mesa-Lago (2004b) except Dominican Republic; 2004 from AIOS (2005); BCU (2005); CONSAR (2005); SAFJP (2005); SAFP (2005); SBC (2005); SBS (2005); SIPEN (2005); SP (2005); SPVS (2005); SUPEN (2005).

Reasons for declining compliance rates include the following:

(a) many affiliates have abandoned the labor force or are unemployed;
(b) affiliates who had formal employment have shifted to the informal sector;
(c) some employers keep the withheld contributions instead of transferring them to the private system (in Chile the employer's debt for that reason rose six times in 1990–2002, it was equivalent to 1 percent of the total pension fund in 2002, and 43 percent of it was uncollectible);
(d) many members contribute just the minimum necessary to qualify for the minimum pension and maximize the state subsidy to such benefit and then stop contributing; and
(e) the significant size of the worker's contribution and its increase in six countries (largely as the result of the elimination or reduction of employers' contributions) have generated incentives for evasion and payment delays (Mesa-Lago 2005).

## 4.3 Imperfect Competition among Management Firms

Competition is the foundation of the private system because it eliminates the monopoly of the public system and allegedly promotes greater efficiency. It is assumed that fund management firms will compete for members and that individuals will have the necessary information and skills to choose the best ones—that is, those charging the lowest commission and offering the highest rates of capital return, because this will result in higher sums in the individual's account and pension. There is evidence, however, that competition is not working, or working imperfectly, in most of the countries. For instance, Gill *et al.* (2005) have found that the heavy regulations and tight restrictions on switching between management firms have created a captive clientele for each pension fund firm and institutionalized what was *de facto* already an oligopoly.

Competition depends to a large extent on the size of the market of insured persons: the more there are of these, the more pension management firms there will be, and vice versa. Table 33.3 shows that, at the end of 2004, Mexico had 33 million

Table 33.3 Size of insured market, number of administrative firms, and concentration in the largest two and three firms, December 2004[1]

| Country | Affiliates (thousands) | Number of administrative firms | % of affiliates in biggest firms | |
|---|---|---|---|---|
| | | | Two biggest | Three biggest |
| Argentina | 10,008 | 12 | 38 | 52 |
| Bolivia | 878 | 2 | 100 | 100 |
| Chile | 7,080 | 6 | 66 | 80 |
| Colombia | 5,747 | 6 | 53 | 74 |
| Costa Rica | 1,270 | 10 | 66 | n.a. |
| Dominican Rep. | 1,033 | 8 | 63 | 79 |
| El Salvador | 1,166 | 2 | 100 | 100 |
| Mexico | 32,994 | 13 | 31 | 41 |
| Peru | 3,397 | 4 | 52 | 76 |
| Uruguay | 660 | 4 | 67 | 86 |
| Total and averages[2] | 64,233 | 6.7 | 64 | 76 |

*Notes:* n.a.= not available.
[1] Costa Rica, June 2004; Mexico, October 2004.
[2] Non-weighted average estimated by author.
*Sources:* Based on AIOS (2005); BCU (2005); CONSAR (2005); SAFJP (2005); SAFP (2005); SBC (2005); SBS (2005); SIPEN (2005); SP (2005); SPVS (2005); SUPEN (2005).

insured persons and 13 management firms, Argentina 10 million insured persons and 12 firms, Chile 7 million insured persons and six firms, Peru 3 million insured persons and four firms, and Bolivia and El Salvador about 1 million insured persons and two firms respectively. Ecuador and Nicaragua, with 300,000 insured persons and about 1 million insured, respectively, will face severe obstacles in securing a sufficient number of firms. Costa Rica and the Dominican Republic, however, with about 1 million insured persons, had 10 and eight firms respectively, because they have multiple types of firms and their systems have only been operating for a few years.[4] In all the countries the number of firms initially rises and then falls due to mergers: in Argentina the number declined from 25 to 12; in Chile from 21 to six; in Mexico from 17 to 13; in Colombia from ten to six; in Peru from eight to four; in Uruguay from six to four, and in El Salvador from five to two.

Even in countries with a considerable number of management firms, competition may be reduced by excessive concentration. The last two columns of Table 33.3 show the level of concentration of insured persons in the biggest two and three management firms at the end of 2004: concentration was 100 percent in Bolivia and El Salvador because they had only two firms; concentration ranged from 52 to 67 percent in the biggest two firms in seven countries, and from 74 to 86 percent in the biggest three firms in six countries. In Chile, concentration in the biggest three firms rose from 63 to 80 percent in 1983–2004. Mexico had the lowest level of concentration (31 and 41 percent) because the law prevents firms from having more than 20 percent of the total number of members. If the biggest firms are the ones offering the best conditions, with the lowest administrative costs and highest capital returns, then concentration should not be a cause for concern. This had not always been the case over time, as the author has proved in a study of Chile. Surveys of the reforms in various countries show a significant lack of information among the insured population about their individual accounts, commission charged, and capital returns earned. They also lack the skills to select the best firms, and generally choose a scheme on the basis of advertisement and the work of salespeople who are hired and paid commission by the largest firms (Mesa-Lago 2004a).

## 4.4 High and Sustained Managerial Costs

Competition is supposed to reduce management costs, but it has already been seen that many countries lack proper competition. Gill *et al.* (2005) acknowledge that private systems still change a commission that is unacceptably high for a large percentage of the population. Reductions in Chile and a few other countries have been achieved at the cost of restricting individual choice and competition between firms, and only a small fraction in the decline of operating expenses is being passed on to members of schemes in lower commission.

Table 33.4 Managerial cost of the private system: deposit, costs, total deduction, and administrative burden (as percentages of wages), December 2004

| Country | Deposit in individual account | Managerial costs (commission plus premium)[1] | Total deduction | Administrative burden (costs as % of total deduction) |
|---|---|---|---|---|
| Argentina | 4.47 | 2.53 | 7.00 | 36.14 |
| Bolivia | 10.00 | 2.21 | 12.21 | 18.10 |
| Chile | 10.00 | 2.27 | 12.27 | 18.50 |
| Colombia | 10.00 | 3.50 | 13.50 | 25.93 |
| Costa Rica | 4.50 | –[4] | n.a. | n.a. |
| Dominican Rep.[2] | 5.50 | 1.50 | 7.00 | 21.42 |
| El Salvador | 10.00 | 3.00 | 13.00 | 23.17 |
| Mexico | 7.04 | 3.96 | 11.00 | 47.00 |
| Peru | 8.00 | 3.19 | 11.19 | 28.51 |
| Uruguay | 12.17 | 2.83 | 15.00 | 18.87 |
| Averages[3] | 8.57 | 2.78 | 11.35 | 24.49 |

Notes:
[1] Commission charged by the administrator of the old-age program and premium for the insurance company to cover disability and survivor risks.
[2] In addition, 30 percent is charged on the amount that exceeds the average capital return.
[3] Non-weighted average of nine countries (excludes Costa Rica).
[4] There is no commission on wages but a percentage over the gross capital return.

Sources: Bolivia, Dominican Republic, and Mexico, June 2004 from AIOS (2005); rest from BCU (2005); SAFJP (2005); SAFP (2005); SBC (2005); SBS (2005); SP (2005); SPVS (2005).

Table 33.4 presents the percentage deductions from worker's wages that go toward the managerial costs of pensions schemes: these comprise deposits in individual accounts, managerial costs (combining commissions for administrators of old-age pension funds and premiums paid to commercial insurance companies to cover disability and survivor risks), the total deduction, and the administrative burden (costs as a percentage of the total deduction). At the end of 2004, managerial costs varied from 2 to 4 percent of wages with one exception. In Bolivia, Chile, and Uruguay the administrative burden was 18–19 percent of the total deduction, and in the remaining six countries it ranged from 21 to 47 percent, the average in the nine countries being 24 percent. This heavy burden is exclusively financed by the worker (except in Colombia) and, combined with the high level of the worker's contribution, constitutes a strong disincentive to affiliation and compliance. Fixing managerial costs as a set percentage of wages (as in the large majority of countries) does not create incentives for cost reduction, and the serious flaws in competition are additional obstacles. Gill et al. (2005) identify the lowering of management costs as a priority and state that Chile has slowly reduced them, but historical data do not bear this out. The administrative burden was 2.44 percent in 1981, peaked at 3.60 percent in 1984, and declined to 2.27 percent in 2004, only 0.17 points below the starting rate after 23 years of operation.

## 4.5 Significant Accumulation of Capital in the Pension Fund but Questionable Impact on National Saving

According to Gill *et al.* (2005) the regional rate of capital accumulation in pension funds doubled from 7.1 to 13.5 percent of GDP in 1998–2002. Table 33.5 confirms a very significant capital accumulation at the end of 2004, albeit the rate varied greatly among countries due to factors such as the size of the economy, the number of insured individuals, the wage level, capital returns, and the time the system has been in operation. Chile showed the highest figures (US$57,770 million and 63 percent of GDP) and Costa Rica the lowest (US$493 million and 2.1 percent). In the ten countries the total accumulation was US$142,979 million and the average rate of GDP was 11.8 percent. Despite the fact that Brazil does not have a mandated second pillar but voluntary supplementary pension schemes, this country had the highest accumulation in the region (US$80,000 million), although its rate ranked third (18 percent) because it has the second largest economy in the region.

The above figures only take into account the funds accumulated in individual accounts, but do not include the fiscal costs of the transition. They include the operational deficit in the closed public pension system; the value of contributions made to the public system by contributors who moved to the private system; and the minimum pension guaranteed by the state to people insured in the private system whose accumulation in their individual account is insufficient to finance a pension. Other components are the cost of social assistance pensions and the deficit in the armed forces scheme (Mesa-Lago 2004*b*). The World Bank (1994) asserted that pension reform would promote national saving, which in turn would boost economic growth and employment, and eventually make it possible to pay better pensions. Chile is the only country whose reform has been in effect long enough to test such an assumption, and three studies have shown that when fiscal costs were subtracted from savings deposited in individual accounts the net result was negative: an annual average of −2.7 to −3 percent of GDP during the first 16–18 years of the reform. One study has shown a net positive result of 2.3 percent in the first 20 years of the reform but it excluded various transition costs (for details and sources see Mesa-Lago 2004*b*).[5]

Table 33.5 Capital accumulation in the private system in US million dollars in December 2004, and as percentage of GDP in June 2004, and average capital return in December 2003–2004

| Country | Accumulated capital in individual accounts | | Average capital return (%)[1] |
|---|---|---|---|
| | Million US dollars | % of GDP | |
| Argentina | 18,614 | 11.8 | 9.9 |
| Bolivia | 1,716 | 19.5 | 11.1 |
| Chile | 57,770 | 62.6 | 10.3 |
| Colombia | 11,168 | 6.2[2] | 6.9 |
| Costa Rica | 493 | 2.1 | 8.0 |
| Dominican Republic | 245 | 6.6 | n.a. |
| El Salvador | 2,148 | 12.7 | 10.5 |
| Mexico | 41,165 | 5.8 | 8.1 |
| Peru | 7,982 | 11.2 | 7.6 |
| Uruguay | 1,678 | 14.4 | 13.8 |
| Total and averages | 142,979 | 11.8[3] | 9.6[4] |

Notes: n.a.= not available.
[1] From the inception of the system until December 2003, except Argentina and Peru in December 2004.
[2] December 2002.
[3] Excluding Colombia.
[4] Non-weighted average.

Sources: Capital in US million dollars from BCU (2005); CONSAR (2005); SAFJP (2005); SAFP (2005); SBC (2005); SBS (2005); SIPEN (2005); SP (2005); SPVS (2005); SUPEN (2005). Percentage of GDP and capital return from AIOS (2005).

## 4.6 Apparent Development of the Capital Market but Poor Diversification of the Investment Portfolio

It is claimed that structural pension reforms will help to develop capital markets, create new financial instruments, and diversify the investment portfolio to hedge against risks. Gill et al. (2005) evaluate the positive effects of the pension reforms on capital and financial markets, separating these effects from other policies. They pinpoint a number of problems. First, the capital market development in Latin America has been driven largely by state-sponsored modernization of the capital market infrastructure, tax and bankruptcy reforms, and by the regulatory structure for pension funds and other financial institutions. Second, the transparency and integrity in financial markets have dramatically improved but, in principle, these improvements could have taken place independently of the pension reform. Third, the instability created by a large transition debt is an obstacle to the deepening of financial markets and, in the absence of a sustained fiscal effort, transition costs can severely curtail the positive impact of pension funds on capital markets.

Gill *et al.* also evaluate investment of the funds and reach a number of conclusions. The fiscal costs of the transition have forced many governments to set ceilings to investment instruments, restricting foreign securities and favoring public-debt instruments—the main beneficiaries of the growth of pension funds. As a consequence, direct pension fund financing to the private sector through bonds and equities is still relatively low. Moreover, most of the stability in capital markets helped by pension reforms is artificial because it is driven at least in part by portfolio rules that force pension funds to hold mainly domestic assets and in some countries oblige them to invest a minimum percentage in government bonds. Gill *et al.* highlight that in no countries do individuals have investment choice because the firms, under the terms of regulations, decide investment allocation (except in Chile where the insured can choose among five types of instrument) and exhibit a herding instinct. This is particularly worrying because the industry is increasingly concentrated and the dominant investor in capital markets with decisions being placed in fewer hands. Finally, the precarious fiscal position of the governments in the region has—through high interest rates on government debt issues—resulted in high gross returns of the portfolio. This, in turn, raises other concerns: how long these high returns can be maintained where fiscal adjustments have reduced the spread of government debt, the risk of default where fiscal adjustment is low, and falling gross returns coupled with persistently high commissions.

Table 33.6, which shows the distribution of the pension fund portfolio by instruments at the end of 2004, confirms several of the above observations and shows that most of the countries are far from reaching a satisfactory level of diversification. In half of the countries, between 64 to 82 percent was invested in government debt and, in another two countries, 49 and 58 percent. Only Chile, the Dominican Republic, and Peru had a minor share in public debt. Such heavy concentration leads to a dependency on state-fixed interest, dangerous for both future capital returns and the pension level.

Argentina had the highest annual average capital return since the inception of the fund until 2000 (15 percent), because the state interest rate was very high, although it could not be sustained in the long run. Due to strong fiscal pressure, the government compelled pension firms to convert instruments in dollars into 'guaranteed' bonds in pesos, and the supervisory bodies collaborated by raising the ceiling of investment in public debt. The crisis of 2001–2 led to the devaluation of the peso, a reduction in the interest rate, and a drastic fall in both the fund and the projected pension in dollars (Hujo 2004).

Conversely, in Chile, after the crisis of 1982–3 threatened the new pension system, the supervisory bodies played a crucial role in promoting diversification of the portfolio and, after 21 years, cut the share invested in public debt from 50 to 19

Table 33.6 Portfolio diversification: percentage distribution of total pension fund by financial instrument in December 2004[1]

| Country | Government debt | Financial institutions | Non-financial | Stocks | Mutual funds, etc. | Foreign emissions | Others |
|---|---|---|---|---|---|---|---|
| Argentina | 61.2 | 6.3 | 1.9 | 12.7 | 4.1 | 10.3 | 3.5 |
| Bolivia | 68.0 | 5.8 | 16.1 | 7.5 | 0.0 | 0.0 | 2.6 |
| Chile | 18.7 | 29.5 | 6.9 | 14.7 | 2.7 | 27.3 | 0.2 |
| Colombia | 48.5 | 17.4 | 19.6 | 3.6[4] | —[4] | 9.7 | 1.2 |
| Costa Rica | 78.2 | 14.0 | 6.3 | 0.0 | 1.5 | 0.0 | 0.0 |
| Dom. Rep.[2] | 24.4 | 66.5 | 2.4 | 6.5 | 0.0 | 0.0 | 0.2 |
| El Salvador | 83.5 | 10.5 | 4.2 | 0.4 | 0.0 | 1.4 | 0.0 |
| Mexico | 83.0 | 4.5 | 12.5 | 0.0 | 0.0 | 0.0 | 0.0 |
| Peru | 24.2 | 11.4 | 12.1 | 37.1 | 1.4 | 10.2 | 3.6 |
| Uruguay | 57.9 | 36.9 | 5.2 | 0.0 | 0.0 | 0.0 | 0.0 |
| Averages[3] | 54.8 | 20.3 | 8.7 | 8.2 | 1.0 | 5.9 | 1.1 |

Notes: [1] Dominican Republic, June 2004; Mexico, October 2004.
[2] Distribution by AIOS including all pension funds; the individual account fund is all invested in paper from commercial banks and savings associations.
[3] Non-weighted average distribution of total fund by financial instrument.
[4] Unclear distribution between stocks and mutual funds.

Sources: AIOS (2004); BCU (2005); CONSAR (2005); SAFJP (2005); SAFP (2005); SBC (2005); SBS (2005); SIPEN (2005); SP (2005); SPVS (2005); SUPEN (2005).

percent. Despite the promise that reform and capital accumulation would help to finance the private sector, investment in stocks averaged only 8 percent and was significant in only half of the countries (8 to 37 percent). The alternative of investing in foreign instruments was prohibited in several countries: the share averaged 6 percent and was significant in only four countries (10 to 27 percent). Small countries without a capital market or an incipient one face a major barrier to diversifying their portfolios and a high risk of heavy dependence on public debt instruments.

## 4.7 Variable Real Capital Returns

Another assumption of the structural reform is that it generates a high rate of real capital return. The last column of Table 33.5 supports this assumption, although the results vary between countries and according to the period used for the calculations. Average real annual rates of capital return (adjusted for inflation) from the time when the system began to operate up to the end of 2003 were: 14 percent in Uruguay; 10 to 11 percent in Argentina, Bolivia, Chile, and El Salvador; and 6 to 8 percent in the remaining four countries, with a regional average of 9.6 percent. These are gross rates of return; they do not deduct the cost of commission, so that the net return is lower. In 1981–2000, the gross rate of return of the pension fund in Chile averaged 11.9 percentage points less than the Selective Share Price Index of the Santiago Stock Exchange and 3.8 points more than the average interest rate on deposits, but with much greater volatility. In 1993–2000, the pension fund in Peru had an average rate of return below that of bank deposits or Brady Bonds (Mesa-Lago 2004*b*; Gill *et al.* 2005).

These figures refer to the average for the whole period since the reform came into effect, but if we take only the period up to the mid-1990s the average is much higher, while for the period since 1995 it is much lower because of the economic and stock exchange crises of 1995, 1998, and 2001. Thus, the average rate of return in Chile in 1981–94 was three times higher than that of 1995–2004 and negative average rates occurred in 1995 and 1998 (SAFP 2002 and 2005). These fluctuations in rates of return involve a serious risk: if the insured person retires at a peak period in the capital market, his pension will be good, but the amount accumulated in his individual account will go down considerably during a crisis, especially if this is prolonged.

## 4.8 Accentuation in Gender-Based Inequalities

Most of the literature on the impact of structural pension reforms on gender in Latin America concludes that it has increased inequality for a number of reasons. First, private systems require a given number of years of contribution to grant a minimum pension and most of the reforms have increased those years, making it more difficult for women—who have a lower contribution density than men—to gain that pension. Furthermore, the pension is based on contributions during the whole working life, instead of only the last years before retirement, as in most public systems in the region, which further damages the pensions prospects of women whose density of contributions is low. In addition, the annuity is calculated with mortality tables differentiated by gender; since the sum accumulated in the individual account is divided by the average life expectancy, women's pensions are lower than men, who have a shorter life expectancy. Women's pensions are further reduced if they retire five years earlier as legally stipulated in four countries under the reforms. In Chile, in 2000–1, the average pension fund of women was 32–46 percent lower than men's; the female replacement rate was 52–7 percent versus 81–6 percent for men and the average pension of a retired women at age 60 was 60 percent that of a retired men or 87 percent if women retired at 65 (SAFP 2002; Bertranou and Arenas de Mesa 2003; CEPAL 2005).

Gill *et al.* (2005) assessed the gender impact of the reform in eight countries (all those with reforms, except Dominican Republic) in a simulation exercise based on the difference between internal rates of return of women and men, with mixed results. In two countries the return for women increased marginally relative to that of men. In one country the reform reversed distribution returns in favor of women. In three countries reforms replaced subsidized benefits for women by subsidized benefits for men, and in all countries, despite the reforms, women earned lower returns than men. The simulation assumed that men and women had the same work and contributory history, which must have resulted in an overestimation of women's rates of return. In addition, the three experts acknowledged that due to higher life expectancy and sex-specific mortality tables, annuities received by women are lower than men, even if they retire at the same age.

# 5 Conclusions and Directions for Future Research

This chapter has demonstrated that eight of the presumed effects of structural pension reforms in ten Latin American countries have either not materialized or are not validated by empirical evidence.

1. Instead of increasing, labor force coverage declined in all countries from the time of the reform to 2004 and the average coverage in the ten countries decreased from 38 to 26 percent. Clearly, new policies are needed to halt such decline and expand coverage to the informal sector.
2. Rather than stimulating compliance in the payment of contributions, the average proportion of scheme members in all countries who contributed monthly fell from 60 to 41 percent between 1998 and 2004. Again, more research is necessary to identify the causes of non-compliance in order for there to be any prospect of remedying this situation.
3. Competition among management firms—the foundation of a private system—has not worked in small countries and was poor in most of the rest. The concentration of members in the largest three firms ranged from 74 to 100 percent in 2004 (with two exceptions), a trend set to increase.
4. Partly because of the absence of competition, managerial costs have not decreased; instead they are high and have not significantly declined in most countries. These costs as a proportion of total wage deductions ranged from 18 to 47 percent in 2004 and research is required to find the causes of this problem and design alternatives.

5. Confirming the initial assumption, there has been a significant capital accumulation in pension funds, albeit varying from 2 to 63 percent of GDP in the ten countries. However, this accumulation does not take into account the fiscal costs of the transition and, when this is subtracted from capital accumulation, most studies on Chile show an annual negative average of −3 percent of GDP in the first 16–18 years of the reform. This is a crucial area for research in other countries, in order to establish the pattern there.
6. The impact of the reform on the development of capital and financial markets is difficult to measure because it must be separated from other causative factors, and more research is vital to clarify this. Furthermore, there has not been a diversification of the investment portfolio in eight of the ten countries, where investment is highly concentrated on government debt and little or nothing is invested in stocks.
7. Apparently confirming the assumption that capital returns would be higher in private than in public systems, average gross real capital returns ranged from 7 to 14 percent from the start of the reform until 2003–4. However, these returns were lower when the administrative commissions were substracted, underlining the need for accurate estimates of net returns. Furthermore, these averages varied significantly over time, showing a declining trend in several countries.
8. The reforms have accentuated gender-based inequalities because of an increase in the years of contribution required for accessing both minimum and overall pensions. The mortality tables differentiated by sex used by the pension schemes have the result of further lowering pensions for women.

# Notes

The author acknowledges authorization to reproduce material from previous articles: 'An appraisal of a quarter-century of structural pension reforms in Latin America', *ECLAC Review*, 84 (Dec.) 2004, and 'Assessing the World Bank Report Keeping the Promise', *International Social Security Review*, 58/2–3 (2005).

1. This reform involves three stages and the second one—scheduled to begin in 2004—has not been implemented yet.
2. Estimates by the author based on BCU (2005); CONSAR (2005); SAFJP (2005); SAFP (2005); SBC (2005); SBS (2005); SIPEN (2005); SP (2005); SPVS (2005); SUPEN (2005).
3. In 2002 the author estimated an average of 27 percent (Mesa-Lago 2004*b*, 2005), one percentage point higher than in 2004, suggesting a rapid decline in coverage.
4. The Dominican Republic also allows management firms to use the infrastructure of other financial institutions to reduce costs and facilitate entry and greater competition.
5. The estimate of fiscal costs and projections to 2040 in five countries by Gill *et al.* (2005) were contrasted by the author with initial domestic estimates and projections, showing that the former were higher than the latter in three countries (Mesa-Lago 2005). The

three experts warned that, despite improvements, fiscal sustainability is far from assured; pension reforms can create new implicit and explicit liabilities, and produce severe cash-flow problems in excess of initially projected transition costs. In Nicaragua, the implementation of the system was postponed indefinitely in 2004 because, as currently designed, the country cannot finance the transitional fiscal costs.

# References

Arenas de Mesa, A., and Hernández, H. (2001). 'Análisis, evolución y propuestas de ampliación de la cobertura del sistema civil de pensiones en Chile', in F. Betranou (ed.), *Cobertura Previsional in Argentina, Brasil y Chile*. Santiago: OIT.

Asociación Internacional de Organismos de Supervisión de Fondos de Pensiones (AIOS). (1999–2005). *Boletín Estadístico AIOS*, Nos. 1 to 11.

Banco Central del Uruguay (BCU) (2005). Montevideo. www.bcu.gub.uy

Barr, N. (2002). 'Reforming pensions: myths, truths, and policy choices'. *International Social Security Review*, 55/2 (Mar.–June): 3–36.

Bertranou, F., and Arenas de Mesa, A. (eds.) (2003). *Protección social, pensiones y género en Argentina, Brasil y Chile*. Santiago: OIT.

Comisión Económica para América Latina y el Caribe (CEPAL) (2004). *Statistical Yearbook for Latin America and the Caribbean 2003*. Santiago.

—— (2005). *Los sistemas de pensiones en América Latina: un análisis de género*, F. Marco (ed.). Santiago: Cuadernos de la CEPAL, 90.

Comisión Nacional del Sistema de Ahorro para el Retiro (CONSAR) (2005). México D. F. www.consar.gob.mx

Gill, I., Packard, T., and Yermo, J. (with the assistance of Puggart, T.) (2005). *Keeping the Promise of Social Security in Latin America*. Stanford, Calif.: Stanford University Press and the World Bank.

Hujo, K. (2004). 'Reforma previsional y crisis económica: el caso Argentino', in C. Mesa-Lago, K. Hujo, and M. Nitsch (eds.), *¿Públicos o privados? Los sistemas de pensiones en América Latina después de dos décadas*. Caracas: Nueva Sociedad, 135–74.

International Labour Office (ILO) (2003). *Panorama laboral 2003: América Latina y el Caribe*. Lima: Oficina Regional para América Latina y el Caribe.

Mesa-Lago, C. (2002). 'Myth and reality on social security pension reform: the Latin American evidence'. *World Development*, 30/8 (Aug.): 1309–21.

—— (2004a). *Las reformas de pensiones en América Latina y su impacto en los principios de la seguridad social*. Santiago: CEPAL Serie Financiamiento del Desarrollo, 144.

—— (2004b). 'An appraisal of a quarter-century of structural pension reforms in Latin America'. *ECLAC Review*, 84 (Dec.): 59–82.

—— (2005). 'Assessing the World Bank Report Keeping the Promise'. *International Social Security Review*, 58/2–3: 97–117.

Orszag, P., and Stiglitz, J. (2001). 'Rethinking pension reforms: ten myths about social security systems', in R. Holzmann, J. Stiglitz, L. Fox, E. James, and P. Orszag (eds.), *New Ideas about Old Age Security: Towards Sustainable Pension Systems in the 21st Century*. Washington, D.C.: World Bank, 17–56.

SUPERINTENDENCIA BANCARIA DE COLOMBIA (SBC) (2005). Bogotá. www.superbancaria.gov.co

SUPERINTENDENCIA DE ADMINISTRADORAS DE FONDOS DE JUBILACIONES Y PENSIONES (SAFJP) (2005). Buenos Aires. www.safjp.gov.ar

SUPERINTENDENCIA DE ADMINISTRADORAS DE FONDOS DE PENSIONES (SAFP) (2002). *El Sistema Chileno de Pensiones*, 5th edn. Alejandro Ferreiro (ed.). Santiago.

—— (2005). Santiago. www.safp.cl

SUPERINTENDENCIA DE BANCA Y SEGUROS (SBS) (2005). Lima. www.sbs.gob.pe

SUPERINTENDENCIA DE PENSIONES (SIP) (2005). Managua. www.sip.org.ni

SUPERINTENDENCIA DE PENSIONES (SIPEN) (2005). Santo Domingo. www.sipen.gov.do

SUPERINTENDENCIA DE PENSIONES (SP) (2005). San Salvador. www.spensiones.gob.sv

SUPERINTENDENCIA DE PENSIONES (SUPEN) (2005). San José. www.supen.fi.cr

SUPERINTENDENCIA DE PENSIONES, VALORES Y SEGUROS (SPVS) (2005). La Paz. www.spvs.gov.bo

WORLD BANK (1994). *Averting the Old Age Crisis: Policies to Protect the Old and Promote Growth*. New York: Oxford University Press.

# CHAPTER 34

# PRIVATE PENSIONS AND PUBLIC POLICY: THE PUBLIC–PRIVATE DIVIDE REAPPRAISED

## NOEL WHITESIDE

## 1 Introduction

Recent pension debates have focused overwhelmingly on problems of pension finance: on the sustainability of present schemes and the problems posed by rising pension obligations for both public and private sectors. In response to the recommendations of the World Bank (1994) and rising pressures to cut public welfare budgets, many European states have restructured their public pension schemes and, under a range of initiatives, have sought to promote private saving to sustain pensioner income. Reductions in public provision follow a neoliberal economic logic: free markets are the source of efficient distribution of goods and services and state intervention distorts market signals while driving up costs. At the extreme, we might conclude that government should not provide pensions at all (Blinder 1988).

This perspective represents the opposite to that taken in many countries after the Second World War, when state protection for all elderly and infirm was considered a fundamental social obligation. Recent reappraisals of state schemes and the acceptance of the World Bank's multi-pillar approach have justified the desirability of raising personal savings. At the same time, public opposition to the dismantling of state pension systems, a foundation stone of European welfare states, has forced delay, compromise, and political vacillation.

This chapter does not take sides in the debate on the relative strengths and weaknesses of public or private pension provision, but examines the assumptions on which this division is based. In many respects, we might argue that the debate over public versus private is irrelevant to the analysis of pension schemes and the current pension crisis. After all, in one way or another, the solution demands that we (collectively or singly) pay more and that future pensioners work longer or receive less. The following section shows how states, through the law, are deeply implicated in all market systems, which offer but one means of coordinating economic action. It is not possible to conceive of a market without rules and the state, solely sovereign in this matter, governs market actions as much as it governs everything else. The second section explores this proposition empirically and relates it to pension policy developments in the decades following the Second World War. It outlines how governments adapted established private institutions (occupational and complementary pension systems) to public purposes, in response to popular demand for higher pensions. This created quasi-independent hybrids that, being neither state nor market, offered old-age security under varied funding systems while attaching pension receipt to previous earnings. The final section demonstrates the relevance of these debates to our current concerns and discusses possible future research agendas that explore the issue along these lines. The chapter suggests that the genesis of global financial markets is central to many current problems, as market-based systems and conventions are overriding other value judgments that offer alternative bases from which to assess the worth of public services, including welfare.

Much comparative social policy literature on pension development since the Second World War has focused on state provision and has been shaped by Esping-Andersen's seminal study on welfare state regimes (1990). Based on a quantitative analysis of the coverage and redistributive effects of public pensions, this analysis divides welfare states into three basic types: social-democratic in Scandinavia, liberal in Anglo-Saxon countries, conservative-corporate in Continental Europe. One problem with Esping-Andersen's 'worlds' of welfare, however, stems from its rigidity. His comparative theory rests on characterizations of welfare states derived from the prolonged period of economic growth following the Second World War. This limited historical perspective distorts understanding of the instability that preceded and has followed this era; it offers a misleading impression of the permanence of postwar social settlements that were necessarily historically contingent. Even so, this work has proved highly influential. In spite of permanent pressures of austerity, little sign has been found by political scientists of convergence of welfare states (or pension regimes) toward a single, minimal model (Pierson 1998). Wholesale retrenchment and radical welfare reconstruction have been confined to liberal regimes, where state provision has lower public support (Pierson 2001). While embellishing the political factors that underpin the worlds of welfare, path dependency theory still upholds the viability of the model itself.

Not all analysts agree with the premise that welfare reform develops solely along established lines. The view that the Continental European welfare landscape is 'frozen' (Esping-Andersen 1996) is contested (e.g. Bonoli 2000; Bonoli and Palier 1996). There has been a perceptible shift toward the World Bank's recommended multi-pillar pension system within Europe. The European Commission is encouraging the development of a single European market for supplementary pensions, to foster greater cross-national labor mobility while developing a Eurozone-wide pension fund market as a key element in the integration of EU financial markets (Pochet 2003; Connell 2005). With or without the Commission's intervention, EU member states acknowledge the need for private supplementation to bolster shrinking public provision (Myles and Pierson 2001; Palier 2003). This focus on the similar trajectories developed by Bismarckian states (including Sweden) has challenged Esping-Andersen's old geography of welfare regimes as a basis for social analysis (Hinrichs 2001: 2004). Esping-Andersen himself has recently shifted his allegiances, supporting the trend to more neoliberal solutions based on more personal saving in lieu of redistributive, universal systems of the Scandinavian type (Esping-Andersen *et al.* 2002).

The spate of recent reforms thus calls for a new analytical framework. We need a theoretical perspective that explains difference while incorporating a more sophisticated understanding of the dynamics that have provoked modification and change. Further, analyses of developments in global finance on the one hand and of pension reform politics on the other have tended to remain academically separate (exceptions include Deacon and Hulse 1996; Schwartz 2001; Clark 2003). In social policy literature, fiscal and demographic factors that promote welfare state retrenchment receive extensive attention; the strengths and weaknesses of global financial markets receive far less. It is patently obvious that their transfer into private hands does not automatically increase pension resources for future generations. On the contrary, the higher costs generated by competing multiple providers might actually reduce them. Both the promise—and the threat—offered by personal investment on global capital markets as a potential solution to the current pension crisis require more attention. The assumptions underpinning the promotion of market solutions to social problems, moreover, rest on potentially uneasy foundations and to their analysis we now turn.

## 2 Private Pensions and Public Policy: the Theory of the Convention

To analyze current debates over public and private pensions requires an understanding of the neoliberal premises that have informed policy discussion. In the UK, where privatization initiatives developed during the 1980s (earlier than elsewhere in Europe), politicians argued that old-age protection would be most effectively secured by returning to the individual the freedom to choose the savings product best suited to guaranteeing her future. The assumption that action based on personal interest offers the best way forward rests on neoliberal tenets of political economy; these argue that markets, untrammeled by state intervention, automatically secure the most efficient distribution of goods and services. Such arguments assume that rational individuals, left to their own devices, base their actions on optimizing personal interests, seeking out and utilizing pertinent information to secure this end. Within this framework, public sector interventions should be minimal and confined to residual provision for those who, through no fault of their own, are unable to assume responsibility for their own security. If state provision is excessive, the market becomes deformed: high taxation (to fund collective welfare) distorts price signals and the belief that the state will offer universal protection against risk breeds social dependency. At best, market provision offers choices and market competition guarantees that these choices are available at optimally efficient prices. Within an ordered and tractable analytical logic, collective choice thus permits the perfection of efficient provision. This (admittedly crude) summary of how neoliberal market systems can and should shape collective decision-making is based on a model that unifies the private and the personal. It is applied extensively in the social sciences to the analysis of labor productivity, industrial organization—even public policy formation—as well as social protection.

Sociologists and economists working within the theory of the convention offer us a starting point from which to build an alternative analysis. Focusing on the problem of uncertainty and the consequent requirement for coordinated action to enable all to achieve their goals, this approach denies that each individual is an independent agent (the premise of neoliberal market theory). All social and economic actions are interdependent. The chief problem for individuals is to anticipate how others might respond to their initiatives: this generates uncertainty over outcomes. Uncertainty can provoke distrust and non-participation, leading to the breakdown of socio-economic systems. For uncertainty implies no basis for understanding the consequences of an action: if I hand over money on the promise of future goods or services, can I be assured of their receipt? Or if I turn to someone for help when sick, can I be assured of her professional competence? Similarly, if I contribute to a pension fund, can I rest assured that it will provide the expected income in my old age? In the absence of conventions that serve as a basis for coordination, I will not act, as the uncertainty is too strong. Successful action depends essentially on collective trust and mutual expectation that all will know and respect conventions underpinning specific situations. Coordination emerges as the cornerstone of social and economic action, rather than competition between multiple providers.

The term 'uncertainty' is here employed to define a world where outcomes of action are unknowable. It must be distinguished from risk or hazard, the phenomena that form part of the insurance world, where possible adverse outcomes are identifiable and, with the aid of expert diagnosis, a probable consequence of action is predictable and risk can be measured. Actuarial evaluation shapes the calculation of premiums in an insurance environment that offers compensation in the event of action or accident producing a collectively recognized but undesired result—but this outcome is identifiable in advance. Protection against collectively acknowledged risk is necessary to establish confidence for all to participate in entrepreneurial activity. In the world of economic action, risk (multiple but identifiable) lies at one end of the spectrum, uncertainty (infinite and unknowable) at the other. In short, taking a risk implies previous knowledge about (even awareness concerning the likelihood of) adverse outcomes of action, while uncertainty denies the actor any basis for reaching a judgment about the effects of action, if any (Knight 1921). Seen from this perspective, effective action depends on the elimination of uncertainty more than on the containment of risk.

Risk may be insured individually or collectively. Classical mechanisms of social insurance, the foundation stone of many European state pension schemes, allow low risk cases to compensate for the high risk cases. These systems have long protected working people against conventionally defined 'risks' that threaten their livelihood, covering illness, unemployment, invalidity, as well as old age. In different countries and contexts, protection against some or all of such risks is assumed to be a personal, not a collective, responsibility—current renegotiations over pension provision demonstrate how this balance can change. Further, close examination of how such risks are defined (whether retirement, or the achievement of a pre-specified age, or both, is required for receipt of a pension) reveals variation in terms of place, occupation, and time. Identities are constantly reshaped. This fluidity, however, remains hidden behind the convention that this type of risk exists—and that collective agencies (commercial, mutual, state-sponsored) are in place to offer compensation. The identity of the risk (and the nature of the compensation) themselves reflect expectations about behaviors proper to public or private, collective or individual action: these shape the bedrock of conventions sustaining collective trust and define remits of welfare provision. Hence the existence of social protection promotes specific strategies of collective bargaining and manpower management: the use of early retirement and sickness pensions to facilitate industrial restructuring during the 1980s offers one example (Chaskiel et al. 1986).

Systems of coordination and the logics that underpin them vary widely. In the need to justify our actions publicly, to offer explanation or to resolve dispute, different conventions (collectively accepted means of coordinated action) are revealed (Boltanski and Thevenot 1991). Public forms of justification are necessary to explain and coordinate action, as calculation concerning its consequences requires us to anticipate the reaction of others. In simple terms, these action frameworks (or evaluations of worth) are the building blocks of collective understanding and trust. Different evaluations of worth are pertinent to different given objects. Within plural frameworks of social ordering, market-based systems, reliant on competition and dependent on signals of quality and price, distinguish good products from bad, thereby offering one form of coordination. There are others. Standardized forms of measurement and knowledge provide the basis for professional knowledge: these coordinate evaluations in medicine, or technical knowledge—including, for example, actuarial expertise. This 'industrial' world displays the permanent value of certain types of knowledge, measurement, and analysis: the foundations for coordinating future socio-economic development. In similar vein, we can distinguish hierarchies of worth that legitimate the public exercise of authority and distinguish civic virtues from anti-social behaviors that merit collective condemnation. This civic world denotes the varying bases of moral-political evaluations that identify legitimate forms of decision-making and spheres of state power. Other conventions delineate the domestic or familial world: acceptable modes of behavior within households or local communities. Here, the bonds of love and the desire for intimacy foster compliance and conformity with different social practices. As Thevenot argues (2001), these hierarchies of worth are neither permanent nor stable. All are grounded in historical precedent and all are constantly modified in the course of action. All offer different foundations for rational action: while all co-exist, none can be used to denigrate or disqualify any other as all operate within their own terms of reference. Plural coordinating reference points based on different hierarchies of worth form frameworks for individual choice. These reference points are central to the confidence and trust that render coordinated action possible.

Hence social frameworks (collectively respected conventions) are necessary for market activity; individual choices and compromises are made within complex situations. To secure specified outcomes, individuals make decisions based on their expectations concerning the consequences of their actions and the relationship of these to their desired goals. This implies the pre-existence of a collective understanding about right and proper behavior within specific environments; to act, each person requires the common knowledge embedded in conventions shaping different environments (Dupuy 1989). The various hierarchies of worth reflect worlds of moral judgment, which in turn reflect respectable behavior, accepted duties, and civil codes. Here, the common good is found: not a side-product of the collective pursuit of personal interest, but conventions accepted by all as a proper basis for social and economic coordination—including the means by which they are defined and enforced. The need for coordination locates the personal within the collective; conventions are central to the creation of market institutions and to the need for state intervention.

Collective foundations for social action (firms and other institutions) now no longer appear as anomalies in market competition, but instead can be understood as formalized compromises between different hierarchies of worth (Thevenot 2001). For such institutions, market competition, technological and organizational planning, and public relations generate tensions over resources and priorities that require constant re-evaluation and compromise: compromises focused on the nature of the product, the degree of capital investment, the location (and values) of potential consumers. Far from relying solely on product quality and price, real life markets depend on the development of trust between seller and buyer. Here, the nature of the product is crucial. The very term 'marketing' denotes the ambition of creating consumer confidence: the 'Find, Mind, Bind, Grind' of US consultant manuals stresses how customer relations are based on care, to foster trust and confidence as necessary preconditions to the extraction of profit. All markets, including pension markets, are a compromise between different worlds. When choosing complex goods, consumers turn to friends, work colleagues and family for advice—and will be happier choosing the 'good enough' product ratified by intimates than one that appears to offer better value for money (for an historical example, see Whiteside 1997).

To achieve coordination, all markets rely on collectively recognized codes of conduct. Much of this is ratified in law: there exist (implicitly or explicitly) moral orders that reflect collective perceptions of social justice, or the 'proper' way of doing things. The rules of competition and contract, of agency and its just remuneration, have to be known and accepted for market economies to function. Institutional arrangements ensure that rules are observed. The state, the only institution endowed with sovereign powers, acts as the coordinator of last resort: guaranteeing social justice by establishing the rules of the game, by identifying undesirable behaviors, and by protecting the polity from external threat or the sudden alien imposition of new rules (Salais 1998). In all market-based economies, regulation is present; should markets wobble or threaten to fail, the public turns to government for more legislative protection, not less. Hence, to take an example, the collapse of Enron (2002) stimulated demands for international accounting regulations, to enable all investors to be informed of total corporate assets and liabilities. When seen from this angle, the division between 'state' and 'market', so common in neoliberal discussion, becomes hard to sustain, for the state—through the law—remains charged with underwriting market operations to secure the necessary confidence and trust to enable all to participate. As some economists have noted

(Storper and Salais 1997; Dore 2000; Hall and Soskice 2001), contractual relations, the institutions that enforce them, and their underpinning conventions vary widely—between nations, between products, and over time.

From this perspective, pensions also represent institutionalized compromises rooted in agreed principles of social justice (Whiteside 2005). These compromises have been officially ratified in various ways. Governments in different countries have established or sustained very diverse typologies of pension management, requiring different points of state intervention and creating varied patterns of direct and indirect control. In consequence, there is no equivalence between apparently similar institutions or pension schemes embedded in different environments. Comparative assessments based solely on social support provided directly by the state are therefore highly partial. There is no simple way to distinguish between public and private schemes. An examination of pension development in the postwar years illustrates this point.

## 3 OCCUPATION AND SECURITY[1]

In Europe, state-funded pensions formed part of a postwar settlement characterized by a standardized working week and faith in the efficiency of state welfare. These varied schemes were less an economic than a political product: a compromise reached between industrial, labor, and national economic interests underwritten by collective agreements and social legislation (Whiteside and Salais 1998). The agreements reflected specific historical circumstances: an urgent need to rebuild war-shattered economies, to modernize industrial production, to secure democracy, and to establish universal security following the destructive impact of the slump years and total war. American paradigms, stressing economies of scale and the commercial merits of large, integrated production systems, influenced how modernity was conceived. Postwar labor shortages encouraged firms to develop company pensions to foster worker loyalty, a development equally evident in the professional protection already established in fast-expanding public sectors. This drive to rationalize labor distribution and to secure worker cooperation for an agenda based on a specific vision of the future represented an apogee in state-sponsored security (Salais and Whiteside 1998, part III). As postwar living standards rose, so demand increased for the socially dependent—particularly pensioners—to share in rising prosperity. To protect public expenditure from future growing burdens, some European governments decided to promote earnings-related pensions and turned to the extension of company and occupational schemes to meet rising expectations.

Postwar welfare states have been thoroughly documented in both historical and social policy literature; less attention has been directed to earnings-related occupational pensions in the 1950s and 1960s.[2] Here, we can note fundamental differences between European and Scandinavian welfare and pension policies and their Anglo-Saxon counterparts. This is reflected in traditions of joint or tripartite decision-making and the role of government (through labor law) in guaranteeing (and extending) basic employment contracts (Gamet 2000). Continental European labour law enforces the norms governing employment, as reflected in rights and obligations of employers and employed (including compliance with social security legislation). Formal agreements establish minimum standards: pensions agreed through collective bargaining, as well as those stipulated by social security legislation, are given the protection of the law. As a result, the apparent divide between public and private pension provision is less profound in Continental Europe than in Anglo-Saxon countries, where occupational pension schemes may be collectively negotiated, but are still essentially private arrangements. Moreover, European employers' organizations and trade unions administer occupational or enterprise-based systems and state welfare: this reflects long-established conventions of co-determination and corporate governance (strong, for example, in Germany, the Netherlands, and Sweden but less so in France). Such differences are rooted in Bismarckian social insurance, revived after the Second World War.

In the immediate postwar years, occupational or complementary pension schemes grew rapidly. In an era of skilled labor shortages, employers cultivated the loyalty of key employees, to offset the attractions of pensions available to workers in the public sector, and to facilitate internal labor management. Generally, company pensions covered white-collar, professional, and technical staffs who were hard to replace; blue-collar, unskilled, or temporary personnel (the sectors most vulnerable to old-age poverty) tended to be excluded. Fiscal concessions to promote such schemes, originally introduced in the early twentieth century, were extended. However, variance in state social security meant that occupational and professional provision was integrated into the wider sphere of economic and social politics in diverse ways. Legally endowed occupational and professional pension rights formed an institutional heritage highly resistant to change. Postwar processes of establishing (and raising) state pensions necessarily affected previous arrangements. In Europe, the legacy of the war (inflation, industrial devastation, and labor market dislocation) almost required the provision of citizenship pensions (exemplified by Sweden and the Netherlands) independent of contributory record or means test, to prevent the spread of destitution. The contested solidarity embedded in such public schemes (Baldwin 1990) extended to occupational pensions that also involved a pooling of risk, whose governance was, like its public counterpart, vested in representatives of employers and employed.

The 1950s witnessed the emergence of the first pension panic; rising longevity combined with growing prosperity was creating poor pensioners unable to share in rising living standards. Governments in the 1950s and 1960s sought to adapt existing employment-based, earnings-related provision to eradicate future pensioner poverty. This strategy had many advantages. It allowed, by index-linking contributions and benefits, pensioner income to be secured against inflation. Contributory income could be used for the purposes of industrial modernization. Finally, offering higher earnings-related pensions (as deferred salary) could help to contain wage demands. Similar strategies, however, were disguised by the very different roles ascribed to the state (as direct provider, legal guarantor, or participatory administrator) in different national contexts. Even as different governments had created different public agencies for the purposes of postwar economic reconstruction, so these precedents helped to shape the nature of state participation in pension reform, thereby generating varied remits of public and private responsibility, administration, and ownership. A brief review of pension politics in this period reveals how public and private spheres of activity were reconstituted: key cases demonstrate how political processes shaped a public/private division that has subsequently assumed an enormous importance.

In the late 1950s, Germany and Sweden transformed state pension provision to embrace a universal, earnings-related component on all incomes under a specified ceiling. Norway followed the Swedish example in 1966 (Palme 2003: Hinrichs 2004). Following extensive debate, reforms in these countries endowed the state with responsibility for guaranteeing that pensioner income remained linked to current earnings, protecting pensioners against inflation. In Germany, the high replacement ratio guaranteed by the new state scheme (following the 1957 reform, state pensions rose by 70 percent: Hinrichs 2004: 17) did not spell the disappearance of company pensions. On the contrary, German firms continued to promote private schemes. Thanks to the 'book reserve' system, German corporate pensions helped to restrain wage demands while creating funds for the company to invest in future expansion. In the 1990s, two out of three salaried workers were covered by a complementary scheme (Reynaud and Tamburi 1994, ch. 4). In Sweden, following the introduction of the state-run earnings related scheme in 1959 (ATP), additional pension protection was collectively negotiated. A new defined benefit scheme to cover white-collar workers was collectively agreed in 1960 (ITP), with an additional scheme for blue-collar workers created in 1973 (STP). Finally, defined benefit pensions were established for central (SPN) and local government (KPA) employees (Kangas and Palme 1996). This created a multi-tiered hierarchy of guaranteed pensions, offering high levels of old-age income replacement and reducing the need for personal saving until pensions were restructured in the late 1990s (Palme 2003).

In France and the Netherlands, policy reinforced occupational pensions, but the management of earnings-related provision remained outside state hands. In the Netherlands, collective agreements in the early 1950s created funded occupational pension schemes in pre-specified sectors (1953), predating universal state insurance (1957). Sectoral pension funds were invested in postwar reconstruction of the Dutch economy and, from the start, their provision was compulsory for all employers (Van Riel 2003). Coverage grew steadily, reaching 60 percent of Dutch employees in the 1960s and well over 90 percent in the 1990s (Clark and Bennett 2001). In France, social security fractured along occupational lines from its very inception (Palier 2002, ch. 2). The cadres (white-collar and technical staffs in the private sector) supplemented the new state regime of social security created in 1946 with their own earnings-related pension scheme (AGIRC) (Lion 1962). This precedent encouraged other supplementary occupational pensions in the 1950s, to complement state pension benefits that remained very low. Many firms committed to such schemes were small: intense economic modernization forced some to disappear or merge with other companies. Larger umbrella associations guaranteed worker protection. For example, AGRR,[3] established in 1951, covered 99,800 firms with 780,000 members in sugar, textiles, wood, and furniture 20 years later. The largest, UNIRS,[4] founded in 1957, covered 298,000 firms, was paying 1.9 million complementary pensioners, and had 4.3 million subscribing members by 1971. In 1961, under official prompting, a collective agreement created ARRCO,[5] an association covering all complementary occupational pensions below specified earnings (Lyon-Caen 1962). By pooling a proportion of contributions, funds in surplus subsidized those in deficit; employers remained free to offer additional pensions if they wished. By the early 1970s, ARRCO covered all French workers in France and its overseas territories (ARRCO 1972).

These examples show that, through collective agreement and legislative obligation, major European economies consolidated and extended established occupational earnings-related pensions. The object was to guarantee pension security while promoting labor mobility during the years of postwar economic modernization: collective provision protected acquired pension rights. In Sweden, the Netherlands, and even France (where ARRCO and AGIRC initially established large reserves), accumulating pension contributions, invested largely in government securities, were used for state-sponsored programs of modernization—reflecting the public equivalent of what the German book reserve system achieved for the private firm. This formed a foundation for the European social model. Concordance between public and private was not, however, so visible in Anglo-Saxon economies. Debates over pension reform in Australia and the UK illustrate very different political trajectories.

In both Britain and Australia, pension debates also centered on occupational provision—but in both countries official initiatives to extend established schemes were widely (and more successfully) opposed. The reasons behind the opposition were, however, not identical: the foundations of postwar state pensions in the two countries were very different. While Britain had embraced Beveridge's pension model, Australian governments and trade unions had long rejected the contributory principle. In a country whose economy still relied overwhelmingly on the farm and the mine, seasonal employment and mobile labor blurred distinctions between subcontractors, the employed, and those ostensibly working on their own behalf, making contributory systems an unrealistic solution to the coverage of social risks. Social security (including state pensions), introduced by a Labor government in the 1940s, rejected contributions in favor of tax-funded welfare. Postwar Australian pensions were universal and flat-rate, but lightly means tested. When the Liberal (conservative) government tried to introduce a contributory system of national superannuation in 1965, the scheme won no support: an exercise repeated by a Labor administration in the mid-1970s, with the same result. As might be expected, employers and insurance companies opposed state initiatives that threatened their business, for much the same reasons as in Britain. Occupational providers, managed by major companies and financial service institutions, looked askance at competition from a state-sponsored alternative. However, Australian trade unions opposed any scheme that required workers to pay for their own retirement. The virtue of the postwar welfare settlement for Australian workers lay in its redistributive nature: tax-based pensions meant that the well-off paid for the poor. Australian trade unionists argued that solutions to pensioner poverty lay in raising the basic state pension, not in the introduction (or extension) of contributory schemes. In consequence, the world of Australian pensions changed little prior to the 1990s.

Similar resistance to the adaptation of private pensions for public purposes was also encountered in Britain, but the eventual outcome was different. Far from being a liberal measure faced with opposition from organized labor, the British debate was stimulated by two Labour governments and the most persistent resistance to any policy to widen state provision came from within the civil service—from the Treasury. Evidence of continuing pensioner poverty in the midst of growing affluence, coupled with rising earnings-related provision in other European states, stimulated the introduction of a graduated state pension by a Conservative government in 1959. This earnings-related state scheme was, however, misleading: policy combined fiscal incentives and additional insurance contribution rebates to subsidize British employers who introduced private occupational schemes, contracting out of state provision. During the 1960s, occupational cover boomed; pension funds came to represent over one-third of private saving in the UK economy: a proportion higher than that found in the United States (Hannah 1986: 48–51). Occupational protection was also used within collective bargaining, to bypass official wage restraint policies: a trend well supported by public sector unions who therefore looked askance at plans to universalize occupational cover that would negate negotiated and hard-won gains for their members.

Even so, the incoming Labour government in 1964 promised to create a national superannuation scheme, to operate on a funded basis managed by independent trustees, to guarantee an income at 50 percent of previous earnings. The fund so created would allow government, as in Sweden, to influence investments in the public interest—a powerful tool for national planning. The scheme provoked opposition from the union movement, from employers, the financial service sector, and, most effectively, from the Treasury, where the plan was interpreted (to quote one official) as 'nationalisation by the back door'. For these civil servants, the scheme threatened monetary stability and private sector investment. Higher contributions (and consumption among the elderly) would prove inflationary, would disrupt the balance of payments, and damage confidence in sterling. Further, if fund balances were placed in equities, this would inflate market prices, forcing up interest rates on gilt-edged securities and thus the cost of government borrowing. Conversely, if vested in government securities, the new pension obligations would eventually burden the public accounts while simultaneously damaging London's capital markets and internal industrial investment. These arguments persuaded British governments of all political complexions to give monetary stability priority over questions of pensioner security. When the State Earnings Related Pension Scheme (SERPS) was eventually introduced (1976), it assumed a residual role, underwriting around 60,000 private occupational schemes in a manner not witnessed anywhere else in Europe, creating an administrative nightmare in the process.

These limited historical narratives demonstrate how a similar strategy (the promotion of earnings-related complementary pensions) was debated as a potential solution to common problems (pensioner poverty, funding for inward investment, wage restraint) in widely differing combinations of private responsibility and public regulation or provision. From the roots of a common strategy emerges a history of divergent trajectories, as political contingency combined with social necessity to generate multiple public-private productions of old-age security. Varied pathways were taken toward a common goal. We can see that divisions between 'public' and 'private' provision, common to neoliberal discourse, are ill-suited to describing these systems. Different states intervened at different points to promote a common objective. Clear distinctions between Pillars 1 and 2 under the World Bank classification (1994) become hard to sustain and identifying public and private pensions is rendered problematic. Both Dutch and French occupational systems, for example, were established by legislative enactment, but were regarded as essentially private concerns, with ownership and management vested with the members and no direct financial contribution from the state. Nor was the state entirely absent from any of these systems: in both the UK and in Australia, tax advantages effectively subsidized companies sustaining occupational schemes. Hybrid compromises served varied political purposes, linking old-age security to strategies of modernization and growth, with official agencies performing their coordinating role in multiple ways.

## 4 Conclusions

The pension developments described above offer a new perspective on more recent debates. They show how the real world of pension provision does not divide between the public and the private, but has long involved agencies whose management and ownership reflect widely differing arrangements. Yet, with the establishment of the single market, European hybrid systems have been compelled, under the exigencies of EU competition law, to identify themselves either as part of the welfare state (and therefore public) or as private (and therefore commercial). In other words, the introduction of market-based systems into established pension provision has forced conformity with conventions that these institutions do not recognize and into whose evaluative world they do not fit. In consequence, AGIRC, ARRCO, and the Dutch sectoral pension schemes are today legally regarded as part of the public sector, threatening their earlier (and much cherished) independence while throwing into question whether the state is now liable for their continued financial viability. This gives rise to further logical anomalies concerning the position, for example, of other systems of social protection that do not operate on the basis of market competition, but are highly regarded for the services they offer and the ethics they espouse. Should we assume that market discipline will guarantee either their effective conversion into successful commercial operations, or their imminent demise? What values and moral imperatives derived from other hierarchies of worth that formed the foundations of such institutions will be destroyed in the process—and is such destruction desirable? In short, we should be aware of the dangers posed by a myopic addiction to the virtues of the market world at the expense of every other form of evaluation. Complex institutional constructions reflect diverse compromises between different hierarchies of worth that have developed over prolonged periods of time.

Current arguments about the benefits of market-based systems are driven by neoliberal logic (outlined briefly at the beginning of this chapter). This is largely responsible for the compulsion to reduce state welfare budgets and the translation of the state's role from welfare provider to welfare guarantor. However, the adaptation of commercial markets to the provision of social services has not been an unmitigated success. The nature of risk, the plethora of unwritten conventions, and the sheer complexity of market products in financial services have provoked new types of state intervention and regulation, largely to protect new consumers, to foster confidence and trust. In the process, transaction costs rise as administrative complexity increases while signals of quality and price (the hallmark of market value) are obscured by the introduction of official subsidies directed to shape consumer behavior in accordance with current policy preferences. The result has been public uncertainty, opposition, and non-participation (witnessed both in Britain and Germany) or continuing reliance on the state—currently evident in

Sweden, where rising numbers of participants in obligatory personal pension plans vest the state with the responsibility of managing their funds (Hinrichs 2004: 39–40). Moreover, regulatory requirements have not been confined to national boundaries. The growth of global financial markets has forced even the most neoliberal administrations to demand international agreement on collective rules to foster confidence in market operations. The slow and painful birth of a single market for European financial services has required the extensive negotiation and elaboration of its remit and the identification of legal and illegal practices (Lamfalussy process). The negotiation of international accounting standards, rules on disclosure, investment regulations, and so on reflect attempts by a range of official bodies to guarantee coordination by making markets user-friendly, to foster confidence and trust in their activities, to enable the uninitiated to participate. Thus are new institutional hybrids born.

This historical repetition (if it can be so characterized) invites empirical research into claims that supposedly 'private' pensions offer better value to the citizen than the public alternative. Such assertions are in need of serious reappraisal. We have lost sight of Beveridge's strictures based on economies of scale: the cost advantages of collecting compulsory contributions (as opposed to voluntary saving), the 'duplication and waste' (in terms of buildings and personnel) generated by multiple competing providers (Beveridge 1942). The transfer of pensions from state bureaucracy to private enterprise may improve the profile of the public accounts. Does this represent 'better value' for the majority of future pensioners—who ultimately pay not just for multiple managerial hierarchies but also for the unmeasured (because unmeasurable) compliance costs consequent on burgeoning regulation? Do such judgments take account of the high transaction costs (and multiple social consequences) of means-testing claimants who are unable to save for a pension?

Thanks to the genesis of increasingly unified market systems without the control of the state, the pensions agenda is increasingly driven by conventions of international accountancy—which themselves require academic attention. We need to understand the conventions underpinning the real world construction of public accounts. While neoliberal arguments that shape current pension policy are widely understood (if not necessarily accepted), we know far less about how financial accounting practices operate. How is the remit of public expenditure on pensions defined in practice? Are tax concessions offered to employers to fund occupational or professional schemes understood as a public subsidy (and, if not, why not)? What 'counts' as public taxation? Why are compulsory collective premiums (or social insurance contributions) included under this remit while some compulsory personal premiums (car insurance) are not? How do conventions of public accountancy determine the public/private status of Pillar 2 and Pillar 3 pensions? In other words, we should unpick the macroeconomic statistics that fuel the arguments of politicians and academics alike, to understand the political processes involved in their construction and their implications for pension policy. This research agenda is highly complex: conventions of public accountancy have, like all other conventions, evolved over prolonged periods of time. Their political significance has, however, attained an importance in pension deliberations that outstrips nearly all other considerations. Their analysis, therefore, is a matter of urgency if current debates are to become more balanced and the collective costs and benefits of alternative typologies of pension provision are to be understood.[6]

# NOTES

Research for this paper was funded by the ESRC under the Future of Governance Programme (grant no. L 216252020) and by Zurich Financial Services. To both the author extends her thanks; however, the opinions expressed here are purely her own.

1. A more detailed account of the following section can be found in Whiteside (2003).
2. Exceptions include Hannah (1986), Reynaud and Tambouri (1994), Whiteside (2003), Kangas and Palme (1996).
3. Association Générale des Retraites par Repartition.
4. Union des Institutions de Retraites des Salariés.
5. Association des Régimes de Retraites Complémentaires.
6. At the time of writing, the EU Directorate-General for Economic and Financial Affairs is calculating the impact of new conventions of public accounting (forcing governments to conform to recently introduced International Accounting Standards) on the finances of both national social security and schemes involving the state as employer. This implies a new order of magnitude for public debt and deficit. See Oksanen (2004); I am grateful to Bernard Casey for this reference.

# REFERENCES

ARRCO (1972). *Tenth Anniversary Report*. Paris: ARRCO.

BALDWIN, P. (1990). *The Politics of Social Solidarity: Class Bases of the European Welfare State, 1875–1975*. Cambridge: Cambridge University Press.

BEVERIDGE REPORT (1942). *Social Insurance and Allied Services*. Cmd. 6404. London: HMSO.

BLINDER, A. S. (1988). 'Why is the government in the pension business?', in Susan M. Wachter (ed.), *Social Security and Private Pensions*. Lexington, Mass. and Toronto: Lexington Books, 17–34.

BOLTANSKI, L., and THEVENOT, L. (1991). *De la justification: Les economies de la grandeur*. Paris: Gallimard.

—— —— (1999). 'The sociology of critical capacity'. *European Journal of Social Theory*, 2/3: 359–77.

BONOLI, G. (2000). *The Politics of Pension Reform: Institutions and Policy Change in Western Europe.* Cambridge: Cambridge University Press.

—— and PALIER, B. (1996). 'Reclaiming welfare: the politics of French social protection reform'. *South European Society and Politics,* 1: 240–59.

CHASKIEL, P., LHOTEL, H., & VILLEVAL, M.-C. (1986). 'Negotiations et transformations du rapport salarial dans la crise d'une enterprise', in Salais and Thevenot (1986).

CLARK, G. L. (2003). 'Twenty-first-century pension (in)security', in Clark and Whiteside (2003), 225–49.

—— and BENNET, P. (2001). 'Dutch sector-wide supplementary pensions: fund governance, European competition policy, and the geography of finance'. *Environment and Planning A,* 33/1: 27–48.

—— and WHITESIDE, N. (eds.) (2003). *Pension Security in the 21ST Century.* Oxford: Oxford University Press.

CONNELL, M. (2005). 'The Supplementary Pensions Directive: setting the agenda for pension reform in the European Union'. Unpublished paper.

DEACON, B., and HULSE, M. (1996). *The Globalisation of Social Policy.* Leeds: ISPRU.

DORE, R. (2000). *Stock Market Capitalism: Welfare Capitalism: Japan and Germany versus the Anglo-Saxons.* Oxford: Oxford University Press.

DUPUY, J.-P., (1989). 'Convention et common knowledge', *Revue Economique,* No. 2 (Mar.): 361–400.

ESPING-ANDERSEN, G. (1990). *Three Worlds of Welfare Capitalism.* Princeton: Princeton University Press.

—— (1996). "Welfare states without work: the impasse of labour shedding and familialism in continental European social policy', in Esping-Andersen (ed.), *Welfare States in Transition: National Adaptations in Global Economies.* London: Sage.

—— GALLIE, D., and MYLES, J. (2002) *Why We Need a New Welfare State.* Oxford: Oxford University Press.

GAMET, L. (2000). 'Towards a definition of "flexibility in labour law"', in B. Strath (ed.), *After Full Employment.* Brussels: Laing.

HALL, P., and SOSKICE, D. (eds.) (2001). *The Varieties of Capitalism: The Institutional Foundations of Comparative Advantage.* Oxford: Oxford University Press.

HANNAH, L. (1986). *Inventing Retirement.* Cambridge: Cambridge University Press.

HINRICHS, K. (2001). 'Elephants on the move', in S. Leibfried (ed.), *Welfare State Futures.* Cambridge: Cambridge University Press.

—— (2004). *Active Citizens and Retirement Planning: Enlarging Freedom of Choice in the Course of Pensions Reforms in Nordic Countries and Germany.* ZeS-Arbeitspapier No. 11/2004.

KANGAS, O., and PALME, J. (1996). 'The development of occupational pensions in Finland and Sweden', in M. Shalev (ed.), *The Privatization of Social Policy?* Basingstoke and London: Macmillan, 211–40.

KNIGHT, F. H. (1921). *Risk, Uncertainty and Profit.* New York: Kelly.

LION, H. (1962). 'La Convention du 14 mars 1947 et son evolution'. *Droit Social,* 12 (Dec.): 114–23.

LYON-CAEN, G. (1962). 'La co-ordination des régimes complémentaires de retraites'. *Droit Sociale,* 25/7–8: 457–63.

MYLES, J., and PIERSON, P. (2001). 'The comparative political economy of pension reform', in P. Pierson (ed.), *The New Politics of the Welfare State.* Oxford: Oxford University Press.

OKSANEN, H. (2004). 'Public pensions in the national accounts and public finance targets'. EC Directorate-General for Economic and Financial Affairs, Economic Papers No. 207, http://europa.eu.int/comm/economy_finance.
PALIER, B. (2002). *Gouverner la sécurité sociale, les réformes du système français de protection sociale depuis 1945*. Paris: PUF.
—— (2003). 'Facing the pension crisis in France', in Clark and Whiteside (2003), 93–115.
PALME, J. (2003). 'Pension reform in Sweden and the changing boundaries between public and private', in Clark and Whiteside (2003), 144–68.
PIERSON, P. (1998). 'Irresistible forces, immovable objects: post-industrial welfare states confront permanent austerity'. *Journal of European Public Policy*, 5/4: 539–60.
—— (ed.) (2001). *The New Politics of the Welfare State*. Oxford: Oxford University Press.
POCHET, P. (2003). 'Pensions: the European debate', in Clark and Whiteside (2003), 44–64.
REYNAUD, E., and TAMBURI, G. (1994). *Les Retraites Complémentaires en France*. Paris: La Documentation Francaise.
SALAIS, R. (1998). 'A la recherche du fondement conventionnel des insititutions', in R. Salais, E. Chatel, and D. Rivaud-Danset (eds.), *Institutions et Conventions: la reflexivité de l'action économique*. Paris: EHSS, 255–91.
—— et THEVENOT, L. (eds.) (1986). *Le Travail, marchés, règles, conventions*. Paris: Economica.
—— and WHITESIDE, N. (1998). *Governance, Industry and Labour Markets in Britain and France: The Modernising State in the Mid-Twentieth Century*. London: Routledge.
SCHWARTZ, F. W. (2001). 'The viability of advanced welfare states in the international economy', in S. Leibfried (ed.), *Welfare State Futures*. Cambridge: Cambridge University Press.
STORPER, M., and SALAIS, R. (1997). *Worlds of Production: The Action Frameworks of the Economy*. Cambridge, Mass.: Harvard University Press.
THEVENOT, L. (2001). 'Organized complexity: conventions of coordination and composition of economic arrangements'. *European Journal of Social Theory*, 4/4: 405–25.
VAN RIEL, B. (2003). 'Ageing, PAYG and funding: the Dutch discussion in the early 1950s on financing public pensions'. Unpublished paper.
WHITESIDE, N. (1997). 'Regulating markets'. *Public Administration*, 75/3: 467–87.
—— (2003). 'Historical perspectives on the politics of pension reform', in Clark and Whiteside (2003), 21–44.
—— (2005). 'Comparing welfare states: conventions, institutions and political frameworks of pension reform in France and Britain after the Second World War', in J.-C. Barbier and M.-T. Letablier (eds.), *Comparaisons internationales des politiques sociales: enjeux épistémologiques et methodologiques*. Brussels: Peter Laing.
—— and Salais, R. (1998). 'Comparing welfare states: social protection and industrial politics in France and Britain, 1930–60'. *Journal of European Social Policy*, 8/2: 139–55.
WORLD BANK (1994), *Averting the Old Age Crisis: Policies to Protect the Old and Promote Growth*. Oxford: Oxford University Press.

# CHAPTER 35

# UNENDING WORK

## ANNIKA SUNDÉN

## 1 INTRODUCTION

Retirement behavior in the OECD countries has been characterized by a trend toward early retirement in recent decades. Coupled with increasing life expectancy, individuals are spending more of their lives in retirement than ever before. At the same time, population ageing puts financial pressures on public and private pension schemes and, in response, countries around the world are discussing and implementing pension reforms that reduce benefit levels. A possible consequence of the demographic shift is that early retirement comes to a halt and that people start working longer to maintain their standard of living in retirement.

Retirement behavior reflects the intersection between labor supply decisions made by workers and labor demand decisions made by employers. It is only by examining both sides of the decision that it is possible to assess whether individuals will continue working longer. The changing demographic structure with an increasing share of the population aged 65 and older could mean that countries will experience labor shortages in the future and more jobs for older workers may become available. On the other hand, employers have generally been reluctant to hire older workers because of their higher costs, and generous pension schemes that have created incentives for workers to leave the labor force early. Furthermore, many European countries still have mandatory retirement.

This chapter discusses the transition to retirement and how it might evolve in the future to provide adequate income for workers as well as meeting the demands of employers. Several factors are identified as important for workers' willingness to continue working: economic incentives in pension systems, labor market legislation, and flexibility. On the demand side, the cost of older workers and employers' attitudes play a crucial role.

The chapter is organized as follows: the following section summarizes labor force participation among workers approaching retirement in the OECD countries. The next two sections discuss reasons why older workers might be likely to increase their labor supply in the future. Section 5 looks at the demand side and asks whether employers will hire older workers. Section 6 concludes.

## 2 Labor Force Participation Among Workers Approaching Retirement

To what extent do individuals approaching retirement work? The answer appears to be not very much, with a few notable exceptions. Figure 35.1 shows labor force participation rates for individuals aged 55 to 64 in the OECD countries in 2003. Labor force participation is highest in the Nordic countries, Japan, and the United States with around 60 percent of the population aged 55–64 in the workforce (with the exception of Iceland where 90 percent work) while in countries in Continental Europe like Italy, France, Germany, and Belgium only between 30 and 40 percent in the same age group are in the labor force. The ranking of countries is similar if men and women are examined separately—that is, it appears that countries that have the highest labor force participation overall also have high labor force participation rates among women.

The current employment pattern among older workers is a result of the trend toward earlier retirement that has occurred across countries during the past 20 years. As discussed in earlier chapters, an important explanation behind this trend is the development of public and private pension schemes. Increased coverage and generosity of pensions have enabled workers to withdraw from the labor force at earlier and earlier ages. In fact, in almost half of the OECD countries public pension benefits are available at age 60 or earlier and in these countries less than half of men aged 55 to 64 are participating in the labor force (OECD 2004).

However, it appears that the trend toward earlier retirement has come to a halt and labor force participation has started to increase somewhat, in particular in the Scandinavian countries, the United States, and the United Kingdom. But even in some countries in the European Union, for example Italy, with

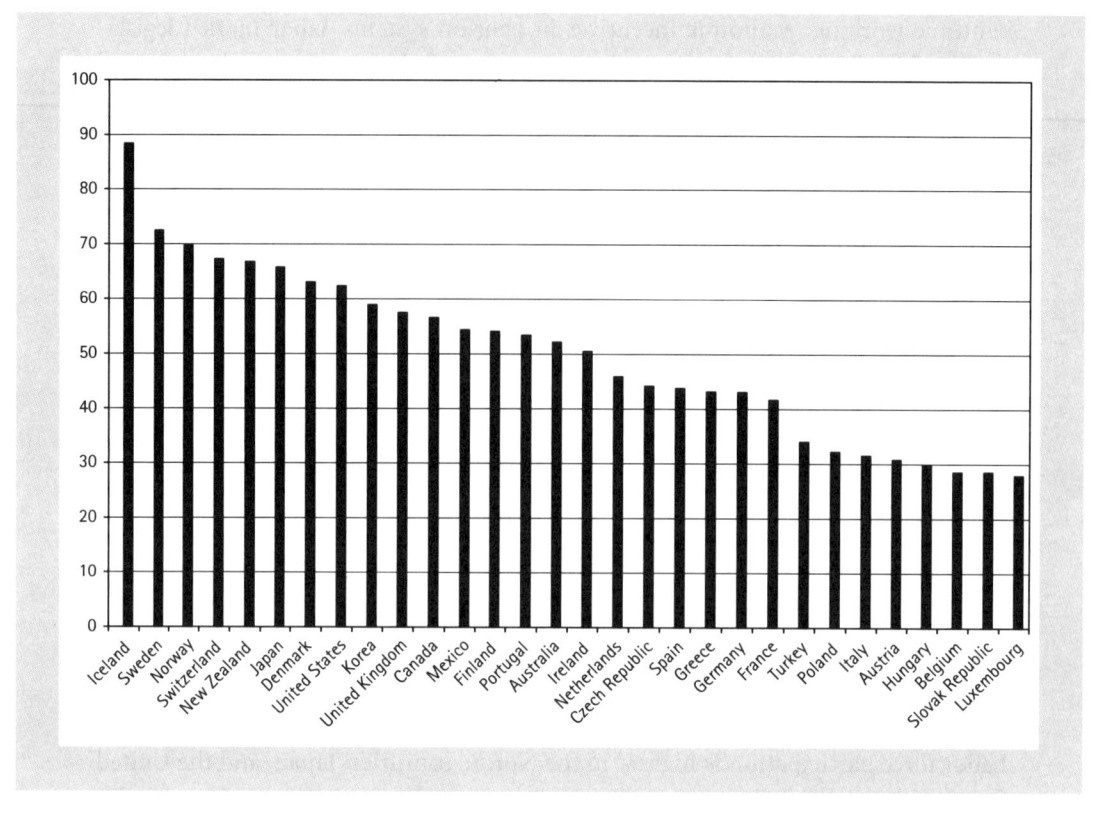

**Fig. 35.1** Labor force participation aged 55–64 in the OECD, 2003

*Source*: OECD (2004).

very low labor force participation among workers aged 55 to 64 it appears that workers have started to delay retirement (Burtless and Quinn 2002; National Social Insurance Board 2000; OECD 2001). However, when it comes to the recent changes in retirement behavior in the Anglo-American countries and northern Europe, researchers have not reached consensus as to whether the leveling off in early withdrawal represents a temporary or permanent shift in the labor force participation among older individuals.[1] And when discussing a possible reversal, it is important to keep in mind that in most countries in Continental Europe the dominant retirement pattern is still to leave the labor force completely before age 60.

However, some evidence suggests that people's attitudes toward work late in life may be changing both in the United States and in Europe. Two decades ago, only half of American workers approaching retirement indicated that they would like to continue working after retirement and if so only for economic reasons (Rix 1999). In a more recent survey by the American Association of Retired Persons (AARP) in the United States, 80 percent of respondents aged 34 to 52 reported that they expect to keep working at least part-time after 65 (Roper Starch Worldwide 1998). Similar results are found for European countries where in 1999 more than 70 percent of workers in Germany and Italy reported that they expect to continue working after retirement (OECD 2001).

Who stays in the labor force? Overall, people who continue working tend to be healthier, better educated, and have higher wealth than average (Haider and Loughran 2001).[2] And evidence from both the United States and the European Union indicates that those who retire early are more likely to be employed in low-skilled occupations.

Will people continue working longer in the future? Several developments indicate that this may be the case. If the recent changes in retirement behavior can be explained by shifts in incentives in pension plans and the reduction in replacement rates in public schemes, workers could be expected to retire later in the future even in countries where labor force participation today is low among those aged 55 and older. The pension schemes in several of the countries where labor force participation among older workers is increasing have been subject to substantial change and reduction in the generosity of benefits. On the other hand, in countries where early retirement is still dominant, for example in France and Belgium, pension reforms have not yet been introduced. But benefit cuts and increased retirement ages are on the political agenda and deemed necessary in the near future to maintain the systems' financial stability in view of population ageing, thus increasing the possibility that workers will continue working longer.

Improved health and education of older workers, the shift to less physically demanding employment, and increases in life expectancy could also imply that workers are willing to work longer. Retirement itself has started to change, at least in some countries. For many, the decision to retire is no longer an all-or-nothing decision, nor is it always permanent. The introduction of phased retirement schemes in the Scandinavian countries and the United States has the potential to improve the options for older workers to stay in the labor force. Of course, these schemes are more likely to evolve in countries where employers are willing to keep older workers in the labor force. In the European countries where a majority of workers leave before age 60, the opportunities for older individuals to continue working at all have often been limited because of weak economic conditions and high unemployment rates among young workers. On the other hand, several of these countries also face labor shortages in the future, and for example in Belgium—one of the countries with the lowest labor force participation among individuals aged 55 to 64 in Europe—a public debate about how to keep individuals aged 55 and older in the workforce has emerged.[3] Thus, several factors point to the likelihood that workers across the OECD countries will continue working longer in the future.

# 3 Pension Plan Design and Pathways to Retirement

No single definition of retirement exists. For example, retirement can be defined as leaving the workforce completely, leaving a career job, or beginning to collect pension benefits. Retirement was until the 1970s generally viewed as an involuntary decision that occurred due to poor health, layoffs, or mandatory retirement. Since then retirement has increasingly been considered a voluntary decision affected by the economic incentives imbedded in public and private pension plans.[4] The design of public and private pension systems therefore has important implications for individuals' willingness to continue to work.

## 3.1 Shift from Defined Benefit to Defined Contribution Plans

Previous chapters have discussed the structure of pension plans and the shift from defined benefit plans to defined contribution plans. This shift has implications for older workers' willingness to continue to work. In traditional pension plans (defined benefit plans) benefits are typically determined by a formula involving number of years in the labor market and average wage. These plans, both public and private, have often included subsidies in their benefit formulas that encouraged early retirement (Gruber and Wise 1999). These subsidies meant that by retiring early (sometimes as early as age 55) a worker received a benefit that was greater than the actuarially fair amount—the benefit at the early retirement age was not reduced to fully reflect the fact that it would be received for a longer time period. As a result, a worker who retired early received larger lifetime benefits than a worker who retired at the normal retirement age, hence encouraging workers to leave early. On the other hand, defined contribution plans do not have incentives to leave the labor force early. In these plans, the benefit is determined by an individual's contributions and the rate of return on these contributions. Thus, such a plan is neutral with respect to retirement age and an additional year's contribution produces a larger benefit. A defining characteristic of defined contribution plans is that much of the risk and responsibility is put on workers (Munnell and Sundén 2004). As a result, benefits provided by this type of plan are less certain and one possible way workers can protect themselves against the risks in these plans is by working longer.

The shift to defined contribution plans is occurring in private as well as in public plans. In the United States, a type of defined contribution plan, the 401(k) plan, is now the dominant employer-sponsored pension plan and several other countries are including defined contribution features in their public and private schemes. One example is Sweden where a major pension reform in 1998 transformed the public defined benefit plan to a notional defined contribution plan—a defined contribution plan financed on a pay-as-you-go basis.[5] The defined contribution model was chosen because an important objective of the Swedish reform was to create strong work incentives and in particular for older workers to continue working. Furthermore, the system has no age limit for earning pension credits so Swedish workers can increase their benefits by working longer for as long as they wish. An individual can also return to work after retirement and continue to earn pension credits and thereby increase pension benefits. The calculation of benefits at retirement includes an automatic adjustment to changes in life expectancy resulting in lower benefits at a given retirement age if life expectancy increases. As a result, workers are going to have to work longer in order to reach a given replacement rate. The Swedish scheme also includes a second pillar of mandatory funded accounts.[6] Interestingly, a few years after the reform, labor force participation among older workers has started to increase in Sweden. A similar pension scheme to the Swedish plan has been introduced in Italy and labor supply among older workers have been inching up in that country as well.

But public schemes that are remaining defined benefit are also implementing changes to make the schemes less generous and thereby making work more attractive. For example, in the United States the normal retirement age is gradually being raised from 65 to 67 in 2022. This is equivalent to an across-the-board benefit cut which increases the attractiveness of work.[7] On the other hand, public pension systems in many countries in Continental Europe have not yet been the subject of reform and still provide generous incentives to leave the labor force early. But the development of a single market for the EU puts pressure on pension policy in Europe to change. A guiding principle of the EU is the free mobility of labor. Today's defined benefit plans with generous incentives for early retirement have limited portability and thus lock in workers in their current jobs—changing jobs late in life could mean a large reduction in pension benefits. Thus, in order to facilitate mobility across countries the EU is encouraging the harmonization of pension plans (Whiteside, Chapter 34 this volume). As a result a continuation in the shift toward defined contribution plans is likely to occur, further reducing the incentives to retire early.

## 3.2 Alternative Pathways

Another strategy to encourage workers to leave the labor force early has been to introduce special programs, for example early retirement windows, or to use other existing social insurance programs to provide early retirement benefits. In European countries it has been common to use disability and unemployment insurance as early retirement programs by loosening eligibility rules. For example, in the Netherlands and Sweden disability benefits were granted to workers approaching retirement without medical testing until the early 1990s. In other countries, for example France, the unemployment program functioned in much the same way. Often older workers were not subject to the same job-search requirement as younger workers and could receive extended unemployment benefits as a bridging benefit until they became eligible for old-age benefits. The reasoning was that by inducing older workers to leave the workforce, employment opportunities for younger workers would become available; thus the policy was a method to reduce youth unemployment. However, beginning in the 1990s, several of the countries that had implemented these early retirement pathways took steps to curb their use by tightening eligibility rules, reducing benefits replacement rates, and making disability insurance more costly to employers.[8] Eliminating or reducing these alternative pathways should have a positive effect on work incentives among older workers in the future. For example, in Sweden the removal of the option to grant disability benefits due to poor labor market conditions has contributed to increased labor force participation among those aged 60 to 64.

# 4 A Flexible Labor Market

The structure of the labor market is important for workers' willingness and opportunities to continue working. During the past 25 years the composition of the labor market across all industrialized countries has changed from physically strenuous manufacturing occupations to less arduous service occupations (Engelen, Chapter 6 this volume). The increase in the service sector has also contributed to increased flexibility because these jobs are often more suited for part-time work. Employment policies in both the United States and Europe during this restructuring phase were focused on retiring older workers whose compensation exceeded their productivity to make room for younger and less expensive workers who entered the labor market.

A common view in many countries in Continental Europe was that a fixed number of jobs existed in the economy and in order to reduce youth unemployment it was necessary for older workers to leave the labor market. The result, as discussed above, was to use the unemployment and disability programs to encourage early retirement among older workers. The Scandinavian countries were an exception. Although the disability program in Sweden functioned as an early retirement scheme, the overarching principle for all workers was the 'principle of work', that is everyone should support him- or herself through work. Consequently, considerable resources were spent in Sweden and the other Scandinavian countries on training programs for older workers to improve their skills in the changing labor market.

A flexible labor market might improve the possibility of older workers remaining in the workforce in the future. Individuals often report that they would be willing to continue working if they could reduce their number of hours. For example, in a survey of Swedish workers more than half reported that a reduction in hours was necessary in order to stay in the workforce (Statistics Sweden 2001). Being able to reduce working hours may avoid health problems and in that way also contribute to continued work. Currently, part-time work is uncommon among workers approaching retirement in the OECD countries (Table 35.1). Typically, no more than 10 percent of men aged 55 to 59 work part-time. The share is somewhat higher in the Netherlands and Japan where between 11 and 18 percent of the population aged 55 to 59 work part-time. For the age group 60 to 64, part-time work is somewhat more prevalent, especially in Japan and Sweden. Among women, part-time work is much more common because women to a large extent work part-time throughout their lives.

However, the increased flexibility for older workers implied by the expansion of the service sector could lead to a more precarious labor market for younger workers.

Table 35.1 Percentage of employees Aged 55 and older working part-time in selected OECD countries, 1999

|  | Age 55-9 | | Age 60-4 | | Age 65 and older | |
| --- | --- | --- | --- | --- | --- | --- |
|  | Men | Women | Men | Women | Men | Women |
| Canada | 5.1 | 13.2 | 6.4 | 9.6 | 3.0 | 1.6 |
| Finland | 5.0 | 9.0 | 6.6 | 6.8 | 2.1 | 0.6 |
| Germany | 2.9 | 21.8 | 3.3 | 7.6 | 2.1 | 1.1 |
| Italy | 2.0 | 3.2 | 1.8 | 0.9 | 0.8 | 0.3 |
| Japan | 10.3 | 23.2 | 15.5 | 17.6 | 13.2 | 8.0 |
| Netherlands | 11.2 | 22.9 | 7.3 | 6.6 | – | – |
| Sweden | 6.7 | 26.3 | 11.8 | 21.3 | – | – |
| United Kingdom | 6.7 | 26.8 | 9.1 | 16.3 | 4.9 | 2.8 |
| United States | 5.4 | 13.2 | 7.8 | 12.4 | 7.6 | 4.9 |

Source: OECD (2001).

Because service sector jobs are more likely to be part-time, temporary, and low paid they are less likely to provide full coverage by pension schemes and other social security protections, thus putting some groups of younger workers at risk of low incomes in old age (Engelen Chapter 6, this volume). Nevertheless, two labor market developments in the countries with the highest labor force participation rates among older workers—United States, Japan, and Sweden—indicate that increased flexibility toward the end of the working life could be important for workers' willingness to continue working: bridge jobs and phased retirement schemes.

## 4.1 Bridge Jobs

In the United States, some evidence shows that workers are increasingly using 'bridge jobs' as a way of leaving the labor market. A bridge job is defined as a job between a worker's full-time career job and complete labor force withdrawal. These types of jobs have become quite common and estimates show that more than one-quarter of men and one-third of women in the United States will change jobs between their career job and complete labor market withdrawal (Quinn 1999*b*). Bridge jobs typically involve a change of industry, a reduction of hours, and often a switch to self-employment. An indication that bridge jobs are important for US retirement behavior is that part-time work and self-employment increase among workers as they approach retirement. In the United States, only 10 percent of men aged 55 to 61 in the labor force work part-time, while 40 percent of those aged 65 to 69 and more than half of those aged 70 and over work part-time. This is a very different pattern compared to countries with low labor force participation among workers approaching retirement—for example in Italy where less than 40 percent of those aged 55 to 64 work, only 6 percent of men aged 60 to 64 work part-time (Table 35.1). Thus, in countries where few individuals over 55 work, retirement is still likely to be an all-or-nothing event.

Self-employment is also more common among older workers in the United States; the self-employed retire later and individuals are more likely to switch to self-employment as they age. Among men aged 65 to 69, almost 20 percent are self-employed compared to 12 percent of men in the age group 55 to 61 (Munnell *et al.* 2004).

Workers in the United States who choose bridge jobs typically fall into two categories: those at the lower end of the earnings distribution and those at the upper end. Thus, workers appear to choose bridge jobs either because they have to support themselves or because they want to continue working although they could afford to retire. Workers with pension coverage are less likely to choose bridge jobs and instead leave the labor force completely, confirming the importance of incentives in pension plans for workers' willingness to remain in the workforce.

## 4.2 Partial Retirement

An alternative to bridge jobs is formal partial or phased retirement schemes. These schemes can be designed in different ways. One possibility is to provide a partial retirement benefit that allows a worker to reduce the number of hours worked and receive a benefit replacing part of the lost earnings. In other instances, phased retirement schemes do not provide an explicit benefit but allow workers to stay in their job half-time at 50 percent of the full-time salary. This can be viewed as a benefit because it often provides higher earnings than if the worker switched to another employer (bridge job) in order to work part-time. A switch of employers often results in a reduction in the hourly wage because a worker's specific human capital would not be valued the same by another employer and wage rates in part-time jobs are usually lower (Allen et al. 2003).

Because many pension schemes require workers to resign in order to receive benefits, partial retirement creates flexibility for workers in leaving the labor force. However, formal partial retirement schemes are relatively uncommon. One of the few countries to introduce partial retirement is Sweden where such a scheme existed within the national pension system between 1976 and 2000. The scheme was quite generous and allowed workers to reduce their hours and receive a benefit that replaced between 50 and 65 percent of the lost earnings. The scheme was popular and 14 percent of individuals aged 60 to 64 collected partial retirement benefits at the peak of the program's popularity in the early 1980s.

Japan is another country with partial retirement. In Japan the rules for calculating pension benefits encourage part-time work for those aged 60 to 65 and almost 16 percent of individuals in this age group work part-time as shown in Table 35.1, a considerably higher proportion than the countries without formal partial retirement schemes.

In the United States, a 1999 survey showed that 16 percent of companies offered some kind of phased retirement scheme and that phased retirement was most common in the educational sector (Watson Wyatt 1999). However, a recent survey of employers showed that almost 75 percent would permit older white-collar workers to reduce their hours although few companies have formal policies (Hutchens 2003). The most common reason for employers' willingness to offer phased retirement is to retain skilled workers and a majority of these employers view partial retirement as a feasible strategy to meet anticipated labor shortages.

The crucial question for whether partial retirement schemes are successful in promoting employment among older workers is if such schemes actually increase the number of hours worked or if they simply act as a subsidy for workers who would like more leisure. The answer depends on who chooses the benefit. The objective with partial retirement schemes is that workers who otherwise would have left the labor force completely remain working and thus contribute to increased labor supply. On the other hand, partial retirement schemes may also induce workers who otherwise would have continued working full-time to reduce their hours and thereby have a negative effect on labor supply. If a phased retirement scheme is going to be successful in terms of increasing the number of hours worked, the first group must dominate. One study for Sweden showed that most workers who collected partial retirement benefits would have continued working full-time in the absence of the program and that the program therefore was not successful in increasing labor supply among older workers (Sundén 1994).

The popularity of phased retirement schemes among older workers will also depend on how they affect old-age benefits. Benefits in defined benefits schemes are typically determined by final salary, which would mean that reducing hours just before retirement would reduce old-age benefits. Even if formal partial retirement schemes are not available, individuals could remain in the labor force if it is possible to combine work with old-age benefits or benefits from other social insurance schemes. One possible explanation for Sweden's high labor force participation rate among older workers is that most social insurance benefits (sickness benefits, disability benefits, and old-age benefits) allow individuals to claim partial benefits while they continue to work during the remaining time. For example, a worker can claim disability benefits for 50 percent of the time and work the other 50 percent.

In the United States, workers cannot claim partial social security benefits but may continue working to supplement their income while collecting benefits. If earnings are above a certain threshold, the social security earnings test reduces benefits, which are repaid through an actuarially fair increase in later benefits. Thus, the earning test should not have a negative effect on the willingness to work but because workers perceive the reduction in benefits while working as permanent it has had a negative effect on work incentives. In 2000, the earnings test for workers above the normal retirement age (65) was eliminated and the result may be a positive effect on work effort in this age group.

# 5 WILL EMPLOYERS HIRE OLDER WORKERS?

In order for older workers to stay in the labor force in the future, employers must be willing to hire them. The ageing of the population together with falling fertility rates implies that many countries will face labor shortages in the future. In the United States, the first cohorts in the baby-boom generation (those born between

1946 and 1964) will approach retirement age in the next five to ten years. At the same time the inflow of young people will remain more or less constant so older workers will constitute an increasing share of the workforce (Bureau of Labor Statistics 2003). Because many European countries are ahead of the United States in the ageing of the population, labor shortages could be imminent in several countries.

Employers can close the gap by using more capital, recruiting younger workers and immigrants, or by hiring older workers. An increase in the amount of capital per worker would increase the productivity of the labor force and thereby offset the need for additional labor. However, it is unlikely that this measure will solve the labor shortage problem because it requires an increase in personal and government spending to make capital available. Many countries have experienced very low savings rates in the past and future demographic development is likely to put downward pressure on savings.[9]

Another option is immigration. During the 1960s and 1970s, labor force immigration was common in Europe but in recent years the nature of immigration has changed and many of today's immigrants to Europe are refugees who have had difficulties establishing themselves on the labor market. On the other hand, the expansion of the European Union allows workers to move more freely within Europe to meet labor demand. Such migration could be encouraged by increased portability of pension rights and other social security benefits across countries. In the United States immigration is already high and unlikely to increase in the future. Consequently, immigration does not appear to be the solution.

Although women's labor force participation has increased dramatically, their labor force participation during prime-age years is still low in many countries and this group is another source of increased labor supply. Hence, it is important to create incentives for women to increase their participation in the labor market. Today family policy and lack of subsidized day care in many countries make it difficult for women of child-rearing age to enter the labor market.[10] For example, in Germany policy-makers are currently discussing the expansion of parental leave in an effort to increase women's labor force participation. The design of pension schemes is another important policy tool that could contribute to women's increased employment. Women have lower pension benefits than men and often lack coverage by supplemental pension schemes (Bajtelsmit, Chapter 7 this volume). A stronger attachment to the labor force could improve women's incomes in retirement but this requires pension systems to provide work incentives by creating a strong link between contributions and benefits. Pension schemes could further encourage women's labor force participation by including child credits as in the current Swedish pension system and thereby not punish child-rearing.

The remaining group to fill the expected labor shortage is older workers. In particular, in countries where most workers leave the labor force completely prior to age 60, older workers are going to be crucial to meet future labor demand.

Several factors imply that older workers could be attractive to employers. Overall, workers approaching retirement today are better educated than previous generations. In the United States, 24 percent of the population aged 25 and older had a bachelor's degree in 2000, a doubling since 1970 (Munnell *et al.* 2004). A similar development has taken place in other countries. In the Scandinavian countries, educational policy has emphasized 'lifelong learning' and workers in all age groups have been offered schooling and training courses to update their skills in response to the changing labor market.

Furthermore, older workers are healthier than in the past making it possible to continue working (Freedman *et al.* 2002). At the same time, jobs have become less strenuous as a result of the decline in manufacturing and increase in the service sector. Thus, workers are more productive and should be attractive to employers. The problem is that the group that is most productive is often the group that is best positioned to retire early (Esping-Andersen and Myles, Chapter 42 this volume).

On the other hand, several barriers make older workers less attractive to employers. First, older workers are more expensive. Their earnings are typically higher than for younger workers in comparable jobs and employer contributions to fringe benefits such as health care, pensions, and disability insurance often increase with an employee's age. The compensation for the higher costs for older workers is if they are also more productive because of skills they have developed on the job. But studies have shown that older workers tend to be less productive than younger workers although they are paid more (Hellerstein *et al.* 1996). Furthermore, older workers' skills may become obsolete in view of changing technology and the costs for training exceed the benefits because of their fewer years left in the labor market. Although employers rate older workers above average when it comes to experience, judgment, commitment to quality, attendance, and punctuality, they also report that older workers are less willing to adapt to changing technology and are more likely to have difficulties learning new skills (OECD 2001).

In order to hire older workers, employers may also need to restructure work to meet older workers' preferences for part-time work. Such adjustments may be easier in industries that are labor intensive and have flexibility in how to organize the workplace, for example the service industry. However, part-time workers are more expensive per hour than full-time workers because they are associated with the same fixed costs for hiring and administration as full-time workers. Phased retirement schemes may reduce these costs somewhat because they allow the firm to keep employees with specialized skills rather than hire new workers. Finally, traditional defined benefit plans create economic incentives for older workers to leave firms completely.

In addition to the higher costs of hiring older workers, employers often have negative attitudes toward older workers as indicated above. In the United States, the Age Discrimination in Employment Act prohibits employers from discriminating against workers aged 40 and older. Similar laws will be in effect in the

European Union in 2006. Age discrimination legislation should improve employment possibilities for older workers but to the extent that such legislation increases employers' costs for older workers it could also reduce opportunities.[11] Despite legislation, older workers in the United States report that age discrimination is still an impediment to employment. In the Health and Retirement Study between 10 and 20 percent of older workers indicate that younger workers are given preference by employers (Munnell *et al.* 2004). Similarly, workers in Europe report that employers have negative attitudes toward older workers. In one survey, more than 80 percent of workers aged 50–64 in Germany, Italy, the Netherlands, Sweden, and the United Kingdom reported that it would be difficult to find a new job (OECD 2001).

# 6 Conclusions

Will workers stay in the labor force longer in the future? Several developments indicate that the trend toward early retirement may be coming to an end. Population ageing puts financial pressure on public pension systems and as a result several countries have implemented or are discussing pension reforms that will reduce replacement rates. As a result individuals will have to work longer to maintain their standard of living in retirement unless their non-pension savings increase. At the same time, older workers are healthier and better educated than ever before putting them in a good position to continue working.

Experiences in a few countries indicate that the retirement process itself is beginning to change. In these countries retirement is no longer an all-or-nothing event and instead workers have started to leave the labor force gradually. However, for phased retirement to be successful, people who partially retire have to come from the group who in absence of the program would have left the labor force completely rather than from the group who would have continued working full-time. If the second group dominates, phased retirement programs simply become a way to subsidize leisure. Only a few studies have examined the labor supply effects of phased retirement schemes and additional research is necessary to evaluate whether these schemes will contribute to increased work effort among older workers. It also has to be kept in mind that in many countries, in particular in Continental Europe, a majority of workers leave the labor force completely between age 55 and 60. For these countries an important goal must be to increase the number of full-time workers rather than promoting gradual retirement. In the Scandinavian countries, training and education of older workers have been important tools in promoting a continued working life and additional evaluations of such programs could provide important lessons for other countries.

On the demand side, the position for older workers has also improved. The demographic shift means that fewer younger workers will be available and several countries, in particular in Europe, are facing labor shortages in the near future. One possibility for firms to fill the gap is to employ older workers. In the past, employers have been reluctant to hire older workers. Older workers are more expensive: they are paid more than younger workers but are often less productive, and the costs for pensions and health care are also higher. And although employers often view older workers as reliable, they also report that they have difficulty adjusting to change and in learning new skills. But few other options to fill expected labor shortages exist so older workers should look more attractive to employers in the future. However, compared to the literature on labor supply, relatively little is known about labor demand and few studies have empirically examined how employers adjust in response to changes in labor supply. One problem has been the lack of matched employee–employer data but in order to better understand the labor market for older workers and how retirement will evolve in the future such studies would be valuable.

Finally, public policy could play a role in reducing the barriers to employing older workers by facilitating training, allowing employers to offer pro rata fringe benefits, and providing health insurance. But it is equally important to create incentive for workers to stay in the labor force by removing generous early retirement incentives in pension schemes.

## Notes

The opinions and conclusions are solely those of the author and should not be construed as representing the opinions or policy of the Swedish Social Security Administration or any agency of the Federal Government, the Center for Retirement Research at Boston College, or the Swedish Social Insurance Agency.

1. See for example Quinn (1999a) and Costa (1998).
2. Haider and Loughran (2001).
3. Séminaire national 'vieillissement actif' (National Seminar on Active Ageing, 30 Sept. 2004), Belgian Social Insurance Agency.
4. Mandatory retirement was eliminated in the United States in 1987 but still exists in European countries. An EU directive that will become effective in 2006 will abolish mandatory retirement within the European Union.
5. Italy has also implemented a notional defined contribution plan.
6. Several other OECD countries have mandatory individual accounts as part of their public pension schemes, among them the Netherlands, Switzerland, and Denmark.

7. The provision of health insurance could be another important factor in the decision to remain in the workforce. In countries like the United States where health insurance is tied to the job, leaving the labor force early could mean that health insurance costs paid by the worker increase dramatically.
8. In the Netherlands, employers are now responsible for the costs of sickness and disability insurance during the first two years when a worker becomes disabled. In addition, disability insurance premiums are experience rated. In Finland, the requirement of pre-funding has increased and thereby contribution rates. More frequent medical reviews have been introduced in the disability program in the United States and several countries are moving toward making disability benefits temporary.
9. The large cohorts who are retiring are drawing down their assets to finance consumption while the increased payouts from public social insurance programs will make it difficult for the government to save.
10. A notable exception is the United States where female labor force participation is high despite the lack of comprehensive family policies.
11. Neumark and Stock (1999) find positive effects of anti-discrimination legislation on employment among older workers while little evidence has been found of increased costs (Neumark 2001).

# References

ALLEN, STEVEN G., CLARK, ROBERT L., and GHENT, LINDA S. (2003). 'Phasing into retirement'. NBER Working Paper 9779. Cambridge, Mass.: National Bureau of Economic Research.

BUREAU OF LABOR STATISTICS (2003). Labor Force Data.

BURTLESS, GARY, and QUINN, JOSEPH F. (2002). 'Is working longer the answer for an aging workforce?' Issue in Brief, Center for Retirement Research, N. 11 (Dec.).

COSTA, DORA L. (1998). *The Evolution of Retirement. An American History 1880–1990*. Chicago: The University of Chicago Press.

FREEDMAN, VICKI A., MARTIN, LINDA G., and SCHOENI, ROBERT (2002). 'Recent trends in disability and functioning among older individuals in the United States: a systematic review'. *Journal of the American Medical Association*, 288/24 (Dec.).

GRUBER, JONATHAN, and WISE, DAVID A. (1999). *Social Security and Retirement around the World*. Chicago: University of Chicago Press.

HAIDER, STEVEN, and LOUGHRAN, DAVID (2001). 'Elderly labor supply: work or play?' Center for Retirement Research at Boston College Working Paper 2001-04. Boston: Center for Retirement Reseach.

HELLERSTEIN, JUDITH K., NEUAMARK, DAVID, and TROSKE, KENNETH R. (1996). 'Wages, productivity, and worker characteristics: evidence from plant-level production functions and wage equations'. Working Paper 5626. Cambridge, Mass.: National Bureau of Economic Research.

HUTCHENS, ROBERT (2003). *The Cornell Study of Employer Phased Retirement Policies: A Report on Key Findings*. Ithaca, NY: Cornell University School of Industrial and Labor Relations.

MUNNELL, ALICIA H., CAHILL, KEVIN E., D. ESCHTRUTH, ANDREW, and SASS, STEVEN A. (2004). *The Graying of Massachusetts: Aging, the New Rules of Retirement, and the Changing Workforce*. Boston: MassINC and the Center for Retirement at Boston College.

—— and SUNDÉN, ANNIKA (2004). *Coming Up Short: The Challenge of 401(k) Plans*. Washington, D.C.: Brookings Institution Press

NATIONAL SOCIAL INSURANCE BOARD (2000). *Social Insurance in Sweden*. Stockholm: National Social Insurance Board.

NEUMARK, DAVID (2001). 'Age Discrimination in the United States'. NBER Working Paper 8152. Cambridge, Mass.: National Bureau of Economic Research.

NEUMARK, DAVID, and STOCK, W. (1999). 'Age discrimination laws and labor market efficiency'. *Journal of Political Economy*, 13/4: 736–61.

OECD (2001). *Ageing and Income: Financial Resources and Retirement in 9 OECD Countries*. Paris: Organization for Economic Cooperation and Development.

—— (2004). OECD Employment Outlook 2004.

QUINN, JOSEPH (1999a). 'Has the early retirement trend reversed?' First Annual Joint Conference for the Retirement Research Consortium (20–1 May). Boston.

—— (1999b). 'Retirement patterns and bridge jobs in the 1990s'. EBRI Issue Brief (Feb.).

RIX, SARAH (1999). *Social Security Reform: Rethinking Retirement Age Policy—A Look at Raising Social Security's Retirement Age*. Washington, D.C.: AARP Public Policy Institute.

ROPER STARCH WORLDWIDE, INC. (1998). 'Boomers look toward retirement'. Presentation for the AARP. Washington (2 June).

STATISTICS SWEDEN (2001). Arbetsmiljöundersökningen (Survey of Working Conditions).

SUNDÉN, ANNIKA (1994). 'Early retirement in the Swedish pension system'. Unpublished Ph.D. diss. Department of Labor Economics, Cornell University.

WATSON WYATT (1999). *Phased Retirement—Reshaping the End of Work*. Washington, D.C.: Watson Wyatt.

# CHALLENGES

CHAPTER 36

# PRODUCTIVITY, COMPENSATION, AND RETIREMENT

## DAVID NEUMARK

The interplay between productivity, compensation, and retirement is central to many core issues regarding pensions and retirement, in particular the life-cycle earnings profile, the structure of pensions, and public policies regarding the employment of older workers and their retirement—including pension regulations, age discrimination laws, and prohibitions of mandatory retirement. Moreover, these core issues are intimately related. One of the most robust findings in labor economics is the increase in compensation (earnings as well as pension wealth) over much of the life cycle. While the empirical relationship is well-established, its interpretation—and specifically the relationship between compensation and productivity over the life cycle—is controversial. But the relationship between compensation and productivity over the life cycle has critical implications for understanding pensions and retirement behavior, for public policies toward pensions, retirement, and age discrimination, and for contemplating the implications of changes in pension arrangements—in particular, the massive shift from defined benefit (DB) to defined contribution (DC) pension plans.

These issues are going to become even more prominent in the coming decades, as the industrialized countries confront rapidly ageing populations and smaller numbers of workers per retiree, posing challenges not only to public pension systems but also potentially to private pension systems as well. And this demographic change will likely bring to the fore issues related to private pensions, as countries respond by reducing the obligations of public pensions and encouraging private pensions—as has already occurred in Germany and Japan, for example (Nyce and Schieber 2005; Poterba 2004).

This chapter proceeds in six steps. First, it discusses alternative models of the relationship between productivity, compensation, and age, focusing on the human capital model and long-term incentive contracts. Second, it considers workers' retirement behavior in these models, as well as employers' interests in retirement and job tenure, and the role of pensions in influencing retirement and tenure. Third, because the alternative models of the relationship between productivity, compensation, and age have different implications for retirement and pensions, it presents evidence on the alternative models. Fourth, it examines the role of public policy regarding age discrimination and mandatory retirement, which can influence the productivity-compensation-retirement nexus. Fifth, it summarizes changes in pensions in the United States. And sixth, it considers the possible implications of the shifts in pensions in the United States in light of the role that pensions play in the links between productivity, compensation, and retirement.

# 1 Models of Productivity, Compensation, and Age

The two main models that relate productivity, compensation, and age are the human capital model and the long-term incentive contract model.

## 1.1 The Human Capital Model

Mincer's (1974) seminal research on the relationship between productivity, compensation, and age documented the pattern of rising wages with time in the labor force over most of the career, and developed models of human capital investment that could explain this empirical regularity. Related work parsed rising wage profiles into a part due to the accumulation of general labor market experience and a part due to the accumulation of tenure with a specific employer. In particular, Becker (1964) developed the distinction between general human capital—which rose with experience and was equally productive at other jobs—and specific human capital—which rose with tenure on the current job and was productive only there.[1]

The human capital model has a few key implications. Most broadly, in the human capital model earnings rise over much of the life cycle because investments in workers increase their productivity; that is, both productivity and wages rise over much of the life cycle. There are, however, richer implications. General human capital investment should be financed by workers, because employers would never pay for investments that are equally valuable elsewhere and hence for which they would have to pay workers commensurately higher wages after the investments are made. Thus, workers pay for this human capital, and their wages rise in step with the resulting increases in productivity. In contrast, specific human capital investments are financed in part by workers and in part by employers. Employers pay part because workers cannot command a higher wage for investments that are not valued by other employers, but employers do not pay for all of the investment since they would lose the investment if the worker left. Thus, employers also share part of the higher productivity associated with specific human capital with workers, in the form of higher wages, to deter separations.[2] When specific human capital is important, productivity and wages still rise over the life cycle, but wages grow more slowly—starting out higher than productivity but ending up lower as productivity rises faster.[3]

## 1.2 The Long-Term Incentive Contract Model

Lazear (1979) provides a quite different model of the age-earnings profile, in which the employer has to solve the problem of extracting effort from the worker, whereas workers have incentives to work less hard, or to 'shirk'. The earnings profile plays the role of a long-term incentive contract which can generate a rising earnings profile even when productivity is flat over the life cycle. Specifically, if the worker is paid less than his marginal product when young, with the promise of earning more than his marginal product later, then the worker effectively posts a bond that guarantees high effort, and receives higher compensation later for having lasted a long time with the employer without shirking. This contract structure (a 'Lazear contract') encourages the worker to exert effort, and as long as the present value of compensation net of the disutility of higher effort is higher under this arrangement than under a 'spot market' wage that equates wages with productivity in each period, the worker gains from this arrangement.

In contrast to the human capital model, in the Lazear model earnings rise faster than productivity over the life cycle. The Lazear model pertains more to earnings growth with tenure than with experience, since subsequent employers would have no reason to compensate a worker for the below-productivity wage earned on a previous job. However, most workers in the US economy settle into long-term jobs (Hall 1982), a finding that has changed little despite some changes in job attachment in US labor markets (Neumark 2000). Thus, the evolution of earnings during workers' tenure with their employer plays an important role in the life-cycle pattern of earnings.

## 2 Retirement and Pensions in the Alternative Models

In a spot labor market in which workers are always paid their marginal product and workers choose when to retire, the standard economic model of retirement predicts that retirement will occur when it is efficient. It is typically assumed that workers' utility of leisure (or disutility of work) rises with age, whether because of rising actual benefits of leisure or the increased difficulty of exerting effort on the job. In this case, workers will retire when the wage no longer exceeds the disutility of work, or the reservation wage. In a spot market, this occurs when the worker's marginal product—which equals the wage—falls below the worker's reservation wage, and this is efficient because after retirement the utility the retiree gets from leisure exceeds what he would have produced on the job.

On the other hand, as discussed in more detail below, it is impossible to observe the complexities of pension arrangements—in particular DB pensions—without suspecting that pensions are used in part to shape retirement behavior. What do the alternative models of rising earnings profiles have to say about retirement and the role of pensions?[4]

In the general human capital model, wages equal marginal product, so the increased productivity that occurred because of investment may delay retirement, but this is efficient. Pensions play no obvious role. But in the standard model of specific human capital investment, wages of older workers are below their marginal products, so workers may prefer to retire too early—at a point where their marginal product exceeds their reservation wage—preventing employers from fully recouping the value of their investments in workers' specific human capital. As Becker (1964) pointed out, employers therefore have an incentive to offer pensions that reward workers for staying on the job until their investments are recouped (and indeed even longer). To satisfy this condition, pensions must involve some form of incomplete vesting or other incentive for long tenure (such as backloading). Defined benefit (DB) pension plans do this quite naturally, by tying benefits to years of service and the high wages earned late in the career.

The Lazear model has direct implications for pensions and retirement. First, part of the delayed payments in Lazear contracts may come in the form of a pension upon retirement. Indeed, the model predicts that even in the last period of employment some delayed payment is required to deter shirking, so in some sense there is always some pension in one of these contracts. More generally, the backloading of DB pension plans provides a way to delay compensation.

Second, the Lazear model implies that employers will want to terminate the employment relationship before the employee would voluntarily retire in the presence of long-term incentive contracts. Because wages of older workers reflect current plus past productivity, wages may exceed the reservation wage for a far longer time than they would in a spot market. But from the employer's perspective, at some point when the wage is still above the reservation wage—so that the employee would like to keep working—the worker's present discounted value of compensation has caught up with his present discounted value of productivity, and continuing the employment relationship (at the same wage or higher) would result in a net loss to the employer on the contract. Thus, the employer has to induce retirement; *ex ante* workers are willing to accept retirement as of the date at which this condition just holds, but *ex post* they would choose to continue working. At the same time, the higher earnings for more-tenured workers implies that the employer has an incentive to terminate employment even earlier, reneging on the long-term incentive contract, and 'pocketing' the difference between earnings and productivity thus far. Lazear argued that reputation effects may deter this behavior; we return to this issue of 'opportunistic' employer behavior below.

Lazear originally argued (1979) that mandatory retirement is used to enforce termination of the employment relationship at the appropriate time. Later, though, he noted that a DB pension plan could be structured that would induce retirement at the same date, by setting the maximum present value of the pension to peak at that date (Lazear 1995). Changes in public policy toward older workers and in pension arrangements may have quite important implications if the Lazear model helps to characterize the relationship between compensation, productivity, and age, because of the potential importance of mandatory retirement and pensions in this model.

## 3 Evidence on the Alternative Models

Because the alternative models of the life-cycle relationship have different implications for retirement and pensions—and hence also for public policy and institutional changes regarding retirement and pensions—it is important to assess the evidence on the models. This is an extensive area of research, but is covered rather quickly in this section. Because the central distinguishing feature of the alternative models of the age-earnings profile is whether earnings rise faster or slower than productivity over the life cycle, the ideal test would use actual data on earnings and productivity. However, such data are difficult to come by, which has prompted tests based on other implications of the models.

The general human capital model predicts that although different workers will choose careers and investments resulting in flatter or steeper age-earnings profiles, in equilibrium (under some conditions), the present value of the profiles for similar workers will be equal (Mincer 1974: 18). In contrast, in the Lazear model steeper age-earnings profiles are associated with higher productivity—because the steepness of the profile is likely to be associated with greater effort—and hence with higher present value of earnings. Neumark and Taubman (1995) use estimates of age-earnings profiles coupled with assumptions needed to calculate the implied present discounted values of earnings profiles to test whether steeper profiles are associated with higher present value of earnings, and find that the evidence is most consistent with the general human capital model.

Another way to test the key implication of the Lazear model that earnings rise faster than productivity is to ask whether owners of firms gain from shedding older workers. If older workers are overpaid, and if they can be shed without loss of reputation that damages the ability of employers to enter into Lazear-type contracts in the future, then in fact owners may gain. Researchers studying corporate takeovers have suggested that one of the motivations for hostile takeovers is to recapture the higher wages paid to older workers (Shleifer and Summers 1988). Such takeovers enable firms to cut employment of older workers, and, perhaps because takeover targets often are resold, or because the employment cuts occur under the burden of heavy debt, reputation effects may be small. Gokhale *et al.* (1995) find evidence supportive of the joint hypothesis that older workers are paid more than their marginal product and that hostile takeovers target these excess payments—consistent with Lazear's model.

Kotlikoff and Gokhale (1992) assess the Lazear model by exploiting the first-order condition from profit maximization that, at hiring, the present discounted value of productivity must equal the present discounted value of earnings. Because they have data on new hires at a single firm, and can observe the future stream of earnings for each hire, they can infer the future stream of productivity of hires at different ages and from this work out productivity at each age. Their evidence suggests that productivity falls with age, and productivity exceeds earnings when young and falls short of earnings when old, as predicted by the Lazear model.

Medoff and Abraham (1980) ask whether the returns to experience in a company-level data set can be accounted for by productivity—as measured by a performance rating—or instead whether more experienced workers are paid more for other reasons, such as those suggested by the Lazear model. They conclude that performance accounts for little of the experience-earnings or tenure-earnings profile, and argue that theories that generate returns to experience without linking experience to productivity have to be given serious credence.

Finally, Hellerstein and Neumark (2004) obtain direct evidence on earnings and productivity over the life cycle. They use data on US manufacturing plants matched to their workers, combining standard data used to estimate production functions with information on labor costs and on the age structure of plants' workforces, which enables them to estimate relative pay and productivity differentials of older versus younger workers. Consistent with the Lazear model, they find that older workers are paid more than younger workers, but are quite a bit less productive, by perhaps 15–20 percent.

The combined evidence does not point to an unambiguous conclusion regarding the correct model of the age-earnings profile. The labor market is quite heterogeneous, and the importance of human capital investment versus the elicitation of effort may vary across industries, occupations, and so on. Moreover, even individual workers may be subject to competing influences of the alternative models. At the same time, the case that Lazear contracts are an important feature of US labor markets is fairly compelling, which has to shape how we view changes in labor market policies and pension arrangements that influence retirement.

# 4 AGE DISCRIMINATION LAWS, EMPLOYMENT, AND RETIREMENT

The 1967 Age Discrimination in Employment Act (ADEA) launched a major attack on discrimination against older workers in the United States, although the evolution of governmental efforts to prohibit such discrimination goes back further to state statutes prohibiting age discrimination as part of states' Fair Employment Practices Acts. The ADEA prohibited discrimination based on age, covering those aged 40 to 65, and including discrimination based on age within this protected age range. In addition to prohibiting discriminatory hiring practices, by covering those aged 40 to 65 the ADEA also forbade mandatory retirement prior to age 65. Amendments in 1978 extended the age range for the protected group to 40 to 70, raised the mandatory retirement age to 70 in the process, and also eliminated mandatory retirement for most federal employees. Finally, 1986 amendments to the ADEA eliminated the upper age range for defining the protected class and hence prohibited mandatory retirement in nearly all cases. It is likely that these policy changes affected both retirement and employment of older workers, and more generally the relationship between productivity, compensation, and retirement, although the effects of these policy changes depend on which model best characterizes the productivity-compensation-retirement nexus.

In the context of the general or specific human capital model, in which older workers are either paid their marginal product, or less than their marginal product, legislation prohibiting age discrimination is likely to increase efficiency. 'Discrimination' in this context refers to the classic sense of the word—differential treatment of identically productive workers (as in Becker 1964). If employers, either because of prejudice or stereotypes, incorrectly view older workers as less productive, then it is likely that they will underpay older workers and limit their employment prospects. This may lead to inefficient allocation of resources (Arrow 1972), with older workers paid less and working less than is optimal given the productivity of their labor and the utility they place on their leisure, and may possibly contribute to premature retirement.

Numerous types of evidence point to discrimination against older workers in the past, including: evidence that negative stereotypes about older workers exist (or existed) and that these appear to be used to rate applicants for jobs; evidence that older workers face difficulties in getting hired; and evidence that age discrimination—as perceived by workers—resulted in older workers leaving their jobs and the workforce (Adams and Neumark 2002). Overall, this research suggests that age discrimination legislation could play a potentially beneficial role in increasing employment and reducing premature retirement of older individuals.

Evidence on the effects of age discrimination laws indicates that these laws boosted employment of older men. This research does not focus solely on estimating the impact of the federal ADEA, because inferring the effect of the federal law solely from changes over time in employment (or retirement) is difficult given other changes in the employment and retirement behavior of older males. By using variation in the timing with which age discrimination laws were introduced across states—including the introduction of the ADEA in those states that had not implemented their own laws by 1967—it is possible to control for the influence of aggregate changes in employment and retirement behavior. Neumark and Stock's (1999) evidence indicates that workers aged 60 and over experienced significantly higher employment rates (by about six percentage points) following passage of an age discrimination law that protected them. When a particular provision also barred mandatory retirement (perhaps up to a certain age), the employment rates of those aged 60 and older were slightly higher still, although this evidence was not statistically significant. Thus, it was mainly simply the existence of an age discrimination prohibition that boosted employment of older men.

Viewed through the prism of Lazear contracts, the links between age discrimination laws, employment, and retirement are potentially more complex. The most obvious impact of the ADEA stems from its raising the age of mandatory retirement and then eliminating it altogether. What is most interesting in thinking about the connection between age discrimination legislation and retirement and employment of older workers in the context of the Lazear model is that such legislation—while seemingly addressing a social evil—may have adverse unintended consequences. In this model, mandatory retirement is part of an efficient long-term incentive contract, and acceptable to older workers *ex ante* (when they were young), although not when they are older. Rather, it is in the interest of older workers to eliminate mandatory retirement. Yet doing so would—Lazear argued—impair the ability of workers and firms to enter into efficient long-term incentive contracts, providing current older workers with a 'small once-and-for-all gain at the expense of a much larger and continuing efficiency loss' (Lazear 1979: 1283–4).

However, mandatory retirement may not have been that critical in ending the employment relationship. As discussed above, under DB pension plans, at least, it was possible to create strong financial incentives to induce retirement at any given age, and empirical work supports the importance of these incentives (Kotlikoff and Wise 1989). Furthermore, subsequent research suggests that mandatory retirement was relatively unimportant in inducing retirement among all but a small percentage of the workforce, because of factors such as pensions and social security retirement incentives (Burkhauser and Quinn 1983).

But if the ADEA had relatively little impact via raising the age for mandatory retirement and then prohibiting it, then its consequences may have been quite different, and its 'blanket' prohibition of age discrimination may have been more important. In particular, in the labor market described by Lazear contracts, as noted earlier, employers have an incentive to renege—firing workers before the age of mandatory retirement when they owe them more in compensation (in present value terms) than the value of their remaining productivity. Although reputation effects may lessen these incentives, they require fairly strong conditions to work; for example, information asymmetries between workers and firms may allow firms to claim that layoffs of older workers are due to changed economic conditions, which workers cannot fully verify. In addition, institutional innovations may arise that allow employers to 'circumvent' damages to reputation stemming from opportunistic behavior, such as hostile takeovers in which Lazear contracts are abrogated but the company is subsequently resold so that the new owner suffers no loss of reputation.[5]

Neumark and Stock (1999) test these alternative interpretations of age discrimination legislation. If age discrimination laws acted predominantly as a rent-seeking mechanism for older workers, their passage would reduce the use of long-term incentive (Lazear) contracts for new labor market entrants, whereas the opposite implication holds if the predominant effect was to strengthen such contracts by reducing opportunistic behavior on the part of employers. They test these alternatives by asking whether age discrimination laws result in flatter or steeper age-earnings profiles of new entrants, with the former corresponding to the rent-seeking hypothesis, and vice versa. The evidence indicates that the predominant effect of age discrimination legislation was to strengthen the employment relationship and hence long-term incentive contracts.

The findings from this research viewed as a whole suggest that the ADEA did not have its principal effects through the prohibition of mandatory retirement, but instead through increasing employment of older workers. Whether this was countering discriminatory attitudes or stereotypes, or incentives for opportunistic behavior by employers, cannot be determined.[6] In either case, age discrimination efforts likely acted to keep older workers in the workforce longer. And in the context of Lazear contracts, it appears that a combination of pensions and other incentives created by public programs combined to largely maintain a pattern of retiring at ages previously specified by mandatory retirement.[7] To the extent that these types of contracts are an important and efficiency-increasing component of labor markets, then, age discrimination legislation may have done no harm and even some good.

## 5 Pensions and Retirement and Pension Changes

As already explained, DB pension plans can be structured to create strong incentives to induce retirement at a given age. This implies that employers and workers may be able to enter into Lazear-type implicit contracts even in the absence of employers' ability to use mandatory retirement. As examples, Kotlikoff and Wise (1989) study a 1979 survey of pension plans, focusing on DB plans that based benefits on past earnings. Pension plans typically specify certain retirement ages, including, for example, early and normal retirement ages. The earlier one takes retirement, the longer benefits are received, but in return benefits are lowered. However, if the benefit reductions are actuarially unfair, so that pensions taken at these retirement ages are not adjusted downward by as much as they should be to compensate for the greater number of years for which they will be received, then after each of these ages pension accrual rates (the rate of growth of pension wealth from period to period) can fall sharply and typically become negative. Kotlikoff and Wise show that such accrual patterns characterize DB pension plans in the United States, and argue that these kinds of patterns in pension wealth suggest explicit attempts to induce retirement at specific ages, as we would expect to arise under Lazear contracts. The other significant feature of DB plans is that they typically create strong incentives for long tenure, because the benefits are tied to years of service and the latest—and usually highest—earnings.

DC plans, on the other hand, do not have either of these features. They do not particularly bind workers to firms, because they are portable. And because they continually grow (as long as the assets in which they are invested grow), they do not serve explicitly to induce retirement. Nonetheless, the system offers other inducements to retire. One is the ability to begin making withdrawals from DC plans at age $59\frac{1}{2}$, which in the presence of liquidity constraints should result in increased reservation wages at that age. A second is the incentives provided by social security for retirement at ages 62 and 65, as already noted with regard to work assessing the importance of mandatory retirement in inducing retirement.

It is also important to point out that employers' ability to use changes in pension wealth to induce retirement is not unrestricted. The 1990 Older Workers Benefits Protection Act (OWBPA) regulated financial inducements to retire. One of the important requirements was that retirement incentive schemes be offered to anyone over a minimum age, rather than to workers in a specific age range, placing some limits on the ability of employers to induce retirement through financial incentives (Issacharoff and Worth Harris 1997). In addition, the OWBPA limited offsets of pensions benefits against severance payments, raising the cost borne by employers when involuntarily terminating older workers. At the same time, the OWBPA codified the types of retirement incentives that can be used and how they can be implemented, such as establishing the 'ground rules' for waivers of workers' rights to sue under the ADEA.[8] In addition, the 1986 Age Discrimination Act lessened the declines in accruals at the age of normal retirement built into pension plans, by requiring that credit continue to be given for years of service following the normal retirement age. Overall, though, this discussion of DB pension plans, coupled with the evidence on the effects of age discrimination legislation presented in the previous section, suggests that, as Lazear (1995) puts it, 'blunt instruments, such as mandatory retirement, can be replaced by more refined ones, such as efficient pension plans' (p. 45).

However, a sea change in pension provision that has occurred since the early 1980s has been a shift from DB to DC pension plans (including 401(k) plans). For example, Papke (1997) reports that for single-employer pension plans with 100 or more participants, the number of DB plans fell from over 22,000 in 1980 to 17,000 in 1992, and the number of active participants fell from 21.9 million to 19.8 million. At the same time, the number of DC plans rose from 13,000 to 38,000, and the number of participants from 15 million to 29 million, while the number of 401(k) plans and participants rose even more strongly. And Friedberg and Webb (2003) report that the percentage of pensioned full-time employees with a DC plan rose from 40 to 79 percent between 1983 and 1998, while the percentage covered by a DB plan fell from 87 to 44 percent over the same period.

The shift in pensions has been attributed to numerous factors. Ippolito (1995) suggests that about half of the shift stems from the loss of employment in large unionized workplaces where DB plans are more common. He also suggests (Ippolito 2002) that changes in tax laws have reduced the attractiveness of DB plans. A tax on reversions from DB plans was imposed in 1986, beginning at 10 percent and increasing to 50 percent by 1990. Although the tax may have discouraged reversions, it should also have decreased the attractiveness of DB plans to employers, by establishing a claim to assets used to overfund pensions and generate a tax deduction.

Finally, the shift to DC plans may reflect the changing nature of the labor market and the workforce. One conjecture is that the shift out of DB plans has been spurred by employers trying to avoid the costs entailed by these plans when the workforce is ageing. Alternatively, with technological and other changes leading to a more mobile workforce, and less value placed on long tenure, the tenure-promoting effects of DB plans may have become less important. Or, if mobility has largely been driven by worker behavior, then encouraging long tenure through DB plans may have become too expensive (Coronado and Copeland 2003).

# 6 Implications of Pension Changes

The shift from DB to DC plans would appear to undermine what has been described in this chapter as one of the principal roles of pensions in the interplay between productivity and compensation.[9] In both the specific human capital model and the Lazear contract model, backloading of pensions plays an important role. DC plans, however, typically do not have backloading, but instead generally result in contributions of a given share of wages, and workers are fully vested relatively quickly (a maximum of six years under 401(k) plans).[10] And in a world of Lazear contracts, DB plans, but not DC plans, can create strong incentives for workers to separate at the right retirement age, from the perspective of the implicit long-term incentive contract.[11] As already pointed out, while mandatory retirement in principle provides an alternative way to ensure that contracts with backholding can be used, by enforcing a termination date, the elimination of mandatory retirement with the later amendments to the ADEA leaves DB pension plans as the principal way for employers to induce retirement.

Thus, the shift in pensions in the US economy could possibly threaten or limit the ability of workers and employers to enter into long-term relationships whose productivity is enhanced by either greater specific human capital investment, or greater incentives to exert effort. This, in turn, raises a couple of key questions. First, if the incentives created by DB plans are beneficial to employers and workers, have changes in pensions been driven in part by changes in the employment relationship, so that perhaps the changes are not as harmful as might be the case if the employment relationship had remained unchanged? And second, is the decline in DB plans likely to pose problems for employers, especially as growing numbers of workers approach retirement ages with the ageing of the baby-boomers?

If the underlying importance of long-term employment relationships—stemming from either specific human capital investment or Lazear-type contracts—has not changed, then the shift in pensions may be alarming. On this view, whatever has spurred the shift to DC plans and away from DB plans ultimately threatens the ability of employers and workers to form these productive long-term relationships. Moreover, with the ageing of the baby boomers, employers may be likely to be hit by rapidly ageing, highly paid workforces, with little leverage with which to encourage retirement, especially given the threat of age discrimination claims. This 'perfect storm' of an increasing burden of highly paid older workers and an inability to 'lock in' younger workers may be viewed as presenting severe challenges to companies in the next couple of decades.

A more sanguine view is that the change in pensions reflects the accumulation of many marginal changes in the costs and benefits of DB and DC plans that have shifted in ways that no longer favor DB plans. It is possible that some of the tax changes that have spurred these changes may have had unintended consequences, and on those grounds merit reconsideration, but at the same time there may be other changes in the economy that make the changes in pensions rational. Many of these issues have already been discussed. For example, the changes in tax laws associated with pension terminations may have made DB plans less attractive, and the restrictions on using DB pensions to induce retirement may have had a similar effect. Similarly, I have emphasized throughout that DB plans provide two levers—one inducing retirement at specific ages, and the other encouraging long tenure. But if workers with low discount rates tend to be those who accumulate longer tenure, then the advent of 401(k) plans may have provided employers with another way to encourage longer-tenure workers to stay with the firm.

Changes in the workforce and in the employment relationship may have also contributed to this trend. As already noted, the decline in unionization likely played a major role in the shift in pensions. As union contracts typically put in place rules that encourage long tenure, it would make sense that unionized employers would tend to offer pension plans that reward long tenure, and the decline in unions would produce a shift toward more portable pension arrangements, especially if unions tended to result in too much tenure relative to what employers regarded as optimal, which seems plausible. Aaronson and Coronado (2004) also present evidence that, across industries, a rising share of workers with lower tenure expectations (such as married women with children) is associated with declines in DB pension coverage and increases in DC pension coverage.

A large literature also addresses the question of whether longer-term attachments between workers and employers are diminishing (Neumark 2000). The findings of this literature vary somewhat, but overall appear to point to moderate declining attachment. Moreover, Valletta (1999) finds declines in job security—that is, increases in dismissals—for more-tenured workers in the 1980s and early 1990s. The combined evidence is interesting. If all we were observing were declines in attachments between workers and firms over the same period in which pensions switched away from DB plans, we would have no idea whether declining attachments decreased the value of DB pensions, or the shift away from DB pensions reduced attachments. But Valletta interprets his evidence of declining job security as consistent with rising employer default on Lazear-type contracts. This behavior might be partly attributable to employers placing less value on such contracts and could explain both the decline in job attachment and also the shift away from DB pensions.[12]

These changes, coupled with the use of hostile takeovers to breach implicit contracts, may have contributed to greater expectations on the part of workers that firms would renege on Lazear-type contracts. In Lazear's model, this would result in less backloading of pay, consistent also with the decline in DB pension plans. An alternative perspective, which does not point to greater default but simply to lower value placed on long-term relationships, is provided by Friedberg and Owyang (2004), who argue that more rapid technological change results in more shocks that reduce value of existing jobs relative to new jobs, thus reducing the appeal of DB pensions (as well as reducing tenure).

In addition, a concern that the shift from DB to DC plans makes it difficult to induce older workers to retire may appear misplaced in some important respects, which instead point to the challenge of trying to keep older individuals employed. We have all heard the evidence on the declining ratios of workers to social security beneficiaries that will be faced as a result of the ageing workforce, better health, and declining work, over the long term, among older individuals (Lumsdaine and Mitchell 1999). From a public policy perspective, increasing employment among older individuals may not help very much with social security solvency unless it is accompanied by increases in ages at which beneficiaries can draw benefits or full benefits—the latter of which is occurring. From a private perspective, employers may face some difficulties in meeting labor demand needs if they cannot induce enough older individuals to remain in the labor market. Thus, the reduced incentives to retire generated by the shift from DB to DC plans may, over the next few decades, offer some advantages because of the need to try to keep older individuals working, even if, in the steady state, the shift in pensions might otherwise pose challenges to employers.

# 7 CONCLUSIONS

Any discussion of issues of public policy and institutional change with regard to pensions and retirement must be filtered through particular—or multiple—perspectives on the relationship between productivity, compensation, and retirement. The nexus between these variables has critical implications for whether employers would like to keep workers in their employ as they age and over what period, and whether or at what point employers establish mechanisms to ease them out of the workforce. Stemming from this, private policies regarding pensions and mandatory retirement, public anti-discrimination policies affecting hiring, dismissals, and other aspects of the employment relationship, and institutional changes regarding pension arrangements that may be driven by both policy and by economic change, have potentially different impacts depending on the productivity-compensation-retirement nexus. The importance of these policy issues will almost certainly be increasingly magnified in coming decades as the industrialized countries generally face rapidly ageing populations.

This chapter has argued that at least some evidence is consistent with the model of long-term incentive contracts developed by Lazear (1979), in which workers are paid less than their productivity when young, and more when old. In turn, this implies that a potentially important role for private pensions, especially in light of the elimination of mandatory retirement, is to induce retirement at some point. At the same time, society has an interest in encouraging continued employment by older individuals, and certainly in discouraging employers from acting on what may sometimes be in their private interest and opportunistically discharging older workers too early. Age discrimination laws appear to have been one vehicle that discouraged this type of opportunistic behavior, without eliminating the ability of employers to induce retirement at later ages through pension incentives.

However, the shift from DB to DC pension plans raises fears that, coupled with the restrictions on employers posed by the ADEA, employers' ability to induce retirement, and hence to structure long-term implicit incentive contracts that are productive, has been impeded. In principle, there are some foundations for this fear. However, the shift in pensions may not be too problematic. First, changes in both the economy and the labor force have reduced the value of these long-term contracts, so that at least some part of the shift in pensions reflects a response to these changes, rather than an exogenously induced change with negative consequences. Second, over the next few decades problems of an ageing population may imply that measures that extend employment into later ages may have benefits that help outweigh some of the costs that the change in pensions might otherwise impose. Ultimately, we cannot be sure. Clearly, though, it remains important to ask whether public policies toward pensions and retirement have created distorted incentives to provide one type of pension over the other, in a way that impinges on the productivity-compensation-retirement nexus so as to entail welfare losses. On the other hand, it is also important to better understand how changes in the economy and the labor force have contributed to changes in pensions and retirement, to avoid policy changes that inhibit adaptations that are welfare-enhancing.

# Notes

1. There is little dispute that labor market experience contributes to rising wages, but some dispute about how much tenure increases wages, because better worker–employer matches result in higher wages and also last longer (Topel 1991).
2. However, Baron *et al.* (1999) present evidence suggesting that much human capital investment is general, yet employers appear to pay for it.
3. Versions of models with specific human capital investment can be constructed in which wages rise faster than productivity (Carmichael 1983).
4. Other theories about why employers provide pensions are not considered here, including: tax incentives because earnings of pension assets are not taxed until benefits are paid; insurance against the risk of living a long time after retirement (for DB plans, a role also played by public pensions); and shifting the risk on retirement-related benefits to employers (in the case of DB plans). See Dorsey *et al.* (1998).
5. Legislation prohibiting age discrimination may offer workers protection against opportunistic behavior by employers by effectively barring dismissals disproportionately weighted toward older workers, and at the same time solving the problem that commitments to adhere to Lazear contracts may be in employers' interests but are not credible when made by employers acting on their own (Neumark and Stock 1999; Jolls 1996).
6. The evidence in Neumark and Stock (1999) suggests the latter, but reductions in simple discrimination that would lengthen time with the employer would also create incentives for more human capital investment, which could lead to faster earnings growth.
7. This may not hold in particular labor markets. For example, Ashenfelter and Card (2002) find that the elimination of mandatory retirement led to relatively sharp reductions in retirements of 70 and 71-year-old university faculty members. This study is restricted to institutions with DC pension plans, where it is more likely that changes in mandatory retirement policies will have an impact because employers cannot use DB pension formulas to induce retirement at specific ages.
8. The Employees Retirement Income Security Act (ERISA) of 1975 also regulated pension (and other) benefits, potentially limiting opportunistic behavior of employers toward older workers.

9. A more recent change is the growth of cash balance plans, which arise most frequently from conversions of DB plans. Cash balance plans operate more like DC plans, in that workers accumulate pension wealth more steadily over their career. But they are like DB plans in that workers do not literally own the pension assets or bear the risks of stock market fluctuations. These plans may pose the same challenge as DC plans with regard to the backloading of pay, although by retaining normal retirement ages, etc., they can still include inducements to retire. But Johnson and Uccello (2004) note that conversions to cash balance plans have often been accompanied by the elimination of subsidies for early retirement in DB pension plans.
10. Bodie *et al.* (1988) point out that in principle a DC plan could be backloaded by increasing the share contributed with age or tenure of the workers. But this could run into IRS restrictions on maximum contributions for older or more-tenured workers, especially for higher-paid workers.
11. Friedberg and Webb (2005) present evidence that the shift to DC plans leads to later retirement ages.
12. Balan (2003) also presents some evidence consistent with declining importance of Lazear-style contracts—in particular, declining returns to tenure for less-experienced workers.

# References

Aaronson, Stephanie, and Coronado, Julia (2004). 'Are firms or workers behind the shift away from DB pension plans?' Unpublished manuscript, Federal Reserve Board of Governors.

Adams, Scott J. (2004). 'Age discrimination legislation and the employment of older workers'. *Labour Economics*, 11/2 (Apr.): 219–41.

—— and Neumark, David (2002). 'Age discrimination in U.S. labor markets: a review of the evidence'. Public Policy Institute of California Working Paper No. 2002-08.

Arrow, Kenneth J. (1972). 'Some mathematical models of race discrimination in the labor market', in A. Pascal (ed.), *Racial Discrimination in Economic Life*. Lexington, Mass.: D.C. Heath, 187–203.

Ashenfelter, Orley, and Card, David (2002). 'Did the elimination of mandatory retirement affect faculty retirement?' *American Economic Review*, 92/4 (Sept.), 957–80.

Balan, David J. (2003). 'Have Lazear-style contracts disappeared?' Federal Trade Commission Working Paper No. 256.

Barron, John M., Berger, Mark C., and Black, Dan A. (1999). 'Do workers pay for on-the-job training'. *Journal of Human Resources*, 34/2 (spring): 235–52.

Becker, Gary S. (1964). *Human Capital*. Chicago: University of Chicago Press.

Bodie, Zvi, Marcus, Alan J., and Merton, Robert C. (1988). 'Defined benefit versus defined contribution pension plans: what are the real trade-offs?', in Zvi Bodie, John B. Shoven, and David A. Wise (eds.), *Pensions in the U.S. Economy*. Chicago: University of Chicago Press, 139–60.

Burkhauser, Richard V., and Quinn, Joseph F. (1983). 'Is mandatory retirement overrated? Evidence from the 1970s'. *Journal of Human Resources*, 18/3 (summer): 337–58.

CARMICHAEL, LORNE (1983). 'Firm-specific human capital and promotion ladders'. *Bell Journal of Economics*, 14/1 (spring): 251–8.

CORONADO, JULIA LYNN, and COPELAND, PHILLIP C. (2003). 'Cash balance pension plan conversions and the new economy'. Unpublished manuscript, Federal Reserve Board of Governors.

DORSEY, STUART, CORNWELL, CHRISTOPHER, and MACPHERSON, DAVID (1998). *Pensions and Productivity.* Kalamazoo, Mich.: W. E. Upjohn Institute for Employment Research.

FRIEDBERG, LEORA, and OWYANG, MICHAEL (2004). 'Explaining the evolution of pension structure and job tenure'. NBER Working Paper No. 10714.

—— and WEBB, ANTHONY (2005). 'Retirement and the evolution of pension structure'. *Journal of Human Resources*, 40/2 (spring): 281–308.

GOKHALE, JAGADEESH, GROSHEN, ERICA L., and NEUMARK, DAVID (1995). 'Do hostile takeovers reduce extramarginal wages? An establishment-level analysis'. *Review of Economics and Statistics*, 77/3 (Aug.): 470–85.

HALL, ROBERT E. (1982). 'The importance of lifetime jobs in the U.S. economy'. *American Economic Review*, 72/4 (Sept.): 716–24.

HELLERSTEIN, JUDITH K., and NEUMARK, DAVID (2004). 'Production function and wage equation estimation with heterogeneous labor: evidence from a new matched employer-employee data set'. National Bureau of Economic Research Working Paper No. 10325.

IPPOLITO, RICHARD A. (1995). 'Toward explaining the growth of defined contribution plans'. *Industrial Relations*, 34/1 (Jan.): 1–20.

—— (2002). 'The reversion tax's perverse result'. *Regulation*, 25/1 (spring): 46–53.

ISSACHAROFF, SAMUEL, and WORTH HARRIS, ERICA (1997). 'Is age discrimination really age discrimination? The ADEA's unnatural solution'. *New York University Law Review*, 72/4: 780–840.

JOHNSON, RICHARD W., and UCCELLO, CORE E. (2004). 'Cash balance plans: what do they mean for retirement security?' *National Tax Journal*, 58/2 (part 1) (June): 315–28.

JOLLS, CHRISTINE (1996). 'Hands-tying and the Age Discrimination in Employment Act'. *Texas Law Review*, 74: 1813–46.

KOTLIKOFF, LAURENCE J., and GOKHALE, JAGADEESH (1992). 'Estimating a firm's age-productivity profile using the present value of workers' earnings'. *Quarterly Journal of Economics*, 107/4 (Nov.): 1215–42.

—— and WISE, DAVID A. (1989). *The Wage Carrot and the Pension Stick.* Kalamazoo, Mich.: W. E. Upjohn Institute for Employment Research.

LAZEAR, EDWARD P. (1979). 'Why is there mandatory retirement?' *Journal of Political Economy*, 86/6 (Dec.): 1261–84.

—— (1995). *Personnel Economics.* Cambridge, Mass.: The MIT Press.

LUMSDAINE, ROBIN L., and MITCHELL, OLIVIA S. (1999). 'New developments in the economic analysis of retirement', in Orley Ashenfelter and David Card (eds.), *Handbook of Labor Economics*, volume 3. Amsterdam: Elsevier Science B.V., 3261–307.

MEDOFF, JAMES L., and ABRAHAM, KATHARINE G. (1980). 'Experience, performance, and earnings'. *Quarterly Journal of Economics*, 95/4 (Dec.): 703–36.

MINCER, JACOB (1974). *Schooling, Experience, and Earnings.* New York: National Bureau of Economic Research.

NEUMARK, DAVID (ed.) (2000). *On the Job: Is Long-Term Employment a Thing of the Past?* New York: Russell Sage Foundation.

—— and STOCK, WENDY A. (1999). 'Age discrimination laws and labor market efficiency'. *Journal of Political Economy*, 107/5 (Oct.): 1081–125.

—— and TAUBMAN, PAUL (1995). 'Why do wage profiles slope upward? Tests of the general human capital model'. *Journal of Labor Economics*, 13/4 (Oct.): 736–61.

NYCE, STEVEN A., and SCHIEBER, SYLVESTER J. (2005). *The Economic Implications of Aging Societies: The Costs of Living Happily Ever After.* Cambridge: Cambridge University Press.

PAPKE, LESLIE E. (1997). 'Quantifying the substitution of 401(k) plans for defined benefit plans: evidence from ongoing employers'. *National Tax Association 89th Annual Conference on Taxation*, 136–44.

POTERBA, JAMES (2004). 'The impact of population aging on financial markets'. NBER Working Paper No. 10851.

SHLEIFER, ANDREI, and SUMMERS, LAWRENCE H. (1988). 'Breach of trust in hostile takeovers', in Alan J. Auerbach (ed.), *Corporate Takeovers: Causes and Consequences.* Chicago: University of Chicago Press, 33–68.

TOPEL, ROBERT (1991). 'Specific capital, mobility, and wages: wages rise with job seniority'. *Journal of Political Economy*, 99/1 (Feb.), 145–76.

VALLETTA, ROBERT G. 1999. 'Declining Job Security.' *Journal of Labor Economics*, 17 (4, Part 2), October, S170–S197.

CHAPTER 37

# POVERTY AND INEQUALITY

## GARY BURTLESS

All of the world's rich countries have made enormous progress over the past 50 years in improving relative well-being and reducing poverty among their aged citizens. During the early post-Second World War era, national governments established or liberalized public retirement systems in order to increase living standards among retirees and their dependents so that they might approach those enjoyed by the working-age population. By the end of the 1980s most OECD countries came close to accomplishing this goal. While significant differences are sometimes observed between the gross incomes of elderly and non-elderly families, these are largely offset by the smaller size of aged households and the more favorable tax treatment of incomes received by the elderly.

The equalization of incomes received by the aged and non-aged is one of the great success stories of postwar social policy, but it has been achieved at high cost. Public expenditures devoted to pensions have risen spectacularly, both absolutely and as a fraction of national incomes. As populations in rich countries grow older, the cost of paying for pensions must rise still further. Only one of the seven largest industrial countries, the United Kingdom, has overhauled its public pensions to hold down future pension spending so that it does not increase sharply as a percentage of national income (Bosworth and Burtless 1998). Future UK retirees are expected to derive much more of their retirement income from privately managed and invested pension accounts than from publicly financed, pay-as-you-go (or 'paygo') pensions. Other leading industrial countries may imitate the UK example or adopt other measures to curtail the growth in public pension spending.

This chapter assesses the impact of national pension systems on inequality and poverty and considers how cost-saving reform in these systems may affect the redistributional effects of pensions. It first explores the inequality-reducing effects of pensions within a one-year time horizon. A pension program collects contributions from active workers and their employers and distributes monthly payments to retired or disabled workers and the dependents of deceased workers. On the whole pension recipients are poorer than contributors, so with a one-year time horizon, pension systems undeniably redistribute from the better off to the less affluent. Most of the cross-national literature on the redistributional impact of pensions focuses on their effects within a one-year accounting framework.

The second section summarizes evidence on how pension systems redistribute resources between different income classes when workers' incomes are measured on a lifetime basis. Viewed over an individual's lifetime a pension program simply reallocates income from periods of high earnings to periods when the worker's earned income is low. The reallocation takes place for covered workers whether they are poor, middle-class, or wealthy. Even though pension formulas are often tilted to favor workers with low lifetime earnings, the amount of lifetime redistribution from rich to poor is much smaller than it seems when redistribution is measured by a single year's income.

The concluding section evaluates the likely effects of reform on the redistribution accomplished by national pension systems. The shifting population age structure of industrialized countries will place growing pressure on legislators to scale back pension promises or find new ways to pay for them. Future reforms will almost certainly change the redistributional impacts of national pension systems, whether redistribution is measured from a one-year or a lifetime perspective.

# 1 Redistribution in a Single Year

The goal of a pension system is to replace labor earnings that are lost as a result of old age, premature death, or invalidity. The usual way rich countries accomplish this goal is through mandatory, publicly financed pensions. The typical public program is a defined-benefit program in which the pension is calculated on the basis of the worker's years of coverage under the system and average covered wages while the worker is contributing to the system (World Bank 1994: 102–9). Benefits are financed largely out of the current contributions of active workers and their employers. Only a few public systems have built up enough reserves to pay for a large percentage of pension obligations. Many countries supplement the basic public pension with a system of voluntary or compulsory occupational pensions. Such pensions are usually capital funded and are often managed in the private sector rather than by public officials.

The amount of redistribution accomplished by a given system depends on details of the contribution and pension formulas as well as benefit eligibility rules. However, almost any pension system with broad worker coverage will redistribute from people with relatively high current income to people with low income, reducing the overall inequality of current incomes. Liebman (2002: 14) has performed illustrative calculations for the US public pension system using income data for 1998. Liebman's tabulations show that Americans with non-pension incomes below two times the poverty line received more benefits than they paid in pension taxes, while people with incomes above that threshold on average paid higher taxes for pensions than they received in public pensions. Using a one-year assessment period for measuring incomes, the US public pension system unquestionably achieved a substantial redistribution from the well-to-do toward people who have low incomes aside from their pensions.

Similar calculations have been performed for other nations. For rich countries these calculations always show that national pension systems transfer resources from households that on average are well-off to households that on average have below-average incomes apart from their pension benefits. Mahler and Jesuit (2004) have used micro-census survey files covering years from the early 1980s through 2000 to examine trends in the Gini coefficient of income inequality for 12 industrialized countries. The Gini coefficient is a measure of inequality that ranges between zero (when all individuals receive the same income) and one (when all income is received by just a single individual). They estimated the impacts of public transfer benefits, on the one hand, and income tax payments and payroll tax contributions, on the other, in reducing inequality below what it would be if household incomes were measured before the addition of transfers or the subtraction of direct tax payments. In one set of calculations they focused on the effects of pension payments alone, including occupational pensions if such pensions were compulsory.

Mahler and Jesuit's estimates are displayed in Table 37.1. Column 2 in the table shows the Gini coefficient of income inequality if household incomes are measured on a before-tax, before-transfer basis. Column 3 shows the Gini coefficient when tax payments are subtracted from income and government transfers, including public pensions, are added. The countries are listed in ascending order from least to most unequal on the basis of after-tax, after-transfer incomes. Column 4 shows the percentage reduction in the Gini coefficient as a result of including taxes and government transfers in the income definition. Column 5 shows the percentage reduction in inequality taking account of pension payments, including compulsory occupational pensions. The inclusion of pension payments in the definition of income reduces measured inequality by 6 percent to 24 percent compared with

Table 37.1 Income inequality and reduction of inequality through government redistribution and pensions in 12 industrialized countries[1]

| Country | Year | Gini coefficient[2] | | Percentage reduction in Gini | |
| --- | --- | --- | --- | --- | --- |
| | | Private income | Income after taxes and transfers | From all government redistribution[3] | From redistribution through pensions[4] |
| | | (1) | (2) | (3) | (4) | (5) |
| Denmark | 1992 | 0.426 | 0.236 | 45 | 13 |
| Finland | 2000 | 0.430 | 0.247 | 43 | 16 |
| Netherlands | 1999 | 0.440 | 0.248 | 44 | 21 |
| Norway | 2000 | 0.406 | 0.251 | 38 | 15 |
| Sweden | 2000 | 0.447 | 0.252 | 44 | 17 |
| Belgium | 1997 | 0.481 | 0.260 | 46 | 22 |
| Germany | 2000 | 0.459 | 0.264 | 42 | 21 |
| France | 1994 | 0.485 | 0.288 | 41 | 24 |
| Canada | 2000 | 0.413 | 0.302 | 27 | 9 |
| Australia | 1994 | 0.452 | 0.311 | 31 | 6 |
| United Kingdom | 1999 | 0.500 | 0.345 | 31 | 8 |
| United States | 2000 | 0.469 | 0.368 | 22 | 6 |

Notes: [1] Countries are listed in ascending order by inequality after accounting for taxes and transfers.
[2] The Gini coefficient is a measure of inequality that ranges between zero (when all individuals receive the same income) and one (when all income is received by just a single individual).
[3] Redistribution through taxation and all government transfers.
[4] Public pensions plus occupational pensions when they are mandated by labor law or a national collective bargaining agreement.

Source: Mahler and Jesuit (2004).

inequality measured on a before-tax, before-transfer basis. In several countries, including Belgium, France, Germany, and the Netherlands, the amount of redistribution accomplished through the pension system accounts for half or more of all redistribution achieved through taxes and government transfers. Even in countries like Canada, the United Kingdom, and the United States, where public redistribution has a smaller impact on the final income distribution, one-quarter or more of the total redistributive effect of government programs is achieved through public pensions.

Pension benefits also have a sizeable impact on destitution among households containing an aged or disabled person. This is hardly surprising, because many pensioners have little or no income aside from their pensions. In a tabulation of the income sources of the aged in nine industrialized countries, Börsch-Supan and

Reil-Held (1998, table 2) found that an overwhelming fraction of the incomes received by elderly people in the bottom half of the income distribution is derived from public pensions. Among unmarried people aged 65 and older who were in the bottom one-fifth of the income distribution, the fraction of income derived from public pensions ranged from a low of 70 percent in Japan to a high of 96 percent in the Netherlands. Elderly married couples derive a larger percentage of their income from sources other than public pensions, but low-income couples rely heavily on pensions.

Pensions clearly play an important role in keeping many low-income elderly out of poverty. Smeeding and Williamson (2001, tables 1 and 5) have estimated poverty rates of the aged and non-aged in 19 industrial countries and measured the effects of public pensions in reducing old-age poverty in eight of these countries. In about half the industrialized countries poverty in old age is roughly equal to or less common than poverty at younger ages. In the other half of countries poverty is somewhat more common among the elderly than the non-elderly. When Smeeding and Williamson's income definition included only private sources of income, such as earnings, income from property and investment, and occupational pensions, an average of 72 percent of elderly households were found to be poor. When public pensions were also included in the income definition, the household poverty rate dropped to just 21 percent. The measured poverty rate dropped still further when means-tested government benefits were included in the income definition, but public pensions are clearly much more important than means-tested benefits in removing aged households from poverty.

The tabulations by Smeeding and Williamson (2001) and the results displayed in Table 37.1 show that the redistributional impact of pensions differs notably from one country to the next. The redistributive effects of the French, German, Dutch, and Swedish pension systems are larger than those of the four English-speaking countries. This is mainly the result of differences in the overall generosity of public pensions, but also reflects the extent to which the nations' pension formulas are tilted toward the poor. The point is illustrated in Figure 37.1, which shows average pension entitlements in relation to workers' past average wages in selected countries. The calculations by Whitehouse (2002) assume workers remain employed until the standard pensionable age and earn a steady wage throughout their careers. Career wages, shown on the horizontal axis, are measured relative to the average earnings of a production worker in each country. Pensions, measured on the vertical axis, are calculated in relation to the worker's average wage while employed.

The pension schedules displayed in Figure 37.1 show wide variation in benefit generosity across countries. The Dutch, French, and Swedish pension formulas are more generous than the UK, US, or Canadian formulas, and they are more generous at every earnings level. In contrast, the French and Swedish formulas are more generous than the Dutch formula for workers earning below-average and average wages, but they are less generous than the Dutch formula for workers who earn high wages. There is a similar crossover in the relative generosity of the

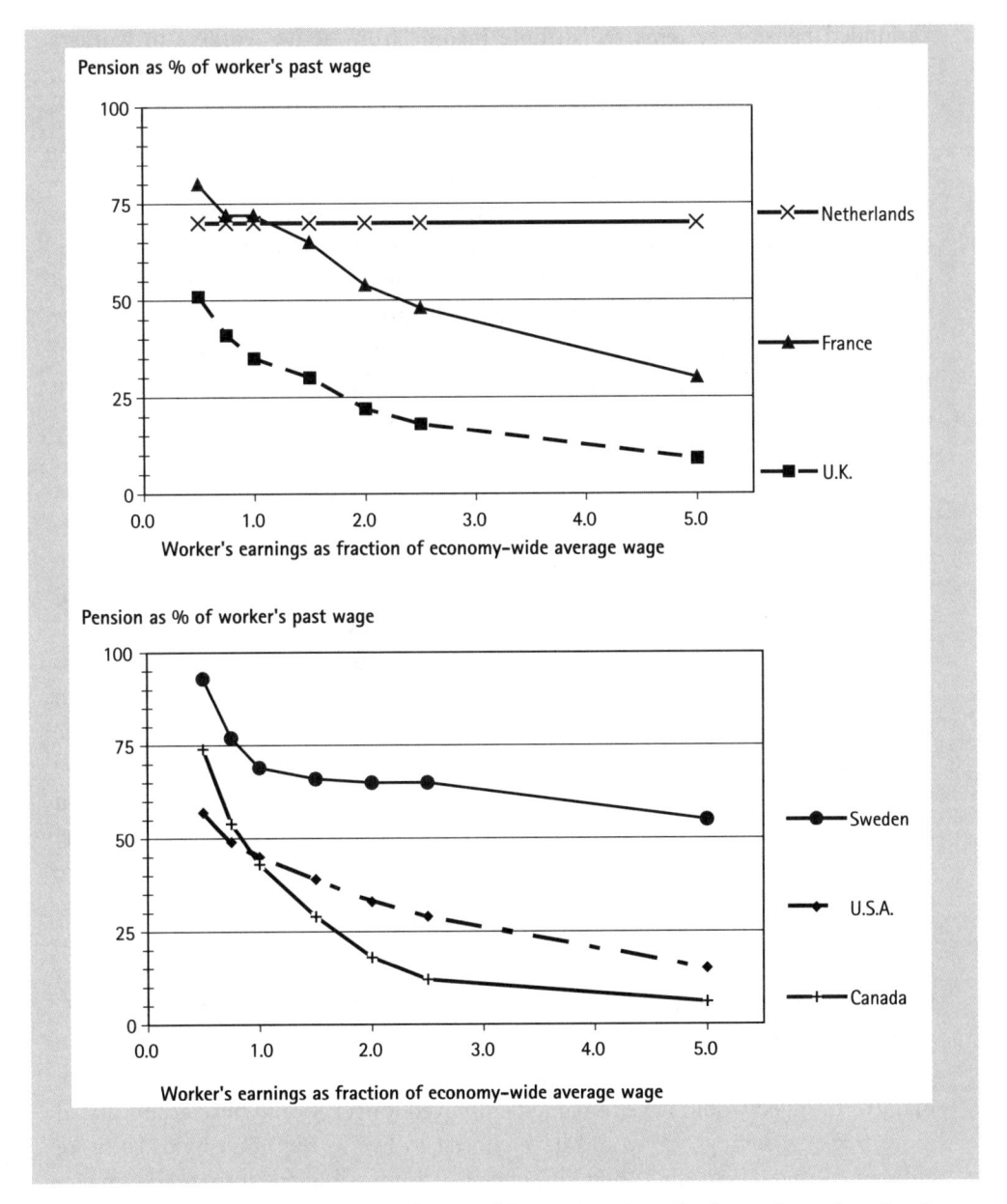

**Fig. 37.1 Relation between pension entitlement and worker's past earnings in six industrialized countries**

*Source:* Whitehouse (2002).

Canadian and US pension formulas. Indeed, Smeeding and Williamson (2001) find much lower old-age poverty rates in Canada than in the United States.

As one would expect, mandatory national systems, funded on a pay-as-you-go basis, involved markedly more redistribution than voluntary funded schemes.

Unfunded pension systems redistribute income from active workers to workers who have stopped working because of invalidity or advanced age. Redistribution through the pension system lowers inequality and old-age poverty in all countries that have broad pension coverage. The redistributive impact is larger in countries that provide more generous benefits to retirees, especially to retirees who earned low wages or suffered lengthy unemployment during their careers. The pension systems of several countries include important voluntary and employer-sponsored programs in addition to the mandatory or state-sponsored components discussed above. Voluntary systems can be sizeable in countries in which the compulsory or state-supported system does not provide generous pensions to a large fraction of the workforce. Where public pensions are low, workers and employers are often eager to establish an alternative system of forced saving so that ageing employees can comfortably retire.

When the voluntary system is capital funded, the redistributional effects of the program are likely to be much smaller than they are under an unfunded state-sponsored or compulsory system. In a compulsory system, highly paid workers can be forced to make excess contributions to the system so that generous benefit payments can be provided to workers who earn low wages or suffer frequent joblessness. In a voluntary pension program it is much harder to collect excess premium contributions from the highly paid. They can always seek jobs with employers who offer pensions calculated under a formula that is more favorable to well-compensated workers. Even a purely voluntary pension plan will have positive redistributional effects if these effects are measured using household income received in a single year. Pensioners typically have modest incomes apart from their pensions, and many of them would be judged poor if their incomes were calculated exclusive of pension income.

The redistributional estimates described so far have been measured relative to the income distribution that would prevail if pensions were subtracted from household income. An unstated assumption behind the calculations is that pensioners' incomes aside from pensions would be unchanged if pensions were eliminated. The assumption is implausible. If pensions had never been developed, many of the aged would have remained employed longer, would have accumulated more personal savings, or would have chosen to live in the households of more affluent relatives, including their children. It is impossible to estimate the precise impact of pensions on the earnings, savings, and living arrangements of the elderly, but it seems likely the effects have been important.

Before pensions became widely available, retirement was comparatively rare. In 1900, four decades before the US Social Security system was established, only about a third of American men past age 65 were retired. By the end of the twentieth century, just 18 percent of US men over 65 were employed or actively seeking a job (US Bureau of the Census 1975: 132 and 2003: 385). The decline in labor force participation among the elderly has not been confined to the United States. It is characteristic of all rich industrialized countries. Aged men in every Western European country except Portugal now have an even lower participation rate than aged men in the United States. Employment rates in old age would almost certainly increase if pensions were eliminated or reduced. One reason that ageing workers in Japan and the United States retire later than Europeans is that Japanese and US pensions are less generous and contain fewer work disincentives than pensions in much of Western Europe (Gruber and Wise 1999). Saving habits among the non-aged and living arrangements among the aged would change if pensions were drastically scaled back. Pensioners would eventually derive more income from their own savings, and some would move in with more affluent non-aged relatives if their pensions were cut. Standard estimates of the redistributional impact of pensions thus overstate their true effect relative to a world in which pensions are absent.

# 2 REDISTRIBUTION WITHIN A LIFETIME PERSPECTIVE

Another perspective on the redistributional impact of pensions is provided by considering the lifetime incomes, pension contributions, and pension benefits of participants in a program. A moment's reflection suggests that this perspective can fundamentally change our interpretation of the relative position of contributors and recipients. Most 70-year-old pensioners have less current income than the average 50-year-old worker. But all 70-year-old retirees were once 50-year-old workers themselves, and at age 50 many of them earned wages that were far above average. Assessing workers' and pensioners' incomes over a full lifetime rather than only a single year can dramatically change their rank in the income distribution. If workers who earn the highest lifetime wages also receive the largest old-age pensions, it is not obvious whether the pension system is responsible for much lifetime redistribution at all.

Many pension systems have minimum contribution requirements that must be satisfied before workers become entitled to benefits. Workers who earn low or erratic wages may not qualify for a pension, even though they are required to contribute to the system while employed. Pension systems with this type of rule reduce the lifetime net incomes of some of the most disadvantaged workers. On the other hand, many systems have features that explicitly favor workers with low average earnings. Many national pension systems offer a minimum pension, which obviously confers an advantage on eligible workers who make the smallest lifetime contributions. In addition, the basic pension may be subject to a means test, as is the case in Canada. Alternatively, the basic formula which determines monthly pensions may be explicitly redistributive, as is the case in the United States. Five of the pension schedules displayed in Figure 37.1 provide bigger benefits in comparison to past wages to workers who have below-average pay. In some cases, though, the apparently favorable tilt for poorly paid workers is partly the result of an upper limit on the pensionable wage. Workers do not receive any pension credits for their earnings above the limit. If highly paid workers do not make contributions on earnings above the wage limit, this feature of the system does not represent an advantage to the poorly paid. High-wage workers receive a pension that is a smaller percentage of their career wages, but they also pay taxes that represent a smaller fraction of career earnings. For a given worker the lifetime redistributional impact of the system depends on the difference between contributions paid and benefits received. Whether the pension schedules in Figure 37.1 offer favorable terms to workers with low lifetime pay depends on the schedule of contributions, which is not shown.

Analysts have long recognized one kind of lifetime redistribution that occurs after a paygo system is established. Early participants receive lifetime benefits that are much bigger than the discounted value of their contributions. Since contributions in a paygo program are scaled to cover current benefit costs, early entrants make modest contributions for a few years and then collect generous pensions over a lengthy retirement. Workers who enter the labor force after all aged retirees have become entitled to full benefits are less fortunate. They must pay high contributions over a full career, and thus they receive smaller net transfers than early participants in the system. This implies that the system redistributes in favor of earlier generations at the expense of later ones.

The extent of these transfers is large. Leimer (1999: 44) calculated the lifetime returns that successive cohorts of Americans have received and can expect under the Old-Age and Survivors Insurance (OASI) program, the most important single component of the US public pension system. His estimates were based on historical tax and benefit payments up through the early 1990s and projected taxes and benefits under the assumption that future contribution rates and pensions would be determined under the 1994 law. For the generation born in 1876 the estimated real rate of return was 36.5 percent. In other words, if workers' contributions and pension payments were converted into constant, inflation-adjusted dollars, $100 dollars of contributions yielded a return of $36.50 per year. Compared with other investment options, this is a spectacular rate of return. The generation born in 1876 was 60 years old when OASI taxes were first collected, so workers made very small lifetime contributions to the program. People born afterwards obtained lower returns. The generation born in 1900 received a real return of 11.9 percent, and the cohorts born in 1925 and 1950 are expected to receive returns of 4.8 per cent and

2.2 per cent, respectively. Later generations will receive even lower returns, because the changing population age structure will eventually force a tax increase or benefit cut to keep the program solvent. Leimer's calculations assume that the tax and benefit schedule embodied in the 1994 law will remain in effect over the lifetimes of current and future workers. If contribution rates are raised or benefits lowered to keep the program solvent, future returns will be worse than his calculations imply.

Many critics of paygo pensions point out that cross-generational redistribution in these systems can lead to perverse transfers. Highly paid workers in an early generation of contributors can receive lifetime transfers at the expense of poorly paid workers in later, less favored generations. What is certain is that the average size of net transfers to successive generations must decline over time. This does not mean that workers with low lifetime wages in later generations must receive poor returns on their contributions. The pension or contribution formula could be tilted in favor of low-wage workers in every generation so they receive good returns on their contributions. It is unlikely, however, that low-wage workers as a class will ever receive the spectacular returns enjoyed by early contributors to a paygo plan, including the high-wage contributors. Making transfers from later to earlier generations, however, has a distributional advantage often overlooked by critics of paygo systems. In all of the rich countries, more recent generations have been wealthier than generations that received large transfers when public pension plans were first established. On balance the cross-generational transfers favored poorer generations at the expense of wealthier ones. Moving to a capital-funded system and phasing out the paygo program would eventually eliminate this kind of cross-generational redistribution and with it a type of redistribution that has historically favored the less well-off.

Lifetime transfers that take place within a single generation are not easy to measure. The information needed to determine a worker's lifetime contributions and lifetime benefits is not available in a single household survey, and it can be difficult to obtain from the records of a pension administrator. Almost all estimates of within-generation redistribution are therefore based on stylized representations of worker contributions and benefits (Leimer 1999; Feldstein and Liebman 2002). Even if the stylized estimates are based on the actual pension files of representative workers, the files rarely contain a complete record of all lifetime benefits. Retirees who are still alive when the records are extracted will collect benefits for an unknown number of future years and may bequeath survivor benefits to one or more dependents. Active workers will retire or become disabled in a future year that analysts do not know, and their future earnings and benefits are uncertain. Pension records can provide reliable data on the earnings rank of each worker, but they usually lack information about the combined earnings of the worker and his or her spouse. Even if the data permit us to calculate net transfers received by each earnings class of worker, it may be impossible to measure the size of transfers within family income classes. If large net transfers are received by secondary earners in dual-earner households, it is technically correct to say the pension system is redistributional in favor of low lifetime earners. It may also be the case that the redistribution favors high-income households containing low-wage secondary earners.

To determine lifetime transfers analysts must predict how long pensioners will collect benefits. Some studies have proceeded under the assumption that all workers have identical life expectancy, at least within the same race and gender (Hurd and Shoven 1985). This is unlikely to be true, since people who have high income tend to live longer than those with lower incomes. Figure 37.2 shows the relationship between life expectancy and family income for a sample of Americans whose annual incomes were ascertained at the end of the 1970s (Rogot et al. 1992). The researchers classified families' incomes within broad income categories and then determined how many respondents in each category died during the next six years. The mortality rates at successive years of age can be converted into estimates of life expectancy at some standard age, say 25. The estimates displayed in the figure imply that low-income men who survive to age 25 die 10.0 years younger than high-income men, while low-income women die 4.3 years younger than high-income women. The estimates also suggest that low-income workers are less likely than high-income workers to live long enough to qualify for an old-age pension.

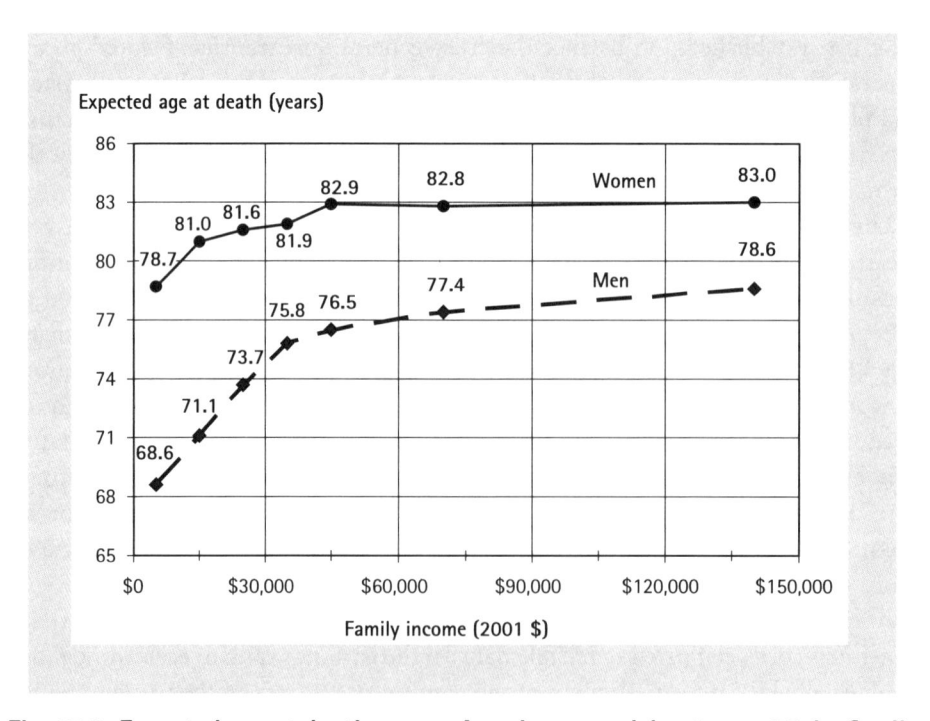

**Fig. 37.2 Expected age at death among Americans surviving to age 25, by family income**

Source: Rogot et al. (1992) calculations based on 1979–85 mortality experiences of white Americans.

When they qualify, they are likely to receive an old-age pension for a smaller number of years.

The positive correlation of income and life expectancy obviously reduces the relative return that low-income workers receive on their old-age pension contributions. Whether the reduction is large enough to offset other redistributional features of the pension formula is an open question. In the United States the balance of empirical evidence suggests that low-wage workers obtain better real returns on their contributions than high-wage workers (Leimer 1999: 45), but this result may not hold in other countries where the pension formula is less tilted in favor of contributors with low wages.

The US results sometimes show that the absolute lifetime transfers to high-wage workers have historically been larger than the transfers received by low-wage or low-wealth workers (Leimer 1999; Hurd and Shoven 1985). Some people will regard this as a perverse kind of redistribution, but it nonetheless represents redistribution in the intended direction. Even though high-wage contributors receive larger lifetime transfers than low-wage workers, the net transfers received by low-wage workers represent a bigger fraction of their lifetime incomes.

Most of the US analysis also shows that the large lifetime transfers to high-wage workers will shrink or disappear. Whether future low-wage workers will continue to receive net transfers depends on the discount factor used to estimate the present value of workers' lifetime tax and benefit payments. Gokhale and Kotlikoff (2002) discounted contributions and benefits using a 5 percent real interest rate. Workers receiving a rate of return on their contributions below 5 percent are classified as 'net taxpayers', workers earning more than 5 percent are 'net transfer recipients'. Under this definition, Gokhale and Kotlikoff predict that all low-income men born after 1945 will be net taxpayers. The US retirement program is nonetheless redistributional in the sense that low-income men in every generation pay lower net tax rates than high-income men in the same generation. If a lower discount rate were applied, low-income contributors to OASI would be reclassified as net transfer recipients rather than net taxpayers.

One reason that old-age pensions appear disadvantageous to short-lived contributors is that most public pensions are provided in the form of life annuities. If part or all of a deceased contributor's taxes were distributed to an heir, the returns on the contributions of short-lived workers would be more favorable. This fact has sometimes been used as an argument in favor of capital-funded pension systems, which are alleged to provide more equitable returns to short-lived (and low-income) contributors. Most defined-contribution, capital-funded pension programs do provide lump-sum distributions to survivors after a contributor dies. On the other hand, many defined-benefit, capital-funded pension plans do not refund the contributions of early decedents. The crucial distinction is not between paygo funding and capital funding, but between payout of benefits in the form of annuities or as some other kind of payment. The main goal of life annuities is to provide workers with longevity insurance—protection against the risk of depleting their assets in extreme old age. Retirement systems that provide lump-sum distributions to the heirs of all early decedents are considerably more expensive than systems which only provide life annuities to workers and their aged spouses. Workers would have to make larger contributions to receive the same level of income protection in old age, though workers who do not expect to live long would certainly derive greater benefits under the more expensive system.

Rather than eliminate forced annuitization because it disadvantages the short-lived, another option is to bundle old-age insurance with types of insurance that are particularly valuable to workers with short life expectancy. This is the approach taken in most rich countries' pension plans. Old-age insurance is combined and closely coordinated with insurance that protects workers against early death and disability. Even though short-lived workers may obtain poor returns on their contributions for old-age insurance, they and their dependents obtain good returns on the entire package of insurance. Most analyses of lifetime redistribution under the US Social Security system focus solely on old-age pensions. They ignore the Disability Insurance (DI) program and OASI benefits paid to surviving dependents who are younger than retirement age. When these benefits are included in the analysis, low-income (and shorter-lived) workers appear to fare much better (Leimer 1999: 45–6).

Many conclusions about the lifetime redistributional impact of national pension systems are based on analyses of the US system. One reason is that US statistical agencies and the Social Security Administration have created and released files that combine detailed demographic information and lifetime records of pension contributions and benefits. Lifetime earnings, tax, and benefits records have been less accessible to researchers in other countries.

Some of the US findings about lifetime redistribution are likely to apply in other countries. Redistribution within a generation is much smaller when measured using lifetime taxes and benefits than it is when measured using tax and pension payments recorded in a single year. The magnitude of net transfers received by early participants in a paygo system is so large that all income classes, including early contributors with high lifetime wages, receive substantial net transfers. The net transfers received by later generations have declined and are virtually certain to shrink further as the ratio of pensioners to contributors rises. Several features of a pension system produce better returns on contributions for low lifetime earners compared with high lifetime earners. Many public programs have pension formulas that explicitly favor low-wage contributors. Public pension systems also offer insurance against early death and invalidity, which is particularly valuable to low earners who tend to have below-average life expectancy and above-average disability rates. On the other hand, a redistributional tilt in the pension formula is needed to compensate low earners for the fact that they will receive old-age pensions over a smaller number of years. Most conclusions about cross-country differences in lifetime redistribution under national pension systems rest on informed speculation. Analysts have not yet created the longitudinal data sets needed to compare lifetime redistribution in two or more countries.

## 3 THE FUTURE OF REDISTRIBUTION

The populations of all the industrialized countries are growing older. Over the next few decades the combined effects of declining fertility and rising longevity will substantially increase the proportion of aged and near-aged people in the population. Generous pension commitments and a growing ratio of retired to active workers have pushed many paygo pension programs toward insolvency. Governments can restore solvency by boosting contribution rates, cutting monthly pensions, or delaying the age at which workers can claim benefits. Many industrialized countries have taken one or more of these steps already, but most public pension systems continue to face a long-term funding shortfall. As a result, several countries are considering more fundamental reforms.

Policy-makers in a few countries have suggested replacing part or all of their public systems with private pensions organized around individual investment accounts. Champions of this kind of reform point to the experience of Chile, where a costly and failing paygo system was replaced by a less expensive private system in the early 1980s. Over the past two decades Chile's reformed pension system has received high marks for sound administration, good returns, and broad political acceptance. The expected surge in public retirement costs in the industrialized countries has made some voters and policy-makers receptive to the idea of adopting a Chilean-style system as a full or partial replacement for a scaled-back paygo system.

A handful of countries, including Sweden, Germany, and Japan, have taken modest steps in this direction. In 2001 the German government enacted a reform that created defined-contribution pensions for millions of active workers. German workers were initially permitted to contribute a maximum of 1 percent of their gross earnings to voluntary pension plans, but the limit will gradually increase to 4 percent of gross earnings. Workers' voluntary contributions will be subsidized with government payments. The subsidies can be quite generous for low-wage workers and workers who have child dependents. At the same time, public pensions under Germany's existing retirement system will be scaled back for younger and middle-aged workers. One goal of the 2001 reform was to limit the future contribution rate for the public retirement system—now about 19 percent of gross pay—and replace the lost retirement benefits with pensions financed out of individual investment accounts.

How does scaling back traditional pensions in favor of funded individual accounts affect the redistribution accomplished under national pension systems? Compared with the redistribution achieved over the past few decades, the redistribution under a partially capital-funded system will almost certainly shrink. The amount of redistribution achieved in the past is an unrealistic benchmark for comparison, however. As noted above, paygo pensions provided massive redistribution in favor of generations in the labor force when they were established. Low-, average-, and high-income workers all received generous lifetime transfers financed by generations that entered the workforce after the pension system was fully mature. The net transfers that future generations will receive must decline and may eventually turn negative. Thus, lifetime transfers under the pension system will decline even if the paygo structure of the system is maintained.

A more meaningful question is whether redistribution under individual investment accounts would be greater or less than redistribution under a reformed paygo system that has been modified to restore long-term solvency. Many current proposals for fundamental reform envision creation of voluntary or compulsory individual retirement accounts. As in the Chilean system, workers would build up retirement savings in individually owned and directed private accounts. Workers could withdraw their funds from the accounts when they became disabled or reached the retirement age, and their heirs could inherit any funds accumulated in the account if the worker died before becoming disabled or reaching retirement age. At the time a worker chose to start receiving a pension, some or all of the funds in the worker's account would be converted into an annuity that would last until the worker died.

Under the revamped system, each worker's retirement benefit would depend solely on the size of the worker's contributions and the success of the worker's investment plan. Workers who make larger contributions would receive bigger pensions, and workers whose investments earned better returns would collect larger pensions than workers who obtained poor returns. Because the connection between individual contributions, investment returns, and pension benefits is very straightforward, an individual-account retirement system offers less scope for redistribution in favor of low-wage workers. Redistribution in favor of low-wage workers must take place outside these accounts. To ensure continued redistribution, an individual account system might top up the contributions of low-wage workers or supplement the pensions from individual retirement accounts with a minimum, tax-financed pension or with public assistance payments.

Many plans for fundamental reform do not envisage the complete elimination of the current paygo system. They propose instead that benefits under the old program be scaled back so that contribution rates can be held down, allowing room for voluntary or mandatory contributions to individual retirement accounts.

If the existing paygo system is preserved, even at a reduced scale, redistribution on behalf of low-wage workers would continue, though perhaps on a smaller scale. It seems likely, however, that the annuities paid out of the individual retirement accounts would be much more unequal than pensions paid by current public pension systems. If workers can voluntarily elect to contribute to retirement accounts, some workers will make the maximum allowed contribution while others will contribute nothing. If workers exercise choice over the investment of their contributions, some will choose assets that yield above-average returns while others will earn poor returns. Assuming the decision to contribute to a pension account and the success of workers' investment plans are positively correlated with workers' wages, the payouts from individual retirement accounts will be even more unequal than the distribution of lifetime earnings. Thus, individual-account annuities can easily magnify rather than reduce lifetime inequality. The redistribution that takes place within the remaining paygo system will have to be very large indeed to offset this effect.

It is not inevitable that individual investment accounts would reduce the redistributional impact of the pension system. Contributions to the accounts could be compulsory rather than voluntary. Workers' investment options might be narrowly circumscribed, reducing differences in investment returns. The retirement accounts held by low-wage or unemployed workers could receive public subsidies on top of the workers' own contributions, as in the new German system. These kinds of measures tilt the redistributional effect of an individual-account system in favor of workers with low lifetime incomes.

Analysts have examined the lifetime distributional effects of specific individual-account reform plans for the United States (Feldstein and Liebman 2002; Bosworth and Burtless 2002). Depending on the elements in the reform plan, individual retirement account reforms may produce either more or less redistribution than the existing system. Bosworth and Burtless (2002) analyzed proposals offered by a US presidential commission that advocated voluntary investment accounts. The new accounts would be financed with contributions that otherwise would go to the Social Security program. The diversion of funds from the traditional system would require a large future cut in traditional benefits. Perhaps surprisingly, Bosworth and Burtless found that the commission's main proposal could slightly favor low-wage workers relative to average- and high-wage workers, at least with respect to old-age insurance benefits. The commission proposed to increase traditional benefits for workers with low but steady lifetime wages, and these workers would thus be spared some benefit cuts that would be imposed if all old-age benefits were cut by the same percentage amount. In addition, the commission's plan limited workers' contributions to individual retirement accounts in a way that would be less favorable for high-wage workers than for low- and average-wage workers. While reducing pensions under the traditional paygo program might seem to be a disadvantage to low-income workers, because the benefit formula in the program is tilted in their favor, the commission's plan contained enough elements that favored low-income workers so that reform had very little effect on redistribution within a single generation.

The impact of individual-account plans on redistribution across generations is uncertain. Many advocates of individual investment accounts believe the elimination of paygo pensions would improve the equity of intergenerational transfers under the pension system. In principle, a capital-funded pension system creates little or no redistribution between generations. Each generation consumes what it produces through its labor income and the stream of capital income earned on its savings. Its retirement consumption is largely financed out of capital-funded pensions, which in turn are derived from labor income saved during a working career plus the investment earnings on that saving. In contrast, a paygo system creates substantial redistribution across generations. Though it is straightforward to compare the long-run path of intergenerational redistribution under the two kinds of retirement system, it is not obvious how redistribution would evolve along the transition path from an unfunded to a capital-funded system. No generation that has already retired with unfunded pension benefits would willingly give up its pension entitlements so that the pensions of younger generations can be funded. It is also implausible to expect older workers to surrender all their accumulated unfunded pension credits so that younger workers can fund their pensions. Some people who favor funded pensions think the transition to a funded system can be achieved by issuing public debt to pay for the pensions of the already retired and soon-to-be-retired, allowing young workers to divert their payroll contributions from the unfunded system to funded pension accounts.

Such an approach still leaves open the question of who will bear the burden of the extra debt. Bosworth and Burtless (2002) concluded that the biggest redistributional impact of adopting the presidential commission's reform plan would be on redistribution across generations. Allowing taxpayers to divert their Social Security contributions to individual retirement accounts deprives the paygo system of revenues, forcing deep cuts in traditional benefits. Workers who retire over the next 10 to 35 years would not have an opportunity to contribute to the new system over a full career, so the annuities that could be purchased with their individual account savings would be too small to offset the benefit cuts that would be triggered if the traditional paygo system were required to balance its annual operating budget. Generations retiring over the next 10 to 35 years would receive smaller retirement benefits and lifetime incomes, although the losses would be reversed by income gains enjoyed by the generations retiring afterwards. A balanced-budget transition path to funded pensions could certainly disadvantage the generations retiring during the next three or four decades. A different budget rule could delay the adverse impact on later generations, but it should be clear that a shift to capital-funded pensions will have sizeable effects on cross-generation transfers. Such redistribution does not necessarily disadvantage the low-lifetime-income workers in any particular generation, but it may reduce voters' willingness to pay for generous transfers to low-income workers when workers who have average- and above-average lifetime incomes are feeling squeezed.

A number of countries adopted pension systems that are substantially capital funded years ago. It would be interesting to learn whether the countries relying more heavily on capital funded programs provide more or less redistribution than countries that rely almost exclusively on paygo financing. Unfortunately, the lifetime redistributional consequences of most pension systems are not known. We are only able to compare the redistributional impact of most national systems using a short period of income assessment (see Table 37.1). The OECD made estimates of the capital funding in national pension systems in 1996 (Disney 1999: 19). Canada, the United Kingdom, and the United States are among the countries with the most capital funding in their compulsory and voluntary pension systems. These countries also provide less redistribution through their pension systems than other countries included in Table 37.1. On the other hand, the OECD statistics show that the Netherlands has the most capital funding of any national pension system, while three Scandinavian countries have at least moderate levels of capital funding. Those four countries achieve above-average amounts of redistribution through their pension systems. On balance, countries with more capital funding are no less likely to provide generous redistribution through their pension systems, at least when redistribution is measured with short-term indicators of income rank.

With few exceptions, rich nations must reform their public pension systems in order to make them more affordable. The reforms will change the distributional impact of these systems. It is far more certain, however, that the change will affect redistribution between generations rather than between rich and poor in the same generation. The introduction and liberalization of compulsory pension systems led to an enormous improvement in the relative income positions of the aged and disabled. It is unlikely that cost-saving pension reform will lead to a major unwinding of this kind of redistribution.

# References

Börsch-Supan, A., and Reil-Held, A. (1998). 'Retirement income: level, risk, and substitution among income components'. OECD Ageing Working Paper 3.7. Paris: OECD.

Bosworth, B. P., and Burtless, G. (1998). 'Population aging and economic performance', in Barry P. Bosworth and Gary Burtless (eds.), *Aging Societies: The Global Dimension*. Washington, D.C.: The Brookings Institution.

—— —— (2002). 'Economic and distributional effects of the proposals of President Bush's Social Security Commission'. Paper for the Annual Conference of the Retirement Research Consortium. Ann Arbor: Michigan Retirement Research Center.

DISNEY, R. (1999). 'OECD public pension programmes in crisis: an evaluation of the reform options'. Social Protection Discussion Paper No. 9921. Washington, D.C.: The World Bank.

FELDSTEIN, M., and LIEBMAN, J. B. (eds.) (2002). *The Distributional Aspects of Social Security and Social Security Reform*. Chicago: University of Chicago Press.

GOKHALE, J., and KOTLIKOFF, L. J. (2002). 'Social Security's treatment of postwar Americans: how bad can it get?', in Feldstein and Liebman (2002).

GRUBER, J., and WISE, David A. (1999). 'Introduction', in J. Gruber and David A. Wise (eds.), *Social Security and Retirement around the World*. Chicago: University of Chicago Press.

HURD, M. D., and SHOVEN, J. B. (1985). 'The distributional impact of social security', in DAVID A. WISE (ed.), *Pensions, Labor, and Individual Choice*. Chicago: University of Chicago Press, 193–221.

LEIMER, D. R. (1999). 'Lifetime redistribution under the social security program: a literature synopsis'. *Social Security Bulletin*, 62/2: 43–51.

LIEBMAN, J. B. (2002). 'Redistribution in the current U.S. social security system', in M. Feldstein and J. B. Liebman (eds.), *The Distributional Aspects of Social Security and Social Security Reform*. Chicago: University of Chicago Press.

MAHLER, V., and JESUIT, D. (2004). 'State redistribution in comparative perspective: a cross-national analysis of the developed countries'. LIS Working Paper No. 392. Luxembourg: Luxembourg Income Study.

ROGOT, E., SORLIE, P. D., and JOHNSON, N. J. (1992). 'Life expectancy by employment status, income, and education in the National Longitudinal Mortality Study'. *Public Health Reports*, 107/4 (July–Aug.): 457–61.

SMEEDING, T. M., and WILLIAMSON, J. (2001). 'Income maintenance in old age: what can be learned from cross-national comparisons'. LIS Working Paper No. 263. Luxembourg: Luxembourg Income Study.

US BUREAU OF THE CENSUS (1975). *Historical Statistics of the United States: Colonial Times to 1970*. Washington: US Government Printing Office.

—— (2003). *Statistical Abstract of the United States: 2003*. Washington, D.C.: US Government Printing Office.

WHITEHOUSE, E. (2002). 'Pension systems in 15 countries compared: the value of entitlements'. Centre for Pensions and Superannuation Discussion paper No. 02/04. Sydney: University of New South Wales.

WORLD BANK (1994). *Averting the Old Age Crisis Policies to Protect the Old and Promote Growth*. Oxford and New York: Oxford University Press.

CHAPTER 38

# THE POLITICS OF PENSION REFORM: MANAGING INTEREST GROUP CONFLICTS

BERNHARD EBBINGHAUS

## 1 INTRODUCTION

Mobilized interest groupings shape pension politics as these provoke and reinforce conflicts of interest. Latent and manifest interests play a role in both the old politics, surrounding the development of retirement income systems, and the new politics concerning reforms under current austerity constraints. From the beginning, pension policies were to respond to the growing dependent labor force and to occupational and social status group differentiations. Theories of welfare state development have assumed that social groups' interests affect retirement income security systems both directly and indirectly. Institutionalized pension systems create their own constituencies. While some interests were mobilized to influence pension politics, both in its historical development and in current restructuring processes, other interests remain largely latent and less politically salient. This chapter delineates some major cleavages posed by these latent and manifest interests in modern (post-)industrial societies. It also compares different modes of overcoming interest conflicts through political and social consensus-building.

In the following section, the chapter reviews the main theoretical perspectives on the development of welfare states that more or less explicitly conceptualize the interests of particular social groups in retirement income systems. In Section 3, the main capital–labor cleavage between the interests of employers and labor movements in such systems is juxtaposed. Then, several intra-class cleavages are presented. These conflicts influence and are reinforced by fragmented pension systems, in particular the difference between blue-collar and white-collar workers as well as between private and public sectors. Weaker labor market groups, in particular the unemployed, and gender issues in retirement income systems are discussed. The section also critically reviews often voiced generational conflicts.

The fourth section moves to the different modes of building political and social consensus. Given the potential impact of interest groups using the electoral route and veto points in political systems, governments may seek to build inter-party or societal alliances to overcome potential reform blockage in political decision-making and implementation. Besides political interest politics, various modes of social governance are discussed: institutional consultation of the social groups, tripartite concertation between governments and the social partners, institutionalized forms of self-administration of pension insurance, and self-regulation via collectively negotiated occupational pensions. The main argument pursued is that governance modes which help build societal consensus for pension reform are that much more important when powerful interest groups have veto power and retirement income systems are based on shared policy-making between government and social partners.

## 2 THEORETICAL PERSPECTIVES

Conflicts of interest arise between various social groups, though the main cleavage in welfare states since industrialization has been between capital and labor. Besides the class conflict, other intra-class cleavages and inter-class alliances have been important in shaping pension policies. These have been analyzed from numerous theoretical angles: modernization theory (both industrialization and democratization theses), state-centered institutionalism, and political mobilization. According to *modernization* theory, industrialization led to massive migration from rural to industrial areas, widespread dependency through wage labor, and decline in traditional support structures, particularly the family. With increasing life expectancy, occupational hazards, and unemployment risks, long-term income loss due to 'old age' and 'invalidity' led to poverty among the growing working class, increasing the pressure on the national state, benevolent employers and workers' associations to provide some form of income support for older and disabled workers (Rimlinger 1971).

*State-centered institutionalist* accounts (Heclo 1974) stress that bureaucratic elites implemented social policies as political strategies, linking welfare state building to nation-state formation. The first social pension insurance was introduced in Bismarck's Germany as a response to the 'workers' question'. It sought to integrate the working class into the new nation-state, while suppressing the growing labor movement with anti-socialist laws. Not only did other Continental European countries introduce similar 'Bismarckian' social insurance schemes, but also the United States enacted Social Security legislation in response to rampant unemployment during the Great Depression.

T. H. Marshall's seminal lectures on 'citizenship and social class' (1950) advance a liberal *democratization* thesis, congruent with gradual development of civil, political, and social citizenship rights in Britain. With increased political participation, democratizing nation-states extended social rights to secure all citizens a basic income in old age. Departing from the German model, Denmark introduced a tax-financed people's pension as early as 1891 and Britain did so in 1908, reflecting broad political alliances beyond organized labor. After the Second World War, the Beveridge reforms in Britain became the model of social citizenship rights for many other welfare states, including the Scandinavian countries and the Netherlands. Yet most reform efforts to introduce universality failed in Continental Bismarckian systems, including Germany, France, and Italy, due to Christian-social and conservative conceptions of subsidiarity.

*Political mobilization* approaches look at the influence of interest groups—notably organized labor, the middle class, and employers—in advancing or hindering pension policy development. The social democracy thesis stresses the importance of organized labor for both social-democratic parties' electoral success and the power of centralized trade union movements, particularly in Scandinavia (for a review see Esping-Andersen and Kersbergen 1992). Comparative studies have investigated the postwar welfare reforms resulting from the strengths or weaknesses of organized labour (Korpi 2001). Similarly, Esping-Andersen (1990) traced the importance of three political ideologies of welfare states—liberal, social democratic, and conservative—to three distinct political movements while acknowledging the legacy of state traditions.

Historical studies stressing the result of cross-class alliances between blue-collar workers, the white-collar urban middle class, and rural small-scale farmers' interests (Baldwin 1990) amended the social democracy thesis. Such alliances led to a significant difference of Beveridge-type pension systems: income-related superannuation schemes were introduced on top of basic pensions, serving middle-class status-maintenance interests. While some countries (e.g. Denmark) failed to introduce an earnings-related second tier in the postwar period, others (e.g. Sweden) moved from a basic pension to a two-tier system (basic plus earnings-related pension) and more recently to a fully integrated earnings-related pension system. Laggards in developing public second-tier pensions left more room for private occupational pensions. Myles and Pierson (2001) also link divergent pension reform trajectories to second-tier systems' early or late institutionalization.

More recently, comparative historical studies have investigated the role of employers, finding that employers are not always against social policies (Mares 2003; Swenson 2002). Against the social democracy thesis of 'politics against markets' and organized labor's fight for redistributive social policies, social protection can also serve productive functions: when early retirement policies help firms restructure their personnel in socially acceptable ways, it may in fact be 'politics for markets'.

# 3 LATENT AND MANIFEST INTERESTS

Institutional legacies and past political compromises reflecting particular interests still affect how current pension systems impact on various social groups, even as demographic, social, and economic changes compel pension reform efforts and inevitably lead to conflicts. Four main issues are contentious: who is covered, who pays, who benefits, and who controls these programs? These issues form the core of major differences among latent interests in society, among mobilized manifest interests via collective organizations, in particular trade unions and social advocacy groups. This section provides an analytical overview of key latent interest groupings affected by changes and the role of manifest interest organizations in shaping past, current, and future pension reforms.

## 3.1 Employers' Interests

In most of the modernization and mobilization theory studies, employers were seen as collectively incapable or politically opposed to providing for social protection in old age. Certainly, paternalist employers provided some company-based social policies, yet these voluntary schemes were too small, scattered and selective to provide a society-wide answer to the consequences of industrialization. Moreover, employers were known to have opposed liability laws and mandatory social insurance. Before the First World War, employer organizations were in fact often found to lobby against progressive social legislation. Recent studies have revisited employers' role in social policy development and their interests in today's welfare state arrangements.

Employer liability for occupational accidents was among the first steps toward social protection, followed by mandatory accident insurance for industrial firms. Employer responsibility is less direct in cases of disability unrelated to industrial accidents or due to long-term occupational risks, personal health, social circumstances, and age. Some early paternalist industrialists voluntarily provided occupational pensions to bind and discipline (semi-)skilled workers and white-collar employees (Shalev 1996). Such employers were therefore against mandatory public pension schemes, while other larger firms and smaller employers without such fringe benefits feared resultant labor cost increases.

Indeed, employers co-finance social contributions (payroll taxes) for public old-age and disability pensions, though there are considerable cross-national variations, from substantial employer contributions (Italy, Sweden, France) to near parity (Germany, United Kingdom, United States) to low mandatory contributions due to tax-financed basic pensions (e.g. Denmark). A parity or larger share paid by employers remains a largely symbolic acknowledgment of partial responsibility since employees bear the final costs. Increasingly, costs are shifted from employers to the insured to increase the visibility of pension costs and the link between individual contributions and benefits.

Employers and their associations have been and are among the most forceful opponents to the introduction and later expansion of public pension schemes, particularly to its mandatory co-financing. Under particular circumstances, some employer organizations were willing to support mandatory pension schemes as the 'second-best' solution, while politicians took employers' interests into account when shaping social policies (Mares 2003; Swenson 2002). Mandatory old-age insurance can take wages out of competition by forcing all employers to contribute, creating a level playing field at least within a nation's industrial sector. Moreover, when social risks are spread unevenly across and between sectors, a wider sectoral or nationwide pooling of resources would spread risks more evenly, often to the advantage of the more powerful larger firms and to the detriment of smaller firms (Mares 2003). The more pension schemes were subsidized by the state or costs could be externalized to third parties, the more firms with voluntary pensions on a defined benefit basis would be relieved (Swenson 2002). A further rationale for employers are opportunities to use public or collective schemes to shed older workers in a socially acceptable way at mandatory retirement age or with the help of early retirement options prior to normal pension age (Ebbinghaus forthcoming). In contrast to a social right to individually choose (early) retirement, employers would prefer to steer exit from work by exercising control over early retirement provisions (Mares 2003). Depending on historical circumstances, intra-class divisions, and strategic moves by employers and unions, public policies may have resulted that do not reflect the employers' first but only second-best preference; nevertheless they affected the outcome.

## 3.2 Organized Labor

The labor movement, the trade unions, and allied political parties had a major influence on social policy indirectly as a threat to the political elite or directly through mobilized collective action and electoral strength. According to the mobilization thesis, organized labor was crucial in expanding solidaristic welfare states (Esping-Andersen 1990; Korpi 2001). There is a correlation between the strength of unions, measured by union density, as well as the electoral power of the left and the welfare states' postwar expansion (Huber and Stephens 2001).

Historically, labor's impact was less direct. The workers' question ('*Arbeiterfrage*')—the threat of political unrest due to social problems—challenged political elites. While trade unions first opposed state-imposed pension insurance and were reluctant to give up their meager efforts at self-help, they soon came to embrace the advantages of mandatory old-age insurance and the potential influence via self-administration. In Bismarckian systems, co-financing of social contributions brought self-administration rights for employers and employee representatives; they helped to provide resources and legitimacy to trade union officials. While the division of contributions between employers and the insured remained variable across countries, societal compromises between capital and labor tended to be maintained or rebalanced as part of social partnership conceptions (Berger and Compston 2002).

Contributions toward pensions, paid by workers and/or employers, were deferred social wages. Economically, the question of distribution of social contributions between employer and workers is secondary, but this is not the case politically or psychologically. Overall, social contributions reduce post-payroll-tax wages for workers and increase non-wage labor costs for employers, whatever the division between the two sides of industry. An increase in social contributions in total will have two negative effects for labor: (*a*) it reduces the bargaining scope and the net wages of workers, and (*b*) it raises overall labor costs to the detriment of employment and competitiveness. Thus, wage negotiations and social policy reforms have to be seen as interdependent, making concertation across both policy fields a necessary strategy in cases where policy responsibility is shared by multiple actors (Ebbinghaus and Hassel 2000). Yet in the past, unions and employers negotiated neo-corporatist income policies by increasing the deferred wage, for example by extending early retirement schemes. Welfare states' expansion during the high days of corporatist income policies suggests an implicit and sometimes explicit political exchange between wage moderation and pension right expansion.

## 3.3 White-Collar versus Blue-Collar Workers

While basic public pensions were inclusive for all citizens but allowed inequality in private pensions, Bismarckian employment-related pensions were often occupationally fragmented. Initially limited to workers with low income, the German pension insurance was joined by a separate scheme for white-collar employees. White-collar associations lobbied in both countries for separate pensions aiming at status maintenance; these reinforced social divisions between the new middle and working classes. In many countries, white-collar interests played a large role in employer-provided or negotiated supplementary occupational pensions (superannuation schemes). Thus, collective agreements on second-tier pensions were made compulsory in all of France and for many sectors in the Netherlands.

Thus far, voluntary occupational pensions, in contrast to mandatory schemes, 'are limited to a sub-group of the population and inequality and discrimination were more or less taken as a given' (Stevens *et al.* 2002: 37). In Germany, but also the Netherlands, employers are free to select categories of workers to whom occupational pensions may be offered, though regulations apply that, within the category, all employees must be granted equal rights. Employers thus may easily use pensions as part of their human resource management strategy as they divide the workforce into categorical groups with and without long-term pension plans. Trade unions and works councils have limited scope to challenge this segmentation in employers' social policies. Even today, the interests of blue-collar workers and white-collar employees may be at odds in pension policy.

## 3.4 Public versus Private Sector

Further intra-class cleavages emerged due to differences between the private and public sectors. Many nation-states installed particular pension schemes for long-term tenured civil servants and other public employees. These schemes were often introduced before the public pension schemes for blue-collar workers. With the postwar expansion of public services, particularly in growing welfare states, public employment in health services and education expanded rapidly until the late 1970s. The expansion of the public sector not only helped to buffer the loss of manufacturing jobs, but also provided well-paid and protected (part-time) employment opportunities for women during and after child-caring years. Since the 1980s, public employment has stagnated and privatization efforts have cut back on public employment, particularly in Britain, but also in Sweden.

With a few exceptions, public sector employees are better organized than private service sector workers (Ebbinghaus and Visser 2000). Union recognition by a benevolent employer, meritocratic recruitment, seniority-based grades, and bureaucratic advancement are all factors conducive to high unionization rates. In some cases, particular categories of civil servants are forbidden to strike or collectively bargain; though for most public sector employees these restrictions do not apply. In return for lifelong loyalty to the state, civil servants in Continental Europe receive retirement pay, often financed by taxes or out of pay-as-you-go pension funds. In Esping-Andersen's (1990) welfare regime comparison, the number of special pensions for public employees and their share in overall pension expenditure serve as major indicators of occupationalist fragmentation (*Corporatism*) and statist legacy (*Etatism*).

These special public sector pensions, which often provided favorable early retirement conditions and high replacement rates, have been difficult to reform, due to public sector trade unions' organizational capacity. The French strike wave in 1995 occurred largely in the public sector in protest over cuts on pension benefits that had already been imposed on private sector workers. In Italy, government and trade unions successfully negotiated to harmonize pensions for public sector employees with the less favorable private sector. However, a long-term trend toward privatization of public services, the fiscal limits on welfare states, and a politically induced harmonization of pension rules will make it difficult to maintain these past privileges.

## 3.5 Weaker Labor Market Groups

Unemployment may negatively affect future pension benefits; unemployment pay may also serve as a quasi early retirement provision. With few exceptions, the unemployed are only sparsely organized by trade unions, while self-help groups emerging in recent years lack the coordination and resources to be politically influential. Only where trade unions remain in charge of administering unemployment insurance (the Ghent system in Nordic countries and Belgium), do workers have more than selective incentives to become members and continue in membership even when unemployed. Long-term unemployment can negatively impact on future pension claims, particularly in systems where public or private pensions are based on contribution years and that grant no pension credits for years of unemployment.

Older workers' unemployment has been widespread in some countries due to age-related low re-employment chances. While special pre-retirement schemes in the 1980s were designed to allow older workers' early retirement in exchange for unemployed workers' employment, today such schemes are seen as counterproductive and costly (Ebbinghaus forthcoming). Long-term unemployment is often the first step on the pathway to early retirement. In Germany, Denmark, the Netherlands, and Sweden, favorable rules for older workers allowed the dismissal of workers into long-term unemployment, bridging several years before an early pension could be drawn (Kohli *et al.* 1991). As part of the major shift from passive to active labor market policies, these quasi-retirement possibilities have been recently reformed (Ebbinghaus forthcoming).

## 3.6 The Gender Dimension

Welfare states, and regime typologies, have been criticized for their strong gender bias (Orloff 1996), as they assume a male breadwinner model to conceptualize social citizenship rights and redistribution. In particular, public or private pension programs that base benefits on contribution years discriminate against women who interrupt or end employment due to marriage or care-giving. Indirect pension claims via spousal pensions and widows' pension programs only provide partial relief, especially when claims depend on legal marriage or are restricted in cases of divorce.

Female employment rates have increased earlier and most rapidly in Nordic countries, somewhat later in Anglo-American economies, and belatedly in Continental Europe. With few exceptions, the reconciliation between child-rearing and work is based on part-time employment, though this may lead to lower (if any) pension benefits compared to male full-time workers. In countries where pension credits are granted for the first child's rearing years, this may add to incentives to withdraw from work with substantial difficulties in re-entering the labor market later. Systems with basic pensions based on citizenship would not discriminate against a care-giving parent withdrawing from work fully or partially. However, in addition to Beveridge-type basic pensions, earnings-related second-tier systems, whether public programs or private occupational pensions, create similar problems as under Bismarckian pension systems. The European Court of Justice stipulated that private occupational pensions cannot discriminate against part-time workers (1986) and that equal treatment rules apply also for men and women (1990).

Except in Nordic countries, women are underrepresented in most union movements. Union density for women only meets or tops that of men in Nordic countries (and today's Britain). In all other countries, women tend to be less organized than men (but often as highly organized in the public sector), partly as a result of the difficulties in recruiting part-time, temporary, and private service workers. Given their low employment rate and low union density in Continental Europe, women are underrepresented in the main union confederation (less than one-third of union membership). Organizations of women and family policy groups are increasingly active in voicing gender and family-related issues in pension politics. However, pensioner organizations still tend to best represent the interests of current pensioners of generations with lower female labor force participation, thus defending the rights of married women and widows against sudden changes in pension policy. For example, while British pensioner groups and organizations of women successfully argued for lower retirement ages for women under the reformed postwar Beveridge scheme, during the 1980s, they were unable to prevent the long-term upward equalization from 60 to 65 years (2010–20), in line with EU gender equality rules.

## 3.7 The Generational Conflict

Conflict between old and young and between current pensioners and the current payers are often claimed, yet surveys show no clear cleavage between generations (EEIG 2003). This is surprising since 'many studies have shown empirically that the social security system does not treat generations equally, is not "actuarially fair", and was most generous to the initial generations of retirees' (Cooley and Soares 1999: 136). One explanation is that each generation of payers has an interest in maintaining the current system until they retire. In fact, pay-as-you-go systems face a double-payer problem: the current generation of payers would have to pay for current pensioners via public obligations and save for their own private pensions if a system reform seeks to shift toward funded pensions (Myles and Pierson 2001). Other reasons why generational conflicts are less likely to occur are family bonds between the old and the young, within-family resource transfers from grandparents to parents and to grandchildren.

Nevertheless, a seniority bias is at stake with the favorable representation of older persons' interests in political parties, in trade unions, and at the workplace. While young people tend to be underrepresented today in voluntary organizations— political parties and trade unions—older people and particularly those approaching retirement are well organized. Moreover, particular interest groups exist for pensioners (Walker and Naegele 1999) and many trade unions organize a considerable share of pensioners (Ebbinghaus and Visser 2000); most notably half of all Italian union members have already retired.

# 4 Political and Social Consensus-Building

The development of retirement income systems and the current pension reform efforts show the importance of both political and social consensus-building. While in the past, inter-class alliances often enabled major reforms, today governments need more than their own political majorities to provide sufficient momentum to overcome vested interests in reforming established pensions systems. The more responsibility for retirement income is divided between the state and society, the more possibilities there are for social interest groups to influence political decision-making processes and implementation. Even if they have no formal institutional right or direct channel, unions may use non-institutionalized veto power, such as mass protests or even general strikes, to fight unilateral pension reforms, as happened at times in France and Italy (Ebbinghaus and Hassel 2000). Such mobilization potential in turn may provide the rationale for the state to consult and even negotiate with the social partners to avoid political and social conflict over state interventions. When the social partners share social policy implementation, unilateral state intervention may lead to blockage in the execution phase. Governments may thus be willing to cooperate with the social partners— unless they are able to reform governance structures in order to regain sufficient control.

Beyond unilateral state intervention, the social partners' involvement ranges from institutionalized consultation of interest groups by policy-makers to concertation between the government and social partners on economic and social policy. Advisory councils are a form of consultation, whereas a 'social pact' agreed in tripartite negotiations is defined as social concertation. Corporatist interest intermediation and the social partners' participation in self-administration should be distinguished since the latter provides less scope for state interference than the former. A further distinction is whether the state devolves self-administrative functions in a semi-public agency to the social groups affected or whether the social partners have assumed self-regulatory functions without state interference. In the case of self-administration, legitimacy derives from the state's delegation of public authority to an agency. By contrast, with self-regulation, the state abstains from intervening in the social actors' self-help, according to the *subsidiarity* principle.

## 4.1 Political Veto Power

Today and in the future, pension reform politics will be about building political consensus within institutional conditions and policy legacies. Past explanations for welfare state expansion are insufficient to explain current reform processes that aim at retrenchment or recalibration. Prominently, Pierson (1996) has argued that the 'new politics' of pension reform under austerity does not mirror the 'old' politics of welfare state expansion. Past policies led to vested interests in these programs' continuation among the public generally and the welfare state clientele in particular. He argues that politicians can no longer claim credit for expanding social rights, but must now anxiously avoid blame for retrenchment. In particular, pay-as-you-go pension systems entail major problems for systemic reform, given the dual-payer problem. Moreover, institutional conditions for advancing or blocking reform policies vary considerably across democratic welfare states. Multiple 'veto points' may exist due to federalism, separation of power, coalition governments, constitutional courts, or binding referendums.

The popularity of existing welfare state arrangements has proven a major obstacle to systemic reforms. Studies on public attitudes to welfare states show widespread support for current public pension systems and indicate limited support for retrenchment and majority support for the status quo (EEIG 2003). Moreover, the public underestimates the cost of public pensions, although they are aware of pension systems' future financial problems (Boeri et al. 2001). Indeed, a large share are welfare state dependents, either as beneficiaries or public employees (Flora 1986). The public opinion's status quo preference and the vested interests of the 'welfare state clientele' provide major political reform obstacles.

To change highly institutionalized retirement systems proves difficult: 'while the benefits of retrenchment for welfare state opponents are generally diffuse and often uncertain, the large core constituencies for the welfare state have a concentrated interest in the maintenance of social provisions' (Pierson 2001: 413). Politicians as vote maximizers are worried about the political costs of changing the pension benefit rules of past payers in pay-as-you-go systems. 'The politics of retrenchment is typically treacherous, because it imposes tangible losses on concentrated groups of voters in return for diffuse and uncertain gains' (Pierson 1996: 145). One political strategy has been to stretch the impact of changes in a gradual way, exempting current retirees or obfuscating through invisible technical changes (Myles and Pierson 2001).

Indeed, political systems provide numerous veto points for interest groups to influence policy-making, if not to block major changes detrimental to their own interests. Particular institutional arrangements account for cross-national variations in the political capacity of governments to unilaterally intervene in the public pension system or regulate private retirement systems. Diverse institutional veto points (Bonoli 2001) include the 'veto' of federalist second chambers (Germany), the need to compromise between national and regional governments (Canada), presidential cohabitation (France), bipartisan checks-and-balances (United States), coalition governments that rely on small parties opposed to a reform (Continental Europe), popular referendums (Switzerland), and Constitutional Courts (Germany). These political institutions allow interest groups that do not represent the majority (the median voter) to block reforms that affect their interests, provided that these veto points can be used in pension policy matters indirectly through political parties or directly by mobilizing or advocating for intervention on their behalf. Governments may consider circumventing these veto points by building large social consensus via consultation or concertation. Or they may have delegated implementation rights to self-administrative bodies or rely on private self-regulation.

## 4.2 Consultation

Institutionalized consultation via formal tripartite bodies or more informal consultative practices has been more common in corporatist countries in Continental Europe and Nordic countries, while in Anglo-American pluralist countries organized labor's influence is more remote, although bipartisan committees in the 1981 pension reform in the United States and royal commissions in Britain provided some indirect possibilities. Particularly in corporatist countries in Continental Europe, conventions or legal mandates ensure that statutory advisory bodies are routinely consulted. In Nordic countries, instead of formal bodies consultation procedures (hearings and commissions) are common in the policy-making process, providing opportunities for organized interests.

The French Social and Economic Council and the Italian Economic and Labor Council remain rather symbolic postwar institutions that provide a forum for deliberation, but largely fail to enhance consensus-building due to their heterogeneity. On contentious matters, the governments seek either unilateral action or direct negotiations with the social partners. In the Scandinavian countries, political actors increasingly bypass the long-standing tradition of social consultation in committees and parliamentary hearings, and governments seek direct consultation of interest organizations, often via party channels. In the Netherlands, government initiatives, bipartite consensus-seeking within the social partners' Foundation of Labor, and ad hoc tripartite concertation have increasingly replaced institutionalized concertation via the Social and Economic Council. In Germany, inter-party consensus-building and parliamentary commissions traditionally play a surrogate role for a formal social consultation body, as in the last consensual 1992 pension reform. Due to the political exigencies of a federalist system with the possibility of second chamber opposition, however, the institutional need to seek consensus has also increased the likelihood of reform blockage.

In general, these institutionalized consultation mechanisms are insufficient to provide the social partners with 'veto power' because their advisory role remains limited, and they are often consulted at a late stage in policy-making. Traditional statutory advisory forums seem too cumbersome and heterogeneous to foster consensus and initiate reforms in social policy areas, whereas more informal institutions (such as the bipartite Dutch Foundation of Labor or the Irish concertation with different negotiation rooms) appear to be more flexible. Consultation institutions' most important function is to develop a shared understanding of particular policy problems and deliberate on joint solutions with long-term positive results for all sides.

## 4.3 Self-Administration and Self-Regulation

Instead of relying on consultation, the social partners may actually find more opportunities to influence pension policy through their role in the self-administration of social insurance (Reynaud 2000). Also, social partners perform self-regulatory functions in (private) occupational pensions (Rein and Wadensjö 1997), involving not only employers, but also unions through collective bargaining. As in the case of formal consultation, there are major differences in self-administration and self-regulation with respect to old-age and disability pension policies. Cross-national differences in social partner involvement reflect historical variations in welfare state development, commonly exemplified by the Bismarckian social insurance and the Beveridge-type welfare state models. Where old-age pensions were introduced as social insurance for industrial workers, benefits tended to be financed and self-administered by both employer and employees. On the other hand, in Beveridge-type welfare states, voluntary self-help was supplanted by state-provided social benefits to all citizens, financed by general or payroll taxes and administered by public agencies. Although these main differences still hold, there are many subtle variations and changes over time within the two models.

There are significant cross-national differences in the degree to which the social partners, particularly the trade unions, assume a self-administrative role in publicly mandated social insurance and/or perform self-regulative functions in private occupational pensions. While participation in self-administrative bodies can provide some decision-making power and control over implementation, the degree to which the state can regulate the benefits and conditions of social insurance schemes varies considerably across welfare regimes (Reynaud 2000). The social partners have traditionally had the most say in the Dutch negotiated second-tier pensions and the French mandatory supplementary pension. These schemes are mandatory by *erga omnes* extension in some industries in the Netherlands or legally mandatory for all workers in France. The influence of German and Italian social partners through self-administration is more symbolic, leaving responsibility for setting financial and regulatory parameters largely to the government, while the occupational pension was traditionally employer-provided.

Among the Beveridge-type welfare states, public welfare schemes in Britain and Ireland as well as the Nordic countries' basic income schemes are government-administered and controlled, with no self-administrative functions delegated to the social partners. Yet, voluntary agreements on supplementary pensions are now common in Scandinavia (Shalev 1996), giving the social partners an amplified role in negotiating not only wages, but also occupational benefits. A similar trend could develop in Bismarckian systems, following recent reforms during the late 1990s that foster a 'second pillar' of private occupational pensions and efforts by unions to enhance their bargaining role (e.g. in Germany and Italy). Nevertheless, the state can use regulatory power and 'incentives' through taxation policy to influence private pensions and thus encroach upon social partner self-regulation. Thus, while shared responsibilities in the social policy arena have made reforms more difficult, particularly their implementation, the state still has considerable authority over important parameters with respect to the public pension system. Moreover, the government can influence occupational pension development by using regulatory frameworks.

## 4.4 Social Concertation

Social concertation—negotiations between governments and social partners—plays an important role in pension reforms where public policy is traditionally shared or when governments do not have the capacity to push through unilateral reforms due to union opposition. If a pension system is based on an earnings-related pay-as-you go model, attempts at radical reforms can provoke resistance by workers and their organizations as this would alter an 'earned' social right. 'Unlike generic schemes for those in "need" or for "citizens," each individual has his or her own contract with the government with specific benefits attached to his or her specific work record, years of contribution, and earnings history' (Myles and Pierson 2001: 321). Bismarckian pension systems should thus provide the most noticeable 'veto power' to unions, while Scandinavian unions would follow, given their organizational strength and role in negotiated supplementary pensions. Lastly, dual pension systems with a liberal basic pension and voluntary occupational pensions exhibit the least union influence.

During recent years, concertation does not necessarily follow corporatist traditions: some corporatist countries have moved away from social concertation, while others with a weak tradition have opted for social concertation (Molina and Rhodes 2002). Concertation *and* social conflict have been present in Europe. The strikes against the pension reform of the Berlusconi government in 1994 and the Juppé government in 1995 indicate that at least in countries with contentious labor relations, unions remain able to muster a political strike (Ebbinghaus and Hassel

2000). However, such mass protest depends on the seriousness of welfare retrenchment and the unions' mobilization capacity. In most cases, governments had good reasons to opt for consensual reform. Concerted reforms were undertaken by government and unions in Italy in 1995 and 1997, an all-party consensus led to the German 1992 reform (but limits were set thereafter), and the French government made concessions in 1993 that prevented such mobilization. Bringing the trade unions into reform coalitions entails phased-in reforms and quid pro quo side-payments.

Concertation does not seem to be limited to countries with self-administrative involvement of the social partners. Thus, Scandinavian trade unions have some influence in political decision-making, in particular the blue-collar unions with special corporative links to the Social Democratic party. However, policy-makers have increasingly circumvented the social partners. Consensus on pension reforms was more limited over the 1990s than earlier. Trade unions have the least institutionalized veto power in the United Kingdom, though employers had some impact on the privatization of pensions under the Conservative government. Although the social partners have no self-administrative role in Ireland, tripartite concertation has become an overarching policy process also increasingly used for pension policy, in particular since collective bargaining partners have to implement the expansion of occupational pensions.

In addition to reforms aimed at cutting benefits and restricting eligibility, governments have also attempted to change social governance more generally, either through changes in self-administration or by changing financing modes. The Dutch government has undertaken both strategies by reorganizing the social partners' involvement in self-administration and shifting responsibilities to private actors, for instance, transferring the costs of sick pay to employers. Similarly, the French government has altered self-administration and budget control. The French state increasingly assumes financial responsibility, thereby gaining more control over policy instruments and circumventing the social partners' interests.

New governance in pension policy entails not merely privatization, but could also include increased state-financed and means-tested benefits. Moreover, the trend toward privatization may increase the potential scope for social partners' self-regulation—similar to the trend in Scandinavian countries, France, and the Netherlands, where social partners have negotiated supplementary benefits. Thus, in countries in which private pensions have gained importance, such as Germany and Italy, the social partners may utilize the opportunity to negotiate private pension improvements in exchange for wage moderation (Ebbinghaus and Hassel 2000). In the two countries with traditional employer-provided occupational pensions (the United Kingdom and Ireland), unions have only recently embraced an increased role in private pensions. Depending on the strength of the collective bargaining parties as well as on legal and general frameworks, unions can seize this opportunity and negotiate comprehensive occupational pensions.

## 5 Conclusion

Retirement income systems affect the interests of most social strata in society. Consequently, these groups have mobilized to influence pension policies in the past and will continue to do so in future. Interest groups have often been singled out as the main defendants of the status quo and as obstacles to the rational redesign of retirement income systems. Yet only rarely are governments in the comfortable position of facing no institutionalized veto points in political systems or to have no need to share policy implementations with diverse social groups. To the degree that they have to overcome blockage by vested interests and to the degree that they have to rely on social partners' cooperation in pension regulation, they need to consider the possibilities for building political and societal consensus. This requires an understanding of the potential conflicts of interests between organized capital and labor, as well as the nature of intra-class cleavages and the potential for inter-class alliances.

Over the long term, retirement income systems affect the vital interests of social groups considerably as they regulate the flows of payments and benefits over the life course. This review of the main latent and manifest interests in pension policy has revealed considerable internal differentiation over time and variation across countries in such arrangements. (The chapter could only sketch the main issues without systematically comparing and explaining these differences.) Similarly, the modes of political and social consensus-building vary considerably between welfare states and over time, depending on institutionalized sharing of public policy between the state and the social partners (or other interest groups). Although our technical knowledge about retirement income systems and the global and domestic challenges has increased greatly over the last two decades, the comparative analysis of ongoing reform processes and the obstacles and opportunities for political and social consensus-building are still in progress. More systematic research is needed to study the specific processes of political influence of veto points, institutionalized consultation of social policy-making, tripartite concertation on pension reform, self-administration of pension insurance, and social partner self-regulation via negotiated pensions.

National legacies and contingent political events challenge generalizations about best practice in managing interest conflicts concerning retirement income systems. There seem to be few opportunities to learn from others how to effectively transfer political and social consensus-building processes from one societal context to another.

## REFERENCES

BALDWIN, P. (1990). *The Politics of Social Solidarity: Class Bases of the European Welfare States 1875–1975*. Cambridge: Cambridge University Press.

BERGER, S., and COMPSTON, H. (eds.) (2002). *Policy Concertation and Social Partnership in Western Europe*. New York: Berghahn Books.

BOERI, T., BÖRSCH-SUPAN, A., and TABELLINI, G. (2001). 'Would you like to shrink the welfare state? A survey of European citizens'. *Economic Policy*, 16/32: 8–50.

BONOLI, G. (2001). *The Politics of Pension Reform: Institutions and Policy Change in Western Europe*. Cambridge: Cambridge University Press.

COOLEY, T. F., and SOARES, J. (1999). 'A positive theory of social security based on reputation'. *Journal of Political Economy*, 107/1: 135–60.

EBBINGHAUS, B. (forthcoming). *Reforming Early Retirement in Europe, Japan and the USA*. Oxford: Oxford University Press.

—— and HASSEL, A. (2000). 'Striking deals: concertation in the reform of Continental European welfare states'. *Journal of European Public Policy*, 7/1: 44–62.

EBBINGHAUS, B., and VISSER, J. (2000). *Trade Unions in Western Europe since 1945*. London: Macmillan.

EEIG (2003). *The Future of Pension Systems: Special Eurobarometer 161/Wave 56.1*. Brussels: European Commission.

ESPING-ANDERSEN, G. (1990). *Three Worlds of Welfare Capitalism*. Princeton: Princeton University Press.

—— and KERSBERGEN, K. VON (1992). 'Contemporary research on social democracy'. *Annual Review of Sociology*, 18: 187–208.

FLORA, P. (1986). 'Introduction', in P. Flora (ed.), *Growth to Limits: The Western European Welfare States since World War II*. Berlin: de Gruyter, pp. xii–xxxvi.

HECLO, H. (1974). *Modern Social Politics in Britain and Sweden: From Relief to Income Maintenance*. New Haven: Yale University Press.

HUBER, E., and STEPHENS, J. D. (2001). *Development and Crisis of the Welfare State: Parties and Policies in Global Markets*. Chicago: University of Chicago Press.

KOHLI, M., REIN, M., GUILLEMARD, A.-M., and VAN GUNSTEREN, H. (eds.) (1991). *Time for Retirement: Comparative Studies on Early Exit from the Labor Force*. New York: Cambridge University Press.

KORPI, W. (2001). 'Contentious institutions: an augmented rational-action analysis of the origins and path dependency of welfare state institutions in Western countries'. *Rationality and Society*, 13/2: 235–83.

MARES, I. (2003). *The Politics of Social Risk: Business and Welfare State Development*. New York: Cambridge University Press.

MARSHALL, T. H. (1950). *Citizenship and Social Class: The Marshall Lectures*. Cambridge: Cambridge University.

MOLINA, O., and RHODES, M. (2002). 'Corporatism: the past, present, and future of a concept'. *Annual Review of Political Science*, 5: 305–31.

MYLES, J., and PIERSON, P. (2001). 'The comparative political economy of pension reform', in P. Pierson (ed.), *The New Politics of the Welfare State*. New York: Oxford University Press, 305–33.

ORLOFF, A. (1996). 'Gender in the welfare state'. *Annual Review of Sociology*, 21: 51–78.

PIERSON, P. (1996). 'The new politics of the welfare state'. *World Politics*, 48/2: 143–79.

—— (2001). 'Coping with permanent austerity: welfare state restructuring in affluent democracies', in P. Pierson (ed.), *The New Politics of the Welfare State*. New York: Oxford University Press, 410–56.

REIN, M., and WADENSJÖ, E. (eds.) (1997). *Enterprise and the Welfare State*. Cheltenham: Edward Elgar.

REYNAUD, E. (ed.) (2000). *Social Dialogue and Pension Reform: United Kingdom, United States, Germany, Japan, Sweden, Italy, Spain*. Geneva: International Labour Office.

RIMLINGER, G. V. (1971). *Welfare Policy and Industrialization in Europe, America, and Russia*. New York: Wiley.

SHALEV, M. (ed.) (1996). *The Privatization of Social Policy? Occupational Welfare and the Welfare State in America, Scandianvia and Japan*. London: Macmillan.

STEVENS, Y., GIESELINK, G., and VAN BUGGENHOUT, B. (2002). 'Towards a new role for occupational pensions in Continental Europe'. *European Journal of Social Security*, 4/1: 25–53.

SWENSON, P. A. (2002). *Capitalists against Markets: The Making of Labor Markets and Welfare States in the United States and Sweden*. New York: Oxford University Press.

WALKER, A., and NAEGELE, G. (eds.) (1999). *The Politics of Old Age in Europe*. Buckingham: Open University Press.

# EMERGING ECONOMIES

# CHAPTER 39

# PENSIONS FOR DEVELOPMENT AND POVERTY REDUCTION

## ARMANDO BARRIENTOS

## 1 INTRODUCTION

A priority for developing countries must be to ensure that public policy contributes to the development process, and to the reduction of poverty. This also applies to the international community, especially as the Millennium Development Goals prioritize halving poverty by the year 2015. It is therefore appropriate to consider pension policy in developing countries within the context of their contribution to development and poverty reduction. The main purpose of this chapter is to review and assess the experience of countries in the South, and especially Latin America, with developing pension programs that can reduce and prevent old-age poverty and contribute to the development process.

In Latin America and other developing regions, the main form of pension provision is through employment-based pension plans for workers in formal employment. The coverage of these plans is limited, as shown by figures for the labor force coverage of pension plans in the 1990s from a World Bank study on 'International patterns of pension provision' (Palacios and Pallarés-Millares 2000) later updated (Schwarz 2003). In Latin America and the Caribbean, the proportion of the labor force contributing to pension plans ranges from around 73 percent in Uruguay and 50 percent in Costa Rica to around 12 percent in Bolivia.

In Brazil and Mexico, the two largest countries, coverage rates are around one-third of the labor force.

In other developing regions, coverage rates are also an issue. Leaving aside Singapore, coverage rates in Asia and the Pacific range from around 50 percent in Korea and Malaysia, to less than 5 percent in Pakistan and Bangladesh. In Sub-Saharan Africa, coverage rates are even lower. Leaving Mauritius aside, coverage rates seldom climb above 20 percent of the labour force, and in over one-half of countries in the region coverage rates fail to reach 5 percent. Moreover, overall trends in employment-based pension plan coverage in these regions show little improvement over time. In Latin America, pension plan coverage rates have declined in the last two decades (Barrientos 2004*b*), and especially after the introduction of pension reforms (see Mesa-Lago, Chapter 33 in this volume). As the share of informal employment in developing countries is high, and rising, there is little prospect that existing employment-based pension plans could be extended to cover a majority of the labor force in these countries, and especially in the poorest and most vulnerable among them. Achieving effective and sustainable old-age support in developing countries requires thinking through alternative forms of pension arrangements. Accelerated population ageing in the South and the spread of labor market liberalization add urgency to this task.

Over the decade since the publication of the World Bank Report on *Averting the Old Age Crisis* (World Bank 1994), the main focus of pension policy for developing countries has been on reforming and strengthening employment-based pension plans. More specifically, pension reform has focused on replacing defined benefit unfunded pension plans with defined contribution funded pension plans, while at the same time facilitating the establishment and growth of pension fund management markets, and channeling savings through capital markets (Barrientos 1999; Mesa-Lago 2002). A number of Latin American countries and transition economies have adopted this route to pension reform, provoking a large and growing literature on its successes and failures, reviewed by Mesa-Lago in this volume and in the World Bank's recent review of pension reform (Holzman *et al.* 2004).

A different route to pension reform in developing countries has focused instead on extending pension provision in the form of public cash transfer programs focused on poor and vulnerable older people and their households. These are tax-financed non-contributory pension programs. In Latin America, a handful of countries have residual assistance to poor older groups, but there is a growing recognition that these have a measurable impact on poverty reduction. In South Asia, India, Nepal, and Bangladesh have recently introduced non-contributory pension programs to support poverty reduction objectives. In Sub-Saharan Africa, South Africa, Botswana, and Namibia have 'social pension' programs in place. Although this route to pension reform has not received the same measure of attention from researchers and policy-makers, it promises to reach the majority of older people in developing countries currently unable to access employment-based pension plans. Research into non-contributory pension programs has shown that they can make an important contribution to reducing and preventing poverty and vulnerability among older people and their households, and in addition they strengthen human capital investment. There is a growing body of evidence supporting the view that non-contributory pension programs can make an important contribution to the development process.

The rest of the chapter is divided into three sections. The next section provides summary information on the incidence and patterns of old-age poverty in developing countries, and the need to extend pension provision. The section that follows discusses the findings from research into the poverty reduction properties of non-contributory pension programs, and the extent to which they contribute to the development process. The following section compares non-contributory pension programs in Latin America and elsewhere in the South, drawing out some findings on design and financing issues. The conclusion draws together the key insights and unanswered questions emerging from the chapter.

## 2 OLD-AGE POVERTY IN THE SOUTH

The absence of reliable and comprehensive indicators of old-age poverty for developing countries has been taken as a reflection of the low priority attached to poverty in later life (Barrientos *et al.* 2003). Table 39.1 sets out old-age poverty indicators from regionally comparable studies. In Latin America, the figures show that poverty rates among older people, defined as those aged 60 and over, vary widely across countries (del Popolo 2001). In countries with lower poverty rates, poverty affects roughly one in 20 older people in Uruguay, one in ten in Chile, and one in five in Costa Rica. In countries with higher poverty rates, roughly one in two older people in Paraguay, Bolivia, and Venezuela are poor. A study for Africa provides contrasting evidence of the incidence of old-age poverty. In African countries with lower poverty rates among those aged 60 and over, Ethiopia, Ghana and Guinea, poverty affects one in two older people. The incidence of old-age poverty is much higher for the rest, eight in ten older people are poor in Zambia (Kakwani and Subbarao 2005). Old-age poverty is significant in developing countries.

It is informative to compare the poverty headcount rates of older people with a measure of poverty for the population as a whole. Older people are overrepresented among the poor if their poverty headcount rate is higher than the aggregate headcount rate, and underrepresented if it is lower. Table 39.1 shows that poverty

## Table 39.1 Old-age poverty indicators for Latin America and Africa

| Country | Share of 60 and over in population | Poverty headcount rate of older people | Poverty headcount rate in multigenerational households with older people | Under- and over-representation of old-age poverty |
|---|---|---|---|---|
| **Latin America** | | | | |
| **(Urban)** | | | | |
| Bolivia | 6.1 | 39 | 43 | 0.79 |
| El Salvador | 7.2 | 42 | 44 | 1.01 |
| Honduras | 5.1 | 70 | 71 | 1.00 |
| Nicaragua | 4.6 | 71 | 71 | 1.08 |
| Paraguay | 5.3 | 39 | 38 | 0.91 |
| Brazil | 7.9 | 14 | 21 | 0.48 |
| Colombia | 6.9 | 37 | 38 | 0.87 |
| Costa Rica | 7.5 | 18 | 18 | 1.06 |
| Ecuador | 7 | 47 | 50 | 0.87 |
| Mexico | 6.9 | 36 | 43 | 0.83 |
| Panama | 7.3 | 15 | 23 | 0.71 |
| Dominican Republic | 6.8 | 37 | 37 | 1.15 |
| Venezuela | 6.6 | 40 | 41 | 0.88 |
| Argentina | 13.3 | 12 | 14 | 0.74 |
| Chile | 10.1 | 10 | 13 | 0.49 |
| Uruguay | 17.1 | 2 | 5 | 0.26 |
| **Africa** | | | | |
| Burundi | 4.1 | 59 | 59 | 0.97 |
| Burkina Faso | 5.7 | 56 | 58 | 1.08 |
| Cote d'Ivoire | 4.3 | 47 | 47 | 1.27 |
| Cameroon | 5.3 | 62 | 67 | 1.02 |
| Ethiopia | 5 | 44 | 44 | 1.07 |
| Ghana | 6.5 | 46 | 52 | 1.04 |
| Guinea | 6.8 | 44 | 43 | 1.15 |
| Gambia | 5.5 | 68 | 72 | 1.10 |
| Kenya | 5 | 54 | 59 | 1.08 |
| Madagascar | 4 | 55 | 61 | 0.89 |
| Mozambique | 4.5 | 66 | 68 | 0.96 |
| Malawi | 4.8 | 72 | 72 | 1.12 |
| Nigeria | 5.2 | 60 | 73 | 0.94 |
| Uganda | 4.9 | 52 | 45 | 1.08 |
| Zambia | 3.5 | 79 | 79 | 1.19 |

*Notes*: Poverty headcount rates were estimated on household survey data, mostly from 1997 for Latin America and 1994–2001 for Africa. The poverty headcount rate is based in Africa on adult equivalent household income, but in Latin America on per capita household income. All rates are based on national poverty lines. Under- and over-representation of old-age poverty is the ratio of the poverty headcount rate of people aged 60 and over to the poverty headcount rate for the population as a whole in Africa, and to the same rate for people aged 10–59 in Latin America.
*Sources*: Information was drawn from several sources: del Popolo (2001); Barrientos *et al.* (2003); Schwarz (2003); Kakwani and Subbarao (2005).

among older people in African countries tracks aggregate poverty rates fairly closely. In the majority of these countries, the elderly are overrepresented among the poor but not greatly. In most Latin American countries, on the other hand, older people appear to be underrepresented among the poor.

The contrast reflects a number of factors, but three are especially significant. First, the living arrangements of the elderly are of some interest here. In low income developing countries the elderly are more likely to live in extended households, and therefore share in the living standards of broader population groups. In African countries, households with only older people are rare (less than 1 percent for all countries in Table 39.1, except Ghana and Nigeria), but they are more common in Latin American countries, especially those with older populations and more extensive pension provision (most countries are in the 5 to 7 percent range, except for Argentina and Uruguay which have a higher incidence of older people living alone). In middle income countries in which a higher proportion of the elderly live independently, poverty rates for the elderly may diverge from aggregate trends. The table also provides figures for the incidence of poverty in multigenerational households containing older people. It is interesting that, except for a handful of countries—Burundi, Uganda, and Costa Rica—poverty incidence is higher for older people living in multigenerational households than for older people living independently.[1]

Second, there are technical issues associated with measuring poverty in households of different size and composition (Barrientos *et al.* 2003) which tend to cloud comparison across studies using different methodologies. Poverty studies focusing on expenditure or income should ideally account for the differential 'costs' of children and adults, and also for the share in household consumption of private and public goods (a household of five needs five meals but does not need five stoves). The differences in measured old-age poverty in Latin America and Africa shown in Table 39.1 also reflect methodological differences. The African poverty rates are based on adult equivalent income (with children taken as 0.5 of an adult, and the second and further adult equivalent household members requiring only a 0.70 increase in expenditure), whereas the figures for Latin America are based on per capita household income (i.e. household income divided by the numbers in the household). The latter understate poverty among older people, who tend to live in smaller households. The figures for Latin America refer to urban populations.

Third, the figures reflect the spread of pension provision. Countries with the lowest incidence of poverty among the elderly population—Brazil, Argentina, Chile, and Uruguay—have more comprehensive and generous pension provision, as noted by Mesa-Lago in this volume. In conclusion, old-age poverty is significant in developing countries; it is higher among lower income countries, countries lacking pension provision, and in multigenerational households with older people.

## 3 NON-CONTRIBUTORY PENSIONS REDUCE POVERTY AND FACILITATE HOUSEHOLD INVESTMENT

Non-contributory pension programs typically pay benefits that are fixed at a low value. Studies have found that pension benefits are shared within beneficiary households (Barrientos and Lloyd-Sherlock 2003). The poverty reduction effectiveness of these programs will therefore show more strongly on the poverty gaps of poor older people than on poverty headcount measures. This is confirmed by studies measuring the incidence of non-contributory pension programs on both the poverty headcount and the poverty gap—that is, the difference between the income or consumption of the poor and the poverty line (Bertranou *et al.* 2002; Barrientos and Lloyd-Sherlock 2003). Nonetheless, there is growing evidence that these programs have measurable effects on poverty. In Brazil, researchers at the *Instituto de Pesquisa Econômica Aplicada* (IPEA) have investigated the incidence of the rural old-age pension and have concluded that the program has large effects on poverty (Delgado and Cardoso 2000b, 2000c; Schwarzer 2000; Schwarzer and Querino 2002). Delgado and Cardoso compared households with a pension beneficiary against households without one, and found that the incidence of poverty was higher among the latter. The proportion of beneficiary households who were poor was 38.1 percent in the Northeast region and 14.3 percent in the South, whereas among non-beneficiary households poverty incidence was 51.5 percent and 18.9 percent respectively (Delgado and Cardoso 2000a).

A different approach to identifying the effects of non-contributory programs on poverty is to compare the incidence of poverty in households with non-contributory pension beneficiaries with the incidence of poverty which would be observed if the pension income is subtracted from the household income. This is equivalent to simulating the effect on poverty of a sudden withdrawal of the program.[2] Table 39.2 below summarizes the results of studies based on household survey data. In Latin America, poverty studies usually focus on two measures of poverty: indigence or extreme poverty applies to individuals with income levels insufficient to meet basic subsistence represented by the cost of a basic basket of food, whereas poverty applies to individuals with income levels insufficient to cover both food and non-food requirements. The poverty line is twice the indigence line.

The findings from these studies confirm the poverty reduction effectiveness of non-contributory pension programs. The withdrawal of pension income would result, in the absence of compensating behavior by household members, in increases in poverty of one percentage point in Argentina, and just over five

Table 39.2 The contribution of non-contributory pension income to poverty reduction

|  | Indigence headcount rate | | | Poverty headcount rate | | |
| --- | --- | --- | --- | --- | --- | --- |
|  | Full income | Without pension income | % point difference | Full income | Without pension income | % point difference |
| Argentina (1997)[1] | 6.9 | 8.2 | 1.3 | 19.6 | 20.6 | 1.0 |
| Chile (2000)[2] | 1.7 | 9.8 | 8.1 | 3.9 | 9.2 | 5.3 |
| Brazil (2002)[3] | 22.0 | 30.9 | 8.9 | 58.5 | 63.9 | 5.4 |

Notes: [1] Figures from Bertranou and Grushka (2002) for households with non-contributory pension beneficiaries aged 65 and over.
[2] Figures from Gana Cornejo (2002) for households with non-contributory pension beneficiaries aged 65 and over.
[3] Figures from Barrientos and Lloyd-Sherlock (2003) estimated on a data set of households with at least one member over the age of 60.

percentage points in Chile and Brazil. The effects are much larger if the focus is on indigence, as subtracting pension income from beneficiary households would raise indigence levels roughly by one-sixth in Argentina, seven times in Chile, and by one-third in Brazil. The figures show that, especially in Chile and Brazil, non-contributory programs are most effective in reducing the number of extreme poor. This finding also underlines the fact that the poverty effectiveness of non-contributory pension programs depends to an important extent on whether they reach the poor. The differences in the poverty reduction effects of such programs in Chile and Brazil on the one hand, and Argentina on the other, are explained by a more effective process for selecting beneficiaries, an issue to be taken up in the next section.

There is also a growing body of evidence showing that non-contributory pension programs can contribute to the development process by facilitating key household investment, in human capital and productive capacity by households. Delgado and Cardoso argue strongly that rural pensions in Brazil have been effective in generating a transformation of subsistence agriculture toward sustainable household production (they define this as production capable of generating a surplus). They find that a significant proportion of beneficiaries of the rural pension in Brazil reported using part of their pension to purchase seeds and tools to support agricultural production (Delgado and Cardoso 2000b). Barrientos and Lloyd-Sherlock did not find a similar effect in South Africa, but findings from qualitative surveys reveal a great deal of informal economic activity among pensioners (Barrientos and Lloyd-Sherlock 2003).

The regularity of pension payments, and the links to financial providers where pension payments are made through the banking system, improve access to credit by beneficiary households. This finding has been reported for South Africa (Ardington and Lund 1995) and for Brazil (Schwarzer and Querino 2002). Schwarzer and Querino note that 'the electronic banking card that each beneficiary receives is often used as proof of creditworthiness' (Schwarzer and Querino 2002: 15). They suggest that access to a regular and reliable source of income can lift credit constraints faced by poor households. Studies in Brazil (Schwarzer 2000) and South Africa (Ardington and Lund 1995) report that beneficiary households invest in improvements in their housing after first receipt of the pension.

There is also strong evidence linking pension beneficiaries to human capital investment. Enrollment rates of school-age children have been found to be higher among pension beneficiary households for South Africa (Duflo 2003) and for Brazil (Carvalho 2000*b*). In South Africa the main reason given by pensioners for sharing their pension benefit with relatives living elsewhere was to finance the costs of education (Barrientos and Lloyd-Sherlock 2003). The health status of children and older people has been found to be higher in beneficiary households in South Africa (Case 2001). Duflo (2000) examined the impact of the old-age pension on the height-for-age of co-resident children, and found that the 'pension improves the nutritional status of children (girls in particular) if it was received by a woman, but not by a man' (Duflo 2000: 9). She estimates that 'pensions received by women improved the height for age Z-scores of girls by 1.16 standard deviations, and their weight for height Z-scores by 1.19 standard deviations' (Duflo 2000: 21).

Other second-order effects of pension receipt are harder to assess in terms of their effects on the welfare of households. Some studies have focused on household dynamics associated with pension receipt. Carvalho finds a propensity for older women pensioners to live independently (Carvalho 2000*a*), although this study cannot distinguish between contributory and non-contributory pensioners. Studies for South Africa find evidence that household dynamics around the time of first pension receipt is consistent with labor migration of younger household members (Edmonds *et al.* 2001; Bertrand *et al.* 2003). And studies for both Brazil and South Africa find a labor supply effect on older people associated with pension receipt (Carvalho 2000*c*; Bertrand *et al.* 2003).

To sum up, a growing body of evidence supports the view that non-contributory pension programs are effective in reducing poverty and vulnerability, and can facilitate investment in productive and human capital, and therefore contribute to the development process.

# 4 Issues of Design, Financing, and Politics of Non-Contributory Pension Programs

Non-contributory pension programs in developing countries show considerable heterogeneity in design and financing. Policy-makers concerned with maximizing the poverty reduction effectiveness of non-contributory programs can draw valuable insights from comparative analyses. Table 39.3 provides summary information on these programs for a range of countries in Latin America and elsewhere. The discussion that follows focuses on three key dimensions: the selection of beneficiaries, financing modes, and the politics of establishing and sustaining non-contributory pension programs.

## 4.1 Selection of Beneficiaries

There are differing views as to whether non-contributory pensions are more effective when targeted on poor older groups (Holzman et al. 2004), or extended to all older people as of right (Willmore 2001; HAI 2004). Aside from cost implications, which will be examined below, this debate provides a direct entry point to different approaches to the nature and functions of non-contributory pension programs. Universal basic pension programs emphasize the redistributive properties of non-contributory pension programs, more specifically a redistribution from younger to older groups. Non-contributory pension programs targeted on the poor emphasize instead the insurance properties of such programs, transferring resources to older persons who are threatened with poverty.[3]

In practice there is a fine gradation in the design of existing non-contributory programs, ranging from universal or citizen pensions as in Mauritius or Namibia, to finely targeted programs such as Chile's. In between, pension programs may require a light needs assessment, as in Argentina, repeated means tests as in South Africa's social pension or Brazil's urban pension, or a community-based ranking of the poorest older people as in Bangladesh or Chile. In terms of poverty reduction effectiveness, the literature examining this issue in the context of non-contributory pension programs comes to well-known conclusions. The more universal the non-contributory programs are, the larger is their coverage of the poor as well as leakages to the non-poor. More targeted programs reduce leakages but at the expense of excluding some of the poor.

Eligibility tests are implemented to reduce leakages to the non-poor, but can have important second-order effects. Means tests normally focus on the income

Table 39.3 Summary information on non-contributory pension programs for selected countries

| Country | Selection instrument | Age | Cost as % of GDP | Financing |
|---|---|---|---|---|
| Argentina | Means tested (personal income threshold) or legislature dispensation | 70 | 0.23 | Tax financed |
| Bangladesh | Means tested (Community ranking—oldest and poorest five men and five women in ward) | Any age | 0.03 | Tax financed |
| Brazil (rural) | Time spent in household (subsistence) economic activity (agriculture, fishing, mining) | W55 M60 | 0.80 | Tax financed (government plus tax on first sale of rural produce) |
| Brazil (urban) | Means tested (threshold is per capita household income $< \frac{1}{4}$ of minimum wage)—review every three years | 67 | 0.2 | Tax financed |
| Chile | Means tested (ranking on proxy index CAS) | 65 | 0.38 | Tax financed |
| Costa Rica | Means tested (personal income threshold is $\frac{1}{2}$ of minimum pension)—review every five years | 65 | 0.18 | Tax financed and employer contributions (approx 46.2%) |
| Mauritius | Universal | 60 | 2 | Tax financed |
| Namibia | Universal | 60 | 2 | Tax financed |
| Nepal | Universal | 75 | | Tax financed |
| South Africa | Means tested (threshold level of income plus assets)—review at regular intervals | W60 M65 | 1.4 | Tax financed |
| Uruguay | Means tested (threshold computed on family group, independently of co-residence, who are expected to provide basic transfers) | 70[1] | 0.62 | Tax financed |

Note: [1] Originally 60, raised to 70 in 1979; lowered to 65 in 1986, raised to 70 in 1995.

Sources: Information was drawn from several sources (Mesa-Lago 2001; Willmore 2001, 2003; Bertranou et al. 2002; Schleberger 2002; Schwarzer and Querino 2002; Barrientos and Lloyd-Sherlock 2003; Begum 2003; Schwarz 2003; Willmore 2003).

and assets of potential recipients, setting a threshold above which entitlement to benefits stops. It is a matter of some significance for the living arrangements of the old whether the means tests apply to their individual, or to household, income. In Latin American countries, the tests set a maximum threshold per capita household income, as in the urban pension program in Brazil which has a threshold of a quarter of the minimum wage. This generates incentives for the poor old to live separately from their better off households to qualify for the benefit. In the South African social pension, linking eligibility to the income and assets of the potential beneficiary and his/her spouse only reduces these adverse incentives. In Uruguay, the responsibility of households to provide for their older members is incorporated in the eligibility test, as the income of all close relatives is taken into account. Means tests are administratively costly to perform, and it is not surprising that they are seldom applied in practice, especially when eligibility is supposed to be reviewed at regular intervals.

The low level of the pension benefit often reflects a concern with minimizing disincentives to contribute to formal pension plans. In Brazil, for example, the level of non-contributory pension benefits, at a minimum wage, is on a par with minimum guaranteed pensions in the contributory programs. Concerns with adverse incentives to participate in social insurance pension plans have been important in maintaining the age of eligibility for non-contributory pensions at 67 in urban areas where participation in formal pension plans is more likely (Schwarzer and Querino 2002). Maintaining a higher age of entitlement for non-contributory pensions is regressive in distributional terms, as the poor are less likely to collect because of their lower life expectancy. Nepal's high age of entitlement suggests the program might be good politics but poor social protection. As many non-contributory programs combine old age and disability qualifications, raising the qualification age for pension benefits may simply raise the share of disability beneficiaries, as in Uruguay (Saldain and Lorenzelli 2002).

## 4.2 Financing and Politics

The financial costs of non-contributory programs are small relative to both contributory programs and to alternative social assistance programs. In terms of overall costs, universal programs are more costly than programs targeting the poor. Mauritius, Namibia, and Nepal have universal programs which absorb roughly 2 percent of GDP. In response to concerns over the cost of the program, and leakages to the non-poor, Namibia has passed legislation introducing a means test which is expected to reduce beneficiaries by one-half (Schleberger 2002). The closest program in terms of cost, the social pension in South Africa, has almost universal coverage among blacks. It absorbs 1.4 percent of GDP and reaches

1.9 million beneficiaries and their households. In Brazil, the combined cost of the rural and urban non-contributory pension programs is estimated at 1 percent of GDP. Together these reach 4.6 million older beneficiaries and their households. In Argentina, Chile, Costa Rica, and Uruguay, the costs of the programs range from 0.23 to 0.62 percent of GDP (Bertranou et al. 2002). Among countries with beneficiary selection, only Costa Rica is considering making its means-tested non-contributory pension program fully universal (Mesa-Lago 2001).

The majority of the programs are fully tax financed, with revenues drawn from central government. There are some exceptions. In Brazil, the rural pension is partly financed through a tax on first sale of agricultural produce, but this source of revenue can only cover 10 percent of the total program expenditure. The remainder is, on paper, financed from a subsidy from the formal social insurance system, but in practice it comes from central government revenues (Schwarzer and Querino 2002). In Costa Rica, almost one-half of expenditure is financed from employer contributions, earmarked taxes on beer, cigarettes, and judicial deposits. On the whole, non-central government revenue sources can at best supplement non-contributory pension programs.

A key sustainability issue is the extent to which expenditure on non-contributory pension programs responds to demographic and macroeconomic conditions. Accelerated population ageing in developing countries will ensure that the share of older people in the population climbs up steeply over the next half a century. Because universal non-contributory pension programs are essentially redistributive, their liabilities will directly reflect demographic changes. Targeted non-contributory programs, on the other hand, will be less directly affected by demographic change but significantly exposed to changes in macroeconomic conditions. In a sense, they are supposed to do this, as their main function is to insure older groups against poverty. Program design parameters may provide degrees of freedom to policy-makers in addressing demographic change. In universal pension programs it is possible to raise the age of entitlement and/or reduce benefit levels in order to dampen upward trends in public liabilities arising from demographic change. Uruguay has changed its age of entitlement several times since the start of the program. There are fewer degrees of freedom in the presence of adverse macroeconomic conditions. Chile applies an annual aggregate expenditure cap to the non-contributory pension program, which restricts the entry of new beneficiaries regardless of their situation. This makes program liabilities more certain, but has the effect of undermining the insurance protection of the program. This prompts consideration of the issue of exit from the program, aside from the death of the beneficiary. Some countries have a review of the means test at regular intervals, but in practice few resources are allocated to this activity. This is important in terms of whether non-contributory pension programs provide an annuity, or simply a time-limited safety net.

Whilst it can be shown that non-contributory pension programs are affordable for the majority of developing countries, and that program design parameters provide some means by which to manage their liabilities to demographic and macroeconomic change, in the final analysis public programs depend on public support and solidarity. The extent to which non-contributory pension programs are affordable for low income countries remains an issue (Smith and Subbarao 2003), and where aid funding might be required, global public support and solidarity are involved. It is the experience of developed and developing countries alike that concerns with old-age poverty and policy responses to it usually take priority over concerns with other vulnerable groups. Mulligan and Sala-i-Martin pursue this issue in detail in the context of contributory programs in developed countries (Mulligan and Sala-i-Martin 1999*b*, 1999*c*, 1999*a*). Attitudinal surveys provide evidence, across societies and age groups, to the effect that concerns over old-age poverty are strong and widely shared. Findings for Latin American countries from *Latinobarometro* confirm that a higher proportion of respondents support greater public expenditure on pensions (83.7 percent) than on unemployment insurance (73.4 percent) or defense (32.4 percent) (de Ferranti *et al.* 2000: 4).

Support for pensions is also shown to be consistent across age groups. Strong concerns about old-age poverty, and greater political support for programs targeted at poor older people, can be rationalized in a number of ways. Atkinson (1995) suggests that support for poor older people by the population at large is more likely to be forthcoming because old age is more easily verifiable and less subject to moral hazard, when compared to unemployment insurance for example. Mulligan and Sala-i-Martin (1999*b*) note the fact that non-contributory pensions are incentive compatible in the sense that recipients are less likely to alter their labor supply or saving behavior. Lund (1999) suggests that support for older people is more likely to be forthcoming as most people expect to be old one day, but perhaps not unemployed, or a single parent, or disabled.

Proposals for the establishment of non-contributory pension programs, and for their sustainability in countries where they exist, may well benefit from a natural reservoir of public support among the population at large. A case study examining the institutional sustainability of non-contributory pension programs in Brazil and South Africa (Barrientos 2004*a*) identified a number of factors. First, the programs embed a range of desirable redistribution. Non-contributory pensions combine redistribution to the poor with life course redistribution. They also combine urban–rural redistribution, which helps reduce migration to urban centers. Second, non-contributory pensions are especially effective in addressing old-age poverty among women, and can therefore play a role in reducing discrimination and exclusion. Third, non-contributory pensions are perceived to be effective, they are reasonably well targeted, abuse of the system is not a significant issue, and the administration of the benefit is reasonably effective and low cost. Fourth, non-contributory pensions have proved flexible in responding to problems arising from social and economic change. HIV/AIDS in South Africa, as well as labor migration, have led to a rise in the share of households in which grandparents take up a primary care role, and the social pension is generally perceived to be an effective instrument in providing support for these highly vulnerable households. In Brazil, it is generally agreed that rural pensions have played an important role in facilitating economic transformation in the rural sector, and in protecting households from the adverse effects of such change (Delgado and Cardoso 2000a).

In the context of developing countries in particular, it is important to consider non-contributory pension programs as a basis on which more encompassing poverty reduction programs can be developed. This involves extending widely shared concerns with old-age poverty to cover other groups. The high incidence of co-residence of older and younger people in developing countries noted above reinforces this as non-contributory pension programs support both older people and their households.[4]

## 5 CONCLUSIONS

The chapter began by arguing that pension policy in developing countries must be considered within the context of development and poverty reduction objectives. Old-age poverty is widespread in developing countries, and pension provision constitutes the key policy response. Pension provision in the South is mainly employment-based, and coverage is restricted to workers in formal employment. In contrast to the experience of today's developed nations, it is unlikely that existing pension provision in the South will gradually extend to cover all sections of the labor force and population. The share of informal employment in developing countries is high and growing, and unfunded pension plans there have been undermined by structural adjustment and crises. Securing effective and sustainable old-age support in the South requires thinking through alternative forms of pension arrangements, and the chapter set out to review and assess the experience of countries in the South, and especially Latin America, with developing pension programs that can reduce and prevent old-age poverty and contribute to the development process.

Non-contributory pension programs are rare in Latin America and other developing regions, but they are increasingly seen as an effective means of providing old-age support in the South. The studies reviewed in this chapter suggest that these programs can be effective in reducing poverty among older people and their households and are most effective in reducing extreme poverty or indigence.

Among selective non-contributory pension programs, poverty reduction effectiveness rises with the effectiveness of the selection instrument. The programs are also effective in facilitating the development process, through supporting investment in human capital and the productive capacity of households. These effects are stronger where the incidence of co-residence of young and old is higher. There is rising awareness that well-designed non-contributory pension programs can be a necessary and effective instrument within a development and poverty reduction strategy for countries in the South (HAI 2004).

A comparative analysis of non-contributory pension programs across a range of countries helps clarify how design and financing features can maximize their poverty reduction effectiveness, and also the conditions in which public support for the programs facilitate their introduction and sustainability. It was found that universal pension programs emphasize redistribution from young to old, and selective or targeted programs emphasize insurance. The selection instruments can have important effects upon incentives relating to saving, work, and living arrangements. Non-contributory pension programs are almost exclusively tax financed from central government revenues. Universal programs are more exposed to liabilities arising from demographic change, while selective or targeted programs are more exposed to macroeconomic conditions. Broadly, the relative costs of non-contributory pension programs are low, around 2 percent of GDP for universal programs, with targeted programs clustered around 0.3 percent. From the experience of developed and developing countries, it appears that social concerns with old-age poverty and with potential responses to it in the form of pension programs are widely shared. Non-contributory pension programs can provide a basis on which more extensive solidarity values can be built in developing countries.

While the discussion in the chapter aimed to provide a succinct and coherent review of non-contributory pension programs, it is important to stress that a number of areas require further research. Without exception, evaluations of non-contributory pension programs have been carried out a long time after the introduction of the program. Applying experimental or quasi-experimental methods of evaluation to newly implemented programs could enable more detailed examination of their effects. Our knowledge is very limited on, for example, household dynamics around the first receipt of pension benefits. These have the potential to both strengthen and undermine the effects of the programs on household welfare. Another important area for further research concerns the financial sustainability of non-contributory pension programs in the context of accelerated population ageing and restrictions on public finances arising from globalization. For low income countries, the potential role of international aid in supporting such programs needs serious consideration, especially in the context of a change in aid modalities favoring general budget support.

## NOTES

1. This is important in assessing the poverty reduction effectiveness of non-contributory pensions in the context of pension sharing.
2. A weakness of this approach is that it ignores household responses to such policy change, and the findings emerging from these studies can only be taken as a measure of first-order effects.
3. This is a very important distinction, even in situations where it appears blurred. All insurance programs generate *ex post* redistribution, from those who pay the policy premium to claimants, but this is different to *ex ante* redistribution, in both financial and political terms. Universal non-contributory pension programs can provide a safety net if benefits are set at an adequate level, but the distinction is still important because universal programs can be regressive if they redistribute from the short-lived poor to the long-lived rich (Barrientos 1998a, 1998b).
4. In countries where co-residence is the norm, counterposing the needs of the old and the young may be misplaced. James, for example, notes that 'one can argue that priority for social assistance should be given to young families with children, who have their entire lives ahead of them' (James 2001). For Brazil, Paes de Barros and Carvalho argue for the need to rebalance social expenditure away from pensions and toward families with children (Paes de Barros and Carvalho 2004), although this involves both contributory and non-contributory pension expenditure.


## REFERENCES

ARDINGTON, E., and LUND, F. (1995). 'Pensions and development: social security as complementary to programmes of reconstruction and development'. *Development Southern Africa*, 12/4: 557–77.

ATKINSON, A. B. (1995). 'Social insurance', in A. B. Atkinson (ed.), *Incomes and the Welfare State: Essays on Britain and Europe*. Cambridge: Cambridge University Press, 205–19.

BARRIENTOS, A. (1998a). *Pension Reform in Latin America*. Aldershot: Ashgate.

—— (1998b). 'Pension reform, personal pensions and gender differences in pension coverage'. *World Development*, 26/1: 125–37.

—— (1999). 'The emerging pension fund management market in Latin America'. *Journal of Pensions Management*, 5/1: 60–8.

—— (2004a). 'Cash transfers for older people reduce poverty and inequality'. Background Paper for WDR 06. Manchester: IDPM, University of Manchester.

—— (2004b). 'Latin America: towards a liberal-informal welfare regime', in I. Gough, G. Wood, A. Barrientos, P. Bevan, P. David, and G. Room (eds.), *Insecurity and Welfare Regimes in Asia, Africa and Latin America*. Cambridge: Cambridge University Press.

—— GORMAN, M., and HESLOP, A. (2003). 'Old age poverty in developing countries: contributions and dependence in later life'. *World Development*, 31/3: 555–70.

—— and LLOYD-SHERLOCK, P. (2003). 'Non-contributory pensions and poverty prevention: a comparative study of Brazil and South Africa'. Report. Manchester: IDPM and HelpAge International.

BEGUM, S. (2003). 'Pension and social security in Bangladesh'. Mimeo. Dhaka: Bangladesh Institute of Development Studies.

BERTRAND, M., MULLAINATHAN, S., and MILLER, D. (2003). 'Public policy and extended families: evidence from pensions in South Africa'. *World Bank Economic Review*, 17/1: 27–50.

BERTRANOU, F., and GRUSHKA, C. O. (2002). 'Beneficios sociales y pobreza en la Argentina', in Bertranou et al. (2002), *contributivas y asistenciales. Argentina, Brasil, Chile, Costa Rica y Uruguay*, 31–62.

——, SOLORIO, C., and VAN GINNEKEN, W. (2002). *Pensiones no-contributivas y asistenciales. Argentina, Brasil, Chile, Costa Rica y Uruguay*. Santiago: ILO.

CARVALHO, I. (2000*a*). 'Elderly women and their living arrangements'. Mimeo. Cambridge, Mass.: MIT.

—— (2000*b*). 'Household income as a determinant of child labor and school enrollment in Brazil: evidence from a social security reform'. Mimeo. Cambridge, Mass.: MIT.

—— (2000*c*). 'Old-age benefits and the labor supply of rural elderly in Brazil'. Mimeo. Cambridge, Mass.: MIT.

CASE, A. (2001). 'Does money protect health status? Evidence from South African pensions'. Mimeo. Princeton: Princeton University.

DE FERRANTI, D., PERRY, G. E., GILL, I. S., and SERVÉN, L. (2000). *Securing our Future in a Global Economy*. Washington, D.C.: The World Bank.

DEL POPOLO, F. (2001). 'Características sociodemográficas y socioeconómicas de las personas de edad en América Latina'. Serie Población y Desarrollo 16. Santiago: CELADE.

DELGADO, G. C., and CARDOSO, J. C. (2000*a*). 'Condicões de reproducão econômica e combate à pobreza', in Delgado and Cardoso (2000*c*).

—— —— (2000*b*). 'Principais Resultados da Pesquisa Domiciliar sobre a Previdência Rural na Região Sul do Brasil'. Discussion Paper 734. Rio de Janeiro: Instituto de Pesquisa Econômica Aplicada (IPEA).

—— —— (eds.) (2000*c*). *A Universalização de Direitos Sociais no Brazil: a Prêvidencia Rural nos anos 90*. Brasilia: IPEA.

DUFLO, E. (2000). 'Grandmothers and granddaughters: old age pension and intrahousehold allocation in South Africa'. Working Paper 8061. Cambridge, Mass.: National Bureau of Economic Research.

—— (2003). 'Grandmothers and granddaughters: old age pensions and intrahousehold allocation in South Africa'. *World Bank Economic Review*, 17/1: 1–25.

EDMONDS, E., MAMMEN, K., and MILLER, D. (2001). 'Rearranging the family? Household composition responses to large pension receipts'. Mimeo. Hanover, N.H.: Darmouth College.

GANA CORNEJO, P. A. (2002). 'Las pensiones no contributivas en Chile: pensiones asistenciales (PASIS)', in Bertranou C. et al. (2002).

HAI (2004). 'Age and security: how social pensions can deliver effective aid to poorer older people and their families'. Report. London: HelpAge International.

HOLZMAN, R., GILL, I. S., HINZ, R., IMPAVIDO, G., MUSALEM, A. R., RUTKOWSKI, M., and SCHWARZ, A. M. (2004). 'Old age income support in the 21st century: the World Bank's perspective on pension systems and reform'. Revised Draft. Washington, D.C.: The World Bank.

JAMES, E. (2001). 'Coverage under old age social security programs and protection for the uninsured: what are the issues?', in N. C. Lustig (ed.), *Shielding the Poor: Social Protection in the Developing World*. Washington, D.C.: Brookings Institution Press and InterAmerican Development Bank, 149–74.

KAKWANI, N., and SUBBARAO, K. (2005). 'Ageing and poverty in Africa and the role of social pensions'. Report. Washington, D.C.: The World Bank.

LUND, F. (1999). 'Understanding South African social security through recent household surveys: new opportunities and continuing gaps'. *Development Southern Africa*, 16/1: 55–67.

MESA-LAGO, C. (2001). 'Social assistance on pensions and health care for the poor in Latin America and the Caribbean', in N. C. Lustig (ed.), *Shielding the Poor: Social Protection in the Developing World*. Washington, D.C.: Brookings Institution Press and InterAmerican Development Bank, 175–216.

—— (2002). 'Myth and reality of pension reform: the Latin American evidence'. *World Development*, 30/8: 1309–21.

MULLIGAN, C. B., and SALA-I-MARTIN, X. (1999*a*). 'Gerontocracy, retirement, and social security'. NBER Working Paper 7117. Cambridge, Mass.: National Bureau of Economic Research.

—— —— (1999*b*). 'Social security in theory and practice (I): facts and political theories'. NBER Working Paper 7118, Cambridge, Mass.: National Bureau of Economic Research.

—— —— (1999*c*). 'Social security in theory and practice (II): efficiency theories, and implications for reform'. NBER Working Paper 7119. Cambridge, Mass.: National Bureau of Economic Research.

PAES DE BARROS, R., and CARVALHO, M. (2004). *Targeting as an Instrument for a More Effective Social Policy*. Washington, D.C.: Foro de Equidad Social.

PALACIOS, R., and PALLARÉS-MILLARES, M. (2000). 'International patterns of pension provision'. Pension Primer Paper. Washington, D.C.: The World Bank.

SALDAIN, R., and LORENZELLI, M. (2002). 'Estudio del programa de pensiones no contributivas an Uruguay', in Bertranou *et al.* (2002), 221–64.

SCHLEBERGER, E. (2002). 'Namibia's universal pension scheme: trends and challenges'. ESS Paper 6. Geneva: International Labour Organization.

SCHWARZ, A. M. (2003). 'Old age security and social pensions'. Mimeo. Washington, D.C.: The World Bank.

SCHWARZER, H. (2000). 'Impactos socioeconômicos do sistema de aposentadorias rurais no Brazil—evidências empíricas de un estudio de caso no estado de Pará'. Discussion Paper 729. Rio de Janeiro: IPEA.

—— and QUERINO, A. C. (2002). 'Non-contributory pensions in Brazil: the impact on poverty reduction'. ESS Paper 11. Geneva: Social Security Policy and Development Branch, ILO.

SMITH, W. J., and SUBBARAO, K. (2003). 'What role for safety net transfers in very low income countries?' Social Protection Discussion Paper 0301. Washington, D.C.: The World Bank.

WILLMORE, L. (2001). 'Universal pensions in low-income countries'. Mimeo. Washington, D.C.: Department for Economics and Social Affairs, United Nations.

—— (2003). 'Universal pensions in Mauritius: lessons for the rest of us'. DESA Discussion Paper 32. New York: United Nations Department of Economic and Social Affairs.

WORLD BANK (1994). *Averting the Old Age Crisis: Policies to Protect the Old and Promote Growth*. Oxford: Oxford University Press.

CHAPTER 40

# RETIREMENT INCOME SYSTEMS IN ASIA

## HANAM S. PHANG

## 1 INTRODUCTION

Traditionally in Asia, the extended family was the major sources of supplemental old-age income support (World Bank 1994: 49–67). Formal social security and pension systems in most of the Asian countries are relatively recent. Perhaps as a consequence, these formal systems are also less developed in both coverage and protection than in other parts of the world at comparable levels of economic development. In most Asian countries, the elderly, living in a welfare regime with minimal social security for retirement, tend to remain economically active until they become very old or disabled.

Two key social policy assumptions have emerged from past welfare regimes in the region. First, East Asian countries in the past had assumed that continued rapid economic growth and consequent reduction in poverty would suffice to take care of any social obligation for old-age income security. Second, policy-makers have generally regarded social security provision for the non-public sector labor force as essentially a private concern for employers, families, and local communities (Phillips 1999). The social security needs of individuals have been considered at most as secondary to economic growth and to the needs of the corporate sector (Asher 2000b). As a consequence, the role of the state in social security provision was very limited or had in large part been delegated to the private sector (ILO 2000: 500–1). This social policy perspective constrained the development of social security pensions for the private sector workforce while very generous public pension programs were the norm for public sector employees (in e.g. Korea, Taiwan, and Singapore).

With the rapid economic development that has characterizes the region in recent years, informal family support is gradually being replaced by public and/or private income security schemes. Industrialization and urbanization has drawn the rural self-employed population that had been engaged in farming into urban labor markets for paid employment. As a result, the number of employees as a percentage of the economically active population has increased significantly.

Countries in the region have developed a range of systems to provide people with income in old age. This chapter describes retirement income systems in East and Southeast Asian countries and discusses policy issues and reform initiatives across the region.

# 2 THE CHARACTERISTICS OF RETIREMENT INCOME SYSTEMS

## 2.1 Retirement Income Systems in Southeast Asian Countries

A striking feature of the region is the reliance on national provident fund systems. Singapore, Malaysia, Indonesia, and Hong Kong each have national provident fund systems which cover employees in the private sector (ILO 2000). Singapore has a Central Provident Fund introduced in the early 1950s by the British to provide social security for the civilian workforce, while adopting an independent pay-as-you-go (PAYG)-based pension scheme for civil servants and public sector employees. Malaysia has the Employee Provident Fund established in 1951 and Indonesia has had its Jamestek Provident Fund since 1992. This is mandatory for workplaces with at least ten workers. Hong Kong has recently introduced Mandatory Provident Fund in 2000.

These national provident funds have some unique features as retirement income systems (Asher 2000*b*). They operate as a sort of mandatory savings scheme based on individual accounts financed by defined contributions from employers and/or employees. As such they lack direct social risk pooling or redistributive mechanisms: whatever benefits individuals receive from the system is strictly dependent on his/her contribution records and wage levels. Second, these provident fund systems are usually designed to fulfill a comprehensive social security function, operating not only as retirement savings but also as a fund for housing, education, health care, disability, and unemployment during the working life (Asher 2000a). Advance withdrawals are normally allowed and more often than not substantial withdrawals are made. As a consequence they fall short of being a retirement pension scheme that provides long-term income after retirement. In many cases the fund is nearly depleted by the time of retirement and if there remains any balance then benefits will be exhausted within a few years (McCarthy et al. 2002).

## 2.2 Retirement Income Systems in East Asian Countries

Japan, China, and Korea have adopted a social insurance principle to provide people with retirement income security by setting up public as well as private pension schemes that cover part or all of their workforce and population.

### 2.2.1 The Japanese System

Japan has the oldest public pension system in East Asian countries. The earliest plan was one for military personnel, which was established in 1890 and later extended to civil servants. In 1942 a mandatory pension program for private sector employees, Employee Pension Insurance, was enacted as a defined benefit plan on a fully funded basis. In terms of coverage, a major improvement was the establishment of the National Pension Insurance (NPI) system in 1961. In a major pension reform in 1986 the NPI became a basic pension for both employed workers and the self-employed. Currently Japan has five social security pension schemes covering different sectors of the population and a set of well-established corporate pension plans of defined benefit (DB) or defined contribution (DC). The majority of private sector employees in Japan are also paid a lump-sum retirement allowance (Conrad 2001; Takayama 2004).

### 2.2.2 The Chinese System

In China, for many years the economic system was mainly socialist and the enterprises were mostly state-owned. The provision of old-age income security for employees was historically the responsibility of each state-owned enterprise (SOE). Workers in the public sector normally stayed at the same enterprise throughout their working lives and retired with very generous retirement pension benefits. The social security pension, first established in 1951, covered the employees of the SOEs, public institutions (schools, universities, healthcare institutions, and so on), plus a portion of urban collectives. This was largely an urban phenomenon as the SOEs were mostly urban-based. The vast population living in rural areas was left out of the system.

China's pension system has been extremely fragmented. Typically, each SOE established and financed its own benefit rates, while the central government controlled the rates for its enterprises. Despite variations between enterprises and regions, however, the overall level of benefit was generous compared even to other developed economies. The retirement age was 60 for men, 50 for non-managerial women, and 55 for managerial women. With a minimum contribution period for pension eligibility set at ten years, the average replacement rate was on average above 80 percent of final salary. The system was financed on a pay-as-you-go basis: a proportion of the operating funds from SOEs was the only source of funds for current retirees' pension benefits (Word Bank 1997).

Following the economic reforms in the 1980s and the move toward a market-based economy, the unfunded enterprise-sponsored pension plans became unsustainable. With many of the old industries declining, the non-competitive SOEs were left with increasing numbers of pensioners but little capacity to pay the defined pension benefits. In contrast, new industries and private enterprises with young workers and no pensioners rapidly developed out of open exports and foreign investments (James 2001). The need to extend the coverage of old-age pensions to include private sector workers and the rural population became pressing, while the pension benefits promised under the old regime were being paid to current state sector retirees (ILO 2000: 506–9).

The New Labor Law of 1994 stipulated that coverage should eventually be extended to all salaried workers regardless of the nature of their employment or ownership of the enterprise. The State Council Decree 26, issued in 1997 on setting up a unified basic old-age pension for urban workers, declared that coverage should be expanded to all enterprises and their workers, as well as to the self-employed. China's pension system is currently in a transition from an enterprise-based, fragmented system to a socially integrated 'safety net' scheme with extended coverage for workers, a transition from a fully pay-as-you-go system to a partially funded one with individual accounts (Whiteford 2001). This will be described in the following section.

### 2.2.3 *The Korean System*

The Korean pension system is relatively recent. The Korean National Pension was only introduced in 1988 and payment of full pension benefit will only start in 2008 when the first pensioners with the minimum contribution requirement of 20 years reach retirement. The National Pension scheme is a partially funded defined benefit plan and covers all private sector employees and the self-employed in both rural (since 1995) and urban areas (since 1999).

Korea has yet to introduce a corporate pension system. However, there is an extensive severance pay system. Under the Labor Standards Act, firms are required to pay workers leaving the firm one month's wages for every year of service. These retirement allowances, paid as a lump sum on retirement, serve a limited role in providing income support after retirement or, in case of job loss, prior to retirement (Phang 2001).

The Korean severance pay system is similar to that in Italy and Japan but with some notable differences. Italy probably comes closest to the Korean system in that severance pay is compulsory for all workers leaving the firm and there is a standard formula for calculating the minimum amount of the lump-sum payment. The Japanese system differs from the Korean RAS (Retirement Allowance Scheme) in that it is paid on a voluntary basis but with no standard formula for calculating these allowances (Keese and Lee 2002).

In 2005, Korea plans to introduce a so-called 'Employee Retirement Income Security Act' by which firms will be allowed to set up corporate pension plans—either DB or DC—that could replace the current RAS (Phang 2004).

# 3 Current Pension Arrangements and Pending Issues

## 3.1 Public and Private Pension Schemes in Japan

The Japanese public pension system is composed of two tiers. The first tier, National Pension Insurance (NPI) is a so-called 'basic pension' which provides a flat-rate benefit to the general population. In principle, all residents between the ages of 20 to 59 are required to make monthly flat-rate contributions to the system and basic pension benefits are based solely on the length of their participation. The system is run on a PAYG basis but one-third of the total benefit expenditure has been subsidized by the general budget. The second tier is an earnings-related defined benefit plan called Employees' Pension Insurance (EPI). It covers most employees in the private and public sectors. Employees in the private sector are insured by Employee Pension Insurance (EPI) and those in the public sector are insured by Mutual Aid Associations of their own.

In order to qualify for the old-age pension, the insured person must satisfy the eligibility conditions, a minimum 25 years of contribution out of a maximum 40 years. The normal retirement age under the National Pension Act is now 65, although the old-age pension is payable from 60 for those who were in the EPI before the 1986 pension reform. Under the provision, both a fixed amount of basic pension and the earnings-related pension benefit is paid from the EPI until the beneficiary reaches 65, after which basic pension is paid out of the NPI.

Japan also has private employer-based occupational pension schemes. There are three main types of company retirement plans in Japan: unfunded severance benefit plans, Employee Pension Funds (EPF), and Tax Qualified Pension Plans (TQPP). The latter two are mostly defined benefit plans and about half of all Japanese full-time employees participate in an EPF or a TQPP. More than 90 percent of all Japanese employees have severance pay plans that relate benefits to years of service and earnings, financed out of corporate operating revenue. Severance benefits are typically paid as lump sums when workers leave their career employers.

A characteristic of the Japanese pension system is that these company-based private pension plans are permitted to partially 'contract out' of the earnings-related part of the public EPI in return for lower contributions to the public system. EPF plans are required to pay a 'supplementary' pension benefit, which must not be less than 30 percent of the EPI (Conrad 2001).

Under the current benefit formula, a worker with 40 years of contributions would receive an earnings-related benefit of 30 percent of average real earnings. The flat-rate benefit for a married worker and spouse provides a total replacement rate of over 50 percent for most retirees (Miyatake 2000). Reforms implemented in 1994 gradually boosted the eligibility age for the NPI flat-rate benefit from 60 to 65, although eligibility for EPI benefits was maintained at 60 throughout the 1990s.

Japanese public pension plans, both the NPI and EPI, were designed to be capital funded. However, they rapidly transformed into a pay-as-you-go unfunded system due to rapid increases in benefit level, backed by the successful economic growth of the 1960s and 1970s, and increasing numbers of pension beneficiaries. Although the fund is substantial, it is insufficient to pay for current retirees and for the accrued benefits earned by current workers without a steep rise in contribution rates in the future. It is projected that if current benefit promises are maintained in the face of a rapidly ageing population, EPI tax rates would have to increase from 17.35 to 34.5 percent by 2025 and contributions to the NPI would have to rise by about 100 percent (Clark and Mitchell 2002).

A comprehensive review of the public pension system was conducted in the pension reform of 2000 and changes will be phased in over time. Future benefits will be cut in various ways: the benefit accrual rate will be cut from 0.75 to 0.715 per year of contribution; the indexation of the EPI and NPI benefits will be switched from wage to price indexation for pensioners aged 65 and over; and the normal retirement age for the EPI pension will be raised from 60 to 65 for both men and women.. The government subsidy to the NPI pension, meanwhile, will be raised from one-third to half of the total annual cost (Takayama 2004).

These changes introduced to improve the long-term viability of the system may create an intergenerational inequity by transferring most of the increasing pension costs to younger generations (Clark and Ogawa 1996). It is estimated that the cohorts born after the 1980s will receive less from the public pension schemes than they will have to pay into the current system. The situation would be worse if the government subsidy to the NPI (worth half the current cost) were taken out of the equation. Those born after the 1960s—the baby-boomers who will retire around 2020—may be worse off for having stayed in the public pension plan (Tajika 2002).

The economic recession in Japan during the 1990s also brought about deteriorating conditions for company-based private occupational pension schemes. Japanese pensions are significantly underfunded and occupational pension plans are therefore faced with a long-term problem of sustainability (Takayama 2004). The 2001 Pension Reform Bill introduced new defined benefit-type and defined contribution-type pension plans—modeled after the US 401(k) plan. The bill has, however, left many transitional issues unsolved (Clark and Mitchell 2002).

## 3.2 China's Public Pension System in Transition

The 1997 reform provisions of the social security pension in China have a two-tier structure. The first tier is a pay-as-you-go defined benefit plan with flat-rate basic benefits guaranteeing a replacement rate of 20 percent of regional wages at retirement. It is based on 15 years of contributions financed on a pay-as-you-go basis by a 13 percent payroll tax on employers. The second-tier pension is a defined contribution plan with individual accounts financed by a payroll tax of 11 percent (7 percent by employers, 4 percent by employees). The final benefit from the second-tier pension would depend on an individual's contribution history and earnings level plus returns from investment, providing a replacement of at least 38.5 percent of final wages for 35 years of contributions. The combined replacement rate of the first- and second-tier pension benefits will, then, be 58.5 percent for average wage-earners with 35 years of contributions, a drop of about 20 percent from the old system.

The success of China's pension reforms will depend critically on how and to what extent the second-tier individual account is funded while the old pension benefits owed to current retirees continue to be paid (Rosegrant 1999). After 1997, many municipalities set up both pooled accounts and individual accounts for enterprise workers. In almost all cases, however, the individual accounts were notional (e.g. these accounts existed on paper and were being credited with a certain rate of interest but no actual money was being saved or invested). Because of inadequate reserves, money that would have gone into individual accounts was going instead to pay pension obligations due to current retirees. In effect, pension benefits for current retirees have been paid out of the contributions collected for the second-tier pension. Actual payment into the second-tier accounts will have to wait until the new system is free of the liabilities under the old unfunded system. Because most individual accounts are empty, China's new pension system is essentially an unfunded pay-as-you-go system. This is a typical case of transition costs falling on the current generation of contributors, a serious challenge to a successful transition from an unfunded to a funded pension system (James 2001; McCarthy and Zheng 1996).

The problems threatening the viability of the new system are compounded by a rapidly ageing population, with increasing numbers of SOE retirees, and declining numbers of SOE sector workers to pay the contributions. The new system is also suffering from widespread non-compliance and corruption while the local and central government agencies lack the means for proper regulatory enforcement.

Underreporting of wages, misuse of early retirement privileges, and overreporting of years of service for retiring workers are reportedly widespread (James 2001). The low rate of compliance and high incidence of irregularity are mainly an outcome of the strong disincentives in the current provision. While transition to a centralized funded system is still incomplete, local enterprises continue to be burdened with paying pension benefits to their retired employees. For the non-SOE private enterprises, the newly applied system means a heavy payroll tax for employers, with part of their contributions being used to subsidize the old SOEs' retired workers' pensions. Their own employees are forced to receive a lower rate of return from the second-tier fund investment where the return rate is centrally administered (Takayama 2002).

China's venture of transforming an enterprise-based unfunded PAYG pension system into a pre-funded, centrally managed system is not an easy mission by any standards. It may simply prove impossible, in a country with a planned economy in transition to a market economy, to finance both the massive pension liabilities from the past and the new earnings-related funded scheme of the present. Current pension contributions in the state sector came to around 23 percent in 1999, while the new scheme requires another 11 percent, making a total contribution rate of around 34 percent of earnings. This is too high even by European standards and is 14 percent above the ceiling of 20 percent laid down by the State Council 2000. The contribution rate may prove too high to be successfully enforced, and more feasible and low-cost reform options should have been considered (Takayama 2002).

## 3.3 Korean Public Pension System at a Crossroads

The National Pension Scheme (NPS) and Special Occupational Pensions (SOP) constitute Korea's public old-age pensions. Since its introduction in 1988, the coverage of the NPS has been extended progressively to cover, in theory, all private sector employees and the self-employed. While coverage is now compulsory for all regular employees in workplaces, it is voluntary for other types of workers such as part-time employees and family workers. Currently, only around 50 percent of the labor force is effectively covered. This large discrepancy between formal and effective coverage of the NPS is in large part due to high rates of system evasion and non-contribution, predominantly among the self-employed (Phang 2004).

The current contribution rate for the NPS, which employer and employee share half-and-half, is set at 9 percent of the standard monthly wage. Contribution rates for the self-employed started from 3.0 percent in 1995, when the system was applicable only to the rural self-employed (farmers), and then increased by 1 percent per year, reaching 9 percent by 2005.

Workers become eligible for old-age pension once they reach 60 years of age and have a contribution record of at least 20 years. For workers with average earnings, the accrual rate is 1.5 percent of earnings per year of contribution and workers with 40 years of contributions will receive 60 percent of their former wages. According to the NPS's benefit formula, the level of an individual's pension benefit depends both on the average wage of all insured persons in the year prior to retirement and on the individual's own wages averaged over the entire period for which contributions were made. The benefit formula has a redistributive element: workers with lower than average earnings receive a benefit that is higher relative to their former earnings than workers with higher than average earnings.

These SOP schemes are all defined benefit schemes that guarantee a maximum 76 percent of the final three-year average salary (for minimum 20-year, maximum 33-year contribution). For certain categories of employee (civil servants, private school teachers and military personnel), a special retirement allowance that amounts to a variable percentage (10–60 percent) of the monthly salary, depending on length of service, is accrued for each year of service, payable as a lump sum at the time of retirement. The contribution rates for the SOP schemes for government employees are currently set at 17 percent, divided equally between the employee and the government.

Recognizing that the system will not be financially sustainable even without the changing demographic situation, in 1998 the Korean government reduced the promised pension benefit by about ten percentage points (from a 70 percent replacement rate to 60 percent). The 2003 reform proposed another benefit cut, further reducing the promised replacement rate from 60 to 55 percent, raising the normal retirement age from 60 to 65, and increasing the contribution rate to over 16 percent by 2025.

These reforms, without which the system was projected to run into deficit by 2047, seem to be unavoidable to improve the long-term sustainability of the National Pension system. Nevertheless, such major changes to a public scheme that has not yet started paying out full pensions has undermined the credibility of the public pension scheme, which may in turn lead to a high rate of evasion and illegal non-contribution (Phang 2004; World Bank 2000). The scheduled increase in contribution rates will also strengthen the incentives to stay out of the system, especially among low income workers.

Being a partially funded system in its early accumulation stage, the NPS will continue to run surpluses and keep accumulating reserves for the next 30 years or so. Even under current contribution rates, the NPS reserves are projected to grow to 50 percent of GDP by around 2040 and up to 100 percent under projected rate increases. While the NPS fund is managed and invested by a government agency, the National Pension Corporation, the important question is to what extent these surpluses will actually be invested productively in the domestic market. The sheer size of the pension fund accumulating will raise important questions about the role of the NPS in capital markets, issues of corporate governance, and pose potential conflicts of interests for the government in its role both as institutional investor and as the regulator of financial markets (World Bank 2000).

The SOP schemes are also suffering from serious under-funding. The Government employee's scheme has been in deficit since 1998 and is financially depleted in 2001. The scale of the underfunding is projected to increase rapidly over time. The SOP for military personnel is worse: the fund was depleted way back in 1977 and has been subsidized by the government. The state of the SOP for private school teachers is a little better than the other two schemes, but it is also projected to run into deficit in 2012 and will be depleted in 2018 if the current scheme continues.

This severe financing problem affecting the SOP schemes is mainly due to poor initial benefit-contribution design, and failure to reform the system at the right time thereafter (Moon 2002). It is projected that, to meet current pension promises, the contribution rate will have to be raised eventually to 30–35 percent. This would place an excessive financial burden on future generations and require an increasing government subsidy.

# 4 THE PROVIDENT FUNDS IN SOUTHEAST ASIAN COUNTRIES

## 4.1 Malaysia: Employee Provident Fund

Malaysia's Employee Provident Fund (EPF) established in 1951 is a funded defined contribution scheme for private sector employees. For civil servants an unfunded defined benefit plan is in place. The contribution rate for the EPF is currently 23 percent (12 percent from the employer and 11 percent from the employee). Within the EPF there are separate accounts for retirement savings (Account One), housing (Account Two), and education and health (Account Three). The identification of these accounts, however, is only nominal and withdrawals are allowed of up to 40 percent of the accumulated fund.

The EPF accumulated assets worth almost 50 percent of the GDP in 2003. The investment portfolio is centrally regulated by the government with a guaranteed minimum rate of return of 2.5 percent per annum. Investment choices are restricted. The majority (70 percent) of the fund is invested by government regulation in Malaysian government securities for social and economic development, while investment in equities is limited to a maximum of 25 percent (Thillainathan 2004).

## 4.2 Singapore: CPF

Singapore, with its high income and rapidly ageing society, is unique in relying on a single mandatory savings scheme, the Central Provident Fund (CPF), to finance retirement income for private sector employees. Established by the British in the early 1950s, the CPF is a multi-purpose fund with a number of schemes: for homeownership, health care, investment in properties, shares, and commodities, and loans for education. For government employees and civil servants there is a Government Pension Fund.

The contribution rate to the CPF varies with age. For the main age group (33–55) the total contribution rate is fairly high at 33 percent (13 percent by the employer; 20 percent by the employee), whereas it is much lower for older age groups (18.5 percent for 55–60; 8.5 percent for 65 and older). About 58 percent of the total labor force is actively contributing to the fund. The CPF has also accumulated assets worth 62 percent of the GDP in Singapore. The CPF is invested in non-marketable government securities with the guarantee of a nominal interest rate of 2.5 percent per annum.

As with Malaysia's EPF, the CPF also has three separate accounts set up for different purposes: Ordinary Account, Medisave Account, and Special Account. Individuals' contributions are distributed to different accounts in predetermined proportions, with the Ordinary Account taking the most. Withdrawals are permitted within a limit. The ratio of withdrawals to contributions over the period 1987–2002, was about 79 percent, which indicates that less than a quarter of the total contributions are available for retirement income purposes (Asher 2004).

## 4.3 Indonesia: JPF

Indonesia, like Malaysia and Singapore, has a provident fund system for private sector employees (Jamsostek Provident Fund: JPF) established in 1992. It is mandatory for workplaces with ten or more employees. The JPF provides a lump-sum payment on retirement at 55. Retirees may choose to take out an annuity if their accumulated fund is more than Rp 3 million. It is funded by employer (3.7 percent) and employee (2 percent) contributions.

The rate of return for the fund is determined by the government. Currently the fund has accumulated assets worth 1.3 percent of GDP, which is very low when compared to the Provident Funds of Malaysia and Singapore. Civil servants make a monthly contribution of 8 percent of their salary to an independent pension scheme for government employees. Any shortfall in benefit expenditure is met by the government.

The Indonesian government proposed a National Security System in 2004 to integrate the various social security programs (provident fund, health maintenance, life insurance, work-accident protection) in one unified system. The proposal needs to be further developed and clear transitional rules need to be specified for each scheme to be included under the unified system (Rachmatarwata 2004).

## 4.4 Hong Kong: MPF

Hong Kong has the second highest percentage of old people in Asia after Japan. With an exceptionally low fertility rate (1.2) and long life expectancy (80), the dependency ratio is expected to roughly triple between 2000 and 2050. There was no mandatory scheme of old-age income protection in Hong Kong before the Mandatory Provident Fund (MPF) was introduced in 1995. Hong Kong instead relied on the Social Security Allowance Scheme (SSAS) and the Comprehensive Social Security Assistance (CSSA) scheme for zero-pillar public assistance. The SSAS provides non-means-tested flat-rate allowances for all elderly individuals (aged 65 and over) and the CSSA is a means-tested scheme for elderly individuals and others in need. The two social safety-net schemes are mutually exclusive (Chi 2004).

The MPF scheme is quite different from the government-run central provident funds. It is a privately managed defined contribution plan for the exclusive purpose of retirement income security. The MPF covers all employees and the self-employed between the ages of 18 and 65. In 2003, about 63 percent of the working population had joined the MPF scheme. Both the employer and the employee contribute 5 percent of payroll. The self-employed pay the employee contribution rate of 5 percent but not the employer contribution rate. Compliance rates of both employers and the self-employed are reported to be reasonably high (above 85 percent).

## 4.5 Other Countries

The Philippines, thanks to its colonial past, is one of a few Southeast Asian countries which has adopted a social insurance principle to provide social security benefits for the general population. The Social Security System (SSS) set up in 1954 and the Government Service Insurance System (GSIS) set up in 1936 are partially funded PAYG systems that administer retirement, death, and disability schemes for private sector employees and for public sector employees respectively.

Thailand's Social Security Act introduced in 1990 purports to provide social security protections against social risks (sickness, maternity, invalidity, and death) for the general public. But its impact, so far, is very limited as the proportion of active contributors to the system has been very low (around 10 percent of the total labor force as of 1993). Only about 20 percent of the labor force is reportedly covered by the retirement pension program introduced in 1999. The social security programs are financed on a tripartite basis, with the employer, employee, and government each paying an equal share of 1.5 percent of wages up to a ceiling of 4.5 percent. The self-employed were recently included in the system (in 1995) and pay their own premium with a matching contribution from the government.

# 5 Evaluations and Future Challenges

## 5.1 The Provident Fund System of the Southeast Asian Countries

The provident pension systems in South East Asian countries can provide only limited security for retirement income. In Malaysia, Singapore, and Indonesia people withdraw a substantial portion of their accumulated provident fund for consumption during their working life and thus undersave for retirement. Between 1994 and 1997, about 80 percent of the withdrawals from the CPF in Singapore, for example, were pre-retirement withdrawals and the median balance was estimated to be only about two years of mean wage (Asher 2004). It is now well recognized that the CPF system, even with its high contribution rate (30 percent) is unlikely to meet the retirement income needs of a significant portion of the population, and the situation with other provident funds in Malaysia and Indonesia is no better (James and Vittas 1996). A further source of risk to the income security of retirees in many Asian countries where life expectancy is rising rapidly is the practice of paying out retirement benefits as a lump sum, rather than as an annuity. This leaves many retirees exposed to the risk of outliving their pension income.

For any pre-funded retirement system, investment policies and performance are of crucial importance. Funds for retirement income should be invested in a prudent yet remunerative manner in the best interests of the contributors. In the provident fund systems currently operating in Asian countries, the government determines the use of the funds and sets the rate of return, making it highly probable that political considerations become involved in setting up investment portfolios. Nevertheless, investment risks are still borne by individual participants. The result is low returns and low public confidence in the system. In addition investment in underdeveloped domestic financial markets has resulted in a lower return to the fund than would have been possible otherwise. These issues have led some experts to call for a reform of the provident fund system so as to provide more choice for members in allocating and investing their balances (Asher 2000*b*).

## 5.2 The Public and Private Pension Systems of East Asian Countries

The most obvious problem with social security or public pension systems in East Asian countries is the very limited coverage of the population and workforce. In many Asian countries the majority of people employed in small enterprises or in the informal sector do not participate in retirement pension plans (ILO 2000: 499–514). China's public pension is among the most limited in its effective coverage. Leaving aside the rural population and the self-employed, who comprise more than 70 percent of the population, only 46 percent of the urban labor force is covered by the system (Chen 2004). It is practically limited to employees of the state-owned enterprises (SOEs).

The problem of very limited coverage is, however, even more serious in many of the Southeast Asian countries. For instance, in Indonesia only about 10 percent of the population or around 20 percent of the labor force is covered by any public provident fund or pension plan (Rachmatarwata 2004). In Thailand only 10 percent of the total labor force actively contribute to the social security schemes (sickness, maternity, invalidity, and death benefits), while about 20 percent of the labor force is covered by the Old-Age Pension Fund newly introduced in 1999 (Kanjanaphoomin 2004).

The problem of non-participation or limited coverage of private sector employees and self-employed people is particularly acute. The majority of them are employed in small enterprises or engaged in subsistence-level small businesses and they are the most vulnerable to the risk of old-age poverty. The expansion of pension coverage in Asian countries will be dependent, in large part, on the growth of waged employment in the formal sector.

Formal coverage is not the only issue. Effective coverage and active contribution also matter a lot for a national pension system to be financially healthy and effective. Pension systems in many East Asian countries are suffering from high rates of evasion and low rates of active participation. For instance, in theory, the coverage of the Korean National Pension is universal but its active participation is considerably lower because of high rates of non-contribution among those working in small businesses. More than 40 percent of the self-employed, even though they are formally covered, are reportedly not contributing to the system for various reasons (such as lack of income, unemployment, having gone out of business). Large-scale underreporting of income by the self-employed, in contrast to the payroll tax of employed workers, is another serious problem undermining the National Pension's policy of social equity (Phang 2004).

The issue of equity between sectors of the population is also important. In Japan, the National Pension Insurance for the self-employed is heavily cross-subsidized by the Employee Pension Fund for employed workers. This occurs because the cost of the basic pension is shared by the NPI and EPI and the share is based on the number of contributors instead of the number of beneficiaries. As the active contribution rate among the self-employed is much lower than that among employed workers, it is argued that salaried workers will keep supporting the self-employed for their old-age income security (Tajika 2002).

Another key issue concerns intergenerational equity. The target replacement rate of the public pension in these countries was set too high and, after a few decades of running, the system is now faced with a serious future funding problem as is the case with Japan, Korea, and China. Their public pension systems started with overly generous pension promises and those promises, in the face of a rapid ageing population and macroeconomic reform, will either not be kept or will be considerably watered down in the future. How to achieve equity between the generations will remain an issue for a long time to come.

Retirement income systems in East Asian countries need to be developed so that public and private pension schemes become more integrated and balanced. In one part of the region (East Asian countries), the social security pension based on the pooling of social risk was designed to be too generous and is often too costly to maintain, leaving little room for private pension providers to step in and share the role (e.g. Korea, China). In other parts of the region (Southeast Asian countries), the pooling of social risk is totally ignored under the mandatory savings scheme based on individual accounts in the national provident fund systems. In an ideal multi-pillar system, old-age income security would be achieved through a balanced sharing of roles between the public and private sectors.

Finally, East Asian Countries will be affected by a rapidly ageing population in the first part of the twenty-first century. In 2000 Japan already had an elderly population of over 23 percent. In the next 20 to 30 years, the population aged over 60 in China and South Korea is projected to rise by 20–25 percent. Hong Kong and Singapore are in a similar situation with their old-age dependency ratios being expected to rise above 30 percent by 2025 and 50 percent by 2050. Such a rapid ageing of the population will pose a serious challenge to the long-term financial sustainability of the pension systems in those countries. Without a properly designed and well-managed old-age income security system, it will be very difficult for East Asian countries to cope with the challenges of supporting their population in their old age (McCarthy and Zheng 1996).

# References

ASHER, M. G. (2000a). 'Social security reforms in Southeast Asia'. Paper presented at WBI Workshop on Pension Reform. Washington, D.C.: World Bank Institute (6–17 Mar.).
—— (2000b). 'South East Asian provident and pension funds: investment policies and performance'. Paper presented at WBI Workshop on Pension Reform. Washington, D.C.: World Bank Institute (6–17 Mar.).
—— (2004). 'Retirement financing dilemmas facing Singapore'. PIE Working Paper 199. Tokyo: IER, Hitotsubashi University.
CHEN, V. Y. (2004). 'A macro analysis of China pension pooling system: incentive issues and financial problem'. PIE Working Paper 195. Tokyo: IER, Hitotsubashi University.
CHI, I. (2004). 'Retirement income protection in Hong Kong'. PIE Working Paper 200. Tokyo: IER, Hitotsubashi University.
CLARK, R. L. and MITCHELL, O. S. (2002). 'Strengthening employment-based pensions in Japan'. Discussion Paper PI-0201. The Pensions Institute, University of London.
—— and OGAWA, N. (1996). 'Public attitudes and concerns about population ageing in Japan'. *Ageing and Society*, 14/4: 190–208.
CONRAD, H. (2001). *The Japanese Social Security System in Transition—An Evaluation of Current Pension Reforms*. Tokyo: Deutsches Institut für Japanstudien.
ILO (2000). 'Regional brief 1: Asia and the Pacific', in C. Gillion, J. Turner, C. Bailey, and D. Latulippe (eds.), *Social Security Pensions: Development and Reform*. Geneva: International Labour Office, 499–514.
JAMES, E. (2001). 'How can China solve its old age security problem? The interaction between pension, SOE and financial market reform'. *Journal of Pension Economics and Finance*, 1/1: 53–75.
—— and VITTAS, D. (1996). 'Mandatory savings schemes: are they an answer to the old age security problem?' in Z. Bodie, O. S. Mitchell, and J. A. Turner (eds.), *Securing Employer-Based Pensions*. Philadelphia: University of Pennsylvania Press, 151–82.
KANJANAPHOOMIN, N. (2004). 'Pension fund, provident fund and social security system in Thailand'. PIE Working Paper 201. Tokyo: IER, Hitotsubashi University.

KEESE, M., and LEE, J. (2002). 'Older but wiser: achieving better labour market prospects for older workers in Korea'. OECD Labour Market and Social Policy Working Paper. Paris: OECD.

McCARTHY, DAVID, MITCHELL, O. and PIGGOTT, J. (2002). 'Asset rich and cash poor: retirement provision and housing policy in Singapore'. *Journal of Pension Economics and Finance*, 1/3: 197–222.

—— and ZHENG, K. (1996). 'Population aging and pension systems: reform options for China'. Policy Research Working Paper 1607. Washington, D.C.: The World Bank.

MIYATAKE, G. (2000). *Social Security in Japan*. Tokyo: Foreign Press Center.

MOON, H. (2002). 'Korean pension system: current state and future agenda'. Paper presented at the INPRS(OECD) Conference on Pensions in Asia (24–5 Oct.), Seoul, Korea.

PHANG, H. (2001). 'Reform options for Korean retirement allowance system'. Paper presented at the International Workshop on Korean Pension Reform in Transition (Mar.), Hong Kong, China.

—— (2004). 'The past and future of Korean pension system: a proposal for coordinated development of public and private pensions'. PIE Working Paper 196. Tokyo: IER, Hitotsubashi University.

PHILLIPS, D. R. (1999). 'Issues and constraints in developing services for old people in the Asia-Pacific region today'. Discussion Paper for the Meeting of the Asia Development Research Forum(ADRF), Seoul (4–5 June).

RACHMATARWATA, I. (2004). 'Indonesian pension system: where to go?' PIE Working Paper 198. Tokyo: IER, Hitotsubashi University.

ROSEGRANT, S. (1999). 'Pension reform in China: weighing the alternatives'. Paper presented at WBI Workshop on Pension Reform. Washington, D.C.: World Bank Institute (6–17 Mar.).

TAJIKA, E. (2002). 'The public pension system in Japan: the consequences of rapid expansion'. WBI Working Paper SN 37203. Washington, D.C.: The World Bank.

—— (2002). 'Pension reform of PRC: incentives, governance and policy options'. Paper presented at the ADB Institute, Conference on Challenges and New Agenda for PRC (5–6 Dec.), Tokyo.

—— (2004). 'The Japanese pension system: how it was and what it will be?' PIE Working Paper 194. Tokyo: IER, Hitotsubashi University.

THILLAINATHAN, R. (2004). 'Malaysia: pension and financial market reforms and key issues on governance'. PIE Working Paper 197. Tokyo: IER, Hitotsubashi University.

WHITEFORD, P. (2001). 'From enterprise protection to social protection: social security reform in China'. Discussion Paper. Paris: OECD.

WORLD BANK (1994). *Averting the Old Age Crisis: Policies to Protect the Old and Promote Growth*. New York: Oxford University Press.

—— (1997). *China 2020: Old Age Security and Pension Reform in China*. Washington, D.C.: World Bank.

—— (2000). 'The Korean pension system at a crossroads'. Report No. 20404-KO. Washington, D.C.: World Bank.

CHAPTER 41

# PENSIONS IN AFRICA

## ANTHONY ASHER

## 1 INTRODUCTION

In providing an outline of pension arrangements in Africa, this chapter is particularly concerned with justice. Justice is the traditional criterion for evaluating the performance of governing structures, and this book is intended to describe the theoretical frameworks used to understand the structure and performance of retirement systems. For our purposes, justice can be evaluated by determining whether the policy concerned strives, in a procedurally just manner, to reconcile five sometimes conflicting objectives: equality, liberty, efficiency, provision for people's basic needs, and recognition of their deserts. The main issues raised in this chapter are those where policy appears to fail in achieving these objectives.

Perhaps the thorniest African issues are those of compulsion and governance. Compulsory contributions are an affront to liberty, but are justified on the ground that they provide for basic needs that people would otherwise not provide for themselves, and on the ground of desert, in that people should pay for benefits that the state would otherwise have to provide. Compulsion is also more efficient in that voluntary contributions invariably attract significant marketing costs. In the informal sector however, compulsion is enormously expensive and creates further inequality by acting as an additional tax on the financial and administrative resources of the poor.

On the issue of governance, many would agree with Barbone and Sanchez (1999) that it is the 'first order of business' for retirement reform in Sub-Sahara particularly. The inefficiency and corruption of many government structures are clearly unjust. A specific issue in pension arrangements is actuarial fairness that requires the accruing value of future benefits to be closely related to contributions—real or notional. This is a question of desert, and departures ought to be justified as a contribution to greater equality, or as the provision of basic needs. In Africa, this is a particular problem with civil service schemes.

The chapter is organized as follows. The next section provides some background on the economies of Africa, a short discussion on the causes of poverty, and a description of the informal sector. This is followed by a relatively detailed description of the South African pension system. Apart from the author's familiarity with South Africa, its subsistence and informal sectors have much in common with the rest of Africa, while both its public and private sectors provide a number of models for potential development. Its policy-makers and entrepreneurs have a growing influence on other African countries, particularly in southern Africa. Section 4 extends the description to other African countries. A final section also raises some research questions.

## 2 Background

### 2.1 African Economies

Africa makes up almost a quarter of the world's land surface, one-eighth of its people, but only 4 percent of its economy even on a purchasing power parity (PPP) basis.[1] For purposes of this chapter, we can divide it into three. South Africa has a diversified modern economy and accounts for some quarter of total economic output, with the balance divided more or less equally between the five Mediterranean countries (including Morocco) and the rest of the continent. In terms of per capita income, on a purchasing power parity basis, South Africa is a medium low income country standing at something under $10,000; the North African countries stand at half of this, while the other Sub-Saharan countries average one-tenth.

All African economies are relatively small and concentrated—often dependent on a single commodity. The implication is that all are volatile, and subject to periodic bouts of currency fluctuations and high inflation, except where there are tight foreign exchange controls. This provides one explanation for extensive government intervention in the economy, with its consequential restrictions on private activity and risk of corruption. Economic instability is also invariably linked to political volatility.

These economic and political risks undermine the security that might be offered by a pension system. It is often not possible to find local investments to provide sufficient diversification. Those that are available will not provide security in times of political and economic uncertainty.

## 2.2 Poverty

Of the various explanations for poverty, Sachs *et al.* (2001) offer little hope in that they suggest that geography is a major cause. The tropics, which include most of the world's poverty and very few prosperous nations, are debilitating environments. In addition, Africa is served by relatively few harbours and navigable rivers, significantly increasing the cost of transport and trade.

Other analyses relate to institutions and culture, which are not immutable. In economically fragile societies with poorly understood informal institutions, apparently sensible reforms can be counterproductive. Institutional obstacles to development have been highlighted recently by De Soto (2000), in particular that most property cannot be sold, so tying people to their existing land rights and preventing land from being used as capital. He also describes the multiple bureaucratic obstacles to business development in all poorer countries, which often goes hand in hand with corruption. On these points, it can be noted that unmarketable land rights do function as retirement assets and alternatives will need to be found if they can be sold. As already noted, the imposition of formal social security contributions contributes to the bureaucratic burden on enterprise.

Of those who focus on cultural and political issues, Landes (1998) mentions openness to science and trade, trust within society, open government, and the value placed on hard work. These are also issues covered by Powelson (1994), who emphasizes the benefits of a diffusion of power in society, both as a counter to corruption and a source of personal responsibility and motivation. The South African experience described later shows that private retirement funds with democratically elected trustees can contribute to such diffusion.

Somavia (2003), Director General of the International Labour Office (ILO), surveys the immediate causes of poverty: malnutrition and illiteracy, lack of access to markets and capital, and corruption. He calls for the transfer of resources to the poor, debt relief, and the extension of a developed legal and institutional framework. The need for a system of social security to break the life-cycle of poverty is a major goal of the ILO.

## 2.3 The Informal Sector

Somavia looks at various elements of the informal economy, which accounts for the overwhelming proportion of employment in Africa, and its interaction with poverty. The informal economy can be defined as that beyond state control: untaxed, unregulated, and not using formal legal or accounting systems. It includes subsistence farmers, micro-scale traders and manufacturers, and many domestic workers.

The disadvantages of the informal economy are obvious. Efficiency is low as the division of labor is much more difficult and economies of scale impossible. Access to credit and insurance is limited by the absence of records and formal dispute resolution mechanisms. The latter is also associated with violence. Literacy is of less value, and is therefore encouraged less in the young, which also means that skills are less likely to be passed on. The smaller tax base limits the ability of governments to develop infrastructure and provide social services.

The informal sector, by definition, precludes formal pension arrangements. Outside formal organizations, wage-related contributions cannot be collected; money cannot be securely invested, and structured payouts cannot be managed. While formal systems have clear advantages over informal arrangements, it is not clear that the ILO and other agencies understand the significant demands they place on participants. If the demands cannot be met, the costs and the disruption of attempting to create formal systems may outweigh the advantages.

There are also unstable smaller employers on the fringe of the informal sector. Yakoboski *et al.* (2001) report the results of their US research which suggests that these employers, and their employees, are reluctant to contribute to formal pension arrangements because of their uncertain future, and the expense of contributing on behalf of lower income individuals. It may be better to use persuasion rather than compulsion to bring them into formal pension schemes.

# 3 South Africa

## 3.1 The First Pillar

The first pillar consists of a flat pension, subsidies to old-age homes, and other support to the needy living alone or with their families. The state's resources are inadequate from many perspectives, but it would seem that the positive social impact does justify the costs.

The main benefit is a monthly old-age pension paid out of general revenue, subject to a means test, to men above the age of 65 and women over 60. Recipients must be South African citizens resident in South Africa. The amount, R740 (R3 is approximately U$1 using PPP) monthly for the 2005 fiscal year, although low by OECD standards, is a generous 45 percent of GDP per capita.

### 3.1.1 *Administration*

The Mothers and Fathers Report (2001) contains the following comments that give a flavor of the African setting:

> The predominant method of pension receipt, namely queuing on particular days at a specified pay-point, and the problems associated with this over-shadowed all other problems faced by the elderly... Security at pay-points is a great concern of pensioners, particularly when they have to return home after dark... The length of time spent in the queue, lack of shelter, seating, insufficient and filthy toilets and lack of water at pay points are problems across the country. Even where there are halls, pensioners are not necessarily allowed into them...
> 
> People continue to arrive very early and to sleep at pay-points. No preference is given to the very frail who have to wait in line along with everyone else... Many pensioners experience rough and insulting treatment by staff at pay-points...
> 
> Money lenders are active at pay points, take IDs (identity documents)... and harass pensioners. Hawkers and liquor vendors also cause problems... A large number of burial societies, largely unregistered, try to recruit pensioners.... Security officers accept bribes to let people jump the queues. There are also allegations that pensioners are short-changed by officials...... Pensioners in hospital have to make their way to pay-points on pension day or face the prospect of losing their pension. Some have died in the queue.

Perhaps the most difficult administration issue arises from the bureaucratic need for rules to determine whether the pensioners are still alive. It seems that such rules often become unreasonable. The South African courts (prompted by non-government organization-funded lawyers) are sufficiently reliable to provide some protection, and have recently found certain pension administration to be unjustifiable. One practice that has been outlawed is stopping payment unilaterally in an attempt to counter fraud, and refusing to make back-payments in an attempt to save money.

### 3.1.2 *Means Tests*

An income test phases out the pension at a rate of 50 percent of other income.[2] Married couples with a combined income over R3,384 do not qualify for any state pension. Those with assets (excluding their homes) of more than R266,000 also do not qualify.[3]

Lund (1993) reports that the mechanism is widely misunderstood and inconsistently applied. This should not be surprising. The difficulties of auditing income are immense. Apart from those who are obviously cheating, one just has to think of determining income from casual jobs and the renting of rooms, and of irregular interest, pensions, and transfer payments, let alone translating income in kind from subsistence farming.[4] The means test is not, and probably cannot be, enforced. Unenforceable policy is bad policy.

If this were not enough, it is also inefficient. The distribution of income and the failure to implement the test mean that the pension is paid to almost 85 percent of old-age pensioners. The Smith Committee (1995) estimated that the costs of abolishing the test would be some R1.5 billion of which two-thirds could be recovered through the tax system. This is entirely dwarfed by tax concessions to retirement funds that are justified by the putative savings created by the means tests. The test also offends vertical equity in that the maximum rate of tax levied on high incomes is currently set at 42 percent while poorer pensioners lose 50 percent of the state old age pension for every rand of private income. Willmore (2001) expresses surprise that it has not been abolished. International agencies suggesting the introduction of means tests may well do more harm than good.

### 3.1.3 *Non-citizens*

Rules to determine the benefits to be enjoyed by immigrants require some balance between equality, need, desert, and affordability. This is of particular concern in South Africa where the state old-age pension is significantly larger than anything offered by its immediate neighbors. As in many similar situations, the rules governing the acquisition of citizenship can be contested at times.

### 3.1.4 *Social Impact*

The Smith Committee (1995) records that the amount payable to whites was some eight times that payable to blacks in the mid-1960s, but subsequent reforms led to final equalization in 1993. Even before equalization, social pensions provided an important source of income, particularly in poor rural areas. Ardington and Lund's (1994) study in Kwazulu Natal found that the pension income made up more than half the income of a third of rural households. Not only does the pension relieve poverty among the elderly, it turns old people into economic assets rather than liabilities to their families, and it seemed unlikely to create incentives that might distort the labor market or fertility behavior. Case (2001) confirmed that families with the pension, if it was shared within the family, enjoyed measurably better nutrition and health.

Bertrand *et al.* (2003) introduce an element of skepticism with their findings that labor market participation of working-age adults in extended families is lower in families with the pension, declining from an already low 24 percent to 21 percent. The effect was largely explained by the participation rates of older men. From one perspective, this is a matter for concern as the pension appears to make subsistence more palatable and to reduce the incentives to move into the formal sector. On the other hand, facilitating dignified early retirement to a rural area can be defended as providing openings for younger workers. The negative labor market incentives do, however, need to be made clear as they undermine the arguments currently made in South Africa by supporters of a basic monthly income grant for all.

### 3.1.5 *Institutions for the Aged*

As in the developed world, long-term care is becoming an increasing problem. It is widely accepted that it is desirable for people to remain outside formal institutions for as long as possible, but increasing numbers will inevitably require admittance. Many who require admittance are unlikely to be able to afford the R4,000 monthly cost.[5] The costs in OECD countries of frail care are much higher. Rappaport (2001) reports them as being as much as $6,000 monthly in the United States. South African costs are lower mainly because the wages of caregivers are lower.

Involvement by government or private charities in these homes is inevitable. Old-age homes for whites were previously given generous subsidies by the Department of Social Development, but these have been significantly reduced in the last decade, so undermining the viability of many organizations. Subsidies can be justified to support particularly needy individuals, but whites are disproportionately represented amongst those in frail care not least because of their longer life expectancy and smaller families. Subsidies that largely benefit whites are difficult to justify politically so soon after the removal of apartheid.

The Mothers and Fathers Report also gives a graphic description of these institutions:

> ... some homes are dirty and pervaded by a strong smell of urine. The quality and quantity of food is often below standard... In some homes residents don't have their own clothing, laundry is not marked and face-cloths and toothbrushes are shared... Many residents seem to spend their days seated in rows around a room or along a veranda—waiting for the next meal.
> ... Staff are generally low-paid and untrained and few qualified nurses are employed to care for elderly residents...
> The high level of theft in homes could be described as endemic and nobody seems to take responsibility for addressing it. Some homes have been targeted by criminal elements...

### 3.1.6 *Other Social Services*

The alternative, 'care in the community', may be little better however, as the report continues:

> (this) has become increasingly difficult for many old people due to the absence of community services in most areas, inadequate housing and unaffordable service charges... Many elderly persons are being abused by their children and grandchildren... Elderly people living alone are dying from malnutrition and neglect... Official agencies do not make home visits to elderly people... A meals on wheels service is run by one national organization but it reaches fewer than 10,000 elderly persons... Specialist geriatric clinics and nurses have been totally phased out. Clinic staff tend to say home care is 'not our business'. Equipment banks and lending depots for wheel-chairs and other aids are not supported by clinics and hospitals and tend to run out of stock...

## 3.2 The South African Private Sector

The private sector consists of employer or occupationally based schemes and voluntary products largely sold by commercial life insurers which provide for top-ups, the needs of the self-employed, and perhaps some of those informally employed. The Financial Services Board (FSB) (2003) shows that group retirement funds for which they were able to provide statistics have almost 9 million members (but over 1 million are retired and there are a number of duplications). Contributions amounted to R60 billion. To these occupational scheme contributions, another R8 billion in contributions to annuity products with life insurers can be added. A large proportion of the R27 billion of regular premium life assurance is also written as endowment policies intended to mature at retirement. Total assets amount to over R900 billion, and appear to account for some half (or more) of the country's total assets.

### 3.2.1 *Coverage in the Organized Formal Sector*

The term 'organized formal sector' is used here to describe businesses registered for tax purposes. These businesses usually belong to one or other labor or employer federation, while self-employed people are likely to be organized in professional associations. While noting that the statistics are invariably unreliable, the South African Institute of Race Relations Survey (2000: 356) reports estimates that this sector accounted for some 75 percent of remunerated employment in 1996.

Those employed in this sector are invariably covered by private pension arrangements, whether as part of their employment contract or voluntarily. The actual extent of retirement fund coverage is debatable. Some surveys—such as AMPS[6]—suggest that only 50 percent of employed people are contributing to a retirement fund. This does not however reconcile with the level of contributions to retirement funds reported to the Financial Services Board, which amount to almost 20 percent of personal remuneration. The 9 million active members reported would exceed the number of formal jobs. The latter figures tend to corroborate the Smith Committee estimates that some 80 percent of formally employed workers are covered by retirement funds. The AMPS survey recipients may have misunderstood the questions asked. Evidence from around the world, such as from Ferris (2000) and Glass (2001), is that the average person finds the design of retirement arrangements too complicated to understand.

### 3.2.2 *Explaining the High Coverage*

The South African second pillar is more efficient and has a greater coverage than that of Chile despite not being compulsory. The unusually wide coverage of the organized formal sector can be explained by a number of factors. Not least of these is the absence of an earnings-related state scheme. Of the other factors, and the one with perhaps most significance outside South Africa, is the focus on group schemes. These have significant advantages over arrangements where individuals have more choice. Relatively generous tax concessions are only available to group schemes where employees have no choice but to join. Such compulsion is an infringement of freedom, but the benefits appear to outweigh this loss.

Foremost of the benefits, and now widely recognized, are cheaper administration and minimal marketing costs. Almost all the information required for administration can be obtained from the employer's personnel records. The contributions are collected in one monthly amount from the employer. Large superannuation funds are also able to negotiate lower investment management fees. The costs of selling group schemes are proportionately much lower than selling to individuals. Keeping charges low can make a difference of 20 percent or more to final pension payouts. Compulsory group schemes also routinely offer life, disability, and health cover without medical questions. Those in poor health who might not be offered cover at all under an individual contract are thus able to obtain significant cover at ordinary rates. This generates further cost savings. The contribution that group schemes can make to industrial democracy is not often considered. Members can participate in the election and monitoring of trustees, who in turn are able to vote the shares owned by the fund. This is not possible with individual retirement contracts.

The South African focus on group schemes arises partly from its early start, with the Pension Funds Act (1956) providing focused regulation. There is a widespread perception amongst employers that offering retirement benefits helps retain staff, while trade unions have seen the intrinsic benefits and the opportunities to use the funds as a focus for organization. This has facilitated a number of industry-wide determinations, in terms of the Labor Relations Act, requiring employers to contribute to an industry fund or set up a company-specific fund. The marketing effort of life insurance companies has often been directed at the employers because of the life companies' influence as major shareholders. This, in turn, has arisen because of their management of retirement fund moneys.

### 3.2.3 *The Informal Sector*

The income over which contributions to retirement or insurance funds become economical is debatable. Participants in the South African industry suggest that monthly administrative costs are unlikely to be kept at below R30, while distribution costs (marketing in the private sector, and enforcement in the public sector) may double this. The costs for someone earning even R1,500 monthly (twice the monthly pension) and contributing 15 percent of their income for retirement would be at least 3 percent of income (and 15 percent of contributions).

Requiring people who earn much below these levels to contribute to retirement savings is equivalent to an additional tax. The South African experience makes this clear. Legislative reforms in the early 1990s freed micro-lenders from the constraints of the Usury Act and led to an explosion of loans at interest rates that vary from 20 percent per annum to 80 percent per annum or more. The statistics suggest that most employed South Africans have such loans. While the morality of such rates is debatable, they reflect the shortage of funds in the low income and informal sector. At the same time, retirement funds earn net returns of some 10 percent per annum. Requiring poor people to borrow at 50 percent and invest at 10 percent is clearly exploitative.

Most people employed in this sector rely on government disability and old-age grants for insurance and retirement cover. The current level of these grants is sufficiently high relative to the earnings of the majority of recipients for them not to need further savings. Funding these benefits through consumption taxes is much more efficient and contributes more to equality than collecting contributions. James (1999) also makes many of these points, suggesting that they may be applicable outside South Africa. She also points out that universal pensions provide support for women who have not been active labor market participants and who gain nothing from contribution-based systems.

Compulsory contributions appear to me to be only in the interest of people employed in the formal financial sector, and here I would include policy-makers and government regulators. Their narrow focus on the formal sector and their self-interest appear to combine to blind them to the cruelty of compulsory requirements.

### 3.2.4 *Benefit Coverage*

In spite of these high levels of coverage, which have been all but universal for the white population for 40 years, over a third of the white population still draws the means-tested old-age pension, with women being disproportionately represented. Two interrelated reasons can be identified. The first is the lack of preservation of benefits on changing employers. The second is that elderly widows suffer because their husbands have spent their withdrawal and lump-sum retirement benefits. This is an international problem—as described in Auerbach and Kotlikoff (1991) in a US study. It is an injustice that deserves urgent consideration in the reform of family law.

### 3.2.5 *Types of Fund*

The earliest South African funds were defined contribution (DC) in that they were funded by endowment policies. They were replaced by defined benefit (DB) funds during the 1960s because of the greater predictability of the benefit in DB funds.

A swing back to DC provident funds (that provided lump sums and not pensions) began in the early 1980s largely in response to pressure from black trade unions. Black South Africans were first allowed to join trade unions in 1979, and in the early 1980s organized a series of strikes over plans by the government to limit pre-retirement withdrawals. As in many countries, trade unions continue to be involved in fund administration.

Kerrigan (1991) describes the unions' objectives: fairer withdrawal benefits, lump sums on retirement, greater influence on investment policy and the power to elect trustees. The DC funds did away with the complicated cross-subsidies of DB, and the lump sums offered greater ease in avoiding the means test that at that stage reduced the state pension by 100 percent of other income.

Employers encouraged the shift to DC benefits. First, they were reluctant to permit newly elected trustees to make decisions that could lead to investment losses. Second, they were not averse to reducing the investment risks inherent in DB design, and toward the end of the 1980s, they saw that AIDS threatened a significant increase in the cost of insurance benefits. The swing gained momentum when the high returns on equity investment were seen to lead to better benefits for members.

## 3.3 Regulation

The standard regulatory structure is based on the Pension Funds Act, which sets up the Registrar of Pensions. The Financial Services Board Act (1990) sets up the FSB, whose chief executive officer assumes the functions of the Registrar. Funds regulated by the FSB are subject to proper governance procedures. They must have a set of rules, a board of management of which 50 percent are elected by the members,[7] report regularly to members, and produce audited accounts and actuarial valuations (if they are self-administered). The board of management or trustees owe their primary fiduciary duties, which derive from the common law, to members.

A South African innovation is the Pension Funds Adjudicator, set up to 'dispose of complaints... in a procedurally fair, economical and expeditious manner'.[8] The intention was to empower members who could not use expensive legal procedures to establish their rights. The first adjudicator was flooded with complaints, not least because of his personal energy and ability to address critical issues in legally creative ways if necessary. Some of the complaints were resolved by mediation, but hundreds have required written rulings.[9] In shifting the balance of power toward members, it seems that the innovation has been resoundingly successful. While few will agree with all his determinations, the office and the approach deserve consideration and perhaps imitation in other countries.

The Pension Funds Act has always provided protection to DB members to ensure that the funds are fully funded. Withdrawal benefits were however considerably less than the actuarial reserve, so penalizing early leavers, and inflation was often allowed to erode the real value of pensions significantly. Members transferring to DC funds also suffered losses. Employers taking contribution holidays benefited from the surpluses thus generated. In a relatively high inflationary environment, these flaws in benefit design accelerated the move to DC. Unprecedented legislation in 2001 requires funds to use their surpluses (where they exist) to go back to 1980 and compensate pensioners and those who have withdrawn.

## 3.4 Government Employees' Schemes

South African government sector employees are generally covered by DB schemes. There is one for central government employees, others for local government, and various para-statal organizations. Unusually, these are actuarially valued and fully funded, although the assets of the DB funds are largely held in government stock.

During the 1980s, however, the funds were removed from actuarial oversight and quickly reduced to half their previous funding levels. The reasons partly arose from the inflationary erosion of fixed interest assets, but also from excessive benefits, particularly the notorious 'buyback' provisions that gave enormous discounts to senior members of the funds. Wassenaar's (1989) exposé which led to the reimposition of proper controls reports that this bounty was limited to about 45,000 more senior public servants. He estimated the cost at R5 billion in 1986 terms, but the total deficits required perhaps ten times that number in additional contributions (and tax concessions) before they were extinguished in the mid-1990s. Another abuse of the system was to artificially inflate final salaries by promotions just before retirement—as the rules based the pension on the last day's salary.

# 4 OTHER AFRICAN COUNTRIES

Many of the South African issues have parallels in other African countries. Detailed information on the benefits available is however not as readily available. One source is 'Trends in Social Security' published by the International Social Security Association (ISSA) and available on their website to members. It gives some indication of the nature of retirement arrangements in different countries by reporting on planned changes. Barbone and Sanchez (1999) give some helpful tables.

## 4.1 Civil Service Schemes

Separate DB schemes for the civil service are the norm internationally. They are frequently overly generous: the problem is not limited to developing countries such as South Africa and Brazil, with the *Actuary* (2004: 14) reporting unfunded liabilities in the United Kingdom of over half that country's GNP. Benefits for the military are often particularly favorable with very young retirement ages. In poor African countries, the pensions of government employees do not have to be particularly generous to absorb a large proportion of the state's resources. ISSA data report retirement ages for civil servants that are being raised to 60 in some countries, and that the contributions required for the Egyptian scheme amount to some 30 percent of remuneration. Both suggest generous scheme benefits.

This is not to object to DB arrangements *per se*, but accruing benefits should be clearly defined and bear a reasonable relationship to current income. Actuarial management is necessary for this, but insufficient to prevent abuse. Reform is particularly difficult as those in the government departments responsible for drafting legislation are frequently the main beneficiaries. They are well placed to defeat the intentions of any reforms—not least by last-minute surreptitious insertions.

## 4.2 National Schemes

Most African countries have set up national schemes for all those of working age, that, as discussed, necessarily exclude those employed in the informal sector. In some cases, this is recognized in the regulations of the scheme. In other cases the informal sector is legally included, in which case the law is often an empty letter or another source of confusion and corruption. Coverage is higher in North Africa where it is reported to exceed 80 percent of the workforce in Tunisia and Egypt, but Barbone and Sanchez show most countries have coverage of less that 10 percent. This may, of course, represent a high proportion of the formal sector outside of government employment.

### 4.2.1 *Provident Funds*

A number of ex-British colonies, as elsewhere in the world, introduced national provident funds around the time of independence. These initially provided lump sums at retirement and some ancillary insurance benefits in return for contributions from private sector employees. Lump sums rather than pensions are particularly attractive to members who do not have access to the banking system in retirement. This is the case for much of Africa, where pensioners in rural areas can be charged exorbitant fees by local shopkeepers to cash cheques—if they arrive at all in an unreliable post. Lump sums can be used to upgrade housing and purchase cattle, traditionally the source of wealth in Sub-Sahara.

A number of African provident funds failed because of inadequate investment returns that reduced payouts to trivial amounts in some cases. Governments make it difficult to make international investments, and there are not enough local opportunities. The funds thus proved vulnerable to all the problems listed in Section 2.1 above: political interference, economic volatility, and inflation. Mounbaga (1995) illustrates from Cameroon. Some of the African funds are now being converted into national pension schemes. Nigeria is an exception having just chosen to follow the Chilean model. The different influences of the ILO and the World Bank have presumably contributed to this difference of approach.

### 4.2.2 *Earnings-Related Schemes*

The ex-French colonies introduced national earnings-related pension schemes for private sector employees. These protect the members from direct investment losses, folding the problem into general government finances, which are thereby placed under further pressure.

One apparent exception, which is described by Chaabane (2002) and receives favorable mention by van Ginneken (2003), is that of Tunisia. Imaginative and energetic action appears to have been successful in extending coverage to the self-employed and informal sector. Chaabane does not however report on the efficiency of the approach taken and the exercise is too recent, and the government too authoritarian, to be confident of ongoing success. Chourouk (2003), in a rather confusing paper, suggests that the Tunisian and other North African schemes are facing financial difficulties.

### 4.2.3 *Non-contributory Schemes*

Willmore (2001) describes the four countries he says have universal systems. Three (Mauritius, Botswana, and Namibia) are in Africa and have been influenced by the South African experience. He reports that the schemes are popular in New Zealand and Mauritius where they have been established for some time, without being too expensive (4 percent and 2 percent of GDP respectively). In spite of the administrative difficulties mentioned in Section 3.1.1 above and acknowledged by Willmore, universal pension schemes are probably the most cost-effective way of getting money to poor and rural areas.

## 4.3 Other Arrangements

### 4.3.1 *Large Private Sector Employers*

The employees of multinational companies are invariably covered by pension funds as part of the companies' worldwide human resources policies. These funds do not always offer the same protection to locals as to expatriates. In some cases, there is discrimination in eligibility for membership; in others different practices on withdrawal.

In Anglophone countries with a less extensive first pillar, particularly Kenya and Zimbabwe, larger local companies also have corporate schemes. As in South Africa, both employers and employees appear to have encouraged the move to DC arrangements—in spite of investment restrictions on international investments. Members have not however benefited from all the legislation of the type mentioned in Section 3.3 above.

Anecdotal evidence is that the mortality experience of group schemes does not reflect the increases expected from AIDS deaths because local employees return to their rural homes to die, and so do not claim their entitlements. The author's experience of South African funds makes this credible: large numbers of retirement fund beneficiaries do not claim. Illiteracy plays a role, as does the cultural reluctance of men to let their wives know of potential life cover benefits.

### 4.3.2 *Voluntary Arrangements*

Van Ginneken (2003), from the ILO, suggests the development of voluntary special schemes to give the self-employed access to pension benefits. He envisages community-based non-profit organizations, such as some of those involved in microfinancing, either offering pensions or acting as agents for large formal institutions. Burial and rotating credit societies provide other examples that clearly flourish in Africa. He suggests that they should be subsidized in order to remain attractive to all members—because they are not actuarially fair.

There are a number of models that have historically provided this type of benefit. 'Industrial' life insurance involves the weekly collection of premiums and pays out lump sums. At its peak in the United Kingdom, more than half the households contributed. It also had some success in South Africa. It has however been phased out, largely because it is impossible to give decent value for money. The costs of collection invariably make up more than 30 percent of the premiums.

Friendly societies provide an alternative, community-based, and therefore cheaper, model that goes back to the European Middle Ages, and has proved itself in a number of social and economic environments. The British version pays disability benefits predominantly, which—if there is no retirement age—is precisely what is required for poorer communities where voluntary retirement is a luxury.

Subsidies to voluntary schemes are likely to be abused, and are regressive in that only the wealthier members of society are likely to be able to save. James (1999) warns specifically against them. The first step rather is to remove obstacles to the formation of voluntary arrangements in the form of inappropriate regulations. Subsequent work is to provide financial and technical advice, and appropriate consumer protections. The need for the latter may not always be evident. Informal arrangements are effectively beyond the reach of formal law and can be unreliable. The detailed interviews with a number of burial society members, reported in Thomson and Posel (2002), illustrate the great difficulty of building trust and enforcing agreements in informal arrangements.

### 4.3.3 *The Extended Family*

Kaseke (1999) writes of the extended African family and its role in the provision of financial and social support to the aged and other needy members. The large families that have characterized the rapid population growth of the last century—and which thereby can be called 'traditional'—do provide a level of financial security through the sharing of risk. Certainly, his view that many children provide security in old age appears to be held widely. The sharing also appears to go beyond the extended family to village communities.

Pensioners too old to work do receive support from their families, but Peil (1992) shows that many do not seem to have contact with adult children. Somavia (2003) reports that more than 40 percent of Africans over 64 are still obliged to work. AIDS has greatly aggravated this problem, which is often made worse by the need to care for orphaned grandchildren. If it can be afforded, even a small old-age grant seems desirable.

## 4.4 Investments

Nineteen African countries have local stock exchanges,[10] although most are small. Plans to rationalize some of them will not only improve liquidity and efficiency, but will also provide potentially more diversity for retirement fund investments. Real diversification will require investment in economies removed geographically, as both economic and political risks can be concentrated regionally. Except in South Africa, the capitalization of these is too small to absorb more than a fraction of funded pension liabilities.

Insulation from political risk would mean that the retirement funds themselves would have to be outside the control of their national government. Anything less would be of limited value, but it is not entirely clear whether governments can be persuaded to lose control of such a large pool of assets.

## 4.5 Governance

In suggesting reforms that will aid governance, Barbone and Sanchez (1999) advocate simplification of institutions, reducing the role of government, and formalizing the management of the national schemes. This should go along with a reduction in regressive subsidies in particular, and with increased competition. Simplification clearly contributes to efficiency, but illiteracy should not be confused with the inability to cope with complexity.

Few would disagree on the need to address the accompanying and more difficult issue of corruption, which might well serve as a heading for this section. Addressing corruption will be easier in simpler systems where accountability is easier to enforce and power is diffused from government to private but accountable institutions. Diop (2003) lauds reforms in Senegal, which have created a more autonomous management of the social security system, and appear to offer greater stability as well as improvements in service. The way in which South African unions have both used pensions as an organizing force and contributed to pension fund democracy provides an interesting model of power diffusion.

Given their resources and temptations, it is doubtful whether public sectors in most Sub-Saharan countries have the capacity to administer even simple national retirement funds. If it is accepted that the overwhelming majority of the population in the informal sector would be better off without compulsory schemes, then there is a strong argument for their abolition. The energies of the state would be better directed toward providing a low level of universal cover and the protection of members in voluntary private sector arrangements. The South African experience shows that these can cover a high proportion of the formal sector.

# 5 Conclusion

## 5.1 Research Questions

We know surprisingly little about the actual and potential effects of pensions and social security benefits on the lives of people, especially those living in the Third World. What are the costs of levying contributions on informal sector workers? Are means tests more effective than suggested here in targeting the poor and ameliorating their deprivation? How do families react to unexpected losses of income and of pension benefits? In order to answer these questions, I believe one has to have panel data as suggested in Asher (2001). Cross-sectional studies record the memories and impressions of those interviewed, which are often unreliable.

Research also has a role in exposing and addressing corrupt practices. Careful analyses of institutional structures and the interests that they serve is a necessary first step to reform. Three South African examples can be provided. Wassenaar's (1989) book provided much of the impetus for the subsequent withdrawal of the over-generous state benefits. The recording and publicity given to administrative corruption over many years have clearly brought some measure of relief to state pensioners. The success of the pensions fund adjudicator has depended partly on adequate research, and on the development of the legal protections available.

The role of retirement funds in the development of local capital markets also requires some exploration. This relates to the management of the investments of national schemes and to exchange controls and other pressures placed on private funds to invest locally. Africa would not appear to provide many role models but experience elsewhere may prove helpful.

## 5.2 Policy Lessons

Justice means, *inter alia*, defending the powerless against the powerful. In Africa, the poor and powerless are to be found mainly in the informal sector. Pension arrangements for them need careful consideration; a number of commentators have come to the conclusion that a universal non-contributory pension is the solution.

African civil services are particularly powerful, and need to be constrained. Actuarial management of their own pension schemes may help to reduce their ability to extract excessive benefits from this source. Limiting their involvement in national schemes and encouraging second pillar group arrangements may help develop countervailing powers.

The interests of women also need consideration. Non-contributory schemes provide more equitably for those who have not worked in the formal sector. Family law reform is particularly necessary to protect married women whose husbands consume more than a fair share of lump-sum benefits.

Finally, it should be said that addressing these issues from outside the continent is fraught with dangers. Injustices provoke indignation, and foreigners might do best to support the indignant who have been wronged by providing the fruits of research and technical if not material support. As the *New International Version* has it: 'speak up for those who cannot speak for themselves...'. Particular examples worth considering are the efforts of the trade unions, the Pensions Fund Adjudicator, and the private support for Court actions in South Africa.

## Notes

1. The statistics in this section are taken from the Nationmaster.com website.
2. The formula for the means tests are set out in the South African *Government Gazette* 18771 of 31 March 1998.
3. The asset test has not been phased in since changes published in the *Government Gazette* 22852 of 23 November 2001.
4. The author has some experience attempting to quantify earnings for tort claims. On one occasion he was able to gather evidence that the in-kind income was ten times higher than that initially claimed.
5. Personal communication from Peter Asher, board of The Association for the Aged, Durban.
6. The All Media and Product Survey conducted by the South African Advertising Research Foundation—private communication.
7. Section 7A of the Pension Funds Act (1956), in force since 15 December 1998.
8. Section 30D.
9. Some 162 are recorded in 2001 on the website: http://www.fsb.co.za/pfa/deter2001.htm
10. Found, October 2004, at http://allafrica.com/businesssol.

## References

*Actuary* (2004). 'Danger—unexploded tax bombshell'. The *Actuary* (Sept.) London: Staple Inn Actuarial Society.

ARDINGTON, LIBBY, and LUND, FRANCIE (1994). 'Pensions and development: the social security system as a complementary track to programmes of reconstruction and development'. Centre for Social and Development Studies. University of Natal.

ASHER, ANTHONY (2001). 'South African Panel Study in Income Dynamics'. Annual convention of the Actuarial Society of South Africa. http://www.assa.org.za

AUERBACH, ALAN J., and KOTLIKOFF, LAURENCE (1991). 'Life insurance inadequacy—evidence from a sample of older widows'. NBER Working Paper No. 3765.

BARBONE, LUCA, and SANCHEZ, LUIS-ALVARO (1999). 'Pensions and social security in Sub-Saharan Africa: issues and options'. Africa Region Working Paper Series No. 4. The World Bank.

BERTRAND, MARIANNE, MULLAINATHAN, SENDHIL, and MILLER, DOUGLAS (2003). 'Public policy and extended families: evidence from pensions in South Africa'. *World Bank Economic Review*, 17/1: 27–50.

CASE, ANNE (2001). 'Does Money protect health status? Evidence from South African pensions'. National Bureau of Economic Research Working Paper 8495.

CHAABANE, MOHAMED (2002). 'Towards the universalization of social security: the experience of Tunisia'. Extension of Social Security Paper No.4. Geneva: International Labour Office.

CHOUROUK, HOUSSI (2003). 'Pensions in North Africa: the need for reform'. *The Geneva Papers on Risk and Insurance*, 28/4: 712–26.

DE SOTO, HERNANDO (2000). *The Mystery of Capital: Why Capitalism Triumphs in the West and Fails Everywhere Else*. London: Bantam.

DIOP, AHMADOU YERI (2003). 'Governance of social security regimes: trends in Senegal'. *International Social Security Review*, 56/3–4: 17–23.

FERRIS, SHAUNA (2000). 'Women making choices'. Macquarie Research Paper. www.actuary.mq.edu.au/research_papers/200001_women_making_choices.pdf

FINANCIAL SERVICES BOARD (2003). Annual Report. http://www.fsb.co.za/

GLASS, RICHARD D. (2001). 'Investment education or advice? That's the wrong question to ask!' *Pensions World* (Mar.): 28–33.

JAMES, ESTELLE (1999). 'Coverage under old age Security programs and protection for the uninsured—what are the issues?' Policy Research Working Paper 2163. The World Bank.

KASEKE, EDWIN (1999). 'Social security and the elderly: the African experience'. *The ACP-EU Courier*, 176: 50–2. http://europa.eu.int/comm/development/body/publications/publications_courier_en.htm

KERRIGAN, GRAEME K. (1991). 'The role of COSATU affiliated trade unions in retirement provisions in SA'. *Transactions of the Actuarial Society of South Africa*, IX/I: 177–98.

LANDES, DAVID S. (1998). *The Wealth and Poverty of Nations: Why are Some So Rich and Others So Poor?* New York: W.W. Norton.

LUND, FRANCIE (1993). 'Social benefits in South Africa'. *International Social Security Review*, 46/1.

MOTHERS AND FATHERS (2001). 'Mothers and fathers of the nation: the forgotten people?' Ministerial Committee on Abuse, Neglect and Ill-Treatment of Older Persons: Executive summary. http://www.polity.org.za/govdocs/reports/welfare/2001/elder.html#-content

MOUNBAGA, EMMANUEL (1995). 'The investment of social security reserves during periods of crisis: the experience of Cameroon'. *International Social Security Review*, 48/2: 49–59.

PEIL, MARGARET (1992). 'Family help for the elderly: a comparative study on Nigeria, Sierra Leone and Zimbabwe'. *Bold, Quarterly Journal of the International Institute on Ageing*, 2/3: 2–4.

POWELSON, JOHN P. (1994). *Centuries of Economic Endeavour: Parallel Paths in Japan and Europe and their Contrast with the Third World*. Ann Arbor: University of Michigan Press.

RAPPAPORT, ANNA M. (2001). 'Setting the stage: an overview of the Retirement 2000 issues'. *North American Actuarial Journal*, 5/1: 1–11.

SACHS, JEFFREY D., MELLINGER, ANDREW D., and GALLUP, JOHN L. (2001). 'The geography of poverty and wealth'. *Scientific American*, 284: 70–6.

SMITH COMMITTEE (1995). 'Report to the Minister of Finance of the Committee on Strategy and Policy Review of Retirement Provision in South Africa'. Cape Town: Government Printer.

SOMAVIA, JUAN (2003). 'Report of the Director-General: Working out of Poverty'. International Labour Conference. Geneva: International Labour Office.

SOUTH AFRICAN INSTITUTE OF RACE RELATIONS SURVEY (2000). Annual Survey 1999/2000. Johannesburg.

THOMSON, ROB J., and POSEL, DEBORAH B. (2002). 'The management of risk by burial societies in South Africa'. *South African Actuarial Journal*, 2: 83–128.

VAN GINNEKEN, WOUTER (2003). 'Extending social security: policies for developing countries'. Extension of Social Security Paper No. 13. Geneva: International Labour Office.

WASSENAAR, ANDREAS D. (1989). *Squandered Assets.* Cape Town: Tafelberg.
WILLMORE, LARRY (2001). 'Universal pensions in low income countries'. Discussion Paper. Initiative for Policy Dialogue, Pensions and Social Insurance Section, Oxford Institute of Ageing.
YAKOBOSKI, PAUL, OSTUW, PAMELA and PIERRON, BILL (2001). 'The 1999 small employer retirement survey: building a better mousetrap is not enough'. *North American Actuarial Journal*, 5/1: 131–2.

# CODA

CHAPTER 42

# SUSTAINABLE AND EQUITABLE RETIREMENT IN A LIFE COURSE PERSPECTIVE

GOSTA ESPING-ANDERSEN
AND JOHN MYLES

## 1 INTRODUCTION

As previous chapters demonstrate, population ageing has been with us for more than a century. What is historically genuinely new is that old age now coincides with *retirement*. Retirement in its contemporary sense—permanent withdrawal from employment prior to physiological decline—was, until recently, the privilege of the few. True, in the past rank-and-file elderly workers were also often 'retired', not because they no longer needed work incomes but rather due to disabilities or to lay-offs.[1] Even as late as the 1960s, 'old age' was practically synonymous with poverty in many industrial democracies. All this has changed in the past quarter century. Old-age incomes have been rising, retirement ages have been falling, and the elimination of old-age poverty is a very realistic prospect for most developed nations.

The coupling of ageing with retirement provokes, as with most new things, uncertainty. As several chapters in this *Handbook* show, if we decide to maintain the status quo, the financial costs will escalate substantially over the coming decades. This is driven by low fertility, continued gains in life expectancy, and the arrival of huge cohorts approaching retirement age. Assuming no serious relaxation of our commitment to retirement welfare, population ageing over the coming three decades will necessitate a pension expenditure increase of roughly 40–50 percent in most OECD countries.

Gains in longevity are producing both qualitative and quantitative changes among the elderly. The fraction of the elderly most at risk of disability, the 'oldest old' (aged 80 and over), grows much faster than the elderly population in general. We must accordingly anticipate a surge in the demand for care. And this will occur against a backdrop of a major decline in the traditional pool of informal caregivers (elderly wives, daughters, and daughters-in-law) who now provide about three-quarters of all care to the frail elderly (OECD 1996: 63). The OECD's (1996) benchmark estimate is that the aged in general consume 3.2 times more health care than the non-aged, but the ratio rises to 4.1 among those aged 75 and over. If care for the frail elderly is mainly non-familial, as in Sweden and Denmark, the cost of universal provision hovers around 3 percent of GDP. Keeping up with demographics would mean a doubling to 6 percent by 2030–40, assuming steady prices for old-age care and assuming steady frailty levels. The former will almost inevitably rise in relative terms because of lagging productivity in care services; the latter may abate in view of the improvements in the health of older citizens (Jacobzone 1999). In brief, substantial additional spending requirements are unavoidable unless we are ready to accept serious welfare erosion among tomorrow's retirees.

## 2 THE THREE WELFARE PILLARS: THE FAMILY, THE MARKET, AND GOVERNMENT

Unsurprisingly, policy-makers fear that the coming decades will necessitate unsustainable levels of public expenditure. One response is to ease the expenditure burden by encouraging private pension savings and by inducing family members (daughters largely) to continue caring for their elderly kin. The retirement literature, unfortunately, is overly focused on public finances and this easily produces potentially fallacious conclusions. If we decide to sustain our welfare commitments, shifting the costs to either market transactions or to familial support will not reduce the amount of additional resources that need to be mobilized. The elderly of the future may perhaps absorb less government expenditure, but that does not mean that they will absorb less of the national GDP.[2]

The sum total of a person's welfare combines inputs from family, market, and government. The family provides services (like care), consumption, and also monetary income. Markets furnish work incomes and savings that can be transformed into retirement wealth, and private providers may sell care services and retirement plans. Governments redistribute income and services across the life course and between families. Most retirees receive a mix of all three welfare inputs. Government redistribution is everywhere the dominant pillar in terms of pension incomes (although in some countries private pension plans are significant).

In many OECD countries, the welfare of the elderly remains dependent on familial provision, in particular with regard to caring services. In Japan, Mediterranean Europe, and also in most Continental European countries, the lion's share of care is given by family members. The Scandinavian countries are unique in terms of the near-universal public coverage of elderly care, while North America stands out with its widespread purchased care services. Cohabitation with children is an indicator of family caregiving, but also of economic sustenance more generally. At one end of the spectrum we find Italy and Spain where, roughly, 30 percent of the elderly live with their children. At the other end lies Denmark where cohabitation between generations is practically extinct. If, as many policy-makers conclude (OECD 2001), maximum female employment is a prerequisite for meeting the challenge of population ageing, then obviously arrangements that concentrate the bulk of care for the elderly within the family are unsustainable.[3]

The role of markets is also variable across countries. 'Private' capital savings inside employer pensions and individual retirement accounts play a large role in most Anglo-Saxon countries, in the Netherlands, and, later this century, they will also loom large in Denmark. Still peripheral in most of Europe, their significance may increase as citizens respond to the trimming of public sector plans and to new tax incentives with larger private savings. Privatization may reduce pressures on the exchequer but it is unlikely to alter the future cost scenario. Public and private pensions are simply alternative ways for working-age individuals to register a claim on future production (Barr 2001). The share of total consumption of the retired will rise irrespective of whether it is financed with public pensions or with investment returns from bonds and equities. As Clark *et al.* show in Chapter 1 of this *Handbook*, private plans inevitably incur far greater transaction costs than their public sector rivals. And, as Thompson (1998: 44) observes, if group or personal advanced funded accounts were indeed to produce the higher returns to contributions that their advocates promise, the effect would be to raise further future retirement spending.

The degree to which the elderly must rely on family support or on markets is undoubtedly a function of government provision—and, of course, vice versa. Still, one does not automatically substitute for another. Family reliance is often a response to both government and market 'failure', that is, the last resort when government provision is inadequate and when market alternatives are unaffordable. But we cannot readily assume that aid from kin is always available. Likewise, market-purchased services are undoubtedly more prominent when government provision is ungenerous but, again, the high entry price implies that they will rarely be perfect substitutes.

Perfect substitutes or not, citizens and institutions adapt to 'failure' in one pillar by reallocating their welfare investments and consumption to the remaining pillars. Thus, the decline of familial support over the past century coincided with greater public or market provision. And similarly, it is hardly accidental that private pension incomes are far more prominent in countries like the United States or the United Kingdom, where public pension systems are rather ungenerous.

Ultimately, the total level of societal resource use for retirement seems to be quite convergent among similarly wealthy countries, irrespective of their 'pillar bias'. This is amply evident from OECD's calculations of net welfare expenditure, but also from data on retirement household incomes. Retirees' disposable income converges almost everywhere at around 80–100 percent of the national average, be it in a very generous welfare state like the Swedish or a in a more market-based model, like the United States.

It follows that less government and more markets will not alter much the future scenario in terms of levels of financing. All it really implies is from which of two pockets we take the money. This means that the welfare mix will affect welfare distributions and will most likely produce different second-order consequences.

There is a relationship, albeit not perfect, between degree of market reliance and old-age poverty. As Table 42.1 illustrates, poverty rates are very high in the United States and Australia, and the United Kingdom falls at the high end of the European poverty rate distribution.[4] The relationship is not perfect for two reasons. First, public pension systems can vary considerably in their distributional impact. Take Italy, where public retirement schemes are unusually generous and where private plans hardly exist at all. Yet, old-age poverty is widespread because Italy's basic pension guarantee for citizens with inadequate contribution entitlements is unusually meager. Second, the prominence of private plans may not produce major inequalities among the elderly if, as in Canada, Denmark, and the Netherlands, there exists a basic public pension guarantee that effectively minimizes the risk of poverty.

Depending on the welfare mix, there may also be important second-order effects. Strong reliance on familial care will translate into lower female employment and, hence, a narrower tax-base. And if women are compelled to interrupt their careers, this will have adverse effects not only on their individual lifetime incomes, but also on household incomes since the income from a second earner is increasingly needed to avert poverty. Since women's employment is key both to long-term financial sustainability and to household welfare, continued reliance on the family seems directly counterproductive.

### Table 42.1 Poverty rates among the population 65+, c. 2000

| < 5% | 5–9% | 10–14% | 15–19% | > 20% |
|---|---|---|---|---|
| | Canada | | | Ireland |
| | Denmark | | | |
| | Finland | Austria | | Australia |
| Sweden | France | Belgium | | United States |
| Netherlands | | | | |
| | Germany | | | |
| | Luxembourg | Italy | | |
| | | Norway | | |
| | Switzerland | Spain | | |
| | | United Kingdom | | |

*Source*: LIS Key Figures, Luxembourg Income Study, 2001. The Danish and French estimates are from the 2001 wave of the European Community Household Panel.

## 3 Toward a New Generational Contract

Most of the debate on ageing has centered on how to ensure long-term financial sustainability. Much suggests that we have allowed ourselves to get bogged down in demographic and actuarial arithmetic at the expense of grander visions of a good, just, and productive society in which, it so happens, the aged loom large. Beginning with actuarialism is like putting the cart before the horse. Accountants are only useful once we have a clear idea of which objectives we wish to pursue.

The challenge is manyfold. We need to identify a stable and equitable intergenerational contract that assures the well-being of the elderly without crowding out resources for the young. The median voter is ageing and, as many fear, this may trigger a generational clash as the balance of power favors the interests of retirees. Again, we need to ensure against adverse second-order effects. If additional financing raises fixed labor costs, for example, the result may be impaired job performance.

The challenge is to define a formula for how to allocate fairly the additional costs associated with population ageing. Considering the total welfare mix, we need to adopt an accounting procedure which is not myopically limited to public expenditure but to total GDP use, be it financed from taxation or from citizens' own pockets. The costs will, roughly speaking, amount to an additional 5–8 percent of GDP over the coming decades. The important questions to answer are (*a*) how can we devise an equitable burden sharing? And (b) what happens if we pursue one or another public-private mix?

If our concern is with equity, there is a lot to be said for the Musgrave rule of fixed proportional shares (Musgrave 1986; Myles 2002). To illustrate its relevance, let us imagine two idealized scenarios. In the first, we continue unabated with the conventional pay-as-you-go (PAYGO), defined benefit pension model. In this case, all the additional costs of ageing will fall on the working population. This will necessitate substantially higher employment taxes. To illustrate, in this scenario German contribution rates are projected to rise from 22 to 38 percent of wages. Imagine now a second scenario where we fix the contribution rate at current levels with no further increments to account for population ageing. In this scenario the additional burden would fall squarely on the retirees themselves. Neither of these two extreme scenarios would ensure equity—and both would inevitably be accompanied by very negative second-order effects. In other words, neither is likely to constitute a viable social contract.

How might a three-generation household committed to intergenerational risk-sharing resolve this dilemma? If citizens are content with the status quo (they are happy with the relative levels of consumption of the generations that now obtain), they would undoubtedly opt for a fixed ratio or fixed relative position (FRP) model akin to that advocated by Musgrave (1986).[5] Contributions and benefits are set so as to hold constant the ratio of per capita earnings of those in the working population (net of contributions) to the per capita benefits (net of taxes) of retirees. Once the ratio is fixed, the tax rate is adjusted periodically to reflect both population and productivity changes. As the population ages, the tax rate rises but benefits also fall so that both parties 'lose' at the same rate (i.e. both net earnings and benefits rise more slowly than they would in the absence of population ageing). Simply put, the Musgrave rule is a means of allocating the additional burden equitably between the generations. Its starting point is to fix proportionally the per capita incomes of old and young, that is, of workers and retirees. Any additional expenditure would, according to the rule, be allocated according to these proportions.

If we shift our perspective from a 'point-in-time' to a life course framework, the case for Musgrave's solution is even more persuasive. What are the implications of the three alternative pension models from the point of view of the *entire* life course of cohorts born today and in the future? What will be the legacy that we leave to our children and grandchildren?

Under existing PAYGO defined benefit rules, future cohorts would experience declining living standards in childhood and during their working years, but then they would enjoy a relatively affluent old age. If contribution rates are fixed, now the strategy in several countries, future generations will enjoy prosperous childhoods and working lives but relative penury in old age. The Musgrave strategy, in contrast, effectively smoothes the change across the entire life course and maintains the status quo with respect to the lifetime distribution of income. In this respect, Musgrave's is a 'conservative' strategy based on the assumption that, on average, the lifetime distribution of income available to current generations should be preserved more or less intact into the future. Future generations may of course disagree with our judgments and conclude that they want a different allocation of income over the life course. The point to note here is that if it is possible to agree on a fair proportionality, the future financial scenario will be stable and also perceived as intergenerationally fair.

But only up to a point. First, the Musgrave rule is easy to apply to a government-dominated pension regime, but encounters obstacles where private occupational schemes and individual accounts proliferate (Engelen, Chapter 6, this volume). Indeed, the equity pursued in the public pension domain may very easily become undone in the private domain. In brief, it is only a realistic solution if private plans are somehow co-integrated into an overall accounting scheme. The often very favorable tax treatment of second- and third-tier retirement plans clearly warrants that they, too, be charged with social goals.

Second, the Musgrave principle will remain equitable only if relative prices in the consumer basket of the young and old also remain stable. This is where the future of pensions and health come together. If health and caring services are prone to price inflation, the intergenerational 'pension' contract will be in jeopardy. Indeed, if so, there is a case to be made that intergenerational equity will require that the elderly receive a larger per capita share of national income.[6] This is all the more so since we know that pension incomes decline with age—although the prevalence of low incomes among the elderly varies hugely by gender (being concentrated among women living alone) and by country.[7] In other words, when care services are most needed is exactly when retirees least can afford them.

Third, the Musgrave rule addresses only the quest for intergenerational equity and thereby ignores the much larger problems of distribution within generations. As Wolfson *et al.* (1998) demonstrate, the enormous heterogeneity within generations (or cohorts) dwarfs the differences between generations in the distribution of 'winners' and 'losers' that can result from population ageing. Indeed, it is possible that policies in favour of intergenerational equity may exacerbate intragenerational inequities. To illustrate this, let us examine the possible ramifications of postponing retirement age, on one hand, and on pension financing, on the other hand.

## 3.1 Working Longer

Most now agree that by far the most effective policy is to postpone the age of retirement (Sundén, Chapter 35, this volume). Considering the gains in longevity, such a strategy is entirely consistent with the Musgrave rule. Assuming that workers will not acquire additional pension claims from additional work years, the OECD (2001: 69) estimates that a ten-month postponement is financially equivalent to a 10 percent cut in pension benefits (OECD 2001: 69). The Danish government's recent Welfare Commission estimates that a one month per year increase in retirement age over the coming three decades (equivalent to a little less than three years in total) would ensure sustainability at present welfare levels (Velfaerdskommissionen 2004). Available prognoses and simulations yield divergent results but, all else constant, a return to age 65 as the norm would probably come close to 'balancing the books'. Delaying retirement is a very effective tool because it cuts both ways: reducing pension years while simultaneously raising contribution years.

Raising the retirement age is equitable from an intergenerational perspective but it may easily produce intragenerational injustice. Just as an additional year of retirement represents a larger proportional gain for someone with a seven-year life expectancy than for someone with a 12-year life expectancy, an additional year of employment represents a proportionately greater loss for those with shorter life expectancies. Since health (life expectancy, disability) and wealth tend to be correlated, the equity problem is compounded. Moreover, the recent gains in longevity have gone disproportionately to the most affluent (Hattersley 1999), thus reinforcing the association.[8] If the 'rich' are the main consumers of future high-cost items, such as pensions, health, and long-term care, systems of finance will need to tax more progressively according to risk—especially according to the probability of survival.[9]

## 3.2 Financing

On the contribution side, today's pay-as-you-go pensions are financed with a payroll tax while income from capital and transfers (including pension income) are exempt.[10] The payroll tax is a flat tax, often with a wage ceiling that makes it regressive. There are typically no exemptions and no allowances for family size. These effects are compounded to the extent that high payroll taxes discourage employment, especially at the lower end of the labor market. In effect, charging the additional costs of ageing to payroll taxes creates a huge problem of intragenerational equity among the working-age population since the distribution of the additional costs in no way reflects ability to pay.

The real challenge we face is that for such a contract to be both stable and broadly legitimate, it will have to establish allocation rules that are also intragenerationally equitable among the retired as well as the working population. If the cost of being old rises disproportionally, then a Musgrave-type fixed proportions rule will end up being unfair. If, moreover, the rich consume more pensions, health, or care services, then, once again, a purely intergenerational contract will result in inequitable burden-sharing.

To ensure equitable burden-sharing, one would clearly need to undertake major revisions of tax and contribution schedules, not only in terms of raising the progressiveness of public revenues targeted to the aged, but also of diminishing the regressive nature of tax susbidies that benefit private retirement plans.

If, as is clearly required, we take a longer perspective, both the future financial burden and its associated distributional consequences will depend primarily on the kinds of lives that the coming cohorts will have. If we begin to reform pension systems today, this will probably not affect today's or even tomorrow's elderly. Those most affected will be our children and grandchildren. At mid-century, those who are now children will approach retirement. The real challenge we face is to realistically project how these new generations will fare in the coming half century. Happily, we can rely on more than fortune tellers and crystal balls.

# 4 Pension Reform with Our Children in Mind: Beyond the Generational Contract

Over a decade ago, political scientist Hugh Heclo (1988) pointed out that the great debate over intergenerational 'class war' and equity in the United States had largely passed Europe by. The difference, he speculated, has to do with Europeans' greater inclination toward 'life course' thinking when tackling issues about inequality: childhood and old age are simply *different moments in the lives of the same people.* Americans, he argued, are more inclined to consider the elderly and children as more or less static, distinct social groups that, in turn, divide into yet other groups based on race, disability status, and so forth. For Americans, thinking about childhood and old age as raising a distributional problem over a single life course seems distinctly foreign.

Whether Heclo has captured the true mindset of Americans and Europeans correctly is not important. His essential point can be illustrated by comparing two historical cohorts. Turning the clock back to the 1950s and 1960s, we would find widespread poverty among the elderly in all OECD countries. They were poor not only because public retirement plans were ungenerous, and private plans underdeveloped, but also because they were 'unlucky' generations. Born at the close of the nineteenth century, their youth was marred by the First World War; their careers straddled the difficult 1920s, the depression of the 1930s, and then came the Second World War. In brief, the retirement cohorts of the 1950s were poor mainly because many had led poor lives.

Moving forward, today's retirees are broadly well-off, with a disposable income of typically around 80 percent of the national mean. They do well in large part because of historical fortune: beginning their careers during the booming postwar decades, generally enjoying job security and rising real wages, most have accumulated substantial savings and resources. As Burtless and Quinn (2001: 385) conclude, the 'simplest and probably most powerful explanation for earlier retirement is rising wealth'. In some nations most of this 'wealth' is stored up in national public pension schemes while in others so-called 'private' employer schemes and individual savings matter more. The remarkable fact is that average living standards of the elderly differ little across countries (OECD 2001), irrespective of which kind of pension mix prevails.

A secure retirement then is very much dependent on how we fared during our working lives and this, in turn, correlates powerfully with the quality of our childhood and youth. The retirement prospects for our children and grandchildren 40 or 50 years from now, as well their ability to finance our retirement and care needs until then, are similarly contingent on the kinds of lives they will have. In short, securing retirement for the year 2040 or 2050 depends more on the quality, quantity, and distribution of the stock of productive assets—physical, human, and environmental—that our children inherit than on any reforms we make now to the design of our pension systems.

To illustrate, consider the retirement prospects of the cohorts likely to retire in 2040. They turn 30 in 2005, old enough for us to discern who will and who won't be well placed to provide themselves (and their aged co-citizens) with a secure retirement. The welfare state edifice that we know today was created in response to a profile of risks and needs that prevailed in the age of our grandparents, parents, and those of us who came to maturity in the postwar decades. Today's young workers face a very different risk profile, and this needs to be factored into our retirement projections for mid-century.

## 5 THE CHANGING LIFE COURSE AND THE NEW INEQUALITIES OF RETIREMENT

In a 1944 League of Nations report on postwar labour needs, a group of Princeton demographers worried about the economic impact of population ageing because they assumed that, in 'industrial societies', maximum productivity is reached by age 35 (Notestein *et al.* 1944). The success of industrial economies depended, in their view, on large numbers of muscular young men. Since the age of leaving the parental home, marriage, and childbirth—markers of achieving economic independence—all fell over the first six decades of the twentieth century, it would seem that industrializing economies did indeed place a high economic value on young workers (Beaujot 2004; Corijn and Klijzing 2001). As a result, the contemporary cohorts of retirees reached social and economic maturity relatively early in the life course.

## 5.1 The Changing Life Course

All this has changed for recent cohorts with dramatic implications for the types of careers and family life they will experience as they progress toward their retirement years. Indeed, the revolution in life course patterns of young adults in the past 40 years—the 'second demographic transition' (Lesthaege 1995)—is as much a part of the phenomenon of 'population ageing' as is the much-vaunted arrival of the baby boom. Since the 1960s all of the age markers of social adulthood have been rising. Marriage and first childbirth now occur in the late twenties just about the time people are beginning to establish themselves in real career jobs.

Postponed independence, longer education, and later union formation inevitably lead to lower levels of child-bearing. Hence the very low fertility of 1.2 or less we now see in many advanced countries, particularly in Southern and Eastern Europe. This is linked to the revolution in female employment and the rise in education and skill requirements on the one hand, and on the other, to deteriorating career opportunities for those with insufficient skills.

As with any major change there is good news for some and bad news for others. Starting later means fewer years in the labor market with less opportunity to save or earn benefits early in the life course. Future cohorts may therefore need to postpone retirement. However, starting late has always been the case among the highly educated. Retirement decisions clearly depend on other factors.

First, while total hours and years worked by individuals have fallen, this is not the case for families since women's labor supply has grown sharply. The rise in 'family' years and hours worked helps pay for more years of retirement (Burtless and Quinn 2001). This implies that stable two-income couples will arrive at age 65 well positioned to enjoy a secure retirement while single-earner households and the rising number of never married and divorced will face greater risks. Butrica *et al.* (2003: 46) estimate that the share of never married and divorced persons among the elderly poor in the United States will rise from its current level of 33 percent to 48 percent when the baby boomers retire.

The second divide that will persist over the working lives of current cohorts has two sources: the division between the educationally advantaged and disadvantaged and the multiplier effect of marital homogamy (Bajtelsmidt, Chapter 7, this volume) in a world of high female labor force participation. Well-educated men and women tend to marry one another, forming families with high earnings and few risks of unemployment. Less-well-educated couples will have lower wages and are far more likely to experience periods without work. Marital selection based on education is rising dramatically and is unlikely to abate. In the 1950s, there were very few highly educated women. The doctor married his nurse or his secretary. Today s/he is more likely to be married to another doctor or to a lawyer.

Morrisette and Johnson (2004) show that while the rise in the earnings gap among more and less educated individual workers has been negligible in Canada, the corresponding family earnings gap rose substantially between 1980 and 2000. Couples where both are university graduates saw their average annual earnings rise by 14 percent to 22 percent, while couples where both had high school education or less had stagnant or declining earnings.

The growing income gap between households will of course be compounded in countries like Britain and the United States where earnings differentials between more and less educated individuals have also widened. Butrica *et al.* (2003), for example, estimate that incomes among top quintile retirees in the United States, currently about eight times those of the bottom quintile, will rise to ten times those of the bottom quintile when the baby boomers retire—simply as a result of greater earnings inequality. Among current US retirees, the income of high school dropouts is 68 percent of the mean of their age cohort. The rising earnings gap means this figure will fall to 53 percent when the baby boomers retire.

It is virtually certain, then, that the stable, dual-earner, university-educated couples of today will be able to retire in relative affluence in 2040 irrespective of what happens to national pension systems. And well-educated childless couples will be the best positioned of all.

The fate of low educated couples is bleak. They have, of course, potentially more working years but they will require high demand for low skilled labor over most of their working lives to accumulate the wealth necessary for retirement at 65. It is also far from certain that more years employed helps to increase people's human capital (Klerman and Karoly 1994).

There are two paradoxes associated with this scenario. First, we will reap the largest economic gains if the most productive workers delay retirement and remain in employment longer; yet they are the very people who will be best positioned to retire early. High income earners with greater pension and private wealth outside public plans will be particularly immune to public sector efforts to induce later retirement.

Second, as we have noted, it is the well educated whose retirement will cost the most simply because their life expectancy is far longer (Hattersley 1999). They will consume a larger share of the national retirement budget and incur the larger health and care costs that arise as a result of increasing frailty at advanced old age. And the childless will require the most assistance of all.

Since, by definition and design, old-age insurance transfers income from those with shorter life expectancy to those with greater life expectancy, these two features raise important questions of intra-cohort distributive justice, in particular because mechanisms of social inheritance help reproduce inequalities from generation to generation.

## 5.2 Life Chances from Childhood

An individual's life chances are to a great extent a product of social origins and early childhood experiences. Children's educational attainment continues to be strongly correlated with parental income and education, and the cognitive skills they develop are similarly related to the parent's cultural resources (Shavit and Blossfeld 1993; Esping-Andersen 2004). As the knowledge intensity of our economies increases, citizens with low education and insufficient cognitive skills will, with growing likelihood, find themselves locked into a life of low wages and precarious employment. The risk of unemployment triples among those with less than secondary education, compared to those with some college (OECD 2003). A problematic working life in the coming decades will raise the likelihood of poverty in old age to a greater degree than among today's retirees.

Intergenerational transfers of wealth (both *inter vivos* while the parents are alive and in the form of bequests on their death) are also influenced by the new demographics. Low fertility raises the potential transfer to the next generation since the parents' wealth will be divided among fewer siblings. Since fertility is inversely related to education and income, inequalities due to social inheritance are likely to be far greater. Since well-off parents have fewer children, they can invest far greater resources per child during childhood and youth and later they will leave disproportionately greater per child bequests.

# 6 Public Policy for Equitable and Sustainable Retirement

Securing retirement for the mid-twenty-first century will depend as much on the quality, quantity, and allocation of our productive assets—physical, human, and environmental—as on any reforms we make now to the design of our pension systems. Higher productivity will help us to pay the additional costs of population ageing but it will not solve the associated distributional issues: high productivity economies are not necessarily the most equitable in distributional terms.

Paradoxically, then, there is a sound argument that good retirement policy must begin with babies. The distribution of welfare among tomorrow's retirees will above all hinge on the inequalities in life chances among today's children. If policy-makers are seriously concerned about equitable retirement in the future, the obvious first step would be to ensure more equality now of cognitive stimulation and educational attainment in childhood.

We are, fortunately, well-positioned to know how to invest effectively in children's life chances. Minimizing child poverty is *sine qua non* and would from a public finance perspective cost very little, in particular if employment among mothers becomes universal (Esping-Andersen 2002). Early intervention programmes, like the US Head Start, can be very effective in minimizing the potential damages of a problematic and underprivileged childhood (Heckman 1999). And it is equally clear that universal, high-quality pre-school care can have a strong leveling effect on children's cognitive and motivational development (Waldvogel 2002; Duncan and Brooks-Gunn 1996). It has been amply demonstrated that social inequalities in school performance and educational attainment have their roots in children's pre-school experience. Hence, early childhood investments equalize opportunities over the entire life course. Childcare provision is a win-win policy as it also helps reconcile motherhood and employment.

But our legacy to the next generation also includes the real welfare gains embedded in the social institutions inherited from the past, including those that enable the young to care for the old. As Schokkaert and Van Parijs (2003) highlight, the traditional family structure in which parents care for children when they are too young to work and children support their parents when they are too old and frail to work are important characteristics of the human species, probably with deep biological roots. Contemporary historiography (Haber and Gratton 1994) confirms that the emergence of mandatory public pensions was as important for the young as for the old, a form of risk-sharing not only against the risk of one's own longevity but also against the risk of one's parents' longevity and the imperative of supporting parents financially through an extended old age. For a species motivated by 'filial piety', old-age insurance is also insurance for the young. Rising pension costs may lead our children to complain about high taxes or to ask us to retire later. It is unlikely, however, that they will be grateful if we expose them to the risk of supporting us directly to the age of 95. Just as intergenerational justice requires us to leave them with a sustainable environment, it also requires us to leave them with institutions at least as good as those we have had to care for our parents in their old age.

If this is our bottom-line criterion for policy, how then might an 'at least as good' institutional environment be assured? As far as pension reform is concerned, most experts agree on a set of core fundamentals. First and foremost, sustainability requires raising the average retirement age (Sundén, Chapter 35, this volume). Most would probably advocate a return to age 65 as a benchmark target. There is much to be said for this: people begin their careers later, the health status of older workers is improving for each new cohort approaching retirement age, and the education and skills gap that until now was huge between older and younger workers is rapidly closing. Put differently, there is good news on both the pull and push side. Workers are less compelled to retire for health reasons, and employers will be less eager to rid themselves of older personnel.

Our institutions need, however, to adapt to postponed retirement. Pension accruals in many countries' retirement systems implicitly urge workers to take early retirement. Also wage bargaining systems based on seniority wage hikes need to be changed to avoid older workers being priced out of the market. An extreme example is France where a 60-year-old worker, simply due to seniority, earns 40 percent more than a worker aged 35. As pension entitlements are increasingly based on full-career earnings, rather than on the years immediately preceding retirement, the pressure behind seniority wages should ease considerably.

Raising the retirement age is one logical ingredient in a Musgrave-inspired Fixed Relative Proportions (FRP) model. But as we have discussed, it may have adverse consequences for equity if applied across the board since life expectancy is positively related to lifetime income. To pursue equity, incentives for delaying retirement would have to be graded positively to income. The dilemma here is that high income earners are likely to have large private pension savings that make them relatively immune to incentives in public schemes. If equity is a serious concern, there is a clear case for some harmonization of public and private pension plans. Since, in any case, private plans enjoy substantial tax subsidies it is legitimate to insist that they, too, act in the common good.

As Guillemard (2003) so persuasively shows, the 'one size fits all' model of retirement of the postwar era is no longer adequate. Its understanding of 'universality' was the product of highly standardized life courses characteristic of the uniformity of working lives in the age of high industrialism. The far more differentiated life courses of post-industrial economies require a different understanding of universality, one that allows for multiple and more flexible pathways into retirement including active labor market and partial retirement instruments.

Second, virtually all are agreed that maximizing future employment levels is key to securing future pensions. Again, this is clearly also a principal ingredient in any sustainable FRP model. The per capita additional burden that will fall on the 'young' will decline in proportion to the number of active workers. In part, the active labor force will automatically increase with delayed retirement. And, in part, the attainment of maximum employment will mainly have to come from female labor supply. This is perhaps the least challenging ingredient in any future scenario, simply because women's labor supply is growing very rapidly everywhere. Pissaridis et al. (2003) have argued that the Italian and Spanish pension systems may be more sustainable than one would think, considering very low fertility, simply because female employment in young cohorts is rapidly approaching universality. However, to ensure maximum female employment, most OECD countries will have to invest heavily in daycare services—at least if they aspire to raise fertility.

Female employment may provoke new dilemmas about equity. It will help close the gap with men in terms of accumulated pension rights. But marital selection implies a widening income gap between high and low earner couples that will influence not only joint pension income but also the age of retirement.

Maximum employment levels may not automatically translate into good and stable careers for all. Indeed, the new economy is likely to create far greater heterogeneity of life chances as wage differentials grow and job security wanes. The challenge here is that future generations may retire on a far more unequal footing in terms of accumulated savings and entitlements. Since those who now start adult life with less than secondary-level schooling or with inadequate cognitive skills face the prospect of a precarious career, they are likely to risk poverty in old age. If we believe that bad careers are mainly self-inflicted, then we need not worry about equity. The evidence, however, suggests otherwise. Clearly, early childhood investments are the most effective policy but it is unrealistic to assume that these will fully eradicate all risks. A good case can therefore be made in favor of some kind of basic pension guarantee financed from general revenue, not payroll taxes, as the bottom tier of any pension regime. As private pension plans grow in importance, this will heighten the degree of insecurity attached to future retirement income. Here, then, is a second good case for a basic pension guarantee. As Myles (2002) shows, this would incur very modest additional public expenditure if the guarantee were to be set just above the poverty line.

A basic pension guarantee, financed from general revenue, is an effective tool against poverty in old age but it has the added advantage of helping to diversify the financial base of pension expenditures. Payroll financing implies a relatively narrow (and potentially regressive) tax base and, indirectly, a narrow system of risk-sharing. And, as spending requirements will rise substantially over the next decades, so will payroll taxes and fixed labor costs.

A system overly reliant on payroll taxation has demonstrably adverse second-order effects, in terms of distribution, equity, and employment. Inducing more private pension plans will of course help to diversify the financial base, but these will hardly satisfy criteria of efficiency and equity and will also, most probably, generate more insecurity. If increased longevity is skewed in favor of the privileged and if, additionally, the current trend toward rising income inequality continues into the future, the case for more progressive financing of benefits is stronger than ever.

And if our first priorities are equity and security in old age it would be logical to propose that publicly financed programs, such as a guaranteed basic pension, should expand in direct proportion to the growth of private plans.

# Notes

Gosta Esping-Andersen's contribution was financially supported by a Spanish Ministry of Science and Technology research grant (MCyT SEC2003-02699). John Myles's contribution was supported by the Canada Research Chair program financed by the Social Science and Humanities Research Council of Canada.

1. US surveys of new retirees conducted by the Social Security Administration in the 1950s found the vast majority—90 percent—had 'retired' because they were laid off by their last employer or due to poor health. Less than 5 percent had 'retired' voluntarily or to enjoy more leisure. By the 1980s, involuntary layoff and poor health accounted for only 35 percent of retirees and the majority claimed to have left work voluntarily (Burtless and Quinn 2001: 384).
2. This conclusion is validated by a recent comparison that includes both public, private, and individual pension contribution financing (Bach *et al.* 2003). They find that adding all three contribution resources results in virtual financial convergence across countries with a very different pension mix.
3. It is often argued that family care is preferable from a welfare point of view. But here we should note two factors. One, increased longevity often implies levels of frailty that require labor-intensive, around-the-clock care. Two, externalizing care responsibilities does not automatically imply that familial solidarity evaporates. On the contrary, the level of interaction between frail elderly and their kind is, in Denmark, very frequent (Sarasa 2004).
4. Poverty rates estimated with the Luxembourg Income Study are measured as the share of population with family incomes less than 50 percent of the median income for all families after adjustment for differences in family size. See http://www.lisproject.org/ for definitions and data sources.
5. The FRP principle, however, would not satisfy a concept of fairness defined by the notion that each generation ought to pay the same proportion of salary to get the same level of pension rights during retirement. On a three-generational 'family farm', for example, the *share* of output required to support ageing parents in retirement under FRP will be larger when there are two producers in the working-age generation than when there are four.
6. This point was first raised by Frank Vandenbroucke (2002).
7. In the United States, 35 percent of those aged 75 and over fall in the lowest income quintile. In Europe, low incomes among households headed by a male aged 75 and over are prevalent only in the United Kingdom (estimates from the ECHP).
8. Recent French estimates show that at age 60, a male manager will live three years longer than a male manual worker (at age 35 the gap is 5.4 years) (Cambois *et al.* 2001, table 3). The gap is even wider (about seven years, and worsening) in Britain according to Wilkinson's (forthcoming) data.

9. The probability of survival is substantially higher among the rich, but so also is their expectancy of disability-free years. At the age of 60, French managers can expect four more disability-free years than a manual worker. Also, it is worth noting that the 'disability gap' between the two groups is widening over time (Cambois *et al.* 2001, table 5).
10. For the purposes of this discussion, we adopt the standard assumption that payroll taxes, even when borne by the employer, are additions to labor costs that are ultimately borne by employees, typically in the form of lower wages.

# References

BACH, J., LAITINEN-KUIKKA, S., and VIDLUND, M. (2003). 'Pension contribution levels in EU countries'. *The Finnish Pension Board: Intergroup Reviews*, No. 7

BARR, N. (2001). *The Welfare State as a Piggy Bank: Information, Risk, Uncertainty and the Role of the State.* Oxford: Oxford University Press.

BEAUJOT, R. (2004). *Delayed Life Transitions: Trends and Implications.* Ottawa: The Vanier Institute of the Family, 1–46.

BURTLESS, G., and QUINN, J. (2001). 'Retirement trends and policies to encourage work among older Americans', in P. Budetti, R. Burkhauser, J. Gregory, and H. A. Hunt (eds.), *Ensuring Health and Income Security for an Aging Workforce.* Kalamazoo, Mich.: Upjohn Institute, 375–416.

BUTRICA, B., IAMS, H., and SMITH, K. (2003). 'It's all relative: understanding the retirement prospects of the baby-boomers'. Center for Retirement Research at Boston College, Working Paper 2003–21. Boston.

CAMBOIS, E., ROBINE, J. M., and HAYWARD, M. (2001). 'Social inequalities in disability-free life expectancy in the French male population, 1980–1991'. *Demography*, 38: 513–24.

CORIJN, M., and KLIJZING, E. (eds.) (2001). *Transition to Adulthood in Europe.* Dordrecht: Kluwer.

DUNCAN, G., and BROOKS-GUNN, J. (1996). *Consequences of Growing up Poor.* New York: Russell Sage Foundation.

ESPING-ANDERSEN, G. (2002). 'A child-centred social investment strategy', in Esping-Andersen *et al.* (2002), 26–67.

—— (2004). 'Untying the Gordian knot of social inheritance'. *Research in Social Stratification and Mobility*, 21: 115–38.

—— D. GALLIE, A. HEMERIJCK, and J. MYLES (eds.), *Why We Need a New Welfare State.* Oxford: Oxford University Press.

GUILLEMARD, ANNE-MARIE (2003). *L'age de L'emploi: Les sociétés a l'épreuve du veillissement.* Paris: Armand Colin.

HABER, C., and GRATTON, B. (1994). *Old Age and the Search for Security: An American Social History.* Bloomington, Ind.: Indiana University Press.

HATTERSLEY, LIN (1999). 'Trends in life expectancy by social class—an update'. *Health Statistics Quarterly*, 2: 16–24.

HECKMAN, J. (1999). 'Doing it right: job training and education'. *The Public Interest* (spring): 86–106.

HECLO, H. (1988). 'Generational politics', in J. Palmer, T. Smeeding, and B. Torrey (eds.), *The Vulnerable*. Washington, D.C.: The Urban Institute, 381–411.

JACOBZONE, S. (1999). 'Ageing and caring for frail elderly persons: a review of international perspectives'. Labour Market and Social Policy Occasional Paper. OECD.

KLERMAN, J., and KAROLY, L. (1994). 'Young men and the transition to stable employment'. *Monthly Labour Review*, 117: 31–48.

LESTHAEGE, RON (1995). 'The second demographic transition in western countries: an interpretation', in K. Oppenheim-Mason and A.-M. Jensen (eds.), *Gender and Family Change in Industrialized Countries*. Oxford: Clarendon.

MORRISETTE, R., and JOHNSON, A. (2004). 'Earnings of couples with high and low levels of education, 1980–2000'. Ottawa: Statistics Canada. Analytical Studies Research Paper Series, No. 230.

MUSGRAVE, R. (1986). *Public Finance in a Democratic Society. Volume II: Fiscal Doctrine, Growth and Institutions*. New York: New York University Press.

MYLES, J. (2002). 'A new social contract for the elderly?', in Esping-Andersen *et al.* (2002), 130–72.

NOTESTEIN, F. (1944). 'The future population of Europe and the Soviet Union'. *Population Projections, 1940–1970*. Geneva: League of Nations.

OECD (1996). *Caring for the Elderly*. Paris: OECD.

—— (2001). *A Caring World*. Paris: OECD.

—— (2003). *Education at a Glance*. Paris: OECD.

PISSARIDIS, C., GARIBALDI, P., OLIVETTI, C., PETRONGOLO, B., and WASMER, E. (2003). 'Women in the labour force: how well is Europe doing?' Report to the Fifth European Conference of the Fondazione Debenedetti (June). Alghero.

SARASA, S. (2004). 'El descenso de la natalidad y los servicios de proteccion social a los ancianos'. *Informacion Comercial Española*, 815: 205–18.

SCHOKKAERT, E., and VAN PARIJS, P. (2003). 'Social justice and the reform of Europe's pension systems'. *Journal of European Social Policy*, 13: 245–63.

SHAVIT, Y., and BLOSSFELD, H. P. (1993). *Persistent Inequalities*. Boulder, Colo.: Westview Press.

THOMPSON, L. (1998). *Older and Wiser: The Economics of Public Pensions*. Washington, D.C.: The Urban Institute.

VANDENBROUCKE, F. (2002). 'Foreword', in Esping-Andersen *et al.* (2002), pp. viii–xxiv.

VELFAERDSKOMMISSIONEN (2004). *Analyserapport*. Copenhagen: Velfaerdskommissionen.

WALDVOGEL, J. (2002). 'Child care, women's employment and child outcomes'. *Journal of Population Economics*, 15: 527–48.

WILKINSON, R. (forthcoming). 'Inequality and health', in A. Giddens and P. Diamond (eds.), *The New Egalitarianism*. Oxford: Polity Press.

WOLFSON, M., ROWE, G., LIN, X., and GRIBBLE, S. (1998). 'Historical generational accounting with heterogeneous populations', in M. Corak (ed.), *Government Finances and Generational Equity*. Ottawa: Statistics Canada, 107–26.

# Index

Figures, notes and tables are indexed in bold e.g. 90f, 215n, 123t. When more than one table appears on the same page they are labeled **a** and **b**.

1/n strategy 608
401(k)plans (USA) 21, 109, 111, 203, 331, 362–363, 365–366, 366f, 367–369, 369f, 375, 377, 385–386, 457, 508, 513, 586, 606, 608, 610–612, 706–707, 731, 732, 733, 805
Aaron, H. 236, 269
Aaron-Samuelson condition 269
Aaronson, Stephanie 734
AASB 119 (Australia) 532
Abel, Andrew B. 565
Abrahams, Katharine G. 726
Abrams, Charles 598n
accident insurance 763
accountability 489–491
accounts 368, 374, 401, 404, 405, 418, 519, 522, 528, 529, 690, 741
    accrual 524
    funded 707
    generational 419, 433–435f, 436, 436t
    individual 434
    profit and loss 530–531, 536
Achenbaum, A. 39
active selection 569–570
actuarial-based systems 130, 146, 284, 402, 508, 511, 521, 524, 530, 537, 565, 843
    *see also* public pensions
    adjustment 318, 318f, 326, 326f, 328, 531
    balance 501–502
    fairness 201, 215, 250, 275–277, 279, 280, 281, 283, 287, 325, 331, 567–568, 575, 768, 816–817
    gains and losses 532, 534–535, 536

    management 828
    neutrality 275, 278, 270, 280, 281, 287
    public pensions 268–287
    reductions 225, 318, 323, 324
    reforms 327f(b)
    tables 521
    valuations 71, 230, 402, 826
Adams, Scott J. 728
Administradores de Fondos de Pensiones (AFPs) (Chile) 586
advanced funded systems 502
adverse selection 250, 567–568, 577
adviser-client relationship 648f
Afflect, A. 403
Africa 8, 62, 63, 73, 233, 783, 784f, 785, 829, 831, 833
    pensions 816–833
ageing 722, 843
    economics 82, 172–175
    medical ethics 640
    normal 640–641
    population 3, 10–11, 24, 63, 93, 151, 152, 153–154, 155, 163–169f, 170–181, 183, 189, 190, 197, 201, 202, 223, 226, 312, 312f, 314, 421, 501, 702, 713, 715, 722, 735, 736, 753, 782, 792, 809, 839, 845, 849, 852
    UK 11–12, 14, 38–39
    USA 343, 352
Age Discrimination Act (1986) (USA) 731
Age Discrimination in Employment Act (1967) (ADEA) (USA) 727–730, 732, 735
age-adjusted rebates (UK) 371

age/risk relationship 197
aged poor (UK) 39
Agnew, Julie 608
agriculture, decline 44
Agulnik, P. 243
aid funding 793, 795
Ainslie, George 610
Aizcorbe, Ana M. 634n
Akerloff, George A. 386
Alcon, Arnaa 135
Alderson, M. 408
Alesina, A. 150
Algeria 130
Allen, F. 484, 490
Allen, Steven G. 554, 555, 710
allocative efficiency 213
Alonso, W. 112
Alternative Secured Pension (UK) 376
altruism 144, 150, 185, 188, 195–196, 198, 567
Alzheimer's disease 641
Ameriks, John 191, 193, 196, 575, 605,
    -606, 610
amortization 506, 510–511
Ando, Albert 626
André, Christopher 627
Andrews, Emily S. 377n
Andrietti, V. 109
Anglo-Saxon countries 18, 19, 24, 78–79,
    83–84, 86–89, 90f, 94, 179, 208, 210,
    488, 492, 495, 505–507, 509, 517, 685,
    692, 694, 704, 767, 771, 841
Anglo-American systems 17, 90, 92f, 93, 148,
    274, 484
Anker, Richard 129
annuities 6, 22, 35, 73, 88, 111, 128, 130,
    134, 145, 232, 249, 286, 365, 376, 377,
    504, 511, 513, 514, 519, 544, 563, 573,
    574t, 575, 580, 588, 595, 633, 754,
    756, 812
  factors 282, 283
  inflation-indexed 565, 573
  markets 250, 562–581
  nominal payouts 573
  pricing 568–569, 571–573, 575, 577, 599
  products 577–578

regulations 578–579
timing 576–577, 578–579
UK 562, 570, 573–575, 576, 578
USA 562, 571–575, 577
taxation 572–573
voluntary 566–567, 573, 577
Apelt, Linda 635n
Apgar, William C. 625
'architecture of allocative mechanisms' 207,
    215
Ardington, E. 788, 821
Arenas de Mesa, A. 668, 679
Argentina 70–73, 134, 232, 247, 248, 260,
    381–382, 587, 590, 663, 665, 666, 667,
    668, 670, 673, 677, 679, 785, 786, 787,
    789, 792
Argyle, M. 644
Arita, F. 187
Arnold, R. D. 176
Arnott, R. 404
Arnsperger, C. 144
Arrondel, L. 185, 187, 192
Arrow, Kenneth J. 728
Arts, W. 152
Artus, P. 198
Ashe, Michael 598n
Ashenfelter, Orley 736n
Asher, M. G. 61, 246, 799, 800, 801, 809, 811,
    812, 833
Asia 4, 54, 56, 57, 59, 62, 63, 73, 170, 233, 246,
    782, 812, 813
  see also incomes, Asia
Asset Liability Management (ALM):
  pension funds 417–419, 422, 423–425, 425t,
    428, 430t, 431f, 433, 436–437, 508, 514
asset pricing models 452
assets 82, 132, 174, 177, 179, 184, 192, 195, 203,
    204, 207, 234, 236, 255, 257, 258, 259,
    260, 260t, 280, 295, 343, 365, 374, 376,
    408, 419, 420, 422, 424, 425, 427–428,
    430, 431, 432, 437, 443, 445–446,
    450–452, 456, 457, 459, 469, 470, 489,
    491, 505, 506, 507, 510, 521, 523,
    524–526, 528, 535, 549, 580, 586, 588,
    619, 621, 623, 625, 754, 791, 848

*see also* pension funds
   strategic asset allocation; tactical asset
   allocation
accumulation 244, 250, 563
allocations 188–189, 189t, 190, 195–197, 210,
   248, 257–258, 262, 264, 403, 411, 429,
   441–452, 457, 463, 466t(a), 466t(b),
   467t, 475, 507, 550, 556, 612, 614
   ceiling 529, 531, 534, 537
   classes 257, 257t, 444, 447, 462, 464
      UK 466t(a), 467
   costs 550–551, 591
   financial 213, 258, 597, 628, 629
   household financial 90, 90f
   long-term 205, 206, 207, 257
   retirement 818
   risk 432f, 446
      financial 191–193, 195–197, 428
assortative mating 136–137
assumptions (financial reports): 405–406
asymmetric information 548, 558, 559, 565,
   592, 594, 604, 729
Attanasio, O. 263, 280
Auerbach, A. J. 174, 433, 825
Ausink, John 333n
austerity 759, 769–771
Australia 17, 34, 38, 39, 41, 42, 62, 63,
   78, 83, 85, 89, 106, 123, 135, 204,
   243, 247, 248, 249, 250, 257, 257t,
   258, 260, 261, 262, 263, 273, 296,
   360, 514, 515, 532, 574, 575, 586,
   614, 623, 624, 627, 638, 694–695,
   696, 842
Austria 304, 306, 504, 505, 507
autonomy 643, 645–647, 650, 651, 652,
   656–657
average premiums 232
average prices 535
*Averting the Old Age Crisis* (World Bank) 72,
   176, 204, 782

baby-boom generation 16, 126, 174, 351, 608,
   712–713, 733, 849
backloading 724–725
Bach, J. 855n

Bader, V. 486
Bailey, Clive 122, 130, 238n
Bailey, J. V. 467
Bailliu, J. 204
Bajtelsmit, Vickie L. 125, 129, 135, 136, 137
Balan, David J. 737n
balance sheets 419, 419f, 420–432, 443–444,
   511, 530, 531, 535
   approach 521–522, 524, 525, 529, 532, 533,
   537
Baldwin, P. 101, 143, 150, 692
Balkans 598
Ball, R. M. 83
Bangladesh 782, 789
banking industry 36–37, 211, 213, 828–829
   pension payments 788
bankruptcy 446, 548–549, 555–556
Banks, James 576
Barberis, N. 418, 419, 429
Barbone, Luca 816, 827, 828, 832
Barr, N. 151, 153, 212, 667, 841
Barrell, Ray 635n
Barrientos, Armando 59, 61, 782, 783, 785,
   786, 787, 788, 793, 796n
Barro, R. 188
Baron, John M. 736n
Barsky, R. B. 190, 191, 194
basic needs 15, 17, 24
basic pensions 854, 855
Basic State Pension (UK) 369–370, 371,
   373, 375
Bateman, H. 89, 261
Bayesian methods 452
Bayly, C. A. 15
Beattie, R. 176
Beaujot, R. 849
Becker, Gary S. 135, 580, 193, 504, 722,
   724, 728
Beckert, J. 99
Beebower, G. L. 475
behavioral economics 607, 609–611, 613,
   614, 705
behavioral finance 198
Belgium 106, 130, 148, 313, 511, 513, 517, 703,
   705, 743, 766

862   INDEX

Bell, D. 102
Belsky, Eric S. 621, 627, 635n
Beltanski, L. 689
benchmarks 462, 467–474, 484, 516
Benediktsson, Haukur C. 585
benefits 4, 8, 9, 13, 15, 19, 42, 63, 73, 83, 86,
    146–147, 151, 155, 156, 177, 178, 215,
    224, 227, 233, 258, 259, 260t, 282, 297,
    299, 303, 310, 317, 328, 364, 366–367,
    387, 434, 436, 488, 489, 505, 510, 512,
    516, 525, 526–527, 549, 564, 570,
    585–586, 596, 705, 707, 712, 730, 741,
    743, 746, 747, 749, 751, 754–755, 763,
    795, 801, 824, 825, 844, 854
  see also social security systems, benefits
  delayed 317, 323, 331
  earned by husband 86
  Latin America 667–680
  phased withdrawal 249
  portability 591
  reduction 16–17, 324, 749
  retirement 243, 244, 247, 269, 286, 303,
    314, 514
  social security 330, 394
  trade unions 386–390
  uprating of overseas 295–296
  UK 11, 15, 61, 63, 328
  USA 68, 325, 364, 367, 387, 394, 485, 505
Beneria, Lourdes 130
Bennett, P. 694
bequests 249, 250, 513, 564, 567, 576, 588,
    626, 851
bereavement benefits (UK) 294
Berger, Mark C. 736n
Berger, S. 764
Berghahn, V. R. 104
Bernasek, Alexandra 135, 136
Bernatzi, Shlomo 264, 606, 608, 613
Bernheim, B. Douglas 124, 187, 204, 264, 576,
    605, 606, 607
Bernstein, Jared 383
Berry, Mike 635n
Bertrand, Marianne 788, 821
Bertranou, Fabio 71, 679, 786, 792
Besley, T. 490, 494

Beveridge, William Henry, 1st Baron
    Beveridge: 66, 68, 274, 280, 694, 761,
    767, 768, 772, 773
*Beveridge Report* (1942) (UK) 15, 42, 66, 73
Bewley, Truman F. 557
Bhattacharya, S. 461
Bicksler, J. 403
bilateral contractual relationships 494
bills 451
Binstock. R. H. 150
biometrics 515
birth rate 233, 237
  see also fertility
Bismarckian Continental systems 78, 82–83,
    90f, 91, 92f, 93, 275, 280, 686, 692,
    761, 764, 765, 772, 773
black women 124
Black, Dan A. 736n
Black, Fischer 403, 443, 446, 447, 453n, 485
Blackburn, Robin 110, 111, 392
Blackley, Canon William 39, 40
Blake, David 68, 371, 372, 452n, 467, 475, 476,
    477, 478n, 580
Blanchet, D. 188
Blau, Francine D. 130
Blinder, A. S. 151, 546, 550, 557, 684, 685
Blöndal, S. 278, 280
Blossfield, H. P. 851
blue-collar employees 44, 80, 83, 765, 760,
    761, 765, 774
Blue Cross plan (USA) 347
Blundell, Richard 557
Broadway, Robin 565
Boardman, Tom 580
Boccuti, C. 340
Bodie, Zvi 2–7, 406, 452n, 453n, 537n,
    556, 737n
Boelhouwer, Peter 634n
Boender, C. G. J. 418
Boeri, T. 11, 153, 279, 770
Bois, J.-P. 43
Bolivia 260, 261, 585, 587, 590, 598, 663,
    664, 665, 666, 669, 670, 673, 674, 679,
    781, 783
Bommier, A. 193

bonds 22, 206, 207, 256, 264, 366, 402–403,
    429, 432, 443, 446, 447, 450, 451,
    452, 466, 470, 508, 545, 572, 625,
    629, 841
  *see also* governments, bonds
  corporate rate 533, 536
  inflation-indexed 231, 250, 255, 265,
    515, 527
  ownership 189, 198, 205
  rates 22
  UK 467
Bonoli, G. 17, 686, 770
bonuses 587
book-reserve pensions 87–88, 504, 505, 595,
    596, 597, 694
Booth, Charles 13, 39, 41
Börsch-Supan, A. 173, 174, 279, 281,
    743, 770
borrowing 544
  increase 263
Bosworth, B. P. 740, 754, 756
Botswana 62, 782, 829
Bourdelais, P. 39
Bovenberg, L. 154
Bowers, H. 408
Bowie, D. 478n
Bowles, S. 150
Brady bonds 679
Brandt, M. W. 418, 453n
Brazil 208, 232, 665, 675, 782, 785, 786, 787,
    788, 791, 792, 793, 828
Brennan, M. J. 418, 452
Brenner, R. 104
Breyer, F. 151
bridge jobs (USA) 710, 711
Brinson, G. P. 475
Britain *see* UK
British Civil Service 79–80
British Empire 41, 61, 233
British Post office Savings Bank 38
Bróder, A. 22
Brooks-Gunn, J. 852
Broverman, Samuel 570
Brown, Geoffrey 476, 477, 565
Brown, Jeffrey 565, 571, 572, 575, 576

Brown, Kyle N. 396n
Brown, R. L. 234
Brugiavini, Agar 11, 280, 281, 576
Brumberg, R. 174, 183, 184
Brunner, Johann 578
Brydon, D. 485
Buchmueller, T. 347
Budd, A. 15
Bulow, Jeremy 331, 406
Buntin, M. B. 347
bureaucracy 33, 36
Burkhauser, Richard V. 557, 729
Burns, S. 175
Burrows, William 452n, 580
Burtless, Gary 136, 704, 740, 754, 756,
    849, 855n
Butrica, Barbara A. 123, 128, 849, 850
Burundi 785
Butler, Gillian 6
buyback provisions 827
Byrne, J. P. 216n

Cahill, K. E. 20, 710, 714, 715
Cambois, E. 855n, 856n
Campbell, John Y. 179, 418, 422, 423, 429,
    450, 451, 452, 453n
Campbell, N. 16
Canada 38, 39, 62, 63, 78, 83, 86, 87, 88, 91,
    106, 123, 173, 174, 187, 188, 205, 228,
    229, 273, 296, 303, 324, 325, 326,
    327–328, 329, 331, 360, 399, 506, 507,
    574, 577, 623, 627, 743, 744, 745, 748,
    757, 770, 842
Cancian, Maria 136
Canner, Glenn B. 625, 635n
Cannon, Edmund 573
capacity *see* competence
capital 106, 174, 188, 206, 386, 485,
    495, 504, 531, 597, 625,
    666, 713
  accumulation (pensions funds) 675–676,
    676t, 677–678, 681
  formation 206, 214
  funded pensions 756–757
  income 90f, 92f, 174

capital (cont'd)
  markets 151–152, 180, 192, 204–207, 214,
      231, 236, 399–412, 545, 559, 677,
      686, 833
    Latin America 675–678
  returns 678–679, 681
  systems, funded 746
Capital Asset Pricing Model (CAPM) 528
Capital Market Line 468
capital-labor ratio 173–174
capitalism 15, 101, 108
Caplin, Andrew 605, 606, 610, 630, 631
Caprio, G. 206
Card, David 736n
Cardinale, Mirko 574
Cardoso, J. C. 786, 787, 794
care, long-term 336–352
care in the community (South Africa)
      822–823
career-average formulas 511
Carhart, M. 476
Caribbean 233, 781
Carino, D. R. 418, 423
Carmichael, Lorne 736n
Carpenter, J. W. 476
Carroll, T. 406
Carruth, A. 554
cartels 207
Carvalho, I. 788, 796n
Case, Anne 788, 821
case law 488, 489
Case, Karl E. 626
Casey, B. 89
cash 20, 35, 42, 363, 386, 403, 429, 466,
      551–552, 558
  balance pension schemes 493, 511
  flows 421, 432, 434, 436, 464–465, 524,
      526–529, 533, 536, 568, 571
    accounting 524
  transfers 782
  wages 382, 544, 545, 548, 549
cash-pension trade-offs 550
Castellini, O. 281
Castles, F. G. 154
Catalan, M. 206

Catte, Pietro 627
Caussat, L. 188
*caveat emptor* 491
Central America 233
Central Europe 243, 492
Cerny, Aleš 559
certainty-equivalent approach 527–528
Certificates of Deposit (CDs) 207
Chabane, Mohamed 827
Chan, Sewin 630, 631
Chandler, A. D. 78, 79, 85
Chapman, J. 347
charitable organizations 15
charities 12
Chaskiel, P. 689
Checkland, D. 654, 655
Chen, K. C. 405, 408, 429
Chen, V. Y. 812
Chi, I. 810
children 851
Chile 71, 73, 134, 204–205, 209–210, 213, 232,
      243, 247–248, 260, 281–382, 574, 586,
      590, 598, 614, 663, 664, 665, 666, 667,
      668, 670, 673, 674, 675, 677–678, 679,
      753, 754, 783, 785, 787, 789, 792, 823
China 41, 61, 169, 170, 179, 244, 501, 801–802,
      805–806, 812, 813
Choi, James 607, 608, 609, 611
choice theory 192, 197, 198, 258, 263–264,
      450
Cifuentes, R. 204
citizenship 6, 98, 490, 761
  entitlements 143, 293–307
  non-citizenship 821
  pensions 99–100, 692
civil rights 302
civil service:
  pensions 36
  schemes 828
Clark, Gordon L. 11, 18, 20, 68, 78, 98, 100,
      155, 393, 483, 484, 488, 489, 490, 497n,
      498n, 503, 686, 694
Clark, Robert 68, 197, 555, 606, 710,
      804, 805
Clark-Murphy, Marilyn 135

class struggles 151
Claus, Iris 634n
clearing house 592
closed-end funds *see* investment, trusts
coalitions 16, 17, 25
Cobb-Douglas production function 214
Cocco, J. 410, 418
Cochrane, David H. 303, 436
codes of behavior 502–503
codes of conduct 516, 690
Coggin, T. D. 473
cognitive functions 641–642
Cohen, Randolph 444
Coile, Courtney 333n
Cold War 16, 24, 25
collateral 404
collective actors 151–152
collective arrangements 152–153, 694
collective bargaining 19, 85, 330, 365, 385, 386, 389–390, 502, 505, 516, 688, 695, 773, 775
collective foundations 690
Colombia 260, 663–664, 666–667, 669, 670, 673, 674
Commonwealth Treasury 81, 83, 89
compensation 87, 129, 317, 386, 544, 546, 550, 553, 556, 558, 721–736
competence 651–653f, 654, 656f, 657, 688
competition:
    private pensions (Latin America) 672, 673, 680
        management costs 673–674t, 675, 680
compulsory retirement systems 81, 243
Compston, H. 764
conflicts of interest 759, 760, 776
Congressional Budget Office (USA) 608
Connell, M. 686
Connolly, E. 263
Consiglio, A. 418
consultation 771–772
consumers 104, 594, 625
consumption 178, 193, 227, 263, 281, 547, 550–551, 575, 577, 580, 605, 625, 841
    household 183, 185, 785
    housing wealth 627, 628

life-cycle planning 564–565
    retirement 187, 231, 234, 236, 242
contracting-out options 21, 67, 68, 89, 504, 611, 804
contracts *see* employment, contracts
contractual savings 206
    *see also* national savings; savings
contributions 87, 109–110, 143, 146, 149, 176, 178–180, 188, 224–229, 231, 232, 233, 235, 247, 249, 258, 259, 260t, 263, 260, 268, 269, 273, 275, 280, 282, 283, 284, 285, 286, 294, 295, 303, 366, 376, 392, 417, 419–420, 426–427, 431, 433–435, 436, 437, 456, 463, 478, 504, 505, 506, 511, 522, 523, 524, 525, 526–527, 529, 543, 586, 587, 593, 595, 609, 613–614, 680, 693, 694, 741, 747, 748–749, 751, 753, 754, 763, 764, 805, 806, 819, 844, 847
    compulsory 244, 247, 698, 816, 825
    increasing 428–429
    Latin America 670, 671t, 679
    non-compliance 670–671
    rates 246, 255, 274, 274f, 286, 402–403, 423, 424, 428, 456–457
contributory pensions systems 4, 15, 18, 19, 23, 39, 40, 41, 61, 66, 67, 68, 71, 72–73, 80, 98, 99
    defined 154, 223, 242
'coordinated market economies' 106
Cooley, T. F. 768
Cooper, R. W. 404
Copeland, Craig 124, 132
Copeland, Phillip C. 732
Corber, W. 654, 655
Cornwell, Christopher 555, 736n
Coronado, J. L. 405, 732, 734
corporation tax 547
corporate bonds 568–569, 571, 625
corporate equities 631
corporate finance 399–412, 489
corporate governance 208, 213, 492
corporate pensions *see* occupational pensions
corporatism 766, 769, 771

correlations 418, 429, 447–448
corruption 816, 817, 832, 833
Corsetti, G. 206
Corijn, M. 849
Costa, Dora L. 716n
Costa Rica 663, 665, 666, 669, 670, 673, 675, 781, 783, 785, 792
costs 14, 22, 24, 42, 91, 93, 109, 110, 164, 180, 204, 327f(a), 327f(b), 328f, 434, 515, 556, 591, 593, 598, 732, 852
  acquisition 591–592, 595, 597
  administrative 110–111, 179, 256, 307, 589, 590–591
  agency 419, 423
  financial 840
  health plans (USA) 344–345
  living 230–231
  pensions 234, 237, 284, 524, 524–532, 536, 537, 550–553, 585, 736, 740, 763
  provider 591–592
  social security 63, 293
  transactions 192, 258, 443–444, 507, 545, 548, 550–551, 559, 590–591, 697, 698
Council of Europe 301, 302
Court of Protection (UK) 654–656
Coward, L. 87, 88
Cox, Samuel H. 580
Craig, Lee 68
Croatia 585
Crocker, Keith J. 579
cross-generational transfers 749–750
Crouch, C. 101, 102, 104
Cuba 665
Cui, J. 418, 433
cultural differences 187, 188, 197, 322
Cyprus 228
Czechoslovakia 41

Da Silva, L. C. 459, 460
d'Ambrosio, Madeline 197, 606
Dammon, Robert M. 447
Daniel, K. 472
D'Arcy, S. P. 404, 405
Dau, Ramadhani 62
Davidoff, Thomas 565

Davis, E. P. 98, 202, 205, 208, 210, 212, 213, 214, 215, 216n, 257, 371, 372, 459, 635n
Daykin, Chris 585, 586
de Ferranti, D. 793
De Gier, Erik 360
De Soto, Hernandez 818
Deacon, B. 686
death 750f
  benefits 134
  insurance 752
debt 204, 206, 209, 230, 401, 411, 445–446, 514, 529, 556, 619, 621, 625
  employer 399, 404, 406
  government debt 677
  public (Chile) 677–678
  transition 677
debt-equity ratios 208, 406
decision-making 689, 692
  impaired 651
  older people, financial 638–657
decumulation phase 248–255, 257, 265
  FDC schemes 251t, 252t, 253t, 254t
deferred benefits 71
deferred wages 18, 387, 504
deficits (pensions) (UK) 410f
defined benefit plans (DB) 19–20, 23, 61, 63, 71, 94, 109, 112, 131–132, 134, 147, 155, 175–177, 201, 233–236, 281, 284, 329, 359–378, 381, 385–387, 399, 429, 441–449, 496, 506, 507, 509–510, 512, 514, 518–519, 522, 528, 543, 549, 553–555, 558, 562, 575, 605, 664, 706–707, 714, 721, 724, 725, 729, 730, 731–734, 751, 763, 782, 807, 808, 825–828, 844
  *see also* occupational pensions
  accounting 521–537
  definition 536
  finance 223–239
  funding ratio 509f
  occupational 509–510, 603
  public 226, 232–235, 237–238, 417–419, 442, 444, 446
  UK 369–378, 543
  unfunded 524

USA 110, 203, 331, 336, 338, 365, 366f, 367–378, 382, 39–392, 457, 512–513, 543, 556, 557, 579
  advantages/disadvantages 368
  conversion trends 365
  coverage statistics 366
defined contribution plans (DC) 20, 99, 109, 112, 131–132, 134, 147, 148, 153, 155, 179, 201, 203, 211, 234, 236, 242, 246–250, 255–262, 264, 265, 359–378, 385, 399, 441–444, 446–447, 457, 477, 492, 493, 495, 496, 512–514, 519, 522, 543, 550, 554–555, 567, 584, 587, 606, 611, 614, 664, 705–706, 721, 731, 733, 734, 741, 753, 782, 800, 801, 825–827
  UK 371, 457, 543–544
  USA 336, 338, 366f, 382, 394, 457, 543–544, 557, 580
  account simulations 368
  advantages/disadvantages 368
  coverage statistics 366
  participant behaviour 368
Del Guercio, D. 208, 460
del Popolo, F. 783
Delgardo, G. S. 786, 787, 794
deliberative model 649–650, 657
dementia 641, 642f(a), 642f(b), 652
Demirgüç-Kunt, A. 206
democratization 34, 761
demography 163–181, 233, 241, 243, 247, 285, 286, 287, 584, 686, 702, 716, 721–722, 762, 792, 793, 807, 843, 848, 849
  ageing 7, 164, 269
  costs 23–24
  trends 164–172, 312, 421, 431
Denmark 13, 16, 18, 34, 41, 42, 103, 108, 109, 111, 148, 247, 296, 329, 399, 504, 506, 507–508, 512, 761–762, 763, 766–767, 840, 841, 842, 846
Dert, C. L. 418, 423
'deserving poor' 13
desire fulfillment theories 644
destitution *see* poverty
developing countries 781–795
Devereux, Stephen 62

De Vries, C. G. 418, 429, 433
Di, Zhu Xiao 621, 624, 635n
Diamond, Peter 151, 176, 177, 656
Dicks-Mireaux, L. 205
Dietze, G. 494
Dilnot, A. 478n
Diop, Ahmadou Yeri 832
Dirven, H.-J. 492
disability 40, 80, 134, 278, 283, 318, 319, 322, 329, 330, 342, 351, 371, 385, 388, 502, 640, 708, 709, 714, 741, 743, 754, 763, 772, 791, 830, 839
disclosures 516, 592, 593, 596
discount rate 186, 188, 193, 277, 278, 368, 403, 418, 421, 422, 424, 428, 431–433, 525, 526, 527, 528, 531, 533, 534, 536, 565, 568, 569, 570, 572, 573, 574, 575, 577, 610, 613, 733, 751
discounters 556–557
discrimination 302, 303, 305–307, 488, 505
  age 714, 721, 722, 733
    legislation 727–730, 735
  non-discrimination 516
  racial 822
  reduction 793
diseases, management 639
Disney, R. 11, 146, 156n, 202, 212, 273, 279, 280, 283, 284, 286, 371, 372, 375, 554, 757
'diversified quality production' 105
divorcees 133
Djelic, M.-L. 104
Dobbelsteen, S. 135
Dobronogov, Anton 585, 590
Dolan, Alex 635n
Doling, John 634n
Dominican Republic 663, 664, 665, 666, 667, 669, 673, 677, 680
Dore, R. 691
Dorsey, Stuart 555, 736n
dot.com bubble 484
Doyle, Suzanne 250, 575
Draper, P. 476, 477
dual-earner households 136, 137
Duflo, Ester 607–608, 788

Duncan, G. 852
Dupuy, J.-P. 689
'Duration Enhances Risk' (DER) 193–194
Durkin, Thomas A. 625, 635n
Dus, Ivica 575
Dushi, Irena 576, 577
Dvornak, Nikola 628, 635n
dynamic rebalancing 421–422

earnings 224–225, 227, 233, 268, 502, 723, 727, 844
  see also salaries; wages
  gap 850
  growth 283
  older people 714, 746
  profile 725–726
earnings-related benefits 61, 63, 66, 67, 68, 71, 86, 90, 242
earnings-related pensions 762, 824, 829
earnings-related supplementary pensions 696
East Asia 8, 169, 799, 800, 801–803, 812–814,
East Europe 63, 73, 492, 849
Ebbinghaus, B. 764, 765, 768, 769, 773, 774
Eckert, J. 99
Eckstein, Zvi 565
economic growth 34, 104, 109, 163–164, 176, 177–178, 180, 201–216, 231, 242–243, 528, 799
economic migrants 293
  see also migration
  economic models 544
economic risks 234–235
economics 33, 34
  see also ageing, population
economies of scale 104, 512, 585, 691, 698
economy 5, 11, 20, 102, 736
Ecuador 663, 665, 673
Edey, M. 17, 204
Edmonds, E. 788
education 131, 283, 512, 613, 714, 788, 800
  children 852
differences 849–850
  financial 264, 590
  older workers 715–716
Edward, Alejandra Cox 134

Edwards, S. 203
efficient market theory 393
efficiency gains 104–105, 519
efficiency within the limits 494
efficiency wage 386
Egypt 828
Eichenbaum, Martin 565
El Mekkaoui-de-Freitas, N. 19, 196
El Salvador 381–382, 663, 664, 665, 666, 667, 669, 673, 679
elderly dependency ratio 501
eligibility 315, 789
  see also retirement age
  USA 315–316, 338
Ellison, Robin 303, 498n
Elsinga, Marja 634n
Ely, J. H. 498n
Emmanuel, E. J. 647
Emmanuel, L. L. 647
emerging market economies (EMEs) 201, 208, 210, 214, 215
emigrés 294–295
Emmerson, Carl 66, 280, 576
*Employee Retirement Income Security Act (1974) (USA) (ERISA)* 87, 88, 131, 367, 485, 488, 505
employer-sponsored retirement plans *see* occupational pensions
employment 16, 43, 62, 77, 99, 101, 102, 103, 106–107, 175, 204, 224, 225, 228, 330, 242, 280, 300, 351, 367, 369, 370, 530, 550, 671, 705, 708, 744, 794, 846, 853
  career 152–153
  contracts 106, 107t, 108, 543, 547, 550–551, 552t, 555
  informal 782
  long-term 733
  older people 632, 703, 712
  part-time 107, 109, 129, 131, 262
  relationship 735
  taxes 844
  temporary 106–107
*Employment Outlook* (OECD) 108
endowments 441, 459, 589–590

enduring power of attorney (EPA) 655–656
Engelen, Ewald 100, 486
England *see* UK
entitlements 16, 17, 21, 23–24, 62, 71, 72, 280, 281, 293–307, 387, 745
   pension 745f
equality movements 130
equitable treatment 23, 767–768, 813, 846, 847, 854, 855
equities 35, 150, 188–189, 191, 197, 198, 205, 206, 207, 211, 229, 257, 264, 368, 374, 403, 406, 411, 423, 426, 429, 443–444, 450, 451, 459, 462, 466, 470, 476, 509, 510f, 528, 531, 545, 556, 588, 597, 628, 632, 841
   allocation 409–410
   markets 208, 213, 257, 258, 447
   returns 533–534
   UK 460t, 467, 475
Eschtruth, A. 710, 714, 715
Esping-Andersen, Gosta 6, 16, 18, 78, 82, 98, 101, 102, 148, 492, 685, 686, 761, 764, 766, 852, 852
Estienne, Jean-François 61
étatism 766
ethical financial decision-making 638–652f, 653–657
Ethiopia 63, 783
Europe 15–16, 17, 18, 21, 24, 33, 35, 36, 39, 44, 62–63, 78, 82, 83, 100, 104, 110, 130, 141, 144, 150, 153, 155, 169, 197, 198, 208, 210, 212, 269, 275, 297, 313, 319, 336, 359, 370, 381, 388, 392, 485, 506, 507, 512, 513, 517, 588, 592, 594, 608, 609, 628, 638, 642, 684, 685, 686, 687, 691, 692, 694, 695, 697, 702, 704, 705, 708, 713, 715, 761, 766, 767, 770, 771, 773, 841, 847
European Code of Social Security 301
European Commission 306
European Community 300
European Convention on Human Rights 301, 302, 305–306
European Court of Human Rights 300–301

European Court of Justice 298, 300–301, 767
European Economic Area (EEA) 299
European social model 694
European Union (EU) 109, 111, 154, 171, 293, 294, 295, 296, 306, 510, 519, 524, 533, 579, 595, 686, 697, 703–704, 705, 713, 714–715, 768
Even, William E. 127, 136
exclusion 100, 112, 793
exclusive benefit rule 483, 486
exit 484
Exley, J. 155, 402, 423, 437n, 478n, 515, 537n
expenditures (pensions) 63, 73, 87, 227, 232

Fabozzi, F. J. 473
Faccio, M. 208
factor productivity 173, 208
   total (TFP) 213
Fama, Eugene F. 450, 470
family 7, 62, 121, 126, 133, 136, 137, 152, 172, 299, 760, 799, 832–833, 840, 841–842, 849, 852
   extended 831
fee-based advice 592–593
fees (pension funds) 258–259
Feldman, D. 42
Feldstein, M. 6, 176, 179, 187, 188, 203, 215n, 242, 279, 280, 405, 406, 749, 754
female labor 106, 107t
Ferris, Shauna 822
Ferson, W. 472
fertility 502, 810
   decline 10, 20, 151, 163, 164–165, 166, 169–172, 201, 243, 285, 377, 712, 753, 840, 851, 854
final salary pensions 20, 526
finance 15, 126, 213, 433, 489, 528, 537, 587, 655, 686
   abuse 639, 657
   behavioral 263
   burden 176, 201, 343
   decision-making for older people 638–657

finance (cont'd)
  innovations 207, 215
  institutions 506, 514, 515
  literacy 135, 197, 513, 605
  pension 684
    increases 230–231
financial markets 4, 11, 22, 24, 110, 179, 185,
    196, 197, 205–208, 243, 249, 257, 365,
    375, 404, 447, 496, 502, 549, 628
  consumer behavior 598
  financial performances 586
  global 21–22, 154, 155, 174, 685, 698
  Latin America 677
  products 20, 264–265, 513, 593
financial performances 586
Financial Reporting Standard 17, 374–375
financial services 5, 20, 23, 489, 490, 491, 502
  European 698
*Financial Services Act* (1986) (UK) 594
Financial Services Authority (UK) 491
Financial Supervisory Authority (UK) 593
financial sustainability 843
Findlater, Alec 574, 580
Finkelstein, Amy 573, 578, 579
Finland 280, 505, 506, 596
first-world retirees 21–22
fiscal budgeting 16
fiscal burden 16, 18
fiscal coherence 298
fiscal implications 320–327f, 328
Fitzgerald, R. 36, 37
Fixed Contribution Rate (FCR) 147
Fixed Relative Position (FRP) 147, 844, 853
Fixed Replacement Rate (FRR) 147
flat-rate benefits 61, 67, 71, 98, 556
Fletcher, Frank 591
Flora, P. 770
flow-through model 522, 523, 537
Fong, Wai Mun 575
Fontaine, J. A. 207, 209
Ford, Janet 634n
Fordism 103
foreign direct investment 174
foreign instruments 678

foreign investments 257
Fornero, E. 281
Fox, L. 283
fragmentation 152–153
France 21, 36, 39, 43, 101, 106, 110, 144, 153,
    187, 188, 191, 196, 223, 224, 232, 243,
    269, 313, 326, 457, 459, 460, 608, 609,
    623, 627, 692, 693, 694, 696, 703, 705,
    708, 743, 744, 761, 763, 765, 766, 769,
    770, 771, 772, 773–774
Franks, J. 459, 460
'fraternal solidarity' 143, 144, 150
  *see also* social solidarity
  redistribution among pensioners 151
Frederick, Shane 610
Freedman, Vicki A. 714
Freeman, Charles 630, 631
Freeman, Richard B. 385
French, Kenneth 350, 470
Friedberg, Leora 734, 737n
Friedman, Benjamin 571
friendly societies 38, 80, 85, 830
front-loading charges 591
Frost, Peter A. 453n
FRS 17 (ASB 2000) 521, 522, 524, 526,
    532–534, 536
Fultz, Elaine 62, 176
funding (pensions) 72, 99, 147, 164, 178, 180,
    201–216, 226, 227, 230, 232, 260, 279,
    283, 368, 400–403, 411, 441, 506, 507,
    508, 756
  growth 210–211, 215
  occupational pensions 509–512
  partial 228–229, 233
  ratios 423, 426–428, 430, 431f, 432, 506,
    507–508
  UK 88, 177–178
  underfunding 430

G-5 205
G-7 210, 459, 623
Gabel, J. R. 345
Galasso, V. 154
Gale, W. 215n
Galer, R. 497n

Galup, John L. 818
Gamet, L. 692
Garibaldi, P. 854
Garrett, Daniel 264, 606
Gaunt, D. 35
gender 6, 106, 121, 123t, 579
   *see also* men; women
   bias 767–768
   differences 122–125, 134–135, 316
      life expectancy 126t
   discrimination 306
   earnings gap 129
   inequalities (Latin America) 679–681
   labor force participation 173
   roles 129–130, 173
   USA 125t, 127t
generality *see* universality
generations *see* intergenerations
geography 6, 818
George, L. K. 150
Germany 13, 18, 37, 40–41, 44, 101, 103, 105,
     106, 108, 110, 147, 148, 153, 171, 177,
     187, 223, 224, 232, 242, 243, 269, 281,
     284, 286, 302, 313, 318, 318f, 319, 319f,
     324–326, 326f, 329, 411, 457, 459, 460,
     503–504, 505, 506, 511, 517, 596, 597,
     623, 627, 692, 693, 703, 705, 713, 715,
     722, 743, 744, 753, 754, 761, 763, 765,
     766–767, 770, 771, 772, 774
Gerrans, Paul 135
Gershuny, J. 102
Gersovitz, M. 404
Ghana 783, 785
Ghent, Linda S. 710
Ghent system 766
Ghilarducci, Teresa 19, 110, 385, 392, 395n
Gieselink, G. 765
gift exchange 386
Gigerenzer, G. 22
Gill, I. S. 176, 586, 587, 667, 668, 669, 670,
     672, 674, 675, 676, 677, 679, 680,
     681n, 782, 789, 793
Gillion, Colin 122, 130, 238
gilt-edged securities 696
Gini coefficients 742

Ginsburg, P. B. 345
Girouard, Nathalie 627
Glaeser, E. 150
Glass, Richard D. 822
Glazer, N. 144
global competition 11, 106
globalization 6, 8, 11, 24, 93, 152, 154–155, 495
Gluck, M. 350
'Golden Age of Capitalism' 102, 108, 112
Gokhale, J. 433, 726, 751
golden rules 174, 485, 486–492, 495
Gollier, C. 193, 194
Goodfellow, Gordon P. 396n
Goodwin, R. 492
Gordon, R. H. 146
Gorman, M. 783, 785
Goswami, Ranadev 61
Gould, G. 418, 422
governance 148, 247–248, 261, 410, 411, 412,
     516–517, 692–693, 774, 816, 826, 832
   *see also* pension funds, governance
governments 691, 692, 693, 841, 842
   bonds 72, 426, 472, 514, 527, 568
   control 831
   Europe 691–692
   investments 696
   pensions 82, 381, 684
      earnings-related (UK) 88–89; limited
         85–86
      USA 382
   regulations 255
   retirement plans (USA) 132
   revenues 328, 792
   spending 242, 326
Graduated Retirement Benefit Programme
     (UK) 89
Granger-causality 206
Graebner, W. 81
Graetz, M. J. 176
Gratton, B. 39, 44, 852
Great Depression 15, 16, 24, 25, 68, 82, 388,
     389, 761
Greece 505
Greenwald, B. C. 207, 215
Gregory, A. 475, 477

Gribble, S. 845
Griffin, J. 644
Griffiths, I. 523
Grinblatt, M. 470, 472, 476, 477
Grint, K. 104
Gronchi, E. 281
Groshen, Erica L. 726
gross domestic product (GDP) 63, 206, 209, 213, 214, 247, 281, 283, 286, 326, 336, 360, 457, 459, 586, 588, 675, 792, 795, 808, 809, 810, 819, 829, 840, 841, 843
gross national product (GNP) 174, 828
Gruber, J. 16, 177, 278, 280, 315, 319, 320, 325, 333n, 706, 747
Grushka, Carlos 71, 792
guarantees:
  government 596
  payouts 588
Guatamala 665
Guillemard, Anne-Marie 853
Guillot, M. 14
Guinea 783
Guiso, L. 190, 191, 194, 196
Gustman, Alan L. 377n, 553, 554, 557, 606

Haber, C. 39, 44, 852
Haider, Steven 705, 716n
Hall, Greg 635n
Hall, P. 11, 105, 691
Hall, Robert E. 723
Hannah, Leslie 18, 80, 81, 83, 86, 89, 377n, 695, 699n
Hansell, S. 209
Hanoch, G. 193
Harbrecht, Paul P. 386, 387
harmonization (pension plans) 707, 766
Harris, T. 537n
Harrison, J. M. 403
Hartel, Charmine E. J. 129
Hassel, A. 764, 769, 773, 774
Hattersley, Lin 846, 850
Hawkins, J. 208
Hawley, J. P. 20, 485
Hayward, J. E. S. 142
Hayward, R. 855n

Headey, B. 492
health 578, 631, 788, 845, 846
  annuity 564
  care 502, 522, 643, 800–801, 840
    long-term 822; older people 714, 853; USA 132, 336–352
  costs 177, 250, 264
  insurance 43, 382, 387, 390, 395, 567, 716
  reduction of work 709
health maintenance organization (HMO) (USA) 341
Hebb, Tessa 393
Heckman, J. 852
Heclo, H. 847
hedge funds 256, 402, 404, 406, 418, 421, 448–449, 451, 452, 464, 514, 515, 528, 534, 545, 547, 553, 676
hedonism 644
Heemskerk, F. 418
Heller, P. S. 177
Hellerstein, Judith K. 714, 727
Hemerijck, A. 154
Hendrick, J. 639
Hendricks, D. 477
Henley, A. 554
Hennock, E. P. 41
Herbertsson, Tryggvi 585, 586, 598n
herding behavior 210
Hernández, H. 668
Herrigel, G. 104
Heslop, A. 783, 785
heterogeneity 152–153
Heuveline, P. 14
Hewitt, C. 151
hierarchies of worth 689–690, 697
Hill, Catherine 131
Hill, J. 478n
Hill, Tomeka 396n
Hinrichs, K. 686, 693, 698
Hinz, Richard P. 134, 262, 266n, 782
Hirsch, Barry 129
HIV/AIDS 166, 794, 826, 830, 831
Hodrick, Robert J. 450
Hoevenaars, R. P. M. M. 418, 422, 429
Hoffa tactic 393

Holzmann, R. 177, 178, 206, 209, 213, 262, 266n, 782, 789
Honduras 665
Hong Kong 247, 627, 628, 800, 810
Hood, L. R. 475
Hope, T. 639
horizon effects 429–431
hostile takeovers 726, 734
'house rich, cash poor' retirees 619, 633, 634
households 135, 136, 152, 194, 279, 740, 787–788
　annuities 575–578
　consumption 625–626
　extended 785
　financial assets 90f, 92f, 135, 183, 190
　income 135–136, 742, 786
　responsibilities 125–126, 130
　retirement planning 548–559, 603–615
　savings 187–188
　single person 564
housing 619, 631, 633, 634, 800
　affordability 624, 629, 630
　bubble (USA) 618, 629–630
　downsizing 631–632
　equity 619, 620–621, 624–625, 632–634
　investment 20–21, 262
　ownership 628–629, 631, 633–634
　　older people 631–632
　partnerships 630–631
　prices 623–624, 627, 629–630
　renting 625, 628–629, 631, 633, 634
　wealth 8, 255, 618–634
Hu, Y. 206, 213, 214, 215
Huber, E. 764
Huberman, Gur 608
Hujo, K. 668, 670, 677
Hulse, M. 686
human capital 174, 195, 196, 711, 722–723, 724, 726, 727, 728, 732, 783, 788, 850
human rights:
　case law 293–295
　international law 300–306
　pensions 300–301
*Human Rights Act 1998* (UK) 301
Hungary 260, 512, 513, 585

Hurd, Michael 605, 608, 609, 750, 751
Hutchens, Robert 710
Hviding, K. 204
hyperinflation 15, 18, 73, 78
Hyslop, Dean R. 136

Iams, Howard M. 123, 128, 849
IAS 19 526, 529, 532–534, 536
Iceland 299, 306, 504, 506, 512, 585, 590, 598, 703
illness 642–643
immigration 20, 153, 237, 502, 713
impaired life annuities 578
Impavido, G. 206, 782, 789
Imperial Austria 41
implicit tax 310, 317, 319–320, 331, 373
implied longevity yield 570–571
　*see also* longevity
incentives 25, 178, 331–332, 503, 703, 733
　retirement 280, 319, 321, 322, 331, 731
　taxation 773
　work 707, 712, 716, 729
incomes 33–35, 40, 128, 131, 143, 185, 298, 443, 514–515, 613, 628, 629, 634, 655, 693, 740, 853
　Asia 799–814
　disposable 848
　distribution 16, 25, 91, 122, 136, 146, 179, 630, 741, 743, 744, 746, 750, 751, 757, 820, 844–845
　future 605, 625
　inequality 23, 136, 743, 743t, 854
　low 37, 41, 343
　older people 83, 93f, 155, 747
　replacement rates 15, 17–18, 23, 24, 67, 98, 255–256, 608, 609
　retirement 124, 144, 146, 255, 264, 359–360, 369, 376, 377, 421, 434, 494, 512, 514, 515, 518, 579, 584, 619, 768–769, 775–776, 799–814, 841
　security 73, 128
　systems 90, 759
　tax 262, 298, 546
　UK 374, 375–376
　USA 122, 136, 363f, 368, 395, 622

874  INDEX

independent financial advisers 646–647
index funds 258
index-linked:
   bonds 155, 451
   policies 588
indexation 207, 268, 281, 283, 285, 286,
       417, 419, 424, 426–430, 433, 436,
       437, 452, 511, 514
India 61, 63, 24, 782
individual responsibility for pensions 24,
   38, 71
individual retirement accounts 543–559,
   586–587
individual savings accounts 61, 100, 137,
       283, 377, 381–382, 802
individualization 104, 149, 152–153, 172–173,
       184, 281, 298, 638
   freedom 584–595
   retirement planning 603–615
Indonesia 800, 809–810, 811, 812
industrial economy 76, 79
industrialization 33, 34, 37, 77, 101–102,
       338, 760, 762, 800, 849, 853
inefficiency 816
inequality 6, 150, 740–757, 816
inflation 71, 227, 230–232, 237, 246, 249,
       377, 389, 419, 421, 423, 427, 432,
       511, 514, 528, 577, 622, 817
   *see also* bonds, inflation-indexed
informal economy 818–819
informal sector 824–825, 832
information 657, 808
informative model 647, 649, 650, 657
insolvency 596, 753
institutions 149, 151–152, 204, 502
insurance 176, 459, 548
   companies 399, 461, 514–515, 548, 562,
       564, 568, 578, 579, 580, 585, 586
   markets 21, 149, 460
   plans 99, 177
insured markets 88, 672, 672t, 673
interest groups 759–776
interest rates 419, 421, 422, 432, 450,
       452, 507, 508, 527–528, 571, 621,
       630

intergenerational 851
   accounts 433–434
   conflicts 760, 768
   contracts 843, 845, 846, 847–848
   distribution 845
   equity 11, 177, 273–275, 280, 281, 282, 287,
       351, 586–587, 813, 845
   imbalances 437
   neutrality 279
   risk-sharing 512, 515
   solidarity 229, 269
   tax component 279
   transfers 188, 851
   younger 20
internal rate of return (IRR) 570, 573
International Labor Office (ILO) 62, 177,
       225, 228, 301, 668, 799, 802, 812, 818,
       819, 830
International Social Security Association
   (ISSA) 301
interpretative model 649, 650, 657
invalidity 760
   benefits 299
   insurance 752
   pensions 225
investments 77, 85, 91, 110, 134, 135, 137, 178,
       208, 213, 231, 233, 243, 257, 258, 262,
       365, 366, 375, 381–382, 403, 408, 417,
       437, 457, 476, 485, 504, 509, 512, 524,
       534, 573, 585–586, 593, 596, 597, 605,
       606, 614, 619, 643, 646, 723, 744, 829,
       831, 842
   accounts 753–754
   funds 244, 247, 456, 666
   international 207, 210, 229
   long-term 449–451, 589
   management 458, 461, 464
   policies 420, 428, 441, 459
   management 458–459, 464, 465
   risk adjusted 468–470
   reserves 229–230
   returns 255–259, 261, 298, 478, 522,
       530–531, 543
   risks 132, 179, 180, 249, 519
   trusts 459

Ippolito, Richard A. 367, 377n, 404, 473, 556, 557, 732
Ireland 35, 106, 109, 273, 505, 507, 513, 608, 609, 623, 772, 774–775
Israel 574
Issacharoff, Samuel 731
Italy 39, 101, 110, 148, 153, 171, 178, 196, 204, 212, 243, 246, 260, 280, 281–283, 284, 286, 313, 315, 320, 459, 512, 513, 623, 627, 703–704, 705, 707, 710, 715, 761, 763, 766, 768, 769, 771, 772, 773–774, 803, 841, 842, 854
Iyengar, Sheena 608
Iyer, S. 228

Jackson, G. 109
Jacoby, Sanford 389
Jacobzone, S. 840
Jafari-Samimi, A. 188
Jagannathan, R. 189, 193, 453n
James, D. 404, 405
James, Estelle 134, 176, 204, 392, 574, 585, 590, 796n, 806, 811, 831
James, R. 392, 802
Japan 37, 61, 89, 105, 169, 170, 171, 176, 177, 179, 187, 188, 208, 210, 228, 229, 243, 312, 313, 399, 401, 407, 411, 457, 504, 509, 511, 532, 533, 623, 627, 628, 703, 709, 711, 722, 744, 747, 753, 801, 803–805, 810, 813, 841
Jenks, Wilfred C. 301
Jensen, M. C. 469, 470, 473, 483
Jensen alpha measures 470–472, 475, 475f
Jesuit, D. 741
Jewish immigrants 42
Jianakkoplos, Nancy A. 125, 129, 134, 135, 136
Jiang, Wei 608
Jin, Li 452n
jobs 16
  mobility 108, 109, 111, 112, 553
    UK 554
  new (older people) 715
  part-time 711
  security 854

tenure 12, 19, 35, 86, 94, 99, 101, 106, 107, 108, 119, 129, 131, 157, 365, 385, 386, 554, 557, 711, 722, 723, 724, 731, 733, 734, 765
turnover 553–555
Johnson, A. 850
Johnson, N. J. 750
Johnson, Paul 38, 44, 66, 478n, 557
Johnson, Richard W. 737n
joint life annuity 564
Jolls, Christine 736n
Jones, D. T. 105
Jones, M. 478n
Jong, de, F. 418, 433
Joss, Richard R. 396n
Jousten, Alain 69
Juster, F. T. 190, 191, 194, 576
justice 150, 816–833

Kahneman, D. 22, 198, 649
Kakwani, N. 783
Kaman, Vicki S. 129
Kangas, O. 693, 699n
Kanjanaphoomin, N. 812
Karoly, L. 850
Kaseke, Edwin 831
Kaufman, Bruce E. 386
Kazakhstan 585
Keese, M. 803
Keilman, N. 166
Kennedy, D. 486
Kennedy, L. 35
Kennickell, Arthur B. 131, 634n
Kent, T. 418, 423
Kenya 62, 63, 630
Kerrigan, Graeme K. 826
Kersbergen, K. von 761
Kim, Tong Suk 450
Kimball, M. S. 190, 191, 194
King, Mervyn A. 197, 205, 452n
Kingston, G. 260
Kitamura, Y. 187
Kitschelt, H. 104
Klein, Jennifer 382
Klerman, J. 850

Klyzing, E. 849
Knight, F. H. 688
Kocherlakota, N. R. 189, 193
Kogelman, S. 419
Kohl, M. 202, 204
Kohler, M. 263, 635n
Kohli, M. 99
Kohn, Sally 303
Komter, A. 152
Kooreman, P. 135
Korpi, W. 761, 764
Korea 505, 782, 800, 801, 802–803, 806–808, 813
Kotlikoff, Laurence J. 174, 175, 331, 332, 433, 557, 580, 726, 729, 730, 751, 825
Kouwenberg, R.R. P. 423
Kritzman, M. 426
Kumar, K. 102

labor 77, 82, 89, 104, 130, 153, 206, 212, 255, 555, 736, 764
    force participation 170, 172, 173, 177–178, 180, 233, 269, 279, 280, 312, 313f , 316, 317f, 329, 321, 323, 323f, 324, 324f, 325–326, 328–330, 332, 377, 502, 631, 703, 704f, 708, 716, 759
    Latin America 668–669t, 670; USA 130f, 136, 137, 310–332, 329, 746; workers of retirement age 703–705
    law 692
    markets 12, 16, 20, 82, 100, 106–108, 110, 111, 121, 125–126, 128–130, 152–153, 185, 189, 215, 231, 236, 329, 330, 374, 545, 551, 553, 557–559, 584, 691, 703, 706, 708–710, 727, 760, 767, 800, 849, 853
    mobility 686, 707
    pensions coverage (Latin America) 680
    unused capacity 321f, 322f
Laboul, A. 505
Lagnado, R. 418
Laibson, David 607, 608, 609, 610, 612
Laitineen-Kuikka, S. 855n
Laitner, John 576
Lakonishok, J. A. 461, 473, 476

Lamfalussy process 698
Lane, Christel 105
Langbein, J. H. 485
Lange, P. 104
Langley, P. 109
Lasfer, M. A. 208
Latimer, M. 78
Latin America 8, 61, 63, 72, 209, 243, 247–249, 261, 381, 585, 586, 663–680, 781, 782, 783, 784t, 785, 786, 789, 791, 793, 794
    *see also* contributions, Latin America
Latupille, Denis 122, 130, 238n
Latvia 178, 270, 281, 283–284
Lazear, E. P. 19, 81, 331, 365, 386, 723, 724, 725, 726, 727, 728, 729, 730, 731, 732, 734, 735
lay-offs 839
Leahy, John 605, 606, 610
Leape, J. I. 197
Lee, J. 803
Lee, Mary 395n
Lefort, F. 206, 209, 210
legacy costs 382, 387, 390–391
legislation 299, 302, 488, 492–496, 502–503, 505, 515
    state pensions 302–304
    UK 303–304, 370, 371, 374, 506
    USA 367, 49, 506
Lehmann, B. 476, 477
Leibfried, S. 108
Leibowitz, M.L. 419
Leimer, D. R. 748, 749, 751
Leisering, L. 108
Levine, Philip 122, 124, 129
Levine, R. 215n
Lesthaege, Ron 849
Li, J. 406
liabilities 154, 390, 399–401, 401t, 402, 403, 404, 405–409, 409f, 412, 418, 419, 420, 421, 422, 424, 428, 429, 430, 431, 432f, 433–435, 435f, 436, 436t, 445, 448, 452, 467–468, 489, 506–508, 514, 515, 516, 519, 521–522, 523, 524–536, 607, 762, 792, 793, 806

'liberal market economies' 105–106
liberalism 685, 686
Lichtenstein, Nelson 384, 392
Liebman, J. 242, 741, 749, 754
Liechtenstein 299, 304
life;
   *see also* longevity
   annuities 751–752
   course redistribution 793
   expectancy 145, 150, 163–164, 166, 184, 185,
      186, 186f, 225, 228, 233, 242, 243, 247,
      249, 282, 284, 511, 514, 515, 521, 530,
      562, 564, 567, 584, 631, 680, 702, 705,
      707, 750, 752, 760, 810, 811–812, 840,
      850–851
      gender differences 126t; housing wealth
      628–629; retirement policy 127;
      women 125–126
   insurance 38, 203, 208, 210, 265, 371, 459,
      506, 514, 574, 587–590, 595, 830
      companies 22, 250, 592; unit-linked
      589t
life-cycle consumption planning 564–565
life-cycle earnings 721, 725–727
Life-Cycle Hypothesis theory (LCH)
   183–185f, 186–186f, 187–190, 198,
   232, 626
life-cycle models 173, 202, 244, 545, 576, 579,
   608, 610
lifetime:
   career 374–375
   earnings 82–83, 128
      individual choice 129–130
   income 134
   portfolio selection theory 190
limited liability 444–446
Lin, Jijia 580
Lin, X. 845
Lindbeck, A. 271
Lindberg, G. 41
Linderman, David 61
Lindert, P. H. 150, 151
Lion, H. 694
liquidation basis 419, 419f
liquidity 207, 210, 249, 447, 491, 514

constraints 185, 203, 271, 550, 731
Litterman, Robert 453n
Liu, Lillian 62
Liu, Xiaodong 624, 635n
living conditions, poor 40
living standards 4, 24, 39, 78, 101, 102, 104,
   128, 164, 185, 376, 740
   older people 86, 122, 176, 229, 230, 702, 715
   pre-retirement 82–83, 91
   retirement 3, 21, 83, 249
Lloyd-Sherlock, P. 786, 787, 788
Lo, Andrew W. 450, 468
loans 625, 632, 825
Loewenstein, George 610
London:
   as financial centre 12
   poverty 12–13
long-term incentive contract model 723–724
longevity 10, 82, 126, 144, 145, 146, 156, 171,
   201, 249, 268, 275, 282, 286, 312, 511,
   512, 514, 528, 575, 578, 693, 752, 753,
   840, 845, 846, 852
Lorenzelli, M. 791
Loughran, David 705, 716n
loyalty 386, 484, 692
Luckett, Charles A. 625, 635n
Luckhaus, Linda 130
lump-sum payments 250, 366, 511, 513, 588,
   751, 752, 801, 803, 804, 812, 829
Lumsdaine, Robin 333n, 734
Lund, F. 788, 793, 820, 821
Lusardi, Annmaria 605, 606
Lush, D. 655, 656
Luss, Richard 396n
Lutz, W. 165
Luxembourg 608, 609
*Luxembourg Income Study* 128
Lynch, A. W. 476
Lyon-Caen, G. 694

Ma, Tongshu 453n
Mackenzie, George 580
MacKinlay, A. Craig 450
Macpherson, David 129, 136, 555, 736n
macro social changes 100

macroeconomics 172, 179, 198, 205, 210, 233, 265, 269, 270, 279, 285, 287, 464, 514, 515, 698, 792, 793
  stability 284, 286
Madigan, K. V. 654, 655
Madrian, Brigitte 264, 607, 608, 609, 611, 612
Mahieu, R. 188
Mahler, V. 741
Maki, D. 264
Malaysia 61, 782, 800, 808–809, 811
male labor 106, 107t
manager herding 248
mandated pension systems 241–265
Mangum, Garth 385, 392
Mankiel, B. 189
Mammen, K. 788
Mantel, J. 189
manufacturing 102
March, J. 483
Marcus, Alan J. 737n
Mares, I. 762, 763
Marglin, S. 102, 104
marital status 123t, 127t, 850, 854
  in retirement 125–128
market-based systems 697
markets 149, 207, 417, 489–491, 493, 494, 495, 594, 690, 841, 842
  capitalization 400, 407, 409, 409f, 410
  completeness 544
  imperfections 196–197
  incompleteness 550–553, 558
  information 188, 302, 489–491, 491, 496, 513
    ratio 469–470
  prices 533, 546, 547, 592–593
  timing 470–471, 471f
  transaction data 524
Markov processes 421
Markovitz, H. 190, 192, 423, 447
Marks, G. 104
Marsh, John 595
Marshall, T. H. 99, 761
Martin, Linda G. 714
Masnick, George S. 621

Mason, A. 170
Mason, J. W. 393
Masini, Carlo Alberto 301
Masson, A. 187, 192
maternity benefits 299
mature funds 428–429
Maurer, Raimond 575
Mauritius 62, 782, 789, 829
Mayer, C. 459, 460
Maxwell, S. 343
Mazuy, F. 471
McAuley, Michael 303
McCarthy, David G. 134, 203, 250, 546, 547, 549, 551, 553, 558, 559n, 574, 801, 806, 814
McCarthy, Jonathan 635n
McDermed, Ann A. 554
McDonnell, Ken 122
McGarry, Kathleen 130, 605
McGillivray, W. 176, 226
McKenzie, E. 476, 477
McLean, Peter 635n
McMillan, H. 404
Mealli, F. 554
mean-variance analysis 442, 447, 448, 450, 451, 460
means-testing 41, 42–43, 63, 69, 73, 81–82, 83, 150, 244, 249, 338, 373, 376, 712, 748, 774, 792, 820–821
  non-contributory pensions 62, 66, 789–790t, 791
  public assistance 66
Medicaid (USA) 336–340, 343, 350, 351
medical ethics 638–640
Medicare (USA) 336–351, 364, 567
  costs 342–343
Medigap (USA) 342
Mediterranean Europe 841
Medoff, James L. 726
Mehta, S. J. B. 155, 402, 423, 515, 537n
Mellinger, Andrew D. 818
men:
  annuities 571–572, 579
    Latin America 680
  benefits (UK) 315–316

hazard rates 315
  USA 316f
 labor force 279, 313, 320
   unused productive capacity 314f
 mortality 569
 part-time work 709
 retirement 319f
   income 122–123
 USA 710, 747, 751
mental health legislation 639, 654
mental state theories 644
Merette, M. 204
Merton, R. C. 145, 157n, 190, 192, 195, 196,
    404, 406, 418, 445, 449, 450, 453n,
    737n
Mesa-Lago, Carmelo 70, 667, 668, 671, 673,
    675, 679, 681n, 782, 792
Metrick, Andrew 607, 608, 609, 612
Mexico 59, 63, 134, 209, 381–382, 585, 663,
    664, 666, 668, 669, 670, 672, 782
Michaelides, L. 537n
microeconomics 189, 198, 208, 234
  behavior 626
middle classes (Europe) 15–16, 20–21
migration 12, 100, 171, 172, 174, 175, 285, 293,
    297, 307, 760, 793, 794
 *see also* economic migrants
Miles, D. K. 211
Milevsky, Moshe 570, 576, 577
Millennium Development Goals 781
Miller, Douglas 788, 821
Miller, Lex 396n
Miller, Merton H. 401, 402, 403, 411, 442
Miller, Paul 385
Mincer, Jacob 722, 726
Minimum Income Guarantee Scheme 21, 370
minimum pensions 249, 283–284,
    747–748
  UK 374, 507
*Minimum Funding Requirement* (1997)
    (UK) (MFR) 595
mining industry 37
mis-selling pensions (UK) 264, 371, 590,
    594, 597
Mishel, Lawrence 383

Mitchell, Olivia S. 122, 124, 129, 248, 250, 264,
    544, 553, 565, 571, 572, 574, 575, 585,
    598n, 734, 801, 804, 805, 806
Mittelstaedt, F. 408
Miyatake, G. 804
mobility 293–307, 367
mobilization theory 762, 764, 771, 774
modernization theory 760, 762
Modigliani, F. 174, 183, 184, 197, 401, 402,
    403, 411, 442, 626
Molenaar, R. D. J. 418, 429
Molina, O. 773
monetary conflicts 104
money purchase accounts 109, 371–373,
    375, 376
'money's worth' calculation 568–572, 572t,
    574t, 575
Montigny, E.-A. 39
Moon, H. 807
Moon, M. 340, 343, 350
Moore, James F. 544
Moore, Kevin B. 634n
Moore, N. 408
moral commitments 494–497
  with back-up 492–493
'moral hazard' 80, 255, 315, 507, 545, 546, 548,
    554
morality 13, 14, 15
Morandé, F. G. 209
Mørck, R, 404, 406
Morgan, C. 418, 422
Morocco 817
Morris, S. 484, 490
Morrisette, R. 850
mortality 151, 165, 166, 172, 277, 402, 404, 421,
    511, 514–515, 564, 568, 569–570,
    571–575, 578, 588, 589, 605, 680
mortgages:
  debt 621–622, 622t, 631–632, 633
  interest repayment 625
  loans 632
  markets 628
  reverse 633
*Mothers and Fathers Report* (2001)
    (South Africa) 820, 822

Mounce, R. 478n
Muffels, R, 492
Mullainathan, Sendhil 821, 788
Mulligan, C. B. 793
multinationals 294, 298
Mulvey, Charles 385, 418, 422
Munnell, Alicia H. 21, 23, 176, 368, 395n, 407, 584, 706, 710, 714, 715
Murakami, Kiyoshi 61
Murphy, K. M. 193
Murtaugh, Christopher 580
Murthi, Mamta 570, 573, 585, 590, 591
Musalem, A. R. 206, 782, 789
Musgrave rules 148, 844–845, 845, 846, 853
Musgrave, R. 147, 844, 845
mutual aid funds 37
mutual funds 21, 38, 42, 43, 258, 366, 375, 459, 476
   underperformance 473–474
mutualist solidarity 143, 144, 145, 149, 150
   *see also* social solidarity
Myers, D. H. 418, 423, 557
Myles, John 73, 150, 153, 156n, 686, 762, 768, 770, 773, 844, 854
Myners, P. 462

Namibia 62, 782, 789, 829
nation-states 5, 6, 8, 11
   *see also* state, pensions
national health system (USA) 338
National Health Service (UK) 83
national insurance:
   contracting out (UK) 371
   contributions (UK) 371
   disability 40
   rebates (UK) 372
   systems (UK) 66
National Insurance (NI) (UK) 370, 545–546
National Insurance Fund (UK) 268
national pensions systems 15, 741, 752–754, 757, 828
   mandatory 745–746
national provident funds 800

national savings 173–174, 202, 204–205, 230, 243
National Savings (Latin America) 675–676
national welfare regimes 492
nationality 99, 293
naturalized citizens, benefit restrictions 42
Naegele, G. 768
Neihaus, G. 406
neoliberalism 153, 684, 686, 687–691, 696, 697, 698
Nepal 782, 791
Netherlands 18, 43, 91, 102, 103, 105, 108, 109, 110, 111, 147, 148, 248, 280, 302–303, 313, 330, 331, 360, 399, 402, 411, 421, 457, 504, 506, 507, 508, 509, 511, 596, 623, 627, 692, 693–694, 696, 697, 708, 709, 715, 743, 744–745, 757, 761, 765, 766–767, 771, 772, 774, 841, 842
Neuberger, A. 203, 250, 553
Neumark, David 714, 717n, 724, 726, 727, 728, 729, 734, 736n
New Zealand 34, 39, 41, 62, 244, 265, 273, 296, 303, 515, 623, 829
Newhouse, J. 347
Nicaragua 663, 664, 673
Nigeria 785
Nikkei 500 (Japan) 407f
Nishigaki, Y. 577
Nisticò, C. 281
nominal bonds 155
non-contributory pensions 42, 43, 62, 67, 69, 782–783, 785–787t, 788–789, 790t, 791–795, 829, 833
Nordic countries 106, 703, 766, 767, 771, 773
'normal retirement age' (NRA) 82
   *see also* retirement age
North Africa 817, 828, 829
North America 21, 638, 841
Northern Europe 187
Norway 299, 507, 693
Notestein, F. 848
notional accounts 281, 283, 285–287
notional contributions 283

notional defined contributions (NDC) 178, 224, 246, 255, 270, 287
nuclear family 101
Nyce, Steven 20, 722

Oberhofer, George 446
objective list theories 644–645
O'Brien, P. 202, 204
occupational pensions 15, 18–19, 21, 33, 34, 61, 66–67, 70, 76–90f, 91–92f, 93–96, 99, 100, 101, 109, 128, 141, 148, 154, 155, 224, 268, 275, 310, 331–332, 359–378, 382, 394, 399, 410, 443, 461, 467t, 477, 502–505, 509, 514, 515, 518, 543–559, 606, 611, 684–699, 707, 744, 763, 767, 772, 781, 801, 803, 804, 823–824, 830, 845
    automatic enrollment 611–612
    design 108–111, 543
    international standards 503, 517
    private 773
    supervising 517–518
    UK 78, 81, 88, 212, 361, 369–376, 463, 476–477, 503–505, 507, 509, 517, 543–544, 554
    USA 68, 78, 81, 84f, 86–87, 131, 361, 362, 365, 369, 381, 382, 395, 504 , 507, 509, 543–544 , 579–580, 614
    women 125, 131, 137
occupational hazards 760
occupational segregation 129, 130, 143, 148
occupations:
    blue-collar 37
    female-dominated 129
O'Donoghue, Ted 610, 611
*OECD Recommendation on the Regulation of Occupational Pensions* 516
Offe, C. 102
Ogawa, N. 168, 804
Oh, P. 404, 405
Oksanen, H. 154
old-age 385, 387, 565, 836
    benefits 299
    incomes 144–145, 370, 760, 799
    insurance 43, 68, 851, 852
    pensions 62, 63, 72, 78, 81–83, 85–86, 87, 562, 751, 752, 763, 772, 802
        formulas 225
        state 294–295
        UK 11–12, 39, 83
        USA 39, 68, 83, 127
Old Age, Survivors and Disabled Institution (OASDI) (USA) 68–69, 187, 748–749, 751, 752
older people 168f, 502, 785, 810
    *see also* poverty, old-age
    as voters 154, 155
    borrowing 632
    employment rates 747
    financial security 620
    labor force 173, 180, 320
    low incomes 176, 179, 744
    mental disorder 641
    pensions 242
        funding 175–181; reduction 753
    retirement income 93f, 122
    rich 176
    UK 41–42
    USA 331
    work 322, 325, 328, 332, 713–714, 722–735
*Older Workers Benefit Protection Act* (1990) (USA) (OWBPA) 731
Olivettim P. 854
Omberg, Edward 450
on-the-job training 555
optimal asset allocation 443, 450
optimal funding strategy 403–404, 411
organized labor 761, 764
    USA 381–395, 545
organized formal sector (South Africa) 823–824
Organization for Economic Cooperation and Development (OECD) 24, 108, 111, 126, 201, 204, 207, 208, 211, 213, 215, 243, 248, 270, 273, 275, 279, 301, 336, 399, 400, 501, 502–505, 508, 509, 511, 512, 517, 518t, 623, 627, 702, 703, 704, 704f, 705, 709, 714, 715, 757, 819, 822, 840, 841, 842, 846, 847, 851, 854
    Working Party on Private Pensions 516, 519

Orloff, A. 767
Orszag, J. Michael 570, 573, 574, 585, 585, 591, 598n
Orszag, Peter R. 205, 570, 573, 585, 586, 591, 667
Ostuw, Pamela 819
outsourcing 105
Øverbye, E. 149
Owyang, Michael 734

Pacific countries 782
Packard, Truman G. 176, 586, 587, 667, 668, 669, 670, 672, 674, 675, 676, 677, 679, 680, 681n
Paes de Barros, R. 796n
Paiella, M. 190, 191, 194, 196
Pakistan 782
Palacios, R. 478n, 781
Palier, B. 686, 694
Pallares-Miralles, M. 478n, 781
Palme, J. 17, 693, 699n
Palmer, E. 178, 283
Palmon, Oded 576, 577
Pampel, Fred 66, 151
Panama 665
Papke, Leslie E. 406, 457, 731
Paraguay 665, 783
Pareto gains 151
Parfit, D. 644
passive selection 570
Pastor, Lubos 452, 453n
Patel, J.
paternalism 15, 485, 647, 649, 650, 657, 762
path dependency 11, 151–152, 155, 686
Patterson, William 393
pay-as-you-go (PAYG) 12–13, 14, 16–19, 20–21, 23, 61, 62, 66, 69, 70, 71, 82, 91, 93, 99, 110, 134, 137, 141, 147, 148, 151–152, 153, 154, 158n, 175–177, 187, 188, 201–202, 203, 204, 206, 212, 213, 214, 215, 223, 226–228, 230–231, 232, 236, 237, 242, 243, 244, 247, 255, 275, 282, 283, 285–287, 311, 370, 377, 392, 502, 596, 664, 740, 745–746, 748, 749, 753, 754–757, 766, 768, 770, 800, 802, 805, 844

*see also* public pensions
finance 231, 233, 234, 237, 268, 269, 272–273, 279–181, 283, 846–847
traditional 241, 265
unfunded 456, 457, 806
payroll taxes 94, 134, 351, 394, 763, 771, 846, 854, 856, 806, 846, 854
Peach, Richard W. 536n
Peagle, Nigel 395n
Pech, Suzanne 578
Peil, Margaret 831
Peled, D. 565
*Pension Act* (1908) (UK) 66
Pension Authority (UK) 14
Pension Benefit Guaranty Corporation (USA) 507
*Pension Benefits Acts* (1965–7) (Canada) 87, 88
pension deals 424t
pension funds 154, 203, 213, 214, 248, 257–258, 263–264, 265, 361t, 368, 382, 399, 408, 446, 456–478, 491, 494, 510f, 514, 516, 528, 587, 593, 597, 688
  adjudicators 833
  administration 506
    AFPs (Latin America) 247–248, 261
  contractual negotiations 490
  deficits 521–522, 524, 525, 529–530, 535
  firms 672
  governance 483–497, 493f, 505, 774
  management 258, 458–459t, 463t, 464–465, 467, 477–478
    bespoke 461–462; fees 461, 461t, 462; pooled 461–462
  regulation 483–497
  surpluses 521, 524, 525, 529–530, 535
  transfers 516
  trustees 484, 488, 489
  UK 459, 465, 466t(a), 466t(b), 474t(a), 475f, 476–477
  USA 459
Pension Protection Fund (UK) 549
*Pension Act* (PRA) (1995) (UK) 488, 505
pension reforms 16, 17, 62–63, 72, 173, 201, 204–205, 209–210, 212, 213, 214, 215, 242–243, 280, 311, 322, 324, 325,

326, 327, 326f, 328, 328f, 330, 346, 381, 501, 702, 770–771, 782, 848, 851–853
pension-wage trade-off 555
pensions *see* assets, pension funds; basic pensions; defined benefit plans; defined contribution plans; non-contributory pensions; occupational pensions; private pensions; state, pensions; universality, pensions
Pensions Commission (UK) 155, 239n
*Pensions Funds Act* (1956) (South Africa) 824
Peracchi, F. 11
performance statements 525, 530, 535–536
Perold, A. F. 419
Perry, G. E. 793
personal pensions *see* private pensions
personal savings 13, 14, 202, 204, 214, 685, 693, 746
Persson, T. 271
Peru 663, 664, 665, 666, 667, 668, 670, 673, 677, 679
Pesandro, J. E. 203
Petersen, Jeffrey S. 385, 392
Petersen, Mitchell 457
Petrongolo, B. 854
Phang, H. 803, 807, 813
phased retirement schemes 705, 711–712, 714
Phelps, E. S. 174
Philippines 225, 613, 811
Philips, Peter 385, 392
Philipson, Thomas 580
Phillips, D. R. 799
Phillips, John 122, 124, 129
physician-patient relationships 639–640
Pieris, Badhi 62
Pierron, Bill 819
Pierson, Paul 62, 70, 152, 686, 762, 768, 769, 770, 773
Piggott, John 89, 250, 261, 575, 801, 806
Piore, M. 105
Pissaridis, C. 854

Pizzorni, A. 104
plan sponsors 441–442, 484, 488, 490, 505, 506–507, 512
Pfleiderer, P. 461
Pochet, P. 686
Poland 178, 260, 269, 281, 283–284, 512, 513, 585
Polanyi, K. 100, 101
polarization 594
policies 61–63, 179, 513
political economy 100–103, 687
political mobilization 760, 761–762
politics 34, 233, 236
 pension reforms 760
 veto 769–772, 774
Pollitz, K. 351
Ponds, E. H. M. 145, 418, 433, 436
poor 43, 150
 health 385
 relief 34, 38, 41
 undeserving 66
*Poor Law* (UK) 66, 293, 294, 307
population growth 164–166, 173; *see also* ageing population
 by region 167f
 Europe 166
 North America 166
 over 60 170f
 world 165f
Porter, T. M. 112
portfolios 205, 207, 418, 447–448, 451–452, 467, 469–472, 477, 508, 513, 516, 528, 544, 545, 546, 549–550, 565, 607, 608, 612, 625, 629, 681
 allocation 183–184, 187, 190, 193, 508, 570
 influence of age 190–192, 195
 constraints 443–444
 diversification 678t
Portugal 280, 399, 513, 608, 609, 747
Posel, Deborah B. 831
Posner, R. 491, 495, 497
Poterba, J. 203, 452n, 457, 547, 563, 565, 571, 572, 573, 575, 578, 580, 722

poverty 15, 43, 166, 180, 580, 669–670,
    740–757, 792, 818, 833
  old-age 13–14, 23, 38, 40, 41, 73, 110, 123,
      133, 156, 176, 746, 760, 781, 783–785,
      783, 784t, 785, 786, 789, 793, 813, 821,
      839, 842, 843t, 847
  pensioner 3, 11, 23–24, 695, 696, 745
  reduction (developing countries)
      781–795, 787t, 788, 789, 794–795,
      799
  UK 12–13
  USA 68, 124t, 338, 742
Powelson, John P. 818
Prakken, Joel 627, 635n
Prat, A. 490, 494
prescription drugs (USA) 341, 342, 349, 350
Preston, S. H. 14
price:
  indexation 17, 147, 154, 370, 402
  inflation 284
  strategies 105
  volatility 210
Price, Robert 627
principal-agent relationship 502
'principle of work' 709
private initiatives 173–174, 178–179
private insurance 4
  health plans 344, 346, 351
  market (USA) 338, 341, 348–349
  voluntary 301
private pensions 6, 16, 19, 21, 24, 71, 100, 137,
    204, 243, 298, 301, 377, 477, 489, 502,
    503, 504, 512, 515, 516, 584–598,
    684–699, 703, 707, 721, 742, 753, 767,
    768, 774–775, 799–800, 812–814, 840,
    841–842, 845, 853, 855
  see also occupational pensions
  costs 584–598
  funding 458t
  Latin America 664, 666–667, 671t
  OECD countries 518t
  political interference 71–72
  UK 66–67, 371–372, 374, 376, 457, 474t(b),
      475, 512, 554, 585, 591–592, 740
  USA 68–69, 310, 374

private plans:
  health (USA) 344–352
  retirement (USA) 132
private savings 15, 34, 40, 110, 204, 263, 280,
    502, 606
  see also savings
privatization 112, 372, 687, 765
productivity 174, 382, 385, 504, 721–736, 722,
    723, 725, 726, 727, 732, 788, 848–849,
    852
  pensions 554–555, 577
Profeta, P. 154
property 144, 198, 205, 257, 303–304, 466, 524,
    531, 588, 628–629, 744, 818
  residential 619, 628–629
prosperity 82, 691, 693
provident funds 61, 62, 73, 233, 246, 808–811,
    813, 828–829
'prudent person' standard 506, 508
Prussia 36, 37, 40
public pensions 16, 63, 66, 72, 73, 74, 81–83,
    88–89, 99, 134, 146, 148, 151, 153–154,
    155, 183–184, 187, 189, 197, 212, 213,
    223–227, 231, 235, 256, 268, 269–271,
    273, 278, 280, 287, 359, 360, 501,
    502, 519, 580, 584–585, 603, 606,
    607, 608, 609, 614, 684–699, 703,
    707, 721, 722, 740, 742, 744, 746,
    749, 752, 575, 765, 763, 765–767,
    799–800, 804–807, 812–814, 841,
    852, 853
  see also actuarial-based systems,
      public pensions; pay-as-you-go
      (PAYG)
  expenditure 67–68, 72–73, 840, 854 (1990)
      64f; growth (1960–1989) 65f
  finance 232–233, 404, 741
  old age 86, 93
  Latin America 663–680
  tax-financed 268–286
  UK 66, 740
  USA 66, 68–70, 134, 137, 310, 742
public policy 722, 735
public retirement schemes 100, 233, 242
public social insurance 62, 68, 78

public welfare 82, 87, 268
Pudney, S. 554
purchasing power 145, 817
'push-marketing' 632

Quadagno, Jill 73
Querino, A. C. 786, 788, 791, 792
Quigley, John M. 626
Quinn, Joseph F. 557, 704, 710, 716n, 729, 849, 855n
quality strategies 105

Rabin, Matthew 611
Rachmatarwata, I. 810, 812
Rahman, S. 473
Ralston, N. 478n
Rangel, Antonio 607
Ransom, R. 37
Raphael, M. 36, 80
Rappaport, Anna M. 822
rational choice theory 142
Rauh, J. 408
Rawls, J. 149, 156n
Rea, Samuel A. 579
real estate *see* property
Reed, Deborah 136
reforms *see* policy, reforms
regression 406
*Regulation 1408/71* (EU) 298, 299
regulations 488, 502–503, 505–508, 511–512, 516, 519, 593, 594, 596, 597–598, 666, 826–827, 831
   international standards 515–517
Reil-Held, A. 744
Rein, M. 772
Reisen, H. 204
remunerations 595
rental income:
   risks 146
Repetto, Andrea 609, 610
Republic of Korea 169, 170
Rescher, N. 486, 487
residency 99, 293, 297
   overseas pension freeze (UK) 295
Retail Price Index (UK) 370

retirees 202, 223
retirement age 277, 282, 284, 286, 315, 324–326, 327f, 605–606, 703, 704, 705, 712, 753, 766, 839–840
   delayed 278, 322–323, 323f, 850, 853
   early 153, 173, 203, 211, 225, 243, 262, 312, 314, 316–318, 319, 320, 321f, 332, 403, 688, 702, 705, 707–708, 715, 763, 766–767, 821
   increase in 73, 153, 179, 225, 237, 328, 364, 705, 707, 729, 753, 845–846
   mandatory 35, 41–42, 81, 248, 363, 702, 722, 725, 729, 730, 732, 735
   partial 853
   USA 310, 315, 320, 325, 326, 329, 707, 713
retirement policies 245f
'retirement posts' 37
return smoothing arrangements 512
*Revenue Act* (1942) (USA) 85, 88
Reynaud, E. 693, 699n, 772
Rhodes, M. 773
'Ricardian neutrality' *see* altruism
Rich, D. 426
Richards, T. M. 467
Rider, Barry 598n
Rimlinger, G. V. 561
risks 21, 38, 99–100, 142, 143–146, 156, 177, 181, 183–184, 227, 236–237, 403, 446, 549, 458, 502, 504, 512, 578–580, 593, 596, 692–693, 697, 706, 817, 854
   adjustment 527–528
   aversion 135, 149, 155, 184, 188, 189, 190, 191–194, 197–198, 528, 534, 547, 549, 567, 575
   background 193–196, 198
   basis 547–548
   collective 141–142, 144–145, 146–150, 688
   management 409, 421–422, 508, 514–515, 516, 517, 529, 536
   mismatch 431–432
   retirement 145t
   tolerance 191, 194
Ritter, G. 37, 41
Rix, Sarah 704
Robine, J. M. 855n, 856n

Robinson, Derek 128
Rochet, J.-C. 193
Roe, M. 492
Rofman, Rafael 71
Rogot, E. 750
Rohwedder, S. 263, 280
Roland, David 635n
Roll, R. 470
Romano, R. 484
Roos, D. 104
Rosanvallon, P. 101, 156n
Rose, M. 102
Rosegrant, S. 805
Ross, T. 404
Rossi, N. 204
Rothschild, Casey 579
Rowe, G. 845
rule-based decision-making 486–488, 497
Russell, A. 36
Russia 210
Russian Federation 232
Rutkowski, M. 782, 789

Sabel, C. 104, 105
Sachs, Jeffrey D. 818
Saez, Emmanuel 607, 608
safety net pensions 249
Sala-i-Martin, X. 793
Salais, R. 690, 691
salaries 77, 129, 528
  increases 533, 536
Saldain, R. 791
Samuelson, P. A. 151, 190, 192, 236, 269, 418, 449, 453n
Samwick, A. A. 204
Sanchez, Luis-Alvaro 816, 827, 828, 832
sanctions policy 488
Sanderson. W. 165
Sandstrom, Susanna 128
Santa-Clara, P. 418
Sarasa, S. 855n
Sass, S. 18, 77, 80, 81, 83, 86, 87, 88, 100, 369, 373, 377n, 389, 391, 710, 714, 715
Savage, M. 37
Savarino, James E. 453n

Save More Tomorrow plan (USA) 613–614
savings 37–40, 42, 61, 62, 77, 112, 124, 133, 134, 137, 144, 150, 174, 176, 178, 188, 192, 201–216, 231, 262, 281, 367, 586, 625, 849
  *see also* private savings
  accounts 268
  among poor 39–40
  behavior 191–192, 197, 604, 606, 612–614
  determinants 183–186
  discretionary 202–203
  for pensions 21, 23, 262
  forced 244, 255, 263
  incentives 279
  increase 205, 214
  individual 72, 99, 369
  older people 746, 747
  plans 604–605, 608–615
  rates 187, 188, 197, 198, 202, 213, 264, 280
  retirement 264, 272, 279, 280, 286, 513, 603–615, 604, 606–609, 618–634, 800, 808–809
Savulescu, J. 639, 645
'scaled premium system' 228
Scandinavia 35, 101, 283, 502, 685, 686, 692, 705, 708–709, 714, 715–716, 757, 761, 771, 773, 774, 841
Scarpetta, S. 278, 280
Schadt, R. W. 472
Schelling, Thomas 608, 609, 610
Scherbov, S. 165
Schieber, Sylvester 20, 396n, 512, 722
Schmidt-Hebbel, K. 206, 209, 213
Schmitt, Jon 383
Schoeni, Robert 714
Schokkaert, E. 150, 852
Scholz, John Karl 124, 204
Schor, J. 102, 104
Schotman, P. C. 418, 429
Schrager, Allison 580
Schroder, Mark 450
Schuknecht, L. 10, 16
Schwartz, E. S. 418
Schwartz, F. W. 686
Schwarz, A. M. 782, 789

Schwarzer, H. 786, 788, 791, 792
Scobie, Grant 634n
Scott, Jason 606
scientific management 103–104
Seaward, Mary R. 130
Second World War *see* World War II
sectoral changes (USA) 117a1, 118a1, 119a1, 120f
securities 201, 207, 230, 443, 464, 508, 515, 524, 547, 549, 550, 580, 625
Securities Exchange Commission (USA) 491
Security Market Line 468–469, 473
securitization 207
self-employment 196, 299, 306, 710, 830
    contributions 226, 247
    Latin America 668, 669, 669t
self-regulation 516
Segal, M. 343
Seligman, S. 406
Senegal 832
senior citizens *see* older people
SERPS *see* State Earnings Related Pensions Scheme (UK)
Servén, L. 793
service sector 102, 103, 106, 108, 113n, 710
Seth-Iyengar, S. 263
Settergren, O. 177
settlements, costs 530
SFAS 87 (USA) 526, 532, 533, 534, 535, 536
Shahar, S. 35
Shalev, M. 151, 763, 773
Shapiro, C. 504
Shapiro, M. D. 190, 191, 194
share markets 159t
shareholders 155, 441–445
Sharpe, S. 405
Sharpe, W. F. 400, 402, 403, 421, 445, 468, 472, 549
Shavit, Y. 851
Shaw, Lois 131
Shea, D. 264, 611, 612
Sheshinski, E. 271
Shiller, Robert J. 22, 145, 385, 450, 484, 626
Shin, H. S. 484, 490

Shleifer, A. 461, 373, 476, 726
Shoven, J. 179, 452n, 580, 750, 751
Sialm, Clemens 452n
Sias, R. W. 211
sickness benefits 283, 299, 502, 688–689
    insurance 41, 43, 80
Siebert, H. 6
Silberfield, M. 654, 655
Silvers, Damon 393
Simon, J. 17, 204
Singapore 61, 169–170, 179, 246, 249, 574, 575, 782, 800, 809, 811
single-person households 152, 785
single premium immediate life annuity 563–564
    *see also* annuities
Sinha, Tapen 576
Sinn, H. W. 151
Sires, R. 12
Skiadas, Costis 450
Skinner, J. 187
Skocpol, T. 36
Sloane, Arthur 392
Smalhout, James 585, 590, 596
Smeeding, T. M. 123, 128, 131, 744, 745
Smith, A. D. 155, 402, 423, 515, 537n
Smith, K. 849
Smith, W. J. 793
Smolkin, Sheryl 303
Snow, Arthur 579
Soares, J. 768
social benefits (Prussia) 40–41
social concertation 773–775
social democracy 151, 685, 762
social dependency 687
social impact (South Africa) 821
social insurance 13, 62, 63, 70, 74, 82, 143, 156, 204, 269, 275, 302, 330, 586, 688, 708, 791, 811
    self-administration 772–773
    UK 41–42, 66
*Social Insurance Act* (1946) (UK) 66
social justice 11, 23, 691
social policy 14–15, 761, 762–763, 764
social sciences 12–13

social security systems 12, 16, 21, 71, 123, 175, 205, 230, 235, 293, 298, 319, 325, 330, 363, 492, 501–502, 503, 504, 505, 513, 567, 584, 605, 688–689, 694, 729, 731, 756, 759, 799–801, 812, 818, 832
  see also costs, social security; pay-as-you-go (PAYG)
  benefits 227, 293, 294, 299, 310, 315, 316–317, 326, 328, 606
  government intervention 565
  pensions 6, 122, 158n, 164, 172, 187, 226, 229, 301, 562
  reforms 8, 175, 325
  rights 107, 108, 110, 111–112
  UK 15, 16, 21, 24, 177, 294–296, 544
  unfunded 203, 214
  USA 122, 132–133, 204, 332, 336, 363–364t, 365, 377, 388–390, 394–395, 544, 557, 712, 746, 754, 761
*Social Security Act* (1935) (USA) 69–70, 78, 310
*Social Security Act* (1975) (UK) 370
*Social Security Amendments* (1950) (USA) 83, 86
social solidarity 141–158, 494
social welfare 83, 275
Solomon, Joel 381
Solorio, C. 786
solvency 506–508, 595, 596, 597
Somavia, Juan 818, 831
Song, Xue 574
Sorian, R. 351
Sorlie, P. D. 750
sorting behavior 136–137
Soskice, D. 11, 105, 691
Soto, M. 20, 407
South Africa 62, 208, 296, 623, 782, 788, 789, 791, 793, 794, 817, 818, 819–827, 828, 829, 830, 831, 832, 833
South America 232, 233
South Asia 782
South Europe 849
Southeast Asia 169, 800–801, 808–811, 812
Soviet Union 225, 232
  see also Russia

Spain 109, 153, 313, 329, 459, 504, 505, 512, 513, 608, 609, 623, 627, 841, 854
Spatt, Chester H. 447
Speed, C. 478n
Spicker, P. 142
Spiers, T. 478n
Spillman, Brenda 580
Spivak, Avia 576, 577, 580
spot labor markets 544, 545, 551, 723, 724
Sri Lanka 61
SSAP 24 (UK) 523
stability 108, 110, 112
Stacy, C. 418, 423
stakeholders 148, 235, 417–419, 423, 424, 428, 429, 433, 436, 486
  pensions (UK) 66, 373, 375, 513, 595
Stambaugh, Robert F. 452, 453n
standards, harmonization 536
standards (IAS 19) 510, 511, 532–533, 536
  pension costs 521–537
Starr, P. 112
state bonds (Chile) 71
State Earnings Related Pension Scheme (SERPS) (UK) 66–68, 89, 305–306, 370, 371–373, 377, 696
state pensions 4, 15, 17, 33–34, 38–39, 71, 78, 88–89, 98, 232, 295, 304, 685
  UK 14–15, 66, 83
State Second Pension (UK) 67, 373, 375
state-centered institutionalism 760, 761
Statement of Recognized Gains and Losses (STRGL) (UK) 532
statutory rules 488–490
Stedman Jones, Gareth 12
Steenkamp, T. B. M. 418, 422, 429
Steil, B. 210, 459
Stein, Gregory 606
Steinmeier, Thomas 377n, 553, 554, 557, 606
Stephens, J. 104, 764
Stevens, Beth 369
Stevens, Y. 765
Stiglitz, J. 22, 177, 205, 207, 215, 504, 667
Stimpson, A. 108
Stjernø, S. 142
stochastic models 422, 423, 436

Stock, James H. 332, 333n
Stock, Wendy A. 717n, 729, 736n
stocks 366, 444, 449, 451, 470–471, 475, 476, 605, 625, 629
    company 368
    exchanges 831
    markets 206, 208, 213, 214, 367, 405, 511, 587, 630
        bubble 507; prices 521; wealth 622–623, 626–628
    ownership 189, 190, 191, 197
    publicly traded 620
    USA 628
Stocks, Wendy A. 728
Storper, M. 691
Stoughton, N. M. 461
strategic asset allocation 442, 449–450, 451–452, 464
Streeck, W 99, 105
Strotz, Robert 610
structural pension reforms (Latin America) 663–680
Strunk, B. C. 345
Sturrock, T. 405
Studebaker pension plan (1963) 88
sub-Saharan Africa 782, 816, 817, 829, 832
Subbarao, K. 783, 793
subsidiarity 761, 769
Summers, Laurence H. 406, 726
Sundén, Annika A. 21, 23, 131, 134, 287n, 368, 598n, 706, 712
Sundaresan, S. 403
superannuation 249, 695–696
supplementary earnings 44
supplementary pensions 590–597, 686, 765
    rights 300
    UK 591–592, 595
    USA 595
supplementary public support 83, 244
Supplementary Security Income (USA) 69
Surette, B. J. 134
surplus funds 420f
surplus risks 431
*Survey of Consumer Finances* (Kennickell and Sundén) 131

survivor bonds 580
survivorship 299, 477, 846
Sutch, R. 37
Sutcliffe, C. 402
Swaziland 62
Sweden 17, 18, 42, 101, 103, 105, 106, 108, 110, 123, 147, 177, 178, 212, 260, 261, 270, 281, 283, 284, 285, 286, 313, 324, 329, 381, 502, 504, 513, 590, 592, 596, 598, 608, 609, 614, 623, 686, 692, 693, 694, 696, 697–698, 707, 708, 709, 711, 712, 713, 715, 744, 753, 761–762, 763, 765, 766–767, 840, 842
Swenson, P. A. 762, 763
Switzerland 18, 243, 247, 248, 399, 504, 505, 506, 509, 574, 596, 770
Sylvanus, M. 418, 423
system design 8, 279
Szykman, Lisa 608

Tabellini, G. 153, 279, 770
tactical asset allocation 442, 451, 464
Taiwan 800
Tajika, E. 805, 813
Takayama, N. 176, 177, 178, 187, 801, 804, 805, 806
Tamburi, G. 693, 699n
Tanzania 62, 587
Tanzi, V. 10, 16
Taubenfield, R. 301
Taubenfield, S. 301
Taubman, Paul 726
Taverne, Dick 597
tax force to retire 320, 321f, 322f
tax-and-transfer systems 177, 268, 269, 287, 502
tax-deferred contributions 137
tax-qualified plans 87
taxation 41, 69, 85, 98, 153, 231, 244, 256, 263, 268, 298, 350, 403, 433, 443, 511, 513, 514, 551–552, 557, 570, 592, 687, 698, 732, 740, 742, 743, 816, 854
    advantages 586, 603
    effective components 271, 279
    incentives 179, 203, 310, 515, 519

taxation (cont'd)
  increase 178–179, 230, 243, 749
  pensions 261–263, 298, 546–547
  rates 277–278, 321f, 847
  regimes 16, 24, 73, 78
  revenues 325, 326
  UK 369–370, 544, 546
  USA 544, 546
taxpayers 442, 446–447
Taylor, Frederick W. 103
Taylorism 103–106
Teamsters (USA) 392–393
technology 502, 506–507
Tepper, I. 403, 443, 446, 447
terminal bonuses 587
Teulings, C. N. 418, 429, 433
Thailand 811
Thaler, R. H. 22, 264, 606, 608, 613
Thane, P. 11, 36, 40, 42, 43
Thevenot, L. 689, 690
Thies, C. F. 405
Thillainathan, R. 809
Thomas, A. 475
Thomas, K. 351
Thompson, L. 150, 231, 237, 841
Thomson, D. 36, 38, 39, 41
Thomson, Rob J. 831
Thrift, N. 484
Thullen, P. 228
Tickell, A. 484
Tierney, D. E. 467
Timmermann, A. 467, 476, 477
Titman, S. 470, 472, 476, 477
Tkac, P. A. 460
Tobacman, Jeremy 609, 610
Todd, R. 22
Tonks, I. 463, 475, 477, 573
Topel, Robert 736n
Townley, Peter 565
Tracy, Joseph 628, 630, 631
trade unions 85–86, 154, 212, 261, 362, 369,
    386, 404, 556, 733–734, 761, 763–768,
    772, 773, 774, 832
  black 826
  solidarity 385–386

  USA 381, 382–393
training, of older workers 715–716
transparency 22, 201, 248, 261, 406, 417,
    433, 436, 437, 444, 467, 529, 592–593,
    676
Treasury bills 191
Treasury bonds 571, 572, 573
treatment decisions *see* medical ethics
Treaty of Rome 109, 297, 299
Tressel, T. 206
Treynor, Jack L. 445, 453n, 468, 469, 471
Troske, Kenneth R. 714
Troyansky, D. G. 36
trust institution 485
trust law 88, 488
  USA 485
trusts 248, 506
Tunisia 130, 828, 829
Turkey 505
Turner, A. L. 418, 423
Turner, John A. 122, 127, 130, 134,
    238n, 472
Tversky, A. 22, 198, 649
two-tier pension systems 761–762, 765, 767

Uccello, Cori E. 124, 737n
Uganda 785
UK 21, 38, 44, 85, 86, 91, 105–106, 108, 109, 111,
    123, 155, 177, 187, 197, 202, 211, 212,
    244, 248, 249, 258, 260, 263, 264, 268,
    273, 293, 294–297, 305, 306, 307, 331,
    371t, 401, 405–406, 408, 409f, 410f,
    445, 459, 475, 511, 513, 545, 569, 590,
    598, 623, 627, 638, 639, 652, 687, 694,
    696, 703–704, 715, 743, 744, 757, 761,
    763, 765, 767–768, 771, 773, 774–775,
    830, 842, 850
  *see also* under benefits; equities;
    legislation; mis-selling pensions;
    occupational pensions; pension
    funds; private pensions; social
    insurance; social security systems;
    state pensions
uncertainty 687–688, 697, 839–840
under-employment 16, 36–37

underfunding:
  pensions 506–508, 512, 549, 555–556, 746, 808
  retirement 603
unemployment 15, 16, 18, 43, 77, 104, 150, 180, 194, 225, 232, 236, 283, 299, 319, 322, 329, 388, 551, 671, 705, 708, 760, 761, 793, 801, 851
union pension premium 385–386
unit credit method 526, 533, 536
unit trusts *see* mutual funds
unit-linked policies 587, 588–589, 592
  life insurance 589t
United Nations 166, 168, 171, 201
*Universal Declaration of Human Rights* (Council of Europe) 301
universal life insurance *see* unit-linked policies
universality 17–18, 21, 382, 486–487, 761, 854
  pensions 42, 98, 99, 244, 789, 795, 829, 853
urbanization 800
Uruguay 663, 665, 666, 673, 674, 679, 781, 783, 785, 791, 792
US Social Security Administration 132
USA 15, 36, 39, 44, 63, 68, 69f , 78, 85, 88, 91, 101, 102, 103, 104, 105, 105–106, 108, 124t, 126, 127t, 128–130, 130f, 134–138, 144, 150, 155, 171, 187, 188, 197, 198, 202, 208, 211, 215, 228, 244, 250, 258, 264, 273, 295–296, 327–328, 332, 370, 401, 405–406, 408, 409, 445, 459, 472, 507, 511, 533, 534, 569, 608, 609, 618, 627, 639, 652, 703–705, 707, 708, 711, 712–713, 714, 715, 722, 724, 727, 743, 744, 745, 748, 750, 752, 754, 757, 763, 770, 771, 822, 842, 847, 849, 850
  *see also under* 401(k) plans; actuarial-based systems, fairness; annuities; benefits; defined benefit plans; defined contribution plans; health, care; labor force; legislation; Medicaid; Medicare; men; occupational pensions; old age; organized labor; poverty; private pensions; private plans; public pensions; retirement age; social security systems
utility functions 192–196, 197, 403, 423, 447, 449, 575
utility models, discounted 544, 545
Utkus, S. 264

Valdes, Salvador 598n
Valdes Prieto, S. 204, 285, 286
Valletta, Robert G. 734
Van Aalst, P. C. 418
Van Buggenhout, B. 765
Vandenbroucke, Frank 855n
vanDerhee, Jack 124
van Ginneken, W. 786, 827, 830
Van Parijs, R. 150, 852
Van Riel, B. 154, 694
van Zyl, Elize 62
variable annuities (USA) 563
Varian, H. R. 146
Varoufakis, Y. 144
vascular disease 641
vector autoregressive models (VAR) 422, 424
'veil of ignorance' 149–150
Venezuela 665, 783
Venti, Steven F. 203, 629
Verburg, R. 152
vesting requirements 87, 89, 109
veterans' pensions (USA) 36
Viceira, L. M. 418, 422, 423, 429, 450, 451, 452, 453n
Vidlund, M. 855n
Villeval, M.-C. 689
Visco, I. 204
Vishny, R. W. 461, 473, 476
Visser, J. 154, 765, 768
Vittas, Dimitri 574, 585, 590, 811
voice 385, 484
volatilities 407, 418, 429, 431, 447–448, 533
Volpin, P. 410
voluntary bequests 188
voluntary pensions 746, 830–831
Vuolteenaho, Tuomo O. 451

Wadensjö, E. 772
Wadswoth, Mike 580
wage path 145
wages 23, 77, 80, 104, 128, 131, 146, 147, 154,
    178, 189, 212, 230, 284, 316, 317, 404,
    427, 452, 514, 545, 547, 551, 554, 556,
    723, 741, 746, 747, 854
  *see also* deferred wages; earnings; salaries
  average 706
  indexation 17, 154, 285–286
  labor 760
  low 751
  rising 722
Wagner, J. 418
Wahal, S. 208
Waidmann, T. 351
Waite, Linda J. 127
Wakefield, M. 156n
Waldvogel, J. 852
Wales *see* UK
Walker, A. 768
Walker, E. 206, 209, 210
Walters, Simon 293
Warshawsky, Mark 571, 572, 575, 580
Wasmer, E. 854
Wassenaar, Andreas D. 827, 833
Watanabe, K. 418, 423
wealth 134, 189, 191–193, 195, 202, 485, 545,
    567, 577, 580, 619, 736, 846
  accumulation 190, 195, 205, 277, 620,
    624–626, 627, 628, 633
  composition 184–186f, 189
  distribution (USA) 136, 136–137
  effect 187, 194
  older homeowners 621t, 633
  pensions 278t, 280, 282
  productivity shocks 449–450
Weaver, Carolyn 69
Webb, Anthony 576, 577, 731, 737n
Weinberg, S. 187
welfare 16, 73, 98, 146, 152, 153, 279, 281,
    404, 421, 485–486, 494, 495,
    496–497, 568, 491, 594, 639, 685,
    697, 840, 841, 848
  capitalism (USA) 387–388

distribution 852
mix 842, 843–844
old-age 9, 23–24, 72, 799
regimes 799
retrenchment 686, 774
states 6, 11, 16, 18, 101, 104, 154, 388,
    685–686, 691, 692, 759, 760, 761, 764,
    765, 769, 770, 772, 773
systems 15, 16
well-being (of clients) 644, 646–647,
    656–657
Wermers, R. 473
West Europe 73, 225, 228, 232, 588, 625, 638,
    747
Western economies 484, 497
Weyns, G. 537n
white-collar workers 44, 80, 83, 369, 711, 765,
    760, 761, 763, 765
Whiteford, E. A. 100, 110, 802
Whitehouse, Edward 260, 266n, 370, 371,
    372, 744
Whiteside, N. 6, 18, 78, 82, 83, 86, 690, 691,
    699n
Whitley, R. 105
widowers 133
widows 86, 133
Wilkie, A. D. 422
Wilkie, C. 281
Williams, A. 485
Williams, A. T. 20
Williams, H. 478n
Williams, M. 246
Williamson, J. B. 123, 131, 151, 154, 246,
    744, 745
Williamson, John 66
Williamson, Samuel 68
Willmore, Larry 821, 827
Wilson, Jack 68
Wise, David A. 16, 177, 203, 278, 280, 315, 319,
    320, 325, 331, 332, 333n, 557, 629, 706,
    729, 730, 747
with-profits policies 587–588
Wójcik, D. 11
Wolfson, M. 845
Womack, J. P. 105

women 279, 283, 502, 579, 825, 833, 841
  annuities 571–573
    Latin America 680
  as savers 37, 40
  benefits 154
  earnings (USA) 128f
  employment 767, 842, 849–850, 853–854
  Hispanic 124
  labor force participation 93, 180, 713
  mortality 569
  old age 38, 86, 91, 133
  part-time work 709
  retirement age 768
  UK 315–316, 370
  USA 137, 130f
Wong, Rebeca 134
Wooten, James E. 391
work 20, 23, 42–43, 84, 87, 99, 106–107, 109, 163, 702–716;
  see also older people, work
  adults (of working age) 93f
  classes 39–40
  low-wage 154, 370, 757
  organization 103
  penalties 329, 330
workers 514, 556
  associations 85
  active, decline 234
  employers 734
  flexibility 703
  individual pension accounts 233, 242, 244, 247
  older 310, 702–716, 721
  part-time 107, 109, 129, 370, 709t, 714, 767
  pension coverage 384t
  USA 605
  young 849
working classes 761

World Bank 72, 100, 150, 157n, 176, 177, 204, 213, 243–244, 246, 255, 262, 266n, 584–585, 667, 670, 675, 684, 685, 686, 696, 741, 781, 782, 799, 802, 807, 808
*World Population Policies 2003* (United Nations) 166
World War II 10, 15, 16, 19, 24, 44, 45, 46, 76, 78, 81, 82, 83, 85, 104, 151, 241, 242, 362, 370, 389, 390, 504, 505, 685, 692, 740, 761, 847
Worth Harris, Erica 731

Xia, Yihong 418, 450, 453n

Yaari, Menahem 564, 565
Yagi, T. 577
Yakoboski, Paul 819
Yamada, A. 91
Yang, S. T. 248
Yang, Yi 624, 635n
Yermo, J. 176, 508, 519n, 586, 587, 667, 668, 669, 670, 672, 674, 675, 676, 677, 679, 680, 681n
Young, Peter 635n

Zambia 62, 783
Zapatero, F. 403
Zeckhauser, R. 193, 194, 477
Zeitlin, J. 104
Zeldes, S. P. 191, 192, 196
Zelenka, A. 301
Zenios, S. A. 418
zero coupn bonds 531
Zervos, S. 215n
Zhang, Harold H. 447
Zheng, K. 806, 814
Zhu, Yukun 61
Ziemba, T. Z. 418, 422, 423
Zimbabwe 830
Zissimopoulos, Julie 608, 609